5e

ACCOUNTING INFORMATION SYSTEMS

JAMES A. HALL
LEHIGH UNIVERSITY

THOMSON
™
SOUTH-WESTERN

Australia · Brazil · Canada · Mexico · Singapore · Spain · United Kingdom · United State

THOMSON
SOUTH-WESTERN

Accounting Information Systems, Fifth Edition
James A. Hall

VP/Editorial Director:
Jack W. Calhoun

Publisher:
Rob Dewey

Acquisitions Editor:
Matt Filimonov

Developmental Editor:
Aaron Arnsparger

Marketing Manager:
Chris McNamee

Production Project Manager:
Brian Courter

Manager of Technology, Editorial:
Vicky True

Technology Project Editor:
Sally Nieman

Web Coordinator:
Scott Cook

Manufacturing Coordinator:
Doug Wilke

Production House:
GEX Publishing Services

Printer:
Transcontinental
Louiseville, Quebec CANADA

Art Director:
Bethany Casey

Internal Designer:
Jen2 Design

Cover Designer:
Jen2 Design

Cover Images:
© Getty Images

Library of Congress Control Number:
2005935614

For more information about our
products, contact us at:

Thomson Learning Academic Resource
Center

1-800-423-0563

Thomson Higher Education
5191 Natorp Boulevard
Mason, OH 45040
USA

Brief Table of Contents

Table of Contents

Preface

WELCOME TO THE FIFTH EDITION

The fifth edition of *Accounting Information Systems* includes a full range of new and revised homework assignments, up-to-date content changes, as well as several reorganized chapters based on reviewer feedback. All of these changes add up to more student and instructor enhancements than ever before. As this preface makes clear, we have made these changes to keep students and instructors as current as possible on issues such as business processes, systems development methods, IT governance and strategy, security, internal controls, and relevant aspects of Sarbanes-Oxley legislation.

FOCUS AND FLEXIBILITY IN DESIGNING YOUR AIS COURSE

Among accounting courses, accounting information systems (AIS) courses tend to be the least standardized. Often the objectives, background, and orientation of the instructor, rather than adherence to a standard body of knowledge, determines the direction the AIS course takes. Therefore, we have designed this text for maximum flexibility:

- This textbook covers a **full range of AIS topics** to provide instructors with flexibility in setting the direction and intensity for their courses.

- At the same time, for those who desire a **structured model**, the first nine chapters of the text, along with the chapters on electronic commerce and computer controls, provide what has proven to be a **successful template for developing an AIS course.**

- Earlier editions of this book have been used successfully in **introductory, advanced, and graduate-level AIS courses.**

- The **topics in this book are presented from the perspective of the managers' and accountants' AIS-related responsibilities under the Sarbanes-Oxley Act.**

- While the book was written primarily to meet the needs of accounting majors about to enter the modern business world, we have also developed it to be an **effective text for general business and industrial engineering students who seek a thorough understanding of AIS and internal control issues as part of their professional education.**

KEY FEATURES

CONCEPTUAL FRAMEWORK

This book employs a **conceptual framework** to emphasize the professional and legal responsibility of accountants, auditors, and management for the design, operation, and control of AIS applications. This responsibility pertains to business events that are narrowly defined as financial transactions. Systems that process nonfinancial transactions are not subject to the new standards of internal control under Sarbanes-Oxley legislation. Supporting the information needs of all users in a modern organization, however, requires systems that integrate both accounting and nonaccounting functions. While providing the organization with unquestioned benefit, a potential consequence of such integration is a loss of control due to the blurring of the lines that traditionally separate AIS from non-AIS functions. **The conceptual framework presented in this book distinguishes AIS applications that are legally subject to specific internal control standards.**

EVOLUTIONARY APPROACH

Over the past 50 years, accounting information systems have been represented by a number of different approaches or models. Each new model evolved because of the shortcomings and limitations of its predecessor. An interesting feature in this evolution is that older models are not immediately replaced by the newest technique. Thus, at any point in time, various generations of legacy systems exist across different organizations and often coexist within a single enterprise. The modern accountant needs to be familiar with the operational characteristics of all AIS approaches that he or she is likely to encounter. **Therefore, this book presents the salient aspects of five models that relate to both legacy and state-of-the-art systems:**

1. manual processes
2. flat-file systems
3. the database approach
4. the resources, events, and agents (REA) model
5. enterprise resource planning (ERP) systems

EMPHASIS ON INTERNAL CONTROLS

The book presents a **conceptual model for internal control** based on COSO and *Statement on Auditing Standards (SAS) No. 78.* This model is used to discuss control issues for both manual processes and computer-based information systems (CBIS). **Three chapters (Chapters 15, 16 and 17) are devoted to the control of CBIS.** Special emphasis is given to the following areas:

- computer operating systems

- database management systems

- electronic data interchange (EDI)

- electronic commerce systems

- ERP systems

- systems development and program change processes

- the organization of the computer function

- the security of data processing centers

- verifying computer application integrity

EXPOSURE TO SYSTEMS DESIGN AND DOCUMENTATION TOOLS

The book examines various approaches and methodologies used in **systems analysis and design,** including the following:

- structured design

- object-oriented design

- computer-aided software engineering (CASE)

- prototyping

In conjunction with these general approaches, professional systems analysts and programmers use a number of documentation techniques to specify the key features of systems. The modern auditor works closely with systems professionals during IT audits and must learn to communicate in their language. **The book deals extensively with documentation techniques such as data flow diagrams (DFDs), entity relationship diagrams (ERDs), as well as system, program, and document flowcharts.** The book contains **numerous systems design and documentation cases and assignments** intended to develop the students' competency with these tools.

SIGNIFICANT CHANGES IN THE FIFTH EDITION

Chapter 3, "Ethics, Fraud, and Internal Control"

A revised internal control model based on the COSO framework. This framework was recommended by both the SEC and the PACAOB as the preferred model for achieving compliance with Sarbanes-Oxley control requirements.

Chapter 4, "The Revenue Cycle"; Chapter 5 "The Expenditure Cycle Part I: Purchases and Cash Disbursements Procedures"; Chapter 6, "The Expenditure Cycle Part II: Payroll Processing and Fixed Asset Procedures"; and Chapter 8, "General Ledger, Financial Reporting, and Management Reporting Systems"

All the transaction processing and financial reporting chapters have been reorganized and revised to create a better balance between the treatments of manual and computer systems. Accounting systems are presented first conceptually in a technologically neutral setting. The objective is to focus on the tasks to be performed, the risks, and the control issues. The reader then moves on to examine the physical system. At this juncture, some instructors prefer to teach manual systems before moving on to computer applications. Others favor moving directly to computer-based systems. The chapters have been redesigned to accommodate both teaching styles. The reader may continue with the review of manual systems or, without loss of technical content, bypass this material and go directly to computer-based systems.

Chapter 15, "IT Controls Part I: Sarbanes-Oxley and IT Governance"; Chapter 16, "IT Controls Part II: Security and Access Control"; and Chapter 17, "IT Controls Part III: Systems Development, Program Changes, and Application Controls"

These three chapters have been completely rewritten to comply with the COSO framework for internal controls as prescribed by the PCAOB. Chapter 15 provides an overview of management and auditor responsibilities under Section 404 as well as the general control and audit issues related to IT governance issues. Chapter 16 addresses control and audit issues related to operating systems, networks, and database access and security. Chapter 17 focuses on the control and audit of systems development and program change procedures. The chapter also presents application controls and audit procedures.

GLOBAL CHANGES

- The end-of-chapter problems have been significantly revised throughout.

- All of the internal control cases in the revenue and expenditure cycle chapters have been replaced with new cases.

ORGANIZATION AND CONTENT

PART 1: OVERVIEW OF ACCOUNTING INFORMATION SYSTEMS

Chapter 1, "The Information System: An Accountant's Perspective"

This chapter places the subject of accounting information systems in perspective for accountants. It is divided into four major sections, each dealing with a different aspect of information systems.

- The first section explores the *information environment of the firm*. It introduces basic systems concepts, identifies the types of information used in business, and describes the flows of information through an enterprise. This section also presents a framework for viewing accounting information systems in relation to other information systems components.

- The second section of the chapter deals with the *impact of organizational structure on AIS*. The centralized and distributed models are used to illustrate extreme cases in point.

- The third section reviews the evolution of *information systems models*. Accounting information systems have been represented by a number of different approaches or models. *Five dominant models* are examined: manual processes; flat-file systems; the database approach; the resources, events, agents (REA) model; and enterprise resource planning (ERP) systems.

- The final section discusses the *role of accountants as users, designers, and auditors of AIS*. The nature of the responsibilities shared by accountants and computer professionals for developing AIS applications are examined.

Chapter 2, "Introduction to Transaction Processing"

The second chapter expands on the subject of transaction cycles introduced in Chapter 1. While the operational details of specific transaction cycles are covered in subsequent chapters, this chapter presents material that is common to all cycles. Topics covered include:

- the relationship between source documents, journals, ledgers, and financial statements in both manual and computer-based systems;

- system documentation techniques, such as data flow diagrams, entity relationship (ER) diagrams, document systems, and program flowcharts; and

- data processing techniques, including batch and real-time processing.

The techniques and approaches presented in this chapter are applied to specific business cycle applications in later chapters. The chapter is supported by material in the appendix and on the web site.

Chapter 3, "Ethics, Fraud, and Internal Control"

Chapter 3 deals with the related topics of ethics, fraud, and internal control.

- **The chapter first examines ethical issues related to business and specifically to computer systems.** The questions raised are intended to stimulate class discussions.

- **The chapter then addresses the subject of fraud.** There is perhaps no area of greater controversy for accountants than their responsibility to detect fraud. Part of the problem stems from confusion about what constitutes fraud. This section distinguishes between management fraud and employee fraud. The chapter presents techniques for identifying unethical and dishonest management and for assessing the risk of management fraud. Employee fraud can be prevented and detected by a system of internal controls. The section discusses several fraud techniques that have been perpetrated in both manual and computer-based environments. The results of a research study conducted by the Association of Certified Fraud Examiners as well as the provisions of the Sarbanes-Oxley Act are presented.

- **The final section of the chapter describes the internal control structure and control activities specified in SAS 78 and the COSO framework.** The control concepts discussed in this chapter are applied to specific applications in chapters that follow.

PART 2: TRANSACTION CYCLES AND BUSINESS PROCESSES

Chapters 4, 5, and 6, The Revenue and Expenditure Cycles

The approach taken in all three chapters is similar. First, the business cycle is reviewed conceptually using data flow diagrams to present key features and control points of each major subsystem. At this point the reader has the choice of either continuing within the context of a manual environment or moving directly to computer-based examples. Each system is examined under two alternative technological approaches:

- First examined is automation, which preserves the basic functionality by replacing manual processes with computer programs.

- Next, each system is reengineered to incorporate real-time technology.

Under each technology, the effects on operational efficiency and internal controls are examined. This approach provides the student with a solid understanding of the business tasks in each cycle and an awareness of how different technologies influence changes in the operation and control of the systems.

Chapter 7, "The Conversion Cycle"

Manufacturing systems represent a dynamic aspect of AIS. **Chapter 7 describes several manufacturing environments,** including the following:

- traditional mass production (batch) processing

- just-in-time production systems

- computer-integrated manufacturing

These environments are driven by information technologies such as materials requirements planning (MRP) and manufacturing resources planning (MRP II). The chapter addresses the shortcomings of traditional accounting models and the advantages of activity-based accounting (ABC) in assessing value-added business activities.

Chapter 8, "Financial Reporting and Management Reporting Systems"

Chapter 8 begins with a review of data coding techniques used in transaction processing systems and for general ledger design. It explores several coding schemes and their respective advantages and disadvantages. Next it **examines the objectives, operational features, and control issues of three related systems: the general ledger system (GLS), the financial reporting system (FRS), and the management reporting system (MRS)**. The emphasis is on operational controls and the use of advanced computer technology to enhance efficiency in each of these systems. The chapter distinguishes the MRS from the FRS in one key respect: financial reporting is *mandatory* and management reporting is *discretionary*. Management reporting information is needed for planning and controlling business activities. Organization management implements MRS applications at their discretion, based on internal user needs.

The chapter examines a number of factors that influence and shape information needs. These include management principles, decision type and management level, problem structure, reports and reporting methods, responsibility reporting, and behavioral issues pertaining to reporting.

PART 3: ADVANCED TECHNOLOGIES IN ACCOUNTING INFORMATION

Chapter 9, "Database Management Systems"

Chapter 9 deals with the design and management of an organization's data resources.

- It begins by demonstrating how problems associated with traditional flat-file systems are resolved under the database approach.

- The second section describes in detail the functions and relationships among four primary elements of the database environment: the users, the database management system (DBMS), the database administrator (DBA), and the physical database.

- The third section is devoted to an in-depth explanation of the characteristics of the relational model. A number of database design topics are covered, including data modeling, deriving relational tables from ER diagrams, the creation of user views, and data normalization techniques.

- The fourth section concludes the chapter with a discussion of distributed database issues. It examines **three possible database configurations in a distributed environment:** centralized, partitioned, and replicated databases.

Chapter 10, "The REA Approach to Business Process Modeling"

Chapter 10 presents the REA model as a means of specifying and designing accounting information systems that serve the needs of all users within an organization. The chapter is composed of three major sections.

- The first section introduces the REA approach and describes how it overcomes a number of problems associated with traditional accounting practice.

- The second section examines traditional database applications and their limitations. Although superior to flat-file systems, traditional database systems suffer from serious problems that limit their usefulness. A limitation of particular importance is their almost exclusive support of financial information users and their inadequacy at meeting the growing need for nonfinancial information. A second problem is their inability to respond to noneconomic events that may be of extreme importance to an organization.

- The third section provides a detailed review of the steps involved in developing an REA model. This approach is then compared to the traditional ER approach to modeling business processes.

Chapter 11, "Enterprise Resource Planning Systems"

This chapter presents a number of issues related to the implementation of enterprise resource planning (ERP) systems. It is composed of five major sections.

- The first section outlines the key features of a generic ERP system by comparing the function and data storage techniques of a traditional flat file or database system to that of an ERP.

- The second section describes various ERP configurations related to servers, databases, and bolt-on software.

- Data warehousing is the topic of the third section. A data warehouse is a relational or multidimensional database that supports on-line analytical processing (OLAP). A number of issues are discussed, including data modeling, data extraction from operational databases, data cleansing, data transformation, and loading data into the warehouse.

- The fourth section examines risks associated with ERP implementation. These include "big bang" issues, opposition to change within the organization, choosing the wrong ERP model, choosing the wrong consultant, cost overrun issues, and disruptions to operations. The fifth section reviews several control and auditing issues related to ERPs. The discussion follows the SAS 78 framework.

- The chapter appendix provides a review of the leading ERP software products including SAP, Oracle, PeopleSoft, J.D. Edwards, and BAAN.

Chapter 12, "Electronic Commerce Systems"

Driven by the Internet revolution, electronic commerce is dramatically expanding and undergoing radical changes. While electronic commerce promises enormous opportunities for consumers and businesses, its effective implementation and control are urgent challenges facing organization management and accountants. To properly evaluate the potential exposures and risks in this environment, the modern accountant must be familiar with the technologies and techniques that underlie electronic commerce. **This chapter and the associated appendix deal with several aspects of electronic commerce.**

- The body of the chapter examines Internet commerce including business-to-consumer and business-to-business relationships. It presents the risks associated with electronic commerce and reviews security and assurance techniques used to reduce risk and to promote trust.

- The chapter concludes with a discussion of how Internet commerce impacts the accounting and auditing profession. The internal usage of networks to support distributed data processing and traditional business-to-business transactions conducted via EDI systems are presented in the appendix.

PART 4: SYSTEMS DEVELOPMENT ACTIVITIES

Chapter 13, "Managing the Systems Development Life Cycle" and Chapter 14, "Construct, Deliver, and Maintain Systems Projects"

These chapters examine the accountant's role in the systems development process.

- **Chapter 13** begins with an overview to the systems development life cycle (SDLC). This multistage process guides organization management through the development and/or purchase of information systems.

- Next, Chapter 13 presents the key issues pertaining to developing a systems strategy, including its relationship to the strategic business plan, the current legacy situation, and feedback from the user community. The chapter provides a methodology for assessing the feasibility of proposed projects and for selecting individual projects to go forward for construction and delivery to their users. The chapter concludes by reviewing the role of accountants in managing the SDLC.

- **Chapter 14** covers the many activities associated with in-house development, which fall conceptually into two categories: (1) construct the system and (2) deliver the system. Through these activities, systems selected in the project initiation phase (discussed in Chapter 13) are designed in detail and implemented. This involves creating input screen formats, output report layouts, database structures, and application logic. Finally, the completed system is tested, documented, and rolled out to the user.

- Chapter 14 then examines the increasingly important option of using commercial software packages. Conceptually, the commercial software approach also consists of construct and delivery activities. In this section we examine the pros, cons, and issues involved in selecting off-the-shelf systems.

- Chapter 14 also addresses the important activities associated with systems maintenance and the associated risks that are important to management, accountants, and auditors.

- **Several comprehensive cases designed as team-based systems development projects are available on the web site.** These cases have been used effectively by groups of three or four students working as a design team. Each case has sufficient details to allow analysis of user needs, preparation of a conceptual solution, and the development of a detailed design, including user views (input and output), processes, and databases.

PART 5: COMPUTER CONTROLS AND AUDITING

Chapters 15, "IT Controls Part I: Sarbanes-Oxley and IT Governance"

This chapter provides an overview of management and auditor responsibilities under Sections 302 and 404 of the Sarbanes-Oxley Act (SOX). The design, implementation, and assessment of internal control over the financial reporting process form the central theme for this chapter and the two chapters that follow. This treatment of internal control complies with the Committee of Sponsoring Organizations of the Treadway Commission (COSO) control framework. Under COSO, IT controls are divided into application controls and general controls. Chapter 15 presents risks, controls and tests of controls related to IT governance including organizing the IT function, controlling computer center operations, and designing an adequate disaster recovery plan.

Chapter 16, "IT Controls Part II: Security and Access"

Chapter 16 continues the treatment of IT controls as described by the COSO control framework. The focus of the chapter is on SOX compliance regarding the security and control of operating systems, database management systems, and communication networks. This chapter examines the risks, controls, audit objectives, and tests of controls that may be performed to satisfy either compliance or attest responsibilities.

Chapter 17, "IT Controls Part III: Systems Development, Program Changes, and Application Controls"

This chapter concludes our treatment of IT controls as outlined in the COSO control framework. The focus of the chapter is on SOX compliance regarding systems development, program changes, and applications controls. This chapter examines the risks, controls, audit objectives, and tests of controls that may be performed to satisfy compliance or attest responsibilities. The chapter examines **five computer-assisted audit tools and techniques** (CAATT) for testing application controls:

- the test data method
- base case system evaluation
- tracing
- integrated test facility
- parallel simulation

It also reviews two substantive testing techniques: embedded audit modules and generalized audit software.

SUPPLEMENTS

Product Web Site

Additional teaching and learning resources, including access to additional **internal control and systems development** cases are available by download from the book's web site at: **http://hall.swlearning.com**.

The *Instructor's Manual*, updated by Georgia Smedley of the University of Nevada–Las Vegas, was written with the first-time instructor in mind. This resource contains lecture notes for each chapter and also suggests which parts of the chapter to cover in class and which to leave to the students for independent study. The manual also includes a helpful assignment grid indicating subject content and degree of difficulty of each exercise.

PowerPoint® Slides

The PowerPoint® slides, prepared and completely updated by Patrick Wheeler of University of South Florida, provide colorful lecture outlines of each chapter of the text, incorporating text graphics and flowcharts where needed.

Test Bank

The *Test Bank*, written and updated by the text author, contains true/false, multiple-choice, short answer, and essay questions. It is available in both print and computerized ExamView® versions.

Solutions Manual

The *Solutions Manual*, written by the author, contains solutions to all end-of-chapter problems and cases. Adopting instructors may download the *Solutions Manual* under password protection at the Instructor's Resource page of the book's web site.

Instructor's Resource CD-ROM with ExamView®

Key instructor ancillaries (*Solutions Manual*, *Instructor's Manual*, Test Bank, and PowerPoint® presentation slides) are provided on CD-ROM—giving instructors the ultimate tool for customizing lectures and presentations. The Test Bank files on the CD are provided in ExamView® format. This program is an easy-to-use test creation software compatible with Microsoft® Windows. Instructors can add or edit questions, instructions, and answers, and select questions (randomly or numerically) by previewing them on the screen. Instructors can also create and administer quizzes online, whether over the Internet, a local area network (LAN), or a wide area network (WAN).

ACKNOWLEDGMENTS

I want to thank the Institute of Internal Auditors, Inc., and the Institute of Certified Management Accountants for permission to use problem materials from past examinations. I would also like to thank Zhen Zhou for her work on the text and the verification of the Solutions Manual. Finally, I would like to extend special thanks to Georgia Smedley, Ph.D., UNLV, for her help in providing additional problem materials for select chapters.

I am grateful to the following people for reviewing the book in development and for providing helpful comments for this new edition:

Beth Brilliant
Kean University

Kevin E. Dow
Kent State University

H.P. Garsombke
University of Nebraska, Omaha

Alan Levitan
University of Louisville

Sakthi Mahenthiran
Butler University

Jeff L. Payne
University of Kentucky

In addition, I would like to thank recent reviewers of the text:

Sarah Brown
University of North Alabama

H. Sam Riner
Southern Arkansas University

David M. Cannon
Grand Valley State University

Helen M. Savage
Youngstown State University

James Holmes
University of Kentucky

Jerry D. Siebel
University of South Florida

Frank Ilett
Boise State University

Richard M. Sokolowski
Teikyo Post University

Andrew D. Luzi
California State University, Fullerton

Patrick Wheeler
University of Missouri, Columbia

Srini Ragothaman
University of South Dakota

James A. Hall
Lehigh University

Dedication

To my wife Eileen, and my children Elizabeth and Katie

part 1

OVERVIEW OF ACCOUNTING INFORMATION SYSTEMS

chapter 1

The Information System: An Accountant's Perspective

LEARNING OBJECTIVES

After studying this chapter, you should:

- Understand the primary information flows within the business environment.
- Understand the difference between accounting information systems and management information systems.
- Understand the difference between a financial transaction and a nonfinancial transaction.
- Know the principle features of the general model for information systems.
- Be familiar with the functional areas of a business and their principle activities.
- Understand the stages in the evolution of information systems.
- Understand the relationship between external auditing, internal auditing, and IT auditing.

Unlike many other accounting subjects, such as intermediate accounting, **accounting information systems (AIS)** lacks a well-defined body of knowledge. Much controversy exists among college faculty as to what should and should not be covered in the AIS course. To some extent, however, the controversy is being resolved through recent legislation. The Sarbanes-Oxley (SOX) Act of 2002 established new corporate governance regulations and standards for public companies registered with the Securities and Exchange Commission (SEC). This wide-sweeping legislation impacts public companies, their management, and their auditors. Of particular importance to students of AIS is SOX's impact on internal control standards and related auditing procedures. Whereas SOX does not define the entire content of the AIS course, it does identify critical areas of study for accountants that need to be included in it. These topics and more are covered in several chapters of this text.

The purpose of this chapter is to place the subject of accounting information systems in perspective for accountants. Toward this end, the chapter is divided into four major sections, each dealing with a different aspect of information systems. The first section explores the information environment of the firm. It introduces basic systems concepts, identifies the types of information used in business, and describes the flows of information through an organization. This section also presents a framework for viewing accounting information systems in relation to other information systems components. The second section of the chapter deals with the impact of organizational structure on AIS. Here we examine the business organization as a system of functional areas. The accounting function plays an important role as the purveyor of financial information for the rest of the organization. The third section reviews the evolution of information systems. Over the years, AIS has been represented by a number of different approaches or models. Five AIS models are examined. The final section discusses the role of accountants as users, designers, and auditors of AIS.

THE INFORMATION ENVIRONMENT

We begin the study of AIS with the recognition that information is a business resource. Like the other business resources of raw materials, capital, and labor, information is vital to the survival of the contemporary business organization. Every business day, vast quantities of information flow to decision makers and other users to meet a variety of internal needs. In addition, information flows out from the organization to external users, such as customers, suppliers, and stakeholders who have an interest in the firm. Figure 1-1 presents an overview of these internal and external **information flows.**

The pyramid in Figure 1-1 shows the business organization divided horizontally into several levels of activity. Business operations form the base of the pyramid. These activities consist of the product-oriented work of the organization, such as manufacturing, sales, and distribution. Above the base level, the organization is divided into three management tiers: operations management, middle management, and top management. Operations management is directly responsible for controlling day-to-day operations. Middle management is accountable for the short-term planning and coordination of activities necessary to accomplish organizational objectives. Top management is responsible for longer-term planning and setting organizational objectives. Every individual in the organization, from business operations to top management, needs information to accomplish his or her tasks.

Notice in Figure 1-1 how information flows in two directions within the organization: horizontally and vertically. The horizontal flow supports operations-level tasks with highly detailed information about the many business transactions affecting the firm. This

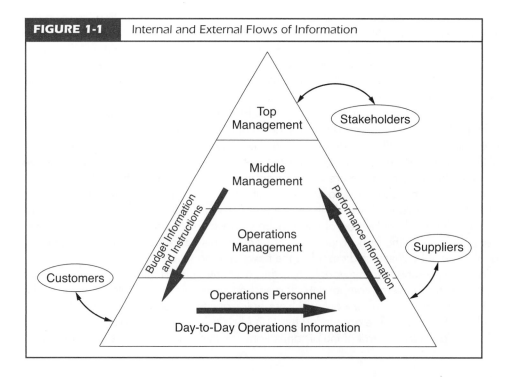

FIGURE 1-1   Internal and External Flows of Information

includes information on events such as the sale and shipment of goods, the use of labor and materials in the production process, and internal transfers of resources from one department to another. The vertical flow distributes summarized information about operations and other activities upward to managers at all levels. Management uses this information to support its various planning and control functions. Information also flows downward from senior managers to junior managers and operations personnel in the form of instructions, quotas, and budgets.

A third flow of information depicted in Figure 1-1 represents exchanges between the organization and users in the external environment. External users fall into two groups: **trading partners** and **stakeholders**. Exchanges with trading partners include customer sales and billing information, purchase information for suppliers, and inventory receipts information. Stakeholders are entities outside (or inside) the organization with a direct or indirect interest in the firm. Stockholders, financial institutions, and government agencies are examples of external stakeholders. Information exchanges with these groups include financial statements, tax returns, and stock transaction information. Inside stakeholders include accountants and internal auditors.

All user groups have unique information requirements. The level of detail and the nature of the information they receive differ considerably. For example, managers cannot use the highly detailed information needed by operations personnel. Management information is thus more summarized and oriented toward reporting on overall performance and problems rather than routine operations. The information must identify potential problems in time for management to take corrective action. External stakeholders, on the other hand, require information very different from that of management and operations users. Their financial statement information, based on generally accepted accounting principles, is accrual-based and far too aggregated for most internal uses.

WHAT IS A SYSTEM?

For many, the term **system** generates mental images of computers and programming. In fact, the term has much broader applicability. Some systems are naturally occurring, whereas others are artificial. Natural systems range from the atom—a system of electrons, protons, and neutrons—to the universe—a system of galaxies, stars, and planets. All life forms, plant and animal, are examples of natural systems. Artificial systems are man-made. These systems include everything from clocks to submarines and social systems to information systems.

Elements of a System

Regardless of their origin, all systems possess some common elements. The following definition specifies:

> A system is a group of two or more interrelated components or subsystems that serve a common purpose.

Let's analyze this general definition to gain an understanding of how it applies to businesses and information systems.

Multiple Components. A system must contain more than one part. For example, a yo-yo carved from a single piece of wood and attached to a string is a system. Without the string, it is not a system.

Relatedness. A common purpose relates the multiple parts of the system. Although each part functions independently of the others, all parts serve a common objective. If a particular component does not contribute to the common goal, then it is not part of the system.

For instance, a pair of ice skates and a volleyball net are both components. They lack a common purpose, however, and thus do not form a system.

System versus Subsystem. The distinction between the terms *system* and *subsystem* is a matter of perspective. For our purposes, these terms are interchangeable. A system is called a **subsystem** when it is viewed in relation to the larger system of which it is a part. Likewise, a subsystem is called a system when it is the focus of attention. Animals, plants, and other life forms are systems. They are also subsystems of the ecosystem in which they exist. From a different perspective, animals are systems composed of many smaller subsystems, such as the circulatory subsystem and the respiratory subsystem.

Purpose. A system must serve at least one purpose, but it may serve several. Whether a system provides a measure of time, electrical power, or information, serving a purpose is its fundamental justification. When a system ceases to serve a purpose, it should be replaced.

An Example of an Artificial System

An automobile is an example of an artificial system that is familiar to most of us and that satisfies the definition of a system provided above. To simplify matters, let's assume that the automobile system serves only one purpose: providing conveyance. To do so requires the harmonious interaction of hundreds or even thousands of subsystems. For simplicity, Figure 1-2 depicts only a few of these.

Figure 1-2 illustrates two points of particular importance to the study of information systems: system decomposition and subsystem interdependency.

System Decomposition. Decomposition is the process of dividing the system into smaller subsystem parts. This is a convenient way of representing, viewing, and understanding the

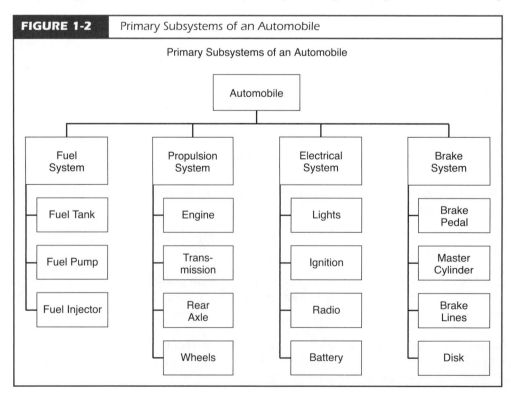

FIGURE 1-2   Primary Subsystems of an Automobile

relationships among subsystems. By decomposing a system, we can present the overall system as a hierarchy and view the relationships between subordinate and higher-level subsystems. Each subordinate subsystem performs one or more specific functions to help achieve the overall objective of the higher-level system. Figure 1-2 shows an automobile decomposed into four primary subsystems: the fuel subsystem, the propulsion subsystem, the electrical subsystem, and the braking subsystem. Each contributes in a unique way to the system's objective, conveyance. These second-level subsystems are decomposed further into two or more subordinate subsystems at a third level. Each third-level subsystem performs a task in direct support of its second-level system.

Subsystem Interdependency. A system's ability to achieve its goal depends on the effective functioning and harmonious interaction of its subsystems. If a vital subsystem fails or becomes defective and can no longer meet its specific objective, the overall system will fail to meet its objective. For example, if the fuel pump (a vital subsystem of the fuel system) fails, then the fuel system fails. With the failure of the fuel system (a vital subsystem of the automobile), the entire system fails. On the other hand, when a nonvital subsystem fails, the primary objective of the overall system can still be met. For instance, if the radio (a subsystem of the electrical system) fails, the automobile can still convey passengers.

Designers of all types of systems need to recognize the consequences of subsystem failure and provide the appropriate level of control. For example, a systems designer may provide control by designing a backup (redundant) subsystem that comes into play when the primary subsystem fails. Control should be provided on a cost-benefit basis. It is neither economical nor necessary to back up every subsystem. Backup is essential, however, when excessive negative consequences result from a subsystem failure. Hence, virtually every modern automobile has a backup braking system, whereas very few have backup stereo systems.

Like automobile designers, information system designers need to identify critical subsystems, anticipate the risk of their failure, and design cost-effective control procedures to mitigate that risk. As we shall see in subsequent chapters, accountants feature prominently in this activity.

AN INFORMATION SYSTEMS FRAMEWORK

The **information system** is the set of formal procedures by which data are collected, processed into information, and distributed to users.

Figure 1-3 shows the information system of a hypothetical manufacturing firm decomposed into its elemental subsystems. Notice that two broad classes of systems emerge from the decomposition: the *accounting information system (AIS)* and the *management information system (MIS)*. We will use this framework to identify the domain of AIS and distinguish it from MIS. Keep in mind that Figure 1-3 is a conceptual view; physical information systems are not typically organized into such discrete packages. More often, MIS and AIS functions are integrated to achieve operational efficiency.

The distinction between AIS and MIS centers on the concept of a transaction, as illustrated by Figure 1-4. The information system accepts input, called transactions, which are converted through various processes into output information that goes to users. Transactions fall into two classes: *financial transactions* and *nonfinancial transactions*. Before exploring this distinction, let's first broadly define the term *transaction*:

> A **transaction** is an event that affects or is of interest to the organization and is processed by its information system as a unit of work.

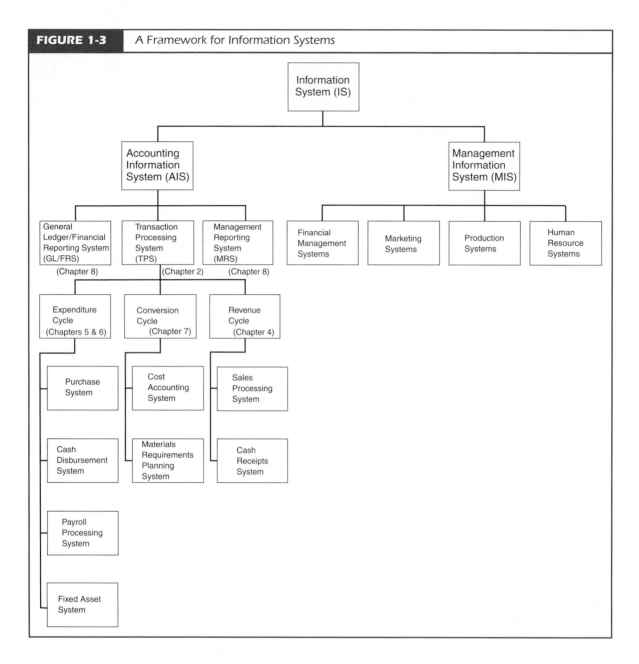

FIGURE 1-3   A Framework for Information Systems

This definition encompasses both financial and nonfinancial events. Since financial transactions are of particular importance to the accountant's understanding of information systems, we need a precise definition for this class of transaction:

A **financial transaction** is an economic event that affects the assets and equities of the organization, is reflected in its accounts, and is measured in monetary terms.

Sales of products to customers, purchases of inventory from vendors, and cash disbursements and receipts are examples of financial transactions. Every business organization is legally bound to correctly process these types of transactions.

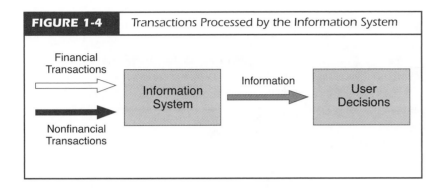

FIGURE 1-4   Transactions Processed by the Information System

Nonfinancial transactions are events that do not meet the narrow definition of a financial transaction. For example, adding a new supplier of raw materials to the list of valid suppliers is an event that may be processed by the enterprise's information system as a transaction. Important as this information obviously is, it is not a financial transaction, and the firm has no legal obligation to process it correctly—or at all.

Financial transactions and nonfinancial transactions are closely related and are often processed by the same physical system. For example, consider a financial portfolio management system that collects and tracks stock prices (nonfinancial transactions). When the stocks reach a threshold price the system places an automatic buy or sell order (financial transaction). Buying high and selling low is not against the law, but it is bad for business. Nevertheless, no law requires company management to design optimal buy and sell rules into their system. Once the buy or sell order is placed, however, the processing of this financial transaction must comply with legal and professional guidelines.

The Accounting Information System

AIS subsystems process financial transactions and nonfinancial transactions that directly affect the processing of financial transactions. For example, changes to customers' names and addresses are processed by the AIS to keep the customer file current. Although not technically financial transactions, these changes provide vital information for processing future sales to the customer.

The AIS is composed of three major subsystems: (1) the **transaction processing system (TPS)**, which supports daily business operations with numerous reports, documents and messages for users throughout the organization; (2) the **general ledger/financial reporting system (GL/FRS)**, which produces the traditional financial statements, such as the income statement, balance sheet, statement of cash flows, tax returns, and other reports required by law; and (3) the **management reporting system (MRS)**, which provides internal management with special-purpose financial reports and information needed for decision making such as budgets, variance reports, and responsibility reports. We examine each of these subsystems later in this chapter.

The Management Information System

Management often requires information that goes beyond the capability of AIS. As organizations grow in size and complexity, specialized functional areas emerge, requiring additional information for production planning and control, sales forecasting, inventory warehouse planning, market research, and so on. The **management information system (MIS)** processes nonfinancial transactions that are not normally processed by traditional AIS. Table 1-1 gives examples of typical MIS applications related to functional areas of a firm.

TABLE 1-1	Examples of MIS Applications in Functional Areas

Function	Examples of MIS Applications
Production	Production Planning and Control Systems Job Scheduling Systems
Finance	Portfolio Management Systems Capital Budgeting Systems
Marketing	Market Analysis New Product Development Product Analysis
Distribution	Warehouse Organization and Scheduling Delivery Scheduling Vehicle Loading and Allocation Models
Personnel	Human Resource Management Systems • Job skill tracking system • Employee benefits system

Why is it Important to Distinguish between AIS and MIS?

Sarbanes-Oxley legislation requires that management designs and implements controls over the entire financial reporting process. This includes the financial reporting system, the general ledger system, and the transaction processing systems that supply the data for financial reporting. SOX further requires that management certify these controls and that the external auditors express an opinion on control effectiveness. Because of the highly integrative nature of modern information systems, management and auditors need a conceptual view of the information system that distinguishes key processes and areas of risk and legal responsibility from the other (non-legally binding) aspects of the system. Without such a model, critical management and audit responsibilities under SOX may not be met.

AIS SUBSYSTEMS

We devote separate chapters to an in-depth study of each AIS subsystem depicted in Figure 1-3. At this point, we shall briefly outline the role of each subsystem.

Transaction Processing System

The transaction processing system (TPS) is central to the overall function of the information system by:

● Converting economic events into financial transactions.

● Recording financial transactions in the accounting records (journals and ledgers).

● Distributing essential financial information to operations personnel to support their daily operations.

The transaction processing system deals with business events that occur frequently. In a given day, a firm may process thousands of transactions. To deal efficiently with such volume, similar types of transactions are grouped together into *transaction cycles*. The TPS consists of three transaction cycles: the *revenue cycle*, the *expenditure cycle*, and the *conversion cycle*. Each cycle captures and processes different types of financial transactions. Chapter 2 provides an overview of transaction processing. Chapters 4, 5, 6, and 7 deal with the revenue, expenditure, and conversion cycles.

General Ledger/Financial Reporting Systems

The general ledger system (GLS) and the financial reporting system (FRS) are two closely related subsystems. However, because of their operational interdependency, they are generally viewed as a single integrated system—the GL/FRS. The bulk of the input to the GL portion of the system comes from the transaction cycles. Summaries of transaction cycle activity are processed by the GLS to update the general ledger control accounts. Other, less frequent events, such as stock transactions, mergers, and lawsuit settlements, for which there may be no formal processing cycle in place, also enter the GLS through alternate sources.

The financial reporting system measures and reports the status of financial resources and the changes in those resources. The FRS communicates this information primarily to external users. This type of reporting is called *nondiscretionary* because the organization has few or no choices in the information it provides. Much of this information consists of traditional financial statements, tax returns, and other legal documents.

Management Reporting System

The management reporting system (MRS) provides the internal financial information needed to manage a business. Managers must deal immediately with many day-to-day business problems, as well as plan and control their operations. Managers require different information for the various kinds of decisions they must make. Typical reports produced by the MRS include budgets, variance reports, cost-volume-profit analyses, and reports using current (rather than historical) cost data. This type of reporting is called discretionary reporting because the organization can choose what information to report and how to present it.

A GENERAL MODEL FOR AIS

Figure 1-5 presents the **general model for viewing AIS applications**. This is a general model because it describes all information systems, regardless of their technological architecture. The elements of the general model are end users, data sources, data collection, data processing, database management, information generation, and feedback.

End Users

End users fall into two general groups: *external* and *internal*. External users include creditors, stockholders, potential investors, regulatory agencies, tax authorities, suppliers, and customers. Institutional users such as banks, the SEC, and the IRS receive information in the form of financial statements, tax returns, and other reports that the firm has a legal obligation to produce. Trading partners (customers and suppliers) receive transaction-oriented information including purchase orders, billing statements, and shipping documents.

Internal users include management at every level of the organization, as well as operations personnel. In contrast to external reporting, the organization has a great deal of latitude in the way it meets the needs of internal users. Although there are some well-accepted conventions and practices, internal reporting is governed primarily by what gets the job done. System designers, including accountants, must balance the desires of internal users against legal and economic concerns such as adequate control and security, proper accountability, and the cost of providing alternative forms of information. Thus internal reporting poses a less structured and generally more difficult challenge than external reporting.

FIGURE 1-5	General Model for Accounting Information Systems

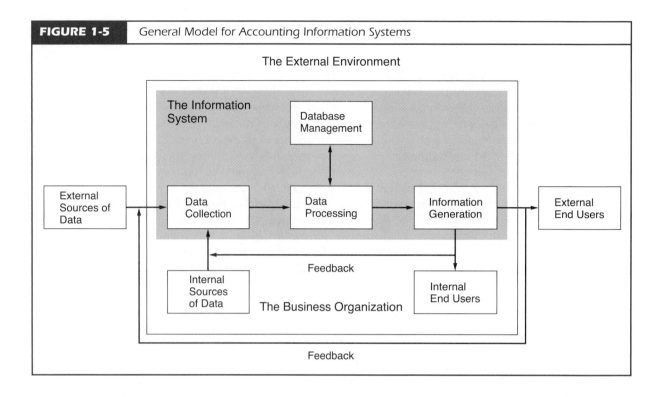

Data versus Information.

Data versus Information. Before discussing the data sources portion of Figure 1-5, we must make an important distinction between the terms *data* and *information*. **Data** are facts, which may or may not be processed (edited, summarized, or refined) and have no direct effect on the user. By contrast, **information** causes the user to take an action that he or she otherwise could not, or would not, have taken. Information is often defined simply as processed data. This is an inadequate definition. Information is determined by the *effect* it has on the user, not by its physical form. For example, a purchasing agent receives a daily report listing raw material inventory items that are at low levels. This report causes the agent to place orders for more inventory. The facts in this report have information content for the purchasing agent. However, this same report in the hands of the personnel manager is a mere collection of facts, or data, causing no action and having no information content.

We can see from this example that one person's information is another person's data. Thus, information is not just a set of processed facts arranged in a formal report. Information allows users to take action to resolve conflicts, reduce uncertainty, and make decisions. We should note that action does not necessarily mean a physical act. For instance, a purchasing agent who receives a report showing that inventory levels are adequate will respond by ordering nothing. The agent's action to do nothing is a conscious decision, triggered by information and different from doing nothing because of being uninformed.

The distinction between data and information has pervasive implications for the study of information systems. If output from the information system fails to cause users to act, the system serves no purpose and has failed in its primary objective.

Data Sources

Data sources are financial transactions that enter the information system from both internal and external sources. *External financial transactions* are the most common source of data for most organizations. These are economic exchanges with other business entities and individuals outside the firm. Examples include the sale of goods and services, the purchase of inventory, the receipt of cash, and the disbursement of cash (including payroll). *Internal financial transactions* involve the exchange or movement of resources within the organization. Examples include the movement of raw materials into work-in-process (WIP), the application of labor and overhead to WIP, the transfer of WIP into finished goods inventory, and the depreciation of plant and equipment.

Data Collection

Data collection is the first operational stage in the information system. The objective is to ensure that event data entering the system are valid, complete, and free from material errors. In many respects, this is the most important stage in the system. Should transaction errors pass through data collection undetected, the system may process the errors and generate erroneous and unreliable output. This, in turn, could lead to incorrect actions and poor decisions by the users.

Two rules govern the design of data collection procedures: *relevance* and *efficiency*. The information system should capture only relevant data. A fundamental task of the system designer is to determine what is and what is not relevant. He or she does so by analyzing the user's needs. Only data that ultimately contribute to information (as defined previously) are relevant. The data collection stage should be designed to filter irrelevant facts from the system.

Efficient data collection procedures are designed to collect data only once. These data can then be made available to multiple users. Capturing the same data more than once leads to data redundancy and inconsistency. Information systems have limited collection, processing, and data storage capacity. Data redundancy overloads facilities and reduces the overall efficiency of the system. Inconsistency among redundant data elements can result in inappropriate actions and bad decisions.

Data Processing

Once collected, data usually require processing to produce information. Tasks in the **data processing** stage range from simple to complex. Examples include mathematical algorithms (such as linear programming models) used for production scheduling applications, statistical techniques for sales forecasting, and posting and summarizing procedures used for accounting applications.

Database Management

The organization's **database** is its physical repository for financial and nonfinancial data. We use the term *database* in the generic sense. It can be a filing cabinet or a computer disk. Regardless of the database's physical form, we can represent its contents in a logical hierarchy. The levels in the data hierarchy—*attribute, record,* and *file*—are illustrated in Figure 1-6.

Data Attribute. The data attribute is the most elemental piece of potentially useful data in the database. An attribute is a logical and relevant characteristic of an entity about which the firm captures data. The attributes shown in Figure 1-6 are *logical* because they all relate sensibly to a common entity—accounts receivable. Each attribute is also *relevant* because it contributes to the information content of the entire set. As proof of this, the absence of any single relevant attribute diminishes or destroys the information content of the set. The addition of irrelevant or illogical data would not enhance the information content of the set.

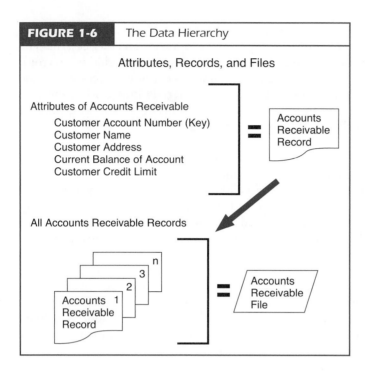

FIGURE 1-6   The Data Hierarchy

Attributes, Records, and Files

Attributes of Accounts Receivable

Customer Account Number (Key)
Customer Name
Customer Address
Current Balance of Account
Customer Credit Limit

= Accounts Receivable Record

All Accounts Receivable Records

Accounts Receivable Record 1 2 3 n

= Accounts Receivable File

Record. A record is a complete set of attributes for a single occurrence within an entity class. For example, a particular customer's name, address, and account balance is one occurrence (or record) within the accounts receivable class. To find a particular record within the database, we must be able to identify it uniquely. Therefore, every record in the database must be unique in at least one attribute.[1] This unique identifier attribute is the *primary key*. Because no natural attribute (such as customer name) can guarantee uniqueness, we typically assign artificial keys to records. The key for the accounts receivable records in Figure 1-6 is the customer account number. This is the only unique identifier in this record class. The other attributes possess values that may also exist in other records. For instance, multiple customers may have the same name, sales amounts, credit limits, and balances. Using any one of these as a key to find a record in a large database would be a difficult task. These nonunique attributes are, however, often used as *secondary keys* for categorizing data. For example, the account balance attribute can be used to prepare a list of customers with balances greater than $10,000.

Files. A file is a complete set of records of an identical class. For example, *all* the accounts receivable records of the organization constitute the accounts receivable file. Similarly, files are constructed for other classes of records such as inventory, accounts payable, and payroll. The organization's database is the entire collection of such files.

Database Management Tasks. **Database management** involves three fundamental tasks: *storage*, *retrieval*, and *deletion*. The storage task assigns keys to new records and stores them in their proper location in the database. Retrieval is the task of locating and extracting an existing record from the database for processing. After processing is

---

1   When we get into more advanced topics, we will see how a combination of nonunique attributes can be used as a unique identifier.

complete, the storage task restores the updated record to its place in the database. Deletion is the task of permanently removing obsolete or redundant records from the database.

Information Generation

Information generation is the process of compiling, arranging, formatting, and presenting information to users. Information can be an operational document such as a sales order, a structured report, or a message on a computer screen. Regardless of physical form, useful information has the following characteristics: *relevance, timeliness, accuracy, completeness,* and *summarization.*

Relevance. The contents of a report or document must serve a purpose. This could be to support a manager's decision or a clerk's task. We have established that only data relevant to a user's action have information content. Therefore, the information system should present only relevant data in its reports. Reports containing irrelevancies waste resources and may be counterproductive to the user. Irrelevancies detract attention from the true message of the report and may result in incorrect decisions or actions.

Timeliness. The age of information is a critical factor in determining its usefulness. Information must be no older than the time period of the action it supports. For example, if a manager makes decisions daily to purchase inventory from a supplier based on an inventory status report, then the information in the report should be no more than a day old.

Accuracy. Information must be free from material errors. However, materiality is a difficult concept to quantify. It has no absolute value; it is a problem-specific concept. This means that, in some cases, information must be perfectly accurate. In other instances, the level of accuracy may be lower. Material error exists when the amount of inaccuracy in information causes the user to make poor decisions or to fail to make necessary decisions. We sometimes must sacrifice absolute accuracy to obtain timely information. Often, perfect information is not available within the user's decision time frame. Therefore, in providing information, system designers seek a balance between information that is as accurate as possible, yet timely enough to be useful.

Completeness. No piece of information essential to a decision or task should be missing. For example, a report should provide all necessary calculations and present its message clearly and unambiguously.

Summarization. Information should be aggregated in accordance with the user's needs. Lower-level managers tend to need information that is highly detailed. As information flows upward through the organization to top management, it becomes more summarized. We shall look more closely at the effects that organizational structure and managerial level have on information reporting later in this chapter.

Feedback

Feedback is a form of output that is sent back to the system as a source of data. Feedback may be *internal* or *external* and is used to initiate or alter a process. For example, an inventory status report signals the inventory control clerk that items of inventory have fallen to, or below, their minimum allowable levels. Internal feedback from this information will *initiate* the inventory ordering process to replenish the inventories. Similarly, external feedback about the level of uncollected customer accounts can be used to *adjust* the organization's credit-granting policies.

Information System Objectives

Each organization must tailor its information system to the needs of its users. Therefore, specific information system objectives may differ from firm to firm. However, three fundamental objectives are common to all systems. They are:

1. *To support the stewardship function of management.* Stewardship refers to management's responsibility to properly manage the resources of the firm. The information system provides information about resource utilization to external users via traditional financial statements and other mandated reports. Internally, management receives stewardship information from various responsibility reports.
2. *To support management decision making.* The information system supplies managers with the information they need to carry out their decision-making responsibilities.
3. *To support the firm's day-to-day operations.* The information system provides information to operations personnel to assist them in the efficient and effective discharge of their daily tasks.

ACQUISITION OF INFORMATION SYSTEMS

We conclude this section with a brief discussion of how organizations obtain information systems. Usually, they do so in two ways: (1) they develop customized systems from scratch through in-house systems development activities, and (2) they purchase preprogrammed commercial systems from software vendors. Larger organizations with unique and frequently changing needs engage in in-house development. The formal process by which this is accomplished is called the **system development life cycle**. Smaller companies and larger firms that have standardized information needs are the primary market for commercial software. Three basic types of commercial software are turnkey systems, backbone systems, and vendor-supported systems.

Turnkey systems are completely finished and tested systems that are ready for implementation. Typically, they are general-purpose systems or systems customized to a specific industry. In either case, the end user must have standard business practices that permit the use of "canned" or "off-the-shelf" systems. The better turnkey systems, however, have built-in software options that allow the user to customize input, output, and processing through menu choices. However, configuring the systems to meet user needs can be a formidable task. Enterprise resource planning (ERP) systems such as *Oracle, SAP, J.D. Edwards*, and *PeopleSoft* are examples of this approach to systems implementation. ERP systems are discussed later in this chapter.

Backbone systems consist of a basic system structure on which to build. The primary processing logic is preprogrammed, and the vendor then designs the user interfaces to suit the client's unique needs. A backbone system is a compromise between a custom system and a turnkey system. This approach can produce satisfactory results, but customizing the system is costly.

Vendor-supported systems are custom (or customized) systems that client organizations purchase commercially rather than develop in-house. Under this approach, the software vendor designs, implements, and maintains the system for its client. This is a popular option with health-care and legal services organizations that have complex systems requirements but are not of sufficient magnitude to justify retaining an in-house systems development staff. Indeed, this has become a popular option for many organizations that traditionally have relied on in-house development but have chosen to outsource these activities. In recent years, public accounting firms have expanded their involvement in the vendor-supported market.

ORGANIZATIONAL STRUCTURE

The structure of an organization reflects the distribution of responsibility, authority, and accountability throughout the organization. These flows are illustrated in Figure 1-7. Firms achieve their overall objectives by establishing measurable financial goals for their operational units. For example, budget information flows downward. This is the mechanism by which senior management conveys to their subordinates the standards against which they will be measured for the coming period. The results of the subordinates' actions, in the form of performance information, flow upward to senior management. Understanding the distribution pattern of responsibility, authority, and accountability is essential for assessing user information needs.

BUSINESS SEGMENTS

Business organizations consist of functional units or **segments.** Firms organize into segments to promote internal efficiencies through the specialization of labor and cost-effective resource allocations. Managers within a segment can focus their attention on narrow areas of responsibility to achieve higher levels of operating efficiency. Three of the most common approaches include segmentation by:

1. *Geographic Location.* Many organizations have operations dispersed across the country and around the world. They do this to gain access to resources, markets, or lines of distribution. A convenient way to manage such operations is to organize the management of the firm around each geographic segment as a quasi-autonomous entity.
2. *Product Line.* Companies that produce highly diversified products often organize around product lines, creating separate divisions for each. Product segmentation allows the organization to devote specialized management, labor, and resources to segments separately, almost as if they were separate firms.
3. *Business Function.* Functional segmentation divides the organization into areas of specialized responsibility based on tasks. The functional areas are determined according

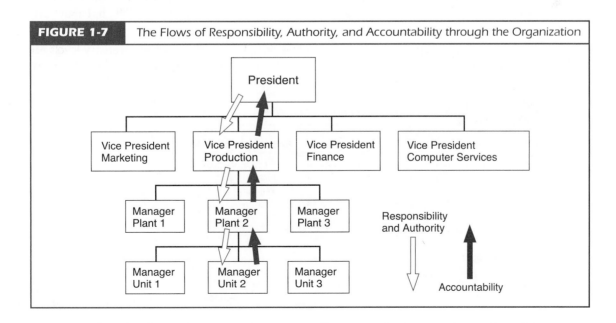

FIGURE 1-7   The Flows of Responsibility, Authority, and Accountability through the Organization

to the flow of primary resources through the firm. Examples of business function segments are marketing, production, finance, and accounting.

Some firms use more than one method of segmentation. For instance, an international conglomerate may segment its operations first geographically, then by product within each geographic region, and then functionally within each product segment.

FUNCTIONAL SEGMENTATION

Segmentation by business function is the most common method of organizing. To illustrate it, we will assume a manufacturing firm that uses these resources: materials, labor, financial capital, and information. Table 1-2 shows the relationship between functional segments and these resources.

The titles of functions and even the functions themselves will vary greatly among organizations, depending on their size and line of business. A public utility may have little in the way of a marketing function compared to an automobile manufacturer. A service organization may have no formal production function and little in the way of inventory to manage. One firm may call its labor resource *personnel*, whereas another uses the term *human resources*. Keeping in mind these variations, we will briefly discuss the functional areas of the hypothetical firm shown in Figure 1-8. Because of their special importance to the study of information systems, the accounting and IT functions are given separate and more detailed treatment.

Materials Management

The objective of materials management is to plan and control the materials inventory of the company. A manufacturing firm must have sufficient inventories on hand to meet its production needs and yet avoid excessive inventory levels. Every dollar invested in inventory is a dollar that is not earning a return. Furthermore, idle inventory can become obsolete, lost, or stolen. Ideally, a firm would coordinate inventory arrivals from suppliers such that they move directly into the production process. As a practical matter, however, most organizations maintain safety stocks to carry them through the lead time between placing the order for inventory and its arrival. We see from Figure 1-8 that materials management has three subfunctions:

Purchasing is responsible for ordering inventory from vendors when inventory levels fall to their reorder points. The nature of this task varies among organizations. In some cases,

TABLE 1-2	**Functions from Resources**
Resource	**Business Function**
Materials	Inventory Management Production Marketing Distribution
Labor	Personnel
Financial Capital	Finance
Information	Accounting Information Technology

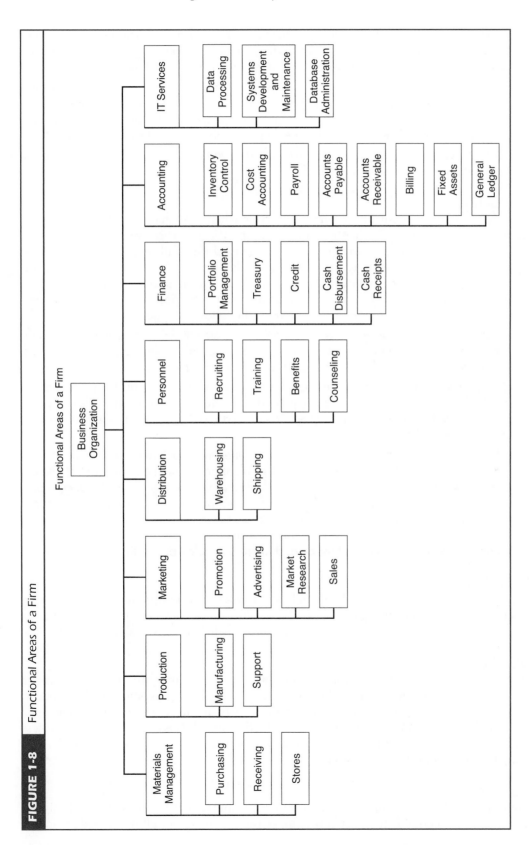

FIGURE 1-8   Functional Areas of a Firm

purchasing is no more than sending a purchase order to a designated vendor. In other cases, this task involves soliciting bids from a number of competing vendors. The nature of the business and the type of inventory determines the extent of the purchasing function.

Receiving is the task of accepting the inventory previously ordered by purchasing. Receiving activities include counting and checking the physical condition of these items. This is an organization's first, and perhaps only, opportunity to detect incomplete deliveries and damaged merchandise before they move into the production process.

Stores takes physical custody of the inventory received and releases these resources into the production process as needed.

Production

Production activities occur in the conversion cycle where raw materials, labor, and plant assets are used to create finished products. The specific activities are determined by the nature of the products being manufactured. In general they fall into two broad classes: (1) primary manufacturing activities and (2) production support activities. Primary manufacturing activities shape and assemble raw materials into finished products. Production support activities ensure that primary manufacturing activities operate efficiently and effectively. These include, but are not limited to, the following types of activities:

Production planning involves scheduling the flow of materials, labor, and machinery to efficiently meet production needs. This requires information about the status of sales orders, raw materials inventory, finished goods inventory, and machine and labor availability.

Quality control monitors the manufacturing process at various points to ensure that the finished products meet the firm's quality standards. Effective quality control detects problems early to facilitate corrective action. Failure to do so may result in excessive waste of materials and labor.

Maintenance keeps the firm's machinery and other manufacturing facilities in running order. The manufacturing process relies on its plant and equipment and cannot tolerate breakdowns during peak production periods. Therefore, the key to maintenance is prevention—the scheduled removal of equipment from operations for cleaning, servicing, and repairs. Many manufacturers have elaborate preventive maintenance programs. To plan and coordinate these activities, maintenance engineers need extensive information about the history of equipment usage and future scheduled production.

Marketing

The marketplace needs to know about, and have access to, a firm's products. The marketing function deals with the strategic problems of product promotion, advertising, and market research. On an operational level, marketing performs such daily activities as sales order entry.

Distribution

Distribution is the activity of getting the product to the customer after the sale. This is a critical step. Much can go wrong before the customer takes possession of the product. Excessive lags between the taking and filling of orders, incorrect shipments, or damaged merchandise can result in customer dissatisfaction and lost sales. Ultimately, success depends on filling orders accurately in the warehouse, packaging goods correctly, and shipping them quickly to the customer.

Personnel

Competent and reliable employees are a valuable resource to a business. The objective of the personnel function is to effectively manage this resource. A well-developed personnel function includes recruiting, training, continuing education, counseling, evaluating, labor relations, and compensation administration.

Finance

The finance function manages the financial resources of the firm through banking and treasury activities, portfolio management, credit evaluation, cash disbursements, and cash receipts. Because of the cyclical nature of business, many firms swing between positions of excess funds and cash deficits. In response to these cash flow patterns, financial planners seek lucrative investments in stocks and other assets and low-cost lines of credit from banks. The finance function also administers the daily flow of cash in and out of the firm.

THE ACCOUNTING FUNCTION

The accounting function manages the financial information resource of the firm. In this regard, it plays two important roles in transaction processing. First, accounting captures and records the financial effects of the firm's transactions. These include events such as the movement of raw materials from the warehouse into production, shipments of the finished products to customers, cash flows into the firm and deposits in the bank, the acquisition of inventory, and the discharge of financial obligations.

Second, the accounting function distributes transaction information to operations personnel to coordinate many of their key tasks. Accounting activities that contribute directly to business operations include inventory control, cost accounting, payroll, accounts payable, accounts receivable, billing, fixed-asset accounting, and the general ledger. We deal with each of these specifically in later chapters. For the moment, however, we need to maintain a broad view of accounting to understand its functional role in the organization.

The Value of Information

The value of information to a user is determined by its **reliability**. We saw earlier that the purpose of information is to lead the user to a desired action. For this to happen, information must possess certain attributes—relevance, accuracy, completeness, summarization, and timeliness. When these attributes are consistently present, information has reliability and provides value to the user. Unreliable information has no value. At best, it is a waste of resources; at worst it can lead to dysfunctional decisions. Consider the following example:

> A marketing manager signed a contract with a customer to supply a large quantity of product by a certain deadline. He made this decision based on information about finished goods inventory levels. However, because of faulty record keeping, the information was incorrect. The actual inventory levels of the product were insufficient to meet the order, and the necessary quantities could not be manufactured by the deadline. Failure to comply with the terms of the contract may result in litigation.

This bad sales decision was a result of flawed information. Effective decisions require information that has a high degree of reliability.

Accounting Independence

Information reliability rests heavily on the concept of accounting **independence**. Simply stated, accounting activities must be separate and independent of the functional areas that maintain custody of physical resources. For example, accounting monitors and records the movement of raw materials into production and the sale of finished goods to customers. Accounting authorizes purchases of raw materials and the disbursement of cash payments to vendors and employees. Accounting supports these functions with information but does not actively participate in the physical activities.

THE INFORMATION TECHNOLOGY FUNCTION

Returning to Figure 1-8, the final area to be discussed is the information technology (IT) function. Like accounting, the IT function is associated with the information resource. Its activities can be organized in a number of different ways. One extreme structure is the *centralized data processing* approach; at the other extreme is the *distributed data processing* approach. Most organizational structures fall somewhere between these extremes and embody elements of both.

Centralized Data Processing

Under the **centralized data processing** model, all data processing is performed by one or more large computers housed at a central site that serve users throughout the organization. Figure 1-9 illustrates this approach in which IT activities are consolidated and managed as a shared organization resource. End users compete for these resources on the basis of need. The IT function is usually treated as a cost center whose operating costs are charged back to the end users. Figure 1-10 shows the IT areas of operation in more detail. These include database administration, data processing, and systems development and maintenance. The key functions of each of these areas are described next.

Database Administration. Centrally organized companies maintain their data resources in a central location that is shared by all end users. In this shared data arrangement, a special independent group—database administration—headed by the database administrator is responsible for the security and integrity of the database. We explore the database concept and the role of the database administrator in Chapter 9.

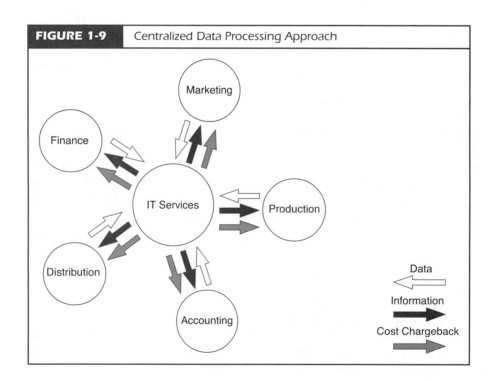

| FIGURE 1-9 | Centralized Data Processing Approach |

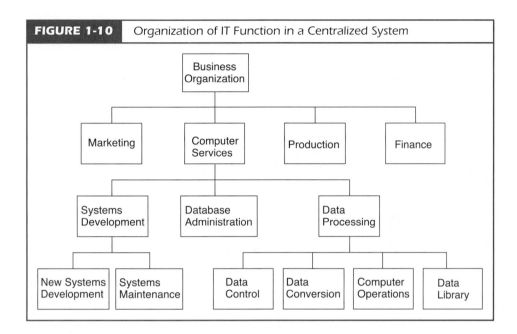

FIGURE 1-10   Organization of IT Function in a Centralized System

Data Processing. The data processing group manages the computer resources used to perform the day-to-day processing of transactions. It may consist of the following functions: *data control, data conversion, computer operations,* and the *data library.*

Some organizations have older legacy systems that use a *data control* group as a liaison between the end user and data processing. Data control is responsible for receiving batches of transaction documents for processing from end users and then distributing computer output (documents and reports) back to the users. The *data conversion* function transcribes transaction data from source (paper) documents to digital media (tape or disk) suitable for computer processing by the central computer, which is managed by the *computer operations group.* Accounting applications are usually run according to a strict schedule that is controlled by the central computer.

The *data library* is a room adjacent to the computer center that provides safe storage for the off-line data files, such as magnetic tapes and removable disk packs. A data librarian who is responsible for the receipt, storage, retrieval, and custody of data files controls access to the library. The librarian issues tapes to computer operators and takes custody of files when processing is completed. The move to real-time processing and direct access files (discussed in Chapter 2) has reduced or eliminated the role of the data librarian in most organizations.

Systems Development and Maintenance. The information needs of users are met by two related functions: systems development and systems maintenance. The former group is responsible for analyzing user needs and for designing new systems to satisfy those needs. The participants in system development include systems professionals, end users, and stakeholders.

Systems professionals include systems analysts, database designers, and programmers who design and build the system. Systems professionals gather facts about the user's problem, analyze the facts, and formulate a solution. The product of their efforts is a new information system.

End users are those for whom the system is built. They are the managers who receive reports from the system and the operations personnel who work directly with the system as part of their daily responsibilities.

Stakeholders are individuals inside or outside the firm who have an interest in the system but are not end users. They include management, internal auditors, and consultants who oversee systems development.

Once a new system has been designed and implemented, the systems maintenance group assumes responsibility for keeping it current with user needs. Over the course of the system's life (often several years), between 80 and 90 percent of its total cost will be attributable to maintenance activities.

Distributed Data Processing

An alternative to the centralized model is the concept of **distributed data processing (DDP)**. The topic of DDP is quite broad, touching on such related topics as end-user computing, commercial software, networking, and office automation. Simply stated, DDP involves reorganizing the IT function into small *information processing units* (IPUs) that are distributed to end users and placed under their control. IPUs may be distributed according to business function, geographic location, or both. Any or all of the IT activities represented in Figure 1-10 may be distributed. Figure 1-11 shows a possible new organizational structure following the distribution of all data processing tasks to the end-user areas.

Notice that the central IT function has been eliminated from the organization structure. Individual operational areas now perform this role. In recent years DDP has become an economic and operational feasibility that has revolutionized business operations. DDP is, however, a mixed bag of advantages and disadvantages. Some of the more important of these are discussed next.

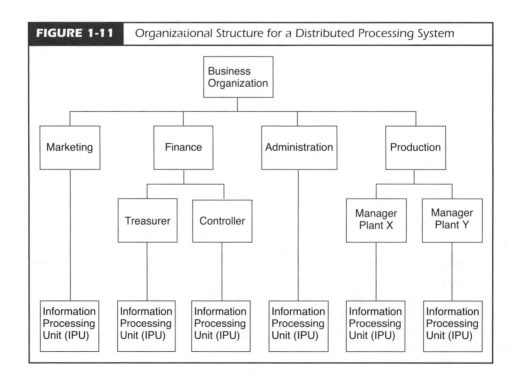

FIGURE 1-11   Organizational Structure for a Distributed Processing System

Disadvantages of DDP. We should bear in mind that the disadvantages of DDP might also be described as the advantages of a centralized approach. The discussion focuses on important issues that carry control implications that accountants should recognize. The loss of control is one of the most serious disadvantages of DDP. Other potential problems include the inefficient use of resources, the destruction of audit trails, inadequate segregation of duties, an increased potential for programming errors and systems failures, and the lack of standards. Specific problems are examined in the following section.

Mismanagement of organizationwide resources. Some argue that when organization-wide resources exceed a threshold amount, say 5 percent of the total operations budget, they should be controlled and monitored centrally. Information processing services (such as computer operations, programming, data conversion, and database management) represent a significant expenditure for many organizations. Those opposed to DDP argue that distributing responsibility for these resources will inevitably lead to their mismanagement and suboptimal utilization.

Hardware and software incompatibility. Distributing the responsibility for hardware and software purchases to user management can result in uncoordinated and poorly conceived decisions. Working independently, decision makers may settle on dissimilar and incompatible operating systems, technology platforms, spreadsheet programs, word processors, and database packages. Such hardware and software incompatibilities can degrade and disrupt communications between organizational units.

Redundant tasks. Autonomous systems development activities distributed throughout the firm can result in each user area reinventing the wheel. For example, application programs created by one user, which could be used with little or no change by others, will be redesigned from scratch rather than shared. Likewise, data common to many users may be re-created for each IPU, resulting in a high level of data redundancy.

Consolidating incompatible activities. The distribution of the IT function to individual user areas results in the creation of many very small units that may not permit the necessary separation of incompatible functions. For example, within a single IPU, the same person may program applications, perform program maintenance, enter transaction data into the computer, and operate the computer equipment. This situation represents a fundamental violation of internal control.

Hiring qualified professionals. End-user managers may lack the knowledge to evaluate the technical credentials and relevant experience of candidates applying for a position as a computer professional. Also, if the organizational unit into which a new employee is entering is small, the opportunity for personal growth, continuing education, and promotion may be limited. For these reasons, IPU managers sometimes experience difficulty attracting highly qualified personnel, which increases the risk of programming errors and systems failures.

Lack of standards. Because of the distribution of responsibility in the DDP environment, standards for developing and documenting systems, choosing programming languages, acquiring hardware and software, and evaluating performance may be unevenly applied or nonexistent. Opponents of DDP argue that the risks associated with the design and operation of a data processing system are made tolerable only if such standards are consistently applied. This requires that standards be imposed centrally.

Advantages of DDP. The most commonly cited advantages of DDP are related to cost savings, increased user satisfaction, and improved operational efficiency. Specific issues are discussed in the following section.

Cost reductions. In the past, achieving economies of scale was the principal justification for the centralized approach. The economics of data processing favored large, expensive, powerful computers. The wide variety of needs that such centralized systems had to satisfy called for computers that were highly generalized and employed complex operating systems.

Powerful yet inexpensive small scale, which can cost effectively perform specialized functions, have changed the economics of data processing dramatically. In addition, the unit cost of data storage, which was once the justification for consolidating data in a central location, is no longer the prime consideration. Moreover, the move to DDP can reduce costs in two other areas: (1) data can be entered and edited at the IPU, thus eliminating the centralized tasks of data conversion and data control; and (2) application complexity can be reduced, which in turn reduces development and maintenance costs.

Improved cost control responsibility. Managers assume the responsibility for the financial success of their operations. This requires that they be properly empowered with the authority to make decisions about resources that influence their overall success. Therefore, if information-processing capability is critical to the success of a business operation, then should not management be given control over these resources? This argument counters the argument presented earlier favoring the centralization of organizationwide resources. Proponents of DDP argue that the benefits from improved management attitudes outweigh the additional costs incurred from distributing these resources.

Improved user satisfaction. Perhaps the most often cited benefit of DDP is improved user satisfaction. This derives from three areas of need that too often go unsatisfied in the centralized approach: (1) as previously stated, users desire to control the resources that influence their profitability; (2) users want systems professionals (analysts, programmers, and computer operators) who are responsive to their specific situation; and (3) users want to become more actively involved in developing and implementing their own systems. Proponents of DDP argue that providing more customized support—feasible only in a distributed environment—has direct benefits for user morale and productivity.

Backup. The final argument in favor of DDP is the ability to back up computing facilities to protect against potential disasters such as fires, floods, sabotage, and earthquakes. One solution is to build excess capacity into each IPU. If a disaster destroys a single site, its transactions can be processed by the other IPUs. This requires close coordination between decision makers to ensure that they do not implement incompatible hardware and software at their sites.

The Need for Careful Analysis

DDP carries a certain leading-edge prestige value that, during an analysis of its pros and cons, may overwhelm important considerations of economic benefit and operational feasibility. Some organizations have made the move to DDP without fully considering whether the distributed organizational structure will better achieve their business objectives. Some DDP initiatives have proven ineffective, and even counterproductive, because decision makers saw in these systems virtues that were more symbolic than real. Before taking such an aggressive step, decision makers should assess the true merits of DDP for their organization. Accountants have an opportunity and an obligation to play an important role in this analysis.

THE EVOLUTION OF INFORMATION SYSTEM MODELS

Over the past 50 years, accounting information systems have been represented by a number of different approaches or models. Each new model evolved because of the shortcomings and limitations of its predecessor. An interesting feature in this evolution is that older models are not immediately replaced by the newest technique. Thus, at any point in time, various generations of systems exist across different organizations and may even coexist within a single enterprise. The modern auditor needs to be familiar with the operational features of all AIS approaches that he or she is likely to encounter. This book deals extensively with five such models: manual processes, flat-file systems, the database approach, the REA (resources, events, and agents) model, and ERP (enterprise resource planning) systems. Each of these is briefly outlined in the following section.

THE MANUAL PROCESS MODEL

The manual process model is the oldest and most traditional form of accounting systems. Manual systems constitute the physical events, resources, and personnel that characterize many business processes. This includes such tasks as order-taking, warehousing materials, manufacturing goods for sale, shipping goods to customers, and placing orders with vendors. Traditionally, this model also includes the physical task of record keeping. Often, manual record keeping is used to teach the principles of accounting to business students. This approach, however, is simply a training aid. These days, manual records are never used in practice.

Nevertheless, there is merit in studying the manual process model before mastering computer-based systems. First, learning manual systems helps establish an important link between the AIS course and other accounting courses. The AIS course is often the only accounting course in which students see where data originate, how they are collected, and how and where information is used to support day-to-day operations. By examining information flows, key tasks, and the use of traditional accounting records in transaction processing, the students' bookkeeping focus is transformed into a business processes perspective.

Second, the logic of a business process is more easily understood when it is not shrouded by technology. The information needed to trigger and support events such as selling, warehousing, and shipping is fundamental and independent of the technology that underlies the information system. For example, a shipping notice informing the billing process that a product has been shipped serves this purpose whether it is produced and processed manually or digitally. Once students understand what tasks need to be performed, they are better equipped to explore different and better ways of performing these tasks through technology.

Finally, manual procedures facilitate understanding internal control activities, including segregation of functions, supervision, independent verification, audit trails, and access controls. Because human nature lies at the heart of many internal control issues, we should not overlook the importance of this aspect of the information system.

THE FLAT-FILE MODEL

The flat-file approach is most often associated with so-called **legacy systems**. These are large mainframe systems that were implemented in the late 1960s through the 1980s. Organizations today still use these systems extensively. Eventually, they will be replaced by modern database management systems, but in the meantime accountants must continue to deal with legacy system technologies.

The **flat-file model** describes an environment in which individual data files are not related to other files. End users in this environment *own* their data files rather than *share* them with other users. Data processing is thus performed by standalone applications rather than integrated systems.

When multiple users need the same data for different purposes, they must obtain separate datasets structured to their specific needs. Figure 1-12 illustrates how customer sales data might be presented to three different users in a durable goods retailing organization. The accounting function needs customer sales data organized by account number and

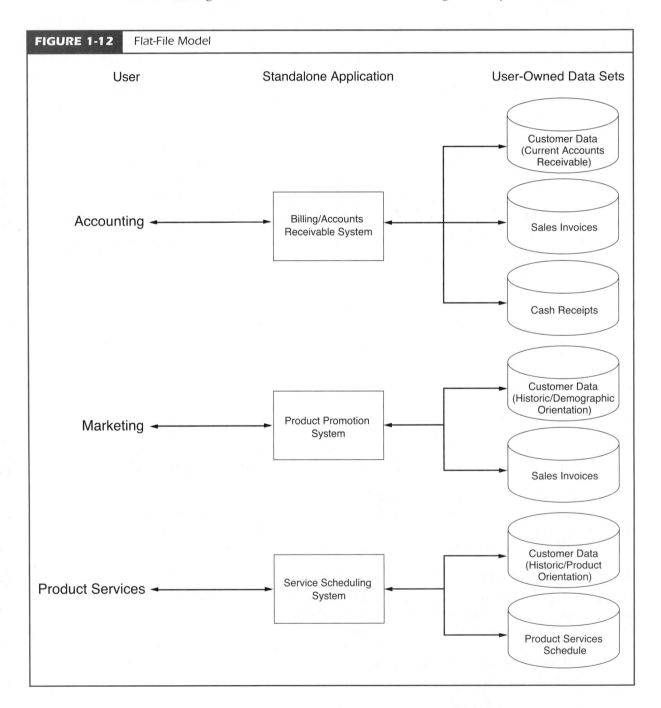

FIGURE 1-12   Flat-File Model

structured to show outstanding balances. This is used for customer billing, accounts receivable maintenance, and financial statement preparation. Marketing needs customer sales history data organized by demographic keys. They use this for targeting new product promotions and for selling product upgrades. The product services group needs customer sales data organized by products and structured to show scheduled service dates. Such information is used for making after-sales contacts with customers to schedule preventive maintenance and to solicit sales of service agreements.

The data redundancy demonstrated in this example contributes to three significant problems in the flat-file environment: **data storage, data updating,** and **currency of information.** These and other problems associated with flat files are discussed in following sections.

Data Storage
An efficient information system captures and stores data only once and makes this single source available to all users who need it. In the flat-file environment, this is not possible. To meet the private data needs of users, organizations must incur the costs of both multiple collection and multiple storage procedures. Some commonly used data may be duplicated dozens, hundreds, or even thousands of times.

Data Updating
Organizations have a great deal of data stored in files that require periodic updating to reflect changes. For example, a change to a customer's name or address must be reflected in the appropriate master files. When users keep separate files, all changes must be made separately for each user. This adds significantly to the task and the cost of data management.

Currency of Information
In contrast to the problem of performing multiple updates is the problem of failing to update all the user files affected by a change in status. If update information is not properly disseminated, the change will not be reflected in some users' data, resulting in decisions based on outdated information.

Task-Data Dependency
Another problem with the flat-file approach is the user's inability to obtain additional information as his or her needs change. This problem is called **task-data dependency.** The user's information set is constrained by the data that he or she possesses and controls. Users act independently rather than as members of a user community. In such an environment, it is very difficult to establish a mechanism for the formal sharing of data. Therefore, new information needs tend to be satisfied by procuring new data files. This takes time, inhibits performance, adds to data redundancy, and drives data management costs even higher.

Flat Files Limit Data Integration
The flat-file approach is a single-view model. Files are structured, formatted, and arranged to suit the specific needs of the *owner* or primary user of the data. Such structuring, however, may exclude data attributes that are useful to other users, thus preventing successful integration of data across the organization. For example, because the accounting function is the primary user of accounting data, these data are often captured, formatted, and stored to accommodate financial reporting and GAAP. This structure, however, may be useless to the organization's other (nonaccounting) users of accounting data, such as the marketing, finance, production, and engineering functions. These users are presented with three options: (1) do not use accounting data to support decisions; (2) manipulate and massage the existing data structure to suit their unique needs; or (3) obtain additional private sets of the data and incur the costs and operational problems associated with data redundancy.

In spite of these inherent limitations, many large organizations still use flat files for their general ledger and other financial systems. Most members of the data processing community assumed that the end of the century would see the end of legacy systems. Instead, corporate America invested billions of dollars making these systems year-2000 (Y2K) compliant. Legacy systems continue to exist because they add value for their users, and they will not be replaced until they cease to add value. Students who may have to work with these systems in practice should be aware of their key features.

THE DATABASE MODEL

An organization can overcome the problems associated with flat files by implementing the **database model** to data management. Figure 1-13 illustrates how this approach centralizes the organization's data into a common database that is shared by other users. With the organization's data in a central location, all users have access to the data they need to achieve their respective objectives. Access to the data resource is controlled by a **database management system (DBMS)**. The DBMS is a special software system that is programmed to know which data elements each user is authorized to access. The user's program sends requests for data to the DBMS, which validates and authorizes access to the database in accordance with the user's level of authority. If the user requests data that he or she is not authorized to access, the request is denied. Clearly, the organization's procedures for assigning user authority are an important control issue for auditors to consider.

The most striking difference between the database model and the flat-file model is the pooling of data into a common database that is shared by all organizational users. With access to the full domain of entity data, changes in user information needs can be satisfied without obtaining additional private datasets. Users are constrained only by the limitations of the data available to the entity and the legitimacy of their need to access it. Through data sharing, the following traditional problems associated with the flat-file approach *may* be overcome.

Elimination of data redundancy. Each data element is stored only once, thereby eliminating data redundancy and reducing data collection and storage costs. For example, customer data exists only once, but is shared by accounting, marketing, and product services users. To accomplish this, the data are stored in a generic format that supports multiple users.

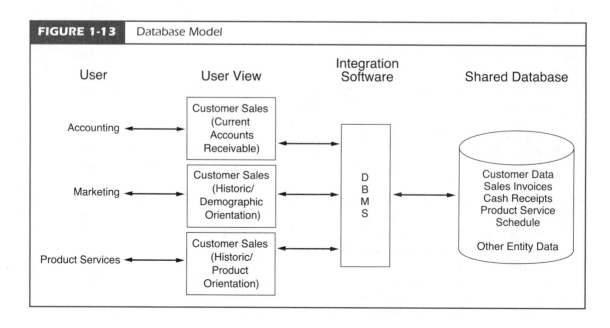

FIGURE 1-13   Database Model

Single update. Because each data element exists in only one place, it requires only a single update procedure. This reduces the time and cost of keeping the database current.

Current values. A single change to a database attribute is automatically made available to all users of the attribute. For example, a customer address change entered by the billing clerk is immediately reflected in the marketing and product services views.

Flat-file and early database systems are called **traditional systems**. Within this context, the term "traditional" means that the organization's information systems applications (its programs) function independently of each other rather than as an integrated whole. Early database management systems were designed to interface directly with existing flat-file programs. Thus when an organization replaced its flat files with a database it did not have to spend millions of dollars rewriting its existing programs. Indeed, early database applications performed essentially the same independent functions as their flat files counterparts. Another factor that limited integration was the structured database models of the era. These models were inflexible and did not permit the degree of data sharing that is found in modern database systems. Whereas some degree of integration was achieved with this type of database, the primary and immediate advantage to the organization was the reduction in data redundancy.

True integration, however, would not be possible until the arrival of the **relational database model**. This flexible database approach permits the design of integrated systems applications capable of supporting the information needs of multiple users from a common set of integrated **database tables**. We should note, however, that the relational database model merely permits integration to occur; integration is not guaranteed. Poor systems design can occur under any model. In fact, most organizations today that employ a relational database run applications that are traditional in design and do not make full use of relational technology. The two remaining models to be discussed (REA and ERP) employ relational database technology more effectively.

THE REA MODEL

REA is an accounting framework for modeling an organization's critical *Resources*, *Events*, and *Agents* (REA) and the relationships between them. Once specified, both accounting and nonaccounting data about these phenomena can be identified, captured, and stored in a relational database. From this repository, user views can be constructed that meet the needs of all users in the organization. The availability of multiple views allows flexible use of transaction data and permits the development of accounting information systems that promote, rather than inhibit, integration.

The REA model was proposed in 1982 as a theoretical model for accounting.[2] Advances in database technology have focused renewed attention on REA as a practical alternative to the classical accounting framework. The key elements of the REA model are summarized as follows.

Resources

Economic **resources** are the assets of the organization. They are defined as objects that are both scarce and under the control of the enterprise. This definition departs from the traditional model because it does not include accounts receivable. An account receivable is an artifact record used simply to store and transmit data. Because it is not an essential element of the system, it need not be included in the database. Instead, accounts receivable

---

2   W. E. McCarthy, "The REA Accounting Model: A Generalized Framework for Accounting Systems in a Shared Data Environment." *The Accounting Review* (July 1982): 554–557.

are derived from the difference between sales to customers and the cash received in payment of sales.

Events

Economic **events** are phenomena that affect changes in resources. They can result from activities such as production, exchange, consumption, and distribution. Economic events are the critical information elements of the accounting system and should be captured in a highly detailed form to provide a rich database.

Agents

Economic **agents** are individuals and departments that participate in an economic event. They are parties both inside and outside the organization with discretionary power to use or dispose of economic resources. Examples of agents include sales clerks, production workers, shipping clerks, customers, and vendors.

The REA model requires that accounting phenomena be characterized in a manner consistent with the development of multiple user views. Business data must not be preformatted or artificially constrained and should reflect all relevant aspects of the underlying economic events. As such, REA procedures and databases are structured around events rather than accounting artifacts such as journals, ledgers, charts of accounts, and double-entry accounting. Under the REA model, business organizations prepare financial statements directly from the event database. The following sales and cash receipts events for a hypothetical retailer can be used to illustrate the inherent differences between classical and REA accounting:

> Sept. 1: Sold 5 units of product X21 @ $30 per unit and 10 units of product Y33 @ $20 per unit to customer Smith (Total sale = $350). The unit cost of the inventory is $16 and $12, respectively (Total CGS = $200).

> Sept. 30: Received $200 cash from customer Smith on account, check number 451.

In flat-file or non-REA database systems, the two events would be recorded in a set of classical accounts like those shown in Figure 1-14. This involves summarizing the events to accommodate the account structure. The details of the transactions are, however, not captured under this approach.

An REA accounting system would capture these transactions in a series of relational database tables that emphasize events rather than accounts. This is illustrated in Figure 1-15. Each table deals with a separate aspect of the transaction. Data pertaining to the customer, the invoice, specific items sold, and so on, can thus be captured for multiple uses and users. The tables of the database are linked via common attributes called primary keys (PK) and embedded foreign keys (FK) that permit integration. In contrast, the files in the traditional system are independent of each other and thus cannot accommodate such detailed data gathering. As a result, traditional systems must summarize event data at the loss of potentially important facts.

Traditional accounting records including journals, ledgers, and charts of accounts do not exist as physical files or tables under the REA model. For financial reporting purposes, views or images of traditional accounting records are constructed from the event tables. For example, the amount of Smith's account receivable balance is derived from {total sales (Quant sold * Sale price) less cash received (Amount) = 350 − 200 = 150}. If necessary or desired, journal entries and general ledger amounts can also be derived from these event tables. For example, the cost of goods sold control account balance is (Quant sold * Unit cost) summed for all transactions for the period.

| FIGURE 1-14 | Classical Accounting Records in a Non-REA System |

Account Receivable File

Customer Number	Customer Name	Debit	Credit	Balance
23456	Smith	350	200	150

Cost of Goods Sold File

Acct Number	Debit	Credit
5734	270	

Sales File

Acct Number	Credit
4975	350

REA is a conceptual model, not a physical system. Many of its tenets, however, are found within advanced database systems. The most notable application of REA philosophy is seen in the proliferation of ERP systems, which are discussed in the following section.

ERP Systems

Enterprise resource planning (ERP) is an information system model that enables an organization to automate and integrate its key business processes. ERP breaks down traditional functional barriers by facilitating data sharing, information flows, and the introduction of common business practices among all organizational users. The implementation of an ERP system can be a massive undertaking that can span several years. Because of their complexity and size, few organizations are willing or able to commit the necessary financial and physical resources and incur the risk of developing an ERP system in-house. Hence, virtually all ERPs are commercial products. The recognized leaders in the market are SAP, Oracle, Baan, J.D. Edwards & Co., and PeopleSoft Inc.

ERP packages are sold to client organizations in modules that support standard processes. Some common ERP modules include:

Asset Management
Financial Accounting
Human Resources
Industry-Specific Solutions
Plant Maintenance
Production Planning
Quality Management
Sales and Distribution
Inventory Management

One of the problems with standardized modules is that they may not always meet the organization's exact needs. For example, a textile manufacturer in India implemented an

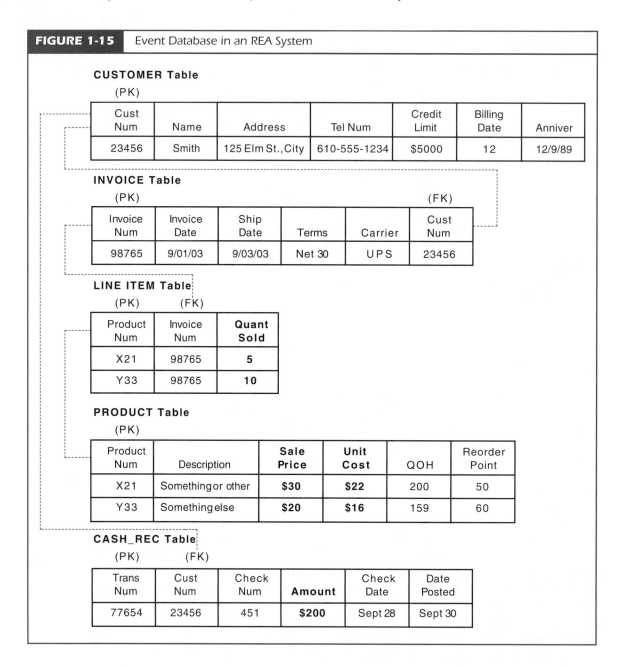

FIGURE 1-15   Event Database in an REA System

CUSTOMER Table

Cust Num (PK)	Name	Address	Tel Num	Credit Limit	Billing Date	Anniver
23456	Smith	125 Elm St., City	610-555-1234	$5000	12	12/9/89

INVOICE Table

Invoice Num (PK)	Invoice Date	Ship Date	Terms	Carrier	Cust Num (FK)
98765	9/01/03	9/03/03	Net 30	UPS	23456

LINE ITEM Table

Product Num (PK)	Invoice Num (FK)	Quant Sold
X21	98765	5
Y33	98765	10

PRODUCT Table

Product Num (PK)	Description	Sale Price	Unit Cost	QOH	Reorder Point
X21	Something or other	$30	$22	200	50
Y33	Something else	$20	$16	159	60

CASH_REC Table

Trans Num (PK)	Cust Num (FK)	Check Num	Amount	Check Date	Date Posted
77654	23456	451	$200	Sept 28	Sept 30

ERP package only to discover that extensive, unexpected, and expensive modifications had to be made to the system. The ERP would not allow the user to assign two different prices to the same bolt of cloth. The manufacturer charged one price for domestic consumption, but another (four times higher) for exported products. That particular ERP system, however, provided no way to assign two prices to the same item while maintaining an accurate inventory count.

Organizations that hope to successfully implement an ERP will need to modify their business processes to suit the ERP, modify the ERP to suit their business or, more likely, modify both. Often, additional software applications need to be connected to the ERP to handle unique business functions, particularly industry-specific tasks. These applications, often called bolt-ons, are not always designed to communicate with ERP packages. The process of creating a harmonious whole can be quite complex and sometimes fails, resulting in significant losses to the organization. ERP packages are enormously expensive, but the savings in efficiencies should be significant. Organization management should exercise great care in deciding which, if any, ERP is best for them.

The evolution of information systems models outlined in this section provides a framework for much of the material contained this book. Chapters 2 through 8 deal with business processes, security, fraud, controls, and a variety of other issues related to traditional (manual, flat-file, and early database) systems. Chapters 9 through 12 examine advanced database systems, the REA model, ERP, and other emerging technologies.

THE ROLE OF THE ACCOUNTANT

The final section of this chapter deals with the accountant's relationship to the information system. Accountants are primarily involved in three ways: as system *users*, as system *designers*, and as system *auditors*.

ACCOUNTANTS AS USERS

In most organizations, the accounting function is the single largest user of IT. All systems that process financial transactions impact the accounting function in some way. As end users, accountants must provide a clear picture of their needs to the professionals who design their systems. For example, the accountant must specify accounting rules and techniques to be used, internal control requirements, and special algorithms such as depreciation models. The accountant's participation in systems development should be active rather than passive. The principle cause of design errors that result in system failure is the absence of user involvement.

ACCOUNTANTS AS SYSTEM DESIGNERS

An appreciation of the accountant's responsibility for system design requires a historic perspective that predates the computer as a business information tool. Traditionally, accountants have been responsible for key aspects of the information system, including assessing the information needs of users, defining the content and format of output reports, specifying sources of data, selecting the appropriate accounting rules, and determining the controls necessary to preserve the integrity and efficiency of the information system.

These traditional systems were physical, observable, and unambiguous. The procedures for processing information were manual, and the medium for transmitting and storing data was paper. With the arrival of the computer, manual procedures were replaced by computer programs, and paper records were stored digitally. The role to be played by accountants in this new era became the subject of much controversy. Lacking computer skills, accountants were generally uncertain about their status and unwilling to explore this emerging technology.

Many accountants relinquished their traditional responsibilities to the new generation of computer professionals who were emerging in their organizations. Computer programmers, often with no accounting or business training, assumed full responsibility for the design of accounting information systems. As a result, many systems violated accounting principles and lacked necessary controls. Large system failures and computer frauds marked this period in accounting history. By the mid-1970s, in response to these problems, the accounting profession began to reassess the accountant's professional and legal responsibilities for computer-based systems.

Today, we recognize that the responsibility for systems design is divided between accountants and IT professionals as follows: the accounting function is responsible for the *conceptual system*, and the IT function is responsible for the *physical system*. To illustrate the distinction between conceptual and physical systems, consider the following example:

> The credit department of a retail business requires information about delinquent accounts from the accounts receivable department. This information supports decisions made by the credit manager regarding the creditworthiness of customers.

The design of the **conceptual system** involves specifying the criteria for identifying delinquent customers and the information that needs to be reported. The accountant determines the nature of the information required, its sources, its destination, and the accounting rules that need to be applied. The **physical system** is the medium and method for capturing and presenting the information. The computer professionals determine the most economical and effective technology for accomplishing the task. Hence, systems design should be a collaborative effort. Because of the uniqueness of each system and the susceptibility of systems to serious error and even fraud, the accountant's involvement in systems design should be pervasive. In later chapters, we shall see that the active participation of accountants is critical to the system's success.

ACCOUNTANTS AS SYSTEM AUDITORS

Auditing is a form of independent attestation performed by an expert—the auditor—who expresses an opinion about the fairness of a company's financial statements. Public confidence in the reliability of internally produced financial statements rests directly on their being validated by an independent expert auditor. This service is often referred to as the **attest function**. Auditors form their opinions based on a systematic process that will be explained in Chapter 15.

Audits are conducted by both internal and external auditors. External auditing is often called "independent auditing" because it is performed by certified public accounting (CPA) firms that are independent of the client organization's management. External auditors represent the interests of third-party stakeholders in the organization, such as stockholders, creditors, and government agencies.

External Auditing

Historically the external accountant's responsibility as a systems **auditor** was limited to the attest function described previously. In recent years this role has been expanded by the broader concept of assurance. The "Big Four" public accounting firms have now renamed their traditional audit functions "assurance services."

Assurance. **Assurance services** are professional services, including the attest function, that are designed to improve the quality of information, both financial and nonfinancial, used by decision makers. For example, a client may contract assurance services to obtain an opinion as to the quality or marketability of a product. Alternatively, a client may need information about the efficiency of a production process or the effectiveness of their network security system. A gray area of overlap exists between assurance and consulting services, which auditors must avoid. They were once allowed to provide consulting services to audit clients. This is now prohibited under SOX legislation. These issues are discussed in later chapters.

IT Auditing. **IT auditing** is usually performed as part of a broader financial audit. The organizational unit responsible for conducting (IT) audits may fall under the assurance services group or be independent. Typically they carry a name such as *IT Risk Management, Information Systems Risk Management,* or *Global Risk Management.* The IT auditor attests to the effectiveness of a clients IT controls to establish their degree of compliance with prescribed standards. Because most modern organizations' internal are essentially computerized, the IT audit may be a large portion of the overall audit. We examine IT controls, risks, and auditing issues in Chapters 15, 16, and 17.

Internal Auditing

Internal auditing is an appraisal function housed within the organization. Internal auditors perform a wide range of activities on behalf of the organization, including conducting financial statement audits, examining an operation's compliance with organizational policies, reviewing the organization's compliance with legal obligations, evaluating operational efficiency, detecting and pursuing fraud within the firm, and conducting IT audits. As you can see, the tasks performed by external and internal auditors are similar. The feature that most clearly distinguishes the two groups is their respective constituencies. External auditors represent third-party outsiders, whereas internal auditors represent the interests of management.

SUMMARY

The first section of the chapter introduced basic systems concepts and presented a framework for distinguishing between accounting information systems and management information systems. This distinction is related to the types of transactions these systems process. AIS applications process financial transactions, and MIS applications process nonfinancial transactions. The section then presented a general model for accounting information systems. The model is composed of four major tasks that exist in all AIS applications: data collection, data processing, database management, and information generation.

The second section examined the relationship between organizational structure and the information system. It focused on functional segmentation as the predominant method of structuring a business and examined the functions of a typical manufacturing firm. The section presented two general methods of organizing the IT function: the centralized approach and the distributed approach.

The third section reviewed the evolution of AIS models. Each new model evolved because of the shortcomings and limitations of its predecessor. As new approaches evolved, however, the predecessor or legacy systems often remained in service. Thus, at any point in time, various generations of systems coexist across different organizations and even within a single enterprise. Five AIS models were examined.

The final section of the chapter examined three roles of accountant as (1) users of AIS, (2) designers of AIS, and (3) auditors of AIS. In most organizations, the accounting function is the single largest user of the AIS. The IT function is responsible for designing the physical system and the accounting function is responsible for specifying the conceptual system. Auditing is an independent attestation performed by the auditor, who expresses an opinion about the fairness of a company's financial statements. One form of auditing conducted by both external and internal auditors is the information technology (IT) audit. The IT auditor attests to the effectiveness of a client's IT controls to establish their degree of compliance with prescribed standards.

KEY TERMS

accounting information systems (AIS) (3)

agents (32)

assurance services (36)

attest function (36)

auditing (36)

auditor (36)

backbone systems (16)

centralized data processing (22)

conceptual system (36)

currency of information (29)

data (12)

data collection (13)

data processing (13)

data sources (12)

data storage (29)

data updating (29)

database (13)

database management (14)

database management system (DBMS) (30)

database model (30)

database tables (31)

distributed data processing (DDP) (24)

end users (11)

enterprise resource planning (ERP) (33)

events (32)

feedback (15)

financial transaction (8)

flat-file model (28)

general ledger/financial reporting system (GL/FRS) (9)

general model for viewing AIS applications (11)

independence (21)

information (12)

information flows (4)

information generation (15)

information system (7)

internal auditing (37)

IT auditing (36)

legacy systems (27)

management information system (MIS) (9)

management reporting system (MRS) (9)

nonfinancial transactions (9)

physical system (36)

REA (31)

relational database model (31)

reliability (21)

resources (31)

segments (16)

stakeholders (5)

subsystem (6)

system (5)

system development life cycle (16)

task-data dependency (29)

trading partners (5)

traditional systems (31)

transaction (7)

transaction processing system (TPS) (9)

turnkey systems (16)

vendor-supported systems (16)

REVIEW QUESTIONS

1. What are the four levels of activity in the pyramid representing the business organization? Distinguish between horizontal and vertical flows of information.
2. Distinguish between natural and artificial systems.
3. What are the elements of a system?
4. What is system decomposition and subsystem interdependency? How are they related?
5. What is the relationship among data, information, and an information system?
6. Distinguish between AIS and MIS.
7. What are the three cycles of transaction processing systems?
8. What is discretionary reporting?
9. What are the characteristics of good or useful information?
10. What rules govern data collection?
11. What are the levels of data hierarchy?
12. What are the three fundamental tasks of database management?

13. What is feedback and how is it useful in an information system?

14. What are the fundamental objectives of all information systems?

15. What does stewardship mean and what is its role in an information system?

16. Distinguish between responsibility, authority, and accountability. Which flow upward and which flow downward?

17. Distinguish between turnkey, backbone, and vendor-supported systems.

18. List each of the functional areas and their subfunctions.

19. What are the roles of internal and external auditors?

20. What is the role of a database administrator?

21. Name the three most common ways to segment an organization.

22. What is the role of the accounting function in an organization?

23. Distinguish between the centralized and distributed approaches to organizing the IT function.

24. What is the role of the data control group?

25. What is distributed data processing?

26. What are the advantages and disadvantages of distributed data processing?

27. What types of tasks become redundant in a distributed data processing system?

28. What is a flat-file system?

29. What are the three general problems associated with data redundancy?

30. Define the key elements of the REA model.

31. What is an ERP system?

32. What three roles are played by accountants with respect to the information system?

33. Define the term *attest function*.

34. Define the term *assurance*.

35. What is IT auditing?

36. Distinguish between conceptual and physical systems.

DISCUSSION QUESTIONS

1. Discuss the differences between internal and external users of information and their needs and demands on an information system. Historically, which type of user has the firm catered to most?

2. Comment on the level of detail necessary for operations management, middle management, and stockholders.

3. Distinguish between financial and nonfinancial transactions. Give three examples of each.

4. Why have reengineering efforts been made to integrate AIS and MIS?

5. Do you think transaction processing systems differ significantly between service and manufacturing industries? Are they equally important to both sectors?

6. Discuss the difference between the financial reporting system and general ledger system.

7. Examine Figure 1-5 and discuss where and how problems can arise that can cause the resulting information to be "bad" or ineffective.

8. Discuss how the elements of efficiency, effectiveness, and flexibility are crucial to the design of an information system.

9. Discuss what is meant by the statement "The accounting system is a conceptual flow of information that represents the physical flows of personnel, raw materials, machinery, and cash through the organization."

10. Discuss the importance of accounting independence in accounting information systems. Give an example of where this concept is important (use an example other than inventory control).

11. Discuss why it is crucial that internal auditors report solely to the uppermost level of management (either to the chief executive officer or the audit committee of the board of directors) and answer to no other group.

12. Contrast centralized data processing with distributed data processing. How do the roles of systems professionals and end users change? What do you think the trend is today?

13. Discuss how conceptual and physical systems differ and which functions are responsible for each of these systems.

14. If accountants are viewed as providers of information, then why are they consulted as system users in the systems development process?

15. Do you agree with the statement "The term *IT auditor* should be considered obsolete because it implies a distinction between 'regular' auditors

and auditors who examine computerized AIS"? Why or why not?

16. What are the primary reasons for segmenting organizations?

17. Why is it important to organizationally separate the accounting function from other functions of the organization?

18. What is the most likely system acquisition method—in-house, turnkey, backbone, or vendor-supported—for each of the following situations?

  - A plumbing supply company with 12 employees that sells standard products to wholesale customers in a local community needs a system to manage its affairs.
  - A major oil company with diverse holdings, complex oil leases, and esoteric accounting

practices needs a system that can coordinate its many enterprises.

  - A municipal government needs a system that complies with standard government accounting practices but can be integrated with other existing systems.

19. The REA model is based on the premise that "business data must not be preformatted or artificially constrained and must reflect all relevant aspects of the underlying economic events." What does this mean and how is it applied?

20. ERP systems are composed of a highly integrated set of standardized modules. Discuss the advantages and potential disadvantages of this approach.

MULTIPLE-CHOICE QUESTIONS

1. CMA Adapted
   Accounting systems are designed to
   a. analyze and interpret information.
   b. allow managers to manage by exception.
   c. provide information required to support decisions.
   d. record and report business transactions.
   e. create database management systems.

2. CMA Adapted
   One of the ingredients of the primary quality of relevance is
   a. verifiability.
   b. predictive value.
   c. neutrality.
   d. due process.
   e. representational faithfulness.

3. CMA Adapted
   Accounting information that users can depend on to represent the economic conditions or events that it purports to represent best defines
   a. relevance.
   b. timeliness.
   c. feedback value.
   d. reliability.
   e. verifiability.

4. CMA Adapted
   Accounting information that is capable of making a difference in a decision by helping users to confirm or correct expectations best defines
   a. neutrality.
   b. timeliness.
   c. accuracy.
   d. verifiability.
   e. relevance.

5. CMA Adapted
   One of the ingredients of the primary quality of reliability is
   a. verifiability.
   b. feedback value.
   c. timeliness.
   d. comparability.
   e. consistency.

6. CMA Adapted
   A database is
   a. essential for storage of large data sets.
   b. a collection of related files.
   c. a real-time system.
   d. a network of computer terminals.
   e. a task-oriented file system.

7. When viewed from the highest to most elemental level, the data hierarchy is
   a. attribute, record, file.
   b. record, attribute, key.
   c. file, record, attribute.
   d. file, record, key.
   e. key, record, file.

8. Which is NOT an accountant's primary role in information systems?
   a. system user
   b. system auditor
   c. system designer
   d. system programmer

9. Which is NOT a primary function of an AIS transaction processing system?
   a. converting economic events into financial transactions
   b. distributing financial information to operations personnel to support their daily operations
   c. monitoring external economic events
   d. recording financial transactions in the accounting records

10. Which of the following best describes the activities of the materials management function?
    a. purchasing, receiving, and inventory control
    b. receiving, sales, distribution, and purchasing
    c. receiving, storage, purchasing, and accounts payable
    d. purchasing, receiving, and storage
    e. purchasing, storage, and distribution

11. Which of the following best describes the activities of the production function?
    a. maintenance, inventory control, and production planning
    b. production planning, quality control, manufacturing, and cost accounting
    c. quality control, production planning, manufacturing, and payroll
    d. maintenance, production planning, storage, and quality control
    e. manufacturing, quality control, and maintenance

12. Which of the following best describes the activities of the accounting function?
    a. inventory control, accounts payable, fixed assets, and payroll
    b. fixed assets, accounts payable, cash disbursements, and cost accounting
    c. purchasing, cash receipts, accounts payable, cash disbursements, and payroll
    d. inventory control, cash receipts, accounts payable, cash disbursements, and payroll
    e. inventory control, cost accounting, accounts payable, cash disbursements, and payroll

13. Which statement best describes the issue of distributed data processing (DDP)?
    a. The centralized and DDP approaches are mutually exclusive; an organization must choose one approach or the other.
    b. The philosophy and objective of the organization's management will determine the extent of DDP in the firm.
    c. In a minimum DDP arrangement, only data input and output are distributed, leaving the tasks of data control, data conversion, database management, and data processing to be centrally managed.
    d. The greatest disadvantage of a totally distributed environment is that the distributed IPU locations are unable to communicate and coordinate their activities.
    e. Although hardware (such as computers, database storage, and input/output terminals) can be effectively distributed, the systems development and maintenance tasks must remain centralized for better control and efficiency.

14. CMA Adapted
    A major disadvantage of distributed data processing is
    a. the increased time between job request and job completion.
    b. the potential for hardware and software incompatibility among users.
    c. the disruption caused when the mainframe goes down.
    d. that users are not likely to be involved.
    e. that data processing professionals may not be properly involved.

PROBLEMS

1. Users of Information

Classify the following users of information as either:

I—internal user
T—external user: trading partner
S—external user: stakeholder

a.   Internal Revenue Service
b.   Inventory control manager
c.   Board of directors
d.   Customers
e.   Lending institutions
f.   Securities and Exchange Commission
g.   Stockholders
h.   Chief executive officer
i.   Suppliers
j.   Bondholders

2. Subsystems

Use the human body system to illustrate the concepts of system decomposition and subsystem interdependency. Draw a hierarchical chart similar to the one in Figure 1-2 and discuss the interdependencies.

3. AIS Model

Examine the diagram below and determine what essential mechanism is missing. Once you have identified the missing element, discuss its importance.

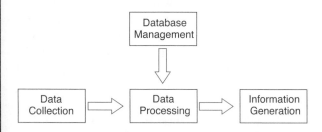

4. AIS & MIS Features

List some AIS and MIS information from which salespeople may benefit. Clearly indicate whether the information item would be an output of a traditional AIS or MIS system. Finally, discuss the benefits of integrating this information.

5. Information System Categorization

Classify the following items as either:

TPS—transaction processing system
FRS—financial reporting system
MRS—management reporting system

a.   Variance reports
b.   Sales order capture
c.   Balance sheet
d.   Budgets
e.   Purchase order preparation
f.   Tax returns
g.   Sales summary by product line
h.   Cash disbursements preparation
i.   Annual report preparation
j.   Invoice preparation
k.   Cost-volume-profit analysis

6. Organizational Chart

Draw an organizational chart for your college or university. What is the "output" for a college or university, and hence what are the "production" departments?

7. Organization Functions

Based on Figure 1-8, draw a diagram of functional segments for an oil company that has the following operations:

a.   A head office in New York City responsible for international and national marketing, acquisition of leases and contracts, and corporate reporting.

b.   Two autonomous regional facilities in Tulsa, Oklahoma, and New Orleans, Louisiana. These facilities are responsible for oil exploration, drilling, refining, storage, and the distribution of petroleum products to corporate service stations throughout the country and abroad.

8. Organization Functions

Based on Figure 1-8, draw a diagram of functional segments for a manufacturer of diversified products. The general characteristics of the firm are as follows:

a.   The organization produces three unrelated products: lawn and garden furniture for sale in home improvement centers and department stores; plastic packaging products for the electronics and medical supply industries; and paper products (e.g., plates, cups, and napkins) for the fast-food industry.

b. Although the manufacturing facilities are located within a single complex, none of the three products share the same suppliers, customers, or physical production lines.

c. The organization's functional activities include design, production, distribution, marketing, finance, human resources, and accounting.

9. Functional Segmentation

The current organization structure of Blue Sky Company, a manufacturer of small sailboats, is presented below.

Required:

a. What operational problems (inefficiency, errors, fraud, etc.) do you think Blue Sky could experience because of this structure?

b. Draw a new diagram reflecting an improved structure that solves the problems you identified. If necessary, you may add up to two new positions.

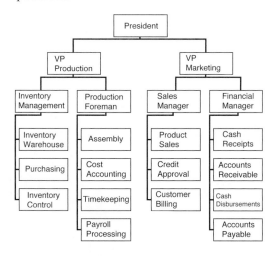

10. Communications

Before the mid-1970s, systems programmers and businesspeople (including accountants) did not communicate well with one another. The programmers were criticized for using too much jargon, and the businesspeople were criticized for not adequately expressing their needs. Efforts have been made to overcome this communication gap, but room for improvement still exists. What problems do you think resulted from this communication gap? What do you think you can do to help close the gap even more when you enter the workforce?

11. Characteristics of Useful Information

All records in a database must be uniquely identifiable in at least one attribute, which is its primary key. Drawing on your general knowledge of accounting, identify the primary key for the following types of accounting records. To illustrate, the first record is done for you.

Record Type	Primary Key
Record Type	*Primary Key*
Accounts Receivable	Customer Number
Accounts Payable	
Inventory	
Customer Sales Orders	
Purchase Orders to vendors	
Cash Receipts (checks) from customers	
Cash Disbursements (checks) to vendors	
Employee Payroll Earnings records	

12. Data Attributes

Drawing from your basic accounting knowledge, list the relevant data attributes that constitute the record types below. Identify which attribute is the primary key for the record.

Accounts Payable record
Inventory record
Customer Sales Orders record
Purchase Orders to vendors
Cash Receipts (checks) from customers
Employee Payroll Earnings records

13. CMA (Adapted) 1288-5Y6
Distributed Data Processing

In the last two decades, there has been a transition from a centralized mainframe computer environment to a distributed network for which an organization has the ability to share computer processing. One of the fastest-growing segments of the computer industry is the local area network (LAN), which is said to be the wave of the future. LANs permit the transfer of information between microcomputers, word processors, data storage devices, printers, voice devices, and telecommunication devices. Current opinion holds that the flow of organizational communications has been enhanced by the transition from the optimization of computers experienced in the traditional distributed network to the optimization of human resources in the LAN environment.

Required:

a. Describe the reasons why an organization would choose a distributed network over the traditional centralized computer environment.

b. Compare and contrast the characteristics of a traditional distributed computer network with those of a local area network as they are related to the:

   i. utilization of computer hardware.

   ii. user interaction and the sharing of electronic information.

c. Identify and explain three problems that can result from the use of local area networks.

d. Explain the hardware characteristics associated with a computer modem as they relate to distributed information processing.

chapter 2

Introduction to Transaction Processing

LEARNING OBJECTIVES

After studying this chapter, you should:

- Understand the broad objectives of transaction cycles.
- Recognize the types of transactions processed by each of the three transaction cycles.
- Know the basic accounting records used in transaction processing systems.
- Understand the relationship between traditional accounting records and their magnetic equivalents in computer-based systems.
- Be familiar with the documentation techniques used for representing manual and computer-based systems.
- Understand the differences between batch and real-time processing and the impact of these technologies on transaction processing.

Chapter 1 introduced the transaction processing system (TPS) as an activity consisting of three major subsystems called cycles: the revenue cycle, the expenditure cycle, and the conversion cycle. While each cycle performs different specific tasks and supports different objectives, they share common characteristics. For example, all three TPS cycles capture financial transactions, record the effects of transactions in accounting records, and provide information about transactions to users in support of their day-to-day activities. In addition, transaction cycles produce much of the raw data from which management reports and financial statements are derived. Because of their financial impact on the firm, transaction cycles command much of the accountant's professional attention.

The purpose of this chapter is to present some preliminary topics that are common to all three transaction processing cycles. In subsequent chapters, we will draw heavily from this material as we examine the individual subsystems of each cycle in detail. The chapter is organized into four major sections. The first is an overview of transaction processing. This section defines the broad objective of the three transaction cycles and specifies the roles of their individual subsystems. The second section describes the relationship among accounting records in forming an audit trail in both manual and computer-based systems. The third section examines documentation techniques used to represent systems. This section presents several documentation techniques for manual and computer-based systems. The fourth section of this chapter addresses computer-based systems. It reviews the fundamental features of batch and real-time technologies and their implication for transaction processing.

AN OVERVIEW OF TRANSACTION PROCESSING

TPS applications process financial transactions. A financial transaction was defined in Chapter 1 as:

> An economic event that affects the assets and equities of the firm, is reflected in its accounts, and is measured in monetary terms.

The most common financial transactions are economic exchanges with external parties. These include the sale of goods or services, the purchase of inventory, the discharge of financial obligations, and the receipt of cash on account from customers. Financial transactions also include certain internal events such as the depreciation of fixed assets; the application of labor, raw materials, and overhead to the production process; and the transfer of inventory from one department to another.

Financial transactions are common business events that occur regularly. For instance, thousands of transactions of a particular type (sales to customers) may occur daily. To deal efficiently with such volume, business firms group similar types of transactions into transaction cycles.

TRANSACTION CYCLES

Three transaction cycles process most of the firm's economic activity: the expenditure cycle, the conversion cycle, and the revenue cycle. These cycles exist in all types of businesses— both profit-seeking and not-for-profit. For instance, every business (1) incurs expenditures in exchange for resources (expenditure cycle), (2) provides value added through its products or services (conversion cycle), and (3) receives revenue from outside sources (revenue cycle). Figure 2-1 shows the relationship of these cycles and the resource flows between them.

THE EXPENDITURE CYCLE

Business activities begin with the acquisition of materials, property, and labor in exchange for cash—the **expenditure cycle**. Figure 2-1 shows the flow of cash from the organization to the various providers of these resources. Most expenditure transactions are based on a credit relationship between the trading parties. The actual disbursement of cash takes place at some point after the receipt of the goods or services. Days or even weeks may pass between these two events. Thus, from a systems perspective, this transaction has two parts: a physical component (the acquisition of the goods) and a financial component (the cash disbursement to the supplier). Each component is processed by a separate subsystem of the cycle. The major subsystems of the expenditure cycle are outlined below. Because of the extent of this body of material, two chapters are devoted to the expenditure cycle. Purchases/accounts payable and cash disbursements systems are the topics of Chapter 5. Payroll and fixed asset systems are examined in Chapter 6.

> *Purchases/accounts payable system.* This system recognizes the need to acquire physical inventory (such as raw materials) and places an order with the vendor. When the goods are received, the purchases system records the event by increasing inventory and establishing an account payable to be paid at a later date.

> *Cash disbursements system.* When the obligation created in the purchases system is due, the cash disbursements system authorizes the payment, disburses the funds to the vendor, and records the transaction by reducing the cash and accounts payable accounts.

> *Payroll system.* The payroll system collects labor usage data for each employee, computes the payroll, and disburses paychecks to the employees. Conceptually, payroll is a

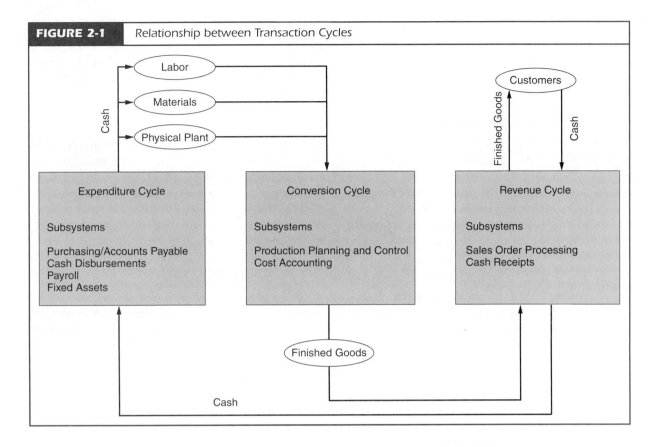

FIGURE 2-1 Relationship between Transaction Cycles

special-case purchases and cash disbursements system. Because of accounting complexities associated with payroll, most firms have a separate system for payroll processing.

Fixed asset system. A firm's fixed asset system processes transactions pertaining to the acquisition, maintenance, and disposal of its fixed assets. These are relatively permanent items that collectively often represent the largest financial investment by the organization. Examples of fixed assets include land, buildings, furniture, machinery, and motor vehicles.

THE CONVERSION CYCLE

The **conversion cycle** is composed of two major subsystems: the production system and the cost accounting system. The production system involves the planning, scheduling, and control of the physical product through the manufacturing process. This includes determining raw material requirements, authorizing the work to be performed and the release of raw materials into production, and directing the movement of the work in process through its various stages of manufacturing. The cost accounting system monitors the flow of cost information related to production. Information produced by this system is used for inventory valuation, budgeting, cost control, performance reporting, and management decisions, such as "make or buy" decisions. We examine the basic features of these systems in Chapter 7.

Manufacturing firms convert raw materials into finished products through formal conversion cycle operations. The conversion cycle is not usually formal and observable in service and retailing establishments. Nevertheless, these firms still engage in conversion cycle activities that culminate in the development of a salable product or service. These activities include the readying of products and services for market and the allocation of resources such as depreciation, building amortization, and prepaid expenses to the proper accounting period. However, unlike manufacturing firms, merchandising companies do not process these activities through formal conversion cycle subsystems.

THE REVENUE CYCLE

Firms sell their finished goods to customers through the **revenue cycle**, which involves processing cash sales, credit sales, and the receipt of cash following a credit sale. Revenue cycle transactions also have a physical and a financial component, which are processed separately. The primary subsystems of the revenue cycle, which are the topics of Chapter 4, are briefly outlined below.

> *Sales order processing.* The majority of business sales are made on credit and involve tasks such as preparing sales orders, granting credit, shipping products (or rendering of a service) to the customer, billing customers, and recording the transaction in the accounts (accounts receivable, inventory, expenses, and sales).

> *Cash receipts.* For credit sales, some period of time (days or weeks) passes between the point of the sale and the receipt of cash. Cash receipts processing includes collecting cash, depositing cash in the bank, and recording these events in the accounts (accounts receivable and cash).

ACCOUNTING RECORDS

MANUAL SYSTEMS

This section describes the purpose of each type of **accounting record** used in transaction cycles. We begin with traditional records used in manual systems (documents, journals, and ledgers) and then examine their magnetic counterparts in computer-based systems.

Documents

A document provides evidence of an economic event and may be used to initiate transaction processing. Some documents are a result of transaction processing. In this section, we discuss three types of documents: source documents, product documents, and turnaround documents.

Source Documents. Economic events give rise to some documents being created at the beginning (the source) of the transaction. These are called source documents. **Source documents** are used to capture and formalize transaction data needed for processing by the transaction cycle. Figure 2-2 shows the creation of a source document.

The economic event (the sale) causes the sales clerk to prepare a multipart sales order, which is formal evidence that a sale occurred. Copies of this source document enter the sales system and are used to convey information to various functions, such as billing, shipping, and accounts receivable. The information in the sales order triggers specific activities in each of these departments.

Product Documents. **Product documents** are the result of transaction processing rather than the triggering mechanism for the process. For example, a payroll check to an employee is a product document of the payroll system. Figure 2-3 extends the example in Figure 2-2 to illustrate that the customer's bill is a product document of the sales system. We will study many other examples of product documents in later chapters.

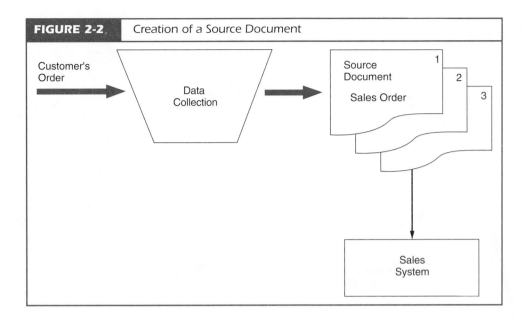

FIGURE 2-2.   Creation of a Source Document

Turnaround Documents. **Turnaround documents** are product documents of one system that become source documents for another system. This is illustrated in Figure 2-4. The customer receives a perforated two-part bill or statement. The top portion of this document is the actual bill, and the bottom portion is the remittance advice. When customers make a payment, they remove the remittance advice and return it to the company along with their check. A turnaround document contains important information about a customer's account to help the cash receipts system process the check. One of the problems faced by designers of cash receipts systems is matching customer payments to the correct

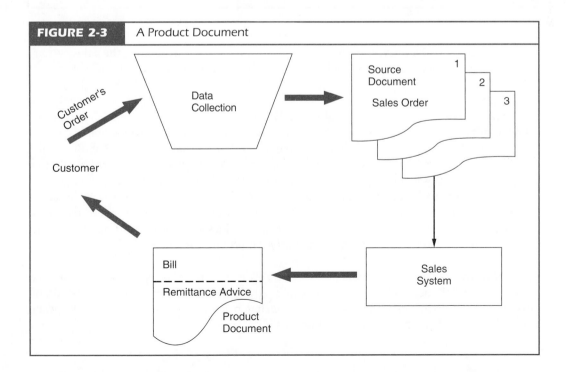

FIGURE 2-3   A Product Document

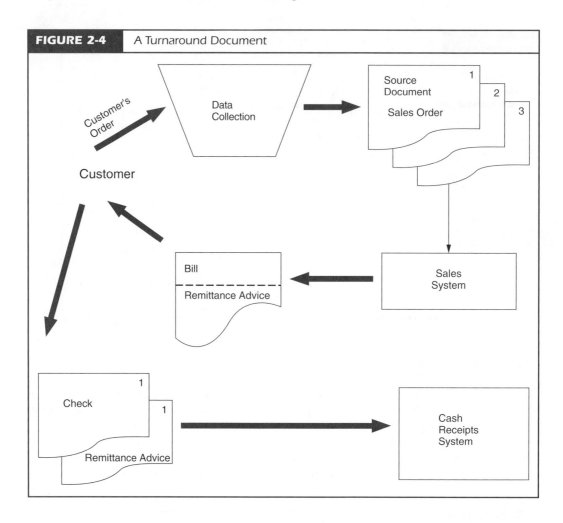

FIGURE 2-4   A Turnaround Document

customer accounts. By providing this needed information as a product of the sales system, we can be sure of its accuracy when it is received by the cash receipts system.

Journals

A **journal** is a record of a chronological entry. At some point in the transaction process, when all relevant facts about the transaction are known, the event is recorded in a journal in chronological order. Documents are the primary source of data for journals. Figure 2-5 shows a sales order being recorded in the sales journal (see the discussion of special journals on the following page). Each transaction requires a separate journal entry, reflecting the accounts affected and the amounts to be debited and credited. Often, there is a time lag between initiating a transaction and recording it in the accounts. The journal holds a complete record of transactions processed by the organization and thus provides a means for posting to accounts. There are two primary types of journals: *special journals* and *general journals*.

Special Journals. Special journals are used to record specific classes of transactions that occur in high volume. Such transactions can be grouped together in a special journal and processed more efficiently than a general journal permits. Figure 2-6 shows a special (sales) journal for recording sales transactions.

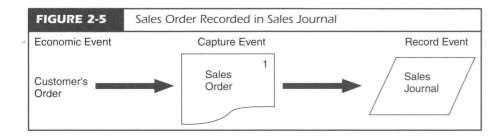

FIGURE 2-5 | Sales Order Recorded in Sales Journal

Economic Event   Capture Event   Record Event

Customer's Order → Sales Order (1) → Sales Journal

As you can see, the sales journal provides a specialized format for recording only sales transactions. At the end of the processing period (month, week, or day), a clerk posts the amounts in the columns to the ledger accounts indicated (see the discussion of ledgers in this chapter). For example, the total of sales will be posted to account number 401. Most organizations use several other special journals, including the cash receipts journal, cash disbursements journal, purchases journal, and the payroll journal.

Register. The term *register* denotes certain types of special journals. For example, the payroll journal is often called the *payroll register*. However, we also use the term register to denote a log. For example, a receiving register is a log of all receipts of raw materials or merchandise ordered from vendors. Similarly, a shipping register is a log that records all shipments to customers.

General Journals. Firms use the general journal to record nonrecurring, infrequent, and dissimilar transactions. For example, we usually record periodic depreciation and closing entries in the general journal. Figure 2-7 shows one page from a general journal. Note that the columns are nonspecific, allowing any type of transaction to be recorded. The entries are recorded in chronological order.

FIGURE 2-6 | Sales Journal

Date	Customer	Invoice Num.	Acct. Num.	Post	Debit Acct. Rec. #102	Credit Sales #401
Sept. 1	Hewitt Co.	4523	1120		3300	3300
15	Acme Drilling	8821	1298		6825	6825
Oct. 3	Buell Corp.	22987	1030		4000	4000
10	Check Ltd.	66734	1110		8500	8500

FIGURE 2-7	General Journal

GENERAL JOURNAL   PAGE

	DATE	DESCRIPTION	POST. REF.	DEBIT					CREDIT					
1	Sept. 1, 2004	Depreciation Expense	520	5	0	0	0							1
2		Accumulated Depreciation	210						5	0	0	0		2
3														3
4	Sept. 2, 2004	Insurance Expense	525	1	2	0	0							4
5		Prepaid Insurance	180						1	2	0	0		5
6														6
7	Sept. 3, 2004	Cash	101	1	1	0	0	0						7
8		Capital Stock	310						1	1	0	0	0	8
9														9
10														10
11														11
12														12

As a practical matter, most organizations have replaced their general journal with a journal voucher system. A journal voucher is actually a special source document that contains a single journal entry specifying the general ledger accounts that are affected. Journal vouchers are used to record summaries of routine transactions, nonroutine transactions, adjusting entries, and closing entries. The total of journal vouchers processed is equivalent to the general journal. Subsequent chapters discuss the use of this technique in transaction processing.

Ledgers

A **ledger** is a book of financial accounts that reflects the financial effects of the firm's transactions after they are posted from the various journals. Whereas journals show the chronological effect of business activity, ledgers show activity by account type. A ledger indicates the increases, decreases, and current balance of each account. Organizations use this financial information to prepare financial statements, support daily operations, and prepare internal reports. Figure 2-8 shows the flow of financial information from the source documents to the journal and into the ledgers.

There are two basic types of ledgers: (1) *general ledgers*, which contain the firm's account information in the form of highly summarized control accounts, and (2) *subsidiary ledgers*, which contain the details of the individual accounts that constitute a particular control account.[1]

---

1   Not all control accounts in the general ledger have corresponding subsidiary accounts. Accounts such as sales and cash typically have no supporting details in the form of a subsidiary ledger.

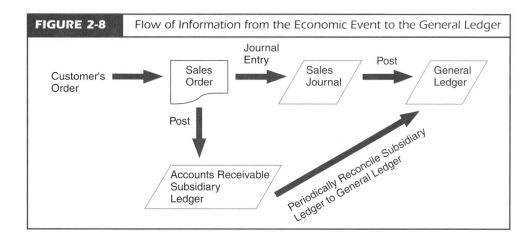

FIGURE 2-8   Flow of Information from the Economic Event to the General Ledger

General Ledgers. The general ledger summarizes the activity for each of the organization's accounts. The general ledger department updates these records from journal vouchers prepared from special journals and other sources located throughout the organization. The general ledger presented in Figure 2-9 shows the beginning balances, the changes, and the ending balances as of a particular date for several different accounts.

The general ledger provides a single value for each control account, such as accounts payable, accounts receivable, and inventory. This highly summarized information is sufficient for financial reporting, but it is not useful for supporting daily business operations. For example, for financial reporting purposes, the firm's total accounts receivable value must be presented as a single figure in the balance sheet. This value is obtained from the accounts receivable control account in the general ledger. However, to actually collect the cash represented by this asset, the firm must have certain detailed information about the customers that is not provided by this summary figure. It must know which customers owe money, how much each customer owes, when the customer last made payment, when the next payment is due, and so on. The accounts receivable subsidiary ledger contains these essential details.

Subsidiary Ledgers. Subsidiary ledgers are kept in various accounting departments of the firm, including inventory, accounts payable, payroll, and accounts receivable. This separation provides better control and support of operations. Figure 2-10 illustrates that the total of account balances in a subsidiary ledger should equal the balance in the corresponding general ledger control account. Thus, in addition to providing financial statement information, the general ledger is a mechanism for verifying the overall accuracy of accounting data that has been processed by separate sources. Any event incorrectly recorded in a journal or subsidiary ledger will cause an out-of-balance condition that should be detected during the general ledger update. By periodically reconciling summary balances from subsidiary accounts, journals, and control accounts, the completeness and accuracy of transaction processing can be formally assessed.

THE AUDIT TRAIL

The accounting records described previously provide an **audit trail** for tracing transactions from source documents to the financial statements. Of the many purposes served by the audit trail, most important to accountants is the year-end audit. While the study of financial auditing falls outside the scope of this text, the following thumbnail sketch of the audit process will demonstrate the importance of the audit trail.

FIGURE 2-9	General Ledger

Cash   ACCOUNT   NO. 101

DATE		ITEM	POST. REF.	DEBIT	CREDIT	BALANCE	
						DEBIT	CREDIT
Sept.	10		S1	3 3 0 0		3 3 0 0	
	15		S1	6 8 2 5		1 0 1 2 5	
Oct.	3		S1	4 0 0 0		1 4 1 2 5	
	10		CD1		2 8 0 0	1 1 3 2 5	

Accounts Receivable   ACCOUNT   NO. 102

DATE		ITEM	POST. REF.	DEBIT	CREDIT	BALANCE	
						DEBIT	CREDIT
Sept.	1		S1	1 4 0 0		1 4 0 0	
	8		S1	2 6 0 5		4 0 0 5	
	15		CR1		1 6 5 0	2 3 5 5	

Accounts Payable   ACCOUNT   NO. 201

DATE		ITEM	POST. REF.	DEBIT	CREDIT	BALANCE	
						DEBIT	CREDIT
Sept.	1		P1		2 0 5 0 0		2 0 5 0 0
	10		CD1	2 8 0 0			1 7 7 0 0

The external auditor periodically evaluates the financial statements of publicly held business organizations on behalf of its stockholders and other interested parties. The auditor's responsibility involves, in part, the review of selected accounts and transactions to determine their validity, accuracy, and completeness. Let's assume an auditor wishes to verify the accuracy of a client's accounts receivable (AR) as published in its annual financial statements. The auditor can trace the AR figure on the balance sheet to the general ledger AR control account.

FIGURE 2-9	(Continued)

Purchases   ACCOUNT   NO. *502*

DATE		ITEM	POST. REF.	DEBIT	CREDIT	BALANCE	
						DEBIT	CREDIT
Sept.	*1*		P1	2 0 5 0 0		2 0 5 0 0	

FIGURE 2-10	Relationship between the Subsidiary Ledger and the General Ledger

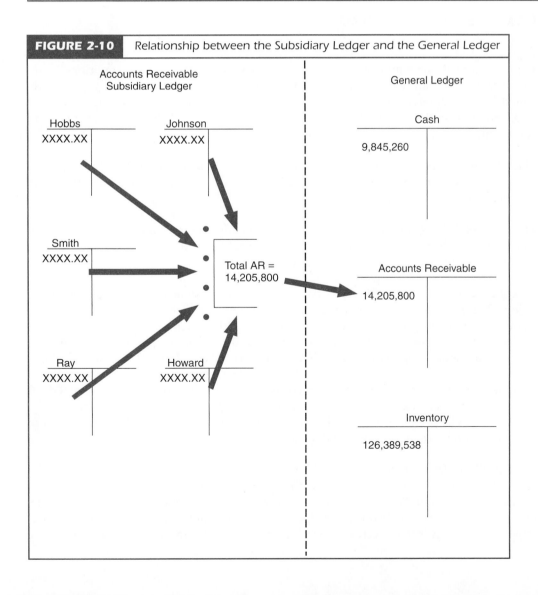

This balance can then be reconciled with the total for the AR subsidiary ledger. Rather than examining every transaction that affected the AR account, the auditor will use a sampling technique to examine a representative subset of transactions. Following this approach, the auditor can select a number of accounts from the AR subsidiary ledger and trace these back to the sales journal. From the sales journal, the auditor can identify the specific source documents that initiated the transactions and pull them from the files to verify their validity and accuracy.

The audit of AR often includes a procedure called confirmation. This involves contacting selected customers to determine if the transactions recorded in the accounts actually took place and that customers agree with the recorded balance. Information contained in source documents and subsidiary accounts enables the auditor to identify and locate customers chosen for confirmation. The results from reconciling the AR subsidiary ledger with the control account and from confirming customers' accounts help the auditor form an opinion about the accuracy of accounts receivable as reported on the balance sheet. The auditor performs similar tests on all of the client firm's major accounts and transactions to arrive at an overall opinion about the fair presentation of the financial statement. The audit trail plays an important role in this process.

COMPUTER-BASED SYSTEMS

Types of Files

While audit trails in computer-based systems are less observable than in traditional manual systems, they still exist. Accounting records in computer-based systems are represented by four different types of magnetic files: master files, transaction files, reference files, and archive files. Figure 2-11 illustrates the relationship of these files in forming an audit trail.

Master File. A **master file** generally contains account data. The general ledger and subsidiary ledgers are examples of master files. Data values in master files are updated from transactions.

Transaction File. A **transaction file** is a temporary file holding transaction records that will be used to change or update data in a master file. Sales orders, inventory receipts, and cash receipts are examples of transaction files.

Reference File. A **reference file** stores data that are used as standards for processing transactions. For example, the payroll program may refer to a tax table to calculate the proper amount of withholding taxes for payroll transactions. Other reference files include price lists used for preparing customer invoices, lists of authorized suppliers, employee rosters, and customer credit files for approving credit sales. The reference file in Figure 2-11 is a credit file.

Archive File. An **archive file** contains records of past transactions that are retained for future reference. These transactions form an important part of the audit trail. Archive files include journals, prior-period payroll information, lists of former employees, records of accounts written off, and prior-period ledgers.

The Digital Audit Trail

Let's walk through the system represented in Figure 2-11 to illustrate how computer files provide an audit trail. We begin with the capture of the economic event. In this example, sales are recorded manually on source documents, just as in the manual system. The next step in this process is to convert the source documents to digital form. This is done in the

| **FIGURE 2-11** | Accounting Records in a Computer-Based System |

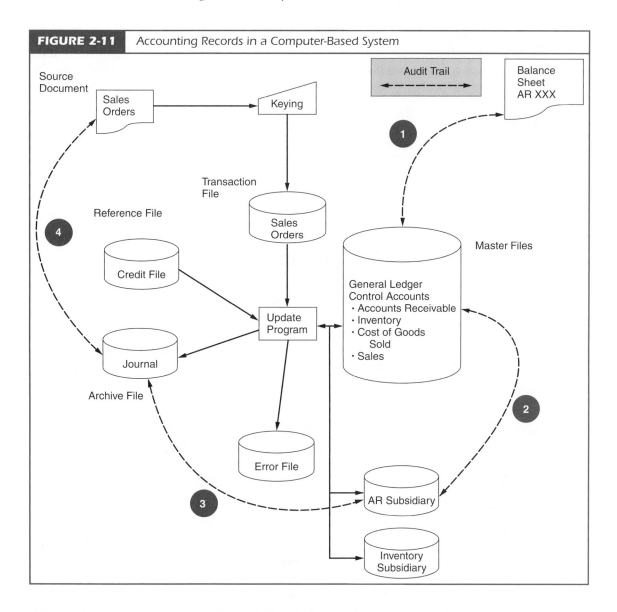

data input stage, where the transactions are edited and a transaction file of sales orders is produced. Some computer systems do not use physical source documents. Instead, transactions are captured directly on digital media. The next step is to update the various master file subsidiary and control accounts that are affected by the transaction. During the update procedure, additional editing of transactions takes place. Some transactions may prove to be in error or invalid for such reasons as incorrect account numbers, insufficient quantities on hand, or customer credit problems. In this example, the system determines the available credit for each customer from the credit file before processing the sale. Any records that are rejected for credit problems are transferred to the error file. The remaining good records are used to update the master files. Only these transactions are added to the archive file that serves as the sales journal. By copying the valid transactions to the journal, the original transaction file is not needed for audit trail purposes. This file can now be erased (scratched) in preparation for the next batch of sales orders.

Like the paper trail, this digital audit trail allows transaction tracing. Again, an auditor attempting to evaluate the accuracy of the accounts receivable figure published in the balance sheet could do so via the following steps, which are identified in Figure 2-11.

1. Compare the accounts receivable balance in the balance sheet with the master file AR control account balance.
2. Reconcile the AR control figure with the AR subsidiary account total.
3. Select a sample of update entries made to accounts in the AR subsidiary ledger and trace these to transactions in the sales journal (archive file).
4. From these journal entries, identify specific source documents that can be pulled from their files and verified. If necessary, the auditor can confirm the accuracy and propriety of these source documents by contacting the customers in question.

DOCUMENTATION TECHNIQUES

The old saying that a picture is worth a thousand words is extremely applicable when it comes to documenting systems. A written description of a system can be wordy and difficult to follow. Experience has shown that a visual image can convey vital system information more effectively and efficiently than words do. As both systems designers and auditors, accountants use system documentation routinely. The ability to document systems in graphic form is thus an important skill for accountants to master. Six basic documentation techniques are introduced in this section: data flow diagrams, entity relationship (ER) diagrams, document flowcharts, system flowcharts, program flowcharts, and record layout diagrams.

DATA FLOW DIAGRAMS AND ENTITY RELATIONSHIP DIAGRAMS

Two commonly used systems design and documentation techniques are the entity relationship (ER) diagram and the data flow diagram (DFD). This section introduces the principal features of these techniques, illustrates their use, and shows how they are related.

Data Flow Diagrams

The **data flow diagram** (DFD) uses symbols to represent the entities, processes, data flows, and data stores that pertain to a system. Figure 2-12 presents the symbol set most commonly used.

Entities in a DFD are external objects at the boundary of the system being modeled. They represent sources of and destinations for data. Entities may be other interacting systems or functions, or they may be external to the organization, such as customers and suppliers.

DFDs are used to represent systems at different levels of detail from very general to highly detailed. In Chapter 14 we will study the construction of multilevel DFDs. At this point, a single-level DFD is sufficient to demonstrate its use as a documentation tool. We see an example of this in Figure 2-13. The accounting records used in each process are represented as data stores, and the data flows between processes are represented by labeled arrows.

DFDs are used extensively by systems analysts to represent the logical elements of the system. However, this technique does not represent the physical system. In other words, DFDs show what logical tasks are being done, but not how they are done or who (or what) is performing them. For example, the DFD does not show whether the sales approval process is separated physically from the billing process in compliance with internal control objectives.

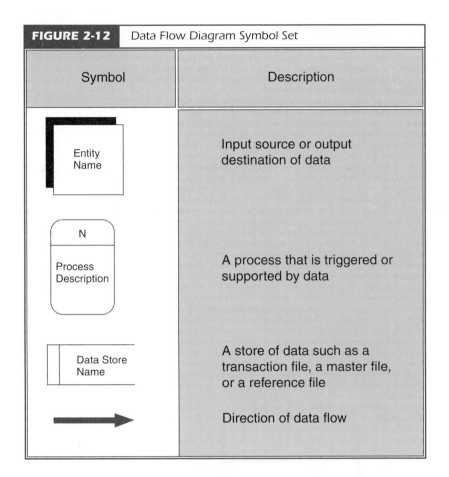

FIGURE 2-12   Data Flow Diagram Symbol Set

Symbol	Description
Entity Name	Input source or output destination of data
N Process Description	A process that is triggered or supported by data
Data Store Name	A store of data such as a transaction file, a master file, or a reference file
→	Direction of data flow

Processes in the DFD should be labeled with a descriptive verb such as *Ship* Goods, *Update* Records, or *Receive* Customer Order. Process objects should not be represented as nouns like Warehouse, Accounts Receivable Dept., or Sales Dept. The labeled arrows connecting the process objects represent flows of data such as Sales Order, Invoice, or Shipping Notice. Each data flow label should be unique. In other words, the same label should not be attached to two different flow lines in the same DFD. When data flow into a process and out again (to another process), they have, in some way, been changed by the process. This is true even if the data have not been physically altered. For example, consider the Approve Sales process in Figure 2-13, where Sales Order is examined for completeness before being processed further. It flows into the process as Sales Order and out of it as Approved Sales Order.

Entity Relationship Diagrams

An **entity relationship (ER) diagram** is a documentation technique used to represent the relationship between entities. **Entities** are physical resources (automobiles, cash, or inventory), events (ordering inventory, receiving cash, shipping goods), and agents (salesperson, customer, or vendor) about which the organization wishes to capture data. One common use for ER diagrams is to model an organization's database, which we examine in detail in Chapter 9.

Figure 2-14 shows the symbol set used in an ER diagram. The square symbol represents entities in the system. The labeled connecting line represents the nature of the relationship between two entities. The degree of the relationship is called **cardinality**. This is

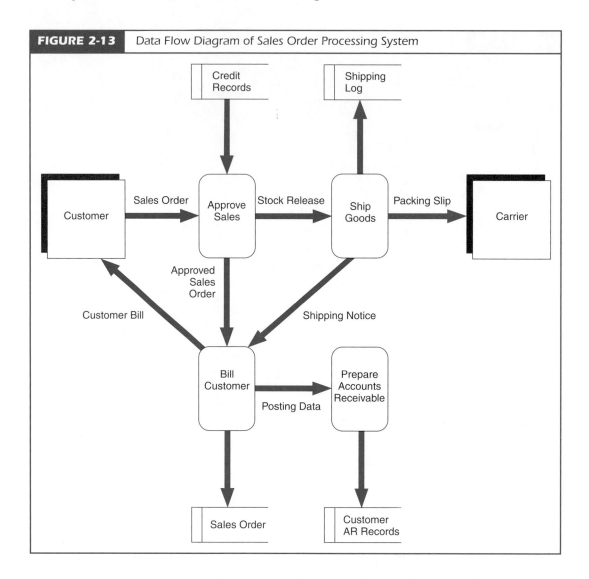

FIGURE 2-13 | Data Flow Diagram of Sales Order Processing System

the numerical mapping between entity instances. A relationship can be one-to-one (1:1), one-to-many (1:M), or many-to-many (M:M).[2] If we think of entities in the ER diagram as files of records, cardinality is the maximum number of records in one file that are related to a single record in the other file and vice versa.

Cardinality reflects normal business rules as well as organizational policy. For instance, the 1:1 cardinality in the first example in Figure 2-14 suggests that each salesperson in the organization is assigned one automobile. If instead the organization's policy were to assign a single automobile to one or more salespersons who share it, this policy would be reflected by a 1:M relationship. Similarly, the M:M relationship between vendor and inventory in Figure 2-14 implies that the organization buys the same type of products from one or more vendors. A company policy to buy particular items from a single vendor would be reflected by a 1:M cardinality.

---

2   We will study variants of these three basic cardinalities in Chapter 9 when we examine data modeling in greater detail. At that time a more precise documentation technique for representing cardinality will be introduced.

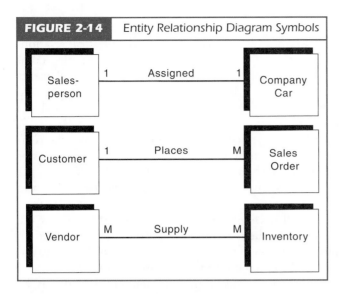

FIGURE 2-14   Entity Relationship Diagram Symbols

System designers identify entities and prepare a model of them, similar to the one presented in Figure 2-15. This **data model** is the blueprint for what ultimately will become the physical database. The data model presented in our example is not, however, sufficiently refined to be the plan for a workable database. Constructing a realistic data model is an advanced topic that involves understanding and applying techniques and rules that are beyond the scope of this chapter. We revisit this topic in Chapter 9, where it will be treated in sufficient detail to model and design a practical database.

Relationship between ER Diagrams and Data Flow Diagrams

Data flow diagrams and ER diagrams depict different aspects of the same system, but they are related and can be reconciled. A DFD is a model of system processes and the ER diagram models the data used in or affected by the system. The two diagrams are related through data; each data store in the DFD represents a corresponding data entity in the ER diagram. Figure 2-15 presents the ER diagram for the DFD in Figure 2-13.

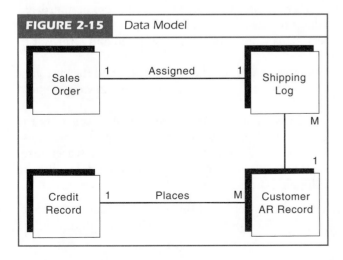

FIGURE 2-15   Data Model

FLOWCHARTS

A flowchart is a graphical representation of a system that describes the *physical* relationship between its key entities. Flowcharts can be used to represent manual activities, computer processing activities, or both. A **document flowchart** is used to depict the elements of a *manual system*, including accounting records (documents, journals, ledgers, and files), organizational departments involved in the process, and activities (both clerical and physical) that are performed in the departments.

System flowcharts portray the computer aspects of a system. They depict the relationships between input (source) data, transaction files, computer programs, master files, and output reports produced by the system. System flowcharts also describe the type of media being used in the system, such as magnetic tape, magnetic disks, and terminals.

The dichotomy between document flowcharts and system flowcharts reflects the dichotomy that traditionally existed between the manual and the computer aspects of an information system. Today, the human–machine interface is far more fluid than it was in the past. For example, transactions may be entered into the system directly by end users, processing often occurs in real time on the user's desktop computer, and output may be delivered to the user via a terminal rather than paper reports. Thus, modern systems are composed of both manual and computer operations.

The flowcharting examples that follow will illustrate the use of traditional *document flowcharts* to represent manual systems and *system flowcharts* to describe systems that employ both manual and computer operations. *Program flowcharts* that describe the internal logic of computer programs are explained last.

Document Flowcharts

To demonstrate the preparation of a document flowchart, let's assume that an auditor needs to flowchart a sales order system to evaluate its internal controls and procedures. The auditor will begin by interviewing individuals involved in the sales order process to determine what they do. This information will be captured in a set of facts similar to those below. Keep in mind that the purpose here is to demonstrate flowcharting. Thus, for clarity, the system facts are intentionally simplistic.

1. A clerk in the sales department receives customer orders by mail and prepares four copies of a sales order.
2. Copy 1 of the sales order is sent to the credit department for approval. The other three copies and the original customer order are filed temporarily, pending credit approval.
3. The credit department clerk validates the customer's order against credit records kept in the credit department. The clerk signs Copy 1 to signify approval and returns it to the sales clerk.
4. When the sales clerk receives credit approval he or she files Copy 1 and the customer order in the department. The clerk sends Copy 2 to the warehouse and Copies 3 and 4 to the shipping department.
5. The warehouse clerk picks the products from the shelves, records the transfer in the stock records, and sends the products and Copy 2 to the shipping department.
6. The shipping department receives Copy 2 and the goods from the warehouse, attaches Copy 2 as a packing slip, and ships the goods to the customer. Finally, the clerk files Copies 3 and 4 in the shipping department.

Based on these facts the auditor can create a flowchart of this partial system. It is important to note that flowcharting is as much an art form as it is a technical skill, giving the flowchart author a great deal of license. Nevertheless, the primary objective should be to provide an unambiguous description of the system. With this in mind, certain rules and conventions need to be observed:

- The flowchart should be labeled to clearly identify the system that it represents.

- The correct symbols should be used to represent the entities in the system.

- All symbols on the flowchart should be labeled.

- Lines should have arrowheads to clearly show the process flow and sequence of events.

- If complex processes need additional explanation for clarity, a text description should be included on the flowchart or in an attached document referenced by the flowchart.

Lay Out the Physical Areas of Activity. Remember that a flowchart reflects the physical system, which is represented as vertical columns of events and actions separated by lines of demarcation. Generally, each of these areas of activity is a separate column with a heading. From the system facts above we see that there are four distinct areas of activity—sales department, credit department, warehouse, and shipping department. The first step in preparing the flowchart is to lay out these areas of activity and label each of them. This step is illustrated in Figure 2-16.

| **FIGURE 2-16** | Flowchart Showing Areas of Activity |

| Sales Department | Credit Department | Warehouse | Shipping Department |

Transcribe the Written Facts into Visual Format. At this point we are ready to start representing the system facts using visual objects. These will be selected from the symbols set presented in Figure 2-17. We begin with the first stated fact:

1. *A clerk in the sales department receives customer orders by mail and prepares four copies of a sales order.*

Figure 2-18 illustrates how this fact could be represented. The customer is the source of the order but is not part of the system. The oval object is typically used to convey a data source or recipient that is apart from the system being flowcharted. The document symbol entering the sales department signifies the customer order and is labeled accordingly. The bucket-shaped symbol represents a manual process. In this case, the clerk in the sales department prepares four copies of the sales order. Notice that the clerk's task, not the clerk, is depicted. The arrows between the objects show the direction of flow and the sequence of events.

By transcribing each fact in this way a flowchart is systematically constructed. See how the second and third facts restated below add to the flowchart in Figure 2-19.

2. *Copy 1 of the sales order is sent to the credit department for approval. The other three copies and the original customer order are filed temporarily, pending credit approval.*
3. *The credit department clerk validates the customer's order against credit records kept in the credit department. The clerk signs Copy 1 to signify approval and returns it to the sales clerk.*

Two new symbols are introduced in this figure. First, the upside-down triangle symbol represents the temporary file mentioned in fact 2. This is a physical file of paper documents such as a drawer in a filing cabinet or desk. Such files are typically arranged

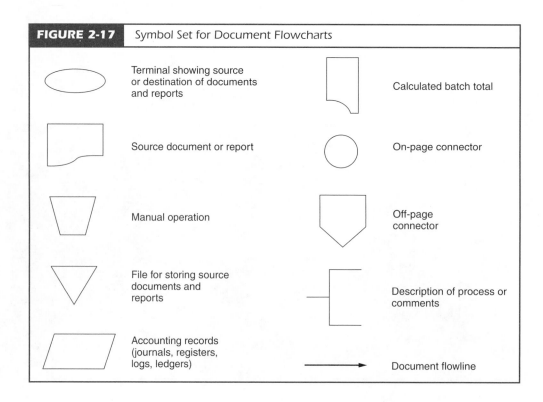

FIGURE 2-17	Symbol Set for Document Flowcharts

Terminal showing source or destination of documents and reports		Calculated batch total
Source document or report		On-page connector
Manual operation		Off-page connector
File for storing source documents and reports		Description of process or comments
Accounting records (journals, registers, logs, ledgers)		Document flowline

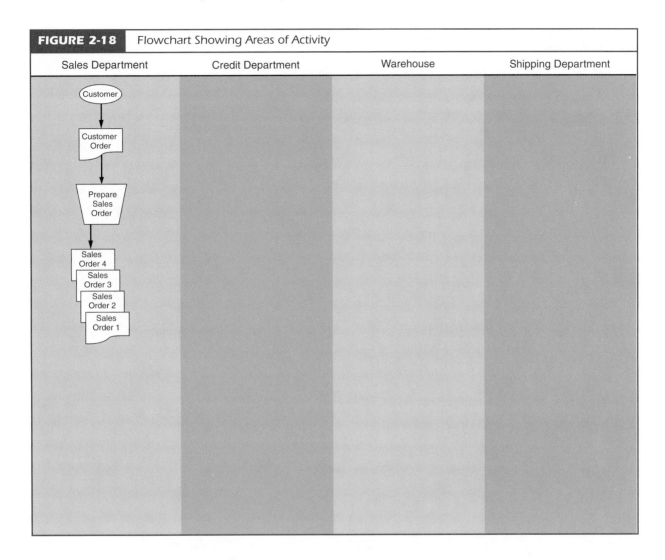

FIGURE 2-18   Flowchart Showing Areas of Activity

| Sales Department | Credit Department | Warehouse | Shipping Department |

according to a specified order. To signify the filing system used the file symbol will usually contain an "N" for numeric (invoice number), "C" for chronological (date), or "A" for alphabetical order (customer name). Secondly, the parallelogram shape represents the credit records mentioned in fact 3. This symbol is used to depict many types of accounting records such as journals, subsidiary ledgers, general ledgers, and shipping logs.

Having laid these foundations, let's now complete the flowchart by depicting the remaining facts.

4. *When the sales clerk receives credit approval he or she files Copy 1 and the customer order in the department. The clerk sends Copy 2 to the warehouse and Copies 3 and 4 to the shipping department.*
5. *The warehouse clerk picks the products from the shelves, records the transfer in the stock records, and sends the products and Copy 2 to the shipping department.*
6. *The shipping department receives Copy 2 and the goods from the warehouse, attaches Copy 2 as a packing slip, and ships the goods to the customer. Finally, the clerk files Copies 3 and 4 in the shipping department.*

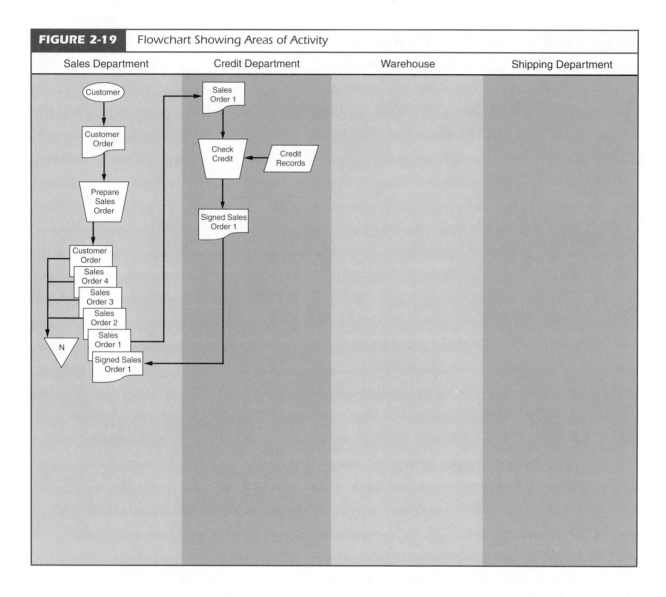

FIGURE 2-19   Flowchart Showing Areas of Activity

Sales Department	Credit Department	Warehouse	Shipping Department

The completed flowchart is presented in Figure 2-20. Notice the circular symbol labeled "A." This is an on-page connector used to replace flowchart lines that otherwise would cause excessive clutter on the page. In this instance, the connector replaces the lines that signify the movement of Copies 3 and 4 from the sales department to the shipping department. Lines should be used whenever possible to promote clarity. Restricted use of connectors, however, can improve the readability of the flowchart. Notice also that the physical products or goods mentioned in facts 4 and 5 are not shown on the flowchart. The document (Copy 2) that accompanies and controls the goods is shown. Some purists argue that a document flowchart should show only the flow of *documents*, not physical assets. On the other hand, if showing the physical asset improves the understandability of the flowchart, then its inclusion adds value.

Finally, for visual clarity, document flowcharts show the processing of a single transaction only. You should keep in mind that transactions usually pass through manual procedures in batches (groups). Before moving on to the next documentation technique, we need to examine some important issues related to batch processing.

FIGURE 2-20   Flowchart Showing Areas of Activity

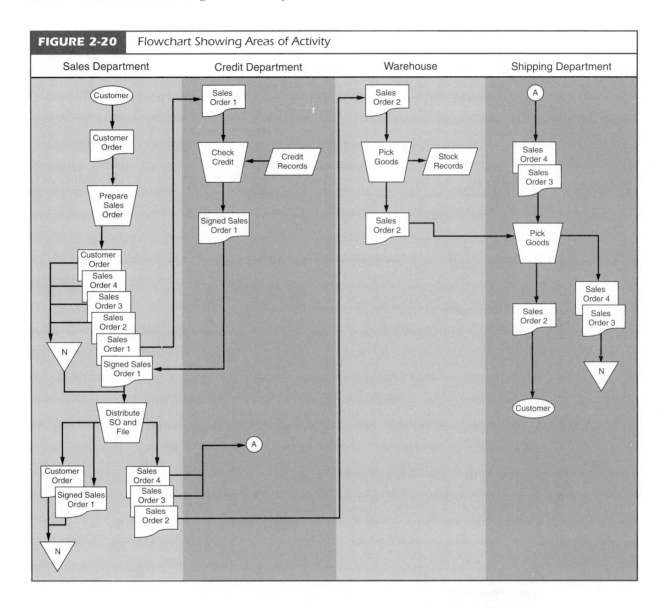

Batch Processing

Batch processing permits the efficient management of a large volume of transactions. A **batch** is a group of similar transactions (such as sales orders) that are accumulated over time and then processed together. There are two general advantages to batch processing. First, organizations improve efficiency by grouping together large numbers of transactions into batches rather than processing each event separately. Thus a business can achieve an efficient allocation of its processing resources by employing specialized, cost-effective procedures to deal with these batches. Batch processing is an economical method of high-volume transaction processing.

Second, batch processing provides control over the transaction process. The accuracy of the process can be established by periodically reconciling the batch against the control figure. For example, assume that the total value of a batch of sales orders is $100,000. This number can be recorded when the batch is first assembled and then recalculated at various points during its processing. If an error occurs during processing (e.g., a sales order is lost), then the recalculated batch total will not equal the original batch total and the problem will be detected.

Both of these advantages have implications for designing batch systems. The first is that economies are derived from having batches that are as large as possible. The cost of processing each transaction is reduced when the fixed costs of data processing are allocated across a large number of transactions. The second implication is that finding an error in a very large batch may prove difficult. When a batch is small, error identification is much easier. In designing a batch system, the accountant should seek a balance between the economic advantage of large batches and the troubleshooting advantage of small batches. There is no magic number for the size of a batch. This decision is based on a number of operational, business, and economic factors. Among these are the volume of transactions, the competitiveness of the industry, the normal frequency of errors, the financial implications of an undetected error, and the costs of processing. Depending on these factors, a system might process small batches (50 to 100 items) several times a day or an entire day's activity as a single batch.

System Flowcharts

We now examine the use of a system flowchart to represent a system that includes both manual and computer processes. The symbol set used to construct the system flowchart will come from Figure 2-17 and Figure 2-21. Again, our example is based on a sales order system that is described by the following facts.

1. A clerk in the sales department receives customer orders by mail and enters the information into a computer terminal that is attached to a computer program in the computer operations department. The original customer order is filed in the sales department. Facts 2, 3, and 4 relate to activities that occur in the computer operations department.
2. A computer program edits the transactions, checks the customers' credit by referencing a credit history file, and produces a transaction file of sales orders.
3. The sales order transaction file is then processed by an update program that posts the transactions to the account receivables (AR) and inventory files.
4. Finally, the update program produces three paper copies of the sales order. Copy 1 is sent to the warehouse and Copies 2 and 3 are sent to the shipping department.
5. The warehouse clerk picks the products from the shelves, records the transfer in the stock records, and sends the products and Copy 1 to the shipping department.
6. The shipping department receives Copy 1 and the goods from the warehouse, attaches Copy 1 as a packing slip, and ships the goods to the customer. Finally, the clerk files Copies 2 and 3 in the shipping department.

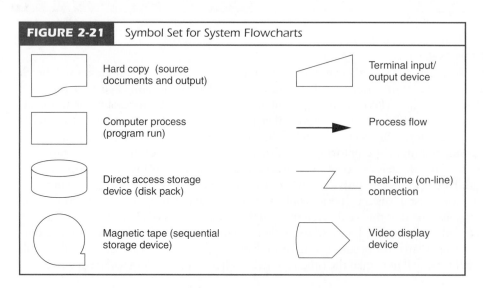

FIGURE 2-21   Symbol Set for System Flowcharts

Hard copy (source documents and output)

Terminal input/output device

Computer process (program run)

Process flow

Direct access storage device (disk pack)

Real-time (on-line) connection

Magnetic tape (sequential storage device)

Video display device

Lay Out the Physical Areas of Activity. The flowcharting process begins by creating a template that depicts the areas of activity similar to the one in Figure 2-16. The only difference is that this system has a computer operations department and does not have a credit department.

Transcribe the Written Facts into Visual Format. As with the document flowchart, the next step is to systematically transcribe the written facts into visual objects. Figure 2-22 illustrates how facts 1, 2, and 3 translate visually.

The customer, customer order, and file symbols in this flowchart are the same as in the previous document flowchart example. The sales clerk's activity, however, is now automated and the manual process symbol has been replaced with a computer terminal symbol. Also, since this is a data *input* operation the arrowhead on the flowchart line points in the direction of the edit and credit check program. If the terminal was also used to receive output (the facts do not specify such an operation), arrowheads would be on both ends of the line.

As with the document flowchart, the emphasis here is on the physical system. For example, the terminal used by the sales clerk to enter customer orders is physically located in the

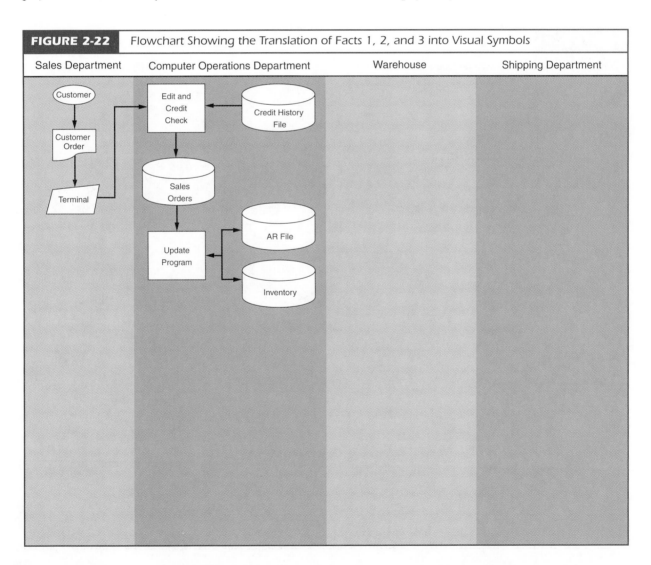

FIGURE 2-22   Flowchart Showing the Translation of Facts 1, 2, and 3 into Visual Symbols

| Sales Department | Computer Operations Department | Warehouse | Shipping Department |

sales department, but the programs that process the transactions and the files that are used, created, and updated by these events are stored in a separate computer operations department.

Notice how the flowchart line points from the credit history file to the edit program. This indicates that the file is read (referenced) but not changed (updated) by the program. In contrast, the interactions between the update program and the AR and inventory files are two-way. Records are read by the program, updated to reflect the transactions, and then written back to the files. The logic of a file update is explained later in the chapter.

Let's now translate the remaining facts into visual symbols. The update program in fact 4 produces three hard-copy documents in the computer operations department, which are then distributed to the warehouse and shipping departments. The activities described by facts 5 and 6 and the symbols that represent them are very similar to those described in the previous document flowchart example. Figure 2-23 illustrates the completed system flowchart.

Program Flowcharts

The system flowchart in Figure 2-23 shows the relationship between two computer programs, the files they use, and the outputs they produce. However, this level of documentation

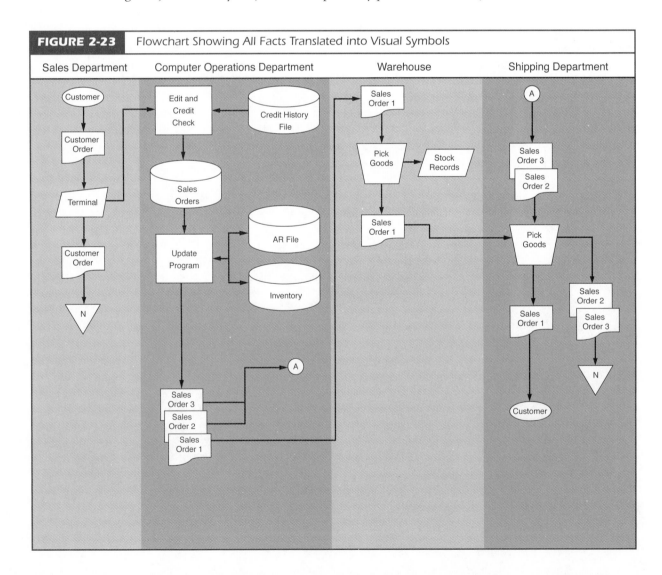

FIGURE 2-23   Flowchart Showing All Facts Translated into Visual Symbols

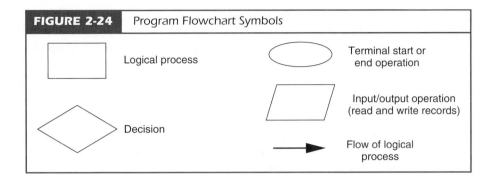

FIGURE 2-24   Program Flowchart Symbols

Logical process

Decision

Terminal start or
end operation

Input/output operation
(read and write records)

Flow of logical
process

does not provide the operational details that are sometimes needed. For example, an auditor wishing to assess the correctness of the edit program's logic cannot do so from the system flowchart. This requires a **program flowchart**. The symbol set used for program flowcharts is presented in Figure 2-24.

Every program represented in a system flowchart should have a supporting program flowchart that describes its logic. Figure 2-25 presents the logic of the edit program

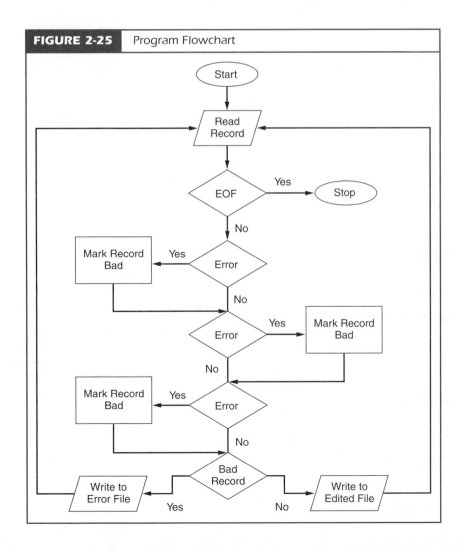

FIGURE 2-25   Program Flowchart

shown in Figure 2-26. Each step of the program's logic is represented by a separate symbol, and each symbol represents one or more lines of computer program code. The connector lines between the symbols establish the logical order of execution. Tracing the flowchart downward from the start symbol, the program performs the following logical steps in the order listed:

1. The program retrieves a single record from the unedited transaction file and stores it in memory.
2. The first logical test is to see if the program has reached the end-of-file (EOF) condition for the transaction file. Most file structures use a special record or marker to indicate an EOF condition. When EOF is reached, the edit program will terminate and the next program in the system (in this case, the update program) will be executed. As long as there is a record in the unedited transaction file, the result of the EOF test will be "no" and process control is passed to the next logical step in the edit program.
3. Processing involves a series of tests to identify certain clerical and logical errors. Each test, represented by a decision symbol, evaluates the presence or absence of a condition. For example, an edit test could be to detect the presence of alphabetic data in a field that should contain only numeric data. We examine specific edit and validation tests in Chapter 17.
4. Error-free records are sent to the edited transaction file.

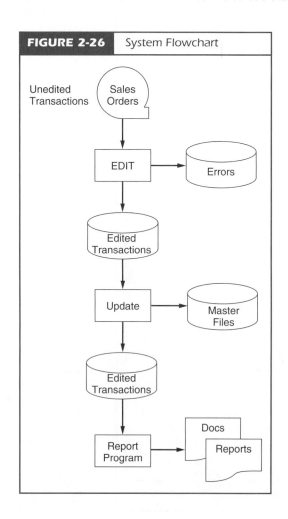

FIGURE 2-26   System Flowchart

5. Records containing errors are sent to the error file.
6. The program loops back to Step 1 and the process is repeated until the EOF condition is reached.

Accountants sometimes use program flowcharts to verify the correctness of program logic. They compare flowcharts to the actual program code to determine whether the program is actually doing what the documentation describes. Program flowcharts provide essential details for conducting information technology (IT) audits, which we examine in Chapters 15, 16 and 17.

RECORD LAYOUT DIAGRAMS

Record layout diagrams are used to reveal the internal structure of the records that constitute a file or database table. The layout diagram usually shows the name, data type, and length of each attribute (or field) in the record. Detailed data structure information is needed for such tasks as identifying certain types of system failures, analyzing error reports, and designing tests of computer logic for debugging and auditing purposes. A simpler form of record layout, shown in Figure 2-27, suits our purposes best. This type of layout shows the content of a record. Each data attribute and key field is shown in terms of its name and relative location.

FIGURE 2-27	Record Layout Diagram for Customer File

Customer File

Key

Customer Number	Customer Name	Street Address	City	State	Zip Code	Credit Limit

COMPUTER-BASED ACCOUNTING SYSTEMS

The final section in this chapter examines alternative computer-based transaction processing models. Computer-based accounting systems fall into two broad classes: batch systems and real-time systems. A number of alternative configurations exist within each of these classes. Systems designers base their configuration choices on a variety of considerations. Table 2-1 summarizes some of the distinguishing characteristics of batch and real-time processing that feature prominently in these decisions.

DIFFERENCES BETWEEN BATCH AND REAL-TIME SYSTEMS

Time Lag

Batch systems assemble transactions into groups for processing. In this approach, there is always a time lag between the point at which an economic event occurs and the point at which it is reflected in the firm's accounts. The amount of lag depends on the frequency of batch processing. Time lags can range from minutes to weeks. Payroll processing is an example of a typical batch system. The economic events—the application of employee labor—occur continuously throughout the pay period. At the end of the period, the paychecks for all employees are prepared together as a batch.

TABLE 2-1	Characteristic Differences between Batch and Real-Time Processing	
	DATA PROCESSING METHODS	
	Batch	**Real-Time**
Information Time Frame	Lag exists between time when the economic event occurs and when it is recorded.	Processing takes place when the economic event occurs.
Resources	Generally, fewer resources (hardware, programming, training) are required.	More resources are required than for batch processing.
Operational Efficiency	Certain records are processed after the event to avoid operational delays.	All records pertaining to the event are processed immediately.

Real-time systems process transactions individually at the moment the event occurs. As records are not grouped into batches, there are no time lags between occurrence and recording. An example of real-time processing is an airline reservations system, which processes requests for services from one traveler at a time while he or she waits.

Resources

Generally, batch systems demand fewer organizational resources (such as programming costs, computer time, and user training) than real-time systems. For example, batch systems can use sequential files stored on magnetic tape. Real-time systems use direct access files that require more expensive storage devices, such as magnetic disks. In practice, however, these cost differentials are disappearing. As a result, business organizations typically use magnetic disks for both batch and real-time processing.

The most significant resource differentials are in the areas of systems development (programming) and computer operations. As batch systems are generally simpler than their real-time counterparts, they tend to have shorter development periods and are easier for programmers to maintain. On the other hand, as much as 50 percent of the total programming costs for real-time systems are incurred in designing the user interfaces. Real-time systems must be friendly, forgiving, and easy to work with. Pop-up menus, online tutorials, and special "help" features require additional programming and add greatly to the cost of the system.

Finally, real-time systems require dedicated processing capacity. Real-time systems must deal with transactions as they occur. Some types of systems must be available 24 hours a day whether they are being used or not. The computer capacity dedicated to such systems cannot be used for other purposes. Thus, implementing a real-time system may require either the purchase of a dedicated computer or an investment in additional computer capacity. In contrast, batch systems use computer capacity only when the program is being run. When the batch job completes processing, the freed capacity can be reallocated to other applications.

Operational Efficiency

Real-time processing in systems that handle large volumes of transactions each day can create operational inefficiencies. A single transaction may affect several different accounts. Some of these accounts, however, may not need to be updated in real time. In fact, the task of doing so takes time that, when multiplied by hundreds or thousands of transactions, can cause significant processing delays. Batch processing of noncritical accounts, however, improves operational efficiency by eliminating unnecessary activities at critical points in the process. This is illustrated with an example later in the chapter.

Efficiency versus Effectiveness

In selecting a data processing mode, the designer must consider the trade-off between efficiency and effectiveness. For example, users of an airline reservations system cannot wait until 100 passengers (an efficient batch size) assemble in the travel agent's office before their transactions are processed. When immediate access to current information is critical to the user's needs, then real-time processing is the logical choice. When time lags in information have no detrimental effects on the user's performance and operational efficiencies can be achieved by processing data in batches, then batch processing is probably the superior choice.

ALTERNATIVE DATA PROCESSING APPROACHES

Legacy Systems versus Modern Systems

Not all modern organizations use entirely modern information systems. Some firms employ legacy systems for certain aspects of their data processing. When legacy systems are used to process financially significant transactions, auditors need to know how to evaluate and test them. We saw in Chapter 1 that legacy systems tend to have the following distinguishing features: they are mainframe-based applications; they tend to be batch oriented; early legacy systems use flat files for data storage, however, hierarchical and network databases are often associated with later-era legacy systems. These highly structured and inflexible storage systems promote a single-user environment that discourages information integration within business organizations.

Modern systems tend to be client-server (network) based and process transactions in real time. While this is the trend in most organizations, the reader should note that many modern systems are mainframe based and use batch processing. Unlike their predecessors, modern systems store transactions and master files in relational database tables. A major advantage of database storage is the degree of process integration and data sharing that can be achieved.

While legacy system configurations no longer constitute the defining features of AIS, they are still of marginal importance to accountants. Therefore, for those who seek further understanding of legacy system issues, detailed material on transaction processing techniques using flat-file structures is provided in Section B of the appendix to this chapter.

The remainder of the chapter focuses on modern system technologies used for processing accounting transactions. Some systems employ a combination of batch and real-time processing, while others are purely real-time systems. In several chapters that follow, we will examine how these approaches are configured to support specific functions such as sales order processing, purchasing, and payroll.

Updating Master Files from Transactions

Whether batch or real-time processing is being used, updating a master file record involves changing the value of one or more of its variable fields to reflect the effects of a transaction. Figure 2-28 presents record structures for a sales order transaction file and two associated master files, accounts receivable (AR) and inventory. The primary key (PK)—the unique identifier—for the inventory file is INVENTORY NUMBER. The primary key for accounts receivable is ACCOUNT NUMBER. Notice that the record structure for the sales order file contains a primary key (SALES ORDER NUMBER) and two secondary key (SK) fields, ACCOUNT NUMBER and INVENTORY NUMBER. These

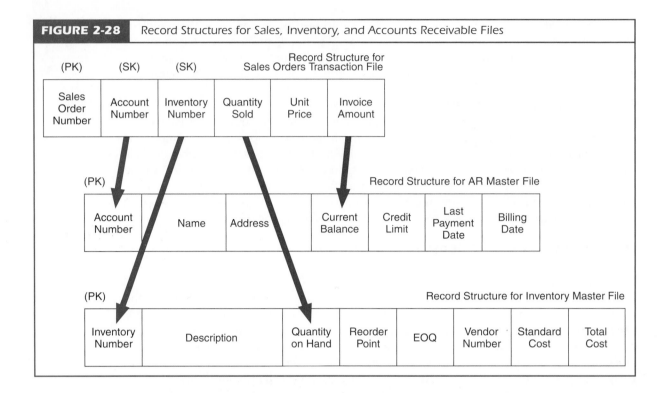

FIGURE 2-28   Record Structures for Sales, Inventory, and Accounts Receivable Files

secondary keys are used for locating the corresponding records in the master files. To simplify the example, we assume that each sale is for a single item of inventory. In Chapter 9 we examine database structures in detail. At that time we study the database complexities associated with more realistic business transactions.

The update procedure in this example involves the following steps:

1. A sales order record is read by the system.
2. ACCOUNT NUMBER is used to search the AR master file and retrieve the corresponding AR record.
3. The AR update procedure calculates the new customer balance by adding the value stored in the INVOICE AMOUNT field of the sales order record to the CURRENT BALANCE field value in the AR master record.
4. Next, INVENTORY NUMBER is used to search for the corresponding record in the inventory master file.
5. The inventory update program reduces inventory levels by deducting the QUANTITY SOLD value in a transaction record from the QUANTITY ON HAND field value in the inventory record.
6. A new sales order record is read and the process above is repeated.

Database Backup Procedures

Each record in a database file is assigned a unique disk location or *address* (see Section A of the chapter appendix) that is determined by its primary key value. Because only a single valid location exists for each record, updating the record must occur in place. Figure 2-29 shows this technique.

In this example, an account receivable record with a $100 current balance is being updated by a $50 sale transaction. The master file record is permanently stored at a disk

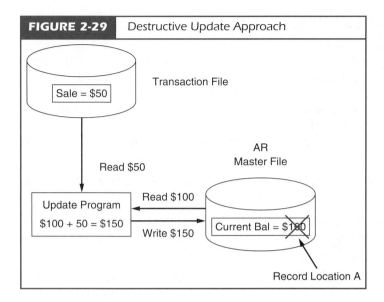

FIGURE 2-29 | Destructive Update Approach

address designated Location A. The update program reads both the transaction record and the master file record into memory. The receivable is updated to reflect the new current balance value of $150 and then returned to Location A. The original current balance value of $100 is destroyed when replaced by the new value of $150. This technique is called *destructive update*.

The destructive update approach leaves no backup copy of the original master file. Only the current value is available to the user. If the current master becomes damaged or corrupted in some way, no backup version exists from which to reconstruct the file. To preserve adequate accounting records, separate backup procedures, such as those shown in Figure 2-30, must be implemented.

Prior to each batch update or periodically (e.g., every 15 minutes), the master file being updated is copied to create a backup version of the original file. Should the current master be destroyed after the update process, reconstruction is possible in two stages. First, a special recovery program uses the backup file to create a pre-update version of the master file. Second, the file update process is repeated using the previous batch of transactions to restore the master to its current condition. Because of the potential risk to accounting records, accountants are naturally concerned about the adequacy of all backup procedures. In Chapter 15 we examine many issues related to file backup.

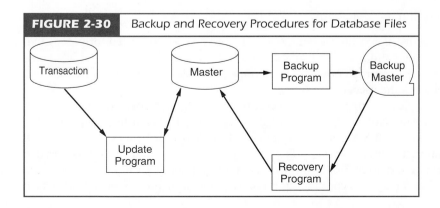

FIGURE 2-30 | Backup and Recovery Procedures for Database Files

BATCH PROCESSING USING REAL-TIME DATA COLLECTION

A popular data processing approach, particularly for large operations, is to electronically capture transaction data at the source as they occur. By distributing data input capability to users, certain transaction errors can be prevented or detected and corrected at their source. The result is a transaction file that is free from most of the errors that plague older legacy systems. The transaction file is later processed in batch mode to achieve operational efficiency. Figure 2-31 illustrates this approach with a simplified sales order system such as that used in a department store. Key steps in the process are:

- The sales department clerk captures customer sales data pertaining to the item(s) being purchased and the customer's account.

- The system then checks the customer's credit limit from data in the customer record (account receivable subsidiary file) and updates his or her account balance to reflect the amount of the sale.

- Next the system updates the quantity on-hand field in the inventory record (inventory subsidiary file) to reflect the reduction in inventory. This provides up-to-date information to other clerks as to inventory availability.

- A record of the sale is then added to the sales order file (transaction file), which is processed in batch mode at the end of the business day. This batch process records each transaction in the sales journal and updates the affected general ledger accounts.

You may be wondering at this point why the sales journal and general ledger accounts are being processed in batch mode. Why not update them in real time along with the subsidiary accounts? The answer is to achieve operational efficiency. We now examine what that means.

Let's assume that the organization using the sales order system configuration illustrated in Figure 2-31 is large and capable of serving hundreds of customers concurrently. Also assume that 500 sales terminals are distributed throughout its many large departments.

Each customer sale affects the following six accounting records:

- Customer account receivable (Subsidiary—unique)

- Inventory item (Subsidiary—almost unique)

- Inventory control (GL—common)

- Account receivable control (GL—common)

- Sales (GL—common)

- Cost of good sold (GL—common)

To maintain the integrity of accounting data, once a record has been accessed for processing, it is locked by the system and made unavailable to other users until processing of it is complete. Using the effected records above as an example, consider the implications that this data-locking rule has on the users of the system.

When processing a customer account receivable subsidiary record, the rule has no implications for other users of the system. Each user accesses only his or her unique record. For example, accessing John Smith's account does not prevent Mary Jones from accessing her account. Updating the inventory subsidiary record is almost unique. Since it is possible that both Mary Jones and John Smith are independently purchasing the same item at the same time, Mary Jones may be kept waiting a few seconds until John Smith's transaction

FIGURE 2-31	Batch Processing with Real-Time Data Collections

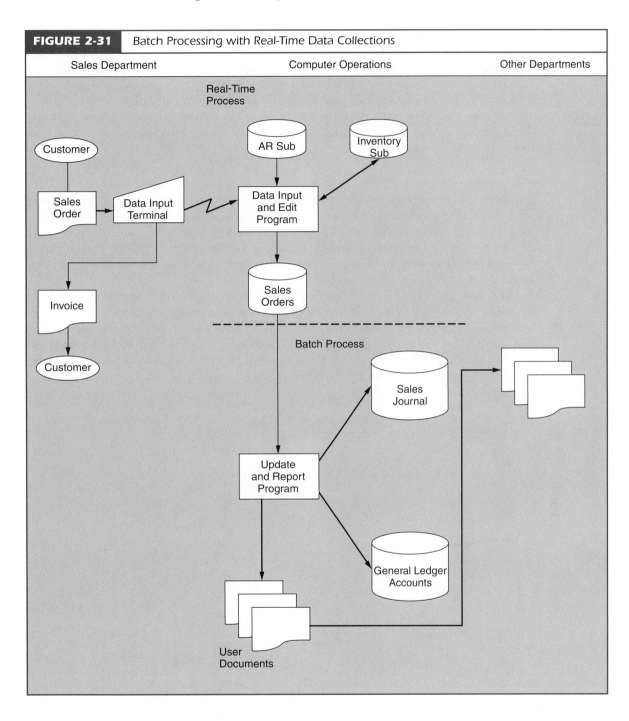

Sales Department | Computer Operations | Other Departments

releases the lock on the inventory account. This will be a relatively rare event, and any such conflicts will be of little inconvenience to customers. As a general rule, therefore, master file records that are unique to a transaction such as customer accounts and individual inventory records can be updated in real time without causing operational delays.

Updating the records in the general ledger is a different matter. All general ledger accounts previously listed need to be updated by every sales transaction. If the processing of John Smith's transaction begins before Mary Jones', then she must wait until all six records have been updated before her transaction can proceed. The 20- or 30-second delay brought about by this conflict will, however, probably not inconvenience Mary Jones. This problem becomes manifest as transaction volumes increase. A 20-second delay in each of 500 customer transactions would create operational inefficiency on a chaotic level. Each of the 500 customers must wait until the person ahead of him or her in the queue has completed processing their transaction. The last person in the queue will experience a delay of 500 $\times$ 20 seconds = 2¾ hours.

REAL-TIME PROCESSING

Real-time systems process the entire transaction as it occurs. For example, a sales order processed by the system in Figure 2-32 can be captured, filled, and shipped the same day. Such a system has many potential benefits, including improved productivity, reduced inventory, increased inventory turnover, decreased lags in customer billing, and enhanced customer satisfaction. Since transaction information is transmitted electronically, physical source documents can be eliminated or greatly reduced.

Real-time processing is well suited to systems that process lower transaction volumes and those that do not share common records. These systems make extensive use of local area network (LAN) and wide area network (WAN) technology. Terminals at distributed sites throughout the organization are used for receiving, processing, and sending information about current transactions. These must be linked in a network arrangement so users can communicate. The operational characteristics of networks are examined in Chapter 12.

FIGURE 2-32   Real-Time Processing of Sales Orders

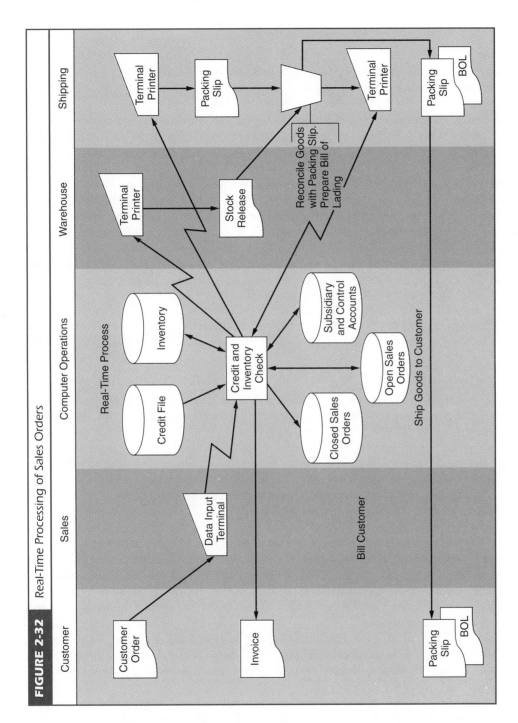

FIGURE 2-32   Real-Time Processing of Sales Orders

Summary

This chapter divided the treatment of transaction processing systems into four major sections. The first section provided an overview of transaction processing, showing its vital role as an information provider for financial reporting, internal management reporting, and the support of day-to-day operations. To deal efficiently with large volumes of financial transactions, business organizations group together transactions of similar types into transaction cycles. Three transaction cycles account for most of a firm's economic activity: the revenue cycle, the expenditure cycle, and the conversion cycle. The second section described the relationship among accounting records in both manual and computer-based systems. The third section of the chapter presented an overview of documentation techniques used to describe the key features of systems. Accountants must be proficient in the use of documentation tools to perform their professional duties. Six types of documentation are commonly used for this purpose: data flow diagrams, entity relationship diagrams, document flowcharts, system flowcharts, program flowcharts, and record layout diagrams. Finally, the chapter examined two computer techniques used for transaction processing: (1) batch processing using real-time data collection, and (2) real-time processing. The section also examined the operational efficiency issues associated with each configuration.

Appendix

Section A: Secondary Storage

A computer's secondary storage includes devices used to store and retrieve system software, application software, and data on magnetic or optical media, such as magnetic tape, hard or floppy disks, and CD-ROMs.

Magnetic Tape

As a secondary storage medium, magnetic tape has some important advantages. For example, large amounts of data can be stored on magnetic tape at a relatively low cost, and magnetic tape is reusable. The primary disadvantage is that data recorded on magnetic tape use the sequential access method; thus the retrieval of information from magnetic tape is slower than with other storage media.

Magnetic tapes for mainframes range in width from one-half to one inch and in length from 2,400 to 3,600 feet. A byte of data (representing a character, digit, or special symbols) is recorded on the tape along its width. (One byte equals eight binary digits, or bits. A bit is the smallest possible unit of electronic information, either a 0 or a 1.) A logical sequence of characters makes up a *field*, and several fields make up a *record*. The number of characters that can be recorded on one inch of tape is known as the tape's *density*. The density of magnetic tape ranges from 1,600 to several thousand bytes per inch. One magnetic tape might contain several million characters of data.

A tape drive is used to record bits of data onto magnetic tape. The tape drive reads and writes blocks of data at a time. Each block is separated by an interblock gap, which instructs the tape drive to stop reading or writing the data until another block is requested. Figure 2-33 shows records blocked together on a magnetic tape.

The tape drives used today in conjunction with microcomputers are usually programmed to back up (copy) the data on the hard disk. If the computer "crashes" (that is, if the data on the disk are destroyed), a duplicate of the data will be available.

Magnetic Disks

The data stored on magnetic disks (hard disks or floppy disks) are considered to be nonvolatile. The data will reside in a certain location on the magnetic surface until they are replaced with different data or erased. Data can be recorded to magnetic disks using either of the access methods described earlier.

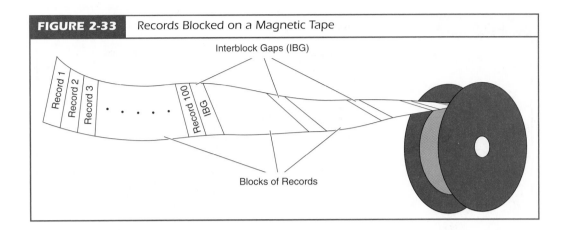

FIGURE 2-33 | Records Blocked on a Magnetic Tape

Interblock Gaps (IBG)

Record 1
Record 2
Record 3

· · · · ·

Record 100
IBG

Blocks of Records

To get the disk ready to receive data, its surface must be formatted. An operating system utility program formats the disk by dividing it into circular tracks and wedge-shaped sectors, which cut across the tracks. The number of bytes that can be stored at a particular track and sector determines the disk's density.

Disks are known as *direct access storage devices* because a piece of data can be accessed directly on the disk. Database management systems and application software work with the operating system to determine the location of the required data.

A disk has a rotating magnetic surface and a read-write head. The read-write head is on an access arm that moves back and forth over the magnetic surface. The time that elapses from when the operating system requests a piece of data to when it is read into the computer is called *access time*. The access time of a particular hard disk is a function of several factors: (1) the seek time—how fast the read-write head moves into position over a particular track, (2) the switching time—the time needed to activate the read-write head, (3) the rotational delay time—the time it takes to rotate the disk area under the read-write head, and (4) the data transfer time—the time it takes for the data to be transferred from the disk track to primary storage. Most microcomputer hard disks have an access time of 5 to 60 milliseconds.

The *file allocation table* is an area on the disk that keeps track of the name of each file, the number of bytes in the file, the date and time it was created, the type of file, and its location (address) on the disk. A file may be stored in only one place on the disk, or it may be spread across several locations. In the latter case, the disk's read-write head must skip among various addresses to read the entire file into the primary memory.

We have used the term *address* several times to represent a disk storage location. Let's now examine the elements of a disk address.

Disk Address. As we have seen, the surface of a disk is divided into magnetized tracks that form concentric circles of data. The floppy disk for a microcomputer may have 40 or 80 tracks on a surface, while the surface of a mainframe disk could contain several hundred tracks. These tracks are logically divided into smaller blocks or record locations where data records reside. Each location is unique and has an address—a numerical value. Depending on the disk's size and density, hundreds or thousands of records may be stored on a single track. Figure 2-34 shows data storage on a disk. For illustration purposes, the physical size of the records is greatly exaggerated.

The concept of an address applies to all types of magnetic disks, including individual floppy disks and hard disks used in microcomputers and the larger mainframe disk-packs. A difference lies in the way the disks are physically arranged. Mainframe disks are often stacked on top of one another in a disk-pack arrangement that resembles a stack of phonograph records. Figure 2-35 illustrates this technique. The disks are mounted to a central spindle that rotates at over 3,500 revolutions per minute. Each disk surface is provided with a separate read-write head that is used for storing and retrieving data.

FIGURE 2-34	How Data Is Stored on a Disk

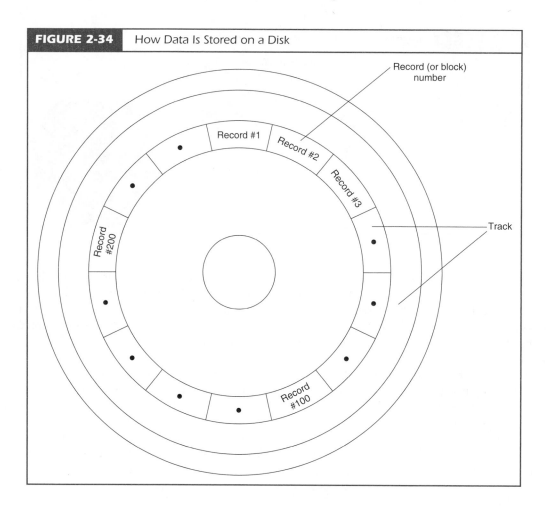

Data Storage on a Disk-Pack. Every disk in a disk-pack has two surfaces with the same number of tracks on each surface. Figure 2-35 shows that Track 100 exists on the top and bottom surfaces of each disk in the disk-pack. Therefore, this disk-pack containing 11 disks has 22 occurrences of Track 100. To protect the data from exposure to damage, the very top and bottom surfaces of the disk-pack are not used, yielding 20 data storage surfaces for Track 100.

When viewed collectively, the same track on each surface in the disk-pack is called a *cylinder*. Therefore, in our example, Cylinder 100 contains 20 tracks of data. However, the cylinders on a microcomputer's floppy disk or hard disk contain only two tracks because these disks have only two surfaces.

Locating a Record Based on Its Address. A disk address consists of three components: the cylinder number, the surface number, and the record (or block) number. To find a record, the system must know the numeric value for each of these components. For example, if a record's address is Cylinder 105, Surface 15, and Record Block 157, the record in question could be directly accessed as follows: First, the disk-pack control device moves the read-write heads into position above Track 105 on each surface (Cylinder 105). Next, it activates the read-write head for Surface 15. Finally, as Record Block 157 passes under the active read-write head, it is either read or written.

The key task in direct access storage and retrieval is ascertaining the record's address. This may be determined from tables or calculations based on its primary key. Several direct access techniques are examined in Chapter 9.

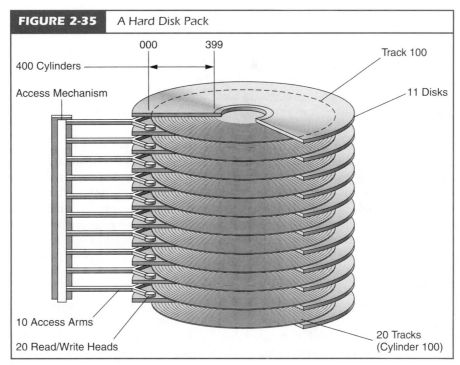

FIGURE 2-35 | A Hard Disk Pack

400 Cylinders

000   399

Track 100

11 Disks

Access Mechanism

10 Access Arms

20 Read/Write Heads

20 Tracks
(Cylinder 100)

The access mechanism can position itself to access data from each of the four hundred cylinders. A cylinder is a set of all tracks with the same distance from the axis about which the disk-pack rotates. In this example, there are twenty tracks in each cylinder.

Optical Disks

Optical disks are growing in popularity. The advantage of optical disks is that they can store very large amounts of data. A compact disc, one type of optical disk, is as portable as a floppy disk but can store more than 600 MB of data. There are several types of optical disk storage systems, including CD-ROM, WORM, and erasable optical disks.

A *CD-ROM (compact disc read-only memory)* is a secondary storage device that contains data or programs imprinted by the manufacturer. The CD-ROM is a read-only device; that is, the user cannot write to (alter) the data on the CD. The *write-once, read-many (WORM)* disk is a secondary storage device that allows the user to write to the disk one time. An *erasable optical disk* allows the user to store and modify data on the disk many times.

Section B: Legacy Systems

A defining feature of legacy systems is their use of flat files for data storage. The following section presents a review of data structures and the flat-file processing techniques that evolved from them. It then examines data processing methodologies that employ these flat-file structures. The section concludes with a detailed explanation of the program logic underlying flat-file update procedures.

Data Structures

Data structures constitute the physical and logical arrangement of data in files and databases. Understanding how data are organized and accessed is central to understanding transaction processing. Data structures have two fundamental components: organization and access method. **Organization** refers to the way records are physically arranged on the secondary storage device (e.g., a disk). This may be either *sequential* or *random*. The records in sequential files are stored in contiguous locations that occupy a specified area of disk space. Records in random files are stored without regard for their physical relationship to other records of the same file. In fact, random files may have records distributed throughout a disk. The **access method** is the technique used to locate records and to navigate through the database or file.

No single structure is best for all processing tasks, and selecting a structure involves a trade-off between desirable features. The file operation requirements that influence the selection of the data structure are listed in Table 2-2.

In the following section, we examine several data structures that are used in flat-file systems. Recall from Chapter 1 that the flat-file model describes an environment in which individual data files are not integrated with other files. End users in this environment own their data files rather than share them with other users. Data processing is thus performed by standalone applications rather than integrated systems. The **flat-file approach** is a single-view model that characterizes legacy systems in which data files are structured, formatted, and arranged to suit the specific needs of the *owner* or primary user of the system. Such structuring, however, may omit or corrupt data attributes that are essential to other users, thus preventing successful integration of systems across the organization.

Sequential Structure

Figure 2-36 illustrates the **sequential structure**, which is typically called the **sequential access method**. Under this arrangement, for example, the record with key value 1875 is placed in the physical storage space immediately following the record with key value 1874. Thus all records in the file lie in contiguous storage spaces in a specified sequence (ascending or descending) arranged by their primary key.

Sequential files are simple and easy to process. The application starts at the beginning of the file and processes each record in sequence. Of the file processing operations in Table 2-2, this approach is efficient for Operations 4 and 5, which are, respectively, reading an entire file and finding the next record in the file. Also, when a large portion of the file (perhaps 20 percent or more) is to be processed in one operation, the sequential structure is efficient for record updating (Operation 3 in Table 2-2). Sequential files are not efficient when the user is interested in locating only one or a few records on a file. A simple analogy can be made with an audio cassette. If you want to listen to only the tenth song on the tape, you must fast-forward to the point at which you think the song is located and then press the play button. Some searching is usually required to find the beginning of the song. However, if you are interested in hearing all the songs on the tape, you can simply play it from the beginning. An example of a sequential file application is payroll processing, whereby 100 percent of the employee records on the payroll file are processed each payroll period. Magnetic tape is a cheap, effective, and commonly used storage medium for sequential files. Sequential files may also be stored on magnetic disks.

TABLE 2-2	Typical File Processing Operations

1. Retrieve a record from the file based on its primary key value.

2. Insert a record into a file.

3. Update a record in the file.

4. Read a complete file of records.

5. Find the next record in a file.

6. Scan a file for records with common secondary keys.

7. Delete a record from a file.

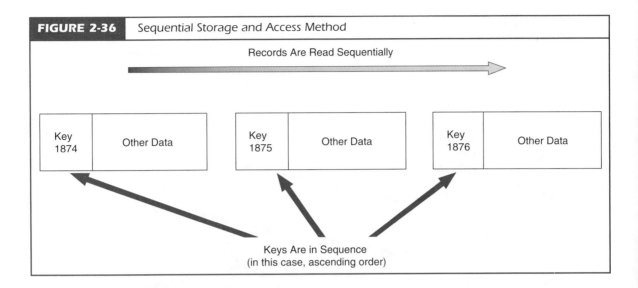

FIGURE 2-36 Sequential Storage and Access Method

The sequential access method does not permit accessing a record directly. Applications that require direct access operations need a different data structure. The techniques described next address this need.

Direct Access Structures

Direct access structures store data at a unique location, known as an address, on a hard disk or floppy disk. The disk address is a numeric value that represents the cylinder, surface, and block location on the disk.[3] The operating system uses this address to store and retrieve the data record. Using our music analogy again, the direct access approach is similar to the way songs are stored on a compact disc. If the listener chooses, he or she can select a specific song directly without searching through all the other songs.

An important part of the direct access approach is in determining the disk address, which is based on the record's primary key. Bank account numbers, social security numbers, credit card numbers, and license plate numbers are examples of primary keys that are translated into addresses to store and retrieve data by different business applications. The following techniques are examples of data structures that have direct access capability.

Indexed Structure

An **indexed structure** is so named because, in addition to the actual data file, there exists a separate index that is itself a file of record addresses. This index contains the numeric value of the physical disk storage location (cylinder, surface, and record block) for each record in the associated data file. The data file itself may be organized either sequentially or randomly. Figure 2-37 presents an example of an indexed random file.

Records in an **indexed random file** are dispersed throughout a disk without regard for their physical proximity to other related records. In fact, records belonging to the same file may reside on different disks. A record's physical location is unimportant as long as the operating system software can find it when needed. Searching the index for the desired key value, reading the corresponding storage location (address), and then moving the disk read-write head to the address location accomplish this. When a new record is added to the file, the data management software selects a vacant disk location, stores the record, and adds the new address to the index.

The physical organization of the index itself may be either sequential (by key value) or random. Random indexes are easier to maintain, in terms of adding records, because new key records are simply added to the end of the index without regard to their sequence. Indexes in sequential order are more difficult to maintain because new record keys must be inserted between existing keys. One advantage of a sequential index is that it can be

---

3   For further explanation about disk addresses, see Section A of the chapter appendix titled "Secondary Storage."

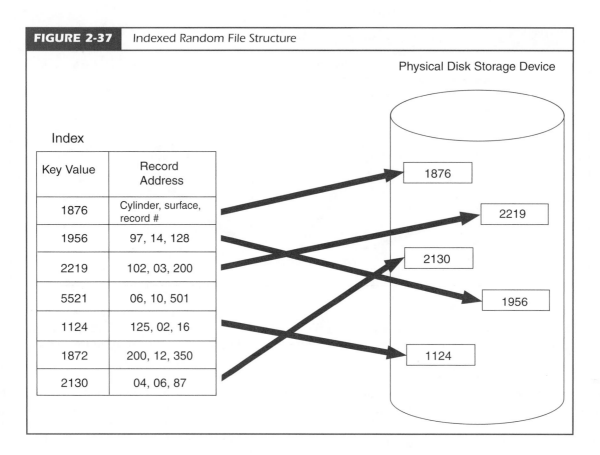

FIGURE 2-37   Indexed Random File Structure

searched rapidly. Because of its logical arrangement, algorithms can be used to speed the search through the index to find a key value. This becomes particularly important for large data files with associated large indexes.

The principal advantage of indexed random files is in operations involving the processing of individual records (Operations 1, 2, 3, and 6 in Table 2-2). Another advantage is their efficient use of disk storage. Records may be placed wherever there is space without concern for maintaining contiguous storage locations. However, random files are not efficient structures for operations that involve processing a large portion of a file. A great deal of access time may be required to access an entire file of records that are randomly dispersed throughout the storage device. Sequential files are more efficient for this purpose.

VSAM Structure

The **virtual storage access method (VSAM)** structure is used for very large files that require routine batch processing and a moderate degree of individual record processing. For instance, the customer file of a public utility company will be processed in batch mode for billing purposes and directly accessed in response to individual customer queries. Because of its sequential organization, the VSAM structure can be searched sequentially for efficient batch processing. Figure 2-38 illustrates how VSAM uses indexes to allow direct access processing.

The VSAM structure is used for files that often occupy several cylinders of contiguous storage on a disk. To find a specific record location, the VSAM file uses a number of indexes that describe in summarized form the contents of each cylinder. For example, in Figure 2-38, we are searching for a record with the key value 2546. The access method goes first to the overall file index, which contains only the highest key value for each cylinder in the file, and determines that Record 2546 is somewhere on Cylinder 99. A quick scan of the surface index for Cylinder 99 reveals that the record is on Surface 3 of Cylinder 99. VSAM indexes do not provide an exact physical address for a single record. However, they identify the

---

FIGURE 2-38 | VSAM Used for Direct Access

VSAM—Virtual Storage Access Method

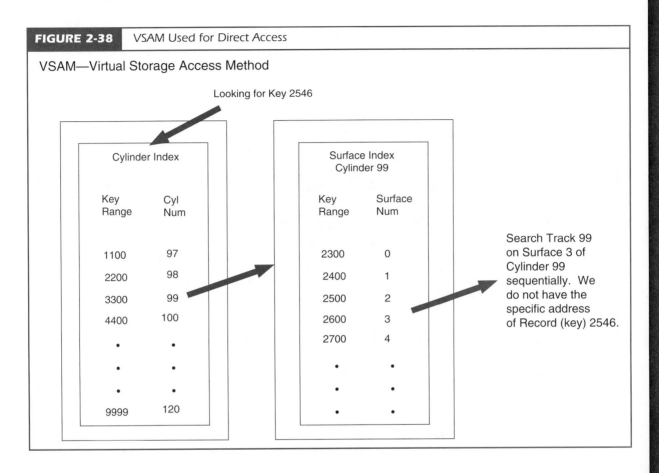

Looking for Key 2546

Cylinder Index	
Key Range	Cyl Num
1100	97
2200	98
3300	99
4400	100
.	.
.	.
.	.
9999	120

Surface Index Cylinder 99	
Key Range	Surface Num
2300	0
2400	1
2500	2
2600	3
2700	4
.	.
.	.
.	.

Search Track 99 on Surface 3 of Cylinder 99 sequentially. We do not have the specific address of Record (key) 2546.

---

disk track on which the record in question resides. The last step is to search the identified track sequentially to find the record with key value 2546.

The VSAM structure is moderately effective for Operations 1 and 3 in Table 2-2. Because VSAM must read multiple indexes and search the track sequentially, the average access time for a single record is slower than the indexed sequential or indexed random structures. Direct access speed is sacrificed to achieve very efficient performance in Operations 4, 5, and 6.

The greatest disadvantage with the VSAM structure is that it does not perform record insertion operations (Operation 2) efficiently. Because the VSAM file is organized sequentially, inserting a new record into the file requires the physical relocation of all the records located beyond the point of insertion. The indexes that describe this physical arrangement must, therefore, also be updated with each insertion. This is extremely time consuming and disruptive to operations. One method of dealing with this problem is to store new records in an overflow area that is physically separate from the other data records in the file. Figure 2-39 shows how this is done.

A VSAM file has three physical components: the indexes, the prime data storage area, and the overflow area. Rather than inserting a new record directly into the prime area, the data management software places it in a randomly selected location in the overflow area. It then records the address of the location in a special field (called a *pointer*) in the prime area. Later, when searching for the record, the indexes direct the access method to the track location on which the record *should* reside. The pointer at that location reveals the record's *actual* location in the overflow area. Thus accessing a record may involve searching the indexes, searching the track in the prime data area, and finally searching the overflow area. This slows data access time for both direct access and batch processing.

| FIGURE 2-39 | Inserting a Record into a VSAM File |

Insert New Record with Key Value = 237

Periodically, the VSAM file must be reorganized by integrating the overflow records into the prime area and then reconstructing the indexes. This involves time, cost, and disruption to operations. Therefore, when a file is highly volatile (records are added or deleted frequently), the maintenance burden associated with the VSAM approach tends to render it impractical. However, for large, stable files that need both direct access and batch processing, the VSAM structure is a popular option.

Hashing Structure

A **hashing structure** employs an algorithm that converts the primary key of a record directly into a storage address. Hashing eliminates the need for a separate index. By calculating the address, rather than reading it from an index, records can be retrieved more quickly. Figure 2-40 illustrates the hashing approach.

This example assumes an inventory file with 100,000 inventory items. The algorithm divides the inventory number (the primary key) into a prime number. Recall that a prime number is one that can be divided only by itself and 1 without leaving a residual value. Thus the calculation will always produce a value that can be translated into a storage location. Hence, the residual 6.27215705 becomes Cylinder 272, Surface 15, and Record 705. The hashing structure uses a random file organization because the process of calculating residuals and converting them into storage locations produces widely dispersed record addresses.

The principal advantage of hashing is access speed. Calculating a record's address is faster than searching for it through an index. This structure is suited to applications that require rapid access to individual records in performing Operations 1, 2, 3, and 6 in Table 2-2.

The hashing structure has two significant disadvantages. First, this technique does not use storage space efficiently. The storage location chosen for a record is a mathematical function of its primary key

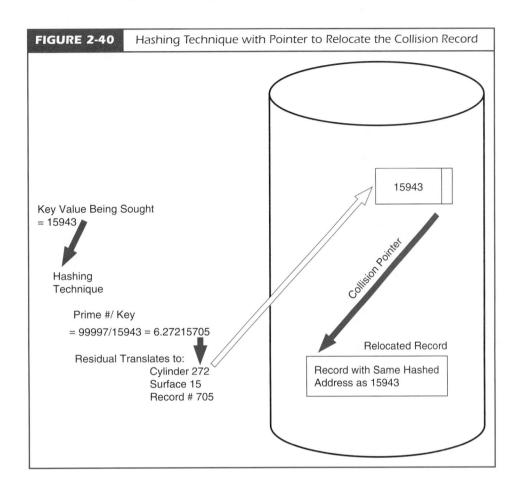

FIGURE 2-40 | Hashing Technique with Pointer to Relocate the Collision Record

Key Value Being Sought
= 15943

Hashing
Technique

Prime #/ Key
= 99997/15943 = 6.27215705

Residual Translates to:
Cylinder 272
Surface 15
Record # 705

15943

Collision Pointer

Relocated Record

Record with Same Hashed
Address as 15943

value. The algorithm will never select some disk locations because they do not correspond to legitimate key values. As much as one-third of the disk-pack may be wasted.

The second disadvantage is the reverse of the first. Different record keys may generate the same (or similar) residual, which translates into the same address. This is called a *collision* because two records cannot be stored at the same location. One solution to this problem is to randomly select a location for the second record and place a pointer to it from the first (the calculated) location. The dark arrow in Figure 2-40 represents the use of this technique.

The collision problem slows access to records. Locating a record displaced in this manner involves first calculating its theoretical address, searching that location, and then determining the actual address from the pointer contained in the record at that location. This has an additional implication for Operation 7 in Table 2-2—deleting a record from a file. If the first record is deleted from the file, the pointer to the second (collision) record will also be deleted and the address of the second record will be lost. This can be dealt with in two ways: (1) After deleting the first record, the collision record can be physically relocated to its calculated address, which is now vacant; or (2) the first record is marked "deleted" but is left in place to preserve the pointer to the collision record.

Pointer Structure

Figure 2-41 presents the **pointer structure**, which in this example is used to create a *linked-list file*. This approach stores in a field of one record the address (pointer) of a related record. The pointers provide connections between the records. In this example, Record 124 points to the location of Record 125,

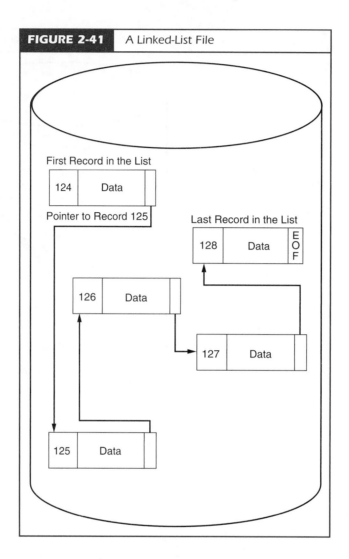

FIGURE 2-41   A Linked-List File

Record 125 points to 126, and so on. As each record is processed, the computer program reads the pointer field to locate the next one. The last record in the list contains an end-of-file marker. The records in this type of file are spread over the entire disk without concern for their physical proximity with other related records. Pointers used in this way make efficient use of disk storage space and are efficient structures for applications that involve Operations 4, 5, and 6 in Table 2-2.

Types of Pointers. Figure 2-42 shows three types of pointers: physical address, relative address, and logical key pointers. A **physical address pointer** contains the actual disk storage location (cylinder, surface, and record number) needed by the disk controller. This physical address allows the system to access the record directly without obtaining further information. This method has the advantage of speed, since it does not need to be manipulated further to determine a record's location. However, it also has two disadvantages: First, if the related record is moved from one disk location to another, the pointer must be changed. This is a problem when disks are periodically reorganized or copied. Second, the physical pointers bear no logical relationship to the records they identify. If a pointer is lost or destroyed and cannot be recovered, the record it references is also lost.

A **relative address pointer** contains the relative position of a record in the file. For example, the pointer could specify the 135th record in the file. This must be further manipulated to convert it to the actual physical

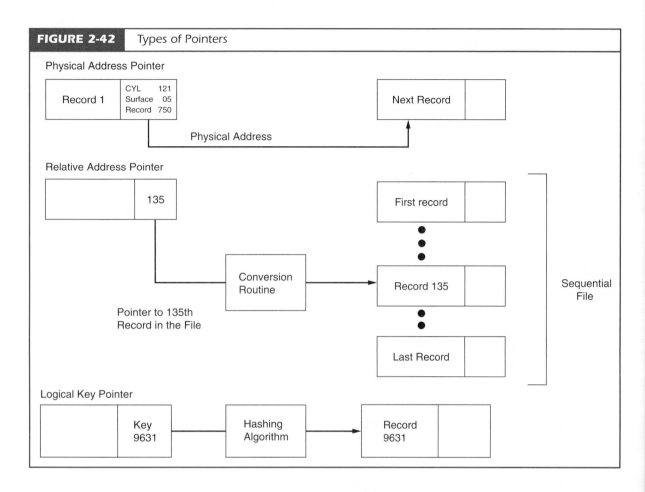

FIGURE 2-42 | Types of Pointers

address. The conversion software calculates this by using the physical address of the beginning of the file, the length of each record in the file, and the relative address of the record being sought.

A **logical key pointer** contains the primary key of the related record. This key value is then converted into the record's physical address by a hashing algorithm.

BATCH PROCESSING USING SEQUENTIAL FILES

The most basic computer-processing configuration is batch mode using sequential file structures. Figure 2-43 illustrates this method.

Each program in a batch system is called a **run**. In this example, there is an edit run, an AR file update run, an inventory file update run, and two intermediate sort runs. The entire file or batch of records is processed through each run before it moves to the next run. When the last run finishes processing the batch, the session terminates.

A prominent feature of this system is the use of sequential files, which are simple to create and maintain. Although sequential files are still used by organizations for backup purposes, their presence in data processing is declining. This file structure is effective for managing large files, such as those used by federal and state agencies that have a high activity ratio. The activity ratio of a file is defined as the percentage of records on the file that are processed each time the file is accessed. For example, a federal payroll file has an activity ratio of 1:1. Each time the payroll file is accessed (payday), all the records on it are processed because everyone gets a paycheck.

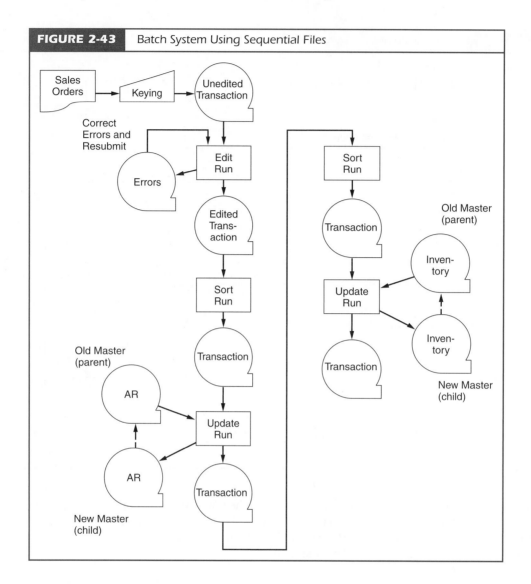

FIGURE 2-43   Batch System Using Sequential Files

The sequential files in the system shown in Figure 2-43 are represented in the flowchart as tapes, but remember that disks are also a common medium for sequential files. The operational description that follows applies equally to both types of media.

Keystroke

The first step in this process is keystroke. In this example, clerks transcribe source documents (sales orders) to magnetic tape for processing later. The transaction file created in this step contains data about customer sales. These data are used to update the appropriate customer and inventory records. As an internal control measure, the keystroke clerks calculate control totals for the batch based on the total sales amount and total number of inventory items sold. This information will be used by the system to maintain the integrity of the process. After every processing run, control totals are recalculated and compared to the previously calculated value. Thus if a record is incompletely processed, lost, or processed more than once, the batch totals calculated after the run will not equal the beginning batch totals. Once the system detects an out-of-balance condition, it sends error reports to users and data control personnel. We examine batch control techniques in Chapter 17.

Edit Run

At a predetermined time each day, the data processing department executes this batch system. The edit program is the first to be run. This program identifies clerical errors in the batch and automatically removes these records from the transaction file. Error records go to a separate error file, where an authorized person corrects and resubmits them for processing with the next day's batch. The edit program recalculates the batch total to reflect changes due to the removal of error records. The resulting "clean" transaction file then moves to the next program in the system.

Sort Runs

Before updating a sequential master file, the transaction file must be sorted and placed in the same sequence as the master file. Figure 2-44 presents record structures for the sales order transaction file and two associated master files, accounts receivable and inventory.

Notice that the record structure for the sales order file contains a primary key (PK)—a unique identifier—and two secondary key (SK) fields, ACCOUNT NUMBER and INVENTORY NUMBER. ACCOUNT NUMBER is used to identify the customer account to be updated in the AR master file. INVENTORY NUMBER is the key for locating the inventory record to be updated in the inventory master file. To simplify the example, we assume that each sale is for a single item of inventory. Because the AR update run comes first in the sequence, the sales order file must first be sorted by ACCOUNT NUMBER and then sorted by INVENTORY NUMBER to update inventory.

Update Runs

Updating a master file record involves changing the value of one or more of its variable fields to reflect the effects of a transaction. The system in our example performs two separate update procedures. The AR update program recalculates customer balances by adding the value stored in the INVOICE AMOUNT field of a transaction record to the CURRENT BALANCE field value in the associated AR record. The inventory update program reduces inventory levels by deducting the QUANTITY SOLD value of a transaction record from the QUANTITY ON HAND field value of the associated inventory record.

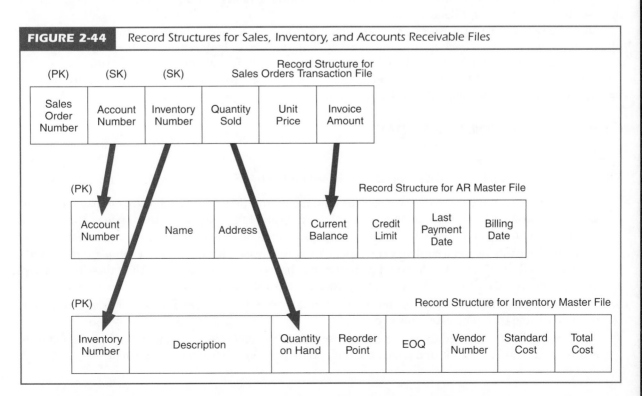

FIGURE 2-44   Record Structures for Sales, Inventory, and Accounts Receivable Files

Sequential File Backup Procedures

An important characteristic of the sequential file update process is that it produces a new physical master file. The new file contains all of the records from the original file, including those that were updated by transactions and those that were not updated. The original master continues to exist. This feature provides an automatic backup capability called the *grandparent-parent-child* approach. The parent is the original master file, and the child is the newly created (updated) file. With the next batch of transactions, the child becomes the parent, the original parent becomes the grandparent (the backup), and a new child is created. Should the current master file (the child) become lost, damaged, or corrupted by erroneous data, a new child can be created from the original parent and the corresponding transaction file. We examine this control technique in Chapter 15.

BATCH PROCESSING USING DIRECT ACCESS FILES

Changing the file structures from sequential to direct access greatly simplifies the system. Figure 2-45 shows a system that is functionally equivalent to the one presented in Figure 2-43 but has been redesigned to use **direct access files**. Notice the use of disk symbols to represent direct access storage device (DASD) media.

The shift to direct access files causes two noteworthy changes to this system. The first is the elimination of the sort programs. A disadvantage of sequential file updating is the need to sort the transaction file before each update run. Sorting consumes a good deal of computer time and is error-prone when very large files are involved. Using direct access files eliminates the need to sort transactions into a predetermined sequence.

The second change is the elimination of automatic file backup in this system. Direct access update does not produce a new physical master as a by-product of the process. Instead, changes to field values are made to the original physical file. Providing file backup requires separate procedures.

Direct Access File Update and Backup Procedures

Each record in a direct access file is assigned a unique disk location or *address* that is determined by its key value. Since only a single valid location exists for each record, updating the record must occur in place using a destructive update approach similar to that for database tables. See Figure 2-29 and the associated discussion in the chapter for details.

Direct access file backup issues are also similar to modern database systems. Since the destructive update approach leaves no backup copy of the original master file, only the current value is available to the user. If the current master becomes damaged or corrupted in some way, no backup version exists from which to reconstruct the file. To preserve adequate accounting records, special backup procedures need to be implemented like those illustrated in Figure 2-30.

GENERAL LOGIC FOR FILE UPDATE

Sequential File-Update

The logic of a sequential file update procedure is based on the following assumptions and conditions:

1. The transaction (T) file contains fewer records than the master (M) file. An organization may have thousands of customers listed in its customer (accounts receivable) file, but only a small percentage of these customers actually purchased goods during the period represented by the current batch of transactions.

2. More than one transaction record may correspond to a given master file record. For example, a department store sells its RCA 27-inch TV to several customers during a one-day special offer. All of these transactions are separate records in the batch and must be processed against the same inventory master file record.

3. Both transaction file and master file must be in the same sequential order. For purposes of illustration, we will assume this to be ascending order.

4. The master file is presumed to be correct. Therefore, any sequencing irregularities are presumed to be errors in the transaction file and will cause the update process to terminate abnormally.

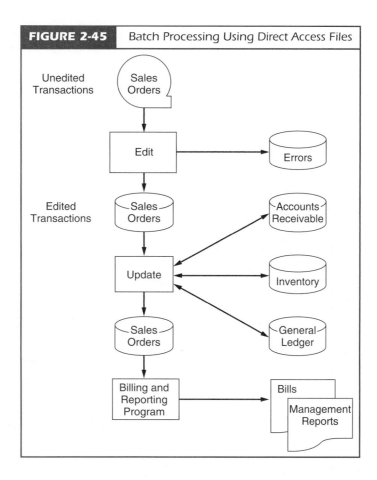

FIGURE 2-45   Batch Processing Using Direct Access Files

With these assumptions in mind, let's walk through the update logic presented in Figure 2-46. This logic is divided into three sections: start-up, update loop, and end procedures.

Start-Up
The process begins by reading the first transaction (T) and the first master (M) record from their respective files into the computer's memory. The T and M records in memory are designated as the *current records*.

Update Loop
The first step in the update loop is to compare the key fields of both records. One of three possible conditions will exist: T = M, T > M, or T < M.

T = M. When the key of T is equal to that of M, the transaction record matches the master record. Having found the correct master, the program updates the master from the transaction. The update program then reads another T record and compares the keys. If they are equal, the master is updated again. This continues until the key values change; recall that under Assumption 2, there may be many Ts for any M record.

T > M. The normal change in the key value relationship is for T to become greater than M. This is so because both T and M are sorted in ascending order (Assumption 3). The T > M relation signifies that processing on the current master record is complete. The updated master (currently stored in computer memory) is then written to a new master file—the child—and a new M record is read from the original (parent) file.

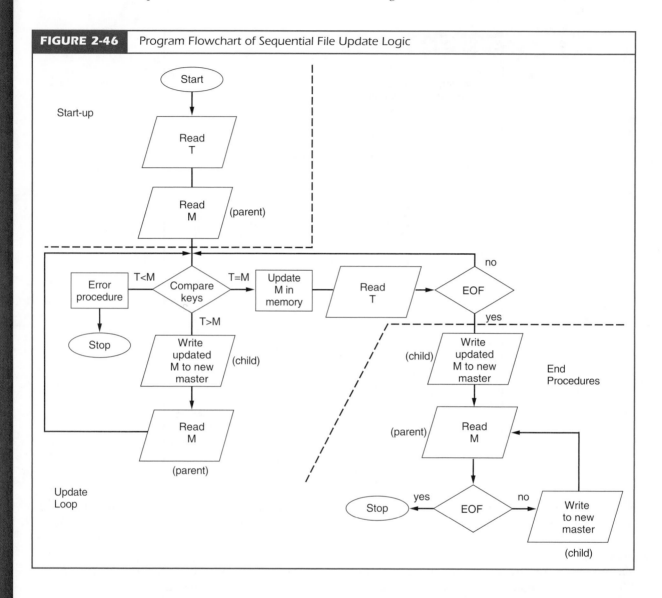

FIGURE 2-46 Program Flowchart of Sequential File Update Logic

Because the transaction file represents a subset of the master (Assumption 1), there normally will be gaps between the key values of the transaction records. Figure 2-47 illustrates this with sample transactions and corresponding master file records. Notice the gap between Key 1 and Key 4 in the transaction file. When Key 4 is read into memory, the condition T > M exists until Master Record 4 is read. Before this, Master Records 2 and 3 are read into memory and then immediately written to the new master without modification.

T < M. The T < M key relationship signifies an error condition. The key of the current T record should only be smaller than that of the current M record if a T record is out of sequence (Assumption 4). To illustrate, refer to Figure 2-47. Notice that the record with Key Value 10 in the transaction file is out of sequence. This goes undetected until the next T record (Key 7) is read. At this point, the computer's memory contains M Record 10 (M10), and the previous M records (M6 through M9) have been read and then written, unchanged, to the new master. Reading Record T7 produces the condition T < M. It is now impossible to update Records M7 and M9 from their corresponding T records. The sequential file update

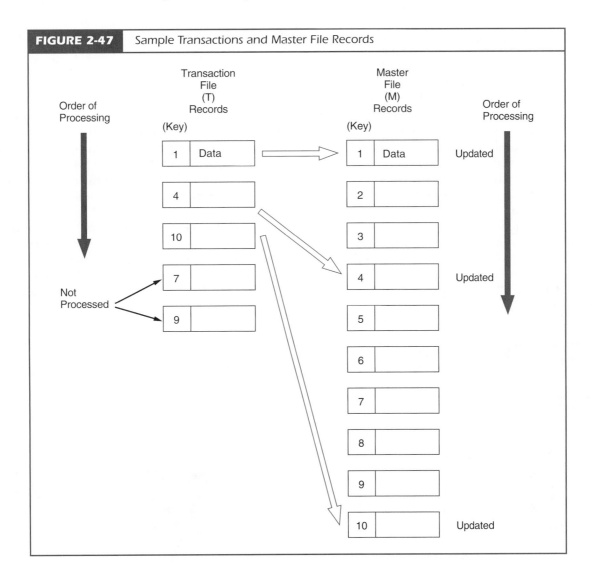

FIGURE 2-47 Sample Transactions and Master File Records

process can only move forward through the files. Skipped records cannot be recovered and updated out of sequence. Because of this, the update process will be incomplete, and the data processing department must execute special error procedures to remedy the problem. We examine various error handling techniques in Chapter 16.

End Procedures

When the last T record is read and processed, the update loop procedure is complete. This is signaled by a special EOF record in the transaction file. At this point, one of two possible conditions will exist:

1. The M record in memory is the last record on the M file, or;
2. There are still unprocessed records on the M file.

Assuming the second condition is true, the remaining records on the M file must be copied to the new master file. Some file structures indicate EOF with a record containing high key values (that is, the key field is filled with 9s) to force a permanent T > M condition, in which case all remaining M records will be read and copied to the new file. Other structures use a special EOF marker. The logic in this example assumes the latter approach. When the EOF condition is reached for the master and all the M records are copied, the update procedure is terminated.

Direct Access File-Update

Figure 2-48 presents the general logic for updating direct access files. The two sample files of data provided will be used to illustrate this process. Notice that this logic is simpler than that used for sequential files. There are three reasons for this. First, since record sequencing is irrelevant, the logic does not need to consider the relationship between the T and M key values. Consequently, the update program does not need to deal explicitly with the problem of multiple T records for a given M record. Second, unprocessed master records are not copied to a new master file. Third, complex procedures for searching the master file and retrieving the desired M record are performed by the computer's operating system rather than by the update program.

The transaction file in Figure 2-48 is read from top to bottom. Each record is processed as it is encountered and without regard for its key sequence. First, T9 is read into memory. The operating system then searches for and retrieves the corresponding record (M9) from the master file. The current record is updated in memory and immediately written back to its original location on the master file. Records T2, T5, and T3 are all processed in the same manner. Finally, the second T9 transaction is processed just as the first, resulting in M9 being updated twice.

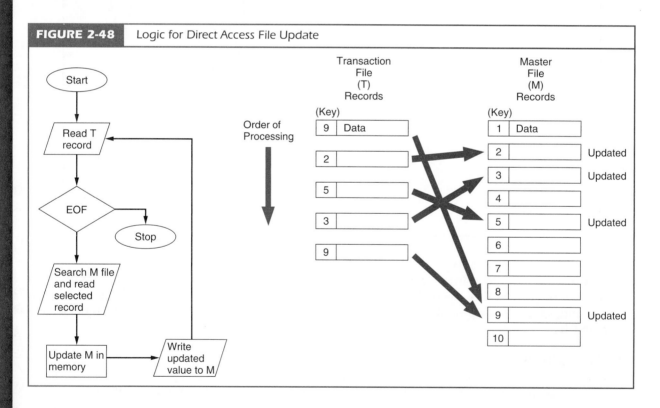

| **FIGURE 2-48** | Logic for Direct Access File Update |

KEY TERMS

access method (86)

accounting record (48)

archive file (56)

audit trail (53)

batch (67)

batch systems (73)

cardinality (59)

conversion cycle (47)

data flow diagram (58)

data model (61)

data structures (85)

direct access files (96)

direct access structures (87)

document flowchart (62)

entities (59)

entity relationship (ER) diagram (59)

expenditure cycle (46)

flat-file approach (86)

hashing structure (90)

indexed random file (87)

indexed structure (87)

journal (50)

ledger (52)

logical key pointer (93)

master file (56)

organization (85)

physical address pointer (92)

pointer structure (91)

product documents (48)

program flowchart (71)

real-time systems (74)

record layout diagrams (73)

reference file (56)

relative address pointer (92)

revenue cycle (48)

run (93)

sequential access method (86)

sequential files (86)

sequential structure (86)

source documents (48)

system flowcharts (62)

transaction file (56)

turnaround documents (49)

virtual storage access method (VSAM) (88)

REVIEW QUESTIONS

1. What three transaction cycles exist in all businesses?
2. Name the major subsystems of the expenditure cycle.
3. Identify and distinguish between the physical and financial components of the expenditure cycle.
4. Name the major subsystems of the conversion cycle.
5. Name the major subsystems of the revenue cycle.
6. Name the three types of documents.
7. Name the two types of journals.
8. Distinguish between a general journal and journal vouchers.
9. Name the two types of ledgers.
10. What is an audit trail?
11. What is the confirmation process?
12. Computer-based systems employ four types of files. Name them.
13. Give an example of a record that might comprise each of the four file types found in a computer-based system.
14. What is the purpose of a digital audit trail?
15. Give an example of how cardinality relates to business policy.
16. Distinguish between entity relationship diagrams, data flow diagrams, document flowcharts, and system flowcharts.
17. What is meant by cardinality in entity relationship diagrams?
18. For what purpose are ER diagrams used?
19. What is an entity?

20. Distinguish between batch and real-time processing.

21. Distinguish between the sequential file and database approaches to data backup.

22. Is a DFD an effective documentation technique for identifying who or what performs a particular task? Explain.

23. Is a flowchart an effective documentation technique for identifying who or what performs a particular task? Explain.

24. How may batch processing be used to improve operational efficiency?

25. Why might an auditor use a program flowchart?

26. How are system flowcharts and program flowcharts related?

27. What are the distinguishing features of a legacy system?

28. What are the two data processing approaches used in modern systems?

29. How is backup of database files accomplished?

30. What information is provided by a record layout diagram?

31. In one sentence, what does updating a master file record involve?

32. Comment on the following statement: "Legacy systems always use flat-file structures."

33. Explain the technique known as *destructive update.*

34. What factor influences the decision to employ real-time data collection with batch updating rather that purely real-time processing? Explain.

35. What are the advantages of real-time data processing?

36. What are the advantages of real-time data collection?

DISCUSSION QUESTIONS

1. Discuss the flow of cash through the transaction cycles. Include in your discussion the relevant subsystems and any time lags that may occur.

2. Explain whether the cost accounting system primarily supports internal or external reporting.

3. Discuss the role of the conversion cycle for service and retailing entities.

4. Can a turnaround document contain information that is subsequently used as a source document? Why or why not?

5. Would the write-down of obsolete inventory be recorded in a special journal or the general journal? Why?

6. Are both registers and special journals necessary?

7. Discuss the relationship between the balance in the accounts payable general ledger control account and what is found in the accounts payable subsidiary ledger.

8. What role does the audit trail play in the task of confirmation?

9. Explain how the magnetic audit trail functions.

10. Are large batch sizes preferable to small batch sizes? Explain.

11. Discuss why an understanding of legacy system technologies is of some importance to auditors.

12. If an organization processes large numbers of transactions that use common data records, what type of system would work best (all else being equal)?

13. If an organization processes transactions that have independent (unique) data needs, what type of system would work best (all else being equal)?

14. Explain how a hashing structure works and why it's quicker than using an index. Give an example. If it's so much faster, why isn't it used exclusively?

15. Describe a specific accounting application that could make use of a VSAM file.

16. Explain the following three types of pointers: physical address pointer, relative address pointer, and logical key pointer.

17. Should an auditor wishing to assess the adequacy of separation of functions examine a data flow diagram, a document flowchart, or a system flowchart? Why?

MULTIPLE-CHOICE QUESTIONS

1. Which statement is not true?
   a. Business activities begin with the acquisition of materials, property, and labor in exchange for cash.
   b. The conversion cycle includes the task of determining raw materials requirements.
   c. Manufacturing firms have a conversion cycle but retail firms do not.
   d. A payroll check is an example of a product document of the payroll system.
   e. A journal voucher is actually a special source document.

2. A documentation tool that depicts the physical flow of information relating to a particular transaction through an organization is a
   a. document flowchart.
   b. program flowchart.
   c. decision table.
   d. work distribution analysis.
   e. systems survey.

3. Sequential file processing will not permit
   a. data to be edited on a separate computer run.
   b. the use of a database structure.
   c. data to be edited in an off-line mode.
   d. batch processing to be initiated from a terminal.
   e. data to be edited on a real-time basis.

4. The production subsystem of the conversion cycle includes all of the following EXCEPT
   a. determining raw materials requirements.
   b. make or buy decisions of components parts.
   c. release of raw materials into production.
   d. scheduling the goods to be produced.

5. Which of the following files is a temporary file?
   a. transaction file
   b. master file
   c. reference file
   d. none of the above

6. A documentation tool used to represent the logical elements of a system is a(n)
   a. programming flowchart.
   b. entity relationship diagram.
   c. document flowchart.
   d. data flow diagram.

7. Which of the following is NOT an advantage of real-time processing files over batch processing?
   a. shorter transaction processing time
   b. reduction of inventory stocks
   c. improved customer service
   d. they are all advantages

8. Which statement is NOT correct?
   a. Legacy systems may process financially significant transactions.
   b. Some legacy systems use database technology.
   c. Mainframes are exclusive to legacy systems, while modern systems use only the client-server model.
   d. All the above are true.

9. Which statement is NOT correct?
   a. Indexed random files are dispersed throughout the storage device without regard for physical proximity with related records.
   b. Indexed random files use disk storage space efficiently.
   c. Indexed random files are efficient when processing a large portion of a file at one time.
   d. Indexed random files are easy to maintain in terms of adding records.

10. Which statement is NOT correct? The indexed sequential access method
    a. is used for very large files that need both direct access and batch processing.
    b. may use an overflow area for records.
    c. provides an exact physical address for each record.
    d. is appropriate for files that require few insertions or deletions.

11. Which statement is true about a hashing structure?
    a. The same address could be calculated for two records.
    b. Storage space is used efficiently.
    c. Records cannot be accessed rapidly.
    d. A separate index is required.

12. In a hashing structure
   a. two records can be stored at the same address.
   b. pointers are used to indicate the location of all records.
   c. pointers are used to indicate location of a record with the same address as another record.
   d. all locations on the disk are used for record storage.

13. An advantage of a physical address pointer is that
   a. it points directly to the actual disk storage location.
   b. it is easily recovered if it is inadvertently lost.
   c. it remains unchanged when disks are reorganized.
   d. all of the above are advantages of the physical address pointer.

14. Which of the following is not true of a turnaround document?
   a. They may reduce the number of errors made by external parties.
   b. They are commonly used by utility companies (gas, power, water).
   c. They are documents used by internal parties only.
   d. They are both input and output documents.

15. Which of the following is not a true statement?
   a. Transactions are recorded on source documents and are posted to journals.
   b. Transactions are recorded in journals and are posted to ledgers.
   c. Infrequent transactions are recorded in the general journal.
   d. Frequent transactions are recorded in special journals.

16. Which of the following is true of the relationship between subsidiary ledgers and general ledger accounts?
   a. The two contain different and unrelated data.
   b. All general ledger accounts have subsidiaries.
   c. The relationship between the two provides an audit trail from the financial statements to the source documents.
   d. The total of subsidiary ledger accounts usually exceeds the total in the related general ledger account.

17. Real-time systems might be appropriate for all of the following except:
   a. airline reservations.
   b. payroll.
   c. point-of-sale transactions.
   d. air-traffic control systems.
   e. all of these applications typically utilize real-time processing.

18. ⬡ is the document flowchart symbol for:
   a. on-page connector.
   b. off-page connector.
   c. home base.
   d. manual operation.
   e. document.

PROBLEMS

1. Transaction Cycle Identification

Categorize each of the following activities into the expenditure, conversion, or revenue cycles and identify the applicable subsystem.

a. Preparing the weekly payroll for manufacturing personnel
b. Releasing raw materials for use in the manufacturing cycle
c. Recording the receipt of payment for goods sold
d. Recording the order placed by a customer
e. Ordering raw materials
f. Determining the amount of raw materials to order

2. Types of Files

For each of the following records, indicate the appropriate related file structure: master file, transaction file, reference file, or archive file.

a. customer ledgers
b. purchase orders
c. list of authorized vendors
d. records related to prior pay periods
e. vendor ledgers
f. hours each employee has worked during the current pay period
g. tax tables
h. sales orders that have been processed and recorded

3. Document Flowchart

Figure 2-4 illustrates how a customer order is transformed into a source document, a product document, and a turnaround document. Develop a similar flowchart for the process of paying hourly employees. Assume time sheets are used and the payroll department must total the hours. Each hour worked by any employee must be charged to some account (a cost center). Each week, the manager of each cost center receives a report listing the employee's name and the number of hours charged to this center. The manager is required to verify that this information is correct by signing the form and noting any discrepancies, then sending this form back to payroll. Any discrepancies noted must be corrected by the payroll department.

4. Entity Relationship Diagram

Shown below is a partial ER diagram of a purchase system. Describe the business rules represented by the cardinalities in the diagram.

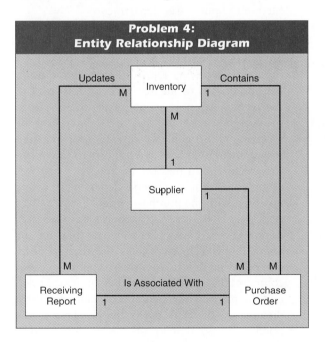

5. Entity Relationship Diagram

Refer to the ER diagram in Problem 4.

Modify the diagram to deal with payments of merchandise purchased. Explain the business rules represented by the cardinalities in the diagram. (You may wish to refer to Chapter 5.)

6. Entity Relationship Diagram

Prepare an ER diagram, in good form, for the expenditure cycle, which consists of both purchasing and cash disbursements. Describe the business rules represented by the cardinalities in the diagrams. (You may wish to refer to Chapter 4).

7. System Flowchart

Using the diagram below, answer the following questions:

a. What do Symbols 1 and 2 represent?

b. What does the operation involving Symbols 3 and 4 depict?

c. What does the operation involving Symbols 4 and 5 depict?

d   What does the operation involving Symbols 6, 8, and 9 depict?

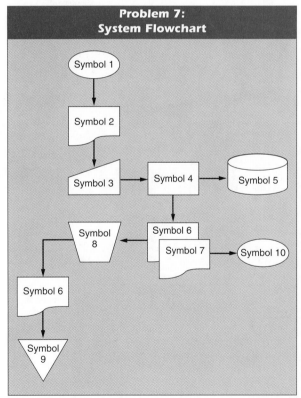

8. System Flowchart

Analyze the system flowchart on the following page and describe in detail the processes that are occurring.

9. System Flowcharts and Program Flowchart

From the diagram in Problem 8, identify three types of errors that may cause a payroll record to be placed in the error file. Use a program flowchart to illustrate the edit program.

10. Data Flow Diagram

Dataflow diagrams employ four different symbols. What are these symbols and what does each symbol represent?

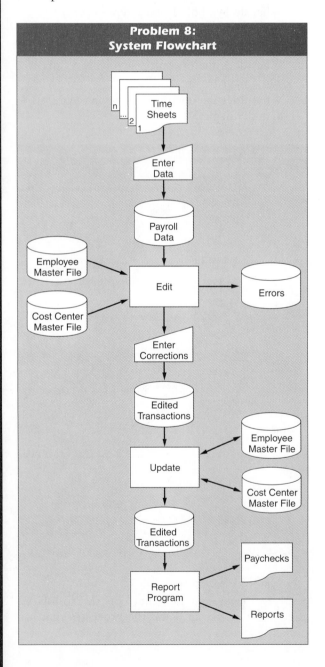

11 Transaction Cycle Relationship

Refer to Figure 2-1, which provides a generic look at relationships between Transaction Cycles. Modify this figure to reflect the Transaction Cycles you might find at your dentist's office.

12. System Documentation— Expenditure Cycle

The following describes the expenditure cycle procedures for a hypothetical company.

● The inventory control clerk examines the inventory records for items that must be replenished and prepares a two-part purchase requisition. Copy 1 of the requisition is sent to the purchases department and Copy 2 is filed.

● Upon receipt of the requisition, the purchases clerk selects a supplier from the valid vendor file (reference file) and prepares a three-part purchase order. Copy 1 is sent to the supplier, Copy 2 is sent to the accounts payable department where it is filed temporarily, and Copy 3 is filed in the purchases department.

● A few days after the supplier ships the order, the goods arrive at the receiving department. They are inspected and the receiving clerk prepares a three-part receiving report describing the number and quality of the items received. Copy 1 of the receiving report accompanies the goods to the warehouse, where they are secured and the receiving report is filed. Copy 2 is sent to inventory control, where the clerk posts to the inventory records and files the document. Copy 3 is sent to the accounts payable department, where it is filed with the purchase order.

● A day or two later, the accounts payable (AP) clerk receives the supplier's invoice (bill) for the items shipped. The clerk pulls the purchase order and receiving report from the temporary file and compares the quantity ordered, quantity received, and the price charged. After reconciling the three documents, the clerk enters the purchase in the purchases journal and posts the amount owed to the accounts payable subsidiary account.

● On the payment due date, the AP clerk posts to the AP subsidiary account to remove the liability and prepares a voucher authorizing payment to the vendor. The voucher is then sent to the cash disbursements clerk.

● Upon receipt of the voucher, the cash disbursements clerk prepares a check and sends it to the supplier. The clerk records the check in the check register and files a copy of the check in the department filing cabinet.

Required:
Prepare a data flow diagram and a document flowchart of the expenditure cycle procedures previously described.

13. Record Structures for Receipt of Items Ordered

Refer to Figure 2-28 and the discussion about updating master files from transaction files. The discussion presents the record structures for a sales transaction. Prepare a diagram (similar to Figure 2-28) that presents the record structure for the receipt (Receiving Report) of items ordered. Presume a purchase order file exists and will be updated through information collected via a receiving report. Further, presume the purchase was made on account and involves the receipt of inventory items.

14. System Documentation—Payroll

The following describes the payroll procedures for a hypothetical company.
- Every Thursday, the timekeeping clerk sends employee time cards to the payroll department for processing.
- Based on the hours worked as indicated by the time cards, the employee pay rate and

withholding information in the employee file, and the tax-rate reference file, the payroll clerk calculates gross pay, withholdings, and net pay for each employee. The clerk then prepares paychecks for each employee, files copies of the paychecks in the payroll department, and posts the earnings to the employee records. Finally, the clerk prepares a payroll summary and sends it and the paychecks to the cash disbursement (CD) department.
- The CD clerk reconciles the payroll summary with the paychecks and records the transaction in the cash disbursements journal. The clerk then files the payroll summary and sends the paychecks to the treasurer for signing.
- The signed checks are then sent to the paymaster, who distributes them to the employees on Friday morning.

Required:
Prepare a data flow diagram and a flowchart of the payroll procedures previously described.

15. System Documentation—Payroll

Required:
Assuming the payroll system described in Problem 14 uses database files and computer processing procedure, prepare a data flow diagram, an ER diagram, and a systems flowchart.

LEGACY SYSTEMS PROBLEMS

16. Access Methods

For each of the following file processing operations, indicate whether a sequential file, indexed random file, virtual storage access method (VSAM), hashing, or pointer structure would work best. You may choose as many as you wish for each step. Also indicate which would perform the least optimally.
a. Retrieve a record from the file based on its primary key value.
b. Update a record in the file.
c. Read a complete file of records.
d. Find the next record in a file.
e. Insert a record into a file.
f. Delete a record from a file.
g. Scan a file for records with secondary keys.

17. File Organization

For the following situations, indicate the most appropriate type of file organization. Explain your choice.

a. A local utility company has 80,000 residential customers and 10,000 commercial customers. The monthly billings are staggered throughout the month and, as a result, the cash receipts are fairly uniform throughout the month. For 99 percent of all accounts, one check per month is received. These receipts are recorded in a batch file, and the customer account records are updated biweekly. In a typical month, customer inquires are received at the rate of about 20 per day.

b. A national credit card agency has 12 million customer accounts. On average, 30 million purchases and 700,000 receipts of payments are processed per day. Additionally, the customer support hotline provides information to approximately 150,000 credit card holders and 30,000 merchants per day.

c. An airline reservations system assumes that the traveler knows the departing city. From that point, fares and flight times are examined based on the destination. When a flight is identified as being acceptable to the traveler the availability is checked and, if necessary, a seat is reserved. The volume of transactions exceeds one-half million per day.

d. A library system stocks over 2 million books and has 30,000 patrons. Each patron is allowed to check out five books. On average, there are 1.3 copies of each title in the library. Over 3,000 books are checked out each day, with approximately the same amount being returned daily. The checked out books are posted immediately, as well as any returns of overdue books by patrons who wish to pay their fines.

18. Manual System Accounting Records

The Manual System section of this text presents the documents, journals, and ledgers typically used for the revenue cycle of a manual system. Using this discussion as a guideline, present the documents, journals, and ledgers for an expenditure cycle. Presume the expenditure in question is the receipt of and payment for inventory items. Further, presume there is a time lag between the purchase of inventory and the payment for inventory.

a. What are the documents that will be used by this cycle?

b. For each document stated above, is this a source, product, or turnaround document?

c. What are the journals that will be used in this cycle?

d. For each journal stated, is this a general or special journal?

e. What are the ledgers that will be used in this cycle?

f. For each ledger stated, is this a subsidiary or general ledger?

19. Backup and Recovery Procedures for Database Files

Figure 2-30 provides a backup and recovery system for files that are updated using a destructive update approach. Now think about a specific situation that might use this approach. A company creates its sales order transaction file in batches. Once a day a sales clerk compiles a transaction file by entering data from the previous day's sales orders to the transaction file. When these transactions have all been entered and the transaction file passes editing, the transaction file is used to destructively update both the sales and the accounts receivable master files. Each of these master files is then backed up to a magnetic tape. The magnetic tapes are stored (off-line) in a remote location. Now consider what might happen if, in the middle of an update of the sales master file, lightning hit the company's building resulting in a power failure that caused the computer to corrupt both the transaction file and the master files.

a. Which, if any, files contain noncorrupted data (transaction file, accounts receivable master file, sales master file, or backup master files)?

b. Will a clerk have to reenter any data? If so, what data will have to be reentered?

c. What steps will the company have to take to obtain noncorrupted master files that contain the previous day's sales data?

20. Hashing Algorithm

The systems programmer uses a hashing algorithm to determine storage addresses. The hashing structure is 9,997/key. The resulting number is then used to locate the record. The first two digits after the decimal point represent the cylinder number, while the second two digits represent the surface number. The fifth, sixth, and seventh digits after the decimal point represent the record number. This algorithm results in a unique address 99 percent of the time. What happens the remainder of the time when the results of the algorithm are not unique? Explain in detail the storage process when Key=3 is processed first, Key=2307 at a later date, and shortly thereafter Key=39.

21. Update Process

Examine the diagram on the next page, which contains the processing order for a transaction file and a master file for a sequential file update process. Indicate the order in which the transactions are processed. Indicate which master file records are updated and which are read and written, unchanged, into the new master file. Also illustrate the relationship between the transaction file and the master file, that is, $T = M$, $T < M$, and $T > M$, in your answer.

How would the update change if a direct access file is used instead?

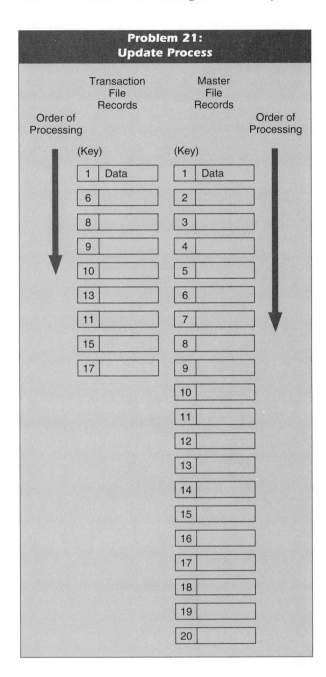

Problem 21:
Update Process

Transaction File Records

Master File Records

Order of Processing

Order of Processing

(Key)

(Key)

Transaction File Records:
Key	Data
1	Data
6	
8	
9	
10	
13	
11	
15	
17	

Master File Records:
Key	Data
1	Data
2	
3	
4	
5	
6	
7	
8	
9	
10	
11	
12	
13	
14	
15	
16	
17	
18	
19	
20	

chapter 3

Ethics, Fraud, and Internal Control

LEARNING OBJECTIVES

After studying this chapter, you should:

- Understand the broad issues pertaining to business ethics.
- Have a basic understanding of ethical issues related to the use of information technology.
- Be able to distinguish between management fraud and employee fraud.
- Be familiar with common types of fraud schemes.
- Be familiar with the key features of SAS 78 / COSO internal control framework.
- Understand the objects and application of physical controls.

This chapter examines three closely related areas of concern, which are specifically addressed by the Sarbanes-Oxley Act (SOX) and important to accountants and management. These are ethics, fraud, and internal control. We begin the chapter by surveying ethical issues that highlight the organization's conflicting responsibilities to its employees, shareholders, customers, and the general public. Organization managers have an ethical responsibility to seek a balance between the risks and benefits to these constituents that result from their decisions. Management and accountants must recognize the new implications of information technologies for such historic issues as working conditions, the right to privacy, and the potential for fraud. The section concludes with a review of code of ethics requirements mandated by SOX.

The second section is devoted to the subject of fraud and its implications for accountants. Although the term *fraud* is very familiar in today's financial press, it is not always clear what constitutes fraud. In this section, we discuss the nature and meaning of fraud, differentiate between employee fraud and management fraud, explain fraud-motivating forces, review some common fraud techniques, and outline the key elements of the reform framework legislated by SOX to remedy these problems.

The final section in the chapter examines the subject of internal control. Both managers and accountants should be concerned about the adequacy of the organization's internal control structure as a means of deterring fraud and preventing errors. In this section, internal control issues are first presented on a conceptual level. We then discuss internal control within the context of the COSO / SAS 78 framework recommended for SOX compliance.

ETHICAL ISSUES IN BUSINESS

Ethical standards are derived from societal mores and deep-rooted personal beliefs about issues of right and wrong that are *not* universally agreed upon. It is quite possible for two individuals, both of whom consider themselves to be acting ethically, to be on opposite sides of an issue. Often, we confuse ethical issues with legal issues. When the Honorable Gentleman from the state of ——, who is charged with ethical misconduct, stands before Congress and proclaims that he is "guilty of no wrongdoing," is he really saying that he did not break the *law*?

We have been inundated with scandals in the stock market, stories of computer crimes and viruses, and almost obscene charges of impropriety and illegalities by corporate executives. Using covert compensation schemes, Enron's CFO Andy Fastow managed to improve his personal wealth by approximately $40 million. Similarly, Dennis Kozowski of Tyco, Richard Scrushy of HealthSouth, and Bernie Ebbers of WorldCom all became wealthy beyond imagination while driving their companies into the ground. Indeed, during the period from early 1999 to May 2002, the executives of 25 companies extracted $25 billion worth of special compensation, stock options, and private loans from their organizations while their companies' stock plummeted 75 percent or more.[1]

A thorough treatment of ethics issues is impossible within the space available. Instead, the objective of this section is to heighten the reader's awareness of ethical concerns relating to business, information systems, and computer technology.

BUSINESS ETHICS

Ethics pertains to the principles of conduct that individuals use in making choices and guiding their behavior in situations that involve the concepts of right and wrong. More specifically, **business ethics** involves finding the answers to two questions:

1. How do managers decide on what is right in conducting their business?
2. Once managers have recognized what is right, how do they achieve it?

Ethical issues in business can be divided into four areas: equity, rights, honesty, and the exercise of corporate power. Table 3-1 identifies some of the business practices and decisions in each of these areas that have ethical implications.

Making Ethical Decisions

Business organizations have conflicting responsibilities to their employees, shareholders, customers, and the public. Every major decision has consequences that potentially harm or benefit these constituents. For example, implementing a new computer information system within an organization may cause some employees to lose their jobs, while those who remain enjoy the benefit of improved working conditions. Seeking a balance between these consequences is the managers' **ethical responsibility**. The following ethical principles provide some guidance in the discharge of this responsibility.[2]

Proportionality. The benefit from a decision must outweigh the risks. Furthermore, there must be no alternative decision that provides the same or greater benefit with less risk.

> **Justice.** The benefits of the decision should be distributed fairly to those who share the risks. Those who do not benefit should not carry the burden of risk.

---

1   Robert Prentice, Student Guide to the Sarbanes-Oxley Act, Thomson Publishing, 2005. p. 23
2   M. McFarland, "Ethics and the Safety of Computer System," *Computer* (February 1991).

TABLE 3-1	Ethical Issues in Business
Equity	Executive Salaries Comparable Worth Product Pricing
Rights	Corporate Due Process Employee Health Screening Employee Privacy Sexual Harassment Diversity Equal Employment Opportunity Whistle-Blowing
Honesty	Employee and Management Conflicts of Interest Security of Organization Data and Records Misleading Advertising Questionable Business Practices in Foreign Countries Accurate Reporting of Shareholder Interests
Exercise of Corporate Power	Political Action Committees Workplace Safety Product Safety Environmental Issues Divestment of Interests Corporate Political Contributions Downsizing and Plant Closures

SOURCE: Adapted from: The Conference Board, "Defining Corporate Ethics," in P. Madsen and J. Shafritz, *Essentials of Business Ethics* (New York: Meridian, 1990), 18.

Minimize risk. Even if judged acceptable by the principles, the decision should be implemented so as to minimize all of the risks and avoid any unnecessary risks.

COMPUTER ETHICS

The use of information technology in business has had a major impact on society and thus raises significant ethical issues regarding computer crime, working conditions, privacy, and more. **Computer ethics** is "the analysis of the nature and social impact of computer technology and the corresponding formulation and justification of policies for the ethical use of such technology. . . . [This includes] concerns about software as well as hardware and concerns about networks connecting computers as well as computers themselves."[3]

One researcher has defined three levels of computer ethics: pop, para, and theoretical.[4] *Pop* computer ethics is simply the exposure to stories and reports found in the popular media regarding the good or bad ramifications of computer technology. Society at large needs to be aware of such things as computer viruses and computer systems designed to aid handicapped persons. *Para* computer ethics involves taking a real interest in computer ethics cases and acquiring some level of skill and knowledge in the field. All systems professionals need to reach this level of competency so they can do their jobs

[3]   J. H. Moor, "What Is Computer Ethics?" *Metaphilosophy* 16 (1985): 266–75.
[4]   T. W. Bynum, "Human Values and the Computer Science Curriculum" (Working paper for the National Conference on Computing and Values, August 1991).

effectively. Students of accounting information systems should also achieve this level of ethical understanding. The third level, *theoretical* computer ethics, is of interest to multidisciplinary researchers who apply the theories of philosophy, sociology, and psychology to computer science with the goal of bringing some new understanding to the field.

A New Problem or Just a New Twist on an Old Problem?

Some argue that all pertinent ethical issues have already been examined in some other domain. For example, the issue of property rights has been explored and has resulted in copyright, trade secret, and patent laws. Although computer programs are a new type of asset, many feel that they should be considered no differently from other forms of property. A fundamental question arising from such debate is whether computers represent new ethical problems or just create new twists on old problems. Where the latter is the case, we need only to understand the generic values that are at stake and the principles that should then apply.[5] However, a large contingent vociferously disagrees with the premise that computers are no different from other technology. For example, many reject the notion of intellectual property being the same as real property. There is, as yet, no consensus on this matter.

Several issues of concern for students of accounting information systems are discussed in the following section. This list is not exhaustive, and a full discussion of each of the issues is beyond the scope of this chapter. Instead, the issues are briefly defined, and several trigger questions are provided. One hopes that these questions will provoke thought and discussion in the classroom.

Privacy

People desire to be in full control of what and how much information about themselves is available to others, and to whom it is available. This is the issue of **privacy**. The creation and maintenance of huge, shared databases makes it necessary to protect people from the potential misuse of data. This raises the issue of **ownership** in the personal information industry.[6] Should the privacy of individuals be protected through policies and systems? What information about oneself does the individual "own"? Should firms that are unrelated to individuals buy and sell information about these individuals without their permission?

Security (Accuracy and Confidentiality)

Computer **security** is an attempt to avoid such undesirable events as a loss of confidentiality or data integrity. Security systems attempt to prevent fraud and other misuse of computer systems; they act to protect and further the legitimate interests of the system's constituencies. The ethical issues involving security arise from the emergence of shared, computerized databases that have the potential to cause irreparable harm to individuals by disseminating inaccurate information to authorized users, such as through incorrect credit reporting.[7] There is a similar danger in disseminating accurate information to persons unauthorized to receive it. However, increasing security can actually cause other problems. For example, security can be used both to protect personal property and to undermine freedom of access to data, which may have an injurious effect on some individuals. Which is the more important goal? Automated monitoring can be used to detect intruders or other misuse, yet it can also be used to spy on legitimate users, thus diminishing their privacy.

---

5   G. Johnson, "A Framework for Thinking about Computer Ethics," in J. Robinette and R. Barquin (eds.), *Computers and Ethics: A Sourcebook for Discussions* (Brooklyn: Polytechnic Press, 1989): 26–31.

6   W. Ware, "Contemporary Privacy Issues" (Working paper for the National Conference on Computing and Human Values, August 1991).

7   K. C. Laudon, "Data Quality and Due Process in Large Interorganizational Record Systems," *Communications of the ACM* (1986): 4–11.

Where is the line to be drawn? What is an appropriate use and level of security? Which is most important: security, accuracy, or confidentiality?

Ownership of Property
Laws designed to preserve real property rights have been extended to cover what is referred to as intellectual property, that is, software. The question here becomes what an individual (or organization) can own. Ideas? Media? Source code? Object code? A related question is whether owners and users should be constrained in their use or access. Copyright laws have been invoked in an attempt to protect those who develop software from having it copied. Unquestionably, the hundreds and thousands of program development hours should be protected from piracy. However, many believe the copyright laws can cause more harm than good. For example, should the "look and feel" of a software package be granted copyright protection? Some argue that this flies in the face of the original intent of the law. Whereas the purpose of copyrights is to "promote the progress of science and the useful arts," allowing a user interface the protection of copyright may do just the opposite. The best interest of computer users is served when industry standards emerge; copyright laws work against this. Part of the problem lies in the uniqueness of software, its ease of dissemination, and the possibility of exact replication. Does software fit with the current categories and conventions regarding ownership?

Equity in Access
Some barriers to access are intrinsic to the technology of information systems, but some are avoidable through careful system design. Several factors, some of which are not unique to information systems, can limit access to computing technology. The economic status of the individual or the affluence of an organization will determine the ability to obtain information technology. Culture also limits access, for example, where documentation is prepared in only one language or is poorly translated. Safety features, or the lack thereof, have limited access to pregnant women, for example. How can hardware and software be designed with consideration for differences in physical and cognitive skills? What is the cost of providing equity in access? For what groups of society should equity in access become a priority?

Environmental Issues
Computers with high-speed printers allow for the production of printed documents faster than ever before. It is probably easier just to print a document than to consider whether it should be printed and how many copies really need to be made. It may be more efficient or more comforting to have a hard copy in addition to the electronic version. However, paper comes from trees, a precious natural resource, and ends up in landfills if not properly recycled. Should organizations limit nonessential hard copies? Can *nonessential* be defined? Who can and should define it? Should proper recycling be required? How can it be enforced?

Artificial Intelligence
A new set of social and ethical issues has arisen out of the popularity of expert systems. Because of the way these systems have been marketed, that is, as decision makers or replacements for experts, some people rely on them significantly. Therefore, both knowledge engineers (those who write the programs) and domain experts (those who provide the knowledge about the task being automated) must be concerned about their responsibility for faulty decisions, incomplete or inaccurate knowledge bases, and the role given to computers in the decision-making process.[8] Further, because expert systems attempt to

---

8   R. Dejoie, G. Fowler, and D. Paradice (eds.), *Ethical Issues in Information Systems* (Boston: Boyd & Fraser, 1991).

clone a manager's decision-making style, an individual's prejudices may implicitly or explicitly be included in the knowledge base. Some of the questions that need to be explored are: Who is responsible for the completeness and appropriateness of the knowledge base? Who is responsible for a decision made by an expert system that causes harm when implemented? Who owns the expertise once it is coded into a knowledge base?

Unemployment and Displacement

Many jobs have been and are being changed as a result of the availability of computer technology. People unable or unprepared to change are displaced. Should employers be responsible for retraining workers who are displaced as a result of the computerization of their functions?

Misuse of Computers

Computers can be misused in many ways. Copying proprietary software, using a company's computer for personal benefit, and snooping through other people's files are just a few obvious examples.[9] Although copying proprietary software (except to make a personal backup copy) is clearly illegal, it is commonly done. Why do people feel that it is not necessary to obey this law? Are there any good arguments for trying to change this law? What harm is done to the software developer when people make unauthorized copies? A computer is not an item that deteriorates with use, so is there any harm to the employer if it is used for an employee's personal benefit? Does it matter if the computer is used during company time or outside of work hours? Is there a difference if some profit-making activity takes place rather than, for example, using the computer to write a personal letter? Does it make a difference if a profit-making activity takes place during or outside of working hours? Is it okay to look through paper files that clearly belong to someone else? Is there any difference between paper files and computer files?

SARBANES-OXLEY ACT AND ETHICAL ISSUES

Public outcry surrounding ethical misconduct and fraudulent acts by executives of Enron, Global Crossing, Tyco, Adelphia, WorldCom, and others, spurred Congress into passing the American Competitiveness and Corporate Accountability Act of 2002. This wide-sweeping legislation, more commonly known as the *Sarbanes-Oxley Act* (SOX), is the most significant securities law since the SEC Acts of 1933 and 1934. SOX has many provisions designed to deal with specific problems relating to capital markets, corporate governance, and the auditing profession. Several of these are discussed later in the chapter. At this point we are concerned primarily with Section 406 of the act, which pertains to ethical issues.

Section 406—Code of Ethics for Senior Financial Officers

Section 406 of SOX requires public companies to disclose to the SEC whether they have adopted a code of ethics that applies to the organization's CEO, CFO, controller, or persons performing similar functions. If the company has not adopted such a code, it must explain why it has not. A public company may disclose its code of ethics in several ways: (1) included as an exhibit to its annual report, (2) as a posting to its website, or (3) by agreeing to provide copies of the code upon request.

Whereas Section 406 applies specifically to executive and financial officers of a company, a company's code of ethics should apply equally to all employees. Top management's attitude toward ethics sets the tone for business practice, but it is also the

---

9   K. A. Forcht, "Assessing the Ethic Standards and Policies in Computer-Based Environments," in R. Dejoie, G. Fowler, and D. Paradice (eds.), *Ethical Issues in Information Systems* (Boston: Boyd & Fraser, 1991).

responsibility of lower-level managers and nonmanagers to uphold a firm's ethical standards. Ethical violations can occur throughout an organization from the board-room to the receiving dock. Methods must therefore be developed for including all management and employees in the firm's ethics schema. The SEC has ruled that com-pliance with Section 406 necessitates a written code of ethics that address the follow-ing ethical issues:

Conflicts of Interest. The company's code of ethics should outline procedures for dealing with actual or apparent conflicts of interest between personal and professional relationships. One should note that the issue here is in "dealing with" conflicts of interest not prohibiting them. Whereas avoidance is the best policy, sometimes conflicts are unavoidable. Thus, one's handling and full disclosure of the matter becomes the ethical concern. Managers and employees alike should be made aware of the firm's code of ethics, be given decision models, and participate in training programs that explore conflicts of interest issues.

Full and Fair Disclosures. This provision states that the organization should provide full, fair, accurate, timely, and understandable disclosures in the documents, reports, and financial statements that it submits to the SEC and to the public. Overly complex and mis-leading accounting techniques were used to camouflage questionable activities that lie at the heart of many recent financial scandals. The objective of this rule is to ensure that future disclosures are candid, open, truthful, and void of such deceptions.

Legal Compliance. Codes of ethics should require employees to follow applicable gov-ernmental laws, rules, and regulations. As stated previously, we must not confuse ethical issues with legal issues. Nevertheless, doing the right thing requires sensitivity to laws, rules, regulations, and societal expectations. To accomplish this, organizations must pro-vide employees with training and guidance.

Internal Reporting of Code Violations. The code of ethics must provide a mechanism to permit prompt internal reporting of ethics violations. This provision is similar in nature to Sections 301 and 806, which were designed to encourage and protect whistleblowers. Employee ethics hotlines are emerging as the mechanism for dealing with these related requirements. Because SOX requires this function to be confidential, many companies are outsourcing their employee hotline service to independent vendors.

Accountability. An effective ethics program must take appropriate action when code vio-lations occur. This will include various disciplinary measures including dismissal. An employee hotline must be seen by employees as credible, or it will not be used. Section 301 directs the organization's audit committee to establish procedure for receiving, retain-ing, and treating such complaints about accounting procedures and internal control viola-tions. Audit committees will also play an important role in oversight of ethics enforcement activities.

FRAUD AND ACCOUNTANTS

Perhaps no major aspect of the independent auditor's role has caused more controversy than their responsibility detecting fraud during an audit. In recent years, the structure of the U.S. financial reporting system has become the object of scrutiny. The SEC, the courts, and the public, along with Congress, have focused on business failures and questionable practices by the management of corporations that engage in alleged fraud. The question often asked is, "Where were the auditors?"

The passage of SOX has had a tremendous impact on the external auditor's responsibilities for fraud detection during a financial audit. It requires the auditor to test controls specifically intended to prevent or detect fraud likely to result in the material misstatement of the financial statements. The current authoritative guidelines on fraud detection are presented in **SAS No. 99,** *Consideration of Fraud in a* **Financial Statement Audit.** The objective of SAS 99 is to seamlessly blend the auditor's consideration of fraud into all phases of the audit process. In addition, SAS 99 requires the auditor to perform new steps such as a brainstorming during audit planning to assess the potential risk of material misstatement of the financial statements from fraud schemes.

DEFINITIONS OF FRAUD

Although fraud is a familiar term in today's financial press, its meaning is not always clear. For example, in cases of bankruptcies and business failures, alleged fraud is often the result of poor management decisions or adverse business conditions. Under such circumstances, it becomes necessary to clearly define and understand the nature and meaning of fraud.

Fraud denotes a false representation of a material fact made by one party to another party with the intent to deceive and induce the other party to justifiably rely on the fact to his or her detriment. According to common law, a fraudulent act must meet the following five conditions:

1. *False representation.* There must be a false statement or a nondisclosure.
2. *Material fact.* A fact must be a substantial factor in inducing someone to act.
3. *Intent.* There must be the intent to deceive or the knowledge that one's statement is false.
4. *Justifiable reliance.* The misrepresentation must have been a substantial factor on which the injured party relied.
5. *Injury or loss.* The deception must have caused injury or loss to the victim of the fraud.

Fraud in the business environment has a more specialized meaning. It is an intentional deception, misappropriation of a company's assets, or manipulation of its financial data to the advantage of the perpetrator. In accounting literature, fraud is also commonly known as "white-collar crime," "defalcation," "embezzlement," and "irregularities." Auditors encounter fraud at two levels: *employee fraud* and *management fraud.* Because each form of fraud has different implications for auditors, we need to distinguish between the two.

Employee fraud, or fraud by nonmanagement employees, is generally designed to directly convert cash or other assets to the employee's personal benefit. Typically, the employee circumvents the company's internal control system for personal gain. If a company has an effective system of internal control, defalcations or embezzlements can usually be prevented or detected.

Employee fraud usually involves three steps: (1) stealing something of value (an asset), (2) converting the asset to a usable form (cash), and (3) concealing the crime to avoid detection. The third step is often the most difficult. It may be relatively easy for a storeroom clerk to steal inventories from the employer's warehouse, but altering the inventory records to hide the theft is more of a challenge.

Management fraud is more insidious than employee fraud because it often escapes detection until irreparable damage or loss has been suffered by the organization. Usually management fraud does not involve the direct theft of assets. Top management may engage in fraudulent activities to drive up the market price of the company's stock. This may be done to meet investor expectations or to take advantage of stock options that have been loaded into the manager's compensation package. The Commission on Auditors' Responsibilities calls this "performance fraud," which often involves deceptive practices to inflate earnings or to forestall the recognition of either insolvency or a decline in earnings. Lower-level management fraud typically involves materially misstating financial data and internal reports to gain additional compensation, to garner a promotion, or to escape the penalty for poor performance. Management fraud typically contains three special characteristics:[10]

1. The fraud is perpetrated at levels of management above the one to which internal control structures generally relate.
2. The fraud frequently involves using the financial statements to create an illusion that an entity is more healthy and prosperous than, in fact, it is.
3. If the fraud involves misappropriation of assets, it frequently is shrouded in a maze of complex business transactions, often involving related third parties.

The preceding characteristics of management fraud suggest that management can often perpetrate irregularities by overriding an otherwise effective internal control structure that would prevent similar irregularities by lower-level employees.

FACTORS THAT CONTRIBUTE TO FRAUD

According to one study, people engage in fraudulent activity as a result of an interaction of forces both within an individual's personality and the external environment. These forces are classified into three major categories: (1) *situational pressures,* (2) *opportunities,* and (3) *personal characteristics (ethics).* Figure 3-1 graphically displays the interplay of these three fraud-motivating forces.[11]

Figure 3-1 suggests that a person with a high level of personal ethics and limited pressure and opportunity to commit fraud is most likely to behave honestly. Similarly, an individual with lower ethical standards, when placed in situations with increasing pressure and given the opportunity, is most likely to commit fraud.

Whereas these factors, for the most part, fall outside of the auditors' sphere of influence, auditors can develop a *red-flag* checklist to detect possible fraudulent activity. To that end, a questionnaire approach could be used to help external auditors uncover motivations for committing fraud. Some of the larger public accounting firms have developed checklists to help uncover fraudulent activity during an audit. Questions for such a checklist might include:[12]

- Do key executives have unusually high personal debt?
- Do key executives appear to be living beyond their means?
- Do key executives engage in habitual gambling?
- Do key executives appear to abuse alcohol or drugs?
- Do any of the key executives appear to lack personal codes of ethics?
- Are economic conditions unfavorable within the company's industry?

---

10 R. Grinaker, "Discussant's Response to a Look at the Record on Auditor Detection of Management Fraud," *Proceedings of the 1980 Touche Ross University of Kansas Symposium on Auditing Problems* (Kansas City: University of Kansas, 1980).
11 M. Romney, W. S. Albrecht, and D. J. Cherrington, "Auditors and the Detection of Fraud," *Journal of Accountancy* (May 1980).
12 *Ibid.*

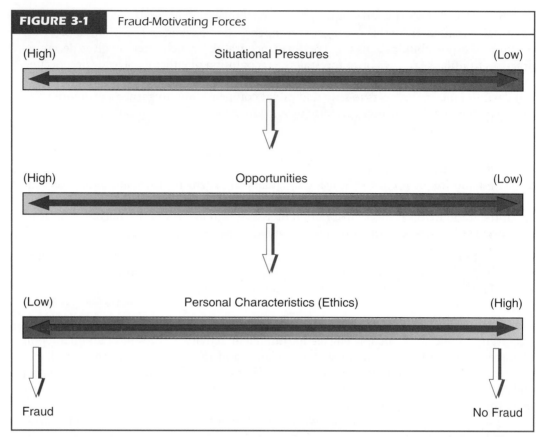

FIGURE 3-1 | Fraud-Motivating Forces

(High)   Situational Pressures   (Low)

(High)   Opportunities   (Low)

(Low)   Personal Characteristics (Ethics)   (High)

Fraud   No Fraud

SOURCE: Adapted from W. S. Albrecht and M. B. Romney, "Auditing Implications Derived from a Review of Cases and Articles Relating to Fraud," *Proceedings of the 1980 Touche Ross University of Kansas Symposium on Auditing Problems* (Kansas City: University of Kansas, 1980).

- Does the company use several different banks, none of which sees the company's entire financial picture?

- Do any key executives have close associations with suppliers?

- Is the company experiencing a rapid turnover of key employees, either through resignation or temination?

- Do one or two individuals dominate the company?

A review of some of these questions suggests that the contemporary auditor may use special investigative agencies to run a complete but confidential background check on the key managers of existing and prospective client firms.

FINANCIAL LOSSES FROM FRAUD

A research study conducted by the Association of Certified Fraud Examiners (ACFE) in 2004 estimates losses from fraud and abuse to be 6 percent of annual revenues. This translates to approximately $660 billion. The actual cost of fraud is difficult to quantify for a number of reasons: (1) not all fraud is detected; (2) of that detected, not all is reported; (3) in many fraud cases, incomplete information is gathered; (4) information is not properly distributed to management or law enforcement authorities; and (5) too often, business organizations decide to take no civil or criminal action against the perpetrator(s) of fraud. In addition to the direct economic loss to the organization, indirect costs including reduced productivity, the cost of legal action, increased unemployment, and business disruption due to investigation of the fraud need to be considered.

Of the 508 cases examined in the ACFE study, more than half of the frauds cost their victim organizations at least $100,000, and 15 percent caused losses of $1 million or more. The distribution of dollar losses is presented in Table 3-2.

THE PERPETRATORS OF FRAUDS

The ACFE study examined a number of factors that characterized the perpetrators of the frauds, including position within the organization, collusion with others, gender, age, and education. The median financial loss was calculated for each factor. The results of the study are summarized in Tables 3-3 through 3-7.

Fraud Losses by Position within the Organization

Table 3-3 shows that 68 percent of the reported fraud cases were committed by nonmanagerial employees, 34 percent by managers, and 12 percent by executives or owners. Although the number of reported fraud incidents perpetrated by employees is twice that of managers and five times that of executives, the average losses per category are inversely related.

Fraud Losses and the Collusion Effect

Collusion among employees in the commission of a fraud is difficult to both prevent and detect. This is particularly true when the collusion is between managers and their subordinate employees. Management plays a key role in the internal control structure of an organization. They are relied upon to prevent and detect fraud among their subordinates. When they participate in fraud with the employees over whom they are supposed to provide oversight, the organization's control structure is weakened, or completely circumvented, and the company becomes more vulnerable to losses.

Table 3-4 compares the median losses from frauds committed by a single individual (regardless of position) and those involving collusion. This includes both internal collusion and schemes in which an employee or manager colludes with an outsider such as a vendor or a customer. Although fraud committed by a single perpetrator is far more common (65 percent of cases), the median loss from collusion is $200,000 as compared to $58,000 for frauds perpetrated by an individual working alone.

TABLE 3-2	Distribution of Losses
Amount of Loss	**Percent of Frauds**
$1–$999	1.4%
$1,000–$9,999	12.3%
$10,000–$49,999	22.8%
$50,000–$99,999	12.9%
$100,000–$499,999	29.2%
$500,000–$999,999	6.8%
$1,000,000–and up	14.6%

SOURCE: Adapted from: The Conference Board, "Defining Corporate Ethics," in P. Madsen and J. Shafritz, *Essentials of Business Ethics* (New York: Meridian, 1990), 18.

TABLE 3-3	Losses from Fraud by Position	
Position	**Percent of Frauds**	**Loss**
Owner/Executive	12	$900,000
Manager	34	140,000
Employee	68	62,000

*The sum of the percentages exceeds 100% because some of the reported frauds involved multiple perpetrators from more than one category.

TABLE 3-4	Losses from Fraud by Collusion
Perpetrators	**Loss**
Two or more (34.9%)	$200,000
One (65.1%)	58,500

TABLE 3-5	Losses from Fraud by Gender
Gender	**Loss**
Male	$160,000
Female	60,000

TABLE 3-6	Losses from Fraud by Age
Age Range	**Loss**
< 25	$ 18,000
26–30	25,000
31–35	75,000
36–40	80,000
41–50	173,000
51–60	250,000
> 60	527,000

TABLE 3-7	Losses from Fraud by Educational Level
Education Level	**Loss**
High school	$ 50,000
College	150,000
Post graduate	325,000

Fraud Losses by Gender

Table 3-5 shows that the median loss per case caused by males ($160,000) was almost three times that caused by females ($60,000).

Fraud Losses by Age

Table 3-6 indicates that perpetrators 25 years of age or younger caused median losses of about $18,000, while employees 60 and older perpetrated frauds that were on average 29 times larger—$527,000.

Fraud Losses by Education

Table 3-7 shows the median loss from frauds relative to the perpetrator's education level. Frauds committed by high school graduates averaged only $50,000, whereas those with bachelor's degrees averaged $150,000. Perpetrators with advanced degrees were responsible for frauds with a median loss of $325,000.

Conclusions to Be Drawn

Unless we intend to eliminate all managers and male employees over the age of 25 who have received degrees in higher education, the fraud classification scheme appears on the surface to provide little in the way of antifraud decision-making criteria. Upon closer examination, however, a common thread appears. Notwithstanding the importance of personal ethics and situational pressures, *opportunity* is the factor that most engenders fraud. Opportunity can be defined as control over assets or access to assets. Indeed, control and access are essential elements of opportunity. The financial loss differences associated with the previous classifications are explained by the opportunity factor.

- *Gender.* Whereas the demographic picture is changing, more men than women occupy positions of authority in business organizations, which provide them greater access to assets.

- *Position.* Those in the highest positions have the greatest access to company funds and assets.

- *Age.* Older employees tend to occupy higher-ranking positions and therefore generally have greater access to company assets.

- *Education.* Generally, those with more education occupy higher positions in their organizations and therefore have greater access to company funds and other assets.

- *Collusion.* One reason for segregating occupational duties is to deny potential perpetrators the opportunity they need to commit fraud. When individuals in critical positions collude, they create opportunities to control or gain access to assets that otherwise would not exist.

FRAUD SCHEMES

Fraud schemes can be classified in a number of different ways. For purposes of discussion, this section presents the classification format derived by the Association of Certified Fraud Examiners. Three broad categories of fraud schemes are defined: fraudulent statements, corruption, and asset misappropriation.[13]

---

13   Report to the Nation: Occupational Fraud and Abuse. (Association of Fraud Examiners, 2004): 31–34.

Fraudulent Statements

Fraudulent statements are associated with management fraud. Whereas all fraud involves some form of financial misstatement, to meet the definition under this class of fraud scheme the statement itself must bring direct or indirect financial benefit to the perpetrator. In other words, the statement is not simply a vehicle for obscuring or covering a fraudulent act. For example, misstating the cash account balance to cover the theft of cash is not financial statement fraud. On the other hand, understating liabilities to present a more favorable financial picture of the organization to drive up stock prices does fall under this classification.

Table 3-8 shows that whereas fraudulent statements account for only 8 percent of the fraud cases covered in the ACFE fraud study, the median loss due to this type of fraud scheme is significantly higher than losses from corruption and asset misappropriation.

Appalling as this type of fraud loss appears on paper, these numbers fail to reflect the human suffering that parallels them in the real world. How does one measure the impact on stockholders as they watch their life savings and retirement funds evaporated after news of the fraud breaks? The underlying problems that permit and aid these frauds are found in the boardroom, not the mail room. In this section we examine some prominent corporate governance failures and the legislation to remedy them.

The Underlying Problems. The series of events symbolized by the Enron, WorldCom, and Adelphia debacles caused many to question whether our existing federal securities laws were adequate to assure full and fair financial disclosures by public companies. The following underlying problems are at the root of this concern.

1. *Lack of Auditor Independence.* Auditing firms who are also engaged by their clients to perform nonaccounting activities such as actuarial services, internal audit outsourcing services, and consulting lack independence. They are essentially auditing their own work. The risk is that as auditors they will not bring to management's attention detected problems that may adversely affect their consulting fees. For example, Enron's auditors—Arthur Andersen—were also their internal auditors and their management consultants.
2. *Lack of Director Independence.* Many boards of directors are composed of individuals who are not independent. Examples of lack of independence are directors who have a personal relationship by serving on the boards of other directors' companies, have a business trading relationship as key customers or suppliers of the company, have a financial relationship as primary stockholders or have received personal loans from the company, or have an operational relationship as employees of the company.

    A notorious example of corporate inbreeding is Adelphia Communications, a telecommunications company. Founded in 1952, it went public in 1986 and grew rapidly through a series of acquisitions. It became the sixth largest cable provider in the

TABLE 3-8	Losses from Fraud by Scheme Type	
Scheme Type	**Percent of Frauds***	**Loss**
Fraudulent statements	8	$1,000,000
Corruption	30	250,000
Asset misappropriation	92	93,000

*The sum of the percentages exceeds 100% because some of the reported frauds in the ACFE study involved more than one type of fraud scheme.

United States before an accounting scandal came to light. The founding family (John Rigas, CEO and chairman of the board; Timothy Rigas, CFO, CAO, and chairman of the audit committee; Michael Rigas, VP for operation; and J.P. Rigas, VP for strategic planning) perpetrated the fraud. Between 1998 and May 2002, the Rigas family successfully disguised transactions, distorted the company's financial picture, and engaged in embezzlement that resulted in a loss of more than $60 billion to shareholders.

Whereas it is neither practical nor wise to establish a board of directors that is totally void of self-interest, popular wisdom suggests that a healthier board of directors is one in which the majority of directors are independent outsiders with the integrity and the qualifications to understand the company and objectively plan its course.

3.   *Questionable Executive Compensation Schemes.* A survey by Thomson Financial revealed the strong belief that executives have abused stock-based compensation.[14] The consensus is that fewer stock options should be offered than currently is the practice. Excessive use of short-term stock options to compensate directors and executives may result in short-term thinking and strategies aimed at driving up stock prices at the expense of the firm's long-term health. In extreme cases, financial statement misrepresentation has been the vehicle to achieve the stock price needed to exercise the option.

As a case in point, Enron's management was a firm believer in the use of stock options. Nearly every employee had some type of arrangement where they could purchase shares at a discount, or were granted options based on future share prices. At Enron's headquarters in Houston, televisions were installed in the elevators so employees could track Enron's (and their own portfolio's) success. Before the firm's collapse, Enron executives added millions of dollars to their personal fortunes by exercising stock options.

4.   *Inappropriate Accounting Practices.* The use of inappropriate accounting techniques is a characteristic common to many financial statement fraud schemes. Enron made elaborate use of special-purpose entities (SPEs) to hide liabilities through off-balance-sheet accounting. SPEs are legal, but their application in this case was clearly intended to deceive the market. Enron also employed income-inflating techniques. For example, when the company sold a contract to provide natural gas for a period of two years, they would recognize all the future revenue in the period when the contract was sold.

WorldCom was another culprit of the improper accounting practices. In April 2001, WorldCom management decided to transfer transmission line costs from current expense accounts to capital accounts. This allowed them to defer some operating expenses and report higher earnings. Also, through acquisitions they seized the opportunity to raise earnings. WorldCom reduced the book value of hard assets of MCI by $3.4 billion and increased goodwill by the same amount. Had the assets been left at book value, they would have been charged against earnings over four years. Goodwill, on the other hand, was amortized over a much longer period. In June 2002, the company declared a $3.8 billion overstatement of profits because of falsely recorded expenses over the previous five quarters. The size of this fraud increased to $9 billion over the following months as additional evidence of improper accounting came to light.

Sarbanes-Oxley Act and Fraud. To address plummeting institutional and individual investor confidence triggered in part by business failures and accounting restatements, Congress enacted into law the **Sarbanes-Oxley Act** (SOX) in July 2002. This landmark

14   Howard Stock, "Institutions Prize Good Governance: Once Bitten, Twice Shy, Investors Seek Oversight and Transparency," *Investor Relations Business* (New York: November 4, 2002).

legislation was written to deal with problems related to capital markets, corporate governance, and the auditing profession and has fundamentally changed the way public companies do business and how the accounting profession performs its attest function. Some SOX rules became effective almost immediately and others were phased in over time. In the short time since it was enacted, however, SOX is now largely implemented.

The Act establishes a framework to modernize and reform the oversight and regulation of public company auditing. Its principal reforms pertain to (1) the creation of an accounting oversight board, (2) auditor independence, (3) corporate governance and responsibility, (4) disclosure requirements, and (5) penalties for fraud and other violations. These provisions are discussed in the following section.

1. *Accounting Oversight Board.* The Sarbanes-Oxley Act creates a **Public Company Accounting Oversight Board (PCAOB).** The PCAOB is empowered to set auditing, quality control, and ethics standards; to inspect registered accounting firms; to conduct investigations; and to take disciplinary actions.

2. *Auditor Independence.* The Act addresses auditor independence by creating more separation between a firm's attestation and nonauditing activities. This is intended to specify categories of services that a public accounting firm cannot perform for its client. These include the following nine functions:
   (1) Bookkeeping or other services related to the accounting records or financial statements;
   (2) Financial information systems design and implementation;
   (3) Appraisal or valuation services, fairness opinions, or contribution-in-kind reports;
   (4) Actuarial services;
   (5) Internal audit outsourcing services;
   (6) Management functions or human resources;
   (7) Broker or dealer, investment adviser, or investment banking services;
   (8) Legal services and expert services unrelated to the audit; and
   (9) Any other service that the PCAOB determines is impermissible.

   Whereas the Sarbanes-Oxley Act prohibits auditors from providing the above services to their audit clients, they are not prohibited from performing such services for nonaudit clients or privately held companies.

3. *Corporate Governance and Responsibility.* The Sarbanes-Oxley Act requires all audit committee members to be independent and requires the audit committee to hire and oversee the external auditors. This provision is consistent with many investors who consider the board composition to be a critical investment factor. For example, a Thomson Financial survey revealed that most institutional investors want corporate boards to be composed of at least 75 percent independent directors.[15]

   Two other significant provisions of the act relating to corporate governance are: (1) public companies are prohibited from making loans to executive officers and directors; and (2) the act requires attorneys to report evidence of a material violation of securities laws or breaches of fiduciary duty to the CEO, CFO, or the PCAOB.

4. *Issuer and Management Disclosure.* The Sarbanes-Oxley Act imposes new corporate disclosure requirements including:

   • Public companies must report all off-balance-sheet transactions.

---

15 *Ibid.*

- Annual reports filed with the SEC must include a statement by management asserting that it is responsible for creating and maintaining adequate internal controls and asserting to the effectiveness of those controls.

- Officers must certify that the company's accounts "fairly present" the firm's financial condition and results of operations. Knowingly filing a false certification is a criminal offence.

5. *Fraud and Criminal Penalties.* The Sarbanes-Oxley Act imposes a range of new criminal penalties for fraud and other wrongful acts. In particular, the Sarbanes-Oxley Act creates new federal crimes relating to the destruction of documents or audit work papers, securities fraud, tampering with documents to be used in an official proceeding, and actions against whistleblowers.

Corruption

Corruption involves an executive, manager, or employee of the organization in collusion with an outsider. The CFE study identifies four principal types of corruption: bribery, illegal gratuities, conflicts of interest, and economic extortion. Corruption accounts for about 10 percent of occupational fraud cases.

Bribery. **Bribery** involves giving, offering, soliciting, or receiving things of value to influence an official in the performance of his or her lawful duties. Officials may be employed by government (or regulatory) agencies or by private organizations. Bribery defrauds the entity (business organization or government agency) of the right to honest and loyal services from those employed by it. The following is an example of bribery.

> The manager of a meat-packing company offers a U.S. health inspector a cash payment. In return, the inspector suppresses his report of health violations discovered during a routine inspection of the meat-packing facilities. In this situation, the victims are those who rely on the honest reporting of the inspector. The loss is salary paid to the inspector for work not performed and any damages that result from failure to perform.

Illegal Gratuities. An **illegal gratuity** involves giving, receiving, offering, or soliciting something of value because of an official act that has been taken. This is similar to a bribe, but the transaction occurs after the fact. The following is an example of an illegal gratuity.

> The plant manager in a large corporation uses his influence to ensure that a request for proposals is written in such a way that only one contractor will be able to submit a satisfactory bid. As a result, the favored contractor's proposal is accepted at a noncompetitive price. In return, the contractor secretly makes a financial payment to the plant manager. The victims in this case are those who expect a competitive procurement process. The loss is the excess costs incurred by the company because of the noncompetitive pricing of the construction.

Conflicts of Interest. Every employer should expect that his or her employees will conduct their duties in a way that serves the interests of the employer. A **conflict of interest** occurs when an employee acts on behalf of a third party during the discharge of his or her duties or has self-interest in the activity being performed. When the employee's conflict of interest is unknown to the employer and results in financial loss, then fraud has occurred. The preceding examples of bribery and illegal gratuities also constitute conflicts of interest. This type of fraud can exist, however, when bribery and illegal payments are not present, but the employee has an interest in the outcome of the economic event. The following is an example.

A purchasing agent for a building contractor is also part owner in a plumbing supply company. The agent has sole discretion in selecting vendors for the plumbing supplies needed for buildings under contract. The agent directs a disproportionate number of purchase orders to his company, which charges above-market prices for its products. The agent's financial interest in the supplier is unknown to his employer.

Economic Extortion. **Economic extortion** is the use (or threat) of force (including economic sanctions) by an individual or organization to obtain something of value. The item of value could be a financial or economic asset, information, or cooperation to obtain a favorable decision on some matter under review. The following is an example of economic extortion.

A contract procurement agent for a state government threatens to blacklist a highway contractor if he does not make a financial payment to the agent. If the contractor fails to cooperate, the blacklisting will effectively eliminate him from consideration for future work. Faced with a threat of economic loss, the contractor makes the payment.

Asset Misappropriation

The most common form of fraud scheme involves some type of asset misappropriation. Ninety-two percent of the frauds included in the ACFE study fall in this category. Assets can be misappropriated either directly or indirectly for the perpetrator's benefit. Certain assets are more susceptible than others to misappropriation. Transactions involving cash, checking accounts, inventory, supplies, equipment, and information are the most vulnerable to abuse. Examples of fraud schemes involving asset misappropriation are described in the following sections.

Charges to Expense Accounts. The theft of an asset creates an imbalance in the basic accounting equation (assets = equities), which the criminal must adjust if the theft is to go undetected. The most common way to conceal the imbalance is to charge the asset to an expense account and reduce equity by the same amount. For example, the theft of $20,000 cash could be charged to a miscellaneous operating expense account. The loss of the cash reduces the firm's assets by $20,000. To offset this, equity is reduced by $20,000 when the miscellaneous expense account is closed to retained earnings, thus keeping the accounting equation in balance. This technique has the advantage of limiting the criminal's exposure to one period. When the expense account is closed to retained earnings, its balance is reset to zero to begin the new period.

Lapping. **Lapping** involves the use of customer checks, received in payment of their accounts, to conceal cash previously stolen by an employee. For example, the employee first steals and cashes a check for $500 sent by Customer A. To conceal the accounting imbalance caused by the loss of the asset, Customer A's account is not credited. Later (the next billing period), the employee uses a $500 check received from Customer B and applies this to Customer A's account. Funds received in the next period from Customer C are then applied to the account of Customer B, and so on.

Employees involved in this sort of fraud often rationalize that they are simply borrowing the cash and plan to repay it at some future date. This kind of accounting cover-up must continue indefinitely or until the employee returns the funds. Lapping is usually detected when the employee leaves the organization or becomes sick and must take time off work. Unless the fraud is perpetuated, the last customer to have funds diverted from his or her account will be billed again, and the lapping technique will be detected. Employers can deter lapping by periodically rotating employees into different jobs and forcing them to take scheduled vacations.

Transaction Fraud. **Transaction fraud** involves deleting, altering, or adding false transactions to divert assets to the perpetrator. This technique may be used to ship inventories to the perpetrator in response to a fraudulent sales transaction or to disburse cash in payment of a false liability.

A common type of transaction fraud involves the distribution of fraudulent paychecks to nonexistent employees. For example, an employee who has left the organization is kept on the payroll by her immediate supervisor. Each week, the supervisor continues to submit time cards to the payroll department just as if the employee was still working for the firm. The fraud works best in organizations where the supervisor is responsible for distributing paychecks to employees. The supervisor may then forge the ex-employee's signature on the check and cash it. Although the organization has lost cash, the fraud can go undetected because the credit to the cash account is offset by a debit to payroll expense.

Computer Fraud Schemes. Because computers lie at the heart of most organizations' accounting information systems today, the topic of **computer fraud** is of special importance to auditors. Whereas the objectives of the fraud are the same—misappropriation of assets—the techniques used to commit computer fraud vary greatly.

No one knows the true extent of business losses each year to computer fraud, but estimates reaching $100 billion per year give some indication of the problem's magnitude. One reason for uncertainty in loss estimates is that computer fraud is not well defined. For example, we saw in the ethics section of this chapter that some people do not view copying commercial computer software to be unethical. On the other side of this issue, software vendors consider this a criminal act. Regardless of how narrowly or broadly computer fraud is defined, most agree that it is a rapidly growing phenomenon.

For our purposes, computer fraud includes the following:

- The theft, misuse, or misappropriation of assets by altering computer-readable records and files.

- The theft, misuse, or misappropriation of assets by altering the logic of computer software.

- The theft or illegal use of computer-readable information.

- The theft, corruption, illegal copying, or intentional destruction of computer software.

- The theft, misuse, or misappropriation of computer hardware.

The general model for accounting information systems shown in Figure 3-2 conceptually portrays the key stages of an information system. Each stage in the model—data collection, data processing, database management, and information generation—is a potential area of risk for certain types of computer fraud.

Data Collection. **Data collection** is the first operational stage in the information system. The objective is to ensure that event data entering the system are valid, complete, and free from material errors. In many respects, this is the most important stage in the system. Should transaction errors pass through data collection undetected, the organization runs the risk that the system will process the errors and generate erroneous and unreliable output. This, in turn, could lead to incorrect actions and poor decisions by the users.

Two rules govern the design of data collection procedures: relevance and efficiency. The information system should capture only relevant data. A fundamental task of the system designer is to determine what is and what is not relevant. He or she does so by analyzing the user's needs. Only data that ultimately contribute to information are relevant. The data collection stage should be designed to filter irrelevant facts from the system.

| FIGURE 3-2 | The General Model for Accounting Information Systems |

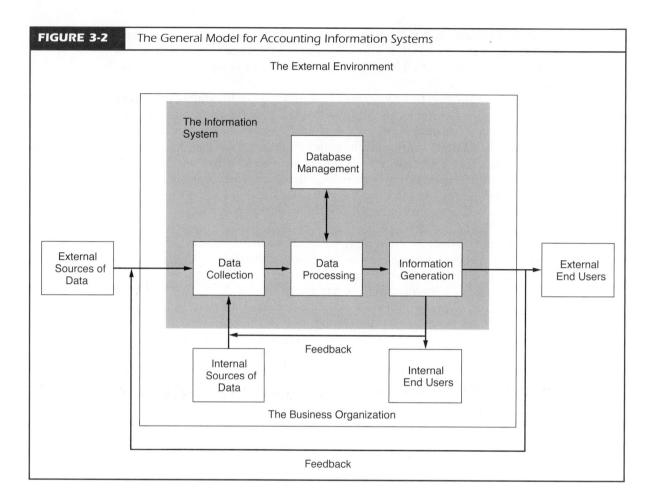

Efficient data collection procedures are designed to collect data only once. These data can then be made available to multiple users. Capturing the same data more than once leads to data redundancy and inconsistency. Information systems have limited collection, processing, and data storage capacity. Data redundancy overloads facilities and reduces the overall efficiency of the system. Inconsistency among data elements can result in inappropriate actions and bad decisions.

The simplest way to perpetrate a computer fraud is at the data collection or data entry stage. This is the computer equivalent of the transaction fraud discussed previously. Frauds of this type require little or no computer skills. The perpetrator need only understand how the system works to enter data that it will process. The fraudulent act involves falsifying data as it enters the system. This can be to delete, alter, or add a transaction. For example, to commit payroll fraud, the perpetrator may insert a fraudulent payroll transaction along with other legitimate transactions. Unless the insertion is detected by internal controls, the system will generate an additional paycheck for the perpetrator. A variation on this type of fraud is to change the Hours Worked field in an otherwise legitimate payroll transaction to increase the amount of the paycheck.

Still another variant on this fraud is to disburse cash in payment of a false account payable. By entering fraudulent supporting documents (purchase order, receiving report, and supplier invoice) into the data collection stage of the accounts payable system, a perpetrator can fool the system into creating an accounts payable record for a nonexistent purchase. Once the record is created, the system will presume it is legitimate and, on the due date, will disperse funds to the perpetrator in payment of a bogus liability.

Networked systems expose organizations to transaction frauds from remote locations. "Masquerading," "piggybacking," and "hacking" are examples of such fraud techniques. Masquerading involves a perpetrator gaining access to the system from a remote site by pretending to be an authorized user. This usually requires first gaining authorized access to a password. Piggybacking is a technique in which the perpetrator at a remote site taps in to the telecommunications lines and latches on to an authorized user who is logging into the system. Once in the system, the perpetrator can masquerade as the authorized user. Hacking may involve piggybacking or masquerading techniques. Hackers are distinguished from other computer criminals because their motives are not usually to defraud for financial gain. They are motivated primarily by the challenge of breaking in to the system rather than the theft of assets. Nevertheless, hackers have caused extensive damage and loss to organizations. Many believe that the line between hackers and the more classic computer criminals is thin.

Data Processing. Once collected, data usually require processing to produce information. Tasks in the data processing stage range from simple to complex. Examples include mathematical algorithms (such as linear programming models) used for production scheduling applications, statistical techniques for sales forecasting, and posting and summarizing procedures used for accounting applications.

Data processing frauds fall into two classes: program fraud and operations fraud. **Program fraud** includes the following techniques: (1) creating illegal programs that can access data files to alter, delete, or insert values into accounting records; (2) destroying or corrupting a program's logic using a computer virus; or (3) altering program logic to cause the application to process data incorrectly. For example, the program a bank uses to calculate interest on its customers' accounts will produce rounding errors. This happens because the precision of the interest calculation is greater than the reporting precision. Therefore, interest figures that are calculated to a fraction of one cent must be rounded to whole numbers for reporting purposes. A complex routine in the interest-calculation program keeps track of the rounding errors so that the total interest charge to the bank equals the sum of the individual credits. This involves temporarily holding the fractional amounts left over from each calculation in an internal memory accumulator. When the amount in the accumulator totals one cent (plus or minus), the penny is added to the customer's account that is being processed. In other words, one cent is added to (or deleted from) customer accounts randomly. A type of program fraud called the *salami fraud* involves modifying the rounding logic of the program so it no longer adds the one cent randomly. Instead, the modified program always adds the plus cent to the perpetrator's account but still adds the minus cent randomly. This can divert a considerable amount of cash to the perpetrator, but the accounting records stay in balance to conceal the crime.

Operations fraud is the misuse or theft of the firm's computer resources. This often involves using the computer to conduct personal business. For example, a programmer may use the firm's computer time to write software that he sells commercially. A CPA in the controller's office may use the company's computer to prepare tax returns and financial statements for her private clients. Similarly, a corporate lawyer with a private practice on the side may use the firm's computer to search for court cases and decisions in commercial databases. The cost of accessing the database is charged to the organization and hidden among other legitimate charges.

Database Management. The organization's database is its physical repository for financial and nonfinancial data. Database management involves three fundamental tasks: storage, retrieval, and deletion. The *storage* task assigns keys to new records and stores them in their proper location in the database. *Retrieval* is the task of locating and extracting an existing record from the database for processing. After processing is complete, the storage task restores the updated record to its place in the database. *Deletion* is the task of permanently removing obsolete or redundant records from the database.

Database management fraud includes altering, deleting, corrupting, destroying, or stealing an organization's data. Because access to database files is an essential element of this fraud, it is usually associated with transaction or program fraud. The most common technique is to access the database from a remote site and browse the files for useful information that can be copied and sold to competitors. Disgruntled employees have been known to destroy company data files simply to harm the organization. One method is to insert a destructive routine called a *logic bomb* into a program. At a specified time, or when certain conditions are met, the logic bomb erases the data files that the program accesses. For example, a disgruntled programmer who was contemplating leaving an organization inserted a logic bomb into the payroll system. Weeks later, when the system detected that the programmer's name had been removed from the payroll file, the logic bomb was activated and erased the payroll file.

Information Generation. Information generation is the process of compiling, arranging, formatting, and presenting information to users. Information can be an operational document such as a sales order, a structured report, or a message on a computer screen. Regardless of physical form, useful information has the following characteristics: **relevance, timeliness, accuracy, completeness,** and **summarization.**

- *Relevance.* The contents of a report or document must serve a purpose. This could be to support a manager's decision or a clerk's task. We have established that only data relevant to a user's action have information content. Therefore, the information system should present only relevant data in its reports. Reports containing irrelevancies waste resources and may be counterproductive to the user. Irrelevancies detract attention from the true message of the report and may result in incorrect decisions or actions.

- *Timeliness.* The age of information is a critical factor in determining its usefulness. Information must be no older than the time period of the action it supports. For example, if a manager makes decisions daily to purchase inventory from a supplier based on an inventory status report, then the information in the report should be no more than a day old.

- *Accuracy.* Information must be free from material errors. However, materiality is a difficult concept to quantify. It has no absolute value; it is a problem-specific concept. This means that in some cases, information must be perfectly accurate. In other instances, the level of accuracy may be lower. Material error exists when the amount of inaccuracy in information causes the user to make poor decisions or to fail to make necessary decisions. We sometimes must sacrifice absolute accuracy to obtain timely information. Often perfect information is not available within the decision time frame of the user. Therefore, in providing information, system designers seek a balance between information that is as accurate as possible, yet timely enough to be useful.

- *Completeness.* No piece of information essential to a decision or task should be missing. For example, a report should provide all necessary calculations and present its message clearly and unambiguously.

- *Summarization.* Information should be aggregated in accordance with a user's needs. Lower level managers tend to need information that is highly detailed. As information flows upward through the organization to top management, it becomes more summarized. Later in this chapter, we will look more closely at the effects that organizational structure and managerial level have on information reporting.

A common form of fraud at the information generation stage is to steal, misdirect, or misuse computer output. One simple but effective technique called **scavenging** involves searching through the trash of the computer center for discarded output. A perpetrator can often obtain useful information from the carbon sheets removed from multipart reports or from paper reports that were rejected during processing. Sometimes output reports are misaligned on the paper or slightly garbled during printing. When this happens, the output must be reprinted and the original output is often thrown in the trash.

Another form of fraud called **eavesdropping** involves listening to output transmissions over telecommunications lines. Technologies are readily available that enable perpetrators to intercept messages being sent over unprotected telephone lines and microwave channels. Most experts agree that it is practically impossible to prevent a determined perpetrator from accessing data communication channels. Data encryption can, however, render useless any data captured through eavesdropping.

INTERNAL CONTROL CONCEPTS AND TECHNIQUES

With the backdrop of ethics and fraud in place, let's now examine internal control concepts and techniques for dealing with these problems. **Internal control system** comprises policies, practices, and procedures employed by the organization to achieve four broad objectives:

1. To safeguard assets of the firm.
2. To ensure the accuracy and reliability of accounting records and information.
3. To promote efficiency in the firm's operations.
4. To measure compliance with management's prescribed policies and procedures.[16]

Modifying Assumptions

Inherent in these control objectives are four modifying assumptions that guide designers and auditors of internal controls.[17]

Management Responsibility. This concept holds that the establishment and maintenance of a system of internal control is a **management responsibility**. This point is made eminent in SOX legislation.

Reasonable Assurance. The internal control system should provide **reasonable assurance** that the four broad objectives of internal control are met in a cost-effective manner. This means that no system of internal control is perfect and the cost of achieving improved control should not outweigh its benefits.

Methods of Data Processing. Internal controls should achieve the four broad objectives regardless of the data processing method used. The control techniques used to achieve these objectives will, however, vary with different types of technology.

---

16   American Institute of Certified Public Accountants, *AICPA Professional Standards*, vol. 1 (New York: AICPA, 1987), AU Sec. 320.30-35.

17   American Institute of Certified Public Accountants, Committee on Auditing Procedure, Internal Control—Elements of a Coordinated System and Its Importance to Management and the Independent Public Accountant, *Statement on Auditing Standards* No. 1, Sec. 320 (New York: AICPA, 1973).

Limitations. Every system of internal control has limitations on its effectiveness. These include (1) the possibility of error—no system is perfect, (2) circumvention—personnel may circumvent the system through collusion or other means, (3) management override—management is in a position to override control procedures by personally distorting transactions or by directing a subordinate to do so, and (4) changing conditions—conditions may change over time so that existing controls may become ineffectual.

Exposures and Risk

Figure 3-3 portrays the internal control system as a shield that protects the firm's assets from numerous undesirable events that bombard the organization. These include attempts at unauthorized access to the firm's assets (including information); fraud perpetrated by persons both within and outside the firm; errors due to employee incompetence, faulty computer programs, and corrupted input data; and mischievous acts, such as unauthorized access by computer hackers and threats from computer viruses that destroy programs and databases.

FIGURE 3-3	Internal Control Shield

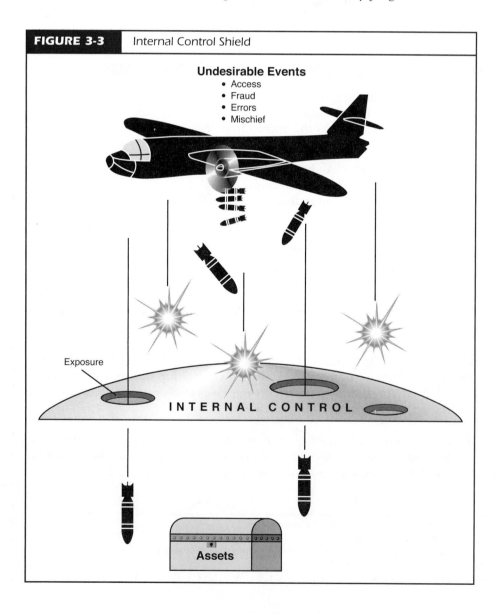

The absence or weakness of a control is called an **exposure**. Exposures, which are illustrated as holes in the control shield in Figure 3-3, increase the firm's risk to financial loss or injury from undesirable events. A weakness in internal control may expose the firm to one or more of the following types of risks:

1. Destruction of assets (both physical assets and information).
2. Theft of assets.
3. Corruption of information or the information system.
4. Disruption of the information system.

The Preventive-Detective-Corrective Internal Control Model

Figure 3-4 illustrates that the internal control shield is composed of three levels of control: preventive controls, detective controls, and corrective controls. This is the Preventive-Detective-Corrective (PDC) control model.

Preventive Controls. Prevention is the first line of defense in the control structure. **Preventive controls** are passive techniques designed to reduce the frequency of occurrence of undesirable events. Preventive controls force compliance with prescribed or desired actions and thus screen out aberrant events. When designing internal control systems, an ounce of prevention is most certainly worth a pound of cure. Preventing errors and fraud is far more cost-effective than detecting and correcting problems after they occur. The vast majority of undesirable events can be blocked at this first level. For example, a well-designed source document is an example of a preventive control. The logical layout of the

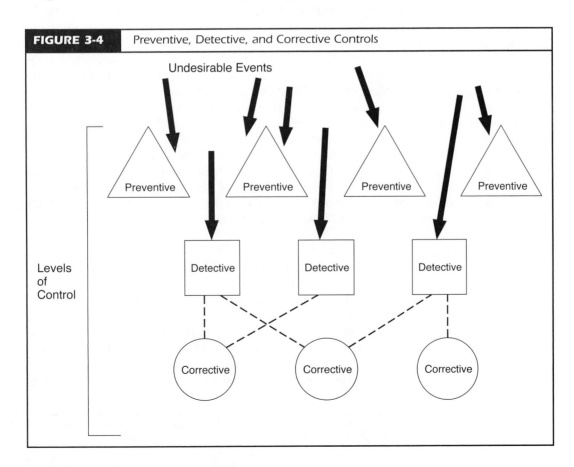

FIGURE 3-4   Preventive, Detective, and Corrective Controls

document into zones that contain specific data, such as customer name, address, items sold, and quantity, forces the clerk to enter the necessary data. The source documents can therefore prevent necessary data from being omitted. However, not all problems can be anticipated and prevented. Some will elude the most comprehensive network of preventive controls.

Detective Controls. **Detective controls** form the second line of defense. These are devices, techniques, and procedures designed to identify and expose undesirable events that elude preventive controls. Detective controls reveal specific types of errors by comparing actual occurrences to pre-established standards. When the detective control identifies a departure from standard, it sounds an alarm to attract attention to the problem. For example, assume a clerk entered the following data on a customer sales order:

Quantity	Price	Total
10	$10	$1,000

Before processing this transaction and posting to the accounts, a detective control should recalculate the total value using the price and quantity. Thus the error in total price would be detected.

Corrective Controls. **Corrective controls** are actions taken to reverse the effects of errors detected in the previous step. There is an important distinction between detective controls and corrective controls. Detective controls identify anomalies and draw attention to them; corrective controls actually fix the problem. For any detected error, however, there may be more than one feasible corrective action, but the best course of action may not always be obvious. For example, in viewing the error above, your first inclination may have been to change the total value from $1,000 to $100 to correct the problem. This presumes that the quantity and price values on the document are correct; they may not be. At this point, we cannot determine the real cause of the problem; we know only that one exists.

Linking a corrective action to a detected error, as an automatic response, may result in an incorrect action that causes a worse problem than the original error. For this reason, error correction should be viewed as a separate control step that should be taken cautiously.

The PDC control model is conceptually pleasing but offers little practical guidance for designing specific controls. For this, we need a more precise framework. The current authoritative document for specifying internal control objectives and techniques is the **Statement on Auditing Standards No. 78,**[18] which is based on the COSO framework. We discuss the key elements of these documents in the following section.

Sarbanes-Oxley and Internal Control

Sarbanes-Oxley legislation requires management of public companies to implement an adequate system of internal controls over their financial reporting process. This includes controls over transaction processing systems that feed data to the financial reporting systems. Management's responsibilities for this are codified in Section 302 and 404 of SOX. Section 302 requires that corporate management (including the CEO) certify their organization's internal controls on a quarterly and annual basis. In addition, Section 404 requires the management of public companies to assess the effectiveness of their organization's internal controls. This entails providing an annual report addressing the following

18   American Institute of Certified Public Accountants, SAS No. 78—Consideration of Internal Control in a Financial Statement Audit: An Amendment to SAS No. 55 (New York: AICPA, 1995).

TABLE 3-9	Generally Accepted Auditing Standards	
General Standards	**Standards of Field Work**	**Reporting Standards**
1. The auditor must have adequate technical training and proficiency.	1. Audit work must be adequately planned.	1. The auditor must state in the report whether financial statements were prepared in accordance with generally accepted accounting principles.
2. The auditor must have independence of mental attitude.	2. The auditor must gain a sufficient understanding of the internal control structure.	2. The report must identify those circumstances in which generally accepted accounting principles were not applied.
3. The auditor must exercise due professional care in the performance of the audit and the preparation of the report.	3. The auditor must obtain sufficient, competent evidence.	3. The report must identify any items that do not have adequate information disclosures.
		4. The report shall contain an expression of the auditor's opinion on the financial statements as a whole.

points: (1) A statement of management's responsibility for establishing and maintaining adequate internal control; (2) an assessment of the effectiveness of the company's internal controls over financial reporting; (3) a statement that the organizations external auditors has issued an attestation report on management's assessment of the company's internal controls; (4) an explicit written conclusion as to the effectiveness of internal control over financial reporting;[19] and (5) a statement identifying the framework used in their assessment of internal controls.

Regarding the control framework to be used, both the PCAOB and the SEC have endorsed the framework put forward by the Committee of Sponsoring Organizations of the Treadway Commission (COSO). Further, they require that any other framework used should encompass all of COSO's general themes.[20] The COSO framework was the basis for SAS 78, but was designed as a management tool rather than an audit tool. SAS 78, on the other hand, was developed for auditors and describes the complex relationship between the firm's internal controls, the auditor's assessment of risk, and the planning of audit procedures. Apart from their audience orientation, the two frameworks are essentially the same and interchangeable for SOX compliance purposes. The key elements of the SAS 78 / COSO framework are presented in the following section.

SAS 78 / COSO INTERNAL CONTROL FRAMEWORK

The SAS 78 / COSO framework consists of five components: the control environment, risk assessment, information and communication, monitoring, and control activities.

---

19   Management may not conclude that internal controls are effective if one or more material weaknesses exist. In addition, management must disclose all material weaknesses that exist as of the end of the most recent fiscal year.

20   A popular competing control framework is *Control Objectives for Information and related Technology* (COBIT®) published by the IT Governance Institute (ITGI). This framework maps into COSO's general themes.

The Control Environment

The **control environment** is the foundation for the other four control components. The control environment sets the tone for the organization and influences the control awareness of its management and employees. Important elements of the control environment are:

- The integrity and ethical values of management.

- The structure of the organization.

- The participation of the organization's board of directors and the audit committee, if one exists.

- Management's philosophy and operating style.

- The procedures for delegating responsibility and authority.

- Management's methods for assessing performance.

- External influences, such as examinations by regulatory agencies.

- The organization's policies and practices for managing its human resources.

SAS 78 requires that auditors obtain sufficient knowledge to assess the attitude and awareness of the organization's management, board of directors, and owners regarding internal control. The following paragraphs provide examples of techniques that may be used to obtain an understanding of the control environment.

1. Auditors should assess the integrity of the organization's management and may use investigative agencies to report on the backgrounds of key managers. Some of the "Big Five" public accounting firms employ ex-FBI agents whose primary responsibility is to perform background checks on existing and prospective clients. If cause for serious reservations comes to light about the integrity of the client, the auditor should withdraw from the audit. The reputation and integrity of the company's managers are critical factors in determining the auditability of the organization. Auditors cannot function properly in an environment in which client management is deemed unethical and corrupt.

2. Auditors should be aware of conditions that would predispose the management of an organization to commit fraud. Some of the obvious conditions may be lack of sufficient working capital, adverse industry conditions, bad credit ratings, and the existence of extremely restrictive conditions in bank or indenture agreements. If auditors encounter any such conditions, their examination should give due consideration to the possibility of fraudulent financial reporting. Appropriate measures should be taken, and every attempt should be made to uncover any fraud.

3. Auditors should understand a client's business and industry and should be aware of conditions peculiar to the industry that may affect the audit. Auditors should read industry-related literature and familiarize themselves with the risks that are inherent in the business.

4. The board of directors should adopt, as a minimum, the provisions of the Sarbanes-Oxley Act. In addition, the following guidelines represent established best practices.

    - *Separate CEO and Chairman.* The roles of CEO and board chairman should be separate. Executive sessions give directors the opportunity to discuss issues without management present, and an independent chairman is important in facilitating such discussions.

    - *Set ethical standards.* The board of directors should establish a code of ethical standards from which management and staff will take direction. At a minimum, a code of ethics should address such issues as outside employment conflicts, acceptance of gifts that could be construed as bribery, falsification of financial and/or performance data, conflicts of interest, political contributions, confidentiality of company and customer data, honesty in dealing with internal and external auditors, and membership on external boards of directors.

- *Establish an Independent Audit Committee.* The audit committee is responsible for selecting and engaging an independent auditor, for ensuring that an annual audit is conducted, for reviewing the audit report, and for ensuring that deficiencies are addressed. Large organizations with complex accounting practices may need to create audit subcommittees that specialize in specific activities.

- *Compensation Committees.* The compensation committee should not be a rubber stamp for management. Excessive use of short-term stock options to compensate directors and executives may result in decisions that influence stock prices at the expense of the firm's long-term health. Compensation schemes should be carefully evaluated to ensure that they create the desired incentives.

- *Nominating Committees.* The board nominations committee should have a plan to maintain a fully staffed board of directors with capable people as it moves forward for the next several years. The committee must recognize the need for independent directors and have criteria for determining independence. For example, under its newly implemented governance standards, General Electric (GE) considers directors independent if the sales to, and purchases from, GE total less than 1 percent of the revenue of the companies where they serve as executives. Similar standards apply to charitable contributions from GE to any organization on which a GE director serves as officer or director. In addition, the company has set a goal that two-thirds of the board will be independent nonemployees.[21]

- *Access to Outside Professionals.* All committees of the board should have access to attorneys and consultants other than the corporation's normal counsel and consultants. Under the provisions of the Sarbanes-Oxley Act, the audit committee of an SEC reporting company is entitled to such representation independently.

Risk Assessment
Organizations must perform a **risk assessment** to identify, analyze, and manage risks relevant to financial reporting. Risks can arise or change from circumstances such as:

- Changes in the operating environment that impose new or changed competitive pressures on the firm.

- New personnel that hold a different or inadequate understanding of internal control.

- New or reengineered information systems that affect transaction processing.

- Significant and rapid growth that strains existing internal controls.

- The implementation of new technology into the production process or information system that impacts transaction processing.

- The introduction of new product lines or activities with which the organization has little experience.

---

21 Rachel E. Silverman, " GE Makes Changes in Board Policy," *The Wall Street Journal* (New York: November 8, 2002)

- Organizational restructuring resulting in the reduction and/or reallocation of personnel such that business operations and transaction processing are affected.

- Entering into foreign markets that may impact operations (i.e., the risks associated with foreign currency transactions).

- Adoption of a new accounting principle that impacts the preparation of financial statements.

SAS 78 requires that auditors obtain sufficient knowledge of the organization's risk assessment procedures to understand how management identifies, prioritizes, and manages the risks related to financial reporting.

Information and Communication

The accounting information system (AIS) consists of the records and methods used to initiate, identify, analyze, classify, and record the organization's transactions and to account for the related assets and liabilities. The quality of information generated by the AIS impacts management's ability to take actions and make decisions in connection with the organization's operations and to prepare reliable financial statements. An effective accounting information system will:

- Identify and record all valid financial transactions.

- Provide timely information about transactions in sufficient detail to permit proper classification and financial reporting.

- Accurately measure the financial value of transactions so their effects can be recorded in financial statements.

- Accurately record transactions in the time period in which they occurred.

SAS 78 requires that auditors obtain sufficient knowledge of the organization's information system to understand:

- The classes of transactions that are material to the financial statements and how those transactions are initiated.

- The accounting records and accounts that are used in the processing of material transactions.

- The transaction processing steps involved from the initiation of a transaction to its inclusion in the financial statements.

- The financial reporting process used to prepare financial statements, disclosures, and accounting estimates.

Monitoring

Management must determine that internal controls are functioning as intended. **Monitoring** is the process by which the quality of internal control design and operation can be assessed. This may be accomplished by separate procedures or by ongoing activities.

An organization's internal auditors may monitor the entity's activities in separate procedures. They gather evidence of control adequacy by testing controls, and then communicate control strengths and weaknesses to management. As part of this process, internal auditors make specific recommendations for improvement to controls.

Ongoing monitoring may be achieved by integrating special computer modules into the information system that capture key data and/or permit tests of controls to be conducted as part of routine operations. Imbedded modules thus allow management and auditors to maintain constant surveillance over the functioning of internal controls. In Chapter 17, we examine a number of embedded module techniques.

Another technique for achieving ongoing monitoring is the judicious use of management reports. Timely reports allow managers in functional areas such as sales, purchasing, production, and cash disbursements to oversee and control their operations. By summarizing activities, highlighting trends, and identifying exceptions from normal performance, well-designed management reports provide evidence of internal control function or malfunction. In Chapter 8, we review the management reporting system and examine the characteristics of effective management reports.

Control Activities

Control activities are the policies and procedures used to ensure that appropriate actions are taken to deal with the organization's identified risks. Control activities can be grouped into two distinct categories: *IT controls* and *physical controls.*

IT Controls. IT controls relate specifically to the computer environment. They fall into two broad groups: general controls and application controls. **General controls** pertain to entitywide concerns such as controls over the data center, organization databases, systems development, and program maintenance. **Application controls** ensure the integrity of specific systems such as sales order processing, accounts payable, and payroll applications. Chapters 15, 16, and 17 are devoted to this extensive body of material. In the several chapters that follow, however, we shall see how physical control concepts apply in specific systems.

Physical Controls. This class of controls relates primarily to the human activities employed in accounting systems. These activities may be purely manual, such as the physical custody of assets, or they may involve the physical use of computers to record transactions or update accounts. Physical controls do not relate to the computer logic that actually performs accounting tasks. Rather, they relate to the human activities that trigger and utilize the results of those tasks. In other words, physical controls focus on people, but are not restricted to an environment in which clerks update paper accounts with pen and ink. Virtually all systems, regardless of their sophistication, employ human activities that need to be controlled.

Our discussion will address the issues pertaining to six categories of physical control activities: transaction authorization, segregation of duties, supervision, accounting records, access control, and independent verification.

Transaction Authorization. The purpose of **transaction authorization** is to ensure that all material transactions processed by the information system are valid and in accordance with management's objectives. Authorizations may be general or specific. General authority is granted to operations personnel to perform day-to-day operations. An example of general authorization is the procedure to authorize the purchase of inventories from a designated vendor only when inventory levels fall to their predetermined reorder points. This is called a *programmed procedure* (not necessarily in the computer sense of the word) where the decision rules are specified in advance, and no additional approvals are required. On the other hand, specific authorizations deal with case-by-case decisions associated with nonroutine transactions. An example of this is the decision to extend a particular customer's credit limit beyond the normal amount. Specific authority is usually a management responsibility.

Segregation of Duties. One of the most important control activities is the segregation of employee duties to minimize incompatible functions. **Segregation of duties** can take many forms, depending on the specific duties to be controlled. However, the following three objectives provide general guidelines applicable to most organizations. These objectives are illustrated in Figure 3-5.

Objective 1. The segregation of duties should be such that the authorization for a transaction is separate from the processing of the transaction. For example, purchases should not be initiated by the purchasing department until authorized by the inventory control department. This separation of tasks is a control to prevent the purchase of unnecessary inventory by individuals.

Objective 2. Responsibility for the custody of assets should be separate from the record-keeping responsibility. For example, the department that has physical custody of finished goods inventory (the warehouse) should not keep the official inventory records. Accounting for finished goods inventory is performed by inventory control, an accounting function. When a single individual or department has responsibility for both asset custody and record keeping, the potential for fraud exists. Assets can be stolen or lost, and the accounting records falsified to hide the event.

Objective 3. The organization should be structured so that a successful fraud requires collusion between two or more individuals with incompatible responsibilities. For example, no individual should have sufficient access to accounting records to perpetrate a fraud. Thus journals, subsidiary ledgers, and the general ledger are maintained separately. For most people, the thought of approaching another employee with the proposal to collude in a fraud presents an insurmountable psychological barrier. The fear of rejection and subsequent disciplinary action discourages solicitations of this sort. However, when employees with incompatible responsibilities work together daily in close quarters, the resulting familiarity tends to erode this barrier. For this reason, the segregation of incompatible tasks should be physical as well as organizational. Indeed, concern about personal familiarity on the job is the justification for establishing rules prohibiting nepotism.

FIGURE 3-5   Segregation of Duties Objectives

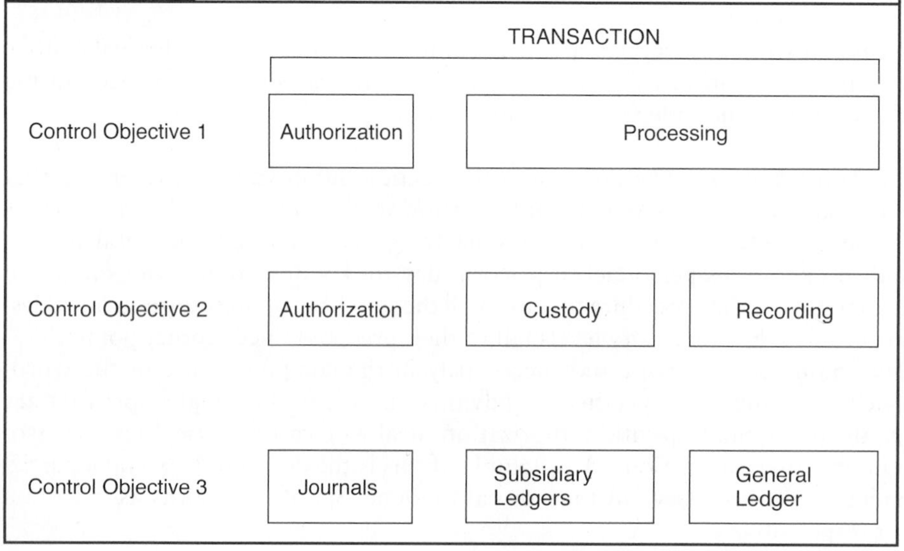

Control Objective 1: Authorization | Processing (TRANSACTION)

Control Objective 2: Authorization | Custody | Recording

Control Objective 3: Journals | Subsidiary Ledgers | General Ledger

Supervision. Implementing adequate segregation of duties requires that a firm employ a sufficiently large number of employees. Achieving adequate segregation of duties often presents difficulties for small organizations. Obviously, it is impossible to separate five incompatible tasks among three employees. Therefore, in small organizations or in functional areas that lack sufficient personnel, management must compensate for the absence of segregation controls with close **supervision**. For this reason, supervision is often called a *compensating control.*

An underlying assumption of supervision control is that the firm employs competent and trustworthy personnel. Obviously, no company could function for long on the alternative assumption that its employees are incompetent and dishonest. The "competent and trustworthy employee" assumption promotes supervisory efficiency. Firms can thus establish a managerial span of control whereby a single manager supervises several employees. In manual systems, maintaining a span of control tends to be straightforward because both manager and employees are at the same physical location.

Accounting Records. The **accounting records** of an organization consist of source documents, journals, and ledgers. These records capture the economic essence of transactions and provide an audit trail of economic events. The audit trail enables the auditor to trace any transaction through all phases of its processing from the initiation of the event to the financial statements. Organizations must maintain audit trails for two reasons. First, this information is needed for conducting day-to-day operations. The audit trail helps employees respond to customer inquiries by showing the current status of transactions in process. Second, the audit trail plays an essential role in the financial audit of the firm. It enables external (and internal) auditors to verify selected transactions by tracing them from the financial statements to the ledger accounts, to the journals, to the source documents, and back to their original source. For reasons of both practical expedience and legal obligation, business organizations must maintain sufficient accounting records to preserve their audit trails.

Access Control. The purpose of **access controls** is to ensure that only authorized personnel have access to the firm's assets. Unauthorized access exposes assets to misappropriation, damage, and theft. Therefore, access controls play an important role in safeguarding assets. Access to assets can be direct or indirect. Physical security devices, such as locks, safes, fences, and electronic and infrared alarm systems, control against direct access. Indirect access to assets is achieved by gaining access to the records and documents that control the use, ownership, and disposition of the asset. For example, an individual with access to all the relevant accounting records can destroy the audit trail that describes a particular sales transaction. Thus, by removing the records of the transaction, including the account receivable balance, the sale may never be billed and the firm will never receive payment for the items sold. The access controls needed to protect accounting records will depend on the technological characteristics of the accounting system. Indirect access control is accomplished by controlling the use of documents and records and by segregating the duties of those who must access and process these records.

Independent Verification. **Verification procedures** are independent checks of the accounting system to identify errors and misrepresentations. Verification differs from supervision because it takes place after the fact, by an individual who is not directly involved with the transaction or task being verified. Supervision takes place while the activity is being performed, by a supervisor with direct responsibility for the task. Through independent verification procedures, management can assess (1) the performance of individuals, (2) the integrity of the transaction processing system, and (3) the correctness of data contained in accounting records. Examples of independent verifications include:

- Reconciling batch totals at points during transaction processing.
- Comparing physical assets with accounting records.
- Reconciling subsidiary accounts with control accounts.
- Reviewing management reports (both computer and manually generated) that summarize business activity.

The timing of verification depends on the technology employed in the accounting system and the task under review. Verifications may occur several times an hour or several times a day. In some cases a verification may occur daily, weekly, monthly, or annually.

SUMMARY

This chapter began by examining ethical issues that societies have pondered for centuries. It is increasingly apparent that good ethics is a necessary condition for the long-term profitability of a business. This requires that ethical issues be understood at all levels of the firm, from top management to line workers. In this section, we identified several ethical issues of direct concern to accountants and managers. SOX legislation has addressed directly these issues.

The next section examined fraud and its relationship to auditing. Fraud falls into two general categories: employee fraud and management fraud. Employee fraud is generally designed to convert cash or other assets directly to the employee's personal benefit. Typically, the employee circumvents the company's internal control structure for personal gain. However, if a company has an effective system of internal control, defalcations or embezzlements can usually be prevented or detected. Management fraud typically involves the material misstatement of financial data and reports to attain additional compensation or promotion or to escape the penalty for poor performance. Managers that perpetrate fraud often do so by overriding the internal control structure. The underlying problems that permit and aid these frauds are frequently associated with inadequate corporate governance. In this section we examined some prominent corporate governance failures and outlined the key elements of the Sarbanes-Oxley Act, which was legislated to remedy them. Finally, several well-documented fraud techniques were reviewed.

The third section examined the subject of internal control. The adequacy of the internal control structure is an issue of great importance to both management and accountants. Internal control was examined first using the PDC control model that classifies controls as preventive, detective, and corrective. Next, the SAS 78 / COSO framework recommended for compliance with SOX was examined. This consists of five levels: control environment, risk assessment, information and communication, monitoring, and control activities. In this section we focused on physical control activities including transaction authorization, segregation of duties, supervision, adequate accounting records, access control, and independent verification.

KEY TERMS

access controls (143)
accounting records (143)
accuracy (132)
application controls (141)
bribery (127)
business ethics (112)
completeness (132)
computer ethics (113)
computer fraud (129)
conflict of interest (127)
control activities (141)
control environment (138)
corrective controls (136)
data collection (129)
database management fraud (132)
detective controls (136)
eavesdropping (133)
economic extortion (128)
employee fraud (118)
ethical responsibility (112)
ethics (112)
exposure (135)
fraud (118)
general controls (141)
illegal gratuity (127)
internal control system (133)

lapping (128)
management fraud (118)
management responsibility (133)
monitoring (140)
operations fraud (131)
ownership (114)
preventive controls (135)
privacy (114)
program fraud (131)
Public Company Accounting Oversight
    Board (PCAOB) (126)
reasonable assurance (133)
relevance (132)
risk assessment (139)
Sarbanes-Oxley Act (125)
scavenging (133)
security (114)
segregation of duties (142)
Statement on Auditing Standards No. 78 (136)
summarization (132)
supervision (143)
timeliness (132)
transaction authorization (141)
transaction fraud (129)
verification procedures (143)

REVIEW QUESTIONS

1. What is ethics?
2. What is business ethics?
3. What are the four areas of ethical business issues?
4. What are the main issues to be addressed in a business code of ethics required by the SEC?
5. What are three ethical principles that may provide some guidance for ethical responsibility?
6. What is computer ethics?
7. How do the three levels of computer ethics—pop, para, and theoretical—differ?
8. Are computer ethical issues new problems or just a new twist on old problems?
9. What are the computer ethical issues regarding privacy?
10. What are the computer ethical issues regarding security?
11. What are the computer ethical issues regarding ownership of property?
12. What are the computer ethical issues regarding equity in access?
13. What are the computer ethical issues regarding the environment?
14. What are the computer ethical issues regarding artificial intelligence?
15. What are the computer ethical issues regarding unemployment and displacement?

16. What are the computer ethical issues regarding misuse of computers?
17. What is the objective of SAS 99?
18. What are the five conditions that constitute fraud under common law?
19. Name the three fraud-motivating forces.
20. What is employee fraud?
21. What is management fraud?
22. What three forces within an individual's personality and the external environment interact to promote fraudulent activity?
23. How can external auditors attempt to uncover motivations for committing fraud?
24. What is lapping?
25. What is collusion?
26. What is bribery?
27. What is economic extortion?
28. What is conflict of interest?
29. What is computer fraud and what types of activities does it include?
30. At which stage of the general accounting model is it easiest to commit computer fraud?
31. What are the four broad objectives of internal control?
32. What are the four modifying assumptions that guide designers and auditors of internal control systems?
33. Give an example of a preventive control.
34. Give an example of a detective control.
35. Give an example of a corrective control.
36. What are management responsibilities under section 302 and 404?
37. What are the five internal control components described in the SAS 78 / COSO framework
38. What are the six broad classes of physical control activities defined by SAS 78?

DISCUSSION QUESTIONS

1. Distinguish between ethical issues and legal issues.
2. Some argue against corporate involvement in socially responsible behavior because the costs incurred by such behavior place the organization at a disadvantage in a competitive market. Discuss the merits and flaws of this argument.
3. Although top management's attitude toward ethics sets the tone for business practice, sometimes it is the role of lower-level managers to uphold a firm's ethical standards. John, an operations-level manager, discovers that the company is illegally dumping toxic materials and is in violation of environmental regulations. John's immediate supervisor is involved in the dumping. What action should John take?
4. When a company has a strong internal control structure, stockholders can expect the elimination of fraud. Comment on the soundness of this statement.
5. Distinguish between employee fraud and management fraud.
6. The estimates of losses annually due to computer fraud vary widely. Why do you think obtaining a good estimate of this figure is difficult?
7. How has the Sarbanes-Oxley Act had a significant impact on corporate governance?
8. Discuss the concept of exposure and explain why firms may tolerate some exposure.
9. If detective controls signal error flags, why shouldn't these types of controls automatically make a correction in the identified error? Why are corrective controls necessary?
10. Discuss the nonaccounting services that external auditors are no longer permitted to render to audit clients.
11. Discuss whether a firm with fewer employees than there are incompatible tasks should rely more heavily on general authority than specific authority.
12. An organization's internal audit department is usually considered an effective control mechanism for evaluating the organization's internal control structure. The Birch Company's internal auditing function reports directly to the controller. Comment on the effectiveness of this organizational structure.
13. According to SAS 78, the proper segregation of functions is an effective internal control procedure. Comment on the exposure (if any) caused by combining the tasks of paycheck preparation and distribution to employees.
14. Explain the five conditions necessary for an act to be considered fraudulent.

15. Distinguish between exposure and risk.

16. Explain the characteristics of management fraud.

17. The text identifies a number of personal traits of managers and other employees that might help uncover fraudulent activity. Discuss three.

18. Give two examples of employee fraud and explain how the thefts might occur.

19. Discuss the fraud schemes of bribery, illegal gratuities, and economic extortion.

20. Explain at least three forms of computer fraud.

21. Why are the computer ethics issues of privacy, security, and property ownership of interest to accountants?

22. A profile of fraud perpetrators prepared by the Association of Certified Fraud Examiners revealed that adult males with advanced degrees commit a disproportionate amount of fraud. Explain these findings.

23. Explain why collusion between employees and management in the commission of a fraud is difficult to both prevent and detect.

24. Because all fraud involves some form of financial misstatement, how is fraudulent statement fraud different?

25. Explain the problems associated with lack of auditor independence.

26. Explain the problems associated with lack of director independence.

27. Explain the problems associated with questionable executive compensation schemes.

28. Explain the problems associated with inappropriate accounting practices.

29. Explain the purpose of the PCAOB.

30. Why is an independent audit committee important to a company?

31. What are the key points of the "Issuer and Management Disclosure" of the Sarbanes-Oxley Act?

32. In this age of high technology and computer-based information systems, why are accountants concerned about *physical* (human) controls?

MULTIPLE-CHOICE QUESTIONS

1. Management can expect various benefits to follow from implementing a system of strong internal control. Which of the following benefits is least likely to occur?
   a. reduction of cost of an external audit
   b. prevention of employee collusion to commit fraud
   c. availability of reliable data for decision-making purposes
   d. some assurance of compliance with the Foreign Corrupt Practices Act of 1977
   e. some assurance that important documents and records are protected

2. Which of the following situations is not a segregation of duties violation?
   a. The treasurer has the authority to sign checks but gives the signature block to the assistant treasurer to run the check-signing machine.
   b. The warehouse clerk, who has the custodial responsibility over inventory in the warehouse, selects the vendor and authorizes purchases when inventories are low.
   c. The sales manager has the responsibility to approve credit and the authority to write off accounts.
   d. The department time clerk is given the undistributed payroll checks to mail to absent employees.
   e. The accounting clerk who shares the record-keeping responsibility for the accounts receivable subsidiary ledger performs the monthly reconciliation of the subsidiary ledger and the control account.

3. The underlying assumption of reasonable assurance regarding implementation of internal control means that
   a. by the control that fraud has not occurred in the period.
   b. auditors are reasonably assured that employee carelessness can weaken an internal control structure.
   c. implementation of the control procedure should not have a significant adverse effect on efficiency or profitability.

d. management assertions about control effectiveness should provide auditors with reasonable assurance.

e. a control applies reasonably well to all forms of computer technology.

4. To conceal the theft of cash receipts from customers in payment of their accounts, which of the following journal entries should the bookkeeper make?

	DR	CR
a.	Miscellaneous Expense	Cash
b.	Petty Cash	Cash
c.	Cash	Accounts Receivable
d.	Sales Returns	Accounts Receivable
e.	None of the above	

5. Which of the following controls would best prevent the lapping of accounts receivable?

a. Segregate duties so that the clerk responsible for recording in the accounts receivable subsidiary ledger has no access to the general ledger.

b. Request that customers review their monthly statements and report any unrecorded cash payments.

c. Require customers to send payments directly to the company's bank.

d. Request that customers make checks payable to the company.

6. Providing timely information about transactions in sufficient detail to permit proper classification and financial reporting is an example of

a. the control environment.

b. risk assessment.

c. information and communication.

d. monitoring.

7. Ensuring that all material transactions processed by the information system are valid and in accordance with management's objectives is an example of

a. transaction authorization.

b. supervision.

c. accounting records.

d. independent verification.

8. Which of the following is often called a compensating control?

a. transaction authorization

b. supervision

c. accounting records

d. independent verification

9. Which of the following is NOT a necessary condition under common law to constitute a fraudulent act?

a. injury or loss

b. material fact

c. written documentation

d. justifiable reliance

10. The fraud scheme that is similar to the "borrowing from Peter to pay Paul" scheme is

a. expense account fraud.

b. bribery.

c. lapping.

d. transaction fraud.

PROBLEMS

1. Fraud Scheme

A purchasing agent for a home improvement center is also part owner in a wholesale lumber company. The agent has sole discretion in selecting vendors for the lumber sold through the center. The agent directs a disproportionate number of purchase orders to his company, which charges above-market prices for its products. The agent's financial interest in the supplier is unknown to his employer.

Required:
What type of fraud is this and what controls can be implemented to prevent or detect the fraud?

2. Fraud Scheme

A procurement agent for a large metropolitan building authority threatens to blacklist a building contractor if he does not make a financial payment to the agent. If the contractor does not cooperate, the contractor will be denied future work. Faced with a threat of economic loss, the contractor makes the payment.

Required:
What type of fraud is this and what controls can be implemented to prevent or detect the fraud?

3. Mail Room Fraud and Internal Control

Sarat Sethi, a professional criminal, took a job as a mail room clerk at Benson & Abernathy and Company, a large department store. The mail room was an extremely hectic work environment consisting of 45 clerks and one supervisor. The clerks were responsible for handling promotional mailings, catalogs, and interoffice mail, as well as receiving and distributing a wide range of outside correspondence to various internal departments. One of Sethi's jobs was to open cash receipts envelopes from customers making payments on their credit card balances. He separated the remittance advices (the bills) and the checks into two piles. He then sent remittance advices to the accounts receivable department where the customer accounts were updated to reflect the payment. He sent the checks to the cash receipts department where they were recorded in the cash journal and then deposited in the bank. Batch totals of cash received and accounts receivable updated were reconciled each night to ensure that everything was accounted for. Nevertheless, over a one-month period Sethi managed to steal $100,000 in customer payments and then left the state without warning.

The fraud occurred as follows: Because the name of the company was rather long, some people had adopted the habit of making out checks simply to "Benson." Sethi had a false ID prepared in the name of John Benson. Whenever he came across a check made out to "Benson" he would steal it along with the remittance advice. Sometimes people would even leave the payee section on the check blank. These checks he also stole. He would then modify the checks to make them payable to "J. Benson" and cash them. Because the accounts receivable department received no remittance advice, the end-of-day reconciliation with cash received disclosed no discrepancies.

Required:

a. This seems like a foolproof scheme. Why did Sethi limit himself to only one month's activity before leaving town?

b. What controls could Benson & Abernathy implement to prevent this from happening again in the future?

4. CMA1288 3-23

Segregation of Duties

Explain why each of the following combinations of tasks should, or should not, be separated to achieve adequate internal control.

a. Approval of bad debt write-offs and the reconciliation of the accounts receivable subsidiary ledger and the general ledger control account.

b. Distribution of payroll checks to employees and approval of employee time cards.

c. Posting of amounts from both the cash receipts and the cash disbursements journals to the general ledger.

d. Writing checks to vendors and posting to the cash account.

e. Recording cash receipts in the journal and preparing the bank reconciliation.

5. Expense Account Fraud

While auditing the financial statements of Petty Corporation, the certified public accounting firm of Trueblue and Smith discovered that its client's legal expense account was abnormally high. Further investigation of the records indicated the following:

- Since the beginning of the year, several disbursements totaling $15,000 had been made to the law firm of Swindle, Fox, and Kreip.

- Swindle, Fox, and Kreip were not Petty Corporation's attorneys.

- A review of the canceled checks showed that they had been written and approved by Mary Boghas, the cash disbursements clerk.

- Boghas's other duties included performing the end-of-month bank reconciliation.

- Subsequent investigation revealed that Swindle, Fox, and Kreip are representing Mary Boghas in an unrelated embezzlement case in which she is the defendant. The checks had been written in payment of her personal legal fees.

Required:

a. What control procedures could Petty Corporation have employed to prevent this unauthorized use of cash? Classify each control procedure in accordance with the SAS 78 framework (authorization, segregation of functions, supervision, and so on).

b. Comment on the ethical issues in this case.

6. Tollbooth Fraud

Collectors at Tollbooths A and B (see the following figure) have colluded to perpetrate a fraud. Each day, Tollbooth Collector B provides A with a number of toll tickets pre-stamped from Tollbooth B. The price of the toll from Point B to Point A is 35 cents. The fraud works as follows:

Drivers entering the turnpike at distant points south of B will pay tolls up to $5. When these drivers leave the turnpike at Point A, they pay the full amount of the toll printed on their tickets. However, the tollbooth collector replaces the tickets collected from the drivers with the 35-cent tickets provided by B, thus making it appear that the drivers entered the turnpike at Point B. The difference between the 35-cent tickets submitted as a record of the cash receipts and the actual amounts paid by the drivers is pocketed by Tollbooth Collector A and shared with B at the end of the day. Using this technique, Collectors A and B have stolen more than $20,000 in unrecorded tolls this year.

Required:

What control procedures could be implemented to prevent or detect this fraud? Classify the control procedures in accordance with SAS 78.

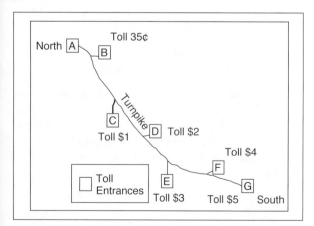

7. CMA 1289 3-Y6
Causes of Fraud

The studies conducted by the National Commission on Fraudulent Financial Reporting (the Treadway Commission) revealed that fraudulent financial reporting usually occurs as the result of certain environmental, institutional, or individual influences and opportune situations. These influences and opportunities, present to some degree in all companies, add pressures and motivate individuals and companies to engage in fraudulent financial reporting. The effective prevention and detection of fraudulent financial reporting requires an understanding of these influences and opportunities, while evaluating the risk of fraudulent financial reporting that these factors can create in a company. The risk factors to be assessed include not only internal ethical and control factors but also external environmental conditions.

Required:

a. Identify two situational pressures in a public company that would increase the likelihood of fraud.

b. Identify three corporate circumstances (opportune situations) where fraud is easier to commit and detection is less likely.

c. For the purpose of assessing the risk of fraudulent financial reporting, identify the external environmental factors that should be considered in the company's

    i.   industry.

    ii. business environment.

    iii. legal and regulatory environment.

d. List several recommendations that top management should incorporate to reduce the possibility of fraudulent financial reporting.

8. CMA 1289 3-4
Evaluation of Internal Control

Oakdale, Inc., is a subsidiary of Solomon Publishing and specializes in the publication and distribution of reference books. Oakdale's sales for the past year exceeded $18 million, and the company employed an average of 65 employees. Solomon periodically sends a member of the internal audit department to audit the operations of each of its subsidiaries, and Katherine Ford, Oakdale's treasurer, is currently working with Ralph Johnson of Solomon's internal audit staff.

Johnson has just completed a review of Oakdale's investment cycle and prepared the following report.

General

Throughout the year, Oakdale has made both short-term and long-term investments in securities; all securities are registered in the company's name. According to Oakdale's bylaws, long-term investment activity must be approved by its board of directors, whereas short-term investment activity may be approved by either the president or the treasurer.

Transactions

All purchases and sales of short-term securities were made by the treasurer. The long-term security purchases were approved by the board, whereas the long-term security sale was approved by the president. Because the treasurer is listed with the broker as the company's contact, all revenue from these investments (dividends and interest) is received by this individual, who then forwards the checks to accounting for processing.

Documentation

Purchase and sale authorizations, along with the broker's advices, are maintained in a file by the treasurer. The certificates for all long-term investments are kept in a safe deposit box at the local bank; only the president of Oakdale has access to this box. An inventory of this box was made, and all certificates were accounted for. Certificates for short-term investments are kept in a locked metal box in the accounting office. Other documents, such as long-term contracts and legal agreements, are also kept in this box. The three keys to the box are held by the president, the treasurer, and the accounting manager. The accounting manager's key is available to all accounting personnel should they require documents kept in this box. Documentation for two of the current short-term investments could not be located in this box; the accounting manager explained that some of the investments are for such short periods of time that formal documentation is not always provided by the broker.

Accounting Records

The accounting department records deposits of checks for interest and dividends earned on investments, but these checks could not be traced to the cash receipts journal, which is maintained by the

individual who normally opens, stamps, and logs incoming checks. These amounts are journalized monthly in an account for investment revenue. The treasurer authorizes checks drawn for investment purchases. Both the treasurer and the president must sign checks in excess of $15,000. When securities are sold, the broker deposits the proceeds directly in Oakdale's bank account by an electronic funds transfer.

Each month, the accounting manager and the treasurer prepare the journal entries required to adjust the short-term investment account. There was insufficient backup documentation attached to the journal entries reviewed to trace all transactions; however, the balance in the account at the end of last month closely approximates the amount shown on the statement received from the broker. The amount in the long-term investment account is correct, and the transactions can be clearly traced through the documentation attached to the journal entries. There are no attempts made to adjust either account to the lower of aggregate cost or market.

Required:

To achieve Solomon Publishing's objective of sound internal control, the company believes the following four controls are basic for an effective system of accounting control:

- Authorization of transactions

- Complete and accurate record keeping

- Access control

- Internal verification
  a. Describe the purpose of each of the four controls listed above.
  b. Identify an area in Oakdale's investment procedures that violates each of the four controls listed above.
  c. For each of the violations identified, describe how Oakdale can correct each weakness.

9. Financial Aid Fraud

Harold Jones, the financial aid officer at a small university, manages all aspects of the financial aid program for needy students. Jones receives requests for aid from students, determines whether the students meet the aid criteria, authorizes aid payments, notifies the applicants that their request has been either approved or denied, writes the financial aid checks on the account he controls, and requires that the students come to his office to receive the checks in person. For years, Jones has used his position of authority to perpetrate the following fraud.

Jones encourages students who clearly will not qualify to apply for financial aid. Although the students do not expect aid, they apply on the "off chance" that it will be awarded. Jones modifies the financial information in the students' applications so that it falls within the established guidelines for aid. He then approves aid and writes aid checks payable to the students. The students, however, are informed that aid was denied. Because the students expect no aid, the checks in Jones's office are never collected. Jones forges the students' signatures and cashes the checks.

Required:
Identify the internal control procedures (classified per SAS 78) that could prevent or detect this fraud.

10. Kickback Fraud

The kickback is a form of fraud often associated with purchasing. Most organizations expect their purchasing agents to select the vendor that provides the best products at the lowest price. To influence the purchasing agent in his or her decision, vendors may grant the agent financial favors (cash, presents, football tickets, and so on). This activity can result in orders being placed with vendors that supply inferior products or charge excessive prices.

Required:
Describe the controls that an organization can employ to deal with kickbacks. Classify each control as either preventive, detective, or corrective.

11. Evaluation of Controls

Gaurav Mirchandaniis is the warehouse manager for a large office supply wholesaler. Mirchandaniis receives two copies of the customer sales order from the sales department. He picks the goods from the shelves and sends them and one copy of the sales order to the shipping department. He then files the second copy in a temporary file. At the end of the day, Mirchandaniis retrieves the sales orders from the temporary file and updates the inventory subsidiary ledger from a terminal in his office. At that time he identifies items that have fallen to low levels, selects a supplier, and prepares three copies of a purchase order. One copy is sent to the supplier, one is sent to the accounts payable clerk, and one is filed in the warehouse. When the goods arrive from the supplier, Mirchandaniis reviews the attached packing slip, counts and inspects the goods, places them on the shelves, and updates the inventory ledger to reflect the receipt. He then prepares a receiving report and sends it to the accounts payable department.

Required:
a. Prepare a systems flowchart of the procedures previously described.
b. Identify any control problems in the system.
c. What sort of frauds are possible in this system.

12. Evaluation of Controls

Matt Demko is the loading dock supervisor for a dry cement packaging company. His work crew is composed of unskilled workers who load large transport trucks with bags of cement, gravel, and sand. The work is hard and the employee turnover rate is high. Employees record their attendance on separate timecards. Demko authorizes payroll payments each week by signing the timecards and submitting them to the payroll department. The paychecks are then prepared by payroll and distributed to Demko, who distributes them to his work crew.

Required:
a. Prepare a systems flowchart of the procedures described above.
b. Identify any control problems in the system.
c. What sort of frauds are possible in this system?

Internal Control Cases

1. Bern Fly Rod Company

Bern Fly Rod Company is a small manufacturer of high-quality graphite fly-fishing rods. It sells its products to fly-fishing shops throughout the United States and Canada. Bern began as a small company with four salespeople, all family members of the owner. Due to the high popularity and recent growth in fly-fishing, Bern now employs a sales force of 16, and for the first time employs nonfamily members. The salespeople travel around the country giving fly-casting demos of their new models. Once the sales orders are generated, inventory availability is determined and, if necessary, the salesperson sends the order directly to the manufacturing department for immediate production. Sales staff compensation is tied directly to their sales figures. Bern's financial statements for the December year-end reflect unprecedented sales, 35 percent higher than last year. Further, sales for December account for 40 percent of all sales. Last year, December sales accounted for only 20 percent of all sales.

Required:

Analyze the previous situation and assess any potential internal control issues and exposures. Discuss some preventive measures this firm may wish to implement.

2. Breezy Company

(This case was prepared by Elizabeth Morris, Lehigh University)

Breezy Company of Bethlehem, Pennsylvania, is a small wholesale distributor of heating and cooling fans. The company deals with retailing firms that buy small to medium quantities of fans. The president, Chuck Breezy, was very pleased with the marked increase in sales over the past couple of years. Recently, however, the accountant informed Chuck that although net income has increased, the percentage of uncollectibles has tripled. Due to the small size of the business, Chuck fears he may not be able to sustain these increased losses in the future. He asked his accountant to analyze the situation.

Background

In 1998, the sales manager, John Breezy, moved to Alaska, and Chuck hired a young college graduate to take over the position. The company had always been a family business and, therefore, measurements of individual performance had never been a large consideration. The sales levels had been relatively constant because John had been content to sell to certain customers with whom he had been dealing for years. Chuck was leery about hiring outside of the family for this position. To try to keep sales levels up, he established a reward incentive based on net sales. The new sales manager, Bob Sellmore, was eager to set his career in motion and decided he would attempt to increase the sales levels. To do this, he recruited new customers while

keeping the old clientele. After one year, Bob had proved himself to Chuck, who decided to introduce an advertising program to further increase sales. This brought in orders from a number of new customers, many of whom Breezy had never done business with before. The influx of orders excited Chuck so much that he instructed Jane Breezy, the finance manager, to raise the initial credit level for new customers. This induced some customers to purchase more.

Existing System

The accountant prepared a comparative income statement to show changes in revenues and expenses over the last three years, shown in Exhibit A. Currently, Bob is receiving a commission of 2 percent of net sales. Breezy Company uses credit terms of net 30 days. At the end of previous years, bad debt expense amounted to approximately 2 percent of net sales.

As the finance manager, Jane performs credit checks. In previous years, Jane had been familiar with most clients and approved credit on the basis of past behavior. When dealing with new customers, Jane usually approved a low credit amount and increased it after the customer exhibited reliability. With the large increase in sales, Chuck felt that the current policy was restricting a further rise in sales levels. He decided to increase credit limits to

---

EXHIBIT A
BREEZY COMPANY
COMPARATIVE INCOME STATEMENT
FOR YEARS 2002, 2003, 2004

	2002	2003	2004
Revenues:			
Net sales	350,000	500,000	600,000
Other revenue	60,000	60,000	62,000
Total revenue	410,000	560,000	662,000
Expenses:			
Cost of goods sold	140,000	200,000	240,000
Bad debt expense	7,000	20,000	36,000
Salaries expense	200,000	210,000	225,000
Selling expense	5,000	15,000	20,000
Advertising Expense	0	0	10,000
Other expenses	20,000	30,000	35,000
Total expenses	372,000	475,000	566,000
Net Income	38,000	85,000	96,000

eliminate this restriction. This policy, combined with the new advertising program, should attract many new customers.

Future

The new level of sales impresses Chuck and he wishes to expand, but he also wants to keep uncollectibles to a minimum. He believes the amount of uncollectibles should remain relatively constant as a percentage of sales. Chuck is thinking of expanding his production line, but wants to see uncollectibles drop and sales stabilize before he proceeds with this plan.

Required:

Analyze the weaknesses in internal control and suggest improvements.

3. Whodunit?

(This case was prepared by Karen Collins, Lehigh University)
The following facts relate to an actual embezzlement case.

Someone stole more than $40,000 from a small company in less than two months. Your job is to study the following facts, try to figure out who was responsible for the theft, how it was perpetrated, and (most important) suggest ways to prevent something like this from happening again.

Facts

Location of company: a small town on the eastern shore of Maryland. Type of company: crabmeat processor, selling crabmeat to restaurants located in Maryland. Characters in the story (names are fictitious):

- John Smith, president and stockholder (husband of Susan).
- Susan Smith, vice president and stockholder (wife of John).
- Tommy Smith, shipping manager (son of John and Susan).
- Debbie Jones, office worker. She began working part time for the company six months before the theft. (At that time, she was a high school senior and was allowed to work afternoons through a school internship program.) Upon graduation from high school (several weeks before the theft was discovered), she began working full time. Although she is not a member of the family, the

Smiths have been close friends with Debbie's parents for more than ten years.

Accounting Records

All accounting records are maintained on a microcomputer. The software being used consists of the following modules:

1. A general ledger system, which keeps track of all balances in the general ledger accounts and produces a trial balance at the end of each month.
2. A purchases program, which keeps track of purchases and maintains detailed records of accounts payable.
3. An accounts receivable program, which keeps track of sales and collections on account and maintains individual detailed balances of accounts receivable.
4. A payroll program.

The modules are not integrated (that is, data are not transferred automatically between modules). At the end of the accounting period, summary information generated by the purchases, accounts receivable, and payroll programs must be entered into the general ledger program to update the accounts affected by these programs.

Sales

The crabmeat processing industry in this particular town was unusual in that selling prices for crabmeat were set at the beginning of the year and remained unchanged for the entire year. The company's customers, all restaurants located within 100 miles of the plant, ordered the same quantity of crabmeat each week. Because prices for the crabmeat remained the same all year and the quantity ordered was always the same, the weekly invoice to each customer was always for the same dollar amount.

Manual sales invoices were produced when orders were taken, although these manual invoices were not prenumbered. One copy of the manual invoice was attached to the order shipped to the customer. The other copy was used to enter the sales information into the computer.

When the customer received the order, the customer would send a check to the company for the amount of the invoice. Monthly bills were not sent to customers unless the customer was behind in payments (that is, did not make a payment for the invoiced amount each week).

Note: The industry was unique in another way: many of the companies paid their workers with cash each week (rather than by check). It was, therefore, not unusual for companies to request large sums of cash from the local banks.

When Trouble Was Spotted

Shortly after the May 30 trial balance was run, Susan began analyzing the balances in the various accounts. The balance in the cash account agreed with the cash balance she obtained from a reconciliation of the company's bank account.

However, the balance in the accounts receivable control account in the general ledger did not agree with the total of the accounts receivable subsidiary ledger (which shows a detail of the balances owed by each customer). The difference was not very large, but the balances should be in 100 percent agreement.

At this point, Susan asked me if I would help her locate the problem. In reviewing the computerized accounts receivable subsidiary ledger, I noticed the following:

1. The summary totals from this report were not the totals that were entered into the general ledger program at month end. Different amounts had been entered. No one could explain why this had happened.
2. Some sheets in the computer listing had been ripped apart at the bottom. (In other words, the listing of the individual accounts receivable balances was not a continuous list but had been split at several points.)
3. When an adding machine tape of the individual account balances was run, the individual balances did not add up to the total at the bottom of the report.

Susan concluded that the accounts receivable program was not running properly. My recommendation was that an effort be made to find out why the accounts receivable control account and the summary totals per the accounts receivable subsidiary ledger were not in agreement and why we were finding problems with the accounts receivable listing. Because the accounts receivable subsidiary and accounts receivable control account in the general ledger had been in agreement at the end of April, the effort should begin with the April ending balances for each customer by manually updating all

of the accounts. The manually adjusted May 30 balances should then be compared with the computer-generated balances and any differences investigated.

After doing this, Susan and John found several differences. The largest difference was the following: Although they found the manual sales invoice for Sale #2, Susan and John concluded (based on the computer records) that Sale #2 did not take place. I was not sure, so I recommended that they call this customer and ask him the following:

1. Did he receive this order?
2. Did he receive an invoice for it?
3. Did he pay for the order?
4. If so, did he have a copy of his canceled check?

Although John felt that this would be a waste of time, he called the customer. He received an affirmative answer to all of his questions. In addition, he found that the customer's check was stamped on the back not with the normally used "for deposit only" stamp of the company but with an address stamp giving only the company's name and city. When questioned, Debbie said that she sometimes used this stamp.

Right after this question, Debbie, who was sitting nearby at the computer, called Susan to the computer and showed her the customer's account. She said that the payment for $5,000 was in fact recorded in the customer's account. I came over to the computer and looked at the account. The payments were listed like this:

Amount	Date of Payment
$5,000	May 3
$5,000	May 17
$5,000	May 23
$5,000	May 10

I questioned the order of the payments—why was a check supposedly received on May 10 entered in the computer after checks received on May 17 and 23? About 30 seconds later, the computer malfunctioned and the accounts receivable file was lost. Every effort to retrieve the file gave the message "file not found."

About five minutes later, Debbie presented Susan with a copy of a bank deposit ticket dated May 10 with several checks listed on it, including the check that the customer said had been sent to the company. The deposit ticket, however, was not stamped by the bank (which would have verified that the deposit had been received by the bank)

Performance of Key Functions by Individual(s)

John, president
Susan, vice president
Tommy, son and shipping manager
Debbie, office worker

		Individual(s) Performing Task	
		Most of the Time	Sometimes
1.	Receiving order from customers	John	All others
2.	Overseeing production of crabmeat	John or Tommy	—
3.	Handling shipping	Tommy	John
4.	Billing customers (entering sales into accounts receivable program)	Debbie	Susan
5.	Opening mail	John	All others
6.	Preparing bank deposit tickets and making bank deposits	Susan or Debbie	All others
7.	Recording receipt of cash and checks (entering collections of accounts receivable into accounts receivable program)	Debbie	Susan
8.	Preparing checks (payroll checks and payments of accounts payable)	Susan or Debbie	—
9.	Signing checks	John	—
10.	Preparing bank reconciliations	John	—
11.	Preparing daily sales reports showing sales by type of product	Susan	—
12.	Summarizing daily sales reports to obtain monthly sales report by type of product	Susan or Debbie	—
13.	Running summaries of AR program, AP program, and payroll program at month end and inputting summaries into GL program	Susan or Debbie	—
14.	Analyzing trial balance at month end and analyzing open balances in accounts receivable and accounts payable	Susan	—

and did not add up to the total at the bottom of the ticket (it was off by 20 cents).

At this point, being very suspicious, I gathered all documents I could and left the company to work on the problem at home, away from any potential suspects. I received a call from Susan about four hours later saying that she felt much better. She and Debbie had gone to Radio Shack (the maker of their computer program) and Radio Shack had confirmed Susan's conclusion that the computer program was malfunctioning. She and Debbie were planning to work all weekend reentering transactions into the computer. She said that everything looked fine and not to waste my time working on the problem.

I felt differently. How do you feel?

Required:

a. If you were asked to help this company, could you conclude from the evidence presented that an embezzlement took place? What would you do next?

CUSTOMER ACCOUNT PER MANUAL RECONSTRUCTION			
Dr.		Cr.	
Sale #1	5,000	Pmt. #1	5,000
Sale #2	5,000	Pmt. #2	5,000
Sale #3	5,000	Pmt. #3	5,000
Sale #4	5,000	—	—
Ending Balance	5,000		

CUSTOMER ACCOUNT PER MANUAL RECONSTRUCTION			
Dr.		Cr.	
Sale #1	5,000	Pmt. #1	5,000
Sale #3	5,000	Pmt. #2	5,000
Sale #3	5,000	Pmt. #3	5,000
Ending Balance	0		

b. Who do you think was the embezzler?

c. How was the embezzlement accomplished?

d. What improvements would you recommend in internal control to prevent this from happening again? In answering this question, try to identify at least one suggestion from each of the six classes of internal control activities discussed in this chapter (under the section "Control Activities"): transaction authorization, segregation of duties, supervision, accounting records, access control, and independent verification.

e. Would the fact that the records were maintained on a microcomputer aid in this embezzlement scheme?

chapter 4

The Revenue Cycle

LEARNING OBJECTIVES

After studying this chapter, you should:

- Understand the fundamental tasks performed in the revenue cycle, regardless of the technology in place.
- Be able to identify the functional departments involved in revenue cycle activities and trace the flow of revenue transactions through the organization.
- Be able to specify the documents, journals, and accounts that provide audit trails, promote the maintenance of historical records, support internal decision making, and sustain financial reporting.
- Understand the risks associated with the revenue cycle and recognize the controls that reduce these risks.
- Be aware of the operational and control implications of technology used to automate and reengineer the revenue cycle.

Economic enterprises, both for-profit and not-for-profit, generate revenues through business processes that constitute their revenue cycle. In its simplest form, the revenue cycle is the direct exchange of finished goods or services for cash in a single transaction between a seller and a buyer. More complex revenue cycles process sales on credit. Many days or weeks may pass between the point of sale and the subsequent receipt of cash. This time lag splits the revenue transaction into two phases: (1) the physical phase, involving the transfer of assets or services from the seller to the buyer; and (2) the financial phase, involving the receipt of cash by the seller in payment of the account receivable. As a matter of processing convenience, most firms treat each phase as a separate transaction. Hence, the revenue cycle actually consists of two major subsystems: (1) the sales order processing subsystem and (2) the cash receipts subsystem.

This chapter is organized into two main sections. The first section presents the conceptual revenue cycle system. It provides an overview of key activities and the logical tasks, sources and uses of information, and movement of accounting information through the organization. The section concludes with a review of internal control issues. The second section presents the physical system. A manual system is first used to reinforce key concepts previously presented. Next, it explores large-scale computer-based systems. The focus is on alternative technologies used to achieve various levels of organizational change from simple automation to reengineering the work flow. The section concludes with a review of PC-based systems and control issues pertaining to end-user computing.

THE CONCEPTUAL SYSTEM

OVERVIEW OF REVENUE CYCLE ACTIVITIES

In this section we examine the revenue cycle conceptually. Using dataflow diagrams (DFDs) as a guide, we will trace the sequence of activities through three processes that constitute the revenue cycle for most retail, wholesale, and manufacturing organizations. These are: sales order procedures, sales return procedures, and cash receipts procedures. Service companies such as hospitals, insurance companies, and banks would use different industry-specific methods.

This discussion is intended to be technology neutral. In other words, the tasks described may be performed manually or by computer. At this point our focus is on *what* (conceptually) needs to be done, not *how* (physically) it is accomplished. At various stages in the processes we will examine specific documents, journals, and ledgers as they are encountered. Again, this review is technology neutral. These documents and files may be physical (hard copy) or digital (computer generated). In the next section we examine examples of physical systems.

Sales Order Procedures

Sales order procedures include the tasks involved in receiving and processing a customer order; filling the order and shipping products to the customer; billing the customer at the proper time; and correctly accounting for the transaction. The relationships between these tasks are presented with the DFD in Figure 4-1 and described in the following section.

Receive Order. The sales process begins with the receipt of a **customer order** indicating the type and quantity of merchandise being demanded. At this point, the customer order is not in a standard format and may or may not be a physical document. Orders may arrive by mail, by telephone, or from a field representative who visited the customer's place of business. When the customer is also a business entity, the order is often a copy of the customer's purchase order. A purchase order is an expenditure cycle document, which is discussed in Chapter 5.

Because the customer order is not in the standard format needed by the seller's order processing system, the first task is to transcribe it into a formal **sales order,** an example of which is presented in Figure 4-2.

The sales order captures vital information such as the name and address of the customer; the customer's account number; the name, number, and description of the items sold; and the quantities and unit prices of each item sold. At this point, financial information such as taxes, discounts, and freight charges may or may not be included. After creating the sales order, a copy of it is placed in the **customer open order file** for future reference. The task of filling an order and getting the product to the customer may take days or even weeks. During this period customers may contact their suppliers to check the status of their orders. The customer record in the open order file is updated each time the status of the order changes such as credit approval, on back-order, and shipment. The open order file thus enables customer service employees to respond promptly and accurately to customer questions.

Check Credit. Before processing the order further, the customer's creditworthiness needs to be established. The circumstances of the sale will determine the nature and degree of the credit check. For example, new customers may undergo a full financial investigation to establish a line of credit. Once a credit limit is set, however, credit checking on subsequent sales may be limited to ensuring that the customer has a history of paying his or her bills and that current sale does not exceed the pre-established limit.

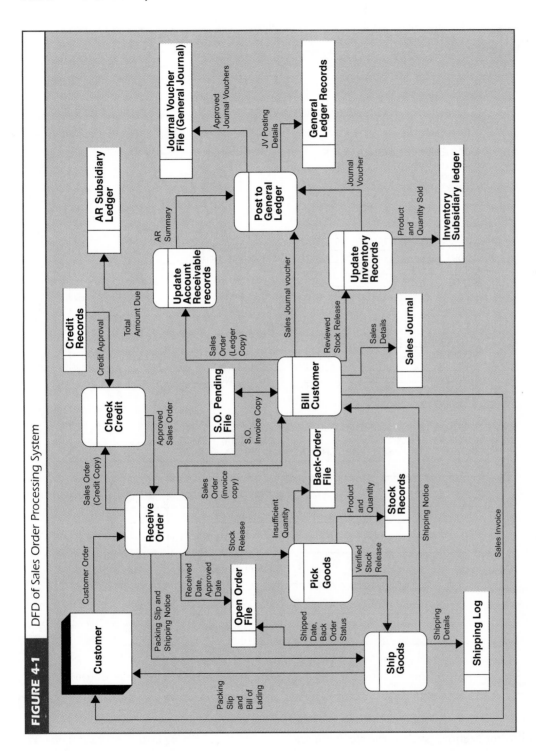

FIGURE 4-1   DFD of Sales Order Processing System

The credit approval process is an authorization control and should be performed as a function separate from the sales activity. In our conceptual system, the receive-order task sends the **sales order (credit copy)** to the check-credit task for approval. The returned **approved sales order** then triggers the continuation of the sales process by releasing sales order information simultaneously to various tasks. Several documents mentioned in the

FIGURE 4-2	Sales Order

CREDIT SALE INVOICE

MONTEREY PENINSULA CO-OP
527 River Road
Chicago, IL 60612
(312) 555-0407

INVOICE NUMBER _____

SOLD TO
FIRM NAME _____
ATTENTION OF _____
ADDRESS_____
CITY_____
STATE _____ ZIP _____

INVOICE DATE _____
PREPARED BY _____
CREDIT TERMS_____

CUSTOMER PURCHASE ORDER
NUMBER_____
DATE_____
SIGNED BY_____

SHIPMENT DATE _____
SHIPPED VIA _____
B.O.L. NO._____

QUANTITY ORDERED	PRODUCT NUMBER	DESCRIPTION	QUANTITY SHIPPED	UNIT PRICE	TOTAL
			TOTAL SALE		
			CUSTOMER ACCT. NO.		
			VERIFICATION		

following sections, such as the *stock release*, *packing slip*, *shipping notice*, and *sales invoice* are simply special-purpose copies of the sales order and are not illustrated separately.

Pick Goods. The receive-order activity forwards the **stock release** document (also called the *picking ticket*) to the pick-goods function, in the warehouse. This document identifies the items of inventory that must be located and picked from the warehouse shelves. It also provides formal authorization for warehouse personnel to release custody of the specified items. After picking the stock, the order is verified for completeness and accuracy and the **verified stock release** document, along with the goods, is sent to the ship goods task. If inventory levels are insufficient to fill the order, a warehouse employee adjusts the verified stock release to reflect the amount actually going to the customer. The employee then prepares a **back-order** record, which stays on file until the inventories arrive from the supplier (not shown in this diagram). Back-ordered items are shipped before new sales are processed.

Finally, the warehouse employee adjusts the **stock records** to reflect the reduction in inventory. These stock records are *not* the formal accounting records for controlling inventory assets. They are used for warehouse management purposes only. Assigning asset custody and accounting record-keeping responsibility to the warehouse clerk would violate a key principle of internal control. The formal accounting inventory records are maintained by the inventory control function, which is discussed later.

Ship Goods. Before the arrival of the goods and the verified stock release document, the shipping department receives the **packing slip** and **shipping notice** from the receive order function. The packing slip will ultimately travel with the goods to the customer to describe the contents of the order. The shipping notice will later be forwarded to the billing function as evidence that the customer's order was filled and shipped. This document conveys pertinent new facts such as the date of shipment, the items and quantities actually shipped, the name of the carrier, and freight charges. In some systems, the shipping notice is a separate document prepared within the shipping function.

Upon receiving the goods from the warehouse, the shipping clerk reconciles the physical items with the stock release, the packing slip, and the shipping notice to verify the correctness of the order. The ship goods function thus serves as an important independent verification control point and is the last opportunity to detect errors before shipment. The shipping clerk packages the goods, attaches the packing slip to the container, completes the shipping notice, and prepares a **bill of lading**. The bill of lading is a formal contract between the seller and the shipping company (carrier) to transport the goods to the customer. This document establishes legal ownership and responsibility for assets in transit. Figure 4-3 shows a bill of lading. Once custody of the goods is transferred to the carrier, the shipping clerk records the shipment in the shipping log, forwards the shipping notice to the bill customer function as proof of shipment, and updates the customer's open order file.

Bill Customer. The shipment of goods marks the completion of the economic event and the point at which the customer should be billed. Billing before shipment encourages inaccurate record keeping and inefficient operations. When the customer order is originally prepared, some details such as inventory availability, prices, and shipping charges may not be known with certainty. In the case of back-orders, for example, suppliers do not typically bill customers for out-of-stock items. Billing for goods not shipped causes confusion, damages relations with customers, and requires additional work to make adjustments to the accounting records.

To prevent such problems, the billing function awaits notification from shipping before it bills. Figure 4-1 shows that upon credit approval, the bill-customer function receives the **sales order (invoice copy)** from the receive-order task. This document is placed in a **S.O. pending file** until receipt of the shipping notice, which describes the products that were actually shipped to the customer. Upon arrival, the items shipped are reconciled with those ordered and unit prices, taxes, and freight charges are added to

FIGURE 4-3   Bill of Lading

UNIFORM STRAIGHT BILL OF LADING — Domestic

Monterey Peninsula Co-Op
527 River Road
Chicago, IL 60612
(312) 555-0407

Document No._____

Shipper No._____

Carrier No._____

Date_____

TO:

Consignee_____

Street_____

City/State_____

Zip Code_____

_____
(Name of Carrier)

Route:		Vehicle		
No. Shipping Units	Kind of packaging, description of articles, special marks and exceptions	Weight	Rate	Charges

TOTAL CHARGES $

The agreed or declared value of the property is hereby specifically stated by the shipper to be not exceeding:

$ _____ per_____

IF WITHOUT RECOURSE:
The carrier shall not make delivery of this shipment without payment of freight

_____
(Signature of Consignor)

FREIGHT CHARGES
Check appropriate box:
[ ] Freight prepaid
[ ] Collect
[ ] Bill to shipper

Signature below signifies that the goods described above are in apparent good order, except as noted. Shipper hereby certifies that he is familiar with all the bill of lading terms and agrees with them.

SHIPPER   Monterey Peninsula Co-op   CARRIER

PER   PER   DATE

(This bill of lading is to be signed
by the shipper and agent of the
carrier issuing same.)
CONSIGNEE

the invoice copy of the sales order. The completed **sales invoice** is the customer's bill, which formally depicts the total amount of charges to the customer. In addition, the billing function performs the following record-keeping related tasks:

● Records the sale in the sales journal.

● Forwards the ledger copy of the sales order to the Update Accounts Receivable task.

● Sends the stock release document to Update Inventory Records task.

The **sales journal** is a special journal used for recording completed sales transactions. The details of sales invoices are entered in the journal individually. At the end of the period, these entries are summarizes into a **sales journal voucher,** which is sent to the general ledger task for posting to the following accounts:

	DR	CR
Accounts Receivable—Control	XXXX.XX	
Sales		XXXX.XX

Figure 4-4 illustrates a journal voucher. Each journal voucher represents a general journal entry and indicates the general ledger accounts affected. Summaries of transactions, adjusting entries, and closing entries are all entered into the general ledger via this method. When properly approved, journal vouchers are an effective control against unauthorized entries to the general ledger. The journal voucher system eliminates the need for a formal general journal, which is replaced by a **journal voucher file.**

Update Inventory Records. The inventory control function updates **inventory subsidiary ledger** accounts from information contained in the stock release document. In a perpetual inventory system, every inventory item has its own record in the ledger containing, at a minimum, the data depicted in Figure 4-5. Each stock release document reduces the quantity on hand of one or more inventory accounts. Periodically, the financial value of the total reduction in inventory is summarized in a journal voucher and sent to the general ledger function for posting to the following accounts:

	DR	CR
Cost of Goods Sold	XXX.XX	
Inventory—Control		XXX.XX

FIGURE 4-4	Journal Voucher

Journal Voucher	Number: *JV6-03*
	Date: *10/7/2004*

Account Number	Account Name	Amount DR.	CR.
20100	*Accounts Receivable*	*5,000*	
50200	*Sales*		*5,000*

Explanation: *to record total credit sales for 10/7/2004*

Approved by: *JRM*   Posted by: *MJJ*

Update Accounts Receivable. Customer records in the **accounts receivable (AR) subsidiary ledger** are updated from information provided by the sales order (**ledger copy**). Every customer has an account record in the AR subsidiary ledger containing, at minimum, the following data: customer name; customer address; current balance; available credit; transaction dates; invoice numbers; and credits for payments, returns, and allowances. Figure 4-6 presents an example of an AR subsidiary ledger record.

Periodically, the individual account balances are summarized in a report that is sent to the general ledger. The purpose for this is discussed next.

Post to General Ledger. By the close of the transaction processing period, the general ledger function has received journal vouchers from the billing and inventory control tasks and an account summary from the AR function. This information set serves two purposes:

First, the general ledger uses the journal vouchers to post to the following control accounts:

	DR	CR
Accounts Receivable Control	XXXX.XX	
Cost of Goods Sold	XXX.XX	
Inventory Control		XXX.XX
Sales		XXXX.XX

Because general ledger accounts are used to prepare financial statement, they contain only summary figures (no supporting detail) and require only summary posting information.

Second, this information supports an important independent verification control. The AR summary, independently provided by the accounts receivable function, is used to verify the accuracy of the journal vouchers from billing. The AR summary figures should equal the total debits to AR reflected in the journal vouchers for the transaction period. By reconciling these figures the general ledger function can detect many types of errors. We examine this point more fully in a later section dealing with revenue cycle controls.

SALES RETURN PROCEDURES

An organization can expect that a certain percentage of its sales will be returned. This occurs for a number of reasons:

- The company shipped the customer the wrong merchandise.

FIGURE 4-5   Inventory Subsidiary Ledger

Perpetual Inventory Record – Item # 86329

Item Description	Date	Units Received	Units Sold	Qnty On Hand	Reorder Point	EOQ	Qnty On Order	Purch Order #	Vendor Number	Standard Cost	Total Inven. Cost
3" Pulley	9/15		50	950	200	1,000	—	—	—	2	1,900
	9/18		300	650							1,300
	9/20		100	550							1,100
	9/27		300	250							500
	10/1		100	150	200	1,000	1,000	87310	851	2	300
	10/7	1,000		1,150			—				2,300

FIGURE 4-6	Accounts Receivable Subsidiary Ledger

Name: *Howard Supply* Account Number *1435*
Address: *121 Maple St.*
Winona, NY 18017

Date	Explanation	Invoice Number	Payment (CR)	Sale (DR)	Account Balance	Credit Limit	Available Credit
9/27	3" Pulley (300 Units)	92131		600.00	600.00	1000.00	400.00
10/7			600.00		0.00		1000.00

- The goods were defective.
- The product was damaged in shipment.
- The seller shipped the goods too late or they were delayed in transit, and the buyer refused delivery.

When a return is necessary, the buyer requests credit for the unwanted products. This involves reversing the transaction accounted for previously in the sales order procedure. Using the DFD in Figure 4-7, let's now review the procedures for approving and processing returned items.

Prepare Return Slip. When items are returned, the receiving department employee counts, inspects, and prepares a **return slip** describing the items. The goods, along with a copy of the return slip, go to the warehouse where they are restocked on the shelves. The second copy of the return slip is sent to the sales function where a credit memo is prepared.

Prepared Credit Memo. Upon receipt of the return slip, the sales employee prepares a **credit memo.** This document is the authorization for the customer to receive credit for the merchandise returned. Figure 4-8 illustrates a credit memo. Note that the credit memo is similar in appearance to a sales order. Some systems may actually use a copy of the sales order marked "credit memo."

In cases where *specific* authorization is required (i.e., the amount of the return or circumstances surrounding the return exceed the sales employee's general authority to approve), the credit memo goes to the credit manager for approval. However, if the clerk has sufficient general authority to approve the return, the credit memo is sent directly to the billing function where the customer sales transaction is reversed.

Approve Credit Memo. The credit manager evaluates the circumstances of the return and makes a judgment to grant (or disapprove) credit. The manager then returns the **approved credit memo** to the sales department.

Update Sales Journal. Upon receipt of the approved credit memo, the transaction is recorded in the sales journal as a contra entry. The credit memo is then forwarded to the inventory control function for posting. At the end of the period, total sales returns are summarized in a journal voucher and sent to the general ledger department.

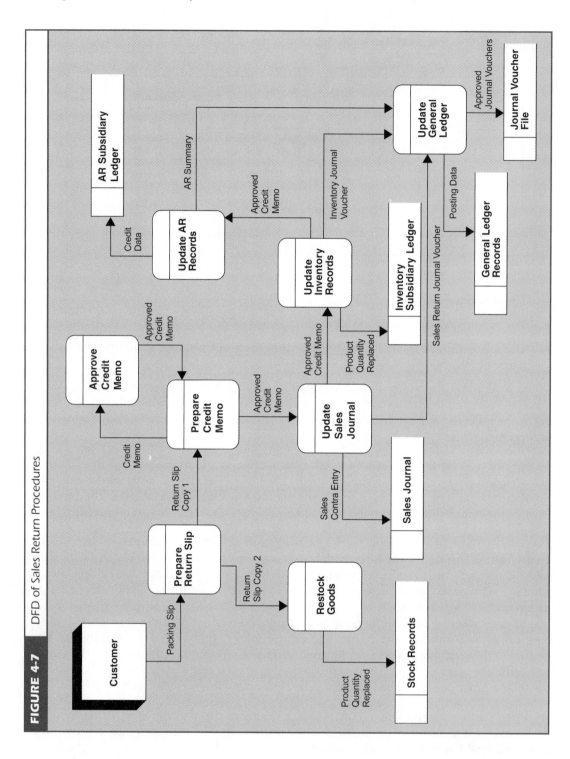

FIGURE 4-7   DFD of Sales Return Procedures

Update Inventory and AR Records. The inventory control function adjusts the inventory records and forwards the credit memo to accounts receivable, where the customer's account is also adjusted. Periodically, inventory control sends a journal voucher summarizing the total value of inventory returns to the general ledger update task. Similarly, accounts receivable submits an AR account summary to the general ledger function.

FIGURE 4-8	Credit Memo

Credit Memo

Monterey Peninsula Co-Op
527 River Road
Chicago, IL 60612
(312) 555-0407

Customer
Invoice # _____

Received from _____

Address _____

City _____

State _____ Zip _____

Reason for Return

_____

_____

_____

Product Number	Description	Quantity Returned	Unit Price	Total
Approved By:			Total Credit	

Update General Ledger. Upon receipt of the journal voucher and account summary information, the general ledger function reconciles the figures and posts to the following control accounts:

	DR	CR
Inventory—Control	XXX.XX	
Sales Returns and Allowances	XXXX.XX	
Cost of Goods Sold		XXX.XX
Accounts Receivable—Control		XXXX.XX

CASH RECEIPTS PROCEDURES

The sales order procedure described a credit transaction that resulted in the establishment of an account receivable. Payment on the account is due at some future date, which is determined by the terms of trade. Cash receipts procedures apply to this future event. They involve receiving and securing the cash; depositing the cash in the bank; matching the payment with the customer and adjusting the correct account; and properly accounting for and reconciling the financial details of the transaction. The data flow diagram in Figure 4-9 shows the relationship between these tasks. They are described in detail in the following section.

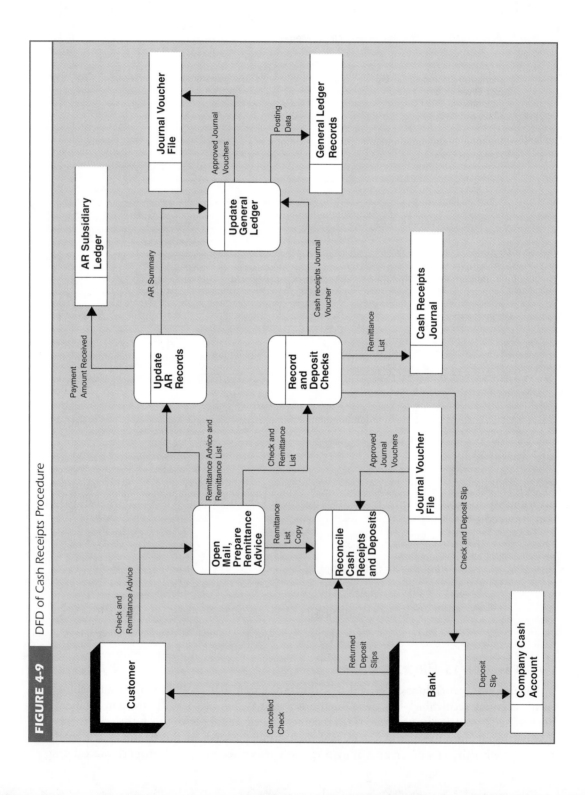

FIGURE 4-9   DFD of Cash Receipts Procedure

Open Mail and Prepare Remittance Advice. Incoming mail is delivered to the mail room and a mail room employee extracts the customer's check along with a document called the **remittance advice** from the envelope. Remittance advices contain information needed to service individual customer's accounts. This includes payment date, account number, amount paid, and customer check number. Figure 4-10 presents an example of a remittance advice. Only the upper portion (above the perforated line) is the remittance advice, which is removed and returned by the customer with the payment check. In some systems, the lower portion of the document is a customer statement periodically sent out by the billing department. In other cases this could be the original customer invoice, which was described in the sales order procedures.

The remittance advice is a form of a turnaround document, as described in Chapter 2. Its importance is most apparent in firms that process large volumes of cash receipts daily. For example, processing a check from John Smith in payment of his account with no supporting details would require a time-consuming and costly search through perhaps thousands records to find the correct John Smith. This task is greatly simplified when the customer provides the seller with the necessary account number and posting information. Because of the possibility of transcription errors and omissions, however, sellers do not rely on their customers to provide this information directly on their checks. Errors are avoided and operational efficiency is greatly improved by providing customers with accurate and reliable posting information on their statement or invoice, which they can easily return with their check.

Mail room personnel route the checks and remittance advices to an administrative clerk who endorses the checks "For Deposit Only" and reconciles the amount presented on each remittance advice with the corresponding check. The clerk then records each check on a form called a **remittance list** (or *cash prelist*). The remittance list is a record of all cash received. In this instance, the clerk prepares three copies of the remittance list. The original copy is sent along with the checks to the record and deposit checks function. The second goes with the remittance advices to the update accounts receivable function. The third goes to a reconciliation task.

Record and Deposit Checks. A cash receipts employee verifies the accuracy and completeness of the checks against the prelist. Any checks that should get lost or misdirected between the mail room and this function would be thus identified. After reconciling the prelist to the checks, the employee records the check in the **cash receipts journal.** All cash receipts transactions, including cash sales, miscellaneous cash receipts, and cash received on account, are recorded in the cash receipts journal. Figure 4-11 illustrates this with an example of each type of transaction. Notice that each check received from a customer is listed as a separate line item in the cash receipts journal.

Next, the clerk prepares a bank **deposit slip** showing the total amount of the day's receipts and forwards this along with the checks to the bank. Upon deposit of the funds, the bank teller validates the deposit slip and returns it to the company for reconciliation. At the end of the day, the cash receipts employee summarizes the journal entries and sends the following journal voucher entry to the general ledger function.

	DR	CR
Cash	XXXX.XX	
Accounts Receivable Control		XXXX.XX

Update Accounts Receivable. The remittance advices are used to post to the customers' accounts in the AR subsidiary ledger. Periodically, the changes in account balances are summarized and forwarded to the general ledger function.

FIGURE 4-10   Remittance Advice

Send To: Monterey Peninsula Co-Op   Page: 1
                         527 River Road
                         Chicago, IL 60612
                         (312) 555-0407

Remittance Advice:

Date	Customer No.	Amount Pd.	Check No.
10/4/07	811901	125.00	2002

- -

Please return the upper portion with your payment — Thank You

        John Smith
To: R.D. #2, Box 312   Due Date   Customer No.   Amount Due
        Prunedale, CA 09278–5704

Due Date	Customer No.	Amount Due
10/10/07	811901	125.00

Date	Invoice Number	Description	Amount Due	
9/28/07	6112115	Cleaning Supplies	125.00	

Thank you for giving Monterey Peninsula the opportunity to serve you

Previous Bal. _____ 300.00 _____
Payments _____ 300.00 _____
Sales _____ 125.00 _____
Late Fees _____ — _____
Tax _____ — _____
Ending Bal. _____ 125.00 _____

FIGURE 4-11	Cash Receipts Journal

Cash Receipts Journal

Date	Account	Post Ref	Check #	Cash Acct. # 101 (Debit)	Sales Discounts Acct. # 430 (Debit)	Accounts Receivable Acct. # 102	Sales Acct. # 401 Credit	Sundry Accounts Debit (Credit)
9/3	Capital Stock	301	2150	14,000				14,000
9/5	Ogment Supply	✓	6712	2,970	30	3,000		
9/9	Marvin Co.		3491	1,000			1,000	

Update General Ledger. Upon receipt of the journal voucher and the account summary, the general ledger function reconciles the figures, posts to the cash and accounts receivable control accounts, and files the journal voucher.

Reconcile Cash Receipts and Deposits. Periodically (weekly or monthly), a clerk from the **controller's** office (or an employee not involved with the cash receipts procedures) reconciles cash receipts by comparing the following documents: (1) a copy of the prelist, (2) deposit slips received from the bank, and (3) related journal vouchers.

REVENUE CYCLE CONTROLS

Chapter 3 defined six classes of internal control activities that guide us in designing and evaluating transaction processing controls. They are transaction authorization, segregation of duties, supervision, accounting records, access control, and independent verification. Table 4-1 summarizes these control activities as they apply in the revenue cycle.

Transaction Authorization

The objective of transaction authorization is to ensure that only valid transactions are processed. In the following sections we see how this objective applies in each of the three systems.

Credit Check. Credit checking of prospective customers is a credit department function. This department ensures the proper application of the firm's credit policies. The principal concern is the creditworthiness of the customer. In making this judgment, the credit department may employ various techniques and tests. The complexity of credit procedures will vary depending on the organization, its relationship with the customer, and the materiality of the transaction. Credit approval for first-time customers may take time. Credit decisions that fall within a sales employee's general authority (such as verifying that the current transaction does not exceed the customer's credit limit) may be dealt with very quickly. Whatever level of test is deemed necessary by company policy, the transaction should not proceed further until credit is approved.

TABLE 4-1	Summary of Revenue Cycle Controls

CONTROL POINTS IN THE SYSTEM

Control Activity	Sales Processing	Cash Receipts
Transactions authorization	Credit check Return policy	Remittance list (cash prelist)
Segregation of duties	Credit is separate from processing; inventory control is separate from warehouse; AR subsidiary ledger is separate from general ledger	Cash receipts are separate from AR and cash account; AR subsidiary ledger is separate from GL
Supervision		Mail room
Accounting records	Sales orders, sales journals, AR subsidiary ledger, AR control (general ledger), inventory subsidiary ledger, inventory control, sales account (GL)	Remittance advices, checks, remittance list, cash receipts journal, AR subsidiary ledger, AR control account, cash account
Access	Physical access to inventory; access to accounting records above	Physical access to cash; access to accounting records above
Independent verification	Shipping department, billing department, general ledger	Cash receipts, general ledger, bank reconciliation

Return Policy. Because credit approval is generally a credit department function, that department authorizes the processing of sales returns as well. An approval determination is based on the nature of the sale and the circumstances of the return. The concepts of specific and general authority also influence this activity. Most organizations have specific rules for granting cash refunds and credits to customers based on the materiality of the transaction. As materiality increases, credit approval becomes more formal.

Remittance List (Cash Prelist). The cash prelist provides a means for verifying that customer checks and remittance advices match in amount. The presence of an extra remittance advice in the accounts receivable department or the absence of a customer's check in the cash receipts department would be detected when the batch is reconciled with the prelist. Thus, the prelist authorizes the posting of a remittance advice to a customer's account.

Segregation of Duties

Segregating duties ensures that no single individual or department processes a transaction in its entirety. The number of employees and the volume of transactions being processed influence how the segregation is accomplished. Recall from Chapter 3 that three rules guide systems designers in this task:

Rule 1. Transaction authorization should be separate from transaction processing.

Within the revenue cycle, the credit department is segregated from the rest of the process, so formal authorization of a transaction is an independent event. The importance of this separation is clear when one considers the potential conflict in objectives between the individual salesperson and the organization. Often, compensation for sales staff is based on their individual sales performance. In such cases, sales staff have an incentive to maximize sales volume and thus may not adequately consider the creditworthiness of prospective customers. By acting in an independent capacity, the credit department may objectively detect risky customers and disallow poor and irresponsible sales decisions.

Rule 2. Asset custody should be separate from the task of asset record keeping.

The physical assets at risk in the revenue cycle are inventory and cash, hence the need to separate assets custody from record-keeping responsibility over them. The inventory warehouse has physical custody of inventory assets, but inventory control (an accounting function) maintains records of inventory levels. To combine these tasks would open the door to fraud and material errors. A person with combined responsibility could steal or lose inventory and adjust the inventory records to conceal the event.

Similarly, the cash receipts department takes custody of the cash asset, while updating AR records is an accounts receivable (accounting function) responsibility. The cash receipts department typically reports to the treasurer, who has responsibility for financial assets. Accounting functions report to the controller. Normally these two general areas of responsibility are performed independently.

Rule 3. The organization should be structured so that the perpetration of a fraud requires collusion between two or more individuals.

The record-keeping tasks need to be carefully separated. Specifically, the subsidiary ledgers (AR and inventory), the journals (sales and cash receipts), and the general ledger should be separately maintained. An individual with total record-keeping responsibility, in collusion with someone with asset custody, is in a position to perpetrate fraud. By separating these tasks, collusion must involve more people, which increases the risk of detection and therefore is less likely to occur.

Supervision

Some firms have too few employees to achieve an adequate separation of functions. These firms must rely on supervision as a form of compensating control. By closely supervising employees who perform potentially incompatible functions, a firm can compensate for this exposure.

Supervision can also provide control in systems that are properly segregated. For example, the mail room is a point of risk in most cash receipts systems. The individual who opens the mail has access both to cash (the asset) and to the remittance advice (the record of the transaction). A dishonest employee may use this opportunity to steal the check, cash it, and destroy the remittance advice, thus leaving no evidence of the transaction. Ultimately, this sort of fraud will come to light when the customer complains after being billed again for the same item and produces the canceled check to prove that payment was made. By the time the firm gets to the bottom of this problem, however, the perpetrator may have committed the crime many times and left the organization. Detecting crimes after the fact accomplishes little; prevention is the best solution. The deterrent effect of supervision can provide an effective preventive control.

Accounting Records

Chapter 2 described how a firm's source documents, journals, and ledgers form an audit trail that allows independent auditors to trace transactions through various stages of processing. This control is also an important operational feature of well-designed accounting systems. Sometimes transactions get lost in the system. By following the audit trail, management can discover where an error occurred. Several specific control techniques contribute to the audit trail.

Prenumbered Documents. **Prenumbered documents** (sales orders, shipping notices, remittance advices, and so on) are sequentially numbered by the printer and allow every transaction to be identified uniquely. This permits the isolation and tracking of a single event (among many thousands) through the accounting system. Without a unique tag, one transaction looks very much like another. Verifying financial data and tracing transactions would be difficult or even impossible without prenumbered source documents.

Special Journals. By grouping similar transactions together into special journals, the system provides a concise record of an entire class of events. For this purpose, revenue cycle systems use the sales journal and the cash receipts journal.

Subsidiary Ledgers. Two subsidiary ledgers are used for capturing transaction event details in the revenue cycle: the inventory and accounts receivable subsidiary ledgers. The sale of products reduces quantities-on-hand in the inventory subsidiary records and increases the customers' balances in the accounts receivable subsidiary records. The receipt of cash reduces customers' balances in the AR subsidiary records. These subsidiary records provide links back to journal entries and to the source documents that captured the events.

General Ledgers. The general ledger control accounts are the basis for financial statement preparation. Revenue cycle transactions affect the following general ledger accounts: sales, inventory, cost of goods sold, accounts receivable, and cash. Journal vouchers that summarize activity captured in journals and subsidiary ledgers flow into the general ledger to update these accounts. Thus we have a complete audit trail from the financial statements to the source documents via the general ledger, subsidiary ledgers, and special journals.

Files. The revenue cycle employs several temporary and permanent files that contribute to the audit trail. The following are typical examples:

Open sales order file shows the status of customer orders.

Shipping Log specifies orders shipped during the period.

Credit records file provides customer credit data.

Sales order pending file contains open orders not yet shipped or billed.

Back-order file contains customer orders for out-of-stock items.

Journal voucher file is a compilation of all journal vouchers posted to the general ledger.

Access Controls

Access controls prevent and detect unauthorized and illegal access to the firm's assets. The physical assets at risk in the revenue cycle are inventories and cash. Limiting access to these items includes:

- Warehouse security, such as fences, alarms, and guards.
- Depositing cash daily in the bank.
- Using a safe or night deposit box for cash.
- Locking cash drawers and safes in the cash receipts department.

Information is also an important asset at risk. Access control over information involves restricting access to documents that control physical assets including source documents, journals, and ledgers. An individual with unrestricted access to records can effectively manipulate the physical assets of the firm. The following are examples of access risks in the revenue cycle:

1. An individual with access to the AR subsidiary ledger could remove his or her account (or someone else's) from the books. With no record of the account, the firm would not send the customer monthly statements.
2. Access to sales order documents may permit an unauthorized individual to trigger the shipment of a product.
3. An individual with access to both cash and the general ledger cash account could remove cash from the firm and cover the act by adjusting the cash account.

Independent Verification

The objective of independent verification is to verify the accuracy and completeness of tasks performed by other functions in the process. To be effective, independent verifications must occur at key points in the process where errors can be detected quickly and corrected. Independent verification controls in the revenue cycle exist at the following points:

1. The shipping function verifies that the goods sent from the warehouse are correct in type and quantity. Before the goods are sent to the customer, the stock release document and the packing slip are reconciled.
2. The billing function reconciles the original sales order with shipping notice to ensure that customers are billed for only the quantities shipped.
3. Prior to posting to control accounts, the general ledger function reconciles journal vouchers and summary reports prepared independently in different functional areas. The billing function summarizes the sales journal, inventory control summarizes changes in the inventory subsidiary ledger, the cash receipts function summarizes the cash receipts journal, and accounts receivable summarizes the AR subsidiary ledger.

Discrepancies between the numbers supplied by these various sources will signal errors that need to be resolved before posting to the GL can take place. For example, a sales transaction that has been entered in the sales journal but not posted to the customer's account in the AR subsidiary ledger would be detected by the general ledger function. The journal voucher from billing, summarizing total credit sales, would not equal the total increases posted to the AR subsidiary ledger. The specific customer account causing the out-of-balance condition would not be determinable at this point, but the error would be noted. Finding it may require examining all the transactions processed during the period. Depending on the technology in place, this could be a tedious task.

PHYSICAL SYSTEMS

In this section we examine the physical system. This begins with a review of manual procedures and then moves on to deal with several forms of computer-based systems. The inclusion of manual systems in this age of computer technology is controversial. We do so for three reasons. First, manual systems serve as a visual training aid to promote a better understanding of key concepts. Manual (document) flowcharts depict information as the flow of physical documents. Their source, routing, destination, and sequence of events are visually discernable from the flowchart. In computer-based systems flows of digital documents are not easily represented on flowcharts and may be difficult for novice AIS students to follow. Second, manual system flowcharts reinforce the importance of segregations of duties through clearly defined departmental boundaries. In computer-based systems, these segregations are often accomplished through computer programming techniques and password controls that cannot be represented visually on a flowchart. Indeed, a single box (program icon) on a system flowchart may consolidate tasks of many different organizational units. Finally, manual systems are a fundamental component of the framework for viewing technology innovations. The shortcomings and failings of current generation technology become the design imperative for the next. The first generation of computer technology emerged out of the manual environment. An argument can be made that understanding what used to be state-of-the-art improves one's understanding of what led us to where we are now.

For these reasons, some instructors prefer to teach manual systems before moving on to computer applications. Others favor moving directly to computer-based systems. This section has been organized to accommodate both teaching styles. At this juncture, the reader may continue below with the review of manual systems or, without loss of technical content, bypass this material and go directly to computer-based systems located on page 186.

MANUAL SYSTEMS

The purpose of this section is to support the system concepts presented in the previous section with tangible models depicting people, organizational units, and physical documents and files. This section should help the reader envision the segregation of duties and independent verifications, which are essential to effective internal control regardless of the technology in place. In addition, we highlight inefficiencies intrinsic to manual systems, which gave rise to improved technologies used by modern systems.

SALES ORDER PROCESSING

The document flowchart in Figure 4-12 shows the procedures and the documents typical to a manual sales order system. In manual systems, maintaining physical files of source documents is critical to the audit trail. As we walk through the flowchart, notice that in each department, after completion of the assigned task, one or more documents are filed as evidence that the task was completed.

Sales Department
The sales process begins with a customer contacting the sales department by telephone, mail, or in person. The sales department captures the essential details of this event on a sales order. This information will later trigger many tasks, but for the moment is held in a file pending credit approval.

Credit Department Approval
To provide independence to **credit authorization** process, the credit department is organizationally and physically segregated from the sales department. When credit is approved, the sales department clerk pulls the various copies of the sales orders from the pending file and releases them to the billing, warehouse, and shipping departments. The customer order and credit approval are then placed in the open order file

Warehouse Procedures
The next step is to ship the merchandise, which should be done as soon after credit approval as possible. The warehouse clerk receives the stock release copy of the sales

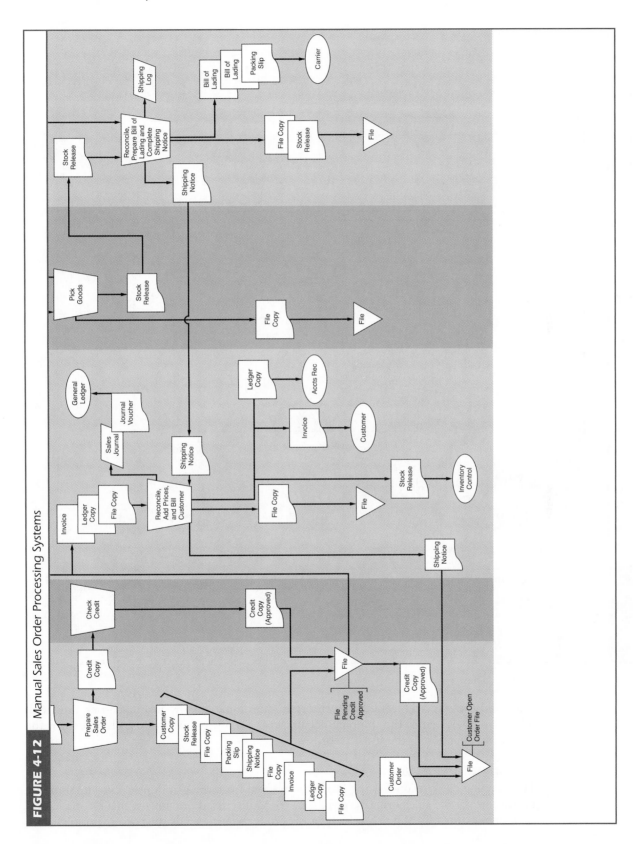

FIGURE 4-12   Manual Sales Order Processing Systems

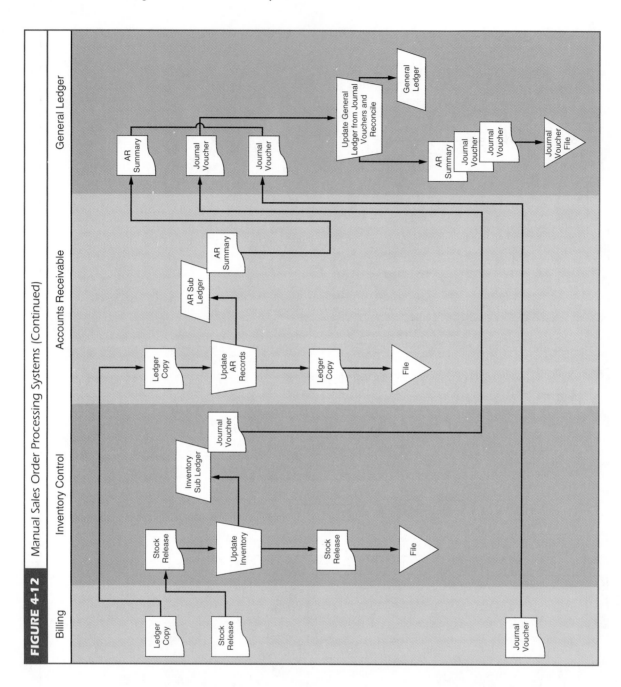

FIGURE 4-12 Manual Sales Order Processing Systems (Continued)

order and uses this to locate the inventory in question. The physical inventory and stock release are then sent to the shipping department. Finally, the warehouse clerk records the inventory reduction in the stock records.

The Shipping Department
The shipping clerk reconciles the products received from the warehouse with the shipping notice copy of the sales order received earlier. As discussed previously, this reconciliation is an important control point, which ensures that the firm sends the correct products and

quantities to the customer. Assuming all is well with the order, a bill of lading is prepared, and the products are packaged and shipped via common carrier to the customer. The clerk then enters the transaction into the shipping log and sends the shipping notice to the billing department.

The Billing Department

The shipping notice is proof that the product has been shipped and is the trigger document that initiates the billing process. Upon receipt or the shipping notice, the billing clerk compiles the relevant facts about the transaction (product prices, handling charges, freight, taxes, and discount terms) and bills the customer. The billing clerk then enters the transaction into the sales journal and distributes documents to the accounts receivable and inventory control departments. Periodically, the clerk summarizes all transactions into a journal voucher and sends this to the general ledger department.

Accounts Receivable, Inventory Control, and General Ledger Departments

Upon receipt of sales order copies from the billing department the AR and inventory control clerks update their respective subsidiary ledgers. Periodically they prepare journal vouchers and account summaries, which they send to the general ledger department for reconciliation and posting to the control accounts.

SALES RETURN PROCEDURES

Figure 4-13 illustrates the procedures and documents used for processing sales returns.

Receiving Department

The process begins in the receiving department where returned products are received by personnel, counted, inspected for damage, and sent to the warehouse for storage. The receiving clerk prepares a return slip, which is forwarded to the sales department for processing.

Sales Department

Upon receipt of the return slip the clerk prepares a credit memo. Depending on the materiality and circumstance of the return, company policy will dictate whether credit department approval (not shown) is required.

Processing the Credit Memo

The objective of the sales returns system is to reverse the effects of the original sales transaction. Billing does this by recording a contra entry into Sales Return and Allowance Journal Inventory control debits the inventory records to reflect the return of goods and the AR clerk credits the customer account. All departments periodically prepare journal vouchers and account summaries, which are then sent the general ledger for reconciliation and posting to the control accounts.

CASH RECEIPTS PROCEDURES

Figure 4-14 presents a document flowchart depicting the cash receipts procedures.

Mail Room

Customer payments arrive at the mail room, where the envelopes are opened. The checks are sent to the cashier in the cash receipts department, and the remittance advices are sent to the accounts receivable department.

FIGURE 4-13   Sales Returns Procedures

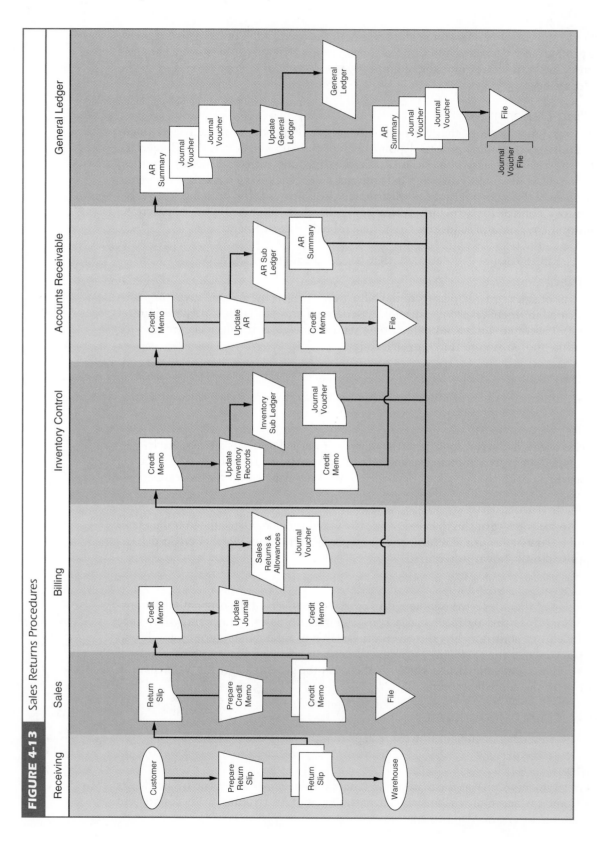

FIGURE 4-14 Flowchart of Cash Receipts System

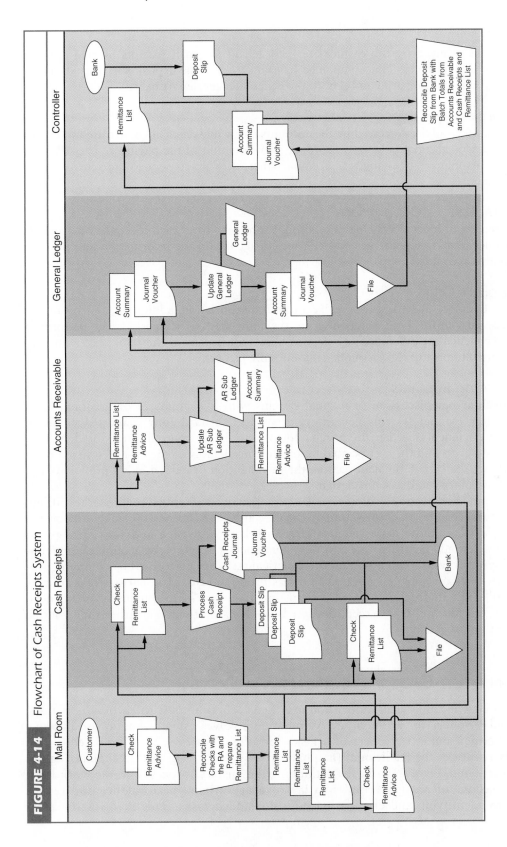

Cash Receipts

The checks received by the cashier are recorded in the cash receipts journal and are promptly sent to the bank, accompanied by two copies of the deposit slip. Periodically, a journal voucher is prepared and sent to the general ledger department.

Accounts Receivable

The remittance advices received by the accounts receivable department are used to reduce the customers' account balances according to the amount of the payment. The AR clerk prepares a summary of changes in account balances, which is sent to the general ledger department.

General Ledger Department

Upon receipt of journal voucher and account summary from cash receipts and accounts receivable, respectively, the general ledger clerk reconciles the information and posts to the control accounts.

Controller's Office

Because cash is a liquid asset and subject to misappropriation, additional controls over it are necessary. In this case, someone from the controller's office periodically performs a bank reconciliation by comparing deposit slips returned from the bank, account summaries used to post to the accounts, and journal vouchers.

Concluding Remarks

We conclude our discussion of manual systems with two points of observation. First, notice how manual systems generate a great deal of hard-copy (paper) documents. Physical documents need to be purchased, prepared, transported, and stored. Hence, these documents and their associated tasks add considerably to the cost of system operation. As we shall see in the next section, their elimination or reduction is a primary objective of computer-based systems design.

Second, for purposes of internal control many functions such as the billing, accounts receivable, inventory control, cash receipts, and the general ledger are located in physically separate departments. These are labor-intensive and thus error-prone activities that add greatly to the cost of system operation. When we examine computer-based systems you should note that these clerical tasks are performed by computer programs, which are much cheaper and far less prone to error. The various departments may still exist in computer-based system, but their tasks are refocused on financial analysis and dealing with exception-based problems that emerge rather than routine transaction processing.

COMPUTER-BASED ACCOUNTING SYSTEMS

We can view technological innovation in AIS as a continuum with *automation* at one end and *reengineering* at the other. **Automation** involves using technology to improve the efficiency and effectiveness of a task. Too often, however, the automated system simply replicates the traditional (manual) process that it replaces. **Reengineering**, on the other hand, involves radically rethinking the business process and the work flow. The objective of reengineering is to improve operational performance and reduce costs by identifying and eliminating nonvalue-added tasks. This involves replacing traditional procedures with procedures that are innovative and often very different from those that previously existed.

In this section we review automation and reengineering techniques applied to both sales order processing and cash receipts systems. We also review the key features of point-of-sale (POS) systems. Next, we examine electronic data interchange (EDI) and the Internet as alternative techniques for reengineering the revenue cycle. Finally, we look at some issues related to PC-based accounting systems.

AUTOMATING SALES ORDER PROCESSING WITH BATCH TECHNOLOGY

The file structures used to illustrate the following automated system are presented in Figure 4-15. The relationship between key data in the transaction files and master files that it updates is represented with arrows. Notice also that the sales order file has three key fields—Sales Order Number, Account Number, and Inventory Number. Sales Order Number is the primary key (PK) because it is the only field that uniquely identifies each record in the file. This is the preprinted number on the physical source document that is transcribed during the keystroke operation. In systems that do not use physical source documents, this unique number is automatically assigned by the system. The primary key is critical in preserving the audit trail. It provides the link between digital records stored on a computer disk and the physical source documents.

Account Number and Inventory Number are both secondary keys (SK) as neither of these keys uniquely identifies sales order records. For instance, there may be more than one sales order for a particular customer. Similarly, the same inventory item type may be sold to more than one customer. Hence, the values for these keys are not unique. Their purpose is to locate the corresponding records in the AR subsidiary and inventory master files.

A simplifying assumption in this hypothetical system is that each sales order record is for a single item of inventory. This one-to-one relationship is unrealistic because in reality one sales order could include many different inventory items. In Chapter 9, we will examine more complex file structures that permit the representation of "one-to-many" and "many-to-many" relationships that are frequently found in business transactions. At this point, however, avoiding this complicating factor will facilitate understanding both automated and reengineered systems.

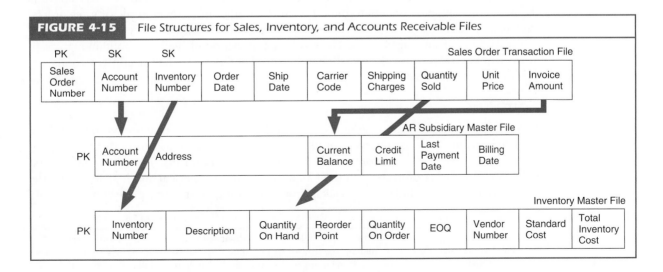

FIGURE 4-15   File Structures for Sales, Inventory, and Accounts Receivable Files

Figure 4-16 illustrates an automated sales order system that employs batch processing.[1] The greatest impact from this low-end technology is seen in billing, inventory control, accounts receivable, and general ledger. These previously manual bookkeeping tasks have been automated. The two principal advantages of this are cost savings and error reduction. By automating accounting tasks, a firm can reduce its clerical staff and its exposure to many forms of errors. Other clerical and operational tasks including sales order taking, credit checking, warehousing, and shipping are performed manually in this system. The tasked presented in Figure 4-16 are described below.

Sales Department

The sales process begins with a customer contacting the sales department and placing and order. The sales clerk captures the essential details and prepares a multiple copies of a sales order, which are held pending credit approval.

Credit Department Approval

When credit is approved, the sales department releases copies of the sales order to the billing, warehouse, and shipping departments. The customer order and credit approval are then placed in the open order file.

Warehouse Procedures

Next the warehouse clerk receives the stock release copy of the sales order and uses this to pick the goods. The inventory and stock release are then sent to the shipping department.

The Shipping Department

The shipping clerk reconciles the products received from the warehouse with the shipping notice received earlier. Assuming no discrepancies exist, a bill of lading is prepared, and the products are packaged and shipped via common carrier to the customer. The clerk then sends the shipping notice to the computer department.

KEYSTROKE

The automated element of the system begins with the arrival of batches of shipping notices from the shipping department. These documents are verified copies of the sales orders that contain information about the customer and the items shipped. The keystroke clerk converts the hard-copy shipping notices to digital form to produce a transaction file of sales orders. This is a continuous process. Several times throughout the day, the keystroke clerk transcribes batches of shipping notices. The resulting transaction file will thus contain many separate batches of records. For each batch stored on the file, batch control totals are automatically calculated.[2]

EDIT RUN

Periodically, the sales order system is executed. Depending on transaction volume and the need for current information, this could be a single end-of-day task or performed several times per day. The system is composed of a series of program runs. The edit program first validates all transaction records in the batch by performing clerical and logical test on the data. Typical tests include field checks, limit tests, range tests, and price-times-quantity

---

1   A variant on this system, which uses sequential flat files, is discussed in the appendix to this chapter.

2   Batch controls are designed to manage the flow of large numbers of records through the system. They consist of summary figures pertaining to the number of records in the batch, total dollar amount of the batch, and a hash total of a non-numeric field. See Chapter 17 for a detailed discussion.

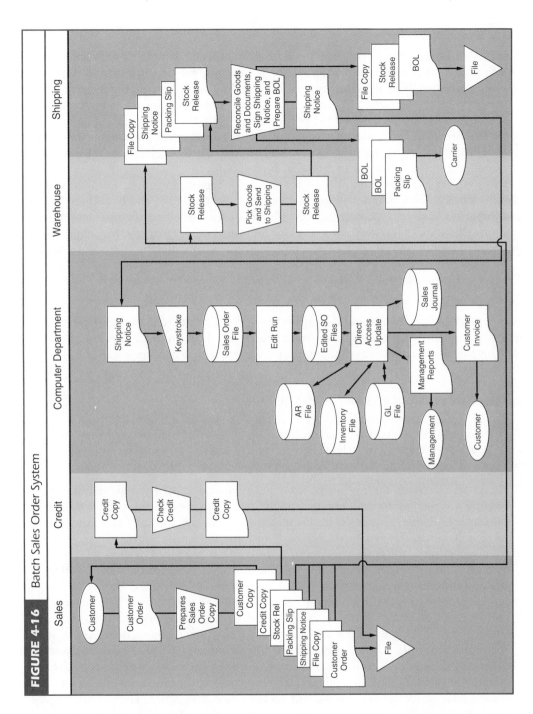

FIGURE 4-16   Batch Sales Order System

extensions.[3] Recall from Chapter 2 that detected errors are removed from the batch and copied to a separate error file (not shown in Figure 4-16), which are later corrected and resubmitted for processing with the next day's business. The edit program recalculates the batch control totals to reflect any changes due to the removal of error records. The edited sales order file is then passed to the file update run.

---

3   Chapter 17 provides a complete discussion of computer application controls.

UPDATE PROCEDURES

Figure 4-17 illustrates the direct access update process using sample data. Starting at the top of the edited sales order file, the update program posts the first transaction to the corresponding inventory and accounts receivable subsidiary records using the secondary keys (Inventory Number and Account Number) to locate the records directly. This transaction is then recorded in the journal, and the program moves to the next transaction record and repeats the process. This continues until all records in the transaction file have been posted. The general ledger accounts are typically updated after each batch. When the program reaches the end of the transaction file, it terminates.

This system generates a number of management reports including sales summaries, inventory status reports, transaction listings, journal voucher listings, and budget and performance reports. Quality management reports play a key role in helping management monitor operations to ensure that controls are in place and functioning properly. In Chapter 8, we examine management information needs and management reporting techniques in detail.

REENGINEERING SALES ORDER PROCESSING WITH REAL-TIME TECHNOLOGY

Figure 4-18 illustrates a real-time sales order system. Many of the manual procedures and physical documents of the previous system are replaced by interactive computer terminals. This system provides real-time input and output with batch updating of only some master files.

TRANSACTION PROCESSING PROCEDURES

Sales Procedures. Under real-time processing, sales clerks receiving orders from customers process each transaction separately as it is received. Using a computer terminal connected to a sales order system, the clerk performs the following tasks in real-time mode:

1. The system accesses the inventory subsidiary file and checks the availability of the inventory. It then performs a credit check by retrieving the customer credit data in the Customer (AR) file. This file contains information such as the customer's credit limit, current balance, date of last payment, and current credit status. Based on programmed criteria, the customer's request for credit is approved or denied.
2. If credit is approved, the system updates the customer's current balance to reflect the sale and reduces inventory by the quantities of items sold to present an accurate and current picture of inventory on hand and available for sale.
3. The system automatically transmits a digital stock release document to the warehouse, a digital shipping notice to the shipping department, and records the sale in the open sales order file. The structure of this file includes a CLOSED field that contains either the value N or Y to indicate the status of the order. Closed records (those containing the value Y) have been shipped, so the customer can now be billed. This field is used later to identify closed records to the batch procedure. The default value in this field when the record is created is N. It is changed to Y when the goods are shipped to the customer. The sales clerk can determine the status of an order in response to customer inquiries by viewing the records.

Warehouse Procedures. The warehouse clerk's terminal immediately produces a hardcopy printout of the electronically transmitted stock release document. The clerk then picks the goods and sends them, along with a copy of the stock release document, to the shipping department.

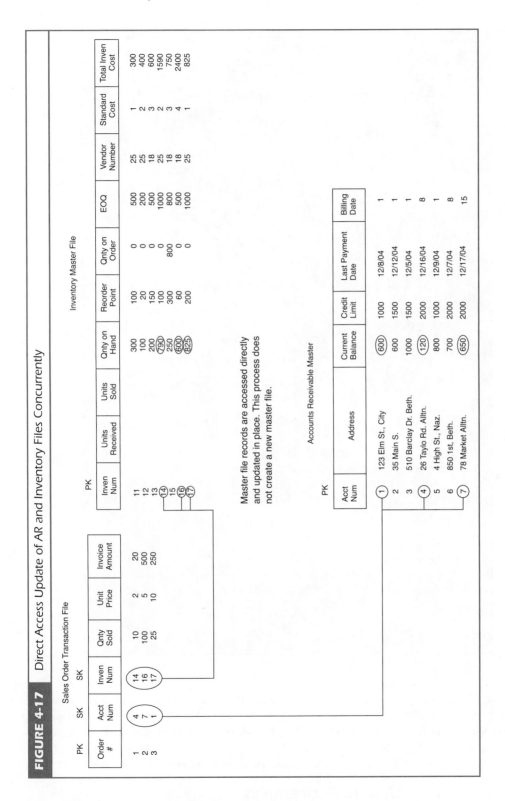

FIGURE 4-17   Direct Access Update of AR and Inventory Files Concurrently

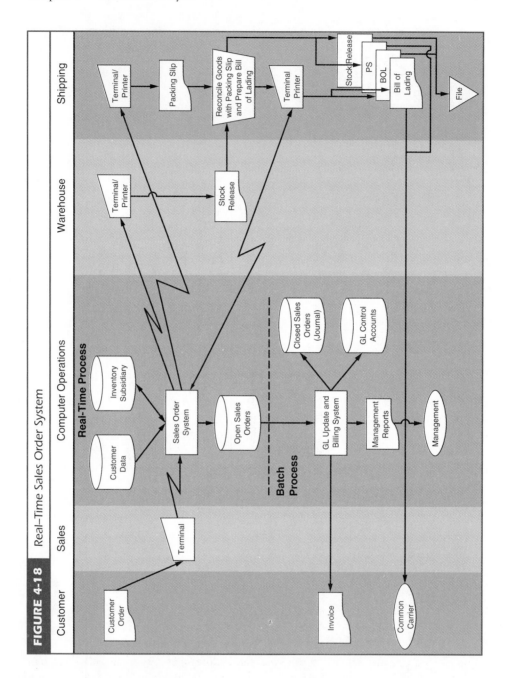

FIGURE 4-18   Real–Time Sales Order System

Shipping Department. A shipping clerk reconciles the goods, the stock release document, and the hard-copy packing slip produced on the terminal. The clerk then selects a carrier and prepares the goods for shipment. From the terminal, the clerk transmits a shipping notice containing shipping date and freight charges. The system updates the open sales order record in real time and places a Y value in the CLOSED field, thus *closing* the sales order.

GENERAL LEDGER UPDATE PROCEDURES

At the end of the day, the batch update program searches the open sales order file for records marked closed and updates the following general ledger accounts: Inventory—Control, Sales,

AR—Control, and Cost of Goods Sold. The inventory subsidiary and AR subsidiary records were updated previously during the real-time procedures. Recall from Chapter 2 that batch updating of general ledger records is done to achieve operational efficiency in high-volume transaction processing systems. An alternative approach is to update the general ledger accounts in real time, if doing so poses no significant operational delays. Finally, the batch program prepares and mails customer bills and transfers the closed sales records to the **closed sales order file** (Sales Journal).

Advantages of Real-Time Processing

Reengineering the sales order processes to include real-time technology can significantly reduce operating costs while increasing revenues. The following advantages make this approach an attractive option for many organizations:

1. Real-time processing greatly shortens the cash cycle of the firm. Lags inherent in batch systems can cause delays of several days between taking an order and billing the customer. A real-time system with remote terminals reduces or eliminates these lags. An order received in the morning may be shipped by early afternoon, thus permitting same-day billing of the customer.
2. Real-time processing can give the firm a competitive advantage in the marketplace. By maintaining current inventory information, sales staff can determine immediately whether the inventories are on hand. This enhances the firm's ability to maximize customer satisfaction, which translates into increased sales. In contrast, batch systems do not provide salespeople with current information. As a result, a portion of the order must sometimes be back ordered, causing uncertainty for the customer.
3. Manual procedures tend to produce clerical errors, such as incorrect account numbers, invalid inventory numbers, and price-quantity extension miscalculations. These errors may go undetected in batch systems until the source documents reach data processing, by which time the damage may have already been done. For example, the firm may find that it has shipped goods to the wrong address, shipped the wrong goods, or promised goods to a customer at the wrong price. Real-time editing permits the identification of many kinds of errors as they occur and greatly improves the efficiency and the effectiveness of operations.
4. Finally, real-time processing reduces the amount of paper documents in a system. Hardcopy documents are expensive to produce and clutter the system. The permanent storage of these documents can become a financial and operational burden. Documents in digital form are efficient, effective, and adequate for audit trail purposes.

Automated Cash Receipts Procedures

Cash receipts procedures are natural batch systems. Unlike sales transactions, which tend to occur continuously throughout the day, cash receipts are discrete events. Checks and remittance advices arrive from the postal service in batches. Likewise, the deposit of cash receipts in the bank usually happens as a single event at the end of the business day. The cash receipts system in Figure 4-19 uses technology that automates manual procedures. The following discussion outlines the main points of this system.

Mail Room. The mail room clerk separates the checks and remittance advices and prepares a remittance list. These checks and a copy of the remittance list are sent to the cash receipts department. The remittance advices and a copy of the remittance list are sent to the accounts receivable department.

FIGURE 4-19   Automated Cash Receipts System

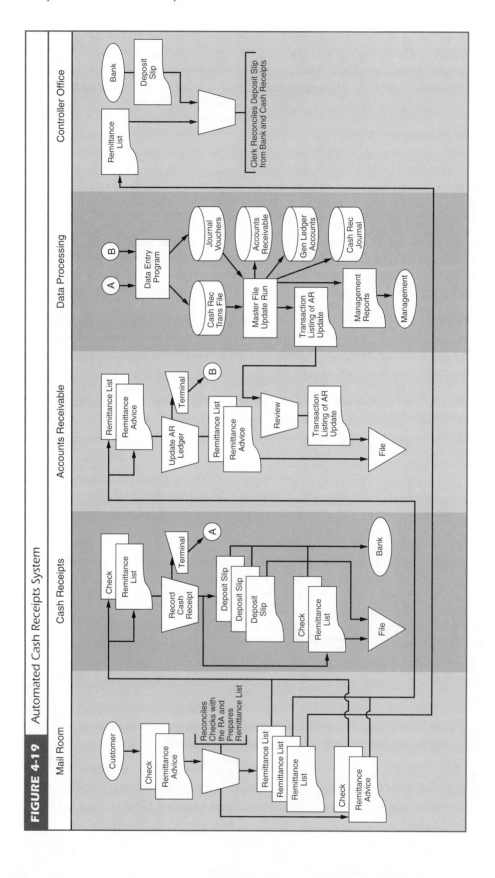

Cash Receipts Department. The cash receipts clerk reconciles the checks and the remittance list and prepares the deposit slips. Via terminal, the clerk creates a journal voucher record of total cash received. The clerk files the remittance list and one copy of the deposit slip. At the end of the day, the clerk deposits the cash in the bank.

Accounts Receivable Department. The accounts receivable clerk receives and reconciles the remittance advices and remittance list. Via terminal, the clerk creates the cash receipts transaction file based on the individual remittance advices. The clerk then files the remittance advices and the remittance list.

Data Processing Department. At the end of the day, the batch program reconciles the journal voucher with the transaction file of cash receipts, and updates the AR subsidiary and the general ledger control accounts (AR—Control and Cash). This process employs the direct access method described earlier. Finally, the system produces a transaction listing that the accounts receivable clerk will reconcile against the remittance list.

REENGINEERED CASH RECEIPTS PROCEDURES

The task of opening envelopes and comparing remittance advices against customer checks is labor intensive, costly, and creates a control risk. Some organizations have reengineered their mail room procedures to effectively reduce the risk and the cost.

The mail room clerk places batches of unopened envelopes into a machine that automatically opens them and separates their contents into remittance advices and checks. Simple logic is used to make the distinction. Because the remittance advice contains the address of the payee organization, the customer will need to place it at the front of the envelope so it can be displayed through the window. When the envelope is opened, the machine knows that the first document in the envelope is the remittance advice. The second is, therefore, the check. The process is performed internally and, once the envelopes are opened, mail room staff cannot access their contents.

The system uses special transaction validation software that employs artificial intelligence capable of reading handwriting. The system scans the remittance advices and the checks to verify that the dollar amounts presented on each are equal and that the checks are signed. Any items that are inconsistent or cannot be interpreted by the validation system are rejected and processed separately by hand. The system prepares a computer-readable file of cash receipts, which is then posted to the appropriate customer and general ledger accounts. Batches of checks are sent to the cash receipts department for deposit in the bank. Transaction listings are sent to management in the accounts receivable, cash receipts, and general ledger departments for review and audit purposes.

The advantages of improved control and reduced operating costs can be achieved by organizations with sufficient transaction volume to justify the investment in hardware and software. The system works best when a high degree of consistency between remittance advices and customer checks exists. Partial payments, multiple payments (a single check covering multiple invoices), and clerical errors on customer checks complicate the process and may cause rejections that require separate processing.

POINT-OF-SALE (POS) SYSTEMS

The revenue cycle systems that we have examined so far are used by organizations that extend credit to their customers. Obviously, this assumption is not valid for all types of business enterprises. For example, grocery stores do not usually function in this way. Such businesses exchange goods directly for cash in a transaction that is consummated at the point of sale.

Point-of-sale (POS) systems like the one shown in Figure 4-20 are used extensively in grocery stores, department stores, and other types of retail organizations. In this example, only cash, checks, and bank credit card sales are valid. The organization maintains no customer accounts receivable. Inventory is kept on the store's shelves, not in a separate warehouse. The customers personally pick the items they wish to buy and carry them to the check-out location, where the transaction begins.

DAILY PROCEDURES

First, the check-out clerk scans the **universal product code (UPC)** label on the items being purchased with a laser light scanner. The scanner, which is the primary input device of the POS system, may be handheld or mounted on the check-out table. The POS system is connected online to the inventory file from which it retrieves product price data and displays this on the clerk's terminal. The inventory quantity on hand is reduced in real time to reflect the items sold. As items fall to minimum levels, they are automatically reordered.

When all the UPCs are scanned, the system automatically calculates taxes, discounts, and the total for the transaction. In the case of credit card transactions, the sales clerk obtains transaction approval from the credit card issuer via an online connection. When the approval is returned, the clerk prepares a credit card voucher for the amount of the sale, which the customer signs. The clerk gives the customer one copy of the voucher and secures a second copy in the cash drawer of the register. For cash sales, the customer renders cash for the full amount of the sale, which the clerk secures in the cash drawer.

The clerk enters the transaction into the POS system via the register's keypad and a record of the sale is added to the sales journal in real time. The record contains the following key data: date, time, terminal number, total amount of sale, cash or credit card sale, cost of items sold, sales tax, and discounts taken. The sale is also recorded on a two-part paper tape. One copy is given to the customer as a receipt; the other is secured internally within the register and cannot be accessed by the clerk. This internal tape is later used to close out the register when the clerk's shift is over.

At the end of the clerk's shift, a supervisor unlocks the register and retrieves the internal tape. The cash drawer is removed and replaced with a new cash drawer containing a known amount of start-up cash (float) for the next clerk. The supervisor and the clerk whose shift has ended take the cash drawer to the cash room (treasury), where the contents are reconciled against the internal tape. The cash drawer should contain cash and credit card vouchers equal to the amount recorded on the tape. Often, small discrepancies will exist because of errors in making change for customers. Organizational policy will specify how cash discrepancies are handled. Some organizations require sales clerks to cover all cash shortages via payroll deductions. Other organizations establish a materiality threshold. Cash shortages within the threshold are recorded but not deducted from the employee's pay. However, excess shortages should be reviewed for possible disciplinary action.

When the contents of the cash drawer have been reconciled, the cash receipts clerk prepares a cash reconciliation form and gives one copy to the sales clerk as a receipt for cash remitted and records cash received and cash short/over in the cash receipts journal. The clerk files the credit card vouchers and secures the cash in the safe for deposit in the bank at the end of the day.

END-OF-DAY PROCEDURES

At the end of the day, the cash receipts clerk prepares a three-part deposit slip for the total amount of the cash received. One copy is filed and the other two accompany the cash to the bank. Because cash is involved, armed guards are often used to escort the funds to the bank repository.

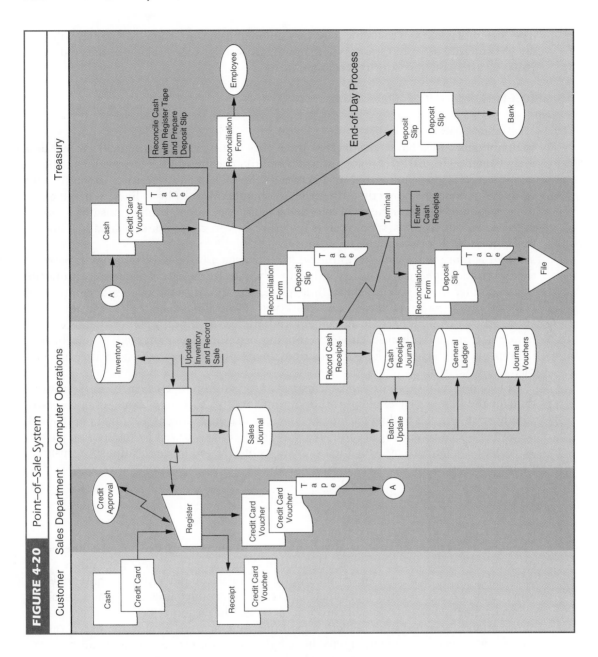

FIGURE 4-20 Point-of-Sale System

Finally, a batch program summarizes the sales and cash receipts journals, prepares a journal voucher, and posts to the general ledger accounts as follows:

	DR	CR
Cash	XXXX.XX	
Cash Over/Short	XX.XX	
Accounts Receivable (credit card)	XXX.XX	
Cost of Goods Sold	XXX.XX	
Sales		XXXX.XX
Inventory		XXX.XX

The accounting entry in the table may vary among businesses. Some companies will treat credit card sales as cash. Others will maintain an account receivable until the credit card issuer transfers the funds into their account.

REENGINEERING USING EDI

Doing Business via EDI

Many organizations have reengineered their sales order process through **electronic data interchange (EDI)**. EDI technology was devised to expedite routine transactions between manufacturers and wholesalers, and between wholesalers and retailers. The customer's computer is connected directly to the seller's computer via telephone lines. When the customer's computer detects the need to order inventory, it automatically transmits an order to the seller. The seller's system receives the order and processes it automatically. This system requires little or no human involvement.

EDI is more than just a technology. It represents a business arrangement between the buyer and seller in which they agree, in advance, to the terms of their relationship. For example, they agree to the selling price, the quantities to be sold, guaranteed delivery times, payment terms, and methods of handling disputes. These terms are specified in a trading partner agreement and are legally binding. Once the agreement is in place, no individual in either the buying or selling company actually authorizes or approves a particular EDI transaction. In its purest form, the exchange is completely automated.

EDI poses unique control problems for an organization. One problem is ensuring that, in the absence of explicit authorization, only valid transactions are processed. Another risk is that a trading partner, or someone masquerading as a trading partner, will access the firm's accounting records in a way that is unauthorized by the trading partner agreement. Chapter 12 presents the key features of EDI and its implications for business. EDI control issues are discussed in Chapter 16.

REENGINEERING USING THE INTERNET

Doing Business on the Internet

Thousands of organizations worldwide are establishing home pages on the Internet to promote their products and solicit sales. By entering the seller's home page address into the Internet communication program from a personal computer (PC), a potential customer can access the seller's product list, scan the product line, and place an order. Typically, Internet sales are credit card transactions. The customer's order and credit card information is attached to the seller's e-mail file. An employee reviews the order, verifies credit, and enters the transaction into the seller's system for processing in the normal way. Because of the need to review the e-mail file before processing, the turnaround time for processing Internet sales is sometimes longer than for telephone orders. Research is currently underway to develop intelligent agents (software programs) that review and validate Internet orders automatically as they are received.

Unlike EDI, which is an exclusive business arrangement between trading partners, the Internet connects an organization to the thousands of potential business partners with whom it has no formal agreement. In addition to unprecedented business opportunities, risks for both the seller and the buyer accompany this technology. Connecting to the Internet exposes the organization to threats from computer hackers, viruses, and transaction fraud. Many organizations take these threats seriously and implement controls including password techniques, message encryption, and firewalls to minimize their risk.

The technology of networks is discussed in the appendix to Chapter 12. In Chapter 16, we examine techniques for controlling these technologies.

CONTROL CONSIDERATIONS FOR COMPUTER-BASED SYSTEMS

The remainder of this section looks at the relationship between internal controls under alternative processing technologies. The purpose of this discussion is to identify the nature of new exposures and gain some insight into their ramifications. Solutions to many of these problems are beyond the scope of discussion at this point. Chapters 15, 16, and 17 present these general control issues as well as management and auditor responsibilities under Sarbanes-Oxley legislation.

Authorization

Transaction authorization in real-time processing systems is an automated task. Management and accountants should be concerned about the correctness of the computer-programmed decision rules and the quality of the data used in this decision.

In POS systems, the authorization process involves validating credit card charges and establishing that the customer is the valid user of the card. After receiving online approval from the credit card company, the clerk should match the customer's signature on the sales voucher with the one on the credit card.

Segregation of Duties

Tasks that would need to be segregated in manual systems are often consolidated within computer programs. For example, a computer application may perform such seemingly incompatible tasks as inventory control, accounts receivable updating, billing, and general ledger posting. In such situations, management and auditor concerns are focused on the integrity of the computer programs that perform these tasks. They should seek answers to such questions as: Is the logic of the computer program correct? Has anyone tampered with the application since it was last tested? Have changes been made to the program that could have caused an undisclosed error?

Answers to the questions lie, in part, in the quality of the general controls over segregation of duties related to the design, maintenance, and operation of computer programs. Programmers who write the original computer programs should not also be responsible for making program changes. Both of these functions should also be separate from the daily task of operating the system.

Supervision

In an earlier discussion, we examined the importance of supervision over cash-handling procedures in the mail room. The individual who opens the mail has access both to cash (the asset) and to the remittance advice (the record of the transaction). A dishonest employee has an opportunity to steal the check and destroy the remittance advice. This risk exists in both manual systems and computer-based systems where manual mail room procedures are in place.

In a POS system, where both inventory and cash are at risk, supervision is particularly important. Customers have direct access to inventory in the POS system, and the crime of shoplifting is of great concern to management. Surveillance cameras and shop floor security personnel can reduce the risk. These techniques are also used to observe sales clerks handling cash receipts from customers. In addition, the cash register's internal tape is a form of supervision. The tape contains a record of all sales transactions processed at the register. Only the clerk's supervisor should have access to the tape, which is used at the end of the shift to balance the cash drawer.

Access Control

In computerized systems, digital accounting records are vulnerable to unauthorized and undetected access. This may take the form of an attempt at fraud, an act of malice by a disgruntled employee, or an honest accident. Additional exposures exist in real-time systems, which often maintain accounting records entirely in digital form. Without physical source documents for backup, the destruction of computer files can leave a firm with inadequate accounting records. To preserve the integrity of accounting records, Sarbanes-Oxley legislation requires organization management to implement controls that restrict unauthorized access. Also at risk are the computer programs that make programmed decisions, manipulate accounting records, and permit access to assets. In the absence of proper access controls over programs, a firm can suffer devastating losses from fraud and errors. Thus current laws require management to implement such controls.

Because POS systems involve cash transactions, the organization must restrict access to cash assets. One method is to assign each sales clerk to a separate cash register for an entire shift. When the clerk leaves the register to take a break, the cash drawer should be locked to prevent unauthorized access. This can be accomplished with a physical lock and key or by password. At the end of the clerk's shift, he or she should remove the cash drawer and immediately deposit the funds in the cash room. When clerks need to share registers, responsibility for asset custody is split among them and accountability is reduced.

Inventory in the POS system must also be protected from unauthorized access and theft. Both physical restraints and electronic devices are used to achieve this. For example, steel cables are often used in clothing stores to secure expensive leather coats to the clothing rack. Locked showcases are used to display jewelry and costly electronic equipment. Magnetic tags are attached to merchandise, which will sound an alarm when removed from the store.

Accounting Records

Digital Journals and Ledgers. Digital journals and master files are the basis for financial reporting and many internal decisions. Accountants should be skeptical about accepting, on face value, the accuracy of computer-produced hard-copy printouts of digital records. The reliability of hard-copy documents for auditing rests directly on the quality of the controls that protect them from unauthorized manipulation. The accountant should, therefore, be concerned about the quality of controls over the programs that update, manipulate, and produce reports from these files.

File Backup. The physical loss, destruction, or corruption of digital accounting records is a serious concern. The data processing department should perform separate file-backup procedures (discussed in Chapter 2). Typically these are behind-the-scenes activities that may not appear on the system flowchart. The accountant should verify that such procedures are, in fact, performed for all subsidiary and general ledger files. Although backup requires significant time and computer resources, it is essential in preserving the integrity of accounting records.

Independent Verification

The consolidation of many accounting tasks under one computer program removes some of the traditional independent verification control from the system. Independent verification is restored somewhat by performing batch control balancing after each run and by producing management reports and summaries for end users to review.

PC-BASED ACCOUNTING SYSTEMS

The software market offers hundreds of PC-based accounting systems. In contrast to mainframe and client/server systems that are frequently custom designed to meet the specific user requirements, PC applications tend to be general-purpose systems that serve a wide range of needs. This strategy allows software vendors to mass-produce low-cost and error-free standard products. Not surprisingly, PC accounting systems are popular with smaller firms, which use them to automate and replace manual systems and thus become more efficient and competitive. PC systems have also made inroads with larger companies that have decentralized operations.

Most PC systems are modular in design. Typical business modules include sales order processing and accounts receivable, purchases and accounts payable, cash receipts, cash disbursements, general ledger and financial reporting, inventory control, and payroll. Their modular design provides users with some degree of flexibility in tailoring systems to their specific needs. Many vendors target their products to the unique needs of specific industries, such as health care, transportation, and food services. By so doing, these firms forgo the advantages of flexibility to achieve a market niche. The modular design technique is illustrated in Figure 4-21.

The central control program provides the user interface to the system. From this control point, the user makes menu selections to invoke application modules as needed. By selecting the sales module, for instance, the user can enter customer orders in real time. At the end of the day, in batch mode, the user can enter cash receipts, purchases, and payroll transactions.

Commercial systems usually have fully integrated modules. This means that data transfers between modules occur automatically. For example, an integrated system will ensure that all transactions captured by the various modules have been balanced and posted to subsidiary and general ledger accounts before the general ledger module produces the financial reports.

PC CONTROL ISSUES

PC accounting systems create unique control problems for accountants. The risks arise from inherent weaknesses in the PC environment. These are discussed in the following paragraphs.

Segregation of Duties

PC systems tend to have inadequate segregation of duties. A single employee may be responsible for entering all transaction data, including sales orders, cash receipts, invoices, and disbursements. In a manual system, this degree of authority would be similar to assigning accounts receivable, accounts payable, cash receipts, and cash disbursements responsibilities to the same person. The exposure is compounded when the individual is also responsible for programming or tailoring the application he or she runs.

Often little can be done in small companies to avoid such conflicts of duties. Controlling the PC environment requires a high degree of supervision, adequate management reports (such as detailed listings of all transactions), and frequent independent verification. For example, the supervisor should reconcile daily transaction details with the affected subsidiary and control accounts.

Access Control

PC systems generally provide inadequate control over access to data files. While some applications achieve modest security through password control to files, accessing data files

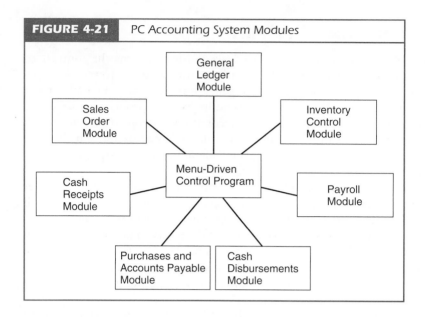

FIGURE 4-21 | PC Accounting System Modules

directly via the operating system can often circumvent this control. Solutions for dealing with the problem include data encryption, disk locks, and physical security devices.

Accounting Records

The PC environment is plagued by data losses that threaten accounting records and audit trails. Computer disk failure is the primary cause of data loss. When this happens, recovery of data stored on the disk may be impossible. Formal procedures for creating backup copies of data files and programs can reduce this threat considerably. In the mainframe environment, backup is provided automatically. Backup of PC data files relies on a conscious action by the users, who too often fail to appreciate the importance of the act.

SUMMARY

This chapter examined conceptually the revenue cycle of a typical merchandising firm and focused on the following areas: (1) the functional areas and the flow of transaction information that triggers key tasks; (2) the documents, journals, and accounts that support audit trails, decision making, and financial reporting; and (3) the exposure to risks in the revenue cycle and the control techniques that reduce them.

The chapter examined the operational and control implications of different degrees of technology. First, we examined the manual system depicting people, organizational units, and physical documents and files. The purpose of this was to help the reader envision the segregation of duties and independent verifications, which are essential to effective internal control regardless of the technology in place. In the process we highlighted inefficiencies intrinsic to manual systems, which gave rise to improved technologies and techniques used by modern systems.

Next we examined automated data processing techniques. While these systems improve record-keeping efficiency and effectiveness, they do little to advance an organization's business strategy. We then examined reengineered system. This involves rethinking traditional business approach to achieve competitive advantage by improving operational effectiveness. We then turned to control issues in the digital environment and found that computer processing consolidates many tasks, thus removing some traditional segregation of duties. The integrity of the computer programs that now perform these tasks becomes a matter of great concern to the organization. Similarly, organization management must control access to digital accounting files and ensure that adequate backup procedures are in place.

Finally, the chapter dealt with the subject of PC accounting systems. The modular design of these systems allows users to tailor the system to their specific needs. This feature has resulted in a tremendous growth in end-user computing that is changing the way many organizations do business. The PC environment poses some unique exposures that accountants must recognize. Three of the most serious exposures are (1) the lack of properly segregated duties; (2) PC-operating systems that do not have the sophistication of mainframes and expose data to unauthorized access; and (3) computer failures and inadequate backup procedures that rely too heavily on human intervention and thus threaten the security of accounting records.

APPENDIX

BATCH PROCESSING USING SEQUENTIAL FILES

Figure 4-22 illustrates a legacy sales order system that uses batch processing and sequential files. Because this system uses the sequential file structure for its accounting records, either tapes or disks may be employed as the physical storage medium. For day-to-day operations, however, tapes are inefficient because someone must mount them on a tape drive and then dismount the tape when the job ends. This approach is labor intensive and expensive. The constant decline in the per-unit cost of disk storage in recent years has destroyed the economic advantage of using tapes. Typically, an organization using sequential files will now employ disk storage devices. The operational features of sequential files are the same for both tape and disk media, but the disk storage devices can be left online for ease of access requiring no human intervention. Today, tapes are used primarily as backup devices and for storing archive data. For these purposes, they are an efficient and effective storage medium.

The computer processing phases of a batch system with sequential files was discussed in detail in the appendix to Chapter 2. The main points of that discussion are briefly reviewed in the following paragraphs.

Keystroke
The process begins with the arrival of batches of shipping notices from the shipping department. These documents are copies of the sales orders that contain accurate information about the number of units shipped and information about the carrier. The keystroke clerk converts the shipping notices to magnetic media to produce a transaction file of sales orders. This is a continuous process. Several times throughout the day, the keystroke clerk receives and converts batches of shipping notices. The resulting transaction file will thus contain many separate batches of sales orders. **Batch control totals** are calculated for each batch on the file.

Edit Run
Periodically, the batch sales order system is executed. In our example, we will assume that this occurs at the end of each business day. The edit program is the first run in the batch process. This program validates transactions by testing each record for the existence of clerical or logical errors. Typical tests include field checks, limit tests, range tests, and (price x quantity) extensions. Recall from Chapter 2 that detected errors are removed from the batch and copied to a separate error file. Later, these are corrected by an authorized person and resubmitted for processing with the next day's business. The edit program recalculates the batch control totals to reflect changes due to the removal of error records. The "clean" transaction file is then passed to the next run in the process.

Sort Run
At this point, the sales order file is in no useful sequence. Remember from an earlier discussion that a transaction file must be placed in the same sequence as the master file it is updating. The first sort run in this system rearranges the sales order file by order of the secondary key—Account Number.

FIGURE 4-22   Batch Processing with Sequential Files

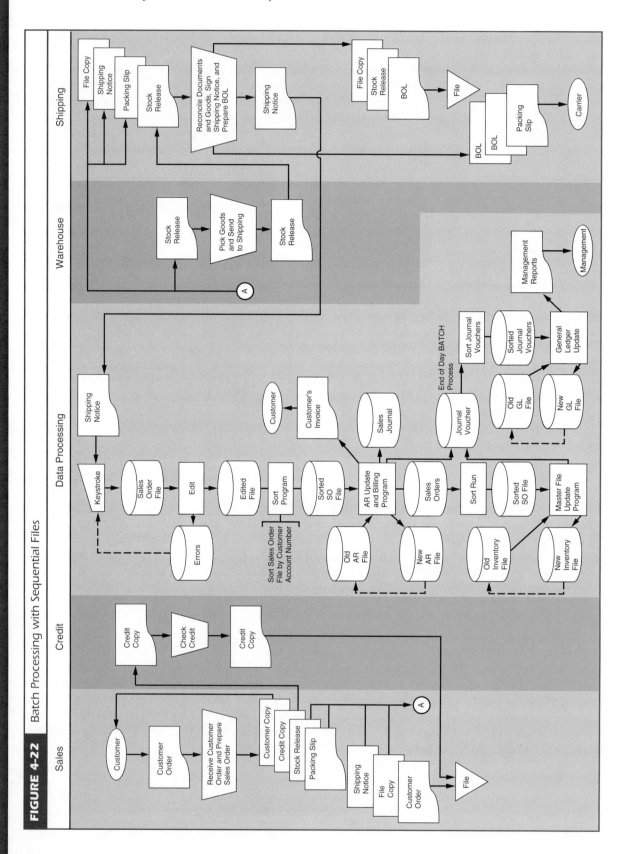

AR Update and Billing Run

The AR update program posts to accounts receivable by sequentially matching the Account Number key in each sales order record with the corresponding record in the AR subsidiary master file. This procedure creates a new AR subsidiary master file that incorporates all the changes to customer accounts affected by the transaction records. The original AR subsidiary master file remains complete and unchanged by the process. This automatic backup feature is an advantage of sequential file processing. Figure 4-23 illustrates this method with some sample records.

Each sales transaction record processed is added to the sales journal file. At the end of the run, these are summarized and an entry is made to the journal voucher file to reflect total sales and total increases to accounts receivable.

To spread the billing task evenly over the month, some firms employ **cycle billing** to bill their customers. The update program searches the billing date field in the AR subsidiary master file for those customers to be billed on a certain day of the month and prepares statements for the selected accounts. The statements are then mailed to the customer.

Sort and Inventory Update Runs

The procedures for the second sort and inventory update runs are similar to those previously described. The sort program sorts the sales order file on the secondary key—Inventory Number. The inventory update program reduces the Quantity On Hand field in the affected inventory records by the Quantity Sold field in each sales order record. A new inventory master file is created in the process. Figure 4-24 illustrates the process.

In addition, the program compares values of the Quantity On Hand and the Reorder Point fields to identify inventory items that need to be replenished. This information is sent to the purchasing department. Finally, a journal voucher is prepared to reflect cost of goods sold and the reduction in inventory.

General Ledger Update Run

Under the sequential file approach, the general ledger master file is not updated after each batch of transactions. To do so would result in the re-creation of the entire general ledger every time a batch of transactions (such as sales orders, cash receipts, purchases, cash disbursements, and so on) is processed. Firms using sequential files typically employ separate end-of-day procedures to update the general ledger accounts. This technique is depicted in Figure 4-22.

At the end of the day, the general ledger system accesses the journal voucher file. This file contains journal vouchers reflecting all of the day's transactions processed by the organization. The journal vouchers are sorted by general ledger account number and posted to general ledger in a single run, and a new general ledger is created.

The end-of-day procedures will also generate a number of management reports. These may include sales summaries, inventory status reports, transaction listings, journal voucher listings, and budget and performance reports. Quality management reports play a key role in helping management monitor operations to ensure that controls are in place and functioning properly. In Chapter 8, we examine management information needs and management reporting techniques.

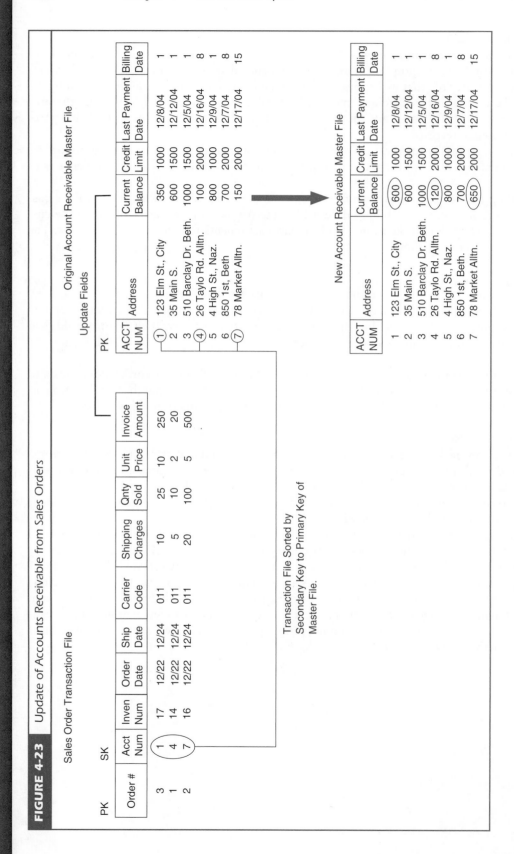

FIGURE 4-23 Update of Accounts Receivable from Sales Orders

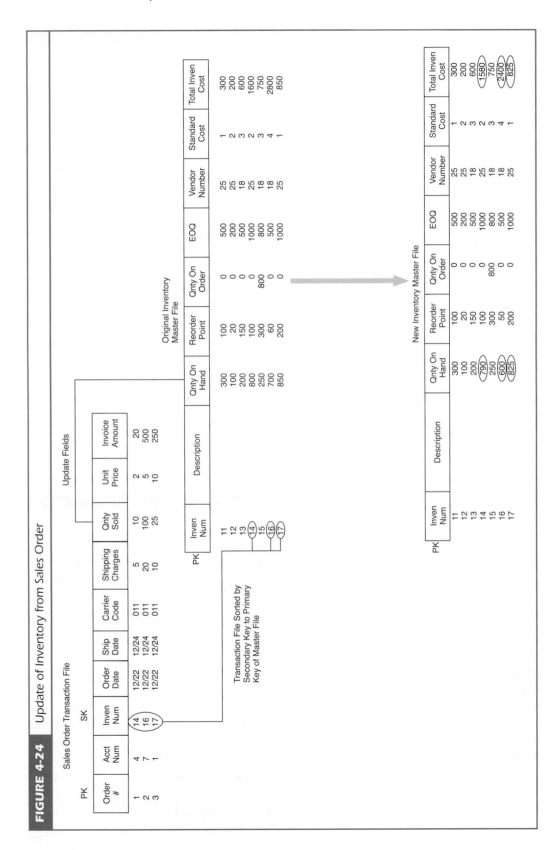

FIGURE 4-24   Update of Inventory from Sales Order

KEY TERMS

accounts receivable subsidiary ledger (168)

automation (186)

back-order (165)

batch control totals (203)

bill of lading (165)

cash receipts journal (173)

closed sales order file (193)

controller (175)

credit authorization (180)

credit memo (169)

customer open order file (162)

customer order (162)

cycle billing (205)

deposit slip (173)

electronic data interchange (EDI) (198)

inventory subsidiary ledger (167)

journal voucher (167)

journal voucher file (167)

ledger copy (168)

open sales order file (178)

packing slip (165)

point-of-sale (POS) systems (196)

prenumbered documents (178)

reengineering (186)

remittance advice (173)

remittance list (173)

sales invoice (167)

sales journal (167)

sales order (162)

shipping notice (165)

shipping log (178)

stock release (picking ticket) (164)

universal product code (UPC) (196)

REVIEW QUESTIONS

1. What document initiates the sales process?
2. Distinguish between a packing slip, a shipping notice, and a bill of lading.
3. What function does the receiving department serve in the revenue cycle?
4. The general ledger clerk receives summary data from which departments? What form of summary data?
5. What are three authorization controls?
6. What are the three rules that ensure that no single employee or department processes a transaction in its entirety?
7. At which points in the revenue cycle are independent verification controls necessary?
8. What is automation and why is it used?
9. What is the objective of reengineering?
10. Distinguish between an edit run, sort run, and update run.
11. What are the key features of a point-of-sale system?
12. How is the primary key critical in preserving the audit trail?
13. What are the advantages of real-time processing?
14. Why does billing receive a copy of the sales order when the order is approved but does not bill until the goods are shipped?
15. Why was EDI devised?
16. What types of unique control problems are created by the use of PC accounting systems?
17. In a manual system, after which event in the sales process should the customer be billed?
18. What is a bill of lading?
19. What document initiates the billing process?
20. Where in the cash receipts process does supervision play an important role?

Discussion Questions

1. Why do firms have separate departments for warehousing and shipping? What about warehousing and inventory control? Doesn't this just create more paperwork?

2. Distinguish between the sales order, billing, and accounts receivable departments. Why can't the sales order or accounts receivable departments prepare the bills?

3. Explain the purpose of having mail room procedures.

4. In a manual accounting system, what advantage does the journal voucher system have over the traditional general journal system?

5. How could an employee embezzle funds by issuing an unauthorized sales credit memo if the appropriate segregation of duties and authorization controls were not in place?

6. What task can the accounts receivable department engage in to verify that all checks sent by the customers have been appropriately deposited and recorded?

7. Why is access control over revenue cycle documents just as important as the physical control devices over cash and inventory?

8. How can reengineering of the sales order processing subsystem be accomplished by using the Internet?

9. What financial statement misrepresentations may result from an inconsistently applied credit policy? Be specific.

10. Give three examples of access control in a point-of-sale (POS) system.

11. Discuss the trade-off in choosing to update the general ledger accounts in real time.

12. Discuss how the nature of the necessary internal control features is affected by switching from a manual system to:

    a large-scale PC-based accounting system, or

    a PC-based accounting system.

13. Under what circumstances will automated mail room procedures provide the most benefit? The least benefit?

14. What makes point-of-sale systems different from revenue cycles of manufacturing firms?

15. Is a point-of-sale system that uses bar coding and a laser light scanner foolproof against inaccurate updates? Discuss.

16. How is EDI more than technology? What unique control problems may it pose?

17. Discuss the key segregation of duties related to computer programs that process accounting transactions.

Multiple-Choice Questions

1. Which document is NOT prepared by the sales department?
   a. packing slip
   b. shipping notice
   c. bill of lading
   d. stock release

2. Which document triggers the update of the inventory subsidiary ledger?
   a. bill of lading
   b. stock release
   c. sales order
   d. shipping notice

3. Which function should NOT be performed by the billing department?
   a. Record the sales in the sales journal.

   b. Send the ledger copy of the sales order to accounts receivable.
   c. Send the stock release document and the shipping notice to the billing department as proof of shipment.
   d. Send the stock release document to inventory control.

4. When will a credit check approval most likely require specific authorization by the credit department?
   a. when verifying that the current transaction does not exceed the customer's credit limit
   b. when verifying that the current transaction is with a valid customer

c. when a valid customer places a materially large order

d. when a valid customer returns goods

5. Which type of control is considered a mitigating control?

a. segregation of duties

b. access control

c. supervision

d. accounting records

6. Which of the following is NOT an independent verification control?

a. The shipping department verifies that the goods sent from the warehouse are correct in type and quantity.

b. General ledger clerks reconcile journal vouchers that were independently prepared in various departments.

c. The use of prenumbered sales orders.

d. The billing department reconciles the shipping notice with the sales invoice to ensure that customers are billed for only the quantities shipped.

7. CMA Adapted 684 3-29
Which of the following poses the biggest threat with respect to potential losses?

a. The petty cash custodian has the ability to steal petty cash. Documentation for all disbursements from the fund must be submitted with the request for replenishment of the fund.

b. An inventory control clerk at a manufacturing plant has the ability to steal one completed television set from inventory a year. The theft probably will never be detected.

c. An accounts receivable clerk, who approves sales returns and allowances, receives customer remittances and deposits them in the bank. Limited supervision is maintained over the employee.

d. A clerk in the invoice processing department fails to match a vendor's invoice with its related receiving report. Checks are not signed unless all appropriate documents are attached to a voucher.

e. An accounting clerk has the ability to record unauthorized journal entries. All journal entries are reviewed by an accounting department supervisor each month.

8. CMA 1288 3-26
In a well-designed internal control structure in which the cashier receives remittances from the mail room, the cashier should not

a. endorse the checks.

b. prepare the bank deposit slip.

c. deposit remittances daily at a local bank.

d. prepare a list of mail receipts.

e. post the receipts to the accounts receivable subsidiary ledger.

9. CMA 689 3-15
Which of the following situations represents an internal control weakness in accounts receivable?

a. Internal auditors confirm customer accounts periodically.

b. Delinquent accounts are reviewed only by the sales manager.

c. The cashier is denied access to customers' records and monthly statements.

d. Customers' statements are mailed monthly by the accounts receivable department.

e. Customers' subsidiary records are maintained by someone who has no access to cash.

PROBLEMS

1. Systems Description
Describe the procedures, documents, and departments involved when insufficient inventory is available to fill a customer's approved order.

2. Batch Processing
Refer to Figure 4-21 in the chapter and explain where the journal vouchers come from and which accounts in the general ledger are affected in the end-of-day batch process.

3. CMA Adapted 1287 5-7 through 5-12
Document Flowchart Analysis
Use the flowchart on the next page to answer the following questions.

a. The customer checks accompanied by the control tape (refer to Symbol A) would be forwarded to whom?

b. The appropriate description that should be placed in Symbol B would be what?

c.   The next action to take with the customer remittance advices (refer to Symbol C) would be to do what?

d.   The appropriate description that should be placed in Symbol D would be what?

e.   The appropriate description that should be placed in Symbol E would be what?

f.   The flowchart can be best described as representing what type of processing system?

4. CMA Adapted 690 5-1 through 5-5
Document Authorization and Transfer
Marport Company is a manufacturing company that uses forms and documents in its accounting information systems for record keeping and internal control. The departments in Marport's organizational structure and their primary responsibilities are shown in the table on the next page.

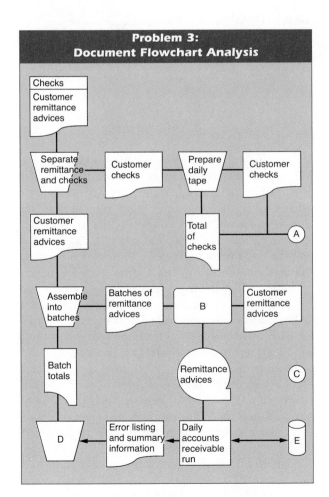

Problem 3:
Document Flowchart Analysis

Required:
Using this information, answer the following questions.

● The initiation of the purchase of materials and supplies would be the responsibility of what department?

● The document generated by the department identified in (a) to initiate the purchasing process would be what?

● Multiple copies of the purchase order are prepared for record keeping and distribution with one copy sent to the vendor and one retained by the purchasing department. In addition, for proper information flow and internal control purposes, a version of the purchase order would be distributed to what other departments?

● What documents must the accounts payable department review before it can properly authorize payment for the purchase of materials and supplies?

● Which document is used to transfer responsibility for goods between the seller of goods and a common carrier?

5. CMA Adapted
Segregation of Functions
Refer to the Marport Company in Problem 4 and determine whether the following situations represent a proper segregation of functions in the processing of orders from customers.

a.   Invoice preparation by the billing department and posting to the customers' accounts by the accounts receivable department.

b.   Approval of a sales credit memo because of a product return by the sales department with subsequent posting to the customer's account by the accounts receivable department.

c.   Shipping of goods by the shipping department that have been retrieved from stock by the finished goods storeroom department.

d.   Posting to the appropriate general ledger accounts by general accounting on the basis of batch totals prepared and verified by the billing department.

6. CMA 688 5-2
Internal Controls
Jem Clothes, Inc., is a 25-store chain concentrated in the Northeast that sells ready-to-wear clothes for

---

PROBLEM 4   Document Authorization and Transfer

Accounts payable—authorize payments and prepare vouchers	Payroll—compute and prepare the company payroll
Accounts receivable—maintain customer accounts	Personnel—hire employees, as well as maintain records on job positions and employees
Billing—prepare invoices to customers for goods sold	Purchasing—place orders for materials and supplies
Cashier—maintain a record of cash receipts and disbursements	Production—manufacture finished goods
Credit department—verify the credit rating of customers	Production planning—decide the types and quantities of products to be produced
Cost accounting—accumulate manufacturing costs for all goods produced	Receiving—receive all materials and supplies
Finished goods storeroom—maintain the physical inventory and related stock records of finished goods	Sales—accept orders from customers
General accounting—maintain all records for the company's general ledger	Shipping—ship goods to customers
Internal audit—appraise and monitor internal controls, as well as conduct operational and management audits	Stores control—safeguard all materials and supplies until needed for production
Inventory control—maintain perpetual inventory records for all manufacturing materials and supplies	Timekeeping—prepare and control time worked by hourly employees
Mail room—process incoming, outgoing, and interdepartmental mail	

---

young men and women. Each store has a full-time manager and an assistant manager, both of whom are paid a salary. The cashiers and sales personnel are typically young people working part time who are paid an hourly wage plus a commission based on sales volume. The accompanying flowchart on page 213 depicts the flow of a sales transaction through the organization of a typical store. The company uses unsophisticated cash registers with four-part sales invoices to record each transaction. These sales invoices are used regardless of the payment type (cash, check, or bank card).

On the sales floor, the salesperson manually records his or her employee number and the transaction (clothes, class, description, quantity, and unit price), totals the sales invoice, calculates the discount when appropriate, calculates the sales tax, and prepares the grand total. The salesperson then gives the sales invoice to the cashier, retaining one copy in the sales book.

The cashier reviews the invoice and inputs the sale. The cash register mechanically validates the invoice by automatically assigning a consecutive number to the transaction. The cashier is also responsible for getting credit approval on charge sales and approving sales paid by check. The cashier gives one copy of the invoice to the customer and retains the second copy as a store copy and the third for a bank card, if deposit is needed. Returns are handled in exactly the reverse manner, with the cashier issuing a return slip.

At the end of each day, the cashier sequentially orders the sales invoices and takes cash register totals for cash, bank card, and check sales, and cash and bank card returns. These totals are reconciled by the assistant manager to the cash register tapes, the total of the consecutively numbered sales invoices, and the return slips. The assistant manager prepares a daily reconciliation report for the store manager's review.

Cash, check, and bank card sales are reviewed by the manager, who then prepares the daily bank deposit (bank card sales invoices are included in the deposit). The manager makes the deposit at the bank and files the validated deposit slip.

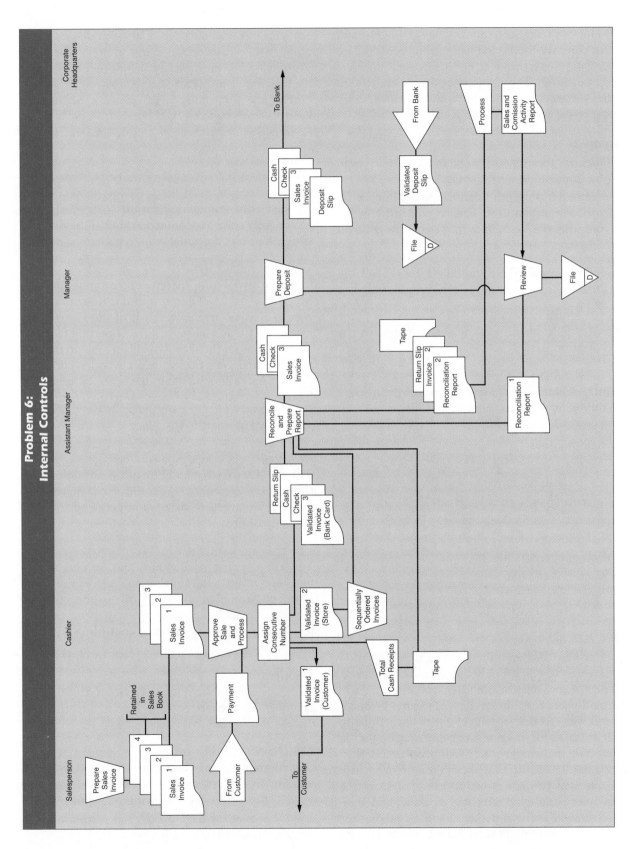

Problem 6:
Internal Controls

The cash register tapes, sales invoices, and return slips are forwarded daily to the central data processing department at corporate headquarters for processing. The data processing department returns a weekly sales and commission activity report to the manager for review.

Required:

a. Identify six strengths in the Jem Clothes system for controlling sales transactions.

b. For each strength identified, explain what problem(s) Jem Clothes has avoided by incorporating the strength in the system for controlling sales transactions.

Use the following format in preparing your answer.

1. *Strength*   2. *Problem(s) Avoided*

7. Internal Control Evaluation
Identify the control weaknesses depicted in the flowchart on page 215.

8. Stewardship
Identify which department has stewardship over the following journals, ledgers, and files.

a. Customer open order file
b. Sales journal
c. Journal voucher file
d. Cash receipts journal
e. Inventory subsidiary ledger
f. Accounts receivable subsidiary ledger
g. Sales history file
h. Shipping report file
i. Credit memo file
j. Sales order file
k. Closed sales order file

9. Control Weaknesses
For the past 11 years, Elaine Wright has been an employee of the Star-Bright Electrical Supply store. Elaine is a very diligent employee who rarely calls in sick and takes her vacation days staggered throughout the year so that no one else gets bogged down with her tasks for more than one day. Star-Bright is a small store that employs only four people other than the owner. The owner and one of the employees help customers with their electrical needs. One of the employees handles all receiving, stocking, and shipping of merchandise. Another employee handles the purchasing, payroll, general ledger, inventory, and accounts payable functions. Elaine handles all of the point-of-sale cash receipts and prepares the daily deposits for the business. Furthermore, Elaine opens the mail and deposits all cash receipts (about 30 percent of the total daily cash receipts). Elaine also keeps the accounts receivable records and bills the customers who purchase on credit.

Required:
Point out any control weaknesses you see in the scenario.

List some recommendations to remedy any weaknesses you have found working under the constraint that no additional employees can be hired.

10. Internal Control
Iris Plant owns and operates three floral shops in Magnolia, Texas. The accounting functions have been performed manually. Each of the shops has a manager who oversees the cash receipts and purchasing functions for the shop. All bills are sent to the central shop and are paid by a clerk who also prepares payroll checks and maintains the general journal. Iris is seriously considering switching to a computerized system. With so many information systems packages on the market, Iris is overwhelmed.

Required:
Advise Iris as to which business modules you think her organization could find beneficial. Discuss advantages, disadvantages, and internal control issues.

11. Internal Control
You are investing your money and opening a fast-food Mexican restaurant that accepts only cash for payments. You plan on periodically issuing coupons through the mail and in local newspapers. You are particularly interested in access controls over inventory and cash.

Required:
Design a carefully controlled system and draw a document flowchart to represent it. Identify and discuss the key control issues.

12. System Configuration
The computer processing portion of a sales order system is represented by the flowchart on page 216. Answer the following questions.

a. What type of data processing system is this? Explain, and be specific.

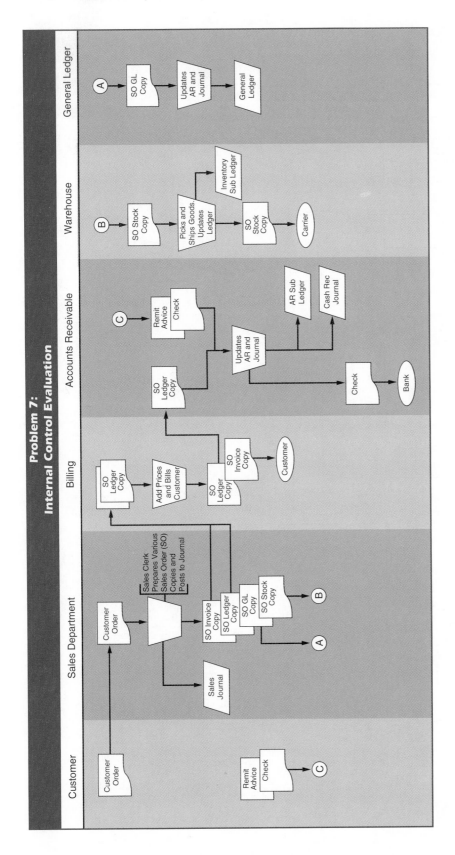

**Problem 7:
Internal Control Evaluation**

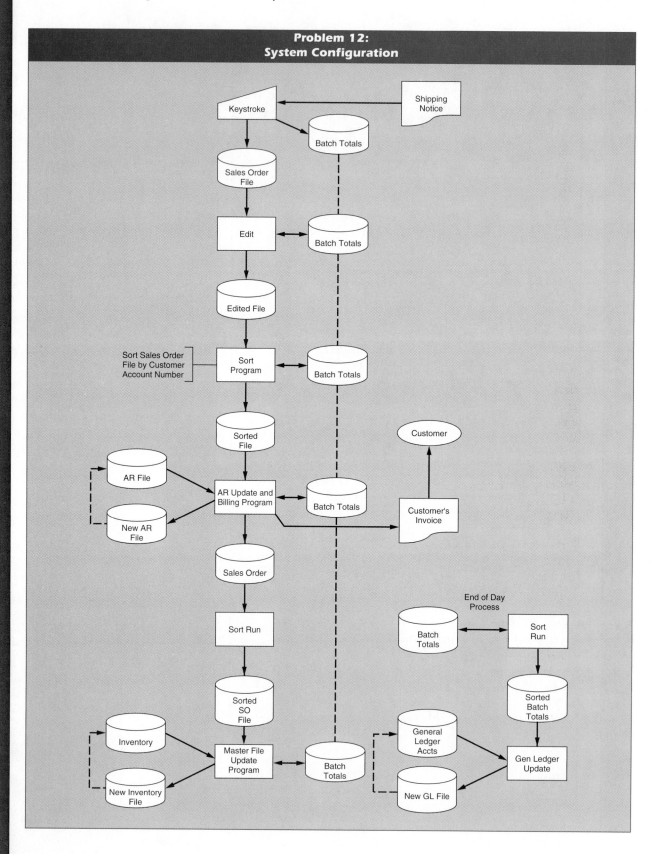

Problem 12:
System Configuration

b. The auditor suggests that this system can be greatly simplified by changing to direct access files. Explain the major operational changes that would occur in the system if this were done.

c. The auditor warns of control implications from this change that must be considered. Explain the nature of the control implications.

d. Sketch a flowchart (the computerized portion only) of the proposed new system. Use correct symbols and label the diagram.

13. System Configuration

The computer processing portion of a sales order system is represented by the flowchart below. Answer the following questions.

a. What type of data processing system is this? Explain, and be specific.

b. The marketing manager suggests that this system can be greatly improved by processing all files in real time. Explain the major operational changes that would occur in the system if this were done.

c. The auditor warns of operational efficiency implications from this change that must be considered. Explain the nature of these implications.

d. Sketch a flowchart of the proposed new system. Use correct symbols and label the diagram.

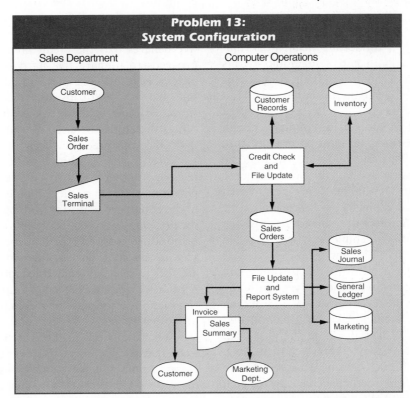

INTERNAL CONTROL CASES

1. Walker Books, Inc.
(Prepared by Matt Wisser, Lehigh University)

Company Background
Walker Books, Inc. is currently one of the largest book distributors in the United States. Established in 1981 in Palo Alto, California, Walker Books was originally a side project of founder and current president Curtis Walker, who at the time was employed by a local law firm. Because reading was much more than just a hobby of his, he decided to use some of his savings to buy out an abandoned restaurant and convert it into a neighborhood bookstore, mainly selling used books that were

donated from friends and family. When the doors first opened, Walker's wife, Lauren, was the only employee during the week; Curtis was the only employee on the weekends.

As the years passed, Curtis quit the law firm and began concentrating fully on his bookstore. More employees were hired, more books were traded in, and more sales were attained each year that passed. However, during the mid-1990s, Walker was faced with two problems: many large, upscale bookstores were being built in the area and the use of the Internet for finding and ordering books was becoming cheaper and more popular for current customers. In 1995, Walker's sales finally started to decline. Deciding to take a risk because of the new-found competition, he closed his doors to the neighborhood, invested more money to expand the current property, and transformed his company from simply selling used books to being a distributor of new books. Publishers send books to his warehouse, in which he stores them and resells them to large bookstore chains upon request.

Walker Books, Inc. has rapidly become one of the largest book distributors in the country. Though they are still at their original location in Palo Alto, California, they distribute books to each of the 50 states and because of that, the company now sees sales of about $105,000,000 per year. When Mr. Walker is asked about his fondest memory, he always responds that he will never forget how the little bookstore, with two employees, has expanded to now have more than 145 employees.

As mentioned, all of Walker's customers are large-chain bookstores who themselves see many millions of dollars in revenue per year. However, some of these bookstores have been having bad relationships with Walker Books in the past year. There have been many disputes between them, such as books that were ordered from Walker but were never sent, poor inventory management by Walker, and the inability of Walker to provide legitimate documentation of transactions. According to projections of this year's financials, the sour relationship that Walker Books and many of its customers have is going to take a toll on year-end revenue. Curtis Walker has stated time after time that because of his law background, he "clearly knows the difference between right and wrong, including those of internal controls." You have been hired to inspect the internal controls currently in place at

Walker Books, Inc. to determine if the customers have a legitimate claim against the company.

Revenue Cycle
Sales Order Processing System

At Walker Books, Inc., the sales order process begins when a customer calls in his or her order to an experienced sales representative, who then transcribes the necessary customer information and also the quantity and type of goods requested onto a formal customer order document. Because of recent problems the company has been having with overstated accounts receivable, Walker Books has set up a computer terminal in the department for the sales representative to check the customer's credit before going any further. If the credit is below the sales representative's subjective assessment, the transaction is not allowed; however, if the sales representative believes that the credit limit is acceptable, he proceeds to prepare five hard copies of the sales order. Because five copies must be made for each sale, blank sales forms are always available in a storage cabinet in the break room across from his office; therefore, there is never an issue of running out. Once prepared, one copy of the sales order is sent over to the warehouse to be used as the stock release. Another copy of the sales order, the shipping notice, is sent to the shipping department. Two of the copies are sent to the billing department, and the final copy of the sales order is stapled to the corresponding customer order where they are then filed in the sales department. Once the documents are sent to their designated locations, the sales representative updates the sales journal to record the transaction. A journal voucher is prepared and sent to the general ledger department.

When the clerk in the warehouse receives the stock release copy, he checks over the document for clerical accuracy. If everything looks right, he records the appropriate decrease in inventory into the stock records that are maintained in the warehouse. Once recorded, he hands off the stock release to the inventory manager, who is the only person that has access to the physical inventory. The manager picks the goods from the shelves to the degree that they are actually in inventory on that given day. The warehouse manager then sends the goods and the stock release document to the shipping department.

Once the shipping department receives the shipping notice from the sales department, the clerk takes the time to make sure the document was filled out in accordance with company standards. When the clerk receives the goods and the stock release, he hands the two documents (shipping notice and stock release) to the shipping supervisor to make sure that both documents reconcile. If they do, the supervisor logs on to a computer terminal and opens up a new relational database developed by interns that the company hired last summer. The supervisor enters the data from the documents into the program, which automatically produces a packing slip and a bill of lading. The supervisor proceeds to print out these two documents, placing the packing slip in the box with the physical goods, and giving the bill of lading to the carrier who then delivers the box of goods to the customer. When the carrier takes the goods away, the supervisor goes back to his computer with the shipping notice and stock release documents in hand for reference, and sends an electronic notification to the billing department, letting them know that the goods have been sent. The shipping notice is filed in the shipping department, while the stock release is sent to inventory control.

The billing department clerk receives the customer invoice and ledger copy of the sales order from the sales department. Because the clerk's job is very important, he has his own computer terminal where he waits to receive notification from the shipping department that the goods have been sent. When the notification is received, he compares what is on the computer screen to the invoice and the ledger copy of the sales order to make sure that everything reconciles correctly. If everything is correct, he adds the tax and final prices to the two documents. The invoice is then sent out to the customer as his bill and the ledger copy of the sales order is sent to the accounts receivable department.

Because of their importance, the company hires only the most skilled and competent individuals for their inventory control and accounts receivable departments. In inventory control, there are only two clerks; the first clerk receives the stock release document from the shipping department and updates the inventory subsidiary ledger to reflect the change. He then hands the stock release to the second clerk who updates the general ledger via a computer terminal. The computer is password protected to ensure that only this clerk can update the general ledger and no one else. The stock release is then filed by the second clerk.

In the accounts receivable department, there is only one clerk who both receives the ledger copy of the sales order and then proceeds to update the accounts receivable subsidiary ledger. Each ledger copy is filed in the department and then at the end of the day, an accounts receivable summary is prepared by the clerk and sent to the general ledger department.

Upon the receipt of the journal voucher from the sales department and the accounts receivable summary, the general ledger department clerk reconciles and updates the appropriate general ledger control accounts via his computer terminal. The two documents are then filed in the department.

Cash Receipts System

Because Walker Books receives both payments from customers and also a lot of junk mail from publishers, the company has decided to set up two separate mail rooms with different PO box addresses. Mail room A is staffed with many employees who have the responsibility of receiving and opening routine mail (catalogs, advertisements). Mail room B has only four employees who only receive customer payments. Because there are more employees working in the more hectic mail room A, the company has decided to concentrate supervision duties here and not in mail room B because there are very few employees who are each highly trusted by management. When customer payments are received by a clerk in mail room B, the clerk opens the envelope and pulls out the check and remittance advice contained inside. The clerk reconciles the two together and then updates the remittance list file via computer terminal in the mail room. At the end of the day, the finished remittance list is automatically sent to the clerk in the cash receipts department. The check is then sent to the cash receipts department and the remittance advice is sent to the accounts receivable department.

When the check is received by the cash receipts clerk, he accesses the remittance list via computer and prints out a hard copy. As long as the amount on the check reconciles to the amount on the remittance list, the clerk endorses the check and signs it "For Deposit Only." The check amount is then recorded in the cash receipts journal and then the clerk prepares a voucher, which is sent to the general ledger department. He then takes the check and the remittance list and sends them over to the accounts receivable department.

Once received by the accounts receivable clerk, the remittance advice is reconciled with the remittance list and the check; next, the clerk updates the accounts receivable subsidiary ledger to recognize the customer's payment. The clerk then prepares an accurate deposit slip and sends it along with the check to the company's bank. At the end of the day, the department prepares an account summary which is then sent to the general ledger department. The remittance list and remittance advice are filed in the accounts receivable department.

The general ledger department receives both the account summary and the journal voucher from the accounts receivable department and cash receipts, respectively. The clerk takes look over the two documents and then updates the general ledger accounts reflected through his terminal. The account summary and journal voucher are then filed by the clerk.

Required:

a. Create a data flow diagram of the current system.

b. Create a document flowchart of the existing system.

c. Analyze the internal control weaknesses in the system. Model your response according to the six categories of physical control activities specified in SAS 78.

d. Prepare a system flowchart of a redesigned computer-based system that resolves the control weaknesses that you identified.

2. A&V Safety, Inc

(Prepared by Adam Johnson and Aneesh Varma, Lehigh University)

A&V Safety Inc. is a growing company specializing in the sales of safety equipment to commercial entities. It currently employs 200 full-time employees who all work out of their headquarters in San Diego, California. During the summer the company expands to include about 10 summer interns who are delegated smaller jobs and other errands. A&V currently competes with Office Safety Inc. and X-Safe who leads the industry. Suppliers for A&V include Halotron Extinguishers, Kadelite, and Exit Signs Inc and there have been no issues requiring redress. The terms of trade used by A&V are 2–10 net 30 with FOB delivery. This is used with all suppliers and inventory is kept at a level that will service two weeks. This level has shown to avoid stock outs and the excess inventory is held a warehouse in a suburb of San Diego.

The company has growing revenue, which has recently topped $23 million and has a Return on Investment of 14 percent and Net Margin of slightly over 20 percent. While the company has been operating efficiently in the past, new systems problems have arisen due to the strain put on these legacy systems from recent growth.

Revenue Cycle

A&V Safety Inc. has one sales department at its headquarters in San Diego, however, their sales people do go out to visit prior and potential clients. Due to the nature of the business, sales always go through a salesperson. The customer and the salesperson write out the customer order (CO) together. From here the CO is returned to the office where the Sales Clerk completes a purchase order (PO). Here the sales clerk performs a credit check and either authorizes or rejects the order. If the credit is authorized the CO is entered into the companies centralized computer system. Once the order is entered an electronic copy is sent to the customer, warehousing, shipping, and billing. Once this is done a hard copy of the CO is filed in the open sales order file.

Warehousing receives the copy of the CO, prints one copy, and uses it as a stock release form to collect the order. Once the goods are picked the warehousing clerk removes the items from the inventory subledger electronically. This automatically updates the general ledger. He then files the electronic sales order in the completed order file, signs the printed stock release, and files it in the picked goods file.

The picked goods are then sent to the shipping department where the goods are reconciled with the electronic sales order. Two copies of the sales order are printed. One copy is sent to the carrier with the goods. The second copy has billing information added to it and is electronically entered into the computer system as a shipping slip. Once this is done bills of lading are prepared electronically. Two copies go to billing and the third is filed in shipping.

Upon receipt of the shipping slip and the two bills of lading the billing clerk prepares a sales invoice from the shipping slip. This is then printed with any other charges and sent to the customer as their bill. An invoice copy is sent back to sales to close the open order file. Once the bill is sent the sale is electronically recorded in the sales journal by billing and an invoice copy goes to AR where the AR sub ledger is updated. Both automatically update the general ledger.

Mail is received in the 20-person mail room, which is overseen by one manager. Here the checks and remittance advices are split after being reconciled. The remittance advices are sent to the AR department, where they are compiled into an electronic remittance list. One copy is electronically sent to Cash Receipts, where the remittance list is reconciled with the checks sent from the mail room. The cashier then signs the checks and prepares deposit slips. One deposit slip is sent to an accountant in charge of cash receipts who updates the cash receipts journal electronically. This then automatically updates the general ledger. Once the cash receipts journal is updated the checks and two copies of the deposit slip are sent through an armored carrier to the bank. One copy of the deposit slip is filed with a copy of the remittance list. A final copy of the deposit slip is sent to the AR department where it is reconciled with the remittance list on file. Once the reconciliation is complete the AR subledger is updated electronically, which automatically updates the general ledger.

Required:

a. Create a data flow diagram of the current system.

b. Create a document flowchart of the existing system.

c. Analyze the internal control weaknesses in the system. Model your response according to the six categories of physical control activities specified in SAS 78.

d. Prepare a system flowchart of a redesigned computer-based system that resolves the control weaknesses that you identified.

3. Premier Sports Memorabilia General Scenario

(Prepared by Chris Polchinski, Lehigh University)

Premier Sports Memorabilia is a medium-sized, rapidly growing online and catalogue-based retailer centered in Brooklyn, New York. The company was founded in 1990 and specializes in providing the customer with authentic yet affordable sports memorabilia from their favorite players and teams past and present. The company gets most of its sales from the northeast region of the United States, but recently has been undergoing a campaign to spread out and increase its customer base. The company is unique that it has a wide range of competitors such as online apparel retailers like EastBay, retail stores such as Sports Authority, and online memorabilia retailers such as the Danbury Mint. The reason for this comes from Premier's wide range of offerings including everything from team jerseys and hats, to autographed balls, plaques, and bats, to sports cards and figurines. The firm's sales have been slowly increasing over the years and last year reported a satisfying $95 million. The company currently employs 205 employees who are spread out among its three warehouses and two offices in the tri-state area.

Premier has been well known for their close relations with their suppliers and have only had a few minor communication problems since the company was started, none which have disrupted the ordinary course of business. The firm uses a wide base of manufacturers and memorabilia dealers around the country and is always looking for additional contacts that have new or rare items to offer. The company uses a series of low-tech computer assistance to assist with its various daily manual tasks and maintains controlled access to relevant data within the organization. As the company continues to expand many of these manual tasks will most likely be replaced with a more advanced computer technology system, but currently they serve their purpose and have not hindered business as a whole.

Revenue Cycle Procedures

Premier's revenue process is initiated with the placement of a customer order by a customer either online, by mail, or through a telephone representative. The order is then manually entered into the computer system for mail or telephone orders, while online orders are automatically entered upon arrival. Upon being entered into the system a sales representative is required to perform a credit check on the customer who has placed the order. If the credit is approved, a sales order is created and entered into the system for further processing. If credit is denied, the process ends and the customer is notified of the automatic cancellation.

Four copies of each sales order are created. The first is simply entered into the terminal in the sales department and filed. A second is sent electronically to the computer terminal in the billing department where it is further processed. A third is sent to the computer terminal in the warehouse for further processing. A final copy is sent to the customer as a receipt stating that their order has been received and processed. In addition to creating sales orders, every time a sale is approved, the sales records are updated and the entries are electronically posted to the sales journal file.

Upon the arrival of the sales order at the warehouse terminal, it is used as a stock release in authorizing a warehouse clerk to go and physically get the requested items from the shelves. When the goods have been obtained, the clerk prepares a bill of lading, packing slip, and shipping notice for the goods that are being sent. The shipping notice is entered into the terminal, while the other two forms are sent to the carrier along with the goods. If a certain item is out of stock or on back-order, this is specified in the shipping notice so that the Billing Department and Accounts Receivable can later be informed. The clerk then sends a copy of the Shipping Notice to the Billing Department.

After the Billing Department has received both a copy of the Sales Order and the Shipping Notice they are reconciled and the order is priced with all of the appropriate charges and taxes for the preparation of the Invoice. Two copies of the invoice are created. One copy is sent to the customer in the form of a bill, the other is sent electronically to Accounts Receivable for further processing.

Upon the arrival of the Invoice at the Accounts Receivable computer terminal, the Accounts receivable records are updated by posting to the Accounts Receivable Journal File.

After the customer has received both the goods and the bill they send payment to Premier, which is received via the mail room. Payment consists of both a customer check and a remittance advice, which are opened and sorted by clerks in the mail room. The Check is sent to the Cash receipts department where the payment is recorded in the Cash Receipts journal file. Two copies of a deposit slip are created after the amount is recorded. One copy is entered into the system via the cash receipts terminal, and the other copy along with the customer check is sent to the bank to be deposited. The remittance advice is sent from the mail room to the Accounts Receivable department where it is used to update the Accounts Receivable files.

Finally, at the end of each day both the Sales department and the Accounts Receivable department prepare journal vouchers stating the total effects of the day's transactions. These vouchers are sent to the Accounts Receivable Department, which also acts as the company's general ledger department due to a lack of personnel. Here both vouchers are reconciled and recorded in the general ledger's control accounts.

Required:

a. Create a data flow diagram of the current system.

b. Create a document flowchart of the existing system.

c. Analyze the internal control weaknesses in the system. Model your response according to the six categories of physical control activities specified in SAS 78.

d. Prepare a system flowchart of a redesigned computer-based system that resolves the control weaknesses that you identified.

4. Jasmine Tea!
(Prepared by Meridith Coyne and Gaby Keely, Lehigh University)

Jasmine Tea! is the largest coffee distributor in the Northeast. They distribute specialty tea leaves to coffee shops, cafes, and restaurants. The company headquarters is located in Newark, New Jersey; in addition there are two distribution warehouses located in Philadelphia and Boston.

Established in 1985, the company's first warehouse was located in Newark. Jasmine Tea! began by purchasing and distributing from one Chinese tea supplier. Within two years, sales had doubled and they were seeking more varieties of tea. They now have dozens of suppliers and over 50 varieties of tea. Currently there are 155 employees and annual sales of over $50 million. Last year was their most successful year with an annual sales growth of 6.5 percent.

Jasmine Tea! has been receiving complaints from customers and suppliers about billing, shipping, and payment problems. Under the current operating system each department has independent computer terminals. The complaints and inefficient computer system have triggered the management team to seek alternative solutions that will enable them to better serve their customers and meet the demands.

Sales Procedures

Jasmine Tea's revenue cycle begins when a customer places an order with a sales representative. Orders can be placed by phone or fax. The sales department enters the customer order into a standard sales order format at a computer terminal. This generates six documents, three copies of sales order, a stock release, a shipping notice, and a packing slip. The billing department receives a copy of the sales order, the warehouse receives the stock release and a copy of the sales order and the shipping department receives a shipping notice and packing slip. The sales clerk files a copy of the sales order in the open customer order file.

Upon receipt of the sales order, the billing department creates an invoice and sends it to the customer. The billing clerk enters the sale into the computer terminal. This process records the sale in the sales journal and in the account receivable journal. The journal summaries are sent to the general ledger and the information is posted to the general ledger.

The warehouse receives a copy of the sales order and stock release. A warehouse employee picks the product. The sales order is filed in the warehouse and the product and stock release is sent to the shipping department. A warehouse clerk updates the inventory records at the warehouse computer terminal. The inventory summary is then posted to the general ledger by the general ledger department.

The shipping department receives a shipping notice and packing slip from the sales department. Upon receipt of goods and stock release the shipping clerk prepares the bill of lading at a computer terminal. Two copies of the bill of lading and packing slip are sent with the product to the carrier. The shipping notice is filed. The billing department receives the stock release reconciles with the invoice to determine if the customer was billed for the correct quantity and prices.

Cash Receipts Procedure

The mail room has five employees who open and sort all mail. Each employee has two bins, one for remittance advice and one for checks. The mail clerk opens the mail and separates the remittance advice and the check. The clerk reconciles the check and remittance advice before separating them.

The remittance advice is sent to the accounts receivable. The AR clerk records each remittance advice on the remittance list and then sends a copy to the cash receipts department. The AR clerk updates the customer account and the accounts receivable at a computer terminal. The summary is sent to the general ledger department where it is posted to the general ledger.

The check is sent to the cash receipts department which endorses each check with "for deposit only" and verifies the checks with the remittance list and then records the cash receipts in the cash receipts journal. The clerk sends the check to the bank.

The general ledger department posts all journal summaries at a computer terminal upon receiving them. Copies of the account summaries are kept in the general ledger department.

Required:

a.   Create a data flow diagram of the current system.

b.   Create a document flowchart of the existing system.

c.   Analyze the internal control weaknesses in the system. Model your response according to the six categories of physical control activities specified in SAS 78.

d.   Prepare a system flowchart of a redesigned computer-based system that resolves the control weaknesses that you identified.

5. Music Source, Inc
(Prepared by Jeff Davis, Gen Feldman, and Denise Nuccio, Lehigh University)

Company Information
Music Source, Inc. is a manufacturer of stereo equipment with six sales offices nationwide and one manufacturing plant in Pennsylvania. Currently, employment is at approximately 200 employees. Music Source focuses on the production of high-quality stereo equipment for resale by retailers. Its larger competitors include Sony, Panasonic, and Aiwa. Music Source's suppliers are Nalequip, Inc. and Uniview. Production includes speakers, bases, subwoofers, and other equipment. Currently Music Source is operating at $135,000,000 in annual sales with revenue growth at a rate of 3 percent. Unfortunately, the company has recently been experiencing several operational problems that may be fixed through the improvement of its systems.

Revenue Cycle

Music Source, Inc. has sales departments with seven full-time employees and several part-time sales clerks at each of its sales offices disbursed throughout the nation. The retailers can use different methods to order stereo equipment from Music Source. They can come to the sales centers where they can see the equipment on display before they place an order and they can even purchase the merchandise that day. Retailers can also place their orders by phone or through Music Source's website. Orders start in the sales department, as a customer order comes in from new and past customers, the sales clerk first checks to see if the customer is already has a customer record on file. The sales clerk enters the customer order into the computer as a new sales order along with the orders that have come in since the last computer entry. The sales clerks enter the customer orders into a computerized sales order system periodically throughout the day. As soon as the sales orders are entered, electronic copies of the sales order are sent to the customer, manufacturing plant, and shipping department, and one is filed in the sales department in the open sales order file.

The manufacturing plant makes two hard copies of the sales order. These copies are used as stock release forms that are used to collect raw materials needed and to ensure correct production of the ordered goods. They are sent along with the finished goods to the shipping department. The clerk in the manufacturing department confirms that the correct goods are being moved to the shipping department, signs the two copies of the stock release, and files the electronic copy of the sales order in the completed order file. After filing the sales order, the clerk inputs the updated amount of inventory used for that order into the computer terminal which then generates a journal voucher that will be used to update the general ledger.

When the shipping department receives two copies of the stock release forms from the manufacturing plant, they are verified with the electronic sales order from the sales department. After verification, one stock release form is used as the packing slip and is sent with the goods to the carrier. The other copy of the stock release has shipping charges and other relevant information needed by the billing department added on to it and becomes a shipping slip that is sent on to the billings/Accounts Receivable Department as proof

that the order has been sent. In the shipping department, three copies of the bill of lading are prepared. Two copies of the bill of lading are sent with the packing slip and the goods to the carrier and the other is filed in the shipping department. The electronic copy of the sales order is filed in the shipping department as well.

Once the shipping slip arrives in the billing/Accounts Receivable Department the customer can be billed. The billings clerk prepares a sales invoice from the information on the shipping slip. One copy is sent to the customer as an official bill. The electronic copy is filed in the billings/Accounts Receivable Department in the open invoice file. The shipping document is sent back to the sales department to be used to close the open sales order file. After the sales invoice is sent, the information from the sales invoice is input in to the computer terminal to update the sales journal and the accounts receivable subsidiary ledger and generates a journal voucher that will be used to update the general journal.

Required:

a. Create a data flow diagram of the current system.

b. Create a document flowchart of the existing system.

c. Analyze the internal control weaknesses in the system. Model your response according to the six categories of physical control activities specified in SAS 78.

d. Prepare a system flowchart of a redesigned computer-based system that resolves the control weaknesses that you identified.

6. Aggressive Ski Company
(Prepared by Vlad Yunger, Lehigh University)
Aggressive Ski Company, based out of Aspen, Colorado, manufactures high-performance skis and bindings. Founded in 1973 by a famous retired Olympic skier, the company experienced rapid growth, particularly in the past few years. Aggressive Ski presently holds a 20 percent market share on high-performance skis throughout the world. The company has more than 200 employees. Aggressive ski has offices and manufacturing facilities on both the East and West coasts and is particularly proud of its strong relations with its suppliers and conviction to its clients. The company is always working to

increase the effectiveness of its supply chain for the good of the company and its customers. To maintain a healthy relationship with its customers, Aggressive Ski offers a 2/10 net 30 to its preeminent customers.

The company is looking to implement a new computer-based system that will help relieve some of the problems in the revenue cycle and wants to ensure it has all the proper controls in place, in compliance with the Sarbanes Oxley Act.

Revenue Cycle (Prepared by Vlad Yunger)
Sales Order Processing System

The revenue cycle begins with the customer placing an order. Because most of the customers are buying in bulk for rentals and ski schools, the orders tend to be very large; however, they are not extremely frequent. Thus, a person could handle taking the orders instead or processing by machines. Also a salesperson is able to give customers necessary help to place the correct order, this adds to customer satisfaction. Once the salesperson receives the order, he performs a credit check using the company's credit records. Once the check is complete, he processes the order, puts it in to different formats, and sends them out to different parts of the company. The salesperson prepares six documents using the information from the customer order and the credit records from the credit department. (1) Credit copy, (2) Customer copy, (3) Stock Release, (4) Shipping notice, (5) Packing Slip, and (6) Invoice. Once the documents are prepared the salesperson files the customer order and the authorized credit copy in the customer open order file and sends the customer copy to the customer to check for errors. Then the salesperson sends the stock release document to the warehouse department, the shipping notice and the packing slip to the shipping department, and the invoice to the billing department.

The warehouse manager uses the stock release document to pick out the skis requested by the customer and sends the skis to the shipping department; additionally, he sends the stock release to the inventory department. The shipping clerk receives the shipping notice and the packing slip from the sales department and waits to receive the goods from the warehouse. Once he receives the goods he packages them, prepares a bill of lading, and updates the shipping log. Then he gives the packaged goods along with the bill of lading and the packing slip to the delivery person who comes to pick up outgoing goods everyday.

The shipping notice is sent back to the sales department where it is filed in the customer open order file. A copy of the shipping notice is also sent to the billing department, which triggers the billing process.

The billing department receives the invoice from the sales department and waits for the shipping notice. Once the shipping notice is received by the billing clerk he adds up the prices and finalizes the invoice. He then sends the invoice to the customer and sends a copy of the invoice to the accounts receivable department.

The inventory clerk receives the stock release and updates the inventory subsidiary ledger along with the general ledger. The accounts receivable clerk receives the invoice and updates the accounts receivable records and updates the general ledger.

Cash receipts system

When the customers are billed, they get a postage paid envelope to use when they are sending in their payment. This envelope is yellow to enable the mail clerks to identify envelopes containing payments. The clerks send these directly to the cash receipts department. The clerk opens the envelopes, reconciles the remittance advice with the check, prepares a remittance list, and sends it to the controller. A copy of the remittance advice and the remittance list also are sent to the accounts receivable department. Next, the cash receipts clerk processes the cash receipts by preparing deposit slips for the checks and sends them along with the actual checks to the bank. Two deposit slips are sent to the bank so that once the bank processes the check, one deposit slip is sent back to the company.

Upon receipt of the remittance list and the remittance advice, the accounts receivable clerk accesses the centralized data entry application from a terminal and creates a cash receipts transaction file. The remittance advice and the remittance list are then filed in the department.

A batch program in the data processing department uses the cash receipts transaction file to update the AR subsidiary ledger, update the general ledger, post the transaction to the cash receipts journal and prepare journal vouchers. Also the program yields a management report of cash receipts and a transaction listing of accounts receivable.

The controller receives the remittance list and waits to receive the deposit slip from the bank which signifies that the check has cleared. The controller reconciles the two documents and makes sure there are no discrepancies.

Required:

a. Create a data flow diagram of the current system.

b. Create a document flowchart of the existing system.

c. Analyze the internal control weaknesses in the system. Model your response according to the six categories of physical control activities specified in SAS 78.

d. Prepare a system flowchart of a redesigned computer-based system that resolves the control weaknesses that you identified.

7. Green Mountain Coffee Roasters, Inc.

(Prepared by Lisa McCutchean, Lehigh University)

Green Mountain Coffee Roasters, Inc., was founded in 1981 and began as a small cafe in Waitsfield, Vermont, roasting and serving premium coffee on the premises. Green Mountain blends and distributes coffee to a variety of customers, including cafes, delis, and restaurants, and currently has about 6,700 customer accounts reaching states across the nation. As the company has grown, several beverages have been added to the product line, including signature blends, light and heavy roasts, decaffeinated coffee and teas, and herbal teas. Green Mountain Coffee Roasters, Inc., has been publicly traded since 1993 and had sales in excess of $84 million for the fiscal year ended September 2002.

Green Mountain Coffee has a warehouse and manufacturing plant located in Wilton, Vermont, where it presently employees 250 full- and part-time workers. The company receives its beans in bulk from a select group of distributors located across the world, with their largest supplier being Columbia Beans Co. Green Mountain Coffee also sells accessories that complement their products, including mugs, thermoses, and coffee containers that they purchase from their supplier Coffee Lovers Inc. In addition to selling coffee and accessories, Green Mountain uses paper products such as coffee bags, coffee cups, and stirrers to distribute to their customers and package the coffee that they purchase from Save the Trees Inc.

Sales Order System

The sales process begins when a customer sends a customer order to the sales clerk. The sales clerk first does a credit check using the customer sales history records to authorize the transaction. The sales clerk then prepares a customer copy, a stock release, a file copy, a packing slip, an invoice, and a ledger copy of the sales order. All documents, including the customer order, are filed. Then the invoice, ledger copy, and file copy are sent to the billing department.

The billing department enters all the information from the source documents into the computer, adds prices, and bills the customer. The computer updates the sales journal and a journal voucher is prepared (at end of day) and sent to Vic, the general ledger clerk. The file copy is then filed and the stock release is sent to Sara in the warehouse. A copy of the invoice is mailed to the customer and the ledger copy is sent to the accounts receivable clerk in the accounting department.

Sara then uses the stock release to pick the goods from the shelf. A PC-based inventory system is used to update the inventory subsidiary ledger from the stock release copy. The file copy is filed and the stock release is sent to the shipping department. At the end of the day Sara prepares a journal voucher, which is sent to the general ledger clerk. The shipping clerk, who reconciles the stock release along with the packing slip and file copy, then prepares a bill of lading. The shipping log is updated and the stock release and file copy are filed. The bill of lading and packing slip are given to the carrier along with the goods.

In the accounting department, relevant information taken from the ledger (sent from billing) is entered into the computer to update the accounts receivable records. A summary (end of day) is sent to Vic. The ledger copy is then filed in the accounting department. Vic reconciles the accounts receivable summary with the journal vouchers and updates the general ledger. All documents are then filed.

Cash Receipts System

The mail room clerk receives the checks and remittance advices from the customer. He reconciles the checks with the remittance advices and prepares two copies of a remittance list. The checks and a remittance list are then sent to John, the cash receipts clerk in the accounting department. John uses a PC to process the cash receipts, update the cash receipts journal, and prepare a journal voucher and three deposit slips. The journal voucher is sent to Vic, the general ledger clerk. The checks and two deposit slips are sent to the bank to be deposited into Green Mountain Coffee's account. The third deposit slip and the remittance list are filed. The second remittance list and the remittance advices are sent to Mary, another cash receipts clerk who, using a separate PC, updates the accounts receivable subsidiary ledger and prepares an account summary, which is sent to Vic. The remittance list and the remittance advice are then filed. Vic uses the journal voucher and the account summary to update the general ledger. These two documents are then filed.

Required:

a. Create a data flow diagram of the current system.

b. Create a document flowchart of the existing system.

c. Analyze the internal control weaknesses in the system. Model your response according to the six categories of physical control activities specified in SAS 78.

d. Prepare a system flowchart of a redesigned computer-based system that resolves the control weaknesses that you identified.

8. USA Cycle Company

(Prepared by Byung Hee Pottenger, Lehigh University)

USA Cycle Company is one of the fastest-growing bicycle distributors in the United States, with headquarters in Chicago. Their primary business is distribution of bicycles assembled in China, but they also have a smaller, custom-order business for which they build bicycles from parts purchased from various suppliers. Their product line includes mountain, road, and comfort bikes as well as a juvenile line with up to 24" frames. They also distribute BMX bicycles as well as tricycles and trailer bikes. In addition, they distribute various bicycle accessories such as helmets, clothing, lights, and spare parts for all models they carry.

Established in 1975, the company's first warehouses were in Illinois and Wisconsin and supplied retail bicycle outlets primarily in the Midwest. One year ago, USA Cycle Company expanded, adding two additional facilities in Sacramento, California, and Redmond, Washington, to meet the growing demand for their bicycles. They now also sell customized bicycles direct to retailers through the Internet as well as by conventional means.

The company's expansion to the West Coast was coupled with a planned increase in reliance on suppliers in China. Although this resulted in decreased costs, some problems regarding inventory levels arose due to unexpected delays in shipping, primarily attributable to miscommunication and shipping conditions. Because the company does not want to carry excess inventory, they are sometimes forced to seek local suppliers at an increased cost.

USA Cycle Company uses limited computer technology to process business transactions and record accounting data, but the data is distributed and not shared throughout the company. This has caused data redundancy and associated problems of data currency, and these problems have been exacerbated by the company's recent rapid expansion on the West Coast.

Initially USA Cycle Company was a family-owned business. In need of capital for expansion, the company went public when they added the two facilities on the West Coast. The number of employees rose from 100 to 200 during the expansion. Gross sales also rose from $10 million to $20 million.

Description of Sales Order Procedures

The USA Cycle Company sales order process begins when a sales representative takes an order from the customer over the phone or fax (for established customers) and prepares the customer order. The sales clerk uses a PC to input the customer order into one of two different data files, either the custom-design order file or the regular order file. The system manager in the sales department periodically checks the web server for orders that come in through the Internet and prints these orders for the sales clerk to enter as sales orders.

At the end of the day, the sales clerk updates the customer file from the regular sales order file and the custom-design sales order file, and prints three copies of the sales orders, including a factory order for each custom-design order. The clerk forwards the sales orders to the warehouse where goods are retrieved from inventory and shipped to the customer. The clerk also sends the factory orders for custom-design bicycles to the factory for assembly. One copy of the sales order is filed in the open customer order file for use in answering customer inquires. The last copy of the sales order is sent to the billing department for preparation of the sales invoice.

Once the warehouse receives a sales order, a warehouse worker retrieves the goods and accesses the warehouse department PC to update the inventory and general ledger using an inventory management application program. Another worker packs the goods and prepares two copies of the bill of lading as well as a packing slip. The packing slip is attached to the shipping container and the two copies of the bill of lading are sent to the shipping company along with the goods. The worker also prepares a shipping notice that is sent to the billing department along with a bill of lading, sales order, and a factory order (if the goods were for a custom-designed bicycle).

When the factory receives a factory order for a custom-designed bicycle from the sales department, a factory worker prepares a material-release form and sends it to the warehouse for the materials. After the worker assembles the product according to the specifications of the order, the factory order and the finished product are sent to the warehouse where the shipping documents are prepared and the goods are shipped to the customer in the same way as other sales orders.

After receiving the sales order from the sales department, the billing/accounts receivable department clerk files it in a temporary file until the shipping notice, the bill of lading, and the sales order or factory order have arrived from the warehouse. Once the shipping notice and other documents have arrived, the clerk reviews these documents along with the sales order from the temporary file and prepares two copies of the sales invoice using the billing/accounts receivable department PC, which automatically records the sale in the sales journal and updates the accounts receivable subsidiary ledger and the general ledger. One copy of the sales invoice is mailed to the customer and the other is forwarded to the sales department, which closes the open customer order file. After closing the open customer order

file, all documents in the file are sent to the billing/accounts receivable department. These documents are then filed in the accounts receivable pending file along with other documents received by the billing/accounts receivable department to await customer payment.

Description of Sales Return Procedures

When goods are returned to the receiving department, the receiving clerk counts and inspects the returned goods, and then prepares two returned goods slips. Following this, the manager in the receiving department evaluates the circumstances of the return and decides whether to grant credit, and stamps the slips accordingly. Afterward, the goods are sent to the warehouse with one of the stamped return slips. In the warehouse, a warehouse employee enters the information on the warehouse department PC, which updates the inventory records and automatically posts to the general ledger. The second stamped slip is sent to the billing/accounts receivable department where the sales journal, accounts receivable subsidiary ledger, and general ledger are automatically updated by crediting the customer account. Both return slips are filed by billing/accounts receivable in the returned goods file for future business evaluation.

Description of Cash Receipts Procedures

All of USA Cycle's mail arrives in the mail room in the cash receipts department. A cash receipts clerk in the mail room opens all the mail and separates the checks and remittance advices and endorses all the checks "for deposit only." Afterward, the clerk records each check on a remittance list, and sends one copy of the remittance list to the billing/accounts receivable department along with the remittance advices. Then the clerk prepares a bank deposit slip and updates the cash receipts journal on the cash receipts department's PC, which automatically posts to the general ledger as well. Later that day, the cash receipts manager deposits the checks in the bank. In the billing/accounts receivable department a clerk updates customer accounts on the department's PC with the information from the remittance advices, which automatically updates the accounts receivable subsidiary and general ledgers. The billing/accounts receivable clerk also closes the accounts receivable pending file for invoices that have been paid in full.

Finally the clerk files all source documents along with the remittance list and remittance advices in the sales history file.

Required:

a.   Create a data flow diagram of the current system.

b.   Create a document flowchart of the existing system.

c.   Analyze the internal control weaknesses in the system. Model your response according to the six categories of physical control activities specified in SAS 78.

d.   Prepare a system flowchart of a redesigned computer-based system that resolves the control weaknesses that you identified.

chapter 5

The Expenditure Cycle Part I: Purchases and Cash Disbursements Procedures

LEARNING OBJECTIVES

After studying this chapter, you should:

- Recognize the fundamental tasks that constitute the purchases and cash disbursements process.
- Be able to identify the functional areas involved in purchases and cash disbursements activities and trace the flow of these transactions through the organization.
- Be able to specify the documents, journals, and accounts that provide audit trails, promote the maintenance of historical records, and support internal decision making and financial reporting.
- Understand the exposures associated with purchases and cash disbursements activities and recognize the controls that reduce these risks.
- Be aware of the operational features and the control implications of technology used in purchases and cash disbursements systems.

The objective of the expenditure cycle is to convert the organization's cash into the physical materials and the human resources it needs to conduct business. In this chapter we concentrate on systems and procedures for acquiring raw materials and finished goods from suppliers. We examine payroll and fixed asset systems in the next chapter.

Most business entities operate on a credit basis and do not pay for resources until after acquiring them. The time lag between these events splits the procurement process into two phases: (1) the physical phase, involving the acquisition of the resource; and (2) the financial phase, involving the disbursement of cash. As a practical matter, these are treated as independent transactions that are processed through separate subsystems.

This chapter examines the principal features of the two major subsystems that constitute the expenditure cycle: (1) the purchases processing subsystem, and (2) the cash disbursements subsystem. The chapter is organized into two main sections. The first section provides an overview of the conceptual system including the logical tasks, the key entities, the sources and uses of information, and the flow of key documents through an organization. The second section deals with the physical system. We first use a manual system to reinforce the readers understanding of key concepts. We then examine several computer-based systems, focusing on the operational and control implications of alternative data processing methods.

THE CONCEPTUAL SYSTEM

OVERVIEW OF PURCHASES AND CASH DISBURSEMENTS ACTIVITIES

In this section we examine the expenditure cycle conceptually. Using dataflow diagrams (DFDs) as a guide, we will trace the sequence of activities through two of the processes that constitute the expenditure cycle for most retail, wholesale, and manufacturing organizations. These are: purchases processing and cash disbursements procedures. Payroll and fixed asset systems, which also support the expenditure cycle, are covered in Chapter 6.

As in the previous chapter, this discussion is intended to be technology neutral. The tasks described in this section may be performed manually or by computer. At this point our focus is on *what* (conceptually) needs to be done, not *how* (physically) it is accomplished. At various stages in the processes we will examine specific documents, journals, and ledgers as they are encountered. Again, this review is technology neutral. These documents and files may be physical (hard copy) or digital (computer generated). Later in the chapter we examine examples of physical systems.

Purchases Processing Procedures

Purchases procedures include the tasks involved in identifying inventory needs, placing the order, receiving the inventory, and recognizing the liability. The relationships between these tasks are presented with the DFD in Figure 5-1. In general, these procedures apply to both manufacturing and retailing firms. A major difference between the two business types lies in the way purchases are authorized. Manufacturing firms purchase raw materials for production and their purchasing decisions are authorized by the production planning and control function. These procedures are described in Chapter 7. Merchandising firms purchase finished goods for resale. The inventory control function provides the purchase authorization for this type of firm.

Monitor Inventory Records. Firms deplete their inventories by transferring raw materials into the production process (the conversion cycle) and by selling finished goods to customers (revenue cycle). Our illustration assumes the latter case, in which inventory control monitors and records finished goods inventory levels. When inventories drop to a predetermined reorder point, a **purchase requisition** is prepared and sent to the prepare purchase order function to initiate the purchase process. Figure 5-2 presents an example of a purchase requisition.

While procedures will vary from firm to firm, typically a separate purchase requisition will be prepared for each inventory item as the need is recognized. This can result in multiple purchase requisitions for a given vendor. These purchase requisitions need to be combined into a single purchase order (discussed next), which is then sent to the vendor. In this type of system, each purchase order will be associated with one or more purchase requisitions.

Prepare Purchase Order. The prepare purchase order function receives the purchase requisitions, which are sorted by vendor if necessary. Next, a **purchase order** (PO) is prepared for each vendor, as illustrated in Figure 5-3. A copy of the PO is sent to the vendor. In addition, a copy is sent to the set up accounts payable function for filing temporarily in the AP pending file and a *blind copy* is sent to the receive goods function, where it is held until the inventories arrive. The last copy is filed in the **open/close purchase order file**.

To make the purchasing process efficient, the inventory control function will supply much of the routine ordering information needed by the purchasing department directly

FIGURE 5-1   DFD for Purchase System

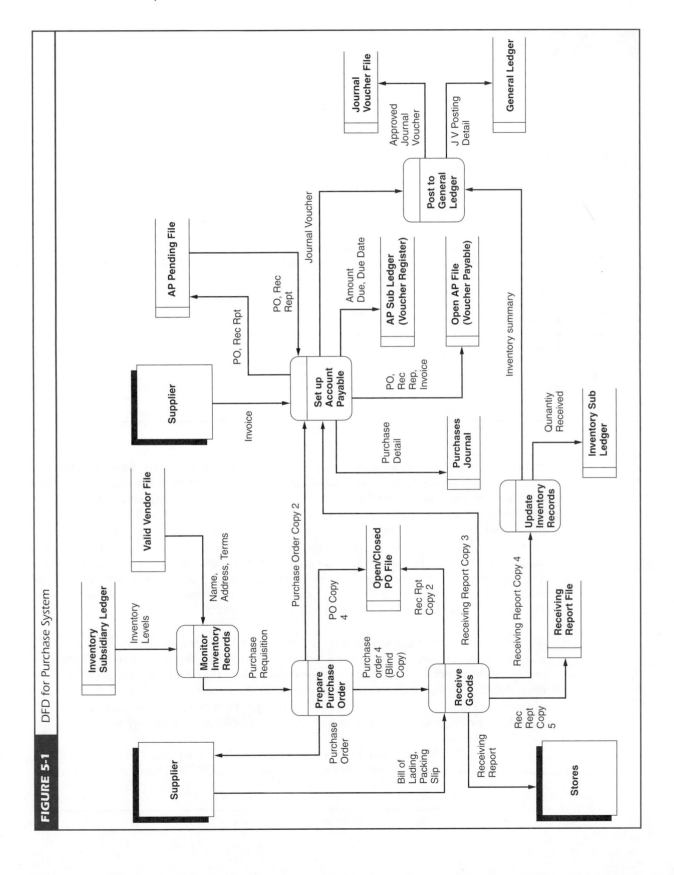

FIGURE 5-2 Purchase Requisition

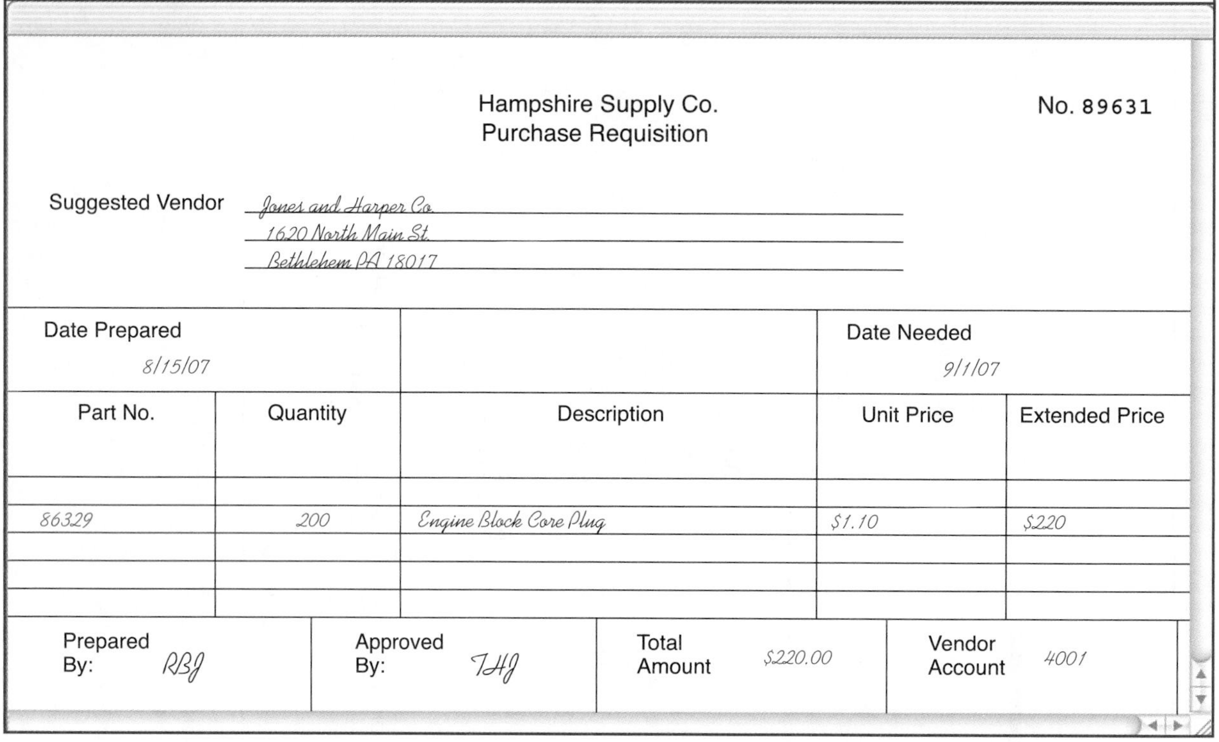

from the inventory and **valid vendor** files. This information includes the name and address of the primary supplier, the economic order quantity (EOQ)[1] of the item, and the standard or expected unit cost of the item. This allows the purchasing department to devote its efforts to meeting scarce, expensive, or unusual inventory needs. To obtain the best prices and terms on special items, the purchasing department may need to prepare detailed product specifications and request bids from competing vendors. Dealing with routine purchases as efficiently as good control permits is desirable in all organizations. The valid vendor file contributes to both control and efficiency by listing only those vendors approved to do business with the organization. This reference helps to reduce certain vendor fraud schemes discussed in Chapter 3.

Receive Goods. Most firms encounter a time lag (sometimes a significant one) between placing the order and receiving the inventory. During this time, the copies of the PO reside in temporary files in various departments. Note that no economic event has yet occurred. At this point, the firm has received no inventories and incurred no financial obligation. Hence, there is no basis for making a formal entry into any accounting record. However, firms often make memo entries of pending inventory receipts and associated obligations.

The next event in the expenditure cycle is the receipt of the inventory. Goods arriving from the vendor are reconciled with the blind copy of the PO. The **blind copy**, illustrated

---

1 The economic order quantity model and other inventory models are covered in Chapter 7.

FIGURE 5-3	Purchase Order

Hampshire Supply Co.
Purchase Order

No. 23591

Please show the
above number on all
shipping documents
and invoices

To :   *Jones and Harper Co.*
        1620 North Main St.
        Bethlehem PA 18017

Vendor Number	Date Ordered		Date Needed	Purchasing Agent	Terms
4001		*8/15/07*	*9/1/07*	*J. Buell*	*2/10, n/30*

Purchase Req. No.	Part No.	Quantity	Description	Unit Price	Extended Price
89631	*86329*	*200*	*Engine Block Core Plug*	*$ 1.10*	*$220.00*
89834	*20671*	*100*	*Brake Shoes*	*9.50*	*950.00*
89851	*45218*	*10*	*Spring Compressors*	*33.00*	*330.00*

Prepared By : *BKG*	Approved By : *RMS*	Total Amount *$1,500.00*

in Figure 5-4, contains no quantity or price information about the products being received. The purpose of the blind copy is to force the receiving clerk to count and inspect inventories prior to completing the receiving report. At times, receiving docks are very busy and receiving staff under pressure to unload the delivery trucks and sign the bill of lading so the truck drivers can go on their way. If receiving clerks are provided with quantity information, they may be tempted to accept deliveries on the basis of this information alone, rather than verify the quantity and condition of the goods being received. Shipments that are short or contain damaged or incorrect items must be detected before the goods are accepted by the firm and placed into inventory. The blind copy is an important device in reducing this exposure.

Upon completion of the physical count and inspection, the receiving clerk prepares a **receiving report** stating the quantity and condition of the inventories. Figure 5-5 contains an example of a receiving report. One copy of the receiving report accompanies the physical inventories to either the raw materials storeroom or finished goods warehouse for safekeeping. Another copy is filed in the Open/closed PO file to close out the purchase order. A third copy of the receiving report is sent to the accounts payable department, where it is filed in the **accounts payable pending file**. A fourth copy of the receiving report is sent to inventory control for updating the inventory records. Finally, a copy of the receiving report is placed in the **receiving report file**.

Update Inventory Records. Depending on the inventory valuation method in place, the inventory control procedures may vary somewhat among firms. Organizations that use a **standard cost system** carry their inventories at a predetermined standard value regardless

FIGURE 5-4	Blind Copy Purchase Order

Hampshire Supply Co.
Purchase Order

No. 23591

Please show the
above number on all
shipping documents
and invoices

To :   Jones and Harper Co.
        1620 North Main St.
        Bethlehem PA 18017

Vendor Number	Date Ordered		Date Needed	Purchasing Agent	Terms
4001		8/15/07	9/1/07	J. Buell	2/10, n/30

Purchase Req. No.	Part No.	Quantity	Description	Unit Price	Extended Price
89631	86329		Engine Block Core Plug		
89834	20671		Brake Shoes		
89851	45218		Spring Compressors		

Prepared By :	BKG	Approved By :	RMS	Total Amount	

FIGURE 5-5	Receiving Report

Hampshire Supply Co.
Receiving Report

No. 62311

Vendor	Jones and Harper Co.	Shipped Via :	Vendor
Purchase Order No.	23591	Date Received	9/1/07

Part No.	Quantity	Description	Condition
86329	200	Engine Block Core Plug	Good
20671	100	Brake Shoes	Good
45218	10	Spring Compressors	Ear on one unit bent

Received By:	Inspected By:	Delivered To:
RTS	LEW	DYT

of the price actually paid to the vendor. Figure 5-6 presents a copy of a standard cost inventory ledger.

Posting to a standard cost inventory ledger requires only information about the quantities received. Because the receiving report contains quantity information, it serves this purpose. Updating an **actual cost inventory ledger** requires additional financial information, such as a copy of the supplier's invoice when it arrives.

Set Up Accounts Payable. During the course of this transaction, the set up accounts payable function has received and temporarily filed copies of the purchase order and receiving report. The organization has received inventories from the vendor and has incurred (realized) an obligation to pay for the goods.

At this point in the process, however, the firm has not received the **supplier's invoice**[2] containing the financial information needed to record the transaction. The firm will thus defer recording (recognizing) the liability until the invoice arrives. This common situation creates a slight lag (a few days) in the recording process, during which time the firm's liabilities are technically understated. As a practical matter, this misstatement is a problem only at period end when the firm prepares financial statements. To close the books, the accountant will need to estimate the value of the obligation until the invoice arrives. If the estimate is materially incorrect, an adjusting entry must be made to correct the error. Because AP procedures are typically triggered by the receipt of the invoice, accountants need to be aware that unrecorded liabilities may exist at period-end closing.

When the invoice arrives, the accounts payable clerk reconciles the financial information with the receiving report and purchase order in the pending file. This is called a threeway match, which verifies that what was ordered was received and is fairly priced. Once the reconciliation is complete, the transaction is recorded in the purchases journal and posted to the supplier's account in the **accounts payable subsidiary ledger**. Figure 5-7 shows the relationship between these accounting records.

Recall that the inventory valuation method will determine how inventory control will have recorded the receipt of inventories. If the firm is using the actual cost method, the

FIGURE 5-6	Inventory Subsidiary Ledger Using Standard Cost

HAMPSHIRE MACHINE CO.

Perpetual Inventory Record Item   #86329

Item Description	Units Received	Units Sold	Qnty On Hand	Reorder Point	Qnty On Order	EOC	Vendor Number	Standard Cost	Total Inven. Cost
Engine Block Core Plug	200		200	30		200	4001	1.10	220
		30	170						187
		20	150						165

2 Note that the supplier's invoice in the buyer's expenditure cycle is the sales invoice of the supplier's revenue cycle.

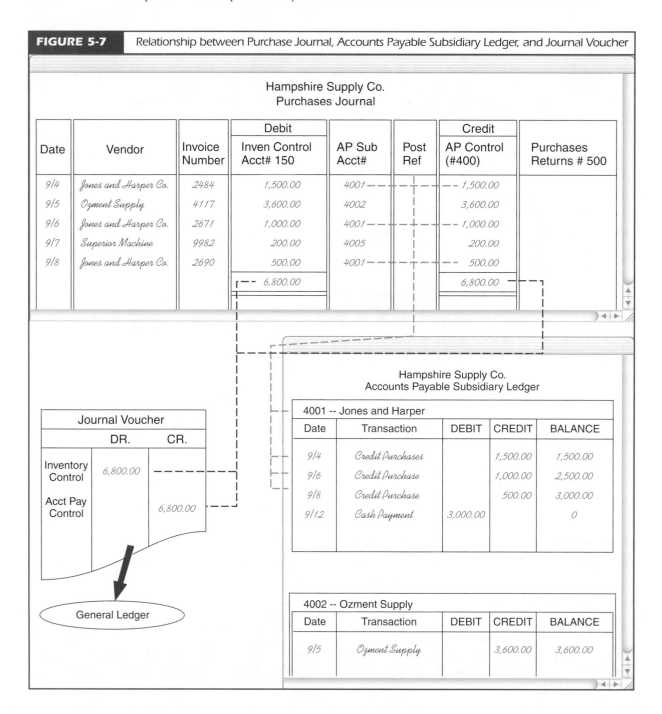

FIGURE 5-7   Relationship between Purchase Journal, Accounts Payable Subsidiary Ledger, and Journal Voucher

accounts payable clerk would send a copy of the supplier's invoice to inventory control. If standard costing is used, this step is not necessary.

After recording the liability, the accounts payable clerk transfers all source documents (purchase order, receiving report, and invoice) to the **open accounts payable file.** Typically, this file is organized by payment due date and scanned daily to ensure that debts are paid on the last possible date without missing due dates and losing discounts. We examine cash disbursements procedures later in this section. Finally, the accounts payable clerk summarizes the entries in the purchases journal for the period (or batch) and prepares a journal voucher for the general ledger function (see Figure 5-7). Assuming the organization uses the perpetual inventory method, the journal entry will be:

	DR	CR
Inventory—Control	6,800.00	
Accounts Payable—Control		6,800.00

If the periodic inventory method is used, the entry will be:

	DR	CR
Purchases	6,800.00	
Accounts Payable—Control		6,800.00

Vouchers Payable System

Rather than the accounts payable procedures described in the previous section, many firms use a **vouchers payable system**. Under this system, the accounts payable department uses **cash disbursement vouchers** and maintains a voucher register. After the AP clerk performs the three-way match, he or she prepares a cash disbursement voucher to approve payment. Vouchers provide improved control over cash disbursements and allow firms to consolidate several payments to the same supplier on a single voucher, thus reducing the number of checks written. Figure 5-8 shows an example of a voucher.

Each voucher is recorded in the **voucher register,** as illustrated in Figure 5-9. The voucher register reflects the accounts payable liability of the firm. The sum of the unpaid vouchers in the register (those with no check numbers and paid dates) is the firm's total accounts payable balance. The accounts payable clerk files the cash disbursement voucher, along with supporting source documents, in the **vouchers payable file.** This file is

FIGURE 5-8   Cash Disbursement Voucher

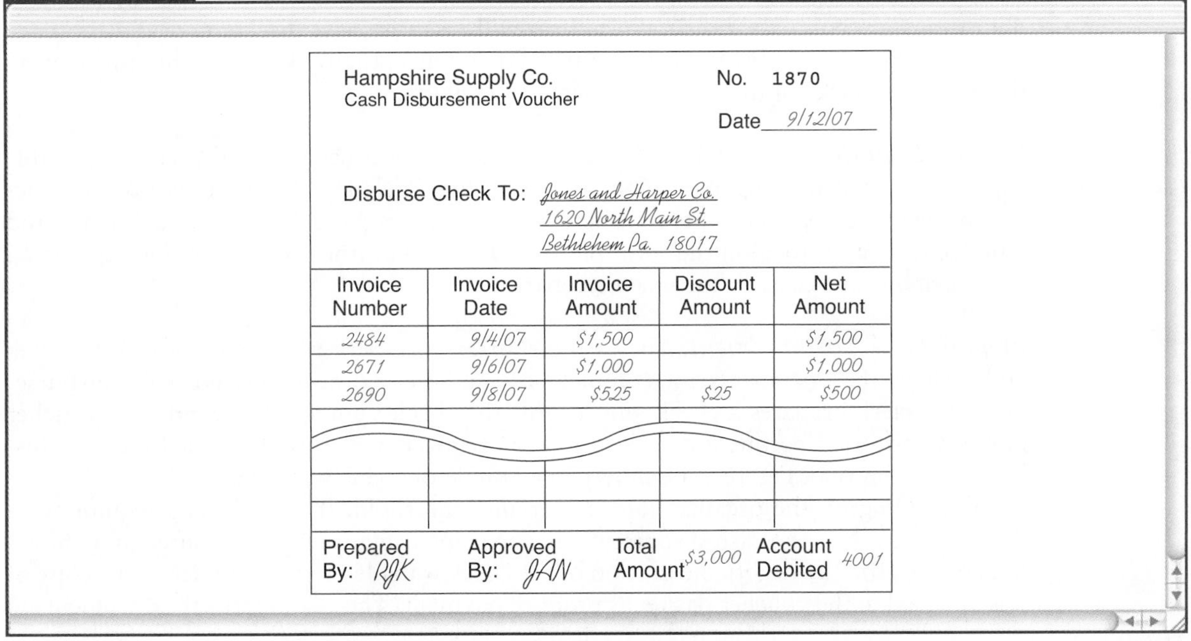

Hampshire Supply Co.
Cash Disbursement Voucher

No.   1870

Date 9/12/07

Disburse Check To: Jones and Harper Co.
1620 North Main St.
Bethlehem Pa. 18017

Invoice Number	Invoice Date	Invoice Amount	Discount Amount	Net Amount
2484	9/4/07	$1,500		$1,500
2671	9/6/07	$1,000		$1,000
2690	9/8/07	$525	$25	$500

Prepared By: RJK	Approved By: JAN	Total Amount $3,000	Account Debited 4001

FIGURE 5-9	Voucher Register

Hampshire Supply Co.
Voucher Register

Date	Voucher No.	Paid		Voucher Payable (credit)	Merchandise Debit	Supplies Debit	Selling Expense Debit	Administrative Expense Debit	Fixed Assets Debit	Misc. Debits	
		Check No.	Date							Acct. No.	Amount
9/12/07	1870	104	9/14	3,000	3,000						
9/13/07	1871			3,600		3,600					
9/14/07	1872	105	9/15	500			500				

equivalent to the open accounts payable file discussed earlier and also is organized by due date. The DFD in Figure 5-1 illustrates both liability recognition methods.

Post to General Ledger. The general ledger function receives a journal voucher from the accounts payable department and an account summary from inventory control. The general ledger function posts from the journal voucher to the inventory and accounts payable control accounts and reconciles the inventory control account and the inventory subsidiary summary. The approved journal vouchers are then posted to the journal voucher file. With this step, the purchases phase of the expenditure cycle is completed.

THE CASH DISBURSEMENTS SYSTEMS

The cash disbursements system processes the payment of obligations created in by purchases system. The principal objective of this system is to ensure that only valid creditors receive payment and that amounts paid are timely and correct. If the system makes payments early, the firm forgoes interest income that it could have earned on the funds. If obligations are paid late, however, the firm will lose purchase discounts or may damage its credit standing. Figure 5-10 presents a DFD conceptually depicting the information flows and key tasks of the cash disbursements system.

Identify Liabilities Due. The cash disbursements process begins in the accounts payable department by identifying items that have come due. Each day, the accounts payable function reviews the open accounts payable file (or vouchers payable file) for such items and sends payment approval in the form of a **voucher packet** (the voucher and/or supporting documents) to the cash disbursements department.

Prepare Cash Disbursement. The cash disbursements clerk receives the voucher packet and reviews the documents for completeness and clerical accuracy. For each disbursement, the clerk prepares a check and records the check number, dollar amount, voucher number, and other pertinent data in the **check register**, which is also called the **cash disbursements journal**. Figure 5-11 shows an example of a check register.

Depending on the organization's materiality threshold, the check may require additional approval by the cash disbursements department manager, or treasurer (not shown in Figure 5-10). The negotiable portion of the check is mailed to the supplier, and a copy of it is attached to the voucher packet as proof of payment. The clerk marks the documents in

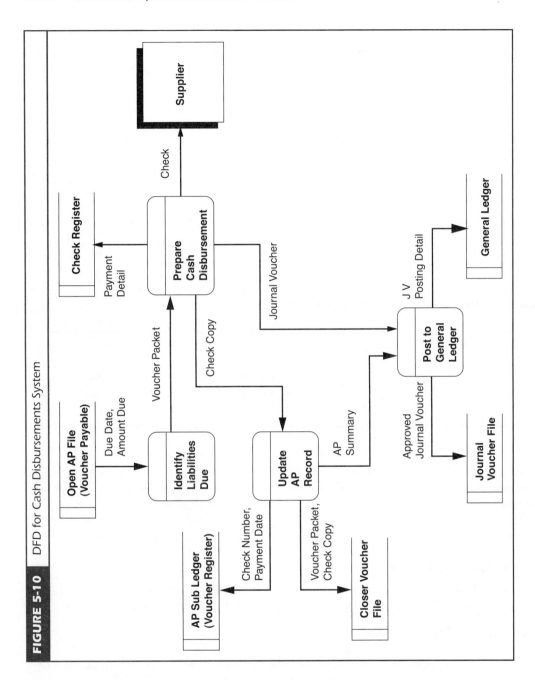

FIGURE 5-10   DFD for Cash Disbursements System

the voucher packets paid and returns them to the accounts payable. Finally, the cash disbursements clerk summarizes the entries made to the check register and sends a journal voucher with the following journal entry to the general ledger department:

	DR	CR
Accounts Payable	XXXX.XX	
Cash		XXXX.XX

| FIGURE 5-11 | Cash Disbursements Journal (Check Register) |

Cash Disbursements Journal

Date	Check No.	Voucher No.	Description	Credit		GL / Subsidiary Account Debited	Posted	Vouch Pay 401	Freight-in 516	Op Expen 509	Other	Posted
				Cash	Purch. Disc.							
9/4/07	101	1867	Martin Motors	500		Auto					500	✓
9/4/07	102	1868	Pen Power	100		Utility	✓			100		
9/12/07	103	1869	Acme Auto	500		Purchases					500	✓
9/14/07	104	1870	Jones and Harper	3,000				3,000				

Update AP Record. Upon receipt of the voucher packet, the accounts payable clerk removes the liability by debiting the AP subsidiary account or by recording the check number and payment date in the voucher register. The voucher packet is filed in the **closed voucher file** and an account summary is prepared and sent to the general ledger function.

Post to General Ledger. The general ledger function receives the journal voucher from cash disbursements and the account summary from accounts payable. The voucher shows the total reductions in the firm's obligations and cash account as a result of payments to suppliers. These numbers are reconciled with the AP summary and the accounts payable control and cash accounts in the general ledger are updated accordingly. The approved journal voucher is then filed. This concludes the cash disbursements procedures.

EXPENDITURE CYCLE CONTROLS

This section describes the primary internal controls in the expenditure cycle according to the control procedures specified in SAS 78. The main points are summarized in Table 5-1.

Transaction Authorization

Purchases Subsystem. The inventory control function continually monitors inventory levels. As inventory levels drop to their predetermined reorder points, inventory control formally authorizes replenishment with a purchase requisition.

Formalizing the authorization process promotes efficient inventory management and ensures the legitimacy of purchases transactions. Without this step, purchasing agents could purchase inventories at their own discretion, being in a position both to authorize and to process the purchase transactions. Unauthorized purchasing can result in excessive inventory levels for some items, while others go out of stock. Either situation is potentially damaging to the firm. Excessive inventories tie up the organization's cash reserves, and stock-outs cause lost sales and manufacturing delays.

TABLE 5-1	Summary of Expenditure Cycle Controls	
CONTROL POINTS IN THE EXPENDITURE CYCLE		
Control Activity	**Purchases Processing System**	**Cash Disbursements System**
Transactions authorization	Inventory control.	Accounts payable authorizes payment.
Segregation of duties	Inventory control separate from purchasing and inventory custody. AP subsidiary ledger separate from the general ledger.	Separate AP subsidiary ledger, cash disbursements, and general ledger functions.
Supervision	Receiving area.	
Accounting records	AP subsidiary ledger, general ledger, purchases requisition file, purchase order file, receiving report file.	Voucher payable file, AP subsidiary ledger, cash disbursements journal, general ledger cash accounts.
Access	Security of physical assets. Limit access to the accounting records above.	Proper security over cash. Limit access to the accounting records above.
Independent verification	Accounts payable reconciles source documents before liability is recorded. General ledger reconciles overall accuracy of process.	Final review by cash disbursements. Overall reconciliation by general ledger. Periodic bank reconciliation by controller.

Cash Disbursements Subsystem. The accounts payable function authorizes cash disbursements via the cash disbursement voucher. To provide effective control over the flow of cash from the firm, the cash disbursements function should not write checks without this explicit authorization. A cash disbursements journal (check register) containing the voucher number authorizing each check (see Figure 5-11) provides an audit trail for verifying the authenticity of each check written.

Segregation of Duties

Segregation of Inventory Control from the Warehouse. Within the purchases subsystem, the primary physical asset is inventory. Inventory control keeps the detailed records of the asset, while the warehouse has custody. At any point, an auditor should be able to reconcile inventory records to the physical inventory.

Segregation of the General Ledger and Accounts Payable from Cash Disbursements. The asset subject to exposure in the cash disbursements subsystem is cash. The records controlling this asset are the accounts payable subsidiary ledger and the cash account in the general ledger. An individual with the combined responsibilities of writing checks, posting to the cash account, and maintaining accounts payable could perpetrate fraud against the firm. For instance, an individual with such access could withdraw cash and then adjust the cash account accordingly to hide the transaction. Also, he or she could establish fraudulent accounts payable (to an associate in a nonexistent vendor company) and then write checks to discharge the phony obligations. By segregating these functions we greatly reduce this type of exposure.

Supervision

In the expenditure cycle, the area that most benefits from supervision is the receiving department. Large quantities of valuable assets flow through this area on their way to the warehouse. Close supervision here reduces the chances of two types of exposure: (1) failure to properly inspect the assets and (2) the theft of assets.

Inspection of Assets. When goods arrive from the supplier, receiving clerks must inspect items for proper quantities and condition (damage, spoilage, and so on). For this reason, the receiving clerk receives a blind copy of the original purchase order from purchasing. A blind purchase order has all the relevant information about the goods being received except for the quantities and prices. To obtain quantities information, which is needed for the receiving report, the receiving personnel are forced to physically count and inspect the goods. If receiving clerks were provided with quantity information via an open purchase order, they may be tempted to transfer this information to the receiving report without performing a physical count.

Inspecting and counting the items received protects the firm from incomplete orders and damaged goods. Supervision is critical at this point to ensure that the clerks properly carry out these important duties. Incoming goods are often accompanied by a packing slip containing quantity information that could be used to circumvent the inspection process. A supervisor should take custody of the packing slip while receiving clerks count and inspect the goods.

Theft of Assets. Receiving departments are sometimes hectic and cluttered during busy periods. In this environment, incoming inventories are exposed to theft until they are securely placed in the warehouse. Improper inspection procedures coupled with inadequate supervision can create a situation that is conducive to the theft of inventories in transit.

Accounting Records

The control objective of accounting records is to maintain an audit trail adequate for tracing a transaction from its source document to the financial statements. The expenditure cycle employs the following accounting records: accounts payable subsidiary ledger, voucher register, check register, and general ledger. The auditor's concern in the expenditure cycle is that obligations may be materially understated on financial statements because of unrecorded transactions. This is a normal occurrence at year-end closing simply because some supplier invoices do not arrive in time to record the liabilities. This also happens, however, as an attempt to intentionally misstate financial information. Hence, in addition to the routine accounting records, expenditure cycle systems must be designed to provide supporting information, such as the purchase requisition file, the purchase order file, and the receiving report file. By reviewing these peripheral files, auditors may obtain evidence of inventory purchases that have not been recorded as liabilities.

Access Controls

Direct Access. In the expenditure cycle, a firm must control access to physical assets such as cash and inventory. These control concerns are essentially the same as in the revenue cycle. Direct access controls include locks, alarms, and restricted access to areas that contain inventories and cash.

Indirect Access. A firm must limit access to documents that control its physical assets. For example, an individual with access to purchase requisitions, purchase orders, and receiving reports has the ingredients to construct a fraudulent purchase transaction. With the proper supporting documents, a fraudulent transaction can be made to look legitimate to the system and could be paid.

Independent Verification

Independent Verification by Accounts Payable. The accounts payable function plays a vital role in the verification of the work done by others in this system. Copies of key source documents flow into this department for review and comparison. Each document contains unique facts about the purchase transaction, which the accounts payable clerk must reconcile before the firm recognizes an obligation. These include:

1. The purchase order, which shows that the purchasing agent ordered only the needed inventories from a valid vendor.[3] This document should reconcile with the purchase requisition.
2. The receiving report, which is evidence of the physical receipt of the goods, their condition, and the quantities received. The reconciliation of this document with the purchase order signifies that the organization has a legitimate obligation.
3. The supplier's invoice, which provides the financial information needed to record the obligation as an account payable. The accounts payable clerk verifies that the prices on the invoice are reasonable compared with the expected prices on the purchase order.

Independent Verification by the General Ledger Department. The general ledger function provides an important independent verification in the system. It receives journal vouchers and summary reports from inventory control, accounts payable, and cash disbursements. From these sources, the general ledger function verifies that the total obligations recorded equal the total inventories received and that the total reductions in accounts payable equal the total disbursements of cash.

PHYSICAL SYSTEMS

In this section we examine the physical system. This begins with a review of manual procedures and then moves on to deal with several forms of computer-based systems. As mentioned in the previous chapter, manual systems are covered here as a visual training aid to promote a better understanding of the concepts presented in the previous section. From this point, therefore, the reader may continue with the review of manual systems or, without loss of technical content, bypass this material and go directly to computer-based systems located on page 249.

A MANUAL SYSTEM

The purpose of this section is to support the conceptual treatment of systems presented in the previous section. This should help the reader envision the relationships between organizational units, the segregation of duties, and the information flows essential to operations and effective internal control. In addition, we will highlight inefficiencies intrinsic to manual systems, which gave rise to improved technologies and techniques used by modern systems. The following discussion is based on Figure 5-12, which presents a flowchart of a manual purchases system.

---

3   Firms often establish a list of valid vendors with whom they do regular business. Purchasing agents must acquire inventories only from valid vendors. This technique deters certain types of fraud such as an agent buying from suppliers with whom he or she has a relationship (a relative or friend) or buying at excessive prices from vendors in exchange for a kickback or bribe.

FIGURE 5-12   Manual Purchase System

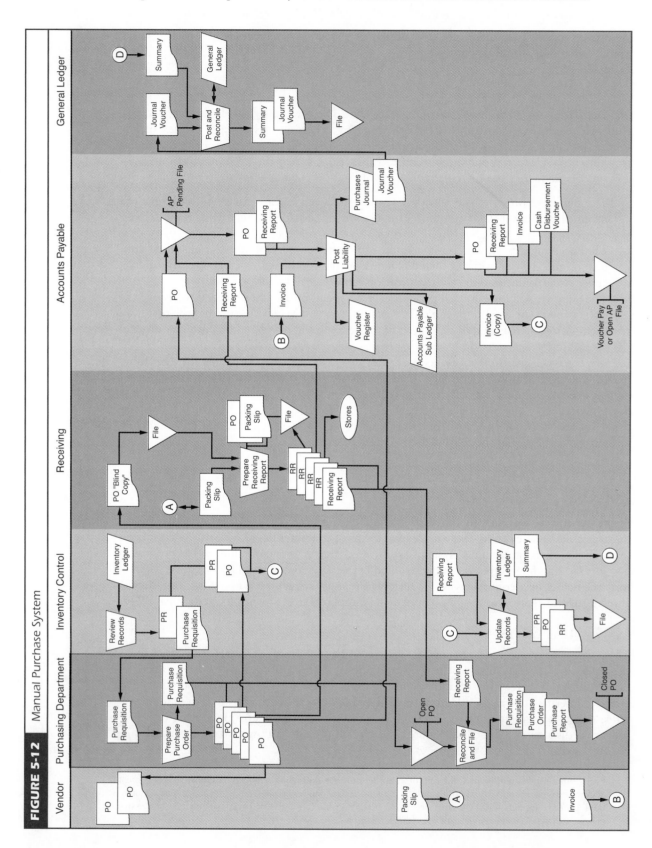

Inventory Control

When inventories drop to a predetermined reorder point, the clerk prepares a **purchase requisition**. One copy of the requisition is sent to the purchasing department, and one copy is placed in the **open purchase requisition file**. Note that to provide proper authorization control, the inventory control department is segregated from the purchasing department, which executes the transaction.

Purchasing Department

The purchasing department receives the purchase requisitions, sorts them by vendor, and prepares a multipart **purchase order** (PO) for each vendor. Two copies of the PO are sent to the vendor. One copy of the PO is sent to inventory control, where the clerk files it with the open purchase requisition. One copy of the PO is sent to accounts payable for filing in the AP pending file. One copy (the *blind copy*) is sent to the receiving department, where it is filed until the inventories arrive. The clerk files the last copy along with the purchase requisition in the **open purchase order file**.

Receiving

Goods arriving from the vendor are reconciled with the blind copy of the PO. Upon completion of the physical count and inspection, the receiving clerk prepares a multipart **receiving report** stating the quantity and condition of the inventories. One copy of the receiving report accompanies the physical inventories to storeroom. Another copy is sent to the purchasing department, where the purchasing clerk reconciles it with the open PO. The clerk closes the open PO by filing the purchase requisition, the PO, and the receiving report in the **closed purchase order file**.

A third copy of the receiving report is sent to inventory control where (assuming a standard cost system) the inventory subsidiary ledger is updated. A fourth copy of the receiving report is sent to the accounts payable department, where it is filed in the accounts payable pending file. The final copy of the receiving report is filed in the receiving department.

Accounts Payable Department

When the invoice arrives, the accounts payable clerk reconciles the financial information with the documents in the pending file, records the transaction in the purchases journal, and posts it to the supplier's account in the accounts payable subsidiary ledger (voucher register). After recording the liability, the accounts payable clerk transfers the source documents (purchase order, receiving report, and invoice) to the **open vouchers payable (accounts payable) file**.

General Ledger Department

The general ledger department receives a journal voucher from the accounts payable department and an account summary from inventory control. The general ledger clerk reconciles these and posts to the inventory and accounts payable control accounts. With this step, the purchases phase of the expenditure cycle is completed.

THE CASH DISBURSEMENTS SYSTEMS

A detailed document flowchart of a manual cash disbursements system is presented in Figure 5-13. The tasks performed in each of the key processes are discussed in the following section.

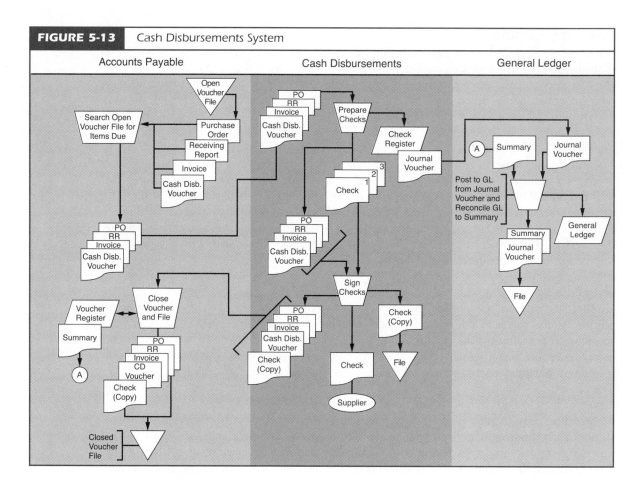

FIGURE 5-13 | Cash Disbursements System

Accounts Payable Department
Each day, the accounts payable clerk reviews the open vouchers payable (accounts payable) file for items due and sends the vouchers and supporting documents to the cash disbursements department.

Cash Disbursements Department
The cash disbursements clerk receives the voucher packets and reviews the documents for completeness and clerical accuracy. For each disbursement, the clerk prepares a three-part check and records the check number, dollar amount, voucher number, and other pertinent data in the **check register**.

The check, along with the supporting documents, goes to the cash disbursements department manager, or treasurer, for his or her signature. The negotiable portion of the check is mailed to the supplier. The clerk returns the voucher packet and check copy to the accounts payable department and files one copy of the check. Finally, the clerk summarizes the entries made to the check register and sends a journal voucher to the general ledger department.

Accounts Payable Department
Upon receipt of the voucher packet, the accounts payable clerk removes the liability by recording the check number in the voucher register and filing the voucher packet in the

closed voucher file. Finally, the clerk sends an AP summary to the general ledger department.

General Ledger Department

Based on the journal voucher from cash disbursements and the account summary from accounts payable, the general ledger clerk posts to the GL control accounts and files the documents. This concludes the cash disbursements procedures.

Concluding Remarks

We conclude our discussion of manual systems with two points of observation. First, notice how manual expenditure cycle systems generate a great deal of paper documentation. Buying, preparing, transporting, and filing physical documents add considerably to the cost of system operation. As we shall see in the next section, their elimination or reduction is a primary objective of computer-based systems design.

Second, for purposes of internal control many functions such as the inventory control, purchasing, accounts payable, cash disbursements, and the general ledger are located in physically separate departments. These labor-intensive activities also add greatly to the cost of system operation. In computer-based systems, these clerical tasks are performed by computer programs, which are much cheaper and far less prone to error. Although the classic department structure may still exist in computer-based environments, personnel responsibilities are refocused. Rather than being involved in day-to-day transaction processing, these departments are now involved with financial analysis and exception-based problem solving. As a result, these departments are smaller and more efficient than their manual system counterpart.

COMPUTER-BASED PURCHASES AND CASH DISBURSEMENTS APPLICATIONS

Now that we have covered the fundamental operational tasks and controls that constitute the expenditure cycle, let's examine the role of computers. In Chapter 4 we presented a technology continuum with *automation* at the low-end and *reengineering* at the high end. Recall that automation involves using technology to improve the efficiency and effectiveness of a task, while the objective of reengineering is to eliminate nonvalue-added tasks. Reengineering involves replacing traditional procedures with innovative procedures that are often very different from those previously in place. In this section we see how both automation and reengineering techniques apply in purchases and cash disbursement systems

AUTOMATING PURCHASES PROCEDURES USING BATCH PROCESSING TECHNOLOGY

The automated batch system presented in Figure 5-14 has many manual procedures similar to those presented in Figure 5-12. The principal difference is that accounting (bookkeeping) tasks are now automated. The following section describes the sequence of events as they occur in this system.

Data Processing Department: Step 1

The purchasing process begins in the data processing department, where the inventory control function is performed. When inventories are reduced by sales to customers or usage in production, the system determines if the affected items in the **inventory subsidiary file** have

FIGURE 5-14   Batch Purchases System

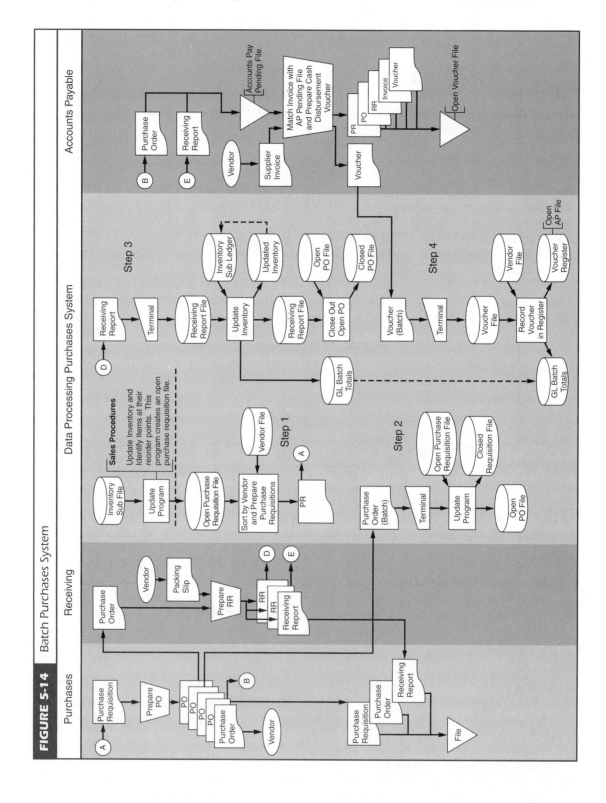

FIGURE 5-14   Batch Purchases System (Continued)

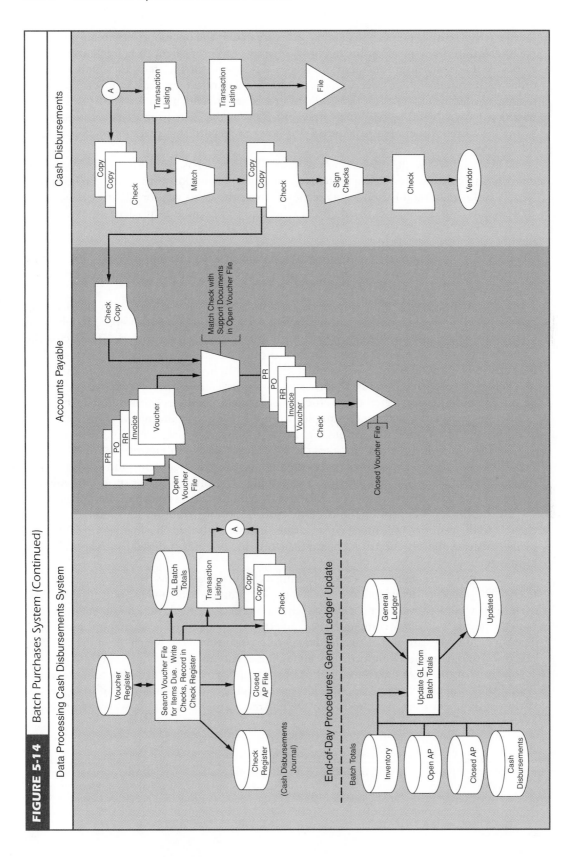

fallen to their reorder points.[4] If so, a record is created in the open purchase requisition file. Each record in the requisition file defines a separate inventory item to be replenished. The record contains the inventory item number, a description of the item, the quantity to be ordered, the standard unit price, and the vendor number of the primary supplier. The information needed to create the requisition record is selected from the inventory subsidiary record, which is then flagged "On Order" to prevent the item from being ordered again before the current order arrives. Figure 5-15 shows the record structures for the files used in this system.

At the end of the day, the system sorts the open purchase requisition file by vendor number and consolidates multiple items from the same vendor onto a single requisition. Next, vendor mailing information is retrieved from the **valid vendor file** to produce purchase requisition documents (hard copy), which go to the purchasing department.

Purchasing Department

Upon receipt of the purchase requisition, the purchasing department prepares a multipart purchase order. Copies are sent to the vendor, accounts payable, receiving, data processing, and the purchasing department's file.

The system in Figure 5-14 employs manual procedures as a control over the ordering process. A computer program identifies inventory requirements and prepares traditional purchase requisitions, but the purchasing agent reviews the requisitions before placing the order. Some firms do this to reduce the risk of placing unnecessary orders with vendors because of a computer error. Such manual intervention, however, does create a bottleneck and delays the ordering process. If sufficient computer controls are in place to prevent or detect purchasing errors, then more efficient ordering procedures can be implemented.

Before continuing with our example, we need to discuss alternative approaches for authorizing and ordering inventories. Figure 5-16 illustrates three common methods.

In *alternative one,* the system takes the procedures shown in Figure 5-14 one step further. This system automatically prepares the purchase order documents and sends them to the purchasing department for review and signing. The purchasing agent then mails the approved purchase orders to the vendors and distributes copies to other internal users.

Alternative two expedites the ordering process by distributing the purchase orders directly to the vendors and internal users, thus bypassing the purchasing department completely. Instead, the system produces a transaction list of items ordered for the purchasing agent's review.

Alternative three represents a reengineering technology called *electronic data interchange (EDI)*. The concept was introduced in Chapter 4 to illustrate its application to the revenue cycle. This method produces no physical purchase orders. Instead, the computer systems of both the buying and selling companies are connected via a dedicated telecommunications link. The buyer and seller are parties to a trading partner arrangement in which the entire ordering process is automated and unimpeded by human intervention.

In each of the three alternatives, the tasks of authorizing and ordering are integrated within the computer system. Because physical purchase requisitions have no purpose in such a system, they are not produced. Digital requisition records, however, would still exist to provide an audit trail.

---

4   This may be batch or real time, depending on the revenue and conversion cycle systems that interface with the expenditure cycle. The raw materials and finished goods inventory files link these three transaction cycles together. The design of one system influences the others. For example, if sales processing (revenue cycle) reduces inventories in real time, the system will naturally identify inventory requirements in real time also. This is true even if the purchases system is batch oriented.

FIGURE 5-15	Record Structures for Expenditure Cycle Files

Inven Num	Description	Qnty on Hand	Reorder Point	**Qnty On Order***	EOQ	Vendor Number	Standard Cost	Total Inven. Cost	Inventory Master File

Pur Req Number	Inven Num	Qnty on Order	Vendor Number	Unit Standard Cost	Purchase Requisition File

Vendor Number	Address	Terms of Trade	Date of Last Order	Lead Time	Vendor File

PO Num	Pur Req Number	Inven Num	Qnty On Order	Vendor Number	Address	Standard Cost	Expected Invoice Amount	Rec Flag	Inven Flag	Open (and Closed) Purchase Order File

Voucher Number	Check Num	Invoice Num	Invoice Amount	Acct Cr	Acct DR	Vendor Number	Open Date	Due Date	Close Date

Voucher Register (Open AP File)

Rec Rpt Number	PO Num	Carrier Code	Date Received	Condition Code	Rec Report File

* A value in this field is a "flag" to the system not to order item a second time.   When inventories are received, the flag is removed by changing this value to zero.

Data Processing Department: Step 2
Returning to Figure 5-14, a copy of the purchase order is sent to data processing and used to create a record in the open purchase order file. The associated requisitions are then transferred from the open purchase requisition file to the closed purchase requisition file.

Receiving Department
When the goods arrive from vendors, the receiving clerk prepares a receiving report and sends copies to purchasing, accounts payable, and data processing.

Data Processing Department: Step 3
The data processing department creates the receiving report file from data provided by the receiving report documents. Then a batch program updates the inventory subsidiary file from the receiving report file. The program removes the "On Order" flag from the updated inventory records and calculates batch totals of inventory receipts, which will

FIGURE 5-16   Alternative Inventory Ordering Procedures

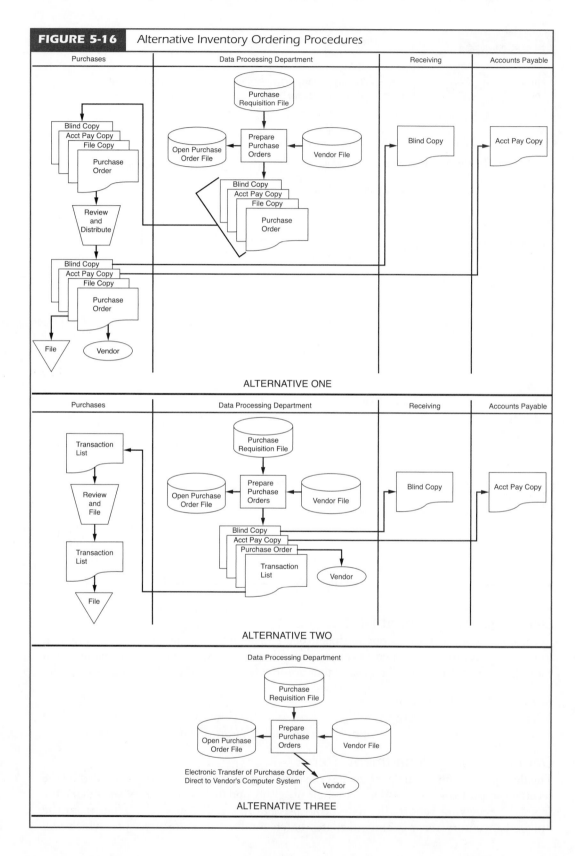

later be used in the general ledger update procedure. Finally, the associated records in the open purchase order file are transferred to the closed purchase order file.

Accounts Payable
When the accounts payable clerk receives the supplier's invoice, he or she reconciles it with the supporting documents that were previously placed in the accounts payable pending file. The clerk then prepares a voucher, files it in the open voucher file, and sends a copy of the voucher to data processing.

Data Processing Department: Step 4
The voucher file is created from the voucher documents. A batch program validates the voucher records against the valid vendor file and adds them to the voucher register (open accounts payable subsidiary file). Finally, batch totals are prepared for subsequent posting to the accounts payable control account in the general ledger.

CASH DISBURSEMENTS PROCEDURES

Data Processing Department
Each day, the system scans the Due Date field of the voucher register (see Figure 5-15) for items due. Checks are printed for these items, and each check is recorded in the check register (cash disbursements journal). The check number is recorded in the voucher register to close the voucher and transfer the items to the **closed accounts payable file**. The checks, along with a transaction listing, are sent to the cash disbursements department. Finally, batch totals of closed accounts payable and cash disbursements are prepared for the general ledger update procedure.

At the end of the day, batch totals of open (unpaid) and closed (paid) accounts payable, inventory increases, and cash disbursements are posted to the accounts payable control, inventory control, and cash accounts in the general ledger. The totals of closed accounts payable and cash disbursements should balance.

Cash Disbursements Department
The cash disbursements clerk reconciles the checks with the transaction listing and submits the negotiable portion of the checks to management for signing. The checks are then mailed to the suppliers. One copy of each check is sent to accounts payable, and the other copy is filed in cash disbursements along with the transaction listing.

Accounts Payable
Upon receipt of the check copies, the accounts payable clerk matches them with open vouchers and transfers these now closed items to the closed voucher file. This concludes the expenditure cycle process.

REENGINEERING THE PURCHASES/CASH DISBURSEMENTS SYSTEM
The automated system described in the previous section simply replicates many of the procedures in a manual system. In particular, the accounts payable task of reconciling supporting documents with supplier invoices is labor intensive and costly. The following example shows how reengineering this activity can produce considerable savings.

The Ford Motor Company employed more than 500 clerks in its North American accounts payable department. Analysis of the function showed that a large part of the clerks' time was devoted to reconciling discrepancies among supplier invoices, receiving reports, and purchase orders. The first step in solving the problem was to change the business environment. Ford initiated trading partner agreements with suppliers in which they agreed in advance to terms of trade such as price, quantities to be shipped, discounts, and lead times. With these sources of discrepancy eliminated, Ford reengineered the work flow to take advantage of the new environment. The flowchart in Figure 5-17 depicts the key features of a reengineered system.

Data Processing

The following tasks are performed automatically.

1. The inventory file is searched for items that have fallen to their reorder points.
2. A record is entered in the purchase requisition file for each item to be replenished.
3. Requisitions are consolidated according to vendor number.
4. Vendor mailing information is retrieved from the valid vendor file.
5. Purchase orders are prepared and added to the open purchase order file.
6. A transaction listing of purchase orders is sent to the purchasing department for review.

Receiving Department

When the goods arrive, the receiving clerk accesses the open purchase order file in real time by entering the purchase order number taken from the packing slip. The receiving screen, illustrated in Figure 5-18, then prompts the clerk to enter the quantities received for each item on the purchase order.

Data Processing

The following tasks are performed automatically by the system.

1. Quantities of items received are matched against the open purchase order record, and a "Y" value is placed in a logical field to indicate the receipt of inventories.
2. A record is added to the receiving report file.
3. The inventory subsidiary records are updated to reflect the receipt of the inventory items.
4. The general ledger inventory control account is updated.
5. The record is removed from the open purchase order file and added to the open accounts payable file, and a due date for payment is established.

Each day, the Due Date fields of the accounts payable records are scanned for items due to be paid. The following procedures are performed for the selected items.

1. Checks are automatically printed, signed, and distributed to the mail room for mailing to vendors. EDI vendors receive payment by electronic funds transfer (EFT). EFT is discussed in the appendix to Chapter 12.
2. The payments are recorded in the check register file.
3. Items paid are transferred from the open accounts payable file to the closed accounts payable file.
4. The general ledger accounts payable and cash accounts are updated.
5. Reports detailing these transactions are transmitted via terminal to the accounts payable and cash disbursements departments for management review and filing.

Because the financial information about purchases is known in advance from the trading partner agreement, the **vendor's invoice** provides no critical information that cannot be derived from the receiving report. By eliminating this source of potential discrepancy, Ford was able to eliminate the task of reconciling vendor invoices with the supporting documents for the majority of purchase transactions. As a result of its reengineering effort, Ford was able to reduce its accounts payable staff from 500 to 125.

FIGURE 5-17	Reengineered Purchases/Cash Disbursements System

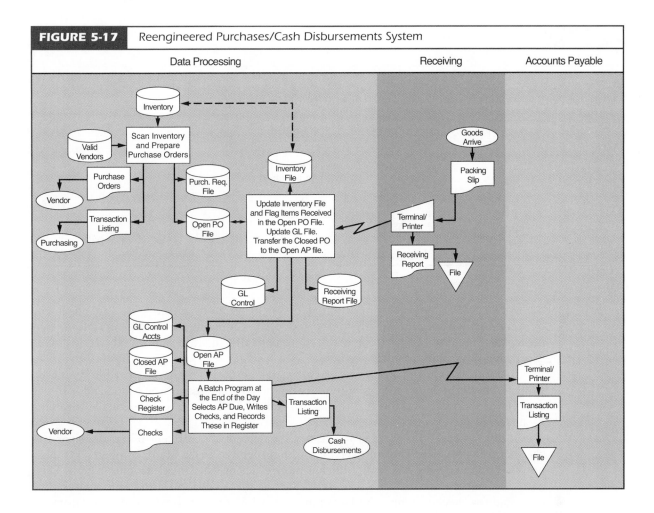

CONTROL IMPLICATIONS

The general control issues raised in Chapter 4 pertain also to the expenditure cycle and are not revisited here. A full treatment of this material is provided in Chapters 15 through 17. In the following we examine only the issues specific to the expenditure cycle by focusing on the differences between automated versus a reengineered systems.

The Automated System

Improved Inventory Control. The greatest advantage of the automated system over its manual counterpart is improved ability to manage inventory needs. Inventory requirements are detected as they arise and are processed automatically. As a result, the risks of accumulating excessive inventory or of running out of stock are reduced. With this advantage, however, comes a control concern. Authorization rules governing purchase transactions are embedded within a computer program. Program errors or flawed inventory models can cause firms to find themselves suddenly inundated with inventories or desperately short of stock. Therefore, monitoring automated decisions is extremely important. A well-controlled system should provide management with adequate summary reports about inventory purchases, inventory turnover, spoilage, and slow-moving items.

| FIGURE 5-18 | Receiving Screen |

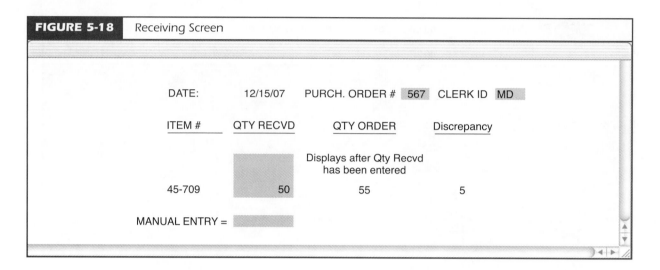

Better Cash Management. The automated system promotes effective cash management by scanning the voucher file daily for items due, thus avoiding early payments and missed due dates. In addition, by writing checks automatically, the firm reduces labor cost, saves processing time, and promotes accuracy.

To control against unauthorized payments, all additions to the voucher file should be validated by comparing the vendor number on the voucher against the valid vendor file. If the vendor number is not on file, the record should be diverted to an error file for management review.

In this system, a manager in the cash disbursements department physically signs the checks, thus providing control over the disbursement of cash. Many computer systems, however, automate check signing, which is more efficient when check volume is high. This, naturally, injects risk into the process. To offset this exposure, firms set a materiality threshold for check writing. Checks in amounts below the threshold are signed automatically while those above the threshold are signed by an authorized manager or the treasurer.

Time Lag. A lag exists between the arrival of goods in the receiving department and recording inventory receipts in the inventory file. Depending on the type of sales order system in place, this lag may negatively affect the sales process. When sales clerks do not know the current status of inventory, sales may be lost.

Purchasing Bottleneck. In this automated system, the purchasing department is directly involved in all purchase decisions. For many firms this creates additional work, which extends the time lag in the ordering process. A vast number of routine purchases could be automated, thus freeing purchasing agents from routine work such as preparing purchase orders and mailing them to the vendors. Attention can then be focused on problem areas (such as special items or those in short supply) and the purchasing staff can be reduced.

Excessive Paper Documents. The automated system is laden with paper documents. All operations departments create documents, which are sent to data processing and which data processing must then convert to magnetic media. Paper documents add costs because they must be purchased, stored, prepared, handled by internal mail carriers, and converted by data processing personnel. Organizations with high volumes of transactions benefit considerably from reducing or eliminating paper documents in their systems.

The Reengineered System

The reengineered system addresses many of the operational weaknesses associated with the automated system. Specifically, the improvements in this system are that (1) it uses real-time procedures and direct access files to shorten the lag time in record keeping, (2) it eliminates routine clerical procedures by distributing terminals to user areas, and (3) it achieves a significant reduction in paper documents by utilizing digital communications between departments and by digitally storing records. These operational improvements, however, have the following control implications.

Segregation of Duties. This system removes the physical separation between authorization and transaction processing. Here, computer programs authorize and process purchase orders as well as authorize and issue checks to vendors. To compensate for this exposure, the system provides management with detailed transaction listings and summary reports. These documents describe the automated actions taken by the system and allow management to spot errors and any unusual events that warrant investigation.

Accounting Records and Access Controls. Advanced systems maintain accounting records on digital storage media, with little or no hard-copy backup. Sarbanes-Oxley legislation requires organization management to implement adequate control security measures to protect accounting records from unauthorized access and destruction.

SUMMARY

The chapter examined procurement procedures involving the acquisition of raw materials and finished goods. Because most organizations conduct these activities on a credit basis, the information system needs to be designed to properly recognize and record obligations as they arise and to discharge them when they come due. Two expenditure cycle subsystems accomplish these tasks: the purchases system and the cash disbursements system. This chapter focused on the following areas:

1. The processes of each subsystem and the flow of information between them.
2. The documents, journals, and accounts needed to provide audit trails, maintain historical records, and support internal decision making and financial reporting.
3. The areas of exposure and the control techniques that reduce these risks.

The chapter examined the impact of technology on items 1, 2, and 3 above. From this perspective, we saw that automated systems use computers to replicate traditional manual tasks. Reengineered systems, however, involve and require new and innovative ways of dealing with traditional problems. Any technological solution carries control implications. Computers remove a fundamental separation of functions between authorizing and processing transactions. Also at risk is the integrity of accounting records. To control these risks, systems must be designed to provide users with documents and reports that permit independent verification and support audit trail needs.

KEY TERMS

accounts payable pending file (235)

actual cost inventory ledgers (237)

blind copy (234)

cash disbursement vouchers (239)

cash disbursements journal (240)

check register (240)

closed accounts payable file (255)

closed purchase order file (247)

closed voucher file (242)

inventory subsidiary file (249)

open accounts payable file (238)

open purchase order file (247)

open purchase requisition file (247)

open vouchers payable file (247)

purchase order (232)

purchase requisition (232)

receiving report (235)

receiving report file (235)

standard cost system (235)

supplier's invoice (237)

valid vendor file (252)

vendor's invoice (256)

vouchers payable system (239)

voucher register (239)

vouchers payable file (239)

REVIEW QUESTIONS

1. Differentiate between a purchase requisition and a purchase order.

2. What purpose does a purchasing department serve?

3. Distinguish between an accounts payable file and a vouchers payable file.

4. What are the three logical steps of the cash disbursements system?

5. What general ledger journal entries are triggered by the purchases system? From which departments do these journal entries arise?

6. What two types of exposure can close supervision of the receiving department reduce?

7. How can a manual purchases cash disbursements system be reengineered to reduce discrepancies, be more accurate, and reduce processing costs?

8. What steps of independent verification does the general ledger department perform?

9. What is (are) the purpose(s) of maintaining a valid vendor file?

10. How do computerized purchasing systems help to reduce the risk of purchasing bottlenecks?

11. What is the purpose of the blind copy of a purchase order?

12. Give one advantage of using a vouchers payable system.

DISCUSSION QUESTIONS

1. What three documents must accompany the payment of an invoice? Discuss where these three documents originate and the resulting control implications.

2. Are any time lags in recording economic events typically experienced in cash disbursements systems? If so, what are they? Discuss the accounting profession's view on this matter as it pertains to financial reporting.

3. Discuss the importance of supervision controls in the receiving department and the reasons behind blind fields on the receiving report, such as quantity and price.

4. Why do the inventory control and general ledger departments seem to "disappear" in computer-based purchasing systems (Figure 5-14)? Are these functions no longer important enough to have their own departments?

5. How does the procedure for determining inventory requirements differ between a basic batch-processing system and batch processing with real-time data input of sales

and receipts of inventory? What about for the procedures used by the receiving department?

6. What advantages are achieved in choosing
   a. a basic batch computer system over a manual system?
   b. a batch system with real-time data input over a basic batch system?

7. Discuss the major control implications of batch systems with real-time data input. What compensating procedures are available?

8. Discuss some specific examples in which information systems can reduce time lags and how the firm is positively affected by such time lags.

9. You are conducting an end-of-year audit. Assume that the terms of trade between a buyer and a seller are **FOB destination**. What document provides evidence that a liability **exists** and **may** be unrecorded?

10. Describe a three-way match.

Multiple-Choice Questions

1. Which document helps to ensure that the receiving clerks actually count the number of goods received?
   a. packing list
   b. blind copy of purchase order
   c. shipping notice
   d. invoice

2. When the goods are received and the receiving report has been prepared, which ledger may be updated?
   a. standard cost inventory ledger
   b. inventory subsidiary ledger
   c. general ledger
   d. accounts payable subsidiary ledger

3. Which statement is NOT correct for an expenditure system with proper internal controls?
   a. Cash disbursements maintains the check register.
   b. Accounts payable maintains the accounts payable subsidiary ledger.
   c. Accounts payable is responsible for paying invoices.
   d. Accounts payable is responsible for authorizing invoices.

4. Which duties should be segregated?
   a. matching purchase requisitions, receiving reports, and invoices and authorizing payment
   b. authorizing payment and maintaining the check register
   c. writing checks and maintaining the check register

   d. authorizing payment and maintaining the accounts payable subsidiary ledger

5. Which documents would an auditor most likely choose to examine closely to ascertain that all expenditures incurred during the accounting period have been recorded as a liability?
   a. invoices
   b. purchase orders
   c. purchase requisitions
   d. receiving reports

6. Which task must still require human intervention in an automated purchases/cash disbursements system?
   a. determination of inventory requirements
   b. preparation of a purchase order
   c. preparation of a receiving report
   d. preparation of a check register

7. CMA 689 3-17
   Which of the following situations represents a strength in the internal control for purchasing and accounts payable?
   a. Prenumbered receiving reports are issued randomly.
   b. Invoices are approved for payment by the purchasing department.
   c. Unmatched receiving reports are reviewed annually.
   d. Vendors' invoices are matched against purchase orders and receiving reports before a liability is recorded.
   e. The purchasing department reconciles the accounts payable subsidiary vendor ledger with the general ledger control account.

PROBLEMS

1. Unrecorded Liabilities

You are auditing the financial statements of a New York City company that buys a product from a manufacturer in Los Angeles. The buyer closes its books on June 30. Assume the following details:

Terms of trade FOB shipping point

June 10, buyer sends purchase order to seller

June 15, seller ships goods

July 5, buyer receives goods

July 10, buyer receives seller's invoice

Required:

a. Could this transaction have resulted in an unrecorded liability in the buyer's financial statements?

b. If "yes," what documents provide audit trail evidence of the liability?

c. On what date did the buyer realize the liability?

d. On what date did the buyer recognize the liability?

New assumption:

Terms of trade FOB destination

e. Could this transaction have resulted in an unrecorded liability in the buyer's financial statements?

f. If "yes," what documents provide audit trail evidence of the liability?

g. On what date did the buyer realize the liability?

h. On what date did the buyer recognize the liability?

2. Inventory Ordering Alternatives

Refer to Figure 5-16 in the text, which illustrates three alternative methods of ordering inventory.

Required:

a. Distinguish between a purchase requisition and a purchase order.

b. Discuss the primary advantage of alternative two over alternative one. Be specific.

c. Under what circumstances can you envision management using alternative one rather than alternative two?

3. Document Preparation

Create the appropriate documents (purchase requisition, purchase order, receiving report, inventory record, and disbursement voucher) and prepare any journal entries needed to process the following business events for Jethro's Boot & Western Wear Manufacturing Company (this is a manual system).

a. On October 28, 2005, the inventory subsidiary ledger for Item 2278, metal pins, indicates that the quantity on hand is 4,000 units (valued at $76), the reorder point is 4,750, and units are on order. The economic order quantity is 6,000 units. The supplier is Jed's Metal Supply Company (vendor number 83682). The customer number is 584446. The current price per unit is $0.02. Inventory records are kept at cost. The goods should be delivered to Inventory Storage Room 2.

b. On November 8, the goods were received (the scales indicated that 4,737 units were received).

c. On November 12, an invoice (number 9886) was received for the above units, which included freight of $6. The terms were 1/10, net 30. Jethro's likes to keep funds available for use as long as possible without missing any discounts.

4. Flowchart Analysis

Examine the diagram on the following page and indicate any incorrect initiation and/or transfer of documentation. What problems could this cause?

5. Accounting Records and Files

Indicate which department—accounts payable, cash disbursements, data processing, purchasing, inventory, or receiving—has ownership over the following files and registers:

a. open purchase order file

b. purchase requisition file

c. open purchase requisition file

d. closed purchase requisition file

e. inventory

f. closed purchase order file

g. valid vendor file

h. voucher register

i. open vouchers payable file

j. receiving report file

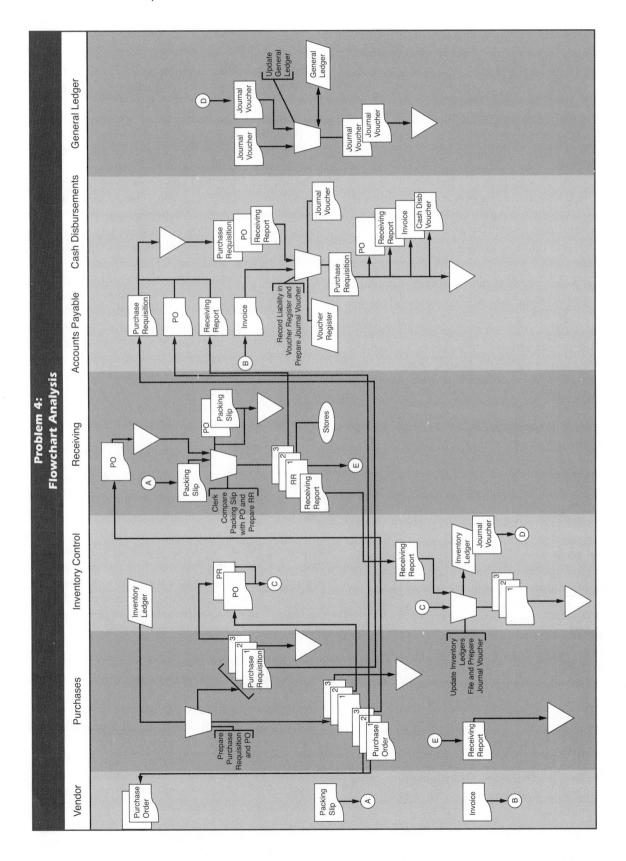

**Problem 4:
Flowchart Analysis**

k.   closed voucher file

l.   check register (cash disbursements journal)

6. Source Documents Identification

Explain, in detail, the process by which the information is obtained and the source of information for each of the fields in the expenditure cycle files. (See Figure 5-15 for a complete listing of files and fields.)

7. Data Processing

Explain how the processing procedures would differ, if at all, for the transactions listed in Problem 1 if a computer-based system with

a.   a basic batch-processing system were implemented.

b.   a batch-processing system with real-time data input were used.

8. Internal Control

Using the flowchart of a purchases system on page 265, identify six major control weaknesses in the system. Discuss and classify each weakness in accordance with SAS 78.

9. Purchase Discounts Lost

Estimate the amount of money that could be saved by the accounts payable and cash disbursements departments if a basic batch-processing system were implemented. Assume that the clerical workers cost the firm $12 per hour, that 13,000 vouchers are prepared, and that 5,000 checks are written per year. Assume that total cash disbursements to vendors amount to $5 million per year. Due to sloppy bookkeeping, the current system takes advantage of only about 25 percent of the discounts offered by vendors for timely payments. The average discount is 2 percent if payment is made within ten days. Payments are currently made on the 15th day after the invoice is received. Make your own assumptions (and state them) regarding how long specific tasks will take. Also discuss any intangible benefits of the system. (Don't worry about excessive paper documentation costs.)

10. Data Processing Output

Using the information provided in Problem 9, discuss all transaction listings and summary reports that would be necessary for a batch system with real-time input of data.

11. CMA 1288 5-3
Internal Control

Lexsteel is a leading manufacturer of steel furniture. While the company has manufacturing plants and distribution facilities throughout the United States, the purchasing, accounting, and treasury functions are centralized at corporate headquarters.

While discussing the management letter with the external auditors, Ray Lansdown, controller of Lexsteel, became aware of potential problems with the accounts payable system. The auditors had to perform additional audit procedures to attest to the validity of accounts payable and cutoff procedures. The auditors have recommended that a detailed systems study be made of the current procedures. Such a study would not only assess the exposure of the company to potential embezzlement and fraud, but would also identify ways to improve management controls.

Landsdown has assigned the study task to Dolores Smith, a relatively new accountant in the department. Because Smith could not find adequate documentation of the accounts payable procedures, she interviewed those employees involved and constructed a flowchart of the current system. This flowchart is presented on page 266. A description of the current procedures follows.

Computer Resources Available

The host computer mainframe is located at corporate headquarters with interactive, remote job-entry terminals at each branch location. In general, data entry occurs at the source and is transmitted to an integrated database maintained on the host computer. Data transmission is made between the branch offices and the host computer over leased telephone lines. The software allows flexibility for managing user access and editing data input.

Procedures for Purchasing Raw Materials

Production orders and appropriate bills of materials are generated by the host computer at corporate headquarters. Based on these bills of materials, purchase orders for raw materials are generated by the centralized purchasing function and mailed directly to the vendors. Each purchase order instructs the vendor to ship the materials directly to the appropriate manufacturing plant. Assuming that the necessary purchase orders have been issued, the manufacturing

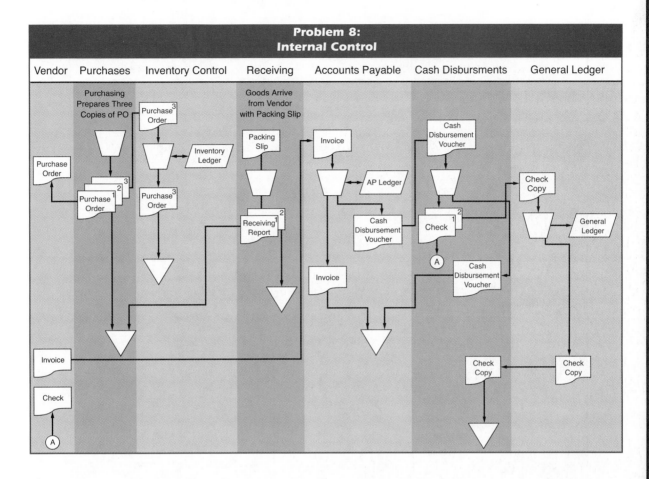

plants proceed with the production orders received from corporate headquarters.

When goods are received, the manufacturing plant examines and verifies the count to the packing slip and transmits the receiving data to accounts payable at corporate headquarters. In the event that raw material deliveries fall behind production, each branch manager is given the authority to order materials and issue emergency purchase orders directly to the vendors. Data about the emergency orders and verification of materials receipt are transmitted via computer to accounts payable at corporate headquarters. Because the company employs a computerized perpetual inventory system, physical counts of raw materials are deemed not to be cost-effective and are not performed.

Accounts Payable Procedures
Vendor invoices are mailed directly to corporate headquarters and entered by accounts payable

personnel when received; this often occurs before the receiving data are transmitted from the branch offices. The final day of the invoice term for payment is entered as the payment due date. This due date must often be calculated by the data entry person using information listed on the invoice.

Once a week, invoices due the following week are printed in chronological entry order on a payment listing, and the corresponding checks are drawn. The checks and the payment listing are sent to the treasurer's office for signing and mailing to the payee. The check number is printed by the computer and displayed on the check, and the payment listing is validated as the checks are signed. After the checks are mailed, the payment listing is returned to accounts payable for filing. When there is insufficient cash to pay all the invoices, certain checks and the payment listing are retained by the treasurer until all checks can be paid. When the remaining checks are mailed, the listing is then returned to accounts payable. Often, weekly check

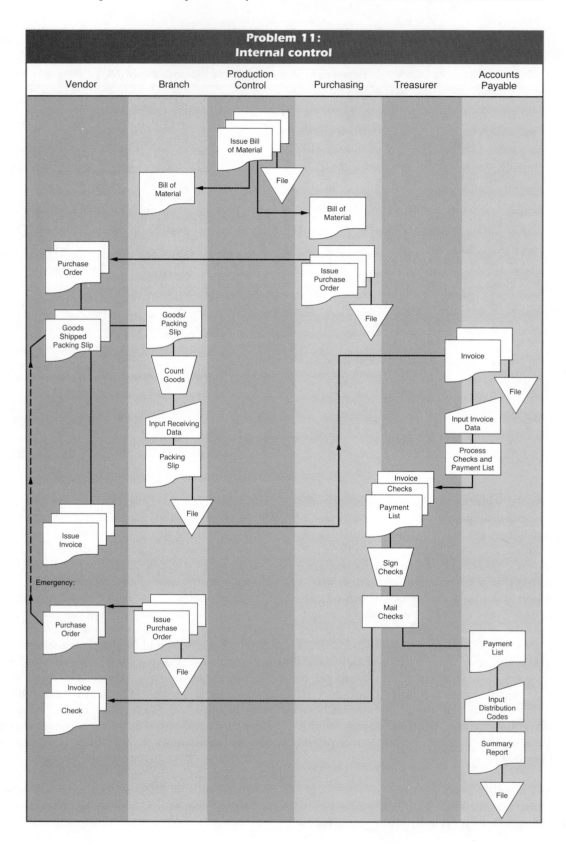

mailings include a few checks from the previous week, but rarely are there more than two weekly listings involved.

When accounts payable receives the payment listing back from the treasurer's office, the expenses are distributed, coded, and posted to the appropriate plant or cost center accounts. Weekly summary performance reports are processed by accounts payable for each cost center and branch location reflecting all data entry to that point.

Required:

a. Identify and discuss three areas where Lexsteel Corporation may be exposed to fraud or embezzlement due to weaknesses in the procedures described, and recommend improvements to correct these weaknesses.

b. Describe three areas where management information could be distorted due to weaknesses in the procedures, and recommend improvements to correct these weaknesses.

c. Identify three strengths in the procedures described and explain why they are strengths.

INTERNAL CONTROL CASES

1. Walker Books, Inc.
(Prepared by Chris Cariello, Lehigh University)

Company Background
Walker Books, Inc. is currently one of the largest book distributors in the United States. Established in 1981 in Palo Alto, California, Walker Books was originally a side project of founder and current president Curtis Walker, who at the time was employed by a local law firm. Because reading was much more than just a hobby of his, he decided to use some of his savings to buy out an abandoned restaurant and convert it into a neighborhood bookstore, mainly selling used books that were donated from friends and family. When the doors first opened, Walker's wife, Lauren, was the only employee during the week; Curtis was the only employee on the weekends. At the end of the first fiscal year, Walker Books had grossed $20,000 in sales.

As the years passed, Curtis Walker quit the law firm and began concentrating fully on his bookstore. More employees were hired, more books were traded in, and more sales were attained each year that passed. However, during the mid-1990s, Walker was faced with two problems: many large, upscale bookstores were being built in the area and the use of the Internet for finding and ordering books was becoming cheaper and more popular for current customers. In 1995, Walker's sales finally started to decline. Deciding to take a risk because of the new-found competition, he closed his doors to the neighborhood, invested more money to expand the current property, and transformed his company from simply selling used books to being a distributor of new books. Publishers send books to his warehouse, in which he stores them and resells them to large bookstore chains upon request.

Walker Books, Inc. has rapidly become one of the largest book distributors in the country. Though they are still at their original location in Palo Alto, California, they distribute books to each of the 50 states and because of that, the company now sees sales of about $105,000,000 per year. When Mr. Walker is asked about his fondest memory, he always responds that he will never forget how the little bookstore, with two employees, has expanded to now have more than 145 employees.

As mentioned, all of Walker's customers are large-chain bookstores who themselves see many millions of dollars in revenue per year. However, some of these bookstores have been having bad relationships with Walker Books in the past year. There have been many disputes between them, such as books that were ordered from Walker but were never sent, poor inventory management by Walker, and the inability of Walker to provide legitimate documentation of transactions. According to projections of this year's financials, the sour relationship that Walker Books and many of its customers have is going to take a toll on year-end revenue. Curtis Walker has stated time after time that because of his law background, he "clearly knows the difference between right and wrong, including those of internal controls." You have been hired as an independent expert to inspect the internal controls currently in place at Walker Books, Inc.

Expenditure Cycle
Purchases System

The purchases process begins with the purchasing agent, who monitors the levels of books available. Upon noticing a deficiency in one inventory item, the agent generates five copies of a purchase order: one is sent to accounts payable, two are sent to the vendor, one is sent to the receiving department, and the last is filed in the purchases pending file.

When goods are received in the receiving department they are usually reconciled against the PO and packing slip, but not always. When not reconciled, the PO is trusted as is. After unloading the goods a receiving report is generated, with one copy going with the inventory items to their destination and another sent to the purchasing department. In the purchasing department, a clerk closes the purchases pending file, sending one copy to accounts payable. The last copy is filed within the receiving department.

The accounts payable department receives the PO and the receiving report but waits until the invoice is received before doing anything. Upon receipt of the invoice, the AP clerk reconciles it with the supporting documents in the pending file and the liability is recorded. All documents are placed into the open accounts payable file and a journal voucher is created, with one copy being filed and one copy being sent to the general ledger department.

Upon notification from the accounts payable department, information from the invoice is posted to the inventory and accounts payable control accounts via a computer terminal, thus ending the purchase process.

Cash Disbursements System

The AP clerk reviews the open accounts payable file for liabilities that are due. Upon finding an open accounts payable file in need of payment, a check is generated for the amount due and the accounts payable ledger is updated. The check number, dollar amount, and other pertinent data are recorded in the check register (cash disbursements journal). The check and supporting documents are sent to the supervisor of the department and are approved and signed.

After the check is signed, it is sent to the supplier. A copy of the check is attached to the supporting documents, which are marked as paid and then filed in the closed accounts payable file. Finally, a journal voucher is created and sent to the general ledger department, where information is posted to the accounts payable and cash control accounts via a computer terminal, completing the cash disbursements process.

Required:

a. Create a data flow diagram of the current system.

b. Create a document flowchart of the existing system.

c. Analyze the internal control weaknesses in the system. Model your response according to the six categories of physical control activities specified in SAS 78.

d. Prepare a system flowchart of a redesigned computer-based system that resolves the control weaknesses that you identified.

2. A&V Safety, Inc
(Prepared by Adam Johnson and Aneesh Varma, Lehigh University)

A&V Safety Inc. is a growing company specializing in the sales of safety equipment to commercial entities. It currently employs 200 full-time employees who all work out of their headquarters in San Diego, California. During the summer the company expands to include about 10 summer interns who are delegated smaller jobs and other errands. A&V currently competes with Office Safety Inc. and X-Safe who leads the industry. Suppliers for A&V include Halotron Extinguishers, Kadelite, and Exit Signs Inc and there have been no issues requiring redress. The terms of trade used by A&V are 2–10 net 30 with FOB delivery. This is used with all suppliers and inventory is kept at a level that will service two weeks. This level has shown to avoid stock-outs and the excess inventory is held a warehouse in a suburb of San Diego.

The company has growing revenue, which has recently topped $23 million and has a return on investment of 14% and net margin of slightly over 20%. While the company has been operating efficiently in the past, new systems problems have arisen due to the strain put on these legacy systems from recent growth.

Expenditure Cycle

The expenditure cycle consists of purchasing procedure and cash disbursements procedure. The company has allocated its purchasing to three departments: warehouse, purchasing, and accounting.

The company has to buy safety devices such as fire extinguishers, exit signs, and sensors. The company maintains a basic inventory control process with triggers. When a certain product is low in inventory, the inventory clerk prepares a standard purchase order (PO). The clerk then sends this PO to the respective vendor from where the current supply of the product was obtained. A copy of this PO is also sent to the general ledger and the receiving department to verify the goods when they arrive. When the required shipment arrives from the vendor, it first goes to the docks of the receiving department. The clerk at the receiving department matches the packing slip in the shipment to the PO that was sent by the inventory clerk earlier. After comparing the numbers on the packing slip to the numbers required on the PO, he signs the PO, which moves to the accounting department. The receiving clerk also prepares a receiving report that is sent to the inventory department where the update program adds this information to inventory ledger.

Meanwhile, the supplier sends an invoice of the goods that were just shipped. Upon reaching A&V Safety this is sent to the accounting department. The accounting department has previously received the signed purchase order from the receiving clerk that indicates that such goods were received. The invoice is then matched and reconciled against the receiving clerk's signed purchase order. The clerk in the accounting department then updates accounts payable subsidiary ledger for these new liabilities and the purchasing journal using this information.

The cash disbursements procedure involves the accounts payable department, the cash disbursements department and the general ledger. The accounts payable reviews the liabilities that are due by searching the accounts payable subsidiary ledger. Those items that are due are then written up into a cash disbursements voucher and a matching accounts payable summary is made that is sent to the general ledger. The cash disbursements voucher is sent to the cash disbursements department. Here the checks are prepared payable to the vendor. The check register is updated to reflect the amounts, check number, and payee information. A summary of this information is also sent to the general ledger. The prepared checks are then approved by the cash disbursements department. The original check is mailed to the vendor. A copy of the check is locally filed at the cash disbursements department. Another copy of the check and the original cash disbursements voucher for the check are sent to the accounts payable department.

At the accounts payable department, the cash disbursements voucher and the copy of the check are used to update the cash disbursements voucher register. The accounts payable subsidiary ledger is also updated to close out the liability that was originally placed. These documents are then locally filed. At the general ledger, all summaries that are received from each department are used to update the general ledger through the update program. Eventually a summary of the update is prepared and filed locally.

Required:

a. Create a data flow diagram of the current system.

b. Create a document flowchart of the existing system.

c. Analyze the internal control weaknesses in the system. Model your response according to the six categories of physical control activities specified in SAS 78.

d. Prepare a system flowchart of a redesigned computer-based system that resolves the control weaknesses that you identified.

3. Premier Sports Memorabilia General Scenario

(Prepared by Chris Polchinski, Lehigh University)

Premier Sports Memorabilia is a medium-sized, rapidly growing online and catalogue-based retailer centered in Brooklyn, New York. The company was founded in 1990 and specializes in providing the customer with authentic, yet affordable sports memorabilia from their favorite players and teams past and present. The company gets most of its sales from the northeast region of the United States, but recently has been undergoing a campaign to spread out and increase its customer base. The company is unique that it has a wide range of competitors such as online apparel retailers like

EastBay, retail stores such as Sports Authority, and online memorabilia retailers such as the Danbury Mint. The reason for this comes from Premier's wide range of offerings including everything from team jerseys and hats, to autographed balls, plaques, and bats, to sports cards and figurines. The firm's sales have been slowly increasing over the years and last year reported a satisfying $95 million. The company currently employs 205 employees that are spread out among its three warehouses, and two offices in the tri-state area.

Premier has been well known for their close relations with suppliers and have only had a few minor communication problems since the company was started, none which have disrupted the ordinary course of business. The firm uses a wide base of manufacturers and memorabilia dealers around the country and is always looking for additional contacts that have new or rare items to offer. The company uses a series of low-tech computer assistance to assist with its various daily manual tasks and maintains controlled access to relevant data within the organization. As the company continues to expand many of these manual tasks will most likely be replaced with a more advanced computer technology system, but currently they serve their purpose and have not hindered business as a whole.

Purchase System Procedures

Premier's purchase transactions are initiated when its inventory levels for a certain item falls below the designated reorder point. This is electronically monitored through Premier's Inventory Update Program that it directly linked to the Inventory File, which are housed within the Inventory Control Department's systems. Once an item falls below the reorder point, an open requisition file is automatically created in addition to a purchase requisition. A valid vendor file is used both to retrieve stored vendor information as well as to check that items are being ordered through a pre-approved vendor that the company has done business with in the past. The purchase requisition is made available to the clerks in the Inventory Control department via the computer terminal. A copy is sent to the Purchasing department terminal for further processing.

When the purchasing department receives the requisition it is used to prepare five copies of the purchase order (PO). One copy is entered into

the system and kept on file. A second is sent electronically to the computer terminal in the receiving department. A third is sent to the terminal in the accounts payable department. A fourth copy is sent to the inventory control department's terminal. A final copy is sent to the vendor and acts as the actual placement of the order.

Upon receiving the PO, the inventory control department's requisition update program automatically brings up the open requisition file and closes it out. In addition the program automatically creates a pending open Purchase file.

Shortly after receiving the PO, the vendor will send out both the goods and a packing slip to Premier's receiving department. After the receiving department has both the purchase order and the packing slip they are used to physically inspect the condition of the goods and check that both the type and quantity received is correct. After the receiving clerk has successfully done this, they are then responsible for creating three copies of a receiving report. One copy is entered into the system via the terminal for filing purposes. The second is sent to accounts payable for reconciliation. The third is sent to the inventory control department.

When the Inventory Control department electronically obtains the receiving report, the system's Purchase Update Program automatically pulls up the pending open purchase file and closes it out. In addition, the event triggers the automatic updating of the inventory files by posting the entries to the Inventory file.

In the meantime, the accounts payable department has now received the PO and receiving report from other areas of the company. Upon the arrival of the vendor invoice a department clerk manually reconciles all three forms to make sure that the information matches up correctly, and then proceeds to update the Accounts Payable files.

Finally at the end of each day the inventory control department and the accounts payable department create an Inventory Summary and A/P journal voucher respectively totaling out the effects of all of the day's transactions. These are both sent electronically to the joint Accounts receivable-general ledger department where they are reconciled against one another and posted to their specific control accounts within the general ledger file.

Required:

a. Create a data flow diagram of the current system.

b. Create a document flowchart of the existing system.

c. Analyze the internal control weaknesses in the system. Model your response according to the six categories of physical control activities specified in SAS 78.

d. Prepare a system flowchart of a redesigned computer-based system that resolves the control weaknesses that you identified.

4. Jasmine Tea!
(Prepared by Meridith Coyne and Gaby Keely, Lehigh University)

Jasmine Tea! is the largest coffee distributor in the Northeast. They distribute specialty tea leaves to coffee shops, cafes, and restaurants. The company headquarters is located in Newark, New Jersey; in addition there are two distribution warehouses located in Philadelphia and Boston.

Established in 1985, the company's first warehouse was located in Newark. Jasmine Tea! began by purchasing and distributing from one Chinese tea supplier. Within two years, sales had doubled and they were seeking more varieties of tea. They now have dozens of suppliers and over 50 varieties of tea. Currently there are 155 employees and annual sales of over $50 million. Last year was their most successful year with an annual sales growth of 6.5 percent.

Jasmine Tea! has been receiving complaints from customers and suppliers about billing, shipping, and payment problems. Under the current operating system each department has independent computer terminals. The complaints and inefficient computer system has triggered the management team to seek alternative solutions that will enable them to better serve their customers and meet the demands.

Purchasing Process
The purchasing agent monitors the inventory and decides when more tea supplies are needed. Once the inventory level falls to the reorder point, the purchasing agent begins the purchasing process by making a purchase requisition. The purchasing agent then decides on a supplier by searching online for the best prices and inputting the purchasing requisition into their computer terminal. The computer terminal generates three copies of a purchase order (PO). One copy is sent to the supplier, one copy is sent to the cash disbursements department, and the third copy is sent to the purchasing department. Once the purchasing agent has entered the purchase requisition into the computer terminal they file one copy of the purchase requisitions and send the other copy to cash disbursements.

When the goods are received in Newark, the receiving department verifies them using a copy of the PO and the packing slip, which was attached to the goods. The goods are verified and sent to the warehouse for storage. The receiving clerk then updates the inventory and sends the inventory summary to the general ledger department for posting to the general ledger.

Cash Disbursements
The cash disbursements clerk receives the PO and reconciles it with the purchase requisition. Then the clerk posts the liability to the purchases journal, and voucher register. Each day, the clerk visually searches the system for open invoices that have come due. The clerk then reviews the purchase order, purchase requisition, and invoice and prepares the check. From a computer terminal, the clerk updates the check register, voucher register, and posts to the general ledger. The negotiable portion of the check is mailed to the vendor, and a check copy is filed. The purchases requisition, invoice and purchase order are then filed in a closed voucher file.

Required:

a. Create a data flow diagram of the current system.

b. Create a document flowchart of the existing system.

c. Analyze the internal control weaknesses in the system. Model your response according to the six categories of physical control activities specified in SAS 78.

d. Prepare a system flowchart of a redesigned computer-based system that resolves the control weaknesses that you identified.

5. Music Source, Inc

(Prepared by Jeff Davis, Gen Feldman, and Denise Nuccio, Lehigh University)

Company Information

Music Source, Inc. is a manufacturer of stereo equipment with six sales offices nationwide and one manufacturing plant in Pennsylvania. Currently, employment is at approximately 200 employees. Music Source focuses on the production of high-quality stereo equipment for resale by retailers. Its larger competitors include Sony, Panasonic, and Aiwa. Music Source's suppliers are Nalequip, Inc. and Uniview. Production includes speakers, bases, subwoofers, and other equipment. Currently Music Source is operating at $135,000,000 in annual sales with revenue growth at a rate of 3 percent. Unfortunately, the company has recently been experiencing several operational problems that may be fixed through the improvement of its systems.

Expenditure Cycle

Music Source reduces its inventory by transferring raw materials into the production process in the manufacturing plant and through the sale of finished equipment to the customers. Music Source's purchasing department works along with the inventory and production control functions to provide the most efficient level of inventory for use in production. Inventory levels and material reorder points are closely monitored by the purchasing department. As soon as the inventory level drops below the reorder point, the purchasing function inputs a purchase order (PO) in to the computer. An electronic notification is sent to accounts payable and the receiving department to notify them of the order and provide them access to view the inputted data on their computer terminals. The accounts payable department moves the PO to the open accounts payable file once the notification of the PO is received. Two copies of each PO are mailed to the vendor by the purchasing clerk.

When the raw materials are received, the receiving department reconciles the goods with the order on the computer. The clerk inputs and saves in the computer a multipart receiving report stating the condition of the materials received. An electronic notification, granting access to view the document, is sent to purchasing and inventory control, where the report is reconciled with the open PO file and inventory and the general ledger are updated. Another notification is sent to accounts payable, where the viewed document is moved to the open accounts payable file.

The accounts payable clerk enters data into the computer terminal to record the liability and prepares a cash disbursement voucher when the electronic notification is received from the receiving department. Once the vendor invoice is received, the accounts payable clerk reconciles Music Source's records with those of the vendor. The computer terminal is used to generate a journal voucher that will be used to update the general ledger accounts.

The accounts payable department sends electronic notification to the cash disbursements department that it is granted access to view a new accounts payable voucher and the associated PO and receiving report.

The notification is received by the cash disbursements clerk who reviews the document for clerical accuracy. The clerk then prepares a check and records the voucher in the check register. The clerk prints the PO and receiving report and sends them along with the check to the manager for a signature. The negotiable portion of the check is mailed to the vendor and a copy of the check is filed. The voucher packet and a copy of the check are sent back to the accounts payable department. Once received the accounts payable clerk records the check number in the voucher register and files the voucher in the closed voucher file. The general ledger accounts payable control accounts are updated when the cash disbursement voucher information is entered into the computer.

Required:

e. Create a data flow diagram of the current system.

f. Create a document flowchart of the existing system.

g. Analyze the internal control weaknesses in the system. Model your response according to the six categories of physical control activities specified in SAS 78.

h. Prepare a system flowchart of a redesigned computer-based system that resolves the control weaknesses that you identified.

6. Aggressive Ski Company
(Prepared by Ryan Murray, Lehigh University)

Aggressive Ski Company, based out of Aspen, Colorado, manufactures high-performance skis and bindings. Founded in 1973 by a famous retired Olympic skier, the company experienced rapid growth, particularly in the past few years. Aggressive Ski presently holds a 20 percent market share on high-performance skis throughout the world. The company has over 200 employees. Aggressive ski has offices and manufacturing facilities on both the east and west coasts and is particularly proud of its strong relations with its suppliers and conviction to its clients. The company is always working to increase the effectiveness of its supply chain for the good of the company and its customers. To maintain a healthy relationship with its customers, Aggressive Ski offers a 2/10 net 30 to its preeminent customers.

The company is looking to implement a new computer-based system that will help relieve some of its manual operations in the expenditure cycle and wants to ensure it has all the proper controls in place, in compliance with the Sarbanes Oxley Act.

Expenditure Cycle (Prepared by Ryan Murray)
Purchasing System

The inventory control department is responsible for checking inventory levels on an hourly basis to see if inventory levels are getting low. Once a clerk feels inventory is too low, they choose a supplier and create a purchase order (PO) on a company computer. An electronic notification will be sent to accounts payable and receiving, giving the clerks of each department access to view the PO through their terminals. The clerk in inventory control will also create an open purchase order file. All computers throughout the company are networked to each other so that each terminal has secured access to the company's database.

When the raw materials arrive on the unloading dock, a clerk prints a copy of the PO and reconciles it to the packing slip. The clerk then creates a receiving report on a company computer. An electronic notification is sent to accounts payable and inventory control giving the clerks of each department access to view the receiving report. Inventory control updates its records and then prepares a summary for the general ledger department. The receiving report and the PO are then stored in data disk space.

As soon as accounts payable views the copy of the PO from inventory control, a clerk records the liability. When the invoice is received from the vendor, a clerk reconciles the invoice with the liability and then prepares a cash disbursements voucher. The cash disbursement voucher, invoice, receiving report, and PO are all put into the open accounts payable file. The clerk also updates the accounts payable subsidiary ledger and records the liability amount in the purchase journal.

The general ledger department receives and reviews the account summaries from both the inventory control department and accounts payable. The information is then reconciled for accuracy and is posted in the accounts payable and inventory control accounts.

Required:

a. Create a data flow diagram of the current system.

b. Create a document flowchart of the existing system.

c. Analyze the internal control weaknesses in the system. Model your response according to the six categories of physical control activities specified in SAS 78.

d. Prepare a system flowchart of a redesigned computer-based system that resolves the control weaknesses that you identified.

7. Green Mountain Coffee Roasters, Inc.
(Prepared by Ronica Sharma, Lehigh University)

Green Mountain Coffee Roasters, Inc., was founded in 1981 and began as a small cafe in Waitsfield, Vermont, roasting and serving premium coffee on the premises. Green Mountain blends and distributes coffee to a variety of customers, including cafes, delis, and restaurants, and currently has about 6,700 customer accounts reaching states across the nation. As the company has grown, several beverages have been added to their product line, including signature blends, light and heavy roasts, decaffeinated coffee and teas, and herbal teas. Green Mountain Coffee Roasters, Inc., has been publicly traded since 1993 and had sales in excess of $84 million for the fiscal year ended September 2002.

Green Mountain Coffee has a warehouse and manufacturing plant located in Wilton, Vermont, where it presently employees 250 full- and part-time workers. The company receives its beans in bulk from a select group of distributors located across the world, with their largest supplier being Columbia Beans Co. Green Mountain Coffee also sells accessories that complement their products, including mugs, thermoses, and coffee containers that they purchase from their supplier Coffee Lovers Inc. In addition to selling coffee and accessories, Green Mountain uses paper products such as coffee bags, coffee cups, and stirrers to distribute to their customers and package the coffee that they purchase from Save the Trees Inc.

Purchases System

Currently Green Mountain employs a manual purchases system with minimal computer technology. Green Mountain Coffee purchases beans and blends from other companies and then sells them to other stores. Bean inventory fluctuates with respect to sales of blends to stores. Sara is in charge of inventory management in the warehouse. She reviews periodic inventory status reports to identify inventory needs. When items fall to their pre-established reorder point, she prepares a purchase requisition. She keeps a copy for herself in her department, files one in the open purchase requisition file, and sends a copy to accounts payable. At the end of the day, a three-part purchase order (PO) is prepared. One copy is filed and two are sent to the supplier.

When the goods arrive, Sara inspects and counts them and sends the packing slip to Fayth in the accounting department. Using a PC, Sara updates the inventory subsidiary ledger and, at the end of day, sends an account summary to Vic in the general ledger department. After checking that the purchase requisitions exist to support the packing slip, Fayth files the documents in the accounts payable pending file. The supplier's invoice is mailed directly to Fayth, who checks it against the documents in the pending file. Using a computer system, she updates the accounts payable subsidiary ledger and records the transaction in the purchases journal. At the end of the day she prepares a journal voucher, which is sent to Vic in the general ledger department. Using a separate computer system, Vic updates the control accounts

affected by the transactions and files the summary and journal vouchers.

Cash Disbursements System Summary

Using the computer, Fayth reviews the accounts payable file for items due for payment, waiting to the last date to make a payment but still take advantage of the discount. She then updates (closes) the appropriate AP subsidiary record, prints a two-part check, and records the payment in the check register file. Fayth has signature authority for payments under $5,000. Checks for amount greater than $5,000 are sent to Stuart, Green Mountain Coffee's treasurer, who co-signs them and returns them to Fayth. At the close of day, Fayth mails the check to the supplier, files a copy, and prepares a journal voucher, which goes to Vic. Vic records the transaction in the affected general ledger accounts and files the journal voucher.

Required:

a. Create a data flow diagram of the current system.

b. Create a document flowchart of the existing system.

c. Analyze the internal control weaknesses in the system. Model your response according to the six categories of physical control activities specified in SAS 78.

d. Prepare a system flowchart of a redesigned computer-based system that resolves the control weaknesses that you identified.

8. USA Cycle Company

(Prepared by Kim Hancy, Lehigh University)
USA Cycle Company is one of the fastest-growing bicycle distributors in the United States, with headquarters in Chicago, Illinois. Their primary business is distribution of bicycles assembled in China, but they also have a smaller, custom-order business for which they build bicycles from parts purchased from various suppliers. Their product line includes mountain, road, and comfort bikes as well as a juvenile line with up to 24-inch frames. They also distribute BMX bicycles as well as tricycles and trailer bikes. In addition, they distribute various bicycle accessories such as helmets, clothing, lights, and spare parts for all models they carry.

Established in 1975, the company's first warehouses were in Illinois and Wisconsin and supplied retail bicycle outlets primarily in the Midwest. One year ago, USA Cycle Company expanded, adding two additional facilities in Sacramento, California, and Redmond, Washington, to meet the growing demand for their bicycles. They now also sell customized bicycles direct to retailers through the Internet as well as by conventional means.

The company's expansion to the West Coast was coupled with a planned increase in reliance on suppliers in China. Although this resulted in decreased costs, some problems regarding inventory levels arose because of unexpected delays in shipping, primarily attributable to miscommunication and shipping conditions. Because the company does not want to carry excess inventory, they are sometimes forced to seek local suppliers at an increased cost.

USA Cycle Company uses limited computer technology to process business transactions and record accounting data, but the data is distributed and not shared throughout the company. This has caused data redundancy and associated problems of data currency, and these problems have been exacerbated by the company's recent rapid expansion on the West Coast.

Initially, USA Cycle Company was a family-owned business. In need of capital for expansion, the company went public when they added the two facilities on the West Coast. The number of employees rose from 100 to 200 during the expansion. Gross sales also rose from $10 million to $20 million.

Description of Purchases Procedures

The USA Cycle Company purchases process begins when a clerk in the warehouse reviews inventory records. When it is determined that inventory is needed, the clerk inputs the information on the warehouse department microcomputer. This automatically inserts the information into a purchase record file. Four copies of the purchase order (PO) are printed. One copy is filed in the open PO file, two copies are sent to the supplier, and one copy is forwarded to the accounts payable department and filed in the accounts payable pending file.

When the goods are received in the warehouse, the PO is pulled from the open PO file and a clerk inspects, counts, and reconciles the goods to the packing slip and what was ordered. If many orders are received at the same time, the clerk tends to skip the reconciliation process to save time. The clerk places the goods on the warehouse shelves and uses the computer to prepare the receiving report. The information is saved in the receiving record file and two copies of the receiving report are printed. One copy is forwarded to the accounts payable department. The second copy, along with the purchase order and packing slip, is used to update the inventory subsidiary records. The general ledger is automatically updated when changes are made to these records. The source documents are then filed in the closed PO file.

When the receiving report is received in the accounts payable department it is filed in the accounts payable pending file with the purchase order. When the invoice is received from the supplier, both documents are pulled from the accounts payable pending file. A clerk uses these documents to add the record to the purchases journal and post the liability. The PO, receiving report, and invoice are filed in the open accounts payable file. When the liability is recorded, the accounts payable subsidiary ledger, purchases journal, and general ledger are automatically updated.

Description of Cash Disbursements Process

Using the open accounts payable file, in which the source documents are arranged by payment date, a clerk in the accounts payable/cash disbursements department searches for accounts coming due. When payments are due, the clerk removes the PO, receiving report, and invoice from the file to prepare the checks. The checks are used to subsequently update the check register and accounts payable subsidiary ledger. The general ledger is automatically updated. The checks are sent to be signed by the supervisor, who generally signs the checks without much examination. A copy of each check is filed with the purchase order, receiving report, and invoice in the closed accounts payable file. The supervisor then mails the checks to the supplier.

Required:

a. Create a data flow diagram of the current system.

b. Create a document flowchart of the existing system.

c. Analyze the internal control weaknesses in the system. Model your response according to the six categories of physical control activities specified in SAS 78.

d. Prepare a system flowchart of a redesigned computer-based system that resolves the control weaknesses that you identified.

9. Comprehensive Case: New Born Candy Company

(Prepared by Gaurav Mirchandani and Matthew Demko, Lehigh University)

New Born Candy Company is the premier manufacturer and marketer of one of the best-selling candies today. They manufacture and market a variety of sugar-intense candies. James Born, the current CEO of New Born Candy Company, took control of the family-run business in the 1970s, although New Born Candy Company has been in existence since the mid-1930s. The company has grown to two plants on the East Coast and 209 employees across the country.

As of the fiscal year ended 2000, New Born Candy Company experienced gross sales of almost $100 million. A major contributor was its line of Leeps candies and Mike and Wike, among the two most popular sugar candies today. Compared to its competitors, New Born Candy Company performed well. In spite of it relative success, the CEO and management team are concerned about recent increases in costs. For example, the rate of increase in cost of goods sold has been disproportionate with growth in sales. Additionally, they are concerned that if they do not implement essential changes and upgrades to their technology platform, they will no long be able to compete with larger manufacturers. Changes in the environment have drastically affected their production and ability to manufacture and market to larger customers such as Walgreens and CVS, big revenue-producers for the candy company.

As a result, James Born and his management team have decided to hire GMD Consulting Group to examine and identify current weaknesses in accounting and operations and to make suggestions for changes in the future. The following describes the relevant business cycles to be reviewed by GMD.

Revenue Cycle Description

New Born Candy Company receives orders from one of two places: they either are mailed in where they are received and sorted by the mail room, or the sales personnel receive them directly. After the mail is received and sorted by the mail room it is passed on to the sales personnel. GMD Consulting looked further into mail room procedures and operations and made some interesting findings. Jonathan, the supervisor of the mail room, explained to GMD Consulting that there are so many orders (due to the rapid growth of the business and the 6000 + customers) that they have trouble sorting through all of the mail and getting it to the appropriate department. Jonathan explained that people in the mail room have been working a lot of overtime to process the mail, and they still frequently fall behind.

Once the sales personnel receive orders, whether via phone, mail, or other means, they then process the order. In talking with Suzanne, a veteran salesperson for New Born Candy Company, it was discovered that sales orders from the mail room are frequently received a few days, and sometimes a week, after they are received. She also told GMD Consulting that during busy times it is very difficult to process all of the daily orders. After receiving the orders, the sales personnel perform a credit check. When completed, the credit copy is placed into a file along with the customer order. The billing copy is sent to the computer department and the stock release, packing slip, shipping notice, and file copy are sent to the warehouse. Here the goods are picked and sent to shipping along with a copy of the stock release. Shipping then takes the file copy, shipping notice, packing slip, and the stock release and reconciles the goods and documents, signs the shipping notice, and prepares the bill of lading. The prepared bill of lading, along with a packing slip, is given to the carrier. The carrier then ships the goods to the customer. Additionally, a file copy, a copy of the stock release, and a copy of the bill of lading is placed in a shipping file. It is important to note that in examining the shipping department it was found that they have been receiving an increasing number of complaints from customers. Some key documents (found on pages 278–281) shed some light on this issue.

The billing copy that was generated by the sales department is now in the computer department. Here a keystroke places the data into a sales order file. Then an edit run is performed. After the edit run, the data is placed into the edit sales order file. The updated data is put into a sales journal, accounts receivable file, general ledger file, and inventory file. Additionally, a management report is created and sent to management. Lastly, the customer invoice is printed and sent to the customer.

Expenditure Cycle Description

In the computer department of New Born Candy Company, the inventory computer file is reviewed. From this review a requisition list is created and sent to purchases. This requisition list is then made into a purchase order (PO). Multiple POs are prepared and sent to the vendor. While POs are being prepared a copy of the requisition list is placed into a file. Upon further review of purchases and inventory control it was discovered that the New Born Candy Company uses a periodic inventory system. The status of the inventory is taken twice a week, on Mondays and Thursdays. Based on the information generated from the inventory count the necessary purchases are made. Additionally, Sammy, who is a manager in the manufacturing department, said that occasionally they run out of certain raw materials necessary for the production of the candy. As a result they do not always produce to capacity.

When the vendor receives the order from purchases they send the goods and a copy of the PO to the receiving department. Here the PO is placed into a file and the receiving report is prepared. After the receiving report is prepared a copy of the purchase order and a copy of the packing slip are placed into a file. One copy of the receiving report is sent to the purchasing department, where it is placed into a file, and another copy is sent to accounts payable, where it is also placed into a file. A requisition is performed based on the receiving report and the invoice that was sent by the vendor. After the requisition the invoice is placed into a file, a journal voucher is sent to the general ledger department, and the disbursements voucher is sent to the computer department. In the computer department, the disbursements voucher is put into the accounts payable computer file via a keystroke.

The journal voucher that was sent from accounts payable to the general ledger department, along with the summary of entries, is posted and reconciled. It is then put into a general ledger computer file. Additionally, the summary and journal voucher are also placed into a file.

Required:

a. Create data flow diagrams of the revenue and expenditure procedures.

b. Create system flowcharts of the current revenue and expenditure procedures.

c. Analyze the internal control and operational weaknesses and in the system.

d. Prepare system flowcharts of a redesigned system that resolves the control and operational weaknesses that you have identified.

Problem 9:
Cash Disbursements Report For Months May and June

Date	Vendor Name	Check No	Invoice No	Invoice Amount	Payment Discount	Amount
5/1/07	Hall Sugar Company	601	121	$5,200		$5,200
5/8/07	Ray Packaging	602	782	$1,200	$180	$1,020
5/15/07	Brown Chemicals	603	52	$1,875		$1,875
5/16/07	Sinclair Labs	604	122	$2,300		$2,300
5/23/07	Sinclair Labs	605	132	$2,300	$345	$1,995
5/30/07	Sugar Suppliers, Inc.	606	888	$1,275		$1,725
5/30/07	Hallies Sugar Company	607	212	$5,275		$5,272
6/1/07	Color Candies, Inc.	608	222	$1,000		$1,000
6/8/07	Hall Sugar Company	609	121	$5,200		$5,200
6/15/07	Candy Wrappers & Co.	610	787	$1,150		$1,150

Problem 9:
Shipping Report For Months Ended May and June

Date	Customer Name	Customer Shipping Address	Invoice No	Invoice Address	Payment	Date Shipped
11/2/07	James McGuire	12 Maple Avenue, Englewood, NJ 07631	556	12 Maple Avenue, Englewood, NJ 07631	$850	11/2/07
11/2/07	The Hall Candy Store	72 E.4th Street, Easton, PA 18042	233	72 E.4th Street, Easton, PA 18042	$1,975	11/2/07
11/2/07	Smiles Candies & Co.	112 Packard Circle, Easton, PA 18042	428	112 Packard Circle, Easton, PA 18042	$1,290	11/12/07
11/2/07	The Candy Guy, Inc.	47 Cresent Avenue, Allentown, PA 18103	166	47 Cresent Avenue, Allentown, PA 18103	$2,895	11/2/07
11/9/07	Candies & Treats	104 W. 48th Street, New York, NY 10017	983	1694 Corporate Way, Clifton, NJ 07014	$6,800	11/9/07
11/9/07	Kathleen Hallaway	118 Cordes Street, Bedford, NH 03110	108	118 Cordes Street - Bedford, NH 03110	$925	11/9/07
11/10/07	Lehigh University	39 University Drive, Bethlehem, PA 18015	191	39 University Drive, Bethlehem, PA 18015	$11,200	11/10/07
11/10/07	Philadelphia Candy Company	100 Mulbury Street, Philadelphia, PA 19103	333	100 Mulbury Street, Philadelphia, PA 19103	$2,650	11/10/07
11/10/07	Timothy Klienman	18 Heatherspoon Way, Bethlehem, PA 18015	445	18 Heatherspoon Way, Bethlehem, PA 18015	$750	11/10/07
11/16/07	The Candy Store At the Hilton	1810 Beach Way, Boca Raton, FL 33432	972	1810 Beach Way, Boca Raton, FL 33432	$8,200	11/16/07

Problem 9:
Invoice

INVOICE

Sugar Suppliers, Inc.
Billing Department
181 Sugar Plant Way
Allentown, PA 18103

To: New Born Candy Company   **Date:** 8/28/07
1332 Rockaway Avenue   **Invoice #:** 888
24th Floor
Bethlehem, PA 18015

Order Number	Quantity	Description	Total Price
1234	1000 Lbs.	Sugar Qty Code SJRT	$1,275.00
		Total Amount Due	$1,275.00

Prepared by: SKM
Approved by: JAH

Please make payment immediately. Please DO NOT SEND CASH.

Failure to pay within 30 days results in additional late charges.

For additional billings questions please contact us at 1-888-NewBorn

Problem 9:
Invoice

INVOICE
New Born Candy Company
Billing Department
1332 Roackaway Avenue
Bethlehem, PA 18015

To: **Customer Shipping Address:**   **Invoice #:** 983
                                                                     Date of Invoice: 11/30/07

         Candies & Treats
         1694 Corporate Way
         Clifton, NJ 07014

Customer Name	Customer No.	Shipping Date	Amount Due
Candies & Treats	1234	11/09/07	$6,800.00
		Total Amount Due	$6,800.00

Prepared by: SKM
Approved by: JAH

Please make payment immediately. Please DO NOT SEND CASH.

Failure to pay within 30 days results in additional late charges.

For additional billings questions please contact us at 1-888-NewBorn

chapter 6

The Expenditure Cycle Part II: Payroll Processing and Fixed Asset Procedures

LEARNING OBJECTIVES

After studying this chapter, you should:

- Recognize the fundamental tasks that constitute the payroll and fixed asset processes.
- Be able to identify the functional departments involved in payroll and fixed asset activities and trace the flow of these transactions through the organization.
- Be able to specify the documents, journals, and accounts that provide audit trails, promote the maintenance of historical records, and support internal decision making and financial reporting.
- Understand the exposures associated with payroll and fixed asset activities and recognize the controls that reduce these risks.
- Be aware of the operational features and the control implications of technology used in payroll and fixed asset systems.

This chapter is divided into two major sections. The first begins with a conceptual overview of the payroll process emphasizing logical tasks, key entities, sources and uses of information, and the flow of key documents through an organization. We illustrate these features first with a manual system and then consider the operational and control issues related to computer-based alternatives. The second section examines fixed asset systems. Fixed assets are the property, plant, and equipment used in the operation of a business. This discussion focused on processes pertaining to the acquisition, maintenance, and disposal of its fixed assets. Finally, we illustrate these concepts with a real-time example.

THE CONCEPTUAL PAYROLL SYSTEM

Payroll processing is actually a special case purchases system in which the organization purchases labor rather than raw materials or finished goods for resale. The nature of payroll processing, however, creates the need for specialized procedures, for the following reasons:

1. A firm can design general purchasing and disbursement procedures that apply to all vendors and inventory items. Payroll procedures, however, differ greatly among classes of employees. For example, different procedures are needed for hourly employees, salaried employees, piece workers, and commissioned employees. Also, payroll processing requires special accounting procedures for employee deductions and withholdings for taxes that do not apply to trade accounts.

2. General expenditure activities constitute a relatively steady stream of purchasing and disbursing transactions. Business organizations thus design purchasing systems to deal with their normal level of activity. Payroll activities, on the other hand, are discrete events in which disbursements to employees occur weekly, biweekly, or monthly. The task of periodically preparing large numbers of payroll checks in addition to the normal trade account checks can overload the general purchasing and cash disbursements system.

3. Writing checks to employees requires special controls. Combining payroll and trade transactions can encourage payroll fraud.

Although specific payroll procedures vary among firms, Figure 6-1 presents a DFD depicting the general tasks of the payroll system in a manufacturing firm. The key points of the process are described below.

Personnel Department

The personnel department prepares and submits **personnel action forms** to the prepare payroll function. These documents identify employees authorized to receive a paycheck and are used to reflect changes in hourly pay rates, payroll deductions, and job classification. Figure 6-2 shows a personnel action form used to advise payroll of an increase in an employee's salary.

Production Department

Production employees prepare two types of time records: job tickets and time cards. **Job tickets** capture the total amount of time that individual workers spend on each production job. These documents are used by cost accounting to allocate direct labor charges to WIP accounts. **Time cards** capture the total time the employee is at work. These are sent to the prepare payroll function for calculating the amount of the employee's paycheck. Figure 6-3 illustrates a job ticket, and Figure 6-4 illustrates a time card.

Each day at the beginning of the shift, employees place their time cards in a special clock that records arrivals and departures. Typically they "clock out" for lunch period and at the end of the shift. This time card is the formal record of daily attendance. At the end of the week, the supervisor reviews the time cards, signs them, and sends them to the payroll department.

Update WIP Account

After cost accounting allocates labor costs to the work-in-process (WIP) accounts, the charges are summarized in a **labor distribution summary** and forwarded to the general ledger function.

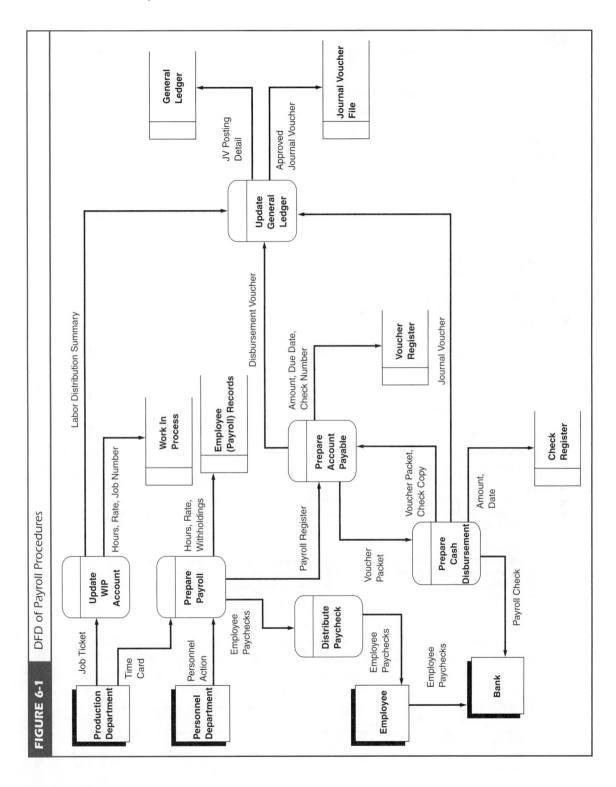

FIGURE 6-1   DFD of Payroll Procedures

FIGURE 6-2   Personnel Action form

Salary Increase Recommendation

Based on the attached appraisal form, the following recommendation is made for:

Name: *Jane Doe*
Position: *Accounting Clerk*
Social Security Number: *111 – 22 – 3333*

Current Salary: *23,520.00*
Current Bonus Level: *00%*
Last Increase Date: *08/22/06*
Next Increase Date: *08/22/07*

Current Performance Rating:
(from attached appraisal)   *good*

Salary Increase Guidelines:
Outstanding: 6–9%   9–12 months
Superior: 4–6%   12 months
Good: 3–4%   12–15 months
Provisional: 0%   Review again in 90 days.

In view of the Current Performance and the Salary Increase Guidelines, I recommend the following salary treatment:

Percentage Increase: *4*   %
New Salary: $ *24,460*
Effective Date: *8* / *22* / *07*

Promotions:
In the case of a promotion, a standard 5% increase for the promotion and a pro-rated merit increase (based on time since last merit increase) are appropriate. The next increase will be considered from the date of promotion.

Other Considerations:
In some situations, it is possible to advance a salary beyond the above guidelines as an exception, with the President's approval. Some typical situations are, but are not limited to, equity adjustment and job reevaluation. If such is the case here, please provide justification below:

Approvals: *J. R. Johnson* _____ Supervisor
                  H. M. Màãāi _____ Director of Personnel

Exception approval if needed: _____ *N/A* _____ President

FIGURE 6-3   Job Ticket

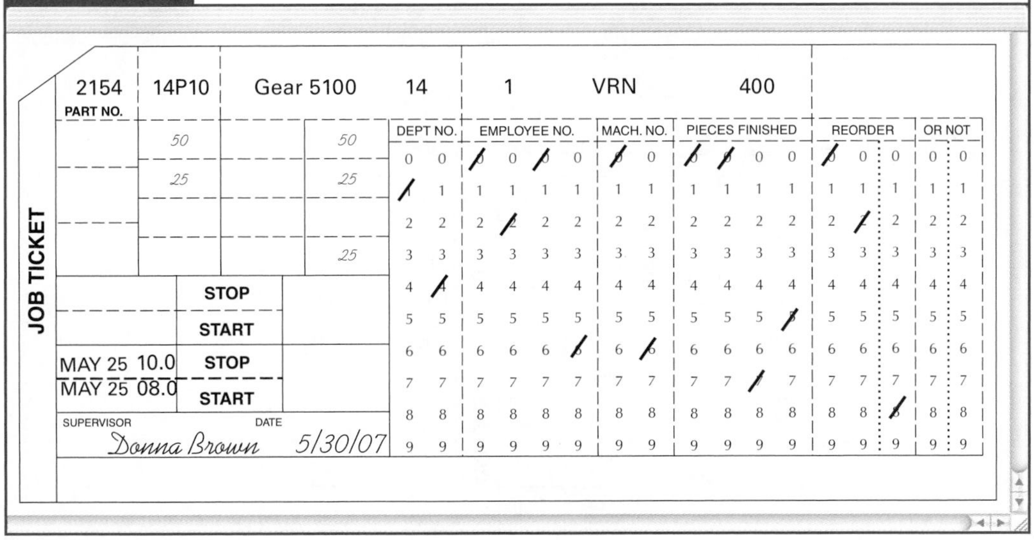

Prepare Payroll

The payroll department receives pay rate and withholding data from the personnel department and hours-worked data from the production department. A clerk in payroll then performs the following tasks.

1. Prepares the **payroll register** (Figure 6-5) showing gross pay, deductions, overtime pay, and net pay.
2. Enters the above information into the **employee payroll records** (Figure 6-6).
3. Prepares **employee paychecks** (Figure 6-7).
4. Sends the paychecks to the distribute paycheck function.
5. Files the time cards, personnel action form, and copy of the payroll register (not shown).

Distribute Paycheck

A form of payroll fraud involves submitting time cards for non-existent employees. To prevent this, many companies use a paymaster to distribute the paychecks to employees. This individual is independent of the payroll process—not involved in payroll authorization or preparation tasks. If a particular paycheck goes unclaimed by a valid employee, the paymaster returns it to payroll. The reason the check went unclaimed can then be investigated.

Prepare Accounts Payable

The accounts payable clerk reviews the payroll register for correctness and prepares copies of a cash disbursement voucher for the amount of the payroll. The clerk records the voucher in the voucher register and submits the voucher packet (voucher and payroll register) to cash disbursements. A copy of the disbursement voucher is sent to the general ledger function.

Prepare Cash Disbursement

Upon receipt of the voucher packet, the cash disbursements function prepares a single check for the entire amount of the payroll and deposits it the **payroll imprest account**. The employee paychecks are drawn on this account, which is used only for payroll. Funds

FIGURE 6-4   Time card

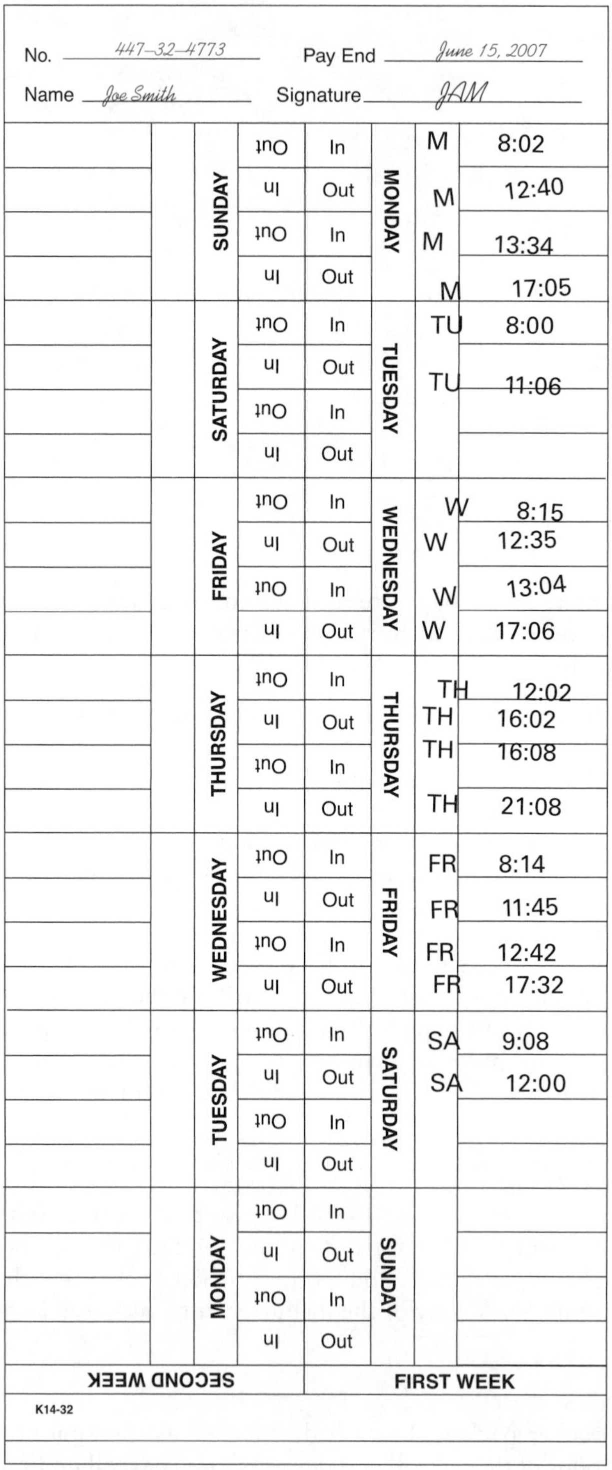

No. _447–32–4773_   Pay End _June 15, 2007_

Name _Joe Smith_   Signature _JAM_

			Out	In			
		SUNDAY	Out	In	**MONDAY**	M	8:02
			In	Out		M	12:40
			Out	In		M	13:34
			In	Out		M	17:05
		SATURDAY	Out	In	**TUESDAY**	TU	8:00
			In	Out		TU	11:06
			Out	In			
			In	Out			
		FRIDAY	Out	In	**WEDNESDAY**	W	8:15
			In	Out		W	12:35
			Out	In		W	13:04
			In	Out		W	17:06
		THURSDAY	Out	In	**THURSDAY**	TH	12:02
			In	Out		TH	16:02
			Out	In		TH	16:08
			In	Out		TH	21:08
		WEDNESDAY	Out	In	**FRIDAY**	FR	8:14
			In	Out		FR	11:45
			Out	In		FR	12:42
			In	Out		FR	17:32
		TUESDAY	Out	In	**SATURDAY**	SA	9:08
			In	Out		SA	12:00
			Out	In			
			In	Out			
		MONDAY	Out	In	**SUNDAY**		
			In	Out			
			Out	In			
			In	Out			

SECOND WEEK	FIRST WEEK

K14-32

FIGURE 6-5	Payroll Register

H₂C HAMPSHIRE SUPPLY COMPANY

Payroll register for period ending   10/31/07
Checks: All
Employee(s): All

Check# 5000   Paid to Emp# CAS : CASEY, SUE

PAY	Hours	Rate	Gross	DEDUCTIONS	
Regular	173.33		1,000.00	SD SDI	9.00
Overtime			0.00	HL INSUR	100.00
Sick			0.00	SV SAVINGS	100.00
Holiday			0.00		0.00
Vacation			0.00	Fed. withholding	16.25
			0.00	Addl. fed. withholding	0.00
				State withholding	21.77
Totals	173.33		1,000.00	Social Security	62.00
				Medicare	14.50
Days worked	21			NET PAY	676.48

Check# 5001   Paid to Emp# JON : JONES, JESSICA

PAY	Hours	Rate	Gross	DEDUCTIONS	
Regular	173.33	15.00	2,599.95	SD SDI	23.40
Overtime		30.00	0.00	HL INSUR	100.00
Sick		15.00	0.00	SV SAVINGS	260.00
Holiday		45.00	0.00		0.00
Vacation		15.00	0.00	Fed. withholding	256.24
			0.00	Addl. fed. withholding	0.00
				State withholding	116.98
Totals	173.33		2,599.95	Social Security	161.20
				Medicare	37.70
Days worked	21			NET PAY	1,644.43

Check# 5002   Paid to Emp # ROB : ROBERTS, WILLIAM

Regular	173.33	15.00	2,599.95	SD SDI	23.40
Overtime		30.00	0.00	HL INSUR	100.00
Sick		15.00	0.00	SV SAVINGS	260.00
Holiday		45.00	0.00		0.00
Vacation		15.00	0.00	Fed. withholding	396.07
			0.00	Addl. fed. withholding	0.00
				State withholding	208.04
Totals	173.33		2,599.95	Social Security	161.20
				Medicare	37.70
Days worked	21			NET PAY	1,413.54

FIGURE 6-6	Employee Payroll Record

HᴄB HAMPSHIRE SUPPLY COMPANY

Employee pay and earnings information

Period Ending   10/31/07

Emp# : JON   SS# : 682–63–0897   JESSICA JONES

Rate: 15.00/ hour

Addl   FITW/ check: 0.00

Normal deduction(s)			Amount
Ded 1 SD	%	0.9000	0.00
Ded 2 HL	%	0.0000	100.00
Ded 3 SV	%	10.0000	0.00
Ded 4	%	0.0000	0.00

Earnings:	– Quarter to date –		— Year to date —	
	Hours	Amount	Hours	Amount
Regular	173.3	2,599.95	173.3	2,599.95
Overtime	0.0	0.00	0.0	0.00
Sick	0.0	0.00	0.0	0.00
Vacation	0.0	0.00	0.0	0.00
Holiday	0.0	0.00	0.0	0.00
	0.0	0.00	0.0	0.00
Withholding:				
FIT		256.24		256.24
SIT		116.98		116.98
Social Security		161.20		161.20
Medicare		37.70		37.70
Deductions:				
SDI		23.40		23.40
HEALTH INSUR		100.00		100.00
SAVINGS		260.00		260.00
		0.00		0.00

FIGURE 6-7	Employee paycheck

H₂C HAMPSHIRE SUPPLY COMPANY

| HOURS | | RATE | REGULAR EARNINGS | OVERTIME EARNINGS | OTHER PAY | | | GROSS | PERIOD ENDING |
REGULAR	OVERTIME				UNITS	RATE	AMOUNT		
173.33	00.00	R 15/Hr	$2,599.95	$00.00	Holiday	45.00	00.00	2,599.95	10/31/07
		OT 30/Hr			Sick	15.00	00.00		TOTAL GROSS
					Vacat.	15.00	00.00		2,599.95

DEDUCTIONS

F.I.C.A.	FED. W/H	STATE W/H			CONTROL NUMBER
161.20	256.24	116.98			682-63-0897
37.70					TOTAL DEDUCTIONS
					955.52

YEAR TO DATE

F.I.C.A.	FED. W/H	STATE W/H	OTHER		NET PAY
161.20	256.24	116.98	SDI	23.40	1,644.43
			HI	100.00	
			SAV	260.00	

EMPLOYEE'S NAME AND SOC. SEC. NO.

JONES, JESSICA
682-63-0897

H₂C HAMPSHIRE SUPPLY COMPANY
406 LAKE AVE.   PH. 323-555-7448
SEATTLE, CA 92801

No. 5001

H₂C HAMPSHIRE SUPPLY COMPANY
406 LAKE AVE.   PH. 323-555-7448
SEATTLE, CA 92801

STATE BANK
4000 PENNSYLVANIA AVE.
UMA CA 98210

PAY: One Thousand Six Hundred Forty-Four and 43/100 dollars
TO THE
ORDER OF

AMOUNT $*******1,644.43

JESSICA JONES
72 N. LOTUS AVE #1
SAN GABRIEL CA 91775-8321

DATE
October 31, 2007

must be transferred from the general cash account to this imprest account before the paychecks can be cashed. The clerk sends a copy of the check along with the disbursement voucher and the payroll register to the accounts payable department, where they are filed (not shown). Finally, a journal voucher is prepared and sent to the general ledger function.

Update General Ledger

The general ledger function receives the labor distribution summary from cost accounting, the disbursement voucher from accounts payable, and the journal voucher from cash disbursements. With this information, the general ledger clerk makes the following accounting entries:

FROM THE LABOR DISTRIBUTION SUMMARY

	DR	CR
Work-in-Process (Direct labor)	XXX.XX	
Factory Overhead (Indirect labor)	XXX.XX	
Wages Payable		XXX.XX

FROM DISBURSEMENT VOUCHER

	DR	CR
Wages Payable	XXX.XX	
Cash		XXX.XX
Fed. Income Tax Withholdings Payable		XXX.XX
State Income Tax Withholdings Payable		XXX.XX
FICA Income Tax Withholdings Payable		XXX.XX
Group Insurance Premiums Payable		XXX.XX
Pension Fund Withholdings Payable		XXX.XX
Union Dues Payable		XXX.XX

The debits and credits from these entries must equal. If they do not, there is an error in the calculation of either labor distribution charges or payroll. When the equality has been verified, the clerk files the voucher and labor distribution summary.

PAYROLL CONTROLS

Transaction Authorization

A form of payroll fraud involves submitting time cards to payroll for employees who no longer work for the firm. To prevent this, the personnel action form helps payroll keep the employee records current. This document describes additions, deletions, and other changes to the employee file and acts as an important authorization control to ensure that only the time cards of current and valid employees are processed.

Segregation of Duties

The time-keeping function and the personnel function should be separated. The personnel function provides payroll with pay-rate information for authorized hourly employees. Typically, an organization will offer a range of valid pay rates based on experience, job classification, seniority, and merit. If this information were to be provided by the production (time-keeping) department, an employee might submit a higher rate and perpetrate a fraud.

For purposes of operational efficiency, the payroll function performs several tasks. Some of these are in contradiction with basic internal control objectives. For example, the payroll function has both asset custody (employee paychecks) and record-keeping responsibility (employee payroll records). This is equivalent in the general purchases system of assigning accounts payable and cash disbursement responsibility to the same person.[1] Control is returned to the process by segregating key aspects of the payroll transaction between accounts payable and cash disbursement functions. Accounts payable reviews the work done by payroll (payroll register) and approves payment. Cash disbursements then writes the check to cover the total payroll. None of the employee paychecks prepared by the payroll function is a negotiable instrument until the payroll check is deposited into the imprest account.

Supervision
Sometimes employees will "clock in" for another worker who is late or absent. Supervisors should observe the time-keeping process and reconcile the time cards with actual attendance.

Accounting Records
The audit trail for payroll includes the following documents:

1. Time cards, job tickets, and disbursement vouchers.
2. Journal information, which comes from the labor distribution summary and the payroll register.
3. Subsidiary ledger accounts, which contain the employee records and various expense accounts.
4. The general ledger accounts: payroll control, cash, and the payroll clearing (imprest) account.

Access Controls
The assets associated with the payroll system are labor and cash. Both can be misappropriated through improper access to accounting records. A dishonest individual can misrepresent on the time cards the number of hours worked and thus embezzle cash. Similarly, control over access to all journals, ledgers, and source documents in the payroll system is important, as it is in all expenditure cycle systems.

Independent Verification
The following are examples of independent verification controls in the payroll system:

1. *Verification of time*. Before sending time cards to payroll, the supervisor must verify their accuracy and sign them.
2. *Paymaster*. The use of an independent paymaster to distribute checks (rather than the normal supervisor) helps verify the existence of the employees. The supervisor may be party to a payroll fraud by pretending to distribute paychecks to nonexistent employees.
3. *Accounts payable*. The accounts payable clerk verifies the accuracy of the payroll register before creating a disbursement voucher that transfers funds to the imprest account.
4. *General ledger*. The general ledger department provides verification of the overall process by reconciling the labor distribution summary and the payroll disbursement voucher.

---

1   This opens the opportunity for the person to create a false liability to himself (or an agent), approve payment, and write the check.

THE PHYSICAL PAYROLL SYSTEM

In this section we examine the physical payroll system. This begins with a very brief review of manual procedures.[2] We then move on to review examples of automated and reengineered payroll systems.

FIGURE 6-8	Manual Payroll System

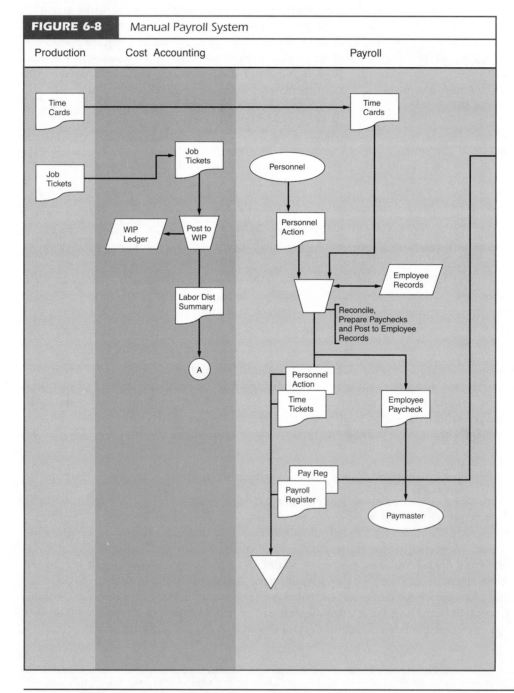

MANUAL PAYROLL SYSTEM

Figure 6-8 presents a flowchart detailing the previous procedures in the context of a manual system. The following key tasks are discussed.

1. Payroll authorization and hours worked enter the payroll department from two different sources: personnel and production.

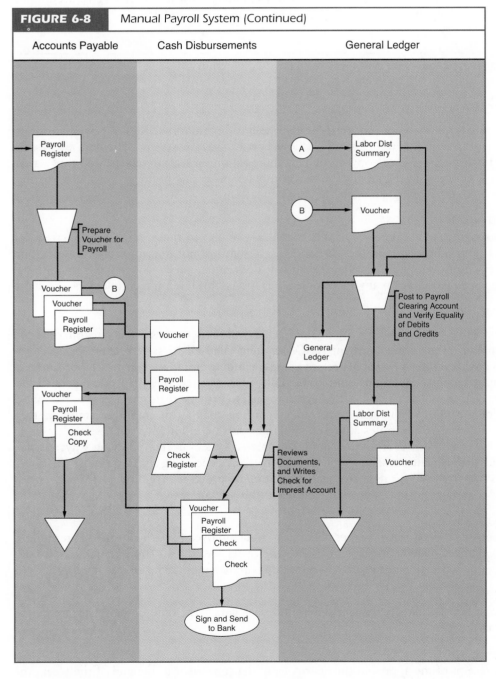

FIGURE 6-8   Manual Payroll System (Continued)

2. The payroll department reconciles this information, calculates the payroll, and distributes paychecks to the employees.

3. Cost accounting receives information regarding the time spent on each job from production. This is used for posting to the work-in-process (WIP) account.
4. Accounts payable receives payroll summary information from the payroll department and authorizes the cash disbursements department to deposit a single check, in the amount of the total payroll, in a bank imprest account on which the payroll is drawn.
5. The general ledger department reconciles summary information from cost accounting and accounts payable. Control accounts are updated to reflect these transactions.

COMPUTER-BASED PAYROLL SYSTEMS

AUTOMATING THE PAYROLL SYSTEM USING BATCH PROCESSING

Because payroll systems run periodically (weekly or monthly), they are well suited to batch processing. Figure 6-9 shows a flowchart for such a system. The data processing department receives hard copy of the personnel action forms, job tickets, and time cards, which it converts to digital files. Batch computer programs perform the check writing, detailed record keeping, and general ledger functions.

Control Implications
The strengths and weaknesses of this system are similar to those in the batch system for general expenditures discussed earlier. This system promotes accounting accuracy and reduces check-writing errors. Beyond this, it does not significantly enhance operational efficiency; however, for many types of organizations, this level of technology is adequate.

REENGINEERING THE PAYROLL SYSTEM

For moderate-sized and large organizations, payroll processing is often integrated within the **human resource management (HRM) system.** The HRM system captures and processes a wide range of personnel-related data, including employee benefits, labor resource planning, employee relations, employee skills, personnel actions (pay rates, deductions, and so on), as well as payroll. HRM systems need to provide real-time access to personnel files for purposes of direct inquires and recording changes in employee status as they occur. Figure 6-10 illustrates a payroll system as part of an HRM system.

This system differs from the simple automated system in the following ways: (1) the various departments transmit transactions to data processing via terminals, (2) direct access files are used for data storage, and (3) many processes are now performed in real time. We discuss the key operating features of this system next.

Personnel
The personnel department makes changes to the employee file in real time via terminals. These changes include additions of new employees, deletions of terminated employees, changes in dependents, changes in withholding, and changes in job status (pay rate).

Cost Accounting
The cost accounting department enters job cost data (real time or daily) to create the **labor usage file.**

Time-keeping
Upon receipt of the approved time cards from the supervisor at the end of the week, the time-keeping department creates the current **attendance file.**

FIGURE 6-9   Batch Payroll System

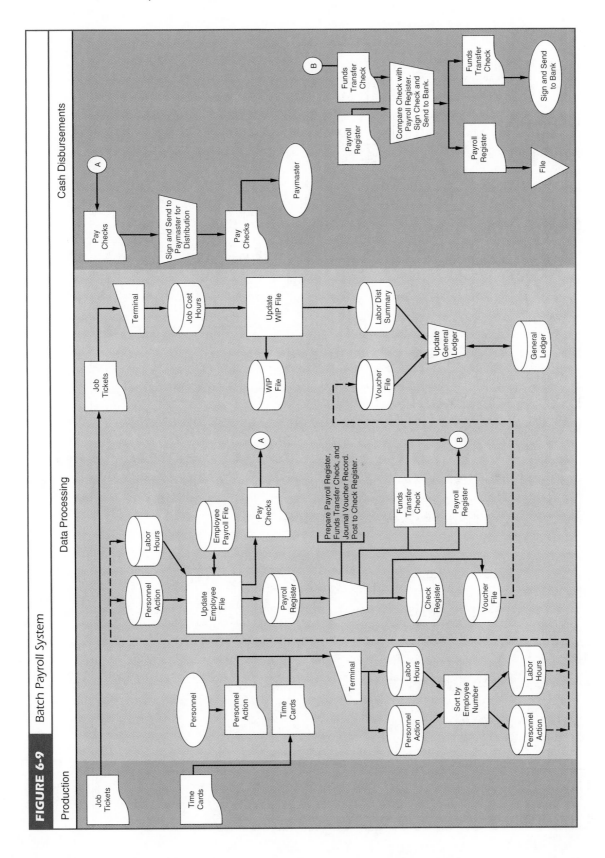

Production | Data Processing | Cash Disbursements

FIGURE 6-10   Payroll System with Real-Time Elements

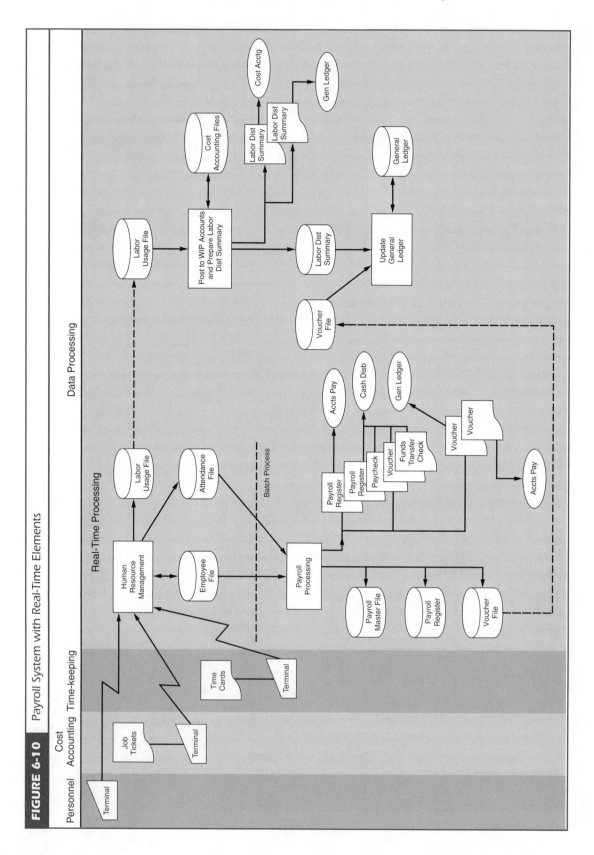

Data Processing

At the end of the work period, the following tasks are performed in a batch process:

1. Labor costs are distributed to various work-in-process, overhead, and expense accounts.
2. An online labor distribution summary file is created. Copies of the file are sent to the cost accounting and general ledger departments.
3. An online payroll register is created from the attendance file and the **employee file**. Copies of the files are sent to the accounts payable and cash disbursements departments.
4. The employee records file is updated.
5. Payroll checks are prepared and signed. They are sent to the treasurer for review and reconciliation with the payroll register. The paychecks are then distributed to the employees.[3]
6. The disbursement voucher file is updated and a check is prepared for the funds transfer to the imprest payroll account. The check and a hard copy of the disbursement voucher are sent to cash disbursements. One copy of the voucher is sent to the general ledger department, and the final copy is sent to accounts payable.
7. At the end of processing, the system retrieves the labor distribution summary file and the disbursements voucher file and updates the general ledger file.

Control Implications

The real-time features of the payroll system provide many of the operational benefits discussed earlier, including reductions paper, clerical labor, and in the lag time between event occurrence and recording them. As mentioned before, these features carry control implications. Computer-based systems must produce adequate records for independent verification and audit purposes. Also, controls must be implemented to protect against unauthorized access to data files and computer programs.

THE CONCEPTUAL FIXED ASSET SYSTEM

Fixed assets are the property, plant, and equipment used in the operation of a business. These are relatively permanent items that often collectively represent the largest financial investment by the organization. Examples of fixed assets include land, buildings, furniture, machinery, and motor vehicles. A firm's fixed asset system processes transactions pertaining to the acquisition, maintenance, and disposal of its fixed assets. The specific objectives of the fixed asset system are to:

1. Process the acquisition of fixed assets as needed and in accordance with formal management approval and procedures.
2. Maintain adequate accounting records of asset acquisition, cost, description, and physical location in the organization.
3. Maintain accurate depreciation records for depreciable assets in accordance with acceptable methods.
4. Provide management with information to help plan for future fixed asset investments.
5. Properly record the retirement and disposal of fixed assets.

The fixed asset system shares some characteristics with the expenditure cycle presented in Chapter 5, but two important differences distinguish these systems. First, the expenditure

---

3   For added internal control, many companies encourage their employees to have their checks directly deposited into their bank accounts.

cycle processes routine acquisitions of raw material and finished goods inventories. The fixed asset system processes nonroutine transactions for a wider group of users in the organization. Managers in virtually all functional areas of the organization make capital investments in fixed assets, but these transactions occur with less regularity than inventory acquisitions. Because fixed asset transactions are unique, they require specific management approval and explicit authorization procedures. In contrast, organizations often automate the authorization procedures for routine acquisitions of inventories.

The second difference between these systems is that organizations usually treat inventory acquisitions as an expense of the current period, while they capitalize fixed assets that yield benefits for multiple periods. Because the productive life of a fixed asset extends beyond one year, its acquisition cost is apportioned over its lifetime and depreciated in accordance with accounting conventions and statutory requirements. Therefore, fixed asset accounting systems include cost allocation and matching procedures that are not part of routine expenditure systems.

THE LOGIC OF A FIXED ASSET SYSTEM

Figure 6-11 presents the general logic of the fixed asset system. The process involves three categories of tasks: asset acquisition, asset maintenance, and asset disposal.

Asset Acquisition

Asset acquisition usually begins with the departmental manager (user) recognizing the need to obtain a new asset or replace an existing one. Authorization and approval procedures over the transaction will depend on the asset's value. Department managers typically have authority to approve purchases below a certain materiality limit. Capital expenditures above the limit will require approval from the higher management levels. This may involve a formal cost-benefit analysis and the formal solicitation of bids from suppliers.

Once the request is approved and a supplier is selected, the fixed asset acquisition task is similar to the expenditure cycle procedures described in Chapter 5, with two noteworthy differences. First, the receiving department delivers the asset into the custody of the user/manager rather than a central store or warehouse. Second, the fixed asset department, not inventory control, performs the record-keeping function.

Asset Maintenance

Asset maintenance involves adjusting the fixed asset subsidiary account balances as the assets (excluding land) depreciate over time or with usage. Common depreciation methods in use are straight line, sum-of-the-years' digits, double-declining balance, and units of production. The method of depreciation and the period used should reflect, as closely as possible, the asset's actual decline in utility to the firm. Accounting conventions and IRS rules sometimes specify the depreciation method to be used. For example, businesses must depreciate new office buildings using the straight-line method and use a period of at least 40 years. The depreciation of fixed assets used to manufacture products is charged to manufacturing overhead and then allocated to WIP. Depreciation charges from assets not used in manufacturing are treated as expenses in the current period.

Depreciation calculations are transactions that the fixed asset system must be designed to anticipate internally when no external event (source document) triggers the action. An important record used to initiate this task is the **depreciation schedule**. A separate depreciation schedule, such as the one illustrated in Figure 6-12, will be prepared by the system for each fixed asset in the fixed asset subsidiary ledger.

A depreciation schedule shows when and how much depreciation to record. It also shows when to stop taking depreciation on fully depreciated assets. This information in a management report is also useful for planning asset retirement and replacement.

FIGURE 6-11 DFD for Fixed Asset System

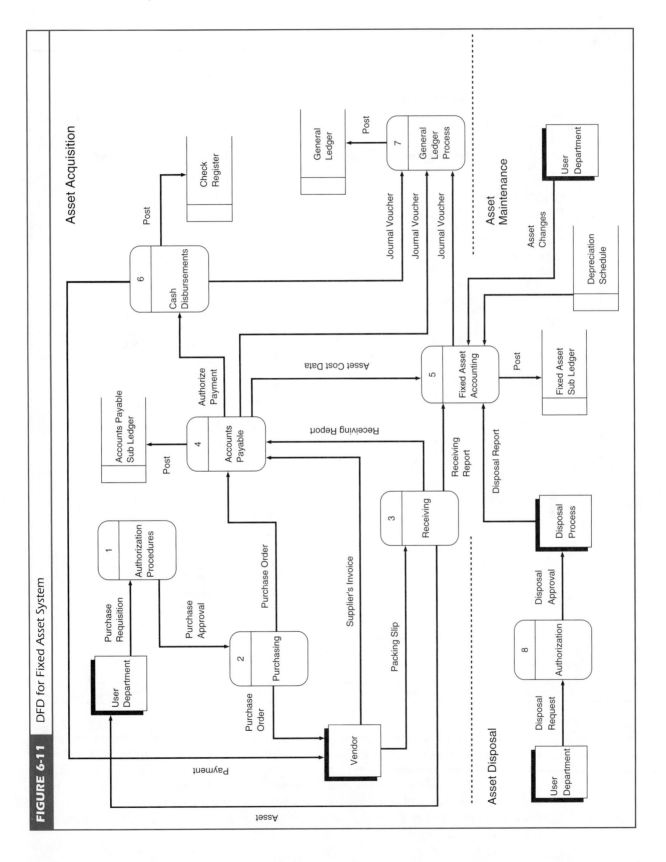

FIGURE 6-12	Depreciation Schedule

OZMENT'S INDUSTRIAL SUPPLY
ASSET LISTING WITH DEPRECIATION SCHEDULES
FROM 200 THROUGH 200

Code	Type	Description	Month#	Depn. exp.	Acc. depn.	Book value
200	OFF&F					

OFFICE FURNITURE
Depn. method: SYD
Life in years: 5
Date acquired 2/01/07
Date retired
Cost   5,500.00
Residual   500.00
Acc. Depn. 2,222.23

Month#	Depn. exp.	Acc. depn.	Book value
1	138.89	138.89	5,361.11
2	138.89	277.78	5,222.22
3	138.89	416.67	5,083.33
4	138.89	555.56	4,944.44
5	138.89	694.45	4,805.55
6	138.89	833.34	4,666.66
7	138.89	972.23	4,527.77
8	138.89	1,111.12	4,388.88
9	138.89	1,250.01	4,249.99
10	138.89	1,388.90	4,111.10
•	•	•	•
•	•	•	•
•	•	•	•
52	27.78	4,777.80	722.20
53	27.78	4,805.58	694.42
54	27.78	4,833.36	666.64
55	27.78	4,861.14	638.86
56	27.78	4,888.92	611.08
57	27.78	4,916.70	583.30
58	27.78	4,944.48	555.52
59	27.78	4,972.26	527.74
60	27.78	5,000.04	499.96

Assets listed: 1

Asset maintenance also involves adjusting asset accounts to reflect the cost of physical improvements that increase the asset's value or extend its useful life. Such enhancements, which are themselves capital investments, are processed as new asset acquisitions.

Finally, the fixed asset system must promote accountability by keeping track of the physical location of each asset. Unlike inventories, which are usually consolidated in secure areas, fixed assets are distributed throughout the organization and are subject to risk from theft and misappropriation. When one department transfers custody of an asset to another department, information about the transfer should be recorded in the fixed asset subsidiary ledger. Each subsidiary record should indicate the current location of the asset. The ability to locate and verify the physical existence of fixed assets is an important component of the audit trail.

Asset Disposal

When an asset has reached the end of its useful life or when management decides to dispose of it, the asset must be removed from the fixed asset subsidiary ledger. The bottom left portion of Figure 6-11 illustrates the **asset disposal** process. It begins when the responsible manager issues a request to dispose of the asset. Like any other transaction, the disposal of an asset requires proper approval. The disposal options open to the firm are to sell, scrap, donate, or retire the asset in place. A disposal report describing the final disposition of the asset is sent to the fixed asset accounting department to authorize its removal from the ledger.

THE PHYSICAL FIXED ASSET SYSTEM

COMPUTER-BASED FIXED ASSET SYSTEM

Because many of the tasks in the fixed asset system are similar in concept to the purchases system in Chapter 5, we will dispense with a review of manual procedures. Figure 6-13 illustrates a computer-based fixed asset system, which demonstrates real-time processing. The top portion of the flowchart presents the fixed asset acquisition procedures, the center portion presents fixed asset maintenance procedures, and the bottom portion presents the asset disposal procedures. To simplify the flowchart and focus on the key features of the system, we have omitted the processing steps for accounts payable and cash disbursements.

Acquisition Procedures

The process begins when the fixed asset accounting clerk receives a receiving report and a cash disbursement voucher. These documents provide evidence that the firm has physically received the asset and show its cost. From the computer terminal a clerk creates a record of the asset in the fixed asset subsidiary ledger. Figure 6-14 presents a possible record structure for this file.

Notice that in addition to the historic cost information, the record contains data specifying the asset's useful life, its salvage (residual) value, the depreciation method to be used, and the asset's location in the organization.

The fixed asset system automatically updates the fixed asset control account in the general ledger and prepares journal vouchers for the general ledger department as evidence of the entry. The system also produces reports for accounting management. Figure 6-15 illustrates the fixed asset status report showing the cost, the accumulated depreciation (if any), and residual value for each of the firm's fixed assets.

Based on the depreciation parameters contained in the fixed asset records, the system prepares a depreciation schedule for each asset when its acquisition is originally recorded. The schedule is stored on computer disk to permit future depreciation calculations.

Asset Maintenance

The fixed asset system uses the depreciation schedules to record end-of-period depreciation transactions automatically. The specific tasks include (1) calculating the current period's depreciation, (2) updating the accumulated depreciation and book value fields in

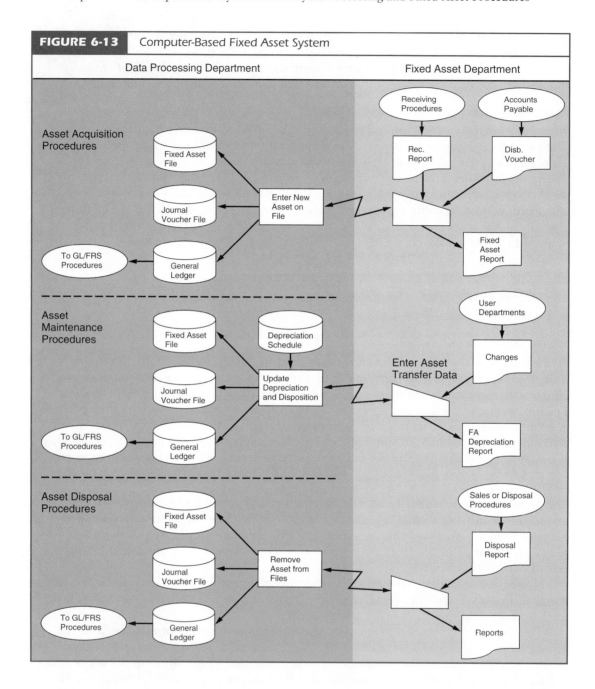

FIGURE 6-13   Computer-Based Fixed Asset System

the subsidiary records, (3) posting the total amount of depreciation to the affected general ledger accounts (depreciation expense and accumulated depreciation), and (4) recording the depreciation transaction by adding a record to the journal voucher file. Finally, a fixed asset depreciation report, shown in Figure 6-16, is sent to the fixed asset department for review.

Department managers must report any changes in the custody or status of assets to the fixed asset department. From a computer terminal a clerk records such changes in the fixed asset subsidiary ledger.

FIGURE 6-14	Fixed Asset Record Structure

ITEM NUMBER	LOCATION	DESCRIP.	ASSET TYPE	ASSET LIFE/ MONTHS	COST	RESIDUAL VALUE	DEPR. METHOD	PERIOD/ MONTH	RETIRE DATE	ACCUM. DEPN.	BOOK VALUE
200	Rm. 182	Photocopier	Off&F	60	5,500.00	500.00	SYD	5	N/A	694.45	4,805.55

Disposal Procedures

The disposal report formally authorizes the fixed asset department to remove from the ledger an asset disposed of by the user department. When the clerk deletes the record from the fixed asset subsidiary ledger, the system automatically (1) posts an adjusting entry to the fixed asset control account in the general ledger, (2) records any loss or gain associated with the disposal, and (3) prepares a journal voucher. A fixed asset status report containing details of the deletion is sent to the fixed asset department for review.

CONTROLLING THE FIXED ASSET SYSTEM

Because of the similarities between the fixed asset system and the expenditure cycle, many of the controls are the same and have already been discussed. Our discussion of fixed asset controls will thus focus on three areas of principal difference between these systems: authorization, supervision, and independent verification.

Authorization Controls

Fixed asset acquisitions should be formal and explicitly authorized. Each transaction should be initiated by a written request from the user or department. In the case of high-value items, there should be an independent approval process that evaluates the merits of the request on a cost-benefit basis.

Supervision Controls

Because capital assets are widely distributed throughout the organization, they are more susceptible to theft and misappropriation than inventories that are secured in a warehouse. Therefore, management supervision is an important element in the physical security of fixed assets. Supervisors must ensure that fixed assets are being used in accordance with the organization's policies and business practices. For example, microcomputers purchased for individual employees should be secured in their proper location and should not be removed from the premises without explicit approval. Company vehicles should be secured in the organization's motor pool at the end of the shift and should not be taken home for personal use unless authorized by the appropriate supervisor.

FIGURE 6-15   Asset Status Report

OZMENT'S INDUSTRIAL SUPPLY
ASSET LISTING

Code	Type	Description
100	OFF&F	
	COMPUTER SYSTEM	
	Depn. method: SL	
	Life in years: 5	
	Date acquired 1/01/07	
	Date retired	
	Cost	40,000.00
	Residual	4,000.00
	Acc. Depn.	10,800.00
200	OFF&F	
	OFFICE FURNITURE	
	Depn. method: SL	
	Life in years: 5	
	Date acquired 2/01/07	
	Date retired	
	Cost	5 ,500.00
	Residual	500.00
	Acc. Depn.	2,222.23
300	MACH	
	SNOWBLOWER	
	Depn. method: DDB	
	Life in years: 5	
	Date acquired 2/01/07	
	Date retired	
	Cost	1 ,000.00
	Residual	0.00
	Acc. Depn.	499.96
400	MACH	
	TRUCK	
	Depn. method: SL	
	Life in years: 3	
	Date acquired 12/01/07	
	Date retired	
	Cost	2 ,000.00
	Residual	0.00
	Acc. Depn.	2,333.31

FIGURE 6-16	Fixed Asset Depreciation Report

OZMENT'S INDUSTRIAL SUPPLY
DEPRECIATION CALCULATIONS LISTING THROUGH
6/30/07 POSTED AS BATCH #1327

Code	Method		Description	Depn. Expense
100	SL	5 yr	COMPUTER SYSTEM	3,600.00
200	SYD	5 yr	OFFICE FURNITURE	694.44
300	DDB	5 yr	SNOWBLOWER	133.33
400	SL	3 yr	DELIVERY TRUCK	0.00
500	SL	3 yr	DELIVERY TRUCK	0.00
600	SL	3 yr	TRUCK	2,333.31

Assets listed: 6			Total	6,761.08

GL summary:

615	DEPRECIATION EXPENSE	6,761.08	
151	ACCUM DEPN. EQUIPMENT		6,761.08

Independent Verification Controls

Periodically, the internal auditor should review the asset acquisition and approval procedures to determine the reasonableness of factors used in the analysis. These include the useful life of the asset, the original financial cost, the proposed cost savings as a result of acquiring the asset, the discount rate used, and the capital budgeting method used in the analysis.

The internal auditor should verify the location, condition, and fair value of the organization's fixed assets against the fixed asset records in the subsidiary ledger. In addition, the automatic depreciation charges calculated by the fixed asset system should be reviewed and verified for accuracy and completeness. System errors that miscalculate depreciation can result in the material misstatement of operating expenses, reported earnings, and asset values.

SUMMARY

The chapter began with an examination of payroll procedures. The discussion focused on fundamental tasks; the functional departments; and the documents, journals, and accounts that constitute the payroll system. Common exposures and controls that reduce risks inherent in payroll activities were explained. In addition, the operational features and the control implications of technology used in payroll systems were reviewed.

The second section of the chapter presented the typical features of the fixed asset system. Fixed asset accounting involves three classes of procedures: asset acquisition, asset maintenance, and asset disposal. We examined the files, procedures, and reports that constitute the fixed asset system. We concluded our discussion by reviewing the principal risks and controls in the system.

KEY TERMS

asset acquisition (300)

asset disposal (303)

asset maintenance (300)

attendance file (296)

depreciation schedule (300)

employee file (299)

employee payroll records (287)

fixed assets (299)

human resource management (HRM) system (296)

job tickets (284)

labor distribution summary (284)

labor usage file (296)

paychecks (287)

payroll imprest account (287)

payroll register (287)

personnel action form (284)

time cards (284)

REVIEW QUESTIONS

1. Which document is used by cost accounting to allocate direct labor charges to work in process?
2. Which department authorizes changes in employee pay rates?
3. Why should the employee's supervisor not distribute paychecks?
4. Why should employee paychecks be drawn against a special checking account?
5. Why should employees clocking on and off the job be supervised?
6. What is a personnel action form?
7. What tasks does a payroll clerk perform upon receipt of hours-worked data from the production department?
8. What documents are included in the audit trail for payroll?
9. What are the strengths and weaknesses of a batch process with sequential files?
10. What are the strengths and weaknesses of a batch system with direct access files?

11. What are the objectives of a fixed asset system?
12. How do fixed asset systems differ from purchases systems?
13. What are three tasks of the fixed asset system?
14. What information is found on the depreciation schedule? How can this information be verified?
15. Why is it crucial to the integrity of the financial statements that the fixed asset department be informed of asset improvements and disposals?
16. What is the auditor's role with respect to the fixed asset system?
17. Which department performs the formal record-keeping function for fixed assets?
18. What document shows when fixed assets are fully depreciated?
19. Who should authorize disposal of fixed assets?
20. Assets used for production are secured in a warehouse. Who has custody of fixed assets?

DISCUSSION QUESTIONS

1. What is the importance of the job ticket? Illustrate the flow of this document and its information from inception to impact on the financial statements.

2. Are any time lags in recording economic events typically experienced in payroll systems? If so, what are they? Discuss the accounting profession's view on this matter as it pertains to financial reporting.

3. What advantages are achieved in choosing a basic batch computer system over a manual system? A batch system with real-time data input over a basic batch system?

4. Discuss the major control implications of batch systems with real-time data input. What compensating procedures are available?

5. Discuss some specific examples in which information systems can reduce time lags and how the firm is positively affected by such time lags.

6. Discuss some service industries that may require their workers to use job tickets.

7. Payroll is often used as a good example of when batch processing by using magnetic tapes is considered appropriate. Why is payroll typically considered a good application for this type of storage device?

8. If an asset that is not fully depreciated is sold or disposed, but the fixed asset records are not adjusted, what effect will this have on the financial statements?

9. Discuss the fundamental risk and control issues associated with fixed assets that are different from raw materials and finished goods.

10. Describe an internal control that would prevent an employee from removing a computer and then reporting it as scrapped.

11. Describe an internal control that would prevent the payment of insurance premiums on an automobile that is no longer owned by the company.

12. Describe an internal control that would prevent the charging of depreciation expense to the maintenance department for a sweeper that is now located in and used by the engineering department.

13. Describe an internal control that would prevent the acquisition of office equipment that is not needed by the firm.

14. What negative consequences result when fixed asset records include assets that are no longer owned by the firm?

MULTIPLE-CHOICE QUESTIONS

1. The document that captures the total amount of time that individual workers spend on each production job is called a
   a. time card.
   b. job ticket.
   c. personnel action form.
   d. labor distribution form.

2. An important reconciliation in the payroll system is
   a. the general ledger department compares the labor distribution summary from cost accounting to the disbursement voucher from accounts payable.
   b. the personnel department compares the number of employees authorized to receive a paycheck to the number of paychecks prepared.
   c. the production department compares the number of hours reported on job tickets to the number of hours reported on time cards.
   d. the payroll department compares the labor distribution summary to the hours reported on time cards.

3. Which internal control is not an important part of the payroll system?
   a. supervisors verify the accuracy of employee time cards
   b. paychecks are distributed by an independent paymaster

c. the accounts payable department verifies the accuracy of the payroll register before transferring payroll funds to the general checking account

d. the general ledger department reconciles the labor distribution summary and the payroll disbursement voucher

4. Which duties should be segregated?

a. matching purchase requisitions, receiving reports, and invoices and authorizing payment

b. authorizing payment and maintaining the check register

c. writing checks and maintaining the check register

d. authorizing payment and maintaining the accounts payable subsidiary ledger

5. CMA Adapted
In a well-designed internal control structure, two tasks that should be performed by different persons are

a. preparation of purchase orders and authorization of monthly payroll.

b. preparation of bank reconciliations and recording of cash disbursements.

c. distribution of payroll checks and approval of credit sales.

d. posting of amounts from both the cash receipts journal and cash disbursements journal to the general ledger.

e. posting of amounts from the cash receipts journal to the general ledger and distribution of payroll checks.

6. Which transaction is not processed in the fixed asset system?

a. purchase of building

b. repair of equipment

c. purchase of raw materials

d. sale of company van

7. Depreciation

a. is calculated by the department that uses the fixed asset.

b. allocates the cost of the asset over its useful life.

c. is recorded weekly.

d. results in book value approximating fair market value.

8. Depreciation records include all of the following information about fixed assets except the

a. economic benefit of purchasing the asset.

b. cost of the asset.

c. depreciation method being used.

d. location of the asset.

9. Which control is not a part of the fixed asset system?

a. formal analysis of the purchase request

b. review of the assumptions used in the capital budgeting model

c. development of an economic order quantity model

d. estimates of anticipated cost savings

10. Objectives of the fixed asset system do not include

a. authorizing the acquisition of fixed assets.

b. recording depreciation expense.

c. computing gain and/or loss on the disposal of fixed assets.

d. maintaining a record of the fair market value of all fixed assets.

11. Which of the following is not a characteristic of the fixed asset system?

a. acquisitions are routine transactions requiring general authorization

b. retirements are reported on an authorized disposal report form

c. acquisition cost is allocated over the expected life of the asset

d. transfer of fixed assets among departments is recorded in the fixed asset subsidiary ledger

PROBLEMS

1. Payroll Fraud

John Smith worked in the stockyard of a large building supply company. One day he unexpectedly and without notice left for California, never to return. His foreman seized the opportunity to continue to submit time cards for John to the payroll department. Each week, as part of his normal duties, the foreman received the employee paychecks from payroll and distributed them to the workers on his shift. Because John Smith was not present to collect his paycheck, the foreman forged John's name and cashed it.

Required:
Describe two control techniques to prevent or detect this fraud scheme.

2. Payroll Controls
Refer to the flowchart below.

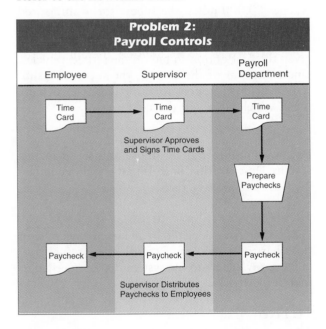

**Problem 2:
Payroll Controls**

Required:
a. What risks are associated with the payroll procedures depicted in the flowchart?
b. Discuss two control techniques that will reduce or eliminate the risks.

3. Payroll Controls
Sherman Company employs 400 production, maintenance, and janitorial workers in eight separate departments. In addition to supervising operations, the supervisors of the departments are responsible for recruiting, hiring, and firing workers within their areas of responsibility. The organization attracts casual labor and experiences a 20 to 30 percent turnover rate in employees per year. A portion of Sherman Company's payroll procedures is described in the following section.

Employees clock on and off the job each day to record their attendance on time cards. Each department has it own clock machine that is located in an unattended room away from the main production area. Each week, the supervisors gather the time cards, review them for accuracy, and sign and submit them to the payroll department for processing. In addition, the supervisors submit personnel action forms to reflect newly hired and terminated employees. From these documents, the payroll clerk prepares payroll checks and updates the employee records. The supervisor of the payroll department signs the paychecks and sends them to the department supervisors for distribution to the employees. A payroll register is sent to accounts payable for approval. Based on this approval, the cash disbursements clerk transfers funds into a payroll clearing account.

Required:
Discuss the risks for payroll fraud in the Sherman Company payroll system. What controls would you implement to reduce the risks? Use the SAS 78 framework of control activities to organize your response.

4. Internal Control
Discuss any control weaknesses found in the flowchart on the next page. Recommend any necessary changes.

5. Human Resource Data Management
In a payroll system with real-time processing of human resource management data, control issues become very important. List some items in this system that could be very sensitive or controversial. Also describe what types of data must be carefully guarded to ensure that they are not altered. Discuss some control procedures that might be put into place to guard against unwanted changes to employees' records.

6. Payroll Flowchart Analysis
Discuss the risks depicted by the payroll system flowchart on page 313. Describe the internal control improvements to the system that are needed to reduce these risks.

7. Comprehensive Flowchart Analysis
Discuss the internal control weaknesses in the expenditure cycle flowchart on page 314. Structure your answer in terms of the SAS 78 control activities covered in Chapters 5 and 6.

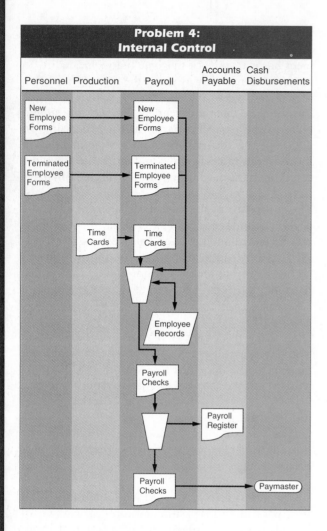

Problem 4: Internal Control

8. Fixed Asset System

The fixed asset acquisition procedures for Turner Brothers, Inc., are as follows:

Supervisors in the user departments determine their fixed asset needs and submit bids or orders directly to contractors, vendors, or suppliers. In the case of competitive bidding, the user makes the final selection of the vendor and negotiates the prices paid. The assets are delivered directly to the user areas. The users inspect and formally receive the assets. They submit the invoice to the cash disbursements department for payment.

Required:
Discuss the risks associated with this process. Describe the controls that should be implemented to reduce these risks.

9. Fixed Asset System

Holder Co. maintains a large fleet of automobiles, trucks, and vans for use by their service and sales force. Supervisors in the various departments maintain the fixed asset records for these vehicles, including routine maintenance, repairs, and mileage information. This information is periodically submitted to the fixed asset department, which uses it to calculate depreciation on the vehicle. To ensure a reliable fleet, the company disposes of vehicles when they accumulate 80,000 miles of service. Depending on usage, some vehicles reach this point sooner than others. When a vehicle reaches 80,000 miles, the supervisor is authorized to use it in trade for a new replacement vehicle or to sell it privately. Employees of the company are given the first option to bid on the retired vehicles. Upon disposal of the vehicle, the supervisor submits a disposal report to the fixed asset department, which writes off the asset.

Required:
Discuss the potential for abuse and fraud in this system. Describe the controls that should be implemented to reduce the risks.

10. Fixed Asset Flowchart Analysis

Discuss the risks depicted by the fixed asset system flowchart on page 315. Describe the internal control improvements to the system that are needed to reduce these risks.

11. Fixed Asset System

The treatment of fixed asset accounting also includes accounting for mineral reserves, such as oil and gas, coal, gold, diamonds, and silver. These costs must be capitalized and depleted over the estimated useful life of the asset. The depletion method used is the units of production method. An example of a source document for an oil and gas exploration firm is presented on page 316. The time to drill a well from start to completion may vary from 3 to 18 months, depending on the location. Further, the costs to drill two or more wells may be difficult to separate. For example, the second well may be easier to drill because more is known about the conditions of the field or reservoir, and the second well may be drilled to help extract the same reserves more quickly or efficiently.

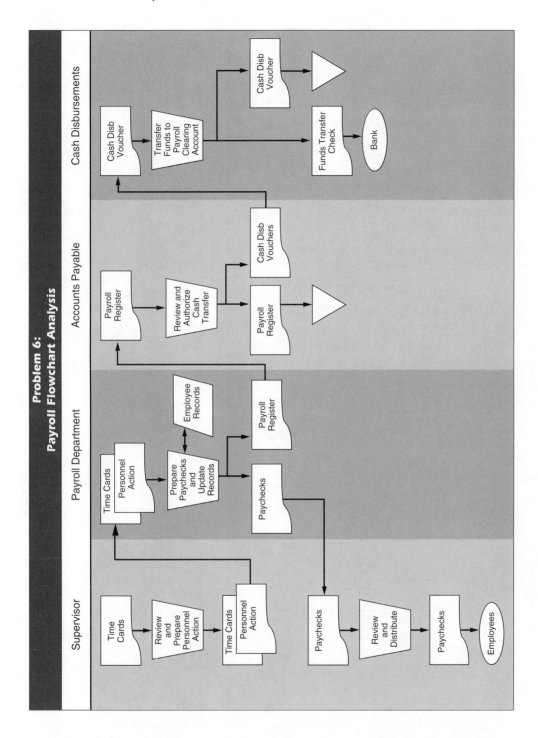

Problem 6:
Payroll Flowchart Analysis

Required:

a. In Figure 6-11, the source documents for the fixed asset accounting system come from the receiving department and the accounts payable department. For an oil and gas firm, where do you think the source documents come from?

b. Assume that a second well is drilled to help extract the reserves from the field. How would you allocate the drilling costs?

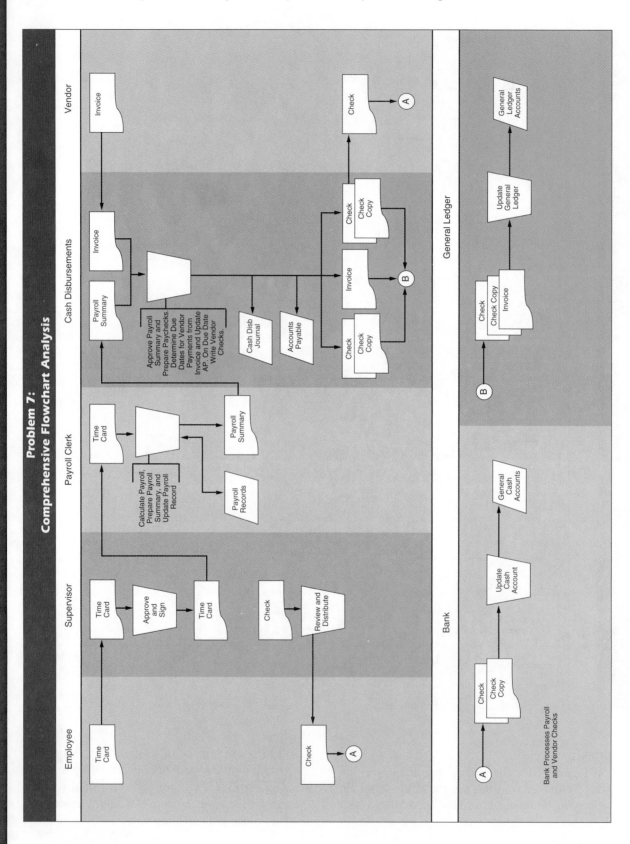

**Problem 7:
Comprehensive Flowchart Analysis**

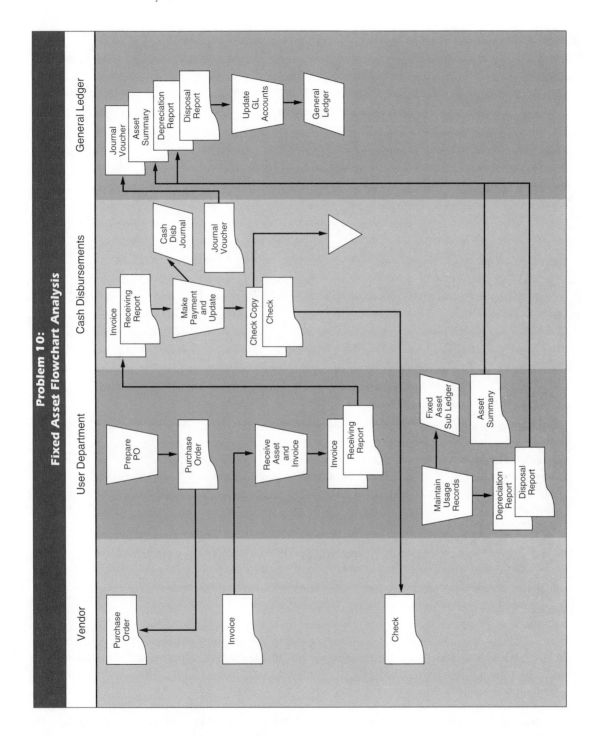

c. The number of reserves to be extracted is an estimate. These estimates are constantly being revised. How does this affect the fixed asset department's job? Does Figure 6-13 need to be altered to reflect these adjustments?

d. How does the auditor verify the numbers calculated by the fixed asset department at the end of the period?

Problem 11:
Fixed Asset System

WILDCAT EXPLORATION COMPANY
P.O. Box 5478
Baton Rouge, Louisiana 56758

JOINT INTEREST BILLING

INVOICE DATE: August 23, 2007
INVOICE NO.: DNS3948
TERM: net 20 days from receipt
BILLING PERIOD: September 19 A ugust 19, 2007
Property: Dutch North Sea—K71
Percentage Interest: .1875

DESCRIPTION	TOTAL AMOUNT	PERCENTAGE DUE
Tubing	$291,876.69	$ 37,851.88
Wellhead Assembly	976.25	183.05
Installation Cost	6,981.38	1,309.01
Permits	3,297.28	618.24
Site Prep & Cleanup	4,298.78	806.02
Contract Drilling	415,345.82	77,877.34
Bits	7,394.12	1,386.40
Equipment Rental	8,109.33	1,520.50
Communications	812.77	152.49
Testing and Drafting	15,980.23	2,996.29
Inspection	3,980.13	746.27
Completion Costs	1 ,980.11	371.27
TOTAL	$761,032.89	$125,818.76

12. Payroll Procedures

When employees arrive for work at Harlan Manufacturing, they punch their time cards at a time clock in an unsupervised area. Mary, the time-keeping clerk, tries to keep track of the employees, but is often distracted by other things. Every Friday, she submits the time cards to Marsha, the payroll clerk.

Marsha copies all time cards and files the copies in the employees' folders. She uses employee wage records and tax tables to calculate the net pay for each employee. She sends a copy of the payroll register to the accounts payable department and files a copy in the payroll department. She updates the employee records with the earnings, and prepares the payroll summary and sends it to the cash disbursements department along with the paychecks.

After receiving the payroll summary, John, an accounts payable clerk, authorizes the cash disbursements department to prepare paychecks. John then updates the cash disbursements journal. The treasurer signs the paychecks and gives them to the supervisors for distribution. The supervisors distribute the checks to the employees and keep the falsified ones. Finally, both the accounts payable and cash disbursements departments send a summary of transactions to the general ledger department.

Required:

a. Analyze the internal control weaknesses in the system. Model your response according to the six categories of physical control activities specified in SAS 78.

b. Make recommendations for improving the system.

13. Fixed Asset System

Fittipaldi Company recently purchased a patent for a radar detection device for $8 million. This radar detection device has been proven to detect three times better than any existing radar detector on the market.

Fittipaldi expects four years to pass before any competitor can devise a technology to beat its device.

Required:

a. Why does the $8 million represent an asset? Should the fixed asset department be responsible for its accounting?

b. Where would the source documents come from?

c. What happens if a competitor comes out with a new model in two years rather than four?

d. How does the auditor verify the numbers calculated by the fixed asset department at the end of the period? Is it the auditor's responsibility to be aware of external regulatory conditions that might affect the value of the patent? For example, what if seven more states prohibit the use of radar detectors? (Two states now prohibit their use.)

INTERNAL CONTROL CASES

1. Walker Books, Inc.—Payroll and Fixed Asset Systems

(Prepared by Alex Moser, Lehigh University)

Walker Books, Inc. is currently one of the largest book distributors in the United States. Established in 1981 in Palo Alto, California, Walker Books was originally a side project of founder and current president Curtis Walker, who at the time was employed by a local law firm. Because reading was much more than just a hobby of his, he decided to use some of his savings to buy out an abandoned restaurant and convert it into a neighborhood bookstore, mainly selling used books that were donated from friends and family. When the doors first opened, Walker's wife, Lauren, was the only employee during the week; Curtis was the only employee on the weekends. At the end of the first fiscal year, Walker Books had grossed $20,000 in sales.

As the years passed, Curtis Walker quit the law firm and began concentrating fully on his bookstore. More employees were hired, more books were traded in, and more sales were attained each year that passed. However, during the mid-1990s, Walker was faced with two problems: many large, upscale bookstores were being built in the area and the use of the Internet for finding and ordering books was becoming cheaper and more popular for current customers. In 1995, Walker's sales finally started to decline. Deciding to take a risk because of the new-found competition, he closed his doors to the neighborhood, invested more money to expand the current property, and transformed his company from simply selling used books to being a distributor of new books. Publishers send books to his warehouse, in which he stores them and resells them to large bookstore chains upon request.

Walker Books, Inc. has rapidly become one of the largest book distributors in the country. Though they are still at their original location in Palo Alto, California, they distribute books to each of the 50 states and because of that, the company now sees sales of about $105,000,000 per year. When Mr. Walker is asked about his fondest memory, he always responds that he will never forget how the little bookstore, with two employees, has expanded to now have more than 145 employees.

As mentioned, all of Walker's customers are large-chain bookstores who themselves see many millions of dollars in revenue per year. However, some of these bookstores have been having bad relationships with Walker Books in the past year. There have been many disputes between them, such as books that were ordered from Walker but were never sent, poor inventory management by Walker, and the inability of Walker to provide legitimate documentation of transactions. According to projections of this year's financials, the sour relationship that Walker Books and many of its customers have is going to take a toll on year-end revenue. Curtis Walker has stated time after time that because of his law background, he "clearly knows the difference between right and wrong, including those of internal controls." You have been hired as an independent expert to inspect the internal controls currently in place at Walker Books, Inc.

Fixed Asset and Payroll Procedures

In the various Walker Books business departments, employees clock in and out at the beginning and end of each day using their timesheets, which they are responsible for keeping at their desks or on their persons until Thursdays, when they are approved by the manager or supervisor of their department. The manager or supervisor then forwards these timesheets to Debby, the payroll clerk who prepares personalized checks for each employee's approved timesheet. She then posts to employee records, and the payroll register using a laptop computer, which she is allowed to bring home for work. A copy of the check is made, and filed in the payroll department, then the check is mailed to the employee. Two summaries of the payroll register are printed, one of which is sent to the accounts payable department, the other of which is sent to the general ledger department.

Any fixed assets needed by each individual division are reported to the manager of that division, who decides if it's necessary. The manager submits a form stating the funds required for the fixed asset acquisition, which he or she must personally sign showing approval, to the purchasing department. Any fixed asset request requiring more than $10,000 is reviewed by the top manager of the fixed asset department, who is knowledgeable regarding fixed asset transactions. The purchasing department clerk receives requests for funds and prepares a purchase order (PO). Two copies of the PO are then made, one is sent to the supplier, and one is filed in the purchasing department. Finally, the purchasing department sends a fixed asset change report to the fixed asset department.

The accounts payable clerk receives the payroll summary and the fixed asset purchase order, and writes a check to the imprest account for the exact summation of the payroll and fixed asset allowances, and writes a check to the supplier. Finally, when fixed assets are received, the packing slip, invoice, and completed blind copy are forwarded from the receiving department to the accounts payable department, where the clerk reconciles them and posts to a journal voucher, which is subsequently sent to the general ledger department.

The general ledger clerk posts journal vouchers and payroll summaries to the general ledger using a microcomputer terminal. Any time a fixed asset shows significant signs that is has come to the end of its useful life, the top manager is sent a disposal request form from the respective division's manager or supervisor. The top-level manager is solely in charge of deciding which assets are capitalized, and which are expensed, and is in charge of disposal of any fixed asset of value greater than $250. The top manager then approves or rejects the disposal, and files a fixed asset change report. The fixed asset department clerk makes additions or deletions to the fixed asset files, and updates the ledger via stand-alone microcomputer.

Required:

a. Create a data flow diagram of the current system.

b. Create a document flowchart of the existing system.

c. Analyze the internal control weaknesses in the system. Model your response according to the six categories of physical control activities specified in SAS 78.

d. Prepare a system flowchart of a redesigned computer-based system that resolves the control weaknesses that you identified.

2. A&V Safety, Inc.—Payroll Processing System

(Prepared by Aneesh Varma, Lehigh University)
The payroll systems consists of the accounting and cash disbursements departments. Supervisors collect and check time cards (including those from interns during the summer). These are then sent to the accounting department. Based on the employee ID on the time cards, the wage rates are pulled from the reference personnel file. Interns do not receive employee IDs because they are only there for 10 weeks. Their wage rates are written in on the time cards by their supervisors.

The accounting department then prepares the checks and updates the payroll register. A copy of the payroll register is sent to the accounts payable department, which duly updates the AP Ledger. A summary report is sent from the accounting department to the general ledger, which shows the distribution of wages across departments and projects. The used time cards are stored in a local file within the accounting department. The checks are then sent from the accounting department to the cash disbursement department, which signs them and returns them to supervisors who distribute them to respective employees in their departments. A copy of the check is also sent to the accounts payable department where they are matched to the payroll register and filed locally. The cash disbursements department also sends a verified list of recipients to the accounts payable which updates the AP ledger to close out the payable salary accounts. A copy of the list of recipients is also sent from cash disbursements to the general ledger where after verification of with the summary report the general ledger is updated. Cash disbursements also sends a list of employees that received paychecks for that period to the bank.

Required:

a. Create a data flow diagram of the current system.

b. Create a document flowchart of the existing system.

c. Analyze the internal control weaknesses in the system. Model your response according to the six categories of physical control activities specified in SAS 78.

d. Prepare a system flowchart of a redesigned computer-based system that resolves the control weaknesses that you identified.

3. Music Source, Inc.—Payroll and Fixed Assets

(Prepared by Jeff Davis, Gen Feldman, Denise Nuccio, Lehigh University)

Company Information

Music Source, Inc. is a manufacturer of stereo equipment with six sales offices nationwide and one manufacturing plant in Pennsylvania. Currently, employment is at approximately 200 employees. Music Source focuses on the production of high-quality stereo equipment for resale by retailers. Its larger competitors include Sony, Panasonic, and Aiwa.

Payroll System

All six sales offices and the manufacturing plants payrolls are processed biweekly through the same system. Every two weeks the employees enter data from their time cards into a terminal. The computer then runs a check on each of the employees through the employee history file to ensure that all the employees that have entered time are valid employees. After the verification, a personnel action form is created and forwarded to the payroll clerk in the payroll department. The payroll clerk in the main office in Pennsylvania receives the time cards and the personnel action form from the manufacturing plants production department and the sales offices general managers' office. The payroll clerk enters the information from these source documents into the employee records and then adds the employee hours to a payroll register reflecting employee pay rates, deductions, and job classification. One copy of the payroll register, along with the time cards, is filed in the payroll department and one copy is sent to the accounts payable department. Next the employee paychecks are prepared and sent to the cash disbursements department by the payroll clerk. The checks are signed and distributed to the employees by the cash disbursements clerk. The accounts payable department prepares a cash disbursements voucher. A copy of the voucher and a copy of the payroll register are sent to the cash disbursements department and are posted to the general ledger. The cash disbursements clerk writes a check for the entire payroll and deposits it in the general cash account. A copy of the check, the disbursement voucher and the payroll register are sent back to the accounts payable department where they are filed.

Fixed Asset System

Asset acquisition begins when the department manager recognizes the need to obtain or replace an existing fixed asset. The manager prepares two copies of a purchase requisition; one is filed in the department and one is sent to the purchasing department. The purchasing department uses the purchase requisition to prepare three copies of a purchase order. One copy of the purchase order is sent to the supplier, another copy is sent to the accounts payable department, and the third copy is filed in the purchasing department. The accounts payable department receives the goods with an invoice and a packing slip from the vendor. The purchase order received from the purchasing department is reconciled by the accounts payable clerk with the packing slip and invoice. The information is input into the computer terminal by the clerk and a liability is posted, the purchase journal is updated, and hard copies of a journal voucher and cash disbursement voucher are printed out. The journal voucher is sent to the general ledger department and the cash disbursements voucher and the supplier's invoice is sent to the cash disbursements department. The purchase order and the packing slip are filed in accounts payable. The cash disbursements clerk prepares and posts a check to the check register using the information from the supplier's invoice and the cash disbursements voucher and prints a hard copy of the check that is sent to the vendor. The cash disbursements voucher is sent on to the general ledger department.

The department manager also handles asset maintenance and asset disposal. The manager adjusts the fixed asset subsidiary account balances as the assets depreciate over time and when an asset has reached the end of its useful life, a disposal report is prepared. The department manager sends a summary to the general ledger. The general ledger department clerk reconciles the cash disbursements voucher, the journal voucher, and the fixed asset summary from the department manager and posts to the general ledger accounts and files the documents.

Required:

a. Create a data flow diagram of the current system.

b. Create a document flowchart of the existing system.

c. Analyze the internal control weaknesses in the system. Model your response according to the six categories of physical control activities specified in SAS 78.

d. Prepare a system flowchart of a redesigned computer-based system that resolves the control weaknesses that you identified.

4. Green Mountain Coffee Roasters, Inc.— Payroll and Fixed Asset Systems
(Prepared by Christina Brown, Lehigh University)

Company Background
Green Mountain Coffee Roasters, Inc., was founded in 1981 and began as a small cafe in Waitsfield, Vermont, roasting and serving premium coffee on the premises. Green Mountain blends and distributes coffee to a variety of customers, including cafes, delis, and restaurants, and currently has about 6,700 customer accounts reaching states across the nation. As the company has grown, several beverages have been added to their product line, including signature blends, light and heavy roasts, decaffeinated coffee and teas, and herbal teas. Green Mountain Coffee Roasters, Inc., has been publicly traded since 1993 and had sales in excess of $84 million for the fiscal year ended September 2002.

Green Mountain Coffee has a warehouse and manufacturing plant located in Wilton, Vermont, where it presently employees 250 full- and part-time workers. The company receives its beans in bulk from a select group of distributors located across the world, with their largest supplier being Columbia Beans Co. Green Mountain Coffee also sells accessories that complement their products, including mugs, thermoses, and coffee containers that they purchase from their supplier Coffee Lovers Inc. In addition to selling coffee and accessories, Green Mountain uses paper products such as coffee bags, coffee cups, and stirrers to distribute to their customers and package the coffee that they purchase from Save the Trees Inc.

Payroll System
In the Green Mountain production departments, each worker fills out a time card each day recording the number of hours they have worked. The supervisor, Toni Holland, is responsible for watching employees clock in their hours and sending the time cards to the payroll department. Using a stand-alone microcomputer, the payroll department clerk inputs the time cards to prepare hard copies of the paychecks and post to employee records. The employee checks are given to the supervisor, Toni, to review and distribute to the employees, and the time cards are filed in payroll.

The payroll department also prepares three copies of a payroll register. Copies one and two are sent to accounts payable and the general ledger department, respectively, and the third copy is filed in payroll. Accounts payable uses the payroll register to write a check for the imprest account. One copy of the check is signed and sent to the bank and the other copy is filed. The general ledger department clerk inputs the payroll register information into a stand-alone microcomputer to post to the payroll clearing account and update the general ledger control accounts. The payroll register is then filed.

Fixed Asset System
Asset acquisition begins when the departmental manager (the user) recognizes the need to obtain a new or replace an existing fixed asset. The user prepares two copies of a purchase requisition, filing one copy in the user department and sending one copy to the purchasing department. The purchases department uses the purchase requisition to prepare three copies of a purchase order. One copy of the purchase order is sent to the supplier, one to the accounts payable department, and the last copy is filed in purchases with the purchase requisition. Accounts payable receives the goods along with an invoice and a packing slip from the vendor. The purchase order sent from purchases is reconciled on a stand-alone microcomputer by the accounts payable clerk with the packing slip and invoice. The clerk uses the information to post a liability, update the purchases journal, and print hard copies of a journal voucher and cash disbursements voucher. The journal voucher is sent to the general ledger department and the cash disbursements voucher is sent to the cash disbursements department with the supplier's invoice. The remaining documents, the purchase order and the packing slip, are filed in accounts payable. The cash disbursements clerk uses a stand-alone microcomputer to prepare and post a check to the check register using the information contained in the supplier's invoice and the cash disbursements voucher and prints a hard copy of the check to send to the vendor. The cash disbursements voucher is then sent to the general ledger department.

Asset maintenance and disposal are handled by the department manager in the user department. The manager adjusts the fixed asset subsidiary account balances as the assets depreciate over time

and when an asset has reached the end of its useful life (in which case a disposal report is prepared). The user sends a summary to the general ledger. The general ledger department clerk reconciles the cash disbursements voucher, the journal voucher, and the fixed asset summary from the user with a stand-alone microcomputer, posts to the general ledger accounts, and files the remaining documents.

Required:
a. Create a data flow diagram of the current system.

b. Create a document flowchart of the existing system.

c. Analyze the internal control weaknesses in the system. Model your response according to the six categories of physical control activities specified in SAS 78.

d. Prepare a system flowchart of a redesigned computer-based system that resolves the control weaknesses that you identified.

5. Sinclair's Chair Company—Fixed Assets and Payroll Systems
(Prepared by Sam Succop, Lehigh University)
Sinclair's Chair Company (SSC) was established in 1951 as a family-run manufacturer of plastic chairs, largely distributed to small universities and colleges. It has three manufacturing plants, located in Bethlehem, Pennsylvania; Pittsburgh, Pennsylvania; and Jersey City, New Jersey.

Fixed Asset System
With three manufacturing plants and lots of machinery, SCC must account for a large amount of fixed assets. To keep up with the acquisition, maintenance, and disposal of assets, the company has slowly begun to adapt to a computer-based system to control the fixed asset accounts. Incorporated in the company is a fixed asset department and a data processing department. When a fixed asset is purchased, the fixed asset department gets a receiving report and a cash disbursements voucher. With these documents, a fixed asset report is created, documenting necessary information about the asset such as its cost and the appropriate depreciation method to be used. The fixed asset clerk then creates a record of the asset in the fixed assets subsidiary ledger, which automatically updates the asset account in the general ledger.

Thanks to the new computer system, the maintenance and record of the asset has now become much easier for SCC. A computerized depreciation schedule is created, making future depreciation calculations fast and simple. The depreciation and disposition of the asset is automatically maintained and updated to the general ledger. Periodically, the fixed asset department is able to get a copy of the depreciation report for review.

If there is any indication that a fixed asset has come to the end of its useful life, the respective department manager sends a request to dispose of the asset. The fixed asset department clerk deletes the asset from the files, which automatically adjusts the fixed asset's account in the ledger. A disposal report is created for the department to review.

Payroll Processing System

All three manufacturing plants' payrolls are processed biweekly through the same system. The payroll clerk in SCC's main plant in Bethlehem receives the time cards from the production department. The payroll clerk enters the information from these time cards into the employee records and then adds the employee hours to a payroll register reflecting employee pay rates, necessary deductions, and job classification. A copy of the payroll register, along with the time cards, is filed in the payroll department and a copy is sent to the accounts payable department. The payroll clerk then prepares the employee paychecks and sends them to the cash disbursements department. The cash disbursements clerk signs the checks and distributes them to the employees. The accounts payable department prepares a cash disbursements voucher. A copy of the disbursements voucher, along with a copy of the payroll register, is sent to the cash disbursements department and is posted to the general ledger. With this, the cash disbursements clerk writes a check for the entire payroll and deposits it in the imprest account. A copy of the check for the imprest account, along with the disbursement voucher and the payroll register, are sent back to the accounts payable department and filed.

Required:

a. Create a data flow diagram of the purchases and payroll systems.
b. Create a document flowchart of the purchases and payroll systems.
c. Analyze the internal control weaknesses in both systems. Model your response according to the six categories of physical control activities specified in SAS 78.

7. Orbits—Comprehensive Case

(Prepared by Jaime Hesser, William Levien, and Rachel Sapir, Lehigh University)

In 1997, J.D. Orbits opened a cell phone accessory manufacturing plant named *Orbits*. Although the company began its operations at the local level with only 40 employees, 3 vendors, and 5 main customers, it experienced rapid success. By 2001, gross sales tripled and the enterprise expanded its customer, vendor, and employee base, and they now serve all major cell phone manufacturers. The success of Orbits is attributed to retention of talented employees and solicitation of large accounts.

Employees: Currently, Orbits has a total of 120 employees.

Executives: J.D. Orbits is the top executive. In 1999, he hired four people to serve as executive directors.

Executive Directors: The directors provide the independent verification control function by monitoring operating procedures. They are also responsible for the sales forecast and production schedule.

Sales Representatives: Sales representatives are crucial to the growth of Orbits. The company retained 10 members of the original staff and hired 30 more to represent the company. The sales representatives of Orbits visit customer sites and take orders over the phone or receive orders online.

Office Personnel: Twenty people serve as office personnel to facilitate the paperwork involved in manual processes. Most of these employees work in the office facility but a small portion work in the company warehouse. These individuals ensure that the inventory control account is properly measured.

Production Staff: Fifty people work on the manufacturing processes. This figure includes individuals that operate machinery, individuals that transport goods to the warehouse, testers, and maintenance staff.

Customers: Orbits sells to the outlet stores of distributors of Verizon, MCI, Cingular, and AT&T cellular phones, in the tri-state area.

Materials and Suppliers: Manufacturing hands-free cell phone devices requires a number of different materials, none of which are made in-house. Orbits purchases most parts from 25 vendors. The more complex components used in the manufacturing process are purchased through contracts with vendors. Pre-made circuitry and software (games), the microphone, and the battery pack are purchased. Everything else is assembled in the plant. Parts that are required to assemble the antennae, buttons, facade, and the wiring are relatively inexpensive. These components are made of either plastic or rubber. The raw materials are purchased from vendors according to price and no formal contract is drawn.

PPE (Fixed Assets):

Equipment:

Plastic Molding Machine

Button Stamping Machine

Robotics Assembly Machines

Buildings:

Office Facility: Occupied by executives, sales representatives, office personnel, and programmers

Warehouse: Stores finished goods (awaiting sale or ready to ship), occupied by parts of office personnel and production staff

Factory Building: Occupied by production staff

Purchases System

The purchases/inventory department prepares a purchase requisition when inventory levels drop below a predetermined reorder point. One copy of the purchase requisition is sent to accounts payable, where the AP clerk files it in the accounts payable pending file. A multi-part purchase order is prepared for each vendor. One copy of the PO is sent to accounts payable where it is filed in the accounts payable pending file and two copies are sent to the vendor. One PO and the purchase requisition are used to update the inventory records and then are filed in the closed purchase order file. The receiving department inspects and counts the goods arriving from the vendor and prepares the receiving report. One copy of the receiving report is sent with the inventory to the raw materials storeroom and another copy is sent to the purchasing/inventory department where it is filed. Another copy is sent to the accounts payable

department where it is filed in the accounts payable pending file. The final copy is filed in the receiving department. Once the accounts payable department receives the purchase requisition, purchase order, and receiving report, the firm records the liability in the purchases journal and posts it to the supplier's account in the AP subsidiary ledger. The purchase requisition, purchase order, and receiving report are transferred to the open accounts payable file. The AP clerk summarizes the transactions in the purchases journal for the period and prepares a journal voucher for the general ledger department. The general ledger department receives an account summary from the purchases/inventory department and the invoice from the vendor. The clerk posts to the inventory and AP control accounts.

Payroll System
Production

Employees who work on the production floor are required to clock in and clock out on a computer every day while supervised by a production manager. The production manager uses the information from the computer to compile time cards and job tickets. Time cards are a record of the total time an employee works and job tickets are a record of the amount of time each worker spends on a specific job. Job tickets are sent to the cost department and time cards are sent to the payroll department.

Cost

The cost department uses the job tickets to allocate labor and manufacturing overhead costs to the work-in-process (WIP) account.

Payroll

The payroll department receives the time cards and uses them to update the employee payroll records. The payroll department also prepares employee paychecks and creates a payroll register. The payroll register shows gross pay, overtime pay, net pay, and commission. A copy of the payroll register is sent to the accounts payable department and the paychecks are signed and sent to employees.

Accounts Payable

The accounts payable department uses the payroll register to create a cash disbursements voucher. The voucher and the payroll register are sent to the cash disbursements department.

Cash Disbursements

The cash disbursements department uses the payroll register and the cash disbursements voucher to write a check for an imprest payroll account. The check is signed and sent to the bank in an amount equal to wages payable.

General Ledger

The general ledger uses the cash disbursements voucher to update payroll. The voucher is then filed.

Fixed Asset System

The acquisition, maintenance, and disposal of fixed assets demand special attention. Purchasing a fixed asset is much different from purchasing supplies for normal operations. Fixed assets are a larger investment for the company and they are bought for long-term use. They also decrease in value as they expend their useful life and their maintenance relies on a depreciation schedule. Executives must approve disposal of a fixed asset. It is possible for the sale of a fixed asset to result in a gain or a loss.

At Orbits, the purchasing/ordering department is responsible for monitoring the needs of user departments. Ordering determines if a user department needs a new fixed asset based on the estimated remaining useful life of the current asset and/or the ability of the asset to generate revenue/increase productivity. In certain circumstances, such as obsolescence or necessity, ordering will approve direct requests from user departments.

Acquiring a Fixed Asset
Ordering Department

The ordering department determines when Orbits' user departments need to acquire new fixed assets. They create a purchase order and send a copy to the vendor. (When the vendor receives the order, they send an invoice to the accounts payable department. The vendor sends the fixed asset and a packing slip to the ordering department.)

Accounts Payable Department

The accounts payable department receives a copy of the vendor invoice and places it in the accounts payable pending file.

Paying for a Fixed Asset
Ordering Department

The vendor ships the fixed asset and the packing slip to the ordering department. When the fixed asset is received, the ordering department creates a receiving report. The receiving report and the packing slip are sent to the accounts payable department.

Accounts Payable Department

The receiving report is placed in the accounts payable pending file with the vendor invoice. When the payment is due, the records are pulled from the accounts payable pending file, a cash disbursement voucher is created, and the accounts payable subsidiary ledger is updated. The voucher is sent to the cash disbursements department and the invoice and packing slip are filed. A copy of the receiving report is sent to the fixed asset department.

Fixed Asset Department

At Orbits, the records of all fixed assets are kept in the fixed asset department. This department designates the method of depreciation and also estimates the salvage value and useful life. In turn, they create a depreciation schedule, a disposal report, and a record of physical location.

Cash Disbursements Department

The cash disbursements department is responsible for paying the vendor the amount that is recorded on the cash disbursements voucher. After the cash disbursements voucher is received, a check is prepared and sent to the vendor. The cash disbursements voucher is sent to the general ledger department.

General Ledger Department

After the general ledger department receives the cash disbursements voucher, accounts are updated and the document is filed.

Maintaining a Fixed Asset

The fixed asset subsidiary ledger and the general ledger are updated throughout the useful life of the asset based on the depreciation schedule. Depreciation adjustments are made by debiting depreciation expense and crediting accumulated depreciation. Accumulated depreciation is a contra account and it reduces the value of the fixed asset.

Disposing of a Fixed Asset

There are a number of ways to retire an asset that is no longer useful to the company. Fixed assets can be sold, scrapped, or donated. In each case, the fixed asset account and the corresponding accumulated depreciation account must be eliminated. A gain or a loss on the disposal should also be recorded and it will appear on the income statement. To record a disposal, accumulated depreciation is debited and fixed asset is credited (loss/gain may also be debited/credited).

Sales Order System

A customer places an order with an operator, who inputs the order information into the order form. The sales order is filed in a database. A stock release, invoice, ledger copy, packing slip, and a shipping notice are all printed. The invoice and ledger copy are sent to billing where the prices and information are added from the database, and the sales journal is updated via a user terminal. The invoice is then sent to the customer, and the ledger copy is sent to accounts receivable. The stock release is then sent to the warehouse, where the goods are picked and the stock records are updated in the database at a terminal. The stock release is sent to shipping where it is reconciled with the packing slip, the shipping notice and bill of lading are prepared, and the shipping log is updated. The shipping notice is filed, and the bill of lading, product, and packing slip are the sent to the customer. The stock release is sent to accounts receivable where it is reconciled with the ledger copy from billing. There the general ledger, accounts receivable, and inventory records are updated at a terminal, and a management summary is produced.

Cash Receipts System

The mail room receives the customer's check along with the remittance advice. Each check is recorded on a remittance list. One copy and the checks are sent to the cash receipts department. A second copy and the remittance advice are transferred to the accounts receivable department. The third copy is sent to the controller department. The cash receipts department reconciles the checks and the remittance list and records the cash receipts in the cash receipts journal. The clerk then prepares a bank deposit slip and transfers the checks and two copies of the deposit slip to the bank. After the funds are deposited, the bank returns a deposit slip to the controller department. The accounts receivable department reviews the remittance advices and updates the accounts receivable subsidiary ledger. Then the AR

clerk summarizes the account and sends it to the general ledger. The general ledger department reviews the account summary and the journal voucher and updates the accounts receivable subsidiary ledger and general ledger and then files the source documents. Frequently, the controller department reconciles the cash receipts by comparing the remittance list, two deposit slips, and the journal vouchers.

Required:

a. Create a data flow diagram of the current system.

b. Create a document flowchart of the existing system.

c. Analyze the internal control weaknesses in the system. Model your response according to the six categories of physical control activities specified in SAS 78.

8. Green Leaf Produce Company— Comprehensive Case

(Prepare Glenn Adams and Nausheena Rahim, Lehigh University)

Green Leaf Produce Company, a wholesale distributor nestled in the coal-mining regions of Pennsylvania, generates revenues of $90 million per year and currently employs 187 people while servicing the northeastern United States. Its customer base is composed of restaurants, public schools, universities, and hospitals. This family-owned operation competes against the likes of national food distributors, Sysco and US Foods. The competition among these rivals can be fierce at times, as pricing strategies are employed to gain market share.

Green Leaf Produce Company first opened its doors to the general public in the 1930s. The local ice company in town rented a small storefront to Green Leaf, giving birth to this mom-and-pop operation. During this time, small merchant businesses were on the rise as they tried their hand at entrepreneurship. Green Leaf succeeded, as it captured the local market selling fruits and vegetables to the people of bustling Main Street.

Through the 1930s until the late 1950s, Green Leaf Produce continued to expand its operations to meet the ever-changing demands of its customers. Land, building, trucks, and equipment were purchased as revenues and earnings increased substantially. Over the years its product base was expanded to include a line of frozen foods, seafood, and fresh meats to enhance the company's product mix.

Green Leaf Produce purchases its inventory items from growers, manufacturers, and processors domestically and from around the world. Since the company's inception, Green Leaf Produce has formed strategic partnerships with more than 47 different suppliers, including industry giants such as Frosty Acres, Tyson Food, H.J Heinz, and Iceland Seafood.

Following another 40 years of growth servicing restaurants, public schools, universities, and hospitals, Green Leaf Produce relocated once again to its new 100,000-square-foot state-of-the-art distribution center. The new facility has a refrigeration capacity of more than 2 million cubic feet, which will position them to meet the challenges of the twenty-first century.

Sales Order Processing

Green Leaf's credit approval system operates in a real-time processing environment. The sales order process begins with the receipt of customer orders indicating the type of product and quantity being requested. Green Leaf receives customer orders two ways, via an 800-number in which a customer service representative keys the order into the computer system, and from a sales representative located in the field who transmits the order to the plant from a wireless laptop. Customer records are then matched with the company's database and checked for flags and credit limits before an approval is generated. If the customer's account has been flagged a message appears that notifies the representative that the account is under review by the credit department. The customer is notified at this point that a decision will be rendered within the hour. In real time the flagged account is transmitted to the credit manager's queue to ensure that proper application of the firm's credit policies and procedures are followed. One aspect of the credit manager's job function is to review customer accounts regularly for creditworthiness and to set appropriate high credit limits. A "second look," also performed by the credit manager, is a process of reviewing customer orders for possibly missed sales opportunities or to give proper attention to past-due accounts. Once a decision has been made regarding the order placed, the credit manager overrides the system, the sales order file is updated, and the customer is notified of the decision made.

A normal business day ends at 5 PM and no new orders are accepted for delivery the next day. A manager in the computer operations department who maintains and operates the system sorts and compiles the orders that were processed and approved during the course of that day's business transactions. At this point the sales journal is updated. Once the orders have been compiled, records are matched against inventory levels to confirm whether the items are in stock or unavailable. An inventory report is then generated and sent to purchasing, notifying them of unavailable items to replenish inventory levels.

The sorted and compiled sales orders are then downloaded to the logistics department where the sales orders are segregated according to geographic area. The groupings of sales orders are determined by the logistics program and are assigned to a truck. Once the sales orders have been routed they are uploaded to the mainframe in computer operations and stored in the routed deliveries file. The manager of the logistics department then runs the billing/invoice program from his terminal. The billing program accesses the records in computer operations and produces a three-part invoice along with the truck summary report detailing the customer stops. Copy 1 of the invoices is sent to the credit department, is temporarily filed, and acts as a control copy in case of missing invoices.

Copies 2 and 3 of the invoice and the truck summary report are sent to shipping and temporarily filed. When the billing/invoice program is run, the accounts receivable and inventory records are updated in computer operations along with the journal voucher file.

The clerk in the computer operations department then accesses the routed delivery file and runs the order-picking program that generates the stock release and picking labels that go to the warehouse.

The labels, which contain customer number, name, truck to be loaded, product name, number, and quantity, are distributed to warehouse workers, and based on the information contained on the labels goods are picked and loaded onto skids and shrink-wrapped. The stock release is filed in the warehouse and the picked goods are sent directly to shipping where the skids are loaded onto the trucks in reverse of customer delivery.

Once the trucks are loaded with the customer orders, the shipping clerk pulls invoice copies

2 and 3, along with the truck summary report, and hands them to the driver with the deliveries for the day. After the driver unloads the orders, the driver has copy 2 of the invoice signed by the customers, which acts as Green Leaf's binding contract, and gives copy 3 of the invoice to the customer. At the end of the day the driver returns with the truck summary report and copy 2 of all the invoices and delivers them to the credit department.

A clerk in the credit department then reconciles the truck summary report and the invoice copy. Once they have been reconciled the invoice is imaged into the optical control reader and stored in the imaged file. This allows invoices to be viewed online to answer customer questions about billing. In addition, this added feature provides internal controls by affording Green Leaf the capability of running spot checks by querying invoices by account number, customer name, amount, or date of invoice.

At 4 AM, the computer operations manager begins the end-of-day batch update process. The journal vouchers are sorted and the general ledger program is run to update the general journal for the previous day's business transactions. After the general journal is updated, three management reports are produced: the sales recap report and the truck recap report that are sent to the controller, and the account receivable control summary that is distributed to the credit manager.

Cash Receipts Procedures

Green Leaf's receptionist, Helen, greets all incoming visitors as they arrive. Each day the mail carrier delivers all the mail for the entire plant, which includes customer payments from orders previously delivered. Helen sorts the mail, separating customer payments from the rest of the mail. As each payment is opened, Helen carefully records the account number along with the business name in the memo section of the check and disposes of the remittance advice. Helen then delivers all the checks documented with customer account number and name to the accounting department to be posted to the respective accounts.

The accounts receivable clerk posts the payments to each of the customers' accounts and updates the accounts receivable ledger and cash receipts journal by entering the information into the computer terminal. All records and files are stored in the data processing department. After all payments are posted, two copies of the payment posting summary are generated. One is sent to the controller's office, and will later be reconciled with the validated deposit slip from the bank. The other payment summary is delivered to the manager of the accounts receivable department. Next the clerk prepares three deposit slips, one of which will accompany the deposit to the bank. One of the copies is filed within the department and the other is sent with the summary report to the controller's office. When the validated deposit slip arrives from the bank, the controller reconciles the payment summary report and deposit slip against the validated deposit slip from the bank. The general journal and control accounts are updated.

Purchases System

The purchasing agent reviews stock reports by category to determine what needs to be ordered based on sales demand and seasonal demand. The order quantity is determined by sales demand/frequency and quantity on hand from the inventory file via a terminal. A full weekly stock reorder report is prepared. The purchasing agent then calls all the suppliers on the suppliers list for prices. The supplier with the best price is contracted and a purchase order is sent. Two copies of the purchase order are made; one is attached to the stock reorder report and both are permanently filed. The other purchase order is sent to the receiving area.

Once the goods arrive in the receiving area, the receiving clerk compares the purchase order to the goods, and notes any discrepancies. A receiving report is prepared and a copy is made. The receiving report, packing slip, and bill of lading are sent to the accounts payable department where they are temporarily filed, awaiting the invoice. Another copy is sent to the purchasing department with the purchase order, where they are reconciled with the stock reorder report in the open purchases file; the documents are then permanently filed. Inventory records are updated via a terminal to the inventory file and the goods are sent to the warehouse. A journal voucher is prepared by the receiving clerk and sent to the general accounting clerk to key in to the general ledger control account file.

After the invoice is received from the supplier by the accounts payable department, it is reconciled with the packing slip and receiving report. Once reconciled, the purchases journal is posted to and the supplier's account is updated in the accounts payable subsidiary ledger. The invoice is than filed by due date. The accounts payable clerk prepares a summary of the entries in journal voucher form and sends it to the general accounting clerk to key in to the general ledger control account file.

Current Cash Disbursements System
As the due dates approach, the accounts payable clerk writes a check to the supplier indicating the invoice number and amount due. The check is sent to the general accounting department comptroller for a signature. The check is signed, a copy made, and the check mailed. The check copy is stamped as "paid" and is sent back to accounts payable. The accounts payable clerk then updates the accounts payable subsidiary ledger to reflect the payments, prepares and sends an account summary to the general ledger, and permanently files the documents. The accounts payable clerk also updates the check register, summarizes it, and sends a journal voucher to the general accounting clerk for keying in to the general ledger control account file via a terminal.

The Fixed Asset System
Daniel Jefferson has been the fixed asset manager for 16 years. He is a trusted employee of Green Leaf Produce and has been given greater responsibility in recent years. Daniel is in charge of the acquisition, maintenance, and time logging of the fixed assets that the company owns. In his tenure, he has implemented a program to buy all delivery trucks rather than lease them. The added equity that owning provides over leasing has allowed Green Leaf Produce to employ leverage in acquiring new assets. Recently, however, management has become concerned about the rise in maintenance costs. The average maintenance bill has increased by 15 percent over the last two years. Management is considering leasing once again, and selling the trucks that they now own. Before taking any major steps, they have decided to investigate the fixed asset department.

Daniel Jefferson is responsible for selecting repair companies and negotiating maintenance and repair contracts. Daniel selected Fix 'Em All Repairs for all the needed work. Jessica Jefferson, his wife, is the office manger of the repair shop. Daniel fills out the work orders as maintenance comes due and repairs are needed. Fix 'Em All Repairs bills Green Leaf Produce at the end of the month for services rendered. Upon receipt of the bill, the accounts payable department processes the payment, which takes five business days. Daniel makes the necessary entries to the general ledger.

Payroll System
Management at Green Leaf Produce trusts the employees to be accurate in recording hours worked. Jim Richmond, treasurer of the company, has been working in the accounting department since the early 1960s. Because of his extended service, he has been entrusted with many responsibilities. One of his responsibilities is to maintain the personnel files. He supplies this information for payroll processing purposes.

The employees prepare their timesheets when they arrive, and note when they leave. At the end of the work week, each department sends the employee timesheets to Jim for approval. After he approves the timesheets, he sends them and the personnel action form to the payroll office to be processed. The paychecks are drawn on the company's general cash account. After preparing the payroll register, the payroll department sends the paychecks and the payroll register to the accounts payable department for review. Accounts payable then sends a journal voucher to the general ledger department, files the payroll register, and sends the paychecks to Jim for signing and distribution to the employees.

Required:
a. Create a data flow diagram for the fixed asset and payroll systems.
b. Create a document flowchart for the fixed asset and payroll systems.
c. Analyze the internal control weaknesses in each of the two systems. Model your response according to the six categories of physical control activities specified in SAS 78.
d. Prepare a system flowchart for each of the two redesigned computer-based systems that resolves the control weaknesses that you identified.

chapter 7

The Conversion Cycle

LEARNING OBJECTIVES

After studying this chapter, you should:

- Understand the basic elements and procedures encompassing a traditional production process.
- Understand the data flows and procedures in a traditional cost accounting system.
- Be familiar with the accounting controls found in a traditional environment.
- Understand the operating features, philosophies, and technologies that characterize a world-class company.
- Understand the objectives of just-in-time systems and recognize the implications of maintaining excessive inventories in the world-class environment.
- Recognize the importance of quality in the world-class environment.
- Understand the shortcomings of traditional accounting methods in the world-class environment.
- Be familiar with the characteristics of a world-class information system.

A company's conversion cycle transforms (converts) input resources, such as raw materials, labor, and overhead, into finished products or services for sale. The conversion cycle is most formal and apparent in manufacturing firms. However, this cycle exists, conceptually, in certain service industries, such as health care, consulting, and public accounting. In this discussion of the conversion cycle, we shall assume a manufacturing environment.

U.S. manufacturers are in a period of dynamic transformation. Rapid swings in consumer demands, shorter product life cycles, and foreign competition have radically changed the rules of the marketplace. In an attempt to cope with these changes, manufacturers are beginning to conduct business in a dramatically new way. The term "world-class" defines this new era of business. Figure 7-1 presents the manufacturing environment as a continuum with traditional firms at one end and world-class firms at the other. At points along this line are firms in various stages of transformation as they move toward world-class status.

Relatively few firms have achieved world-class status. Many are moving in that direction; many more remain traditional. To deal with the diversity of practices, this chapter has been divided into four major sections. The first outlines the defining characteristics of a world-class organization. The second section describes the traditional manufacturing environment. It examines the batch-production process and the traditional accounting information system within this setting. The third section deals with the world-class manufacturing environment. Here, we become acquainted with the significant assumptions, philosophies, objectives, and technologies associated with world-class firms. The fourth section addresses the implications for accounting and AIS. Here, we will see how world-class competition is influencing changes in accounting techniques, information reporting, and information systems. The chapter concludes by presenting the key features of a world-class information system.

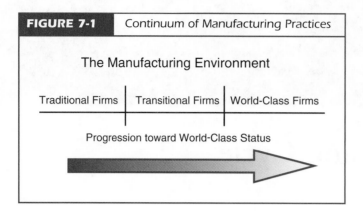

FIGURE 7-1   Continuum of Manufacturing Practices

The Manufacturing Environment

| Traditional Firms | Transitional Firms | World-Class Firms |

Progression toward World-Class Status

WORLD-CLASS COMPANIES

The **world-class company** is a company that has achieved high standards and has undergone fundamental changes from traditional forms of organization and management. This type of company continuously pursues improvement in all aspects of its operations, including its manufacturing procedures. Let's examine some of the characteristics that distinguish world-class manufacturers from traditional firms.

A world-class company profitably meets the needs of its customers. Its goal is not simply to satisfy customers, but to positively delight them. This is not something that can be done once and then forgotten. With competitors aggressively seeking new ways to increase market share, a world-class firm must continue to delight its customers.

The philosophy of customer satisfaction permeates the world-class firm. All of its activities, from the acquisition of raw materials (RM) to selling the finished product, form a "chain of customers." Each activity is dedicated to serving its customer, that is, the next activity in the process. The final paying customer is the last in the chain.

Products in a world-class company are produced in teams comprising members from all functional areas within the firm—engineering and production to marketing and procurement. To activate the talents of everyone on the team, decisions in this setting are pushed to the lowest level in the organization. The result is a flat organizational structure requiring high-quality, cross-functional information.

Achieving world-class status carries significant implications for accounting and accounting-information systems. Traditional information produced under conventional accounting techniques does not adequately support the needs of the world-class firm. These companies need new accounting methods and new information systems that:

1. Show what matters to its customers (such as quality and service).
2. Identify profitable products.
3. Identify profitable customers.
4. Identify opportunities for improvement in operations and products.
5. Encourage the adoption of value-added activities and processes within the organization and identify those that do not add value.
6. Efficiently support multiple users with both financial and nonfinancial information.

The role played by accounting information is a critical determinant in a firm's success as a world-class competitor and will be a major focus of this chapter.

THE TRADITIONAL MANUFACTURING ENVIRONMENT

The traditional conversion cycle consists of two subsystems: the production system and the cost accounting system. The **production system** involves the planning, scheduling, and control of the physical product through the manufacturing process. This includes determining RM requirements, authorizing the release of RM into production and work to be performed, and directing the movement of work-in-process (WIP) through the various stages of manufacturing. The **cost accounting system** monitors the flow of cost information related to production. Information produced by this system is used for inventory valuation, budgeting, cost control, performance reporting, and such management decisions as "make-or-buy" decisions.

In the traditional **manufacturing environment** these subsystems tend to be separate rather than integrated. Therefore, we will examine them separately.

THE PRODUCTION SYSTEM

Depending on the product being manufactured, a company will employ one of the following production methods:

Continuous processing creates a homogeneous product through a continuous series of standard procedures. Cement and petrochemicals are produced by this manufacturing method. Typically, under this approach firms attempt to maintain finished-goods inventory at levels needed to meet expected sales demand. The sales forecast in conjunction with information on current inventory levels triggers this process.

Batch processing produces discrete groups (batches) of product. Each item in the batch is similar and requires the same RM and operations. To justify the cost of setting up and retooling for each batch run, the number of items in the batch is usually large. This is the most common method of production. It is used to manufacture products such as automobiles, household appliances, and computers. The triggering mechanism for this process is the need to maintain finished-goods inventory levels in accordance with projected sales requirements.

Make-to-order processing involves the fabrication of discrete products in accordance with customer specifications. This process is initiated by sales orders rather than depleted inventory levels.

The actual procedures that make up the production system will vary with the manufacturing method in use. The following discussion will focus on the batch-processing system. This system determines in advance the exact quantity and type of input materials, as well as the physical operations required to produce each batch.

Documents in the Batch Processing System

Let's begin our study of the batch processing system with an examination of the documents that trigger and support batch activities. The most common of these are briefly described below.

1. The **sales forecast** shows the expected demand for the firm's finished goods (FG) for a given period. The marketing function usually produces a forecast of annual demand by product. For firms with seasonal swings in sales, this is broken down into shorter periods (quarterly or monthly) that can be revised in accordance with prevailing economic conditions. In many industries, the sales forecast is an essential production planning document.
2. The **production schedule** is the formal plan and authorization to begin production. This document describes the specific products to be made, the quantities to be produced in each batch, and the manufacturing timetable for starting and completing production. Figure 7-2 contains an example of a production schedule.

FIGURE 7-2	Production Schedule

ABC COMPANY   PRODUCTION SCHEDULE   JAN 2004

Batch Num	Qnty Units	OPER #1 Start	OPER #1 Complete	OPER #2 Start	OPER #2 Complete	OPER #3 Start	OPER #3 Complete
1237	800	1/2/04	1/5/04			1/8/04	1/23/04
1567	560	1/3/04	1/8/04	1/9/04	1/15/04	1/16/04	1/18/04
1679	450			1/2/04	1/5/04	1/8/04	1/10/04
4567	650	1/5/04	1/10/04	1/11/04	1/15/04	1/16/04	1/23/04
5673	1000	•	•	•	•	•	•
•	•	•	•	•	•	•	•
•	•	•	•	•	•	•	•

3. The **bill of materials** (BOM), an example of which is illustrated in Figure 7-3, specifies the types and quantities of the RM and subassemblies used in producing a single unit of finished product. The RM requirements for an entire batch are determined by multiplying the BOM by the number of items in the batch.

4. A **route sheet**, illustrated in Figure 7-4, shows the production path a particular batch of product follows during manufacturing. It is similar conceptually to a BOM. Whereas the BOM specifies material requirements, the route sheet specifies the sequence of operations (machining or assembly) and the standard time allocated to each task.

5. The **work order** (or production order) draws from BOMs and route sheets to specify the materials and production (machining, assembly, and so on) for each batch. These,

FIGURE 7-3	Bill of Materials

BILL OF MATERIALS

PRODUCT ENGINE TR6 2500 CC		NORMAL BATCH QNTY 100
Material Item Num	**Description**	**Quantity Reg/Unit Product**
28746	Crank shaft	1
387564	Main bearing set	4
735402	Piston	6
663554	Connecting rods	6
8847665	Rod bearing set	6
663345	Core plug 2"	6
663546	Core plug 1 1/2"	4

FIGURE 7-4 | Route Sheet

ROUTE SHEET

PRODUCT
ENGINE TR6
2500 CC

| Work Center | Operation | Description | Standard Time/Unit | |
			Set Up	Process
101	1a	Mill block and fit studs	.6	1.6
153	4a	Clean block and fit crank	.3	1.5
154	1	Fit pistons and bearings	.1	.7
340	2	Fit water pump, fuel pump, oil pump, and cylinder head	.1	1.4

---

together with move tickets (described next), initiate the manufacturing process in the production departments. Figure 7-5 presents a work order.

6. A **move ticket,** shown in Figure 7-6, records work done in each work center and authorizes the movement of the job or batch from one work center to the next.

7. A **materials requisition** authorizes the storekeeper to release materials (and subassemblies) to individuals or work centers in the production process. This document usually specifies only standard quantities. Materials needed in excess of standard amounts require separate requisitions that may be identified explicitly as excess materials

---

FIGURE 7-5 | Work Order

WORK ORDER #5681

PART NAME: Drawing #
ENGINE CRANK SHAFT   CS-87622

MATERIAL:
CRANK CASTING

| Work Center | Operation | Description | Standard Hrs | | Actual Proc | Unit Compltd | Units Scrap | Insp # |
			Set Up	Proc				
184	21	Draw castings from stores		2 .2	2.5	100	0	
186	23	Turn journals and main bearings per specs	2.3	14.9	16.00	99	1	
156	01	Balance crank	4.0	21.5	32.00	99	0	
¥	¥	¥	¥	¥	¥	¥	¥	¥
¥	¥	¥	¥	¥	¥	¥	¥	¥

FIGURE 7-6   Move ticket

MOVE TICKET

Batch Num: **1292**
Units: **100**

Move to:	Work Center 153
Operation:	4a
Start Date:	1/8/04
Finish Date:	1/10/04
Qnty Received:	100
Received By:	_____

---

requisitions. This allows for closer control over the production process by highlighting excess material usage. In some cases, less than the standard amount of material is used in production. When this happens, the work centers return the unused materials to the storeroom accompanied by a materials return ticket. Figure 7-7 presents a format that could serve all three purposes.

The Batch Production Process

The flowchart in Figure 7-8 (pages 336–337) illustrates the flow of information through a typical batch production system. The functions and interrelationships of each phase in the production system are briefly described. Let's first look at the production planning and control phase of the system. This phase involves two main procedures: the specification of **materials and operations requirements** and production scheduling.

Establishing the raw material requirements for a batch of any given product entails analyzing what is needed against what is available in the RM inventory. Operations

---

FIGURE 7-7   Materials Requisition, Excess Materials Requisition, and Materials Return Ticket

MATERIALS REQUISITION/RETURNS

Issued To: _____   **Work Order Number** _____
Date: _____

Material Item #	Description	Quantity Issued	Unit Cost	Extended Cost

Authorized By: _____
Received By: _____
Cost Accounting: _____

requirements are determined by examining the machining and other manufacturing tasks needed to produce a unit of finished product. Primary determinants for both materials and operations requirements are the sales forecast, inventory status report, and engineering specifications for the finished product.

When producing nonstandard batches or custom products, the specification of materials and operations requirements can become quite involved due to the detailed analysis necessary to prepare the BOMs and route sheets. For standard products, however, the BOMs and route sheets can be prepared in advance and filed. Clerks can simply retrieve these as needed from the BOM and route sheet files, thus reducing the complexity of this phase in the production process. Also produced in the planning and control step are the purchase requisitions (if needed) for additional RM. Procedures for preparing purchase orders and acquiring inventories are the same as those described in Chapter 5.

The second procedure carried out under planning and control is production scheduling. The schedule for a production run is prepared by the production scheduling clerk and is based on the information provided in BOMs and route sheets. The scheduling clerk also prepares work orders, move tickets, and materials requisitions for each batch in the production run. Before releasing these documents to the various work centers, the clerk creates an open work order file and sends a copy of the work order to cost accounting.

The work orders, move tickets, and materials requisitions prepared by the scheduling clerk flow through the various work centers in accordance with the route sheet. To provide a simplified illustration of the manufacturing phase of the production system, Figure 7-8 shows only one work center.

The manufacturing phase begins when workers obtain RM from storekeeping in exchange for materials requisitions. These materials, as well as the machining and the labor required to manufacture the product, are applied in compliance with the work order. When the task is complete, the supervisor or other authorized person fills out and signs the move ticket for that work center. The completed move ticket authorizes the batch to proceed to the next work center. As evidence that this stage of production has been completed, a copy of the move ticket is sent back to production planning and control to update the open work order file. Upon receipt of the last move ticket, the open work order file is closed. The finished product along with a copy of the work order is sent to the FG warehouse. Also, a copy of the work order is sent to inventory control to update the FG inventory records.

As one might expect, work centers also fulfill an important role in recording labor time costs. This task is handled by work center supervisors, who, at the end of each work week, send employee time cards and job tickets to the payroll and cost accounting departments, respectively.

The remaining phase of the production system is inventory control, which has three main functions in the production process. First, it triggers the entire process by providing production planning and control with an inventory status report of RM and FG. Second, inventory control personnel are continually involved in updating the RM inventory records from materials requisitions, excess materials requisitions, and materials return tickets. Finally, upon receipt of the work order from the last work center, inventory control records the completed production in the FG inventory records.

THE ECONOMIC ORDER QUANTITY MODEL

The objective of inventory control is to minimize total inventory cost while ensuring that adequate inventories exist to meet current demand. Inventory models used for achieving this objective help answer two fundamental questions:

1. When should inventory be purchased?
2. How much inventory should be purchased?

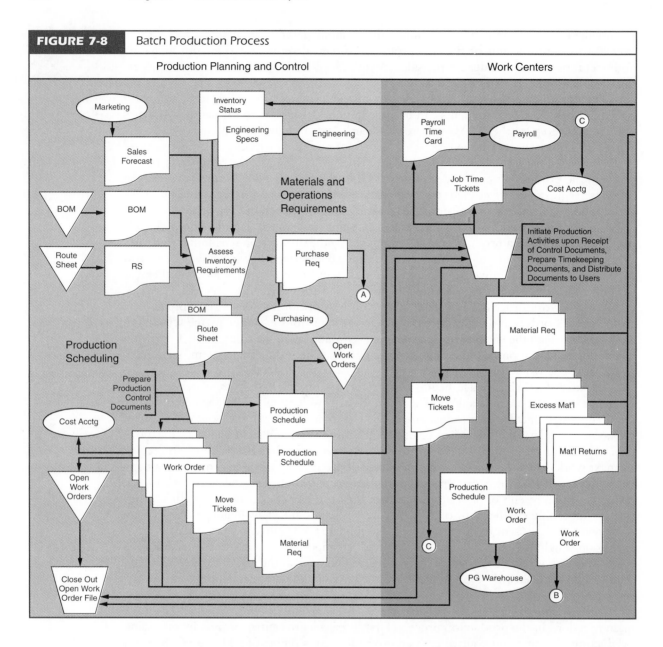

FIGURE 7-8   Batch Production Process

The simplest and most commonly used inventory model is the **economic order quantity (EOQ) model**. However, the EOQ model is based on assumptions that may not always reflect the economic reality. These assumptions are:

1. Demand for the product is constant and known with certainty.
2. The lead time—the time between placing an order for inventory and its arrival—is known and constant.
3. All inventories in the order arrive at the same time.
4. The total cost per year of placing orders is a variable that decreases as the quantities ordered increase. Ordering costs include the cost of preparing documentation, contacting vendors, processing inventory receipts, maintaining vendor accounts, and writing checks.

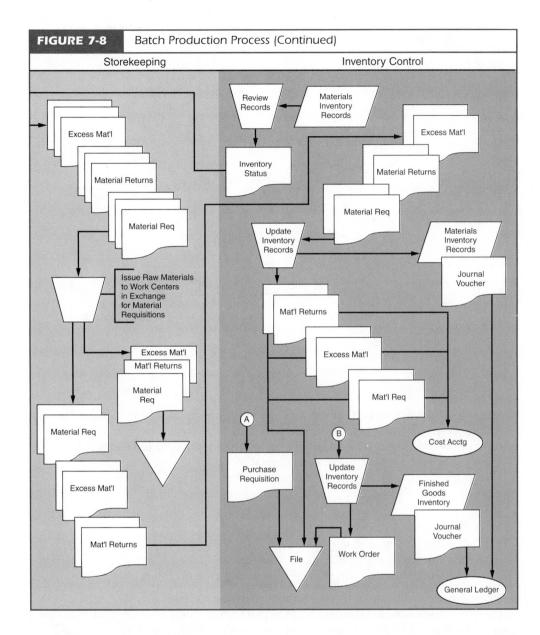

FIGURE 7-8   Batch Production Process (Continued)

5. The total cost per year of holding inventories (carrying costs) is a variable that increases as the quantities ordered increase. These costs include the opportunity cost of invested funds, storage costs, property taxes, and insurance.

6. There are no quantity discounts. Therefore, the total purchase price of inventory for the year is constant.

The objective of the EOQ model is to reduce total inventory costs. The significant parameters in this model are the carrying costs and the ordering costs. Figure 7-9 illustrates the relationship between these costs and order quantity. As the quantity ordered increases, the number of ordering events decreases, causing the total annual cost of ordering to decrease. However, as the quantity ordered increases, average inventory on hand increases, causing the total annual inventory carrying cost to increase. Because the total purchase price of inventory is constant

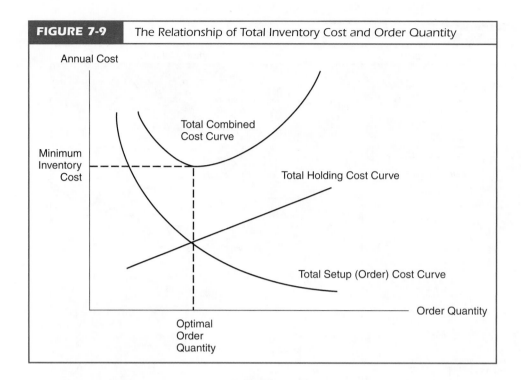

FIGURE 7-9   The Relationship of Total Inventory Cost and Order Quantity

(Assumption 6), we minimize total inventory costs by minimizing the total carrying cost and total ordering costs. The point at which the combined total cost curve is minimized is the intersection of the ordering-cost curve and the carrying-cost curve. This is the EOQ.

The following equation is used to determine the EOQ:

$$Q = \sqrt{\frac{2DS}{H}}$$

Where: Q = economic order quantity
         D = annual demand in units
         S = the fixed cost of placing each order
         H = the holding or carrying cost per unit per year

To illustrate the use of this model, consider the following example:

A company has an annual demand of 2,000 units, a per-unit order cost of $12, and a carrying cost per unit of $0.40. Using these values, we calculate the EOQ as follows:

$$Q = \sqrt{\frac{2DS}{H}}$$

$$Q = \sqrt{\frac{2(2,000)(12)}{0.40}}$$

$$Q = \sqrt{120,000}$$

$$Q = 346$$

Now that we know how much to purchase, let's consider the second question: When do we purchase?

The **reorder point** (ROP) is usually expressed as follows:

ROP = I × d

where :   I = lead time
          d = daily demand (total demand/number of working days)

In simple models, both I and d are assumed to be known with certainty and are constant. For example, if:

d = 5 units, and
I = 8 days, then
ROP = 40 units.

The assumptions of the EOQ model produce the saw-toothed inventory usage pattern illustrated in Figure 7-10. Values for Q and ROP are calculated separately for each type of inventory item. Each time inventory is reduced by sales or used in production, its new quantity on hand (QOH) is compared to its ROP. When QOH = ROP, an order is placed for the amount of Q. In our example, when inventory drops to 40 units, the firm orders 346 units.

If the parameters d and I are stable, the firm should receive the ordered inventories just as the quantity on hand reaches zero. However, if either or both parameters are subject to variation, then additional inventories called "**safety stock**" must be added to the reorder point to avoid unanticipated stockout conditions. Figure 7-11 shows an additional 10 units of safety stock to carry the firm through a lead time that could vary from eight to ten days. The new reorder point is 50 units. Stockouts result in either lost sales or back-orders. A back-order is a customer order that cannot be filled because of a stockout and will remain unfilled until the supplier receives replenishment stock.

When an organization's inventory usage and delivery patterns depart significantly from the assumptions of the EOQ model, more sophisticated models such as the *back-order quantity model* and the *production order quantity model* may be used. However, a discussion of these models is beyond the scope of this text.

THE COST ACCOUNTING SYSTEM

The cost accounting subsystem of the conversion cycle records the financial effects of the events occurring in the production process. Figure 7-12 on page 341 represents typical information flows and tasks in the cost accounting system. The cost accounting process for a given production run begins when the production planning and control department sends

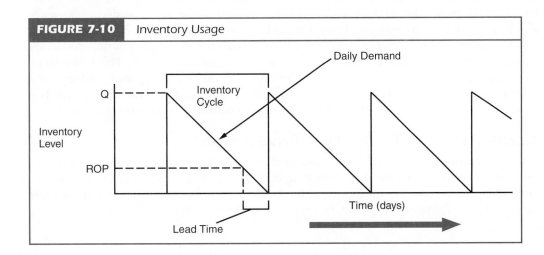

FIGURE 7-10   Inventory Usage

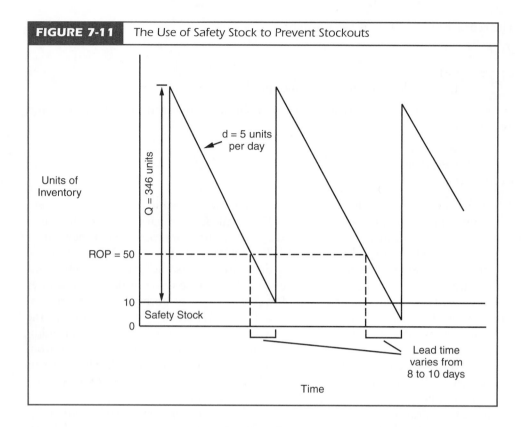

FIGURE 7-11   The Use of Safety Stock to Prevent Stockouts

a copy of the original work order to the cost accounting department. The clerk creates a new cost record for the batch that is beginning production and files this in the WIP file. This file acts as the subsidiary ledger for the WIP control account in the general ledger (GL).

As materials and labor are added throughout the production process, documents reflecting these events flow into cost accounting. Inventory control sends copies of materials requisitions, excess materials requisitions, and materials returns. The various work centers send job tickets and completed move tickets. These documents, along with standards provided by the standard cost file, enable cost accounting clerks to update the affected WIP accounts with the standard charges for direct labor, material, and manufacturing overhead (MOH). Deviations from standard usage are recorded in variance accounts. Common calculated variances include material usage, direct labor, and MOH.

The receipt of the last move ticket for a batch signals the completion of the production process. At this point, the clerk removes the cost sheet from the WIP file. This represents a transfer of product from WIP to the FG inventory. Periodically, summary information regarding charges (debits) to WIP, reductions (credits) to WIP, and variances are recorded on a journal voucher and sent to the GL department for posting to the control accounts.

CONTROLS IN THE TRADITIONAL ENVIRONMENT

Recall from previous chapters the six general classes of internal control activities: transaction authorization, segregation of duties, supervision, access control, accounting records, and independent verification. Specific controls as they apply to the conversion cycle are summarized in Table 7-1 and further explained in the following section.

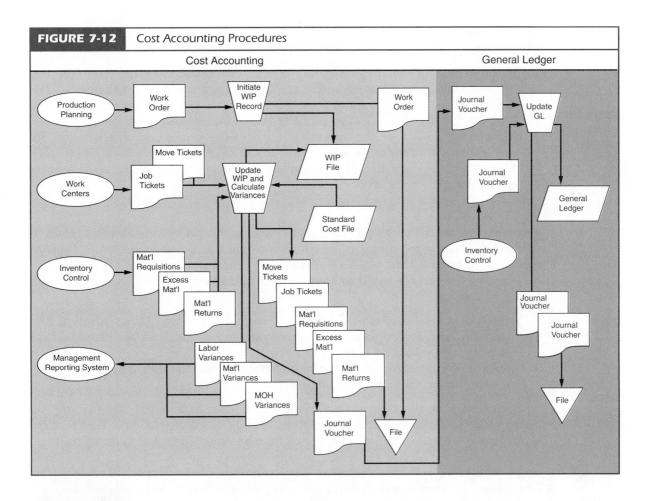

FIGURE 7-12   Cost Accounting Procedures

TABLE 7-1	Summary of Conversion Cycle Controls
Control Class	**Control Points in the System**
Transaction authorization	Work orders, move tickets, and materials requisitions.
Segregation of duties	1. Inventory control separate from RM and FG inventory custody.
	2. Cost accounting separate from work centers.
	3. GL separate from other accounting functions.
Supervision	Supervisors oversee usage of RM and timekeeping.
Access	Limit physical access to FG, RM stocks, and production processes. Use formal procedures and documents to release materials into production.
Accounting records	Work orders, cost sheets, move tickets, job tickets, materials requisitions, WIP records, FG inventory file.
Independent verification	Cost accounting function reconciles all cost of production.
	GL reconciles overall system.

Transaction Authorization

The following describes the transaction authorization procedure in the conversion cycle.

1. In the traditional manufacturing environment, the production activity is authorized by production planning and control via a formal work order. This document reflects production requirements, which are the difference between the expected demand for products (based on the sales forecast) and the FG inventory on hand.
2. Move tickets signed by the supervisor in each work center authorize activities for each batch and for the movement of products through the various work centers.
3. Materials requisitions and excess materials requisitions authorize the storekeeper to release materials to the work centers.

Segregation of Duties

One objective of this control procedure is to separate the tasks of transaction authorization and transaction processing. As a result, the production planning and control department is organizationally segregated from the work centers.

Another control objective is to segregate record keeping from asset custody. The following separations apply:

1. Inventory control maintains accounting records for RM and FG inventories. This activity is kept separate from the materials storeroom and from the FG warehouse functions, which have custody of these assets.
2. Similarly, the cost accounting function accounts for WIP and should be separate from the work centers in the production process.

Finally, to maintain the independence of the GL function as a verification step, the GL department must be separate from departments keeping subsidiary accounts. Therefore, the GL department is organizationally segregated from inventory control and cost accounting.

Supervision

The following supervision procedures apply to the conversion cycle:

1. The supervisors in the work centers oversee the usage of RM in the production process. This helps to ensure that all materials released from stores are used in production and that waste is minimized. Employee time cards and job tickets must also be checked for accuracy.
2. Supervisors also observe and review time-keeping activities. This promotes accurate employee time cards and job tickets.

Access Control

The conversion cycle allows both direct and indirect access to assets.

Direct Access to Assets. The nature of the physical product and the production process influences the type of access controls needed.

1. Firms often limit access to sensitive areas, such as storerooms, production work centers, and FG warehouses. Control methods used include identification badges, security guards, observation devices, and various electronic sensors and alarms.
2. The use of standard costs provides a type of access control. By specifying the quantities of material and labor authorized for each product, the firm limits unauthorized access to those resources. To obtain excess quantities requires special authorization and formal documentation.

Indirect Access to Assets. Assets, such as cash and inventories, can be manipulated through access to the source documents that control them. In the conversion cycle, critical documents include materials requisitions, excess materials requisitions, and employee time cards. A method of control that also supports an audit trail is the use of prenumbered documents.

Accounting Records

As we have seen in preceding chapters, the objective of this control technique is to establish an audit trail for each transaction. In the conversion cycle this is accomplished through the use of work orders, cost sheets, move tickets, job tickets, materials requisitions, the WIP file, and the FG inventory file. By prenumbering source documents and referencing these in the WIP records, a company can trace every item of FG inventory back through the production process to its source. This is essential in detecting errors in production and record keeping, locating batches "lost" in production, and performing periodic audits.

Independent Verification

Verification steps in the conversion cycle are performed as follows:

1. Cost accounting reconciles the materials and labor usage taken from materials requisitions and job tickets with the prescribed standards. Cost accounting personnel may then identify departures from prescribed standards, which are formally reported as variances. In the traditional manufacturing environment, calculated variances are an important source of data for the management reporting system.

2. The GL department also fulfills an important verification function by checking the total movement of products from WIP to FG. This is done by reconciling journal vouchers from cost accounting and summaries of the inventory subsidiary ledger from inventory control.

3. Finally, internal and external auditors periodically verify the RM and FG inventories on hand through a physical count. They compare actual quantities against the inventory records and make adjustments to the records when necessary.

THE WORLD-CLASS MANUFACTURING ENVIRONMENT

The traditional conversion cycle just described still represents procedures in many manufacturing firms in the United States. In the past two decades, however, manufacturing has seen radical changes as firms seek world-class status. In this section, we explore the nature of these changes. We begin with a brief account of factors influencing the world-class environment.

In the mid-1950s, the United States was the undisputed leader in manufacturing among industrialized nations. Mass-production processes, perfected early in the century, provided economies of scale that gave U.S. industry a distinct competitive advantage. Firms achieved low unit costs by producing a narrow range of products in large lot sizes. Demand for these products was stable over time, yielding an extended period for cost recovery. In many respects, this was a seller's market. A line attributed to Henry Ford characterizes the mass-production philosophy: "Americans can have any color Model T they want, as long as it's black."

Today, the dominance of foreign goods in U.S. stores reflects a world very different from 20 or 30 years ago. U.S. industries have seen an erosion of their market shares and a blunting of their competitive edge. The automobile and electronics industries are clear examples of this phenomenon. One argument for the change in status quo asserts that significantly lower labor costs have given foreign firms a competitive advantage. Perhaps true at the beginning of the decline, wage competition now explains only a small portion of the total picture. A better explanation is found in the market factors that have redefined competitive advantage, factors that U.S. industry failed to recognize immediately.

Since the mid-1970s, the factors that govern competitive advantage have shifted away from an emphasis on costs alone to an emphasis on customer satisfaction, product diversity, and the ability to respond rapidly to changing consumer demand. Figure 7-13 portrays the trends in competitive advantage factors over time.

For many years U.S. manufacturers ignored these trends and continued with "business as usual," while foreign competitors seized the leadership role. Through innovations in business philosophy, production processes, and technology, along with a relentless pursuit of customer satisfaction, foreign competitors emerged as serious contenders in an arena once dominated by the United States. Today, U.S. manufacturers are responding to changes they can no longer ignore by achieving manufacturing flexibility.

MANUFACTURING FLEXIBILITY

Modern consumers want quality products, they want them quickly, and they want variety of choice. This demand profile imposes a fundamental conflict on traditional manufacturers, whose structured and inflexible orientation renders them ineffective in this environment.

In contrast, world-class competitors meet the challenges of modern consumerism through flexible manufacturing systems. Consider the following examples of flexibility among world-class automobile manufacturers. One firm has the flexibility to completely retool for a change from one model to another in 2.5 minutes. One manufacturer can produce 600 different end items on a single production line. Another firm can switch paint

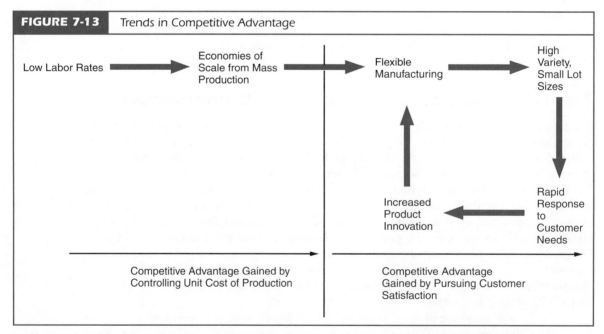

FIGURE 7-13 | Trends in Competitive Advantage

Low Labor Rates → Economies of Scale from Mass Production → Flexible Manufacturing → High Variety, Small Lot Sizes → Rapid Response to Customer Needs → Increased Product Innovation → Flexible Manufacturing

Competitive Advantage Gained by Controlling Unit Cost of Production

Competitive Advantage Gained by Pursuing Customer Satisfaction

SOURCE: Adapted from J. D. Blackburn, "Trends in Manufacturing," *Cost Accounting, Robotics, and the New Manufacturing Environment* (Sarasota, Fla.: American Accounting Association, 1987).

colors on its production line in a few seconds. This allows customized painting to customer orders without having to run a whole batch of vehicles through at one color.

Achieving **manufacturing flexibility** incorporates four operational characteristics: (1) physical reorganization of the production facilities; (2) automation of the manufacturing process; (3) reduction of inventories; and (4) high, product quality. Let's consider each of these characteristics and look at some emerging trends.

PHYSICAL REORGANIZATION OF THE PRODUCTION FACILITIES

Traditional manufacturing processes tend to evolve in piecemeal fashion over years into snakelike sequences of activities. Products move back and forth across shop floors, and upstairs and downstairs through different activities. Figure 7-14 shows a traditional factory layout. The inefficiencies inherent in the layout of traditional plants add handling costs, conversion time, and even inventories to the manufacturing process. Furthermore, because production activities are usually organized along functional lines, there is a tendency for parochialism among employees. This "us-versus-them" mentality is contrary to a team attitude and creates bottlenecks in the process.

A flexible manufacturing system is a much simplified process. Figure 7-15 illustrates this idea. The flexible production system is organized into flows. Computer-controlled machines, robots, and manual tasks that constitute the flow activities are grouped together physically into factory units called *cells*. This arrangement shortens the physical distances between the activities, which reduces setup and processing time, handling costs, and inventories in the flow.

AUTOMATION OF THE MANUFACTURING PROCESS

Automation is at the heart of a well-functioning manufacturing environment. By replacing labor with automation, a firm can be more efficient and, therefore, more competitive. Automation also contributes directly to the other operating characteristics of inventory reduction and increased quality. However, the deployment of automation among U.S. manufacturers varies considerably. Figure 7-16 presents automation as a continuum with the traditional manufacturing model at one end and the fully computer-integrated manufacturing (CIM) model at the other.

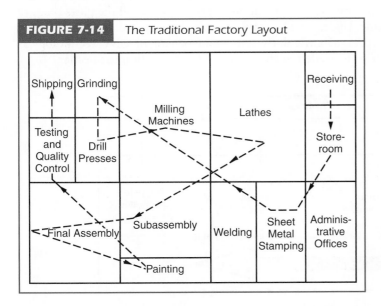

FIGURE 7-14   The Traditional Factory Layout

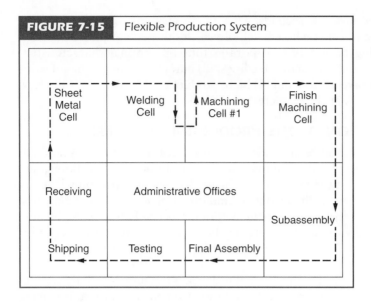

FIGURE 7-15   Flexible Production System

Sheet Metal Cell	Welding Cell	Machining Cell #1	Finish Machining Cell
Receiving	Administrative Offices		
			Subassembly
Shipping	Testing	Final Assembly	

Traditional Manufacturing

The traditional manufacturing environment consists of a range of different types of machines, each controlled by a single operator. Because these machines require a great deal of setup time, the cost of setup must be absorbed by large production runs. The machines and their operators are organized into functional departments, such as milling, grinding, and welding. The WIP follows a circuitous route through the different operations across the factory floor.

Islands of Technology

"**Islands of technology**" describes an environment where modern automation exists in the form of islands that stand alone within the traditional setting. The islands employ **computer numerical controlled (CNC)** machines that can perform multiple operations with little human involvement. CNC machines contain computer programs for all the parts that are manufactured by the machine. Under a CNC configuration, humans still load, set up, and unload the machines. However, a particularly important benefit of CNC technology is that little setup time (and cost) is needed to change from one operation to another.

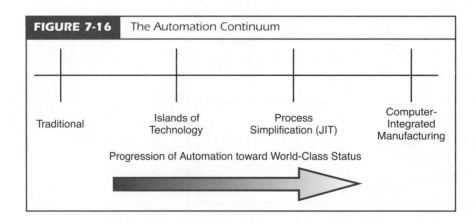

FIGURE 7-16   The Automation Continuum

Traditional — Islands of Technology — Process Simplification (JIT) — Computer-Integrated Manufacturing

Progression of Automation toward World-Class Status

Process Simplification

Process simplification focuses on reducing the complexity of the physical manufacturing layout of the shop floor. Various types of CNC machines are arranged in **cells** to produce an entire part from start to finish in one location. Unlike standard CNC machines, there is no human involvement in a cell. For example, Nissan employs a multioperation cell in the manufacture of heavy-duty truck axles. The machine takes an 800-pound axle and performs more than 40 operations (turning, grinding, drilling, and so on) without any human involvement. The less complex physical layout of a cell reduces the distance a part must travel in manufacturing. This in turn saves on production time and significantly reduces inventories in transit.

Computer-Integrated Manufacturing

Computer-integrated manufacturing (CIM) is a completely automated environment. A CIM facility is organized into group technology cells using no human labor in the manufacturing process. In addition to CNC machines, the process employs automated storage and retrieval systems and robotics. Figure 7-17 shows the physical relationship between these technologies.

Automated Storage and Retrieval Systems (AS/RS). Many firms have increased productivity and profitability by replacing traditional forklifts and their human operators with **automated storage and retrieval systems (AS/RS)**. Harley-Davidson went from 60 forklift operators down to 5. AS/RS are computer-controlled conveyor systems that carry RM from stores to the shop floor and finished products to the warehouse. The operational advantages of AS/RS technology over manual systems include reduced errors, improved inventory control, and lower storage costs.

Robotics. **Robotics** involves the use of robots, special CNC machines, that are useful in hazardous environments or for performing dangerous and monotonous tasks that are prone to causing accidents.

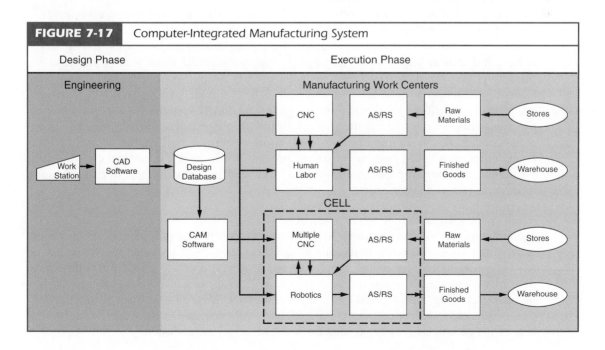

FIGURE 7-17   Computer-Integrated Manufacturing System

The remainder of the section outlines a number of information technologies used to plan and control the production process. These are computer-aided design (CAD), computer-aided manufacturing (CAM), manufacturing resources planning (MRP II), enterprise resource planning (ERP), and electronic data interchange (EDI). Manufacturing and nonmanufacturing firms employ ERP and EDI technologies. Hence, they will be examined within a broader context later, in separate chapters.

Computer-Aided Design

Engineers use **CAD** to design better products faster. CAD systems increase engineers' productivity, improve accuracy by automating repetitive design tasks, allow firms to be more responsive to market demands, and interface with the CAM and MRP II systems, as well as the external environment. The relation between these systems is shown in Figure 7-18.

Product design has been revolutionized through CAD technology. The technology was first applied to the aerospace industry in the early 1960s but has since been adopted by every industry. CAD technology has been extended to the design and evaluation of the manufacturing *process* for new products. This results in the specification of detailed steps and procedures (routing information) for the work center personnel. Advanced CAD systems can design both product and process simultaneously. Thus, aided by CAD, management can evaluate the technical feasibility of the product and determine its "manufacturability."

Computer-aided design technology greatly shortens the time frame between initial and final design. This allows firms to adjust their production quickly to changes in market demand. It also allows them to respond to customer requests for unique products. The CAD system's interface to the external communication network, or EDI, is required so that the world-class manufacturer can share its product design specifications with its vendors and customers. This communications link also allows the world-class manufacturer to receive product design specifications electronically from its customers and suppliers for its review.

Computer-Aided Manufacturing

Computer-aided manufacturing focuses on the shop floor and the use of computers to control the physical manufacturing process. At one time, the most common type of machines in manufacturing were general-purpose machines, such as drill presses, lathes, and milling machines. The objective of early automation was to increase the productivity of labor. Today, CAM provides greater precision, speed, and control than human production processes. The objective behind CAM is to *replace* labor through automation. As shown in Figure 7-19 on page 350, CAM systems monitor and control the production process and routing through the use of process control, numerical control, and robotics equipment. A world-class manufacturer will derive several benefits from deploying a CAM system: improved process productivity, improved cost and time estimates, improved process monitoring, improved process quality, decreased setup times, and reduced labor costs.

MRP II, EDI, and ERP

Manufacturing resources planning (**MRP II**) is an extension of a simpler concept still in use called "**materials requirements planning**" (**MRP**). Figure 7-20 on page 351 illustrates an MRP system, which "explodes" individual work orders to create a BOM and determine inventory requirements in advance of production. This approach was designed to minimize inventory-carrying costs in mass-production industries. MRP is simply an automated version of a traditional production planning and control process. On the other hand, MRP II is a reengineering technique that integrates several business processes.

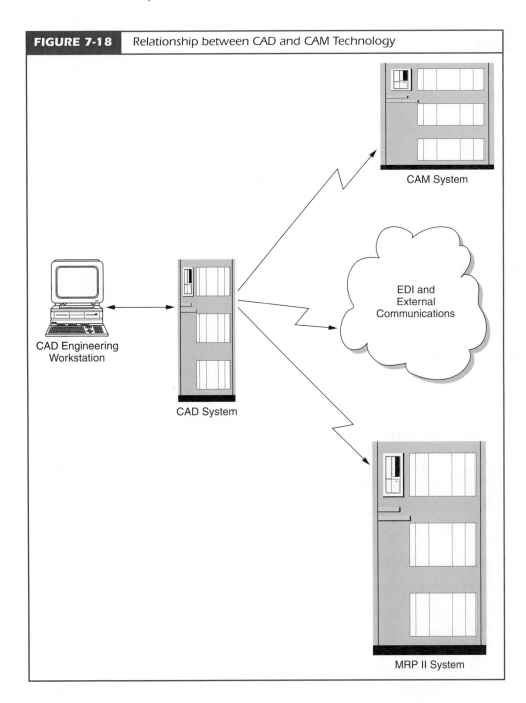

FIGURE 7-18   Relationship between CAD and CAM Technology

CAM System

EDI and
External
Communications

CAD Engineering
Workstation

CAD System

MRP II System

MRP II is not confined to the management of inventory. It is both a system and a philosophy for coordinating the activities of the entire firm. As such, MRP II systems incorporate techniques to execute the production plan, provide feedback, and control the process. Figure 7-21 shows the integration of systems under an MRP II environment.

The MRP II system will produce a BOM for the product, fit the production of the product into the master production schedule, produce a rough-cut capacity plan based

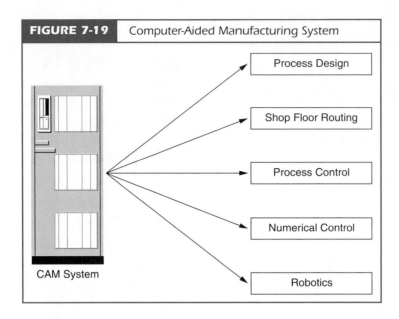

FIGURE 7-19   Computer-Aided Manufacturing System

on machine and labor availability, produce a materials requirements plan that will schedule the delivery of the RM on a just-in-time basis, design a final capacity plan for the factory, and manage the RM and FG inventories. Figure 7-22 on page 353 shows in detail the highly integrated nature of the MRP II concept. MRP II integrates product design and the factory production process with the order entry, accounting information, and activity-based costing (ABC) systems, all of which will allow the world-class manufacturer to establish, communicate, and execute production schedules while controlling costs and maintaining the lowest level of inventory possible. The world-class manufacturer can realize a considerable number of significant benefits from a highly integrated MRP II system, including the following:

- Improved customer service
- Reduced inventory investment
- Increased productivity
- Improved cash flow
- Assistance in achieving long-term strategic goals
- Help in managing change (i.e., new product development or specialized product development for customers or by vendors)
- Flexibility in the production process

MRP II has evolved into the large suites of software called **enterprise resource planning (ERP)** systems. These commercial packages support the information needs of the entire organization, not just the manufacturing functions. An ERP can calculate resource requirements, schedule production, manage changes to product configurations, allow for future planned changes in products, and monitor shop floor production. In addition, the ERP provides order entry, cash receipts, procurement, and cash disbursement functions along with full financial and managerial reporting capability.

A world-class organization will have an ERP system that is capable of external communications with its customers and suppliers through **EDI**. The EDI communications link

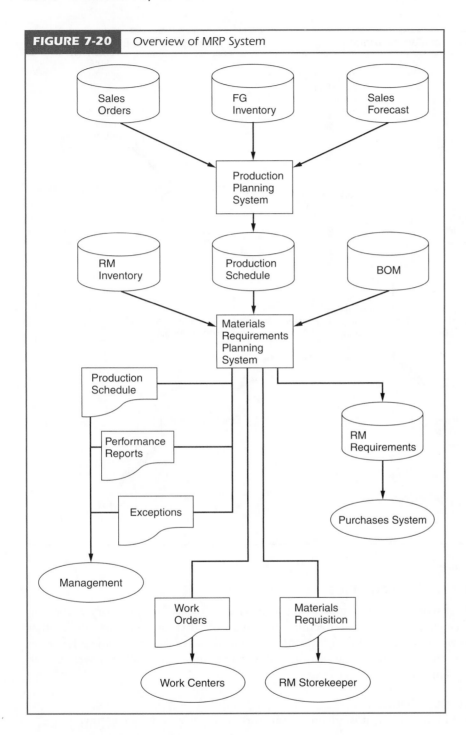

FIGURE 7-20   Overview of MRP System

(either via Internet or direct connection) will allow the firm to electronically receive sales orders and cash receipts from customers, send invoices to customers, send purchase orders to vendors, receive invoices from vendors and pay them, as well as send and receive shipping documents. EDI is a central element of many electronic commerce systems. We will revisit this important topic in Chapter 12.

| FIGURE 7-21 | The Integration of Manufacturing and Financial Systems within the MRP II Environment |

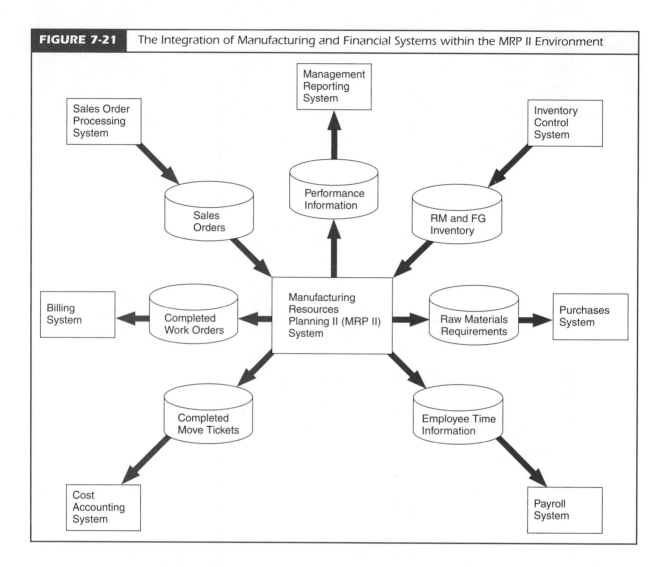

REDUCTION OF INVENTORIES

The hallmark of world-class manufacturing firms is their success in inventory reduction. Such firms often experience annual inventory turnovers of 100 times per year. While other firms carry weeks and even months of inventories, world-class firms have only a few days or sometimes even a few hours of inventory. Why is this important? What is wrong with maintaining inventories?

The Evils of Inventories

There are three main reasons it is advantageous for a company to reduce its inventories.

1. Inventories cost money. Inventories represent an investment in materials, labor, and overhead that cannot be realized until they are sold. Also, there are other costs associated with inventory that are often hidden. Inventories must be transported throughout the factory. They must be handled, stored, and counted. In addition, inventories lose their value through obsolescence.

FIGURE 7-22 | MRP II System: Production Capability Planning Modules

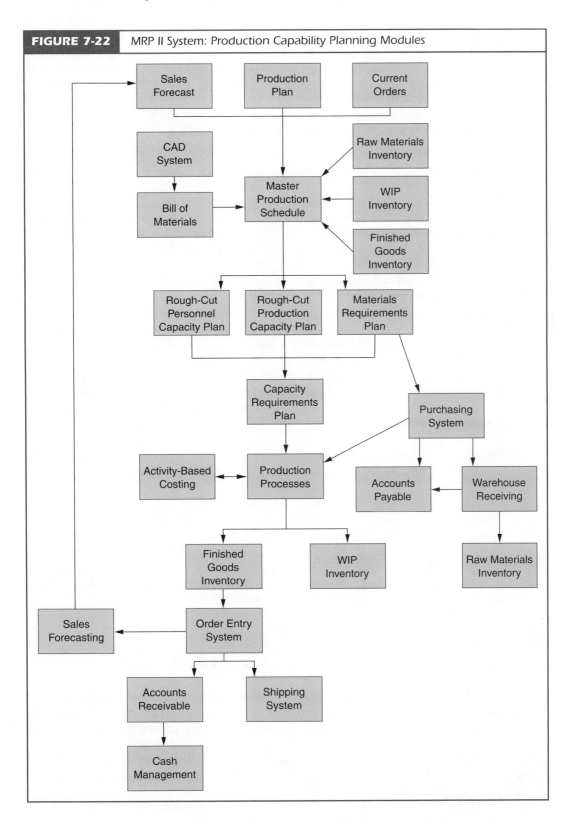

2. Inventories camouflage production problems. If machine capacity imbalances in the manufacturing process are causing bottlenecks, work-in-process inventory builds up at the bottlenecks. If customer orders and production are out of sync, inventories build up.
3. Willingness to maintain inventories can precipitate overproduction. Because of setup cost constraints, firms tend to overproduce inventories in large batches to absorb the allocated costs and create the image of improved efficiency. The true cost of this dysfunctional activity is hidden in excess inventories.

These inventory-driven problems promote inefficiency, reduce profitability, and erode a firm's competitiveness. Many manufacturing problems can be solved by reducing inventories.

How Can Firms Reduce Their Inventories?

Firms have successfully reduced their inventories by adopting the **just-in-time** (**JIT**) manufacturing model. However, JIT is more than an inventory reduction technique: it is a philosophy that attacks the manufacturing problems previously described through process simplification as well as inventory reduction.

Under the JIT approach, inventories arrive in small quantities from vendors several times per day "just in time" to go into production. JIT supports a pull manufacturing process. As production capacity upstream becomes available, the manufacturing process pulls small batches (or a single item) of product into the next work center. Rather than periodically taking in large batches, JIT promotes a continuous flow of production through the process pulled along by idle capacity. Unlike the traditional push process, JIT does not create batches of semifinished inventories at bottlenecks. In fact, under this philosophy, the firm eliminates bottlenecks and reduces the distances between cells and work centers. Hence, fewer inventories are in transit at any point in time. The JIT concept rests heavily on the following assumptions[1]:

Zero Defects. Continuous processing requires RM, WIP, and FG with zero defects. Some world-class manufacturing firms define this as fewer than 200 defects per million parts produced.

Zero Setup Time. Long machine setup procedures add cost and delays to the process. Firms should strive to reduce setup time to less than five minutes.

Small Lot Sizes. To achieve a machine utilization of about 95 percent and a continuous flow of product through the process, lot sizes must be small. Some should be no more than one day's worth of inventory in the production cycle.

Zero Inventories. To reiterate a subtle but important point made earlier, JIT is not simply an inventory reduction technique. Rather, JIT depends on inventory reduction. A successful JIT firm may achieve inventory turnover of 100 times a year.

Zero Lead Times and Reliable Vendors. A JIT firm must have established and cooperative relationships with vendors. Late deliveries, defective RM, or incorrect orders will shut down production immediately. There are no inventory reserves to draw on in a JIT system.

Team Attitude. JIT relies heavily on the team attitude of all employees involved in the process. This includes those in purchasing, receiving, manufacturing, shipping—everyone.

---

1   R. D' Amore, "Just in Time Systems," in *Cost Accounting, Robotics, and the New Manufacturing Environment* (Sarasota, Fla.: American Accounting Association, 1987).

Each employee must be vigilant of problems that threaten the continuous flow operation of the production line. JIT requires a constant state of quality control along with the authority to take immediate action.

When Toyota first introduced JIT, its production employees had the authority to shut down the line when defects were discovered. In the early days, the line was often shut down to bring attention to a problem. Whether a defective part from a vendor or a faulty machine in a cell, the problem was properly addressed so that it did not recur. After an adjustment period, the process stabilized.

PRODUCT QUALITY

There are two basic reasons why quality is important to a world-class manufacturer. First, poor quality is very expensive to the firm. Consider the cost of scrap, reworking, scheduling delays, extra inventories to compensate for defective parts, warranty claims, and field service. These costs can represent between 25 to 35 percent of total product cost. Second, quality is a basis on which world-class manufacturers compete. Quality has ceased to be a tradeoff against price. Consumers demand quality and seek the lowest-priced quality product.

How Can Firms Improve Quality?

One way firms can improve quality is to place control points throughout the manufacturing process to identify "out of control" operations as they happen. Through early detection of problems, firms can better manage the situation. The alternative is the traditional end-of-process quality control procedure. Under this approach, products are examined upon their completion. The manufacturer may discover, too late, that an entire batch of product is scrap.

Statistical process control is a method for controlling automated production systems. A single manufacturing process may employ hundreds of control points that are monitored for out-of-control conditions. Many firms have used this method with great success.

IMPLICATIONS FOR ACCOUNTING AND AIS

The new manufacturing environment carries profound implications for accounting and AIS. In this section, we examine the nature of the changes underway and on the horizon. This discussion addresses two areas of reformation: (1) changes in accounting techniques and (2) changes in information reporting.

CHANGES IN ACCOUNTING TECHNIQUES

What's Wrong with Traditional Accounting Information?

Traditional cost-accounting information emphasizes financial performance rather than manufacturing performance. The techniques and conventions used for so many years do not support the new objectives of world-class manufacturing firms. The following are the most commonly cited deficiencies of traditional accounting systems.

Inaccurate Cost Allocations. Traditional accounting systems do not accurately trace costs to products and processes. One consequence of new technologies is a restructuring of manufacturing cost patterns. Figure 7-23 shows the changing relationship between direct labor, direct materials, and overhead cost in different manufacturing environments. In the traditional manufacturing environment, direct labor is a much larger component of total manufacturing costs than in the CIM environment. Overhead, on the other hand, is a far more significant element of cost in advanced technology manufacturing. In this

| FIGURE 7-23 | Changes in Cost Structure between Different Manufacturing Environments |

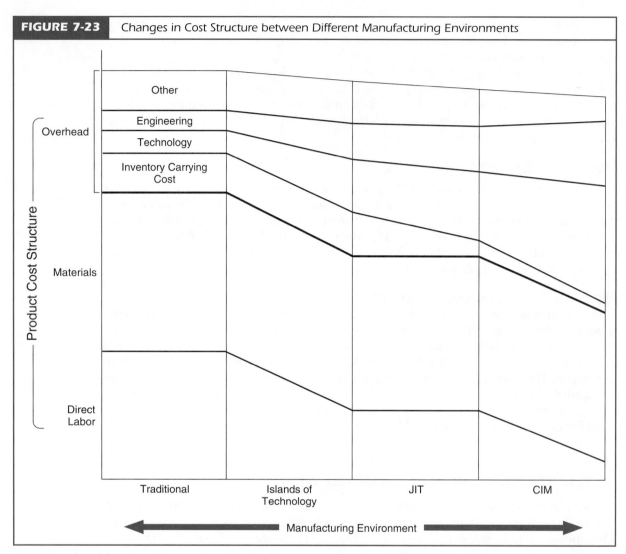

SOURCE: Adapted from J. A. Brimson, "Bringing Cost Management up to Date," Manufacturing Engineering (June 1988): 49.

setting, traditional cost accounting procedures are grossly inadequate. To understand the problem, let's consider how overhead charges are traditionally applied to products. All components of overhead, such as indirect labor, depreciation of machinery, utilities, and insurance, are pooled. This cost pool is then allocated to production on the basis of direct labor hours. The following characteristics of the CIM environment show us why the traditional allocation of overhead is inadequate.

1. In traditional manufacturing, the overhead cost component is relatively small—about 10 to 40 percent of total manufacturing cost. However, overhead is the largest component in CIM.
2. Direct labor charges in CIM are substantially smaller—between 1 to 10 percent of total cost—than they are in traditional manufacturing.
3. Direct labor charges are not easily traced to products in the CIM environment. An advantage of CIM is flexible batch sizes. It is not necessary to produce lots of predetermined

amounts. Products can even be manufactured in single-item lots. In addition, operators may be assigned to more than one machine at a time. It becomes very difficult to assign labor time accurately to individual products being produced simultaneously in variable quantities.

For traditional allocations to be correct, there must be a direct relationship between labor and technology. In CIM, this relationship is diametric rather than complementary. If the cost pool is large and the allocation method ambiguous, any miscalculation in assigning labor is magnified many times in the calculation of overhead. Figure 7-24 illustrates the significance of this problem. The figure shows the product cost profile common to many companies. The curved line represents the products' true cost, as calculated under the ABC method[2]; the straight line represents the allocated cost using conventional accounting. For low-volume, high-variety products, the true cost is as much as 600 percent of the allocated cost. Errors of this magnitude can devastate a company's ability to make crucial decisions. Without accurate cost information, firms cannot:

1. Focus on profitable markets.
2. Service profitable customers.

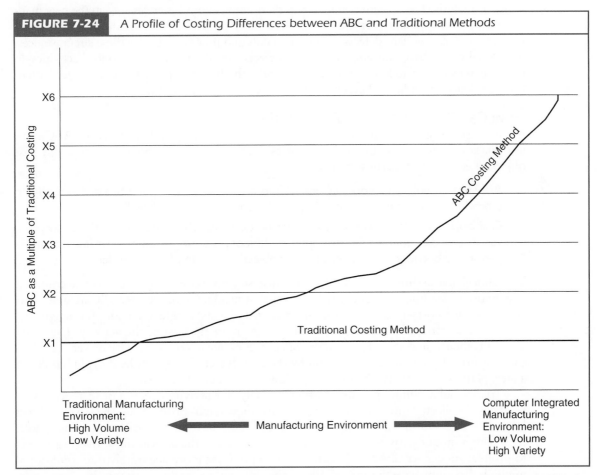

FIGURE 7-24   A Profile of Costing Differences between ABC and Traditional Methods

SOURCE: Adapted from P. B Turney, *Common cents: The ABC Breakthrough* (Hillsboro, Ore.: Cost Technology, 1991): 5.

2   We discuss ABC later in the chapter.

3. Accurately measure the cost of product designs.
4. Accurately measure the cost of process designs.

Time Lag. Traditional accounting data for management reporting is essentially historic. Data lag behind the actual manufacturing activities on the assumption that control can be applied after the fact to correct errors. However, shop floor managers in a JIT setting need immediate information about abnormal deviations. They must know in real time about a machine breakdown or a robot out of control. After-the-fact information is too late to be useful.

Financial Orientation. The orientation of traditional accounting information does not adequately identify defective products or processes. Accounting data use dollars as a standard unit of measure for comparability between items being evaluated. Decisions linking functional areas and different management levels in the firm demand information that has no common basis. These include the functionality of a product or process, improving product quality, and shortening delivery time. Attempts to force these data into a common financial measure may distort the problem and promote bad decisions.

Emphasis on Standard Costs. Conventional accounting emphasizes standard costs and variance analysis. The objectives underlying these conventions lose relevance in the new manufacturing environment. As we have seen, modern production methods are capital-intensive and assume zero defects in both materials and processes. Under these circumstances, traditional variances are insignificant. When defects, deviations, or out-of-control activities do occur, managers need to know immediately. Under the JIT concept such problems need attention long before a traditional accounting system can generate a variance report.

How Can We Solve These Problems?

Many world-class companies have found solutions to these problems in **ABC**. ABC is an information system that provides managers with information about activities and cost objects. Let's first define these terms:

Activities describe the work performed in a firm. Preparing a purchase order, readying a product for shipping, or operating a lathe are examples of activities.

Cost objects are the reasons for performing activities. These include products, services, vendors, and customers. For example, the task of preparing a sales order (the activity) is performed because a customer (the cost object) wishes to place an order.

The underlying assumptions of ABC contrast sharply with traditional cost accounting assumptions. Traditional accounting assumes that products cause costs. ABC assumes that activities cause costs and products (and other cost objects) create a demand for activities.

The first step in the ABC approach is to determine the cost of the activity. The activity cost is then assigned to the relevant cost object by means of an **activity driver**. This factor measures the activity consumption by the cost object. For example, if drilling holes in a steel plate is the activity, the number of holes is the activity driver.

Traditional accounting systems often use only one activity driver. For instance, overhead costs, collected into a single cost pool, are allocated to products on the basis of direct labor hours. A world-class company using ABC may have dozens of activity cost pools, each with a unique activity driver. Figure 7-25 illustrates the allocation of overhead costs to products under ABC. ABC allocates costs to products more accurately than traditional methods. To emphasize the magnitude of the difference possible between these methods, review Figure 7-25. With improved cost information, firms are better able to analyze such critical decisions as pricing, product mix, product design, and process design.

| FIGURE 7-25 | Allocation of Manufacturing Costs under ABC |

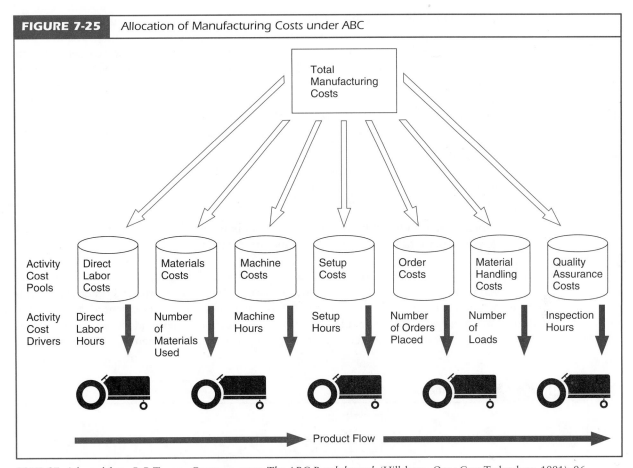

SOURCE: Adapted from P. B Turney, *Common cents: The ABC Breakthrough* (Hillsboro, Ore.: Cost Technology, 1991): 96.

CHANGES IN INFORMATION REPORTING

We are on the threshold of significant change in the role of management accounting information. Historically, the management accounting function was limited to reporting financially oriented information relating to operations. Today, serving the needs of a world-class management team means breaking out of these narrow confines. Management accountants must now provide new information on the state of business activities that is very different from those traditionally produced.

Activity Management

In some organizations, managing business activities is merely a custodial task. This can never be the case in a world-class company. Activity management must be a relentless and continuous quest for improvement. Managers must understand which activities should be performed and how best to perform them. Two underlying objectives guide managers in this challenge:

1. Managers should deploy resources to activities that yield maximum benefit.
2. Managers should seek to improve those factors most important to their customers.

The following discussion provides examples of activity management tasks that require support from a new class of accounting information.

Evaluating Manufacturing Activities. The need for information about operations has led to the development of a second generation of ABC. Figure 7-26 illustrates the new ABC model, which has two dimensions. The vertical dimension is the cost assignment model that we examined in Figure 7-25. It shows the allocation of costs to activities first and then to cost objects. The horizontal dimension is the process model. It reflects the organization's need for a new category of information about the cause of activities and performance measures for those activities. The ABC process model can provide critical information about cost drivers and performance measures to help managers answer such questions as:

1. Which activities require the most resources?
2. What types of resources are required?
3. Where can costs be reduced?

The information produced by the process model is primarily nonfinancial and falls well outside the domain of traditional accounting information.

Identifying Nonessential Activities. Activities are either essential or not. Essential activities add value in one of two ways. First, the activity has value to the customer. For example, balancing the wheels of each car off the production line is essential because the customer demands a car that rides smoothly. Second, the activity adds value to the organization. For example, the activity of preparing financial statements has no immediate

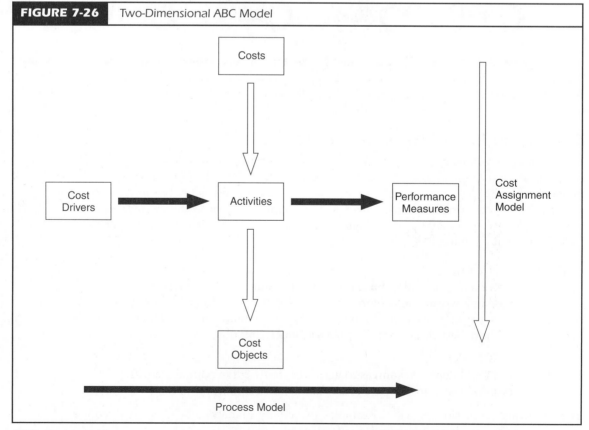

FIGURE 7-26 Two-Dimensional ABC Model

SOURCE: Adapted from P. B Turney, *Common cents: The ABC Breakthrough* (Hillsboro, Ore.: Cost Technology, 1991): 98.

value for the customer. However, because of the firm's legal obligation to do so, this activity has value to the firm and is essential. Nonessential activities add no value and should be eliminated. For example, in a zero defects manufacturing environment, traditional quality control activities at the end of the process become nonessential. Likewise, in this setting, the traditional accounting activities of calculating material usage variances and accounting for scrap are of no value to the organization.

Identifying Cost Drivers. The reduction of unnecessary activities rests on the proper identification of cost drivers. The **cost driver** is the cause of the cost. Managers cannot manage unnecessary activities unless they understand their driving forces. For instance, if the movement of WIP from one operation to another adds no value, it should be eliminated. How do we do this? We must first identify the cost driver for this activity. In this case, it is the physical distance between operations. By reorganizing the need to place these activities in physical sequence, the firm removes the cost driver (distance) and the nonessential activity (moving the product).

Comparing Activities to Benchmarks. In assessing the value added by activities, managers often compare key activities with similar activities elsewhere in the firm or in other firms. This is called **benchmarking.** For example, the firm may rate its key activities on such factors as quality, lead times, flexibility, cost, and customer satisfaction and compare these against the best practices of an industry leader.

Establishing Links between Key Activities. In the previous section, we discussed the importance of team effort in managing a world-class company. From the shop floor to the CEO, each manager (armed with the appropriate information) must act quickly and decisively within his or her sphere of activity. It becomes essential that members of the team, at all levels, understand their performance measures, can spot a problem as it emerges, and recognize their roles in its resolution. Effective coordination requires information that links decision making and performance measures to the firm's **critical success factors** (CSFs). CSFs are items of such importance that failure to meet any one of them would cause the firm to fail. Although specific CSFs vary among firms, the following general categories apply to most manufacturing companies[3]:

- *Product quality.* The firm's product must meet or exceed the customer's expectations.
- *Process quality.* The firm must minimize the amount of process variation that results in scrap or reworking the product.
- *Customer service.* The firm must adequately meet the customer's demand for finished products. The customer may be either the end consumer or an internal customer, such as the next department in the manufacturing process.
- *Resource management.* The firm must optimize the use of RM, labor, and fixed assets in the manufacture of its products.
- *Flexibility.* The firm must be responsive and adaptable to changes in its environment. This includes changes in the product market, in suppliers, and in the legal environment.

No single individual can influence a CSF. Improving a CSF comes from coordinated action at each decision point. Figure 7-27 shows an example of how this can be accomplished for the resource management CSF. The diagram shows some of the performance measures that

3   M. E. Beischel and R. K. Smith, "Linking the Shop Floor to the Top Floor," *Management Accounting* (October 1991): 25, 26.

FIGURE 7-27   Linking Performance Measure at Levels throughout the Organization

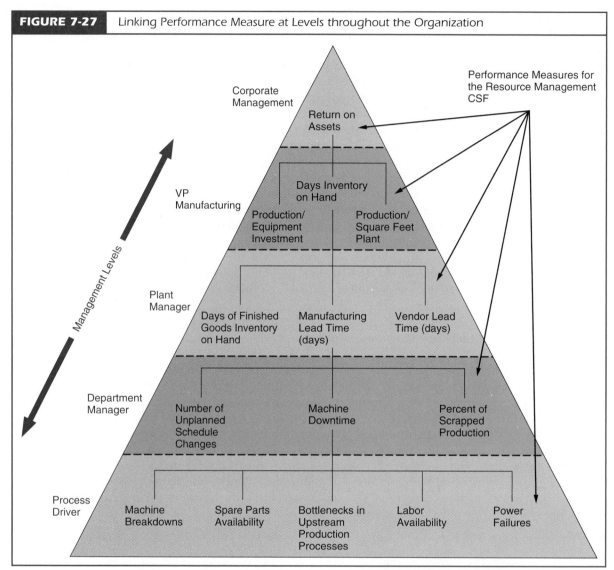

SOURCE: Adapted from M. E. Beischel and R. K. Smith, "Linking the shop Floor to the Top Floor," *Management Accounting* (October 1991): 26.

influence the *resource management* CSF at each management level. To improve this CSF, each manager must control his or her performance measures and recognize the influence they have on the next level in the organization. For example, when the department manager properly manages specific items, e.g., machine downtime, percent of scrapped production, and the number of unplanned schedule changes, the manager knows he or she is contributing to the overall resource management goal of the firm.

Note two additional points to be made from Figure 7-27. First, at higher management levels, performance measures are broader and more aggregated, while at lower levels they are more detailed and specific. Second, this approach integrates financial and nonfinancial information within a common reporting structure, which extends the role of accounting beyond its traditional boundary. Accommodating the broader spectrum of management needs with both financial and nonfinancial information has been the topic of much interest. However, doing so requires a new accounting model that can support multiple user views. Such a model is called "resources, events, and agents" (REA), which is examined at length in Chapter 10.

THE WORLD-CLASS INFORMATION SYSTEM

The key to a world-class information system (WCIS) is the integration of all the system's functional and technological components. Integration is the glue that binds the system together and includes basic accounting applications, ABC, MRP, capacity planning, inventory control, BOM, the master production schedule, forecasting, order entry, CAD, CAM, and EDI communications links.

In this section we introduce the concept of a WCIS. It begins with a review of the traditional information system to illustrate the sharp contrast with a world-class system. As an example of a WCIS, we overview the general features of a system called SAP. SAP is the market leader among a class of information systems known as *enterprise resource planning* (ERP) systems. In recent years, SAP has secured a prominent position and is regarded by many as the standard by which other ERPs are judged. Because of the importance of ERP to accounting information systems, we continue the treatment of this material in Chapter 11. This section concludes with a review of control issues related to WCIS.

CHARACTERISTICS OF THE TRADITIONAL INFORMATION SYSTEM

In the traditional manufacturing environment, technology is generally employed in a haphazard fashion and without a plan. The objective is often to solve a specific, recurring problem for a specific department without regard to integrating the technology into the whole process. The result is isolated islands of technology that are not integrated and often can be integrated only at considerable expense. This is true not only of shop-floor automation technology, but also of information systems and business applications.

Information technology employed by a traditional manufacturer will likely consist of a mainframe to handle the primary accounting functions, such as the sales order processing, purchases processing, and payroll. These basic accounting applications may or may not be integrated. The mainframe applications will be primarily batch-oriented, and only a few real-time systems will exist.

The mainframe will probably have some type of job costing and inventory control systems for FG and RM. However, in many traditional manufacturing environments, the cost accounting system is kept on a separate personal computer (PC), which requires a considerable amount of manual data entry to keep it up to date. In fact, the cost accounting system may be nothing more than a spreadsheet.

Generally, PCs are used by traditional manufacturers to solve standalone business problems, and connectivity to the mainframe through networking is an afterthought and cumbersome. Many of the PCs were purchased by the various functional departments to solve their own business problems and are deployed haphazardly. Unlike the mainframe applications, which generate authorization documents and reports in support of the organization's internal control system, PC-based systems have little or no internal controls placed on them. Therefore, the potential for errors and irregularities (fraud) is significant.

The traditional manufacturer's information system depends heavily on paper-based transactions, which must be entered and re-entered as the paper moves from one department or work center to the next. The duplication of effort is substantial in this environment, which increases the chance of data entry errors and promotes a rather poor level of data integrity.

Finally, the traditional manufacturer's telecommunications network is usually confined to the firm's internal environment. Normally, there is no external communications capability, or even desire to possess the capability, unless the firm is forced to implement EDI by a customer or a supplier. Not only is the traditional manufacturer's implementation of technology a series of isolated islands, the traditional manufacturer itself is an isolated island in relation to the global business community.

SAP: AN EXAMPLE OF A WORLD-CLASS INFORMATION SYSTEM

SAP AG is a German company that was founded in 1972 in Waldorf, Germany, by a couple of IBM employees. Opening their operation, the goal was to create an integrated business package to serve large organizations in the manufacturing industry. The software, also named SAP, supports key business processes related to sales, marketing, manufacturing, and human resources. In English, the term SAP stands for *Systems, Applications, and Products in Data Processing.*

SAP R/3

SAP's primary product is called R/3. This is a client/server-based system (the specifics of this type of network architecture are discussed in Chapter 12) that runs under a number of operating systems and network configurations. SAP R/3 works on multiple hardware platforms including Windows NT PCs, UNIX Systems (multiuser workstations), and the IBM AS 400 (minicomputers). R/3 also supports multiple databases including Informix, Oracle, DB2, ADABAS D, MS SQL, and DB2/4000. It can be customized to interact with EDI and other systems written in standard languages such as C, C++, COBOL, and SQL.

The R/3 architecture is a hierarchical structure. The underlying basis is the first layer in the foundation on which the R/3 system is built. This includes the application modules, the network architecture, and the hardware platform. The database, which may be distributed among multiple computers, is the lowest layer in the system. The database tables contain the transaction details needed to support multiple user needs. The data dictionary describes the *views* of the multiple users of the system. This layer provides the mapping of data relationships between the business entities.

R/3 provides predefined business modules that support hundreds of business processes organized in the following four general categories: financial, logistics, human resources, and business process support. A few years ago, organizations would have had to design and program custom applications in-house to support these functions. R/3 users can, however, mix and match prefabricated software components to assemble an ERP application that meets their business requirements. One of the driving forces behind the ERP revolution is the desire by many organizations to move closer to world-class status through business processes reengineering. An integrated R/3 system can improve customer service, reduce production time of products, increase productivity, and improve decision making. The operational features of R/3 and several other world-class ERP systems are presented in Chapter 11.

CONTROL ISSUES IN THE WCIS

The high degree of automation associated with a WCIS creates a number of unique control issues of concern to accountants. Our objective at this point is to draw attention to the potential risks that must be addressed by management and accountants. Because the solutions to these problems involve an understanding of technologies that we have not yet studied, our discussion of control techniques must be deferred to Chapters 15 and 16, where these issues and their solutions will be revisited.

The Paperless Environment

A WCIS can virtually eliminate the traditional paper flow in the order-delivery-invoice-payment cycle because the system enables transactions to be initiated, recorded, approved, and executed electronically. Paper documents are extremely expensive in terms of handling costs and data entry errors. Therefore, paper documents are printed, handled, and filed only when absolutely necessary. A portion of the paper reduction comes from the extensive use of source data automation, particularly bar-coding. Where feasible, all RM and FG inventory items should be bar-coded. The ideal situation is to have the RM bar-coded by the supplier. To track and monitor labor charges as well as authorizations and security considerations, employees use either barcoded or magnetic strip-encoded identification cards. In fact, all resources (i.e., materials, portable equipment, and employees) that move around the factory floor should be bar-coded for tracking and monitoring purposes.

The paperless environment has a significant impact on a firm's internal control system. It results in control evidence being found in machine-readable formats that may be at locations that transcend traditional organizational boundaries. There may be no traditional documents for the internal or external auditors to examine.

Automatic Transactions

The extensive use of EDI for processing transactions eliminates traditional source documents bearing signatures and evidencing authorization of transactions. Based on the occurrence of an event such as the receipt of a sales order or inventories falling to their reorder point, transactions are automatically initiated by the MRP system and transmitted by EDI. Given the lack of human involvement in the transaction processing system, the control concerns focus on the validity, completeness, and accuracy of automatically generated transactions. The only paper document may be the original contract between the trading parties. Management and accountants seek the following assurances regarding the system's performance:

- The system places orders only when inventory is needed.

- Inventory orders are placed only with approved vendors.

- The quantity of items ordered is correct for the needs of the organization.

- Programmed procedures correctly match electronic control documents (i.e., the purchase order, receiving report, and invoice) before initiating the payment function.

Networking Considerations

A WCIS will be designed around a series of local area networks, minicomputers, and/or mainframes, depending on the needs of the manufacturer. The network architecture may involve the distribution of databases and/or transaction processing responsibility among various users at multiple locations. Distributed technology has implications for the accuracy and consistency of accounting records. For example, auditors are concerned that the GL accounts accurately reflect the sum total of transactions processed at multiple distributed locations. We examine distributed databases in Chapter 9 and network architectures in Chapter 12.

SUMMARY

This chapter has examined the conversion cycle, whereby a company transforms input resources (i.e., materials, labor, and capital) into marketable products and services. The principal aim has been to highlight the changing manufacturing environment of the contemporary business world and to show how it calls for a shift away from traditional forms of business organization and activities toward a "world-class" way of doing business. We have seen how companies that are attempting to achieve world-class status must pursue manufacturing flexibility through increased automation, inventory reduction, and improved product quality.

We have also seen that achieving world-class status requires significant departures from traditional accounting techniques. In response to deficiencies in traditional accounting methods, world-class companies have adopted ABC, which provides a more precise and accurate allocation of costs to products. New techniques in activity management complement ABC and enable managers to better understand the nature of activities and cost drivers. New accounting models are needed that allow organizations to combine both financial and nonfinancial data in an integrated database that will support the needs of multiple users. Finally, we examined the key features of a world-class information system and briefly addressed potential control issues.

KEY TERMS

activities (358)

activity-based costing (ABC) (358)

activity driver (358)

automated storage and retrieval systems (AS/RS) (347)

benchmarking (361)

bill of materials (BOM)(332)

cells (347)

computer-aided design (CAD) (348)

computer-aided manufacturing (CAM) (348)

computer-integrated manufacturing (CIM) (347)

computer numerical controlled (CNC) (346)

cost accounting system (331)

cost driver (361)

cost objects (358)

critical success factors (361)

economic order quantity (EOQ) model (336)

electronic data interchange (EDI) (350)

enterprise resource planning (ERP) (350)

islands of technology (346)

just-in-time (JIT) (354)

manufacturing environment (331)

manufacturing flexibility (345)

manufacturing resources planning II (MRP II) (348)

materials and operations requirements (334)

materials requirements planning (MRP) (348)

materials requisition (333)

move ticket (333)

process simplification (347)

production schedule (331)

production system (331)

reorder point (339)

robotics (347)

route sheet (332)

safety stock (339)

sales forecast (331)

statistical process control (355)

work order (332)

world-class company (330)

REVIEW QUESTIONS

1. What is a world-class firm? What characteristics do world-class information systems need to have to provide sufficient information to world-class firms?

2. What activities are involved in the production system? The cost accounting system?

3. Distinguish between continuous, batch, and made-to-order processing.

4. What documents trigger and support batch processing systems?

5. What are the primary determinants for both materials and operations requirements?

6. What three main functions does inventory control serve in the production process?

7. What document triggers the beginning of the cost-accounting process for a given production run?

8. What documents are necessary in order for cost-accounting clerks to update the WIP accounts with standard charges?

9. What types of management reports are prepared by the cost-accounting system?

10. What document signals the completion of the production process?

11. What functions should be separated in order to segregate record keeping from asset custody?

12. What are the four operating characteristics U.S. manufacturing firms need to incorporate to regain their competitive advantage?

13. Distinguish between CAD and CAM.

14. What is meant by the statement, "Inventories camouflage production problems and can cause overproduction"? What is wrong with overproduction if you already own the RM?

15. Upon what assumptions does the JIT method heavily depend?

16. Distinguish between activities and cost objects in ABC.

17. Differentiate between essential and nonessential activities.

18. What are some critical success factors common to most manufacturing firms?

19. What are the inputs and outputs of an MRP system?

20. Distinguish between CAD and CAM.

DISCUSSION QUESTIONS

1. Discuss the importance to the cost-accounting department of the move ticket and some of the job duties that the work center supervisor performs.

2. How realistic are the assumptions of the EOQ model? Discuss each assumption individually.

3. Explain why the EOQ is the intersection of the ordering cost curve and the carrying cost curve.

4. Supervisors in the work centers oversee the usage of RM in production; explain why the work centers do not keep the records of the WIP.

5. Explain how prenumbered documents help to provide indirect access control over assets.

6. What role does the GL department play in the conversion cycle?

7. How have U.S. manufacturers adjusted their emphasis in response to competitive factors since the mid-1970s?

8. What is meant by manufacturing flexibility and how do firms achieve it?

9. Identify three areas where CAD software applications are being used directly by the consumer to aid in designing the product.

10. How can poor quality be expensive to the firm, especially if low-cost RM are used to reduce cost of goods sold and raise net income?

11. Discuss how an emphasis on financial performance of cost centers, as measured by traditional cost accounting information may lead to inefficient and ineffective production output.

12. How can ABC be used to switch the management of business activities from a custodial task to a continuous improvement activity?

13. How are cost structures fundamentally different between the traditional and CIM environments?

14. How can a firm control against excessive quantities of RM being used in the manufacturing process?

15. Discuss the key segregation of duties that should exist in the traditional manufacturing environment.

16. Explain how CAD can contribute to a firm's move toward world-class status.

17. Explain how CAM can contribute to a firm's move toward world-class status.

18. Explain why traditional cost allocation methods fail in a CIM environment.

19. Explain how JIT can reduce inventory.

20. Explain the relationship between MRP, MRPII, and ERP.

MULTIPLE-CHOICE QUESTIONS

1. Which of the following is not an advantageous reason to reduce inventories?
   a. Inventories provide a competitive advantage.
   b. Inventories can invite overproduction.
   c. Inventories are expensive to maintain.
   d. Inventories may conceal problems.
   e. All of these are good reasons to reduce inventories.

2. The fundamental EOQ model
   a. provides for fluctuating lead times during reorder cycles.
   b. is relatively insensitive to errors in demand, procurement costs, and carrying costs.
   c. focuses on the trade-off between production costs and carrying costs.
   is stochastic in nature.
   d. is best used in conjunction with a periodic inventory system.

3. Refer to the equation for the EOQ in the text. Car Country, a local Ford dealer, sells 1280 small SUVs each year. Keeping a car on the lot costs Car Country $200 per month, so the company prefers to order as few SUVs as is economically feasible. However, each time an order is placed, the company incurs total costs of $300—$240 of which is fixed and $60 is variable. Determine the company's EOQ.
   a. 8
   b. 16
   c. 18
   d. 56
   e. 62

Questions 4 though 6 are based on the diagram below, which represents the EOQ model.

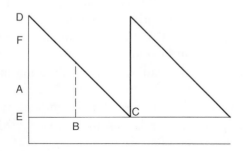

4. Which line segment represents the reorder lead time?
   a. AB
   b. AE
   c. AF
   d. BC
   e. AC

5. Which line segment identifies the quantity of safety stock maintained?
   a. AB
   b. AE
   c. AC
   d. BC
   e. EF

6. Which line segment represents the length of time to consume the total quantity of materials ordered?
   a. DE
   b. BC
   c. AC
   d. AE
   e. AD

7. Which of the following is not a benefit of JIT purchasing?
   a. Increased cash discounts on purchases.
   b. A reduction in the number of suppliers.
   c. A reduction in purchasing paperwork through the use of longer-term contracts with suppliers.
   d. Less checking on quality and quantity of goods received from suppliers.
   e. A reduction in the total value of inventories on hand.

8. All of the following are problems with traditional accounting information except:
   a. Managers in a JIT setting require immediate information.
   b. The measurement principle tends to ignore standards other than money.
   c. Variance analysis may yield insignificant values.

d. The overhead component in a manufacturing company is usually very large.

e. All of these are problems associated with traditional accounting information.

9. Benefits of an MRP II system may include all of the following except

a. reduced inventory investment.

b. improved cash flow.

c. higher quality goods.

d. Higher quality service.

e. Greater flexibility in the production process.

10 Which of the following is NOT an operational characteristic incorporated into manufacturing flexibility?

a. Reduction of inventories.

b. High product quality.

c. Reduction of accounts receivables.

d. Automation of the manufacturing process.

PROBLEMS

1. Document Flowchart

Diagram the sequence in which the following source documents are prepared.

a. bill of materials

b. work order

c. sales forecast

d. materials requisition

e. move ticket

f. production schedule

g. route sheet

2. Economic Order Quantity

Out Camping is a manufacturer of camping supplies and has several divisions, one of which is the tent division. Away From Home is the deluxe tent produced by the tent division; 14,000 of these tents are made each year. This model of tent incorporates two zipping doors in each model. Zippers for these doors are purchased from Zippy Zippers. Out Camping began this year with 500 zippers in inventory, but is now adopting an EOQ approach to inventory. A review of last year's records reveals the following information concerning each order placed with Zippy Zippers: variable labor—$12; variable supplies—$1; fixed computer costs—$4; fixed office expenses—$2; fixed mailing expenses—$2; and fixed supplies— $1. No differences are expected this year. Last year, the cost of carrying one zipper in inventory for the entire year was $1, but Out Camping has recently negotiated a new lease on its warehouse and the cost of carrying each zipper is now expected to increase by $.25. Out Camping also found that it took 7 days from the time an order was sent to Zippy until the zippers were received.

Required:

a. Compute EOQ.

b. Compute ROP, presume Out Camping has a desire to reduce its ending inventory to one half this year's beginning amount and that the company produces the Away From Home model 140 days each year.

3. World-Class Companies

Visit your school's library (either in person or online) and perform a search on the keywords "World-Class Companies" and "manufacturing." Find five companies that claim to be world-class manufacturing companies and state the innovation(s) these companies have undertaken to become world-class.

4. Internal Control

Examine the flowchart on the next page and determine any control threats. Specifically discuss the control problems, the possible dangers, and any corrective procedures you would recommend.

5. Manufacturing Processes

Consider a pizzeria that sells pizza, pasta, lasagna, meatball sandwiches, and sodas. Discuss the methods in which the products would be manufactured under

a. the traditional manufacturing environment.

b. CIM.

6. Zero Defects Process

Playthings, a toy manufacturer specializing in toys for toddlers, is considering switching to a JIT manufacturing process. The CEO has been talking with the production consultants, who tell her that a new philosophy must be embraced: if a defective part of an out-of-control process is detected, no more units

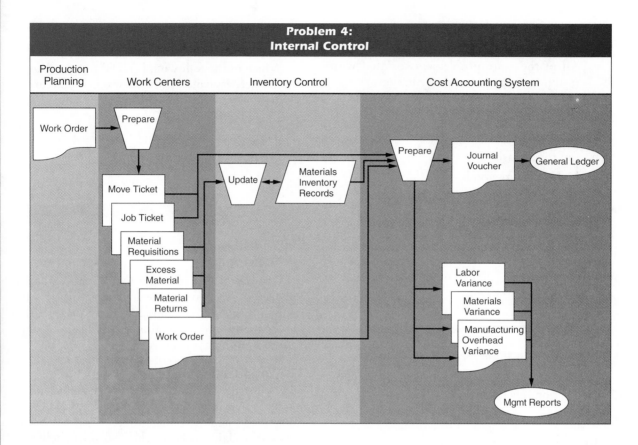

Problem 4:
Internal Control

should be made until the process is corrected. The consultants estimate that the production process may occasionally be shut down anywhere from 30 minutes to 7 hours. Discuss the advantages and disadvantages of such a system.

7. Activity Drivers

Cut It Up, Inc., is a manufacturer of wooden cutting boards that are sold through a chain of kitchen stores. For years, the company has allocated overhead based on total machine hours. A recent assessment of overhead costs has shown that these costs are now in excess of 40 percent of the company's total costs. As an attempt to better control overhead, Cut It Up is adopting an ABC system. Each cutting board goes through the following processes:

a. Cutting—Boards are selected from inventory and are cut to the required width and length. Imperfections in boards (such as knots or cracks) are identified and removed.

b. Assembly—Cut wooden pieces are laid out on clamps, a layer of glue is applied to each piece

and the glued pieces are clamped together until the glue sets.

c. Shaping—Once the glue has set, the boards are sent to the shaping process where they are cut into unique shapes.

d. Sanding—After being shaped, the cutting boards must be sanded smooth.

e. Finishing—Sanded cutting boards receive a coat of mineral oil to help preserve the wood.

f. Packing—Finished cutting boards are placed in boxes of 12. The boxes are sealed, addressed, and sent to one of the kitchen stores.

Required:
What do you suppose are components of overhead for this company? Determine a logical cost driver for each process.

8. JIT Assumptions

Choose a manufactured product (e.g., an automobile or bicycle) and write an essay explaining the implications of underlying JIT assumptions on the manufacturing process of this product.

INTERNAL CONTROL CASES

1. Nautilus Water Pumps, Inc.—Internal Controls Assessment

(Prepared by Scott Pasquale and Kyle Smith, Lehigh University)

Nautilus Water Pumps, Inc., manufactures automotive water pumps. Since 1988 they have supplied the Big Three (Ford Motor Company, General Motors, and Chrysler) North American auto manufacturers. Nautilus has recently broken into the American-made Japanese car market. They now supply Toyota, Nissan, and Honda with automotive water pumps for their assembly operations in North America.

Conversion Cycle

At the start of the year each automobile manufacturer provides Nautilus with an order that is based on budgeted sales predictions. However, this order is guaranteed for only the first month; after that each automobile manufacturer can revise orders on a monthly basis. Nautilus's current system requires orders for RM to be placed with suppliers on a quarterly basis. While the order provides a general idea of what is to be expected, orders from the automobile manufacturers can increase or decrease dramatically after the initial month.

Under the current batch production process in the conversion cycle, the blanket order is sent directly to the production, planning, and control phase. In this phase, the material and operation requirements are determined. It is here that the necessary production documents (bills of materials, route sheets) are created and combined with inventory status reports from inventory control and the required engineering specifications from the engineering department in order to create a purchase requisition. Currently, the production-scheduling phase falls under the responsibility of the work center. At the work center, the supervisor in charge prepares work orders, move tickets, and materials requisitions. These documents are sent to the cost-accounting department and are also used to create an open work order file. The work center also retains copies of these documents so they can be used to initiate production activities. Under the current system, once production is initiated, any excess material is immediately scrapped. The work center also prepares the necessary time-keeping documents (payroll time card and job tickets) and sends this information to the cost-accounting department as well. Upon completion of the production cycle, the production schedule and move tickets are used to close the open work order file, while one copy of the work order is sent to the FG warehouse and another is sent to inventory control.

At the start of the production phase, a copy of the materials requisition is sent to storekeeping so that the necessary RM can be issued to the work center. A copy of the materials requisition is kept on file in storekeeping.

Inventory control is involved in the batch production process throughout the entire operation. It releases the inventory status document to production, planning, and control so that materials and operations requirements can be determined. A copy of the materials requisition document is received from storekeeping so that inventory files can be updated. Once files are updated the materials requisition is sent to cost accounting, while the updated files are also used to prepare a journal voucher that is sent to the GL department. A copy of the materials requisition, purchase requisition, and work order documents are kept on file in inventory control.

Once the cost accounting department has received all the necessary information from the other departments, the work-in-process file is updated. All work center documents (move tickets, job tickets, materials requisitions, excess materials, and materials returns), along with a copy of the work order, are filed in the cost accounting department. At the end of the phase the cost accounting department prepares a journal voucher and sends it to the GL department. This journal voucher along with the one sent by inventory control is used to update the GL. Both journal vouchers are kept on file in the GL department.

Required:

a. Create a data flow diagram of the current system.

b. Create a document flowchart of the existing system.

c. Analyze the internal control weaknesses in the system. Model your response according to the six categories of physical control activities specified in SAS 78.

d. Prepare a system flowchart of a redesigned computer-based system that resolves the control weaknesses that you identified.

2. SAGA Fly Fishing, Inc.— Internal Controls Assessment

SAGA is a manufacturer of high-quality fly fishing equipment that includes rods, reels, fly lines, nets, drift boats, waders, and other equipment. It also produces low-end and moderately priced spinning rods and saltwater fishing equipment, which it sells under a different brand name to protect the high-quality image associated with its Fly Fishing division. Its home office, Fly Fishing production plant is located near Manchester, New Hampshire. The spinning and saltwater manufacturing plants are in upstate New York. In total, SAGA employs 1,500 workers. SAGA distributes its products worldwide through three distribution centers. Sales are currently $200 million per year and growing.

Although equipped with up-to-date production and shop-floor machinery, SAGA's Manchester plant's inventory management, production planning, and control procedures employ little computer technology. These procedures are described below.

The process begins in the storekeeping department, where Mr. Holt controls the inventory and maintains the inventory records. He checks daily on the inventory control files to assess the RM inventory needs, and sends an inventory status report to production planning and control.

The production planning and control department is led by Mr. Brackenbury. Once the inventory status report is received, as well as the sales forecasts from marketing, Mr. Brackenbury takes a copy of the BOM and route sheet and assesses the inventory requirements. If the inventory amounts are adequate, Mr. Brackenbury prepares a production schedule, work order, move tickets, and materials requisitions, which he sends to the work centers. Mr. Brackenbury, then, sends a purchase requisition to the purchasing and storekeeping departments.

Mr. Brackenbury also heads the various work centers, and the supervisors of the different work centers report to him. These supervisors, upon receipt of the above documents, send the materials requisitions

to the storekeeping department, where Mr. Holt sends to the work center the necessary materials. He then files a copy of the materials requisition and updates the RM inventory ledger. At the end of each day, he sends a copy of the materials requisitions to the cost accounting department. He also sends a journal voucher for the use of materials and a journal voucher for FG to the GL department.

In the work centers, the managers of each center collect the employees' time cards and send them to cost accounting, along with a copy to payroll. They also send the job and move tickets, which outline the various costs that have been incurred, to cost accounting.

Ms. Kay, who heads the cost accounting department, collects all of the data, determines the overall cost, compares it to the standard costs, and determines the variances. Only the total variances are compared; the information is then used to evaluate managers and supervisors of the various departments. Ms. Kay updates the work-in-process files and FG inventory files. She then creates a journal voucher and sends it to the GL department.

In the GL department, the information from the journal vouchers is entered into the GL computer program where the files are updated. The journal vouchers are filed.

Required:

a. Create a data flow diagram of the current system.

b. Create a document flowchart of the existing system.

c. Analyze the internal control weaknesses in the system. Model your response according to the six categories of physical control activities specified in SAS 78.

d. Prepare a system flowchart of a redesigned computer-based system that resolves the control weaknesses that you identified.

3. General Manufacturing Inc.— Internal Controls Assessment

The production process at General involves the planning, scheduling, and controlling of the physical products through the manufacturing process. General's manufacturing process begins in the production planning and control department where June determines the materials and operations requirements and combines information from various departments to assess inventory requirements needed to produce a product. Marketing provides the sales forecast, engineering provides the engineering specifications, and the storeroom provides the RM inventory status. June reviews this information to prepare a purchase requisition document, which she sends to purchasing. June then reviews the BOM and route sheets and prepares the following documents: work orders, move tickets, and materials requisitions. Three copies of each document are prepared. One copy of the work order, move ticket, and materials requisitions documents is sent to cost accounting. The remaining two copies are sent to Mike, the supervisor in the work center.

Once Mike receives the production control documents he initiates the production process. Mike sends a copy of the materials requisitions to the inventory storeroom in exchange for necessary RM. When additional RM are need for a job in process, they are obtained with a phone call to Steve, the storeroom clerk. Materials in excess of those needed for production are kept in the work center and used in the future. When the job passes through all production stages and is complete, Mike sends the finished product to the FG warehouse. He files one copy each of the work order, move ticket, and materials requisition, and sends the remaining copies of the work order and move ticket to the cost accounting department. One of Mike's duties is to review the job tickets and the employee timecards, which are sent to cost accounting and payroll, respectively.

Steve, in the inventory storeroom, accepts materials requisitions from the work center employees and releases the RM to the work centers. Steve files a copy of the materials requisitions and updates the RM inventory records. At the end of the day he creates a journal voucher that is sent to Ronica in the cost accounting department.

Ronica receives the following documents: work orders, move tickets, and materials requisitions from the production planning department; job tickets, work orders, and move tickets from the work center; and journal vouchers from the inventory storeroom. Ronica uses these to initiate a work-in-process (WIP) account and to update the WIP as work progresses, to calculate variances, and to update the GL accounts. Ronica files all documents in the department.

Required:
a. Create a data flow diagram of the current system.
b. Create a document flowchart of the existing system.
c. Analyze the internal control weaknesses in the system. Model your response according to the six categories of physical control activities specified in SAS 78.
d. Prepare a system flowchart of a redesigned computer-based system that resolves the control weaknesses that you identified.

4. Bumper Cars, Ltd.—Inventory Management and Control
(Prepared by Julie Fisch and Melinda Bowman, Lehigh University)
In 1983, Mr. Amusement created Bumper Cars, Ltd., a company whose main concern was the manufacture and repair of the exterior shells of bumper cars used in amusement parks. Although the company functioned on a small scale for a few years, it has recently expanded to some new areas, including larger-scale amusement parks like Coney Island. Despite the recent increase in business, Bumper Cars still operates as a small company with limited technology invested in computer systems. Many departments run totally manual systems. Because of the expansion, however, Mr. Amusement has taken a serious look at the setup of his company and determined that some problems exist. The most pressing problem is in the area of inventory management and control.

Inventory Control Department
At Bumper Cars, RM are stored in a warehouse until they are transferred to the production department for manufacturing. The inventory control department, which consists of three workers employed under the inventory manager, Ms. Coaster, work with the inventory at the RM stage. Each worker's responsibilities involve periodic inventory counts, along with the day-to-day jobs of storing and transferring inventory. Each day, when the workers transfer the inventory to WIP, they also attempt to keep track of the levels of inventory to inform the purchasing department to reorder if the stock of materials becomes too low. However, in their attempt to achieve efficient and speedy

transfers of RM to manufacturing, the workers find it difficult and inconvenient to constantly check for low levels of inventory. As a result, the inventory frequently runs out before the workers reorder, which causes a gap in RM needed for production.

Production Department

The production department receives the goods from inventory control, then puts them into production. Recently, Mr. Ferris, the production manager, complained to the president about the inconvenience caused by the lack of RM at crucial periods of production. As he stated at an important managerial meeting:

> Each week, we have a certain number of orders that must be filled, along with an indeterminable and changing number of repair requests. When we receive these orders, we immediately start work in order to fill our quotas on time. Lately, however, my workers have been handicapped by the fact that the RM are not available to put into production at the times we need them. During these lags, production stops, workers become idle, and back-orders pile up. Although we inform the inventory control and purchases departments of the problem right away, it still takes time for them to order and get the inventory to the warehouse. Then, it takes even more time for them to get the inventory to us in production. As a result, when we finally receive the necessary materials, my workers are forced to work overtime and at an unreasonable rate to meet demand. This up-and-down method of working is bad for general morale in my department. My workers tend to become lazy, expecting a lag to occur. Also, requests for repairs become nearly impossible to fulfill because we never know if the materials needed to fix the problem will be available. Usually, we fall so far behind on regular production during these lags that we must concentrate all our efforts just to meet daily demand. As a result, our repair business has dropped steadily over the past year. I feel that these production lags are extremely detrimental to our expanding business and we should immediately work on finding a solution.

Possible Solutions

As a result of Mr. Ferris's complaints, Bumper Cars realized that some changes must be made. Basically, the company determined that both the inventory control and production departments needed reorganization at a reasonable cost. Another managerial meeting of all the department heads took place specifically to discuss this problem. Each manager came to the meeting with his or her own ideas for a possible solution. Mr. Flume, the controller, aggressively suggested that a new companywide computer system be installed. This system would solve the inventory control problems by keeping up-to-date records of the inventory available at any given time. At the same time, the system could be set up to reduce paperwork in the accounting and finance departments. In addition, this computer could link all the departments; and, thus, alleviate communication breakdowns. Finally, the computer could be linked to the company from which Bumper Cars ordered its inventory, so that as soon as materials became low, it could immediately reorder before a problem developed.

At this point in the meeting, the president, Mr. Amusement, jumped up and exclaimed:

> Wait a minute! This system would solve our problems, but as you all know, we are not a large company. The cost of implementing a companywide computer system would be excessive. We would have to consider research, installation, maintenance, and repair costs involved in developing a complex system such as this one. When you take everything into consideration, I'm not sure if the costs would greatly exceed the benefits. Let's search for some other less costly, but still efficient, solutions.

Mr. Ferris, the production manager, then offered a second possible solution. After agreeing that a computer system might be too expensive, he went on to suggest:

> My main problem is meeting demand after a backlog has occurred: another possible solution might be to hire temporary workers to help alleviate the overload problem. These workers would not cost much because they would not receive benefits. Yet they would help solve the immediate problem. They would then be trained for production, so if people leave the production department, it would be easy to find replacements. As a result, production could continue with a minimum of problems and lags.

The managers discussed Mr. Ferris's suggestion for a few minutes. Then, Ms. Coaster, the inventory control manager, stood up and offered a third solution for the inventory problems. She explained:

> Although Mr. Ferris's plan might work, I feel that the real root of the problem lies in my department rather than in the area of production. It seems that the problem is that my employees have too many tasks to perform all at once. Therefore, what we really need are more employees in the inventory control department to continually check and recheck inventory levels. Then my other employees could concentrate solely on the transfer of RM to production. By this separation of tasks, I feel we could efficiently solve our inventory problems. Also, the cost of hiring a few more people would not be excessive.

By the end of the meeting, management still had not made a decision. They had identified the need to reorganize, but they could not decide which approach would be the best for the company.

Required:

Using the information about Bumper Cars, Ltd., along with your own knowledge, either agree or disagree with the various solutions suggested by the company's employees. Then, discuss what you feel is the best solution for the company's inventory problem.

5. Blades R Us—Comprehensive Case
(Prepared by Edward P. Kiernan and Abigail Olken, Lehigh University)

Blades R Us is a growing manufacturing firm that produces high-pressure turbine blades. The company supplies these to airline companies as replacement parts for use in large commercial jet engines. The high-pressure turbine is the segment of the engine that undergoes the most stress and heat. This requires that these parts be replaced frequently, so Blades R Us operates a relatively large firm with constant demand for their products. It operates out of Philadelphia, Pennsylvania, with a workforce of approximately 1000 employees. Its annual output is based on demand, yet at full capacity it has the ability to produce 100,000 blades a year. The company's largest suppliers are casting houses, which take a rough shape of the final product to very demanding specifications given by Blades. Blades R Us then does the final detail work to bring it to FAA regulations.

The general business environment of Blades R Us is one in which it sees expansion in its future. This is because of the recent boom in the commercial airline industry. In addition, with the recent attention to airline safety and the discovery of bogus parts used in engines, the airlines will be doing better checks and needing to replace parts more frequently to insure safety.

Blades R Us has been around for some time, and therefore has no computer-operated accounting systems. Some of the problems the company faces include (a) lack of inventory control; (b) keeping track of items in production or production that was completed in one day; (c) a need for trends and tracking of the largest customers so that future demand might be more accurate; (d) supervisory issues dealing with theft of parts, near substandard parts, and hiding of scrap; and (e) large inventories on hand of both FG and RM.

Procurement Procedures

The company reviewed the records associated with the RM inventory files. Mr. Sampson, the inventory manager, was in charge of this procedure. Once he finished his manual review of the inventory he issued two purchase requisitions. He kept one of the purchase requisitions in the inventory department, filing it in a cabinet. He sent the second purchase requisition to the purchasing department.

Ms. Connolly in the purchasing department would take the requisition and complete a purchase order in triplicate. One copy was sent to the supplier, the second was filed in the purchases department filing cabinet, and the third was sent back to Mr. Sampson in the inventory department. Mr. Sampson would use this PO to update his inventory records so he knew exactly how much inventory was on hand at all times. Once the inventory was updated, the PO was put into the filing cabinet in the inventory department with the original purchase requisition.

The supplier would receive the purchase order and send the requested blades, including a packing slip with the shipment. At the same time shipment was made, the supplier would also send an invoice to the accounts payable department.

In receiving, Mr. Hiro simply used the packing slip that was included with the goods to make three copies of the receiving report. The first copy was sent to the purchasing department where it was filed. The second copy was sent to accounts payable, and the third copy was filed by Mr. Hiro in the filing cabinet.

The accounts payable department would file the receiving report received by Mr. Hiro until the invoice from the supplier arrived. Then, Mr. Maldonado would check both the receiving report and invoice to make sure everything sent was actually received. Mr. Maldonado would then hand off the documents to Mr. Bailey so that he could do the appropriate posting and filing of the checked documents. Mr. Bailey would post the changes to the voucher register and purchases journal, sending a journal voucher to the GL department after the purchases journal was updated. Mr. Bailey would then put the receiving report and invoice in the appropriate file. Also in accounts payable, Mr. Dresden would scan the records to see when it was time to write checks to the different vendors. Whenever a due date arrived, Mr. Dresden would write a check in two copies. The first copy would be filed in the cabinet and the other would be sent to the appropriate vendor. Then Mr. Dresden would update the accounts payable subsidiary ledger, and send an account summary to the GL department.

The GL was a tight ship. Mr. Callahan would receive the account summary and journal voucher and then post the necessary changes to the GL. After posting the documents were filed in the GL department.

Conversion Cycle Procedures

The conversion cycle at Blades R Us begins with the production planning and control department receiving the inventory levels from the FG warehouse. If the number of a given part in the FG warehouse is below the set minimum then production for the part is to be run. The production planning and control department gathers the BOM and the route sheet for that part and makes up the production schedule and work orders. A copy of the work order, route sheet, BOM, and production schedule is filed at the production planning and control department. A copy of the production schedule, work order, and BOM is sent to the work centers.

Once the work centers receive the paperwork from the production planning and control department, production is initiated. The work order is sent to the FG warehouse, and the production schedule and route sheet are filed. Time cards are

filled out and given to the payroll department. Materials requisition forms are filled out in order to attain the necessary materials—one is filed and the other is sent to the inventory control department.

When inventory control receives the materials requisition they send the desired material to the work center, update the inventory records, and then file the material requisition. The inventory control department makes the decision to buy RM based on a predetermined minimum of parts in inventory and a set order number. The inventory records are periodically reviewed, and when the number of a part in inventory falls below the set minimum a purchase requisition is completed. One copy is sent to the purchasing department and the other is filed. The purchasing department sends inventory control a purchase order, which it then uses to update its inventory records. The purchase order is then filed.

Blades R Us has made the decision to try and become a world-class company. It realizes that it will have to make many fundamental changes to achieve this goal. One of the first steps that they have decided to take is to implement an MRP system. They feel this will help them to keep better track of their inventories, WIP, and customer demands and trends. They also realize that there are many weaknesses in the other pieces of their conversion cycles and they would like to take steps in improving those as well.

Required:

a. Create a data flow diagram of the current system.

b. Create a document flowchart of the existing system.

c. Analyze the internal control weaknesses in the system. Model your response according to the six categories of physical control activities specified in SAS 78.

d. Prepare a system flowchart of a redesigned computer-based system that resolves the control weaknesses that you identified.

6. Automotive Component Corporation— Activity-Based Costing Case

(Prepared by Trey Johnston, Lehigh University)
Automotive Component Corporation (ACC) began in 1955 as a small, machine shop supplying

the Big Three automakers. The business is now a $2 billion component manufacturing firm. During the three decades from 1955 to 1985, ACC expanded from a common machine shop to a modern manufacturing operation with CNC machines, automatic guided vehicles (AGVs), and a world-class quality program. Consequently, ACC's direct-labor cost component has decreased significantly since 1955 from 46 percent to 11 percent. ACC's current cost structure is as follows:

Manufacturing overhead	43.6%
Materials	27.1%
Selling and administrative expenses	17.8%
Labor	11.5%

Despite efforts to expand, revenues leveled off and margins declined in the late 1980s and early 1990s. ACC began to question its investment in the latest flexible equipment and even considered scrapping some. Bill Brown, ACC's controller, explains.

> At ACC, we have made a concerted effort to keep up with current technology. We invested in CNC machines to reduce setup time and setup labor and to improve quality. Although we accomplished these objectives, they did not translate to our bottom line. Another investment we made was in AGVs. Our opinion at the time was that the reduction in labor and increased accuracy of the AGVs combined with the CNC machines would allow us to be competitive on the increasing number of small-volume orders. We have achieved success in this area, but once again, we have not been able to show a financial benefit from these programs. Recently, there has been talk of scrapping the newer equipment and returning to our manufacturing practices of the early '80s. I just don't believe this could be the right answer but, as our margins continue to dwindle, it becomes harder and harder to defend my position.

With these sentiments in mind, Bill decided to study the current costing system at ACC in detail. He had attended a seminar recently that discussed some of the problems that arise in traditional cost accounting systems. Bill felt that some of the issues discussed in the meeting directly applied to ACC's situation.

The speaker mentioned that ABC was a tool corporations could use to better identify their true product costs. He also mentioned that better strategic decisions could be made based on the information provided from the activity-based reports. Bill decided to form an ABC team to look at the prospect of implementing ABC at ACC. The team consisted of two other members: Sally Summers, a product engineer with a finance background, and Jim Schmidt, an industrial engineer with an MBA.

Sally had some feelings about the current state of ACC:

> ACC is a very customer-focused company. When the automakers demanded small-volume orders, we did what we could to change our manufacturing processes. The problem is that no one realized that it takes just as long for the engineering department to design a 10-component part and process for a small-volume order as it does for a ten-component large-volume order. Our engineering departments cannot handle this kind of workload much longer. On top of this, we hear rumors about layoffs in the not-too-distant future.

Jim felt similarly:

> Sally is correct. As an industrial engineer, I get involved in certain aspects of production that are simply not volume dependent. For example, I oversee first-run inspections. We run a predetermined number of parts before each full run to ensure the process is under control. Most of the inspections we perform on the automobile components are looking for burrs, which can severely affect fit or function downstream in our assembly process. Many times, we can inspect sample part runs right on the line. The real consumption of resources comes from running a sample batch, not by inspecting each part.

To begin its study, the team obtained a cost report from the plant cost-accountant. A summary of the product costs are as follows:

Product Costs			
	Product		
	101	102	103
Material	$ 5.46	$ 4.37	$ 3.09
Direct labor	1.43	1.55	1.80
Overhead (labor-hour basis)	5.44	5.89	6.85
Total	$12.33	$11.81	$11.74

ACC has been determining product costs basically the same way as it did in 1955. Raw material cost is determined by multiplying the number of components by the standard raw material price. Direct labor cost is determined by multiplying the standard labor hours per unit by the standard labor rate per hour. Manufacturing overhead is allocated to product based on direct labor content.

The team then applied the traditional 20 percent markup to the three products. This represents the target price that ACC tries to achieve on its products. They then compared the target price to the market price. ACC was achieving its 20 percent target gross margin on Product 101, but not on Products 102 or 103, as illustrated below.

Product Costs

	Product		
	101	102	103
Traditional cost	$12.33	$11.81	$11.74
Target selling price	14.79	14.17	14.08
Target gross margin	20%	20%	20%
Market price	14.79	14.05	13.61
Actual gross margin	20%	20%	20%

Bill was concerned; he remembered the conference he had attended. The speaker had mentioned examples of firms headed in a downward spiral because of a faulty cost system. Bill asked the team, "Is ACC beginning to show signs of a faulty cost system?"

Next, the team looked at the manufacturing overhead breakdown (Figure 1). The current cost accounting system allocated 100 percent of this overhead to product based on labor dollars. The team felt ACC could do a better job of tracing costs to products based on transaction volume. Jim explains:

> The manufacturing overhead really consists of the six cost pools shown in Figure 1. Each of these activity cost pools should be traced individually to products based on the proportion of transactions they consume, not the amount of direct labor they consume.

The team conducted the following interviews to determine the specific transactions ACC should use to trace costs from activities to products.

John "Bull" Adams, the supervisor in charge of material movement, provided the floor layout shown in Figure 2 and commented on his department's workload:

> Since ACC began accepting small-volume orders, we have had our hands full. Each time we design a new part, a new program must be written. Additionally, it seems the new small-volume parts we are producing are much more complex than the large-volume parts we produced just a few years ago. This translates into more moves per run. Consequently, we wind up performing AGV maintenance much more frequently. Sometimes I wish we would get rid of those AGVs; our old system of forklifts and operators was much less resistant to change.

Sara Nightingale, the most experienced jobsetter at ACC, spoke about the current status of setups:

> The changeover crew has changed drastically recently. Our team has shifted from mostly mechanically skilled maintenance people to a team of highly trained programmers and mechanically skilled people. This shift has greatly reduced our head count. Yet the majority of our work is still spent on setup labor time.

Phil Johnson, the shipping supervisor, told the team what he felt drove the activity of the shipping department:

> The volume of work we have at the shipping department is completely dependent on the number of trucks we load. Recently, we have been filling more trucks per day with less volume. Our workload has increased, not decreased. We still have to deal with all of the paperwork and administrative hassles for each shipment. Also, the smaller trucks they use these days are side-loaders, and our loading docks are not set up to handle these trucks. Therefore, it takes us a while to coordinate our docks.

Once the interviews were complete, the team went to the systems department to request basic product information on the three products ACC manufactured. The information is shown in Figure 3.

Required:

The team has conducted all of the required interviews and collected all of the necessary information in order to proceed with its ABC pilot study.

a. The first three steps in an activity-based cost implementation is to define the resource categories, activity centers, and first-stage resource drivers. These steps have already been completed at ACC, and the results are displayed in Figure 1. Using the information from the case, perform the next step for the implementation team and determine the second-stage cost drivers ACC should use in its ABC system. Support your choices with discussion.

b.   Using the second-stage cost drivers identified in part (a), compute the new product costs for Products 101, 102, and 103.

c.   Modify Figure 2 and include the cost drivers identified in part (a).

d.   Compare the product costs computed under the current cost accounting system to the product costs computed under the activity-based system.

e.   Explain the differences in product cost.

f.   Given the new information provided by the ABC system, recommend a strategy ACC should pursue to regain its margins and comment on specific improvements that would reduce ACC's overhead burden in the long run.

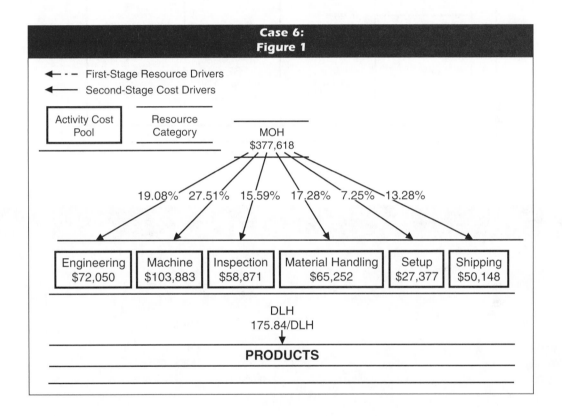

Case 6:
Figure 1

Case 6: Figure 2

Case 6: Figure 3

Basic Product Information

	101	102	103	Total
Production				
Quantity	10,000 units	20,000 units	30,000 units	60,000 units
Runs	10 runs	4 runs	3 runs	17 runs
Shipments				
Quantity	10,000 units	20,000 units	30,000 units	60,000 units
Shipments	20 shipments	4 shipments	3 shipments	27 shipments
Manufacturing cost				
Raw material				
Components	16 components	9 components	6 components	
Cost per component	$0.34 per component	$0.49 per component	$0.52 per component	
Labor usage*				
Setup labor	15.93 hours per run	63.68 hours per run	90.15 hours per run	684 hours
Run labor	0.05 hours per part	0.04 hours per part	0.03 hours per part	2,148 hours
Machine usage**	0.03 hours per part	0.02 hours per part	0.02 hours per part	1,297 hours
Other overhead				
Engineering				$72,050
Inspection				58,871
Material handling				65,252
Material moves	500 feet per run	350 feet per run	250 feet per run	
Shipping				$50,148

*Labor = $40 per hour; including fringe benefits
**Machine cost = $80 per hour

chapter 8

Financial Reporting and Management Reporting Systems

LEARNING OBJECTIVES

After studying this chapter, you should:

- Understand the purpose of data coding and be able to identify the respective features, advantages, and disadvantages of the various numeric and alphabetic coding schemes.
- Understand the operational features of the GLS, FRS, and MRS.
- Be able to identify the principle operational controls governing the GLS and FRS.
- Understand the factors that influence the design of the MRS.
- Understand the elements of a responsibility accounting system.

The chapter begins with a review of data coding techniques used in transaction processing systems and for general ledger design. It explores several coding schemes and their respective advantages and disadvantages. Next, the chapter examines the objectives, operational features, and control issues of two related systems: the general ledger system (GLS) and the financial reporting system (FRS). Finally, the management reporting system (MRS) is examined. The MRS is distinguishable from the FRS in one key respect: financial reporting is *mandatory* and management reporting is *discretionary*. Management reporting information is needed for planning and controlling business activities. Organization management implements MRS applications at their discretion, based on internal user needs.

DATA CODING SCHEMES

In previous chapters we saw how primary and secondary keys link together transaction and master records for file updating. This is one application of data coding. We delve more deeply into this subject here to examine various types of data coding schemes and how they are used in data processing systems. To emphasize the importance of data codes we first consider a hypothetical system that does not use them.

A SYSTEM WITHOUT CODES

Firms process large volumes of transactions that are similar in their basic attributes. For instance, a firm's accounts receivable file may contain accounts for several different customers with the same name and similar addresses. To process transactions accurately against the correct accounts, the firm must be able to distinguish one "John Smith" from another. This task becomes particularly difficult as the number of similar attributes and items in the class increase.

Consider the most elemental item a machine shop wholesaler firm might carry in its inventory—a machine nut. Assume that the total inventory of nuts has only three distinguishing attributes: size, material, and thread type. As a result, this entire class of inventory must be distinguished on the basis of these three features as follows:

1. The size attribute ranges from ¼ inch to 1¾ inches in diameter in increments of ¹⁄₆₄ of an inch, giving 96 sizes of nuts.
2. For each size subclass, four materials are available: brass, copper, mild steel, and case-hardened steel.
3. Each of these size and material subclasses come in three different threads: fine, standard, and coarse.

By these assumptions, this class of inventory could contain 1,152 separate items ($96 \times 4 \times 3$). The identification of a single item in this class thus requires a description featuring these distinguishing attributes. To illustrate, consider the following journal entry to record the receipt of $1,000 worth of half-inch, case-hardened steel nuts with standard threads supplied by Industrial Parts Manufacturer of Cleveland, Ohio.

	DR	CR
Inventory—nut, 1/2 inch, case-hardened steel, standard thread	1,000	
A/P—Industrial Parts Manufacturer, Cleveland, Ohio		1,000

This uncoded entry takes a great deal of recording space, is time consuming to record, and is obviously prone to many types of errors. The negative effects of this approach may be seen in many parts of the organization:

1. *Sales staff.* To properly identify the items sold requires the transcription of large amounts of detail onto source documents. Apart from the time and effort involved, this tends to encourage clerical errors and incorrect shipments.
2. *Warehouse personnel.* Locating and picking goods for shipment are impeded and shipping errors will likely result.
3. *Accounting personnel.* Postings to ledger accounts will require searching through the subsidiary files using lengthy descriptions as the key. This will be painfully slow, and postings to the wrong accounts will be common.

A SYSTEM WITH CODES

These problems are solved, or at least greatly reduced, by using codes to represent each item in the inventory and supplier accounts. Let's assume the inventory item in our previous example had been assigned the numeric code 896, and the supplier in the AP account is given the code number 321. The coded version of the previous journal entry can now be greatly simplified:

ACCOUNT	DR	CR
896	1,000	
321		1,000

This is not to suggest that detailed information about the inventory and the supplier is of no interest to the organization. Obviously it is! These facts will be kept in reference files and used for such purposes as the preparation of parts lists, catalogs, bills of material, and mailing information. The inclusion of such details, however, would clutter the task of transaction processing and could prove dysfunctional as this simple example illustrates. Other uses of data coding in AIS are to:

1. Concisely represent large amounts of complex information that would otherwise be unmanageable.
2. Provide a means of accountability over the completeness of the transactions processed.
3. Identify unique transactions and accounts within a file.
4. Support the audit function by providing an effective audit trail.

The following discussion examines some of the more commonly used coding techniques and explores their respective advantages and disadvantages.

NUMERIC AND ALPHABETIC CODING SCHEMES

Sequential Codes

As the name implies, **sequential codes** represent items in some sequential order (ascending or descending). A common application of numeric sequential codes is the prenumbering of source documents. At printing, hardcopy documents are each given a unique sequential code number. This number becomes the transaction number that allows the system to track each transaction processed and to identify any lost or out-of-sequence documents. Digital documents are similarly assigned a sequential number by the computer when they are created.

Advantages. Sequential coding supports the reconciliation of a batch of transactions, such as sales orders, at the end of processing. If the transaction processing system detects any gaps in the sequence of transaction numbers, it alerts management to the possibility of a missing or misplaced transaction. By tracing the transaction number back through the stages in the process, management can eventually determine the cause and effect of the error. Without sequentially numbered documents, problems of this sort are difficult to detect and resolve.

Disadvantages. Sequential codes carry no information content beyond their order in the sequence. For instance, a sequential code assigned to a raw material inventory item tells us nothing about the attributes of the item (type, size, material, warehouse location, and so on). Also, sequential coding schemes are difficult to change. Inserting a new item at some midpoint requires renumbering the subsequent items in the class accordingly. In applications where record types must be grouped together logically and where additions and deletions occur regularly, this coding scheme is inappropriate.

Block Codes

A numeric **block code** is a variation on sequential coding that in part remedies the disadvantages just described. This approach can be used to represent whole classes of items by restricting each class to a specific range within the coding scheme. A common application of block coding is the construction of a **chart of accounts**.

A well-designed and comprehensive chart of accounts is the basis for the general ledger, and is thus critical to a firm's financial and management reporting systems. The more extensive the chart of accounts, the more precisely a firm can classify its transactions and the greater the range of information it can provide to internal and external users. Figure 8-1 presents an example of a chart of accounts using block codes.

Notice that each account type is represented by a unique range of codes or blocks. Thus balance sheet and income statement account classifications and subclassifications can be depicted. In this example, each of the accounts consists of a three-digit code. The first digit is the "blocking" digit and represents the account classification, for example, current assets, liabilities, or operating expense. The other digits in the code are sequentially assigned.

Advantages. Block coding allows for the insertion of new codes within a block without having to reorganize the entire coding structure. For example, if advertising expense is account number 626, the first digit indicates that this account is an operating expense. As new types of expense items are incurred and have to be specifically accounted for, they may be added sequentially within the 600 account classification. This three-digit code accommodates 100 individual items (X00 through X99) within each block. Obviously, the more digits in the code range, the more items that can be represented.

Disadvantages. As with the sequential codes, the information content of the block code is not readily apparent. For instance, account number 626 means nothing until matched against the chart of accounts, which identifies it as advertising expense.

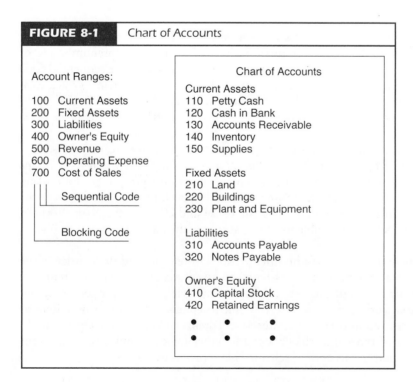

FIGURE 8-1   Chart of Accounts

Group Codes

Numeric **group codes** are used to represent complex items or events involving two or more pieces of related data. The code consists of zones or fields that possess specific meaning. For example, a department store chain might code sales order transactions from its branch stores as follows:

Store Number	Dept. Number	Item Number	Salesperson
04	09	476214	99

Advantages. Group codes have a number of advantages over sequential and block codes, including:

1. They facilitate the representation of large amounts of diverse data.
2. They allow complex data structures to be represented in a hierarchical form that is logical and more easily remembered by humans.
3. They permit detailed analysis and reporting both within an item class and across different classes of items.

Using the previous example to illustrate, Store Number 04 could represent the Hamilton Mall store in Allentown; Dept. Number 09 represents the sporting goods department; Item Number 476214 is a hockey stick; and Salesperson 99 is Jon Innes. With this level of information, a corporate manager could measure profitability by store, compare the performance of similar departments across all stores, track the movement of specific inventory items, and evaluate sales performance by employees within and between stores.

Disadvantages. Ironically the primary disadvantage of group coding results from its success as a classification tool. Because group codes can effectively present diverse information, they tend to be overused. Unrelated data may be linked simply because it can be done. This can lead to unnecessarily complex group codes that cannot be easily interpreted. Finally, overuse can increase storage costs, promote clerical errors, and increase processing time and effort.

Alphabetic Codes

Alphabetic codes are used for many of the same purposes as numeric codes. Alphabetic characters may be assigned sequentially (in alphabetical order) or may be used in block and group coding techniques.

Advantages. The capacity to represent large numbers of items is increased dramatically through the use of pure alphabetic codes or alphabetic characters imbedded within numeric codes (**alphanumeric codes**). The earlier example of a chart of accounts using a three-digit code with a single blocking digit limits data representation to only ten blocks of accounts—0 through 9. Using alphabetic characters for blocking, however, increases the number of possible blocks to 26—A through Z. Furthermore, whereas the two-digit sequential portion of that code has the capacity of only 100 items (10^2), a two-position alphabetic code can represent 676 items (26^2). Thus by using alphabetic codes in the same three-digit coding space, we see a geometric increase in the potential for data representation

(10 blocks × 100 items each) = 1,000 items

to

(26 blocks × 676 items each) = 17,576 items

Disadvantages. The primary drawbacks with alphabetic coding are (1) as with numeric codes, there is difficulty rationalizing the meaning of codes that have been sequentially assigned; and (2) users tend to have difficulty sorting records that are coded alphabetically.

Mnemonic Codes

Mnemonic codes are alphabetic characters in the form of acronyms and other combinations that convey meaning. For example, a student enrolling in college courses may enter the following course codes on the registration form:

Course Type	Course Number
Acctg	101
Psyc	110
Mgt	270
Mktg	300

This combination of mnemonic and numeric codes conveys a good deal of information about these courses; with a little analysis, we can deduce that "Acctg" is accounting, "Psyc" is psychology, "Mgt" is management, and "Mktg" is marketing. The sequential number portion of the code indicates the level of each course. Another example of the use of mnemonic codes is assigning state codes in mailing addresses:

Code	Meaning
NY	New York
CA	California
OK	Oklahoma

Advantages. The mnemonic coding scheme does not require the user to memorize meaning; the code itself conveys a high degree of information about the item that is being represented.

Disadvantages. Although mnemonic codes are useful for representing classes of items, they have limited ability to represent items within a class. For example, the entire class of accounts receivable could be represented by the mnemonic code AR, but we would quickly exhaust meaningful combinations of alphabetic characters if we attempted to represent the individual accounts that make up this class. These accounts would be represented better by sequential, block, or group coding techniques.

THE GENERAL LEDGER SYSTEM

Figure 8-2 characterizes the GLS as a hub connected to the other systems of the firm through spokes of information flows. Transaction cycles process individual events that are recorded in special journals and subsidiary accounts. Summaries of these transactions flow into the GLS and become sources of input for the management reporting system and financial reporting system. The bulk of the flows into the GLS come from the transaction processing subsystems. Note, however, that information also flows from the FRS as feedback into the GLS. We shall explore this point more thoroughly later. In this section we review key elements of the GLS.

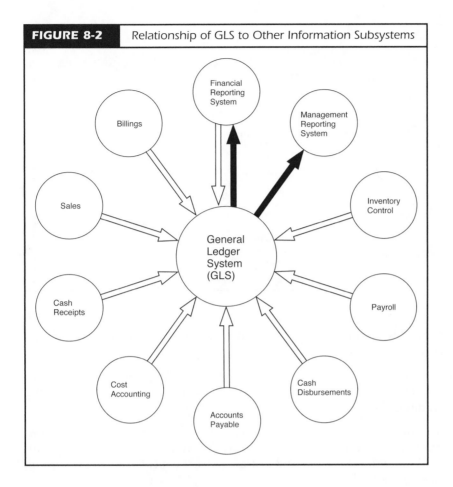

FIGURE 8-2   Relationship of GLS to Other Information Subsystems

THE JOURNAL VOUCHER

The source of input to the general ledger is the *journal voucher* illustrated in Figure 8-3. A journal voucher, which can be used to represent summaries of similar transactions or a single unique transaction, identifies the financial amounts and affected general ledger accounts. Routine transactions, adjusting entries, and closing entries are all entered into the general ledger via journal vouchers. Because journal vouchers must be approved by a responsible manager, they offer a degree of control against unauthorized GL entries.

THE GLS DATABASE

The GLS database includes a variety of files. Whereas these will vary from firm to firm, the following examples are representative.

> The **general ledger master file** is the principle file in the GLS database. This file is based on the organization's published chart of accounts. Each record in the general ledger master is either a separate GL account (for example, sales) or the control account (such as AR—control) for a subsidiary ledger in the transaction processing system. Figure 8-4 illustrates the structure of a typical GL master file. The FRS draws upon the GL master to produce the firm's financial statements. The MRS also uses this file to support internal information reporting.

FIGURE 8-3	Journal Voucher

Journal Voucher		Number:	JV6 - 03
		Date:	6/26/04

Acct Num	Account Name	Amount	
		DR.	CR.
130	Accts Rec.	$5,500	
502	Sales		$5,500

Explanation: To Record Total Credit Sales for 6/26/04.

Approved By:	Posted By:
J. A. Martin	S.D. Smith

The **general ledger history file** has the same format as the GL master. Its primary purpose is to provide historic financial data for comparative financial reports.

The **journal voucher file** is the total collection of the journal vouchers processed in the current period. This file provides a record of all general ledger transactions and replaces the traditional general journal.

The **journal voucher history file** contains journal vouchers for past periods. This historic information supports management's stewardship responsibility to account for resource utilization. Both the current and historic journal voucher files are important links in the firm's audit trail.

The **responsibility center file** contains the revenues, expenditures, and other resource utilization data for each responsibility center in the organization. The MRS draws upon these data for input in the preparation of responsibility reports for management.

Finally, the **budget master file** contains budgeted amounts for revenues, expenditures, and other resources for responsibility centers. These data, in conjunction with the responsibility center file, are the basis for responsibility accounting, which is discussed later in the chapter.

FIGURE 8-4	Record Layout for a General Ledger Master File

Account Number	Account Description	Acct Class A = Asset L = Liab R = Rev E = Expense OE = Equity	Normal Balance D = Debit C = Credit	Beginning Balance	Total Debits This Period	Total Credits This Period	Current Balance

GLS PROCEDURES

As we have seen in previous chapters, certain aspects of GLS update procedures are performed as either a separate operations or integrated within transaction processing systems. Our focus in the next section is on the interrelationship between the GLS and financial reporting. This involves additional updates in the form of reversing, adjusting, and closing entries. Let's now turn our attention to the financial reporting system.

THE FINANCIAL REPORTING SYSTEM

Management's responsibility for providing stewardship information to external parties is dictated by law. This reporting obligation is met via the financial reporting system (FRS). Much of the information provided takes the form of standard financial statements, tax returns, and documents required by regulatory agencies such as the Securities and Exchange Commission.

The primary recipients of financial statement information are external users, such as stockholders, creditors, and government agencies. Generally speaking, outside users of information are interested in the performance of the organization as a whole. Therefore, they require information that allows them to observe trends in performance over time and to make comparisons between different organizations. Given the nature of these needs, financial reporting information must be prepared and presented by all organizations in a manner that is generally accepted and understood by external users.

SOPHISTICATED USERS WITH HOMOGENEOUS INFORMATION NEEDS

Because the community of external users is vast and their individual information needs may vary, financial statements are targeted at a general audience. They are prepared on the proposition that the audience comprises of **sophisticated users** with relatively homogeneous information needs. In other words, it is assumed that users of financial reports understand the conventions and accounting principles that are applied and that the statements have information content that is useful.

FINANCIAL REPORTING PROCEDURES

Financial reporting is the final step in the overall **accounting process** that begins in the transaction cycles. Figure 8-5 presents the FRS in relation to the other information subsystems. The steps illustrated and numbered in the figure are discussed briefly in the following section.

The process begins with a clean slate at the start of a new fiscal year. Only the balance sheet (permanent) accounts are carried forward from the previous year. From this point, the following steps occur:

1. *Capture the transaction.* Within each transaction cycle, transactions are recorded in the appropriate transaction file.
2. *Record in special journal.* Each transaction is entered into the journal. Recall that frequently occurring classes of transactions, such as sales, are captured in special journals. Those that occur infrequently are recorded in the general journal or directly on a journal voucher.
3. *Post to subsidiary ledger.* The details of each transaction are posted to the affected subsidiary accounts.
4. *Post to general ledger.* Periodically, journal vouchers, summarizing the entries made to the special journals and subsidiary ledgers, are prepared and posted to the general

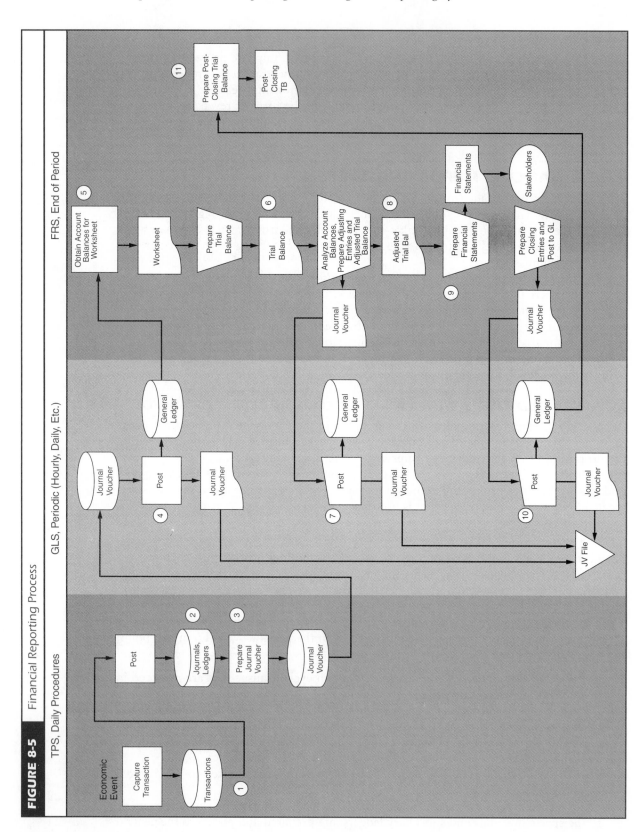

FIGURE 8-5   Financial Reporting Process

ledger accounts. The frequency of updates to the general ledger will be determined by the degree of system integration.

5. *Prepare the unadjusted trial balance.* At the end of the accounting period, the ending balance of each account in the general ledger is placed in a worksheet and evaluated in total for debit-credit equality.
6. *Make adjusting entries.* Adjusting entries are made to the worksheet to correct errors and to reflect unrecorded transactions during the period, such as depreciation.
7. *Journalize and post adjusting entries.* Journal vouchers for the adjusting entries are prepared and posted to the appropriate accounts in the general ledger.
8. *Prepare the adjusted trial balance.* From the adjusted balances, a trial balance is prepared that contains all the entries that should be reflected in the financial statements.
9. *Prepare the financial statements.* The balance sheet, income statement, and statement of cash flows are prepared using the adjusted trial balance.
10. *Journalize and post the closing entries.* Journal vouchers are prepared for entries that close out the income statement (temporary) accounts and transfer the income or loss to retained earnings. Finally, these entries are posted to the general ledger.
11. *Prepare the post-closing trial balance.* A trial balance worksheet containing only the balance sheet accounts may now be prepared to indicate the balances being carried forward to the next accounting period.

The periodic nature of financial reporting in most organizations establishes it as a batch process as illustrated in Figure 8-5. This often is the case for larger organizations with multiple streams of revenue and expense transactions that need to be reconciled before being posted to the general ledger. Many organizations, however, have moved to real-time general ledger updates and financial reporting systems that produce financial statements on short notice. Figure 8-6 presents a FRS using a combination of batch and real-time computer technology.

CONTROLLING THE FRS

Sarbanes-Oxley legislation requires that management designs and implements controls over the financial reporting process. This includes the transaction processing systems that feed data into the FRS. In previous chapters we studied control techniques necessary for the various transaction systems. Here we will examine only the controls that relate to the FRS. The potential risks to the FRS include:

1. A defective audit trail.
2. Unauthorized access to the general ledger.
3. General ledger accounts that are out of balance with subsidiary accounts.
4. Incorrect general ledger account balances because of unauthorized or incorrect journal vouchers.

If not controlled, these risks may result in misstated financial statements and other reports, thus misleading users of this information. The potential consequences are litigation, significant financial loss for the firm, and sanctions specified by SOX legislation.

COSO / SAS 78 CONTROL ISSUES

This discussion of FRS physical controls will follow the COSO / SAS 78 framework, which by now is familiar to you.

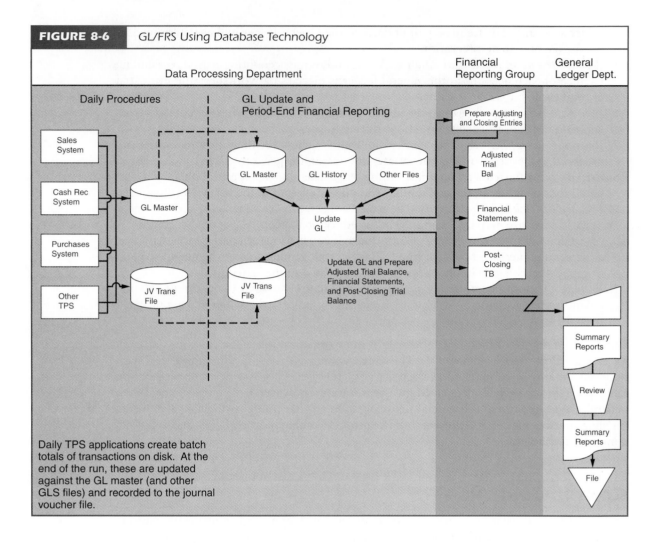

| FIGURE 8-6 | GL/FRS Using Database Technology |

Transaction Authorization

The journal voucher is the document that authorizes an entry to the general ledger. Journal vouchers have numerous sources such as the cash receipts processing, sales order processing, and the financial reporting group. It is vital to the integrity of the accounting records that the journal vouchers be properly authorized by a responsible manager at the source department.

Segregation of Duties

In previous chapters, we have seen how the general ledger provides verification control for the accounting process. To do so, the task of updating the general ledger must be separate from all accounting and asset custody responsibility within the organization. Therefore, individuals with access authority to general ledger accounts should not:

1. Have record-keeping responsibility for special journals or subsidiary ledgers.
2. Prepare journal vouchers.
3. Have custody of physical assets.

Notice that in Figure 8-6 transactions are authorized, processed, and posted directly to the general ledger. To compensate for this potential risk, the system should provide end users and general ledger departments with detailed listings of journal voucher and account activity reports. These documents advise users of the automated actions taken by the system so that errors and unusual events, which warrant investigation, can be identified.

Access Controls

Unauthorized access to the general ledger accounts can result in errors, fraud, and misrepresentations in financial statements. Sarbanes-Oxley explicitly addresses this area of risk by requiring organizations to implement controls that limit database access to only authorized individuals. A number of IT general controls designed to serve this purpose are presented in Chapter 16.

Accounting Records

The audit trail is a record of the path that a transaction takes through the input, processing, and output phases of transaction processing. This involves a network of documents, journals, and ledgers designed to ensure that a transaction can be accurately traced through the system from initiation to final disposition.

An audit trail facilitates error prevention and correction when the data files are conveniently and logical organized. Also, the general ledger and other files which constitute the audit trail should be detailed and rich enough to: (1) to provide the ability to answer inquiries, for example, from customers or vendors; (2) to be able to reconstruct files if they are completely or partially destroyed; (3) to provide historical data required by auditors; (4) to fulfill government regulations; and (5) to provide a means for preventing, detecting, and correcting errors.

Independent Verification

In previous chapters we have portrayed the general ledger function as an independent verification step within the AIS. The FRS produces two operational reports—*journal voucher listing* and the *general ledger change report*—that provide proof of the accuracy of this process. The **journal voucher listing** provides relevant details about each journal voucher posted to the GL. The **general ledger change report** presents the effects of journal voucher postings to the general ledger accounts. Figure 8-7 and Figure 8-8 present examples of these reports.

THE MANAGEMENT REPORTING SYSTEM

Management reporting is often called discretionary reporting because it is not mandated as is financial reporting. One could take issue with the term discretionary, however, and argue that an effective MRS *is* mandated by SOX legislation, which requires that all public companies monitor and report on the effectiveness of internal controls over financial reporting. Indeed, management reporting has long been recognized as a critical element of an organization's internal control structure. An MRS that directs management's attention to problems on a timely basis promotes effective management and thus supports the organization's business objectives.

FACTORS THAT INFLUENCE THE MRS

Designing an effective management reporting system requires an understanding of the information managers need to deal with the problems they face. This section examines several topics that provide insight into factors that influence management information needs. These

FIGURE 8-7	Journal Voucher Listing

Journal Voucher Listing

Date	JV Num	Description	Account Number	Debit	Credit
6/26/07	JV6 - 01	Cash receipts	10100	109,000	
			20100		50,000
			10600		44,000
			10900		15,000
6/26/07	JV6 - 02	Credit sales	20100	505,000	
			50200		505,000
6/26/07	JV6 - 03	Inventory usage	30300	410,000	
			17100		410,000
•	•	•	•	•	•
•	•	•	•	•	•
•	•	•	•	•	•
6/26/07	JV - 12	Cash disbursements	90310	102,100	
			10100		102,100
				6,230,000	6,230,000

are: management principles; management function, level, and decision type; problem structure; types of management reports; responsibility accounting; and behavioral considerations.

MANAGEMENT PRINCIPLES

Management principles provide insight into management information needs. The principles that most directly influence the MRS are formalization of tasks, responsibility and authority, span of control, and management by exception.

Formalization of Tasks

The **formalization of tasks** principle suggests that management should structure the firm around the tasks it performs rather than around individuals with unique skills. Under this principle, organizational areas are subdivided into tasks that represent full-time job positions. Each position must have clearly defined limits of responsibility.

The purpose of formalization of tasks is to avoid an organizational structure in which the organization's performance, stability, and continued existence depend on specific individuals. The **organizational chart** in Figure 8-9 shows some typical job positions in a manufacturing firm.

Although a firm's most valuable resource is its employees, it does not own the resource. Sooner or later, key individuals leave and take their skills with them. By formalizing tasks, the firm can more easily recruit individuals to fill standard positions left open by those who leave. In addition, the formalization of tasks promotes internal control. With employee

FIGURE 8-8	General Ledger Change Report

General Ledger Change Report

Date	Acct	Description	JV Ref	Balance	Debits	Credits	Net Change	New Balance
6/26/07	10100	Cash receipts	JV6 - 01	1,902,300	109,000			
			JV6 - 12			102,100	6,900	1,909,200
6/26/07	20100	Cash receipts	JV6 - 01	2,505,600		50,000		
		Credit sales	JV6 - 02		505,000		455,000	2,960,600
•	•	•	•	•	•	•	•	•
•	•	•	•	•	•	•	•	•
•	•	•	•	•	•	•	•	•
6/26/07	90310	Cash disburs.	JV6 - 12	703,500	102,100		102,100	805,600
6/26/07	17100	Inven. usage	JV6 - 03	1,600,500		410,000	410,000	2,010,500

Control Totals:

	Debits	Credits
Previous Balance	23,789,300	23,789,300
Total Net Change	6,230,000	6,230,000
Current Balance	30,019,300	30,019,300

responsibilities formalized and clearly specified, management can construct an organization that avoids assigning incompatible tasks to an individual.

Implications for the MRS. Formalizing the tasks of the firm allows formal specification of the information needed to support the tasks. Thus when a personnel change occurs, the information needed by the new employee will be essentially the same as for his or her predecessor. The information system must focus on the task, not the individual performing the task. Otherwise, information requirements would need to be reassessed with the appointment of each new individual to the position. Also, internal control is strengthened by restricting information based on need as defined by the task, rather than the whim or desire of the user.

Responsibility and Authority
The principle of **responsibility** refers to an individual's obligation to achieve desired results. Responsibility is closely related to the principle of **authority**. If a manager delegates responsibility to a subordinate, he or she must also grant the subordinate the authority to make decisions within the limits of that responsibility. In a business organization, managers delegate responsibility and authority downward through the organizational hierarchy from superior to subordinates.

Implications for the MRS. The principles of responsibility and authority define the vertical reporting channels of the firm through which information flows. The manager's location

FIGURE 8-9	Organizational Chart for a Manufacturing Firm

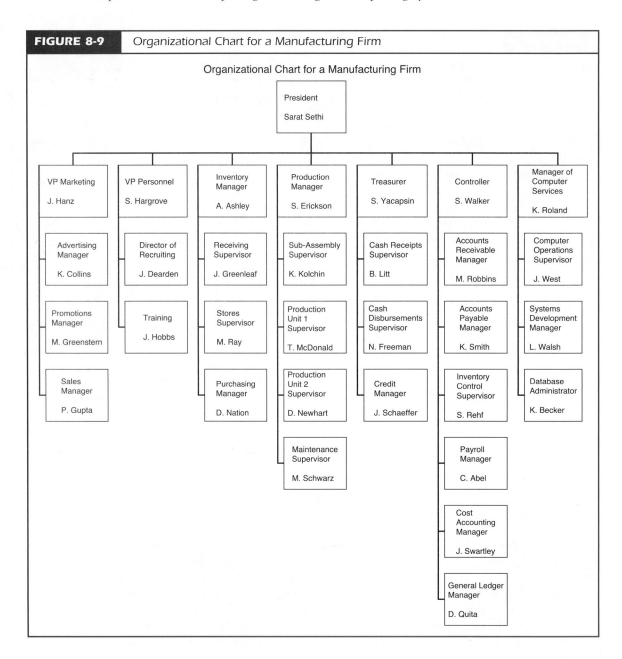

in the reporting channel influences the scope and detail of the information reported. Managers at higher levels usually require more summarized information. Managers at lower levels receive information that is more detailed. In designing a reporting structure, the analyst must consider the manager's position in the reporting channel.

Span of Control

A manager's **span of control** refers to the number of subordinates directly under his or her control. The size of the span has an impact on the organization's physical structure. A firm with a narrow span of control has fewer subordinates reporting directly to managers. These firms tend to have tall, narrow structures with several layers of management.

Firms with broad spans of control (more subordinates reporting to each manager) tend to have wide structures, with fewer levels of management. Figure 8-10 illustrates the relationship between span of control and organizational structure.

Organizational behavior research suggests that wider spans of control are preferable because they allow more employee autonomy in decision making. This may translate into better employee morale and increased motivation. An important consideration in setting the span of control is the nature of the task. The more routine and structured the task, the more subordinates one manager can control. Therefore, routine tasks tend to be associated with a broad span of control. Less structured or highly technical tasks often require a good deal of management participation on task-related problems. This close interaction reduces the manager's span of control.

Implications for the MRS. Managers with narrow spans of control are closely involved with the details of the operation and with specific decisions. Broad spans of control remove managers from these details. These managers delegate more of their decision-making authority to their subordinates. The different management approaches require different information. Managers with narrow spans of control require detailed reports. Managers with broad control responsibilities operate most effectively with summarized information.

Management by Exception

The principle of **management by exception** suggests that managers should limit their attention to potential problem areas (i.e., exceptions) rather than being involved with every activity or decision. Managers thus maintain control without being overwhelmed by the details.

Implications for the MRS. Managers need information that identifies operations or resources at risk of going out of control. Reports should support management by exception by focusing on changes in key factors that are symptomatic of potential problems. Unnecessary details that may draw attention away from important facts should be excluded from reports. For example, an inventory exception report may be used to identify items of inventory that turn over more slowly or go out of stock more frequently than

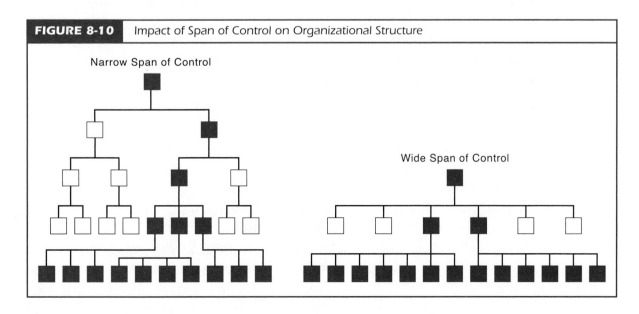

FIGURE 8-10   Impact of Span of Control on Organizational Structure

normal. Management attention must be focused on these exceptions. The majority of inventory items that fluctuate within normal levels should not be included in the report.

MANAGEMENT FUNCTION, LEVEL, AND DECISION TYPE

The management functions of planning and control have a profound effect on the management reporting system. The planning function is concerned with making decisions about the future activities of the organization. Planning can be long range or short range. Long-range planning usually encompasses a period of between one and five years, but this varies among industries. For example, a public utility may plan 15 years ahead in the construction of a new power plant, while a computer manufacturer deals in a time frame of only one or two years in the planning of new products. Long-range planning involves a variety of tasks, including setting the goals and objectives of the firm, planning the growth and optimum size of the firm, and deciding on the degree of diversification among the firm's products.

Short-term planning involves the **implementation** of specific plans that are needed to achieve the objectives of the long-range plan. Examples include planning the marketing and promotion for a new product, preparing a production schedule for the month, and providing department heads with budgetary goals for the next three months.

The control function ensures that the activities of the firm conform to the plan. This entails evaluating the operational process (or individual) against a predetermined standard and, when necessary, taking corrective action. Effective control takes place in the present time frame and is triggered by feedback information that advises the manager about the status of the operation being controlled.

Planning and control decisions are frequently classified into four categories: strategic planning, tactical planning, managerial control, and operational control. Figure 8-11 relates these decisions to managerial levels.

Strategic Planning Decisions

Figure 8-11 shows that top-level managers make **strategic planning decisions,** including:

- Setting the goals and objectives of the firm.

- Determining the scope of business activities, such as desired market share, markets the firm wishes to enter or abandon, the addition of new product lines and the termination of old ones, and merger and acquisition decisions.

- Determining or modifying the organization's structure.

- Setting the management philosophy.

Strategic planning decisions have the following characteristics:

- They have long-term time frames. Because they deal with the future, managers making strategic decisions require information that supports forecasting.

- They require highly summarized information. Strategic decisions focus on general trends rather than detail-specific activities.

- They tend to be nonrecurring. Strategic decisions are usually one-time events. As a result, there is little historic information available to support the specific decision.

- Strategic decisions are associated with a high degree of uncertainty. The decision maker must rely on insight and intuition. Judgment is often central to the success of the decision.

| **FIGURE 8-11** | Management Level and Decision Type |

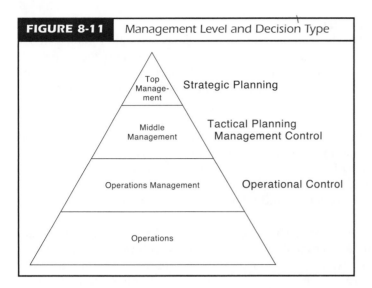

- They are broad in scope and have a profound impact on the firm. Once made, strategic decisions permanently affect the organization at all levels.

- Strategic decisions require external as well as internal sources of information.

Tactical Planning Decisions

Tactical planning decisions are subordinate to strategic decisions and are made by middle management (see Figure 8-11). These decisions are shorter term, more specific, recurring, have more certain outcomes, and have a lesser impact on the firm than strategic decisions. For example, assume that the president of a manufacturing firm makes the strategic decision to increase sales and production by 100,000 units over the prior year's level. One tactical decision that must result from this is setting the monthly production schedule to accomplish the strategic goal.

Management Control Decisions

Management control involves motivating managers in all functional areas to use resources, including materials, personnel, and financial assets, as productively as possible. The supervising manager compares the performance of his or her subordinate manager to pre-established standards. If the subordinate does not meet the standard, the supervisor takes corrective action. When the subordinate meets or exceeds expectations, he or she may be rewarded.

Uncertainty surrounds **management control decisions** because it is difficult to separate the manager's performance from that of his or her operational unit. We often lack both the criteria for specifying management control standards and the objective techniques for measuring performance. For example, assume that a firm's top management places its most effective and competent middle manager in charge of a business segment that is performing poorly. The manager's task is to revitalize the operations of the unit, and doing so requires a massive infusion of resources. The segment will operate in the red for some time until it establishes a foothold in the market. Measuring the performance of this manager in the short term may be difficult. Traditional measures of profit, such as return on investment (which measures the performance of the operational unit itself), would not really reflect the manager's performance. We shall examine this topic in more depth later in the chapter.

Operational Control Decisions

Operational control ensures that the firm operates in accordance with pre-established criteria. Figure 8-11 shows that operations managers exercise operational control. **Operational control decisions** are narrower and more focused than tactical decisions because they are concerned with the routine tasks of operations. Operational control decisions are more structured than management control decisions, more dependent on details than planning decisions, and have a shorter time frame than tactical or strategic decisions. These decisions are associated with a fairly high degree of certainty. In other words, identified symptoms tend to be good indicators of the root problem, and corrective actions tend to be obvious. This degree of certainty makes it easier to establish meaningful criteria for measuring performance. Operational control decisions have three basic elements: setting standards, evaluating performance, and taking corrective action.

Standards. Standards are pre-established levels of performance that managers believe are attainable. Standards apply to all aspects of operations, such as sales volume, quality control over production, costs for inventory items, material usage in the production of products, and labor costs in production. Once established, these standards become the basis for evaluating performance.

Performance Evaluation. The decision maker compares the performance of the operation in question against the standard. The difference between the two is the **variance**. For example, a price variance for an item of inventory is the difference between the expected price—the standard—and the price actually paid. If the actual price is greater than the standard, the variance is said to be unfavorable. If the actual price is less than the standard, the variance is favorable.

Taking Corrective Action. After comparing the performance to the standard, the manager takes action to remedy any out-of-control condition. Recall from Chapter 3, however, that we must apply extreme caution when taking corrective action. An inappropriate response to performance measures may have undesirable results. For example, to achieve a favorable price variance, the purchasing agent may pursue the low-price vendors of raw materials and sacrifice quality. If the lower quality raw materials result in excessive quantities being used in production because of higher than normal waste, the firm will experience an unfavorable material usage variance. The unfavorable usage variance may completely offset the favorable price variance to create an unfavorable total variance.

Table 8-1 classifies strategic planning, tactical planning, management control, and operational control decisions in terms of time frame, scope, level of details, recurrence, and certainty.

PROBLEM STRUCTURE

The structure of a problem reflects how well the decision maker understands the problem. Structure has three elements.[1]

1. Data—the values used to represent factors that are relevant to the problem.
2. Procedures—the sequence of steps or decision rules used in solving the problem.
3. Objectives—the results the decision maker desires to attain by solving the problem.

---

1   Adapted from F. L. Luconi, T. W. Malone, and M. S. Scott Morton, "Expert Systems: The Next Challenge for Managers," *Sloan Management Review* (Summer 1986). Reprinted in P. Gray, W. R. King, E. R. McLean, and H. J. Watson, MOIS: *Management of Information Systems* (Chicago: Dryden Press, 1989): 69–84.

TABLE 8-1	Classification of Decision Types by Decision Characteristics			
	DECISION TYPE			
DECISION CHARACTERISTIC	**Strategic Planning**	**Tactical Planning**	**Management Control**	**Operational Control**
Time frame	Long term	Medium	Medium	Short
Scope	High impact	Medium impact	Lower impact	Lowest impact
Level of details	Highly summarized	Detailed	Moderately summarized	Highly detailed
Recurrence	Nonrecurring	Periodic recurring	Periodic recurring	Frequent recurring
Certainty	Uncertain	Highly certain	Uncertain	Highly certain

When all three elements are known with certainty, the problem is structured. Payroll calculation is an example of a **structured problem:**

1. We can identify the data for this calculation with certainty (hours worked, hourly rate, withholdings, tax rate, and so on).
2. Payroll procedures are known with certainty:

   Gross Pay = Hours worked × Pay rate

   Net pay = Gross Pay − Taxes − Withholdings
3. The objective of payroll is to discharge the firm's financial obligation to its employees.

Structured problems do not present unique situations to the decision maker and, because their information requirements can be anticipated, they are well suited for traditional data processing techniques. In effect, the designer who specifies the procedures and codes the programs solves the problem.

Unstructured Problems

Problems are unstructured when any of the three characteristics identified previously are not known with certainty. In other words, an **unstructured problem** is one for which we have no precise solution techniques. Either the data requirements are uncertain, the procedures are not specified or the solution objectives have not been fully developed. Such a problem is normally complex and engages the decision maker in a unique situation. In these situations, the systems analyst cannot fully anticipate user information needs, rendering traditional data processing techniques ineffective.

Figure 8-12 illustrates the relationship between problem structure and organizational level. We see from the figure that lower levels of management deal more with fully structured problems, whereas upper management deals with unstructured problems. Middle-level managers tend to work with partially structured problems. Keep in mind that these structural classifications are generalizations. Top managers also deal with some highly structured problems, and lower-level managers sometimes face problems that lack structure.

Figure 8-12 also shows the use of information systems by different levels of management. The traditional information system deals most effectively with fully structured problems. Therefore, operations management and tactical management receive the greatest benefit from these systems. Because management control and strategic planning

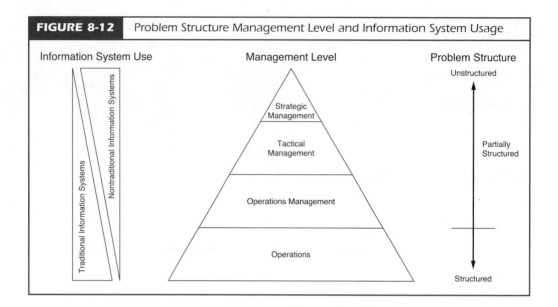

FIGURE 8-12   Problem Structure Management Level and Information System Usage

decisions lack structure, the managers who make these decisions often do not receive adequate support from traditional systems alone.

TYPES OF MANAGEMENT REPORTS

Reports are the formal vehicles for conveying information to managers. The term *report* tends to imply a written message presented on sheets of paper. In fact, a **management report** may be a paper document or a digital image displayed on a computer terminal. The report may express information in verbal, numeric, or graphic form, or any combination of these.

Report Objectives

Chapter 1 made the distinction between information and data. Recall that information leads the user to an action. Therefore, to be useful, reports must have **information content**. Their value is the effect they have on users. This is expressed in two general reporting objectives: (1) to reduce the level of uncertainty associated with a problem facing the decision maker and (2) to influence the decision maker's behavior in a positive way. Reports that fail to accomplish these objectives lack information content and have no value. In fact, reliance on such reports may lead to dysfunctional behavior (discussed later). Management reports fall into two broad classes: programmed reports and ad hoc reports.

Programmed Reporting

Programmed reports provide information to solve problems that users have anticipated. There are two subclasses of programmed reports: scheduled reports and on-demand reports. The management reporting system produces **scheduled reports** according to an established time frame. This could be daily, weekly, quarterly, and so on. Examples of such reports are a daily listing of sales, a weekly payroll action report, and annual financial statements. **On-demand reports** are triggered by events, not by the passage of time. For example, when inventories fall to their pre-established reorder points, the system sends an inventory reorder report to the purchasing agent. Another example is an accounts receivable manager responding to a customer problem over the telephone. The manager can, on demand, display the customer's account history on the computer screen.

Note that this query capability is the product of an anticipated need. This is quite different from the ad hoc reports that we discuss later. Table 8-2 lists examples of typical programmed reports and identifies them as scheduled or on-demand.

Report Attributes

To be effective, a report must possess the following attributes: relevance, summarization, exception orientation, accuracy, completeness, timeliness, and conciseness. Each of these **report attributes** is discussed in the following section.

Relevance. Each element of information in a report must support the manager's decision. Irrelevancies waste resources and may even be dysfunctional by distracting a manager's attention from the information content of the report.

Summarization. Reports should be summarized according to the level of the manager within the organizational hierarchy. In general, the degree of summarization becomes greater as information flows from lower management upward to top management.

Exception Orientation. Control reports should identify activities that are at risk of going out of control and should ignore activities that are under control. For example, consider a purchasing agent with ordering responsibility for an inventory of 10,000 different items. If the agent received a daily report containing the actual balances of every item, he or she would search through 10,000 items to identify a few that need reordering. An exception-oriented report would identify only those inventory items that have fallen to their reorder levels. From this report, the agent could easily prepare purchase orders.

Accuracy. Information in reports must be free of material errors. A material error will cause the user to make the wrong decision (or fail to make a required decision). We often sacrifice accuracy for timely information. In situations that require quick responses, the manager must factor this trade-off into the **decision-making process.**

Completeness. Information must be as complete as possible. Ideally, no piece of information that is essential to the decision should be missing from the report. Like the attribute of accuracy, we sometimes must sacrifice completeness in favor of timely information.

TABLE 8-2	**Examples of Programmed Reports**	
Type of Report	**Scheduled**	**On-Demand**
Planning Reports:		
Financial budgets	X	
Materials requirements reports		X
Sales forecast reports	X	
Production schedules		X
Projected cash flows reports	X	
Control Reports:		
Cost center reports	X	
Profit center reports	X	
Profitability by line of product	X	
Quality control reports		X
Labor distribution reports	X	
Inventory exception reports		X
Equipment utilization reports	X	

Timeliness. If managers always had time on their side, they may never make bad decisions. However, managers cannot always wait until they have all the facts before they act. Timely information that is sufficiently complete and accurate is more valuable than perfect information that comes too late to use. Therefore, the MRS must provide managers with timely information. Usually, information can be no older than the period to which it pertains. For example, if each week a manager decides on inventory acquisitions based on a weekly inventory status report, the information in the report should be no more than a week old.

Conciseness. Information in the report should be presented as concisely as possible. Reports should use coding schemes to represent complex data classifications and provide all the necessary calculations (such as extensions and variances) for the user. In addition, information should be clearly presented with titles for all values.

Ad Hoc Reporting

Managers cannot always anticipate their information needs. This is particularly true for top and middle management. In the dynamic business world, problems arise that require new information on short notice and there may be insufficient time to write traditional computer programs to produce the required information. In the past, these needs often went unsatisfied. Now database technology provides direct inquiry and report generation capabilities. Managers with limited computer background can quickly produce **ad hoc reports** from a terminal or PC, without the assistance of data processing professionals.

Increases in computing power, point-of-transaction scanners, and continuous reductions in data storage costs have enabled organizations to accumulate massive quantities of raw data. This data resource is now being tapped to support ad hoc reporting needs through a concept known as *data mining*.

Data mining is the process of selecting, exploring, and modeling large amounts of data to uncover relationships and global patterns that exist in large databases but are "hidden" among the vast amount of facts. This involves sophisticated techniques such as *database queries* and *artificial intelligence* that model real-world phenomena from data collected from a variety of sources, including transaction processing systems, customer history databases, and demographics data from external sources such as credit bureaus. Managers employ two general approaches to data mining: *verification* and *discovery*.

The **verification model** uses a drill-down technique to either verify or reject a user's hypothesis. For example, assume a marketing manager needs to identify the best target market, as a subset of the organization's entire customer base, for an ad campaign for a new product. The data mining software will examine the firm's historical data about customer sales and demographic information to reveal comparable sales and the demographic characteristics shared by those purchasers. This subset of the customer base can then be used to focus the promotion campaign.

The **discovery model** uses data mining to discover previously unknown but important information that is hidden within the data. This model employs inductive learning to infer information from detailed data by searching for recurring patterns, trends, and generalizations. This approach is fundamentally different from the verification model in that the data are searched with no specific hypothesis driving the process. For example, a company may apply discovery techniques to identify customer-buying patterns and gain a better understanding of customer motivations and behavior.

A central feature of a successful data mining initiative is a **data warehouse** of archived operational data. A data warehouse is a relational database management system that has been designed specifically to meet the needs of data mining. The warehouse is a central location that contains operational data about current events (within the past 24 hours) as well as events that have transpired over many years. Data are coded and stored in the warehouse in detail and at various degrees of aggregation to facilitate identification of recurring patterns and trends.

Management decision making can be greatly enhanced through data mining, but only if the appropriate data have been identified, collected, and stored in the data warehouse. Because many of the important issues related to data mining and warehousing require an understanding of relational database technology, these topics are examined further in Chapters 9 and 11.

RESPONSIBILITY ACCOUNTING

A large part of management reporting involves **responsibility accounting.** This concept implies that every economic event that affects the organization is the responsibility of and can be traced to an individual manager. The responsibility accounting system personalizes performance by saying to the manager, "This is your original budget and this is how your performance for the period compares to your budget." Most organizations structure their responsibility reporting system around areas of responsibility in the firm. A fundamental principle of this concept is that responsibility area managers are accountable only for items (costs, revenues, and investments) that they control.

The flow of information in responsibility systems is both downward and upward through the information channels. Figure 8-13 illustrates this pattern. These top-down and bottom-up information flows represent the two phases of responsibility accounting: (1) creating a set of financial performance goals (budgets) pertinent to the manager's responsibilities, and (2) reporting and measuring actual performance as compared to these goals.

Setting Financial Goals: The Budget Process

The **budget** process helps management achieve its financial objectives by establishing measurable goals for each organizational segment. This mechanism conveys to the segment managers the standards that senior managers will use for measuring their performance. Budget information flows downward and becomes increasingly detailed as it moves to lower levels of management. Figure 8-14 shows the distribution of budget information through three levels of management.

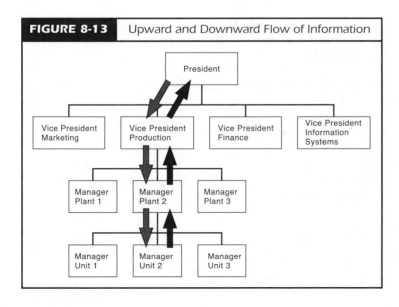

FIGURE 8-13 | Upward and Downward Flow of Information

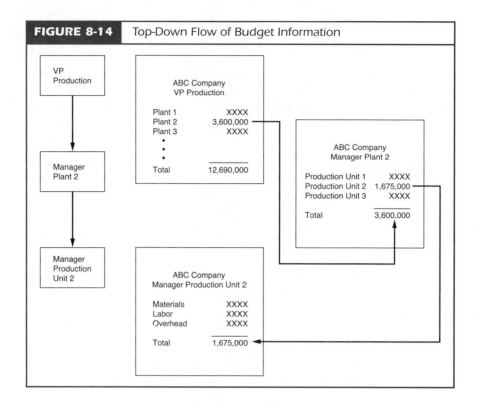

FIGURE 8-14   Top-Down Flow of Budget Information

Measuring and Reporting Performance

Performance measurement and reporting takes place at each operational segment in the firm. This information flows upward as **responsibility reports** to senior levels of management. Figure 8-15 shows the relationship between levels of responsibility reports. Notice how the information in the reports becomes increasingly summarized at each higher level of management.

Responsibility Centers

To achieve accountability, business entities frequently organize their operations into units called **responsibility centers.** The most common forms of responsibility centers are cost centers, profit centers, and investment centers.

Cost Centers. A **cost center** is an organizational unit with responsibility for cost management within budgetary limits. For example, a production department may be responsible for meeting its production obligation while keeping production costs (labor, materials, and overhead) within the budgeted amount. The performance report for the cost center manager reflects its controllable cost behavior by focusing on budgeted costs, actual costs, and variances from budget. Figure 8-16 shows an example of a cost center performance report. Performance measurements should not consider costs that are outside of the manager's control, such as investments in plant equipment or depreciation on the building.

Profit Centers. A **profit center** manager has responsibility for both cost control and revenue generation. For example, the local manager of a national department store chain may be responsible for decisions about:

● Which items of merchandise to stock in the store.

● What prices to charge.

FIGURE 8-15 | The Bottom-Up Flow of Performance Information

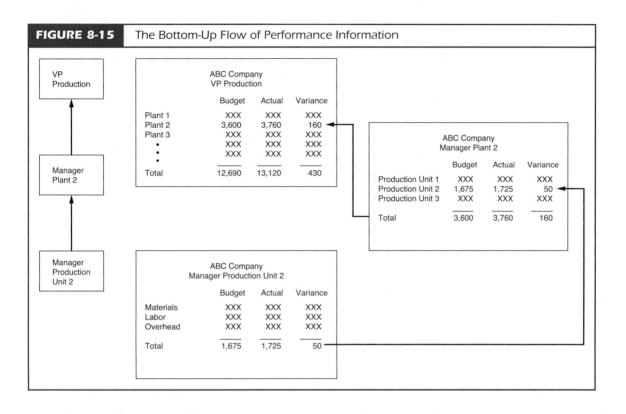

FIGURE 8-16 | Cost Center Performance Report

PLANT UNIT 2
CONTROLLABLE COST REPORT

PLANTWIDE CONTROLLABLE COSTS

	Budget	Actual	Variance
Materials			
Drilling Dept.	XXX	XXX	XX
Milling Dept.	XXX	XXX	XX
Assembly Ship	XXX	XXX	XX
Direct Labor			
Drilling Dept.	XXX	XXX	XX
Milling Dept.	XXX	XXX	XX
Assembly Ship	XXX	XXX	XX
Controllable Overhead			
Drilling Dept.	XXX	XXX	XX
Milling Dept.	XXX	XXX	XX
Assembly Ship	XXX	XXX	XX
Total Controllable Costs	XXXXX	XXXXX	XXX

- The kind of promotional activities for products.

- The level of advertising.

- The size of the staff and the hiring of employees.

- Building maintenance and limited capital improvements.

The performance report for the profit center manager is different from that of the cost center. Nevertheless, the reporting emphasis for both should be on controllable items. Figure 8-17 is an example of a profit center report. Whereas only controllable items are used to assess the manager's performance, the profit center itself is assessed by its contribution after noncontrollable costs.

Investment Centers. The manager of an **investment center** has the general authority to make decisions that profoundly affect the organization. Assume that a division of a corporation is an investment center with the objective of maximizing the return on its investment assets. The division manager's range of responsibilities includes cost management, product development, marketing, distribution, and capital disposition through investments of funds in projects and ventures that earn a desired rate of return. Figure 8-18 illustrates the performance report for an investment center.

BEHAVIORAL CONSIDERATIONS

Goal Congruence

Earlier in this chapter, we touched on the management principles of authority, responsibility, and the formalization of tasks. When properly applied within an organization, these principles promote **goal congruence.** Lower-level managers pursuing their own objectives contribute in a positive way to the objectives of their superiors. For example,

FIGURE 8-17	Profit Center Performance Report

XYZ COMPANY PROFIT STATEMENT			
Sales		XXX	
Less:			
Cost of goods sold	XXX		
Gross profit		XXX	
Less controllable costs:		XXX	
Controllable overhead	XXX		
Controllable operating expenses	XXX		
Controllable operating profit		XXX	(Measure of management performance)
Depreciation on noncontrollable fixed assets	XXX		
Contribution after noncontrollable costs		XXX	(Measure of profit center performance)

| FIGURE 8-18 | Investment Center Performance Report |

XYZ COMPANY DIVISION INCOME STATEMENT

Sales		XXX
Less:		
Cost of goods sold	XXX	
Gross profit		XXX
Less controllable costs:		XXX
Controllable overhead	XXX	
Depreciation on noncontrollable fixed assets	XXX	
Controllable operating profit		XXX (Measure of management performance)
Less noncontrollable costs:		
Divisional overhead	XXX	
Allocated centralized charges	XXX	
Net income before taxes		XXX (Measure of investment center performance)

by controlling costs, a production supervisor contributes to the division manager's goal of profitability. Thus as individual managers serve their own best interests they also serve the best interests of the organization.

A carefully structured management reporting system plays an important role in promoting and preserving goal congruence. On the other hand, a badly designed MRS can cause dysfunctional actions that are in opposition to the organization's objectives. Two pitfalls that cause managers to act dysfunctionally are information overload and inappropriate performance measures.

Information Overload
Information overload occurs when a manager receives more information than he or she can assimilate. This happens when designers of the reporting system do not properly consider the manager's organizational level and span of control. For example, consider the information volume that would flow to the president if the reports were not properly summarized (refer to Figure 8-13). The details required by lower-level managers would quickly overload the president's decision-making process. Although the report may have many of the information attributes discussed earlier (complete, accurate, timely, and concise), it may be useless if not properly summarized.

Information overload causes managers to disregard their formal information and rely on informal cues to help them make decisions. Thus the formal information system is replaced by heuristics (rules of thumb), tips, hunches, and guesses. The resulting decisions run a high risk of being suboptimal and dysfunctional.

Inappropriate Performance Measures
Recall that one purpose of a report is to stimulate behavior consistent with the objectives of the firm. When **inappropriate performance measures** are used, however, the report can

have the opposite effect. Let's see how this can happen using a common performance measure—return on investment (ROI).

Assume that the corporate management of an organization evaluates division management performance solely on the basis of ROI. Each manager's objective is to maximize ROI. Naturally, the organization wants this to happen through prudent cost management and increased profit margins. However, when ROI is used as the single criterion for measuring performance, the criterion itself becomes the focus of attention and object of manipulation. We illustrate this point with the multiperiod investment center report in Figure 8-19. Notice how ROI went up in the second and third years. On the surface, this looks like favorable performance. However, a closer analysis of the cost and revenue figures gives a different picture. Actual sales were below budgeted sales for 2004, but the shortfall in revenue was offset by reductions in discretionary operating expenditures (employee training and plant maintenance). The ROI figure is further improved by reducing investments in inventory and plant equipment (fixed assets) to lower the asset base.

The manager took actions that increased ROI but were dysfunctional to the organization. Usually, such tactics can succeed in the short run only. As the plant equipment starts to wear out, customer dissatisfaction increases (because of stockouts), and employee dissent becomes epidemic. The ROI figure will then begin to reflect the economic reality. By that time, however, the manager may have been promoted based on the perception of good performance, and his or her successor will inherit the problems left behind.

The use of any single criterion performance measure can impose personal goals on managers that conflict with organizational goals and result in dysfunctional behavior. Consider the following examples:

1. The use of price variance to evaluate a purchasing agent can affect the quality of the items purchased.
2. The use of quotas (such as units produced) to evaluate a supervisor can affect quality control, material usage efficiency, labor relations, and plant maintenance.
3. The use of profit measures such as ROI, net income, and contribution margin can affect plant investment, employee training, inventory reserve levels, customer satisfaction, and labor relations.

Performance measures should consider all relevant aspects of a manager's responsibility. In addition to measures of general performance (such as ROI), management should measure trends in key variables such as sales, cost of goods sold, operating expenses, and asset levels. Nonfinancial measures such as product leadership, personnel development, employee attitudes, and public responsibility may also be relevant in assessing management performance.

FIGURE 8-19	Multiperiod Investment Center Report

	ACTUAL			BUDGET
YEAR	**2001**	**2002**	**2003**	**2004**
Sales	1,780.0	2,670.0	3,204.0	3,560.0
Less segment variable costs:				
Materials	445.0	667.5	801.0	890.0
Labor	89.0	133.5	89.0	178.0
Supplies	35.6	53.4	64.1	71.2
Less discretionary costs				
employee training	53.4	62.3	44.5	71.2
Maintenance	89.0	97.9	71.2	106.8
Less segment committed costs:				
Depreciation	213.6	284.8	284.8	356.0
Rent	142.4	178.0	195.8	249.2
Total cost	1,068.0	1,477.4	1,550.4	1,922.4
Contribution	712.0	1,192.6	1,653.6	1,637.6
Investment in assets				
Accounts receivable	178.0	267.0	320.4	356.0
Inventory	356.0	534.0	480.6	712.0
Fixed assets	2,830.2	4,565.7	4,984.0	6,016.4
Less accounts payable	(267.0)	(400.5)	(623.0)	(534.0)
Net investment	3,097.2	4,966.2	5,162.0	6,550.4
Return on investment	23%	24%	32%	25%

SUMMARY

This chapter began by examining the general ledger system and the financial reporting system, two operationally interdependent systems that are vital to the economic activities of the organization. We first learned the importance of data coding schemes and their role in the GLS and TPS as a means of coordinating and managing a firm's transactions. In examining the major types of numeric and alphabetic coding schemes, we saw how each has certain advantages and disadvantages. We then turned to a more direct examination of the GLS, focusing on the files that typically make up a GLS database and on standard GLS procedures. Turning to the FRS, we examined how financial information is provided to both external and internal users. A step-by-step outline of the financial reporting process was presented.

Next, the GLS and the FRS were examined as a single, integrated physical system (GL/FRS). Our principle focus here was on the standard operational controls that govern this system and on the use of computer technology for improved efficiency in reporting and record keeping.

This chapter then examined discretionary reporting systems. Discretionary reporting is not subject to the professional guidelines and legal statutes that govern nondiscretionary financial reporting. Rather, it is driven by several factors, including management principles, management function, level, decision type, problem structure, responsibility accounting, and behavioral considerations The chapter investigated the impact of each factor on the design of the management reporting system.

KEY TERMS

ad hoc reports (404)
alphabetic codes (385)
alphanumeric codes (385)
authority (395)
block code (384)
budget (405)
budget master file (388)
chart of accounts (384)
cost center (406)
data mining (404)
data warehouse (404)
decision-making process (403)
discovery model (404)
formalization of tasks (394)
general ledger change report (393)
general ledger history file (388)
general ledger master file (387)
goal congruence (408)
group codes (385)
implementation (398)
inappropriate performance measures (409)
information content (402)
information overload (409)
investment center (408)
journal voucher history file (388)
journal voucher listing (393)

management by exception (397)
management control decisions (399)
management report (402)
mnemonic codes (386)
on-demand reports (402)
operational control decisions (400)
organizational chart (394)
profit center (406)
programmed reports (402)
report attributes (403)
responsibility (395)
responsibility accounting (405)
responsibility center file (388)
responsibility centers (406)
responsibility reports (406)
scheduled reports (402)
sequential codes (383)
sophisticated users (389)
span of control (396)
strategic planning decisions (398)
structured problem (401)
tactical planning decisions (399)
unstructured problem (401)
variance (400)
verification model (404)

REVIEW QUESTIONS

1. What are some of the more common uses of data codes in AIS?
2. Compare and contrast the relative advantages and disadvantages of sequential, block, group, alphabetic, and mnemonic codes.
3. What information is contained in a journal voucher?
4. How are journal vouchers used as a control mechanism?
5. What information is contained in the general ledger master file?
6. What is the purpose of the general ledger history file?
7. What is the purpose of a responsibility center file?
8. List the primary users of the FRS and discuss their information needs.
9. What are the 11 steps, in order, of the financial reporting process?
10. What assumption is made regarding the external users of financial statements?
11. When are adjusting entries made to the worksheet and what is their purpose? When are the corresponding voucher entries made?
12. What are the purposes of an audit trail? What is meant by a defective audit trail? How can a defective audit trail be prevented?

13. What tasks should the general ledger clerk not be allowed to do?
14. What are two operational reports produced by the FRS that provide proof to the accuracy of the process?
15. Explain which of the four potential exposures in the FRS may be controlled better by a close examination of the journal voucher listing.
16. Explain how the formalization of tasks promotes internal control.
17. Explain why it is important that both responsibility and authority are appropriately assigned to employees.
18. Distinguish between narrow and wide span of control. Give an example of tasks appropriate to each type.
19. How does management by exception help to alleviate information overload by a manager?
20. Identify instances for which feedback becomes useless in helping to control activities.
21. Contrast the four decision types—strategic planning, tactical planning, management control, and operational control—by the five decision characteristics—time frame, scope, level of details, recurrence, and certainty.
22. What are the three elements that distinguish structured and unstructured problems? Give an example of each type of problem. Which type of problem is more suitable to a transaction processing system?

23. What management levels are more likely to deal with unstructured problems? With structured problems? Why?
24. What are two objectives that enable reports to be considered useful?
25. List and define the seven report attributes.
26. What is responsibility accounting?
27. What are the two phases of responsibility accounting?
28. What are the three most common forms of responsibility centers?
29. What is goal congruence?
30. What is data mining?
31. What is a data warehouse?
32. What is information overload?
33. Explain some reporting techniques that may cause dysfunctional behavior by a manager.
34. Explain how ad hoc reports have allowed managers to make more timely and better-quality decisions. Give an example.
35. Explain how exception reporting would be invaluable to the manager of a credit department.
36. What types of variances are found on cost center reports? Explain what each variance is measuring and why this information is important.
37. Distinguish between a profit center and an investment center. Draw a diagram illustrating the relationship between cost, profit, and investment centers.

DISCUSSION QUESTIONS

1. Discuss some of the problems associated with general ledger systems that do not have data coding schemes.
2. For each of the following items, indicate whether a sequential, block, group, alphabetic, or mnemonic code would be most appropriate (you may list multiple methods; give an example and explain why each method is appropriate):
   a. state codes
   b. check number
   c. chart of accounts
   d. inventory item number
   e. bin number (inventory warehouse location)

   f. sales order number
   g. vendor code
   h. invoice number
   i. customer number
3. Discuss any separation of duties necessary to control against unauthorized entries to the general ledger. What other control procedures regarding the general ledger should be employed?
4. Discuss the various sources of data for the FRS output and how these data are processed into information (output) for the different external users.

5. Explain how erroneous journal vouchers may lead to litigation and significant financial losses for a firm.

6. Ultimately, is the purpose of an audit trail to follow a transaction from its input through its processing and finally to the financial statements or vice versa? Explain your answer.

7. Discuss the benefits that may be realized in switching from a computerized batch processing system to a direct access storage system. Also, discuss any additional control implications.

8. Controls are only as good as the predetermined standard on which they are based. Discuss the preceding comment and give an example.

9. If management control and strategic planning decisions do not receive a high level of support from traditional information systems, then how do they get the support?

10. In terms of decision-making capabilities, which type of report do you think is generally more important—scheduled reports or on-demand reports? Explain your answer and give an example of each type of report.

11. Scheduled reports may contain some information that is relevant to some decisions and irrelevant to other decisions. Why are some scheduled reports designed this way, rather than multiple reports being generated for various decision-making purposes?

12. Sometimes a trade-off must be made between information accuracy and timeliness. Give an example where it is imperative to make an estimate now, rather than wait a couple of weeks for an exact number.

13. Figure 8-13 illustrates both upward and downward flows of information. What are the downward flows and their purpose? What about the upward flows? Are the downward and upward flows related?

14. Distinguish between the verification model and the discovery model approaches to data mining.

15. Explain how a data warehouse database is fundamentally different from a transaction processing database.

16. Why are cost centers considered to be more appropriate than profit centers for production departments?

17. Explain how a production quota used to evaluate a supervisor can adversely affect quality control, material usage efficiency, and labor relations.

18. Explain and give an example as to how a manager can manipulate the return on investment figure in the short run. Why are these manipulations bad for the company in the long run? Suggest some alternative performance evaluation and compensation schemes.

19. Comment on the following statement: "More information is always preferred to less; you can never have too much information."

MULTIPLE-CHOICE QUESTIONS

1. CIA 586 III-39
   Sequential access means that
   a. data are stored on magnetic tape.
   b. the address of the location of data is found through the use of either an algorithm or an index.
   c. each record can be accessed in the same amount of time.
   d. to read record 500, records 1 through 499 must be read first.

2. A chart of accounts would best be coded using a(n) _____ coding scheme.
   a. alphabetic
   b. mnemonic
   c. block
   d. sequential

3. Which of the following statements is NOT true?
   a. Sorting records that are coded alphabetically tends to be more difficult for users than sorting numeric sequences.
   b. Mnemonic coding requires the user to memorize codes.
   c. Sequential codes carry no information content beyond their order in the sequence.
   d. Mnemonic codes are limited in their ability to represent items within a class.

4. Which file has as its primary purpose to present comparative financial reports on a historic basis?
   a. journal voucher history file
   b. budget master file
   c. responsibility file
   d. general ledger history file

5. Which of the following statements is true?
   a. Journal vouchers detailing transaction activity flow from various operational departments into the GLS, where they are independently reconciled and posted to the journal voucher history file.
   b. Journal vouchers summarizing transaction activity flow from the accounting department into the GLS, where they are independently reconciled and posted to the general ledger accounts.
   c. Journal vouchers summarizing transaction activity flow from various operational departments into the GLS, where they are independently reconciled and posted to the general ledger accounts.
   d. Journal vouchers summarizing transaction activity flow from various operational departments into the GLS, where they are independently reconciled and posted to the journal voucher history file.

6. Which of the following statements best describes a computer-based GL/FRS?
   a. Most firms derive little additional benefit from a real-time FRS.
   b. Batch processing is typically not appropriate for transaction processing of GLS.
   c. The sequential file approach is an inefficient use of technology.
   d. A batch system with direct access files recreates the entire database each time the file is updated.

7. A coding scheme in the form of acronyms and other combinations that convey meaning is a(n)
   a. sequential code.
   b. block code.
   c. alphabetic code.
   d. mnemonic code.

8. Which of the following is NOT a potential exposure of the FRS?
   a. a defective audit trail

   b. general ledger accounts that are out of balance with subsidiary accounts
   c. unauthorized access to the check register
   d. unauthorized access to the general ledger

9. Which task should the general ledger perform?
   a. update the general ledger
   b. prepare journal vouchers
   c. have custody of physical assets
   d. have record-keeping responsibility for special journals of subledgers

10. CMA Adapted
    Hersh Company uses a performance reporting system that reflects the company's decentralization of decision making. The departmental performance report shows one line of data for each subordinate who reports to the group vice president. The data presented show the actual costs incurred during the period, the budgeted costs, and all variances from budget for that subordinate's department. Hersh Company is using a type of system called
    a. contribution accounting.
    b. cost-benefit accounting.
    c. flexible budgeting.
    d. program budgeting.
    e. responsibility accounting.

11. CMA Adapted
    All of the following are characteristics of the strategic planning process except the
    a. emphasis on both the short and long run.
    b. analysis and review of departmental process.
    c. review of the attributes and behavior of the organization's competition.
    d. analysis of external economic factors.
    e. analysis of consumer demand.

12. CMA Adapted
    Kallert Manufacturing uses budgets only as a planning tool. Management has decided that it would be beneficial to also use budgets for control purposes. To implement this change, the management accountant must
    a. appoint a budget director.
    b. organize a budget committee.
    c. develop forecasting procedures.

d. report daily to operating management any deviations from plan.

e. synchronize the budgeting and accounting system with the organizational structure.

13. CMA adapted

The budgeting process should be one that motivates managers and employees to work toward organizational goals. Which of the following is least likely to motivate managers?

a. setting budget targets at attainable levels

b. participation by subordinates in the budgetary process

c. use of management by exception

d. holding subordinates accountable for the items they control

e. having top management set budget levels

14. CMA adapted

Wong Company uses both strategic planning and operational budgeting. Which of the following items would normally be considered in a strategic plan?

a. setting a target of 12 percent return on sales

b. maintaining the image of the company as the industry leader

c. setting a market price per share of stock outstanding

d. distributing monthly reports for departmental variance analysis

e. tightening credit terms for customers to 2/10, n/30

15. CMA adapted

Long-range planning as a management function is more important

a. at top management levels.

b. at middle management levels.

c. at lower management levels.

d. for staff functions than line functions.

e. for line functions than staff functions.

16. CMA adapted

The basic purpose of a responsibility accounting system is

a. budgeting.

b. motivation.

c. authority.

d. variance analysis.

e. pricing.

17. CMA adapted

A segment of an organization is referred to as a profit center if it has

a. authority to make decisions affecting the major determinants of profit, including the power to choose its markets and sources of supply.

b. authority to make decisions affecting the major determinants of profit, including the power to choose its markets and sources of supply, and significant control over the amount of invested capital.

c. authority to make decisions over the most significant costs of operations, including the power to choose the sources of supply.

d. authority to provide specialized support to other units within the organization.

e. responsibility for combining the raw materials, direct labor, and other factors of production into a final product.

18. CMA adapted

A segment of an organization is referred to as an investment center if it has

a. authority to make decisions affecting the major determinants of profit, including the power to choose its markets and sources of supply.

b. authority to make decisions affecting the major determinants of profit, including the power to choose its markets and sources of supply, and significant control over the amount of invested capital.

c. authority to make decisions over the most significant costs of operations, including the power to choose the sources of supply.

d. authority to provide specialized support to other units within the organization.

e. responsibility for developing markets for and selling of the output of the organization.

PROBLEMS

1. General Ledger System Overview
Draw a diagram depicting the relationship between the general ledger master file, control accounts, subsidiary files, and financial statements.

2. Financial Reporting Process
The following contains the various steps of the financial reporting process. Place these steps in the proper order and indicate whether each step is a function of the TPS, GLS, or FRS.
- Record transaction in special journal
- Make adjusting entries
- Capture the transaction
- Prepare the post-closing trial balance
- Prepare the adjusted trial balance
- Prepare the financial statements
- Journalize and post the adjusting entries
- Post to the subsidiary ledger
- Post to the general ledger
- Journalize and post the closing entries
- Prepare the unadjusted trial balance

3. Coding Scheme
Devise a coding scheme using block and sequential codes for the following chart of accounts for Jensen Camera Distributors.
- Cash
- Accounts Receivable
- Office Supplies Inventory
- Prepaid Insurance
- Inventory
- Investments in Marketable Securities
- Delivery Truck
- Accumulated Depreciation—Delivery Truck
- Equipment
- Accumulated Depreciation—Equipment
- Furniture and Fixtures
- Accumulated Depreciation—Furniture and Fixtures
- Building
- Accumulated Depreciation—Building
- Land
- Accounts Payable
- Wages Payable
- Taxes Payable
- Notes Payable
- Bonds Payable
- Common Stock
- Paid-In Capital in Excess of Par
- Treasury Stock
- Retained Earnings
- Sales
- Sales Returns and Allowances
- Dividend Income
- Cost of Goods Sold
- Wages Expense
- Utility Expense
- Office Supplies Expense
- Insurance Expense
- Depreciation Expense
- Advertising Expense
- Fuel Expense
- Interest Expense

4. Coding Scheme
Devise a coding scheme for the warehouse layout below. Be sure to use an appropriate coding scheme that allows the inventory to be located efficiently from the picking list.

5. Internal Control
Leslie Epstein, an employee of Bormack Manufacturing Company, prepares journal vouchers for general ledger entries. Due to the large number of voided journal vouchers caused by errors, the journal vouchers are not prenumbered by the printer; rather, Leslie numbers them as she prepares each journal voucher. She does, however, keep a log of all journal vouchers written so that she does not assign the same number to two journal vouchers. Biweekly, Leslie posts the journal vouchers to the general ledger and any necessary subsidiary accounts. Bimonthly, she reconciles the subsidiary accounts to their control accounts in the general ledger and makes sure the general ledger accounts balance.

Required:
Discuss any potential control weaknesses and problems in this scenario.

6. Database GL System
Crystal Corporation processes its journal vouchers using batch procedures similar to the process outlined in Figure 8-5. To improve customer satisfaction, the sales system is going to be converted

Problem 4:
Coding Scheme

WAREHOUSE LAYOUT

Three warehouse locations—Warehouses 1, 2, and 3
Each warehouse is organized by aisles.

Aisle A

Aisle B

Aisle C

Aisle D

Aisle E

WAREHOUSE LAYOUT—(CONT.)

Each aisle is separated into a right and left side, with 7 shelves of goods and 17 partitions, with each storage area called a "bin."

7																	
6																	
5																	
4																	
3																	
2																	
1	1	2	3	4	5	6	7	8	9	10	11	12	13	14	15	16	17

to a real-time system. Redraw Figure 8-5 to reflect this change in the financial reporting process.

7. Database GL System

The top management team at Olympia, Inc., wishes to have real-time access to the general ledger. Currently the general ledger is updated nightly via a batch processing system, similar to Figure 8-5 in the text. Adjust Figure 8-5 to accommodate this request by top management, assuming that the nightly updates to the general ledger are sufficient.

8. Internal Control

Expand 8-6 to incorporate the journal voucher listing and general ledger change report as control mechanisms. Also discuss the specific controls they impose on the system.

9. Organizational Chart

Prepare an organizational chart for your university. (Your campus phone directory catalogue may be helpful.)

10. Decision Level

Classify the following decisions as being characteristic of strategic planning, tactical planning, managerial control, or operational control.

- Determining the mix of products to manufacture this year
- Examining whether the number of defective goods manufactured is within a certain range
- Expanding a product line overseas
- Determining the best distribution route
- Examining whether the cost of raw materials is within a certain range
- Examining whether personnel development cost is rising
- Employing more automated manufacturing this year
- Examining whether the amount of scrap material is acceptable
- Building a new plant facility
- Examining whether employees' attitudes are improving
- Examining whether production levels are within a predicted range
- Making purchasing arrangements with a new supplier
- Increasing production capabilities this year by purchasing a more efficient piece of machinery
- Closing a plant

11. Report Categorization

Classify the following reports as being either scheduled or on-demand reports.

- Cash disbursements listing
- Overtime report
- Customer account history
- Inventory stockout report
- Accounts receivable aging list
- Duplicate paycheck report
- Cash receipts listing
- Machine maintenance report
- Vendor delivery record report
- Journal voucher listing
- Investment center report
- Maintenance cost overrun report

12. CMA Adapted—Organizational Structure and Span of Control

Relco Industries recently purchased Arbeck, Inc., a manufacturer of electrical components used by the construction industry. Roland Ford has been

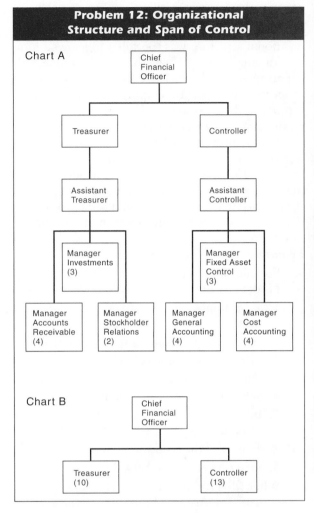

Problem 12: Organizational Structure and Span of Control

appointed as chief financial officer of Arbeck and has been asked by Martha Sanderson, president of Relco, to prepare an organizational chart for his department at Arbeck. The chart that Ford has prepared is shown above.

Ford believes that the treasurer's department should include the following employees: assistant treasurer, manager of accounts receivable and 4 subordinates, manager of investments and 3 subordinates, and manager of stockholder relations and 2 subordinates, for a total of 13 employees besides the treasurer. The controller's department should consist of an assistant controller, a manager of general accounting and 4 subordinates, a manager of fixed asset control and 3 subordinates, and a manager of cost accounting with 4 subordinates, for a total of 15 employees besides the controller.

When Ford presented his plans (Chart A) to Sanderson, she told him that she believed the organizational structure was too tall and showed him, by drawing Chart B, how she had envisioned his department at Arbeck. There would be a reduction in personnel, and 10 employees would report directly to the treasurer, while 13 employees would report directly to the controller.

Ford replied that he believed the span of control was too broad for both the treasurer and the controller and would create problems. Sanderson said that she preferred a flat organizational structure as she believed that its benefits outweighed the problems that could arise from too great a span of control.

Required:

a. For the organizational structure proposed by Ford, chief financial officer, describe the
   1. advantages and disadvantages of that structure.
   2. impact of the resulting span of control.
   3. effect on employee behavior.
b. For the flat organizational structure proposed by Sanderson, president, describe the
   1. advantages and disadvantages of that structure.
   2. impact of the resulting span of control.
   3. effect on employee behavior.
c. When determining the appropriate span of control for Arbeck, Inc., discuss the factors that Ford and Sanderson should consider.

13. CMA Adapted—Organizational Structure and Span of Control

Barnes Corporation recently purchased Parker Machine Company, a manufacturer of sophisticated parts for the aircraft industry. Donald Jenkins has been appointed vice president of production of Parker and has been asked by Beverly Kiner, president of Barnes, to prepare an organizational chart for his department at Parker. The chart that Jenkins prepared is presented in Chart A in the next column.

When Jenkins presented his chart to Kiner, she told him that she preferred a flat organizational structure and showed him how she envisioned his department at Parker by drawing the chart presented in Chart B. Kiner's chart reduced a layer of management personnel and increased the number of

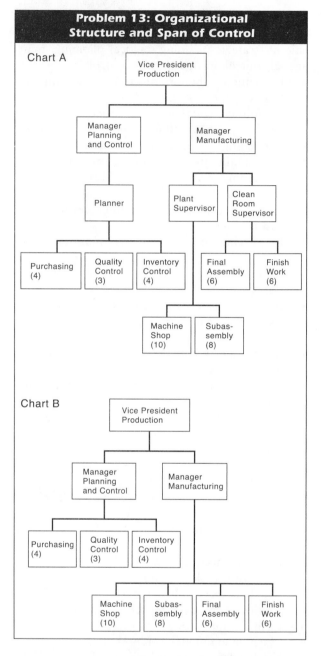

people reporting directly to the manager of planning and control and the manager of manufacturing.

Jenkins expressed concern about the broad span of control depicted in Kiner's chart, as he believed this might cause problems for the two managers. Kiner said that she believed that the benefits of a flat organizational structure outweighed the problems that could arise from too great a span of control.

Required:

a. For the organizational structure proposed by Jenkins, describe
    1. the advantages and disadvantages of that structure.
    2. the impact of the resulting span of control.
    3. the effect of the organizational structure on employee behavior.
b. For the flat organizational structure proposed by Kiner, describe
    1. the advantages and disadvantages of that organizational structure.
    2. the impact of the resulting span of control.
    3. the effect of the organizational structure on employee behavior.
c. When determining the appropriate span of control for Parker Machine Company, discuss the factors that Jenkins and Kiner should consider.

14. CMA Adapted—Organizational Structure

While attending night school to earn a degree in computer engineering, Stan Wilson worked for Morlot Container Company (MCC) as an assembly line supervisor. MCC was located near Wilson's hometown and had been a prominent employer in the area for many years. MCC's main product was milk cartons that were distributed throughout the midwest for use by milk processing plants. The technology at MCC was stable, and the assembly lines were monitored closely. MCC employed a standard cost system because cost control was considered important. The employees who manned the assembly lines were generally unskilled workers who had been with the company for many years; the majority of these workers belonged to the local union.

Wilson was glad he was nearly finished school because he found the work at MCC to be repetitive and boring, even as a supervisor. The supervisors were monitored almost as closely as the line workers, and standard policies and procedures existed that applied to most situations. Most of MCC's management had been with the company for several years and believed in clear lines of authority and well-defined responsibilities. Whereas he knew he had performed well against the company's standards, Wilson also knew that there probably would be little opportunity for advancement or significant compensation increases.

After receiving his degree, Wilson went to work in the research and development department of Alden Computers, a five-year-old company specializing in educational computer systems for elementary schools. The company was customer-oriented and willing to tailor its computer systems to the needs of the end users. The customization of its systems, combined with continual changes in technology, resulted in a job-shop orientation in the company's production facility. The employees who assembled Alden's systems were skilled technicians who worked closely with the engineering staff.

Wilson was gratified by the respect and authority his newly acquired knowledge and skills afforded him at Alden. If changes were required in his area of expertise, Wilson often made recommendations about how the work should proceed and was involved in decisions on new product development. The company's management team frequently "rolled up its sleeves" and worked alongside the technicians when production problems arose; the lines of authority were sometimes difficult to distinguish, and decisions were often made by the expert on the spot. Wilson believed that his skills were appreciated at Alden, and he would be fairly compensated for his professional expertise.

Required:

a. Morlot Container Company and Alden Computers represent two different types of organizational structures. In terms of each of the following points, explain how MCC differs from Alden Computers.
    1. General organizational structure and climate
    2. Bases of authority
    3. Evaluation criteria
    4. Bases of compensation
b. Both structures have potential benefits or can create problems. Discuss the features of the
    1. structure used by Alden Computers that might benefit MCC.
    2. structure used by Alden that might create problems for Alden.
    3. structure used by MCC that might benefit Alden Computers.

15. CMA Adapted—Performance Measures

The Star Paper Division of Royal Industries is located near Los Angeles. A major expansion of the division's only plant was completed in April 2004. The expansion consisted of an addition to the existing building, additions to the production-line machinery, and the replacement of obsolete and fully depreciated equipment that was no longer efficient or cost effective.

On May 1, 2004, George Harris became manager of Star. Harris had a meeting with Marie Fortner, vice president of operations for Royal, who explained to Harris that the company measured the performance of divisions and division managers on the basis of return on gross assets (ROA). When Harris asked if other measures were used in conjunction with ROA, Fortner replied, "Royal's top management prefers to use a single performance measure. Star should do well this year now that it has expanded and replaced all of that old equipment. You should have no problem exceeding the division's historical rate. I'll check with you at the end of each quarter to see how you are doing."

Fortner called Harris after the first quarter results were completed because Star's ROA was considerably below the historical rate for the division. Harris told Fortner that he did not believe that ROA was a valid performance measure for Star. Fortner indicated that she would discuss this with others at headquarters and get back to Harris. However, there was no further discussion of the use of ROA, only reports on divisional performance at the end of the second and third quarters. Now that the fiscal year has ended, Harris has received the memorandum shown in the next column.

Harris is looking forward to meeting with Fortner as he plans to pursue the discussion about the appropriateness of ROA as a performance measure for Star. While the ROA for Star is below historical levels, the division's profits for the year are higher than at any previous time. Harris is going to recommend that ROA be replaced with multiple criteria for evaluating performance—namely, dollar profit, receivable turnover, and inventory turnover.

Required:

a. Identify general criteria that should be used in selecting performance measures to evaluate operating managers.

b. Describe the probable cause of the decline in the Star Paper Division's return on gross assets during the fiscal year ended April 30, 2004.

**Problem 15:
Performance Measures**

TO: George Harris, Star Paper Division
FROM: Marie Fortner, Royal Industries
SUBJECT: Divisional Performance

The operating results for the fourth quarter and for our fiscal year ended on April 30 are now complete. Your fourth quarter return on gross assets was only 9 percent, resulting in a return for the year of slightly under 11 percent. I recall discussing your low return after the first quarter and reminding you after the second and third quarters that this level of return is not considered adquate for the Star Paper Division.

The return on gross assets at Star has ranged from 15 to 18 percent for the past five years. An 11 percent return may be acceptable at some of Royal's other divisions, but not at a proven winner like Star, especially in light of your recently improved facility. Please arrance to meet with me in the near future to discuss ways to restore Star's return on gross assets to its former level.

c. On the basis of the relationship between Fortner and Harris, as well as the memorandum from Fortner, discuss apparent weaknesses in the performance evaluation process at Royal Industries.

d. Discuss whether the multiple performance evaluation criteria suggested by Harris would be appropriate for the evaluation of the Star Paper Division.

16. CMA Adapted—Responsibility Accounting

Family Resorts, Inc., is a holding company for several vacation hotels in the northeastern and mid-Atlantic states. The firm originally purchased several old inns, restored the buildings, and upgraded the recreational facilities. The inns have been well received by vacationing families because many services are provided that accommodate children and afford parents time for themselves. Since the completion of the restoration 10 years ago, the company has been profitable.

Family Resorts has just concluded its annual meeting of regional and district managers. This meeting is held each November to review the

---

Problem 16:
Responsibility Accounting

FAMILY RESORTS, INC.
RESPONSIBILITY SUMMARY
($000 omitted)

Reporting Unit: Family Resorts		Reporting Unit: Maine District	
Responsible Person: President		Responsible Person: District Manager	
Mid-Atlantic Region	$ 605	Harbor Inn	$ 80
New England Region	365	Camden Country Inn	60
Unallocated costs	(160)	Unallocated costs	(35)
Income before taxes	$ 810	Total contribution	$ 105
Reporting Unit: New England Region		Reporting Unit: Harbor Inn	
Responsible Person: Regional Manager		Responsible Person: Innkeeper	
Vermont	$ 200	Revenue	$ 600
New Hampshire	140	Controllable costs	(455)
Maine	105	Allocated costs	(65)
Unallocated costs	(80)		
		Total contribution	$ 80
Total contribution	$ 365		

---

results of the previous season and to help the managers prepare for the upcoming year. Before the meeting, the managers submitted proposed budgets for their districts or regions as appropriate. These budgets have been reviewed and consolidated into an annual operating budget for the entire company. The 2004 budget has been presented at the meeting and was accepted by the managers.

To evaluate the performance of its managers, Family Resorts uses responsibility accounting. Therefore, the preparation of the budget is given close attention at headquarters. If major changes need to be made to the budgets submitted by the managers, all affected parties are consulted before the changes are incorporated. On this page and the next are two pages from the budget booklet that all managers received at the meeting.

Required:

a. Responsibility accounting has been used effectively by many companies, both large and small.
   1. Define responsibility accounting.
   2. Discuss the benefits that accrue to a company using responsibility accounting.
   3. Describe the advantages of responsibility accounting for the managers of a firm.
b. Family Resorts' budget was accepted by the regional and district managers. Based on the

facts presented, evaluate the budget process employed by Family Resorts by addressing the following:
   1. What features of the budget presentation shown are likely to make the budget attractive to managers?
   2. What recommendations, if any, could be made to the budget preparers to improve the budget process? Explain your answer.

17. CMA Adapted—Management by Exception

Some executives believe that it is extremely important to manage "by numbers." This form of management requires that all employees with departmental or divisional responsibilities spend time understanding the company's operations and how they are reflected by the company's financial reports. Because of the managers' increased comprehension of the financial reports and the activities that they represent, their subordinates will become more attuned to the meaning of financial reports and the important signposts that can be detected in these reports. Companies use a variety of numerical measurement systems, including standard costs, financial ratios, human resource forecasts, and operating budgets.

Problem 16:
Responsibility Accounting

FAMILY RESORTS, INC.
CONDENSED OPERATING BUDGET—MAINE DISTRICT
FOR THE YEAR ENDING DECEMBER 31, 2003
($000 OMITTED)

	Family Resorts	Region		New England District					Maine District Inns	
		Mid-Atlantic	New England	Not Allocated[1]	Vermont	New Hampshire	Maine	Not Allocated[2]	Harbor	Camden Country
Net sales	$7,900	$4,200	$3,700		$1,400	$1,200	$1,100		$600	$500
Cost of sales	4,530	2,310	2,220		840	720	660		360	300
Gross margin	$3,370	$1,890	$1,480		$ 560	$ 480	$ 440		$240	$200
Controllable expenses:										
Supervisory	$ 240	$ 130	$ 110		$ 35	$ 30	$ 45	$ 10	$20	$ 15
Training	160	80	80		30	25	25		15	10
Advertising	500	280	220	$ 50	55	60	55	15	20	20
Repairs and maintenance	480	225	255		90	85	80		40	40
Total controllable expenses	$1,380	$ 715	$ 665	$ 50	$ 210	$ 200	$ 205	$ 25	$95	$ 85
Controllable contribution	$1,990	$1,175	$ 815	$(50)	$ 350	$ 280	$ 235	$(25)	$145	$115
Expenses controlled by others:										
Depreciation	$ 520	$ 300	$ 220	$ 30	$ 70	$ 60	$ 60	$ 10	$30	$ 20
Property taxes	200	120	80		30	30	20		10	10
Insurance	300	150	150		50	50	50		25	25
Total expenses controlled by others	$1,020	$ 570	$ 450	$ 30	$ 150	$ 140	$ 130	$ 10	$65	$ 55
Total contribution	$ 970	$ 605	$ 365	$(80)	$ 200	$ 140	$ 105	$(35)	$80	$ 60
Unallocated costs[3]	160									
Income before taxes	$ 810									

[1]Unallocated expenses include a regional advertising campaign and equipment used by the regional manager.
[2]Unallocated expenses include a portion of the district manager's salary, district promotion costs, and a district manager's car.
[3]Unallocated costs include taxes on undeveloped real estate, headquarters' expense, legal fees, and audit fees.

Required:

a. Discuss the following aspects of a standard cost system.

 1. Discuss the characteristics that should be present to encourage positive employee motivation.

 2. Discuss how the system should be implemented to positively motivate employees.

b. The use of variance analysis often results in management by exception.

 1. Explain the meaning of "management by exception."

 2. Discuss the behavioral implications of management by exception.

c. Explain how employee behavior could be adversely affected when actual-to-budget comparisons are used as the basis for performance evaluation.

18. CMA Adapted—Variance Analysis

Engineers Education Association (EEA) is a volunteer membership organization providing educational and professional services to its members. The professional staff is organized into four divisions with a total of 14 operating departments.

EEA adopted an annual budget program many years ago as a means for planning and controlling activities. Each department of EEA prepares an annual budget in consultation with its respective volunteer committee(s). After a series of reviews by both the professional staff and the volunteer structure, the budget is adopted. The professional staff is expected to comply with the budget in conducting its activities and operations.

The EEA's accounting department generates monthly income statements that present actual performance as compared to budget for each department of EEA. The November 2007 statement for the publications department is reproduced in the next column. Accompanying the report this month was a memorandum from EEA's president, Daniel Riley, which is presented on the following page.

Marie Paige, publications manager, was having lunch with Jon Franklin, continuing education manager, when the following conversation about Riley's memorandum took place.

Problem 18: Variance Analysis

EEA—PUBLICATIONS DEPARTMENT
INCOME STATEMENT
FOR THE MONTH ENDED NOVEMBER 30, 2007
($000 OMITTED)

	Budget	Actual	Variance Dollar	Variance Percent
Revenues				
Subscriptions	$ 9.5	$ 8.4	$ (1.1)	(11.6)
Library subscriptions	3.4	3.3	(.1)	(2.9)
Research publications	13.6	15.2	1.6	11.8
Advertising	64.0	50.1	(13.9)	(21.7)
List rentals	15.2	13.9	(1.3)	(8.6)
Total revenue	$105.7	$90.9	$(14.8)	(14.0)
Operating expenses				
Salaries and wages	$ 24.0	$22.0	$ 2.0	8.3
Employee benefits	4.8	4.4	.4	8.3
Temporary help	0.0	1.5	(1.5)	(ERR)
Outside services	1.0	2.5	(1.5)	(150.0)
Education and training	0.5	0.0	.5	100.0
Promotion and advertising	7.5	4.0	3.5	46.6
Typesetting	8.0	12.0	(4.0)	(50.0)
Production printing	46.0	40.4	5.6	12.2
Postage, freight, and handling	12.0	11.0	1.0	8.3
Supplies	1.0	.8	.2	20.0
Total expenses	$104.8	$98.6	$ 6.2	5.9
Contribution	$ .9	$ (7.7)	$ (8.6)	(955.6)

Paige: The volunteers must be giving Riley some static—the memo doesn't sound like him.

Franklin: I think you're right. One of EEA's problems is that membership is down.

Paige: I heard that both growth and retention are bad. This is confirmed by my results. A set percentage of the membership dues of each member is assigned to us each month for the magazine subscription. This amount is down 12 percent. I have no control over this number because only members get the magazine.

Problem 18:
Variance Analysis

December 12, 2007

TO: Department Managers
FROM: Daniel Riley, President
SUBJECT: Performance Analysis

The November 2007 operating results for your department are attached. The results for the entire organization and most departments are unfavorable as compared to budget. In fact, our results for the first three months of this fiscal year are substantially below budget.

I want to determine our problems as quickly as possible. Prepare an explanation of all unfavorable (negative) variances by line item that exceed budget by 5 percent or more, and present a plan to eliminate such variances in the future. Remember that you played a key role in the development of the budget and you have a responsibility to achieve the budget figures. These negative variances must be eliminated if we are to get back on steam.

Please submit your analysis to your divisional director and accounting by noon, Monday, December 17. Divisional directors will meet at 10 A.M. on Tuesday, December 18, to review these analyses.

Franklin: I wonder if the results are really as bad as they look. For instance, accounting has divided all of the annual budget figures by 12 to derive the monthly figures. This is okay for some things but not for most. What about you?

Paige: I agree. I don't know why they do that when we spend so much time up front developing the annual budget. I know what Riley is attempting, but I don't think he is going to get the results he wants. I know he wants to eliminate the negative variances, but some positive variances are really not favorable! We should be analyzing all significant variances—positive and negative.

Franklin: What are you going to do—analyze just the negatives? Should we do anything before we prepare our reports?

Required:

a. The monthly income statements prepared by EEA's accounting department for each department of EEA are a form of communication.
   1. Explain why the departmental income statements are considered a form of communication.
   2. In terms of the format of the income statement presented for the publications department, evaluate EEA's departmental income statement as a communication device.

b. Paige stated that all significant variances should be analyzed because some positive variances are not favorable. Discuss why EEA's departments should be analyzing all significant variances, both positive (favorable) and negative (unfavorable). As support for your answer, identify a positive variance from the publications department's income statement that may not be favorable to EEA's operations and explain why.

c. Recommend a course of action that Paige or Franklin could take to encourage Riley to have all significant variances reviewed.

part 3

ADVANCED TECHNOLOGIES IN ACCOUNTING INFORMATION

chapter 9

Database Management Systems

LEARNING OBJECTIVES

After studying this chapter, you should:

- Understand the operational problems inherent in the flat-file approach to data management that gave rise to the database concept.
- Understand the relationships among the defining elements of the database environment.
- Understand the anomalies caused by unnormalized databases and the need for data normalization.
- Be familiar with the stages in database design including entity identification, data modeling, constructing the physical database, and preparing user views.
- Be familiar with the operational features of distributed databases and recognize the issues that need to be considered in deciding on a particular database configuration.

This chapter deals with the database approach to managing an organization's data resources. The database model is a particular philosophy whose objectives are supported by specific strategies, techniques, hardware, and software that are very different from those associated with flat-file environments.

Chapter 1 drew a distinction between two general data-management approaches: the flat-file model and the database model. Because the best way to present the virtues of the database model is by contrast with the flat-file model, the first section of this chapter examines how traditional flat-file problems are resolved under the database approach. Important features of modern relational databases are covered later in the chapter. The second section describes in detail the functions and relationship between four primary elements of the database environment: the users, the database management system (DBMS), the database administrator (DBA), and the physical database. The third section is devoted to an in-depth explanation of the characteristics of the relational model. A number of database design topics are covered including data modeling, deriving relational tables from ER diagrams, the creation of user views, and data normalization techniques. The fourth section concludes the chapter with a discussion of distributed database issues. It examines three possible database configurations in a distributed environment: centralized, partitioned, and replicated databases.

OVERVIEW OF THE FLAT-FILE VS. DATABASE APPROACH

Figure 9-1 illustrates the **flat-file** approach to data management. In this environment users *own* their data files. Exclusive ownership of data is a natural consequence of two problems associated with the legacy-system era. The first is a business culture that erects barriers between organizational units that inhibits entity-wide integration of data. The second problem stems from limitations in flat-file management technology that requires data files to be structured to the unique needs of the primary user. Thus the same data, used in slightly different ways by different users, may need to be restructured and reproduced in physically different files. To illustrate, the contents of the files in Figure 9-1 are represented conceptually with letters. Each letter could signify a single **data attribute** (field), a record, or an entire file. Note also that data element B is present in all user files. This is called "**data redundancy**," and is the cause of significant data management problems in three areas: **data storage, data updating**, and **currency of information**. Each of these, as well as a fourth problem—**task-data dependency**, which is not directly related to data redundancy—will be examined next.

DATA STORAGE

Chapter 1 showed that an efficient information system captures and stores data only once and makes this single source available to all users who need it. In the flat-file environment this is not possible. To meet the private data needs of users, organizations must incur the costs of both multiple collection and multiple storage procedures. Some commonly used data may be duplicated dozens, hundreds, or even thousands of times, creating excessive storage costs.

DATA UPDATING

Organizations have a great deal of data stored on master files and reference files that require periodic updating to reflect operational and economic changes. For example, a change in a customer's name or address must be reflected in the appropriate master files. This piece of information may be important to several user departments in the organization such as sales, billing, credit, customer services, sales promotion, and catalog sales. When users keep separate files, any such change must be made separately for each user. This adds significantly to the cost of data management.

CURRENCY OF INFORMATION

In contrast to the problem of performing multiple updates is the problem of failing to update the files of all users affected by a change. If update messages are not properly disseminated, then some users may not record the change and will perform their duties and make decisions based on outdated data.

TASK-DATA DEPENDENCY

Another problem with the flat-file approach is the user's inability to obtain additional information as his or her needs change. This problem is called *task-data dependency*. The user's information set is constrained by the data that he or she possesses and controls. For example, in Figure 9-1, if the information needs of User 1 change to include Data L, User 1's program would not have access to these data. Although Data L exists in the files of another user, keep in mind the culture of this environment. Users do not interact as members of a user community. They act independently. As such, User 1 may be unaware of the presence of Data L elsewhere in the organization. In this environment, it is difficult to establish a mechanism for the formal sharing of data. Therefore, Data L would need to be created from scratch. This will take time, inhibit User 1's performance, add to data redundancy, and drive data management costs even higher.

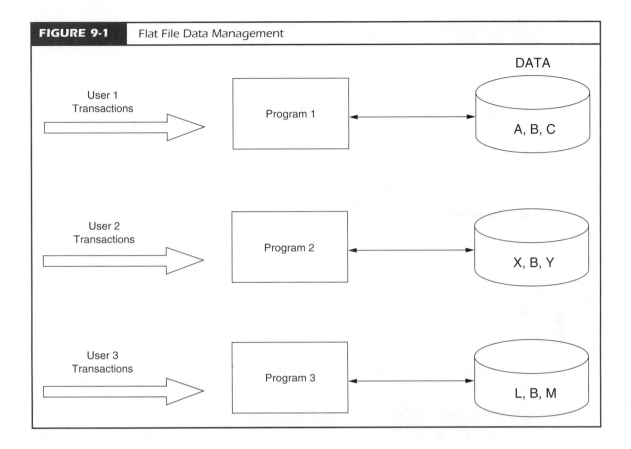

FIGURE 9-1   Flat File Data Management

THE DATABASE APPROACH

Figure 9-2(a) presents a simple overview of the database approach with the same users and data requirements as in Figure 9-1. The most obvious change from the flat-file model is the pooling of data into a common database that is shared by all the users.

FLAT-FILE PROBLEMS SOLVED

Data sharing (the absence of ownership) is the central concept of the database approach. Let's see how this resolves the problems identified.

- *No data redundancy.* Each data element is stored only once, thereby eliminating data redundancy and reducing storage costs.

- *Single update.* Because each data element exists in only one place, it requires only a single update procedure. This reduces the time and cost of keeping the database current.

- *Current values.* A change to the database made by any user yields current data values for all other users. For example, when User 1 records a customer address change User 3 has immediate access to this current information.

- *Task-data independence.* Users have access to the full domain of data available to the firm. As users' information needs expand beyond their immediate domain, the new needs can be more easily satisfied than under the flat-file approach. Users are constrained only by the limitations of the data available to the firm (the entire database) and the legitimacy of their need to access it.

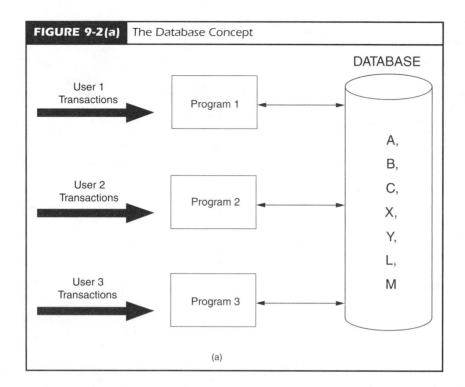

FIGURE 9-2(a)   The Database Concept

(a)

CONTROLLING ACCESS TO THE DATABASE

The database approach places all the firm's information eggs in one basket. It becomes critical, therefore, to take very good care of the basket. The example in Figure 9-2(a) has no provision for controlling access to the database. Assume Data X is sensitive, confidential, or secret information that only User 3 is authorized to access. How can the organization prevent others from gaining unauthorized access to it?

THE DATABASE MANAGEMENT SYSTEM

Figure 9-2(b) adds a new element to Figure 9-2(a). Standing between the users' programs and the physical database is the **database management system** (**DBMS**). The purpose of the DBMS is to provide controlled access to the database. The DBMS is a special software system that is programmed to know which data elements each user is authorized to access. The user's program sends requests for data to the DBMS, which validates and authorizes access to the database in accordance with the user's level of authority. If the user requests data that he or she is not authorized to access, the request is denied. As you might imagine, the organization's procedures for assigning user authority are important control issues for accountants to consider.

THREE CONCEPTUAL MODELS

The database approach is not represented by a single architecture. Early database models are as different from modern database models as they were from traditional flat files. The most common database approaches used for business information systems are the **hierarchical**, the **network**, and the **relational models**. Because of certain conceptual similarities, the hierarchical and network databases are termed **navigational** or **structured models**. The way that data are organized in these early database systems forces users to

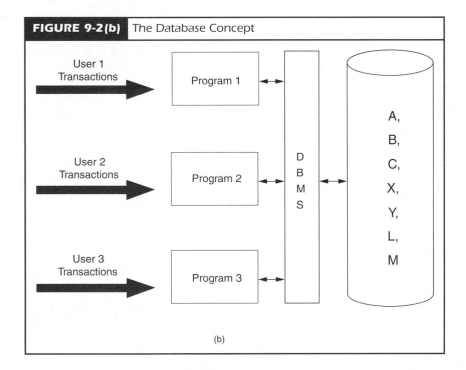

FIGURE 9-2(b) | The Database Concept

navigate between data elements using predefined *structured* paths. The relational model is far more flexible by allowing users to create new and unique paths through the database to solve a wider range of business problems.

Although their limitations are severe and their demise is inevitable, hierarchical and network models still exist as legacy systems that support mission-critical functions in some companies. Most modern systems, however, employ relational databases. The main text of the chapter focuses on the relational model. The key features of structured database models are outlined in the appendix to this chapter.

ELEMENTS OF THE DATABASE ENVIRONMENT

Figure 9-3 presents a breakdown of the database environment into four primary elements: *users*, the *DBMS*, the *database administrator*, and the *physical database*. In this section we examine each of these elements.

USERS

Figure 9-3 shows how **users** access the database in two ways. First, access can be achieved via user programs prepared by systems professionals. User programs send data access requests (calls) to the DBMS, which validates the requests and retrieves the data for processing. Under this mode of access, the presence of the DBMS is transparent to the users. Data processing procedures (both batch and real-time) for transactions such as sales, cash receipts, and purchases are essentially the same as they would be in the flat-file environment.

The second method of database access is via direct query, which requires no formal user programs. The DBMS has a built-in query facility that allows authorized users to process data independent of professional programmers. The query facility provides a

FIGURE 9-3	Elements of the Database Concept

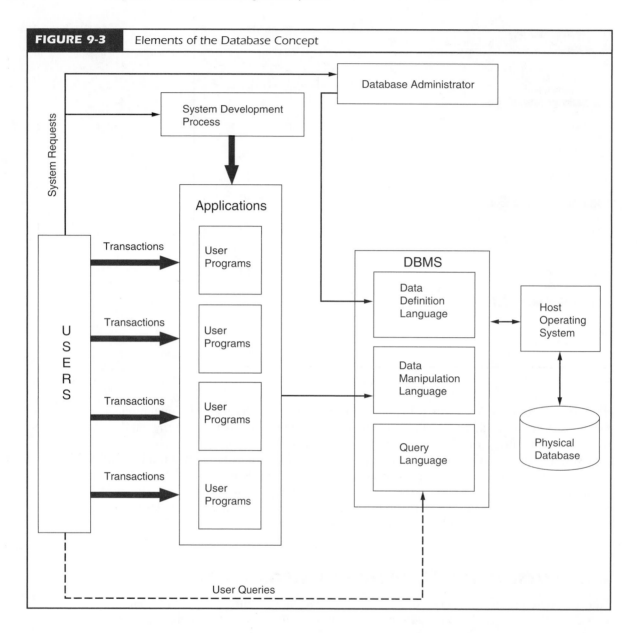

"friendly" environment for integrating and retrieving data to produce ad hoc management reports. This feature is an attractive incentive for users to adopt the database approach.

DATABASE MANAGEMENT SYSTEM

The second element of the database approach depicted in Figure 9-3 is the database management system. The DBMS provides a controlled environment to assist (or prevent) user access to the database and to efficiently manage the data resource. Each DBMS model accomplishes these objectives differently, but some typical features include:

1. *Program development.* The DBMS contains **application development software**. Both programmers and end users may employ this feature to create applications to access the database.

2. *Backup and recovery.* During processing, the DBMS periodically makes backup copies of the physical database. In the event of a disaster (e.g., disk failure, program error, or malicious act) that renders the database unusable, the DBMS can recover an earlier version that is known to be correct. Although some data loss may occur, without the backup and recovery feature the database would be vulnerable to total destruction.
3. *Database usage reporting.* This feature captures statistics on what data are being used, when they are used, and who uses them. The database administrator (DBA) uses this information to help in assigning user authorization and in maintaining the database. We discuss the role of the DBA later in this section.
4. *Database access.* The most important feature of a DBMS is to permit authorized user access to the database. Figure 9-3 shows the three software modules that facilitate this task. These are the data definition language, data manipulation language, and the query language.

Data Definition Language

Data definition language (DDL) is a programming language used to define the physical database to the DBMS. The definition includes the names and the relationship of all data elements, records, and files that constitute the database. There are three levels, called *views*, in this definition: the internal view, the conceptual view (schema), and the user view (subschema). Figure 9-4 shows the relationship between these views.

Internal View. The **internal view** presents the physical arrangement of records in the database. This is the lowest level of representation, which is one step removed from the physical database. The internal view describes the structure of records, the linkages between them, and the physical arrangement and sequence of records in a file. There is only one internal view of the database.

Conceptual View (Schema). The conceptual view or **schema** represents the database logically and abstractly, rather than the way it is physically stored. This view allows users' programs to call for data without knowing or needing to specify how the data are arranged or where the data reside in the physical database. There is only one conceptual view for a database.

User View (Subschema). The **user view** defines how a particular user sees the database. This is the portion of the database that an individual user is authorized to access. To the user, the user view *is* the database. Unlike the internal and conceptual views, there are many distinct user views. For example, a user in the personnel department may view the database as a collection of employee records and is unaware of the supplier and inventory records seen by the users in the inventory-control department.

DBMS Operation. To illustrate the roles of these views, let's look at the typical sequence of events that occurs in accessing data through a DBMS. The following description is hypothetical, and certain technical details are omitted.

1. A user program sends a request (call) for data to the DBMS. The call is written in a special data manipulation language (discussed later) that is embedded in the user program.
2. The DBMS analyzes the request by matching the called data elements against the user view and the conceptual view. If the data request matches, it is authorized and processing proceeds to Step 3. If it does not match the views access is denied.

FIGURE 9-4	Overview of DBMS Operation

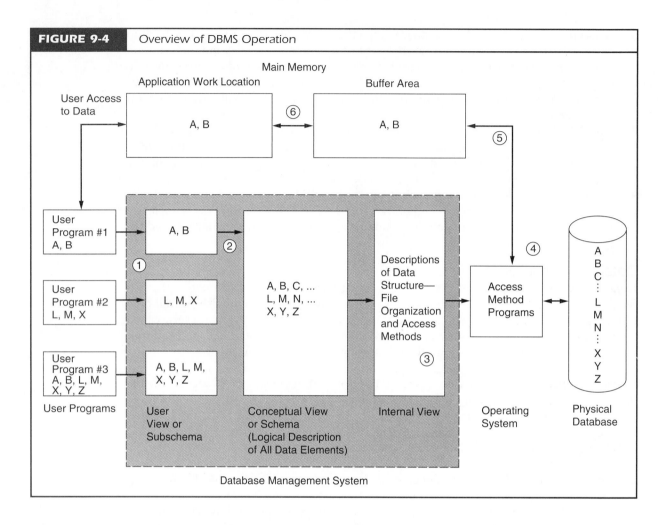

3. The DBMS determines the data structure parameters from the internal view and passes them to the operating system, which performs the actual data retrieval. Data structure parameters describe the organization and **access method** (an operating system utility program) for retrieving the requested data.

4. Using the appropriate access method, the operating system interacts with the disk storage device to retrieve the data from the physical database.

5. The operating system then stores the data in a main memory buffer area managed by the DBMS.

6. The DBMS transfers the data to the user's work location in main memory. At this point, the user's program is free to access and manipulate the data.

7. When processing is complete, Steps 4, 5, and 6 are reversed to restore the processed data to the database.

Data Manipulation Language

Data manipulation language (DML) is the proprietary programming language that a particular DBMS uses to retrieve, process, and store data. Entire user programs may be written in the DML or, alternatively, selected DML commands can be inserted into programs that are written in universal languages, such as PL/1, COBOL, and FORTRAN. Inserting

DML commands enables standard programs, which were originally written for the flat-file environment, to be easily converted to work in a database environment. The use of standard language programs also provides the organization with a degree of independence from the DBMS vendor. If the organization decides to switch its vendors to one that uses a different DML, it will not be necessary to rewrite all the user programs. By replacing the old DML commands with the new commands, user programs can be modified to function in the new environment.

Query Language

The query capability of the DBMS permits end users and professional programmers to access data in the database directly without the need for conventional programs. IBM's **structured query language** (**SQL**, pronounced "*sequel*") has emerged as the standard query language for both mainframe and microcomputer DBMSs. SQL is a fourth-generation, nonprocedural language with many commands that allow users to input, retrieve, and modify data easily. The SELECT command is a powerful tool for retrieving data. The example in Figure 9-5 illustrates the use of the SELECT command to produce a user report from a database called Inventory.

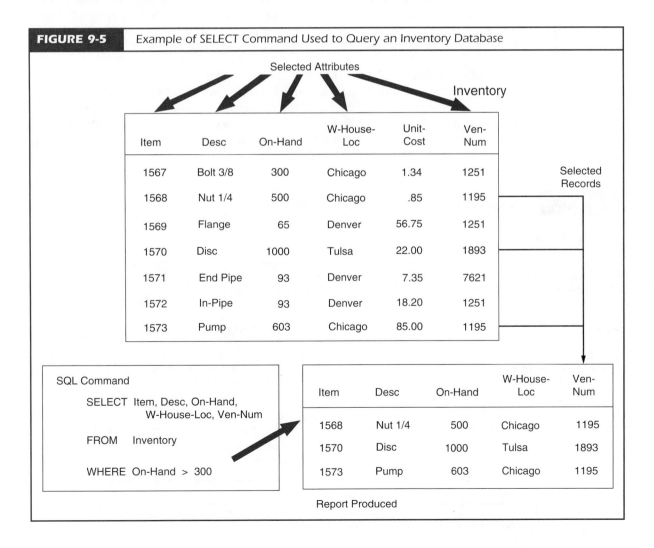

FIGURE 9-5   Example of SELECT Command Used to Query an Inventory Database

SQL is an efficient data-processing tool. Although not a natural English language, SQL requires far less training in computer concepts and fewer programming skills than many languages. In fact, many database query systems require no SQL knowledge at all. Users select data visually by "pointing and clicking" at the desired attributes. The visual user interface then generates the necessary SQL commands automatically. This feature places ad hoc reporting and data-processing capability in the hands of the user/manager. By reducing reliance on professional programmers, managers are better able to deal with problems that "pop up."

DATABASE ADMINISTRATOR

Refer to Figure 9-3 and note the administrative position of **database administrator** (**DBA**). This position does not exist in the flat-file environment. The DBA is responsible for managing the database resource. The sharing of a common database by multiple users requires organization, coordination, rules, and guidelines to protect the integrity of the database.

In large organizations the DBA function may consist of an entire department of technical personnel under the database administrator. In smaller organizations DBA responsibility may be assumed by someone within the computer services group. The duties of the DBA fall into the following areas:[1] database planning, database design, database implementation, database operation and maintenance, and database change and growth. Table 9-1 presents a breakdown of specific tasks within these broad areas.

Organizational Interactions of the DBA

Figure 9-6 shows some of the organizational interfaces of the DBA. Of particular importance is the relationship among the DBA, the end users, and the systems professionals of the organization. Refer again to Figure 9-3 during the examination of this relationship.

As information needs arise, users send formal requests for computer applications to the systems professionals (programmers) of the organization. The requests are handled through

TABLE 9-1	Functions of the Database Administrator
Database Planning:	**Implementation:**
Develop organization's database strategy Define database environment Define data requirements Develop data dictionary	Determine access policy Implement security controls Specify test procedures Establish programming standards
Design:	**Operation and Maintenance:**
Logical database (schema) External users' views (subschemas) Internal view of database Database controls	Evaluate database performance Reorganize database as user needs demand Review standards and procedures
	Change and Growth:
	Plan for change and growth Evaluate new technology

---

1   Adapted from F. R. McFadden and J. A. Hoffer, *Database Management*, 3rd ed. (Redwood City, CA: Benjamin/Cummings Publishing, 1991): 343.

FIGURE 9-6 | Organizational Interactions of the Database Administrator

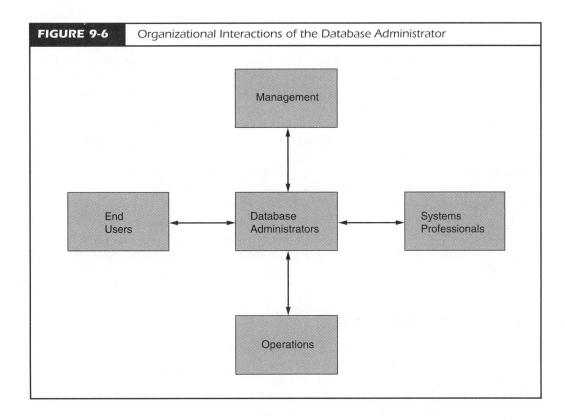

---

formal systems development procedures, which produce the programmed applications. Figure 9-3 shows this relationship as the line from the users block to the systems development process block. The user requests also go to the DBA, who evaluates these to determine the user's database needs. Once this is established, the DBA grants the user access authority by programming the user's view (subschema). This relationship is shown as the lines between the user and the DBA and between the DBA and DDL module in the DBMS. By keeping access authority separate from systems development (application programming), the organization is better able to control and protect the database. Intentional and unintentional attempts at unauthorized access are more likely to be discovered when these two groups work independently. The rationale for this separation of duties is developed in Chapter 15.

The Data Dictionary

Another important function of the DBA is the creation and maintenance of the **data dictionary**. The data dictionary describes every data element in the database. This enables all users (and programmers) to share a common view of the data resource, and greatly facilitates the analysis of user needs.

THE PHYSICAL DATABASE

The fourth major element of the database approach as presented in Figure 9-3 is the **physical database**. This is the lowest level of the database. The physical database consists of magnetic spots on magnetic disks. The other levels of the database (e.g., the user view, conceptual view, and internal view) are abstract representations of the physical level.

At the physical level, the database is a collection of records and files. Relational databases are based on the **indexed sequential file** structure. This structure, illustrated in Figure 9-7, uses an index in conjunction with a sequential file organization. It facilitates both direct access to individual records and batch processing of the entire file. Multiple indexes can be used to create a cross-reference, called an **inverted list**, which allows even more flexible access to data. Two indexes are shown in Figure 9-7. One contains the employee number (primary key) for uniquely locating records in the file. The second index contains record addresses arranged by year-to-date earnings. Using this nonunique field as a secondary key permits all employee records to be viewed in ascending or descending order according to earnings. Alternatively, individual records with selected earnings balances can be displayed. Indexes may be created for each attribute in the file, allowing data to be viewed from a multitude of perspectives.

The next section examines the principles that underlay the relational model and the techniques, rules, and procedures for creating relational tables from indexed sequential files. You will also see how tables are linked to other tables to permit complex, data representations.

THE RELATIONAL DATABASE MODEL

E. F. Codd originally proposed the principles of the relational model in the late 1960s.[2] The formal model has its foundations in relational algebra and set theory, which provide the theoretical basis for most of the data manipulation operations used.

From a purist's point of view, a fully relational system is one that conforms to 12 stringent rules outlined by Codd.[3] As a practical matter, however, not all of Codd's rules are equally important. Some are critical but some are not. Other theorists have, therefore, proposed less rigid requirements for assessing the relational standing of a system.[4] Accordingly, a system is relational if it:

1. Represents data in the form of two-dimensional tables such as the database table, called Customer, shown in Figure 9-8.
2. Supports the relational algebra functions of *restrict*, *project*, and *join*.

FIGURE 9-7	Indexed Sequential File

Emp Num Index

Key Value	Record Address
101	1
102	2
103	3
104	4
105	5

Employee Table

Emp Num	Name	Address	Skill Code	YTD Earnings
101	L. Smith	15 Main St.	891	15000
102	S. Buell	107 Hill Top	379	10000
103	T. Hill	40 Barclay St.	891	20000
104	M. Green	251 Ule St.	209	19000
105	H. Litt	423 Rauch Ave.	772	18000

YTD Earnings Index

Key Value	Address
20000	3
19000	4
18000	5
15000	1
10000	2

2   C. J. Date, *An Introduction to Database Systems*, Vol. 1, 4th ed. (Reading, MA: Addison-Wesley, 1986): 99.
3   For a complete discussion of these rules see McFadden and Hoffer, *Database Management*: 698–703.
4   Date, *An Introduction to Database Systems*: 320–26.

FIGURE 9-8   A Relational Table Called Customer

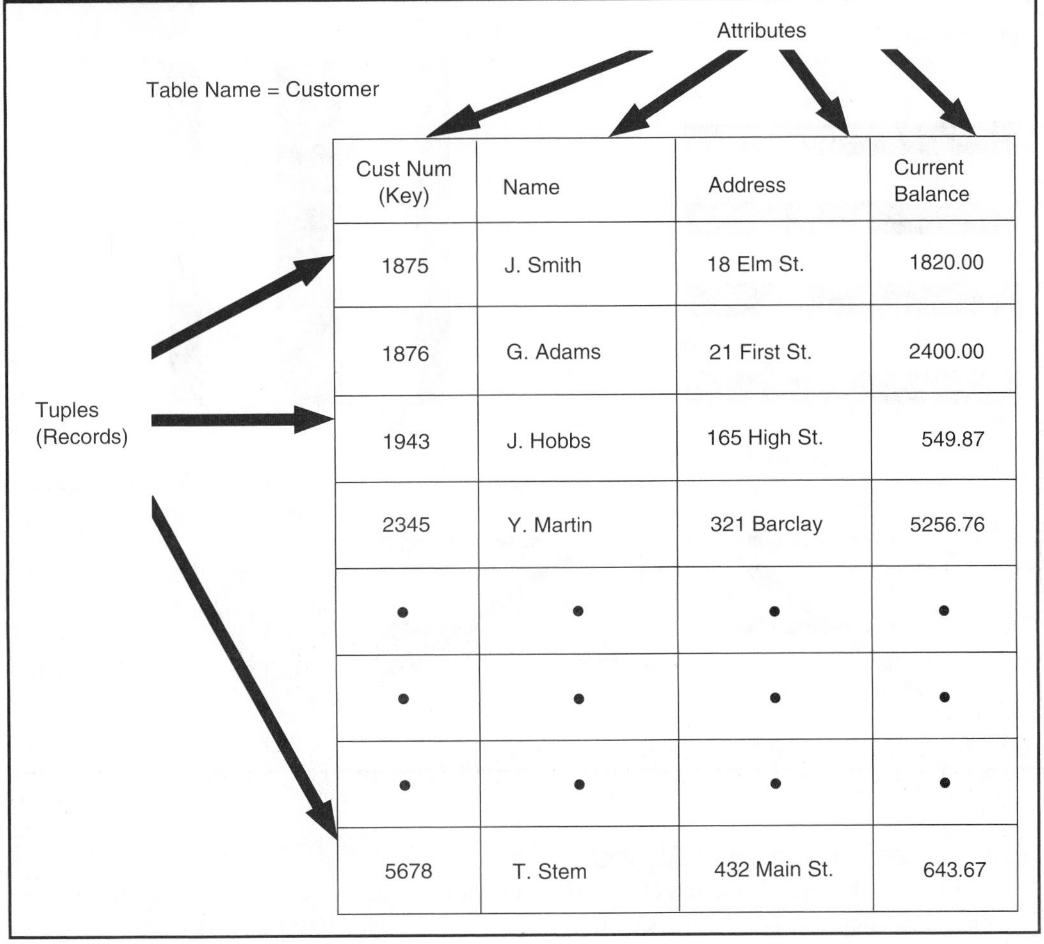

Attributes

Table Name = Customer

Cust Num (Key)	Name	Address	Current Balance
1875	J. Smith	18 Elm St.	1820.00
1876	G. Adams	21 First St.	2400.00
1943	J. Hobbs	165 High St.	549.87
2345	Y. Martin	321 Barclay	5256.76
•	•	•	•
•	•	•	•
•	•	•	•
5678	T. Stem	432 Main St.	643.67

Tuples (Records)

These functions are examined in the following section.

Restrict: Extracts specified rows from a specified table. This operation, illustrated in Figure 9-9(a), creates a virtual table (one that does not physically exist) that is a subset of the original table.

Project: Extracts specified attributes (columns) from a table to create a virtual table. This is presented in Figure 9-9(b).

Join: Builds a new physical table from two tables consisting of all concatenated pairs of rows, from each table. See Figure 9-9(c).

Although restrict, project, and join is not the complete set of relational functions, it is a useful subset that satisfies most business information needs.

RELATIONAL DATABASE CONCEPTS

In this section we review basic concepts, terminology, and techniques common to relational database systems. These building blocks are then used later in the chapter to design a small database from scratch.

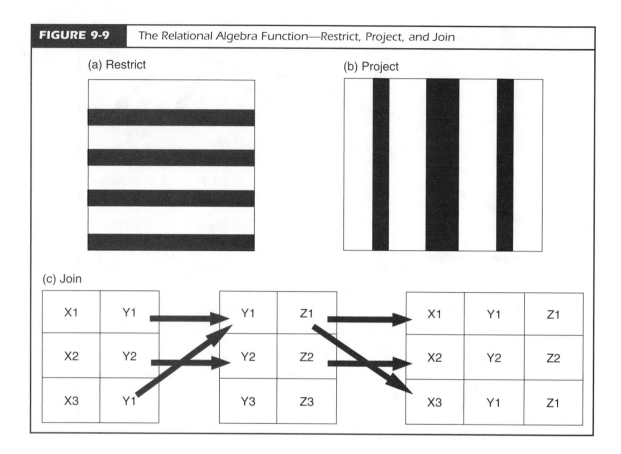

FIGURE 9-9   The Relational Algebra Function—Restrict, Project, and Join

Entity, Occurrence, and Attributes

An **entity** is anything about which the organization wishes to capture data. Entities may be physical, such as inventories, customers, or employees. They may also be conceptual, such as sales (to a customer), accounts receivable, or accounts payable. Systems designers identify entities and prepare a model of them like the one presented in Figure 9-10. This **data model** is the blueprint for ultimately creating the physical database. The graphical representation used to depict the model is called an **entity relationship (ER) diagram**. As a matter of convention, each entity in a data model is named in the singular noun form, such as *Customer* rather than *Customers*. The term **occurrence** is used to describe the number of instances or records that pertain to a specific entity. For example, if an organization has 100 employees, the Employee entity is said to consist of 100 occurrences. **Attributes** are the data elements that define an entity. For example, an Employee entity may be defined by the following partial set of attributes: Name, Address, Job Skill, Years of Service, and Hourly Rate of Pay. Each occurrence in the Employee entity consists of the same types of attributes, but values of each attribute will vary among occurrences. Because attributes are the logical and relevant characteristics of an entity, they are unique to it. In other words, the same attribute should not be used to define two different entities.

Associations and Cardinality

The labeled line connecting two entities in a data model describes the *nature* of the **association** between them. This association is represented with a verb such as ships, requests, or receives. **Cardinality** is the *degree* of association between two entities. Simply

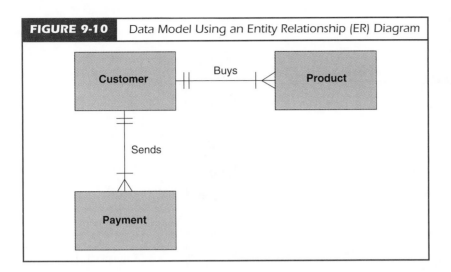

FIGURE 9-10   Data Model Using an Entity Relationship (ER) Diagram

stated, cardinality describes the number of possible occurrences in one table that are associated with a single occurrence in a related table. Four basic forms of cardinality are possible: zero or one (0,1), one and only one (1,1), zero or many (0,M), and one or many (1,M). These are combined to represent logical associations between entities. Figure 9-11 presents several examples of entity associations.

One-to-Zero or One (1:0,1). Assume that a company has 1000 employees but only 100 of them are sales staff. Assume also that each salesperson is assigned a company car. Example 1 in Figure 9-11 shows that for every occurrence (record) in the Employee entity there is a possibility of zero or one occurrence in the Company Car entity.

When defining the cardinality of an entity association, it helps to imagine that you are standing on a single occurrence (record) of one entity and looking at the other entity. What are the minimum and maximum number of records that may be associated with the single record that you have selected? Standing on the Employee entity and looking toward the Company Car entity, we have two possible associations. If the selected employee record is that of a salesperson, then he or she is assigned one (and only one) company car. The Employee record, therefore, is associated with only one record in the Company Car entity. If, however, the selected employee record is not that of a salesperson then he or she is assigned no (zero) car. The record in this case is associated with zero Company Car records. Thus, the minimum cardinality is zero and the maximum is one. A circle and a short line intersecting the line connecting the two entities depict this degree of cardinality. Notice that from the Employee entity perspective, the cardinality is shown at the Company Car end of the association line. Now select a Company Car record and look back at the Employee entity. Because each company car is assigned to only one employee, both the minimum and maximum number of associated records is one. Two short intersecting lines at the Employee end of the association line signify this cardinality.

One-to-One (1:1). Example 2 illustrates a situation in which each record in one entity is always associated with one (and only one) record in the associated entity. In this case, each company laptop computer is assigned to only one manager and every manager is assigned only one computer. Two short lines intersecting the connecting line at both ends depict this cardinality.

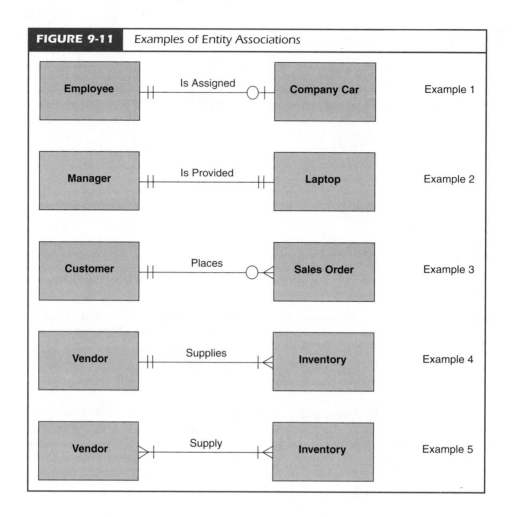

FIGURE 9-11 | Examples of Entity Associations

Employee — Is Assigned — Company Car — Example 1

Manager — Is Provided — Laptop — Example 2

Customer — Places — Sales Order — Example 3

Vendor — Supplies — Inventory — Example 4

Vendor — Supply — Inventory — Example 5

One-to-Zero or Many (1:0,M). The relationship between the Customer and Sales Order entities is presented in Example 3. Notice that the minimum number of Sales Order records per Customer record is zero and the maximum is many. This is because that in any given period (a year or month) to which the Sales Order entity pertains, a particular customer may have purchased nothing (zero Sales Order records) or purchased several times (many records). From the perspective of the Sales Order entity, however, every record is associated with one and only one customer. The *crow's foot* symbol (which gives this form of notation its name) depicts the *many* cardinality.

One-to-Many (1:M). Example 4 represents a situation in which each item of Inventory is supplied by one (and only one) Vendor, and each Vendor supplies one or many different inventory items to the company. This association, which technically is one-and-only-one to one-or-many, is simplified to read one-to-many.

Many-to-Many (M:M). To illustrate the many-to-many association, we again use a Vendor and Inventory relationship in Example 5. This time, however, the company has a policy of purchasing the same types of inventory from multiple suppliers. Management may do this to ensure that they get the best prices or avoid becoming dependent on any one supplier. Under such a policy, each Vendor record is associated with one or many Inventory records and each Inventory record is associated with one or many Vendors. This association (one-or-many to one-or-many) is simplified to read many-to-many.

Examples 4 and 5 demonstrate how cardinality represents the business rules in place within an organization. The database designer must obtain a thorough understanding of how the client-company and specific users conduct business to properly design the data model. If the data model is wrong the resulting database tables will also be wrong. Examples 4 and 5 are both valid but different options and, as we shall see, require different database designs.

The Physical Database Tables

Physical database tables are constructed from the data model with each entity in the model being transformed into a separate physical table. Across the top of each table are attributes forming columns. Intersecting the columns to form the rows of the table are *tuples*. A tuple, which was given a precise definition by Codd when he first introduced it, corresponds approximately to a record in a flat-file system. In accordance with convention, we will use the term *record* or *occurrence* rather than tuple.

Properly designed tables possess the following four characteristics:

1. The value of at least one attribute in each occurrence (row) must be unique. This attribute is the **primary key**. The other (nonkey) attributes in the row need not be unique.
2. Tables must conform to the rules of normalization. This means they must be free of repeating groups, partial dependencies, and transitive dependencies. Normalization is examined in detail later.
3. All attribute values in any column must be of the same class.
4. Each column in a given table must be uniquely named. However, different tables may contain columns with the same name.

Linkages between Relational Tables

Logically related tables need to be physically connected to achieve the associations described in the data model. This is accomplished by embedding the primary key of one table into the related table as a **foreign key**. Use of an embedded foreign key is illustrated in Figure 9-12. For example, the primary key of the Customer table (Cust Num) is embedded as a foreign key in both the Sales Invoice and Cash Receipts tables. Similarly, the primary key in the Sales Invoice table (Invoice Num) is a foreign key in the Line Item table. Note that the Line Item table uses a composite primary key comprising two fields—Invoice Num and Item Num. Both fields are needed to identify each record in the table uniquely, but only the invoice number portion of the key provides the logical link to the Sales Invoice table.

The DBMS makes the physical connection between records in the related tables by searching the specified tables for records with a known key value. For example, if a user wants all the invoices for Customer 1875, the system will search the Sales Invoice table for records with a foreign key value of 1875. We see from Figure 9-12 that there is only one occurrence—invoice number 1921. To obtain the line item details for this invoice, a search is made of the Line Item table for records with a foreign key value of 1921. Two records are retrieved.

The nature of the association between two tables determines the method used for assigning foreign keys. These methods will be examined later.

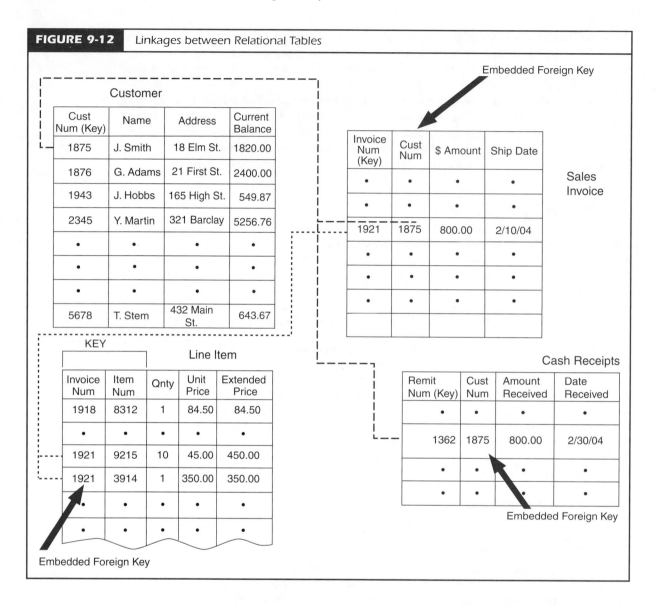

FIGURE 9-12 | Linkages between Relational Tables

User Views

A user view was defined earlier as the set of data that a particular user sees. Examples of user views are computer screens for entering or viewing data, management reports, or source documents such as an invoice. Views may be digital or physical (paper), but in all cases they derive from underlying database tables. Simple views may be constructed from a single table, while more complex views may require several tables. Furthermore, a single table may contribute data to many different views.

A large organization may have thousands of user views supported by thousands of individual tables. The task of identifying all views is a daunting but important aspect of database design. Analysis of individual views reveals the entities and the attributes that must ultimately be translated into physical tables. This is the data normalization process, which we examine next.

THE DATA NORMALIZATION PROCESS

In this section, the **data normalization** process is explored, which involves an understanding of user information needs as well as relevant business rules. The process begins by obtaining views (e.g., output reports, documents, and input screens) required by individual users. Images of these views may be prepared using a word processor, a graphics package, or simply pencil and paper. At this point the view is merely a pictorial representation of the dataset the user will eventually have when the project is completed.

As a matter of efficiency, the views of many users may be normalized together. This is particularly so when the views are derived from common entities. For illustration purposes, however, we will normalize only a single view illustrated in Figure 9-13. This inventory status report provides the purchasing agent with information about inventory items to be ordered and the suppliers (vendors) of the inventory.

The Importance of Data Normalization

Correctly designed database tables are critical to the operational success of the DBMS. Poorly designed tables can cause processing problems that restrict, or even deny, users access to the information they need.

Data normalization is a process that promotes effective database design by grouping data attributes into entities that comply with specific conditions. There are several possible levels of normalization. Designers of business databases normalize to the **third normal form (3NF)** level.

Tables constructed from a data model that has not been normalized are associated with three types of problems called **anomalies**: the *update anomaly*, the *insertion anomaly*, and the *deletion anomaly*. One or more of these anomalies will also exist in tables that are normalized at lower levels such as **first normal form (1NF)** and **second normal form (2NF)**, but tables in 3NF are free of anomalies.

To better demonstrate the impact of anomalies, and the effects of normalization procedures that apply, we need to treat the user view as if were a physical table with records and attribute values. Figure 9-13 has, therefore, been represented in Figure 9-14 as a single

FIGURE 9-13	Inventory Status Report

Ajax Manufacturing Co.
Inventory Status Report

Part Number	Description	Quantity On Hand	Reorder Point	Supplier Number	Name	Address	Telephone
1	Bracket	100	150	22 24 27	Ozment Sup Buell Co. B&R Sup	123 Main St. 2 Broadhead Westgate Mall	555-7895 555-3436 555-7845
2	Gasket	440	450	22 24 28	Ozment Sup Buell Co. Harris Manuf	123 Main St. 2 Broadhead 24 Linden St.	555-7895 555-3436 555-3316
3	Brace	10	10	22 24 28	Ozment Sup Buell Co. Harris Manuf	123 Main St. 2 Broadhead 24 Linden St.	555-7895 555-3436 555-3316
. . .	. . .	. . .	. . .	. . .	. . .	. . .	. . .

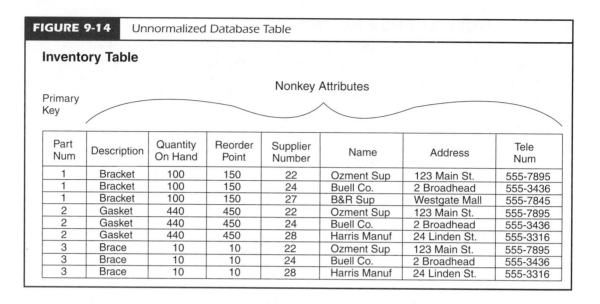

FIGURE 9-14 | Unnormalized Database Table

Inventory Table

Primary Key | | | | | Nonkey Attributes | |

Part Num	Description	Quantity On Hand	Reorder Point	Supplier Number	Name	Address	Tele Num
1	Bracket	100	150	22	Ozment Sup	123 Main St.	555-7895
1	Bracket	100	150	24	Buell Co.	2 Broadhead	555-3436
1	Bracket	100	150	27	B&R Sup	Westgate Mall	555-7845
2	Gasket	440	450	22	Ozment Sup	123 Main St.	555-7895
2	Gasket	440	450	24	Buell Co.	2 Broadhead	555-3436
2	Gasket	440	450	28	Harris Manuf	24 Linden St.	555-3316
3	Brace	10	10	22	Ozment Sup	123 Main St.	555-7895
3	Brace	10	10	24	Buell Co.	2 Broadhead	555-3436
3	Brace	10	10	28	Harris Manuf	24 Linden St.	555-3316

unnormalized table called Inventory. Keep in mind, however, that in practice the normalization process occurs at the entity (data model) level prior to the creation of physical tables. The physical tables are later constructed from the normalized model.

Database Anomalies

While it is possible to derive simple user views from a single 3NF table, complex views typically require more than one table. For example, a single 3NF table cannot produce the Inventory Status Report in Figure 9-13. The unnormalized table depicted in Figure 9-14 can produce this view, but will contain the following anomalies.

Update Anomaly. The **update anomaly** results from data redundancy in an unnormalized table. To illustrate, notice that Supplier Number 22 provides each of the three inventory items (Part Num 1, 2, 3) shown in Figure 9-14. The data attributes pertaining to Supplier Number 22 (Name, Address, and Tele Num) are thus repeated in every record of every inventory item that Supplier Number 22 provides. Any change in the supplier's name, address, or telephone number must be made to each of these records in the table. In the example, this means three different updates. To better appreciate the implications of the update anomaly, consider a more realistic situation where the vendor supplies 10,000 different items of inventory. Any update to an attribute must then be made 10,000 times.

Insertion Anomaly. To demonstrate the effects of the **insertion anomaly**, assume that a new vendor has entered the marketplace. The organization does not yet purchase from the vendor, but may wish to do so in the future. In the meantime, the organization wants to add the vendor to the database. This is not possible because the primary key for the Inventory table is Part Num. Because the vendor does not supply the organization with any inventory items, the supplier data cannot be added to the table.

Deletion Anomaly. The **deletion anomaly** involves the unintentional deletion of data from a table. To illustrate, assume that Supplier Number 27 provides the company with only one item: Part Number 1. If the organization discontinues this item of inventory and deletes it from the table, the data pertaining to Supplier Number 27 will also be deleted.

Although the company may wish to retain the supplier's information for future use, the current table design prevents it from doing so.

The presence of the deletion anomaly is less conspicuous, but potentially more serious than the update and insertion anomalies. A flawed database design that prevents the insertion of records or requires the user to perform excessive updates attracts attention quickly. However, the deletion anomaly may go undetected, and the user may be unaware of the loss of important data until it is too late. A poorly structured database can result in the unintentional loss of critical accounting records and the destruction of the audit trail. Hence, the design of database tables carries internal control significance that accountants need to recognize.

Data Normalization Rules

A normalization process that formally examines anomaly-causing dependencies known as *repeating groups*, *partial dependencies*, and *transitive dependencies* is presented in the appendix to this chapter. Here, an intuitive approach is followed to normalizing data. Simply stated, eliminating the three anomalies involves a process of systematically splitting unnormalized complex tables into smaller tables that meet two conditions:

1. All nonkey attributes in the table are dependent on the primary key.
2. All nonkey attributes are independent of the other nonkey attributes.

In other words, a 3NF table is one in which the primary key of a table wholly and uniquely defines each attribute in the table. Furthermore, none of the table attributes are defined by an attribute other than the primary key. If, however, one or more attributes violate these conditions, they need to be removed and placed in a separate table and assigned an appropriate key.

Splitting Unnormalized Tables

Upon examination of Figure 9-14, we see that not all the data attributes logically relate to the primary key Part Num. In fact, two distinct sets of data reside in this table as it currently stands: data about inventory and data about suppliers. The nonkey attributes of Name, Address, and Tele Num are not dependent on (defined by) Part Num. Rather, these attributes are dependent on the nonkey attribute Supplier Number. The solution is to remove the supplier data from the Inventory table and place them in a separate table, which we will call Supplier. Figure 9-15 shows the two 3NF tables, Inventory and Supplier, along with a third table called Part/Supplier, which links the two. This linking technique will be explained later.

Normalizing the tables has eliminated the three anomalies. First, the update anomaly is resolved because data about each supplier exist in only one location—the Supplier table. Any change in the data about an individual vendor is made only once, regardless of how many items it supplies. Second, the insert anomaly is solved because new vendors can be added to the Supplier table even if they are not currently supplying the organization with inventory. For example, Supplier Number 30 in the table does not supply any inventory items. Finally, the deletion anomaly is eliminated. The decision to delete an inventory item from the database will not result in the unintentional deletion of the supplier data because these data reside independently in different tables.

Linking Normalized Tables

When unnormalized tables are split into multiple 3NF tables, they need to be linked together so the data in them can be related and made accessible to users. The degree of association between the resulting tables (i.e., 1:1, 1:M, or M:M) determines how the linking occurs. The key-assignment rules for linking tables are discussed in the following section.

FIGURE 9-15 | Normalized Database Tables

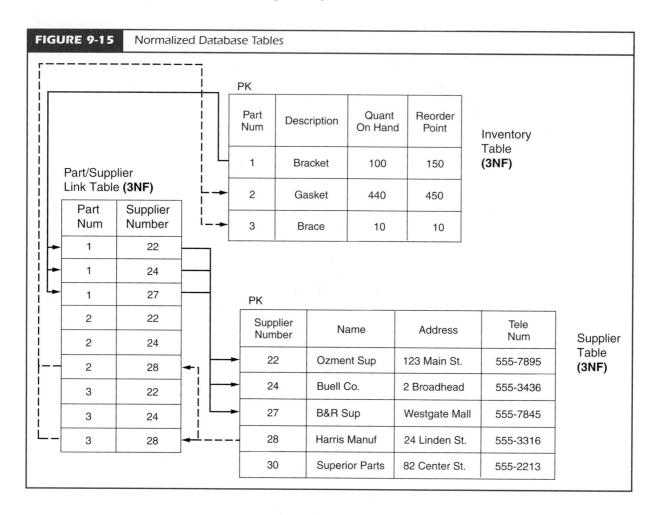

Keys in 1:1 Associations. Where a true 1:1 association exists between tables, either (or both) primary keys may be embedded as foreign keys in the related table. On the other hand, when the lower cardinality value is zero (1:0,1) a more efficient table structure can be achieved by placing the one-side (1:) table's primary key in the zero-or-one (:0,1) table as a foreign key. Using the Employee/Company Car example in Figure 9-11 we see the importance of this key-assignment rule. To illustrate, let's reverse the rule by placing the Company Car (0 side) primary key into the Employee (1 side) table. Because most employees are not assigned a company car, most of the foreign keys in the Employee table will have null (blank) values. While this approach would work, it could cause some technical problems during table searches. Correctly applying the key-assignment rule solves this problem because all Company Car records will have an employee assigned and no null values will occur.

Keys in 1:M Associations. Where a 1:M (or 1:0,M) association exists, the primary key of the 1 side is embedded in the table of the M side. To demonstrate the logic behind this key-assignment rule, consider two alternative business rules for purchasing inventory from suppliers.

Business Rule 1. Each vendor supplies the firm with three (or fewer) different items of inventory, but each item is supplied by only one vendor.

This somewhat unrealistic, but technically possible, business rule describes an upper-bounded 1:M (1:1,3) association between the Supplier and Inventory tables.

To apply this rule the designer will need to modify the Inventory table structure to include the Supplier Number as illustrated in Figure 9-16. Under this approach, each record in the Inventory table will now contain the value of the key field of the vendor that supplies that item. By contrast, Figure 9-17 shows what the table structure might look like if the designer reversed the key-assignment rule by embedding the Part Num key in the Supplier table. Notice that the Supplier table now contains three part number fields each linking to an associated record in the Inventory table. Only the links to part numbers 1, 2, and 3 are shown. Although this technique violates the key-assignment rule, it would work. It does so, however, only because the upper limit of the "many" side of the association is known and is very small (i.e., limited to three). How would this table structure look if we assume a more realistic business rule like the following one?

Business Rule 2. Each vendor supplies the firm with any number of inventory items, but each item is supplied by only one vendor.

This is a true 1:M association in which the upper limit of the "many" side of the association is unbounded. In other words the vendor may supply one item of inventory or 10,000 items. How many fields must we add to the Supplier table structure to accommodate all possible links to the Inventory table? Here we can see the logic behind the 1:M key-assignment rule. The structure in Figure 9-16 still works under this business rule, whereas the technique illustrated in Figure 9-17 does not.

FIGURE 9-16 Applying the 1:M Key-Assignment Rule

(PK) Inventory Table (FK) — "Many" Side

Part Num	Description	Quant On Hand	Reorder Point	Supplier Number
1	Bracket	100	150	22
2	Gasket	440	450	28
3	Brace	10	10	28

(PK) Supplier Table — "1" Side

Supplier Number	Name	Address	Tele Num
22	Ozment Sup	123 Main St.	555-7895
24	Buell Co.	2 Broadhead	555-3436
28	Harris Manuf	24 Linden St.	555-3316

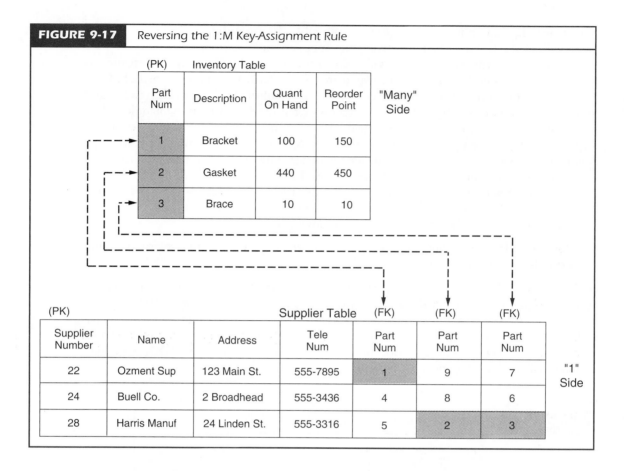

FIGURE 9-17 | Reversing the 1:M Key-Assignment Rule

Keys in M:M Associations. To represent the M:M association between tables, a link table needs to be created. The link table has a combined (composite) key consisting of the primary keys of two related tables. Let's now return to the association in Figure 9-15. These tables illustrate a M:M association described by the following business rule:

Business Rule 3. Each vendor supplies the firm with any number of inventory items and each item may be supplied by any number of vendors.

This business rule is evident by examining the contents of the Inventory Status Report (the user view) in Figure 9-13. Each part number shown has multiple suppliers and each supplier may supply multiple items. For example, Ozment Supply provides items 1, 2, and 3.

Note that an M:M association between tables requires the creation of a separate link table rather than using embedded foreign keys as links. The logic in the previous 1:M example that prevented us from embedding the primary key from the "many" side table of an unbounded 1:M association into the table of the "one" side applies here also. Neither table can donate an embedded key to the other because both are on the "many" side of the association. The solution is to create a new link table containing the key fields of the other two tables.

The link table (Part/Supplier) in Figure 9-15 contains the primary keys for the records in the Inventory table (Part Num) and the related Supplier table (Supplier Number). Via the link table, every inventory record can be linked to each supplier of the item, and every supplier can be linked to the inventory items that it supplies. For example, by searching the Inventory table for Part Num 1, we see that suppliers 22, 24, and 27 supply this item. Searching in the opposite direction, supplier 28 provides part numbers 2 and 3. A separate record in the link table represents each unique occurrence of a supplier/inventory association. For example, if supplier 24 provides 500 different items, 500 link records are needed to depict these associations.

Accountants and Data Normalization

Database normalization is a technical matter that is usually the responsibility of systems professionals. However, the subject has implications for internal control that also make it the concern of accountants. For example, the update anomaly can generate conflicting and obsolete database values; the insertion anomaly can result in unrecorded transactions and incomplete audit trails; and the deletion anomaly can cause the loss of accounting records and the destruction of audit trails. Although most accountants will not be responsible for normalizing an organization's databases, they should have an understanding of the process and be able to determine whether a table is properly normalized.

DESIGNING RELATIONAL DATABASES

This section examines the steps involved in creating a relational database. Keep in mind that database design is a portion of a much larger systems development process that involves extensive analysis of user needs, which are not covered at this time. That body of material is the subject of Chapters 13 and 14. Thus, our starting point normally follows considerable preliminary work that has identified in detail the key elements of the system under development. With this backdrop, the focus will be on six primary phases of database design:

1. Identify entities.
2. Construct a data model showing entity associations.
3. Add primary keys and attributes to the model.
4. Normalize the data model and add foreign keys.
5. Construct the physical database.
6. Prepare the user views.

IDENTIFY ENTITIES

Database design begins by identifying the primary entities of the organization and constructing a data model of their relationships. This involves analysis of business rules and information needs of all users. When the analyst has identified and documented the key operational features of the system, he or she will search for the entities that underlie it. We will demonstrate this complex task with a simplified proposal for a new purchasing system. The key features containing clues to the entities in this proposed new system are as follows:

1. The purchasing agent reviews the inventory status report (Figure 9-13) for items that need to be reordered.
2. The agent selects a supplier and prepares an online purchase order.
3. The agent prints a copy of the purchase order (Figure 9-18a) and sends it to the supplier.
4. The supplier ships inventory to the company. Upon its arrival, the receiving clerk inspects the inventory and prepares an online receiving report (Figure 9-18b). The computer system automatically updates the inventory records.

Recall that entities are things about which the organization wishes to capture data. They are represented as nouns in the system description. A number of candidate entities can be

FIGURE 9-18 Purchase Order and Receiving Report for Purchases System

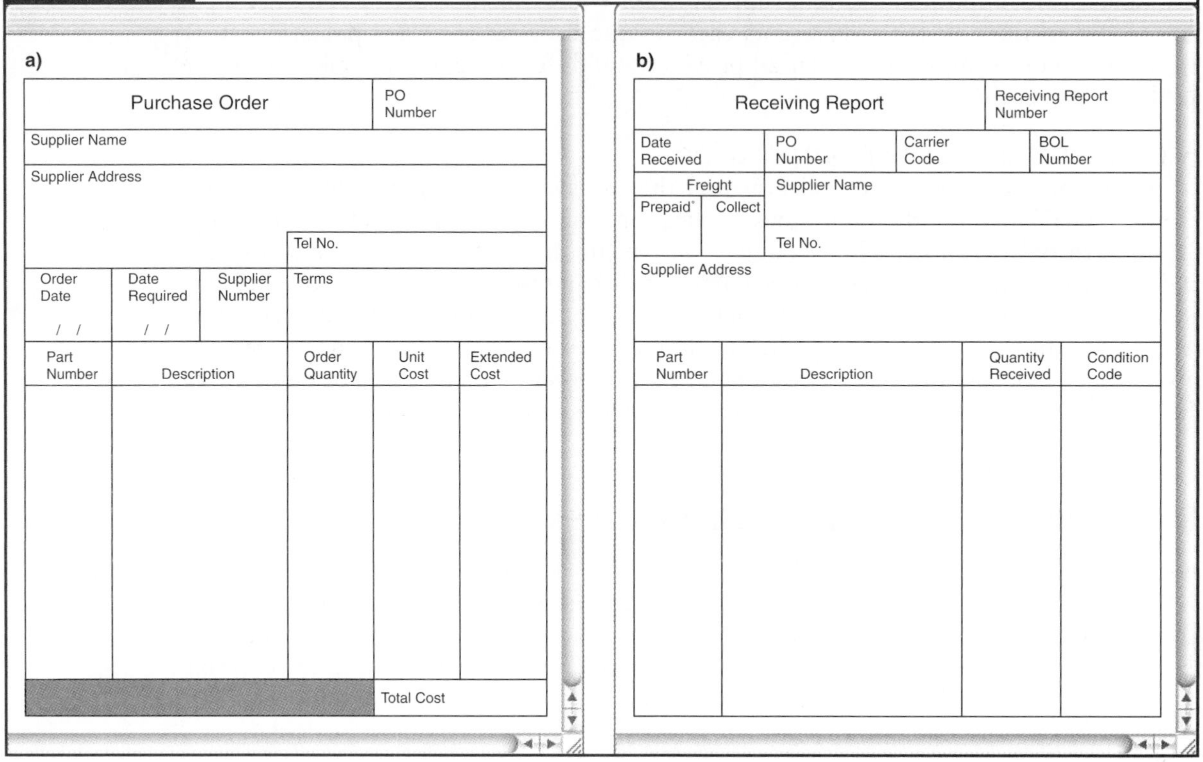

a)

Purchase Order			PO Number	

Supplier Name

Supplier Address

			Tel No.

Order Date	Date Required	Supplier Number	Terms
/ /	/ /		

Part Number	Description	Order Quantity	Unit Cost	Extended Cost
				Total Cost

b)

Receiving Report			Receiving Report Number

Date Received	PO Number	Carrier Code	BOL Number

Freight		Supplier Name
Prepaid	Collect	

	Tel No.

Supplier Address

Part Number	Description	Quantity Received	Condition Code

identified in the previous description: *Purchasing Agent, Receiving Clerk, Inventory, Supplier, Inventory Status Report, Purchase Order*, and *Receiving Report*. Not all of these candidates are true entities that need to be modeled. To pass the valid-entity test, two conditions need be met:

Condition 1. An entity must consist of two or more occurrences.

Condition 2. An entity must contribute at least one attribute that is not provided through other entities.

We need to test these conditions for each candidate to eliminate any false entities.

Purchasing Agent. Assuming that the organization has only one purchasing agent, then the Purchasing Agent candidate fails condition 1. If, however, more than one agent exists, condition 1 is met but condition 2 may be a problem. If we assume that an Employee table already exists as part of a human resources or payroll system, then basic data about the agent as an employee is captured in that table. We need to determine what data about the agent that is unique to his or her role of order placing needs to be captured. Note that we are not referring to data about the order, but data about the agent. Because we have no information on this point in our brief description of the system, we will assume no agent-specific data are captured. Hence, the Purchasing Agent candidate is not an entity to be modeled.

Receiving Clerk. The previous argument applies equally to the Receiving Clerk entity. We will assume that no clerk-specific data need be captured that requires a dedicated table.

Inventory. The Inventory entity meets both conditions. The description suggests that the organization holds many items of inventory, thus the entity would contain multiple occurrences. Also, we can logically assume that the attributes that define the Inventory entity are not provided through other tables. The Inventory entity is, therefore, a true entity that will need to be modeled.

Supplier. The description states that multiple vendors supply inventory, hence the Supplier entity meets the first condition. We can also assume that it meets the second condition since no other entity would logically provide supplier data. The Supplier entity, therefore, will be included the data model.

Inventory Status Report. The Inventory Status Report is a user view derived from the Inventory and Supplier entities (see Figure 9-15). While it contains multiple occurrences, it is not an entity because it does not satisfy condition 2. The view is derived entirely from existing entities, and provides no additional data that requires a separate entity. The view will be carefully analyzed, however, to ensure that all the attributes needed for it are included in the existing entities.

Purchase Order. Like the status report the Purchase Order is a user view. Unlike the status report, however, the Purchase Order pertains directly to a purchase transaction. All transactions are unique events that must be captured in the database. While some purchase order data pertain to existing entities (Inventory and Supplier) in the model, other attributes unique to the purchase event will require one or more additional entities. This view, therefore, will need to be modeled.

Receiving Report. The status of the Receiving Report is similar to the Purchase Order. It is needed to capture transaction-specific data that require additional entities and must be modeled.

At this point our search has revealed four entities: Inventory, Supplier, Purchase Order, and Receiving Report. These will be used to construct a data model and, ultimately, the physical database tables in the sections that follow.

CONSTRUCT A DATA MODEL SHOWING ENTITY ASSOCIATIONS

Next we need to determine the associations between entities and model them in an ER diagram. Recall that associations represent business rules. Sometimes the rules are obvious and are the same for all organizations. For example, the normal association between a Customer entity and a Sales Order entity is 1:M (or 1:0,M). This signifies that one customer may place many orders during a sales period. The association would never be 1:1. This would mean that the organization restricts each customer to a single sale, which is illogical.

Sometimes the association between entities is not apparent because different rules may apply in different organizations. To reiterate an important point made earlier, the organization's business rules directly impact the structure of the database tables. If the database is to function properly, its designers need to understand the organization's business rules as well as the specific needs of individual users. Figure 9-19 illustrates the entity associations in our example. The underlying business rules are explained in the following.

1. There is a 0,M:M association between the Purchase Order and Inventory entities. This means that each inventory item may have been ordered many times or never

FIGURE 9-19	Data Model Showing Entity Associations

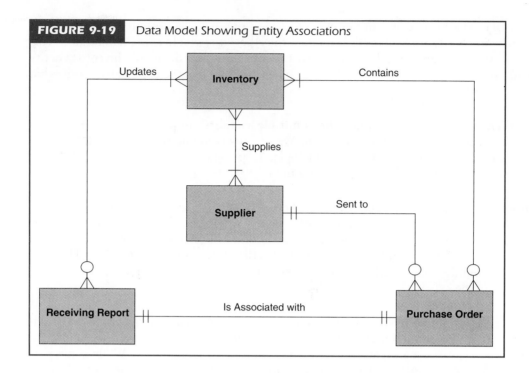

ordered in the current business period. Obviously, every inventory item must have been purchased at least once in the past, so why do we show a 0,M cardinality for the Purchase Order entity? We must keep in mind that transaction entities, such as sales and purchases, are associated with a particular time frame. We will assume that the Purchase Order table for this system will contain records for purchases made in the current period only. Closed purchase orders of past periods will have been removed to an archive table, which is not shown in our example.

2. There is an M:M association between the Inventory and Supplier entities. This means that one or more vendors supply each inventory item, and each of them supplies one or more items of inventory.

3. There is a 1:0,M association between the Supplier and the Purchase Order entities. This means that in the current period each supplier may have received zero or many purchase orders, but each order goes to only one supplier.

4. There is a 1:1 association between the Purchase Order and Receiving Report entities. A single receiving report record reflects the receipt of goods that are specified on a single purchase order record. Multiple purchase orders are not combined on a single receiving report.

5. The association between the Receiving Report and Inventory entities is 0,M:M. This signifies that within the period, each item of inventory may have been received many times or never. Also, each receiving report is associated with at least one and possibly many inventory items.

The many-to-many (M:M and 0,M:M) associations in the data model need to be resolved before the physical databases can be created. We know from previous discussion that these associations signify a missing entity that is needed to link them. We will resolve these problems during the normalization process.

ADD PRIMARY KEYS AND ATTRIBUTES TO THE MODEL

Add Primary Keys. The next step in the process is to assign primary keys to the entities in the model. The analyst should select a primary key that logically defines the nonkey attributes and uniquely identifies each occurrence in the entity. Sometimes this can be accomplished using a simple sequential code such as an Invoice Number, Check Number, or Purchase Order number. Sequential codes, however, are not always efficient or effective keys. Through careful design of block codes, group codes, alphabetic codes, and mnemonic codes, primary keys can also impart useful information about the nature of the entity. These techniques are discussed in detail in Chapter 8. Figure 9-20 presents the four entities in the model with primary keys assigned.

Add Attributes. Every attribute in an entity should appear directly or indirectly (a calculated value) in one or more user views. Entity attributes are, therefore, originally derived and modeled from user views. In other words, if stored data are not used in a document, report, or a calculation that is reported in some way, then it serves no purpose and should not be part of the database. The attributes assigned to each entity in Figure 9-21 are derived from the user views of the Purchase Order and Receiving Report illustrated in Figure 9-18 and from the Inventory Status Report that we normalized previously.

NORMALIZE DATA MODEL AND ADD FOREIGN KEYS

Figure 9-22 presents a normalized data model. The normalization issues that needed resolution are outlined in the following section:

1. **Repeating Group Data in Purchase Order.** The attributes Part Number, Description, Order Quantity, and Unit Cost are **repeating group** data. This means that when a

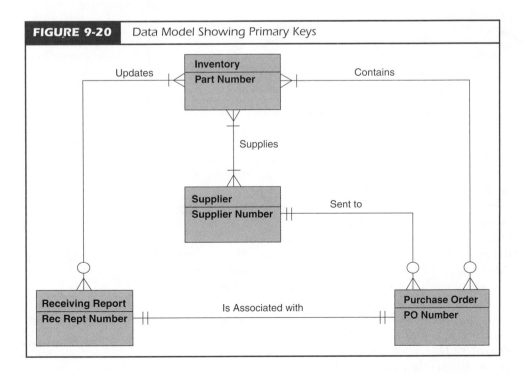

FIGURE 9-20 Data Model Showing Primary Keys

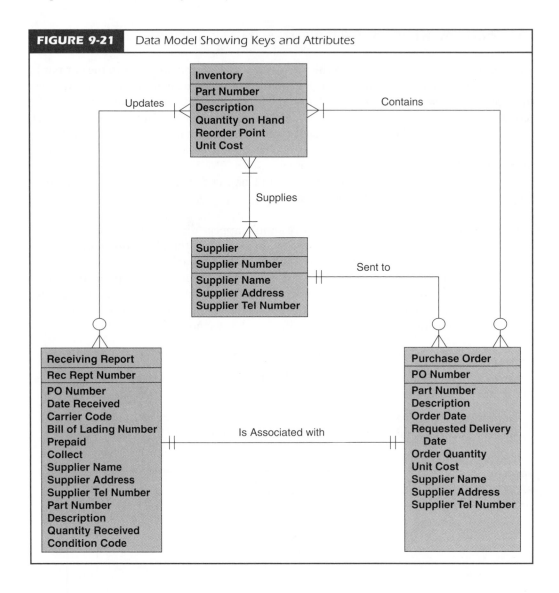

FIGURE 9-21 | Data Model Showing Keys and Attributes

particular purchase order contains more than one item (most of the time), then multiple values will need to be captured for these attributes. To resolve this, these repeating group data were removed to a new PO Item Detail entity. The new entity was assigned a primary key that is a composite of Part Number and PO Number. The creation of the new entity also resolved the M:M association between the Purchase Order and Inventory entities by providing a link.

2. **Repeating Group Data in Receiving Report.** The attributes Part Number, Quantity Received, and Condition Code are repeating groups in the Receiving Report entity and were removed to a new entity called Rec Report Item Detail. A composite key composed of Part Number and Receipt Number was assigned. As in the previous example, creating this new entity also resolved the M:M association between Receiving Report and Inventory.

3. **Transitive Dependencies.** The Purchase Order and Receiving Report entities contain attributes that are redundant with data in the Inventory and Supplier entities.

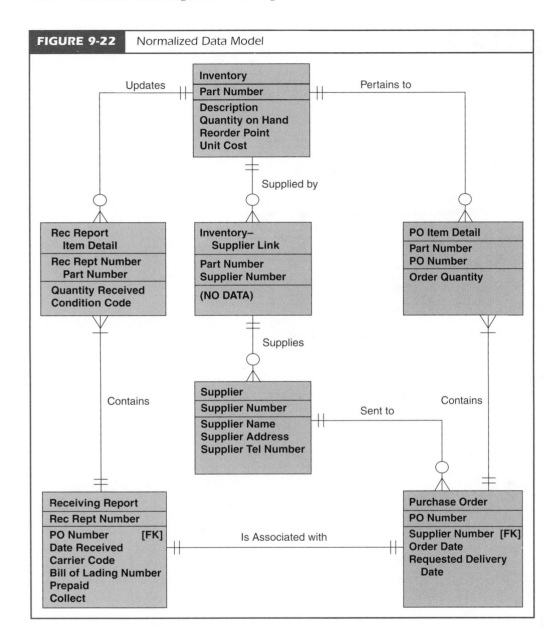

FIGURE 9-22 Normalized Data Model

These redundancies occur because of transitive dependencies (see the appendix of this chapter) in the Purchase Order and Receiving Report entities and are dropped.

CONSTRUCT THE PHYSICAL DATABASE

Figure 9-23 illustrates the 3NF table structures for the database. The primary and foreign keys linking the tables are represented by dotted lines. The following points are worth elaboration.

Each record in the Rec Report Item Detail table represents an individual item on the receiving report. The table has a combined key comprising Rec Rept Number and Part Number. This composite key is needed to uniquely identify the *Quantity Received* and *Condition* attributes of each item-detail record. The Rec Rept Number portion of the key provides the link to the Receiving Report table that contains general data about the

FIGURE 9-23 Normalized Tables

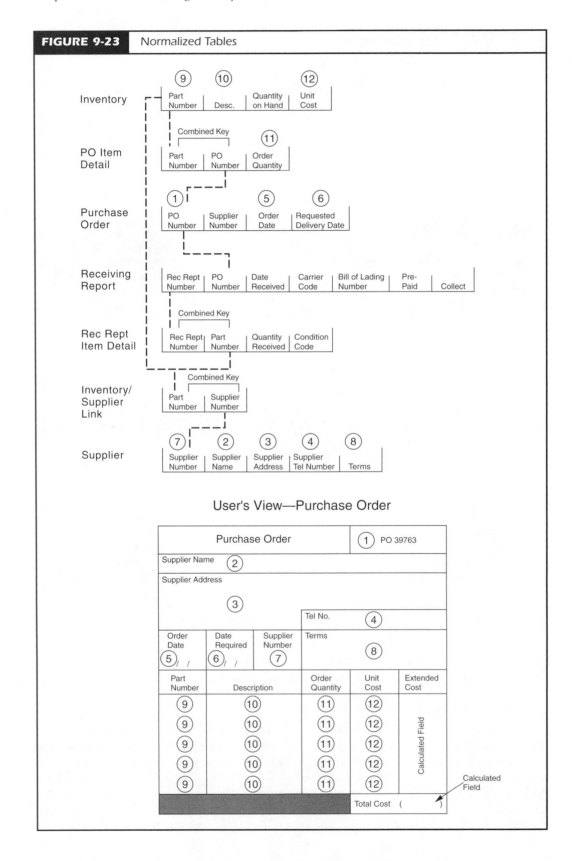

User's View—Purchase Order

receiving event. The Part Number portion of the key is used to access the Inventory table to facilitate updating the Quantity on Hand field from the Quantity Received field of the Item-Detail record.

The PO Item Detail table uses a composite primary key of PO Number and the Part Number to uniquely identify the *Order Quantity* attribute. The PO Number component of the composite key provides a link to the Purchase Order table. The Part Number element of the key is a link to the Inventory table where Description and Unit Cost data reside.

The next step is to create the physical tables and populate them with data. This is an involved step that must be carefully planned and executed, and may take many months in a large installation. Programs will need to be written to transfer organization data currently stored in flat files or legacy databases into the new relational tables. Data currently stored on paper documents will need to be entered into the database tables manually. Once this is done, the physical user views can be produced.

PREPARE THE USER VIEWS

The normalized tables should be rich enough to support the views of all system users. For example, the purchase order in Figure 9-23, which could be the data entry screen for a purchasing clerk, has been constructed from attributes in several tables. To illustrate the relationship, the fields in the user view are cross-referenced via circled numbers to the attributes in the supporting tables. Keep in mind that these tables would also provide data for many other views not shown here, such as the receiving report, purchase requisition listing, inventory status report, vendor purchases activity report.

The query function of a relational DBMS allows the system designer to easily create user views from tables. The designer simply tells the DBMS which tables to use, their primary and foreign keys, and the attributes to select from each table. Older DBMSs require the designer to specify these parameters in SQL. Newer systems allow this to be done visually. The designer simply points and clicks at the tables and the attributes. From this visual representation, the DBMS generates the SQL commands for the query to produce the view.

The Receiving Report, Purchase Order, and Inventory Status Report views would all be created in this way. To illustrate, the SQL commands to produce the inventory status report illustrated in Figure 9-13 are given in the following section.

SELECT inventory.part-num, description, quant-on-hand, reorder-point, EOQ, part-supplier.part-num, part-supplier.supplier-number, supplier.supplier-number, name, address, tele-num,

FROM inventory, part-supplier, supplier

WHERE inventory.part-num=part-supplier.part-num AND part-supplier. supplier-number=supplier.supplier-number AND quant-on hand≤reorder-point

- The SELECT command identifies all the attributes to be contained in the view. When the same attribute appears in more than one table (e.g., part-num) the source table name must also be specified.

- The FROM command identifies the tables used in creating the view.

- The WHERE command specifies how rows in the Inventory, Part-Supplier, and Supplier tables are to be matched to create the view. In this case, the three tables are algebraically joined on the primary keys Part-Num and Supplier-Number.

- Multiple expressions may be linked with the AND, OR, and NOT operators. In this example, the last expression uses AND to restrict the records to be selected with the logical expression *quant-on-hand≤reorder-point*. Only records whose quantities on hand have fallen to or below their reorder points will be selected for the view. The user will not see the many thousands of other inventory items that have adequate quantities available.

These SPL commands will be saved in a user program called a query. To view the Inventory Status report the purchasing agent executes the query program. Each time this is done, the query builds a new view with current data from the Inventory and Vendor tables. By providing the user with his or her personal query, rather than permitting access to the underlying base tables, the user is limited to authorized data only.

A report program is used to make the view visually attractive and easy to use. Column headings can be added, fields summed, and averages calculated to produce a hard-copy or computer screen report that resembles the original user report in Figure 9-13. The report program can suppress unnecessary data from the view such as duplicated fields and the key values in the Inventory/Vendor link table. These keys are necessary to build the view, but are not needed in the actual report.

DATABASES IN A DISTRIBUTED ENVIRONMENT

Chapter 1 introduced the concept of **distributed data processing** (DDP) as an alternative to the centralized approach. Most modern organizations use some form of distributed processing and networking to process their transactions. Some companies process all of their transactions in this way. An important consideration in planning a distributed system is the location of the organization's database. In addressing this issue, the planner has two basic options: databases can be *centralized* or they can be distributed. Distributed databases fall into two categories: *partitioned* and *replicated* databases. This section examines issues, features, and tradeoffs that should be carefully evaluated in deciding how databases should be distributed.

CENTRALIZED DATABASES

Under the **centralized database** approach, remote users send requests via terminals for data to the central site, which processes the requests and transmits the data back to the user. The central site performs the functions of a file manager that services the data needs of the remote users. The centralized database approach is illustrated in Figure 9-24.

Earlier in the chapter, three primary advantages of the database approach were presented: the reduction of data storage costs, the elimination of multiple update procedures, and the establishment of **data currency** (i.e., the firm's data files reflect accurately the effects of its transactions). Achieving data currency is critical to database integrity and reliability. However, in the DDP environment, this can be a challenging task.

Data Currency in a DDP Environment

During data processing, account balances pass through a state of **temporary inconsistency** in which their values are incorrectly stated. This occurs during the execution of any accounting transaction. To illustrate, consider the computer logic for recording the credit sale of $2,000 to customer Jones.

INSTRUCTION	DATABASE VALUES	
	AR-Jones	AR-Control
START		
1 Read AR-Sub account (Jones)	1500	
2 Read AR-Control account		10000

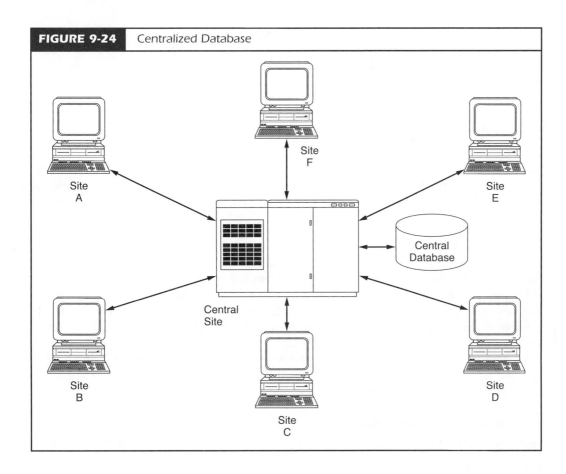

FIGURE 9-24   Centralized Database

3	Write AR-Sub account (Jones) + $2000	3500
4	Write AR-Control account + $2000	12000
	END	

Immediately after the execution of Instruction Number 3, and before the execution of Instruction Number 4, the AR-Control account value is temporarily inconsistent by the sum of $2,000. Only after the completion of the entire transaction is this inconsistency resolved. In a DDP environment, such temporary inconsistencies can result in the permanent corruption of the database. To illustrate the potential for damage, look at a slightly more complicated example. Using the same computer logic as before, consider the processing of two separate transactions from two remote sites: Transaction 1 (T1) is the sale of $2,000 on account to customer Jones from Site A; Transaction 2 (T2) is the sale of $1,000 on account to customer Smith from Site B. The following logic shows the possible interweaving of the two processing tasks and the effect on data currency.

		INSTRUCTION	DATABASE VALUES		
				Central Site	
			AR-Jones	AR-Smith	AR-Control
SITE A	SITE B				
T1	T2	START			
1		Read AR-Sub account (Jones)	1500		
	1	Read AR-Sub account (Smith)		3000	
2		Read AR-Control account			10000

3		Write AR-Sub account (Jones) + $2000	3500		
	2	**Read AR-Control account**			10000
4		Write AR-Control account + $2000			12000
	3	Write AR-Sub account (Smith) + $1000		4000	
	4	Write AR-Control account + $1000 END			11000

Notice that Site B seized the AR-Control data value of $10,000 when it was in an inconsistent state. By using this value to process its transaction, Site B effectively destroyed the record of Transaction T1 that had been processed by Site A. Therefore, instead of $13,000, the new AR-Control balance is misstated at $11,000.

Database Lockout

To achieve data currency, simultaneous access to individual data elements by multiple sites needs to be prevented. The solution to this problem is to use a **database lockout**, which is a software control (usually a function of the DBMS) that prevents multiple simultaneous accesses to data. The previous example can be used to illustrate this technique: immediately upon receiving the access request from Site A for AR-Control (T1, Instruction Number 2), the central site DBMS places a lock on AR-Control to prevent access from other sites until Transaction T1 is complete. Thus, when Site B requests AR-Control (T2, Instruction Number 2), it is placed on "wait" status until the lock is removed. Only then can Site B access AR-Control and complete Transaction T2.

DISTRIBUTED DATABASES

Distributed databases can be distributed using either the partitioned or replicated technique.

Partitioned Databases

The **partitioned database** approach splits the central database into segments or partitions that are distributed to their primary users. The advantages of this approach are:

● Users' control is increased by having data stored at local sites.

● Transaction processing response time is improved by permitting local access to data and reducing the volume of data that must be transmitted between sites.

● Partitioned databases can reduce the potential for disaster. By having data located at several sites, the loss of a single site cannot terminate all data processing by the organization.

The partitioned approach, which is illustrated in Figure 9-25, works best for organizations that require minimal data sharing among users at remote sites. To the extent that remote users share common data, the problems associated with the centralized approach still apply. Requests for data from other sites must now be managed by the primary user. Selecting the optimum host location for the partitions will minimize data access problems. This requires an indepth analysis of end-user data needs.

The Deadlock Phenomenon. In a distributed environment, it is possible that multiple sites will lock out each other, thus preventing each from processing its transactions. For example, Figure 9-26 illustrates three sites and their mutual data needs. Notice that Site 1 has requested (and locked) Data A and is waiting for the removal of the lock on Data C to complete its transaction. Site 2 has a lock on C and is waiting for E. Finally, Site 3 has a lock on E and is waiting for A. A **deadlock** occurs here because there is mutual exclusion to data, and the transactions are in a "wait" state until the locks are removed. This can result

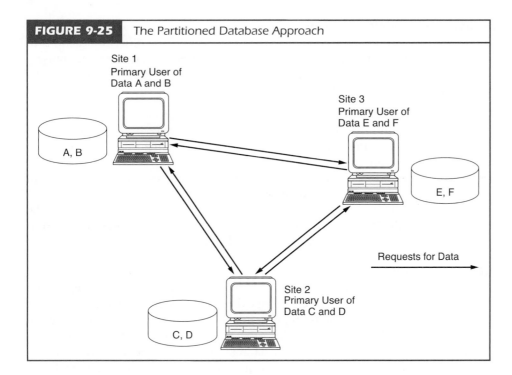

FIGURE 9-25   The Partitioned Database Approach

in transactions being incompletely processed and corruption of the database. A deadlock is a permanent condition that must be resolved by special software that analyzes each deadlock condition to determine the best solution. Because of the implications for transaction processing, accountants should be aware of the issues pertaining to deadlock resolutions.

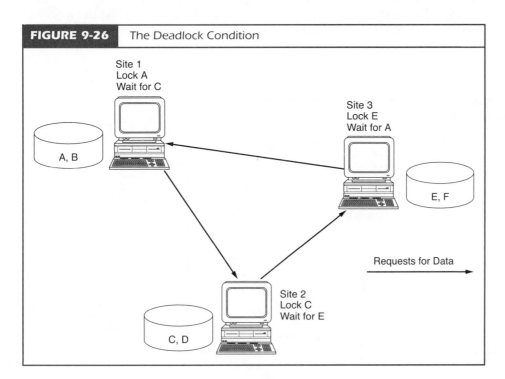

FIGURE 9-26   The Deadlock Condition

Deadlock Resolution. Resolving a deadlock usually involves sacrificing one or more transactions. These must be terminated to complete the processing of the other transactions in the deadlock. The preempted transactions must then be reinitiated. In preempting transactions the deadlock resolution software attempts to minimize the total cost of breaking the deadlock. Although not an easy task to automate, some of the factors that influence this decision are:

1. The resources currently invested in the transaction. This may be measured by the number of updates that the transaction has already performed and that must be repeated if the transaction is terminated.
2. The transaction's stage of completion. In general, deadlock resolution software will avoid terminating transactions that are close to completion.
3. The number of deadlocks associated with the transaction. Because terminating the transaction breaks all deadlock involvement, the software should attempt to terminate transactions that are part of more than one deadlock.

Replicated Databases

In some organizations, the entire database is replicated at each site. **Replicated databases** are effective in companies where there exists a high degree of data sharing but no primary user. Since common data are replicated at each site, the data traffic between sites is reduced considerably. Figure 9-27 illustrates the replicated database model.

The primary justification for a replicated database is to support read-only queries. With data replicated at every site, data access for query purposes is ensured, and lockouts and delays because of network traffic are minimized. However, a problem arises when replicated databases need to be updated by transactions and current copies of the database must be maintained at all sites.

Because each site processes only its local transactions, the common data attributes that are replicated at each site will be updated by different transactions and thus, at any point in time, will possess uniquely different values. Using the data from the earlier example Figure 9-28 illustrates the effect of processing credit sales for Jones at Site A and Smith at Site B. After the transactions are processed, the value shown for the common AR-Control account is inconsistent ($12,000 at Site A and $11,000 at Site B) and incorrect at both sites.

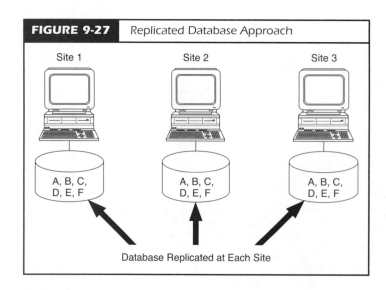

FIGURE 9-27 Replicated Database Approach

Site 1   Site 2   Site 3

A, B, C, D, E, F

Database Replicated at Each Site

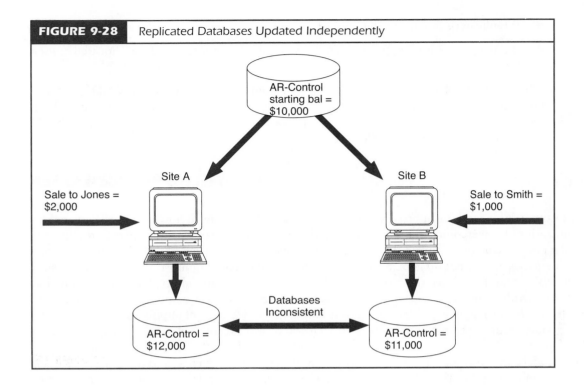

FIGURE 9-28   Replicated Databases Updated Independently

Concurrency Control

Database concurrency is the presence of complete and accurate data at all remote sites. System designers need to employ methods to ensure that transactions processed at each site are accurately reflected in the databases at all other sites. This task, while problematic, has implications for accounting records and is a matter of concern for accountants.

A commonly used method for **concurrency control** is to serialize transactions by time stamping. This involves labeling each transaction by two criteria. First, special software groups transactions into classes to identify potential conflicts. For example, read-only (query) transactions do not conflict with other classes of transactions. Similarly, accounts payable and accounts receivable transactions are not likely to use the same data and do not conflict. However, multiple sales order transactions involving both read and write operations will potentially conflict.

The second part of the control process is to time stamp each transaction. A systemwide clock is used to keep all sites, some of which may be in different time zones, on the same logical time. Each time stamp is made unique by incorporating the site's ID number. When transactions are received at each site, they are examined first for potential conflicts. If conflicts exist, the transactions are entered into a serialization schedule. An algorithm is used to schedule updates to the database based on the transaction time stamp and class. This method permits multiple interleaved transactions to be processed at each site as if they were serial events.

Distributed Databases and the Accountant

The decision to distribute databases is one that should be entered into thoughtfully. There are many issues and tradeoffs to consider. Some of the most basic questions to be addressed are:

- Should the organization's data be centralized or distributed?

- If data distribution is desirable, should the databases be replicated or partitioned?

- If replicated, should the databases be totally replicated or partially replicated?

- If the database is to be partitioned, how should the data segments be allocated among the sites?

The choices involved in each of these questions impact the organization's ability to maintain database integrity. The preservation of audit trails and the accuracy of accounting records are key concerns. Clearly, these are decisions that the modern accountant should understand and influence intelligently.

Summary

This chapter examined the database approach to data management and showed how this approach enables business organizations to overcome data redundancy and the associated problems that plague the flat-file approach to data management. It showed that the database concept is composed of four dynamically interrelated components: users, the database management system, the database administrator, and the physical database. The DBMS stands between the physical database and the user community. Its principal function is to provide a controlled and secure environment for the database. This is achieved through software modules, such as a query language, a data definition language, and a data manipulation language. The DBMS also provides security against human error and natural disaster through various backup and recovery modules.

Database models are abstract representations of data about entities, events, and activities, and their relationships within an organization. The focus of attention was on the relational model. A number of database design topics were covered, including data modeling, the creation of user views from ER diagrams, and data normalization techniques. Finally, the chapter presented a number of issues associated with distributed databases. It examined three possible database configurations in a distributed environment: centralized, partitioned, and the replicated databases.

Appendix

The Hierarchical Database Model

The earliest database management systems were based on the *hierarchical* data model. This was a popular approach to data representation because it reflected, more or less faithfully, many aspects of an organization that are hierarchical in relationship. Also, it was an efficient data-processing tool for highly structured problems. Figure 9-29 presents a data structure diagram showing a portion of a hierarchical database.

The hierarchical model is constructed of sets of files. Each set contains a *parent* and a *child*. Notice that File B, at the second level, is both the child in one set and the parent in another set. Files at the same level with the same parent are called *siblings*. This structure is also called a *tree structure*. The file at the most aggregated level in the tree is the *root* segment, and the file at the most detailed level in a particular branch is called a *leaf*.

A Navigational Database

The hierarchical data model is called a *navigational database* because traversing it requires following a predefined path. This is established through pointers (discussed in Chapter 2) that create explicit linkages between related records. The only way to access data at lower levels in the tree is from the root and via the pointers down the navigational path to the desired records. For example, consider the partial database in Figure 9-30. To retrieve an invoice line-item record, the DBMS must first access the customer record (the root). That record contains a pointer to the sales invoice record, which points to the invoice line-item record.

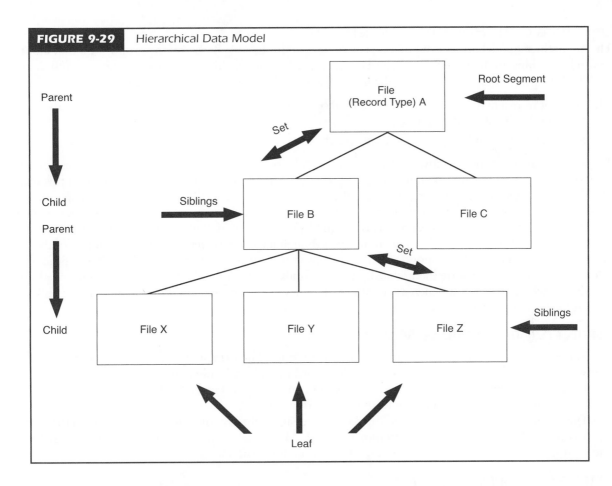

FIGURE 9-29   Hierarchical Data Model

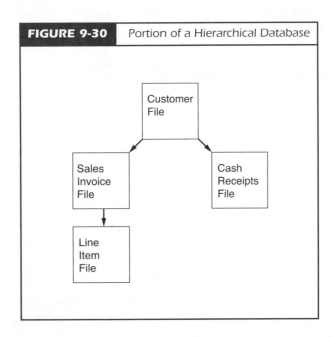

FIGURE 9-30   Portion of a Hierarchical Database

Limitations of the Hierarchical Model

The hierarchical model presents a limited view of data relationships. Based on the proposition that all business relationships are hierarchical (or can be represented as such), this model does not always reflect reality. The following rules, which govern the hierarchical model, reveal its operating constraints:

1. A parent record may have one or more child records. For example, in Figure 9-30, customer is the parent of both sales invoice and cash receipts.
2. No child record can have more than one parent.

The second rule is often restrictive and limits the usefulness of the hierarchical model. Many firms need a view of data associations that permit multiple parents like that represented by Figure 9-31(a). In this example, the sales invoice file has two natural parents: the customer file and the salesperson file. A specific sales order is the product of both the customer's purchase activity and a salesperson's selling efforts. Management, wishing to keep track of sales orders by customer and by salesperson, will want to view sales order records as the logical child of both parents. This relationship, although logical, violates the single parent rule of the hierarchical model. Figure 9-31(b) shows the most common way of resolving this problem. By duplicating the sales invoice file, two separate hierarchical representations are created. Unfortunately, this improved functionality is achieved at a cost—increased data redundancy. The network model, examined next, deals with this problem more efficiently.

THE NETWORK DATABASE MODEL

The *network* model is a variation of the hierarchical model. The principal distinguishing feature between the two is that the network model allows a child record to have multiple parents. The multiple ownership rule is flexible in allowing complex relationships to be represented. Figure 9-31(a) illustrates a simple network model in which the sales invoice file has two parent files—Customer and Salesperson.

The navigational DBMS dominated the data processing industry for many years, although the current trend is overwhelmingly toward the relational model. Many hierarchical and network systems still exist and continue to be maintained and upgraded by their manufacturers.

DATA STRUCTURES

Data structures are the bricks and mortar of the database. The data structure allows records to be located, stored, and retrieved, and enables movement from one record to another. Chapter 2 examined data structures commonly

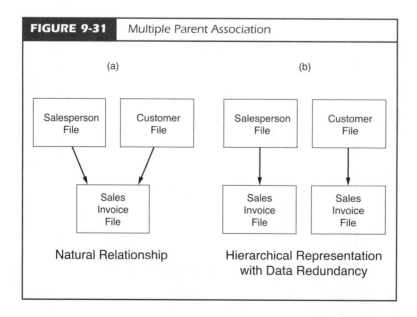

FIGURE 9-31   Multiple Parent Association

(a)

Salesperson File   Customer File

Sales Invoice File

Natural Relationship

(b)

Salesperson File   Customer File

Sales Invoice File   Sales Invoice File

Hierarchical Representation
with Data Redundancy

used by flat file systems. These include *sequential*, *indexed*, *hashing*, and *pointer* structures. These basic structures form the foundation for the more complex *hierarchical* and *network* database structures discussed next.

HIERARCHICAL MODEL DATA STRUCTURE

Figure 9-32 shows the data structures and linkages between files for the partial database in Figure 9-30. Because the purpose is to illustrate the navigational nature of the data structure, the content of the records has been simplified.

Assume that a user of this system is using a query program to retrieve all the data pertinent to a particular sales invoice (Invoice Number 1921) for a customer John Smith (Account Number 1875). The access method used for this situation is the **hierarchical indexed direct access method (HIDAM)**. Under this method, the root segment (customer file) of the database is organized as an indexed file. Lower-level records (e.g., sales invoice, invoice line item, and cash receipts records) use pointers in a linked-list arrangement. This allows both efficient processing of the root records for tasks, such as updating accounts receivable and billing customers, and direct access of detail records for inquiries.

The access method retrieves the primary key—Cust Num 1875—entered by the user via the query program and compares this against the index for the root segment. Upon matching the key with the index, it directly accesses John Smith's customer record. Notice the customer record contains only summary information. The current balance figure represents the total dollar amount owed ($1,820) by John Smith. This is the difference between the sum of all sales to this customer and all cash received in payment on the account. The supporting details about these transactions are contained in the lower-level sales invoice and cash-receipts records. In response to the user's inquiry for data pertaining to Invoice Number 1921, the access method follows the invoice record pointer to the sales invoice file.

The sales invoice file is a randomly organized file of invoices for all customers arranged in a series of linked lists. The records in each linked list have a common property—they all relate to a specific customer. The first record in the list—the head record—has a pointer to the next in the list (if one exists), which points to the next and so on. The pointer in the customer record (the level above) directs the access method to the

FIGURE 9-32   Linkages between Files in a Hierarchical Database

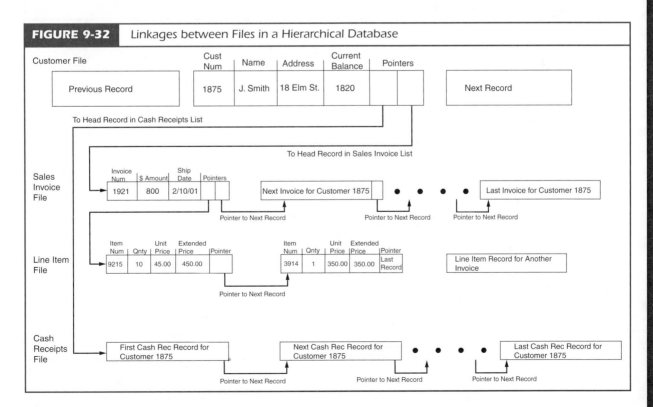

head record in the appropriate linked list. The access method then compares the key value sought (Invoice Number 1921) against each record in the list until it finds a match. The records in the sales invoice file contain only summary information about sales transactions. Pointers in these records identify the supporting detail records (the specific items sold) in the invoice line item file. The structure of the line item file is also a linked-list arrangement. Starting with the head record, the access method retrieves the entire list of line items for Invoice Number 1921. In this list there are two records. The sales invoice and line-item records are returned to the user's application for processing.

NETWORK MODEL DATA STRUCTURE

As with the hierarchical model, the network model is a navigational database with pointers creating explicit linkages between records. Whereas the hierarchical model allows only one path, the network model supports multiple paths to a particular record. Figure 9-33 shows the linkages for the data structure in Figure 9-31(a).

The structure can be accessed at either of the root level records (salesperson or customer) by hashing their respective primary keys (SP Num or Cust Num) or by reading their addresses from an index. A pointer field in the parent record explicitly defines the path to the child record, as discussed earlier. Notice the structure of the sales invoice file. In this example, each child now has two parents and contains explicit links to other records that form linked lists related to each parent. For example, Invoice Number 1 is the child of Salesperson Number 1 and Customer Number 5. This record structure has two links to related records. One of these is a salesperson (SP) link to Invoice Number 2. This represents a sale by Salesperson Number 1 to Customer Number 6. The second pointer is the customer (C) link to Invoice Number 3. This represents the second sale to Customer Number 5, which was processed this time by Salesperson Number 2. Under this data structure, management can track and report sales information pertaining to both customers and sales staff.

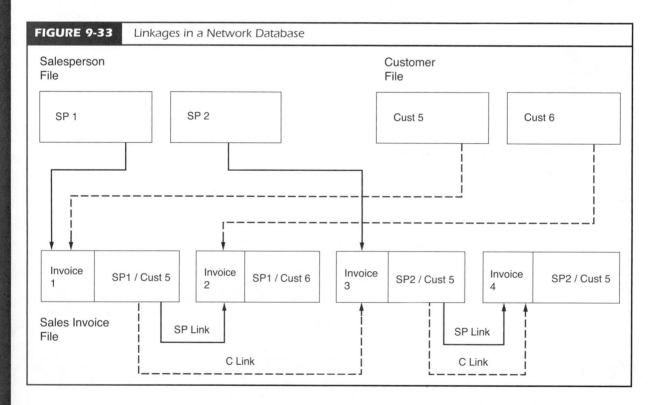

FIGURE 9-33   Linkages in a Network Database

THE DATA NORMALIZATION PROCESS

In this appendix, the normalization process is applied to the unnormalized table in Figure 9-34.[5] The table represents a view of student enrollment data for the registrar of a university. The data, as presented in the unnormalized table, satisfy the registrar's information needs. The current structure of the table, however, does not comply with the requirements of a relational database management system and will not function properly. The table must be normalized to accommodate the needs of both the DBMS and the registrar. Data normalization is the process of systematically reducing a complex table to a set of simple efficient tables that meet two conditions:

1. All nonkey attributes in the table are dependent on (defined by) the primary key.
2. All nonkey attributes are independent of the other nonkey attributes.

When these conditions are met, the table in question is in third normal form (3NF). Although tables can be further normalized to fourth and fifth normal form, these levels of precision are beyond most business needs. Achieving the state of 3NF involves the systematic process presented in Figure 9-35.

Beginning with an unnormalized table, the first step in the process is to identify and remove any repeating groups. Repeating groups are multiple data values at the intersection of rows and columns. When this is done, the table is in first normal form (1NF). The next step is to identify and remove any partial dependencies. These are nonkey attributes that are dependent on (defined by) only part of the primary key. This condition exists only when the primary key is a composite key. At this point, the table is in second normal form (2NF). The last step, which places the table in 3NF, is to remove any transitive dependencies. These are nonkey attributes dependent on another nonkey attribute in the table. With these basic goals in mind, let's now apply the normalization process to the Student Enrollment table.

Remove Repeating Groups

This example contains repeating groups of data. Because a student may take more than one course, the data unique to each additional course constitutes a repeating group. There is no single primary key that defines the repeating group data in an unnormalized table. We can see this clearly in Figure 9-36 by looking at the relationship between Stdnt Num (the candidate primary key) and the other attributes.

There is a 1:1 association between Stdnt Num and the Stdnt and Major attributes.[6] In other words, the two nonkey attributes (Stdnt and Major) are uniquely defined by the primary key (Stdnt Num). There is a 1:M association, however, between Stdnt Num and the other attributes. These repeating-group attributes are not uniquely defined by Stdnt Num. The lack of dependency between Stdnt Num and the repeating-group attributes

FIGURE 9-34	Unnormalized Database of Student Enrollments								
Stdnt Num	**Stdnt**	**Major**	**Course**	**Crse Desc**	**Instr**	**Off Hrs**	**Loc**	**Tel Num**	**Grade**
86432	Sethi	Acctg	Acc 315	Fin Acct	Ray	9–11	442	8-4545	A
			Acc 324	Mgt Acc	Smith	8–10	448	8-8945	A
			Math 21	Calc	Jones	1–3	323	8-2345	B
86789	Archer	Mgt	Mgt 1	Intro Mgt	Buell	4–5	463	8-3436	C
			Hist 1	U.S. Hist		9–11	342	8-2378	B
98653	Mills	Acctg	Acc 371	Ind Stdy	Ray	9–11	442	8-4545	B
			Math 21	Calc	Jones	1–3	323	8-2345	B
			Mgt 1	Intro Mgt	Buell	4–5	463	8-3436	C

---

5   This section is based on an excellent example by McFadden and Hoffer, Database Management: 223–230.
6   This assumes the student is allowed to have only one major at a time.

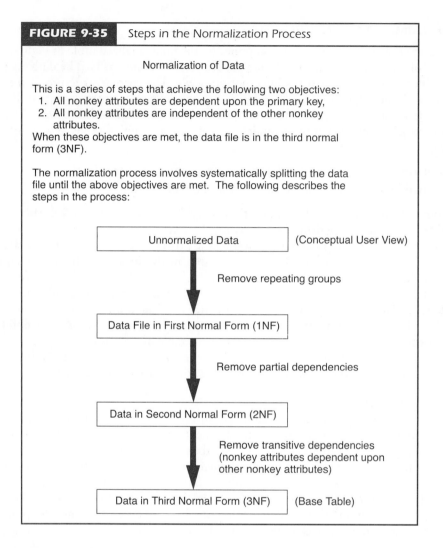

FIGURE 9-35   Steps in the Normalization Process

Normalization of Data

This is a series of steps that achieve the following two objectives:
1. All nonkey attributes are dependent upon the primary key,
2. All nonkey attributes are independent of the other nonkey attributes.

When these objectives are met, the data file is in the third normal form (3NF).

The normalization process involves systematically splitting the data file until the above objectives are met. The following describes the steps in the process:

Unnormalized Data   (Conceptual User View)

Remove repeating groups

Data File in First Normal Form (1NF)

Remove partial dependencies

Data in Second Normal Form (2NF)

Remove transitive dependencies (nonkey attributes dependent upon other nonkey attributes)

Data in Third Normal Form (3NF)   (Base Table)

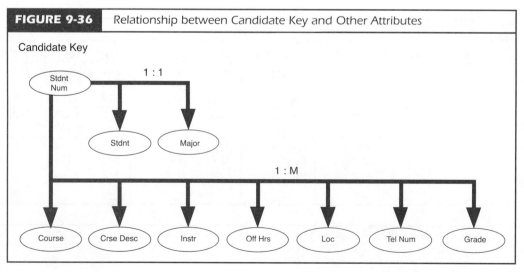

FIGURE 9-36   Relationship between Candidate Key and Other Attributes

Candidate Key

Stdnt Num

1 : 1

Stdnt   Major

1 : M

Course   Crse Desc   Instr   Off Hrs   Loc   Tel Num   Grade

prevents it from being the primary key for the table as it currently exists because the first normalization condition stated has not been met. Note that no other attribute in the table qualifies as the primary key either.

Figure 9-37 shows that the repeating-groups problem is solved by dividing the unnormalized table into two new tables: Student and Course-Grade. The Student table now meets the normalization conditions. The attributes Stdnt and Major are both defined by the primary key Stdnt Num and are independent of each other. This table is in 3NF.

The Course-Grade table is in 1NF. The primary key for this table is a composite key: Stdnt Num and Course. This is the only key that uniquely identifies the attribute Grade. While this table no longer contains repeating groups, a good deal of data redundancy exists. The attributes Instr, Loc, and Off Hrs are repeated for every student in every course the instructor teaches. Data redundancy and the partial relationships in the table (which will be explained shortly) lead to anomalies that negatively affect the performance of the database in three areas: updating records, inserting records, and deleting records. Before moving to the next step in the normalization process, let's briefly examine each of these anomalies.

Update Anomaly. Assume that Mgt 1, Introduction to Management, is an introductory course with 600 students registered. Assume the decision has been made to change the name of the course to Principles of Management. The current course title appears in each student record registered for this course. The user will need to search the entire Course-Grade table for each student enrolled in Mgt 1 and modify the course name 600 times. This is a consequence of data redundancy.

FIGURE 9-37   Removing Repeating Groups from Unnormalized Data

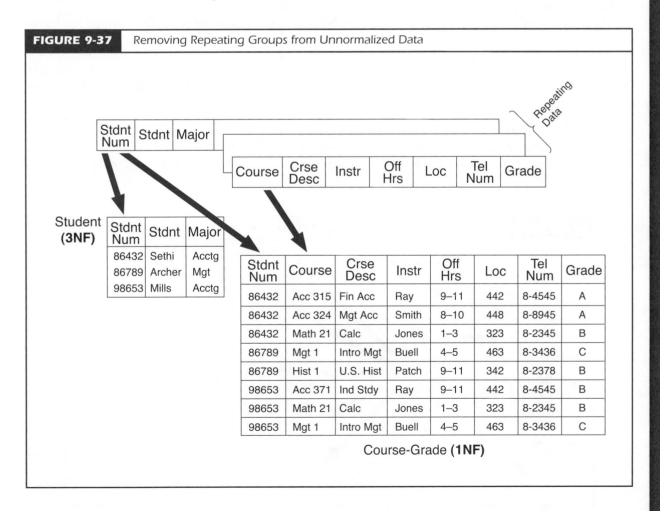

Insertion Anomaly. Suppose the registrar wants to add a new course—Acc 398, Advanced Managerial Topics—to the Course-Grade table. Currently, no students are enrolled in the course. Because Stdnt Num is part of the primary key, the registrar is unable to record this course until at least one student registers.

Deletion Anomaly. Suppose only one student is registered for the course Acc 371, Independent Study. Assume the student permanently leaves the university and is deleted from the Course-Grade table. The data about the course and the instructor will be lost because it cannot exist in the table without the primary key. This is undesirable because the course and the instructor still exist and the registrar wants and needs to retain these data. This problem occurs because the Stdnt Num is part of a composite primary key and the course and instructor data are not defined by this portion of the key. In other words, these data are only *partially* dependent on the primary key.

Remove Partial Dependencies

The next step in the normalization process is to remove all partial dependencies. **Partial dependencies** occur only in tables with a composite primary key. Figure 9-38 shows the relationship between the primary key and the nonkey attributes.

Notice that course and instructor data are dependent only on the Course portion of the composite key. The Grade attribute, however, is dependent on the entire key. For each student in each course, there is a single grade. By removing the partially dependent attributes, we create the two new tables—Stdnt-Grade and Course-Instr—shown in Figure 9-39.

The Stdnt-Grade table meets the conditions for 3NF. The Course-Instr table is in 2NF because it is free of repeating groups and partial dependencies. The three anomalies previously discussed are reduced significantly by this new table. Because of the reduced data redundancy in the table, the most apparent improvement pertains to the update anomaly. Now each course is listed only once, rather than once for every student. Although diminished in the 2NF table, the insertion and deletion anomalies still exist because of transitive dependencies. They are resolved in the next step.

Remove Transitive Dependencies

The instructor attributes (Off Hrs, Loc, Tel Num) are defined not by the course that the instructor teaches, but by the instructor, as illustrated in Figure 9-40. This is a transitive dependency that causes update, insertion, and deletion anomalies similar to those discussed earlier.

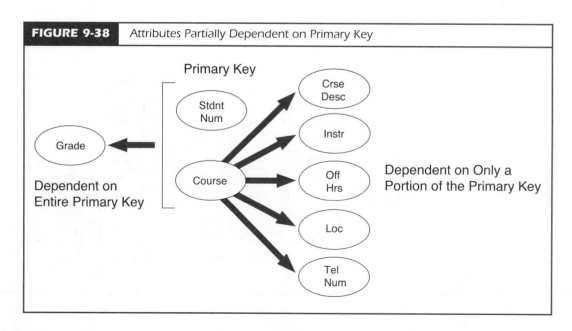

FIGURE 9-38   Attributes Partially Dependent on Primary Key

Primary Key

Stdnt Num

Crse Desc

Instr

Grade

Course

Off Hrs

Loc

Tel Num

Dependent on Entire Primary Key

Dependent on Only a Portion of the Primary Key

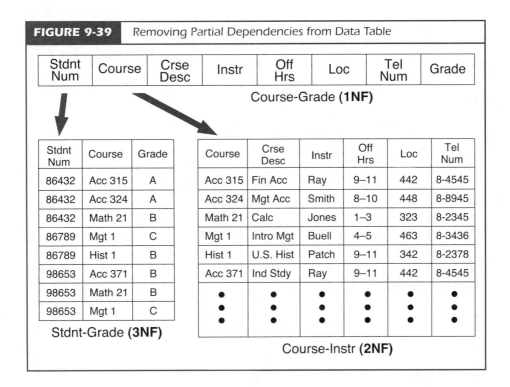

FIGURE 9-39 | Removing Partial Dependencies from Data Table

Stdnt Num	Course	Crse Desc	Instr	Off Hrs	Loc	Tel Num	Grade

Course-Grade (**1NF**)

Stdnt-Grade (**3NF**)

Stdnt Num	Course	Grade
86432	Acc 315	A
86432	Acc 324	A
86432	Math 21	B
86789	Mgt 1	C
86789	Hist 1	B
98653	Acc 371	B
98653	Math 21	B
98653	Mgt 1	C

Course-Instr (**2NF**)

Course	Crse Desc	Instr	Off Hrs	Loc	Tel Num
Acc 315	Fin Acc	Ray	9–11	442	8-4545
Acc 324	Mgt Acc	Smith	8–10	448	8-8945
Math 21	Calc	Jones	1–3	323	8-2345
Mgt 1	Intro Mgt	Buell	4–5	463	8-3436
Hist 1	U.S. Hist	Patch	9–11	342	8-2378
Acc 371	Ind Stdy	Ray	9–11	442	8-4545
⋮	⋮	⋮	⋮	⋮	⋮

Update Anomaly. Under the current table structure, the instructor data must be repeated for every occurrence of a course taught. For example, Ray teaches Acc 315 and Acc 371. In each of these records, Loc, Off Hrs, and Tel Num are listed. Any change in these instructor attributes must be changed for each occurrence.

Insertion Anomaly. The insertion anomaly prevents the registrar from adding data about an instructor unless he or she is currently teaching a course. Therefore, the registrar cannot maintain information about new faculty who are not yet teaching, nor existing faculty on sabbatical leave.

Deletion Anomaly. The deletion anomaly causes the unintentional destruction of data. Assume that an instructor is teaching only one course that for some reason is canceled. By deleting the course from the table, the instructor data is also destroyed.

FIGURE 9-40 | Transitive Relationship between the Nonkey Attribute Instructor and Other Instructor Attributes

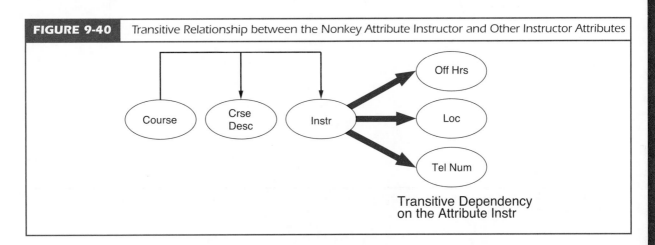

Transitive Dependency on the Attribute Instr

The transitive dependency is resolved by creating two new tables—Course and Instructor—as illustrated in Figure 9-41. Both of these tables are in 3NF. The anomalies associated with the original Course-Instr table no longer exist. Instructor data now reside independently from course data in separate tables that facilitate efficient updates, insertions, and deletions.

Embedded Keys

At this point, we have systematically reduced the unnormalized Stdnt-Grade table to four normalized base-tables: Student, Stdnt-Grade, Course, and Instructor. Figure 9-42 shows how the four base tables are linked together by common attributes. The primary key of one table is an embedded key in the related table. Specifically, Stdnt Num is the common attribute between the Student and Stdnt-Grade tables; Course is common to both the Stdnt-Grade and the Course tables;[7] and Instr is the attribute common to both the Course and Instructor tables. From these four normalized tables the student enrollment information needed by the registrar can be derived. The physical user view that presents this information can take the form of a computer screen or a hard-copy report. The underlying base tables will be transparent to the user.

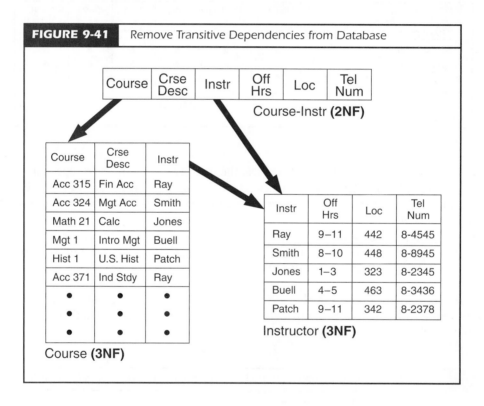

FIGURE 9-41   Remove Transitive Dependencies from Database

Course	Crse Desc	Instr	Off Hrs	Loc	Tel Num

Course-Instr (2NF)

Course (3NF)

Course	Crse Desc	Instr
Acc 315	Fin Acc	Ray
Acc 324	Mgt Acc	Smith
Math 21	Calc	Jones
Mgt 1	Intro Mgt	Buell
Hist 1	U.S. Hist	Patch
Acc 371	Ind Stdy	Ray
•	•	•
•	•	•
•	•	•

Instructor (3NF)

Instr	Off Hrs	Loc	Tel Num
Ray	9–11	442	8-4545
Smith	8–10	448	8-8945
Jones	1–3	323	8-2345
Buell	4–5	463	8-3436
Patch	9–11	342	8-2378

---

7   Remember, Stdnt-Grade has a composite key (Stdnt Num and Course). Thus we can access this table by using the entire key or either component.

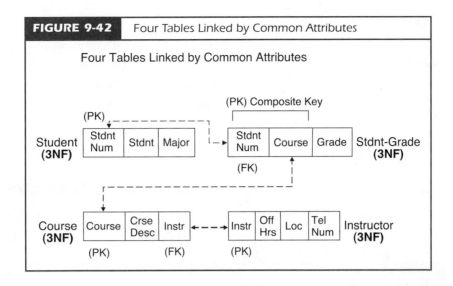

FIGURE 9-42   Four Tables Linked by Common Attributes

Four Tables Linked by Common Attributes

KEY TERMS

access method (436)

anomalies (447)

application development software (434)

association (442)

attributes (442)

cardinality (442)

centralized database (462)

concurrency control (467)

currency of information (430)

data attribute (430)

data currency (462)

data definition language (DDL) (435)

data dictionary (439)

data manipulation language (DML) (436)

data model (442)

data normalization (447)

data redundancy (430)

data storage (430)

data structures (470)

data updating (430)

database administrator (DBA) (438)

database lockout (464)

database management system (DBMS) (430)

deadlock (464)

deletion anomaly (448)

distributed data processing (DDP) (462)

distributed databases (464)

entity (442)

entity relationship (ER) diagram (442)

first normal form (1NF) (447)

flat file (430)

foreign key (445)

hierarchical model (432)

hierarchical indexed direct access method
    (HIDAM) (471)

indexed sequential file (440)

insertion anomaly (448)

internal view (435)

inverted list (440)

join (441)

navigational model (432)

network model (432)

occurrence (442)

partial dependencies (476)

partitioned database (464)

physical database (439)

primary key (445)

project (441)

relational model (432)

repeating group (457)

replicated databases (466)

restrict (441)

schema (conceptual view) (435)

second normal form (2NF) (447)

structured model (432)

structured query language (SQL) (437)

task-data dependency (430)

temporary inconsistency (462)

third normal form (3NF) (447)

transitive dependencies (458)

update anomaly (448)

user view (subschema) (435)

users (433)

REVIEW QUESTIONS

1. Give five general duties of the database administrator.
2. What are the four primary elements of the database environment?
3. How are the network and hierarchical models different?
4. What flat-file data management problems are solved as a result of using the database concept?
5. What are four ways in which database management systems provide a controlled environment to manage user access and the data resources?
6. Explain the relationship between the three levels of the data definition language. As a user, which level would you be most interested in?
7. What is a primary key?
8. What is a foreign key?
9. What is a data dictionary and what purpose does it serve?
10. Give an application for a partitioned database.
11. What is an entity?
12. Give an application for a replicated database.
13. Discuss and give an example of the following types of associations: (1:0,1), (1:1), (1:M), and (M:M).
14. Distinguish between association and cardinality.
15. Explain how a separate linking table works in a many-to-many association.
16. What are the four characteristics of properly designed relational database tables?
17. What do the relational features restrict, project, and join mean?
18. What are the conditions for third normal form (3NF)?
19. Explain how the SELECT and WHERE commands help a user to view the necessary data from multiple database files (tables).
20. What is a data model?
21. How can a poorly designed database result in unintentional loss of critical records?
22. What is a user view?
23. Does a user view always require multiple tables to support it? Explain.
24. What two conditions must valid entities meet?
25. Can two different entities have the same defining attributes? Explain.

DISCUSSION QUESTIONS

1. In the flat-file data management environment users are said to own their data files. What is meant by the "ownership" concept?
2. Discuss the potential aggravations you might face as a student as a result of your university using a flat-file data management environment, that is, different files for the registrar, library, parking, and so on.
3. Discuss why control procedures over access to the data resource become more crucial under the database approach than in the flat-file environment. What role does the DBMS play in helping to control the database environment?
4. What is the relationship between a database table and a user view?
5. Explain how linkages between relational tables are accomplished.

6. Explain the purpose of an ER diagram in database design.

7. SQL has been said to place power in the hands of the user. What does this statement mean?

8. Discuss the importance of the role of the database administrator. In the flat-file environment, why is such a role not necessary? What are the tasks performed by the DBA?

9. As users determine new computer application needs, requests must be sent to both the system programmers and the DBA. Why is it important that these two groups perform separate functions and what are these functions?

10. Why is a separate link table required when a M:M association exits between related tables?

11. As an accountant, why would you need to be familiar with data normalization techniques?

12. How does a database lockout contribute to financial data integrity?

13. How does concurrency control contribute to financial data integrity?

14. In a relational database environment certain accounting records (e.g., journals, subsidiary ledgers, and event general ledger accounts) may not exist. How is this possible?

15. Explain how to link tables in (1:1) association. Why may this be different in a (1:0,1) association?

16. Discuss the accounting implications of the update, insertion, and deletion anomalies associated with improperly normalized tables.

17. Give three examples that illustrate how cardinality reflects an organization's underlying business rules.

18. Discuss the key factors to consider in determining how to partition a corporate database.

19. Distinguish between a database lockout and a deadlock.

20. Replicated databases create considerable data redundancy, which is in conflict with the database concept. Explain the justification of this approach.

MULTIPLE-CHOICE QUESTIONS

1. The data attributes that a particular user has permission to access are defined by the
   b. operating system view.
   b. systems design view.
   c. database schema.
   d. user view.
   e. application program.

2. The database approach has several unique characteristics not found in traditional (flat-file) systems. Which of the following statements does not apply to the database model?
   a. Database systems have data independence; that is, the data and the programs are maintained separately except during processing.
   b. Database systems contain a data-definition language that helps describe each schema and subschema.
   c. The database administrator is the part of the software package that instructs the operating aspects of the program when data are retrieved.
   d. A primary goal of database systems is to minimize data redundancy.
   e. Database systems provide increased accessibility to data and flexibility in its usage.

3. One of the first steps in the creation of a relational database is to
   a. integrate accounting and nonfinancial data.
   b. plan for increased secondary storage capacity.
   c. order data-mining software that will facilitate data retrieval.
   d. create a data model of the key entities in the system.
   e. construct the physical user view using SQL.

4. Database currency is achieved by
   a. implementing partitioned databases at remote sites.
   b. employing data-cleansing techniques.
   c. ensuring that the database is secure from accidental entry.
   d. an external auditor's reconciliation of reports from multiple sites.
   e. a database lockout that prevents multiple simultaneous access.

5. The installation of a database management system is likely to have the least impact on
   a. data redundancy.
   b. entity-wide sharing of common data.

c. exclusive ownership of data.

d. the logic needed to solve a problem in an application program.

e. the internal controls over data access.

6. The functions of a database administrator are

a. database planning, data input preparation, and database design.

b. data input preparation, database design, and database operation.

c. database design, database operation, and equipment operations.

d. database design, database implementation, and database planning.

e. database operations, database maintenance, and data input preparation.

7. A relational database system contains the following inventory data: part number, description, quantity-on-hand, and reorder point. These individual items are called

a. attributes.

b. relations.

c. associations.

d. occurrences.

8. Which of the following is a characteristic of a relational database system?

a. All data within the system are shared by all users to facilitate integration.

b. Database processing follows explicit links that are contained within the records.

c. User views limit access to the database.

d. Transaction processing and data warehousing systems share a common database.

9. Partitioned databases are most effective when

a. users in the system need to share common data.

b. primary users of the data are clearly identifiable.

c. read-only access is needed at each site.

d. all of the above.

10. Database entities

a. may contain zero or many occurrences.

b. are represented as verbs in an ER diagram.

c. may represent both physical assets and intangible phenomena.

d. are often defined by common attributes that also define other entities.

e. are unique to a specific user view.

11. A transitive dependency

a. is a database condition that is resolved through special monitoring software.

b. is a name given to one of the three anomalies that result from unnormalized database tables.

c. can exist only in a table with a composite primary key.

d. cannot exist in tables that are normalized at the 2NF level.

e. is none of the above.

12. A partial dependency

a. is the result of simultaneous user requests for the same data in a partitioned database environment.

b. is a name given to one of the three anomalies that result from unnormalized database tables.

c. can exist only in a table with a composite primary key.

d. may exist in tables that are normalized at the 2NF level.

e. is none of the above.

13. Repeating group data

a. is a form of data redundancy common to replicated databases in a distributed database environment.

b. is a name given to one of the three anomalies that result from unnormalized database tables.

c. can exist only in a table with a composite primary key.

d. cannot exist in tables that are normalized at the 2NF level.

e. is none of the above.

14. The database model most likely to be used in the development of a modern (not legacy) system is:

a. Hierarchical.

b. Structured.

c. Relational.

d. Network.

e. Navigational.

15. Typical DBMS features include all of the following except:
    a. database interface design and development.
    b. backup and recovery.
    c. program development.
    d. database access.
    e. all of these are typical DBMS features.
16. Which of the following is least likely to be an attribute of an employee table in a normalized database?
    a. Employee name
    b. Employee address
    c. Employee number
    d. Employee supervisor's name
    e. All of these would be attributes of the employee table in a normalized database.
17. The advantages to using a partitioned database approach include all of the following except:
    a. The possibility for the deadlock phenomenon is reduced.
    b. User control is increased.
    c. Transaction processing time is decreased.
    d. The potential for wide-scale disaster is reduced.
    e. These are all advantages of partitioned databases.
18. Of the following, select the attribute that would be the best primary key in an inventory table.
    a. Item name
    b. Item location
    c. Item cost
    d. Item number
    e. Item supplier

PROBLEMS

1. DBMS versus Flat-File Processing
Werner Manufacturing Corporation has a flat-file processing system. The information-processing facility is very large. Different applications, such as order processing, production planning, inventory management, accounting systems, payroll, and marketing systems, use separate tape and disk files. The corporation has recently hired a consulting firm to investigate the possibility of switching to a database management system. Prepare a memo to the top management team at Werner explaining the advantages of a DBMS. Also, discuss the necessity of a database administrator and the job functions this person would perform.

2. Access Methods
For each of the following file processing operations, indicate whether a sequential file, indexed random file, indexed sequential access method (ISAM), hashing, or pointer structure works the best. You may choose as many as you wish for each step. Also, indicate which would perform the least optimally.
a. Retrieve a record from the file based upon its primary key value.
b. Update a record in the file.
c. Read a complete file of records.
d. Find the next record in a file.
e. Insert a record into a file.
f. Delete a record from a file.
g. Scan a file for records with secondary keys.

3. Database Design
Design a relational database for a video rental store. The store, which rents only DVDs and has no sales other than DVD rentals, has approximately 5,000 customers and approximately 1200 DVD titles. There are 25 suppliers of DVDs. Business rules include: (1) each DVD title may have many copies; (2) customers use their telephone numbers to uniquely identify themselves for video rentals; (3) a telephone number may apply to anyone in the household; (4) customers may rent more than one copy of any title, but, obviously, a copy of a title can only be rented by one customer at a time; and (5) suppliers may provide many titles and a DVD may be acquired from several different suppliers. Design the necessary database tables. State the primary key for each table as well as all other necessary attributes. Make certain the tables are in third normal form. Mark the attribute you have selected as the primary key (PK) as well as the attributes that serve as foreign keys (FK).

4. Database Design

Sears Roebuck, the most well-known and oldest mail-order retailer in the country, discontinued its mail-order operations a few years ago. Other mail-order marketers are using information systems to trim printing and postage costs of their catalogs. They also want to more effectively target their customers. Explain how an appropriately designed coding system for inventory items (see Chapter 8), incorporated in a relational database system with SQL capabilities, could allow more cost-efficient and effective mail-order operations. Sketch the necessary database table structure.

5. Database Deadlock

How is a lockout different from a deadlock? Give an accounting example to illustrate why a database lockout is necessary and how a deadlock can occur. Use actual table names in your example.

6. Structured Query Language

A vehicle rental company has a database that includes the following tables and attributes within those tables:

Customer Table

Customer number (PK); customer name, customer address, customer phone number, customer credit card number.

Inventory Table

Inventory number (PK); item description; item cost; item rental price; number of days for which an item can be rented.

Rental Form Table

Rental Form number (PK); rental date; customer number (FK).

Rental Line Items Table

Rental Form number (PK); inventory number (PK); due date.

Required:
Using the SQL commands given in this chapter, write the code that would be necessary to generate a report of each customer with rented items that are past due. Customers can rent more than one item at a time, and items may have different rental periods, so this report should only include overdue items. (You may use "Today" to signify the current date.)

7. Distributed Databases

The XYZ company is a geographically distributed organization with several sites around the country. Users at these sites need rapid access to common data for read-only purposes. Which distributed database method is best under these circumstances? Explain your reasoning.

8. Distributed Databases

The ABC Company is a geographically distributed organization with several sites around the country. Users at these sites need rapid access to data for transaction processing purposes. The sites are autonomous; they do not share the same customers, products, or suppliers. Which distributed database method is best under these circumstances? Explain your reasoning.

9. Normalization of Data

A table of data for a library is found on the following page. Normalize this data into the third normal form, preparing it for use in a relational database environment. The library's computer is programmed to compute the due date to be 14 days after the checkout date. Document the steps necessary to normalize the data similar to the procedures found in the chapter. Index any fields necessary and show how the databases are related.

10. Normalization of Data

A college bookstore maintains all of its records on index cards. This has proven to be a very tedious chore, and the manager has asked you to design a database that will simplify this task. The index cards are preprinted and contain the following labels:

Title:
Author(s)
Edition:
Publisher:
Publisher Address:
Publisher Phone #:
Cost of Text:
Selling Price:
Number on Hand:
Professor:
Class:
Semester:
Year:
Professor Phone #:

	Problem 9: Normalization of Data						
Student ID Number	**Student First Name**	**Student Last Name**	**Number of Books Out**	**Book Call No**	**Book Title**	**Date Out**	**Due Date**
678-98-4567	Amy	Baker	4	hf351.j6	Avalanches	09-02-04	09-16-04
678-98-4567	Amy	Baker	4	hf878.k3	Tornadoes	09-02-04	09-16-04
244-23-2348	Ramesh	Sunder	1	i835.123	Politics	09-02-04	09-16-04
398-34-8793	James	Talley	3	k987.d98	Sports	09-02-04	09-16-04
398-34-8793	James	Talley	3	d879.39	Legal Rights	09-02-04	09-16-04
678-98-4567	Amy	Baker	4	p987.t87	Earthquakes	09-03-04	09-17-04
244-23-2348	Ramesh	Sunder	1	q875.i76	Past Heroes	09-03-04	09-17-04

Using your understanding of the business rules that exist in most colleges and for most college bookstores, prepare the base tables (in third normal form) that will be required to translate the index card information into a working database for the bookstore.

11. Normalization of Data
Prepare the base tables, in third normal form, needed to produce the user view below.

12. Normalization of Data
Prepare the base tables, in third normal form, needed to produce the user view on the following page.

13. Normalization of Data
Prepare the 3NF base tables needed to produce the sales report view on the following page.

14. Normalization of Data—Purchase Order
The purchase order on page 487 is used by Acme Plywood Company.

Acme business rules:

(1) Each vendor may supply many items, an item is supplied by only one vendor.

(2) A purchase order may list many items, an item may be listed on many purchase orders.

(3) An employee may complete several purchase orders, but only one employee may fill out an individual PO.

Prepare the 3FN base tables needed to produce this purchase order.

15. Table Linking
Refer to text in Problem 15 on page 487.

16. Defining Entities and Data Modeling—Payroll
Employees at the Sagerod manufacturing company record their hours worked on paper time cards that are inserted into a time clock machine at the beginning and end of each shift. On Fridays the supervisor collects the time cards, reviews and signs them, and

	Problem 11: Normalization of Data									
	USER VIEW									
Part Num	**Description**	**QOH**	**Reorder Point**	**EOQ**	**Unit Cost**	**Ven Num**	**Ven Name**	**Ven Address**	**Tel**	
132	Bolt	100	50	1000	1.50	987	ABC Co.	654 Elm St	555 5498	
143	Screw	59	10	100	1.75	987	ABC Co.	654 Elm St	555 5498	
760	Nut	80	20	500	2.00	742	XYZ Co.	510 Smit	555 8921	
982	Nail	100	50	800	1.00	987	ABC Co.	654 Elm St	555 5498	

Problem 12:
Normalization of Data

USER VIEW

Part Num	Description	QOH	Reorder Point	EOQ	Unit Cost	Ven Num	Ven Name	Ven Address	Tel
132	Bolt	100	50	1000	1.50	987	ABC Co.	654 Elm St	555 5498
					1.55	750	RST Co.	3415 8th St	555 3421
					1.45	742	XYZ Co.	510 Smit	555 8921
982	Nail	100	50	800	1.00	987	ABC Co.	654 Elm St	555 5498
					1.10	742	XYZ Co.	510 Smit	555 8921
					1.00	549	LMN Co.	18 Oak St	555 9987

Problem 13:
Normalization of Data

Sales Report

Customer Number: 19321
Customer Name : Jon Smith
Address : 520 Main St.,City

Invoice Num	Date	Invoice Total	Part Num	Quantity	Unit Price	Ext'd Price
12390	11/11/04	$850	2	5	$20	$100
			1	10	50	500
			3	25	10	250
12912	11/21/04	$300	4	10	$30	$300

Customer Total: $1,150

   ** * *** * *** * *** * *** * *** * ** *

Customer Number: 19322
Customer Name : Mary Smith
Address : 2289 Elm St., City

Invoice Num	Date	Invoice Total	Part Num	Quantity	Unit Price	Ext'd Price
12421	11/13/04	$1,000	6	10	$20	$200
			1	2	50	100
			5	7	100	700
12901	11/20/04	$500	4	10	$30	$300
			2	10	20	200

Customer Total: $1,500

   ** * *** * *** * *** * *** * *** * ** *

Next Customer
   •
   •
   •
Next Customer

Problem 14:
Normalization of Data

Purchase Order

Acme Plywood Co.   P.O. #
1234 West Ave.   Date: __/__/__
Somewhere, OH 000000

Vendor: _____
         _____
         _____

Ship Via: _____   Please refer this P.O. number on all correspondence.

Prepared by: _____

Item #	Description	Quantity	Cost	Extension

Problem 15:
Table Linking

Several related tables with their primary keys (PK) are shown below. Place the foreign key(s) in the tables to link them according to the associations shown (e.g., 1:M and M:M). Create any new table(s) that may be needed.

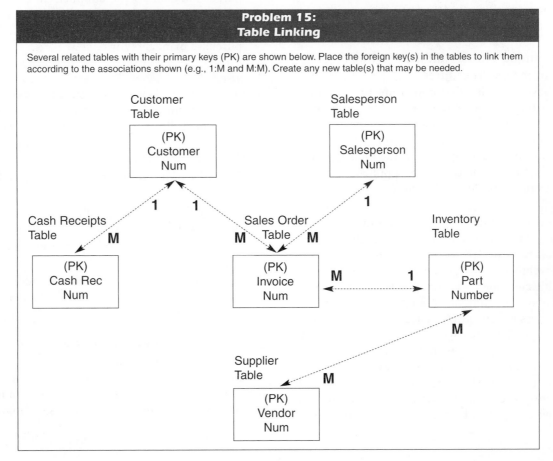

sends them to the payroll clerk. The clerk calculates the pay for each employee and updates the individual earnings records. The clerk then prepares a paycheck for each employee and records it in the check register. Based on these records, the clerk prepares a payroll register, which is sent with the paychecks to the cash disbursements clerk. The clerk reviews the payroll register, updates the cash disbursements journal to record the total payroll, and prepares a check for the total payroll, which is deposited into the imprest account. The clerk then signs the paychecks and distributes them to the employees.

Required:

Assume that this manual system is to be automated using a relational database system. Perform the following tasks. You may need to make assumptions about how certain automated activities will be performed.

a. List all candidate entities in the procedures described.

b. Identify the valid entities and explain why the rejected entities should not be modeled.

c. Create a data model of the process showing entity associations.

17. Defining Entities and Data Modeling— Purchases Procedures

The business rules that constitute the purchases system for the Safe Buy Grocery Stores chain are similar at all the store locations. The purchase manager at each location is responsible for selecting his or her local suppliers. If the manager needs a product he or she chooses a supplier. Each store follows the steps described below.

1. The purchasing function begins with sales representatives from suppliers periodically observing the shelves and displays at each individual location and recognizing the need to restock inventory. Inventory declines by direct sales to the customers or by spoilage of perishable goods. In addition, the supplier's sales representatives review obsolescence reports prepared by the purchase manager that identify slow-moving and dated products that are deemed unsalable at a particular location. These products are returned to the supplier and replaced with more successful products. The sales representatives prepare a hard-copy purchase requisition

and meet with the purchase managers of the individual store locations. Together the sales representative and the purchase manager create a purchase order defining products, the quantity, and the delivery date.

2. At the intended delivery date, Safe Buy Grocery Stores receive the goods from the suppliers. Goods received are unloaded from the delivery trucks and stocked on the shelves and displays by part-time employees.

3. The unloading personnel create a receiving report. Each day a receiving report summary is prepared and sent to the purchase managers for review.

4. The supplier subsequently submits an invoice to the accounts payable department clerk who creates an invoice record. The clerk reconciles the invoice against the receiving report and purchase order and then creates a payment obligation to be paid at a future date, depending on the terms of trade.

5. On the due date a check is automatically prepared and sent to the supplier, and the payment is recorded in the check register. At the end of each day a payment summary is sent to purchase managers for review.

Required:

Assume that the manual system above is to be automated using a relational database system. Perform the following tasks. You may need to make assumptions about how certain automated activities will be performed.

a. List all candidate entities in the procedures described.

b. Identify the valid entities and explain why the rejected entities should not be modeled.

c. Create a data model of the process showing entity associations.

d. Create a fully attributed model by adding primary keys, foreign keys, and data attributes. Normalize the model.

18. Defining Entities and Data Modeling— Fixed Asset Procedures

The business rules that constitute the fixed asset procedures for the Safe Buy Grocery Stores chain are similar at all the store locations. The store manager at each location is responsible for identifying needed fixed assets and for selecting the vendor. Freezers, refrigerators, delivery vans, and store shelving are examples of fixed asset purchases. Once the need has been identified, each store follows the procedure described next.

The manager creates a purchase order, which is sent to the supplier. The supplier delivers the asset to the receiving clerk, who prepares a receiving report. Each week the fixed-asset department clerk reviews the fixed asset receiving report summary and creates a fixed asset inventory record for each receipt. The fixed-asset clerk maintains the inventory records and depreciation schedules. The vendor subsequently submits an invoice to the accounts payable department clerk who creates an invoice record. The clerk reconciles the invoice against the receiving report and purchase order and then creates a payment obligation to be paid at a future date, depending on the terms of trade. On the due date a check is automatically prepared and sent to the vendor, and the payment is recorded in the check register. At the end of each day a payment summary is sent to the accounts payable manager for review.

Required:

Assume that the manual system above is to be automated using a relational database system. Perform the following tasks. You may need to make assumptions about how certain automated activities will be performed.

a. List all candidate entities in the procedures described.

b. Identify the valid entities and explain why the rejected entities should not be modeled.

c. Create a data model of the process showing entity associations.

d. Create a fully attributed model by adding primary keys, foreign keys, and data attributes. Normalize the model.

19. Defining Entities and Data Modeling— Business Rules

Given the following business rules, construct an ER diagram so each rule is captured for the database. Presume each rule is to be treated individually, so construct an ER diagram for each rule.

a. A retail sales company prepares sales orders for its customers' purchases. A customer can make many purchases, but a sales order is written for a single customer.

b. A retail sales company orders inventory using a purchase order. An inventory item may be ordered many times, and a purchase order may be created for more than one inventory item.

c. A company that sells antique cars prepares a sales order for each car sold. The inventory for this company consists of unique automobiles and only one of these automobiles may be listed on a sales order.

d. A grocery store identifies returning customers via a plastic card that the clerk scans at the time of each purchase. The purpose of this card is to track inventory and to maintain a database of customers and their purchases. Obviously, a customer may purchase an unlimited number of items from the grocery store. Items are unique only by a UPC code and each UPC code may be associated with many different customers.

e. A video rental store uniquely identifies each of its inventory items so customers can rent a movie and return the movie via a drop box and the store can identify which copy of the movie was rented and returned. A customer is allowed to rent up to six movies at a time, but a copy of a movie can only be rented by one customer at a time.

20. Comprehensive Case
(Prepared by Katie Daley and Gail Freeston, Lehigh University)

D&F is a distributor of CDs and cassettes that offers benefits such as discount prices and an introductory offer of 10 CDs or cassettes for a penny (not including the shipping and handling costs). Its primary target customers are college students; its main marketing strategy is constant deals to club members. The company's main competitors in the industry are BMG and Columbia House; both offer similar promotions. D&F started in 1993 with an office in Harrisburg, Pennsylvania, initially targeting college students in the surrounding area. The company realized there was a high demand for discounted music merchandise and the convenience of delivery by mail within universities. After its second year, with a constant increase in customer orders, D&F relocated to Philadelphia because it was located near more colleges and universities. The move has had a positive effect on net profits and demand, supporting the decision to continue the growth of the company. D&F recently expanded its facility to be able to fulfill a higher demand for its services. Its customer base ranges from areas as close as Villanova University to as far as Boston College. As of 2003, there were 103 employees. Their prior year's gross sales were $125 million.

D&F's market share is on the rise, but is not yet comparable to the magnitude of BMG and Columbia House. However, the corporation's goals for the upcoming years include establishing itself as an industry player through increased customer satisfaction and loyalty. D&F is also considering the installation of a new information processing system. This system will reengineer their current business functions by reducing loopholes in their internal control problems.

D&F receives CDs and cassettes from various wholesale suppliers and music store chains, totaling 32 suppliers nationwide. The office has its own warehouse, stores its own merchandise, and is responsible for replenishing the inventory. D&F has had no substantial problems in the past with their suppliers. On the other hand, it has encountered problems with excess inventory, stockouts, and discrepancies with inventory records.

Revenue Cycle

Becoming a member of D&F Music Club involves calling the toll-free number and speaking with a sales representative, who establishes a new customer account. A customer's account record contains his or her name, address, phone number, previous orders he or she made with the company, and a sequentially assigned unique customer account number.

Customers place orders by phone with a sales representative, who prepares a sales order record. John, in the billing department, reviews the sales orders, adds prices and shipping charges, and prints a copy (invoice) that is sent to the customer. John then adds a record to the sales journal to record the sale.

Chris, a warehouse employee, verifies the information on the sales order, picks the goods, prints the packing slip, and updates the inventory subsidiary ledger. Chris then prepares the bill of lading for the carrier. The goods are then shipped.

Sandy in accounts receivable updates the customer accounts and general ledger control accounts.

When customers make a payment on account, they send both the remittance advice (that was attached to the invoice) and a check with their account number on it. Scott, a mail room clerk, opens all the cash receipts. He separates the check and remittance advice and prepares a remittance list, which, along with the checks, is sent to the cash receipts department.

Laura, the cash receipts clerk, reconciles the checks with the remittance, updates the customer's account and the general ledger, and then deposits the checks in the bank. She sends the deposit slip to Sandy in the accounting department.

Upon receiving the bank receipt, Sandy files it and updates the cash receipts journal to record the amount deposited. Upon the receipt of the CDs or cassettes ordered, the customer has a 15-day trial period. If, at the end of that period, he or she sends a payment, it is understood that the goods have been accepted. If, on the other hand, the customer is dissatisfied with the product for any reason, he or she can return it to D&F Music Club at no charge. However, to return the CD or cassette, the customer must call the company to obtain an authorization number. When the goods arrive, Chris prepares the return record and updates the inventory subsidiary ledger. Printed copies of the return record are sent to John and Sandy. John reviews the return record and updates the sales journal. Sandy credits the customer's account and updates the general ledger to reverse the transaction.

Expenditure Cycle

The purchases system and the cash disbursements system comprise D&F Music Club's expenditure cycle. The three departments within the purchasing system are the warehouse, purchasing, and accounting. The purchasing function begins in the warehouse, which stores the inventory of CDs and cassettes. Jim, the warehouse manager, compares inventory records with the various demand forecasts of each week, provided by the market research analyst teams, to determine the necessary orders to make. At the end of the week, Jim prepares the purchase requisition record.

Sara, the purchasing clerk, reviews the purchase requisitions, selects the suppliers, and prepares the purchase orders. Copies of the purchase orders are sent to the supplier and accounting.

When the shipment arrives, Chris, the warehouse clerk, working from a blind copy of the purchase order, counts and inspects the goods for damage. He then prepares a receiving report and updates the inventory records.

Upon receipt of the supplier's invoice, Diana, the accounting clerk, compares it to the respective purchase order and receiving report. If the invoice is accurate, Diana creates an accounts payable record, sets a due date to be paid, and updates general ledger accounts.

On the due date Evan, the cash disbursements clerk, closes the accounts payable record, cuts a check, and sends it sent to the supplier. He then updates the check register and the general ledger.

Required:
Assume that the manual system above is to be automated using a relational database system.

Perform the following tasks. You may need to make assumptions about how certain automated activities will be performed.

a. List all candidate entities in the procedures described.

b. Identify the valid entities and explain why the rejected entities should not be modeled.

c. Create a data model of the processes showing entity associations.

d. Create a fully attributed model by adding primary keys, foreign keys, and data attributes. Normalize the model.

e. Prepare a data flow diagram of the system showing the data stores.

chapter 10

The REA Approach to Business Process Modeling*

LEARNING OBJECTIVES

After studying this chapter, you should:

- Recognize the limitations of the traditional database system.
- Be aware of the benefits of adopting an REA approach to information systems compared to a traditional approach.
- Be aware of the implications of REA for the accounting profession.
- Be aware of the steps involved in preparing an REA model of a business process.
- Appreciate the importance of identifying the attributes of entity relations in relational database design.
- Appreciate the difference between an REA model representation of a business process and an ER diagram representation.

This chapter examines the resources, events, and agents (REA) model as a means of specifying and designing accounting information systems that serve the needs of all the users within an organization. The chapter is composed of three major sections. The first introduces the REA approach and identifies a number of problems associated with traditional accounting practice that can be resolved through an REA approach. The second section examines traditional database applications and their limitations. While superior to flat-file systems, traditional database systems suffer from serious problems that limit their usefulness. An important limitation is their almost exclusive support of financial information users and their inadequacy at meeting the growing need for nonfinancial information. A second limitation is their inability to respond to noneconomic events that may be of extreme importance to an organization. The third section provides a detailed examination of the REA model. The steps involved in developing an REA model are presented and compared to the traditional ER approach to modeling business processes.

---

* This chapter was co-authored by Alan Sangster, Open University Business School, Milton Keynes, United Kingdom.

THE REA APPROACH

Central to the REA philosophy is the recognition that information systems should support the information needs of all users of information in the organization. This section addresses the changing information needs of modern management, the limitations of traditional accounting in meeting those needs, and the role of REA as a potential solution.

USER VIEWS

You will recall from Chapter 9 that a **user view** is the set of data that a particular user needs to achieve his or her assigned tasks. For example, a general ledger clerk's user view will include the organization's chart of accounts, but not detailed transaction data. A sales manager's view may include detailed customer sales data organized by product, region, and salesperson. A production manager's view may include finished goods inventory on hand, available manufacturing capacity, and vendor lead times.

A problem arises in meeting these diverse needs when the collection, summarization, storage, and reporting of transaction and resource data are dominated by a single view that is inappropriate for entity-wide purposes. The accounting profession has been criticized in recent years for focusing too narrowly on the role of accounting information. Many believe that the profession should shift its emphasis away from debits, credits, double-entry accounting, and GAAP and move toward providing useful information for decision making and helping organizations identify and control business risk. As the primary providers of information, however, accountants have dictated the set of data used by organizations.

Modern managers need both financial and nonfinancial information in formats and at levels of aggregation that the traditional GAAP-based accounting systems are generally incapable of providing. The response within organizations to the single view of accounting information has been to create separate information systems to support each user's view. This has resulted in organizations with multiple information systems that are frequently unconnected electronically. Virtually all data entered into one system needs to be re-entered into the others. With such widespread duplication of data, accuracy and currency are serious problems. Often, these information systems provide different answers to the same requests for information, which leads to confusion, poor decision making, and inappropriate actions.

Future accountants will increasingly face enterprise-wide information systems that are designed to overcome the information shortcomings outlined above. These systems will be based on the relational database model and will be event oriented rather that account oriented. Such a system is REA. The modern accountant needs to be responsive, proactive, and equipped with an understanding of the REA approach, its power, and its flexibility.

THE REA MODEL

The **REA model** is an alternative accounting framework for modeling an organization's critical resources, events, and agents (REA) and the relationships between them. Once adopted, both accounting and nonaccounting data about these phenomena can be identified, captured, and stored in a centralized database. From this repository, user views can be constructed that meet the needs of all users in the organization. The availability of multiple views allows flexible use of transaction data and enables the development of accounting information systems that are free of the weaknesses identified earlier.

REA was proposed in 1982 as a theoretical model for accounting.[1] At that time, technology was not sufficiently powerful to translate the theory of REA into practice.

1   W. E. McCarthy, "The REA Accounting Model: A Generalized Framework for Accounting Systems in a Shared Data Environment," *The Accounting Review* (July 1982): 554–577.

Advances in database technology have now focused renewed attention on REA as a practical alternative to the traditional accounting framework.

The REA model requires that phenomena be characterized in a manner consistent with the development of multiple user views. Business data must not be preformatted or artificially constrained and must reflect all relevant aspects of the underlying economic events. As such, REA **data modeling** does not include traditional accounting elements such as journals, ledgers, charts of accounts, and double entry (debits and credits) accounting, though it can be used to create any or all of them if required.

Organizations that use REA produce financial statements and reports directly from the event-driven detailed data, rather than from traditional ledgers and journals. The key elements of the REA model are discussed in the following sections.

Resources

Economic **resources** are the assets of the organization. They are defined as objects that are both scarce and under the control of the enterprise. This definition departs from the traditional model since it does not include anything that can be derived from other data, such as accounts receivable, which is an artifact record used simply to store and transmit data. (Accounts receivable is derived as the difference between sales to customers and the cash received in payment of sales.)

It should be noted that when relevant to the planning, evaluation, and control of events, the resources within an REA model include the locations where significant events occur, such as cash tills, inventory records, and inquiry desks.

Events

Economic **events** are phenomena that affect changes in resources. They can result from activities such as production, exchange, consumption, and distribution. Economic events are the critical information elements of the accounting system and should be captured in a highly detailed form to provide a rich database. Under the REA modeling approach, events are divided into three classes, *operating events* (what happens), *information events* (what is recorded), and *decision/management events* (what is done as a result). Only operating events, however, are included in the REA model.

Agents

Economic **agents** are individuals and departments that participate in an economic event. They are parties both inside and outside the organization with discretionary power to use or dispose of economic resources. Examples of agents include sales clerks, production workers, shipping clerks, customers, and vendors.

ADVANTAGES OF THE REA MODEL

Organizations that use the REA approach can derive the following advantages.

More Efficient Operations

Firms using the REA approach may experience improved operational efficiency in three ways:

1. The REA approach to modeling business processes will help managers identify nonvalue-added activities that can be eliminated from operations.
2. The storage of both financial and nonfinancial data in the same central database reduces the need for multiple data collection, storage, and maintenance procedures.
3. Storing financial and nonfinancial data about business events in detailed form permits the support of a wider range of management decisions.

Increased Productivity

Improving the operational efficiency of individual departments by eliminating nonvalue-added activities will generate excess capacity. This additional capacity can be redirected to increase the overall productivity of the firm.

Competitive Advantage

By supporting multiple user views, the REA model provides managers with more relevant, timely, and accurate information. This will translate into better customer service, higher quality products, and flexible production processes.

VALUE CHAIN ANALYSIS

The competitive advantage benefits of adopting the REA approach are most clearly seen from the perspective of the **value chain**. These are the activities that add value or usefulness to an organization's products and services. To remain competitive, most organizations must differentiate between their various business activities, prioritizing them on the basis of their value in achieving organizational objectives. Organizations need to be increasingly adaptable and responsive to changes in the environment in which they operate. This includes their industry, suppliers, customers, and other external influences that impact performance. Furthermore, organization management needs to continuously review and improve the effective and efficient utilization of resources to maximize the attainment of their organization's objectives.

Decision makers need to look beyond the internal operations and functions of their organizations. One approach adopted for this purpose is known as **value chain analysis**. This analysis distinguishes between primary activities—those that create value—and support activities—those that assist in the achievement of the primary activities. Through applying this analysis, an organization is able to look beyond itself and maximize its ability to create value by, for example, incorporating the needs of its customers in its products, or the flexibility of its suppliers in scheduling its production.

Traditional information systems are not well suited to supporting many value chain activities. Organizations that have applied value chain analysis have generally done so outside the traditional accounting information system by providing such information separately to the decision makers. Frequently, this involved the creation of separate information systems with all the resulting problems outlined in the previous section. It is fairly obvious that the adoption of a single information system framework that supplies all the needed information is preferable.

DATABASE APPLICATIONS

Before considering REA modeling further, we need to first look at traditional database applications. Specifically, the operational characteristics of revenue and expenditure cycle applications that use relational databases and how they differ from equivalent flat-file systems will be examined. We shall then be better prepared to look further at REA modeling and understand how an REA model may be used for developing relational databases that support business processes.

ORDER ENTRY AND CASH RECEIPTS SYSTEM

A quick review of the order entry system flowchart in Figure 10-1 shows that the business processes in this database application are not fundamentally different from its legacy flat-file counterpart. Orders are received, credit is checked, goods are shipped, and customers are billed just as with flat files.

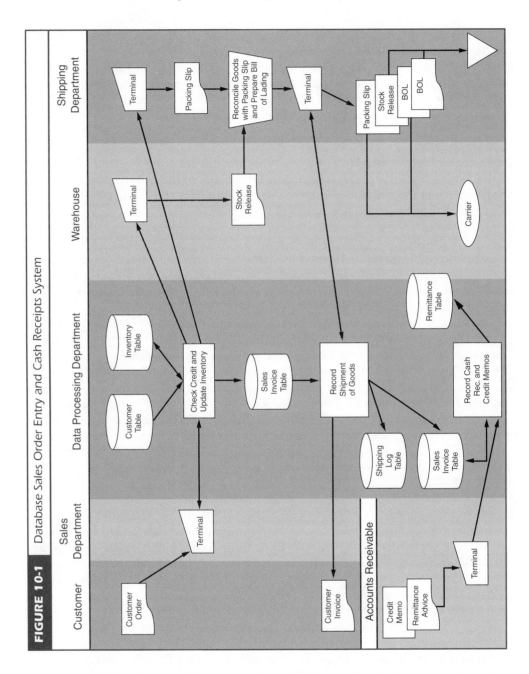

FIGURE 10-1   Database Sales Order Entry and Cash Receipts System

The most significant difference between the two approaches is the method of storing data. Relational tables have replaced the flat files that emulate classical accounting records, including journals, subsidiary ledgers, and the general ledger. The transaction data captured by such systems tend to be artificially structured to meet the needs of financial reporting. These systems are account-based in their orientation. This orientation often results in the loss of rich details that are needed by other users. In a relational database environment it is possible to focus on economic transactions rather than the accounting *artifacts* that merely capture the financial effects of these events. If the transaction is captured in sufficient detail, the financial values needed for financial reporting can be calculated from the transaction database. However, this rich database can also support the needs of other users.

Many organizations adopt a compromise position and maintain both a traditional general ledger for financial reporting and a transaction database for operations support. Figure 10-2 illustrates the structures of the database tables represented in Figure 10-1. An explanation of their usage is given in the following section.

Customer Table

The **Customer table** contains address and credit information about customers. The Credit Limit value is used to validate sales transactions. If the sum of the customer's outstanding account balance and the amount of current sales transaction exceeds the pre-established credit limit, then the transaction is rejected.

Sales Invoice Table

The **Sales Invoice table**, along with the Line Item table (discussed next), captures sales transactions for the period. A sales invoice record is created when credit approval is granted. When the order is shipped to the customer, the date is placed in the Shipped Date field to signify the event and to flag the record "open." When cash receipts are received, they are matched to the open invoice record, which is then closed by placing the current date in the Closed Date field. Also, the Remittance Number, which is the primary key of the Remittance table, is added to the invoice record as a cross-reference.

The Sales Invoice table may be used to replace some traditional accounting records. First, since it contains the total amount due for each invoice, summing the Invoice Amount field for all records in the table yields total sales (equivalent to the sales journal) for the period. The accounts receivable balance (AR subsidiary ledger) for a particular customer is calculated by summing the Invoice Amount fields for all of the customer's open invoices. Total accounts receivable (general ledger, AR—Control) is the sum of all the open invoice records in the entire table.

Line Item Table

The **Line Item table** contains a record of every item sold to the organization's customers. Since a single transaction can involve one or more products, each record in the Sales Invoice table is associated with (linked to) one or more records in this table. Notice that the table contains two primary keys—Invoice Number and Item Number. Both keys are needed to uniquely define each record in the table. They also provide links to related records in the Sales Invoice and Inventory tables.

Cost of goods sold is determined by linking each Line Item table record to the Inventory table and multiplying the Quantity field value in the former by the Unit Cost field value in the latter. This table also supports operational tasks such as billing, customer service, marketing, and auditing. For example, sales details in the table allow marketing to evaluate the demand for the organization's products. These data also provide audit evidence needed to corroborate the accuracy of price multiplied by quantity calculations that are summarized in the sales invoices.

Inventory Table

The **Inventory table** contains quantity, price, supplier, and warehouse location data for each item of inventory. When products are sold, the Quantity On Hand field in the associated records is reduced by the value of the Quantity field in the Line Item record. The Quantity On Hand field is increased by inventory receipts from suppliers.

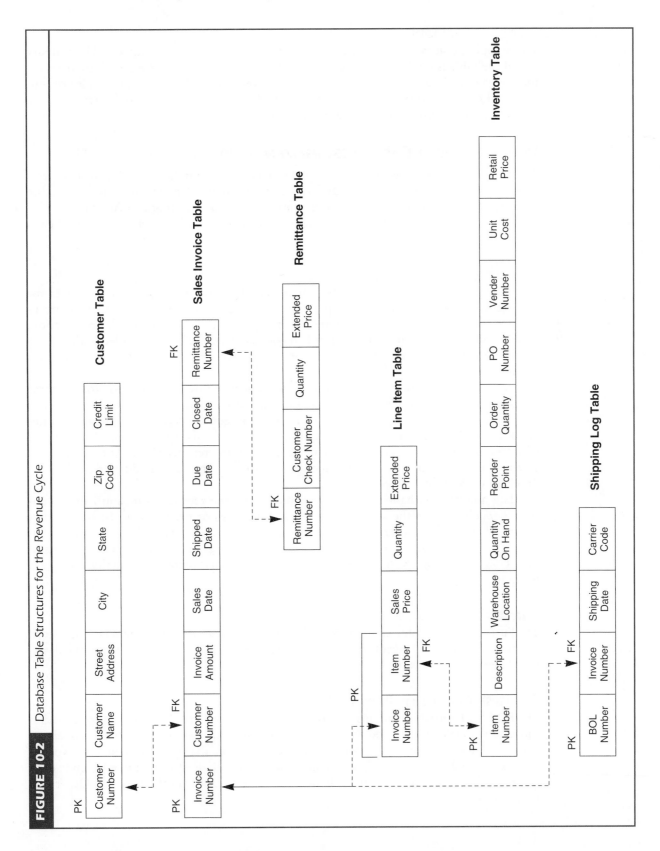

FIGURE 10-2   Database Table Structures for the Revenue Cycle

Shipping Log Table

The **Shipping Log table** is a record of all sales orders shipped to customers. The primary key of the table is the bill of lading number. The data in this table are useful for verifying that all sales reflected in the Sales Invoice table were shipped in the period under review. As a tool for measuring efficiency, shipping log data can also be used to determine if customer orders are being shipped in a timely manner.

PURCHASES AND CASH DISBURSEMENTS SYSTEM

The flowchart in Figure 10-3 shows a database for a purchases and cash disbursements system. Again, the main difference between this approach and the flat-file equivalent is the focus on events rather than classical accounting records. Figure 10-4 depicts the table structures for this system. Following the tables is a discussion of each table in the system.

Inventory Table

The *Inventory table* contains quantity, price, supplier, and warehouse location data for each item of product inventory. The purchasing process begins with a review of the inventory records to identify inventory items that need to be ordered. In a retail organization, this step is performed when sales of finished goods to customers are recorded in the inventory records. In this case, the purchasing process involves replenishing the finished goods inventory.

Purchasing systems of manufacturing firms replenish raw materials inventory as these items are used in the production process. In either case, when inventory items are sold or used in production, the Quantity On Hand field is reduced accordingly by a computer application. With each inventory reduction, the system tests for a "reorder" condition, which occurs when the quantity on hand falls below the reorder point. At that time, the system prepares a purchase order, which is sent to the vendor, and adds a record to the Purchase Order table.

The quantity on hand value will remain below the reorder point until the inventory is received from the supplier. This may take days or even weeks. To signify that the item is on order and prevent it from being reordered each time the computer application detects the same reorder condition, a computer-generated purchase order number is placed in the PO Number field of the inventory record. Normally, this field is blank.

Purchase Order Table

The **Purchase Order table** contains records of purchases placed with suppliers. The record remains open until the inventory arrives. Placing the receiving report number in the designated field closes the record.

Purchase Order Line Item Table

The **PO Line Item table** contains a record of every item ordered. Since a single transaction can involve one or more products, each record in the Purchase Order table is associated with (linked to) one or more records in this table. Notice that the table contains two primary keys—PO Number and Item Number. Both keys are needed to uniquely define each record in the table. They also provide links to related records in the Purchase Order and Inventory tables.

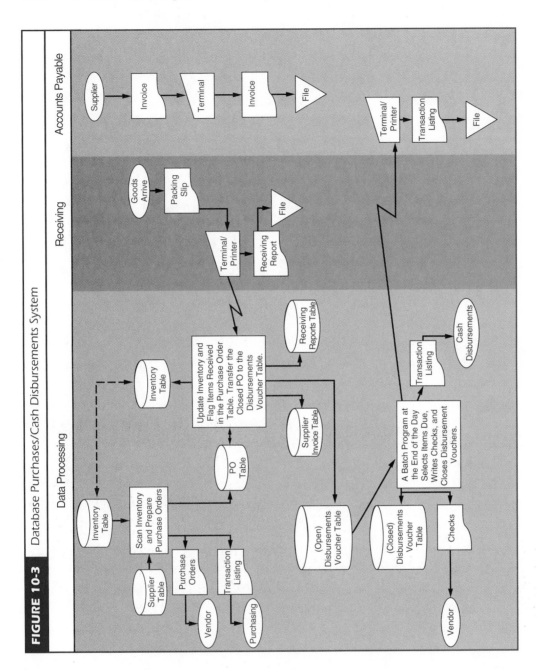

FIGURE 10-3 Database Purchases/Cash Disbursements System

Receiving Report Table

When the ordered items arrive from the supplier, they are counted and inspected and receiving documents are prepared. Via a terminal, the receiving clerk enters information about the items received in the **Receiving Report table**. The system automatically performs the following tasks: (1) increases the Quantity On Hand field in the inventory record(s); (2) removes the reorder condition by resetting the PO Number field to its normal blank state; (3) creates a record in the Receiving Report table; and (4) closes the purchase order record by placing the receiving report number in the designated field.

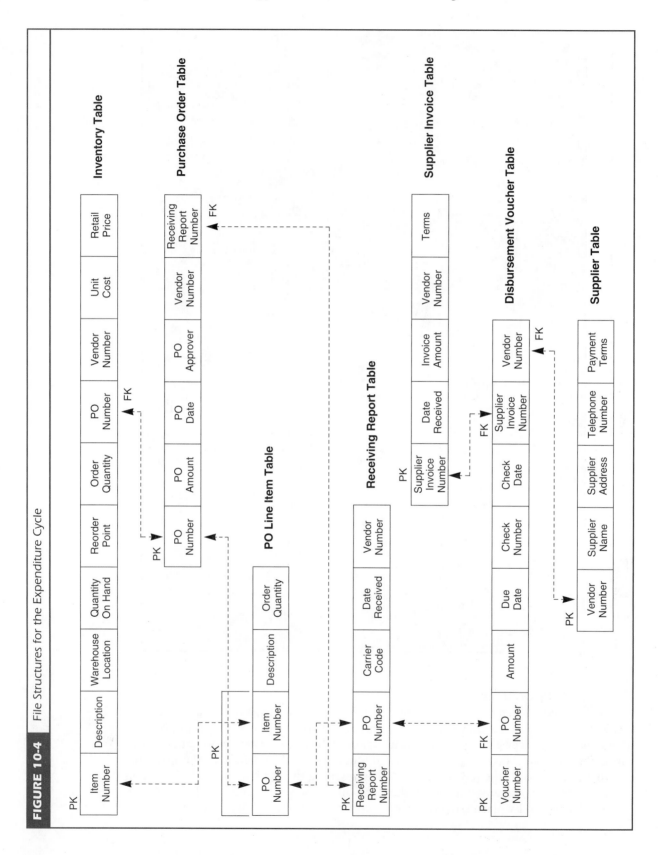

FIGURE 10-4   File Structures for the Expenditure Cycle

Disbursement Voucher Table

For most companies, discrepancies between amounts ordered, received, and billed are legitimate concerns that must be resolved before payment to the vendor is approved. Because of its complexity, this reconciliation is often a manual process that is triggered by receipt of the supplier's invoice. The accounts payable clerk reviews the supporting records in the Purchase Order and Receiving Report tables and compares them to the invoice. If the items, quantities, and prices match, then a cash disbursement voucher is created and a record is added to the Supplier Invoice table. Based on the supplier's terms of trade and the company's payment policy, the payment due date is determined and placed in the disbursement voucher record.

Each payment day, the cash disbursements application automatically selects the items due, flags them "paid" by entering the current date in the Check Date field, and cuts the check, which is then mailed to the supplier.

The **Disbursement Voucher table** provides three important pieces of information that are traditionally contained in formal accounting records. First, it is a record of checks written in payment of trade accounts for the period and thus replaces the traditional cash disbursements journal. Second, the sum of the open items (unpaid vouchers) for a particular vendor is equivalent to the accounts payable subsidiary ledger for the vendor. Finally, the total of all unpaid vouchers in the table constitutes the company's accounts payable (general ledger) balance.

LIMITATIONS OF TRANSACTION-BASED SYSTEMS

While the system just described represents a marked improvement over the traditional flat-file approach, it has serious shortcomings. This system is **transaction-based**, which allows the user to capture detailed information related to *economic events* such as sales to customers and purchases from suppliers. A look at the database tables, however, shows that they are designed to capture only financial transaction data. Nonfinancial data are not captured. Furthermore, *noneconomic events* are ignored by this system. An example of a noneconomic event is a customer who enters a place of business, browses, inquires about products, but does not buy. Information about such customer behavior may be very important to an organization. This type of event would, however, not be captured by a transaction-based system such as the one above. As we will see, REA is an **event-based** (or sometimes called a **pattern-based**) system. The distinction is more than semantic. An REA system is responsive to both economic and noneconomic phenomena, permitting the creation of much richer databases that can support the information needs of all users within the organization.

TRADITIONAL APPROACH TO MODELING BUSINESS PROCESSES

Under the traditional approach to relational database design, an entity relationship (ER) diagram is used to model the relationships between an organization's critical entities. The ER data modeling approach was discussed in Chapter 9. Figure 10-5 shows an unnormalized ER diagram of a manufacturing firm.

The sales procedures are shown in the upper left of the figure surrounded by a dashed border, and the procurement procedures are shown in the top and bottom right surrounded by a dashed border.

This ER data model is suitable when a traditional approach to database design is being followed. A different form of model is developed, however, under the REA approach. This is illustrated in the next section.

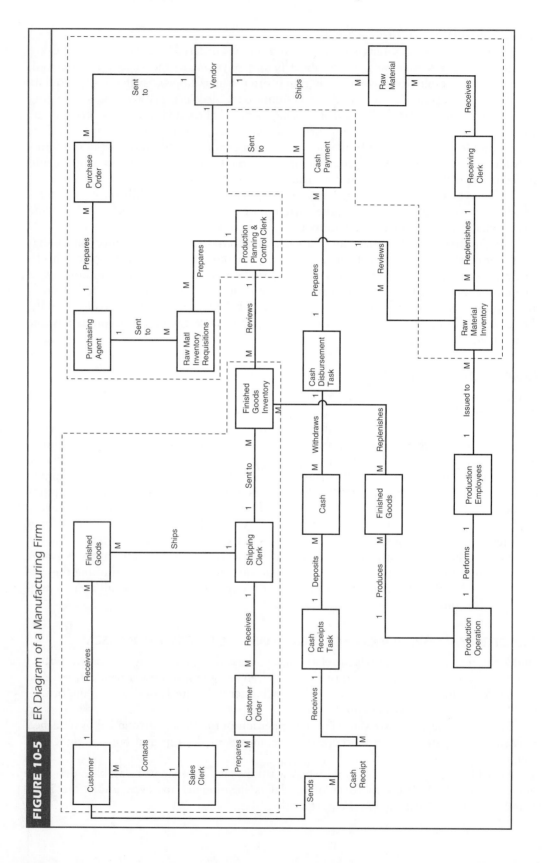

FIGURE 10-5 ER Diagram of a Manufacturing Firm

DEVELOPING AN REA MODEL

Having introduced the basic concepts of the REA model and its potential advantages over the traditional approach, let's now look at how REA models are developed. Central to this approach is the concept of an event. One business process may consist of several events. Before developing an REA model, events must be classified as either:

- **Operating events,** which are activities that produce goods and services.

- **Information events,** which are activities associated with recording, maintaining, and reporting information.

- **Decision/management events,** which are activities that lead to decisions being made and implemented.

These classes of events are all linked in a circular fashion: Decision/management events trigger operating events. Operating events trigger information events. Information events trigger decision/management events, and so on. In a manual information system, it is fairly easy to distinguish between these three classes of events. Unfortunately, the greater complexity of computerized information systems makes it much less clear where one class ends and another begins. Nevertheless, from the perspective of control and relevance to the item of interest, it is important that they are separately identified when an REA model is being developed.

Starting with the most straightforward, it is generally not difficult to identify which are decision/management events. These involve decisions relating to planning, evaluation, and control. For example, to purchase or not to purchase, to sell or not to sell, to hire or not to hire, to request a report, to request information, and to implement a new control measure are all decision/management events.

Information events produce the information that enables decisions to be made. These include the acts of recording, amending, updating, or maintaining. The following are examples of information events:

- recording new customer data,

- updating inventory records following a sale,

- amending the details of a customer who has changed address,

- preparing cost estimates for new products,

- preparing credit rating reports on potential customers,

- preparing an analysis of applicant data for a position in the organization,

- preparing sales invoices,

- preparing purchase orders, and

- preparing divisional performance reports.

Operating events are the physical activities associated with business processes. Because of accounting students' information orientation, they sometimes have difficulty separating operating events from information events. For example, taking a customer's order, shipping the product to the customer, receiving raw materials from the supplier, and paying for inventories received are operating events. Preparing the sales invoice, recording shipments in the shipping log, recording inventory receipts in the ledger, and preparing a cash disbursement voucher for payment to the supplier are the related, but different, information events.

To identify operating events within a business process we can employ an approach used by many disciplines when trying to discover what has occurred. Operating events are revealed through the answers to a series of questioning verbs: Who did it? What happened? When did it happen? Where did it happen? What was involved? How did it happen?

To illustrate the process of developing an REA model, the following case is used.

Horizon Books

Horizon Books is a bookstore in downtown Philadelphia. It carries an inventory of approximately 5,000 books. Customers come in and browse the shelves, select their books, and take them to one of three cashiers positioned in different parts of the store. One of the cashiers is situated at an information desk where customers can discover whether a particular book is in stock, place orders for books not currently available in the bookstore, and collect and pay for books previously ordered. The cashier at the information desk has a book database that is consulted for every query. There are no credit sales. All customers pay for their purchases at the time of purchase.

STEP 1

As a first step, the operating events that are to be included in the model are identified. These are the events that support the strategic objectives of the organization and about which information is needed. At its simplest, the model could have only one event, the sale. But that would mean gathering no data about the time a customer spent browsing before purchase. It would also mean gathering no data about customers who inquired but left without purchasing. To capture these data, an *arrival* event, a *departure* event, and an *inquiry* event need to be included in the model. For the sake of simplicity, assume that Horizon Books does not require information about customer arrivals and departures at this time. Information is needed, however, for a customer payment event and a customer inquiry event.

STEP 2

The operating events identified now need to be organized by sequence of occurrence. While many sales will occur without an inquiry preceding them, whenever an inquiry takes place, it will precede any subsequent sale arising from it. Hence, the sequence of events in the model is inquiry, sale, and payment. This is shown in Figure 10-6. Notice how each event is shown as verb–object. Note also that the verb is represented from the perspective of the organization, not the customer.

STEP 3

Next the resources and agents involved in each operating event must be identified. This is most easily done by answering *who*, *what*, and *where* questions about each event. For example, the following questions may be asked. Who was involved? What was involved? Where did it take place?

In the case of the Answer Query event, the customer and a cashier were involved, the inventory database was involved, and it occurred at the information desk. The make sale event involved the customer, a cashier and the book sold. The event took place at a cash register. The Receive Payment event involved the customer, a cashier, and cash, and took place at a cash register.

This model is presented in Figure 10-7. Notice that resources are illustrated on the left, events in the middle, and agents on the right of the figure. An REA model is typically drawn without the column headings and dividers. They are shown in Figure 10-7 to illustrate the correct placement of the objects. Headings and dividers are not shown in subsequent diagrams.

FIGURE 10-6	Horizon Books REA Sales Model Events of Interest

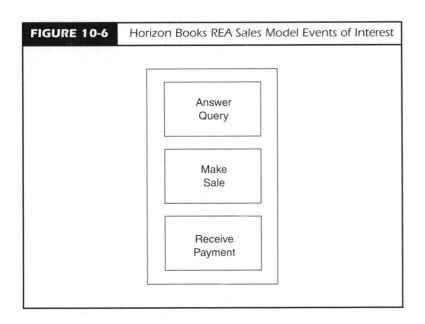

FIGURE 10-7	Horizon Books Resources, Events, and Agents Labeled to Show Their Positions

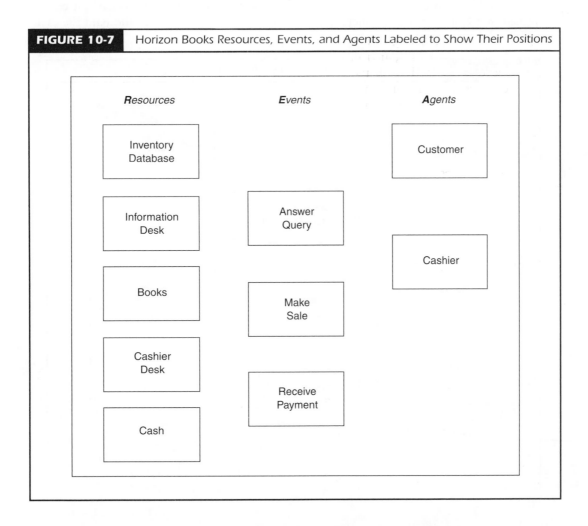

STEP 4

The next step is to identify the links between the resources, events, and agents. Start from each event and connect it to the resources and agents that are involved in the event. Next draw a line connecting events that are logically related. This graphical representation is shown in Figure 10-8.

You learned how to construct relational tables in Chapter 9. Since REA models are used to build relational databases, an REA-based information system exhibits all the features of a relational database. Look at the relational table called Customer in Figure 10-9, which has been reproduced from Chapter 9.

In an REA accounting system, where there is a mixture of cash and credit sales, cash customers can all be assigned the same identifier within the Customer table. In terms of Figure 10-9, this could be represented in the line:

Cust Num	Name	Address	Current Balance
0	Cash	0	0

However, Horizon Books operates a cash-sales-only policy. In a traditional accounting system in which all sales are for cash, no data would be maintained for a customer and there would be no customer data table. When the form of settlement is cash, it can be argued that from a purely financial point of view we need not know who paid the cash.

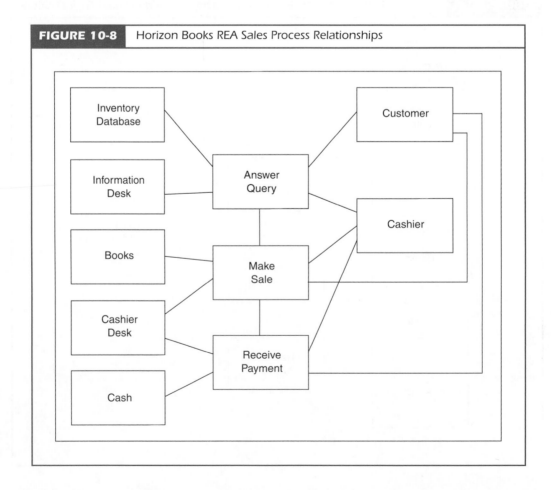

FIGURE 10-8   Horizon Books REA Sales Process Relationships

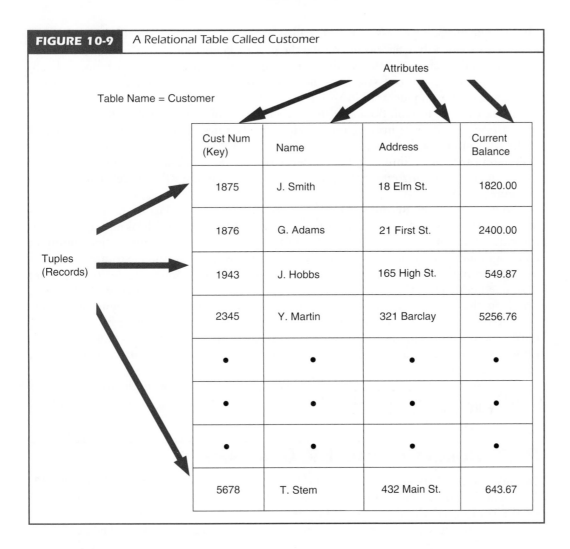

FIGURE 10-9 | A Relational Table Called Customer

We need to know only that cash has been received. If each cash sale is identified uniquely to separate the transactions then there is no need for a Customer table.

On the other hand, an advantage of REA is to capture a far wider range of data about events. These include the age and gender of the customer, the type of books that the customer likes to read, and the customer's name and address. With this information the bookshop can send the customer details of new books and special events. Thus, even where all sales are for cash, under an REA-based information system the Customer table will not only exist but will likely have many more attributes than would typically appear in a traditional information system.

STEP 5

The next step is to assign the **cardinalities** of all the entity relationships. Five forms of associations are used when constructing the REA model. These are zero-to-one (0,1), zero-to-many (0,M), one-to-one (1,1), one-to-many (1,M), and many-to-many (M,M).

Note that the actual design of the relational base tables follows the same process whether they are derived from a traditional ER or an REA model. The advantage of an REA model is that event-based nonfinancial data can be captured that traditional ER diagrams for the same business process ignore. The increased level of detail in the REA model makes it far easier to identify what occurs during the process being modeled. This added information adds to the richness of the database and also improves planning, evaluation, and control of the business processes. Let's now see how this works in practice by further developing the REA model for Horizon Books.

In the case of Horizon Books' *customer:make sale* entity relationship, the existence of one *customer* may result in zero, one, or many *make sales* occurring. This is represented in the REA model of the process using the notation (0,M) to represent the minimum and maximum cardinality. Similarly, the existence of one *make sale* arises from the existence of one and only one *customer* entity, represented as (1,1) in the REA model. This is shown in Figure 10-10.

Sometimes, when defining the cardinalities of an entity relation, it helps to imagine that you are standing on top of one of the entity boxes and looking at the other. Imagine what you see. If you are on top of the customer entity box, what minimum and maximum sales can you see? You can see as few as zero (the customer may wish to buy nothing) or a maximum greater than one (if the customer decides to buy more than one item). Thus the *make sale* entity in this relation is zero-to-many (0,M). Now, stand on the other entity box. How many *customers* do you see buying a specific item? The minimum is one. For the *make sale* entity to exist there must be a *customer*. Furthermore, since only one customer can buy a specific item, the maximum cardinality is also one. The cardinalities of the *customer* entity in this relation is, therefore, one-to-one (1,1).

Using these principles, cardinalities are assigned to the relations in the REA model for the sales process of Horizon Books. These cardinalities are illustrated in Figure 10-11.

REA MODELS VERSUS ER DIAGRAMS

To illustrate the differences between the REA and ER modeling, refer to Figure 10-12. Although not obvious at first glance, this is an REA model of the same process described by the traditional ER diagram in Figure 10-5. The areas modeled in Figure 10-12 correspond to the sales and procurement processes outlined with the dashed borders in Figure 10-5.

The **entities** in both REA models and ER diagrams are represented by rectangles, and lines connect them. The lines connecting the ER diagram entities are labeled with a verb that indicates what occurs in the relationship. In effect, each line represents an event. ER diagrams represent a much broader set of events than do REA models. These include operating events (receives), information events (prepares, updates), and decision

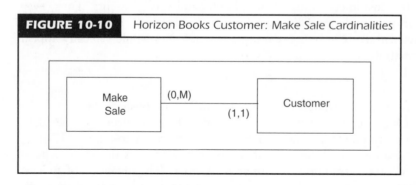

FIGURE 10-10   Horizon Books Customer: Make Sale Cardinalities

Make Sale — (0,M) — (1,1) — Customer

FIGURE 10-11   The REA Model for the Sales Process of Horizon Books

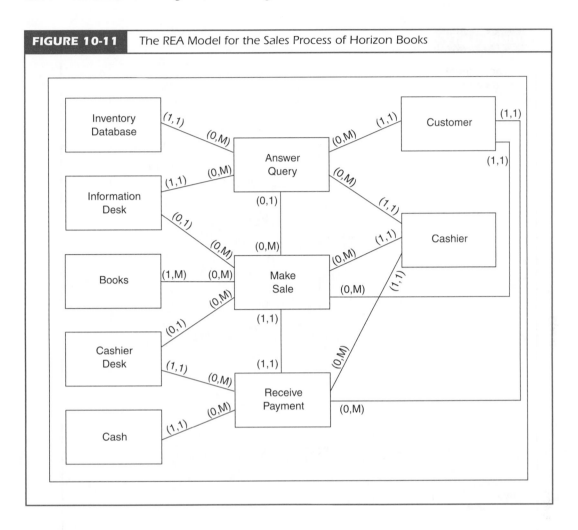

---

events (reviews). In contrast, only operating events are included in an REA model, and only those of strategic importance.

While in some respects the REA model is simpler than the corresponding ER diagram, it provides more relevant information. The REA approach allows the systems designer to focus on key events that facilitate the design and placement of controls. Because information and decision-making events are isolated from the primary operating events, the differing controls required over these classes of events can be more easily identified and inserted into the business process.

It is in these crucial differences that the benefits of preparing an REA model become apparent. The ER diagram is a data-modeling tool that enables organizations to ensure alignment between business processes and the database tables in which data relating to them are stored. Its primary purpose is to identify the data attributes that represent the conceptual user views that must be supported by the base tables. In other words, the ER model is view oriented.

The REA model pinpoints where the organization can plan, evaluate, and control significant operating events within the business process. Since REA focuses on business activities, it is event-oriented.

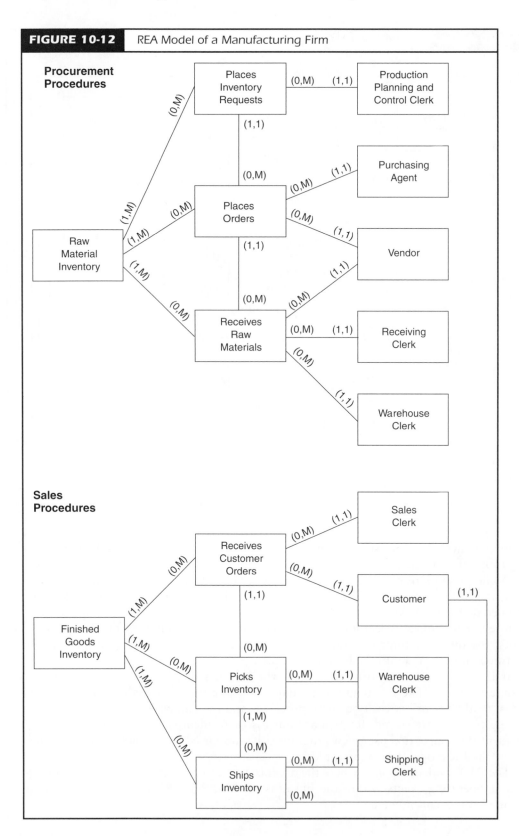

FIGURE 10-12   REA Model of a Manufacturing Firm

DEFINING THE ENTITY ATTRIBUTES

The REA model can be used to define entity **attributes**. Consider the procurement procedures presented in Figure 10-12. The following describes the accounting phenomena associated with this process.

- The operating *events* in the process are placing inventory requests, placing the order, and receiving the inventory. The data elements describing these events should be specified in sufficient detail to support all user needs. To illustrate, the financial and nonfinancial data for the Places Orders event include:

Financial	*Nonfinancial*
Vendor name	Vendor lead time
Vendor address	Carrier used
Inventory item number	On-time delivery record
Quantity to be ordered	Incomplete shipments record
Unit cost	Damaged shipments record
Purchase order number	Price disputes record
Order date	

- Raw materials inventory is the economic *resource* affected by the event. The data attributes needed to specify this resource and the changes that are made to it include:

Financial	*Nonfinancial*
Inventory item number	Turnover rate
Description	Lead time
Quantity on hand	Usage rate
Reorder point	Warehouse location
Economic order quantity	Stockout history
Supplier	Scrap history
	Delayed arrival history

- The primary *agents* are production planning and control clerks, the purchasing agent, the vendor, the receiving clerks, and the warehouse clerks. All of the relevant attributes describing these agents are specified and modeled into the database. Using the vendor as an example, these data include:

Financial	*Nonfinancial*
Vendor name	On-time delivery record
Vendor address	Damaged goods record
Vendor telephone number	Average lead time
Amount owed to vendor	Help line support
Value of total purchases to date	EDI access
Terms of trade offered	Internet access

Consider now the sales procedures in Figure 10-12. The following describes the accounting phenomena associated with this process.

- The *events* in the process are receiving the customer order, picking the finished goods inventory, and shipping the inventory. The data elements describing these events should be specified in sufficient detail to support all user needs. To illustrate, the financial and nonfinancial data for the Receives Customer Order event include:

Financial	*Nonfinancial*
Customer name	Customer credit rating

Customer address
Inventory item number
Quantity ordered
Unit price
Sales order number
Order date

Carrier used
On-time delivery record
Incomplete shipments record
Damaged shipments record
Complaints record

- Finished goods inventory is the economic *resource* affected by the event. The data attributes needed to specify this resource and the changes that are made to it include:

Financial
Inventory item number
Description
Quantity on hand
Production reorder point
Economic order quantity

Nonfinancial
Turnover rate
Lead time
Usage rate
Warehouse location
Stockout history
Scrap history
Delayed production history

- The primary *agents* are the sales clerks, the customer, the warehouse clerks, and the shipping clerks. All of the relevant attributes describing these agents would be specified and modeled into the database. Using the customer as an example, these data include:

Financial
Customer name
Customer address
Customer telephone number
Amount owed by customer
Value of total sales to date
Terms of trade offered

Nonfinancial
Customer credit rating
Damaged goods record
On-time payment record
Customer volume record
EDI access
Internet access

Data requirements of other business processes such as production, cash receipts, and so on, would be obtained in this fashion and combined to produce an overall schema of data requirements. Both accounting and nonaccounting requirements contribute to the overall database. In the process of combining data requirements, it is important to recognize and eliminate any redundancies from the model. For example, the raw materials inventory resource is also an element of the production process. Similarly, the vendor is also an agent in the cash disbursement process.

The data requirements for resources, events, and agents associated with multiple business processes must be integrated, not modeled separately. Hence, while each business process is modeled separately, the same underlying database tables are used across all the models. The same Customer table will be used in the sales model and in the cash collection model, and the same Vendor table will be used in the purchase model as in the cash disbursement model, and so on.

Once the attributes have been defined, the database tables can be designed. The process of assigning primary and foreign keys and table normalization to support user views is no different from that described in Chapter 9, and is not repeated here.

CREATING USER VIEWS

The REA approach can generate an information system capable of supporting multiple views. As a result, the various possible views must be accounted for at an early stage in model development. This is achieved through defining a range of data attributes that cover the desired range of views.

This usually involves an extensive analysis of user information needs. Once the analysis is complete, the designer can derive the set of data attributes (the conceptual user view) necessary to produce these inputs and outputs. As the physical representation of the conceptual user view, the reports, documents, and computer screens are called **physical views**. They help the designer understand key relationships among the data.

Once the attributes have been identified, the forms and procedures to collect event, resources, and agent data can be designed and the base tables can be populated. Once this is done, a query interface can be created to produce views and reports.

The query interface must encompass all conceivable views, and the format for the reports resulting from each query must be determined. Figures 10-13 through 10-15 present examples of the physical views of three users. The first view is for a purchasing agent who needs information about inventory items to be ordered and the suppliers of the inventory. Figure 10-13 depicts the inventory status report that conveys this information. The second user view is for a sales manager who needs a breakdown of daily sales activity organized by customer and product. Figure 10-14 shows the sales report containing this information. Finally, the third view, for the general ledger department, presents a listing of journal vouchers summarizing the day's business activity. The journal voucher report is portrayed in Figure 10-15. These views were all obtained from the same database. They each satisfy the information needs of a user and they show the data at the required level of details.

Flexibility in user view design is one of REA's strengths. User views should be capable of being amended in any way that the individual user wishes. To illustrate, let's return to the Horizon Books example. If the sales manager of the company wants to know whether each sale resulted from an initial customer inquiry, that information could be easily provided in a report. Similarly, as shown in Figure 10-16, a report could be produced for the Horizon Books purchasing manager showing the time spent on each customer inquiry, the nature of the inquiry, whether the inquiry resulted in a sale, and the demographic details of the customer who made the inquiry. This could then be used to identify potential new topics or authors Horizon Books should carry.

FIGURE 10-13	Inventory Status Report

Ajax Manufacturing Co.
Inventory Status Report

Part Number	Description	Quantity On Hand	Reorder Point	Order Quantity	Supplier Number	Name	Address	Telephone
1	Bracket	100	150	500	22 24 27	Ozment Sup Buell Co. B&R Sup	123 Main St. 2 Broadhead Westgate Mall	555-7895 555-3436 555-7845
2	Gasket	440	450	1000	22 24 28	Ozment Sup Buell Co. Harris Manuf	123 Main St. 2 Broadhead 24 Linden St.	555-7895 555-3436 555-3316
3	Brace	10	10	50	22 24 28	Ozment Sup Buell Co. Harris Manuf	123 Main St. 2 Broadhead 24 Linden St.	555-7895 555-3436 555-3316
• • •	• • •	• • •	• • •	• • •	• • •	• • •	• • •	• • •

| FIGURE 10-14 | Sales Report |

Sales Report

Customer Number : 19321
Customer Name : Jon Smith
Address : 520 Main St.,City

Invoice #	Date	Invoice Total	Part Num	Quantity	Unit Price	Ext'd Price
12390	11/11/04	$850	2	5	$20	$100
			1	10	50	500
			3	25	10	250
12912	11/21/04	$300	4	10	$30	$300

Customer Total: $1,150

* * *   * * * *   * * * *   * * * *   * * * *   * * * *   * * *

Customer Number : 19322
Customer Name : Mary Smith
Address : 2289 Elm St., City

Invoice #	Date	Invoice Total	Part Num	Quantity	Unit Price	Ext'd Price
12421	11/13/04	$1,000	6	10	$20	$200
			1	2	50	100
			5	7	100	700
12901						
	11/20/04	$500	4	10	$30	$300
			2	10	20	200

Customer Total: $1,500

* * *   * * * *   * * * *   * * * *   * * * *   * * * *   * * *

Next Customer

- •
- •
- •

Next Customer

| FIGURE 10-15 | Journal Voucher Report |

Journal Voucher Report

JV Num	Date	Title	Acct Num	Debit	Credit
1	9/20/04	Cash Acct Rec Sales	101 103 401	1000 2000	 3000
2	9/20/04	Cost of Goods Sold Inventory	501 108	2500	 2500
•	•	•	•	•	•
•	•	•	•	•	•
•	•	•	•	•	•

| FIGURE 10-16 | Customer Inquiry Report |

Customer Inquiry Report 2/14/04 – 7/14/04

Inq Num	Date	Cust Num	m/f	Age	Topic	Author	In Store	Sale	Time Spent	Comments
483	2/14	217	m	26	collecting	—	yes	yes	5	—
484	2/14	142	f	19	—	Wood, F	no	no	7	—
485	2/14	723	f	54	aerobics	Banks, J	yes	no	3	too expensive
.	.	.	.	.	.	.	.	.	.	.
.	.	.	.	.	.	.	.	.	.	.

SUMMARY

This chapter examined the REA model as a means of specifying and designing accounting information systems that serve the needs of all users in an entity. It began by defining the key elements of REA and outlining its advantages, such as efficient operations, increased productivity, and competitive advantage. The competitive advantage benefits of REA are most clearly seen from the perspective of the value chain. Before delving into REA, the chapter examined the advantages and disadvantages of traditional database design. While superior to flat-file systems, traditional database systems have serious limitations. Foremost among these is that they support primarily the needs of financial information users. Also, they are economic event-driven and unresponsive to noneconomic events that may be of extreme importance to an organization. Next, the chapter examined the steps involved in developing an REA model of a business process. These include the following:

1. Identify the operating events that are to be included in the model. These are the operating events of interest, about which we wish to gather information. Typically, these are the events of strategic significance to the organization.
2. Organize the operating events into their sequence of occurrence.
3. Identify the resources and agents involved in each operating event.
4. Identify the links between these resources, events, and agents.
5. Define the entity relations by assigning cardinalities to them.

Using a manufacturing firm as an example, the REA and ER models of sales and procurement processes were compared. The similarities and differences between the two approaches were highlighted. Based on the REA model of these business processes, a set of financial and nonfinancial data that would meet the need of multiple users was derived. The chapter concluded with a discussion of REA's flexibility in producing and amending user views.

KEY TERMS

agents (495)

attributes (513)

cardinalities (509)

Customer table (498)

data modeling (495)

decision/management events (505)

Disbursement Voucher table (503)

entities (510)

event-based (503)

events (495)

information events (505)

Inventory table (498)

Line Item table (498)

operating events (505)

pattern-based (503)

physical views (515)

PO Line Item table (500)

Purchase Order table (500)

REA model (494)

Receiving Report table (501)

resources (495)

Sales Invoice table (498)

Shipping Log table (500)

transaction-based (503)

user view (494)

value chain (496)

value chain analysis (496)

REVIEW QUESTIONS

1. What is a user view?
2. What other type of information do modern managers need apart from financial information?
3. In the term *REA model*, what does the "R" stand for?
4. In the term *REA model*, what does the "E" stand for?

5. In the term *REA model*, what does the "A" stand for?

6. What form of view is provided by an REA-based information system?

7. Define *economic resources.*

8. Define *economic events.*

9. Define *economic agents.*

10. What is represented by the labeled lines connecting entities in an ER diagram?

11. Value chain analysis distinguishes between which two primary activities?

12. Define *operating event.*

13. Define *information event.*

14. Define *decision/management event.*

15. What criteria do you apply when deciding which operating events are to be included in an REA model?

16. What form of questions do you use to identify the resources and agents involved in each event?

17. List the steps involved in preparing an REA model of a business process.

18. What do you need to do to prepare an REA model for use in the development of a relational database?

DISCUSSION QUESTIONS

1. Discuss the primary differences between flat-file and traditional database systems.

2. Explain how a Sales Invoice table can be used to replace traditional accounting records.

3. Explain how a Disbursement Voucher table can be used to replace traditional accounting records.

4. Discuss the limitations of transaction-based systems.

5. Discuss why adherence by accountants to a single, GAAP-based view is inappropriate.

6. What do you think the implications of accountants' adherence to a single, GAAP-based view are for the accounting profession?

7. Discuss why the REA approach empowers accountants to meet the needs of modern managers.

8. Distinguish between resources, events, and agents.

9. Compare and contrast the appearance and content of an ER diagram with that of an REA model.

10. Discuss the advantages of adopting an REA modeling approach over a traditional approach to information system development.

11. Discuss how adopting a value chain perspective reveals advantages of the REA approach to information system development.

12. Discuss the relationship between operating events, information events, and decision/management events.

13. Discuss the differences between the cardinalities defined in an ER diagram and those defined in an REA model, and their usefulness in the development of relational databases.

MULTIPLE-CHOICE QUESTIONS

1. Advantages of the REA model include all of the following except:
   a. the REA approach may help identify non-value-added activities.
   b. the need for multiple data collection is reduced.
   c. the REA approach may increase productivity.
   d. the REA approach may increase competitive advantages.
   e. all of these are advantages of the REA model.

2. Which of the following is most likely a primary activity of a manufacturing company?
   a. production of accurate accounting information.
   b. production of reliable transportation channels.
   c. production of manufactured goods.
   d. production of quality management reports.
   e. all of these are primary activities of a manufacturing company.

3. Which of the following is not an example of the cardinalities included in an REA model?
   a. one-to-one
   b. many-to-one
   c. many-to-many
   d. none, they all are

4. Which of the following statements is correct?
   a. The REA model requires that phenomena be characterized in a manner consistent with the development of a single user view.
   b. The REA model requires that phenomena be characterized in a manner consistent with the development of selected user views.
   c. The REA model requires that phenomena be characterized in a manner consistent with the development of unique user views.
   d. The REA model requires that phenomena be characterized in a manner consistent with the development of multiple user views.

5. Which of the following events would be least likely to be captured by a transaction-based system?
   a. customer behavior information
   b. sales to a customer
   c. purchases from a vendor
   d. a loan from a bank
   e. all of these events would be captured.

6. Each of the following is an event classification for an REA model except:
   a. operating events.
   b. financing events.
   c. information events.
   d. decision events.
   e. all of the above.

7. When designing an REA model, events need to be organized in sequence of
   a. completion.
   b. length.
   c. ease of analysis.
   d. occurrence.

8. In an REA model, each event is described from the perspective of the
   a. user.
   b. organization.
   c. designer.
   d. customer.

9. Which of the following is not an example of a physical view?
   a. reports
   b. documents
   c. electronic images
   d. data tables

PROBLEMS

1. REA Model Extract

Prepare an REA model depicting the issuance of raw materials into the manufacturing process.

a. List the specific data elements necessary to describe the issuance of raw materials into the manufacturing process.
b. Identify the
   1. economic resources affected.
   2. underlying economic event.
   3. primary agents involved.

2. REA Model Extract

Prepare an REA model depicting the shipping of finished goods to a customer.

a. List the specific data elements necessary to describe the shipping of finished goods to the customer.

b. Identify the
   1. economic resources affected.
   2. underlying economic event.
   3. primary agents involved.

3. REA Model

Prepare an REA model for the customer inquiry business process from the following amended version of the Horizon Books case.

Horizon Books

Horizon Books is a bookstore in downtown Philadelphia. It carries an inventory of approximately 5,000 books. In addition, Horizon Books has an extensive database of out-of-print and used books. Customers come in and browse the shelves, select their books, and take them to the cashier. At the cashier's desk they can also discover whether a particular book is in stock, available via a search of the database as an out-of-print or used book, or whether an out-of-stock book can be ordered new. The catalogue of new books (including those that are out-of-stock) and the catalogue out-of-print or used books exist in separate databases. In addition to answering questions about the availability of books, the cashier can also place orders for books not currently available, produce previously ordered books, and collect for book purchases. There are no credit sales. All customers pay for books at the time of purchase (no advanced sales).

4. REA Model
Prepare an REA model for the sales process from the following amended version of the Horizon Books case.

Horizon Books

Horizon Books is a bookstore in downtown Philadelphia. It carries an inventory of approximately 5,000 books. Customers come in and browse the shelves, select their books, and take them to the cashier. At the cashier's desk they can also discover whether a particular book is in stock, place orders for books not currently available in the bookstore, and collect and pay for books previously ordered. The cashier has a book database that is consulted for every query. There are no credit sales. All customers pay for their purchases at the time of purchase.

5. REA Model
Redraw Figure 10-11 showing the collapsed cardinalities between the entities required for design of a relational database for Horizon Books as per the revision in A.

6. REA Model
(Prepared by Todd Feinman, Coopers & Lybrand LLP)
F&Y is in the industry of computer sales. Its main competition is other major mail-order computer companies. Its market share is small compared to the industry leaders, but it hopes to increase its share by becoming more responsive to its customers' orders through reengineering its sales order processing system. F&Y has 147 employees,

and the main office is located in St. Paul, Minnesota.

F&Y sells desktop computer systems that it primarily manufactures itself, with a few parts purchased from third-party companies. It offers many different packages to accommodate its end-user customers, about 15 different bundles in all. Customers pay on credit terms and receive a satisfaction guarantee for 30 days after receipt of their computers. F&Y's suppliers include a few different microcomputer chip and software manufacturers whose products F&Y packages with its computers. F&Y's warehouse is located at the main office in St. Paul.

Last year, F&Y's market share dropped in comparison to its competition. A survey revealed that one reason was because customers were not getting their computers on time. The lead times were too long and were always a day or two late. Customer orders need to be sent out the day they are received, and inventory records need to be updated as orders are placed to be able to accurately tell customers how long a lead time is or whether a back-order is necessary. The board of directors also suspects that internal control weaknesses exist that might lead to internal fraud.

When customers need to order new computers for their homes or offices, they call F&Y to place an order. All sales are made via an order document. F&Y gives these to its usual customers to complete; it may be mailed or faxed to the company, or a telephone order may be placed. In this case, sales representatives transcribe the order to a formal sales order document. Existing customers pay via credit, usually through existing accounts, while new customers must have a new account established. A customer's account record includes his or her name, address, phone number, background history with the company, and F&Y's formally assigned unique customer number. Usually Sam, from the sales department, will create the formal sales order and send it to Chris in the credit department.

Chris's job is to check the customer's credit and make sure he or she has the funds available to pay for the order. If this is so, the customer receives a credit approval, and Chris creates a stock release so that the order can continue to be processed. Credit that is not approved gets filed, and Chris calls the customer to notify him or her that the order has been canceled. For approved credit,

Chris staples the approved sales order to the stock release and sends it to the warehouse (shipping) department.

Willie, a warehouse employee, receives the stock release, picks the goods, and calls either FedEx, UPS, or a service requested by the customer. Willie then proceeds to update the inventory subsidiary ledger to account for the computers he is going to load on the trucks. When Willie is too busy to ship the computers, he can ask another employee to do it because once inside the warehouse, any employee can transport any item out of the warehouse onto a delivery truck. Due to this easy transportation of goods, F&Y wants to ensure that it is not easy for unauthorized people to get into the warehouse. F&Y implemented codes rather than keys to open the warehouse doors, since keys can be stolen or lost. Willie now prepares the bills of lading and shipping notices. The shipping companies arrive every day at 4:30 PM, and Willie gives them the bill of lading, shipping notice, and computers to be shipped. After he knows the goods are on their way to the customer, the stock release, copy of shipping notice, and sales order are stapled together and sent to Barb in the billing department.

Barb receives and files the stock release, prepares the invoice, makes a copy of it, and mails it to the customer. Every Friday afternoon, Barb updates the sales journal and then sends the original invoice, sales order, stock release, and shipping notice to the accounts receivable department.

Adam in the accounting (accounts receivable) department files the documents that Barb sent him and updates the accounts receivable and general ledger for the customer's account. The accounts receivable is sorted according to customer number for Adam's ease, since each customer number is unique. Every week he goes through the accounts and calls customers who are overdue on the payments. If a customer defaults on payment, Adam reclassifies the account as "doubtful."

When a customer receives his or her goods and invoice, the company is usually mailed a check for payment. Mickey in the mail room receives the checks and sends them to cash receipts. Mickey's boss, Muhammad, also works in the mail room, but is too busy with administrative work in his office behind closed doors to supervise the opening of the mail. This structure allows mail room clerks like Mickey to listen to music while they work and not disturb Muhammad. Mickey also happens to be Adam's (accounts receivable) son. Adam thought it would be wise to get his son's foot in the company's door by getting him a low-level job in the mail room.

Carol, the cash receipts clerk, receives the checks and stores them in her top drawer until the end of the week, at which point she prepares a deposit slip and deposits the checks at the Bank of New York. Carol returns from the bank with a bank receipt, files it, and updates the cash receipts journal.

At the end of each month, Adam makes sure all transactions are reconciled in the general ledger. If they are not, he asks the corresponding department to verify the books and report back to him. Usually the department in question can identify and correct the problem and tell Adam what adjusting entries to make.

Upon receipt of the goods, the customer sends F&Y the payment check as described above.

Required:

a. Prepare the REA model of the sales/collection business process of F&Y.

b. List the information events in the process and classify each of them as either recording, reporting, or maintaining events.

c. List the decision/management events in the process.

7. REA Model
(Prepared by Megan Gillette, Lehigh University)

Horox, Inc. is a manufacturer of portable compact disc (CD) players. It is located outside of Philadelphia, Pennsylvania, and employs 1,500 workers at a centrally located, 15-acre production facility. It distributes its products worldwide through three nearby distribution centers. Sales are currently $20 million per year and growing. Horox was formed 10 years ago; its management was relatively inexperienced and its technical knowledge was lacking. Since 1997, Horox has been expanding into new research areas and in the past three years has reported enormous profits in its financial statements.

Its major competitors for the small market share it has are electronic giants. Horox has managed to edge its way into retail chains and privately owned stores through the aggressiveness and wit of its sales staff. Horox supplies the major electronic chains and department stores, requiring payment for all orders within 30 days of the order or upon receipt.

The salespersons work partly on salary and partly on commissions. Since the salespeople are traveling to retailers most of the time, the purchase orders come in throughout the day over the fax machine or by telephone to Eddie in the sales department. Eddie has been with the company for a long time; he knows the sales process well and performs credit checks simultaneously with sales order processing. Once Eddie prepares copies of the sales order, he sends a copy to billing and two copies to the inventory warehouse. He files one copy.

Once the sales orders reach Rosemary in the inventory warehouse, she prepares the packing slip and collects the CD players from inventory. Rosemary then updates the inventory records and sends the merchandise, a copy of the sales order, and the packing slip to Kelly in the shipping department. She files one copy of the sales order. Once received by the shipping department, Kelly prepares two shipping notices and bills of lading.

Once the order is ready to be distributed to the customer, it is sent out with the bills of lading, shipping notice, and packing slip. Kelly files one copy of the sales order and shipping notice.

In the billing department, the sales order is processed into an invoice with prices. The remittance advice is also created. Both are sent out to the customer as a bill. The sales journal is updated by Tim, the billing clerk. The sales department reconciles with the billing department periodically.

Once the customer receives the bill requesting payment, he or she sends a check along with the remittance advice back to the company. Here the mail room sorts the checks by company and gives the checks and remittance advice accompanying the checks to Katie, the billing department secretary. Katie updates the cash receipts journal and credits the customer's account. Katie deposits the checks in the company account at the bank. She then files the remittance advice in a file for two months, after which she discards them.

Required:
a. Prepare the REA model of the sales/collection business process of Horox, Inc.

b. List the information events in the process and classify each of them as either recording, reporting, or maintaining events.
c. List the decision/management events in the process.

8. REA Model
DVDs For Less, Inc. (DVDs) is a provider of rental DVDs. The company operates several rental locations throughout the greater Phoenix, Arizona, area and employs nearly 2,000 individuals as managers and store clerks. Current annual rental revenue exceeds $25 million, an amount that has increased by about 5 percent for each of the previous six years.

DVDs, of course, faces intense competition for the national video rental chains. The success DVDs has enjoyed is due, primarily, to how well the CEO has predicted the rapid growth in Phoenix. As the population in Phoenix has increased rapidly, the CEO has purchased property for new locations more conveniently accessible for customers than any of the competitors.

DVDs has also initiated a unique method of tracking its customers. Each customer, after passing a rigorous credit check and submitting a credit card to cover delinquent or lost DVDs, is provided with a unique customer number. A key pad is provided at each store's entry, and customers are asked to enter their customer number on the key pad each time they come into a store. This way, DVDs for Less can track the number of times a customer visits the store, whether they made a purchase, whether they inquired about a DVD, or whether a visit was made without any of these activities taking place. In order to encourage customers to provide their customer number with each visit, DVDs has instituted a policy of giving a customer a free rental for every 20 visits.

Prepare an REA Model for customer visits. This model should include customer tracking, sales, credit information, and customer inquiries.

9. REA Model
(Prepared by Heather Racki, Bob's Stores)
The Heatheria Company was founded five years ago by Elizabeth Robinson. It is a retailing company that buys dresses at wholesale and distributes them to upscale stores. The Heatheria expenditure cycle is based on four basic goals: to order goods as

needed, to make sure they are received in good condition, to store the goods without loss, and to record transactions properly and accurately.

A purchase is the first procedure in the expenditure cycle. Every Friday, Susan, a clerk in the inventory control department, checks her accounts to determine the amount to be ordered for the following week. To confirm whether her records are accurate, Susan compares her accounts to John's in receiving. After adjusting her records, Susan prepares a purchase requisition, noting the quantities to be reordered and the requested delivery date. The quantities are determined by the economic order quantity. Susan then sends copies to Heather in purchasing and David in accounts payable and files a copy for herself.

After receiving a purchase requisition, Heather must choose an appropriate supplier and prepare a purchase order. Using the supplier file, Heather is able to select the supplier that best fits her needs. She then gives Beth, a purchasing clerk, all of the information concerning the sale. At the end of the day, Beth prepares a purchase order containing the quantities needed, the expected unit prices, and the terms and conditions negotiated. Copies of the purchase order are sent to the supplier, inventory control, receiving, and accounts payable. Beth files a copy for her department.

As the dresses arrive, John counts them and examines each one for defects. Any goods that are unacceptable are sent back to the supplier. John informs Chuck of the number of dresses that are accepted. Chuck prepares a receiving report and sends copies to accounts payable, purchasing, and inventory control. One copy is kept and filed with the packing slip. Chuck enters the quantity of dresses received into the inventory accounts.

Shortly after the goods are received, an invoice is sent to accounts payable. David compares the purchase order, receiving report, and invoice. If the invoice prices and quantities match those of the purchase order and all the goods have been received, David approves the invoice. If not, David writes the errors onto an error report. The error report is then sent to Jennifer, who settles all discrepancies with the supplier.

Once the invoice is approved, David enters the transactions into the accounts payable ledger and purchases journal. Next, he sends the invoice to Maria, head of the accounts payable department.

Upon receiving the invoice, Maria prepares a prenumbered cash disbursements voucher and signs it. She records all vouchers in the vouchers register and posts them to the general ledger. George in the general accounting department is sent the vouchers for approval. After authorizing them, George places the vouchers in a bin.

Each Friday, Maria collects the unpaid vouchers from George's bin and then prepares prenumbered checks. Upon completing the checks, Maria enters each one into the check register and posts everything to the general ledger. She then sends the checks to George, who signs and mails them.

Required:

a. Prepare the REA model of the acquisition/payment business process of The Heatheria Company.

b. List the information events in the process and classify each of them as either recording, reporting, or maintaining events.

c. List the decision/management events in the process.

10. REA Model

(Prepared by Kate Cannon, Lehigh University)

Horox, Inc. is a manufacturer of portable compact disc (CD) players. It is located outside of Philadelphia, Pennsylvania, and employs 1,500 workers at a centrally located, 15-acre production facility. It distributes its products worldwide through three nearby distribution centers. Sales are currently $20 million per year and growing. Horox was formed 10 years ago; its management was relatively inexperienced and its technical knowledge was lacking. Since 1997, Horox has been expanding into new research areas and in the past three years has reported enormous profits in its financial statements.

Its major competitors for the small market share it has are electronic giants. Horox has managed to edge its way into retail chains and privately owned stores through the aggressiveness and wit of its sales staff. Horox supplies the major electronic chains and department stores, requiring payment for all orders within 30 days of the order or upon receipt.

Within the expenditure cycle, the company needs to purchase raw materials such as plastics and special computer chips and send these materials to the conversion cycle. The expenditure cycle also maintains the payroll department. John, a purchasing department clerk, monitors the inventory levels and determines whether purchases are necessary. He then prepares a purchase requisition. If purchases are needed, he prepares six purchase order forms. Two purchase orders are sent directly to the vendor. One is placed in an open purchase order file in the purchasing department, and the other is used to update the records of the purchasing department. Accounts payable and the receiving department also are sent a purchase order. Upon receiving the goods with a packing slip, the receiving department creates five receiving reports. A receiving report is sent to the stores and the accounts payable department. Two receiving reports are sent to the purchasing department, where one is filed and one is used to update records. The final report is filed in the receiving department with the purchase order and packing slip. Vendors send the accounts payable department invoices, which are updated to the accounts payable subsidiary ledger and the purchases journal and filed. A voucher is created from the purchases journal, and it is sent to the general ledger.

In the cash disbursements department, Larry prepares and signs the checks for the suppliers. He receives the information from the accounts payable department such as the purchase requisition, purchase order, receiving report, invoice, and the cash disbursement voucher. After preparation of the checks, these documents are sent back to the accounts payable department, and a journal voucher is sent to general ledger. A copy of the check is filed after the original is sent to the supplier. Within the general ledger, the journal voucher is reconciled with the summary sent by the accounts payable department. After reconciliation, the voucher and the summary are filed.

Required:

a. Prepare the REA model of the acquisition/payment business process of Horox, Inc.

b. List the information events in the process and classify each of them as either recording, reporting, or maintaining events.

c. List the decision/management events in the process.

11. REA Model
(Prepared by Patrick Gilbride, Fleet Bank)

Lava Typewriter Manufacturing (LTM) is a regional producer of business machines. LTM employs 120 production and office workers. The general accounting record keeping of LTM is predominantly manual. "One Write" style records are maintained for accounts payable, purchases, payroll, cash disbursements, and the general journal. Select information from the general journal and other journals is manually input to a series of Lotus worksheets to produce trial balances and other reports.

Every two weeks, the payroll supervisor initiates the payroll cycles. She calculates each employee's gross pay, overtime pay, taxes, and so forth. These calculations are entered into the payroll register and sent to the accounts payable clerk who checks the calculations and notifies the payroll supervisor of any errors. Errors are corrected immediately in the payroll register. The accounts payable clerk posts the obligations to the payroll subsidiary ledger. The totals from this ledger are sent to the general ledger clerk and entered into the computer. Meanwhile, the payroll supervisor calls Automatic Data Processing (ADP), a service bureau, and faxes it all of the information necessary for the checks. ADP cuts the checks and sends them to the payroll supervisor, along with two copies of a list of payment details for each employee.

The payroll supervisor sends the accounts payable clerk one of the copies of the payment details list and files the other. The accounts payable clerk posts the payments to the payroll subsidiary ledger. The payroll supervisor sends the checks to the payroll clerk who places them in individual envelopes and then mails them to the employees.

At the end of the day on which the checks were mailed, the payroll supervisor sends batch totals of the payments to the general ledger clerk, who posts them to the computer.

Required:

a. Prepare the REA model of the payroll business process of Lava Typewriter Manufacturing (LTM).

b. List the information events in the process and classify each of them as either recording, reporting, or maintaining events.

c. List the decision/management events in the process.

chapter 11

Enterprise Resource Planning Systems

LEARNING OBJECTIVES

After studying this chapter, you should:

- Understand the general functionality and key elements of ERP systems.
- Understand the various aspect of ERP configuration including servers, databases, and the use of bolt-on software.
- Understand the purpose of data warehousing as a strategic tool and recognize the issues related to the design, maintenance, and operation of a data warehouse.
- Recognize the risks associated with ERP implementation.
- Be aware of the key considerations related to ERP implementation.
- Understand the internal control and auditing implications associated with ERPs.
- Be able to identify the leading ERP products and be familiar with their distinguishing features.

Until recently, most large and midsized organizations designed and programmed custom information systems in-house. This resulted in an array of standalone systems that were designed to the unique needs of specific users. While these systems dealt with their designated tasks efficiently, they did not provide strategic decision support at the enterprise level because they lacked the integration needed for information transfer across organization boundaries. Today the trend in information systems is toward implementing highly integrated, enterprise-oriented systems. These are not custom packages designed for a specific organization. Instead, they are generalized systems that incorporate the best business practices in use. Organizations mix and match these prefabricated software components to assemble an **enterprise resource planning (ERP)** system that best meets their business requirements. This means that an organization may need to change the way that it conducts business to take full advantage of the ERP.

This chapter is composed of five major sections and an appendix. The first section outlines the key features of a generic ERP system by comparing the function and data-storage techniques of a traditional flat-file or database system to that of an ERP. The second section describes various ERP configurations related to servers, databases, and bolt-on software. The topic of the third section is data warehousing. A data warehouse is a relational or multidimensional database that supports online analytical processing (OLAP). The fourth section examines risks associated with ERP implementation. The fifth section reviews the internal control and auditing issues related to ERPs and the discussion follows the SAS 78 framework. The chapter appendix reviews the leading ERP software products. Some of the functionality and distinguishing features of these systems are highlighted.

WHAT IS AN ERP?

ERP systems are multiple module software packages that evolved primarily from traditional manufacturing resource planning (MRP II) systems. The term ERP was coined by the Gartner Group and has become widely used in recent years. The objective of ERP is to integrate key processes of the organization such as order entry, manufacturing, procurement and accounts payable, payroll, and human resources. By doing so, a single computer system can serve the unique needs of each functional area. Designing one system that serves everyone is an undertaking of massive proportions. Under the traditional model each functional area or department has its own computer system optimized to the way that it does its daily business. ERP combines all of these into a single, integrated system that accesses a single database to facilitate the sharing of information and to improve communications across the organization.

To illustrate, consider the traditional model for a manufacturing firm illustrated in Figure 11-1. This company employs a **closed database architecture**, which is similar in concept to the basic, flat-file model. Under this approach a database management system is used to provide minimal technological advantage over flat-file systems. The database management system is little more than a private but powerful file system. As with the flat-file approach, the data remains the property of the application. Thus, distinct, separate, and independent databases exist. As is true with the flat-file architecture, there is a high degree of data redundancy in a closed database environment.

When a customer places an order, the order begins a paper-based journey around the company where it is keyed and rekeyed into the systems of several different departments. These redundant tasks cause delays and lost orders, as well as promote data entry errors. During transit through the various systems the status of the order may be unknown at any point in time. For example, responding to a customer query, the marketing department may be unable to look into the production database to determine whether an order has been manufactured and shipped. Instead, the frustrated customer is told, "You will need to call manufacturing." Similarly, the procurement of raw materials from suppliers is not linked to customer orders until they reach the manufacturing stage. This results in delays because manufacturing awaits the arrival of needed materials or in excessive investment in inventories to avoid stockouts.

The lack of effective communication between systems in the traditional model is often the consequence of a fragmented, systems design process. Each system tends to be designed as a solution to a specific operational problem rather than as a part of an overall strategy. Furthermore, because systems designed in-house emerge independently and over time, they are often constructed on different and incompatible technology platforms. Thus, special procedures and programs need to be created so that older mainframe systems using flat files can communicate with newer, distributed systems that use relational databases. Special software "patches" are also needed to enable commercial systems from different vendors to communicate with each other as well as with custom systems that were developed in-house. While communications between such a hodgepodge of systems is possible, it is highly fragmented and not conducive to efficient operations.

ERP systems support a smooth and seamless flow of information across the organization by providing a standardized environment for a firm's business processes and a common operational database that supports communications. An overview of ERP is presented in Figure 11-2. Data in the operational database are modeled, structured, and stored in accordance with the internal attributes of the data. They remain independent of any specific application. Extensive data sharing among users occurs through application-sensitive views that present the data in a way that meets all user needs.

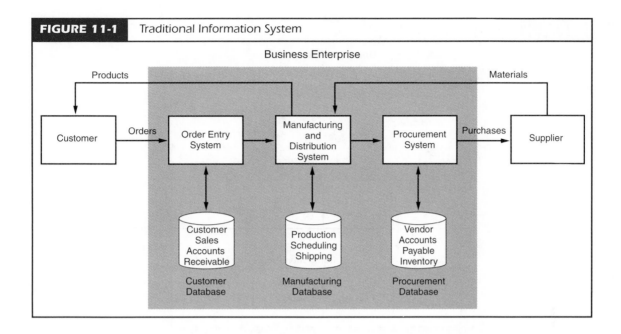

FIGURE 11-1 | Traditional Information System

ERP CORE APPLICATIONS

ERP functionality falls into two general groups of applications: *core applications* and *business analysis applications*. **Core applications** are those applications that operationally support the day-to-day activities of the business. If these applications fail, so does the business. Typical core applications include, but are not limited to, sales and distribution, business planning, production planning, shop floor control, and logistics. Core applications are also called *online transaction processing (OLTP)* applications. Figure 11-2 illustrates these functions applied to a manufacturing firm.

Sales and distribution functions handle order entry and delivery scheduling. This includes checking on product availability to ensure timely delivery and verifying customer credit limits. Unlike the previous example, customer orders are entered into the ERP only once. Because all users access a common database, the status of an order can be determined at any point. In fact, the customer may be able to dial-up over the Internet and check the status of the order directly. Such integration reduces manual activities, saves time, and decreases human error.

Business planning consists of forecasting demand, planning product production, and detailing routing information that describes the sequence and the stages of the actual production process. Capacity planning and production planning can be very complex; therefore, some ERPs provide simulation tools to help managers decide how to avoid shortages in materials, labor, or plant facilities. Once the master production schedule is complete, the data are entered into the MRP (materials requirements planning) module, which provides three key pieces of information: an exception report, materials requirements listing, and inventory requisitions. The exception report identifies potential situations, such as late delivery of materials, that will result in rescheduling production. The materials requirements listing shows the details of vendor shipments and expected receipts of products and components needed for the order. Inventory requisitions are used to trigger material purchase orders to vendors for items not in stock.

Shop floor control involves the detailed production scheduling, dispatching, and job costing activities associated with the actual production process. Finally, the logistics

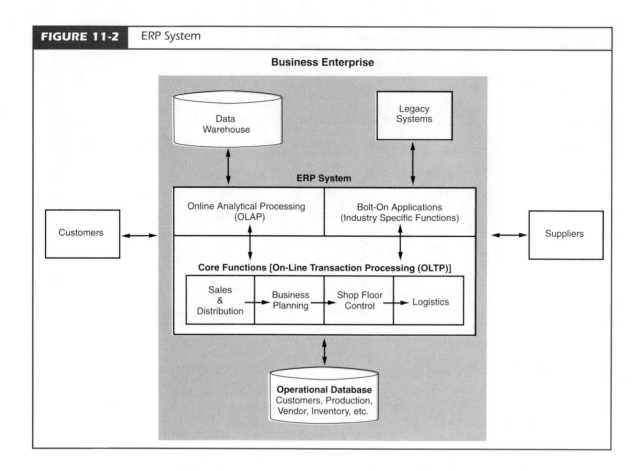

FIGURE 11-2   ERP System

application is responsible for assuring timely delivery to the customer. This consists of inventory and warehouse management, as well as shipping. Most ERPs also include their procurement activities within the logistics function.

Online Analytical Processing

An ERP is more than simply an elaborate transaction processing system. It is a decision support tool that supplies management with real-time information and permits timely decisions that are needed to improve performance and achieve competitive advantage. **Online analytical processing (OLAP)** includes decision support, modeling, information retrieval, ad hoc reporting/analysis, and what-if analysis. Some ERPs support these functions with their own industry-specific modules that can be added to the core system. Other ERP vendors have designed their systems to accept and communicate with specialized *bolt-on* packages that are produced by third-party vendors. Sometimes the user organization's decision support requirements are so unique that they need to integrate in-house legacy systems into the ERP.

However, business analysis applications are obtained or derived and are central to their successful function as a data warehouse. A **data warehouse** is a database constructed for quick searching, retrieval, ad hoc queries, and ease of use. The data is normally extracted periodically from an operational database or from a public information service. An ERP system could exist without having a data warehouse; similarly, organizations that have not implemented an ERP may deploy data warehouses. The trend, however, is that organizations, which are serious about competitive advantage, deploy both. The recommended data architecture for an ERP implementation includes separate operational and data warehouse databases. Issues related to the creation and operation of a data warehouse will be examined later in the chapter.

ERP SYSTEM CONFIGURATIONS

SERVER CONFIGURATIONS

Most ERP systems are based on the **client-server model,** which will be discussed in detail in Chapter 12. Briefly, the client-server model is a form of network topology in which a user's computer or terminal (the client) accesses the ERP programs and data via a host computer called the server. While the servers may be centralized, the clients are usually located at multiple locations throughout the enterprise. Two basic architectures are the *two-tier model* and the *three-tier model,* as described in the following sections.

Two-tier Model

In a typical **two-tier model,** the server handles both application and database duties. Client computers are responsible for presenting data to the user and passing user input back to the server. Some ERP vendors use this approach for local area network (LAN) applications where the demand on the server is restricted to a relatively small population of users. This configuration is illustrated in Figure 11-3.

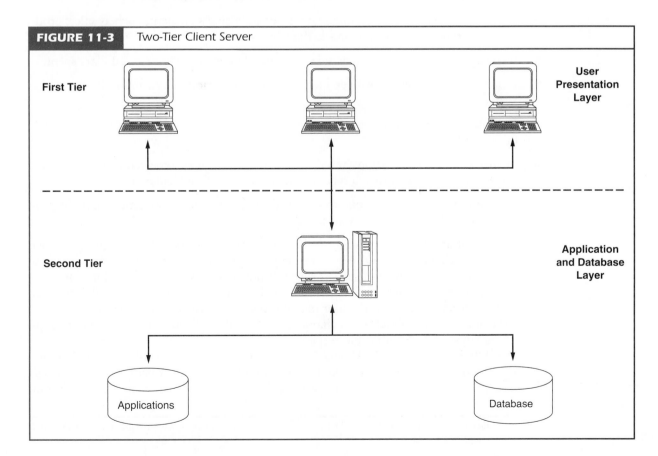

FIGURE 11-3	Two-Tier Client Server

First Tier — User Presentation Layer

Second Tier — Application and Database Layer

Applications   Database

Three-tier Model

The database and application functions are separated in the **three-tier model**. This architecture is typical of large ERP systems that use wide area networks (WANs) for connectivity among the users. Satisfying client requests requires two or more network connections. Initially, the client establishes communications with the application server. The application server then initiates a second connection to the database server. Figure 11-4 presents the three-tier model.

OLTP VERSUS OLAP SERVERS

When implementing an ERP system that will include a data warehouse, a clear distinction needs to be made between the competing types of data processing: *OLTP* and *OLAP*. OLTP events consist of large numbers of relatively simple transactions, e.g., updating accounting records that are stored in several related tables. For example, an order entry system retrieves all of the data relating to a specific customer to process a sales transaction. Relevant data are selected from the Customer table, Invoice table, and a detail Line Item table. Each table contains an embedded key (i.e., customer number), which is used to relate rows between different tables. The transaction processing activity involves updating the customer's current balance and inserting new records into the Invoice and Line Item tables. The relationships between records in such OLTP transactions are generally simple, and only a few records are actually retrieved or updated in a single transaction.

OLAP can be characterized as online transactions that[1]:

- Access very large amounts of data (e.g., several years of sales data).

- Analyze the relationships among many types of business elements such as sales, products, geographic regions, and marketing channels.

- Involve aggregated data such as sales volumes, budgeted dollars, and dollars spent.

- Compare aggregated data over hierarchical time periods (e.g., monthly, quarterly, yearly).

- Present data in different perspectives such as sales by region, by distribution channel, or by product.

- Involve complex calculations among data elements such as expected profit as a function of sales revenue for each type of sales channel in a particular region.

- Respond quickly to user requests so that they can pursue an analytical thought process without being stymied by system delays.

An example of an OLAP transaction is the aggregation of sales data by region, product type, and sales channel. The OLAP query may need to access vast amounts of sales data over a multiyear period to find sales for each product type within each region. The user can further refine the query to identify sales volume by product for each sales channel within a given region. Finally, the user may decide to perform year-to-year or quarter-to-quarter comparisons for each sales channel. An OLAP application must be able to support this analysis online with rapid response.

The difference between OLAP and OLTP can be summarized as follows. OLTP applications support mission-critical tasks through simple queries of operational databases. OLAP applications support management-critical tasks through analytical investigation of

---

1   The Queen's University of Belfast. Data Mining Techniques, http://www.pcc.qub.ac.uk/tec/courses/datamining/stu_notes/dm_book_4.html.

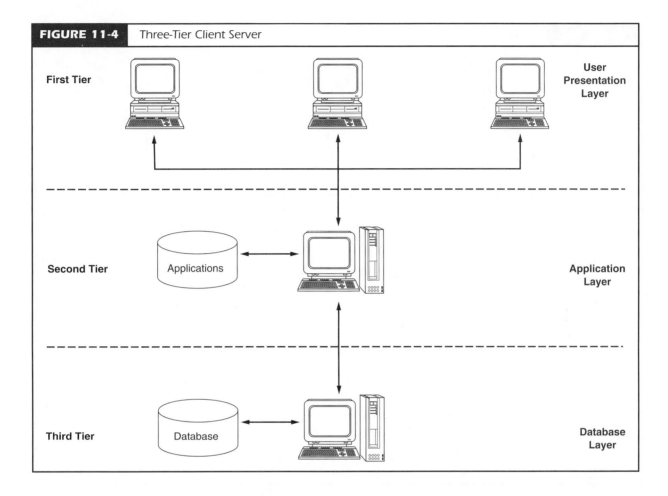

| FIGURE 11-4 | Three-Tier Client Server |

complex data associations that are captured in data warehouses. OLAP and OLTP have specialized requirements that are in direct conflict. Figure 11-5 shows how the client-server architecture enables organizations to deploy separate and specialized application and database servers to resolve these conflicting data management needs. OLAP servers support common analytical operations including *consolidation*, *drill-down*, and *slicing and dicing*.

Consolidation is the aggregation or roll-up of data. For example, sales offices data can be rolled up to districts and districts rolled up to regions.

Drill-down permits the disaggregation of data to reveal the underlying details that explain certain phenomena. For example, the user can drill down from total sales returns for a period to identify the actual products returned and the reasons for their return.

Slicing and dicing enables the user to examine data from different viewpoints. One slice of data might show sales within each region. Another slice might present sales by product across regions. Slicing and dicing is often performed along a time axis to depict trends and patterns.

OLAP servers allow users to analyze complex data relationships. The physical database itself is organized in such a way that related data may be rapidly retrieved across multiple dimensions. Thus, OLAP database servers need to be efficient when storing and processing multidimensional data. Later in the chapter, data modeling and storage techniques that

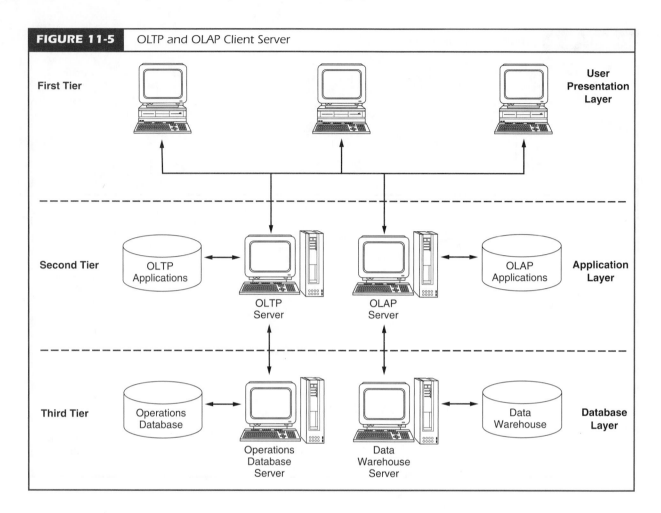

FIGURE 11-5   OLTP and OLAP Client Server

improve data warehouse efficiency will be examined. In contrast, relational databases for operations are modeled and optimized to handle OLTP applications. They concentrate on reliability and transaction processing speed, instead of decision support need.

DATABASE CONFIGURATION

ERP systems are composed of thousands of database tables. Each table is associated with business processes that are coded into the ERP. The ERP implementation team, which includes key users and IT professionals, selects specific database tables and processes by setting switches in the system. Determining how all the switches need to be set for a given configuration requires a deep understanding of the existing processes used in operating the business. Often, however, choosing table settings involves decisions to reengineer the company's processes so that they comply with the best business practices in use. In other words, the company typically changes its processes to accommodate the ERP rather than modifying the ERP to accommodate the company.

BOLT-ON SOFTWARE

Many organizations have found that ERP software alone cannot drive all the processes of the company. These firms use a variety of **bolt-on software** provided by third-party vendors. The decision to use bolt-on software requires careful consideration. Most of the leading ERP vendors have entered into partnership arrangements with third-party vendors that provide specialized functionality. The least risky approach is to choose a bolt-on that is endorsed by the ERP vendor. Some organizations, however, take a more independent approach. Domino's Pizza is a case in point.

Domino's Pizza

Domino's U.S. distribution delivered 338 million pizzas in 1998.[2] The company manufactures an average of 4.2 million pounds of dough per week in its 18 U.S. distribution centers. A fleet of 160 trucks carries the dough along with other food and paper products to the 4,500 U.S. Domino's franchises. Domino's has no cutoff time for ordering supplies. Therefore, a franchise can call and adjust its order even after the truck has rolled away from the distribution center. To help anticipate demand, Domino's uses forecasting software from Prescient Systems Inc., which bolts on to their PeopleSoft ERP system. In addition, they use a system from Manugistics Inc. to schedule and route the delivery trucks. Each truck has an onboard computer system that feeds data into a time-and-attendance system from Kronos Inc., which connects to the PeopleSoft human resources module. Domino's also has an extensive data warehouse. To anticipate its market, Domino's performs data mining with software from Cognos Inc. and Hyperion Solutions Corp.

Domino's had been using these and other applications before it implemented an ERP. The company did not want to retire its existing applications, but discovered that the legacy system required data fields that the ERP did not provide. For instance, the routing system tells the truck drivers which stores to visit and in what order. The ERP system did not have a data field for specifying the delivery stop sequence. This information, however, was needed by the warehousing system to tell loaders what to put in the trucks and in what order. Having confidence in its in-house IT staff, Domino's management decided to take the relatively drastic step of modifying the ERP software to include these fields.

Supply Chain Management

Another development regarding the bolt-on software issue is the rapid convergence between ERP and bolt-on software functionality. **Supply chain management** (SCM) software is a case in point. The supply chain is the set of activities associated with moving goods from the raw materials stage to the consumer. This includes procurement, production scheduling, order processing, inventory management, transportation, warehousing, customer service, and forecasting the demand for goods. SCM systems are a class of application software that supports this task. Successful SCM coordinates and integrates these activities into a seamless process. In addition to the key functional areas within the organization, SCM links all of the partners in the chain, including vendors, carriers, third-party logistics companies, and information systems providers. Organizations can achieve competitive advantage by linking the activities in its supply chain more efficiently and effectively than its competitors.

Recognizing this need, ERP vendors have moved decisively to add SCM functionality to their ERP products. ERP systems and SCM systems are now on converging paths. SAP and Oracle have recently added an SCM module, while Baan and PeopleSoft both have acquired smaller SCM vendors to integrate their SCM software into future releases. On the other hand, SCM software vendors are also expanding their functionality to appear more like ERP systems. As larger ERP vendors move into the midsize company market, the smaller SCM and ERP vendors will likely be pushed out of business.

---

2   Slater, D. "The Ties That Bolt," Enterprise Resource Planning, *CIO Magazine* (April 15, 1999): 4–9.

DATA WAREHOUSING

Data warehousing is one of the fastest growing IT issues for businesses today. Not surprisingly, data warehousing functionality is being incorporated into all leading ERP systems. A *data warehouse* is a *relational* or *multidimensional* database that may consume hundreds of gigabytes or even terabytes of disk storage. When the data warehouse is organized for a single department or function, it is often called a **data mart**. Rather than containing hundreds of gigabytes of data for the entire enterprise, a data mart may have only tens of gigabytes of data. Other than size, we make no distinction between a data mart and a data warehouse. The issues discussed in this section apply to both.

The process of data warehousing involves extracting, converting, and standardizing an organization's operational data from ERP and legacy systems and loading it into a central archive—the data warehouse. Once loaded into the warehouse, data are accessible via various query and analysis tools that are used for *data mining*. Data mining, which was introduced in Chapter 8, is the process of selecting, exploring, and modeling large amounts of data to uncover relationships and global patterns that exist in large databases but are "hidden" among the vast number of facts. This involves sophisticated techniques that use *database queries* and *artificial intelligence* to model real-world phenomena from data collected from the warehouse.

Most organizations implement a data warehouse as part of a strategic IT initiative that involves an ERP system. Implementing a successful data warehouse involves installing a process for gathering data on an ongoing basis, organizing it into meaningful information, and delivering it for evaluation. The data warehousing process has the following essential stages[3]:

- Modeling data for the data warehouse
- Extracting data from operational databases
- Cleansing extracted data
- Transforming data into the warehouse model
- Loading the data into the data warehouse database

MODELING DATA FOR THE DATA WAREHOUSE

Chapters 9 and 10 stressed the importance of data normalization to eliminate three serious anomalies: the *update*, *insertion*, and *deletion anomalies*. Normalizing data in an operational database is necessary to reflect accurately the dynamic interactions among entities. Data attributes are constantly updated, new attributes are added, and obsolete attributes are deleted on a regular basis. While a fully normalized database will yield the flexible model needed for supporting multiple users in this dynamic operational environment, it also adds to complexity in that it translates into performance inefficiency.

The Warehouse Consists of Denormalized Data

Because of the vast size of a data warehouse, such inefficiency can be devastating. A three-way join between tables in a large data warehouse may take an unacceptably long time to complete and may be unnecessary. In the data warehouse model, the relationship among attributes does not change. Because historical data are static in nature, nothing is gained by constructing normalized tables with dynamic links.

3   Fiore, P. Everyone is Talking About Data Warehousing, *Evolving Enterprise,*(Spring 1998): 2.

For example, in an operational database system, Product X may be an element of work-in-process in Department A this month and part of Department B's work-in-process next month. In a properly normalized data model, it would be incorrect to include Department A's work-in-process data as part of a Sales Order table that records an order for Product X. Only the product item number would be included in the Sales Order table as a foreign key linking it to the Product table. Relational theory would call for a join (link) between the Sales Order table and Product table to determine the production status (i.e., which department the product is currently in) and other attributes of the product. From an operational perspective, complying with relational theory is important because the relation changes as the product moves through different departments over time. Relational theory does not apply to a data warehousing system because the Sales Order/Product relation is stable.

Wherever possible, therefore, normalized tables pertaining to selected events may be consolidated into denormalized tables. Figure 11-6 illustrates how sales-order data is reduced to a single denormalized Sales Order table for storage in a data warehouse system.

EXTRACTING DATA FROM OPERATIONAL DATABASES

Data extraction is the process of collecting data from operational databases, flat files, archives, and external data sources. Operational databases typically need to be out of service when data extraction occurs to avoid data inconstancies. Because of their large size and the need for a speedy transfer to minimize the downtime, little or no conversion of data occurs at this point. A technique called **changed data capture** can dramatically reduce the extraction time by capturing only newly modified data. The extraction software compares the current operational database with an image of the data taken at the last transfer of data to the warehouse. Only the data that have changed in the interim are captured.

Extracting Snapshots Versus Stabilized Data

Transaction data stored in the operational database go through several stages as economic events unfold. For example, a sales transaction first undergoes credit approval, then the product is shipped, then billing occurs, and finally payment is received. Each of these events changes the state of the transaction and associated accounts such as inventory, accounts receivable, and cash.

A key feature of a data warehouse is that the data contained in it are in a nonvolatile, stable state. Typically, transaction data are loaded into the warehouse only when the activity on them has been completed. Potentially important relationships between entities may, however, be absent from data that are captured in this stable state. For example, information about cancelled sales orders will probably not be reflected among the sales orders that have been shipped and paid for before they are placed in the warehouse. One way to reflect these dynamics is to extract the operations data in "slices of time." These slices provide snapshots of business activity. For example, decision makers may want to observe sales transactions approved, shipped, billed, and paid, at various points in time along with snapshots of inventory levels at each state. Such data may be useful in depicting trends in the average time taken to approve credit or ship goods that might help explain lost sales.

CLEANSING EXTRACTED DATA

Data cleansing involves filtering out or repairing invalid data prior to being stored in the warehouse. Operational data are "dirty" for many reasons. Clerical, data entry, and computer program errors can create illogical data such as negative inventory quantities, misspelled names, and blank fields. Data cleansing also involves transforming data into standard business terms with standard data values. Data are often combined from multiple systems that use slightly different spellings to represent common terms, such as "cust," "cust_id," or "cust_no." Some

FIGURE 11-6   De-Normalized Data

A. Normalized Representation for an Operational Database System

Customer Table

Customer Number	Name	Street	City	State
34675	John Smith	10 Elm	Bath	PA

Invoice Table

Invoice Number	Invoice Date	Shipped Date	Invoice Amount	Customer Number
8866376	06/12/04	06/23/04	600	34675

Line Item Table

Invoice Number	Item Number	Quantity	Price	Extended Price
8866376	j683	2	200	400
8866376	r223	5	40	200

B. De-Normalized Representation for Data Warehouse System

Sales Order Table

Customer Number	Name	Street	City	State	Invoice Number	Invoice Date	Shipped Date	Invoice Amount	Ite Number	Quantity	Price	xtended Price
34675	John Smith	10 Elm	Bath	PA	8866376	06/12/04	06/23/04	600	j683	2	200	400
34675	John Smith	10 Elm	Bath	PA	8866376	06/12/04	06/23/04	600	r223	5	40	200

operational systems may use entirely different terms to refer to the same entity. For example, a bank customer with a certificate of deposit and an outstanding loan may be called a *Lender* by one system and a *Borrower* by another. The source application may use cryptic or difficult-to-understand terms for a number of reasons. For example, some older legacy systems were designed at a time when programming rules placed severe restrictions on naming and formatting data attributes. Also, a commercial application may assign attribute names that are too generic for the needs of the data warehouse user. Businesses that purchase commercial data, such as competitive performance information or market surveys, need to extract data from whatever format the external source provides and reorganize them according to the conventions used in the data warehouse. During the cleansing process, therefore, the attributes taken from multiple systems need to be transformed into uniform, standard business terms. This tends to be an expensive and labor-intensive activity, but one that is critical in establishing data integrity in the warehouse. Figure 11-7 illustrates the role of data cleansing in building and maintaining a data warehouse.

Transforming Data into the Warehouse Model

A data warehouse is composed of both detail and summary data. To improve efficiency, data can be transformed into summary views before they are loaded into the warehouse. For example, many decision makers may need to see product sales figures summarized weekly, monthly, quarterly, or annually. It may not be practical to summarize information from detail data every time the user needs it. A data warehouse that contains the most frequently requested summary views of data can reduce the amount of processing time during analysis. Referring again to Figure 11-7, we see the creation of summary views over time. These are typically created around business entities such as customers, products, and suppliers. Unlike operational views, which are virtual in nature with underlying base tables, data warehouse views are physical tables. Most OLAP software will, however, permit the user to construct virtual views from detail data when one does not already exist.

A data warehouse will often provide multiple, summary views based on the same detailed data such as customers or products. For example, several different summary

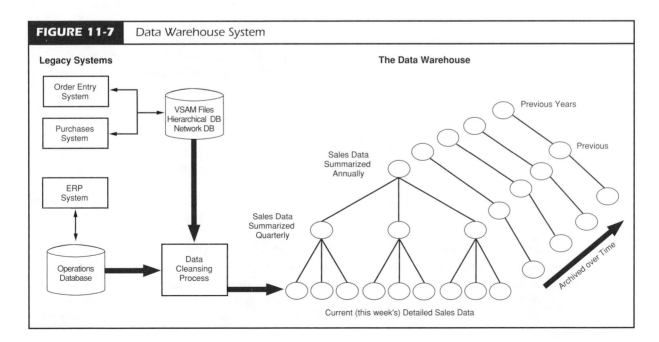

FIGURE 11-7   Data Warehouse System

Legacy Systems   The Data Warehouse

Order Entry System
Purchases System
VSAM Files Hierarchical DB Network DB
ERP System
Operations Database
Data Cleansing Process

Sales Data Summarized Annually
Sales Data Summarized Quarterly
Previous Years
Previous
Archived over Time

Current (this week's) Detailed Sales Data

views may be generated from sales-order detail data. These may include summaries by product, customer, and region. From such views an analyst can drill down into the underlying detail data. Many business problems require a review of detail data to fully evaluate a trend, pattern, or anomaly exhibited in the summarized reports. Also, a single anomaly in detail data may manifest itself differently in different summary views.

LOADING THE DATA INTO THE DATA WAREHOUSE DATABASE

Most organizations have found that data warehousing success requires that the data warehouse be created and maintained separately from the operational (transaction processing) databases. This point is developed further below.

Internal Efficiency

One reason for a separate data warehouse is that the structural and operational requirements of transaction processing and data mining systems are fundamentally different, making it impractical to keep both operational (current) and archive data in the same database. Transaction processing systems need a data structure that supports performance, whereas data mining systems need data organized in a manner that permits broad examination and the detection of underlying trends.

Integration of Legacy Systems

The continued influence of legacy systems is another reason that the data warehouse needs to be independent of operations. A remarkably large number of business applications continue to run in the mainframe environment of the 1970s. By some estimates, more than 70 percent of business data for large corporations still resides in the mainframe environment. The data structures employed by these systems are often incompatible with the architectures of modern, data mining tools. Hence, transaction data that are stored in navigational databases and VSAM systems often end up in large tape libraries that are isolated from the decision process. A separate data warehouse provides a venue for integrating the data from legacy and contemporary systems into a common structure that supports entitywide analysis.

Consolidation of Global Data

Finally, the emergence of the global economy has brought about fundamental changes in business organizational structure and has profoundly changed the information requirements of business entities. Decision makers in the global corporation are challenged by unique business complexities. For example, they need to assess the profitability of products built and sold in multiple countries with volatile currencies. Such challenges add complexity to data mining. A separate centralized data warehouse is an effective means of collecting, standardizing, and assimilating data from diverse sources.

In conclusion, the creation of a data warehouse separate from operational systems is a fundamental data warehousing concept. Many organizations now consider data warehouse systems to be key components of their IS strategy. As such, they allocate considerable resources to build data warehouses concurrently with the operational systems being implemented.

DECISIONS SUPPORTED BY THE DATA WAREHOUSE

By making the data warehouse as flexible and friendly as possible, it becomes accessible by many end users. Some decisions supported by a data warehouse are not fundamentally different from those that are supported by traditional databases. Other information uses, such as multidimensional analysis and information visualization, are not possible with traditional systems. Some users of the data warehouse need routine reports based on traditional queries. When standard reports can be anticipated in advance, they can be provided automatically as a periodic product. Automatic generation of standard information reduces access activity against the data warehouse and will improve its efficiency in dealing with more esoteric needs.

   Drill-down capability is a useful data analysis technique associated with data mining. Drill-down analysis begins with the summary views of data described above. When anomalies or interesting trends are observed, the user "drills down" to lower-level views and ultimately into the underlying detail data. Obviously, such analysis cannot be anticipated like a standard report. Drill-down capability is an OLAP feature of data mining tools available to the user. Tools for data mining are evolving rapidly to satisfy the decision maker's need to understand the business unit's behavior in relation to key entities including customers, suppliers, employees, and products. Standard reports and queries produced from summary views can answer many "what" questions, but drill-down capability answers the "why" and "how" questions. Table 11-1 summarizes some of the applications of data mining in decision support.

SUPPORTING SUPPLY CHAIN DECISIONS FROM THE DATA WAREHOUSE

The primary reason for data warehousing is to optimize business performance. Many organizations feel that more strategic benefit can be gained by sharing data externally. By providing customers and suppliers with the information they need when they need it, the company can improve its relationships and provide better service. The potential gain to the giving organization is seen in a more responsive and efficient supply chain. Using Internet technologies and OLAP applications an organization can share its data warehouse with its trading partners and, in effect, treat them like divisions of the firm. A few examples of this approach are outlined in the following.[4]

TABLE 11-1	Applications of Data Mining
Business Field	**Application**
Banking/Investments	Detect patterns of fraudulent credit card use.
	Identify "loyal" customers and predict those likely to change their credit card affiliation.
	Examine historical market data to determine investors' stock trading rules.
	Predict credit card spending of key customer groups.
	Identify correlations between different financial indicators.
Health Care and Medical Insurance	Predict office visits from historical analysis of historical patient behavior.
	Identify successful and economical medical therapies for different illnesses.
	Identify which medical procedures tend to be claimed together.
	Predict which customers will buy new policies.
	Identify behavior patterns associated with high-risk customers.
	Identify indicators of fraudulent behavior.
Marketing	Identify buying patterns based on historical customer data.
	Identify relationships among customer demographic data.
	Predict response to various forms of marketing and promotion campaigns.

---

4   Davis, B., "Data Warehouses Open Up," *Information Week On Line News in Review* (June 28, 1999).

Western Digital Corporation, a leading manufacturer of hard drives, plans to grant certain suppliers access to its data warehouse so suppliers can view performance data on their parts. Because Western Digital maintains a limited engineering staff, the company relies on its suppliers to act as strategic partners in product development. Providing suppliers with performance data allows them to make improvements and participate in the engineering process. The suppliers improve their parts, which in turn improves Western Digital's products.

The company's data warehouse holds more than 600 gigabytes of raw data collected from more than 100,000 drives that it manufactures each day. Approximately 800 attributes are collected on each drive, which can be analyzed using OLAP software. The systems feeding the warehouse include ERP applications, data from trouble-call centers, data from failure-analysis systems, and field test data from customer sites and service centers. The company routinely searches the data warehouse for failure information on every drive that it manufactures. All failures and their causes can be linked back to the supplier.

GM's supply-chain data warehouse will be available via the Web to more than 5,000 suppliers worldwide. The suppliers can log on to a secure Web site and query information on the quantities of supplies shipped, delivery times, and prices. This information will help GM suppliers optimize their product planning, ability to source materials, and shipping-fulfillment processes.

MIM Health Plans Inc., an independent pharmacy benefits management company, lets its customers view warehouse data to promote better buying decisions. For instance, benefits managers can view reports and drill down into the warehouse to see claims costs, overall costs, the number of prescriptions ordered in a given time period, the number of brand versus generic drugs, and other decision metrics.

RISKS ASSOCIATED WITH ERP IMPLEMENTATION

The benefits from ERP can be significant, but they do not come risk-free to the organization. An ERP system is not a silver bullet that will, by its mere existence, solve an organization's problems. If that were the case, there would never be ERP failures, but there have been many. This section examines some of the risk issues that need to be considered.

BIG BANG VERSUS PHASED-IN IMPLEMENTATION

Implementing an ERP system has more to do with changing the way an organization does business than it does with technology. As a result, most ERP implementation failures are due to cultural problems within the firm that stand in opposition to the objective of process reengineering. Strategies for implementing ERP systems to achieve this objective follow two general approaches: the *big bang* and the *phased-in* approach.

The **big bang** method is the more ambitious and risky of the two. Organizations taking this approach attempt to switch operations from their old legacy systems to the new system in a single event that implements the ERP across the entire company. While this method has certain advantages, it has been associated with numerous system failures. Because the new ERP system means new ways of conducting business, getting the entire organization on board and in sync can be a daunting task. On day one of the implementation no one within the organization will have had any experience with the new system. In a sense, everyone in the company is a trainee learning a new job. The new ERP will initially meet with opposition because using it involves compromise. The legacy systems, which everyone in the organization was familiar with, had been honed over the years to meet exact needs. In most cases, ERP systems have neither the range of functionality nor the familiarity of the legacy systems that they replace. Also, because a single system is now serving the entire organization, individuals at data input points often find themselves entering considerably more data than they did previously with the more narrowly focused legacy system. As a result, the speed of the new system often suffers and causes disruptions to daily operations. These problems are typically experienced whenever any new system is implemented. The magnitude of the problem is the issue under the big bang approach in which everyone in the company is affected. Once the initial adjustment period has passed and the new culture emerges, however, the ERP becomes an effective operational and strategic tool that provides competitive advantage to the firm.

Because of the disruptions associated with the big bang, the **phased-in** approach has emerged as a popular alternative. It is particularly suited to diversified organizations whose units do not share common processes and data. In these types of companies, independent ERP systems can be installed in each business unit over time to accommodate the adjustment periods needed for assimilation. Common processes and data, such as the general ledger function, can be integrated across the organization without disrupting operations throughout the firm.

Organizations that are not diversified can also employ the phased-in approach. The implementation usually begins with one or more key processes, such as order entry. The goal is to get ERP up and running concurrently with legacy systems. As more of the organization's functions are converted to ERP, legacy systems are systematically retired. In the interim the ERP is interfaced to legacy systems. During this period, the objectives of *system integration* and *process reengineering*, which are fundamental to the ERP model, are not achievable. To take full advantage of the ERP, process reengineering will still need to occur. Otherwise, the organization will have simply replaced its old legacy system with a very expensive new one.

OPPOSITION TO CHANGES IN THE BUSINESS'S CULTURE

To be successful, all functional areas of the organization need be involved in determining the culture of the firm and in defining the new system's requirements. The firm's willingness and ability to undertake a change of the magnitude of an ERP implementation is an important consideration. If the corporate culture is such that change is not tolerated or desired, then an ERP implementation will not be successful.

The technological culture must also be assessed. Organizations that lack technical support staff for the new system or have a user base that is unfamiliar with computer technology face a steeper learning curve and a potentially greater barrier to acceptance of the system by its employees.

CHOOSING THE WRONG ERP

Because ERP systems are prefabricated systems, users need to determine whether a particular ERP fits their organization's culture and its business processes. A common reason for system failure is when the ERP does not support one or more important business processes. In one example, a textile manufacturer in India implemented an ERP only to discover afterward that it did not accommodate a basic need. The textile company had a policy of maintaining two prices for each item of inventory that it sold. One price was used for the domestic market and a second price, which was four times higher, was for export sales. The ERP that the user implemented was not designed to allow two different prices for the same inventory item. The changes needed to make the ERP work were both extensive and expensive. Serious system disruptions resulted from this oversight. Furthermore, modifying an ERP program and database can introduce potential processing errors and can make updating the system to later versions difficult.

Goodness of Fit

Management needs to make sure that the ERP they choose is right for its company. No single ERP system is capable of solving all the problems of all organizations. For example, SAP's R/3 was designed primarily for manufacturing firms with highly predictable processes that are relatively similar to those of other manufacturers. It may not be the best solution for a service-oriented organization that has a great need for customer-related activities conducted over the Internet.

Finding a good functionality fit requires a software selection process that resembles a funnel, which starts broad and systematically becomes more focused. It begins with a large number of software vendors that are potential candidates. Evaluation questions are asked of vendors in iterative rounds. Starting with a large population of vendors and a small number of high-level qualifier questions, the number of vendors is reduced to a manageable few. With proper questioning, more than half the vendors are removed from contention with as few as 10 to 20 questions. In each succeeding round, the questions asked become more detailed and the population of vendors decreases.

When a business's processes are truly unique, the ERP system must be modified to accommodate industry-specific (bolt-on) software or to work with custom-built legacy systems. Some organizations, such as telecommunications service providers, have unique billing operations that cannot be satisfied by off-the-shelf ERP systems. Before embarking on the ERP journey, the organization's management needs to assess whether they can and should reengineer their business practices around a standardized model.

System Scalability Issues

If an organization's management expects business volumes to increase substantially during the life of the ERP system, then there is a scalability issue that needs to be addressed. **Scalability** is the system's ability to grow smoothly and economically as user requirements increase. The term *system* in this context refers to the technology platform, application software, network configuration, or database. *Smooth and economical growth* is the ability to increase system capacity at an acceptable incremental cost per unit of capacity without encountering limits that would demand a system upgrade or replacement. *User requirements* pertain to volume-related activities such as transaction processing volume, data entry volume, data output volume, data storage volume, or increases in the user population.

To illustrate scalability, four dimensions of scalability are important: size, speed, workload, and transaction cost. In assessing scalability needs for an organization, each of these dimensions in terms of the ideal of linear scaling must be considered.[5]

Size. With no other changes to the system, if database size increases by a factor of x, then query response time will increase by no more than a factor of x in a scalable system. For example, if business growth causes the database to increase from 100GB to 500GB, then transactions and queries that previously took one second will now take no more than five seconds.

Speed. An increase in hardware capacity by a factor of x will decrease query response time by no less than a factor of x in a scalable system. For example, increasing the number of input terminals (nodes) from 1 to 20 will increase transaction processing time proportionately. Transactions that previously took 20 seconds will now take no more than one second in a system with linear scaling.

5   Winter, R. Scalable Systems: Lexicology of Scale, *Intelligent Enterprise Magazine* (March 2000): 68–74.

Workload. If workload in a scalable system is increased by a factor of x, then response time, or throughput, can be maintained by increasing hardware capacity by a factor of no more than x. For example, if transaction volume increased from 400 per hour to 4,000 per hour, the previous response time can be achieved by increasing the number of processors by a factor of 10 in a system that is linearly scalable.

Transaction cost. In a scalable system, increases in workload do not increase transaction cost. Therefore, an organization should not need to increase system capacity faster than demand. For example, if the cost of processing a transaction in a system with one processor is 10 cents, then it should still cost no more than 10 cents when the number of processors is increased to handle larger volumes of transactions.

Vendors of ERP systems sometimes advertise scalability as if it were a single-dimension factor. In fact, it is a multifaceted issue. Some systems accommodate growth in user populations better than others. Some systems can be scaled to provide more efficient access to large databases when business growth demands it. All systems, however, have their scaling limits. Since infinite scalability is impossible, prospective users need to assess their needs and determine how much scalability they want to purchase up front and what form it should take. The key is to anticipate specific scalability issues before making an ERP investment and before the issues become reality.

CHOOSING THE WRONG CONSULTANT

Implementing an ERP system is an event that most organizations will undergo only once. Success of the projects rests on skills and experience that typically do not exist in-house. Because of this, virtually all ERP implementations involve an outside consulting firm, which coordinates the project, helps the organization to identify its needs, develops a requirements specification for the ERP, selects the ERP package, and manages the cutover. ERP consulting has grown into a $20 billion-per-year market. The fee for a typical implementation is normally between three and five times the cost of the ERP software license.

Consulting firms with large ERP practices have at times been desperately short of human resources. This was especially true in the mid- to late-1990s, when thousands of clients were rushing to implement ERP systems before the new millennium to avoid Y2K problems. As demand for ERP implementations grew beyond the supply of qualified consultants, more and more stories of botched projects materialized.

A frequent complaint is that consulting firms promise experienced professionals, but deliver incompetent trainees. They have been accused of employing a bait-and-switch maneuver to get contracts. At the initial, engagement interview the consulting firm introduces their top consultants, who are sophisticated, talented, and persuasive. The client agrees to the deal with the firm, but incorrectly assumes that these individuals, or others with similar qualifications, will actually implement the system.

The problem has been equated to the airline industry's common practice of overbooking flights. Some suggest that consulting firms, not wanting to turn away business, are guilty of overbooking their consulting staff. The consequences, however, are far graver than the inconvenience of missing a flight—a free hotel room and meal cannot compensate for the damages done. Therefore, before engaging an outside consultant, management should:

- Interview the staff proposed for the project and draft a detailed contract specifying which members of the consulting team will be assigned to which tasks.

- Establish in writing how staff changes will be handled.

- Conduct reference checks of the proposed staff members.

- Align the consultants' interests with those of the organization by negotiating a pay-for-performance scheme based on achieving certain milestones in the project. For example, the actual amount paid to the consultant may be between 85 to 115 percent of the contracted fee, based on whether a successful project implementation comes in under or over schedule.

- Set a firm, termination date for the consultant to avoid consulting arrangements becoming interminable, resulting in dependency and an endless stream of fees.

HIGH COST AND COST OVERRUNS

Total cost of ownership (TCO) for ERP systems varies greatly from company to company. For medium- to large-sized systems implementations, costs range from hundreds of thousands to hundreds of millions of dollars. TCO includes hardware, software, consulting services, internal personnel costs, installation, and upgrades and maintenance to the system for the first two years after implementation. The risk comes in the form of underestimated and unanticipated costs. Some of the more commonly experienced problems occur in the following areas.

Training. Training costs are invariably higher than estimated because management focuses primarily on the cost of teaching employees the new software. This is only part of the needed training. Employees also need to learn new procedures, which is often overlooked during the budgeting process.

System Testing and Integration. In theory, ERP is a holistic model in which one system drives the entire organization. The reality, however, is that many organizations use their ERP as a backbone system that is attached to legacy systems and other bolt-on systems, which support unique needs of the firm. Integrating these disparate systems with the ERP may involve writing special conversion programs or even modifying the internal code of the ERP. Integration and testing are done on a case-by-case basis; thus, the cost is extremely difficult to estimate in advance.

Database Conversion. A new ERP system usually means a new database. Data conversion is the process of transferring data from the legacy system's flat files to the ERP's relational database. When the legacy system's data are reliable, the conversion process may be accomplished through automated procedures. Even under ideal circumstances, a high degree of testing and manual reconciliation is necessary to ensure that the transfer was complete and accurate. More often, the data in the legacy system are not reliable (sometimes called dirty). Empty fields and corrupted data values cause conversion problems that demand human intervention and data rekeying. Also, and more importantly, the structure of the legacy data is likely to be incompatible with the reengineered processes of the new system. Depending on the extent of the process reengineering involved, the entire database may need to be converted through manual data entry procedures.

Develop Performance Measures

Because ERPs are extremely expensive to implement, many managers are often dismayed at the apparent lack of cost savings that they achieve in the short term. In fact, a great deal of criticism about the relative success of ERPs relates to whether they provide benefits that outweigh their cost. To assess benefits, management first needs to know what they want and need from the ERP. They should then establish key performance measures such as reductions in inventory levels, inventory turnover, stockouts, and average order fulfillment time that reflect their expectations. To monitor performance in such key areas, some organizations establish an independent *value assessment group* that reports to top management. Although financial break-even on an ERP will take years, by developing focused and measurable performance indicators, an operational perspective on its success can be developed.

DISRUPTIONS TO OPERATIONS

ERP systems can wreak havoc in the companies that install them. In a Deloitte Consulting survey of 64 Fortune 500 companies, 25 percent of the firms surveyed admitted that they experienced a drop in performance in the period immediately following implementation. The reengineering of business processes that often accompanies ERP implementation is the most commonly attributed cause of performance problems. Operationally speaking, when business begins under the ERP system everything looks and works differently from the way it did with the legacy system. An adjustment period is needed for everyone to reach a comfortable point on the learning curve. Depending on the culture of the organization and attitudes toward change within the firm, adjustment may take longer in some firms than in others. The list of major organizations that have experienced serious disruptions includes Dow Chemical, Boeing, Dell Computer, Apple Computer, Whirlpool Corporation, and Waste Management. The most notorious case in the press was Hershey Foods Corporation, which had trouble processing orders through its new ERP system and was unable to ship products.

As a result of these disruptions, Hershey's 1999 third-quarter sales dropped by 12.4 percent compared to the previous year's sales, and earnings were down by 18.6 percent. Hershey's problem has been attributed to two strategic errors related to system implementation. First, because of schedule overruns, they decided to switch to the new system during their busy season. The inevitable snags that arise from implementations of complex systems like SAP's R/3 are easier to deal with during slack business periods. Secondly, many experts feel that Hershey attempted to do too much in a single implementation. In addition to the R/3 system, they implemented a customer-relations management system and logistics software from two different vendors, which had to interface with R/3. The ERP and these bolt-on components were all implemented using the big bang approach.

IMPLICATIONS FOR INTERNAL CONTROL AND AUDITING

As with any system, the internal control and audit of ERP systems are issues. Key concerns are examined next within the framework of SAS 78.

TRANSACTION AUTHORIZATION

A key benefit of an ERP system is its tightly integrated architecture of modules. This structure, however, also poses potential problems for transaction authorization. For example, the bill of materials drives many manufacturing systems. If the procedures for the creation of the bill of materials are not configured correctly, every component that uses the bill of materials could be affected. Controls need to be built into the system to validate transactions before they are accepted and acted on by other modules. Because of their real-time orientation, ERPs are more dependent on programmed controls than on human intervention, as was the case with legacy systems. The challenge for auditors in verifying transaction authorization is to gain a detailed knowledge of the ERP system configuration as well as a thorough understanding of the business processes and the flow of information between system components.

SEGREGATION OF DUTIES

Operational decisions in ERP-based organizations are pushed down to a point as close as possible to the source of the event. Manual processes that normally require segregation of duties are, therefore, often eliminated in an ERP environment. For example, shop supervisors may order inventories from suppliers and receiving-dock personnel may post inventory receipts to the inventory records in real time. Furthermore, ERP forces together many different business functions, such as order entry, billing, and accounts payable, under a single integrated system. Organizations using ERP systems must establish new security, audit, and control tools to ensure duties are properly segregated.

To help resolve the segregation of duties problem, SAP, the leading ERP system, employs a configuration technique called *user role*. Each role is associated with a specific set of activities that are assigned to an authorized user of the ERP system. SAP currently provides more than 150 predefined user roles, which limit a user's access to only certain functions and associated data. The system administrator assigns roles to users of the system when it is configured. These can be customized as needed. When the user logs onto the system, a role-based menu appears, which limits the user to the specified tasks. Auditors should ensure that roles are assigned in accordance with job responsibilities on a "need-to-know" basis.

SUPERVISION

An often-cited pitfall of an ERP implementation is that management does not fully understand its impact on business. Too often, after the ERP is up and running, only the implementation team understands how it works. Because their traditional roles will be changed, supervisors need to acquire an extensive technical and operational understanding of the new system. Typically, when an organization implements an ERP many decision-making responsibilities are pushed down to the shop floor level. The employee-empowered philosophy of ERP should not eliminate supervision as an internal control. Instead, it should provide substantial efficiency benefits. Supervisors should have more time to manage the shop floor and, through improved monitoring capability, increase their span of control.

ACCOUNTING RECORDS

ERP systems have the ability to streamline the entire financial reporting process. In fact, many organizations can and do close their books daily. OLTP data can be manipulated quickly to produce ledger entries, accounts receivable and payable summaries, and financial consolidation for both internal and external users. Traditional batch controls and audit trails are no longer needed in many cases. This risk is mitigated by improved data entry accuracy through the use of default values, cross-checking, and specified user views of data.

In spite of ERP technology, some risk to accounting record accuracy may still exist. Because of the close interfaces with customers and suppliers, some organizations run the risk that corrupted or inaccurate data may be passed from these external sources and corrupt the accounting database. Additionally, many organizations need to import data from legacy systems into their ERP systems. These data may be laden with problems such as duplicate records, inaccurate values, or incomplete fields. Consequently, strict data cleansing is an important control. Special *scrubber* programs are used as interfaces between the ERP and the exporting systems to reduce these risks and ensure that the most accurate and current data is being received.

ACCESS CONTROLS

Security is perhaps one of the most critical control issues in an ERP implementation. The goal of security in these systems is to provide confidentiality, integrity, and availability of necessary information. Security weaknesses can result in the revealing of trade secrets to competitors and other unauthorized access. Some security professionals argue that computer systems should be restricted to user-specific tasks. Others argue that everyone should have access to all company information. The most sensible resolution to these opposing views is to impose security limitations to data based on a risk assessment. Security administrators should tightly control the more sensitive and risky data within the organization.

Access to the Data Warehouse

Access control is a vital feature of a data warehouse that is shared with customers and suppliers. The organization should establish procedures to oversee the authorization of individuals at customer and supplier sites that will be granted access to their data warehouses. Access privileges should be specified for each outside user and controlled by passwords. User views need to be created to limit outsider access to only approved data. Internet sessions should be managed through a firewall and use encryption and digital signatures to maintain confidentiality.[6] Firewalls, which are a combination of hardware and software that protect the resources of a private network, help to secure data from unauthorized internal and external users. Auditing tools for intrusion detection are available to assist in mitigating security risks. Periodic audits should include a risk assessment and review of access levels granted to both internal and external users based on their job descriptions.

Contingency Planning

In addition to access security, detailed contingency plans must be developed for computer and business operations that can be invoked instantly in the event of a disaster. These plans need to be developed prior to the switch to a new ERP system. Related to this is the need for backup procedures in the event of a server failure. Two general approaches are outlined briefly next, but a more extensive discussion is presented in Chapter 15.

Centralized organizations with highly integrated business units may need a single global ERP system that is accessed via the Internet or private lines from around the world to consolidate data from subsidiary systems. A server failure under this model could leave the entire organization unable to process transactions. To control against this, two linked servers can be connected in redundant backup mode. All production processing is done on one server. If it fails, processing is automatically transferred to the other. Organizations that want more security and resilience may arrange servers in a cluster of three or more that dynamically share the workload. Processing can be redistributed if one or more of the servers in the cluster fail.

Companies whose organizational units are autonomous and do not share common customers, suppliers, or product lines often choose to install regional servers. This approach permits independent processing and spreads the risk associated with server failure. For example, BP Amoco implemented SAP's R/3 into 17 separate business groups.

Independent Verification

Because ERP systems employ OLTP, traditional, independent verification controls such as reconciling batch control numbers are meaningless. Similarly, process reengineering to improve efficiency also changes the nature of independent verification. For example, the traditional three-way match of the purchase order, receiving report, and invoice serves no purpose in an EDI environment in which the vendor's check is cut when the order is

---

6   Firewalls, encryption, and digital signatures are discussed in Chapters 12 and 16.

placed. The focus of independent verification needs to be redirected from the transaction level to one that views overall performance. ERP systems come with canned controls and can be configured to produce performance reports that should be used as assessment tools. Internal auditors also play an important role in this new environment and need to acquire a thorough technical background and comprehensive understanding of the ERP system. Ongoing independent verification efforts can be conducted only by a team well versed in ERP technology.

Auditing the Data Warehouse

As part of an information-system audit the auditor designs a procedure to gather evidence relating to various management assertions pertaining to the firm's financial statements. As part of this procedure the auditor often performs an **analytical review** of account balances to identify relationships between accounts and risks that are not otherwise apparent. Analytical procedures may indicate trends, even in adequately controlled organizations, that lead the auditor to extend the number and nature of substantive tests that he or she subsequently performs.[7] On the other hand, such evidence can provide assurance that transactions and accounts are reasonably stated and complete, and may permit the auditor to reduce substantive testing (this material is discussed in the appendix to Chapter 15).

The vast amount of data contained in the data warehouse is an excellent resource for performing time-series and ratio analysis. In the case of the revenue cycle, an analytical review will provide the auditor with an overall perspective for trends in sales, cash receipts, sales returns, and accounts receivable. For example, the auditor may compare reported sales for the quarter with those for the same period in previous years. Ratio analysis may be used to compare total sales to cost of goods sold, sales to accounts receivable, and allowance for doubtful accounts to accounts receivable. Significant variations in account balances over time, or unusual ratios, may signify financial statement misrepresentations. Accounts receivable may be examined in time slices for changes in balances relative to sales. This can indicate whether the organization's credit policy is being properly and consistently applied. Another useful audit procedure for identifying potential audit risks involves scanning thousands or even millions of records for unusual transactions and abnormal account balances.

In the case of the expenditure cycle, an analytical review can provide the auditor with an overall perspective for trends in accounts payable and related expenses. Current expenses may be compared to historical expenses and management budgets. For example, the auditor may compare current payroll expenses for the quarter with those for the same period in previous years. Unusual trends or variances should be examined for cause.

The auditor may use drill-down techniques to identify unusually high levels of business activity with a particular supplier. Excessive purchases from a single supplier could represent an abnormal business dependency that may prove harmful to the firm if the supplier raises prices or cannot deliver on schedule. It may also signify a fraudulent relationship involving kickbacks to purchasing agents or other management. On the other hand, a large number of vendors with small balances may be evidence of a highly inefficient purchasing process. In such cases management may need to consolidate business activity. Various corporate surveys have estimated the cost of processing a purchase order at

---

7   Substantive tests are tests of details as opposed to tests of controls. For example, an auditor may examine the details of invoices to verify that their amounts were properly calculated and recorded in the accounts. Substantive testing can be time consuming. Extensive, substantive tests will add cost and delays to the audit. The amount of substantive testing performed is influenced in part by the quality of internal controls in place. Based on evidence provided by testing internal controls and analytical reviews, the auditor may decide to reduce or expand the amount of substantive testing to be performed.

between $50 and $125. Restricting the number of vendors with whom the organization does business can reduce this expense.

While an organization's data warehouse is an excellent resource for performing analytical reviews, the auditor needs to understand the procedures used to populate the warehouse. As illustrated, data cleansing is an important phase in the maintenance of a warehouse. To be useful as an OLAP tool the data warehouse needs to be free of contamination. Erroneous data, such as negative inventory values, missing fields, and other clerical errors, that are a natural part of operational databases are identified and repaired, or rejected, in the cleansing process prior to their entering the data warehouse. The auditor must, therefore, be careful of the reliance placed on this resource. Because the data warehouse exists in an artificially pristine state, it may not be a suitable substitute for the operational database when assessing tests of process controls and performing substantive tests.[8]

SUMMARY

This chapter opened by comparing the function and data storage techniques of a traditional flat-file or database system with that of an ERP. An important distinction was drawn between OLTP and OLAP applications. Similarly, the differences between the ERP's operational database and the data warehouse were discussed. Next, ERP configurations were examined related to servers, databases, and bolt-on software. SCM as an area of contention was discussed. ERP vendors are moving quickly to provide SCM functionality. Simultaneously, SCM vendors are encroaching on traditional ERP territory. Data warehousing was the topic of the third section. A data warehouse is a relational or multidimensional database that supports OLAP. A number of data warehouse issues were discussed, including data modeling, data extraction from operational databases, data cleansing, data transformation, and data loading into the warehouse. The fourth section examined common risks associated with ERP implementation. Among these are the risks associated with the big bang approach, internal opposition to changing the way a company does its business, choosing the wrong ERP model, choosing the wrong consultant, cost overrun issues, and disruptions to operations. Also presented were a number of issues to consider when implementing an ERP. These include selecting a system that is a good fit for the organization, understanding that the term "scalability" can mean different things to different people, potential problems associated with customizing the software, the need for assigning performance measures, and the need to control outside consultants. The chapter concluded with a review of the internal control and auditing issues related to ERPs.

APPENDIX*

LEADING ERP PRODUCTS

The ERP market constitutes products from dozens of vendors of all sizes. This appendix reviews the key features and distinguishing characteristics of the industry leaders including SAP, Oracle, Microsoft, and SoftBrands. The purpose is to provide overview and insight into the underlying philosophies of these vendors. Specific system characteristics and functionality, however, undergo changes on a regular basis. To obtain current and detailed information on these products the reader should visit the vendors' Web pages.

---

8   For a more complete discussion of this material see Hall, J. A., *Information Systems Auditing and Assurance* (South-Western College Publishing, 2000).
*   Prepared by Zhen Zhou, graduate student at Lehigh University.

SAP

Founded in 1972, SAP is the leader in providing collaborative business solutions. By April 2005, it had an estimated 12 million users worldwide with more than 88,700 installations and more than 1,500 partners. The customer list consists of firms of all sizes in 20 different industries including aerospace, automobile, banking, chemicals, consumer goods, higher education, post office, and utilities.

For years, SAP R/3® software had been the leading ERP software, providing comprehensive functions that integrate virtually all major business processes within the enterprise. Recently, SAP developed mySAP products as a supplement to R/3. mySAP can be used as an independent software product or in combination with R/3. It is especially centered on cross-over e-business applications, which link the business processes of several companies and coordinate them with one another, and thereby optimize them. SAP is offering upgrades from R/3 to mySAP for current R/3 customers.

Key Features and Functions

mySAP ERP comes with four individual solutions that support key business processes: mySAP ERP Financials, mySAP ERP Operations, mySAP ERP Human Capital Management, and mySAP ERP Corporate Service.

mySAP ERP Financials

Financial and Managerial Accounting. mySAP ERP Financials supports both financial accounting and managerial accounting. Financial accounting functions help users comply with international accounting standards, such as general accepted accounting principles (GAAP) and International Accounting Standards (IAS). It also supports the legal and accounting requirements resulting from European market and currency unification.

Using the financial accounting functions, users can perform the activities of general ledger, accounts receivable and payable, fixed-asset accounting, cash journal accounting, inventory accounting, tax accounting, accrual accounting, fast close, financial statements and parallel valuation.

Using the managerial accounting functions of mySAP ERP Financials, users can perform the activities of profit center accounting, cost center and internal order accounting, project accounting, investment management, product cost accounting, profitability accounting, and transfer pricing.

Corporate Governance. The solution includes new tools that support corporate governance projects, including:

- Management of Internal Controls (MIC)
  It certifies the accuracy of quarterly and annual financial statements and disclosures. Meanwhile, it designs, establishes, and maintains disclosure controls and procedures. Moreover, the solution evaluates and reports the effectiveness of those controls and procedures, as well as indicates any significant changes, including discrepancies that have occurred since the most recent evaluation.

- Management of the Audit Information System (AIS)
  mySAP ERP Financials includes an auditor's toolbox to help users comply with corporate governance requirements, such as sections 302 and 404 of the Sarbanes-Oxley Act. The solution enables audit trails to the document level, tests users' financial system security controls, and provides structure-control reports for better auditing.

- Management of Whistle-blower Complaints
  mySAP ERP Financials includes whistle-blower functions that support section 301 of the Sarbanes-Oxley Act, allowing stakeholders to send and analyze anonymous complaints.

- Management of Capital and Risk
  mySAP ERP Financials supports the requirements of Basel II by enabling users to evaluate the capital-adequacy frameworks used to analyze risk levels and allowing users to create a reporting framework and analytical workbench that operate with central bank data.

Financial Supply Chain Management. mySAP ERP Financials includes features and functions to support financial SCM activities such as electronic invoicing and payments, dispute management, collections management, credit management, cash and liquidity management, and treasury and risk management.

mySAP ERP Operations

mySAP ERP Operations provides solution for procurement and logistics execution, product development and manufacturing, and sales and service. The solution also provides powerful analytic tools for better decision making.

Procurement and Logistics Execution. mySAP ERP Operations enables users to manage end-to-end logistics for complete business cycles, including purchase-to-pay and make-to-order cycles.

Product Development and Manufacturing. mySAP ERP Operations enables core development and manufacturing activities. The solution provides features and functions in production planning, manufacturing execution, asset management, product development and data management.

Sales and Services. mySAP ERP Operations supports core sales and services processes, including sales order management, aftermarket sales and service, and global trade services across SAP and non-SAP systems. It also helps users manage incentive and commission programs.

mySAP ERP Human Capital Management

The solution provides integrated, enterprise-wide functionality in human resource management. It helps users to identify, recruit, and track most qualified employees. With SAP Learning Solution, it enables enterprises to manage and integrate business learning processes. It functions to integrate team and individual goals with corporate-level goals and strategies. Moreover, its performance management could link management objective to performance review, appraisal, and support a performance-oriented compensation process. In addition, mySAP Human Capital Management helps users to implement different reward strategies. Companies can perform comparative compensation-package analysis based on internal and external salary data to ensure competitiveness in the marketplace.

Workforce Process Management. mySAP ERP Human Capital Management supports all basic processes related to personnel and employee information management. Through a centralized database, employees and management have instant access to up-to-date, consistent, complete information. The solution supports key processes for managing and disseminating organizational structure and policy information. It facilitates effective time-management strategies and provides convenient tracking, monitoring, record keeping, and evaluation of time data. It also enables users to handle complex payroll processes.

The solution supports current legal regulations for more than 50 countries worldwide, besides ensuring compliance with regulatory requirements for reporting purposes. Accordingly, it supports all processes involved in international employee relocation, from the planning and preparation of global assignments to personnel administration and payroll for global employees. Advanced features address considerations such as national currency, multiple languages, collective agreements, and reporting.

Workforce Deployment. mySAP ERP Human Capital Management provides comprehensive support for project resource planning that ensures employees are assigned to appropriate jobs, projects, and teams. The solution uses a portfolio management paradigm to unify project management, time tracking, financial data, and employee skills information. It facilitates workforce deployment across other SAP solutions, which enables businesses to create project teams based on skills and availability, monitor project progress, track time, and analyze results. It supports call center scheduling, which is based on forecasted call volume and shift schedules. It schedules retail staff based on customer volume, shift schedules, and skills.

mySAP ERP Corporate Services

mySAP ERP Corporate Services supports and optimizes both centralized and decentralized administrative processes. It can be tailored to meet specific requirements for transparency and control, as well as reduced financial and environmental risk, in the real estate, project portfolio, travel and environment, health and safety management. It also enables a unified approach to total quality management, delivering efficiencies that result from fewer product returns and improved asset utilization. It has strong quality control and maintaining function so that it could react quickly when unexpected issues arise throughout the product life cycle.

ORACLE | PEOPLESOFT

Founded in 1977 by Larry Ellison, Oracle was the first database management system to incorporate the SQL language. Oracle is also the first software company to develop and deploy 100 percent internet-enabled enterprise software across its entire product line: database, business applications, and application development and decision support tools. Oracle is the world's leading supplier of software for information management, and the world's second largest independent software company.

Oracle acquired PeopleSoft on January 18, 2005 (and PeopleSoft completed the acquisition of JD Edwards in July 2003). For the PeopleSoft Enterprise and JD Edwards EnterpriseOne product lines, the combined companies plan to develop and release a subsequent version of each over the next two calendar years. The combined company plan to continue to enhance and support the PeopleSoft product lines until at least 2013, while it is extending support for JD Edwards EnterpriseOne versions XE and 8.0 until February 2007.

Oracle E-Business Suite

Oracle E-Business Suite is a complete and integrated set of enterprise applications. Oracle uses a single, unified data model that stores information for all application in one place. Its Financials Services supports documentation and auditing for compliance with Sarbanes-Oxley and other regulations, and the Manufacturing/High technology provides option-dependent sourcing, automated spare parts return and repair processing, international drop shipment, and distribution planning.

PeopleSoft Enterprise Solutions

PeopleSoft Enterprise is built on its Pure Internet Architecture technology and designed for complex business requirements. It includes Campus Solutions, which is being used by University of Michigan and other universities, Customer Relationship Management, Financial Management, Human Capital Management, Service Automation, Supplier Relationship Management, Supply Chain Management, and All Supply Chain Management Product Modules.

JD Edwards EnterpriseOne

JD Edwards EnterpriseOne is a complete suite of modular, preintegrated, industry-specific business applications designed for rapid deployment and ease of administration on a pure internet architecture. It is ideally suited for organizations that manufacture, construct, distribute, service, or manage products or physical assets. EnterpriseOne includes functionality of Asset Lifecycle Management, Customer Relation Management, Financial Management, Human Capital Management, Manufacturing and Supply Chain Management, Project Management, Supply Management.

MICROSOFT

Microsoft Business Solutions are integrated business applications for small and midsize organizations, and divisions of large enterprises. It provides applications and services for retailers, manufacturers, wholesale distributors, and service companies. Microsoft Business Solutions series includes Great Plains, Axapta, Solomon and others. These solutions are ready to work with widely used productivity applications, like Microsoft Office, and technologies such as Microsoft Windows Server System and Microsoft.NET.

Microsoft Business Solutions–Great Plains

Microsoft purchased Great Plains in 2001. Great Plains focuses on the business-process needs for lower midmarket businesses and is scalable to meet the requirements of complex business processes for upper midmarket and corporate firms. Great Plains offers integrated capabilities for financial management, distribution, manufacturing, project accounting, human resource management, field service management, and business analytics. Great Plains delivers deep access to decision-driving information, a rapid return on investment, as well as expert, dedicated customer service.

Microsoft Business Solutions–Axapta

Axapta is a multilanguage, multicurrency ERP solution with core strengths in manufacturing and e-business together with strong functionality for the wholesale distribution and business services industries.

Axapta's Manufacturing offers the full range of functionality to control manufacturing and production. At any time, users can measure very specific costs associated with employees, machinery, and products. Its capacity on materials planning helps users project long-term needs, foresee fluctuations in demand, and adjust plans accordingly. Users can manage the shop floor more effectively by reducing manual entry and Web-enable employee information such as time registration and payroll. By collecting and analyzing production-related information, such as work hours and production activities, users can improve cost control. For project management, Axapta uses Gantt charts to provide a graphical illustration of schedules. Users can define their own Gantt plans and envision the production flow from one machine to another. Because of the online configuration, products can be generated online and with greater precision. At the same time, users can open the system to customers and vendors so that they can configure their own products, submit orders, and view an expected delivery date via the Internet. The full graphical suite, including version control, helps users design and maintains bills of materials.

Microsoft Business Solutions–Solomon

Solomon is a robust, flexible solution built to meet the needs of project-centric and distribution-driven companies. It also boosts employee efficiency by providing real-time data access through a Web-based interface.

BEST SOFTWARE

Best Software, Inc. offers automated business management solutions including accounting, human resources, payroll, fixed asset management, customer: relationship management, and e-commerce software.

MAS 500 is a complete enterprise management solution that Best Software developed to help companies manage and streamline operations. This SQL server-based software system automates all areas of business management including Core and Advanced Financials, Customer Relationship Management (CRM), Project Accounting (including time and expense tracking), Wholesale Distribution, Discrete Manufacturing, Warehouse Management, Human Resources and Payroll, e-Business and Business Intelligence

MAS 500's recent version 6.3 benchmark processes more than 360,000 sales orders per hour in a multiuser environment. MAS 500 Suite is the only application in the enterprise market developed from the start exclusively for Microsoft platforms, and is designed to support the latest features of current Microsoft releases.

Distinguishing Features and Functions

Manufacturing. Streamlines the entire manufacturing process and helps users respond quickly to customer demands. Advanced capabilities include project management, routings, bill of materials, work orders, MRP, scheduling, job costing, and labor reporting.

Distribution. Ideal for larger distributors with multiple warehouses, MAS 500 optimizes the supply chain, improving productivity and workflow. It also reduces inventory carrying and shipping costs and manage customer returns quickly and efficiently.

Project Accounting. Gives project-driven businesses the control to reduce cost overruns, improve cash flow, closely track progress, and capture every billable hour.

SoftBrands

SoftBrands is a leader in providing next-generation enterprise software for businesses in the hospitality and manufacturing sectors. It has more than 4,000 customers in more than 60 countries.

The Fourth Shift Edition for SAP Business One was provided by SoftBrands to meet the unique needs of dynamic small, midsize businesses. The Fourth Shift Edition enables emerging companies to streamline their operational and managerial processes with SAP-centric solution.

Distinguishing Features and Functions

Custom Products Manufacturing. Custom Products Manufacturing helps users to plan and control make-to-order and engineer-to-order products. Users can price custom products by having retail prices established and, as the custom product is configured, roll up the retail prices for a final sales price. Users can alternatively price custom products based on accumulating the component costs and applying a mark-up. Users can easily estimate and track job costs, schedule production, control inventory and purchasing, manage job configurations, and improve customer order processing. Users can respond quickly to quotation requests and customer inquiries, which improves customer service. Users can promise valid delivery dates based on availability of material, and meet users' promises using Fourth Shift to coordinate purchasing, manufacturing, and shipping activities. The Fourth Shift Edition could help users improve job cost estimating, quicken job configuration process, manage job-related activities, and track job status and actual-versus-estimated job costs.

Trace and Serialization. The functions of Lot Trace and Serialization help users gain control over raw materials and finished goods to improve quality, prevent waste, and provide better customer service. Fourth Shift Edition Lot Trace/Serialization allows users to track lot-traced items throughout the manufacturing process, from receiving through shipping. Serial numbers can be assigned to items at the time of shipment. The Fourth Shift Edition could help users improve quality control, prevent waste and improve customer satisfaction.

For further information, please visit the following companies websites.

1. www.2020software.com
2. www.sap.com
3. www.oracle.com
4. www.peoplesoft.com
5. www.microsoft.com
6. www.softbrands.com
7. www.bestsoftware.com

Key Terms

analytical review (550)

big bang (542)

bolt-on software (534)

changed data capture (537)

client-server model (531)

closed database architecture (528)

consolidation (533)

core applications (529)

data mart (536)

data warehouse (530)

drill-down (533)

enterprise resource planning (ERP) (527)

online analytical processing (OLAP) (530)

online transaction processing (OLTP) (532)

phased-in (543)

scalability (544)

slicing and dicing (533)

supply chain management (SCM) (535)

three-tier model (532)

two-tier model (531)

REVIEW QUESTIONS

1. Define ERP.
2. What is the closed database architecture?
3. Define core applications and give some examples.
4. Define OLAP and give some examples.
5. What is the client-server model?
6. Describe the two-tier client-server model.
7. Describe the three-tier client-server model.
8. What is bolt-on software?
9. What is SCM software?
10. What is changed data capture?
11. What is a data warehouse?
12. What is data mining?
13. What does data cleansing mean?
14. Why are denormalized tables used in data warehouses?
15. What is the drill-down approach?
16. What is the big bang approach?
17. What is scalability?
18. What is a business activator?
19. What is a technology activator?
20. What is Baan's Evergreen Delivery?
21. How is the Oracle database different from relational databases?
22. What is the OLAP operation called "consolidation"?
23. What is the OLAP operation of drill-down?
24. What is meant by the term "slicing and dicing"?

DISCUSSION QUESTIONS

1. How are OLTP and OLAP different? Explain by providing some examples.
2. Distinguish between the two-tier and three-tier client-server models. Describe when each would be used.
3. Why do ERP systems need bolt-on software? Give an example of bolt-on software.
4. Your organization is considering acquiring bolt-on software for your ERP system. What approaches are open to you?
5. Explain why the data warehouse needs to be separate from the operational database.
6. Data in a data warehouse are in a stable state. Explain how this can hamper data mining analysis. What can an organization do to alleviate this problem?
7. This chapter stressed the importance of data normalization when constructing a relational database. Why then is it important to denormalize data in a data warehouse?
8. What problems does the data cleansing step attempt to resolve?
9. How are the summary views in a data warehouse different from views in an operational database?
10. Would drill-down be an effective audit tool for identifying an unusual business relationship between a purchasing agent and suppliers in a large organization with several hundred suppliers? Explain.
11. Disruptions to operations are a common side effect of implementing an ERP. Explain the primary reason for this.
12. ERP systems use the best practices approach in designing their applications. Yet goodness of fit is considered to be an important issue when selecting an ERP. Shouldn't the client just be able to use whatever applications the ERP system provides?
13. Explain the issues of size, speed, workload, and transaction as they relate to scalability.

14. Explain how SAP uses roles as a way to improve internal control.

15. How would you deal with the problem of file-server backup in a highly centralized organization?

16. How would you deal with the problem of file-server backup in a decentralized organization with autonomous divisions that do not share common operational data?

17. Distinguish between the OLAP operations of consolidation and drill-down.

18. When would slicing and dicing be an appropriate OLAP tool? Give an example.

MULTIPLE-CHOICE QUESTIONS

1. Closed database architecture is
   a. a control technique intended to prevent unauthorized access from trading partners.
   b. a limitation inherent in traditional information systems that prevents data sharing.
   c. a data warehouse control that prevents unclean data from entering the warehouse.
   d. a technique used to restrict access to data marts.
   e. a database structure used by many of the leading ERPs to support OLTP applications.

2. Each of the following is a necessary element for the successful warehousing of data except:
   a. cleansing extracted data.
   b. transforming data.
   c. modeling data.
   d. loading data.
   e. all of the above are necessary.

3. Which of the following is typically not part of an ERP's OLAP applications?
   a. decision support systems
   b. information retrieval
   c. ad hoc reporting/analysis
   d. logistics
   e. what-if analysis

4. There are a number of risks that may be associated with ERP implementation. Which of the following was not stated as a risk in the chapter?
   a. A drop in firm performance after implementation because the firm looks and works differently than it did while using a legacy system.
   b. Implementing companies have found that staff members, employed by ERP consulting firms, do not have sufficient experience in implementing new systems.
   c. Implementing firms fail to select systems that properly support their business activities.
   d. The selected system does not adequately meet the adopting firm's economic growth.
   e. ERP's are too large, complex, and generic for them to be well integrated into most company cultures.

5. Which statement is not true?
   a. In a typical two-tier client-server architecture, the server handles both application and database duties.
   b. Client computers are responsible for presenting data to the user and passing user input back to the server.
   c. Two-tier architecture is for local area network (LAN) applications where the demand on the server is restricted to a relatively small population of users.
   d. The database and application functions are separated in the three-tier model.
   e. In three-tier client-server architectures, one tier is for user presentation, one is for database and applications access, and the third is for Internet access.

6. Which statement is not true?
   a. Drill-down capability is an OLAP feature of data mining tools available to the user.
   b. The data warehouse should be separate from operational systems.
   c. Denormalization of data involves dividing the data into very small tables that support detailed analysis.
   d. Some decisions supported by a data warehouse are not fundamentally different from those that are supported by traditional databases.
   e. Data cleansing involves transforming data into standard business terms with standard data values.

7. Which statement is least accurate?

   a. Implementing an ERP system has more to do with changing the way an organization does business than it does with technology.

   b. The phased-in approach to ERP implementation is particularly suited to diversified organizations whose units do not share common processes and data.

   c. Because the primary reason for implementing an ERP is to standardize and integrate operations, diversified organizations whose units do not share common processes and data do not benefit and tend not to implement ERPs.

   d. To take full advantage of the ERP process reengineering will need to occur.

   e. A common reason for ERP failure is that the ERP does not support one or more important business processes of the organization.

8. SAP, one of the leading ERP producers, makes several modules available to adopters. Which of the following is not a SAP module?

   a. Business Process Support

   b. Internet Development Support

   c. Logistics.

   d. E-commerce Support

   e. Human Resources

9. Auditors of ERP systems

   a. need not be concerned about segregation of duties because these systems possess strong computer controls.

   b. focus on output controls such as independent verification to reconcile batch totals.

   c. may be concerned that the data in the data warehouse is too clean and free from errors.

   d. do not see the data warehouse as an audit or control issue at all because financial records are not stored there.

   e. need not review access levels granted to users since these are determined when the system is configured and never change.

10. Which statement is most correct?

   a. SAP is more suited to service industries than manufacturing clients.

   b. J.D. Edwards' ERP is designed to accept the best practices modules of other vendors.

   c. Oracle evolved from a human resources system.

   d. PeopleSoft is the world's leading supplier of software for information management.

   e. Baan's Evergreen Delivery policy ensures free upgrades of bolt-on software.

PROBLEMS

1. Data Warehouse Access Control

You are the CEO of a large organization that implemented a data warehouse for internal analysis of corporate data. The operations manager has written you a memo advocating opening the data warehouse to your suppliers and customers. Explain any merit to this proposal. What are the control issues, if any?

2. Project Implementation

Your organization is planning to implement an ERP system. Some managers in the organization favor the big bang approach. Others are advocating a phased-in approach. The CEO has asked you, as project leader, to write a memo summarizing the advantages and disadvantages of each approach and to make a recommendation. This is a traditional organization with a strong internal hierarchy. The company was acquired in a merger two years ago and the ERP project is an effort on the part of the parent company to standardize business processes

and reporting across the organization. Prior to this the organization had been using a general ledger package that it acquired in 1979. Most of the transaction processing is a combination of manual and batch processing. Most employees think that the legacy system works well. At this point the implementation project is behind schedule.

3. OLTP vs. OLAP Servers

For each of the following processes state whether OLTP or OLAP is appropriate and why.

a. An order entry system that retrieves customer information, invoice information, and inventory information for local sales.

b. An order entry system that retrieves customer information, invoice information, inventory information, and several years of sales information about both the customer and the inventory items.

c. An order entry system that retrieves customer information, invoice information, inventory information, and information to compare the current sale to sales across several geographic regions.

d. An order entry system that retrieves customer information, invoice information, inventory information, and accounts receivable information for sales within one marketing region.

e. An insurance company requires a system that will allow it to determine total claims by region, determine whether a relationship exists between claims and meteorological phenomenon, and why one region seems to be more profitable than another.

f. A manufacturing company has only one factory, but that factory employs several thousand people and has nearly $1 billion in revenue each year. The company has seen no reason to make comparisons about its operations from year to year or from process to process. Its information needs focus primarily on operations, but it has maintained backup of prior-year operations activities. Examination of prior-year financial reports have shown that the company, while profitable, is not growing and ROI is decreasing. The owners are not satisfied with this situation.

4. Selecting a Consultant

You are the chief information officer for a midsized organization that has decided to implement an ERP system. The CEO has met with a consulting ERP firm based on a recommendation from a personal friend at his club. At the interview the president of the consulting firm introduced the chief consultant who was charming, personable, and seemed very knowledgeable. The CEO's first instinct was to sign a contract with the consultant, but he decided to hold off until he had received your input.

Required:

Write a memo to the CEO presenting the issues and the risks associated with consultants. Also, outline a set of procedures that could be used as a guide in selecting a consultant.

5. Auditing ERP Databases

You are an independent auditor attending an engagement interview with the client. The client organization has recently implemented a data warehouse. Management is concerned that the audit tests that you perform will disrupt operations. They suggest that instead of running tests against the live operational database, you draw the data for your analytical reviews and substantive tests of details from the data warehouse. They point out that operational data is copied weekly into the warehouse and everything you need will be contained there. This will enable you to perform your tests without disrupting routine operations. You agree to give this some thought and get back with the client with your answer.

Required:

Draft a memo to the client outlining your response to their proposal. Mention any concerns that you might have.

6. Big Bang vs. Phased-in

The Nevada Department of Motor Vehicles is the agency responsible for licensing both drivers and vehicles in the state of Nevada. Until recently, legacy systems were used for both licensing needs. The legacy system for driver's licenses maintained the following information about each licensed driver: name, age, address, violation, license classification, organ donation, and restrictions. The vehicle licensing system maintained information about each vehicle including cost, taxes, VIN, weight, insurance, and ownership. In the summer of 1999, over a three-day weekend, information from the two legacy systems was transferred to a new ERP, the ERP and all new hardware was installed in every DMV across the state, and when employees returned from their long weekend, an entirely new system was in place. The DMV employees were not well trained on the new system, and the system itself presented a few bugs. As a result of these obstacles, customers at the DMV faced excessively long lines and extended waiting times, several of the employees simply quit their jobs because of frustrations with the system and difficulty dealing with irate customers. Knowing that the waiting times were so long, many drivers simply refused to renew licenses or obtain new licenses. Assume the ERP selected by the DMV was correctly configured and was capable of meeting all requirements of the DMV; consider data warehousing implications, business culture implications, and disruption to operations; and discuss the advantages and disadvantages associated with the decision to implement the new system using the big bang versus the phased-in approach.

7. ERP Failure
When an ERP implementation fails who is to blame? Is it the software manufacture, the client firm, or the implementation strategy?

Required:
Research this issue and write a brief paper outlining the key issues.

8. ERP Market Growth
Because many large corporations implemented ERP systems prior to 2000, what direction will growth of the ERP market take?

Required:
Research this issue and write a brief paper outlining the key issues.

9. ERP Consultants
Do an Internet search of complaints about ERP consultants. Write a report about the most common complaints and cite examples.

10. ERP Bolt-on Software
Go to ten Web sites of companies that supply bolt-on software. Write a report containing URLs that briefly describes the software features and its compatibility with specific ERP systems.

chapter 12

Electronic Commerce Systems

LEARNING OBJECTIVES

After studying his chapter, you should:

- Be acquainted with the topologies that are employed to achieve connectivity across the Internet.
- Possess a conceptual appreciation of protocols and understand the specific purposes served by several Internet protocols.
- Understand the business benefits associated with Internet commerce and be aware of several Internet business models.
- Be familiar with the risks associated with intranet and Internet electronic commerce.
- Understand issues of security, assurance, and trust pertaining to electronic commerce.
- Be familiar with the electronic commerce implications for the accounting profession.

Upon hearing the term "electronic commerce" many people think of browsing an electronic catalogue on the Web or going Internet shopping at a virtual mall. While this may be the predominate component of electronic commerce (EC), it is not the entire story. Electronic commerce involves the electronic processing and transmission of data. This is a broad definition that encompasses many diverse activities, including the electronic buying and selling of goods and services, online delivery of digital products, electronic funds transfer (EFT), electronic trading of stocks, and direct consumer marketing. Electronic commerce is not an entirely new phenomenon. Many companies have engaged in electronic data interchange (EDI) over private networks for decades. Driven by the Internet revolution, however, EC is dramatically expanding and undergoing radical changes. This fast-moving environment has engendered an array of innovative markets and trading communities. While EC promises enormous opportunities for consumers and businesses, its effective implementation and control are urgent challenges facing organization management and accountants.

To properly evaluate the potential exposures and risks in this environment, the modern accountant must be familiar with the technologies and techniques that underlie EC. Hardware failures, software errors, and unauthorized access from remote locations can expose the organization's accounting system to unique threats. For example, transactions can be lost in transit and never processed, altered or rearranged electronically to change their financial effect, corrupted by transient signals on transmission lines, and diverted to or initiated by the perpetrator of a fraud.

In this chapter and its appendix we consider three aspects of EC: (1) the intra-organizational use of networks to support distributed data processing; (2) business-to-business transactions conducted via EDI systems; and (3) Internet-based commerce including business-to-consumer and business-to-business relationships. We examine the technologies, topologies, and applications of

EC in each of these areas. We review the risks associated with EC, examine security and assurance techniques used to reduce risk and promote trust, and conclude with a discussion of EC's implications for the accounting profession.

INTRA-ORGANIZATIONAL NETWORKS AND EDI

Local area networks (LANs), wide area networks (WANs), and EDI are EC technologies that have been with us for decades. As such, these topics are frequently found among the subject matter of introductory systems courses. Because many accounting and information systems students become familiar with these topics before taking an AIS course, this material is covered in the appendix to this chapter. The body of the chapter focuses on the salient issues pertaining to Internet-based EC. Students who have not been exposed to network and EDI topologies and technologies should, however, review the appendix before proceeding as the treatment in the chapter presumes this background.

INTERNET COMMERCE

Internet commerce has enabled thousands of business enterprises of all sizes, as well as millions of consumers to congregate and interact, in a worldwide, virtual shopping mall. Along with enormous opportunities, however, the electronic marketplace has engendered unique risks and problems that need to be resolved. This section of the chapter examines the technologies, benefits, risks, and security issues associated with Internet commerce.

INTERNET TECHNOLOGIES

The Internet is a large network composed of more than 100,000 interconnected, smaller networks located around the world. The Internet was originally developed for the U.S. military, and later became used widely for academic and government research. In recent years the Internet has evolved into a worldwide, information highway. This growth is attributed to three factors. First, in 1995, national commercial telecommunications companies such as MCI, Sprint, and UUNET took control of the backbone elements of the Internet and have continued to enhance their infrastructures. Large Internet service providers (ISPs) can link into these backbones to connect their subscribers, and smaller ISPs can either connect directly to the national backbones or into one of the larger ISPs. Second, online services, e.g., CompuServe and AOL, connect to the Internet for email, which enables users of different services to communicate with each other. Third, the development of graphics-based Web browsers, e.g., Netscape Navigator and Microsoft's Internet Explorer, made accessing the Internet a simple task. The Internet, thus, became the domain of ordinary people with PCs rather than scientists and computer hackers. As a result, the Web has grown exponentially and continues to grow daily.

Packet Switching
The Internet employs communications technologies based on **packet switching**. Figure 12-1 illustrates this technique, whereby messages are divided into small packets for transmission. Individual packets of the same message may take different routes to their destinations. Each packet contains address and sequencing codes so they can be reassembled into the original complete message at the receiving end. The choice of transmission path is determined according to criteria that achieve optimum utilization of the long-distance lines,

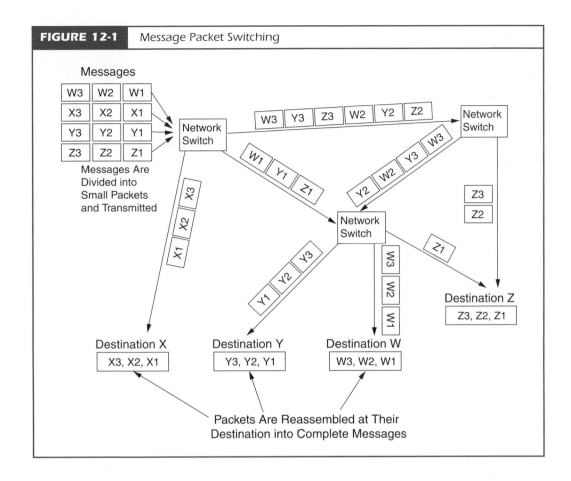

FIGURE 12-1 | Message Packet Switching

including the degree of traffic congestion on the line, the shortest path between the end points, and the line status of the path (i.e., working, failed, or experiencing errors). Network switches provide a physical connection for the addressed packets only for the duration of the message; the line then becomes available to other users. The first international standard for wide area packet switching networks was X.25, which was defined when all circuits were analog and very susceptible to noise. Subsequent packet technologies, such as frame relay and SMDS (Switched Multimegabit Data Service) were designed for today's almost error-free digital lines.

Virtual Private Networks
A **virtual private network** (VPN) is a private network within a public network. For years, common carriers have built VPNs, which are private from the client's perspective, but physically share backbone trunks with other users. VPNs have been built on X.25 and frame-relay technologies. Today, Internet-based VPNs are of great interest. Maintaining security and privacy in this setting, however, requires encryption and authentication controls discussed later in the chapter.

Extranets
Another variant on Internet technology is the **extranet.** This is a password-controlled network for private users rather than the general public. Extranets are used to provide access between trading partner internal databases. Internet sites containing information intended for private consumption frequently use an extranet configuration.

World Wide Web

The World Wide Web (Web) is an Internet facility that links user sites locally and around the world. In 1989, Tim Berners-Lee of the European Center for Nuclear Research (CERN) in Geneva developed the Web as a means of sharing nuclear research information over the Internet. The fundamental format for the Web is a text document called a **Web page** that has embedded Hypertext Markup Language (HTML) codes that provide the formatting for the page as well as hypertext links to other pages. The linked pages may be stored on the same server or anywhere in the world. HTML codes are simple alphanumeric characters that can be typed with a text editor or word processor. Most word processors support Web publishing features that allow text documents to be converted to HTML format.

Web pages are maintained at **Web sites**, which are computer servers that support Hypertext Transfer Protocol (HTTP). The pages are accessed and read via a Web browser such as Netscape Navigator or Internet Explorer. Accessing a Web site requires entering the Uniform Resource Locator (URL) address of the site in the Web browser. When an Internet user visits a Web site, his or her point of entry is typically the site's **homepage**. This HTML document serves as a directory to the site's contents and other pages. Through browsers the Web provides point-and-click access to the largest collection of online information in the world. The Web has also become a multimedia delivery system that supports audio, video, videoconferencing, and 3-D animation. The ease of Web page creation and navigation via browsers has driven the unprecedented growth of the Web. In 1994, there were approximately 500 Web sites in the world; today there are millions.

Internet Addresses

The Internet uses three types of addresses for communications: (1) email addresses, (2) Web site URL addresses, and (3) addresses of individual computers attached to a network (IP address). Each of these is discussed below.

Email Address. The format for an email address is USER NAME@DOMAIN NAME. For example, the address of the author of this textbook is jah0@lehigh.edu. There are no spaces between any of the words. The user name (or in this case user ID) is jah0. A domain name is an organization's unique name combined with a top-level domain (TLD) name. In the example above, the unique name is "lehigh" and TLD is "edu." Following are the TLD names:

.com	commercial
.net	network provider
.org	nonprofit organization
.edu	education and research
.gov	government
.mil	military agency
.int	international intergovernmental

Outside of the United States, the TLD names consist of the country code, such as .uk for the United Kingdom and .es for Spain. The Internet Ad Hoc Committee (IAHC) has introduced a category called a generic top-level domain (gTLD), which includes the following:

.firm	a business
.store	goods for sale
.web	WWW activities
.arts	culture/entertainment

.rec   recreation/entertainment
.info   information service
.nom   individual/personal

The Internet email addressing system allows the user to send email directly to the mailboxes of users of all major online services, e.g., America Online and CompuServe.

URL Address. The **URL** is the address that defines the path to a facility or file on the Web. URLs are typed into the browser to access Web site homepages and individual Web pages, and can be embedded in Web pages to provide hypertext links to other pages. The general format for a URL is **protocol prefix**, **domain name**, **subdirectory name**, and **document name**. The entire URL is not always needed. For example, to access the South-Western Publishing home page, only the following *protocol* and *domain* name are required:

http://www.swlearning.com

The protocol prefix is "http://" and the domain name is "www.swlearning.com." From this home page the user can activate hyperlinks to other pages as desired. The user can go directly to a linked page by providing the complete address and separating the address components with slashes. For example,

http://www.swlearning.com/hall.html

Subdirectories can be several levels deep. To reference them each must be separated with a slash. For example, the elements of the following URL for a hypothetical sporting goods company are described below.

http://www.flyfish.com/equipment/rods/brand_name.html

http://   protocol prefix (most browsers default to HTTP if a prefix is
                   not typed)
www.flyfish.com/   domain name
equipment/   subdirectory name
rods/   subdirectory name
brand_name.html   document name (Web page)

IP Address. Every computer node and host attached to the Internet must have a unique Internet protocol (IP) address. For a message to be sent, the IP addresses of both the sending and the recipient nodes must be provided. Currently, IP addresses are represented by a 32-bit data packet. The general format is four sets of numbers separated by periods. The decomposition of the code into its component parts varies depending on the class to which it is assigned. Class A, class B, and class C coding schemes are used for large, medium, and small networks, respectively. To illustrate the coding technique, the IP address 128.180.94.109 translates into:

128.180   Lehigh University
94   Business Department faculty server
109   A faculty member's office computer (node)

PROTOCOLS

The term **protocol** has been used several times in this section. Let's now take a closer look at the meaning of this term. Protocols are the rules and standards governing the design of hardware and software that permit users of networks, which have been manufactured by different vendors, to communicate and share data. The general acceptance of protocols within the network community provides both standards and economic incentives for the manufacturers of hardware and software. Products that do not comply with prevailing protocols will have little utility to prospective customers.

The data-communications industry borrowed the term *protocol* from the diplomatic community. Diplomatic protocols define the rules by which the representatives of nations communicate and collaborate during social and official functions. These formal rules of conduct are intended to avoid international problems that could arise through the misinterpretation of ambiguous signals passed between diplomatic counterparts. The greatest potential for error naturally exists between nations with vastly dissimilar cultures and conventions for behavior. Establishing a standard of conduct through protocols, which all members of the diplomatic community understand and practice, minimizes the risk of miscommunications between nations of different cultures.

An analogy may be drawn to data communications. A communications network is a community of computer users who also must establish and maintain unambiguous lines of communication. If all network members had homogeneous needs and operated identical systems, this would not be much of a problem; however, networks are characterized by heterogeneous systems components. Typically, network users employ hardware devices (PC, printers, monitors, data storage devices, modems, and so on) and software (user applications, network control programs, and operating systems) that are produced by a variety of vendors. Passing messages effectively from device to device in such a multivendor environment requires ground rules or protocols.

What Functions Do Protocols Perform?

Protocols serve network functions in several ways.[1] First, they facilitate the physical connection between the network devices. Through protocols, devices are able to identify themselves to other devices as legitimate network entities and initiate (or terminate) a communications session.

Second, protocols synchronize the transfer of data between physical devices. This involves defining the rules for initiating a message, determining the data transfer rate between devices, and acknowledging message receipt.

Third, protocols provide a basis for error checking and measuring network performance. This is done by comparing measured results against expectations. For example, performance measures pertaining to storage device access times, data transmission rates, and modulation frequencies are critical to controlling the network's function. Thus, the identification and correction of errors depend on protocol standards that define acceptable performance.

Fourth, protocols promote compatibility among network devices. To transmit and receive data successfully, the various devices involved in a particular session must conform to a mutually acceptable mode of operation, such as synchronous, asynchronous and duplex, or half-duplex. Without protocols to provide such conformity, messages sent between devices will be distorted and garbled.

Finally, protocols promote network designs that are flexible, expandable, and cost effective. Users are free to change and enhance their systems by selecting from the best offerings of a variety of vendors. Manufacturers must, of course, construct these products in accordance with established protocols.

---

1   H. M. Kibirige, *Local Area Networks in Information Management* (Greenwood Press, 1989).

The Layered Approach to Network Protocol

The first networks used several different protocols that emerged in a rather haphazard manner. These protocols often provided poor interfaces between devices and sometimes resulted in irreconcilable incompatibilities. Also, early protocols were structured and inflexible, thus limiting network growth by making system changes difficult. A change in the architecture at a node on the network could have an unpredictable effect on an unrelated device at another node. Technical problems such as these can translate into unrecorded transactions, destroyed audit trails, and corrupted databases. Out of this situation emerged the contemporary model of layered protocols. The purpose of a layered-protocol model is to create a modular environment that reduces complexity and permits changes to one layer without adversely affecting another.

The data communication community, through the **International Standards Organization**,[2] has developed a layered set of protocols called the **Open System Interface (OSI)**. The OSI model provides standards by which the products of different manufacturers can interface with one another in a seamless interconnection at the user level. This seven-layer protocol model is discussed in detail in the appendix to this chapter.

INTERNET PROTOCOLS

Transfer Control Protocol/Internet Protocol (TCP/IP) is the basic protocol that permits communication between Internet sites. It was invented by Vinton Cerf and Bob Kah under contract from the U.S. Department of Defense to network dissimilar systems. This protocol controls how individual packets of data are formatted, transmitted, and received. This is known as a reliable protocol because delivery of all the packets to a destination are guaranteed. If delivery is interrupted by hardware or software failure, the packets are automatically retransmitted.

The TCP portion of the protocol ensures that the total number of data bytes transmitted were received. The IP component provides the routing mechanism. Every server and computer in a TCP/IP network requires an IP address, which is either permanently assigned or dynamically assigned at startup. The IP part of the TCP/IP protocol contains a network address that is used to route messages to different networks.

While TCP/IP is the fundamental communications protocol for the Internet, the following are some of the more common protocols that are used for specific tasks.

File Transfer Protocols

File Transfer Protocol (FTP) is used to transfer text files, programs, spreadsheets, and databases across the Internet. **TELNET** is a terminal emulation protocol used on TCP/IP-based networks. It allows users to run programs and review data from a remote terminal or computer. TELNET is an inherent part of the TCP/IP communications protocol. While both protocols deal with data transfer, FTP is useful for downloading entire files from the Internet; TELNET is useful for perusing a file of data as if the user were actually at the remote site.

Mail Protocols

Simple Network Mail Protocol (SNMP) is the most popular protocol for transmitting email messages. Other email protocols are **Post Office Protocol (POP)** and **Internet Message Access Protocol (IMAP)**.

---

2   The International Standards Organization (ISO) is a voluntary group comprising representatives from the national standards organizations of its member countries. The ISO works toward the establishment of international standards for data encryption, data communications, and protocols.

Security Protocols

Secure Sockets Layer (SSL) is a low-level encryption scheme used to secure transmissions in higher-level HTTP format. **Private Communications Technology (PCT)** is a security protocol that provides secure transactions over the Web. PCT encrypts and decrypts a message for transmission. Most Web browsers and servers support PCT and other popular security protocols such as SSL. **Secure Electronic Transmission (SET)** is an encryption scheme developed by a consortium of technology firms and banks (Netscape, Microsoft, IBM, Visa, MasterCard, etc.) to secure credit card transactions. Customers making credit card purchases over the Internet transmit their encrypted credit card number to the merchant, who then transmits the number to the bank. The bank returns an encrypted acknowledgment to the merchant. The customer need not worry about an unscrupulous merchant decrypting the customer's credit card number and misusing the information. **Privacy Enhanced Mail (PEM)** is a standard for secure email on the Internet. It supports encryption, digital signatures, and digital certificates as well as both private and public key methods (which will be discussed later).

Network News Transfer Protocol

Network News Transfer Protocol (NNTP) is used to connect to Usenet groups on the Internet. Usenet newsreader software supports the NNTP protocol.

HTTP and HTTP-NG

HTTP controls Web browsers that access the Web. When the user clicks on a link to a Web page, a connection is established and the Web page is displayed, then the connection is broken. **Hypertext Transport Protocol-Next Generation (HTTP-NG)** is an enhanced version of the HTTP protocol that will enable it to meet the increasing performance requirements anticipated for the twenty-first century.

HTML

Hyper Text Markup Language (HTML) is the document format used to produce Web pages. HTML defines the page layout, fonts, and graphic elements as well as hypertext links to other documents on the Web. HTML is used to lay out information for display in an appealing manner much like what one sees in magazines and newspapers. The ability to lay out text and graphics (including pictures) is important in terms of appeal to users in general. Even more pertinent is HTML's support for hypertext links in text and graphics that enable the reader to "jump" to another document located anywhere on the World Wide Web.

With advances in Internet technology and connectivity, corporations have moved toward disclosure of corporate financial information in a form compatible with standard Web-browsing tools such as Netscape and Internet Explorer. In this way, investors and analysts may have access to current corporate information. Dissemination of HTML-based financial reports, however, is limited to presentation only. HTML does not support the exchange of information in a relational form such as that commonly employed in EDI applications.[3] Until very recently, no widely accepted standards for business-to-business (B2B) information exchange via the Internet existed. A new generation of markup languages based on XML, which is discussed below, has overcome many limitations of HTML.

---

3   Although EDI can employ the Internet, it is normally limited to specific trading partners in a precontracted trade agreement and is focused on a relatively narrow aspect of overall business operations (e.g., exchange of purchase orders and subsequent payment in electronic form).

XML

eXtensible Markup Language (**XML**) is a metalanguage for describing markup languages. The term *extensible* means that any markup language can be created using XML. This includes the creation of markup languages capable of storing data in relational form in which tags (or formatting commands) are mapped to data values. Thus, XML can be used to model the data structure of an organization's internal database.

The examples illustrated in Figure 12-2 serve to distinguish HTML from XML using a bookstore order formatted in both languages.[4] Although essentially the same information is contained in both examples, and they look similar in structure, important differences exist between them. While, both examples use tags (words that are bracketed by the symbols "<" and ">") and attributes such as "Doe, John," the way in which these tags and attributes are used differs. In the HTML example, the tags have predefined meaning that describes how the attributes will be presented in a document. The book order in this example can only be viewed (similar to a FAX) and must be manually entered into the bookstore's order entry system for processing. In the case of the XML order, the tags are customized to delimit the attributes. Interpretation of the data is performed by the application that reads it. Thus, the bookstore order prepared in XML presents order attributes in a relational form that can be automatically imported into a bookseller's internal database.

XBRL

Recognizing the potential benefits of XML, the AICPA encouraged research into the creation of an accounting-specific markup language based on XML. **eXtensible Business Reporting Language (XBRL)** is an XML-based language that was designed to provide the financial community with a standardized method for preparing, publishing, and automatically exchanging financial information, including financial statements of publicly held companies. XBRL is typically used for reporting aggregated financial data, but can also be applied to communicating information pertaining to individual transactions.

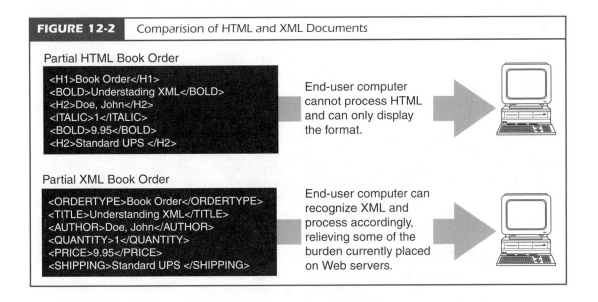

| **FIGURE 12-2** | Comparision of HTML and XML Documents |

Partial HTML Book Order

```
<H1>Book Order</H1>
<BOLD>Understading XML</BOLD>
<H2>Doe, John</H2>
<ITALIC>1</ITALIC>
<BOLD>9.95</BOLD>
<H2>Standard UPS </H2>
```

End-user computer cannot process HTML and can only display the format.

Partial XML Book Order

```
<ORDERTYPE>Book Order</ORDERTYPE>
<TITLE>Understanding XML</TITLE>
<AUTHOR>Doe, John</AUTHOR>
<QUANTITY>1</QUANTITY>
<PRICE>9.95</PRICE>
<SHIPPING>Standard UPS </SHIPPING>
```

End-user computer can recognize XML and process accordingly, relieving some of the burden currently placed on Web servers.

4   http://www.ebusinessforum.gr/links/reports/agency.com/xml.pdf

XBRL taxonomies are classification schemes that are compliant with the XBRL specifications to accomplish a specific information exchange or reporting objective. To date, more than 100 companies and standards organizations are participating on the XBRL Steering Committee to develop XBRL taxonomies for information exchange via the Internet. These projects include regulatory and tax filing responsibilities, such as filing for the Securities and Exchanges Commission's EDGAR System.

With the emergence of XBRL-based taxonomies for exchanging data, business entities can offer expanded financial information instantaneously to all interested parties. Furthermore, companies that use native-XBRL database technology[5] internally, as their primary information storage platform, can further speed up the process of reporting. Consumers of such financial data (e.g., investors and analysts) can readily import XBRL documents into internal databases and analysis tools to greatly facilitate their decision-making processes.

Creating an XBRL Report

Figure 12-3 presents part of a hypothetical company's internal database.[6] This snapshot shows various general ledger accounts and their values. Currently, these data are organized and labeled according to the hypothetical company's internal needs and conventions. To make the data useful to outsiders and comparable with other firms, they need to be organized, labeled, and reported in a manner that is generally accepted by all XBRL users. This involves mapping the organization's internal data to XBRL taxonomy elements to produce an **XBRL instance document**. The process for doing so is described below.[7]

The first step in the process is to select a taxonomy. In essence, the XBRL taxonomy specifies the data to be included in an exchange or report. Currently several taxonomies are being created by the XBRL Standards Committee in hopes that they will be adopted for widespread use. This illustration employs XBRL Taxonomy for Financial Reporting for Commercial and Industrial Companies, referred to as "CI" taxonomy.

The next step is to cross-reference each general ledger account to an appropriate XBRL taxonomy element (tag). This can be accomplished using a simple tool such as Taxonomy Mapper pictured in Figure 12-4.[8] Note how the XBRL tag labeled "Cash, Cash Equivalents and Short Term Investments" is mapped to the database account labeled "Cash in Bank – Canada."

Once the mapping process is complete, each database record will contain a stored tag as depicted by the "Taxonomy Element" field in Figure 12-5. Data mapping needs be done only once, but the tags are used whenever the data are placed in XBRL format for dissemination to outsiders.

From this new database structure, XBRL instance documents (the actual financial reports) can be generated by computer programs that recognize and interpret the tags associated with the data attributes. Figure 12-6 presents an example of an instance document.[9]

The XBRL instance document can now be published to make it available to users. The document can be placed on an intranet server (see the appendix) for internal use; it can be placed on an extranet for limited dissemination to customers or trading partners; or it can be placed on the Internet for public dissemination. In its current state, the instance document is computer readable for analysis and processing. To make it more

---

5   As opposed to the use of a standard databases such as Oracle or Sybase.

6   http://www.xbrlsolutions.com/Public/Demos/FinancialHighlights/Static/00-Overview.htm

7   This illustration is based on an example prepared by Charles Hoffman, member of the XBRL Steering Committee Specification Working Group with assistance from Neal Hannon, XBRL Steering Committee Education co-chair.

8   Ibid.

9   http://www.xbrlsolutions.com/Public/Demos/FinancialHighlights/Static/00-Overview.htm

FIGURE 12-3	Internal Corporate Database

qryMappedTrialBalance : Select Query

FullAccount	TrialBalanceDate	Amount	AccountDescription
000-1100-00	5/31/1999	$608,637.31	Cash - Operating Account
000-1101-00	5/31/1999	$8,957.84	Cash in Bank - Canada
000-1102-00	5/31/1999	$18,302.17	Cash in Bank - Australia
000-1103-00	5/31/1999	$6,007.94	Cash in Bank - New Zealand
000-1104-00	5/31/1999	$7,909.80	Cash in Bank - Germany
000-1105-00	5/31/1999	$12,697.77	Cash in Bank - United Kingdom
000-1106-00	5/31/1999	$7,501.90	Cash in Bank - South Africa
000-1107-00	5/31/1999	$6,963.24	Cash in Bank - Singapore
000-1110-00	5/31/1999	$139,080.67	Cash - Payroll
000-1120-00	5/31/1999	$345.32	Cash - Flex Benefits Program
000-1130-00	5/31/1999	$319.54	Petty Cash
000-1140-00	5/31/1999	$16,316.12	Savings
000-1200-00	5/31/1999	$1,740,867.12	Accounts Receivable
000-1205-00	5/31/1999	$3,871.03	Sales Discounts Available
000-1210-00	5/31/1999	($45,963.30)	Allowance for Doubtful Accounts
000-1220-01	5/31/1999	$22,500.00	Credit Card Receivable-American Express
000-1230-00	5/31/1999	$250.00	Interest Receivable
000-1240-00	5/31/1999	$5,000.00	Notes Receivable
000-1260-00	5/31/1999	$250.00	Employee Advances
000-1271-00	5/31/1999	$26,757.58	Accounts Receivable - Canada
000-1272-00	5/31/1999	$11,164.46	Accounts Receivables - Australia
000-1273-00	5/31/1999	$9,381.79	Accounts Receivable - New Zealand
000-1274-00	5/31/1999	$2,716.40	Accounts Receivable - Germany

Record: 1   of 231

human readable, HTML layout rules can be provided in a separate *style sheet* that is used by Web browsers to present the XBRL information in an visually appealing manner.

XBRL is an important technology that facilitates B2B information exchange while still supporting widespread dissemination via the World Wide Web. In addition, the use of XBRL will facilitate fulfillment of legal requirements stipulated in the Sarbanes-Oxley Act. This sweeping legislation was passed in response to widespread concern and skepticism about financial reporting standards. XBRL can play a role in facilitating earlier reporting of financial statements required under Sarbanes-Oxley.

BENEFITS FROM INTERNET COMMERCE

Virtually all types of businesses have benefited in some way from Internet commerce. Some of the potential significant benefits include:

- Access to a worldwide customer and/or supplier base.

- Reductions in inventory investment and carrying costs.

- The rapid creation of business partnerships to fill market niches as they emerge.

- Reductions in retail prices through lower marketing costs.

- Reductions in procurement costs.

- Better customer service.

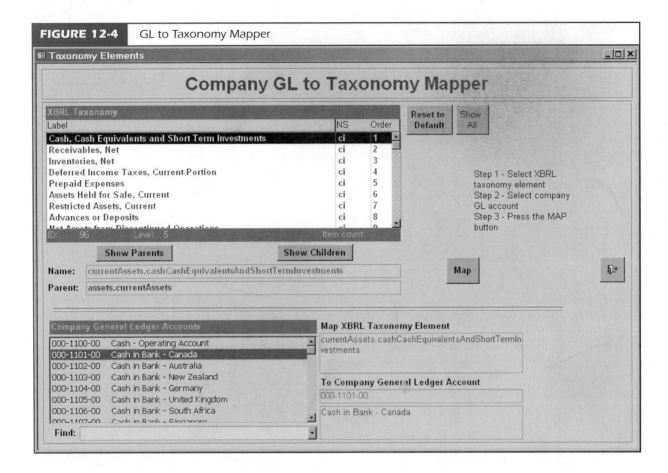

FIGURE 12-4   GL to Taxonomy Mapper

Internet Business Models

Not all organizations enjoy all the benefits listed above. The degree of benefits attained from EC depends on the level of the organization's commitment to it as a business strategy. This can occur on three levels as discussed in the following section.

Information Level. At the **information level** of activity an organization uses the Internet to display information about the company, its products, services, and business policies. This level involves little more than creating a Web site, and it is the first step taken by most firms entering the virtual marketplace. When customers access the Web site, they generally first visit the home Web page. This is an index to the site's contents through other Web pages. Large organizations often create and manage their Web sites internally. Smaller companies have their sites hosted on servers that are maintained by an ISP. To be successful at this level the organization must ensure that:

- Information displayed on the Web site is current, complete, and accurate;

- Customers can find the site and successfully navigate through it;

- An adequate hardware and software infrastructure exists to facilitate quick access during high usage periods; and

- Information stored on the site is accessed only by authorized users.

FIGURE 12-5 Database Structure with XBRL Tag

FullAccount	TrialBalanceDate	Amount	AccountDescription	TaxonomyElement
000-1100-00	5/31/1999	$608,637.31	Cash - Operating Account	cashAndCashEquivalents.cash
000-1101-00	5/31/1999	$8,957.84	Cash in Bank - Canada	currentAssets.cashCashEquivalentsAndShortTermInvestments
000-1102-00	5/31/1999	$18,302.17	Cash in Bank - Australia	currentAssets.cashCashEquivalentsAndShortTermInvestments
000-1103-00	5/31/1999	$6,007.94	Cash in Bank - New Zealand	currentAssets.cashCashEquivalentsAndShortTermInvestments
000-1104-00	5/31/1999	$7,909.80	Cash in Bank - Germany	currentAssets.cashCashEquivalentsAndShortTermInvestments
000-1105-00	5/31/1999	$12,697.77	Cash in Bank - United Kingdom	currentAssets.cashCashEquivalentsAndShortTermInvestments
000-1106-00	5/31/1999	$7,501.90	Cash in Bank - South Africa	currentAssets.cashCashEquivalentsAndShortTermInvestments
000-1107-00	5/31/1999	$6,963.24	Cash in Bank - Singapore	currentAssets.cashCashEquivalentsAndShortTermInvestments
000-1110-00	5/31/1999	$139,080.67	Cash - Payroll	currentAssets.cashCashEquivalentsAndShortTermInvestments
000-1120-00	5/31/1999	$345.32	Cash - Flex Benefits Program	currentAssets.cashCashEquivalentsAndShortTermInvestments
000-1130-00	5/31/1999	$319.54	Petty Cash	currentAssets.cashCashEquivalentsAndShortTermInvestments
000-1140-00	5/31/1999	$16,316.12	Savings	currentAssets.cashCashEquivalentsAndShortTermInvestments
000-1200-00	5/31/1999	$1,740,867.12	Accounts Receivable	accountsReceivableTradeNet.accountsReceivableTradeGross
000-1205-00	5/31/1999	$3,871.03	Sales Discounts Available	accountsReceivableTradeNet.allowanceForDoubtfulAccounts
000-1210-00	5/31/1999	($45,963.30)	Allowance for Doubtful Accounts	accountsReceivableTradeNet.allowanceForDoubtfulAccounts
000-1220-01	5/31/1999	$22,500.00	Credit Card Receivable-American Express	accountsReceivableTradeNet.allowanceForDoubtfulAccounts
000-1230-00	5/31/1999	$250.00	Interest Receivable	receivablesNet.otherReceivablesNet
000-1240-00	5/31/1999	$5,000.00	Notes Receivable	receivablesNet.notesReceivableNet
000-1260-00	5/31/1999	$250.00	Employee Advances	relatedPartyReceivablesNet.employeeReceivablesNet
000-1271-00	5/31/1999	$26,757.58	Accounts Receivable - Canada	currentAssets.receivablesNet
000-1272-00	5/31/1999	$11,164.46	Accounts Receivables - Australia	currentAssets.receivablesNet

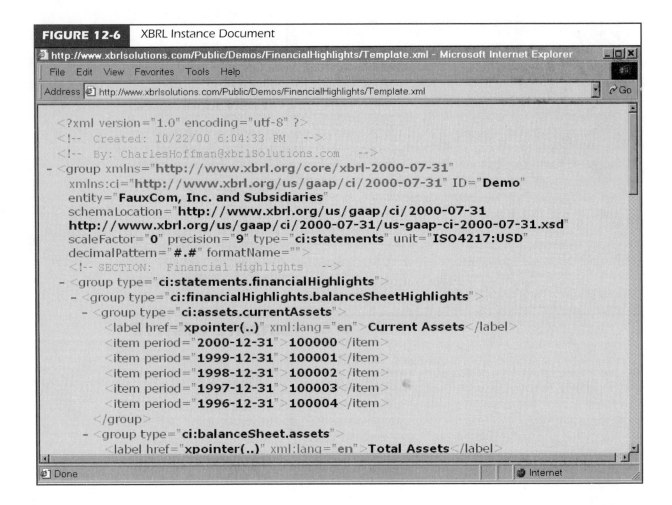

FIGURE 12-6   XBRL Instance Document

Transaction Level. Organizations involved at the **transaction level** use the Internet to accept orders from customers and/or to place them with their suppliers. This involves engaging in business activities with total strangers from remote parts of the world. These may be customers, suppliers, or potential trading partners. Many of the risks that are discussed later in the chapter relate to this (and to the next) level of EC. Success in this domain involves creating an environment of trust by resolving some key concerns. These include:

- Ensuring that data used in the transaction are protected from misuse.

- Verifying the accuracy and integrity of business processes used by the potential customer, partner, or supplier.

- Verifying the identity and physical existence of the potential customer, partner, or supplier.

- Establishing the reputation of the potential customer, partner, or supplier.

Distribution Level. Organizations operating on the **distribution level** are using the Internet to sell and deliver digital products to customers. These include subscriptions to online news services, software products and upgrades, and music and video products. In addition to all the concerns identified at the transaction level, firms involved in this aspect of EC are concerned that products are delivered successfully and only to legitimate customers.

Dynamic Virtual Organizations

Perhaps the greatest potential benefit to be derived from EC is the firm's ability to forge dynamic business alliances with other organizations to fill unique market niches as opportunities arise. These may be long-lasting partnerships or one-time ventures. Electronic partnering of business enterprises forms a **dynamic virtual organization** that benefits all parties involved. For example, consider a company that markets millions of different products including books, music, software, and toys over the Internet. If this were a traditional organization created to serve walk-in customers, it would need a massive warehouse to store the extensive physical inventories of the products that it sells. It would also need to make significant investments in inventory and personnel to maintain stock, fill customer orders, and control the environment. A virtual organization does not need this physical infrastructure. Figure 12-7 illustrates the partnering relationship that is possible in a virtual organization.

FIGURE 12-7   Dynamic Virtual Organization

The selling organization maintains a Web site for advertising product offerings. The products themselves are not physically in the custody of the seller, but are stored at the trading partner organization's (e.g., manufacturers, publishers, and distributors) facilities. The seller provides customers with product descriptions, consumer reports, prices, availability, and expected delivery times. This information comes from trading partners through an Internet connection. The seller validates customer orders placed through the Web site and automatically dispatches these to the trading partner firm, which actually ships the product.

The virtual organization can expand, contract, or shift its product line and services by simply adding or eliminating trading partners. To fully exploit this flexibility, organizations often forge relationships with total strangers. Managers in both firms need to make quick determinations as to the competence, compatibility, and capacity of potential partners to discharge their responsibilities. These and other security-related risks are potential impediments to EC that will be examined later.

RISKS ASSOCIATED WITH ELECTRONIC COMMERCE

As a vehicle for processing business transactions, the potential for EC is almost unlimited. Reliance on EC, however, opens new areas for concern about unauthorized access to confidential information. As LANs become the platform for mission-critical applications and data, proprietary information, customer data, and financial records are at risk. Organizations connected to their customers and business partners via the Internet are particularly exposed. Without adequate protection, firms open their doors to computer hackers, vandals, thieves, and industrial spies both internally and from around the world.

The paradox of networking is that networks exist to provide user access to shared resources, yet the most important objective of any network is to control access. Hence, for every productivity argument in favor of remote access, there is a security argument against it. Organization management must seek a balance between improved performance and the associated risks.

This section opens with a definition of EC risk. We then examine the internal risks posed by intranets and dishonest employees with the technical knowledge and position to perpetrate frauds and malicious acts. Finally, we turn our attention to the Internet and the risks faced by both consumers and business entities in this relatively new business frontier.

WHAT IS RISK?

Business **risk** is the possibility of loss or injury that can reduce or eliminate an organization's ability to achieve its objectives. In terms of EC, risk relates to the loss, theft, or destruction of data as well as the use or generation of data or computer programs that financially or physically harm an organization.

INTRANET RISKS

Intranets consist of small LANs and large WANs that may contain thousands of individual nodes.[10] Intranets are used to connect employees within a single building, between buildings on the same physical campus, and between geographically dispersed locations. Typical intranet activities include email routing, transaction processing between business units, and linking to the outside Internet.

---

10   See the appendix to this chapter for a complete discussion of local area networks (LANs) and wide area networks (WANs).

Intranet threats are spawned internally by unauthorized and illegal employee activities. Their motives for doing harm may be vengeance against the company, the challenge of breaking into unauthorized files, or to profit from selling trade secrets or embezzling assets. The threat from employees (both current and former) is significant because of their intimate knowledge of system controls and the lack of controls. Trade secrets, operations data, accounting data, and confidential information to which the employee has access are at greatest risk. Discharged employees, or those that leave under contentious circumstance, raise particular concerns.

Interception of Network Messages

The individual nodes on most intranets are connected to a shared channel across which travel user IDs, passwords, confidential emails, and financial data files. The unauthorized interception of this information by a node on the network is called "sniffing." The exposure is even greater when the intranet is connected to the Internet. Commercially available sniffer software is routinely used by network administrators to analyze network traffic and to detect bottlenecks. Sniffer software, however, can also be downloaded from the Internet. In the hands of a computer criminal, sniffer software can be used to intercept and view data sent across a shared intranet channel.

Access to Corporate Databases

Intranets connected to central corporate databases increase the risk that data will be viewed, corrupted, changed, or copied by an employee. Social security numbers, customer listings, credit card information, recipes, formulas, and design specifications may be downloaded and sold. Employees with access privileges to financial accounts have been bribed by outsiders to electronically write off an account receivable or erase an outstanding tax bill. A 2002 Computer Security Institute (CSI) study reported that financial fraud losses of this sort averaged $500,000.[11] A previous CSI study found that the average loss from corporate espionage was more than $1 million. Total losses from insider trade secret theft have been estimated to exceed $24 billion per year.

Privileged Employees

We know from earlier chapters that an organization's internal controls are typically aimed at lower-level employees. According to the CSI study, however, middle managers are most often prosecuted for insider crimes.[12] Middle managers often possess access privileges that allow them to override controls. Information systems employees within the organization are another group empowered with override privileges that may permit access to mission-critical data.

Reluctance to Prosecute

A factor that contributes to computer crime is the reluctance by many organizations to prosecute the criminals. According to the CSI study this situation is improving. In 1996, only 17 percent of the firms that experienced an illegal intrusion reported it to a law enforcement agency. In 2002, 75 percent of such crimes were reported. Of the 25 percent that did not report the intrusions, fear of negative publicity was the most common cited justification for their silence.

---

11   Association of Certified Fraud Examiners, "2002 Report to the Nation: Occupational Fraud and Abuse," (2002).

12   Financial Executives Institute, "Safety Nets: Secrets of Effective Information Technology Controls, An Executive Report," (June 1997).

Many computer criminals are repeat offenders. An organization can significantly reduce its hiring risk and avoid criminal acts by performing background checks on prospective employees. In the past, employee backgrounding was difficult to achieve because former employers, fearing legal action, were reluctant to disclose negative information to prospective employers. A "no comment" policy prevailed. The relatively new legal doctrine of *negligent hiring liability* is changing this. This doctrine effectively requires employers to check into an employee's background. Increasingly, courts are holding employers responsible for criminal acts perpetrated by employees both on and off the job that a background check could have prevented. Many states have passed laws that protect a former employer from legal action when providing work-related performance information about a former employee when (1) the inquiry comes from a prospective employer, (2) the information is based on credible facts, and (3) the information is given without malice.[13]

INTERNET RISKS

This section looks at some of the more significant risks associated with Internet commerce. First the risks related to consumer privacy and transaction security are examined. The risk to business entities from fraud and malicious acts are then reviewed.

Risks to Consumers

As more and more people connect to the Web, Internet fraud increases. Because of this, many consumers view the Internet as an unsafe place to do business. In particular, they worry about the security of credit card information left on Web sites and the confidentiality of their transactions. This section examines some of the more common threats to consumers from cyber criminals. The next section will look at some the risks business entities face when doing business on the Web.

Theft of Credit Card Numbers. The perception that the Internet is not secure for credit card purchases is considered to be the biggest barrier to EC. Are Internet companies negligent or even fraudulent in the way they collect, use, and store credit card information? One hacker successfully stole 100,000 credit card numbers with a combined credit limit of $1 billion from an Internet service provider's customer files. He was arrested when he tried to sell the information to an undercover FBI agent.

Another fraud scheme involves establishing a fraudulent business operation that captures credit card information. For example, the company may take orders to deliver flowers on Mother's Day. When the day arrives, the company goes out of business and disappears from the Web. Of course, the flowers are never delivered and the credit card information collected is either sold or used by the perpetrator.

Theft of Passwords. One form of Internet fraud involves establishing a Web site for the purpose of stealing a visitor's password. To access the Web page, the visitor is asked to register and provide an email address and password. Many people use the same password for different applications such as ATM services, email, and employer-network access. In the hopes that the Web site visitor falls into this pattern of behavior, the cyber criminal uses the captured password to break into the victim's accounts.

---

13   M. Greenstein and T. Fineman, Electronic Commerce: Security, Risk Management and Control (Irwin McGraw-Hill, 2000): 146.

Consumer Privacy. Concerns about the lack of privacy are discouraging consumers from engaging in Internet commerce. One poll revealed that:[14]

- Almost two-thirds of non-Internet users would start using the Internet if they could be assured that their personal information was protected; and

- Privacy is the number one reason that individuals are avoiding Internet commerce.

Many coalitions have been formed to lobby for stronger privacy measures. The Center for Democracy and Technology (CDT), Electronic Frontier Foundation (EFF), and Electronic Privacy Information Center (EPIF) are three prominent groups. One aspect of privacy involves the way in which Web sites capture and use "cookies."

Cookies are files containing user information that are created by the Web server of the site being visited and are then stored on the visitor's computer hard drive. Cookies contain the URLs of sites visited by the user. When the site is revisited the user's browser sends the specific cookies to the Web server. The original intent behind the cookie was to improve efficiency in processing return visits to sites where users are required to register for services. For example, on the user's first visit to a particular Web site, the URL and user ID may be stored as a cookie. On subsequent visits, the Web site retrieves the user ID; thus, saving the visitor from rekeying the information.

Cookies allow Web sites to off-load the storage of routine information about vast numbers of visitors. It is far more efficient for a Web server to retrieve this information from a cookie file stored on the user's computer than to search through millions of such records stored at the Web site. Most browsers have preference options to disable cookies or to warn the user before accepting one.

The privacy controversy over cookies relates to what information is captured and how it is used. For example, the cookie may be used to create a profile of user preferences for marketing purposes. The profile could be based on the pages accessed or the options selected during the site visit, the time of day or night of the visit, and the length of time spent at the site. The profile could also include the user's email address, zip code, home phone number, and any other information the user is willing to provide to the Web site.

This type of information is useful to online marketing firms that sell advertising for thousands of Internet firms that sell goods and service. The user profile enables the marketing firm to customize ads and to target them to Internet consumers. To illustrate, let's assume a user visiting an online bookstore browses sports car and automobile racing listings. This information is stored in a cookie and transmitted to the online marketing firm, which then sends JavaScript ads for general automotive products to the bookstore's Web page to entice the visitor to click on the ads. Each time the consumer visits the site, the contents of the cookie will be used to trigger the appropriate ads. User profile information can also be compiled into a mailing list, which is sold and used in the traditional way for solicitation.

Cookies and Consumer Security. Another concern over the use of cookies relates to security. Cookies are text (.txt) files that can be read with any text editor. Some Web sites may store user passwords in cookies. If the passwords are not encrypted (discussed later) before being stored, anyone with access to the computer can retrieve the cookies and the passwords. Thus, when multiple employees share a computer in the workplace, all users of the computer may review the cookies file, which is stored in a common directory.

---

14 "Privacy . . . A Weak Link in the Cyber-Chain," PricewaterhouseCoopers E-Business Leaders Series, www.pcwglobal.com, 1999.

A related form of risk comes from criminal or malicious Web sites. As the user browses the site, a JavaScript program such as the "Frieburg Bug" may be uploaded to the user's computer. The program secretly scans the hard drive for the cookies file and copies it to the Web site where it is reviewed for passwords.

Risks to Businesses

Business entities are also at risk from Internet commerce. IP spoofing, denial of service attacks, and malicious programs are three significant concerns that are examined below.

IP Spoofing. **IP spoofing** is a form of masquerading to gain unauthorized access to a Web server and/or to perpetrate an unlawful act without revealing one's identity. To accomplish this the perpetrator disguises his or her identity by modifying the IP address of the originating device. A criminal may use IP spoofing to make a message appear to be coming from a trusted or authorized source and thus slip through controls systems designed to accept transmissions from certain (trusted) host computers and block out others. This technique could be used to crack into corporate networks to perpetrate frauds, conduct acts of espionage, or destroy data. For example, a hacker may "spoof" a manufacturing firm with a false sales order that appears to come from a legitimate customer. If the spoof goes undetected the manufacturer will incur the costs of producing and delivering a product that was never ordered.

Denial of Service Attacks. A **denial of service attack** is an assault on a Web server to prevent it from servicing users. While such attacks can be aimed at any type of Web site, they are particularly devastating to business entities that cannot receive and process business transactions from their customers.

When a user establishes a connection on the Internet through TCP/IP, a three-way handshake takes place. The connecting server sends an initiation code called a *"SYN" (SYNchronize) packet* to the receiving server. The receiving server then acknowledges the request by returning a **SYNchronize-ACKnowledge (SYN-ACK)** packet. Finally, the initiating host machine responds with an *ACK packet code*. The attack is accomplished by not sending the final acknowledgment to the server's SYN-ACK response, which causes the server to keep signaling for acknowledgement until the server times out.

The individual or organizations perpetrating the denial of service attack transmits hundreds of SYN packets to the targeted receiver, but never responds with an ACK to complete the connection. As a result, the ports of the receiver's server are clogged with incomplete communication requests that prevent legitimate transactions from being received and processed. Organizations under attack have been prevented from receiving Internet messages for days at a time.

If the target organization could identify the server that is launching the attack, a firewall (discussed later) could be programmed to ignore all communication from that site. Such attacks, however, are difficult to prevent because IP spoofing is used to disguise the source of the messages. IP spoofing programs that randomize the source address of the attacker have been written and publicly distributed over the Internet. Therefore, to the receiving site it appears that the transmissions are coming from all over the Internet.

Malicious Programs. Viruses and other forms of malicious programs such as worms, logic bombs, and Trojan horses pose a threat to both Internet and intranet users. These may be used to bring down a computer network by corrupting its operating systems, destroy or corrupt corporate databases, or capture passwords that enable hackers to break into the system. Malicious programs, however, are not exclusively an EC issue; database management, operating systems security, and application integrity are also threatened. Because of the broad-based implications of this class of risk it is examined at length in Chapter 16.

SECURITY, ASSURANCE, AND TRUST

Trust is the catalyst for increasing EC. Both consumers and businesses are drawn to organizations that are perceived to have integrity. Organizations must convey a sense that they are competent and conduct business fairly with their customers, trading partners, and employees. This is a two-pronged problem. First, the company must implement the technological infrastructure and controls needed to provide for adequate security. Second, the company must assure potential customers and trading partners that adequate safeguards are in place and working. According to Forrester Research, organizations are expected to spend the bulk of their security budgets in three key areas: *data encryption*, *digital authentication*, and *firewalls*.[15] These security techniques are outlined below, but are presented in more detail in Chapter 16. This section concludes with a review of *seals of assurance* initiatives underway to promote trust in EC.

ENCRYPTION

Encryption is the conversion of data into a secret code for storage in databases and transmission over networks. The sender uses an encryption algorithm to convert the original message (called "cleartext") into a coded equivalent (called "ciphertext"). At the receiving end the ciphertext is decoded (decrypted) back into cleartext.

The earliest encryption method is called the **Caesar Cipher**, which is said to have been used by Julius Caesar to send coded messages to his generals in the field. Like modern-day encryption, the Caesar Cipher has two fundamental components: a *key* and an *algorithm*. The **key** is a mathematical value that is selected by the sender of the message. The **algorithm** is the simple procedure of shifting each letter in the cleartext message the number of positions indicated by the key value. Thus a key value of +3 would shift each letter three places to the right. For example, the letter "A" in cleartext would be represented as the letter "D" in the ciphertext message. The receiver of the ciphertext message decodes it and recreates the cleartext by reversing the process; in this case shifting each ciphertext letter three places to the left. Obviously, both the sender and receiver of the message must know the key.

Modern-day encryption algorithms are far more complex than that described above, and encryption keys are 40 to 128 bits in length. The more bits in the key the stronger the encryption method. Today, nothing less than 128-bit algorithms are considered truly secure. Two commonly used methods of encryption are data encryption standard (DES) and public key encryption.

The **DES** approach uses a single key known to both the sender and the receiver of the message. To encode a message, the sender provides the encryption algorithm with the key, which produces the ciphertext message. This is transmitted to the receiver's location, where it is decoded using the same key to produce a cleartext message. Because the same key is used for coding and decoding, control over the key becomes an important security issue. The more individuals that need to exchange encrypted data, the greater the chance that the key will become known to an unauthorized intruder who could intercept a message and read it, change it, delay it, or destroy it.

---

15   Forrester Research, Cambridge, Massachusetts, www.forrester.com, 1998.

To overcome this problem, **public key encryption** was devised. This approach uses two different keys: one for encoding messages and the other for decoding them. The recipient has a private key used for decoding that is kept secret. The encoding key is public and published for everyone to use. This approach is illustrated in Figure 12-8.

Receivers never need to share private keys with senders, which reduces the likelihood that they fall into the hands of an intruder. The most trusted public key encryption method is **Rivest-Shamir-Adleman** (**RSA**). This method is, however, computationally intensive and much slower than DES encryption. Sometimes, both DES and RSA are used together in what is called a **digital envelope**.

DIGITAL AUTHENTICATION

Not all security concerns are resolved by encryption alone. For example, how does the supplier (receiver) know for sure that a purchase order (message) for 1,000 units of product sent by a customer (sender) was not intercepted by a hacker during transmission and altered to read 100,000? If such an alteration went undetected, the supplier would incur the labor, material, manufacturing, and distribution costs for the order. Litigation between the innocent parties may ensue.

A **digital signature** is an electronic authentication technique that ensures the transmitted message originated with the authorized sender and that it was not tampered with after the signature was applied. The digital signature is derived from a mathematically computed digest of the document that has been encrypted with the sender's private key. Both the digital signature and the text message are encrypted using the receiver's public key and transmitted to the receiver. At the receiving end, the message is decrypted using the receiver's private key to produce the digital signature (encrypted digest) and the cleartext version of the message. Finally, the receiver uses the sender's public key to decrypt the digital signal to produce the digest. The receiver recalculates the digest from the cleartext using the original, hashing algorithm and compares this to the transmitted digest. If the message is authentic, the two digest values will match. If even a single character of the message was changed in transmission, the digest figures will not be equal.

Another concern facing the receiver is determining if a message was actually initiated by the expected sender. For example, suppose that the supplier receives a purchase order addressed from Customer A for 100,000 units of product, which was actually sent from an unknown computer criminal. Once again, significant costs would accrue to the supplier organization if they act on this fraudulent order.

A **digital certificate** is like an electronic identification card that is used in conjunction with a public key encryption system to verify the authenticity of the message sender. Also called "digital IDs," digital certificates are issued by trusted third parties known as **certification authorities** (**CAs**), e.g., Veri-Sign, Inc. The digital certificate is actually the sender's public key that has been digitally signed by the CA. The digital certificate is transmitted with the encrypted message to authenticate the sender. The receiver uses the CA's public key to decrypt the sender's public key, which is attached to the message, and then uses the sender's public key to decrypt the actual message.

Because public key encryption is central to digital authentication, public key management becomes an important internal control issue. **Public key infrastructure** (**PKI**) constitutes the policies and procedures for administering this activity. A PKI system consists of:

1. A certification authority that issues and revokes digital certificates.
2. A registration authority (RA) that verifies the identity of certificate applicants. The process varies depending on the level of certification desired. It involves establishing

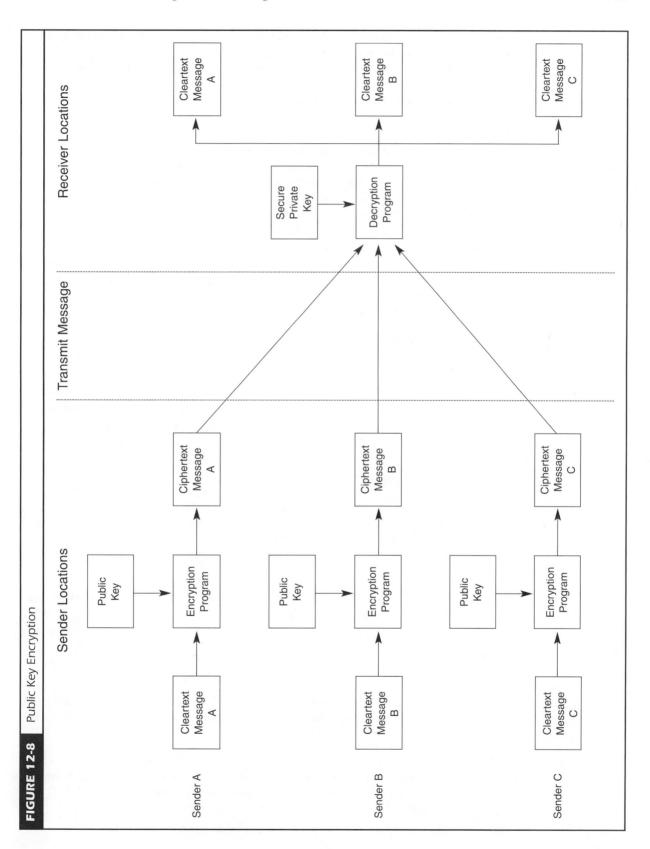

FIGURE 12-8   Public Key Encryption

one's identity with formal documents such as a driver's license, notarization, and fingerprints, and proving one's ownership of the public key.

3. A certification repository (CR), which is a publicly accessible database that contains current information about current certificates and a certification revocation list (CRL) of certificates that have been revoked and the reasons for revocation.

FIREWALLS

A **firewall** is a system used to insulate an organization's intranet from the Internet. It can be used to authenticate an outside user of the network, verify his or her level of access authority, and then direct the user to the program, data, or service requested. In addition to insulating the organization's network from external networks, firewalls can also be used to protect LANs from unauthorized internal access.

A common configuration employs two firewalls: a network-level firewall and an application-level firewall. The **network-level firewall** provides basic screening of low-security messages (e.g., email) and routes them to their destinations based on the source and destination addresses attached. The **application-level firewall** provides high-level network security. These firewalls are configured to run security applications called *proxies* that perform sophisticated functions such as verifying user authentication.

SEALS OF ASSURANCE

In response to consumer demand for evidence that a Web-based business is trustworthy, a number of "trusted" third-party organizations are offering *seals of assurance* that businesses can display on their Web site homepages. To legitimately bear the seal, the company must show that it complies with certain business practices, capabilities, and controls. This section reviews six seal-granting organizations: *Better Business Bureau (BBB)*, *TRUSTe*, *Veri-Sign, Inc.*, *International Computer Security Association (ICSA)*, *AICPA/CICA WebTrust*, and *AICPA/CICA SysTrust*.

Better Business Bureau

The Better Business Bureau (BBB) is a nonprofit organization that has been promoting ethical business practices through self-regulation since 1912. The BBB has extended its mission to the Internet through a wholly owned subsidiary called BBBOnline, Inc. To qualify for the BBBOnline seal an organization must:

- Become a member of the BBB.
- Provide information about the company's ownership, management, address, and phone number. This is verified by a physical visit to the company's premises.
- Be in business for at least one year.
- Promptly respond to customer complaints.
- Agree to binding arbitration for unresolved disputes with customers.

The assurance provided by BBBOnline relates primarily to concern about business policies, ethical advertising, and consumer privacy. BBBOnline does not verify controls over transaction processing integrity and data security issues.

TRUSTe

Founded in 1996, TRUSTe is a nonprofit organization dedicated to improving consumer privacy practices among Internet businesses and Web sites. To qualify for the TRUSTe seal the organization must:

- Agree to follow TRUSTe privacy policies and disclosure standards.

- Post a privacy statement on the Web site disclosing the type of information being collected, the purpose for collecting information, and with whom it is shared.

- Promptly respond to customer complaints.

- Agree to site compliance reviews by TRUSTe or an independent third party.

TRUSTe addresses consumer privacy concerns exclusively and provides a mechanism for posting consumer complaints against its members. If a member organization is found to be out of compliance with TRUSTe standards, its right to display the trust seal may be revoked.

Veri-Sign, Inc.

Veri-Sign, Inc. was established as a for-profit organization in 1995. Veri-Sign, Inc. provides assurance regarding the security of transmitted data. The organization does not verify security of stored data or address concerns related to business policies, business processes, or privacy. Their mission is to "provide digital certificate solutions that enable trusted commerce and communications." Their products allow customers to transmit encrypted data and verify the source and destination of transmissions. Veri-Sign, Inc. issues three classes of certificates to individuals, businesses, and organizations. To qualify for class three certification the individual, business, or organization must provide a third-party confirmation of name, address, telephone number, and Web site domain name.

ICSA

The International Computer Security Association (ICSA) established its Web Certification Program in 1996. ICSA certification addresses data security and privacy concerns. It does not deal with concerns about business policy and business processes. Organizations that qualify to display the ICSA seal have undergone an extensive review of firewall security from outside hackers. Organizations must be recertified on an annual basis and undergo at least two surprise checks each year.

AICPA/CICA WebTrust

The AICPA and CICA established the WebTrust program in 1997. To display the AICPA/CICA WebTrust seal the organization undergoes an examination according to the AICPA's Standards for Attestation Engagements, No. 1, by a specially Web-certified CPA or CA. The examination focuses on the areas of business practices (policies), transaction integrity (business process), and information protection (data security). The seal must be renewed every 90 days.

AICPA/CICA SysTrust

In July 1999, the AICPA/CICA introduced an exposure draft describing a new assurance service called SysTrust. It is designed to increase management, customer, and trading partner confidence in systems that support entire businesses or specific processes. The assurance service involves the public accountant evaluating the system's reliability against four essential criteria: availability, security, integrity, and maintainability.

The potential users of SysTrust are trading partners, creditors, shareholders, and others who rely on the integrity and capability of the system. For example, Virtual Company is considering outsourcing some of its vital functions to third-party organizations. Virtual needs assurance that the third parties' systems are reliable and adequate to provide the contracted services. As part of the outsourcing contract, Virtual requires the servicing organizations to produce a clean SysTrust report every three months.

In theory, the SysTrust service will enable organizations to differentiate themselves from their competitors. Those organizations that undergo a SysTrust engagement will be perceived as competent service providers and trustworthy. They will be more attuned to the risks in their environment and equipped with the necessary controls to deal with the risks.[16]

IMPLICATIONS FOR THE ACCOUNTING PROFESSION

The issues discussed in this chapter carry many implications for auditors and the public accounting profession. As key functions such as inventory procurement, sales processing, shipping notification, and cash disbursements are performed automatically, digitally, and in real time, auditors are faced with the challenge of developing new techniques for assessing control adequacy and verifying the occurrence and accuracy of economic events. The following describes issues of increasing importance to auditors in the EC age.

PRIVACY VIOLATION

Privacy pertains to the level of confidentiality employed by an organization in managing customer and trading partner data. Privacy applies also to data collected by Web sites from visitors who are not customers. Specific concerns include:

- Does the organization have a stated privacy policy?

- What mechanisms are in place to assure the consistent application of stated privacy policies?

- What information on customers, trading partners, and visitors does the company capture?

- Does the organization share or sell its customer, trading partner, or visitor information?

- Can individuals and business entities verify and update the information captured about them?

The growing reliance on Internet technologies for conducting business has placed the spotlight on **privacy violation** as a factor detrimental to a client entity's existence. In response to this threat, several firms have developed assurance services for evaluating their client's *privacy violation risk*. A KPMG white paper examines the importance customers place on their privacy.[17] The paper suggests that developing a set of privacy protection policies may prove to be a significant differentiation factor for commercial companies. As such, particular care needs to be exerted by auditors engaged in certifying management's practices and established privacy policy.

The importance of privacy was reasserted by the **Safe Harbor Agreement** implemented in 1995. The two-way agreement between the United States and the European Union establishes standards for information transmittal. Approved by the European Commission in July 2000, the Safe Harbor principles essentially enable U.S. companies to do business in the European Union by establishing what is deemed to be an "adequate" level of privacy protection. Although the document is still evolving, it establishes that companies need to enter the Safe Harbor Agreement or provide evidence that they are abiding by the privacy regulations set forth in it. Noncompliant organizations may

---

16 American Institute of Certified Public Accountants, Inc. and Canadian Institute of Chartered Accountants, AICPA/CICA SysTrust Principle and Criteria for Systems Reliability (1999): 3.

17 "A New Covenant with Stakeholders: Managing Privacy as a Competitive Advantage, Privacy Risk Management," © 2001 KPMG LLP, the U.S. member firm of KPMG International, a Swiss association: 22–23.

be effectively banned from doing business in the European Union. Compliance with the Safe Harbor Agreement requires that a company meet six conditions:[18]

Notice. Organizations must provide individuals with clear notice of "the purposes for which it collects and uses information about them, the types of third parties to which it discloses the information, and how to contact the company with inquiries or complaints."

Choice. Before any data is collected, an organization must give its customers the opportunity to choose whether to share their sensitive information (e.g., data related to factors such as health, race, or religion).

Onward Transfer. Unless they have the individual's permission to do otherwise, organizations may share information only with those third parties that belong to the Safe Harbor Agreement or follow its principles.

Security and Data Integrity. Organizations need to ensure that the data they maintain is accurate, complete, and current; thus, reliable for use. They must also ensure the security of the information by protecting it against loss, misuse, unauthorized access, disclosure, alteration, and destruction.

Access. Unless they would be unduly burdened or violate the rights of others, organizations must give individuals "access to personal data about themselves and provide an opportunity to correct, amend, or delete such data."

Enforcement. Organizations must "enforce compliance, provide recourse for individuals who believe their privacy rights have been violated, and impose sanctions on their employees and agents for non-compliance."

Audit Implications of XBRL

Although the potential benefits of XBRL and associated Web technologies have been extensively researched, little attention has been given to the audit implications of using XBRL. Areas of specific concern include:

Taxonomy Creation. Taxonomy may be generated incorrectly, which results in an incorrect mapping between data and taxonomy elements that could result in material misrepresentation of financial data. Controls must be designed and in place to ensure the correct generation of XBRL taxonomies.

Validation of Instance Documents. As noted, once the mapping is complete and tags have been stored in the internal database, XBRL instance documents (reports) can be generated. Independent verification procedures need to be established to validate the instance documents to ensure that appropriate taxonomy and tags have been applied before posting to a Web server.

Audit Scope and Timeframe. Currently, auditors are responsible for printed financial statements and other materials associated with the statements. What will be the impact on the scope of auditor responsibility as a consequence of real-time distribution of financial statements across the Internet? Should auditors also be responsible for the accuracy of other related data that accompany XBRL financial statements, such as textual reports?

---

18   Ibid.

Continuous Auditing

Continuous auditing techniques need to be developed that will enable the auditor to review transactions at frequent intervals or as they occur. To be effective, such an approach will need to employ **intelligent control agents** (computer programs) that embody auditor-defined heuristics that search electronic transactions for anomalies. Upon finding unusual events, the control agent will first search for similar events to identify a pattern. If the anomaly cannot be explained, the agent alerts the auditor with an alarm or exception report.

Electronic Audit Trails

In an EDI environment, electronic transactions are generated automatically by a trading partner's computer, relayed across a **value-added network (VAN),**[19] and processed by the client's computer without human intervention. In this setting, audits may need to be extended to all critical systems of the parties involved in the transactions. Validating such transactions may involve the client, its trading partners, and the VAN that connects them. This could take the form of direct review of these systems or collaboration between the auditors of the trading partners and VANs.

Confidentiality of Data

As system designs become increasingly open to accommodate trading partner transactions, mission-critical information is at the risk of being exposed to intruders both from inside and outside the organization. Accountants need to understand the cryptographic techniques used to protect the confidentiality of stored and transmitted data. They need to assess the quality of encryption tools used and the effectiveness of key management procedures used by CAs. Furthermore, the term *mission-critical* defines a set of information that extends beyond the traditional financial concerns of accountants. This broader set demands a more holistic approach to assessing internal controls that ensure the confidentiality of data.

Authentication

In traditional systems, the business paper on which it was written determines the authenticity of a sales order from a trading partner or customer. In EC systems, determining the identity of the customer is not as simple a task. With no physical forms to review and approve, authentication is accomplished through digital signatures and digital certificates. To perform their assurance function, accountants must develop the skill set needed to understand these technologies and their application.

Nonrepudiation

Accountants are responsible for assessing the accuracy, completeness, and validity of transactions that constitute client sales, accounts receivable, purchases, and liabilities. Transactions that can be unilaterally repudiated by a trading partner can lead to uncollected revenues or legal action. In traditional systems, signed invoices, sales agreements, and other physical documents provide proof that a transaction occurred. As with the problem of authentication, EC systems can also use digital signatures and digital certificates to promote nonrepudiation.

Certification Authority Licensing

The purpose of CAs is to have independent and trusted third parties empowered with responsibility to vouch for the identity of organizations and individuals engaging in Internet commerce. The question then becomes who vouches for the CA? How does one

---

19   See the appendix for discussion of value-added networks.

know that the CA, who awarded a seal of authenticity to an individual, is itself reputable and was meticulous in establishing his or her identity? These questions hold specific implications for the accounting profession. Because they enjoy a high degree of public confidence, public accounting firms are natural candidates for CAs.

Data Integrity

A nonrepudiated transaction from an authentic trading partner may still be intercepted and rendered inaccurate in a material way. In a paper-based environment, such alterations are easy to detect. Digital transmissions, however, pose much more of a problem. To assess data integrity, accountants must become familiar with the concept of computing a digest of a document and the role of digital signatures in data transmissions.

Access Controls

Controls need to be in place that prevent or detect unauthorized access to an organization's information system. Organizations whose systems are connected to the Internet are at greatest risk from outside intruders. Accounting firms need to be expert in assessing their clients' access controls. Many firms are now performing penetration tests, designed to assess the adequacy of their clients' access control by imitating known techniques used by hackers and crackers.

A Changing Legal Environment

Accountants have traditionally served their clients by assessing risk (both business and legal) and devising techniques to mitigate and control risk. This risk assessment role is greatly expanded by Internet commerce, whose legal framework is still evolving in a business environment fraught with new and unforeseen risks. To estimate its client's exposure to legal liability in this setting, the public account must understand the potential legal implications (both domestic and international) of actions taken by the client's EC system. The act of creating a Web page from which customers may order goods opens the organization to the national and international business communities and exposes it to multiple and possibly conflicting legal statutes. Legal issues relating to taxes, privacy, security, intellectual property rights, and libel are of particular concern. For example, for tax purposes, where does the sale originate if a company has its corporate headquarters and inventory warehouse in one country and its Internet transaction processing systems in another?

The legal issues associated with EC have and will continue to create new opportunities for the profession. Accounting firms will need to provide their clients with rapid and accurate advice on a wide range of legal questions.

SUMMARY

This chapter focused on Internet commerce, including business-to-consumer and business-to-business relationships. Internet commerce has been the source of intense interest because it enables thousands of business enterprises of all sizes and millions of consumers to congregate and participate in worldwide commerce. The chapter examined Internet technologies, including packet switching, the World Wide Web, Internet addressing, and protocols. Several advantages of Internet commerce were reviewed, including access to worldwide markets, reductions in inventory, creation of business partnerships, reductions in prices, and better customer service.

Electronic commerce is associated with unique risks. The primary concerns posed by intranets (discussed in the appendix) come from employees. Internet risks were characterized as a number of specific, fraud schemes that threaten consumer privacy and the security of transmitted and stored data. Several measures were examined that can reduce risks and promote an environment of security and trust. These include data encryption, digital certificates, firewalls, and third-party trust seals for Web sites.

The chapter concluded with a review of implications for accountants and the profession. The issues covered included privacy issues, continuous process auditing, electronic audit trails, and the auditors' need for new skill sets to deal with highly technical, evidential matter that redefine traditional auditing concerns.

APPENDIX

INTRA-ORGANIZATIONAL ELECTRONIC COMMERCE

Distributed data processing was introduced in Chapter 1 as an alternative to the centralized model. Most modern organizations use some form of distributed processing to process their transactions; some companies process all of their transactions in this way. Networks owned or leased by organizations for internal business use intranets. The section examines several intranet topologies and techniques for network control.

NETWORK TOPOLOGIES

A **network topology** is the physical arrangement of the components (e.g., nodes, servers, communications links, and so on) of the network. In this section, we examine the features of five basic network topologies: star, hierarchical, ring, bus, and client-server. Most networks are a variation on, or combination of, these basic models. However, before proceeding, working definitions are presented for some of the terms that will be used in the following sections.

Local Area Networks and Wide Area Networks

One way of distinguishing between networks is the geographic area covered by their distributed sites. Networks are usually classified as either *local area networks* (LANs) or *wide area networks* (WANs). **LANs** are often confined to a single room in a building, or they may link several buildings within a close geographic area. However, a LAN can cover distances of several miles and connect hundreds of users. The computers connected to a LAN are called nodes.

When networks exceed the geographic limitations of the LAN, they are called **WANs**. Because of the distances involved and the high cost of telecommunication infrastructure (telephone lines and microwave channels), WANs are often commercial networks (at least in part) that are leased by the organization. The nodes of a WAN may include microcomputer workstations, minicomputers, mainframes, and LANs. The WAN may be used to link geographically dispersed segments of a single organization or connect multiple organizations in a trading partner arrangement.

Network Interface Cards

The physical connection of workstations to the LAN is achieved through a **network interface card** (**NIC**), which fits into one of the expansion slots in the microcomputer. This device provides the electronic circuitry needed for internode communications. The NIC works with the network control program to send and receive messages, programs, and files across the network.

Servers

LAN nodes often share common resources such as programs, data, and printers, which are managed through special-purpose computers called **servers** as depicted in Figure 12-9. When the server receives requests for resources, the requests are placed in a queue and are processed in sequence.

In a distributed environment, there is often a need to link networks together. For example, users of one LAN may share data with users on a different LAN. Networks are linked via combinations of hardware and software devices called *bridges* and *gateways*. Figure 12-10 illustrates this technique. **Bridges** provide a means for linking LANs of the same type, e.g., an IBM token ring to another IBM token ring. **Gateways** connect LANs of different types and are also used to link LANs to WANs. With these definitions in mind, we now turn our attention to the five basic network topologies.

Star Topology

The **star topology** shown in Figure 12-11 describes a network of computers with a large central computer (the host) at the hub that has direct connections to a periphery of smaller computers. Communications between the nodes in the star are managed and controlled from the host site.

The star topology is often used for a WAN, in which the central computer is a mainframe. The nodes of the star may be microcomputer workstations, minicomputers, mainframes, or a combination. Databases under this approach may be distributed or centralized. A common model is to partition local data to the nodes and centralize the common data. For example, consider a department store chain that issues its own credit cards. Each node represents a store in a different metropolitan area. In Figure 12-11 these are Dallas,

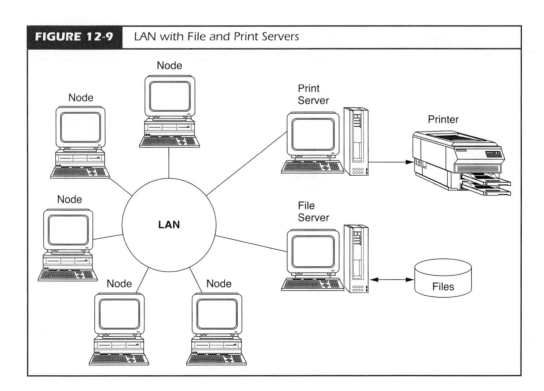

FIGURE 12-9   LAN with File and Print Servers

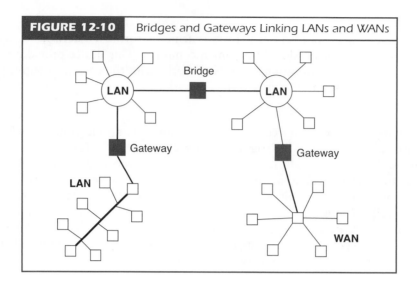

FIGURE 12-10 | Bridges and Gateways Linking LANs and WANs

St. Louis, Topeka, and Tulsa. The nodes maintain local databases such as records for customers holding credit cards issued in their areas and records of local inventory levels. The central site—Kansas City—maintains data common to the entire regional area, including data for customer billing, accounts receivable maintenance, and overall inventory control. Each local node is itself a LAN, with point-of-sales (POS) terminals connected to a minicomputer at the store.

If one or more nodes in a star network fail, communication between the remaining nodes is still possible through the central site. However, if the central site fails, individual nodes can function locally, but cannot communicate with the other nodes.

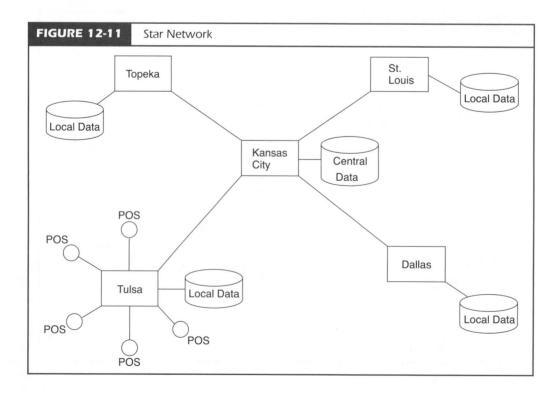

FIGURE 12-11 | Star Network

Transaction processing in this type of configuration could proceed as follows. Sales are processed in real time at the POS terminals. Local processing includes obtaining credit approval, updating the customer's available credit, updating the inventory records, and recording the transaction in the transaction file (journal). At the end of the business day, the nodes transmit sales and inventory information to the central site in batches. The central site updates the control accounts, prepares customer bills, and determines inventory replenishment for the entire region.

The assumption underlying the star topology is that primary communication will be between the central site and the nodes. However, limited communication between the nodes is possible. For example, assume a customer from Dallas was in Tulsa and made a purchase from the Tulsa store on credit. The Tulsa database would not contain the customer's record, so Tulsa would send the transaction for credit approval to Dallas via Kansas City. The approved transaction would then be returned by Dallas to Tulsa via Kansas City. Inventory and sales journal updates would be performed at Tulsa.

This transaction processing procedure would differ somewhat depending on the database configuration. For example, if local databases are partial replicas of the central database, credit queries could be made directly from Kansas City. However, this would require keeping the central database current with all the nodes.

Hierarchical Topology

A **hierarchical topology** is one in which a host computer is connected to several levels of subordinate, smaller computers in a master-slave relationship. This structure is applicable to firms with many organizational levels that must be controlled from a central location. For example, consider a manufacturing firm with remote plants, warehouses, and sales offices like the one illustrated in Figure 12-12. Sales orders from the local sales departments are transmitted to the regional level, where they are summarized and uploaded to the corporate level. Sales data, combined with inventory and plant capacity data from manufacturing, are used to compute production requirements for the period, which are downloaded to the regional production scheduling system. At this level, production schedules are prepared and distributed to the local production departments. Information about completed production is uploaded from the production departments to the regional level, where production summaries are prepared and transmitted to the corporate level.

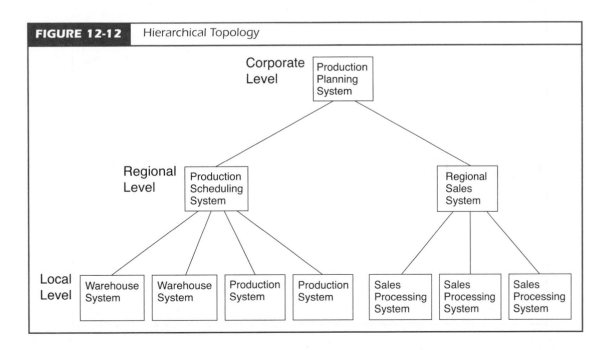

FIGURE 12-12   Hierarchical Topology

Ring Topology

The **ring topology** illustrated in Figure 12-13 eliminates the central site. All nodes in this configuration are of equal status; thus, responsibility for managing communications is distributed among the nodes. Every node on the ring has a unique electronic address, which is attached to messages such as an address on an envelope. If Node A wishes to send a message to Node D, the message is received, regenerated, and passed on by Nodes B and C until it arrives at its destination. The ring topology is a *peer-to-peer arrangement* in which all nodes are of equal status. This is a popular topology for LANs. The peer nodes manage private programs and databases locally. However, common resources that are shared by all nodes can be centralized and managed by a file server that is also a node on the network ring.

   The ring topology may also be used for a WAN, in which case the databases may be partitioned rather than centralized. For example, consider a company with widely separated warehouses, each with different suppliers and customers and each processing its own shipping and receiving transactions. In this case, where there is little common data, it is more efficient to distribute the database than to manage it centrally. However, when one warehouse has insufficient stock to fill an order, it can communicate through the network to locate the items at another warehouse.

Bus Topology

The **bus topology** illustrated in Figure 12-14 is the most popular LAN topology. It is so named because the nodes are all connected to a common cable—the bus. Communications and file transfers between workstations are controlled centrally by one or more servers. As with the ring topology, each node on the bus has a unique address, and only one node may transmit at a time. The technique, which has been used for over two decades, is simple, reliable, and generally less costly to install than the ring topology.

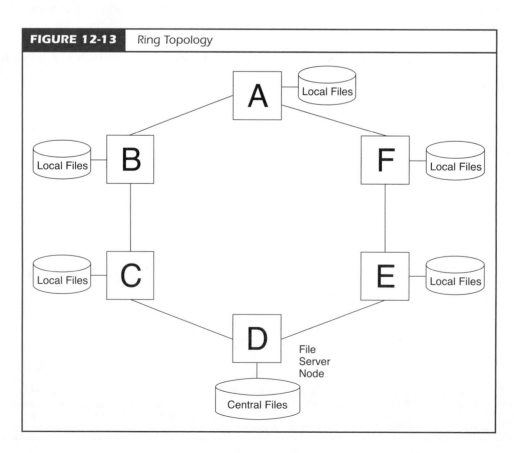

FIGURE 12-13   Ring Topology

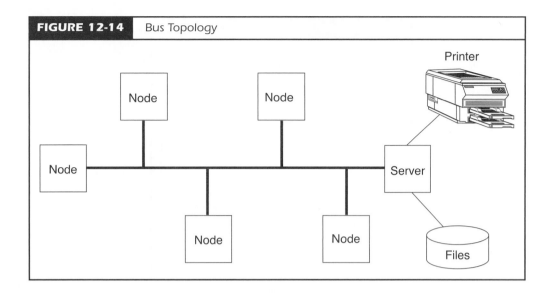

FIGURE 12-14   Bus Topology

Client-Server Topology

The term *client-server* is often misused to describe any type of network arrangement. In fact, the **client-server topology** has specific characteristics that distinguish it from the other topologies. Figure 12-15 illustrates the approach.

To explain the client-server difference let's review the features of a traditional distributed system (DDP). DDP can result in considerable data "traffic jams." Users competing for access to shared data files experience queues, delays, and lockouts. A factor influencing the severity of this problem is the structure of the database in use. For example, assume that User A requests a single record from a database table located at a central site. To meet this request, the file server at the central site must lock and transmit the entire table to User A. The search for the specific record is performed at the remote site by the user's application. When the record is updated, the entire file is then transmitted back to the central site.

The client-server model distributes the processing between User A's (client) computer and the central file server. Both computers are part of the network, but each is assigned functions that it performs best. For example, the record-searching portion of an application is placed at the server, and the data manipulation portion is on the client computer. Thus, only a single record, rather than the entire file, must be locked and sent to the client for processing. After processing, the record is returned to the server, which restores it to the table and removes the lock. This approach reduces traffic and allows more efficient use of shared data. Distributing the record-searching logic of the client's application to the server permits other clients to access different records in the same file simultaneously. The client-server approach can be applied to any topology (i.e., ring, star, or bus). Figure 12-15 illustrates the client-server model applied to a bus topology.

NETWORK CONTROL

In this section, we examine methods for controlling communications between the physical devices connected to the network. **Network control** exists at several points in the network architecture. The majority of network control resides with software in the host computer, but control also resides in servers and terminals at the nodes and in switches located throughout the network. The purpose of network control is to perform the following tasks:

1. Establish a communications session between the sender and the receiver.
2. Manage the flow of data across the network.
3. Detect and resolve data collisions between competing nodes.
4. Detect errors in data caused by line failure or signal degeneration.

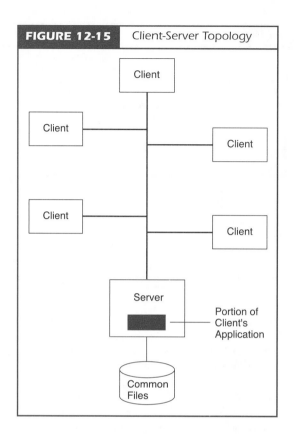

FIGURE 12-15   Client-Server Topology

DATA COLLISION

To achieve effective network control, there must be an exclusive link or session established between a transmitting and a receiving node. Only one node at a time can transmit a message on a single line. Two or more signals transmitted simultaneously will result in a **data collision**, which destroys both messages. When this happens, the messages must be retransmitted. There are several techniques for managing sessions and controlling data collisions, but most of them are variants of three basic methods: polling, token passing, and carrier sensing.

Polling

Polling is the most popular technique for establishing a communication session in WANs. One site, designated the "master," polls the other "slave" sites to determine if they have data to transmit. If a slave responds in the affirmative, the master site locks the network while the data are transmitted. The remaining sites must wait until they are polled before they can transmit. The polling technique illustrated in Figure 12-16 is well suited to both the star and the hierarchical topologies. There are two primary advantages to polling. First, polling is *noncontentious*. Because nodes can send data only when requested by the master node, two nodes can never access the network at the same time. Data collisions are, therefore, prevented. Second, an organization can set *priorities* for data communications across the network. Important nodes can be polled more often than less important nodes.

Token Passing

Token passing involves transmitting a special signal—the token—around the network from node to node in a specific sequence. Each node on the network receives the token, regenerates it, and passes it to the next node. Only the node in possession of the token is allowed to transmit data.

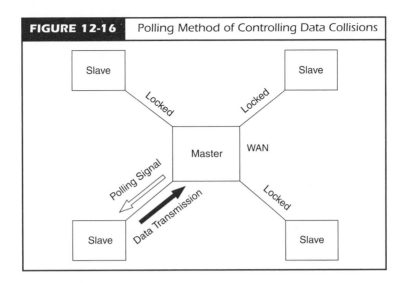

FIGURE 12-16   Polling Method of Controlling Data Collisions

Token passing can be used with either ring or bus topologies. On a ring topology, the token passing sequence is determined by the order in which the nodes are physically connected. With a bus, the sequence is logical, not physical. The token is passed from node to node in a predetermined order to form a logical ring. Token-bus and token-ring configurations are illustrated in Figure 12-17. Because nodes are permitted to transmit only when they possess the token, the node wishing to send data across the network seizes the token upon receiving it. Holding the token blocks other nodes from transmitting and ensures that no data collisions will occur. After the transmitting node sends its message and receives an acknowledgment signal from the receiving node, it releases the token. The next node in sequence then has the option of either seizing the token and transmitting data or passing the token on to the next node in the circuit.

A major advantage of token passing is its *deterministic* access method, which avoids data collisions. This is in contrast with the *random* access approach of carrier sensing (discussed below). IBM's version of token ring is emerging as an industry standard.

Carrier Sensing

Carrier sensing is a random access technique that detects collisions when they occur. This technique, which is formally labeled *carrier sensed multiple access with collision detection (CSMA/CD)*, is used with the bus topology. The node wishing to transmit "listens" to the bus to determine if it is in use. If it senses no transmission in progress (no carrier), the node transmits its message to the receiving node. This approach is not as fail-safe as token passing. Collisions can occur when two or more nodes, unaware of each other's intent to transmit, do so simultaneously when they independently perceive the line to be clear. When this happens, the network server directs each node to wait a unique and random period of time and then retransmit the message. In a busy network data collisions are more likely to occur; thus, it results in delays while the nodes retransmit their messages. Proponents of the token passing approach point to its collision-avoidance characteristic as a major advantage over the CSMA/CD model.

Ethernet is the best-known LAN software that uses the CSMA/CD standard. The Ethernet model was developed by Xerox Corporation in the 1970s. In 1980, Digital Equipment Corporation, in a joint venture with Intel Corporation, published the specifications for a LAN based on the Ethernet model.[20] The greatest advantage of Ethernet is that it is established, reliable, and well understood by network specialists. Ethernet also has a number of economic advantages over token ring: (1) the technology, being relatively

20   "The Ethernet, a Local Area Network Version 1.0." Digital Equipment Corporation, Maynard, MS.; Intel Corporation, Santa Clara, CA.; and Xerox Corporation, Stanford, CN.

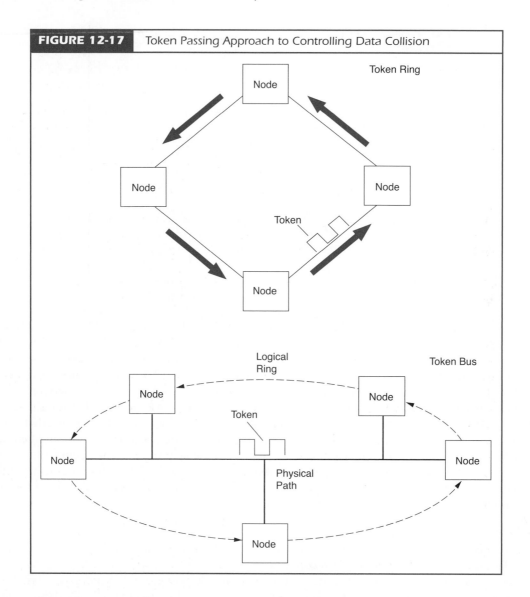

FIGURE 12-17 | Token Passing Approach to Controlling Data Collision

simple, is well suited to the less costly twisted-pair cabling, whereas token ring works best with more expensive coaxial cable; (2) the network interface cards used by Ethernet are much less expensive than those used in the token ring topology; and (3) Ethernet uses a bus topology, which is easier to expand.

ELECTRONIC DATA INTERCHANGE (EDI)

To coordinate sales and production operations and to maintain an uninterrupted flow of raw materials, many organizations enter into a trading partner agreement with their suppliers and customers. This agreement is the foundation for a fully automated business process called **EDI**. A general definition of EDI is:

The intercompany exchange of computer-processable business information in standard format.

The definition reveals several important features of EDI. First, EDI is an interorganization endeavor. A firm does not engage in EDI on its own. Second, the transaction is processed automatically by the information systems of the trading partners. In a pure EDI environment, there are no human intermediaries to approve or authorize transactions. Authorizations, mutual obligations, and business practices that apply to transactions are all specified in advance under the trading partner agreement. Third, transaction information is transmitted in a standardized format. Therefore, firms with different internal systems can exchange information and do business. Figure 12-18 shows an overview of an EDI connection between two companies. Assume that the transaction in Figure 12-18 is the purchase of inventory by the customer (Company A) from the supplier (Company B). Company A's purchases system automatically creates an electronic purchase order (PO), which it sends to its translation software. Here, the PO is converted to a standard format electronic message ready for transmission. The message is transmitted to Company B's translation software, where it is converted to the supplier's internal format. Company B's sales order processing system receives the customer order, which it processes automatically.

Figure 12-18 shows a direct communications link between companies. But many companies choose to use a third-party **value added network (VAN)** to connect to their trading partners. Figure 12-19 illustrates

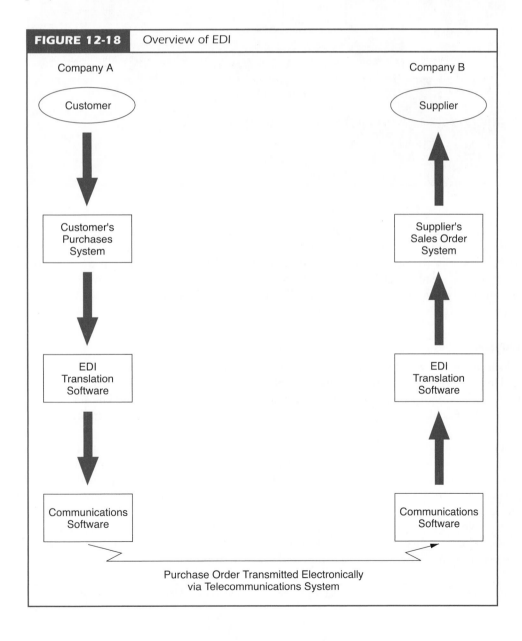

FIGURE 12-18   Overview of EDI

Company A

Customer

Customer's Purchases System

EDI Translation Software

Communications Software

Company B

Supplier

Supplier's Sales Order System

EDI Translation Software

Communications Software

Purchase Order Transmitted Electronically via Telecommunications System

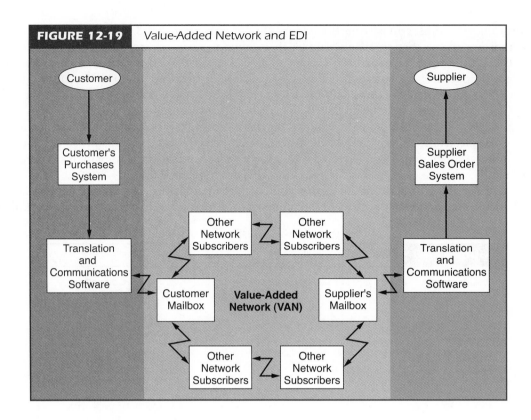

FIGURE 12-19 Value-Added Network and EDI

this arrangement. The originating company transmits its EDI messages to the network rather than directly to the trading partner's computer. The network directs each EDI transmission to its destination and deposits the message in the appropriate electronic mailbox. The messages stay in the mailboxes until the receiving companies' systems retrieve them. The network is a *VAN* because it provides service by managing the distribution of the messages between trading partners. VANs can also provide an important degree of control over EDI transactions. EDI control issues are examined in Chapter 16.

EDI STANDARDS

Key to EDI success is the use of a standard format for messaging between dissimilar systems. Over the years, both in the United States and internationally, a number of formats have been proposed. The standard in the United States is the **American National Standards Institute (ANSI) X.12** format. The standard used internationally is the **EDI For Administration, Commerce, and Transport (EDIFACT)** format. Figure 12-20 illustrates the X.12 format.

The electronic envelope contains the electronic address of the receiver, communications protocols, and control information. This is the electronic equivalent of a traditional paper envelope. A functional group is a collection of transaction sets (electronic documents) for a particular business application, such as a group of sales invoices or purchase orders. The transaction set is the electronic document and is composed of data segments and data elements. Figure 12-21 relates these terms to a conventional document.[21]

Each data segment is an information category on the document, such as part number, unit price, or vendor name. The data elements are specific items of data related to a segment. In the example in Figure 12-21, these include such items as REX-446, $127.86, and Ozment Supply.

---

21   J. M. Cathey, "Electronic Data Interchange: What the Controller Should Know," *Management Accounting* (November 1991): 48.

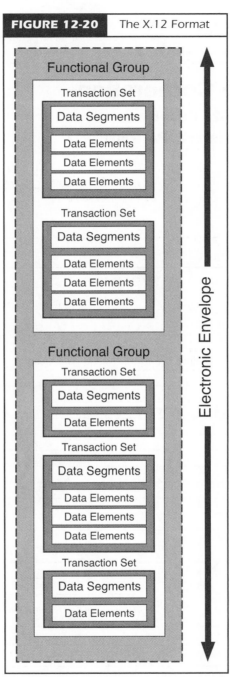

SOURCE: B. K. Stone, One to Get Ready: How to Prepare Your Company for EDI (CoreStates, 1988): 12.

BENEFITS OF EDI

EDI has made considerable inroads in a number of industries, including automotive, groceries, retail, health care, and electronics. The following are some common EDI cost savings that justify the approach.

FIGURE 12-21 Relationship between X.12 Format and a Conventional Source Document

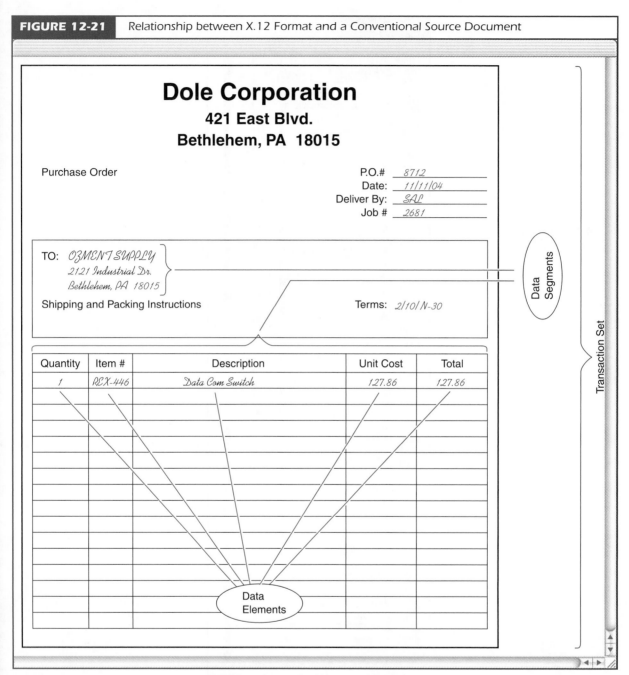

SOURCE: J. M. Cathey, "Electronic Data Interchange: What the Controller Should Know," *Management Accounting* (November 1991): 4.

- *Data keying.* EDI reduces or even eliminates the need for data entry.

- *Error reduction.* Firms using EDI see reductions in data keying errors, human interpretation and classification errors, and filing (lost document) errors.

- *Reduction of paper.* The use of electronic envelopes and documents reduces drastically the paper forms in the system.

- *Postage.* Mailed documents are replaced with much cheaper data transmissions.

- *Automated procedures.* EDI automates manual activities associated with purchasing, sales order processing, cash disbursements, and cash receipts.

- *Inventory reduction.* By ordering directly as needed from vendors, EDI reduces the lag time that promotes inventory accumulation.

FINANCIAL EDI

Using Electronic funds transfer (EFT) for cash disbursement and cash receipts processing is more complicated than using EDI for purchasing and selling activities. **EFT** requires intermediary banks between trading partners. This arrangement is shown in Figure 12-22. Purchase invoices are received and automatically approved for

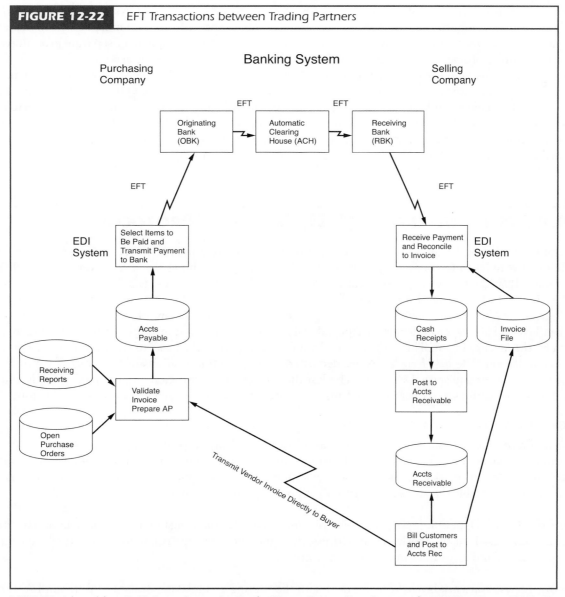

FIGURE 12-22   EFT Transactions between Trading Partners

SOURCE: Adapted from B. K. Stone, *One to Get Ready: How to Prepare Your Company for EDI* (CoreStates, 1988): 62.

payment by the buyer's EDI system. On the payment date, the buyer's system automatically makes an EFT to its originating bank (OBK). The OBK removes funds from the buyer's account and transmits them electronically to the automatic clearing house (ACH) bank. The ACH is a central bank that carries accounts for its member banks. The ACH transfers the funds from the OBK to the receiving bank (RBK), which in turn applies the funds to the seller's account.

Transferring funds by EFT poses no special problem. A check can easily be represented within the X.12 format. The problem arises with the remittance advice information that accompanies the check. Remittance advice information is often quite extensive because of complexities in the transaction. The check may be in payment of multiple invoices or only a partial invoice. There may be disputed amounts because of price disagreements, damaged goods, or incomplete deliveries. In traditional systems, these disputes are resolved by modifying the remittance advice and/or attaching a letter explaining the payment.

Converting remittance information to electronic form can result in very large records. Members of the ACH system are required to accept and process only EFT formats limited to 94 characters of data—a record size sufficient for only very basic messages. Not all banks in the ACH system support the ANSI standard format for remittances, ANSI 820. In such cases, remittance information must be sent to the seller by separate EDI transmission or conventional mail. The seller must then implement separate procedures to match bank and customer EDI transmissions in applying payments to customer accounts.

Recognizing the void between services demanded and those supplied by the ACH system, many banks have established themselves as **value-added banks** (**VABs**) to compete for this market. A VAB can accept electronic disbursements and remittance advices from its clients in any format. It converts EDI transactions to the ANSI X.12 and 820 formats for electronic processing. In the case of non-EDI transactions, the VAB writes traditional checks to the creditor. The services offered by VABs allow their clients to employ a single cash disbursement system that can accommodate both EDI and non-EDI customers.

OPEN SYSTEM INTERFACE (OSI) NETWORK PROTOCOL

The **OSI** model provides standards by which the products of different manufacturers can interface with one another in a seamless interconnection at the user level. Figure 12-23 shows the seven-layer OSI model. The OSI standard has the following general features. First, each layer in the model is independent, which allows the development of separate protocols specifically for each layer. Second, the layers at each node communicate logically with their counterpart layers across nodes. The physical flow of data and parameters pass between layers. Each layer performs specific subtasks that support the layer above it and are in turn supported by the layer below it. Third, the model distinguishes between the tasks of data communications and data manipulation. The first four layers are dedicated to data communications tasks, which are a function of hardware devices and special software. The last three layers support data manipulation, which is a function of user applications and operating systems. The specific function of each layer is described below.

Layer Functions

Physical Layer. The **physical layer**, the first and lowest level in the protocol, defines standards for the physical interconnection of devices to the electronic circuit. This level is concerned with pin connections to devices, the wiring of workstations, and cabling standards. An example of a standard at this layer is the RS-232 connector cable that is used by virtually all microcomputer manufacturers.

Data Link Layer. **Data link layer** protocols are concerned with the transmission of packets of data from node to node based on the workstation address. This includes message origination, acknowledgment of message receipt, and error detection and retransmission.

Network Layer. **Network layer** protocols deal with the routing and relaying of data to different LANs and WANs based on the network address. They specify how to identify nodes on a network and regulate the

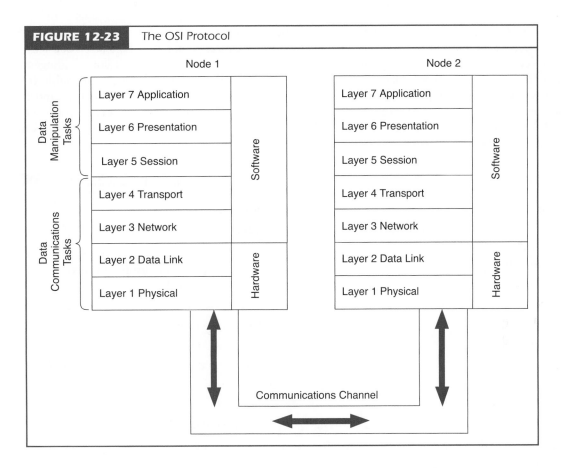

FIGURE 12-23 | The OSI Protocol

sequencing of messages to the nodes. In addition, this third layer describes how packet data are transferred between networks with different architectures, which permits the synchronization of data.

Transport Layer. The purpose of the **transport layer** is to ensure delivery of the entire file or message across individual networks and multiple networks, regardless of the number and type of dissimilar devices involved. If a transmission error is detected, this layer defines the retransmission methods to ensure the complete and accurate delivery of the message.

In addition, the transport layer seeks the connection between users that best meets the users' needs for message packeting and multiplexing messages. These protocols provide the logic for segmenting long messages into smaller units and, at the receiving end, reassembling the packets into the original message.

Session Layer. A **session layer** is a specific connection between two users or entities on the network. The purpose of this layer is to guarantee a correct and synchronized connection. At this level, the protocols for starting a session may require a user password to establish the legitimacy of the connection. Protocols may also determine priorities of sessions and rules for interrupting and reestablishing the session. For example, the transmission of a large document may be interrupted by a transmission of higher priority. Session protocols define the rules for such interrupts and the procedures for resuming the original transmission.

Presentation Layer. In the **presentation layer**, data in transit are often in a format that is very different from that required by the user's application. During transmission, data may be compressed to increase transfer speeds, blocked for efficiency, and encrypted for security. Presentation protocols provide the rules for editing, formatting, converting, and displaying data to the user's system.

Application Layer. The **application layer** provides the overall environment for the user or the user's application to access the network. This layer provides what are called "common application services." These services—common to all communicating applications—include protocols for network management, file transfer, and email. The uniqueness of user applications makes this layer the least amenable to general standards. By their very nature, protocols at this level impinge upon application structure and function. Consequently, these are the least rigorously defined rules. Most of the protocols here tend to be vendor defined. For example, an individual vendor's DBMS may provide the application layer protocols for managing file transfers.

KEY TERMS

algorithm (583)

American National Standards Institute (ANSI) (602)

application layer (608)

application-level firewalls (586)

bridges (593)

bus topology (596)

Caesar cipher (583)

carrier sensing (599)

certification authorities (CAs) (584)

client-server topology (597)

cookies (581)

data collision (598)

data encryption standard (DES) (583)

data link layer (606)

denial of service attack (582)

digital certificate (584)

digital envelope (584)

digital signature (584)

distribution level (576)

document name (567)

domain name (567)

dynamic virtual organization (577)

EDI for Administration, Commerce, and Transport (EDIFACT) (602)

electronic data interchange (EDI) (600)

electronic funds transfer (EFT) (605)

extranet (565)

firewall (586)

File Transfer Protocol (FTP) (569)

gateways (593)

hierarchical topology (595)

homepage (566)

Hypertext Markup Language (HTML) (570)

Hypertext Transfer Protocol (HTTP) (570)

Hypertext Transport Protocol-Next Generation (HTTP-NG_) (570)

Internet Message Access Protocol (IMAP) (569)

information level (574)

intelligent control agents (590)

International Standards Organization (569)

IP spoofing (582)

key (583)

local area networks (592)

network control (597)

network interface card (NIC) (593)

network layer (606)

network-level firewall (586)

network topology (592)

Network News Transfer Protocol (NNTP) (570)

Open System Interface (OSI) (569)

packet switching (564)

Private Communications Technology (PCT) (570)

Privacy Enhanced Mail (PEM) (570)

physical layer (606)

polling (598)

Post Office Protocol (POP) (569)

presentation layer (607)

privacy (588)

privacy violation (588)

protocol (567)

protocol prefix (567)

public key encryption (584)

public key infrastructure (PKI) (584)

ring topology (596)

risk (578)

Rivest-Shamir-Adleman (RSA) (584)

Safe Harbor Agreement (588)

servers (593)

session layer (607)

Secure Electronic Transmission (SET) (570)

Simple Network Mail Protocol (SNMP) (569)

Secure Sockets Layer (SSL) (570)

star topology (593)

subdirectory name (567)

SYNchronize-ACKnowledge (SYN-ACK) (582)

Transfer Control Protocol/Internet Protocol (TCP/IP) (569)

TELNET (569)

token passing (598)

transaction level (576)

transport layer (607)

Uniform Resource Locator (URL) (567)

value-added banks (VAB) (606)

value-added network (VAN) (590)

virtual private network (VPN) (565)

Web page (566)

Web sites (566)

wide area networks (WANs) (592)

XBRL (eXtensible Business Reporting Language) (571)

XBRL instance document (572)

XBRL taxonomies (572)

XML (eXtensible Markup Language) (571)

REVIEW QUESTIONS

1. What is packet switching?
2. What is a VPN?
3. Name the three types of addresses used on the Internet.
4. Describe the elements of an email address.
5. Networks would be inoperable without protocols. Explain their importance and what functions they perform.
6. What is the purpose of the TCP portion of TCP/IP?
7. What does the HTTP protocol do?
8. How do HTTP and HTTP-NG differ?
9. What is XML?
10. What is XBRL?
11. What is the World Wide Web?
12. What is meant by "intranet risk?"
13. What is a cookie?
14. What is a malicious program?
15. What is a digital certificate and what is it used for?
16. What are the two levels of a typical firewall system?
17. What is a seal of assurance?
18. Name and describe an audit implication of XBRL.
19. What is a VAN?
20. What must the accountant become familiar with in order to assess data integrity?
21. As many as three entities may be scrutinized in the audit of an EDI environment. Name them.
22. What is a LAN?
23. What is a WAN?
24. What is a NIC?
25. What is a server?
26. What is meant by the term "client-server topology"?
27. What is meant by data collision?
28. What is the purpose of EDI?
29. What is OSI?

DISCUSSION QUESTIONS

1. What purpose do protocols serve?
2. Explain the purpose of the two elements of the TCP/IP protocol.
3. Distinguish between the FTP and TELNET protocols.

4. Discuss the three levels of Internet business models.

5. What is a dynamic virtual organization?

6. Define risk in an electronic commerce setting.

7. How can Intranet expansion increase risk to an organization?

8. What are cookies and why are the used?

9. What security concerns pertain to cookies?

10. Discuss IP spoofing.

11. Explain a denial of service attack.

12. What is a digital envelope?

13. What is a digital signature?

14. What is a digital certificate? How is it different from a digital signature?

15. Distinguish between a network-level firewall and an application-level firewall.

16. What is a certification authority, and what are the implications for the accounting profession?

17. Discuss the key aspects of the following five seal-granting organizations: Better Business Bureau (BBB), TRUSTe, Veri-Sign, Inc., International

Computer Security Association (ICSA), and AICPA/CICA WebTrust.

18. Discuss three audit implications of XBRL.

19. Differentiate between a LAN and a WAN. Do you have either or both at your university or college?

20. As the information superhighway progresses and EDI increases in popularity, interfaces between organizational computers are becoming a necessity. Discuss what steps are being taken to foster these types of interfaces.

21. EDI systems tied into inventory control models in conjunction with just-in-time inventory systems have been said to be very beneficial in many ways; however, a mistake made by one firm in over ordering can mushroom into overproduction for many firms. Explain how this happen.

22. EFTs are widely used by payroll departments and by individuals to pay their personal bills, so why are they so infrequently used by businesses for cash disbursements?

23. Explain the purpose of each of the layers in the OSI protocol model.

MULTIPLE-CHOICE QUESTIONS

1. Which of the following statements is correct?
   a. TCP/IP is the basic protocol that permits communication between Internet sites.
   b. TCP/IP controls Web browsers that access the Web.
   c. TCP/IP is the document format used to produce Web pages.
   d. TCP/IP is used to transfer text files, programs, spreadsheets, and databases across the Internet.
   e. TCP/IP is a low-level encryption scheme used to secure transmissions in higher-level (HTTP) format.

2. Which of the following best describes a system of computers that connects the internal users of an organization distributed over a wide geographic area?
   a. LAN
   b. Internet
   c. decentralized network
   d. multidrop network
   e. intranet

3. Sniffer software is
   a. used by malicious Web sites to sniff data from cookies stored on the user's hard drive.
   b. used by network administrators to analyze network traffic.
   c. used by bus topology intranets to sniff for carriers before transmitting a message to avoid data collisions.
   d. an illegal program downloaded from the Web to sniff passwords from the encrypted data of Internet customers.
   e. illegal software for decoding encrypted messages transmitted over a shared Intranet channel.

4. Which of the following statements is true?
   a. Cookies were originally intended to facilitate advertising on the Web.
   b. Cookies always contain encrypted data.
   c. Cookies are text files and never contain encrypted data.

d. Cookies contain the URLs of sites visited by the user.

e. Web browsers cannot function without cookies.

5. A message that is contrived to appear to be coming from a trusted or authorized source is called

a. a denial of service attack.

b. digital signature forging.

c. Internet protocol spoofing.

d. URL masquerading.

e. a SYN-ACK packet.

6. A digital signature

a. is the encrypted mathematical value of the message sender's name.

b. is derived from the digest of a document that has been encrypted with the sender's private key.

c. is derived from the digest of a document that has been encrypted with the sender's public key.

d. is the computed digest of the sender's digital certificate.

e. allows digital messages to be sent over an analog telephone line.

7. Which of the following statements about the client-server model is correct?

a. It is best suited to the token-ring topology because the random-access method used by this topology detects data collisions.

b. It distributes both data and processing tasks to the server node. The client-server model can use the bus or ring topology.

c. It is most effective when used as a bus topology because its deterministic access method avoids collisions and prevents data loss during transmissions.

d. It is more efficient than the bus or ring topologies because it transmits an entire file of records to the requesting node rather than only a single record.

e. It is not used in conjunction with either the bus or ring topologies.

8. Which of the following statements is correct?

a. A bridge is used to connect a LAN and a WAN.

b. Packet switching combines the messages of multiple users into a "packet" for transmission. At the receiving end, the packet is disassembled into individual messages and distributed to the user.

c. The decision to partition a database assumes that no identifiable primary user exists in the organization.

d. Message switching is used to establish temporary connections between network devices for the duration of a communications session.

e. A deadlock is a temporary phenomenon that disrupts transaction processing. It will resolve itself when the primary computer completes processing its transaction and releases the data needed by the other nodes.

PROBLEMS

1. Encryption
The coded message that follows is an encrypted message from Brutus to the Roman Senate. It was produced using the Caesar Cipher method in which each letter is shifted by a fixed number of places (determined by the key value).

OHWV GR MXOLXV RQ PRQGDB PDUFK 48

GUHVV: WRJD FDVXDO (EBRG)

Required:
Determine the key used to produce the coded message above and decode it.

2. Encryption
a. Develop a Caesar Cipher-type encryption algorithm with a little more complexity in it. For example, the algorithm could alternatively shift the cleartext letters positive and negative by the amount of the key value. Variations on this are limitless.

b. Select a single-digit key.

c. Code a short message using the algorithm and key.

d. Hand in to your instructor the algorithm, key, cleartext, and ciphertext.

e. Optional: Your instructor will randomly redistribute to the class the ciphertext messages completed in part d above. You are to decode the message you receive as an additional assignment.

3. Seals of Assurance

Visit 10 Web sites that sell products or services and record the following for each:

a. The URL

b. Did the site issue you a cookie?

c. Did the site have a published privacy policy?

d. Does the site reserve the right to distribute or sell customer data?

e. Does the site use encryption for transmission of personal/financial data?

4. XBRL

John Ozment, director of special projects and analysis for Ozment's company, is responsible for preparing corporate financial analyses and monthly statements and reviewing and presenting to upper management the financial impacts of proposed strategies. Data for such financial analyses and are obtained from operations and financial databases through direct queries by Ozment's department staff. Reports and charts for presentations are then prepared by hand and typed. Multiple copies are prepared and distributed to various users. The pressure on Ozment's group has intensified as demand for more and more current information increases. A solution to this reporting problem must be found.

The systems department wants to develop a proprietary software package to produce the reports automatically. The project would require a considerable programming investment by the company. Ozment is concerned about the accuracy, completeness, and currency of data in automatically produced reports. He has heard about a reporting system called XBRL and wonders whether a new system based on this technology would not be more effective and reliable.

Required:

a. Research the current state of XBRL and determine if this technology is appropriate for internal reporting projects such as this.

b. Identify the enhancements to current information and reporting that the company could realize by using XBRL.

c. Discuss any data integrity, internal control, and reporting concerns associated with XBRL.

5. Certification Authority Licensing

Research the current state of certification authority licensing in the United States and Europe. Write a brief report of your findings.

6. Privacy

Visit 10 Web sites that sell products or services and record the URL of each. Evaluate each site's published privacy policy in terms of the conditions need for compliance with the Safe Harbor Agreement. Write a report of your findings.

7. Electronic Data Interchange

The purchase order for one firm is the source document for the sales order of another firm. Consider the following purchase order and sales order data elements stored for two firms. Discuss any differences that may be problematic in transferring information between the two firms.

Purchasing Firm:
GH BETTIS
A Division of Galveston-Houston Corp.
1200 Post Oak Blvd.
P.O. Box 4768
Houston, TX 77637-9877

Data Elements
Vendor Number
Vendor Name
Vendor Address
Vendor City
Vendor State
Vendor Country
Vendor Zip Code
Purchase Order No.
Date
Shipment Destination Code
Vendor Part No.
Item Description
Quantity Ordered
Unit Price
Total

Selling Firm:

Oakland Steel Company
469 Lakeland Blvd.
Chicago, IL 60613-8888

Data Elements

Customer Number
Customer Name
Customer Address
Customer City
Customer State
Customer Country
Customer Zip Code
Purchase Order No.
Sales Order No.
Date
Shipping Company
Vendor Part No.
Item Description
Quantity Ordered
Unit Price
Total
Discount Offered
Tax
Freight Charges

8. Internal Controls Assessment and Electronic Data Interchange:

Gresko Toys Factory
(Prepared by Robertos Karahannas, Lehigh University)

Gresko Toys was started in the early 1960s by Mr. and Mrs. Gresko. Initially, the company was small and few toys were produced. The talent and skills of Mr. Gresko were by far the major assets of the company. Toys were mainly made of wood and had few or no electronic parts; they were mainly manually operated and included toy cars, several kinds of dolls, and toy guns. Gresko toys became part of the Pennsylvania tradition. Kids loved them and parents had no choice but to buy them.

Gresko toys quickly expanded, and by 1969 it reported a sales volume of $400,000, $50,000 of which was profit. Such profits caught the attention of other businesspeople, who began entering the market. The innovative spirit of some competitors through the introduction of fancy, battery-operated toys stole some of Gresko's market share. As the competition became more intense, the Greskos saw their market share declining even further. Children liked battery-operated toys.

Mr. Gresko saw this as both a threat and a challenge. He would not give up, however. He knew that he needed better machinery to make competitive toys. With a loan from the local bank and his savings, he sought and bought what he needed. After a period of training and test marketing, Gresko toys were again in the market and boosting sales. However, the company was generating orders that the factory could not handle. The workforce rose from a low of 50 to a high of 350 people. Most of the workforce was on the factory floor. More equipment was purchased and the company has been expanding since.

Today, the company sells $20 million of toys per year. The president of the company is Mrs. Gresko. Mr. Gresko felt that he should be on the factory floor managing production. Under him are the purchasing agent supervising a buyer, the warehouse manager managing two inventory clerks, a chief engineer, and a supervisor who is in charge of the factory workers. The controller of the company is Randi, the Greskos' elder daughter. An accounting clerk, a cashier, and a personnel manager work for her. Finally, Bob, the Greskos' only son, is the sales manager. A credit manager and two salespeople work for him.

Company Information

At present, the company's profit margin is 9 percent, only 2 percent below the industry average. According to Mr. Gresko, $850,000 in sales was lost last year because of insufficient inventory of parts. Because the seasonal nature of the market and the short popularity span of most toys, Gresko customers require fast delivery of the ordered toys; if the parts are not available, it takes at least two weeks to get the paperwork ready, order the parts, and have them delivered by the suppliers. Some customers cannot wait that long; others order the toys and subsequently cancel the order if it takes too long to complete. Often orders are accepted on the assumption that the parts are readily available in the warehouse; when they are not, orders are delayed for weeks. A missing part not only delays an order, but the whole assembly line.

To alleviate the problem, many parts are rushed in, which raises the cost of the toys tremendously.

The fine quality of the products allows for slight price increases to make up for part of the extra cost, but customers have already complained about such price fluctuations.

The Greskos are on good terms with their suppliers. After all, the market is so competitive that a reliable supplier is crucial to a firm's survival. Most of their major suppliers are located in Pennsylvania, where the Greskos have about 35 percent of the market share. However, those suppliers deal with the Greskos' competitors as well. There are about a dozen suppliers with whom the Greskos deal; eight of them supply about 95 percent of all inventory parts.

Even though good supplier relations are crucial to Gresko Toys, suppliers have often complained about Gresko's promptness in paying. The Greskos demand on-time delivery; the payment of the supplier invoice, however, is usually not timely. Mr. Gresko said that he does not have the time to run from the factory to the accounting department to make sure payments are on time. Late payments, however, also mean a loss of the 2 percent discount offered by the suppliers for early payment.

Besides resulting in lost sales, insufficient inventory of parts also delays the whole assembly line. Workers spend much time switching jobs. A just-in-time inventory system would, according to Mr. Gresko, be more appropriate for the factory. If the parts were available in the warehouse, the machines could be set up on an assembly-line fashion and operated on scheduled runs. But the fact that the necessary parts are frequently missing, forcing production to switch to another job, is a major obstacle to a just-in-time inventory system.

The Purchasing Cycle

Gresko Toys is very involved in purchasing the parts used in the production of toys. The company uses a periodic inventory system. When sales orders are received, Bob Gresko sends a copy to the production floor. This copy is used to trigger production as well as to indicate the potential need of parts not available in inventory. The inventory clerks search for parts; when parts are out of stock, the inventory clerks issue two copies of a purchase requisition. This requisition is approved by Mr. Gresko before a purchase order is issued. One copy is sent to the purchasing manager and the other to the accounting department.

The buyer checks the suppliers' prices for the needed parts. Based on cost as well as past experience

with a particular supplier, two suppliers are recommended. The purchasing manager subsequently decides on the supplier, and a purchase order is issued. Four copies of the purchase order are issued. The first copy is sent to the supplier, the second is filed by the purchasing manager, the third is sent to the warehouse, and the fourth is sent to the accounting department. All purchase order copies are filed by supplier number.

Approximately a week after the initiation of the purchase the parts are received. The warehouse manager, along with the inventory clerks, inspect and count the received parts. The purchase order copy previously received by the purchasing manager is used as the basis of comparison. A receiving report in three parts is prepared. If prices and quantities received agree with those ordered and with the information on the packing slip received by the carrier, the parts are accepted. If any differences exist, Mr. Gresko is called in to decide whether to accept or reject the parts. On many occasions, acceptance of parts will be delayed for days until the suppliers are informed and an agreement is reached.

One copy of the receiving report is sent to the purchasing manager and another to the accounting department. The original copy is kept at the warehouse. The accounting clerk files the receiving report along with the purchase requisition and the purchase order by supplier number. The clerk also prepares the necessary journal entry and credits the related supplier in the subsidiary ledger. When the supplier sends the invoice, the accounting clerk matches the information to the purchase requisition, purchase order, and receiving report and prepares a disbursement voucher. This voucher is used for two purposes. It initiates the journal entry for the disbursement of cash, and it is used by the cashier to issue a check. Randi Gresko, as well as Mrs. Gresko, must sign the checks before they are sent to the suppliers.

Electronic Data Interchange

In search of anything that could improve the present system at the Gresko Toys factory, Mr. Gresko came across the EDI system. One of his suppliers had attended a conference on EDI and had supplied Mr. Gresko with the conference material. Looking at the present system, Mr. Gresko tried to find EDI applications that would benefit the company's operations and at the same time improve its financial position.

For EDI to be implemented, certain databases will need to be established. An inventory master file with all relevant information is the key to the system. Predetermined order quantities and minimum inventory levels will need to be set for each item based on forecasts. At the warehouse, the inventory clerks will be constantly updating this database. When inventory levels drop below acceptable levels, an EDI purchase requisition will be issued to the purchasing department.

A supplier master file with related information on supplier performance will be accessed to identify potential suppliers. Depending on how advanced the system is, the computer or the purchasing manager will choose the proper supplier and issue an EDI order. This means that the factory's suppliers will also need to be using EDI.

Various ways of developing EDI links with suppliers are available. In the Gresko case, developing an independent system seems more appropriate; it is cheaper and perhaps easier to convince suppliers to join in. Software is readily available in the market and is easy to set up. Someone, however, should help set up the EDI links with the suppliers.

Once an EDI order is issued, the supplier will receive the message instantaneously. The open purchase order will be kept in a database until the receipt of the parts. Any changes to the order can be made by accessing the particular transmitted order and making the change. Suppliers can send the parts as well as their invoices more quickly. An EDI invoice can be sent to the Gresko factory upon shipment.

On arrival of the parts, the receiving clerk will prepare a receiving report and file it in a receiving database file. This report will be used to verify prices by accessing the purchase order. Credit terms, volume discounts, trade allowances, and other adjustments to quoted prices can be settled through EDI-transmitted messages. If adjustments from disagreements occur, the transaction is entered into the adjusted database file. The inventory master file is also updated, and the open purchase order is closed. In addition, the supplier-history file and the accounts payable file are updated, and an evaluated receipts settlement (ERS) is established.

An ERS is a database containing records to be used for the payment of suppliers. The EDI order is matched against the receiving and adjusted database files. Such a comparison creates a payment-input file that indicates the scheduled payment date within which any discount can be obtained, the latest possible payment date, and the remittance record for such payments.

At the beginning of every day, the treasurer (who presently does not exist) should receive a listing of the payment input file; this listing will indicate what has to be paid and when. The treasurer will initiate an EDI payment pending the approval of Mrs. Gresko. Upon approval and the transmission of the payment, the supplier records as well as the accounts payable records will be automatically updated. For an EFT to occur, the banks that serve Gresko and its suppliers will also need to be using EDI. If such intermediary banks are not using EDI, Gresko and its suppliers will need to rely on a manual system of cash disbursement to settle their transactions.

Conclusion
Mr. Gresko has hired you to look at the present accounting system and his suggested EDI implementation plan. He wants you to identify the problem areas and look into the feasibility of setting up EDI links with the company's suppliers.

Required:
a. Draw a document flowchart of the present accounting system at Gresko.
b. What control problems, if any, exist in the accounting system?
c. Draw a document flowchart of the accounting system of the Gresko Toys factory using EDI as suggested by Mr. Gresko.
d. Do some research on your own. What EDI options, other than the one suggested by Mr. Gresko, are available to the Gresko Toys factory?
e. Discuss the possible implementation of an EDI system at the Gresko Toys factory. What areas should Mr. Gresko concentrate on, and what are the related issues associated with implementing EDI at the factory?

9. Electronic Fraud
In a recent financial fraud case, city employees in Brooklyn, New York, accessed electronic databases to defraud the city of $20 million. Several employees in collusion with the former deputy tax collector completely erased or reduced $13 million in property taxes and $7 million in accrued interest

owed by taxpayers. In exchange for this service, the taxpayers paid the employees involved bribes of 10 to 30 percent of their bills.

Required.
Discuss the control techniques that could prevent or detect this fraud.

10. Santa's Attic.com

Santa'sAttic.com is an online retailer/manufacturer of children's toys. Its main competitors are larger EC toy companies including Amazon.com; Yahoo Shopping, which includes ToysRUs.com and KBKids.com; and all of the other retail stores with online shopping. It has a low market share compared to the industry leaders, and is possibly a victim of Internet fraud. The CEO of Santa'sAttic.com has noticed that the level of accounts receivable has been quite high in comparison to prior years. He is wondering if this is a sign of weak internal controls. He has also heard through the grapevine that some of his customers were noticing unauthorized charges on their credit cards, and is wondering if there may be online security issues to deal with as well. For this reason, you have been contacted to help Santa'sAttic.com restructure its company to prevent possible company failure.

Santa'sAttic.com employs 100 individuals, 75 of which work directly on the manufacturing line and 25 of which hold administrative positions. Its customer base consists mainly of individuals, but also smaller toy stores, day care centers, and schools. Santa'sAttic.com works on a cash basis with its customers and accepts all major credit cards. It has running credit balances with all of its suppliers. Its credit terms are 2/10, n30. Santa'sAttic.com currently has only one warehouse, which is located in Cooperstown, New York. Being the technical genius that he is, the vice president of marketing took it upon himself to design the company Web site. The Web site has pages where customers can view all of the products and prices. There is a virtual shopping cart available for each customer once he or she has set up a demographical information account. If the customer chooses to make a purchase, he or she simply clicks on the direct link to the shopping cart from the product that he or she wishes to purchase and proceeds to the checkout. Here the customer is prompted to choose a payment method and enter the shipping address. Once this information has been entered, the customer chooses a shipping method. All shipping is

done through U.S. Mail, UPS, Federal Express, Airborne Express, or certified mail. The customer is then informed of the total price and the date to expect shipment.

Within the purchasing system, Santa'sAttic.com purchases raw materials for production, such as plastics, wood, metal, and certain fabrics. There is no formal purchasing department at Santa'sAttic.com. Judy, the inventory clerk in the warehouse department, is responsible for all purchasing activity. Within the warehouse department, Judy has access to the inventory records and knows when certain materials have to be repurchased. If materials are needed, she prepares a single purchase requisition and also five copies of the purchase order form. Judy includes all of the necessary information on all copies of the form, including the material to be purchased, the price of the material, the quantity needed, and the requested delivery date. Once completed, two copies of the form are sent to the vendor along with the order. One is placed in the open purchase order file in the warehouse, and one is used to update the inventory records that are also kept within the warehouse department. The final copy is forwarded to the receiving department.

The materials are received by Harry, the receiving clerk, who creates four copies of a receiving report based on the packing slip and purchase order information. Two of these receiving reports are forwarded to the warehouse, where one is used to update inventory records and the other is filed. One copy of the receiving report is also maintained within the receiving department and is filed along with the packing slip and the purchase order. The final copy is sent to the accounts payable department, where it is reconciled with the vendor invoice.

Once the receiving report and the vendor invoice are reconciled in the accounts payable department, the liability is posted to the purchases journal and the total amount due is paid to the vendor. Finally, both the receiving report and the invoice are filed within the accounts payable department and the liability is posted to the general ledger by Joanna, the accounts payable clerk.

Santa'sAttic.com's production workers each have timecards that they punch at a punch-in station in the morning when they arrive, and again in the evening when they leave. The punch-in station is located at the entrance to the plant and is not monitored. At the end of the week, the supervisor authorizes the timecards by reviewing them and signing them, and then sends the timecards to cash disbursements. Supervisors do not keep their own attendance records. Rose, in cash disbursements, receives the timecards and reconciles them with personnel records on the company database to verify the timecards for accuracy. All personnel records are maintained in a database. Access to the database is restricted. Personnel can update the records only once a year. Rose's only view displays employee demographic information and does not allow access to salary information. Rose prepares the paychecks and signs them. She then prepares the payroll register using only information gained from the timecards. Sally in accounts payable receives a copy of the payroll register and uses it to update the general ledger. Accounts payable receives no information besides the payroll register. Rose, in cash disbursements, hands the prepared paychecks to the supervisors of each department for distribution. All checks are written directly from the company's only cash account. Supervisors distribute the checks directly to the employees and themselves.

Engaging in electronic commerce has exposed Santa'sAttic.com to a whole new nature of risks within its real-time revenue cycle. A customer has the option of paying for the product by credit card or personal check. Upon entering the credit card information, it becomes attached to the customer's email file. This information includes the type of card, the customer's name as it appears on the card, the credit card number, and the expiration date. Once an order is placed, an employee reviews the order in question, verifies credit, and enters the transaction into Santa'sAttic.com's main database.

The main problem with this system is that orders have been placed with the company where the customer in question honestly denies ever submitting orders. It turns out that many of these orders have been placed by their children, without the customer's knowledge. The children were able to gain access to their parent's account after the system recognized cookies in the hard drive. When the children went to the Web site, the page recognized them as the users of the account and gave them authorized access to make purchases.

Another problem with the information in the revenue cycle has been that hackers have been able to enter the database and obtain information concerning customers. This unauthorized access has sent top management into a frenzy knowing that their customer information is insecure.

Required:

a. Discuss the control and security weaknesses in this system.

b. Make specific recommendations for improving controls.

part 4

SYSTEMS DEVELOPMENT ACTIVITIES

chapter 13

Managing the Systems Development Life Cycle*

LEARNING OBJECTIVES

After studying this chapter, you should:

- Be able to identify the key stages in the SDLC.
- Recognize how a firm's business strategy will shape its information system.
- Understand the relationship between strategic systems planning and legacy systems.
- Understand what transpires during systems analysis.
- Understand the TELOS model for assessing project feasibility.
- Be familiar with cost-benefit analysis issues related to information systems projects.
- Understand the role of accountants in the SDLC.

A responsive, user-oriented information system is a valuable asset of the modern business organization. Well-designed systems can increase business performance by reducing inventories, eliminating nonvalue-added activities, improving customer service, and coordinating supply chain activities.

This chapter examines several topics related to the process by which organizations acquire information systems. It begins with an overview to the systems development life cycle (SDLC). This multistage process guides organization management through the development and/or purchase of information systems. Next, the chapter presents the key issues pertaining to developing a systems strategy including its relationship to the strategic business plan, the current legacy situation, and feedback from the user community. The chapter provides a methodology for assessing the feasibility of proposed projects and for selecting individual projects to go forward for construction and delivery to their users. The chapter concludes by reviewing the role of accountants in managing the SDLC.

---

* This chapter was co-authored by Jiri Polak, Ph.D., Deloitte & Touche, and Vojtech Merunka, Ph.D., Deloitte & Touche.

THE SYSTEMS DEVELOPMENT LIFE CYCLE

Moderate and large firms with unique information needs often develop information systems in-house. That is to say that IT professionals within the firm design and program the systems. A greater number of smaller companies and large firms with relatively standardized information needs opt to purchase information systems from software vendors. Both approaches represent significant financial and operational risks. The **SDLC** shown in Figure 13-1 is a model for reducing this risk through careful planning, execution, control, and documentation of key activities. The five phases of this model are outlined below. Systems strategy and project initiation are discussed in this chapter. The remaining phases are the topics of Chapter 14.

FIGURE 13-1 | Systems Development Life Cycle

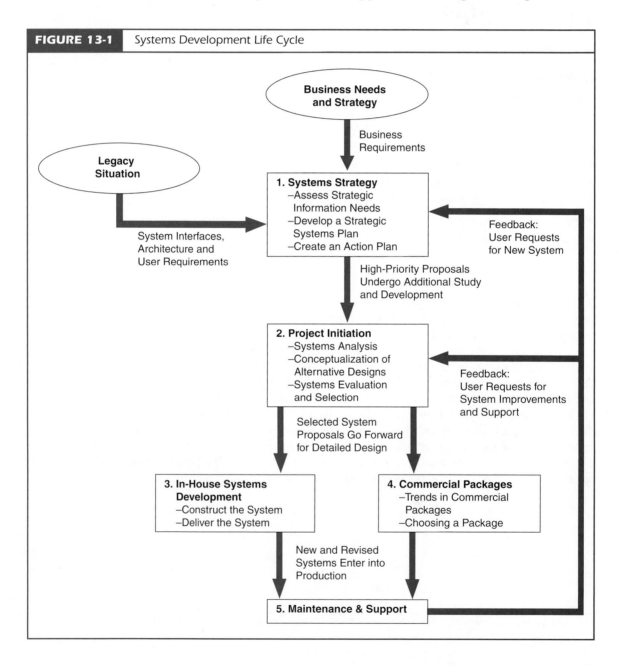

Systems Strategy. The first step in the SDLC is to develop a systems strategy, which requires understanding the strategic business needs of the organization. This may be derived from the organization's mission statement, an analysis of competitive pressures on the firm, and the nature of current and anticipated market conditions. These needs reflect the organization's current position relative to where it needs to be in the long term to maintain strategic advantage. In addition, project management must consider the information systems' implications pertaining to legacy systems and concerns registered through user feedback. A strategic plan for meeting these various and complex needs, along with a timetable for implementation of selected systems, is produced.

Project Initiation. Project initiation is the process by which systems proposals are assessed for consistency with the strategic systems plan and evaluated in terms of their feasibility and cost-benefit characteristics. Alternative conceptual designs are considered and those selected enter the construct phase of the SDLC. Depending upon the nature of the project and the needs of the organization, the proposal will require in-house development, a commercial package, or both.

In-House Development. As mentioned earlier, some organizations have unique information needs that can be adequately met only through internal development. The in-house development step includes analyzing user needs, designing processes and databases, creating user views, programming the applications, and testing and implementing the completed system.

Commercial Packages. When the nature of the project and the needs of the user permit, most organizations will seek a pre-coded commercial software package rather than develop a new system from scratch. A number of advantages accrue to the organization that can implement commercial software. These include lower initial cost, shorter implementation time, better controls, and rigorous testing by the vendor. All of these benefits translate into cost savings to the user. This process, however, is not without risk. Formal procedures need to be followed to ensure that the user gets a package that adequately meets his or her needs and is compatible with existing systems.

Maintenance and Support. Maintenance involves both acquiring and implementing the latest software versions of commercial packages and making in-house modifications to existing systems to accommodate changing user needs. Maintenance may be relatively trivial such as modifying an application to produce a new report, or more extensive, such as programming new functionality into a system. The feedback loops from maintenance to the project initiation and systems strategy steps, respectively, despite these relationships.

Traditionally, systems maintenance was viewed as a separate and distinct stage of the SDLC that could last five to ten years. Modern businesses in highly competitive industries, however, see frequent changes in technology and much shorter system life spans. Indeed, this is becoming the norm for many organizations. Many complex systems today are developed and implemented using an incremental approach that integrates maintenance and new development. System maintenance is often viewed as the first phase of a new development cycle. Existing (maintained) applications are the prototypes for their new versions. Thus, instead of implementing an application in a single "big-bang" release, modern systems are delivered in parts continuously and quickly as smaller releases that can more accurately reflect changing business needs. Another aspect of modern maintenance includes establishing a user support infrastructure. This could include helpdesk services, providing user training and education classes, and documenting user feedback pertaining to problems and system errors.

PARTICIPANTS IN SYSTEMS DEVELOPMENT

The participants in systems development can be classified into three broad groups: systems professionals, end users, and stakeholders.

Systems professionals are systems analysts, systems designers, and programmers. These individuals actually build the system. They gather facts about problems with the current system, analyze these facts, and formulate a solution to solve the problems. The product of their efforts is a new system.

End users are those for whom the system is built. There are the many users at all levels in an organization. These include managers, operations personnel, accountants, and internal auditors. In some organizations, it is difficult to find someone who is not a user. During systems development, systems professionals work with the primary users to obtain an understanding of the users' problems and a clear statement of their needs.

As defined in Chapter 1, **stakeholders** are individuals either within or outside the organization who have an interest in the system but are not end users. These include accountants, internal auditors, external auditors, and the internal steering committee that oversees systems development.[1]

SYSTEMS STRATEGY

The objective of **systems strategy** is to link individual system projects to the strategic objectives of the firm. Firms that take systems strategy seriously establish a steering committee to provide guidance and oversight for systems projects. The composition of the **steering committee** may include the chief executive officer, the chief financial officer, the chief information officer, senior management from user areas, the internal auditor, and senior management from computer services. External parties, such as management consultants and the firm's external auditors, may also supplement the committee. This committee is involved not only in developing system strategy but in every major phase of the SDLC.

The strategy stage in the SDLC consists of three fundamental tasks: assessing the organization's strategic information needs, developing a strategic systems plan, and creating actions plans. The inputs to the systems strategy phase are the business plan, the legacy system situation, and feedback from the user community. In this section we see how these pieces come together to form a comprehensive strategic plan that will generate action plans for selecting and developing individual systems projects.

ASSESS STRATEGIC INFORMATION NEEDS

Strategic systems planning involves the allocation of systems resources at the macro level, which usually deals with a time frame of three to five years. This process is very similar to budgeting resources for other strategic activities, such as product development, plant expansions, market research, and manufacturing technology. For most companies, key inputs in developing a sound systems strategy include the strategic business needs of the organization, the legacy system situation, and user feedback. Each of these is examined next.

---

1 Accountants and auditors are end users of some systems, but are stakeholders in all accounting information systems.

STRATEGIC BUSINESS NEEDS

All functional areas should support the business strategy of the organization. Because this is most certainly true for the information systems function, we begin with an overview of business strategy. We will briefly review some common aspects of business strategy that bear directly on developing a sound systems strategy.

Vision and Mission

Developing a systems strategy requires an understanding of top management's vision, which has shaped the organization's business strategy. Many CEOs communicate their strategic vision through a formal mission statement. In some cases, however, top management's strategic view for the company is not fully articulated or formulated. Organizations without a well-considered mission statement might be managed and directed by individuals who lack a clear vision for the future. Not surprisingly, companies in this situation often lack a viable systems strategy. Consequently, their management is prone to making knee-jerk responses to information systems needs that emerge out of crisis rather than planning.

Industry and Competency Analysis

In addition to needing a durable vision component, the strategic planning process is driven by many dynamic business factors including consolidations, competition, rapidly evolving technology, changes in the regulatory landscape, and increasing demands from stakeholders. Two strategic planning methodologies used to capture information on these factors are *industry analysis* and *competency analysis*.

Industry analysis provides management with an analysis of the driving forces that affect their industry and their organization's performance. Such analysis offers a fact-based perspective on the industry's important trends, significant risks, and potential opportunities that may impact the business's performance.

Competency analysis provides a complete picture of the organization's effectiveness as seen via four strategic filters: resources, infrastructure, products/services, and customers. By assessing these factors, an organization can develop an accurate view of its relative strengths, weaknesses, and core competencies. The analysis helps in developing strategic options, which are based on an understanding of the future environment and the firm's core competencies. Strategic opportunities may include market-entry options or new product development options.

In developing a business strategy many organizations perform competency analysis on their key competitors as well as potential business partners. By knowing the strengths and weaknesses of competitors, management can identify imminent threats and spot new business opportunities for growth. Similarly, by examining the competencies of potential trading partners, strategic gaps and/or synergies from the partnership may materialize.

LEGACY SYSTEMS

Legacy systems are comprised of applications, databases, and business processes that are currently in full operation. Often, these are complicated systems to maintain and enhance. Even in modern companies, the information system is usually a mixture of old and modern technologies, which are critical to the organization's business success.

Legacy components need to be mapped to current business processes to determine the extent to which they support the mission of the company. This evaluation, together with an assessment of future strategic business needs, will enable management to develop the migration strategy needed to move from legacy systems to future systems with minimum disruption to business operations.

Developing an Architecture Description

System architecture is the structure of components, their interrelationships, and the principles and guidelines governing their design and evolution over time. An **architecture description** is a formal description of an information system, organized in a way that identifies the structural properties of the system and defines the components or building blocks that make up the overall information system. This description provides the elements for a plan from which new systems can be developed and commercial packages procured that will work together as harmonious components of the overall system. It also provides the technical foundation for a legacy migration strategy. Finally, the technical advantages that result from an architecture description translate into important business benefits, which are presented in Table 13-1.

USER FEEDBACK

Assessing user feedback involves identifying areas of user needs, preparing written proposals, evaluating each proposal's feasibility and contribution to the business plan, and prioritizing individual projects. User feedback at this point pertains to substantial, perceived problems rather than minor, systems modifications, which are dealt with at a later point in the SDLC. Next, we examine the following key phases of this activity.

1. Recognizing the problem.
2. Defining the problem.
3. Specifying system objectives.
4. Determining project feasibility.
5. Preparing a formal project proposal.

Recognizing the Problem

The need for a new, improved information system may be manifested through various symptoms. In the early stages of a problem, these symptoms may seem vague and innocuous or may go unrecognized. However, as the underlying source of the problem grows in

TABLE 13-1	Business Benefits from Architecture Description

Efficient IT operation
- Lower software development, support, and maintenance costs.
- Increased portability of applications.
- Improved interoperability and easier system and network management.

Ability to address critical enterprise-wide issues.
- Easier upgrade and exchange of system components.
- Better return on existing investment and reduced risk for future investment.
- Reduced complexity in IT infrastructure.
- Maximum return on investment in existing IT infrastructure.
- The flexibility to make, buy, or outsource IT solutions.
- Reduced risk overall in new investment and the costs of IT ownership.

Improved procurement
- Buying decisions are simpler because the information governing procurement is readily available in a coherent plan.
- The procurement process is faster, maximizing procurement speed and flexibility without sacrificing architectural coherence.

severity so do its symptoms, until they are alarmingly apparent. At this point, operations may have reached a state of crisis. Therefore, the point at which the problem is recognized is important. This is often a function of the philosophy of a firm's management. The reactive management philosophy characterizes an extreme position; in contrast with this is the philosophy of proactive management.

Reactive management responds to problems only when they reach a crisis state and can no longer be ignored. This approach creates a great deal of pressure to solve the problem quickly once it has been recognized. Too often, this results in hurried analysis, incomplete problem identification, shortcuts in design, poor user participation, and the final product of a generally suboptimal solution.

Proactive management stays alert to the subtle signs of problems and aggressively looks for ways to improve the organization's systems. This management style is more likely to recognize symptoms early and, therefore, implement better solutions. Early problem detection avoids the crisis stage and provides the necessary time for a complete and thorough study.

Who reports problem symptoms? Typically, lower-level managers and operations personnel first report symptoms. Being in continuous contact with day-to-day operations, these individuals are quick to notice operational difficulties with customers, suppliers, and the financial community. As a result, most systems requests originate with lower-level management.

Defining the Problem

The manager must avoid the temptation to take a leap in logic from symptom recognition to problem definition. One must keep an open mind and avoid drawing conclusions about the nature of the problem that may channel attention and resources in the wrong direction. For example, increased product returns, excessive delays in product shipments to customers, excessive overtime for operations personnel, and slow inventory turnover rates are all problem symptoms. These are evidence of underlying problems, but they do not, in themselves, define the problems. The manager must learn enough about the problem to pursue a solution intelligently. The manager cannot, however, collect all the information needed to define the problem accurately and specify a solution. This would require a detailed system evaluation. The manager must specify the nature of the problem as he or she sees it based on the nature of the difficulties identified.

The manager reports this problem definition to the computer systems professionals within the firm. This begins an interactive process between the systems professionals and the user, which results in a formal project proposal that will go before the steering committee for approval. The following three stages in the planning phase—specifying system objectives, determining project feasibility, and preparing a formal project proposal—represent the cooperative efforts of the manager and the systems professional.

Specifying System Objectives

User information requirements need to be specified in terms of operational objectives for the new information system. For example, the user may need an order entry system that can handle 5,000 transactions per hour, maintain up-to-the-minute inventory status, and allow all orders received by 2 PM to be shipped to the customer by the end of the day. At this point, we need only define the objectives in general terms. More precise system requirements will be developed later in the SDLC.

Preliminary Project Feasibility

A preliminary **project feasibility** study is conducted at this early stage to determine how best to proceed with the project. By assessing the major constraints on the proposed system, management can evaluate the project's feasibility, or likelihood for success, before committing large amounts of financial and human resources. The acronym **TELOS** provides guidance for assessing project feasibility. The term stands for *technical*, *economic*, *legal*, *operational*, and *schedule* feasibility. Each of these issues is described below.

Technical feasibility is concerned with whether the system can be developed under existing technology or if new technology is needed. As a general proposition, the technology in the marketplace is far ahead of most firms' ability to apply it. Therefore, from an availability viewpoint, technical feasibility is not usually an issue. For most firms, the real issue is their desire and ability to apply available technology. Given that technology is the physical basis for most of the system's design features, this aspect bears heavily on the overall feasibility of the proposed system.

Economic feasibility pertains to the availability of funds to complete the project. At this point, we are concerned with management's financial commitment to this project in view of other competing capital projects under consideration. The level of available economic support directly impacts the operational nature and scope of the proposed system. Later, in the system justification and selection step, cost-benefit analysis is used to identify the best system design for the cost.

Legal feasibility involves ensuring that the proposed system is not in conflict with the company's ability to discharge its legal responsibilities. In previous chapters, we have studied the need to comply with the control requirement laid down in the Foreign Corrupt Practices Act of 1977, SAS 78, and Sarbanes-Oxley legislation. In addition, many regulations and statutes deal with invasion of privacy and the confidentiality of stored information. We must be certain the proposed system does not breach any legal boundaries.

Operational feasibility pertains to the degree of compatibility between the firm's existing procedures and personnel skills and the operational requirements of the new system. Implementing the new system may require adopting new procedures and retraining operations personnel. The question that must be answered is: can enough procedural changes be made, personnel retrained, and new skills obtained to make the system operationally feasible?

Schedule feasibility relates to the firm's ability to implement the project within an acceptable time. This feasibility factor impacts both the scope of the project and whether it will be developed in-house or purchased from a software vendor. If the project, as originally envisioned, cannot be produced internally by the target date, then its design, its acquisition method, or the target date must be changed.

Preparing a Formal Project Proposal

The **systems project proposal** provides management with a basis for deciding whether or not to proceed with the project. The formal proposal serves two purposes. First, it summarizes the findings of the study conducted to this point into a general recommendation for a new or modified system. This enables management to evaluate the perceived problem along with the proposed system as a feasible solution. Second, the proposal outlines the linkage between the objectives of the proposed system and the business objectives of the firm. It shows that the proposed, new system complements the strategic direction of the firm. Figure 13-2 shows an example of a project proposal.

DEVELOP A STRATEGIC SYSTEMS PLAN

After collecting and documenting input from the business plan, legacy issues, and user feedback, members of the steering committee and systems professionals evaluate the pros

FIGURE 13-2	System Project Proposal

Project Proposal

Requested by: _____*J.J. Johnson*_____ Date: _*11/13/04*_

Nature of System Requested: _*Inventory Control System*_____

_____

Reason for New System: _*Better manage inventory, reduce obsolescence,*_____
_*increase turnover, and reduce inventory carrying costs*_____

Resource Requirements of New System:

	High	Moderate	Low
Personnel	☐	☐	☑
Hardware	☐	☑	☐
Software	☐	☑	☐

Rate project's feasibility factors on a scale of 1 to 10 where 10 is most feasible:

Technical Feasibility	*9*
Economic Feasibility	*8*
Legal Feasibility	*10*
Operational Feasibility	*10*
Schedule Feasibility	*8*

Project Priority: High _✓_   Moderate ____   Low ____

and cons of each proposal. This involves assessing each potential project's benefits, costs, and strategic implications to the organization. Development will proceed on proposals that show the greatest potential for supporting the organization's business objectives at the lowest cost. Figure 13-3 shows how the merits of competing projects may be presented to provide a sense of relative scale. The vertical dimension shows project priority in terms of organizational need. The horizontal plane shows the expected costs of each project, and the size of the circle reflects the projects' strategic impact. For example, an ERP system is a high-priority project of great strategic importance. Such a project would, however, be extremely costly. On the other hand, the human resources project is of strategic importance also, but at a much lower cost.

CREATE AN ACTION PLAN

An important skill for top management is the ability to translate strategy into action. Although most United States companies are taking measures to decrease the distance between those who formulate the strategy and those who carry it out, translating vision into work is difficult. If organizations want to be successful, however, they must learn to implement strategy and beat the 90 percent failure rates experienced by their peers.[2]

2   D. Norton, "SAP Strategic Enterprise Management," Compass White Paper, (1999).

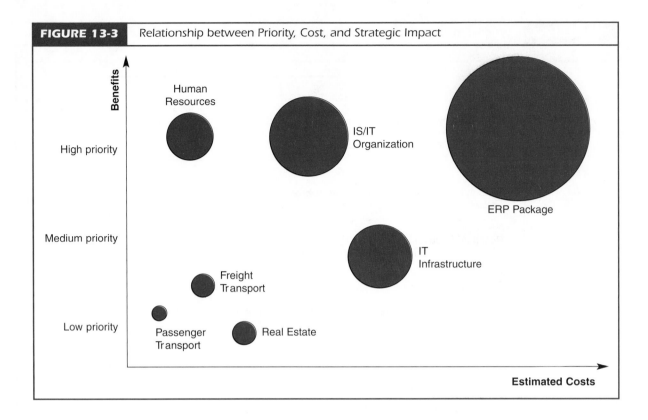

FIGURE 13-3 Relationship between Priority, Cost, and Strategic Impact

The **balanced scorecard** (BSC) is a management system that enables organizations to clarify their vision and strategy and translate them into action. It provides feedback both from internal business processes and external outcomes to continuously improve strategic performance. When fully deployed, the balanced scorecard transforms strategic planning from an academic exercise into operational tasks.

Today, the BSC enjoys increasing attention and is likely to become ubiquitous in senior management circles. Much of the BSC's appeal stems from its ability to integrate financial and operational measures into a single comprehensive framework that can "translate a company's strategic objectives into a coherent set of performance measures."[3]

The BSC approach lends itself especially well to one of the fundamental challenges facing CEOs and IT executives, namely, how to measure, improve, and understand the value that information technology delivers to the business.[4] The BSC can help managers identify opportunities for improvement in IT, and track the impact of improvement initiatives through a wide range of performance indicators.

The BSC suggests that we view the organization from four perspectives. We develop metrics, collect data, and analyze it relative to each of the perspectives. The four perspectives are:

● The learning and growth perspective

● The internal business process perspective

---

3 Robert S. Kaplan and David P. Norton, "Putting the Balanced Scorecard to Work," *Harvard Business Review* (January–February 1996).

4 "IT Efficiency and Business Value," *Compass White Paper* (July 1998).

- The customer perspective
- The financial perspective

THE LEARNING AND GROWTH PERSPECTIVE

Learning and growth constitute the essential foundation for success of any organization. This perspective includes employee training and corporate cultural attitudes related to both individual and corporate self-improvement. In our current climate of rapid technological change, workers need to be in a continuous learning mode. Government agencies often find themselves unable to hire new technical workers and at the same time are showing a decline in training existing employees. Metrics can be developed to guide managers in channeling training funds where they can be of greatest benefit.

THE INTERNAL BUSINESS PROCESS PERSPECTIVE

Metrics based on this perspective allow managers to know how well their business is running, and whether its products and services conform to customer requirements. These metrics have to be carefully designed by those who know these processes most intimately.

THE CUSTOMER PERSPECTIVE

Recent management philosophy has shown an increasing realization of the importance of customer focus in any business. These are leading indicators: if customers are not satisfied, they will eventually find other suppliers that will meet their needs. Poor performance from this perspective predicts future decline, even though the current financial picture may look good. The customer perspective includes objective measurements such as customer retention rate, as well as more subjective criteria such as market research and customer satisfaction surveys.

THE FINANCIAL PERSPECTIVE

The financial perspective includes traditional measurements such as profitability, revenues, and sales. An overemphasis on financial performance, however, may stimulate short-run decisions that create an imbalance with other perspectives.

The power of the BSC model lies in the linkages between these four core measurement perspectives. Consider, for example, a business experiencing poor performance from a financial perspective, as measured by low sales growth, and from a customer perspective, as measured by low customer retention and satisfaction. Using the BSC approach, management can examine measures from the learning and innovation perspective and from the internal process perspective to identify root causes as well as potential solutions to the problem. By identifying imbalances that exist in these measurement areas, the scorecard can be used to take corrective action.

BALANCED SCORECARD APPLIED TO IT PROJECTS

Figure 13-4 illustrates a BSC that measures the business benefits of a hypothetical online banking proposal. The bank's retail customers are producing low profit margins because of the high overhead and service costs of managing their accounts. Electronic banking is seen as a way to address this problem. If a strategic goal is to increase account profitability, performance indicators such as numbers of accounts managed per fulltime employee and cost per transaction are relevant measures. Relationships can be drawn between these measures. For example, hours spent training support staff can have an impact on reducing customer complaints.

Through analysis of BSC indicators, the steering committee can establish priorities to competing proposals based on their strategic impact as viewed from multiple perspectives. They will use these metrics to identify the proposals that go forward to the project

---

FIGURE 13-4 | Balanced Scorecard for On-Line Banking System

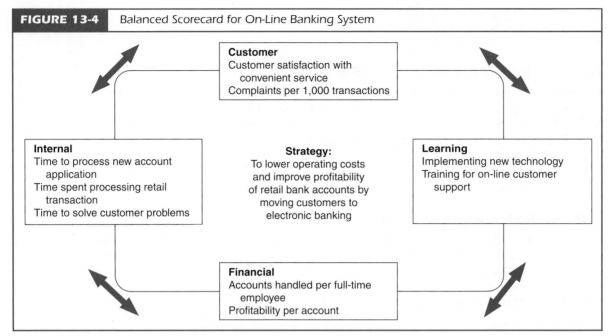

Source: Adapted from The Balanced Scorecard Collaborative, Inc.

initiation phase of the SDLC. This is the first major decision point in a project's life cycle. If the committee approves a proposal, then the proposal will undergo further detailed study and development. If a proposal is rejected, it will not be considered further within the current budget period.

PROJECT INITIATION

Project initiation involves obtaining a detailed understanding of the user problem and proposing multiple alternative solutions. Each of these proposals is assessed in terms of its feasibility and cost-benefit characteristics. The option selected at this step then proceeds to the construct phase of the SDLC. Depending upon the nature of the project and the needs of the organization, a system will require in-house development, a commercial package, or both. These approaches are examined in Chapter 14.

SYSTEMS ANALYSIS

A business problem must be fully understood by the systems analyst before he or she can formulate a solution. An incomplete or defective analysis will lead to an incomplete or defective solution. Therefore, systems analysis is the foundation for the rest of the SDLC. **Systems analysis** is actually a two-step process involving an initial survey of the current system and then an analysis of the user's needs.

THE SURVEY STEP

Most systems are not developed from scratch. Usually, some form of information system and related procedures are currently in place. The analyst often begins the analysis by determining what elements, if any, of the current system should be preserved as part of the new system. This involves a rather detailed **system survey**. Facts pertaining to preliminary questions about the system are gathered and analyzed. As the analyst obtains a greater depth of understanding of the problem, he or she develops more specific questions for which more facts must be gathered. This process may go on through several iterations. When all the relevant facts have been gathered and analyzed, the analyst arrives at an assessment of the current system. Surveying the current system has both disadvantages and advantages.

Disadvantages of Surveying the Current System
Perhaps the most compelling argument against a current system survey centers on a phenomenon known as the *current physical tar pit.*[5] This is the tendency on the part of the analyst to be "sucked in" and then "bogged down" by the task of surveying the current dinosaur system.

Some argue that current system surveys stifle new ideas. By studying and modeling the old system, the analyst may develop a constrained notion about how the new system should function. The result is an improved old system rather than a radically new approach. An example is the implementation of an ERP system. The task of reviewing current organizational procedures may serve no purpose because the successful implementation of an ERP depends on reengineering these processes to employ the best business practices of the industry.

Advantages of Surveying the Current System
There are three advantages to studying the current system. First, it is a way to identify what aspects of the old system should be kept. Some elements of the system may be functionally sound and can provide the foundation for the new system. By fully understanding the current system, the analyst can identify those aspects worth preserving or modifying for use in the new system.

Second, when the new system is implemented, the users must go through a conversion process whereby they formally break away from the old system and move to the new one. The analyst must determine what tasks, procedures, and data will be phased out with the old system and which will continue. To specify these conversion procedures, the analyst must know not only what is to be done by the new system but also what was done by the old one. This requires a thorough understanding of the current system.

Finally, by surveying the current system, the analyst may determine conclusively the cause of the reported problem symptoms. Perhaps the root problem is not the information system at all; it may be a management or employee problem that can be resolved without redesigning the information system. We may not be able to identify the root cause of the problem if we discard the existing system without any investigation into the symptoms.

Gathering Facts
The survey of the current system is essentially a fact-gathering activity. The facts gathered by the analyst are pieces of data that describe key features, situations, and relationships of the system. System facts fall into the following broad classes:

Data Sources. These include external entities, such as customers or vendors, as well as internal sources from other departments.

Users. These include both managers and operations users.

5   W. Keuffel, "House of Structure," Unix Review 9 (February 1991): 36.

Data Stores. Data stores are the files, databases, accounts, and source documents used in the system.

Processes. Processing tasks are manual or computer operations that represent a decision or an action triggered by information.

Data Flows. Data flows are represented by the movement of documents and reports between data sources, data stores, processing tasks, and users.

Controls. These include both accounting and operational controls and may be manual procedures or computer controls.

Transaction Volumes. The analyst must obtain a measure of the transaction volumes for a specified period of time. Many systems are replaced because they have reached their capacity. Understanding the characteristics of a system's transaction volume and its rate of growth are important elements in assessing capacity requirements for the new system.

Error Rates. Transaction errors are closely related to transaction volume. As a system reaches capacity, error rates increase to an intolerable level. Although no system is perfect, the analyst must determine the acceptable error tolerances for the new system.

Resource Costs. The resources used by the current system include the costs of labor, computer time, materials (e.g., invoices), and direct overhead. Any resource costs that disappear when the current system is eliminated are called *escapable costs*. Later, when we perform a cost-benefit analysis, escapable costs will be treated as benefits of the new system.

Bottlenecks and Redundant Operations. The analyst should note points where data flows come together to form a bottleneck. At peak-load periods, these can result in delays and promote processing errors. Likewise, delays may be caused by redundant operations, such as unnecessary approvals or sign-offs. By identifying these problem areas during the survey phase, the analyst can avoid making the same mistakes in the design of the new system.

Fact-Gathering Techniques

Systems analysts use several techniques to gather the above-cited facts. These include *observation*, *task participation*, *personal interviews*, and *reviewing key documents*.

Observation. Observation involves passively watching the physical procedures of the system. This allows the analyst to determine what gets done, who performs the task, when they do it, how they do it, why they do it, and how long it takes.

Task Participation. Participation is an extension of observation, whereby the analyst takes an active role in performing the user's work. This allows the analyst to experience first-hand the problems involved in the operation of the current system. For example, the analyst may work on the sales desk taking orders from customers and preparing sales orders. The analyst can determine that documents are improperly designed, that insufficient time exists to perform the required procedures, or that peak-load problems cause bottlenecks and processing errors. With hands-on experience, the analyst can often envision better ways to perform the task.

Personal Interviews. Interviewing is a method of extracting facts about the current system and user perceptions about the requirements for the new system. The instruments used to gather these facts may be open-ended questions or formal questionnaires.

Open-ended questions allow users to elaborate on the problem as they see it and offer suggestions and recommendations. Answers to these questions tend to be difficult to analyze, but they give the analyst a feel for the scope of the problem. The analyst in this type of interview must be a good listener and able to focus on the important facts. Examples of open-ended questions are: "What do you think is the main problem with our sales order system?" and "How could the system be improved?"

Questionnaires are used to ask more specific, detailed questions and to restrict the user's responses. This is a good technique for gathering objective facts about the nature of specific procedures, volumes of transactions processed, sources of data, users of reports, and control issues.

Reviewing Key Documents. The organization's documents are another source of facts about the system being surveyed. Examples of these include the following:

- Organizational charts.
- Job descriptions.
- Accounting records.
- Charts of accounts.
- Policy statements.
- Descriptions of procedures.
- Financial statements.
- Performance reports.
- System flowcharts.
- Source documents.
- Transaction listings.
- Budgets.
- Forecasts.
- Mission statements.

Following the fact-gathering phase, the analyst formally documents his or her impressions and understanding about the system. This will take the form of notes, system flowcharts, and various levels of data flow diagrams.

THE ANALYSIS STEP

Systems analysis is an intellectual process that is commingled with fact gathering. The analyst is simultaneously analyzing as he or she gathers facts. The mere recognition of a problem presumes some understanding of the norm or desired state. It is therefore difficult to identify where the survey ends and the analysis begins.

System Analysis Report

The event that marks the conclusion of the systems analysis phase is the preparation of a formal **systems analysis report**. This report presents management or the steering committee with the survey findings, the problems identified with the current system, the user's needs, and the requirements of the new system. Figure 13-5 contains a possible format for this report. The primary purpose for conducting systems analysis is to identify user needs and specify requirements for the new system. The report should set out in detail what the system must do rather than how to do it. The requirements statement within the report establishes an understanding between systems professionals, management, users, and other stakeholders. This document constitutes a formal contract that specifies the objectives and goals of the system. The systems analysis report should establish in clear terms the data sources, users, data files, general processes, data flows, controls, and transaction volume capacity.

The systems analysis report does not specify the detailed design of the proposed system. For example, it does not specify processing methods, storage media, record structures, and other details needed to design the physical system. Rather, the report remains at the objectives level to avoid placing artificial constraints on the conceptual design phase. Several possible designs may serve the user's needs, and the development process must be free to explore all of these.

FIGURE 13-5 Outline of Main Topics in a Systems Analysis Report

Systems Analysis Report

I. Reasons for System Analysis
   A. Reasons specified in the system project proposal
   B. Changes in reasons since analysis began
   C. Additional reasons

II. Scope of Study
   A. Scope as specified by the project proposal
   B. Changes in scope

III. Problems Identified with Current System
   A. Techniques used for gathering facts
   B. Problems encountered in the fact-gathering process
   C. Analysis of facts

IV. Statement of User Requirements
   A. Specific user needs in key areas, such as:
      1. Output requirements
      2. Transaction volumes
      3. Response time
   B. Nontechnical terms for a broad-based audience, including:
      1. End users
      2. User management
      3. Systems management
      4. Steering committee

V. Resource Implications
   A. Preliminary assessment of economic effect
   B. Is economic feasibility as stated in proposal reasonable?

VI. Recommendations
   A. Should the project continue?
   B. Has analysis changed feasibility, strategic impact, or priority of the project?

CONCEPTUALIZATION OF ALTERNATIVE DESIGNS

The purpose of the conceptualization phase is to produce several alternative conceptual solutions that satisfy the system requirements identified during systems analysis. By presenting users with a number of plausible alternatives, the project team avoids imposing preconceived constraints onto the new system. These alternative designs then go to the systems selection stage where their respective costs and benefits are compared and a single optimum design is chosen for construction.

HOW MUCH DESIGN DETAIL IS NEEDED?

The conceptual design phase should highlight the differences between critical features of competing systems rather than their similarities. Therefore, system designs at this point should be general. The designs should identify all the inputs, outputs, processes, and special features necessary to distinguish one alternative from another. In some cases, this may be accomplished at the context diagram level. In situations where the important distinctions between systems are subtle, designs may need to be represented by lower-level DFDs and even with structure diagrams. However, detailed DFDs and structure diagrams are more commonly used at the detailed design phase of the SDLC. We shall discuss the transition from detailed DFD to structure diagram in Chapter 14.

Figure 13-6 presents two alternative conceptual designs for a purchasing system. These designs lack the details needed to implement the system. For instance, they do not include such necessary components as:

- Database record structures.

- Processing details.

- Specific control techniques.

- Formats for input screens and source documents.

- Output report formats.

The designs do, however, possess sufficient detail to demonstrate how the two systems are conceptually different in their functions. To illustrate, let's examine the general features of each system.

Option A is a traditional, batch purchasing system. The initial input for the process is the purchase requisition from inventory control. When inventories reach their predetermined reorder points, new inventories are ordered according to their economic order quantity. Transmittal of purchase orders to suppliers takes place once a day via the U.S. mail.

In contrast, Option B employs EDI technology. The trigger to this system is a purchase requisition from production planning. The purchases system determines the quantity and the vendor and then transmits the order online via EDI software to the vendor.

Both alternatives have pros and cons. A benefit of Option A is its simplicity of design, ease of implementation, and lower demand for systems resources than Option B. A negative aspect of Option A is that it requires the firm to carry inventories. On the other hand, Option B may allow the firm to reduce or even eliminate inventories. This benefit comes at the cost of more expensive and sophisticated system resources. It is premature, at this point, to attempt to evaluate the relative merits of these alternatives. This is done formally in the next phase of the SDLC. At this point, system designers are concerned only with identifying plausible alternative designs.

FIGURE 13-6   Alternative Conceptual Designs for a Purchasing System

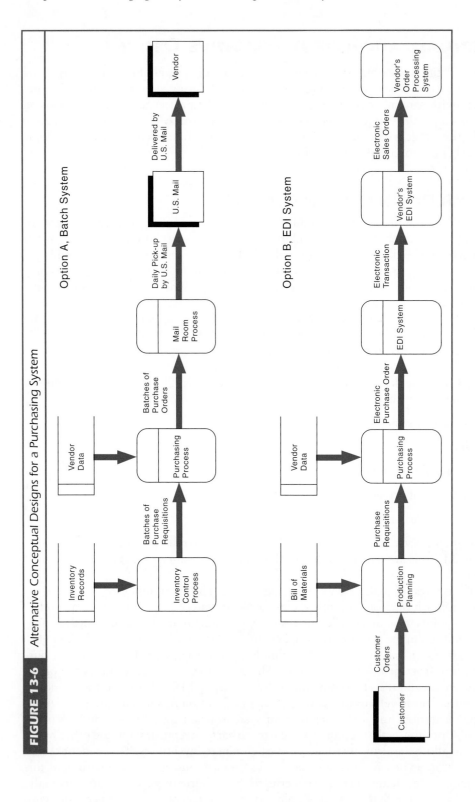

SYSTEMS EVALUATION AND SELECTION

This phase in the SDLC is a formal mechanism for selecting the one system from the set of alternative conceptual designs that will go forward for construction. The **systems evaluation and selection** phase is an optimization process that seeks to identify the best system. This decision represents a critical juncture in the SDLC. At this point there is a great deal of uncertainty about the system, and a poor decision can be disastrous. The purpose of a formal evaluation and selection procedure is to structure this decision-making process and thereby reduce both uncertainty and the risk of making a poor decision.

There is no magic formula to ensure a good decision. Ultimately, the decision comes down to management judgment. The objective is to provide a means by which management can make an informed judgment. This selection process involves two steps:

1. Perform a detailed feasibility study.
2. Perform a cost-benefit analysis.

The results of these evaluations are then reported formally to the steering committee for final system selection.

PERFORM A DETAILED FEASIBILITY STUDY

We begin the system selection process by reexamining the feasibility factors that were evaluated on a preliminary basis as part of the systems proposal. Originally, the scores assigned to these factors were based largely on the judgment and intuition of the systems professional. Now that specific system features have been conceptualized, the designer has a clearer picture of these factors. Also, at the proposal stage, these factors were evaluated for the entire project. Now they are evaluated for each alternative conceptual design.

Informed evaluators should perform the **detailed feasibility study**. Objectivity is essential to a fair assessment of each design. This group should consist of the project manager, a user representative, and systems professionals who have expertise in the specific areas covered by the feasibility study. Also, for operational audit reasons, the group should contain a member of the internal audit staff. The feasibility factors that were introduced in the previous section provide a framework for identifying the key issues that evaluators should consider.

Technical Feasibility

In evaluating technical feasibility, a well-established and understood technology represents less risk than an unfamiliar one. If the systems design calls for established technology, the feasibility score will be high, say 9 or 10. The use of technology that is new (first release) and unfamiliar to systems professionals who must install and maintain it, or that is a hybrid of several vendors' products, is a more risky option. Depending on the number and combination of risk factors, the feasibility score for such technology will be lower.

Legal Feasibility

In financial transaction processing systems, the legality of the system is always an issue. However, legality is also an issue for nonfinancial systems that process sensitive data, such as hospital patient records or personal credit ratings. Different systems designs may represent different levels of risk when dealing with such data. The evaluator should be concerned that the conceptual design recognizes critical control, security, and audit trail issues and that the system does not violate laws pertaining to rights of privacy and/or the use and distribution of information.

Operational Feasibility

The availability of well-trained, motivated, and experienced users is the key issue in evaluating the operational feasibility of a design. If users lack these attributes, the move to a highly technical environment may be risky and will require extensive retraining. This may also affect the economic feasibility of the system. On the other hand, a user community that is comfortable with technology is more likely to make a smooth transition to an advanced technology system. The operational feasibility score of each alternative design should reflect the expected ease of this transition.

Schedule Feasibility

At this point in the design, the system evaluator is in a better position to assess the likelihood that the system will be completed on schedule. The technology platform, the systems design, and the need for user training may influence the original schedule. The systems development technology being used is another influence. The use of CASE and prototyping tools (discussed in Chapter 14) can significantly reduce the development time of any systems design option.

Economic Feasibility

The preliminary economic feasibility study was confined to assessing management's financial commitment to the overall project. This is still a relevant issue. Whether the economic climate has changed since the preliminary study or whether one or more of the competing designs does not have management's support should now be determined.

The original feasibility study could specify the project's costs only in general terms. Now that each competing design has been conceptualized and expressed in terms of its unique features and processes, designers can be more precise in their estimates of the costs of each alternative. The economic feasibility study can now be taken a step further by performing a cost-benefit analysis.

PERFORM COST-BENEFIT ANALYSIS

Cost-benefit analysis helps management determine whether (and by how much) the benefits received from a proposed system will outweigh its costs. This technique is frequently used for estimating the expected financial value of business investments. In this case, however, the investment is an information system, and the costs and benefits are more difficult to identify and quantify than those of other types of capital projects. Although imperfect in this setting, cost-benefit analysis is employed because of its simplicity and the absence of a clearly better alternative. In spite of its limitations, cost-benefit analysis, combined with feasibility factors, is a useful tool for comparing competing systems designs.

There are three steps in the application of cost-benefit analysis: identifying costs, identifying benefits, and comparing costs and benefits. We discuss each of these steps below.

Identify Costs

One method of identifying costs is to divide them into two categories: one-time costs and recurring costs. *One-time costs* include the initial investment to develop and implement the system. *Recurring costs* include operating and maintenance costs that recur over the life of the system. Table 13-2 shows a breakdown of typical one-time and recurring costs.

One-Time Costs

Hardware Acquisition. This includes the cost of mainframe servers, PCs, and peripheral equipment, such as networks and disk packs. The cost figures for items can be obtained from the vendor.

TABLE 13-2	One-Time and Recurring Costs

One-Time Costs
    Hardware acquisition
    Site preparation
    Software acquisition
    Systems design
    Programming and testing
    Data conversion from old system to new system
    Training personnel

Recurring Costs
    Hardware maintenance
    Software maintenance contracts
    Insurance
    Supplies
    Personnel

Site Preparation. This involves such frequently overlooked costs as building modifications, e.g., adding air conditioning or making structural changes; equipment installation, which may include the use of heavy equipment; and freight charges. Estimates of these costs can be obtained from the vendor and the subcontractors who do the installation.

Software Acquisition. These costs apply to all software purchased for the proposed system including operating system software, if not bundled with the hardware; network control software; and commercial applications, such as accounting packages. Estimates of these costs can be obtained from vendors.

Systems Design. These are the costs incurred by systems professionals performing the planning, analysis, and design functions. Technically, such costs incurred up to this point are "sunk" and irrelevant to the decision. The analyst should estimate only the costs needed to complete the detailed design.

Programming and Testing. Programming costs are based on estimates of the personnel hours required to write new programs and modify existing programs for the proposed system. System testing costs involve bringing together all the individual program modules for testing as an entire system. This must be a rigorous exercise if it is to be meaningful. The planning, testing, and analysis of the results may demand many days of involvement from systems professionals, users, and other stakeholders of the system. The experience of the firm in the past is the best basis for estimating these costs.

Data Conversion. These costs arise in the transfer of data from one storage medium or structure to another. For example, the accounting records of a manual system must be converted to digital form when the system becomes computer-based. This can represent a significant task. The basis for estimating conversion costs is the number and size of the files to be converted.

Training. These costs involve educating users to operate the new system. This could be done in an extensive training program provided by an outside organization at a remote site or through on-the-job training by in-house personnel. The cost of formal training can be easily obtained. The cost of an in-house training program includes instruction time, classroom facilities, and lost productivity.

Recurring Costs

Hardware Maintenance. This involves the cost of upgrading the computer (e.g., increasing the memory), as well as preventive maintenance and repairs to the computer and peripheral equipment. The organization may enter into a maintenance contract with the vendor to minimize and budget these costs. Estimates for these costs can be obtained from vendors and existing contracts.

Software Maintenance. These costs include upgrading and debugging operating systems, purchased applications, and in-house developed applications. Maintenance contracts with software vendors can be used to specify these costs fairly accurately. Estimates of in-house maintenance can be derived from historical data.

Insurance. This covers such hazards and disasters as fire, hardware failure, vandalism, and destruction by disgruntled employees.

Supplies. These costs are incurred through routine consumption of such items as printer ribbons and paper, magnetic disks, magnetic tapes, and general office supplies.

Personnel. These are the salaries of individuals who are part of the information system. Some employee costs are direct and easily identifiable, such as the salaries of operations personnel exclusively employed as part of the system under analysis. Some personnel involvement, e.g., the database administrator and computer room personnel, is common to many systems. Such personnel costs must be allocated on the basis of expected incremental involvement with the system.

Identify Benefits

The next step in the cost-benefit analysis is to identify the benefits of the system. These may be both tangible and intangible.

Tangible Benefits. *Tangible benefits* are benefits that can be measured and expressed in financial terms. Table 13-3 lists several types of tangible benefits.

Tangible benefits fall into two categories: those that increase revenue and those that reduce costs. For example, assume a proposed EDI system will allow the organization to reduce inventories and at the same time improve customer service by reducing stockouts. The reduction of inventories is a cost-reducing benefit. The proposed system will use fewer resources (inventories) than the current system. The value of this benefit is the dollar amount of the carrying costs saved by the annual reduction in inventory. The estimated increase in sales because of better customer service is a revenue-increasing benefit.

TABLE 13-3	Tangible Benefits

Increased Revenues
    Increased sales within existing markets
    Expansion into other markets

Cost Reduction
    Labor reduction
    Operating cost reduction (such as supplies and overhead)
    Reduced inventories
    Less expensive equipment
    Reduced equipment maintenance

When measuring cost savings, only escapable costs should be included in the analysis. Escapable costs are directly related to the system and cease to exist when the system ceases to exist. Some costs that appear to be escapable to the user are not truly escapable and, if included, can lead to a flawed analysis. For example, data processing centers often "charge back" their operating costs to their user constituency through cost allocations. The charge-back rate they use for this includes both fixed costs (allocated to users) and direct costs created by the activities of individual users. Figure 13-7 illustrates this technique.

Assume the management in User Area B proposes to acquire a computer system and perform its own data processing locally. One benefit of the proposal is the cost savings derived by escaping the charge-back from the current data processing center. Although the user may see this as a $400,000 annual charge, only the direct cost portion ($50,000) is escapable by the organization as a whole. Should the proposal be approved, the remaining $350,000 of the charge-back does not go away. This cost must now be absorbed by the remaining users of the current system.

Intangible Benefits. Table 13-4 lists some common categories of *intangible benefits.* Although intangible benefits are often of overriding importance in information system decisions, they cannot be easily measured and quantified. For example, assume that a proposed point-of-sale system for a department store will reduce the average time to process a customer sales transaction from eleven minutes to three minutes. The time saved can be quantified and produces a tangible benefit in the form of an operating cost saving. An intangible benefit is improved customer satisfaction; no one likes to stand in long lines to

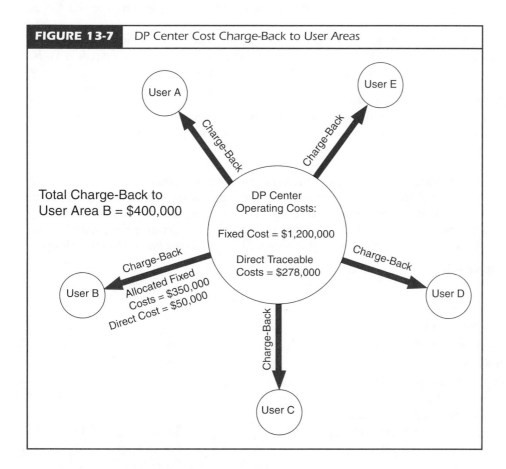

FIGURE 13-7   DP Center Cost Charge-Back to User Areas

TABLE 13-4	Intangible Benefits

Increased customer satisfaction
Improved employee satisfaction
More current information
Improved decision making
Faster response to competitor actions
More efficient operations
Better internal and external communications
Improved planning
Operational flexibility
Improved control environment

pay for purchases. But what is the true value of this intangible benefit to the organization? Increased customer satisfaction may translate into increased sales. More customers will buy at the store—and may be willing to pay slightly more to avoid long checkout lines. But how do we quantify this translation? Assigning a value is often highly subjective.

Systems professionals draw upon many sources in attempting to quantify intangible benefits and manipulate them into financial terms. Some common techniques include customer (and employee) opinion surveys, statistical analysis, expected value techniques, and simulation models. Though systems professionals may succeed in quantifying some of these intangible benefits, more often they must be content to simply state the benefits as precisely as good judgment permits.

Because they defy precise measurement, intangible benefits are sometimes exploited for political reasons. By overstating or understating these benefits, a system may be pushed forward by its proponents or killed by its opponents.

Compare Costs and Benefits

The last step in the cost-benefit analysis is to compare the costs and benefits identified in the first two steps. The two most common methods used for evaluating information systems are net present value and payback.

The Net Present Value Method. Under the **net present value method,** the present value of the costs is deducted from the present value of the benefits over the life of the system. Projects with a positive net present value are economically feasible. When comparing competing projects, the optimal choice is the project with the greatest net present value. Figure 13-8 illustrates the net present value method by comparing two competing designs.

The example is based on the following data:

	Design A	Design B
Project completion time	1 year	1 year
Expected useful life of system	5 years	5 years
One-time costs (thousands)	$300	$140
Recurring costs (thousands) incurred in beginning of Years 1 through 5	$45	$55
Annual tangible benefits (thousands) incurred in end of Years 1 through 5	$170	$135

FIGURE 13-8	Net Present Value Method of Cost-Benefit Analysis

Year Time	Beginning End Year Outflows	Inflows	Beginning Year Time	End Year Outflows	Inflows
0	$(300,000)		0	$(140,000)	
1	(45,000)	170,000	1	(55,000)	135,000
2	(45,000)	170,000	2	(55,000)	135,000
3	(45,000)	170,000	3	(55,000)	135,000
4	(45,000)	170,000	4	(55,000)	135,000
5	(45,000)	170,000	5	(55,000)	135,000
PV Out	$(479,672)		PV Out	$(359,599)	
PV In	$628,428		PV In	$499,089	
NPV	$148,810		NPV	$139,490	
Interest Rate	8.00%				

If costs and tangible benefits alone were being considered, then Design A would be selected over Design B. However, the value of intangible benefits, along with the design feasibility scores, must also be factored into the final analysis.

The Payback Method. The **payback method** is a variation of break-even analysis. The break-even point is reached when total costs equal total benefits. Figures 13-9(a) and (b) illustrate this approach using the data from the previous example.

The total cost curve consists of the one-time costs plus the present value of the recurring costs over the life of the project. The total benefits curve is the present value of the tangible benefits. The intersection of these lines represents the number of years into the future when the project breaks even, or pays for itself. The shaded area between the benefit curve and the total-cost curve represents the present value of future profits earned by the system.

In choosing an information system, payback speed is often a decisive factor. With brief product lifecycles and rapid advances in technology, the effective lives of information systems tend to be short. Using this criterion, Design B, with a payback period of four years, would be selected over Design A, whose payback will take four and a half years. The length of the payback period often takes precedence over other considerations represented by intangible benefits.

PREPARE SYSTEMS SELECTION REPORT

The deliverable portion of the systems selection process is the **systems selection report**. This formal document consists of a revised feasibility study, a cost-benefit analysis, and a list and explanation of intangible benefits for each alternative design. On the basis of this report, the steering committee will select a single system that will go forward to the next phase of the construct phase of the SDLC.

In-House Development or Purchase Commercial Software

Two general options are open to the organization in the construct phase: develop the system in-house or purchase commercial software. At this juncture management should have a good sense as to which option they will follow. Systems that need to meet unique and proprietary business needs are more likely to undergo in-house development. Systems that

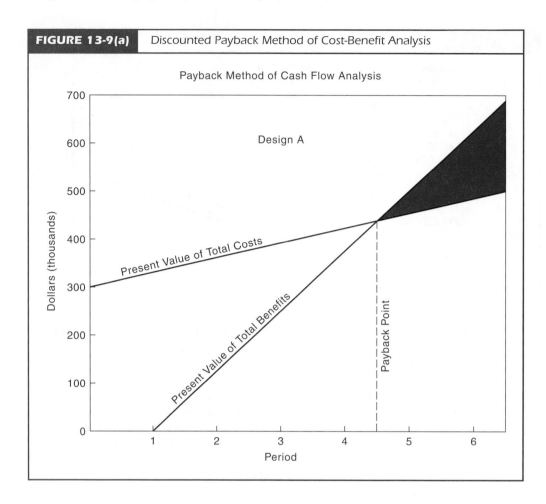

FIGURE 13-9(a)   Discounted Payback Method of Cost-Benefit Analysis

Payback Method of Cash Flow Analysis

Design A

are expected to support "best industry practices" may be better suited to the purchased-software option. A third approach, which involves both options, is to tailor the commercial system to meet the organization's needs. This may require making extensive in-house modifications to the package. The previous analysis of system architecture, TELOS factors, system survey results, and preliminary cost/benefit issues will have revealed to decision makers the suitability of one approach over the other. Both the in-house and the commercial package options are examined in detail in Chapter 14.

Announcing the New System Project

Management's formal announcement of the new system to the rest of the organization is the last and most delicate step in the project initiation phase of the SDLC. This exceedingly important communiqué, if successful, will pave the way for the new system and help ensure its acceptance among the user community.

A new system can sometimes generate considerable political backlash that may threaten its success. For example, not all users may understand the objectives of the new system. In fact, some users may feel threatened by the uncertainty surrounding the system. As we have seen, new systems must improve the productivity and efficiency of operations. These objectives sometimes translate into organizational restructuring that erodes

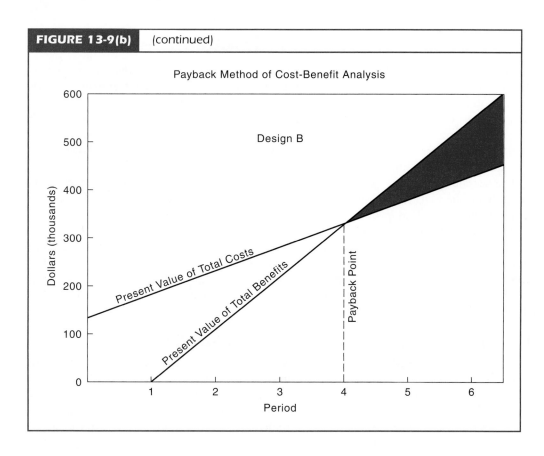

FIGURE 13-9(b)   (continued)

Payback Method of Cost-Benefit Analysis

the personal powerbase of some users. Because a new system brings about operational changes, some employees may be displaced or may be required to undergo retraining to function in the new workplace.

The fears that take root and grow in this environment of uncertainty are often revealed in acts of opposition, both overt and covert, to the new system. To minimize opposition, top management must quell unnecessary fears and fully explain the business rationale for the new system before formal construction begins. If lower-level management and operating staff are assured that the system will be beneficial, the project's chances for success are vastly improved.

USER FEEDBACK

The preceding discussion was based on the assumption that the project under development passed through the strategic planning phase presented in the previous section. Not all systems projects should be, or can be, initiated in this manner. Systems maintenance is an integral component of the modern SDLC environment. This function needs to be receptive to user feedback and responsive to their legitimate needs. Therefore, user requests are also directed to the project initiation phase (refer to Figure 13-1). At this point in the SDLC, user requests involve relatively small enhancements to existing systems rather than major retrofits or entirely new systems. The IT budget must, therefore, be flexible enough to accommodate short term "quick hit" projects that emerge on a daily basis.

THE ACCOUNTANT'S ROLE IN MANAGING THE SDLC

The SDLC process is of interest to accountants for two reasons. First, the creation of an information system represents a significant financial transaction that consumes both financial and human resources. Systems development is like any manufacturing process that produces a complex product through a series of stages. Such transactions must be planned, authorized, scheduled, accounted for, and controlled. Accountants are as concerned with the integrity of this process as they are with any manufacturing process that has financial resource implications.

The second, and more pressing, concern for accountants is with the products that emerge from the SDLC. The quality of accounting information systems rests directly on the SDLC activities that produce them. These systems are used to deliver accounting information to internal and external users. The accountant's responsibility is to ensure that the systems apply proper accounting conventions and rules, and possess adequate controls. Therefore, accountants are concerned with the quality of the process that produces accounting information systems. For example, a sales order system produced by a defective SDLC may suffer from serious control weaknesses that introduce errors into databases and, ultimately, the financial statements.

HOW ARE ACCOUNTANTS INVOLVED WITH SDLC?

Accountants are involved in systems development in three ways. First, accountants are users. All systems that process financial transactions impact the accounting function in some way. Like all users, accountants must provide a clear picture of their problems and needs to the systems professional. For example, accountants must specify accounting techniques to be used; internal control requirements, such as audit trails; and special algorithms, such as depreciation models).

Second, accountants participate in systems development as members of the development team. Their involvement often extends beyond the development of strictly AIS applications. Systems that do not process financial transactions may still draw on accounting data. The accountant may be consulted to provide advice or to determine if the proposed system constitutes an internal control risk.

Third, accountants are involved in systems development as auditors. Accounting information systems must be auditable. Some computer audit techniques require special features that must be designed into the system. The auditor/accountant has a stake in such systems and must be involved early in their design.

THE ACCOUNTANT'S ROLE IN SYSTEMS STRATEGY

Auditors routinely review the organization's systems strategy. History has shown that careful systems planning is a cost-effective activity in reducing the risk of creating unneeded, unwanted, inefficient, and ineffective systems. Both internal and external auditors have vested interests in this outcome.

THE ACCOUNTANT'S ROLE IN CONCEPTUAL DESIGN

The accountant plays an important role in the conceptual design of the system. He or she must recognize control implications of each alternative design and ensure that accounting conventions and legal requirements are understood. These issues need not be specified in detail at this point, but they should be recognized as items to be addressed during the construct phase of the system. Furthermore, the auditability of a system depends in part on its design characteristics. Some computer auditing techniques require systems to be designed with built-in audit features. Such features require resources and need to be considered at conceptual design.

THE ACCOUNTANT'S ROLE IN SYSTEMS SELECTION

The economic feasibility of proposed systems is of primary concern to accountants. Specifically, the accountant should ensure that:

1. Only escapable costs are used in calculations of cost-savings benefits.
2. Reasonable interest rates are used in measuring present values of cash flows.
3. One-time and recurring costs are completely and accurately reported.
4. Realistic useful lives are used in comparing competing projects.
5. Intangible benefits are assigned reasonable financial values.

Errors, omissions, and misrepresentations in the accounting for such items can distort the analysis and result in a suboptimal decision.

SUMMARY

This chapter dealt with managing the SDLC. It began with a review of the key phases of a modern SDLC. The first of these involves strategic systems planning, which derives input from the strategic business plan, the diverse needs and concerns of the user community, and the organization's existing legacy system. The chapter then reviewed the project initiation phase of the SDLC. This includes systems analysis and conceptualization of alternative designs. To ensure a correct systems solution, management must gather and weigh relevant information regarding the various systems alternatives under consideration. Systems evaluation and final selection is accomplished through a detailed feasibility study and careful cost-benefit analysis of these alternative solutions. Because success at this stage depends, in large part, on an accurate identification of prospective costs and benefits, we devoted special attention to the principle of one-time and recurring costs associated with systems and to the various tangible and intangible benefits they can be expected to yield. The chapter concluded with a review of the accountant's role in managing the SDLC.

KEY TERMS

architecture description (626)

balanced scorecard (BSC) (630)

competency analysis (625)

cost-benefit analysis (640)

detailed feasibility study (639)

economic feasibility (628)

end users (624)

industry analysis (625)

legal feasibility (628)

net present value method (644)

operational feasibility (628)

payback method (645)

proactive management (627)

project feasibility (627)

reactive management (627)

schedule feasibility (628)

stakeholders (624)

steering committee (624)

system survey (633)

systems analysis (632)

systems analysis report (635)

systems development life cycle (SDLC) (622)

systems evaluation and selection (639)

systems professionals (624)

systems project proposal (628)

systems selection report (645)

systems strategy (623)

technical feasibility (628)

TELOS (628)

REVIEW QUESTIONS

1. What are the five stages of the systems development life cycle?
2. What is the balanced scorecard?
3. What is the role of the accountant in the SDLC? Why might accountants be called on for input into the development of a nonaccounting information system?
4. What is the learning and growth perspective?
5. Why is it often difficult to obtain competent and meaningful user involvement in the SDLC?
6. Is the SDLC a step-by-step procedure that must be followed precisely, or is it more interactive and recursive? Explain your answer.
7. Explain why a survey of the current system may serve no purpose when an organization is planning to implement an ERP.
8. Why is it crucial that the strategic objectives of the firm be considered when conducting the systems planning phase?
9. Who should sit on the systems steering committee? What are their typical responsibilities?
10. Explain the internal business process perspective.
11. Contrast proactive and reactive management styles. Which style would you prefer for your organization? Why?
12. What purposes do system objectives serve? Should they be broadly or narrowly defined? Why?
13. Why can the formal announcement of a new system technique be crucial?
14. Discuss the various feasibility measures that should be considered. Give an example of each.
15. What are the broad classes of facts that need to be gathered in the system survey?
16. What are the primary fact-gathering techniques?
17. What are the relative merits and disadvantages of a current system survey?
18. What is the primary objective of conceptual design?
19. How much design detail is needed in the conceptual design phase?
20. What is the accountant's primary role in conceptual design?
21. Who should be included in the group of evaluators performing the detailed feasibility study?
22. What makes the cost-benefit analysis more difficult for information systems than most other investments an organization may make?
23. Classify each of the following as either one-time or recurring costs:
    a. training personnel.
    b. initial programming and testing.
    c. systems design.
    d. hardware costs.
    e. software maintenance costs.
    f. site preparation.
    g. rent for facilities.
    h. data conversion from old system to new system.
    i. insurance costs.
    j. installation of original equipment.
    k. hardware upgrades.
24. Distinguish between escapable and inescapable costs. Give an example of each.
25. Distinguish between tangible and intangible benefits.
26. What is a systems selection report?
27. Explain the net present value and the payback methods. Which method do you prefer? Why?
28. What is the role of the accountant in evaluation and selection?

DISCUSSION QUESTIONS

1. Accounting educators are discussing ways to incorporate communication skills, both oral and written, into accounting information systems courses. Why do you think these skills are deemed crucial for proper execution of the SDLC?

2. Comment on the following statement: "The maintenance stage of the SDLC involves making trivial changes to accommodate changes in user needs."

3. Discuss how rushing the system's requirements stage may delay or even result in the failure of a systems development process. Conversely, discuss how spending too long in this stage may result in "analysis paralysis."

4. Discuss the independence issue when audit firms also provide consulting input into the development and selection of new systems.

5. Should the systems development tasks be performed by users of the system or by systems professionals who are trained specifically in systems development techniques? Why?

6. Why are the customer perspective measures important when a company is doing financially well?

7. Some may argue that a company's financial bottom line is all important. Comment on this from the financial perspective of the balanced scorecard approach.

8. Is a good strategic plan detail-oriented?

9. Distinguish between a problem and a symptom. Give an example. Are these usually noticed by upper-, middle-, or lower-level managers?

10. What purposes does the systems project proposal serve? How are these evaluated and prioritized? Is the prioritizing process objective or subjective?

11. Most firms underestimate the cost and time requirements of the SDLC by as much as 50 percent. Why do you think this occurs? In what stages do you think the underestimates are most dramatic?

12. A lack of support by top management has led to the downfall of many new systems projects during the implementation phase. Why is this support so important?

13. Many new systems projects grossly underestimate transaction volumes because they do not take into account how the new, improved system can actually increase demand. Explain how this can happen and give an example.

14. Do you think legal feasibility is an issue for a system that incorporates the use of machines to sell lottery tickets?

MULTIPLE-CHOICE QUESTIONS

1. All of the following individuals would likely be SDLC participants except:
   a. accountants.
   b. shareholders.
   c. management.
   d. programmers.
   e. all of the above.

2. Which of the following represents the correct order in problem resolution?
   a. Define the problem, recognize the problem, perform feasibility studies, specify system objectives, and prepare a project proposal.
   b. Recognize the problem, define the problem, perform feasibility studies, specify system objectives, and prepare a project proposal.
   c. Define the problem, recognize the problem, specify system objectives, perform feasibility studies, and prepare a project proposal.
   d. Recognize the problem, define the problem, specify system objectives, perform feasibility studies, and prepare a project proposal.

3. CIA 584 II-36
   In reviewing a feasibility study for a new computer system, the auditor should ascertain that the study
   a. considered costs, savings, controls, profit improvement, and other benefits analyzed by application area.
   b. provided the preliminary plan for converting existing manual systems and clerical operations.
   c. provided management with assurance from qualified, independent consultants that the use of a computer system appeared justified.
   d. included a report by the internal audit department that evaluated internal control features for each planned application.

4. CMA 686 5-2
   The most important factor in planning for a system change is
   a. having an auditor as a member of the design team.
   b. using state-of-the-art techniques.

c. concentrating on software rather than hardware.

d. involving top management and people who use the system.

e. selecting a user to lead the design team.

5. CMA 678 5-5

In the context of a feasibility study, technical feasibility refers to whether

a. a proposed system is attainable, given the existing technology.

b. the systems manager can coordinate and control the activities of the systems department.

c. an adequate computer site exists for the proposed system.

d. the proposed system will produce economic benefits exceeding its costs.

e. the system will be used effectively within the operating environment of an organization.

6. CMA 678 5-4

A systems survey is being conducted to obtain an accurate perspective on the existing system and to identify weaknesses that can be corrected by the new system. Which of the following steps is NOT considered part of this systems survey?

a. Interviews are conducted with operating people and managers.

b. The complete documentation of the system is obtained and reviewed.

c. Measures of processing volume are obtained for each operation.

d. Equipment sold by various computer manufacturers is reviewed in terms of capability, cost, and availability.

e. Work measurement studies are conducted to determine the time required to complete various tasks or jobs.

7. CMA 1281 5-12

Kesta Company is doing a systems development study. The study started with broad organizational goals and the types of decisions made by organizational executives. This study supports a model of information flow and, ultimately, design requirements. This approach to systems development is called

a. bottom-up.

b. network.

c. top-down.

d. strategic.

e. sequential.

8. The study that determines whether a project can be completed in an acceptable time frame is:

a. a schedule feasibility study.

b. a technical feasibility study.

c. an operational feasibility study.

d. an economic feasibility study.

e. a legal feasibility study.

9. Which of the following is least likely to be an accountant's role in the SDLC?

a. User.

b. Consultant.

c. Auditor.

d. Programmer.

e. All of these are likely roles.

10. CMA 1289 5-8

In determining the need for system changes, several types of feasibility studies can be made. The most commonly recognized feasibility studies are

a. legal, environmental, and economic.

b. environmental, operational, and economic.

c. technical, economic, legal, and practical.

d. practical, technical, and operational.

e. technical, operational, and economic.

11. CMA 1290 4-13

The technique that recognizes the time value of money by discounting the after-tax cash flows for a project over its life to time period zero using the company's minimum desired rate of return is called the

a. net present value method.

b. capital rationing method.

c. payback method.

d. average rate of return method.

e. accounting rate of return method.

12. One-time costs of system development include all of the following except:

a. Site preparation.

b. Hardware maintenance.

c. Programming.

d. Hardware acquisition.

e. Data conversion.

Questions 13 and 14 are based on the following information and deal with a critique of the cost-benefit analysis portion of the feasibility study.

When management decides to implement a management information system in a segment of the company, the decision is often based upon a feasibility study conducted by the systems department. Listed below are terms and examples of them used in the section of the study dealing with the cost-benefit analysis.

Terms	Examples
Tangible cost	Development cost
Intangible cost	Imputed interest
Tangible benefits	Cost displacement
Intangible benefits	Improved decisions

The feasibility study identifies the major benefits of the new management information system. Many of the benefits are intangible, such as improved decision-making capability and effectiveness, better customer relations, and improved employee morale.

13. CMA Adapted 679 5-9
    The estimated category that ordinarily would have the greatest uncertainty as to its precise value is
    a. the tangible costs.
    b. the intangible costs.
    c. the tangible benefits.
    d. the intangible benefits.
    e. none of the above because they are equally precise.

14. CMA Adapted 679 5-10
    Which of the following statements best describes what is usually true regarding the estimates included in feasibility studies?
    a. Development time and cost are usually less than estimated; benefits are stated accurately.
    b. Development time and cost are usually less than estimated; benefits are usually greater than estimated.
    c. Development cost and benefits are usually greater than estimated; development time is usually less than estimated.
    d. Development time and cost are usually greater than estimated; benefits are usually less than estimated.
    e. Development time, cost, and benefits are usually greater than estimated.

PROBLEMS

1. Systems Planning

A new systems development project is being planned for Reindeer Christmas Supplies Company. The invoicing, cash receipts, and accounts payable modules are all going to be updated. The controller, Kris K. Ringle, is a little anxious about this project. The last systems development project that affected his department was not very successful, and the employees in the accounting department did not accept the new system very well at first. He feels that the systems personnel did not interact sufficiently with the users of the systems in the accounting department. Prepare a memo from Ringle to the head of the information systems department, Sandy Klaus. In this memo, provide some suggestions for including the accounting personnel in the systems development project. Give persuasive arguments as to why prototyping would be helpful to the workers in the accounting department.

2. Problem Identification

Classify each of the following as a problem or a symptom. If it is a symptom, give two examples of a possible underlying problem. If it is a problem, give two examples of a possible symptom that may be detected.
a. declining profits
b. defective production process
c. low-quality raw materials
d. shortfall in cash balance
e. declining market share
f. shortage of employees in the accounts payable department
g. shortage of raw material due to a drought in the Midwest
h. inadequately trained workers
i. decreasing customer satisfaction

3. Systems Development and User Involvement

Kruger Designs hired a consulting firm three months ago to redesign the information system used by the architects. The architects will be able to use state-of-the-art CAD programs to help in designing the products. Further, they will be able to store these designs on a network server where they and other architects may be able to call them back up for future designs with similar components. The consulting firm has been instructed to develop the system without disrupting the architects. In fact, top management believes that the best route is to develop the system and then to "introduce" it to the architects during a training session. Management does not want the architects to spend precious billable hours guessing about the new system or putting work off until the new system is working. Thus, the consultants are operating in a backroom under a shroud of secrecy.

Required:

a. Do you think that management is taking the best course of action for the announcement of the new system? Why?

b. Do you approve of the development process? Why?

4. Systems Analysis

Consider the following dialogue between a systems professional, Joe Pugh, and a manager of a department targeted for a new information system, Lars Meyer:

Pugh: The way to go about the analysis is to first examine the old system, such as reviewing key documents and observing the workers perform their tasks. Then we can determine which aspects are working well and which should be preserved.

Meyer: We have been through these types of projects before and what always ends up happening is that we do not get the new system we are promised; we get a modified version of the old system.

Pugh: Well, I can assure you that will not happen this time. We just want a thorough understanding of what is working well and what is not.

Meyer: I would feel much more comfortable if we first started with a list of our requirements. We

should spend some time up-front determining exactly what we want the system to do for my department. Then, you systems people can come in and determine what portions to salvage if you wish. Just don't constrain us to the old system!

Required:

a. Obviously these two workers have different views on how the systems analysis phase should be conducted. Comment on whose position you sympathize with the most.

b. What method would you propose they take? Why?

5. Fact-Gathering Techniques

Your company, Tractors, Inc., is employing the SDLC for its new information system. You have been chosen as a member of the development team because of your strong accounting background. This background includes a good understanding of both financial and managerial accounting concepts and required data. You also possess a great understanding of internal control activities. You do not, however, fully understand exactly what the internal auditors will need from the system in order to comply with Section 404 of the Sarbanes-Oxley Act. Lay out the fact-gathering techniques you might employ to increase your understanding of this important component of your new system.

6. Systems Selection

Your company, Kitchen Works, is employing the SDLC for its new information system. The company is currently performing a number of feasibility studies, including the economic feasibility study. A draft of the economic feasibility study has been presented to you for your review. You have been charged with determining whether only escapable costs have been used, the present value of cash flows is accurate, the one-time and recurring costs are correct, realistic useful lives have been used, and the intangible benefits listed in the study are reasonable. While you are a member of the development team because of your strong accounting background, you have questions about whether some costs are escapable, the interest rates used to perform present value analysis, and the estimated useful lives that have been used. How might you resolve your questions?

7. Cost-Benefit Analysis

Listed below are some probability estimates of the costs and benefits associated with two competing projects.

a. Compute the net present value of each alternative. Round the cost projections to the nearest month. What happens to the answer if the probabilities of the recurring costs are incorrect and a more accurate estimate is as follows:

	A		B
.10	$ 75,000	.4	$ 85,000
.55	95,000	.4	100,000
.35	105,000	.2	110,000

b. Repeat Step (a) for the payback method.

c. Which method do you feel provides the best source of information? Why?

8. Balanced Scorecard

An organization's IT function has the following goals:

- Improve the quality of IT solutions and services to its internal users.
- Increase the ratio of planned-to-realized benefits from systems solutions.
- Fully match IT strategy with enterprise strategies.
- Integrate information systems architectures to minimize database redundancy and increase systems reusability across the user community.

Required:

Develop a BSC depiction specific measures for each of the four BSC perspectives.

Problem 7: Cost-Benefit Analysis

COST OF CAPITAL = .14

	A		B	
	Probability	Amount	Probability	Amount
Project completion time	0.5	12 months	0.6	12 months
	0.3	18 months	0.2	18 months
	0.2	24 months	0.1	24 months
Expected useful life	0.6	4 years	0.5	4 years
	0.25	5 years	0.3	5 years
	0.15	6 years	0.2	6 years
One-time costs	0.35	$200,000	0.2	$210,000
	0.4	250,000	0.55	250,000
	0.25	300,000	0.25	260,000
Recurring costs	0.1	$ 75,000	0.4	$ 85,000
	0.55	95,000	0.4	100,000
	0.35	105,000	0.2	110,000
Annual tangible benefits starting with weighted average completion date	0.3	$220,000	0.25	$215,000
	0.5	233,000	0.5	225,000
	0.2	240,000	0.25	235,000

SYSTEMS DEVELOPMENT CASES

Several systems development cases that draw upon the material in this chapter and Chapter 14 are available online at http://hall.swlearning.com.

chapter 14

Construct, Deliver, and Maintain Systems Project[*]

LEARNING OBJECTIVES

After studying this chapter, you should:

- Be able to identify the sequence of events that constitute the in-house development phase of the SDLC.
- Be familiar with the tools used to improve the success of system construction and delivery activities, including prototyping, CASE tools, and the use of PERT and Gantt charts.
- Understand the distinction between the structured and object-oriented design approaches.
- Understand the use of multi-level DFDs in the design of business processes.
- Be familiar with the different types of system documentation and the purposes they serve.
- Recognize the role of accountants in the construct and delivery of systems.
- Understand the advantages and disadvantages of the commercial software option, and be able to discuss the decision-making process used to select commercial software.

This chapter covers the final three phases of the SDLC. First we examine the many activities associated with in-house development. These activities fall conceptually into two categories: (1) construct the system and (2) deliver the system. Through these activities, systems selected in the project initiation phase (discussed in Chapter 13) are designed in detail and implemented. This involves creating input screen formats, output report layouts, database structures, and application logic. Finally, the completed system is tested, documented, and rolled out to the user. The chapter then examines the increasingly important option of using commercial software packages. The majority of companies today, particularly smaller firms and large firms with standardized information needs, employ pre-written software systems rather than develop in-house systems from scratch. Conceptually the commercial software approach also consists of construct and delivery activities. In this section we examine the pros, cons, and issues involved in selecting off-the-shelf systems. Finally, the chapter addresses the important activities associated with systems maintenance. This stage in the SDLC carries significant financial and operational risks that are of particular importance to management, accountants, and auditors. A trend in systems development, maintenance, and operation within organizations is to outsource part or all system activities. The SDLC does not change in such a case, but its component parts are provided by an outsourcing provider. Therefore, special controls should be introduced to prevent increasing costs, decreasing functionality of systems, and loss of strategic advantage.

---

[*] This chapter was co-authored by Jiri Polak, Ph.D., Deloitte & Touche, and Vojtech Merunka, Ph.D., Deloitte & Touche.

IN-HOUSE SYSTEMS DEVELOPMENT

Organizations usually acquire information systems in two ways: (1) they develop customized systems in-house through formal systems development activities and/or (2) they purchase commercial systems from software vendors. Numerous commercial vendors offer high-quality, general-purpose information systems. These vendors primarily serve organizations with generic information needs. Typically, their client firms have business practices so standardized that they can purchase predesigned information systems and employ them with little or no modifications. However, many organizations require systems that are highly tuned to their unique operations. These firms design their own information systems through in-house systems development activities.

While each approach has advantages and disadvantages, they are not mutually exclusive options. A firm may satisfy some of its information systems needs by purchasing commercial software and developing other systems in-house. This section is concerned with the in-house systems development component of Figure 14-1. Issues pertaining to the purchase of commercial software are discussed in the next section.

TOOLS FOR IMPROVING SYSTEMS DEVELOPMENT

Systems development projects are not always success stories. In fact, by the time they are implemented, some systems are obsolete or defective and must be replaced. Estimates hold that up to 25 percent of all systems projects fail. That is, they are terminated prematurely and never implemented, or they must be redesigned within six months of implementation. Historically, the SDLC has been plagued by three problems that account for most systems failures. These problems are discussed in the following section.

1. *Poorly specified systems requirements.* Systems development is not a precise science. The process involves human communications and the sharing of ideas between users and systems professionals. This information exchange is often imperfect. Mistakes are made in identifying problems and needs, new ideas emerge as the true nature of the problem unfolds, and people simply change their minds about what they really want and need from the system.

   Because of this uncertainty, the SDLC tends not to be a smooth, linear process, where one stage is completed before the next one begins. In reality, the process is iterative or cyclical. For example, it is not uncommon for a systems designer to return to the analysis stage from the construct stage to gather additional information as his or her perception of the problem changes.

   The cyclical nature of this process results in time-consuming false starts, much repeated work, and pressure from all fronts to get the job done. Too often, the result is a system that is poorly designed, over budget, and behind schedule.

2. *Ineffective development techniques.* The problems cited above are amplified by ineffective techniques for presenting, documenting, and modifying systems specifications. In the worst-case scenario, systems development tools are simply paper, pencils, rulers, templates, and erasers. The situation is improved considerably by the use of computer-based graphics software that permits original designs and changes to be made electronically. Nevertheless, days or even weeks of work may need to be redone because of a change in a system's specifications.

3. *Lack of user involvement in systems development.* The major cause of systems failure is the lack of end user involvement during critical development stages. At one time, computer systems development was thought to be the exclusive domain of the systems professionals. During this period, users (including accountants) abdicated their

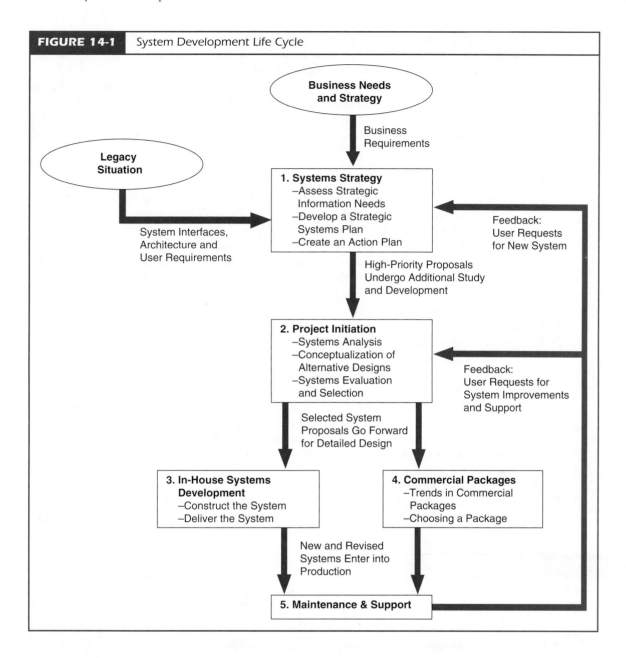

FIGURE 14-1   System Development Life Cycle

traditional responsibility for systems design. Too often, this led to business problems because system designs reflected the analyst's perception of information needs rather than the perception of accountants and other users. Systems often lacked adequate controls and audit trails.

Today, we recognize that user involvement in a system's development is the key to its ultimate success. However, achieving competent user involvement is still difficult to accomplish. There are two reasons for this: (1) users tend to become discouraged when they discover the amount of time they must actually invest and (2) communication between end users and systems professionals is generally not fluent. It is often said that these groups speak different languages. Each tends to resort to its own jargon when communicating with the other. Therefore, much time is spent identifying user problems and needs and formulating acceptable solutions. Miscommunications between users and systems professionals lead to mistakes that, sometimes, are discovered too late.

These problems have led researchers to seek ways to improve the development process. The focus of this effort has been on techniques to reduce development time, facilitate better information transfer, encourage user involvement, and improve overall systems quality. Several widely used techniques for improving systems development are reviewed in the following section.

Prototyping

Prototyping is a technique for providing users a preliminary working version of the system. The prototype is built quickly and inexpensively with the intention that it will be modified. The objective of this technique is for the prototype to represent "an unambiguous functional specification, serve as a vehicle for organizing and learning, and evolve ultimately into a fully implemented" system.[1] As the users work with the prototype and make suggestions for changes, both they and the systems professional develop a better understanding of the true requirements of the system.

The costs of a prototype model are kept low by reducing its features to the essential elements. For example, the prototype system will not contain the complex code necessary to perform transaction validation, exception-handling capabilities, and internal controls. Typically, prototypes are limited to user input screens, output reports, and some principle functions.

When incorporated in the front-end stages of the SDLC, prototyping is an effective tool for establishing user requirements. Once these are obtained, the prototype is discarded. This throwaway prototyping is used for developing structured applications, such as accounting systems.[2] An alternative technique continues the prototyping process until the system is completed. This approach is used for developing decision support systems and expert systems. Figure 14-2 illustrates the prototyping model.

The Case Approach

Computer-aided software engineering (CASE) technology involves the use of computer systems to build computer systems. CASE tools are commercial software products

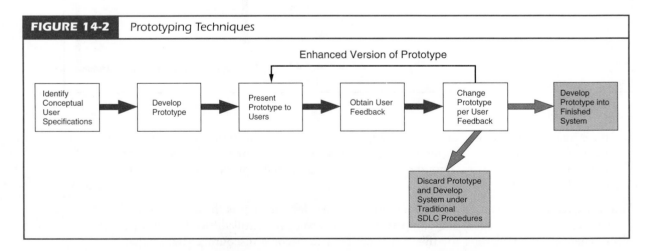

FIGURE 14-2   Prototyping Techniques

Enhanced Version of Prototype

Identify Conceptual User Specifications → Develop Prototype → Present Prototype to Users → Obtain User Feedback → Change Prototype per User Feedback → Develop Prototype into Finished System

Discard Prototype and Develop System under Traditional SDLC Procedures

---

1   J. C. Emery, Management Information Systems: The Critical Strategic Resource (New York: Oxford University Press, 1987): 325.

2   V. Zwass, Management Information Systems (Dubuque, Iowa: Wm. C. Brown, 1992): 740.

consisting of highly integrated applications that support a wide range of SDLC activities. This methodology was developed to increase the productivity of systems professionals, improve systems design quality, and expedite the SDLC.

Most CASE products comprise both upper and lower tools or applications. Upper CASE tools support the conceptual activities of analysis and design. Lower CASE tools support the physical activities associated with application programming and system maintenance. CASE tools are used to define user requirements, create physical databases from conceptual ER diagrams, produce system design specifications, automatically generate computer program code, and facilitate the maintenance of programs created by both CASE and non-CASE techniques. Figure 14-3 illustrates the CASE spectrum of tools as they apply to various stages in the SDLC. The appendix to this chapter presents more detailed discussion of CASE features.

PERT Chart

The project evaluation and review technique (PERT) is a tool for showing the relationship among key activities that constitute the construct and delivery process. Figure 14-4 presents a **PERT chart** for a hypothetical project. The principal features of this diagram are:

1. *Activities*—the tasks to be completed in the project. These are labeled (and lettered A through L) on the lines, along with the time estimate for their completion. For example, the process design activity (C) is estimated to take four weeks.
2. *Events*—mark the completion of one activity and the beginning of the next. The events in this diagram are numbered 1 through 9.
3. *Paths*—routes through the diagram that connect the events from the first to the last.
4. *Critical path*—the path with the greatest overall time. The critical path in this project is C-F-G-J-L, with a total time of 20 (4 + 5 + 3 + 4 + 4) weeks. Any time delays in the activities along this path will extend the overall project time, which is why this path is critical.

Gantt Chart

The **Gantt chart** is a horizontal bar chart that presents time on a horizontal plane and activities on a vertical plane. Figure 14-5 illustrates a Gantt chart for the same project represented by the PERT chart in Figure 14-4. The time associated with each activity is

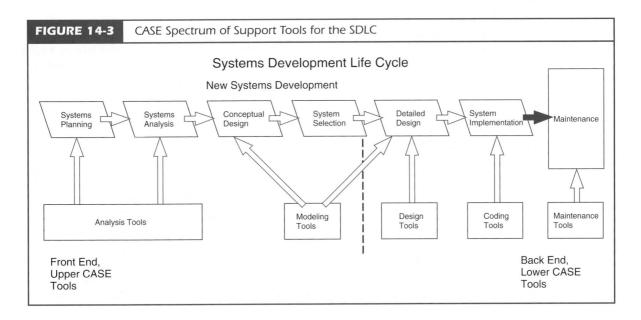

FIGURE 14-3   CASE Spectrum of Support Tools for the SDLC

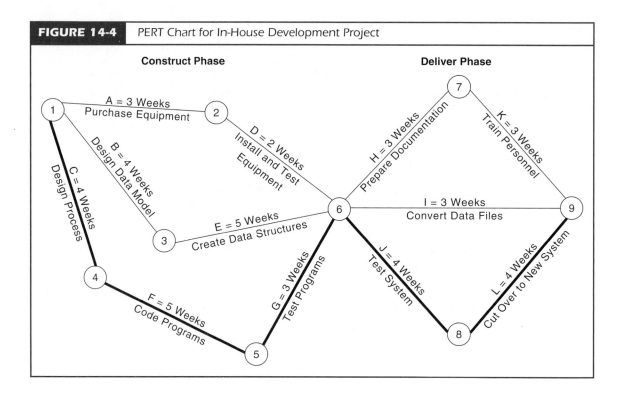

FIGURE 14-4   PERT Chart for In-House Development Project

represented by a bar marking its starting and ending dates. The Gantt chart is popular because it can show the current status of the project at a glance. By comparing projected time and work completed to date, we can see which projects are on, ahead of, or behind schedule.

CONSTRUCT THE SYSTEM

The main goal of the **construct** phase is to design and build working software that is ready to be tested and delivered to its user community. This phase involves modeling the system, programming the applications, and application testing. The design and programming of modern systems follows one of two basic approaches: the *structured approach* and the *object-oriented approach*. We begin this section with a review of these competing methodologies. We then examine construct issues related to system design, programming, and testing.

THE STRUCTURED DESIGN APPROACH

The **structured design** approach is a disciplined way of designing systems from the top down. It consists of starting with the "big picture" of the proposed system that is gradually decomposed into more and more detail until it is fully understood. Under this approach the business process under design is usually documented by dataflow and structure diagrams. Figure 14-6 shows the use of these techniques to depict the top-down decomposition of a hypothetical business process.

We can see from these diagrams how the systems designer follows a top-down approach. The designer starts with an abstract description of the system and, through successive steps, redefines this view to produce a more detailed description. In our

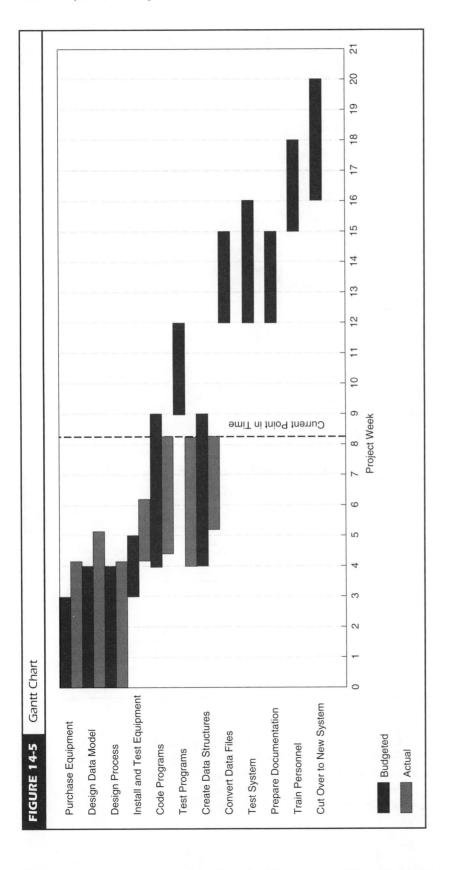

FIGURE 14-5   Gantt Chart

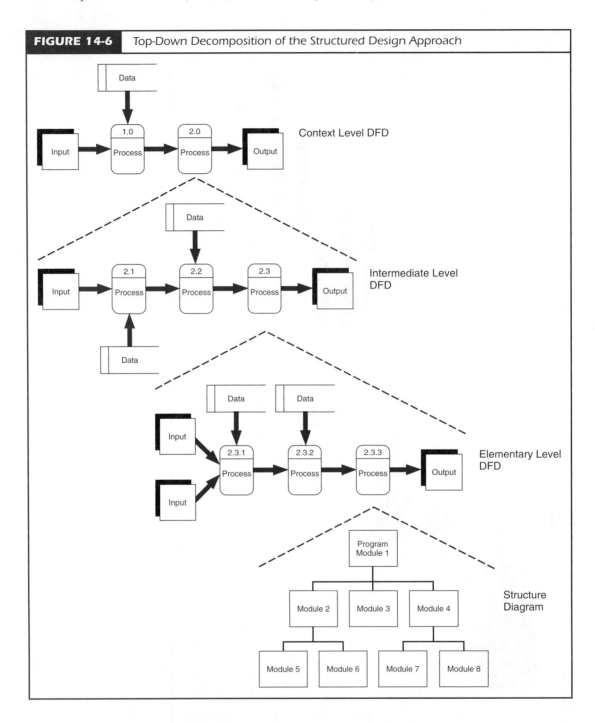

FIGURE 14-6   Top-Down Decomposition of the Structured Design Approach

example, Process 2.0 in the context diagram is decomposed into an intermediate-level DFD. Process 2.3 in the intermediate DFD is further decomposed into an elementary DFD. This decomposition could involve several levels to obtain sufficient details. Let's assume that three levels are sufficient in this case. The final step transforms Process 2.3.3 into a structure diagram that defines the program modules that will constitute the process.

THE OBJECT-ORIENTED DESIGN APPROACH

The **object-oriented design** approach is to build information systems from reusable standard components or objects. This approach may be equated to the process of building an automobile. Car manufacturers do not create each new model from scratch. New models are actually built from standard components that also go into other models. For example, each model of car produced by a particular manufacturer may use the same type of engine, gearbox, alternator, rear axle, radio, and so on. Some of the car's components will be industry-standard products that are used by other manufacturers. Such things as wheels, tires, spark plugs, and headlights fall in to this category. In fact, it may be that the only component actually created from scratch for a new car model is the body.

The automobile industry operates in this fashion to stay competitive. By using standard components, car manufacturers minimize production and maintenance costs. At the same time, they can remain responsive to consumer demands for new products and preserve manufacturing flexibility by mixing and matching components according to the customer's specification.

The concept of reusability is central to the object-oriented design approach to systems design. Once created, standard modules can be used in other systems with similar needs. Ideally, the systems professionals of the organization will create a library (inventory) of modules that can be used by other systems designers within the firm. The benefits of this approach are similar to those stated for the automobile example. They include reduced time and cost for development, maintenance, and testing and improved user support and flexibility in the development process.

Elements of the Object-Oriented Design Approach

A distinctive characteristic of the object-oriented design approach is that both data and programming logic, such as integrity tests, accounting rules, and updating procedures, are encapsulated in modules to represent objects. The following discussion deals with the principle elements of object-oriented approach.

Objects. **Objects** are equivalent to nouns in the English language. For example, vendors, customers, inventory, and accounts are all objects. These objects possess two characteristics: attributes and methods. **Attributes** are the data that describe the objects. **Methods** are the actions that are performed on or by objects that may change their attributes. Figure 14-7 illustrates these characteristics with a nonfinancial example. The object in this example is an automobile whose attributes are make, model, year, engine size, mileage, and color. Methods that may be performed on this object include drive, park, lock, and wash. Note that if we perform a drive method on the object, the mileage attribute will be changed.

Figure 14-8 illustrates these points with an inventory accounting example. In this example, the object is inventory and its attributes are part number, description, quantity on hand, reorder point, order quantity, and supplier number. The methods that may be performed on inventory are reduce inventory (from product sales), review available quantity on hand, reorder inventory (when quantity on hand is less than the reorder point), and replace inventory (from inventory receipts). Again, note that performing any of the methods will change the attribute quantity on hand.

Classes and Instances. An **object class** is a logical grouping of individual objects that share the same attributes and methods. An **instance** is a single occurrence of an object within a class. For example, Figure 14-9 shows the inventory class consisting of several instances or specific inventory types.

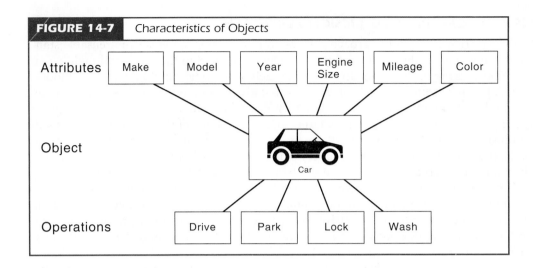

FIGURE 14-7 Characteristics of Objects

Inheritance. **Inheritance** means that each object instance inherits the attributes and methods of the class to which it belongs. For example, all instances within the inventory class hierarchy share the attributes of part number, description, and quantity on hand. These attributes would be defined once and only once for the inventory object. Thus, the object instances of wheel bearing, water pump, and alternator will inherit these attributes. Likewise, these instances will inherit the methods (reduce, review, reorder, and replace) defined for the class.

Object classes can also inherit from other object classes. For example, Figure 14-10 shows an object hierarchy made up of an object class called control and three subclasses called accounts payable, accounts receivable, and inventory. This diagramming technique is an example of unified modeling language (UML). The object is represented as a rectangle with three levels: name, attributes, and methods.

The three object subclasses have certain control methods in common. For example, no account should be updated without first verifying the values Vendor Number, Customer Number, or Part Number. This method (and others) may be specified for the control object (once and only once) and then inherited by all the subclass objects to which this method applies.

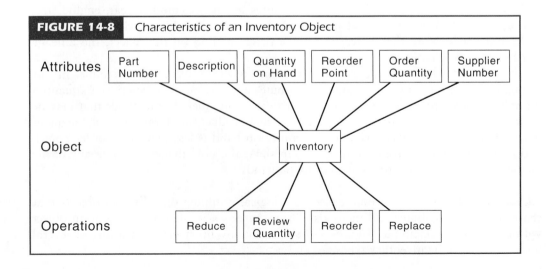

FIGURE 14-8 Characteristics of an Inventory Object

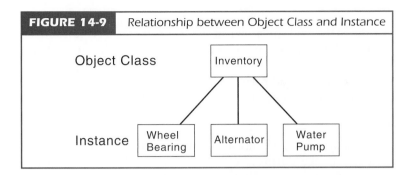

FIGURE 14-9   Relationship between Object Class and Instance

Object Class   Inventory

Instance   Wheel Bearing   Alternator   Water Pump

Because object-oriented designs support the objective of reusability, portions of systems, or entire systems, can be created from modules that already exist. For example, any future system that requires the attributes and methods specified by the existing control module can inherit them by being designated a subclass object.

Finally, the object-oriented approach offers the potential of increased security over the structured model. The functionality (behavior) of each object is determined by its collection of methods, which creates an impenetrable **wall of code** around the data. This means that the internal data of the object can be manipulated only by its methods. Direct access to the object's internal structure is not permitted.

SYSTEM DESIGN

The purpose of the **design phase** is to produce a detailed description of the proposed system that both satisfies the system requirements identified during systems analysis and is in accordance with the conceptual design. In this phase, all system components—user views, database tables, processes, and controls—are meticulously specified. At the end of this phase, these components are presented formally in a detailed design report. This report constitutes a set of "blueprints" that specify input screen formats, output report layouts, database structures, and process logic. These completed plans then proceed to the final phase in the SDLC—system implementation—where the system is physically constructed.

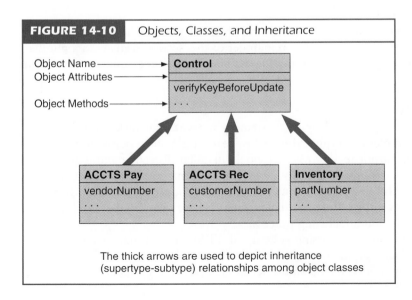

FIGURE 14-10   Objects, Classes, and Inheritance

Object Name ——→ **Control**
Object Attributes ——→
Object Methods ——→ verifyKeyBeforeUpdate
. . .

ACCTS Pay   **ACCTS Rec**   **Inventory**
vendorNumber   customerNumber   partNumber
. . .   .

The thick arrows are used to depict inheritance (supertype-subtype) relationships among object classes

The Design Sequence

The **systems design** phase of the SDLC follows a logical sequence of events: create a data model of the business process, define conceptual user views, design the normalized database tables, design the physical user views (output and input views), develop the process modules, specify the system controls, and perform a system walkthrough. In this section, each of the design steps is examined in detail.

An Iterative Approach

Typically, the design sequence listed in the previous section is not a purely linear process. Inevitably, system requirements change during the detailed design phase, causing the designer to revisit previous steps. For example, a last-minute change in the process design may influence data collection requirements that, in turn, changes the user view and requires alterations to the database tables.

To deal with this material as concisely and clearly as possible, the detailed design phase is presented here as a neat linear process. However, the reader should recognize its circular nature. This characteristic has control implications for both accountants and management. For example, a control issue that was previously resolved may need to be revisited as a result of modifications to the design.

DATA MODELING, CONCEPTUAL VIEWS, AND NORMALIZED TABLES

Data modeling is the task of formalizing the data requirements of the business process as a conceptual model. The primary documentation instrument used for data modeling is the entity relationship (ER) diagram. This technique is used to depict the entities or data objects in the system. Once the entities have been represented in the data model, the data attributes that define each entity can then be described. They should be determined by careful analysis of user needs and may include both financial and nonfinancial data. These attributes represent the **conceptual user views** that must be supported by *normalized database tables*. To the extent that the data requirements of all users have been properly specified in the data model, the resulting databases will support multiple user views. Data modeling, defining user views, and designing normalized base tables were described in Chapter 9 and its appendix. In the interest of space, these procedures are not reexamined here.

DESIGN PHYSICAL USER VIEWS

The physical views are the media for conveying and presenting data. These include output reports, documents, and input screens. The remainder of this section deals with a number of issues related to the design of physical user views. The discussion examines output and input views separately.

Design Output Views

Output is the information produced by the system to support user tasks and decisions. Table 14-1 presents examples of output produced by several AIS subsystems. At the transaction processing level, output tends to be extremely detailed. Revenue and expenditure cycle systems produce control reports for lower-level management and operational documents to support daily activities. Conversion cycle systems produce reports for scheduling production, managing inventory, and cost management. These systems also produce documents for controlling the manufacturing process.

The general ledger/financial reporting system (GL/FRS) and the management reporting system (MRS) produce output that is more summarized. The intended users of these systems are management, stockholders, and other interested parties outside the firm. The

TABLE 14-1	Examples of System Outputs

System	Output
Expenditure cycle	Purchase orders Cash disbursement voucher Payment check Purchases summary report Cash disbursements summary
Revenue cycle	Sales invoice Remittance advice Bill of lading Packing slip Customer statements Deposit slips Cash receipts prelist Sales summary Cash receipts summary
Conversion cycle	Purchase requisitions Work orders Move tickets Materials requisitions Production schedules Job tickets Employee time cards Work-in-process status reports Summary of changes to finish goods
General ledger and financial reporting system	Financial statements Comparative financial statements Tax returns Reports to regulatory agencies

Management Reporting System	Various status and analysis reports such as:
	    Inventory turnover reports
	    Inventory status reports
	    Vendor analysis reports
	    Budget and performance reports

GL/FRS is a nondiscretionary reporting system that produces formal reports required by law. These include financial statements, tax returns, and other reports demanded by regulatory agencies. The output requirements of the GL/FRS tend to be predictable and stable over time and between organizations.

The management reporting system serves the needs of internal management users. MRS applications may be stand-alone systems or they may be integrated in the revenue, conversion, and expenditure cycles to produce output that contains both financial and nonfinancial information. The MRS produces problem-specific reports that vary considerably between business entities.

Output Attributes. Regardless of their physical form, whether operational documents, financial statements, or discretionary reports, output views should possess the following attributes: relevance, summarization, exceptions orientation, timeliness, accuracy, completeness, and conciseness.

Relevance. Each element of information output must support the user's decision or task. Irrelevant facts waste resources and detract attention from the information content of the output. Output documents that contain unnecessary facts tend to be cluttered, take time to process, cause bottlenecks, and promote errors.

Summarization. Reports should be summarized according to the level of the user in the organization. The degree of summarization increases as information flows upward from lower-level managers to top management. We see this characteristic clearly in the responsibility reports represented in Figure 14-11.

Exception Orientation. **Operations control reports** should identify activities that are about to go out of control and ignore those that are functioning within normal limits. This allows managers to focus their attention on areas of greatest need. An example of this is illustrated with the inventory reorder report presented in Figure 14-12. Only the items that need to be ordered are listed on the report.

Timeliness. Timely information that is reasonably accurate and complete is more valuable than perfect information that comes too late to be useful. Therefore, the system must provide the user with information that is timely enough to support the desired action.

Accuracy. Information output must be free of material errors. A material error is one that causes the user to take an incorrect action or to fail to take the correct action. Operational documents and low-level control reports usually require a high degree of accuracy. However, for certain planning reports and reports that support rapid decision making, the system designer may need to sacrifice accuracy to produce information that is timely. Managers cannot always wait until they have all the facts before they must act. The

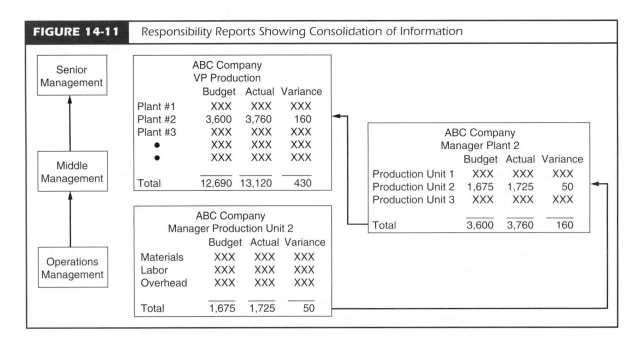

FIGURE 14-11   Responsibility Reports Showing Consolidation of Information

| FIGURE 14-12 | Inventory Reorder Report |

Sports Car Factory
Inventory Reorder Report

\# 12975

Date: 11/22/04

The following inventory items have fallen below normal levels:

Part	Description	Primary Vendor	Order Quantity	Quantity On Hand	Average Daily Usage
47782	Exhaust Header	2378	10	2	1
6671	Wheel Bearing	2378	500	25	20
9981	Ball Joint	2401	200	10	20

designer must seek a balance between the competing needs for accuracy and timeliness when designing output reports.

Completeness. Information must be as complete as possible. Ideally, no piece of information essential to the task or decision should be missing from the output. As with the accuracy attribute, the designer must sometimes sacrifice completeness in favor of timely information.

Conciseness. Information output should be presented as concisely as possible within the report or document. Output should use coding schemes to represent complex data classifications. Also, information should be clearly presented with titles for all values. Reports should be visually pleasing and logically organized.

Output Reporting Techniques. While recognizing that differences in cognitive styles exist among managers, systems designers must determine the output type and format most useful to the user. Some managers prefer output that presents information in tables and matrices. Others prefer information that is visually oriented in the form of graphs and charts. The issue of whether the output should be hard copy (paper) or electronic must also be addressed.

Despite predictions for two decades or more, we have not yet achieved a paperless society. On the contrary, trees continue to be harvested and paper mills continue to be productive. In some firms, top management receives hundreds of pages of paper output each day. Paper documents also continue to flow at lower organizational levels.

On the other hand, many firms are moving to paperless audit trails and support daily tasks with electronic documents. Insurance companies, law firms, and mortgage companies make extensive use of electronic documents. The problems associated with paper documents (purchasing, handling, storage, and disposal) are greatly reduced or eliminated by the use of electronic output. However, the use of electronic output has obvious implications for accounting and auditing.

The query- and report-generating features of modern database management systems permit the manager to quickly create standard and customized output reports. Custom reports can present information in different formats, including text, matrices, tables, and graphs. Section 1 in the chapter appendix examines these formats and provides some examples.

Design Input Views

Data input views are used to capture the relevant facts about the resources, events, and agents involved in business process transactions. In this section, we divide input into two classes: hard-copy input and electronic input.

Design Hard-Copy Input. Businesses today still make extensive use of paper input documents. In designing **hard copy** documents, the system designer must keep in mind several aspects of the physical business process. Several of these are discussed in the following section.

Handling. How will the document be handled? Will it be on the shop floor around grease and oil? How many hands must it go through? Is it likely to get folded, creased, or torn? Input forms are part of the audit trail and must be preserved in legible form. If they are to be subjected to physical abuse, they must be made of high-quality paper.

Storage. How long will the form be stored? What is the storage environment? Length of storage time and environmental conditions will influence the appearance of the form. Data entered onto poor-quality paper may fade under extreme conditions. Again, this may have audit trail implications. A related consideration is the need to protect the form against erasures.

Numbers of Copies. Source documents are often created in multiple copies to trigger multiple activities simultaneously and provide a basis for reconciliation. For example, the system may require that individual copies of sales orders go to the warehouse, the shipping department, billing, and accounts receivable. Manifold forms are often used in such cases. A manifold form produces several carbon copies from a single writing. The copies are normally color-coded to facilitate distribution to the correct users.

Form Size. The average number of facts captured for each transaction affects the size of the form. For example, if the average number of items received from the supplier for each purchase is 20, the receiving report should be long enough to record them all. Otherwise, additional copies will be needed, which will add to the clerical work, clog the system, and promote processing errors.

Standard forms sizes are full-size, 8½ by 11 inches; and half size, 8½ by 5½ inches. Card form standards are 8 by 10 inches and 8 by 5 inches. The use of nonstandard forms can cause handling and storage problems and should be avoided.

Form Design. Clerical errors and omissions can cause serious processing problems. Input forms must be designed to be easy to use and collect the data as efficiently and effectively as possible. This requires that forms be logically organized and visually comfortable to the user. Two techniques used in well-designed forms are zones and embedded instructions.

Zones. **Zones** are areas on the form that contain related data. Figure 14-13 provides an example of a form divided into zones. Each zone should be constructed of lines, captions, or boxes that guide the user's eye to avoid errors and omissions.

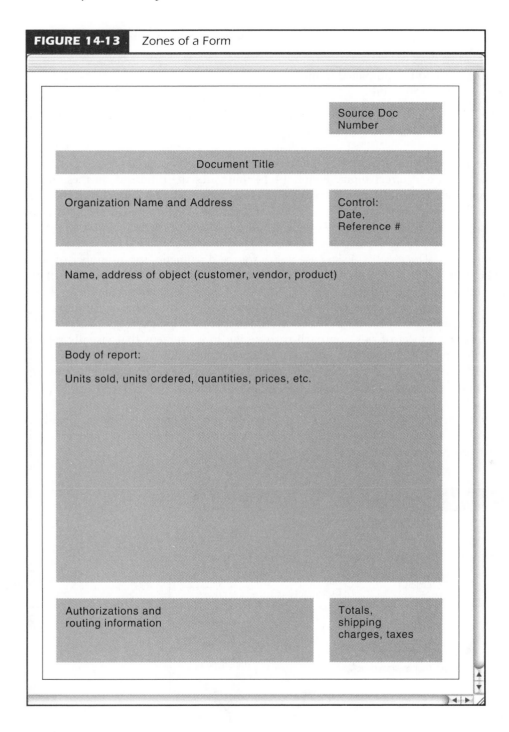

FIGURE 14-13   Zones of a Form

Embedded Instructions. **Embedded instructions** are contained within the body of the form itself rather than on a separate sheet. It is important to place instructions directly in the zone to which they pertain. If an instruction pertains to the entire form, it should be placed at the top of the form. Instructions should be brief and unambiguous. As an instructive technique, active voice is stronger, more efficient (needing fewer words), and less ambiguous than passive voice. For example, the first instruction below is written in passive voice. The second is in active voice.

1. This form should be completed in ink.
2. Complete this form in ink.

Notice the difference: the second sentence is stronger, shorter, and clearer than the first; it is an instruction rather than a suggestion.

Design Electronic Input. **Electronic input techniques** fall into two basic types: input from source documents and direct input. Figure 14-14 illustrates the difference in these techniques. Input from source documents involves the collection of data on paper forms that are then transcribed to electronic forms in a separate operation. Direct input procedures capture data directly in electronic form, via terminals at the source of the transaction.

Input from Source Documents. Firms use paper source documents for a number of reasons. Some firms prefer to maintain a paper audit trail that goes back to the source of an economic event. Some companies capture data onto paper documents because direct input procedures may be inconvenient or impossible. Other firms achieve economies of scale by centralizing electronic data collection from paper documents.

An important aspect of this approach is to design input screens that visually reflect the source document. The captions and data fields should be arranged on the electronic form exactly as they are on the source document. This minimizes eye movement between the source and the screen and maximizes throughput of work.

Direct Input. Direct data input requires that data collection technology be distributed to the source of the transaction. A very common example of this is the point-of-sale terminal in a department store.

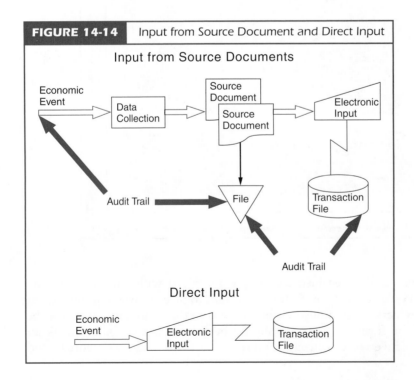

FIGURE 14-14   Input from Source Document and Direct Input

An advantage of direct input is the reduction of input errors that plague downstream processing. By collecting data once, at the source, clerical errors are reduced since the subsequent transcription step associated with paper documents is eliminated. The more times a transaction is manually transcribed, the greater the potential for error.

Direct data collection uses **intelligent forms** for online editing that help the user complete the form and make calculations automatically. The input screen is attached to a computer that performs logical checks on the data being entered. This reduces input errors and improves the efficiency of the data collection procedures. During data entry, the intelligent form will detect transcription errors, such as illegal characters in a field, incorrect amounts, and invalid item numbers. A beep can be used to draw attention to an error, an illegal action, or a screen message. Thus, corrections to input can be made on the spot.

Given minimal input, an intelligent form can complete the input process automatically. For example, a sales clerk need enter in the terminal only the item numbers and quantities of products sold. The system will automatically provide the descriptions, prices, price extensions, taxes, and freight charges and calculate the grand total. Many time-consuming and error-prone activities are eliminated through this technique. Modern relational database packages have a *screen painting* feature that allows the user to quickly and easily create intelligent input forms.

Data Entry Devices. A number of data entry devices are used to support direct electronic input. These include point-of-sale terminals, magnetic ink character recognition devices, optical character recognition devices, automatic teller machines, and voice recognition devices.

DESIGN THE SYSTEM PROCESS

Now that the database tables and user views for the system have been designed, we are ready to design the process component. This starts with the DFDs that were produced in the general design phase. Depending on the extent of the activities performed in the general design phase, the system may be specified at the context level or may be refined in lower-level DFDs. The first task is to decompose the existing DFDs to a degree of detail that will serve as the basis for creating structure diagrams. The structure diagrams will provide the blueprints for writing the actual program modules.

Decompose High-Level DFDs

To demonstrate the decomposition process, we will use the intermediate DFD of the purchases and cash disbursements system illustrated in Figure 14-15. This DFD was decomposed from the context-level DFD (Figure 13–6, Option A) originally prepared in the conceptual design phase. We will concentrate on the accounts payable process numbered 1.4 in the diagram. This process is not yet sufficiently detailed to produce program modules.

Figure 14-16 shows Process 1.4 decomposed into the next level of detail. Each of the resulting subprocesses is numbered with a third-level designator, such as 1.4.1, 1.4.2, 1.4.3, and so on. We will assume that this level of DFD provides sufficient detail to prepare a structure diagram of program modules. Many CASE tools will automatically convert DFDs to structure diagrams. However, to illustrate the concept, we will go through the process manually.

Design Structure Diagrams

The creation of the **structure diagram** requires analysis of the DFD to divide its processes into input, process, and output functions. Figure 14-17 presents a structure diagram showing the program modules based on the DFD in Figure 14-16.

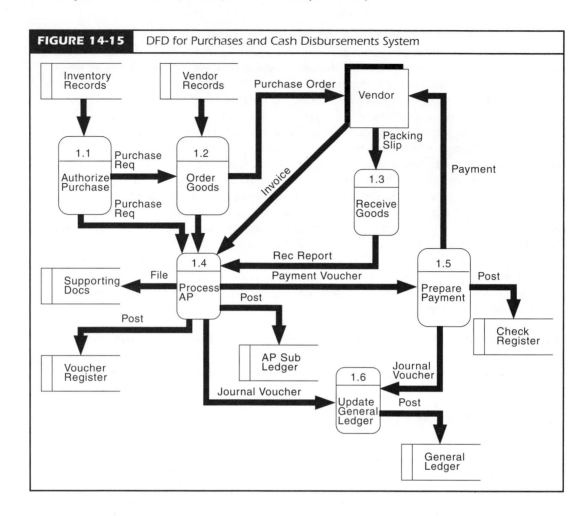

FIGURE 14-15 DFD for Purchases and Cash Disbursements System

The Modular Approach

The modular approach presented in Figure 14-17 involves arranging the system in a hierarchy of small discrete modules, each of which performs a single task. Correctly designed modules possess two attributes: they are loosely coupled, and they have strong cohesion. **Coupling** measures the degree of interaction between modules. Interaction is the exchange of data between modules. A loosely coupled module is independent of the others. Modules with a great deal of interaction are tightly coupled. Figure 14-18 shows the relationship between modules in loosely coupled and tightly coupled designs.

In the loosely coupled system, the process starts with Module A. This module controls all the data flowing through the system. The other modules interact only with this module to send and receive data. Module A then redirects the data to other modules.

Cohesion refers to the number of tasks a module performs. Strong cohesion means that each module performs a single, well-defined task. Returning to Figure 14-17, Module D gets receiving reports and only that. It does not compare reports to open purchase orders, nor does it update accounts payable. These tasks are performed by separate modules.

Modules that are loosely coupled and strongly cohesive are much easier to understand and easier to maintain. Maintenance is an error-prone process, and it is not uncommon for errors to be accidentally inserted into a module during maintenance. Thus, changing a single module within a tightly coupled structure can have an impact on the

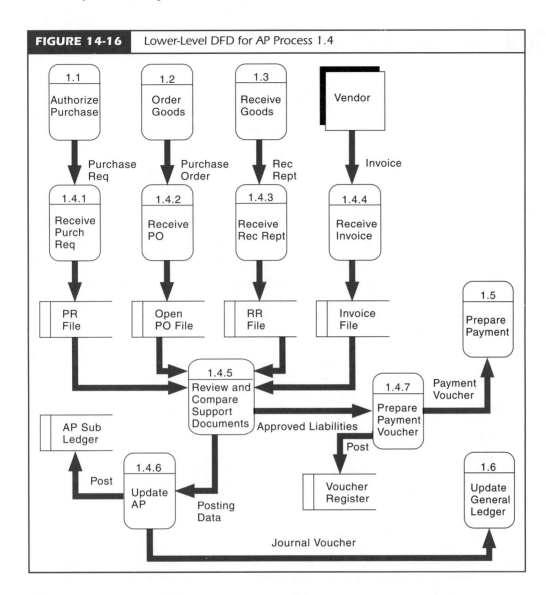

FIGURE 14-16 | Lower-Level DFD for AP Process 1.4

other modules with which it interacts. Look again at the tightly coupled structure in Figure 14-18. These interactions complicate maintenance by extending the process to the other modules. Similarly, modules with weak cohesion—those that perform several tasks—are more complex and difficult to maintain.

Pseudocode the System Modules

Each module in Figure 14-17 represents a separate computer program. The higher-level programs will communicate with lower-level programs through "call" commands. System modules are coded in the implementation phase. When we get to that phase, we will examine programming language options. At this point, the designer must specify the functional characteristics of the modules through other techniques.

Next, we illustrate how **pseudocode** may be used to describe the function of Module F in Figure 14-17. This module authorizes payment of accounts payable by validating the supporting documents.

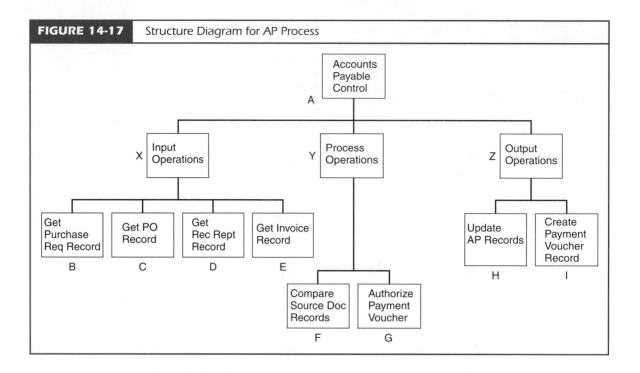

FIGURE 14-17   Structure Diagram for AP Process

COMPARE-DOCS (Module F)
    READ PR-RECORD FROM PR-FILE
    READ PO-RECORD FROM PO-FILE
    READ RR-RECORD FROM RR-FILE
    READ INVOICE-RECORD FROM INVOICE-FILE
    IF ITEM-NUM, QUANTITY-RECEIVED, TOTAL AMOUNT
        IS EQUAL FOR ALL RECORDS
        THEN PLACE "Y" IN AUTHORIZED FIELD OF PO-RECORD
    ELSE READ ANOTHER RECORD

The use of pseudocode for specifying module functions has two advantages. First, the designer can express the detailed logic of the module, regardless of the programming language to be used. Second, although the end user may lack programming skills, he or she can be actively involved in this technical but crucial step.

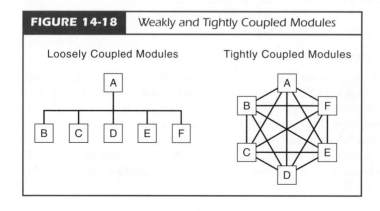

FIGURE 14-18   Weakly and Tightly Coupled Modules

DESIGN SYSTEM CONTROLS

The last step in the design phase is the design of system controls. This includes computer processing controls, database controls, manual controls over input to and output from the system, as well as controls over the operational environment (for example, distributed data processing controls). In practice, many controls that are specific to a type of technology or technique will, at this point, have already been designed, along with the modules to which they relate. This step in the design phase allows the design team to review, modify, and evaluate controls with a systemwide perspective that did not exist when each module was being designed independently. Because of the extensive nature of computer-based system controls, treatment of this aspect of the systems design is deferred to Chapters 15, 16 and 17, where they can be covered in depth.

PERFORM A SYSTEM DESIGN WALKTHROUGH

After completing the detailed design, the development team usually performs a system design **walkthrough** to ensure the design is free from conceptual errors that could become programmed into the final system. Many firms have formal, structured walkthroughs conducted by a **quality assurance group**. This is an independent group of programmers, analysts, users, and internal auditors. The job of this group is to simulate the operation of the system to uncover errors, omissions, and ambiguities in the design. Most system errors emanate from poor designs rather than programming mistakes. Detecting and correcting errors in the design thus reduces costly reprogramming later.

Review System Documentation

The **detailed design report** documents and describes the system to this point. This report includes:

- Designs of all screen outputs, reports, and operational documents.
- Entity relationship (ER) diagrams describing the data relations in the system.
- Third normal form designs for database tables specifying all data elements.
- An updated **data dictionary** describing each data element in the database.
- Designs for all screen inputs and source documents for the system.
- Context diagrams for the overall system.
- Low-level data flow diagrams of specific system processes.
- Structure diagrams for the program modules in the system, including a pseudocode description of each module.

These documents are scrutinized by the quality control group, and any errors detected are recorded in a walkthrough report. Depending on the extent of the system errors, the quality assurance group will make a recommendation. The system design will be either accepted without modification, accepted subject to modification of minor errors, or rejected because of material errors.

At this point, a decision is made either to return the system for additional design or to proceed to the next phase—systems implementation. Assuming the design goes forward, the documents just mentioned constitute the "blueprints" that guide programmers and system designers in constructing the physical system.

PROGRAM APPLICATION SOFTWARE

The next stage of the in-house development is to select a programming language from among the various languages available and suitable to the application. These include *procedural languages* such as COBOL, *event-driven languages* such as Visual Basic, or *object-oriented programming (OOP) languages* such as Java or C++. This section presents a brief overview of various programming approaches. Systems professionals will make their decision based on the in-house standards, architecture, and user needs.

Procedural Languages

A **procedural language** requires the programmer to specify the precise order in which the program logic is executed. Procedural languages are often called **third-generation languages** (3GLs). Examples of 3GLs include COBOL, FORTRAN, C, and PL1. In business (particularly in accounting) applications, COBOL was the dominant language for years. COBOL has great capability for performing highly detailed operations on individual data records and handles large files efficiently. On the other hand, it is an extremely "wordy" language that makes programming a time-consuming task. COBOL has survived as a viable language because many of the "legacy systems" written in the 1970s and 1980s, which were coded in COBOL, are still in operation today. Major retrofits and routine maintenance to these systems need to be coded in COBOL. More than 12 billion lines of COBOL code are executed daily in the United States.

Event-Driven Languages

Event-driven languages are no longer procedural. Under this model, the program's code is not executed in a predefined sequence. Instead, external actions or "events" that are initiated by the user dictate the control flow of the program. For example, when the user presses a key, or "clicks" on an icon on the computer screen, the program automatically executes code associated with that event. This is a fundamental shift from the 3GL era. Now, instead of designing applications that execute sequentially from top to bottom in accordance with the way the programmer *thinks* they should function, the user is in control.

Microsoft's Visual Basic is the most popular example of an event-driven language. The syntax of the language is simple yet powerful. Visual Basic is used to create real-time and batch applications that can manipulate flat files or relational databases. It has a screen-painting feature that greatly facilitates the creation of sophisticated *graphical user interfaces (GUI)*.

Object-Oriented Languages

Central to achieving the benefits of this approach is developing software in an **object-oriented programming (OOP) language**. The most popular true OOP languages are Java and Smalltalk. However, the learning curve of OOP languages is steep. The time and cost of retooling for OOP is the greatest impediment to the transition process. Most firms are not prepared to discard millions of lines of traditional COBOL code and retrain their programming staffs to implement object-oriented systems. Therefore, a compromise, intended to ease this transition, has been the development of hybrid languages, such as Object COBOL, Object Pascal, and C++.

Programming the System

Regardless of the programming language used, modern programs should follow a *modular approach*. This technique produces small programs that perform narrowly defined tasks. The following three benefits are associated with modular programming.

Programming Efficiency. Modules can be coded and tested independently, which vastly reduces programming time. A firm can assign several programmers to a single system. Working in parallel, the programmers each design a few modules. These are then assembled into the completed system.

Maintenance Efficiency. Small modules are easier to analyze and change, which reduces the start-up time during program maintenance. Extensive changes can be parceled out to several programmers simultaneously to shorten maintenance time.

Control. By keeping modules small, they are less likely to contain material errors of fraudulent logic. Because each module is independent of the others, errors are contained within the module.

SOFTWARE TESTING

Programs must be thoroughly tested before they are implemented. Program testing issues of direct concern to accountants are discussed in this section.

Testing Individual Modules

Completed modules should be tested independently by programmers before being implemented. This usually involves the creation of test data. Depending on the nature of the application, this could include test transaction files, test master files, or both. Figure 14-19 illustrates the test data approach. This and several other testing techniques are examined in detail in Chapter 17.

Assume the module under test is the Update AP Records program (Module H) represented in Figure 14-17. The approach taken is to test the application thoroughly within its range of functions. To do this, the programmer must create some test accounts payable master file records and test transactions. The transactions should contain a range of data values adequate to test the logic of the application, including both "good" and "bad" data. For example, the programmer may create a transaction with an incorrect account

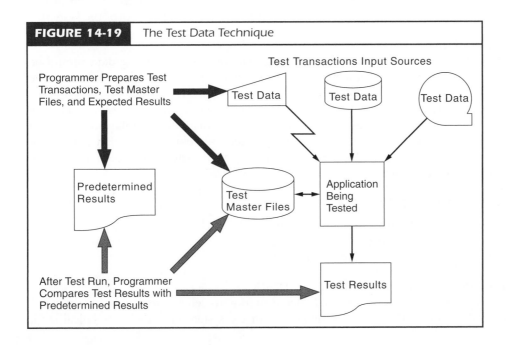

FIGURE 14-19   The Test Data Technique

number to see how the application handles such errors. The programmer will then compare the amounts posted to accounts payable records to see if they tally with precalculated results. Tests of all aspects of the logic will be performed in this way, and the test results will be used to identify and correct errors in the logic of the module.

DELIVER THE SYSTEM

The system is now ready to be implemented. In this phase, database structures are populated with data, equipment is purchased and installed, employees are trained, and the system is documented. This phase concludes with the roll-out of the new system and the termination of the old system.

The implementation process engages the efforts of designers, programmers, database administrators, users, and accountants. All the steps in this stage warrant careful management. Nevertheless, not all steps are part of every system's implementation and not all are of direct concern to accountants. For example, the implementation activities of ordering equipment from vendors, preparing the site, installing equipment, and training employees are not performed with each new system. Moreover, these are technical tasks that do not usually involve the accounting function. This section focuses on those activities that have the greatest direct implications for accountants and auditors.

TESTING THE ENTIRE SYSTEM

When all modules have been coded and tested, they must be brought together and tested as a whole. User personnel should direct systemwide testing as a prelude to the formal system cutover. The procedure involves using the system to process hypothetical data. The outputs of the system are then reconciled with predetermined results, and the test is documented to provide evidence of the system's performance. Finally, when those conducting the tests are satisfied with the results, a formal acceptance document should be completed. This is an explicit acknowledgment by the user that the system in question meets stated requirements. The user acceptance document becomes important in reconciling differences and assigning responsibility during the post-implementation review of the system.

Saving Test Data
The preparation of test data is a tedious, time-consuming activity. These data should be saved for future use by the auditor during system reviews. By preserving the test data, we create what is called a *base case*, which documents how the system performed at a point in time. At any future point, the base case data should generate the same results. The only differences between base case results and current test results will be explained by system changes (maintenance) that have occurred since system implementation. Hence, the base case provides a reference point for analyzing the effects of system changes and eases the burden of creating test data.

DOCUMENTING THE SYSTEM

The system's **documentation** describes how the system works. In this section, we consider the documentation requirements of four groups: systems designers and programmers, computer operators, end users, and accountants.

Designer and Programmer Documentation
Systems designers and programmers need documentation to debug errors and perform maintenance on the system. This group is involved with the system on a highly technical level,

which requires both general and detailed information. Some of this is provided through DFDs, ER diagrams, and structure diagrams. In addition, system flowcharts, program flowcharts, and listings of program code are important forms of documentation. The *system flowchart* shows the relationship of input files, programs, and output files. However, it does not reveal the logic of individual programs that constitute the system. The *program flowchart* provides a detailed description of the sequential and logical operation of the program. Each program in the system's flowchart is represented by a separate program flowchart. From these, the programmer can visually review and evaluate the program's logic. The program code should itself be documented with comments that describe each major program segment.

Operator Documentation

Computer operators use documentation describing how to run the system called a **run manual**. The typical contents of a run manual include:

- The name of the system, such as Purchases System.
- The run schedule (daily, weekly, time of day, and so on).
- Required hardware devices (tapes, disks, printers, or special hardware).
- File requirements specifying all the transaction (input) files, master files, and output files used in the system.
- Run-time instructions describing the error messages that may appear, actions to be taken, and the name and telephone number of the programmer on call, should the system fail.
- A list of users who receive the output from the run.

For security and control reasons, system flowcharts, logic flowcharts, and program code listings are not part of the operator documentation. Operators should not have access to the details of a system's internal logic. We will discuss this point more fully in Chapter 15.

User Documentation

Users need documentation describing how to use the system. User tasks include such things as entering input for transactions, making inquiries of account balances, updating accounts, and generating output reports. The nature of user documentation will depend on the user's degree of sophistication with computers and technology. Thus, before designing user documentation, the systems professional must assess and classify the user's skill level. The following is one classification scheme:

- Novices
- Occasional users
- Frequent light users
- Frequent power users

Novices have little or no experience with computers and may be embarrassed to ask questions. Novices also know little about their assigned tasks. User training and documentation for novices must be extensive and detailed.

Occasional users once understood the system but have forgotten some essential commands and procedures. They require less training and documentation than novices.

Frequent light users are familiar with limited aspects of the system. Although functional, they tend not to explore beneath the surface and lack depth of knowledge. This group knows only what it needs to know and requires training and documentation for unfamiliar areas.

Frequent power users understand the existing system and will readily adapt to new systems. They are intolerant of detailed instructions that waste their time. They like to find shortcuts and use macro commands to improve performance. This group requires only abbreviated documentation.

With these classes in mind, user documentation often takes the form of a user handbook, as well as online documentation. The typical **user handbook** will contain the following items:

- An overview of the system and its major functions
- Instructions for getting started
- Descriptions of procedures with step-by-step visual references
- Examples of input screens and instructions for entering data
- A complete list of error message codes and descriptions
- A reference manual of commands to run the system
- A glossary of key terms
- Service and support information

Online documentation will guide the user interactively in the use of the system. Some commonly found online features include tutorials and help features.

Tutorials. Online tutorials can be used to train the novice or the occasional user. The success of this technique is based on the tutorial's degree of realism. Tutorials should not restrict the user from access to legitimate functions.

Help Features. Online help features range from simple to sophisticated. A simple help feature may be nothing more than an error message displayed on the screen. The user must "walk through" the screens in search of the solution to the problem. More sophisticated help is context related. When the user makes an error, the system will send the message, "Do you need help?" The help feature analyzes the context of what the user is doing at the time of the error and provides help with that specific function (or command).

Accountant (Auditor) Documentation

With responsibility for the design of certain security procedures, accounting controls, and audit trails, accountants are stakeholders in all AIS applications. For these tasks, accountants may draw upon all of the documentation described previously. As internal and external auditors, accountants also require document flowcharts of manual procedures. We have encountered numerous examples of document flowcharts in the chapters dealing with the revenue, expenditure, and conversion cycles. Document flowcharts differ from DFDs in an important way. DFDs describe the overall logic of the system. Document flowcharts show explicitly the flow of information between departments, the departments in which tasks are actually performed, and the specific types and number of documents that carry information. A physical view such as this is needed to understand the segregation of duties, the adequacy of source documents, and the location of files that support the audit trail. Document flowcharts are not always included as part of the system's documentation. When not provided, auditors must create their own during the audit process.

CONVERTING THE DATABASES

Database conversion is a critical step in the implementation phase. This is the transfer of data from its current form to the format or medium required by the new system. The degree of conversion depends on the technology leap from the old system to the new one. Some conversion activities are very labor-intensive, requiring data to be entered into new databases manually. For example, the move from a manual system to a computer system will require converting files from paper to magnetic disk or tape. In other situations, data transfer may be accomplished by writing special conversion programs. A case in point is changing the file structure of the databases from sequential direct access files. In any case, data conversion is risky and must be carefully controlled. The following precautions should be taken:

1. *Validation.* The old database must be validated before conversion. This requires analyzing each class of data to determine whether it should be reproduced in the new database.
2. *Reconciliation.* After the conversion action, the new database must be reconciled against the original. Sometimes this must be done manually, record by record and field by field. In many instances, this process can be automated by writing a program that will compare the two sets of data.
3. *Backup.* Copies of the original files must be kept as backup against discrepancies in the converted data. If the current files are already in magnetic form, they can be conveniently backed up and stored. However, paper documents can create storage problems. When the user feels confident about the accuracy and completeness of the new databases, the paper documents may be destroyed.

CONVERTING TO THE NEW SYSTEM

The process of converting from the old system to the new one is called the **cutover**. A system cutover will usually follow one of three approaches: cold turkey, phased, or parallel operation.

Cold Turkey Cutover

Under the **cold turkey cutover** approach (also called the "Big Bang" approach), the firm switches to the new system and simultaneously terminates the old system. When implementing simple systems, this is often the easiest and least costly approach. With more complex systems, it is the riskiest. Cold turkey cutover is akin to skydiving without a reserve parachute. As long as the main parachute functions properly, there is no problem. But things don't always work the way they are supposed to. System errors that were not detected during the walkthrough and testing steps may materialize unexpectedly. Without a backup system, an organization can find itself in serious trouble.

Phased Cutover

Sometimes an entire system cannot, or need not, be cutover at once. The **phased cutover** begins operating the new system in modules. For example, Figure 14-20 shows how we might implement a system, starting with the sales subsystem, followed by the inventory control subsystem, and finally the purchases subsystem.

By phasing in the new system in modules, we reduce the risk of a devastating system failure. However, the phased approach can create incompatibilities between new subsystems and yet-to-be-replaced old subsystems. This problem may be alleviated by implementing special conversion systems that provide temporary interfaces during the cutover period.

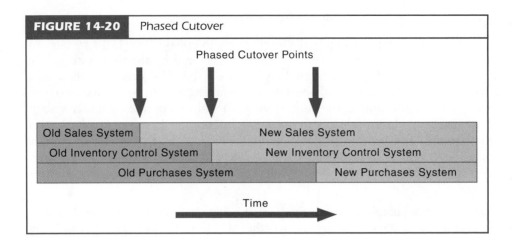

FIGURE 14-20   Phased Cutover

Phased Cutover Points

| Old Sales System | New Sales System |

| Old Inventory Control System | New Inventory Control System |

| Old Purchases System | New Purchases System |

Time

Parallel Operation Cutover

Parallel operation cutover involves running the old system and the new system simultaneously for a period of time. Figure 14-21 illustrates this approach, which is the most time consuming and costly of the three. Running two systems in parallel essentially doubles resource consumption. During the cutover period, the two systems require twice the source documents, twice the processing time, twice the databases, and twice the output production.

The advantage of parallel cutover is the reduction in risk. By running two systems, the user can reconcile outputs to identify errors and debug errors before running the new system solo. Parallel operation should usually extend for one business cycle, such as one month. This allows the user to reconcile the two outputs at the end of the cycle as a final test of the system's functionality.

POST-IMPLEMENTATION REVIEW

The final step in the implementation phase actually takes place some months later in a *post-implementation review*. The objective is to measure the success of the system and of the process after the dust has settled. Although systems professionals strive to produce systems that are on budget, on time, and meet user needs, this does not always happen.

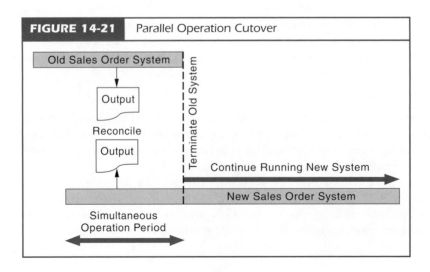

FIGURE 14-21   Parallel Operation Cutover

Old Sales Order System

Output

Reconcile

Output

Terminate Old System

Continue Running New System

New Sales Order System

Simultaneous Operation Period

The post-implementation review of the newly installed system can provide insight into ways to improve the process for future systems. The areas discussed in the following section are of particular concern.

System Design Adequacy

The physical features of the system should be reviewed to see if they meet user needs. The reviewer should seek answers to the following types of questions:

1. Does the output from the system possess such characteristics of information as relevance, timeliness, completeness, accuracy, and so on?
2. Is the output in the format most useful and desired by the user (such as tables, graphs, electronic, hard copy, and so on)?
3. Are the databases accurate, complete, and accessible?
4. Were data lost, corrupted, or duplicated by the conversion process?
5. Are input forms and screens properly designed and meeting user needs?
6. Are the users using the system properly?
7. Does the processing appear to be correct?
8. Can all program modules be accessed and executed properly, or does the user ever get stuck in a loop?
9. Is user documentation accurate, complete, and easy to follow?
10. Does the system provide the user adequate help and tutorials?

Accuracy of Time, Cost, and Benefit Estimates

The task of estimating time, costs, and benefits for a proposed system is complicated by uncertainty. This is particularly true for large projects involving many activities and long time frames. The more variables in the process, the greater the likelihood for material error in the estimates. History is often the best teacher for decisions of this sort. Therefore, a review of actual performance compared to budgeted amounts provides critical input for future budgeting decisions. From such information, we can learn where mistakes were made and how to avoid them the next time. The following questions provide some insight:

1. Were PERT and Gantt chart estimates accurate to within 10 percent?
2. What were the areas of significant departures from budget?
3. Were departures from the budget controllable (internal) in the short run or noncontrollable (for example, supplier problems)?
4. Were estimates of the number of lines of program code accurate?
5. Was the degree of rework due to design and coding errors acceptable?
6. Were actual costs in line with budgeted costs?
7. Are users receiving the expected benefits from the system?
8. Do the benefits seem to have been fairly valued?

THE ROLE OF ACCOUNTANTS

The role of accountants in the construct and deliver phases of the SDLC should be significant. Most system failures are due to poor designs and improper implementation. Being a major stakeholder in all financial systems, accountants must apply their expertise in this process to guide and shape the finished system. Specifically, accountants should get involved in the following ways.

Provide Technical Expertise

The detailed design phase involves precise specifications of procedures, rules, and conventions to be used in the system. In the case of an AIS, these specifications must comply with

GAAP, GAAS, SEC regulations, and IRS codes. Failure to so comply can lead to legal exposure for the firm. For example, choosing the correct depreciation method or asset valuation technique requires a technical background not necessarily possessed by systems professionals. The accountant must provide this expertise to the systems design process.

Specify Documentation Standards

In the implementation phase, the accountant plays a role in specifying system documentation. Because financial systems must periodically be audited, they must be adequately documented. The accountant must actively encourage adherence to effective documentation standards.

Verify Control Adequacy

The applications that emerge from the SDLC must possess controls that are in accordance with the provisions of SAS 78. This requires the accountant's involvement at both the detailed design and implementation phases. Controls may be programmed or manual procedures. Some controls are part of the daily operation of the system, while others are special actions that precede, follow, or oversee routine processing. The extent of control techniques makes it impossible to treat them within this chapter. Instead, we have devoted the next two chapters to the study of control concepts and design.

COMMERCIAL PACKAGES

Thus far we have examined system construction and delivery activities pertaining to in-house development. Not all systems are acquired in this fashion; the trend today is toward purchased software. Faced with many competing packages, each with unique features and attributes, management must choose the system and the vendor that best serves the needs of the organization. Making the optimal choice requires that this be an informed decision.

Before moving on to the next phase of the SDLC, we will examine the issues surrounding the purchase of commercial software. Our discussion will focus primarily on a technique that can help structure and evaluate the many intangible factors that complicate the process of selecting commercial software.

TRENDS IN COMMERCIAL PACKAGES

Four factors have stimulated the growth of the commercial software market: (1) the relatively low cost of general commercial software as compared to customized software; (2) the emergence of industry-specific vendors who target their software to the needs of particular types of businesses; (3) a growing demand from businesses that are too small to afford an in-house systems development staff; and (4) the trend toward downsizing of organizational units and the resulting move toward the distributed data processing environment, which has made the commercial software option more appealing to larger organizations. Indeed, organizations that maintain their own in-house systems development staff will purchase commercial software when the nature of their need permits. Commercial software can be divided into a number of general groups, which are discussed in the following section.

Turnkey Systems

Turnkey systems are completely finished and tested systems that are ready for implementation. Often these are general-purpose systems or systems customized to a specific industry.

Turnkey systems are usually sold only as compiled program modules, and users have limited ability to customize such systems to their specific needs. Some turnkey systems have software options that allow the user to customize input, output, and some processing through menu choices. Other turnkey system vendors will sell their customers the source code if program changes are desired. For a fee, the user or the vendor can then customize the system by reprogramming the original source code. Some examples of turnkey systems are described in the following section.

General Accounting Systems. General accounting systems are designed to serve a wide variety of user needs. By mass producing a standard system, the vendor is able to reduce the unit cost of these systems to a fraction of in-house development costs. Powerful systems of this sort can be obtained for under $2,000.

To provide as much flexibility as possible, general accounting systems are designed in modules. This allows users to purchase the modules that meet their specific needs. Typical modules include accounts payable, accounts receivable, payroll processing, inventory control, general ledger, financial reporting, and fixed asset.

Special-Purpose Systems. Some software vendors have targeted their systems to selected segments of the economy. For example, the medical field, the banking industry, and government agencies have unique accounting procedures, rules, and conventions that general-purpose accounting systems do not always accommodate. Software vendors have thus developed standardized systems to deal with industry-specific procedures.

Office Automation Systems. Office automation is the use of computer systems to improve the productivity of office workers. Examples of office automation systems include word processing packages, database management systems, spreadsheet programs, and desktop publishing systems.

Backbone Systems

As we learned in Chapter 1, **backbone systems** provide a basic system structure on which to build. Backbone systems come with all the primary processing modules programmed. The vendor designs and programs the user interface to suit the client's needs. This approach can produce highly customized systems. But customizing a system is expensive and time-consuming. Many vendors thus employ object-oriented systems design, which takes advantage of reusable modules and thereby reduces the costs of tailoring the system to the user.

Vendor-Supported Systems

Vendor-supported systems are hybrids of custom systems and commercial software. Under this approach, the vendor develops (and maintains) custom systems for its clients. The systems themselves are custom products, but the systems development service is commercially provided. This option is popular in the health care and legal services industries. Because the vendor serves as the organization's in-house systems development staff, the client organization must rely on the vendor to provide custom programming and on-site maintenance of systems. Much of each client's system may be developed from scratch, but by using an object-oriented approach, vendors can produce common modules that can be reused in other client systems. This approach helps to reduce development costs charged to the client firms.

ERP Systems

ERP systems are difficult to classify into a single category because they have characteristics of all of the above. They are prewritten systems, which in some cases are implemented as turnkey applications. On the other hand, they can be modified to meet user needs. An ERP may be installed as a backbone system that interfaces with other legacy systems or it may constitute an entirely new system. Because of their complexity, ERP systems are most often vendor-supported packages that are installed by an outside service provider.

ADVANTAGES OF COMMERCIAL PACKAGES

Implementation Time

Custom systems often take a long time to develop. Months or even years may pass before a custom system can be developed through in-house procedures. Unless the organization successfully anticipates future information needs and schedules application development accordingly, it may experience long periods of unsatisfied need. On the other hand, small commercial software systems can be implemented almost immediately upon recognizing a need. The user does not need to wait. The implementation of a single module of larger systems such as Peoplesoft, SAP, BAAN, MFG/PRO, ORACLE-FIN, or JDE, however, could take from several weeks to a few months. An entire ERP could take years, but this is still much quicker than in-house or outsourced development would take.

Cost

In-house development costs must be wholly absorbed by a single user. However, because the cost of commercial software is spread across many users, the unit cost is reduced to a fraction of the cost of a system developed in house.

Reliability

Most reputable commercial software packages are thoroughly tested before their release to the consumer market. Any system errors not discovered during testing are likely to be uncovered by user organizations shortly after release and corrected. Although no system is certified as being free from errors, commercial software is less likely to have errors than an equivalent in-house system.

DISADVANTAGES OF COMMERCIAL PACKAGES

Independence

Purchasing a vendor-supported system makes the firm dependent on the vendor for maintenance. The user runs the risk that the vendor will cease to support the system or even go out of business. This is perhaps the greatest disadvantage of vendor-supported systems.

The Need for Customized Systems

The prime advantage of in-house development is the ability to produce applications to exact specifications. This advantage also describes a disadvantage of commercial software. Sometimes, the user's needs are unique and complex, and commercially available software is either too general or too inflexible.

Maintenance

Business information systems undergo frequent changes. If the user's needs change, it may be difficult or even impossible to modify commercial software. On the other hand, in-house development provides users with proprietary applications that can be maintained.

CHOOSING A PACKAGE

Having made the decision to purchase commercial software, the systems development team is now faced with the task of choosing the package that best satisfies the organization's needs. On the surface, there may appear to be no clear-cut best choice from the many options available. The following four-step procedure can help structure this decision-making process by establishing decision criteria and identifying key differences between options.

Step 1: Needs Analysis

As with in-house development, the commercial option begins with an analysis of user needs. These are formally presented in a statement of systems requirements that provides a basis for choosing between competing alternatives. For example, the stated requirement of the new system may be to:

1. Support the accounting and reporting requirements of federal, state, and local agencies.
2. Provide access to information in a timely and efficient manner.
3. Simultaneously support both accrual accounting and fund accounting systems.
4. Increase transaction processing capacity.
5. Reduce the cost of current operations.
6. Improve user productivity.
7. Reduce processing errors.
8. Support batch and real-time processing.
9. Provide automatic general ledger reconciliations.
10. Be expandable and flexible to accommodate growth and changes in future needs.

The systems requirements should be as detailed as the user's technical background permits. Detailed specifications enable users to narrow the search to only those packages most likely to satisfy their needs. Although computer literacy is a distinct advantage in this step, the technically inexperienced user can still compile a meaningful list of desirable features that the system should possess. For example, the user should address such items of importance as compliance with accounting conventions, special control and transaction volume requirements, and so on.

Step 2: Send Out the Request for Proposals

Systems requirements are summarized in a document called a **request for proposal (RFP)** that is sent to each prospective vendor. A letter of transmittal accompanies the RFP to explain to the vendor the nature of the problem, the objectives of the system, and the deadline for proposal submission.

The RFP provides a format for vendor responses and thus a comparative basis for initial screening. Some vendors will choose not to respond to the RFP, while others will propose packages that clearly do not meet the stated requirements. The reviewer should attempt to select from these responses those proposals that are feasible alternatives.

Step 3: Gather Facts

In this next step in the selection process, the objective is to identify and capture relevant facts about each vendor's system. The following describes techniques for fact gathering.

Vendor Presentations. At some point during the review, vendors should be invited to make formal presentations of their systems at the user's premises. This provides the principle decision makers and users with an opportunity to observe the product firsthand.

Technical demonstrations are usually given at these presentations using modified versions of the packages that run on microcomputers. This provides an opportunity to obtain answers to detailed questions. Sufficient time should therefore be allotted for an in-depth demonstration followed by a question-and-answer period. If vendor representatives are unable or unwilling to demonstrate the full range of system capabilities or to deal with specific questions from the audience, this may indicate a functional deficiency of the system.

Failure to gain satisfactory responses from vendor representatives may also be a sign of their technical incompetence. The representatives either do not understand the user's problem or their own system and how it relates to the user's situation. In either case, the user has cause to question the vendor's ability to deliver a quality product and to provide adequate support.

Benchmark Problems. One often-used technique for measuring the relative performance of competing systems is to establish a benchmark problem for them to solve. The benchmark problem could consist of important transactions or tasks performed by key components of the system. In the benchmark example illustrated in Figure 14-22, both systems are given the same data and processing task. The results of processing are compared on criteria such as speed, accuracy, and efficiency in performing the task.

Vendor Support. For some organizations, vendor support is an important criterion in systems selection. The desired level of support should be carefully considered. Organizations with competent in-house systems professionals may need less vendor support than firms without such internal resources. Support can vary greatly from vendor to vendor. Some vendors provide full-service support, including:

- Client training.

- User and technical documentation.

- Warranties.

- Maintenance programs to implement system enhancements.

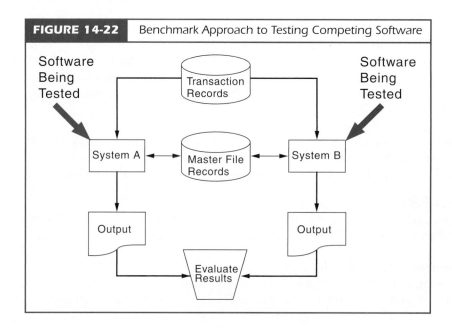

FIGURE 14-22   Benchmark Approach to Testing Competing Software

- Toll-free help numbers.

- Annual seminars to obtain input from users and apprise them of the latest developments.

At the other extreme, some vendors provide virtually no support. The buyer should be wary of a promise of support that seems too good to be true, because it probably is. The level of support the vendor provides can account for a large portion of its product's price. To avoid "dump and run" vendors, the buyer must be prepared to pay for support.

Contact User Groups. A vendor's current user list is an important source of information. The prospective user, not the vendor, should select a representative sample of users with the latest version of the package and with similar computer configurations. A standard set of questions directed to these users will provide information for comparing packages. The following list is an example of the type of questions to ask:

- When did you purchase the package?

- Which other vendors did you review?

- Why did you select this package?

- Are you satisfied with the package?

- Are you satisfied with the vendor support?

- Does the system perform as advertised?

- Were modifications required?

- What type of training did the vendor provide?

- What is the quality of the documentation?

- Have any major problems been encountered?

- Do you subscribe to the vendor's maintenance program?

- If so, do you receive enhancements?

To reiterate an important point, the prospective user, not the vendor, should select the user references. This provides for a more objective appraisal and reduces the possibility of receiving biased information from "showcase" installations.

Step 4: Analyze the Findings and Make a Final Selection

The final step in the selection process is to analyze the facts and choose the best package. The principle problem is dealing with the many qualitative aspects of this decision. A popular technique for structuring and analyzing qualitative variables is the "weighted factor matrix." The technique requires constructing a table similar to the one illustrated in Table 14-2. This table shows a comparison between only two proposals, those of Vendor A and Vendor B. In practice, the approach can be applied to all the vendors under consideration.

The table presents the relevant decision criteria under the heading "Factor." Each decision factor is assigned a weight that implies its relative importance to the user. Two steps are critical to this analysis technique: (1) identify all relevant decision factors and (2) assign realistic weights to each factor. As these factors represent all of the relevant decision criteria, their weights should total 100 percent. These weights will likely vary among decision makers. One reviewer may consider vendor support an important factor and thus assign a high numeric value to its weight. Another decision maker may give this a low weight because support is not important in his or her firm, relative to other factors.

TABLE 14-2	Weighted Factor Matrix				

		PROPOSAL A		**PROPOSAL B**	
Factor	**Weight**	**Raw Score**	**Weighted Score**	**Raw Score**	**Weighted Score**
Response time	10	5	50	4	40
Compatibility	9	3	27	5	45
Reputation and experience	5	3	15	5	25
Ability to deliver on schedule	7	4	28	5	35
Range of capabilities	15	4	60	4	60
Modularity	12	4	48	3	36
User friendliness	15	4	60	3	45
Supports database	9	2	18	5	45
Supports networking	3	2	6	5	15
Vendor support	15	4	60	3	45
Total	100		372		391

After assigning weights, each vendor package is evaluated according to its performance in each factor category. Based upon the facts gathered in the previous steps, each individual factor is scored on a scale of 1 to 5, where 1 is poor performance and 5 is excellent. The weighted scores are computed by multiplying the raw score by the weight for each factor. Using the previous example, a weight of 15 for vendor support is multiplied by a score of 4 for Vendor A and 3 for Vendor B, yielding the weighted scores of 60 and 45, respectively.

The weighted scores are then totaled, and each vendor is assigned a composite score. This is the vendor's overall performance index. Table 14-2 shows a score for Vendor B of 391 and 372 for Vendor A. This composite score suggests that Vendor B's product is rated slightly higher than Vendor A's.

This analysis must be taken a step further to include financial considerations. For example, assume Proposal A costs $150,000 and Proposal B costs $190,000. An overall performance/cost index is computed as follows.

Proposal A: $\frac{372}{\$150,000}$ = 2.48 per $1,000

Proposal B: $\frac{391}{\$190,000}$ = 2.06 per $1,000

This means that Proposal A provides 2.48 units of performance per $1,000 versus only 2.06 units per $1,000 from Proposal B. Therefore, Proposal A provides the greater value for the cost.

The option with the highest performance/cost ratio is the more economically feasible choice. Of course, this analysis rests on the user's ability to identify all relevant decision factors and assign to them weights that reflect their relative importance to the decision. If any relevant factors are omitted or if their weights are misstated, the results of the analysis will be misleading.

MAINTENANCE AND SUPPORT

Maintenance involves both implementing the latest software versions of commercial packages and making in-house modifications to existing systems to accommodate changing user needs. Maintenance may be relatively trivial, such as modifying an application to produce a new report, or more extensive, such as programming new functionality into a system.

Some organizations view systems maintenance services as commodity activities that should be outsourced to third-party vendors on the low-cost bidder basis. The underlying justification for this is short-term economic benefit. By outsourcing maintenance and support, management can channel financial resources into the organization's core competencies. Unfortunately, isolating maintenance activities from the organization also disrupts the flow of system-related knowledge that may be of strategic importance to the organization.

Some organizations take a strategic view of maintenance. Maintenance is an integral part of the SDLC. Rather than representing the end of the line, it can be an incubator for new ideas. If management captures the appropriate data, each currently running system can be the prototype for the next version. To ensure success, the organization needs to collect all relevant data from comments, requests, observed symptoms, and ideas for improvement from the user community.

USER SUPPORT

Typically, the first point of contact for such data transfer is through the user support function. This includes help desk services, user training and education classes, and formally documented user feedback pertaining to problems and system errors. To facilitate data gathering and analysis, **knowledge management** systems are effective maintenance tools.

KNOWLEDGE MANAGEMENT AND GROUP MEMORY

Knowledge management is a concept consisting of four basic processes: *gathering*, *organizing*, *refining*, and *disseminating*. **Gathering** brings data into the system. **Organizing** associates data items with subjects, giving them context. **Refining** adds value by discovering relationships between data, performing synthesis, and abstracting. **Disseminating** gets knowledge to the recipients in a usable form. The most difficult of these processes to automate is refining.

A knowledge management system can be used to create a **group memory**, which makes an organization more effective just as human beings become more effective and mature with the accumulation of thoughts and memories. From a technology viewpoint a knowledge management system is a database-oriented software tool that allows users, developers, and the operations community to contribute to the group memory. Contributors add their comments, suggestions, or complaints about a system or process into forms from their desktop PCs. The knowledge management software uses a parsing utility that takes incoming strings of data and infers relationships from them. A notable strength of the system is that it can deal with both historical and emerging data. The goal of the system is not simply to store information in a central repository for record keeping or archival recall. Rather, it analyzes the heterogeneous data and disseminates information to users and systems management. Group memory is thus a potentially valuable input to the organization's evolving systems strategy.

SUMMARY

The chapter dealt with the construction and delivery of information systems. The first section presented topics and issues related to in-house development. This began with a review of techniques used for improving systems construction, including prototyping, CASE technology, PERT charts, and Gantt charts. Next, two design approaches were discussed: the structured approach and the object-oriented approach. The discussion followed a design sequence that dealt with system components in the following order: create a data model of the business process, define conceptual user views, design the normalized database tables, design the physical user views (output and input views), develop the process modules, specify the system controls, and perform a system walkthrough. The delivery stage involves populating database structures, purchasing and installing equipment, employee training, and system documentation. This phase concludes with the roll-out of the new system and the termination of the old system. The section concluded with a discussion of the accountant's role in in-house development. We next examined issues related to commercial software, an option that businesses are increasingly using. After briefly identifying the pros and cons of commercial software, we examined a four-step procedure that can be employed in the selection of commercial software packages. The chapter concluded with a brief discussion of the strategic role of system maintenance and the importance of group memory as a key input to systems strategy.

APPENDIX

CASE TOOLS

Figure 14-23 presents the CASE spectrum of support in relation to the relevant stages of the SDLC. CASE tools are used to define user requirements, create physical databases from conceptual user views, produce systems design specifications, automatically generate computer program code, and facilitate the maintenance of programs created by both CASE and non-CASE techniques. Figure 14-24 presents an overview diagram of a comprehensive CASE system. The sections below follow the main points of this diagram.

Central Repository
The heart of the CASE system is the **central repository**. Essentially, this is a database of attributes, relations, and elements that describe all the applications created under the CASE system. These items include:

1. Definitions of all databases.
2. Systems documentation, such as context diagrams, data flow diagrams, and structure charts.

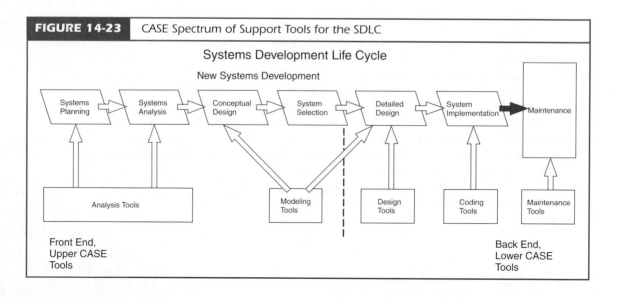

FIGURE 14-23   CASE Spectrum of Support Tools for the SDLC

FIGURE 14-24   Overview of CASE System

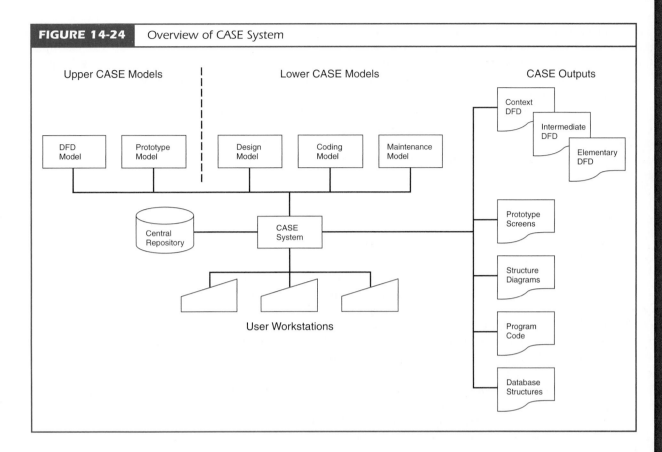

3. The program code.
4. Reusable program modules.
5. User prototype screens.

The central repository system helps to integrate the activities of system designers working on the same project or on separate but related projects. For example, if the size or the name of a data attribute must be changed, then all the applications that use that attribute must also be changed. In a moderate-sized firm, this could involve hundreds of programs. Normally, this would require many days of manual searching to identify the affected programs. However, the central repository system can quickly identify and list the applications that use the attribute being changed. Another example of the integration of activities is the ability to reuse program code. Different applications may use the same routines. These routines can be created, tested, and then used many times. The central repository stores reusable modules for immediate implementation in other systems. This reduces the overall development time of subsequent applications.

CASE Models

CASE products employ several functional models that can be used to support activities in different phases of the SDLC. The following models are representative.

The Dataflow Diagram Model. We introduced the dataflow diagram in Chapter 2. This section presents a more extensive use of this documentation technique. The DFD uses a set of symbols to represent the processes, data sources, dataflows, and process sequences of a current or proposed system.

As a systems design tool, DFDs are used to represent multiple levels of detail. From the most general to the most detailed, these are, respectively, the context level, the intermediate level, and the elementary level.

The Context-Level DFD. The analyst can use the context-level DFD to present an overview model of the business activities and the primary transactions processed by the system. Figure 14-25 presents an example of a context diagram of the revenue cycle for a company. The context diagram is a very high-level representation of the system. It does not include a detailed definition of data files and specific procedures. The focus is on the overall relationship between the entities (data, sources of data, and processes) in the system. This relationship is represented by symbols, lines, and arrows that show the direction of the dataflows.

The Intermediate-Level DFD. The next step is to explode the context-level DFD into one or more intermediate-level DFDs, as illustrated in Figure 14-26. Notice how Process 1.0 in Figure 14-25 is decomposed into the following subprocesses.

- 1.1 Sales Approval
- 1.2 Ship Goods
- 1.3 Bill Customer
- 1.4 Update Accounts Receivable

Several levels of intermediate DFDs may be needed to present enough detail for the systems professional and user to fully understand the system. In this example, we show only one intermediate level.

The Elementary-Level DFD. Figure 14-27 presents the elementary-level DFD for Process 1.3 in Figure 14-26. An elementary-level DFD provides a clear and precise definition of all elements of a portion of the system. In this example, Process 1.3 (bill customer) is explained in detail. Other elementary-level DFDs will be required for Processes 1.1, 1.2, and 1.4.

The preparation of DFDs in a non-CASE environment can be time-consuming for the analyst. Because of inevitable changes in specifications during the system's development, the analyst may produce many versions of the DFD documents before arriving at the final product. The graphics capability of CASE tools greatly expedites this task by providing functions for labeling, modifying, and rearranging the DFD. However, the CASE DFD is more than simply a graphic representation of the system. The elementary-level DFD is the physical input to lower CASE models that automatically produce program code and database tables. Any and all changes to the system during its development and maintenance are thus made directly through the DFD.

The Prototype Model. The prototype model supports the prototyping concept presented earlier. This is a powerful feature that helps ensure that user requirements are being met. Systems professionals can

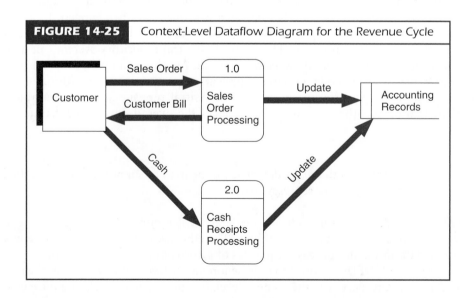

FIGURE 14-25   Context-Level Dataflow Diagram for the Revenue Cycle

FIGURE 14-26 Intermediate-Level Dataflow Diagram for Sales Order Processing System

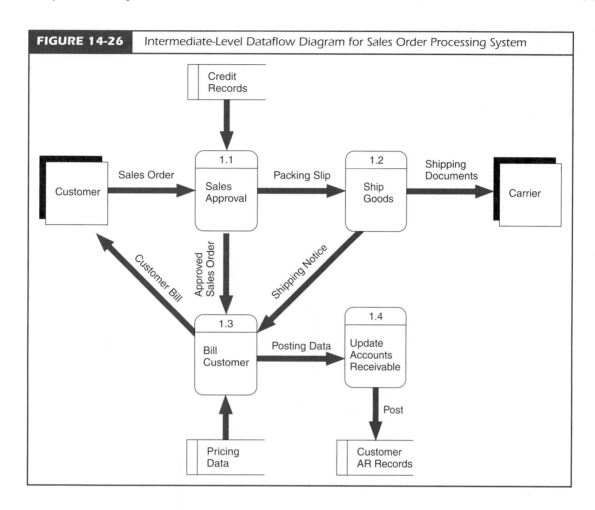

immediately provide users with input screens and report formats. The user can thus visualize certain features of the system before it is actually designed and evaluate the proposed system. Any changes can be implemented before the system is designed and at virtually no cost to the project schedule.

The Design Model. The logic of the design model is based on the concept of system decomposition, which was introduced in Chapter 1. Recall that any system can be decomposed from the top down into smaller and smaller subsystems, each with a specific function. The design model takes the elementary-level DFD as input and produces from this a structure diagram. The DFD is a model of the conceptual system, and the structure diagram is a model of the program code that constitutes the physical system. Figure 14-28 shows a structure diagram for the elementary-level DFD in Figure 14-27. The structure diagram shows the overall relationship between the modules that constitute the system. Each of these modules represents a separate program that must be coded, unless it already exists as a reusable program module. We examine the issue of reusable modules later in the chapter.

Many CASE tools document the details of each module in the form of pseudocode or structured English. Pseudocode explains what the module is supposed to do, regardless of the programming language used.

The Coding Model. One of the great labor-saving advantages of CASE is its facility for transforming the structure diagram into computer modules. Many top-end CASE tools produce program source code, such as COBOL, C, and C++. These source programs must then be compiled (translated) into executable machine code modules.

FIGURE 14-27   Elementary-Level Dataflow Diagram for the Billing Process

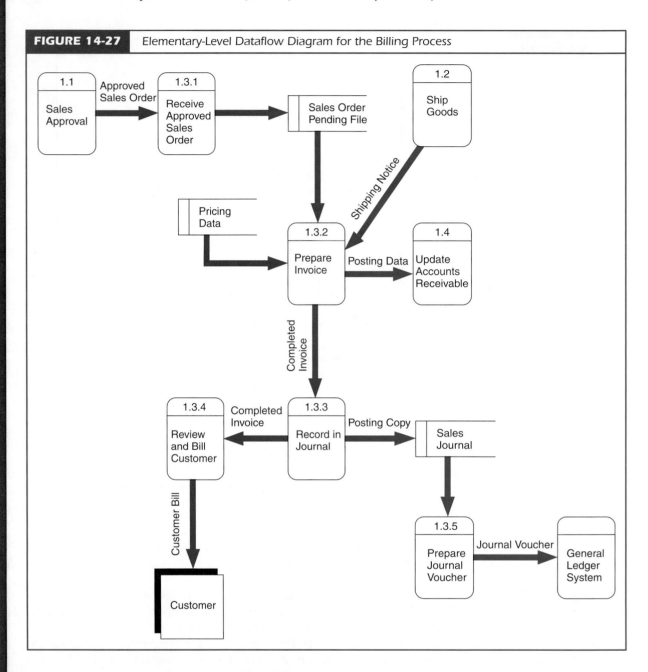

Some CASE tools convert the structure diagrams directly to machine code and eliminate the source-code stage. The reason for this is to preserve the integrity between the conceptual system model (the DFD) and the physical system (the program). Sometimes during maintenance or original development, systems specialists are tempted to make design changes directly to the source code. If these changes are not also made to the DFDs and structure diagrams that specify the system, there will be a discrepancy between documentation that describes what the program does and the actual program. By eliminating the source code, the systems professional is forced to make all systems changes via the DFDs. The CASE tool will then modify the structure diagrams and rewrite the computer (machine level) code automatically. This ensures that the system's description is always consistent with the program code.

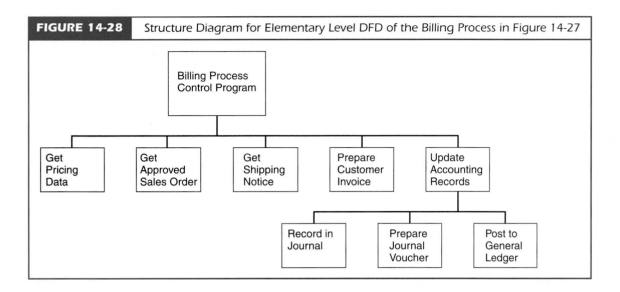

FIGURE 14-28 Structure Diagram for Elementary Level DFD of the Billing Process in Figure 14-27

The nonsource code approach has two implications for accountants, auditors, and management. The first is a potential control issue. The program source code is part of the system documentation. To properly design their test procedures, auditors sometimes need to review the source code. If it is not available, this may hamper testing and force the auditor to employ alternative, less efficient, and more costly procedures. Second, the nonsource code approach can have the effect of committing the firm to a particular CASE tool and vendor. By creating source code as a by-product of the development process, the application remains independent of the CASE system. Should the firm's management decide to switch to another vendor, current applications can still be maintained. Most CASE tools will accept source programs written in standard source code.

The Maintenance Model. Eighty to 90 percent of the total cost of a system is expended during the maintenance phase of the SDLC. This is often referred to as the "iceberg effect." Figure 14-29 illustrates this phenomenon. All systems must be maintained throughout their lives, and some iceberg effect is inevitable.

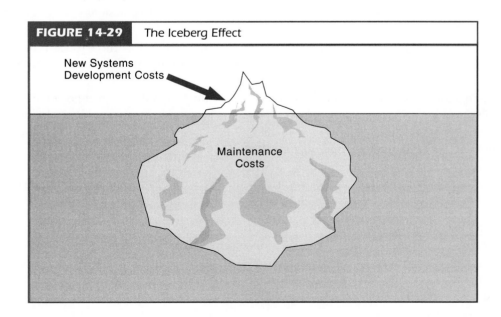

FIGURE 14-29 The Iceberg Effect

However, poorly designed systems can significantly contribute to the problem. To make a change to a computer program in a non-CASE environment, the maintenance programmer must first thoroughly review the program code in an attempt to understand the original programmer's logic. This review often requires a great deal of time and is protracted by awkward, inefficient, and redundant program logic. Even companies that use CASE tools will have some badly designed systems. Often these systems are old and precede CASE usage.

The CASE maintenance model facilitates program maintenance and greatly reduces the iceberg effect. Applications originally developed under CASE are relatively easy to maintain. The maintenance programmer reviews the documentation for the application and makes the required changes, at the conceptual level, to the DFDs. The CASE system then makes the changes to the structure diagrams and program code automatically. Finally, the programmer thoroughly tests and installs the modified application.

CASE tools can also be used to maintain applications that were not originally developed under the CASE system. The CASE maintenance model provides two such tools for this purpose: reverse engineering and reengineering. Reverse engineering extracts from the source code meaningful design specifications that the maintenance programmer can use to understand the application logic. Reengineering restructures and documents the old source code logic to conform to CASE standards. This includes preparing DFDs and structure diagrams. Thus, future maintenance of the system can proceed as if the application were originally created under CASE.

Advantages of CASE

The following is a list of the commonly cited advantages of the CASE approach.

1. *Reduced system complexity.* CASE systems are more easily comprehended than traditional methods and support structured logic concepts.

2. *Increased flexibility.* The systems development process does not usually proceed in a purely linear fashion in which each stage is totally complete before the next one begins. Rather, it tends to be a cyclical process. It will be necessary to return to a previous stage if proceeding to the next stage will result in a flawed design or an improper implementation. As the details of the problem unfold in the downstream stages, it may be necessary to reconsider and revise upstream models. Compared to manual techniques, CASE provides a great deal of flexibility to the analyst in making such revisions.

3. *Capacity to review alternative designs.* Because CASE systems can be rapidly produced and changed, users and systems specialists can review prototypes of many alternative designs before committing to a particular system.

4. *Quicker development process.* The development process under CASE is three to six times faster than traditional methods, depending on the complexity of the system and the degree of CASE expertise within the firm.

5. *Promotion of user involvement.* Through its prototyping features, CASE has great potential for improving user involvement in the development process. We discuss this point in more detail in the following section.

6. *Reusable program code and documentation.* The central repository feature allows CASE systems to share common program modules and documentation.

7. *Reduced maintenance cost.* By maintaining the system at the conceptual level, maintenance time and programming errors are reduced. This translates into a more efficient process that responds more quickly to user needs. The iceberg effect is reduced by as much as 50 percent.

Disadvantages of CASE

In spite of these many virtues, CASE is not without its disadvantages, including:

1. *Product cost.* The cost of a CASE system is proportional to its features and sophistication. Microcomputer CASE tools with limited features may be obtained for hundreds of dollars. Fully equipped CASE tools for a mainframe environment can cost hundreds of thousands of dollars.

2. *Start-up time and cost.* Developing a pool of CASE expertise within the organization takes time. Systems professionals must be trained, and the learning curve for sophisticated CASE systems is steep.

3. *Incompatible CASE tools.* The hundreds of CASE products on the market are often incompatible with one another. This limits a firm's choices when selecting CASE tools and tends to tie the firm to a single product and vendor.

4. *Program inefficiency.* The source code produced by CASE tools is not as efficient as code written by a skilled programmer. To improve program efficiency, programmers often modify the CASE-generated modules. This practice can produce discrepancies between the DFD system logic and the program logic.

OUTPUT REPORTING ALTERNATIVES

This section presents various output design alternatives, along with a number of example output reports.

Tables and Matrices

Tables and matrices can be used to summarize large amounts of information. A *table* is a report arranged in columns and rows, such as the supplier analysis report in Figure 14-30. This table shows columns of evaluation data for suppliers with whom the firm does business. This is an effective means for comparing and contrasting relevant facts.

A *matrix* is a rectangular arrangement of data into rows and columns. Each element (the intersection of a row and a column) is a data value. This form of report is particularly useful for presenting binary state relations—the presence or absence of a state—among elements. Figure 14-31 is a matrix report showing which vendors supply which major inventory items.

Graphs and Charts

Graphs and *charts* present numeric data as geometric shapes. This visual approach to reporting presumes that a picture is worth a thousand words. Certainly this is true when conveying such summarized messages

FIGURE 14-30	Supplier Analysis Report

| Attribute | VENDOR | | | |
	Acme Motors	Morgan Supply	Norton Co.	The Roadster Factory
Yrs in Business	1$\frac{1}{2}$	4	9	3
Terms of Trade	2/10, n/30 offers quantity discounts	40% off retail, no quantity discounts	2/10, n/30, offers quantity discounts	Wholesale price list, no quantity discounts
Price Structure	Competitive	Lowest-priced supplier	Competitive	
Lead Time	5–7 days	7–10 days	7–10 days for most Items	3 days guaranteed
Rush Service	1 day delivery at 3% charge	None	None	Overnight—2% charge
Delivery Reliability	Good	Good	Poor	Good

FIGURE 14-31	Matrix Report Showing Vendors (columns) and Inventory (rows) Provided

Inventory Item Supplied	Vendor			
	Acme Motors	Morgan Supply	Norton Co.	The Roadster Factory
109873 k	X	X	X	X
109873 q	X		X	X
1098745		X		X
1098746	X		X	
•		X		
•				X
•	X		X	
•		X		
•		X		
•	X	X		
•		X		
•			X	
•	X			X
•			X	X
7893279				X
8237419	X			X
9495581	X	X	X	
				X

as "the big picture" and trends over time, and comparing the performance of multiple products. For these purposes, visual reports are far more effective than numeric reports alone. In this section, we examine five visual reporting techniques: line graph, scatter graph, bar graph, pie chart, and layer chart.

Line Graph. The simple line graph is used to show the fluctuations in an item of interest over time. Figure 14-32 illustrates this approach. We can use different colors and different shaped lines to track multiple items. In Figure 14-32, the solid line is projected sales and the dashed line is actual sales. The increments of the scale (sales dollars) should be small enough to detect material fluctuations. However, in using line graphs, we must guard against using a scale that is too small, because it might portray an exaggerated picture to the user.

Scatter Graph. The purpose of a scatter graph is to reveal relationships among underlying data. To illustrate, Figure 14-33 superimposes a line graph and scatter graph. The line graph shows only the movement from Point A to Point B in the form of a trend line that takes the average path through the data. In some instances, this could result in the loss of important information to the user. The points in the scatter graph show the degree of dispersion associated with the underlying activity.

Bar Graph. The purpose of a bar graph is to show the relationship of total quantities or proportions. Figure 14-34 uses a vertical bar graph to show the relationship over time between actual computer usage for a firm and budgeted usage.

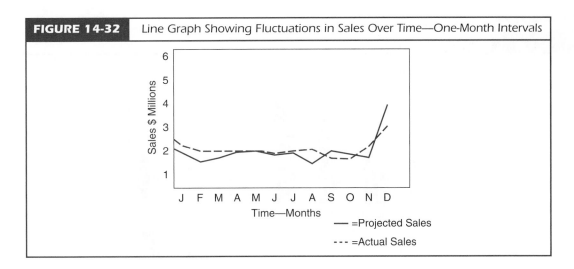

FIGURE 14-32   Line Graph Showing Fluctuations in Sales Over Time—One-Month Intervals

The height of the bars represents the total amount of computer usage. If we were to plot the top points of each bar, we could construct a line graph showing the trend in usage and the relationship between actual and budgeted usage. However, the emphasis of a bar graph is on total amounts at specific points rather than on trends.

The horizontal bar graph is used to compare multiple items in the same time frame. For example, Figure 14-35 compares output from four production plants for the month of January.

Pie Chart. A pie chart presents the proportional relationship of different items to the whole. For example, Figure 14-36 shows the proportions of several items that together constitute total manufacturing cost. We can differentiate the segments by using color or by exploding them slightly from the rest of the pie. To maintain the visual power of the message, however, the designer should attempt to restrict the number of segments. Too many pie wedges make differentiation difficult and complicate the chart.

Layer Chart. A layer chart also shows proportional relationships but allows the addition of another dimension, such as time or condition. Figure 14-37 illustrates this by showing the change in the proportion of individual item costs to total manufacturing cost under different technology bases.

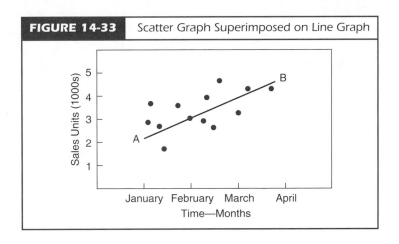

FIGURE 14-33   Scatter Graph Superimposed on Line Graph

FIGURE 14-34 Bar Graph Showing Actual Computer Usage to Budgeted Usage—Shows CPU Hours per Month

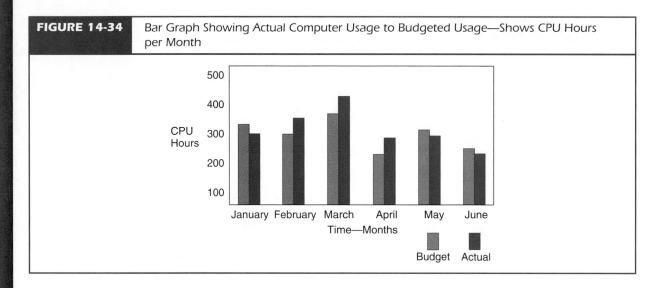

FIGURE 14-35 Horizontal Bar Graph Comparing Production of Multiple Plants

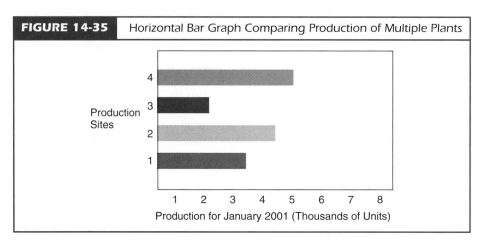

FIGURE 14-36 Pie Chart for Manufacturing Costs

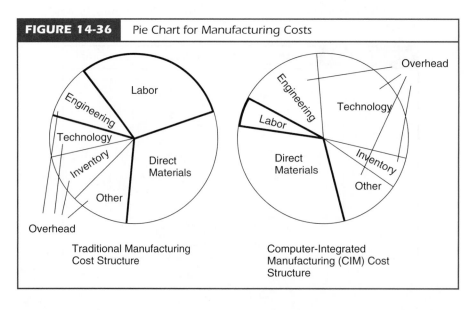

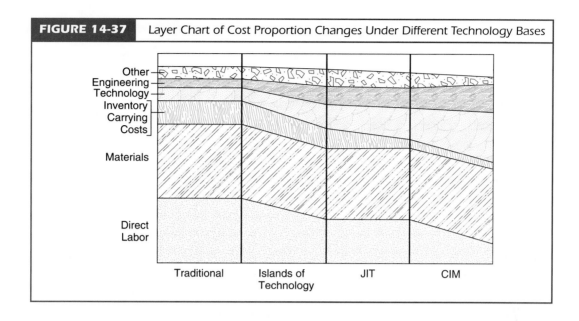

FIGURE 14-37   Layer Chart of Cost Proportion Changes Under Different Technology Bases

Colors

Colors can greatly enhance the usefulness of a report. Choosing colors that are widely spaced on the color spectrum—such as red, green, and blue—provides for the greatest visual discrimination. This approach can be used to present data that are being compared or contrasted within a report. The level of color intensity can be used to emphasize material items or to de-emphasize normal (or less important) data. For example, the variance report in Figure 14-38 shows budgeted amounts, actual amounts, and the variance from budget for each line item.

High-intensity color is used here to draw attention to line items with a material variance (for example, a variance greater than 10 percent). Line items whose variance is under this materiality threshold are deemed under control and are deemphasized by the use of low-intensity color.

FIGURE 14-38   Variance Report Using Intensity to Highlight Material Variances

Sports Car Factory
Cost Variance Report for Production Dept. 6

Date 11/20/04

CVAR 1

Item	Budget	Actual	(Over) Under Budget
Direct labor	36,000	36,800	<800>
Direct materials	122,000	141,600	<19,600>
Job setup	4,000	3,600	400
Supplies	2,200	2,330	<130>
Scheduled maintenance	1,200	1,200	0

KEY TERMS

attributes (665)

backbone systems (689)

central repository (696)

cohesion (676)

cold turkey cutover (685)

computer-aided software engineering (CASE) (660)

conceptual user views (668)

construct (662)

coupling (676)

cutover (685)

data dictionary (679)

data modeling (668)

database conversion (685)

design phase (667)

detailed design report (679)

disseminating (695)

documentation (682)

electronic input techniques (674)

embedded instructions (673)

event-driven languages (680)

Gantt chart (661)

gathering (695)

group memory (695)

hard copy (672)

inheritance (666)

instance (665)

intelligent forms (675)

knowledge management (695)

methods (665)

object class (665)

object-oriented design (665)

object-oriented programming (OOP) language (680)

objects (665)

online documentation (684)

operations control reports (670)

organizing (695)

parallel operation cutover (686)

PERT chart (661)

phased cutover (685)

procedural language (680)

prototyping (660)

pseudocode (677)

quality assurance group (679)

refining (695)

request for proposal (RFP) (691)

run manual (683)

structure diagram (675)

structured design (662)

systems design (668)

third-generation languages (680)

turnkey systems (688)

user handbook (684)

walkthrough (679)

wall of code (667)

zones (672)

REVIEW QUESTIONS

1. How does a prototype differ from the final product? Why discard the prototype? What role does the end user play in prototyping?

2. What functions do CASE tools serve?

3. Distinguish between upper and lower CASE tools.

4. What is a central repository in a CASE system?

5. How can program code be reused?

6. What is a dataflow diagram? What are the different levels from most general to most detailed? Draw the common symbols used.

7. What is the relationship between an elementary-level DFD and a structure diagram? Which must be prepared first?

8. Is pseudocode programming language specific? How about the coding model?

9. What is the difference between source code and machine code? Why is it preferable to have the CASE tools convert the structure diagrams into machine code rather than source code?

10. What is the iceberg effect? How can CASE tools help to minimize this phenomenon?

11. Distinguish between reverse engineering and reengineering.

12. Contrast the advantages and disadvantages of CASE tools. What should determine whether CASE is used?

13. What is an object, and what are its characteristics in the object-oriented approach? Give two examples.

14. Distinguish between object classes and instances.

15. What is meant by inheritance? Give an example.

16. Why is the object-oriented approach particularly suited to ERP system design?

17. What are the four factors that have stimulated the growth of commercial software?

18. Distinguish between turnkey and backbone systems. Which is more flexible?

19. What are the four steps involved in choosing a package?

20. What is an RFP?

21. Discuss the relative merits of in-house programs versus commercially developed software.

22. List, in sequential order, the system components that are designed in the detailed design phase.

23. What is data modeling? What is its primary tool?

24. What are the three basic symbols in an ER diagram?

25. Distinguish between primary and foreign keys.

26. What is a data dictionary?

27. What document is used to determine which tables of data are necessary?

28. Once the conceptual links between tables have been determined, how are the physical links incorporated?

29. What attributes should output views possess?

30. Why is the quality of the paper a major consideration in the design of a hard-copy input?

31. What are the two classes of design input views?

32. What are zones?

33. In what form should embedded instructions be written—active or passive voice? Why?

34. What are the relative merits of input from source documents and direct input?

35. What is pseudocode? Are end users or systems designers involved in this process?

36. What are the controls designated in the systems controls stage?

37. Typically, which is more difficult to detect and more costly to fix—a design flaw in the processes or a programming error?

38. Who is included in the quality assurance group? What are their tasks? What documents do they need to perform their tasks?

39. Which activities during the systems implementation phase have the greatest implications for accountants and auditors?

40. Which chart, a PERT or a Gantt, shows the project status at a glance for a given point in time? Which method illustrates the critical path at a glance?

41. Discuss the relative merits and drawbacks to 3GL. How might changing technology affect some of these issues in the future?

42. What is a hybrid language?

43. What are the advantages to the modular programming approach?

44. Why should test data be saved after it has been used?

45. Explain the importance of documentation by the systems programmers.

46. What documents not typically needed by other stakeholders do accountants and auditors need for the new system?

47. What very important precautions must be taken during the data conversion procedures?

DISCUSSION QUESTIONS

1. Dataflow diagrams are often described as exploding from one level to the next. What is meant by "exploding"? Also, dataflow diagrams must reconcile from the general level to the next level of detail. What is meant by "reconcile"? How do you think CASE tools help in this procedure?

2. What issues are accountants concerned with when determining their preference for CASE tools that convert structure diagrams into machine code or source code? What are the costs associated with each?

3. What documentation techniques are used in the structured design approach to conceptual

design? What is the purpose of each of these documentation techniques, and how do they vary from each other? How much detail is provided?

4. Compare and contrast the structured design approach and the object-oriented design approach. Which do you feel is most beneficial? Why?

5. If a firm decides early to go with a special-purpose system, such as SAP, based upon the recommendations of the external audit firm, should the SDLC be bypassed?

6. Explain how benchmarking works. Should this be conducted on the vendor's computer or the customer's computer? What about technical presentations by the vendor? Why?

7. Discuss the importance of the weights assigned to factors in the final selection process. What method might you suggest be used to investigate the appropriateness of the weights?

8. Who should select the contact user group—the vendor or the prospective user? Why?

9. What processes should be used to develop useful and meaningful output? Who should be involved in the development process?

10. Are input requirements or output requirements examined to determine the attributes of tables? Should all of these attributes physically be in the data file? Why or why not?

11. Are direct input systems (i.e., point-of-sale using bar codes) error free? Why or why not?

12. Why is it necessary to decompose the DFD to a level of high detail before preparing the structure diagram? How do you know when to stop this process?

13. A good structure diagram should be loosely coupled yet strongly cohesive. How can you achieve both characteristics simultaneously? What implications do these characteristics have on error-prone problems during maintenance?

14. Why bother with pseudocode? Why not spend the time developing actual source code?

15. During a test data procedure, why should the developers bother testing "bad" data?

16. During implementation, if the system is behind schedule and if each program module is tested and no problems are found, is it necessary to test all modules in conjunction with one another? Why or why not?

17. Run manuals for computer operators are similar in theory to the checklists that airplane pilots use for takeoffs and landings. Explain why these are important.

18. How might the decision to use CASE tools affect the choice of a programming language?

19. What are the three implementation (cutover) methods? Which appears to be the most costly up front? Which could very likely end up being the most costly in the long run?

20. Who conducts the post-implementation review? When should it be conducted? If an outside consulting firm were hired to design and implement the new system, or a canned software package were purchased, would a post-implementation review still be useful?

21. Discuss the importance of involving accountants in the detailed design and implementation phases. What tasks should they perform?

MULTIPLE-CHOICE QUESTIONS

1. CPA (From Gleim 5.8 # 108, 10th Ed.)
   The proper sequence of activities in the systems development life cycle is
   a. Design, analysis, implementation, and operation.
   b. Design, implementation, analysis, and operation.
   c. Analysis, design, implementation, and operation.
   d. Programming, analysis, implementation, and operation.

2. CMA 1287 5-6
   The process of developing specifications for hardware, software, personnel hours, data resources, and information products required to develop a system is referred to as
   a. systems analysis.
   b. systems feasibility study.
   c. systems maintenance.
   d. systems implementation.
   e. systems design.

3. Which of the following is NOT an output attribute?

   a. relevance

   b. exception orientation

   c. zones

   d. accuracy

4. Which of the following is NOT a principle feature of a PERT chart?

   a. starting and ending dates

   b. events

   c. paths

   d. activities

5. CPA (From Gleim 5.8 # 117, 10th Ed.)

Which of the following is the most appropriate activity for an internal auditor to perform during a review of systems development activity?

   a. Serve on the MIS steering committee that determines what new systems are to be developed.

   b. Review the methodology used to monitor and control the system development function.

   c. Recommend specific automated procedures to be incorporated into new systems that will provide reasonable assurance that all data submitted to an application are converted to machine-readable form.

   d. Recommend specific operational procedures that will ensure that all data submitted for processing are converted to machine-readable form.

6. CMA 691 4-30

The least risky strategy for converting from a manual to a computerized accounts receivable system would be a

   a. direct conversion.

   b. parallel conversion.

   c. pilot conversion.

   d. database conversion.

   e. file conversion.

7. CMA 691 4-29

Errors are most costly to correct during

   a. programming.

   b. conceptual design.

   c. analysis.

   d. detailed design.

   e. implementation.

8. CMA 685 5-22

A useful tool for formatting computer input and file records is a

   a. document flowchart.

   b. printer layout chart.

   c. record layout sheet.

   d. work distribution analysis.

   e. decision table.

9. CMA 1287 5-6

The process of developing specifications for hardware, software, personnel hours, data resources, and information products required to develop a system is referred to as

   a. systems analysis.

   b. systems feasibility study.

   c. systems maintenance.

   d. systems implementation.

   e. systems design.

10. CPA (From Gleim 5.8 # 121, 10th Ed.)

User acceptance testing is more important in an object-oriented development process than in a traditional environment because of the implications of the

   a. absence of traditional design documents.

   b. lack of a tracking system for changes.

   c. potential for continuous monitoring.

   d. inheritance of properties in hierarchies.

11. CMA 1282 5-12

Characteristics of an accounting application that might influence the selection of data entry devices and media for a computerized accounting system are

   a. Timing of feedback needs relative to input, need for documentation of an activity, and the necessity for reliability and accuracy.

   b. cost considerations, volume of input, complexity of activity, and liquidity of assets involved.

   c. need for documentation, necessity for accuracy and reliability, volume of output, and cost considerations.

   d. relevancy of data, volume of input, cost considerations, volume of output, and timing of feedback needs relative to input.

   e. Type of file used, reliability of manufacturer's service, volume of output, and cost considerations.

12. CPA (From Gleim 5.8 # 126, 10th Ed.)

A systems development approach used to quickly produce a model of user interfaces, user interactions with the system, and process logic is called:

a. neural networking.

b. prototyping.

c. reengineering.

d. application generation.

13. CMA 1287 5-26

The program evaluation and review technique (PERT) is widely used to plan and measure progress toward scheduled events. PERT is combined with cost data to produce a PERT-cost analysis to

a. calculate the total project cost inclusive of the additional slack time.

b. evaluate and optimize trade-offs between time of an event's completion and its cost to complete.

c. implement computer-integrated manufacturing concepts.

d. avoid the problem of time variance analysis.

e. calculate expected activity times.

14. CPA (From Gleim 5.8 # 128, 10th Ed.)

All of the following are included in the systems implementation process except:

a. Training.

b. documentation.

c. systems design.

d. Testing and correction.

15. CMA 684 5-21

When using the PERT method for network analysis, the critical path through the network is the

a. shortest path through the network.

b. longest path through the network.

c. path with the most slack.

d. path with the most variability in estimated times.

e. least-cost path.

PROBLEMS

1. CASE Tools

Reeve Lumber Company has a small information systems department consisting of five people. A backlog of approximately 15 months exists for requests for new systems applications to even be considered. Both information users and systems personnel are unhappy with this state of affairs. The users feel that the systems department is not responsive enough to their needs, while the systems personnel feel overworked, frustrated, and unappreciated. Janet Hubert, the manager of the systems department, has decided that she needs to take a proactive measure. She is requesting the funds to purchase a CASE system for approximately $75,000 that takes about two months to install and train workers how to use it. The president of the company, Mike Cassidy, initially responded by questioning the wisdom of taking the systems personnel away from their duties when they are backlogged so they can learn a system. Prepare a memo from Hubert to Cassidy. In the memo, outline the expected benefits of purchasing and using a CASE system and address

Cassidy's concern regarding the two-month training and implementation period.

2. Dataflow Diagrams

Sawicki Music Supply is a mail-order business that accepts merchandise orders by telephone and mail. All payments must be prepaid with a major credit card. Once an order is received, the item is either found in inventory and shipped immediately, the item is not found in inventory and is ordered from the manufacturer, or a notice is sent to the customer indicating the item is no longer stocked.

Required:

Prepare a context-, intermediate-, and elementary-level dataflow diagram for Sawicki Music Supply. For the elementary-level diagram, explode the inventory function.

3. Dataflow Diagrams

Examine the context and intermediate (Level 1) dataflow diagrams on the next page and indicate what is incorrect about them.

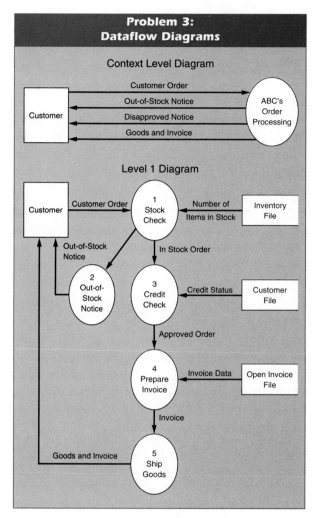

Problem 3:
Dataflow Diagrams

Context Level Diagram

Customer Order
Out-of-Stock Notice
Disapproved Notice
Goods and Invoice

Customer

ABC's Order Processing

Level 1 Diagram

Customer — Customer Order → 1 Stock Check — Number of Items in Stock → Inventory File

Out-of-Stock Notice

In Stock Order

2 Out-of-Stock Notice

3 Credit Check — Credit Status — Customer File

Approved Order

4 Prepare Invoice — Invoice Data — Open Invoice File

Invoice

Goods and Invoice

5 Ship Goods

4. During the system design phase of the SDLC, input interfaces or input views must be sketched out so programmers can capture necessary elements when they program the interfaces the system will use to gain inputted information. Figure 14-12 presents an interface for a Reorder Report. Sketch a similar interface that could be used to program a sales invoice interface. Include areas for a document heading, customer information, shipping information, sales employee information, and items sold.

5. Systems Design
Robin Alper, a manager of the credit collections department for ACME Building Supplies, is extremely unhappy with a new system that was installed three months ago. Her complaint is that the dataflows from the billing and accounts receivable departments are not occurring in the manner origi-

nally requested. Further, the updates to the database files are not occurring as frequently as she had envisioned. Thus, the hope that the new system would provide more current and timely information has not materialized. She claims that the systems analysts spent three days interviewing her and other workers. During that time, she and the other workers thought they had clearly conveyed their needs. She feels as if their needs were ignored and their time was wasted.

Required:
What went wrong during the systems design process? What suggestions would you make for future projects?

6. Attributes and Operations
Prepare a list of attributes and operations for the following items:

a. general ledger
b. accounts payable ledger
c. accounts receivable ledger
d. fixed assets ledger
e. inventory ledger

7. Commercial Software
Robert Hamilton was hired six months ago as the controller of a small oil and gas exploration and development company, Gusher, Inc., headquartered in Beaumont, Texas. Before working at Gusher, Hamilton was the controller of a larger petroleum company, Eureka Oil Company, based in Dallas. The joint interest billing and fixed asset accounting systems of Gusher are outdated, and frequent processing problems and errors have been occurring. Hamilton immediately recognized these problems and informed the president, Mr. Barton, that it was crucial to install a new system. Barton concurred and met with Hamilton and Sally Jeffries, the information systems senior manager. Barton instructed Jeffries to make the new system a top priority. Basically, he told Jeffries to deliver the system to meet Hamilton's needs as soon as possible.

Jeffries left the meeting feeling overwhelmed because the IS department is currently working on two other very big projects, one for the production department and the other for the geological department. The next day, Hamilton sent a memo to Jeffries indicating the name of a system he had 100 percent confidence in—Amarillo Software—and he also indicated that he would very much like this system to be purchased as soon as possible. He stated that the system had been used with much success during the past four years in his previous job.

When commercial software is purchased, Jeffries typically sends out requests for proposals to at least six different vendors after conducting a careful analysis of the needed requirements. However, due to the air of urgency demonstrated in the meeting with the president and the overworked systems staff, she decided to go along with Hamilton's wishes and sent only one RFP, which went to Amarillo Software. Amarillo promptly returned the completed questionnaire. The purchase price ($75,000) was within the budgeted amount. Jeffries contacted the four references provided and was satisfied with their comments. Further, she felt comfortable because the system was for Hamilton, and he had used the system for four years.

The plan was to install the system during the month of July and try it for the August transaction cycle. Problems were encountered, however, during the installation phase. The system processed extremely slowly on the hardware platform owned by Gusher. When Jeffries asked Hamilton how the problem had been dealt with at Eureka, he replied that he did not remember having such a problem. He called the systems manager from Eureka and discovered that Eureka has a much more powerful mainframe than Gusher. Further investigation revealed that Gusher has more applications running on its mainframe than Eureka does, because Eureka uses a two-mainframe distributed processing platform.

Further, the data transfer did not go smoothly. A few data elements being stored in the system were not available as an option in the Amarillo system. Jeffries found that the staff at Amarillo was very friendly when she called, but they could not always identify the problem over the phone. They needed to come out to the site and investigate. Hamilton was surprised at the delays between requesting an Amarillo consultant to come out and the time in which he or she actually arrived. Amarillo explained that it had to fly a staff member from Dallas to Beaumont for each trip. The system finally began to work somewhat smoothly in January, after a grueling fiscal year-end close in October. Hamilton's staff view the project as an unnecessary inconvenience. At one point, two staff accountants threatened to quit. The extra consulting fees amounted to $35,000.

Further, the systems department at Gusher spent 500 more hours during the implementation process than it had expected. These additional hours caused other projects to fall behind schedule.

Required:
Discuss what could have been done differently during the design phase. Why were most of the problems encountered? How might a detailed feasibility study have helped?

8. Dataflow Diagram
The detailed dataflow diagram in Figure 14-16 decomposes the DFD for the expenditure cycle in Figure 14-15. Further decompose the process numbered 1.4.4, Receive Invoice, in detail.

9. PERT Chart
The Peabody Coal Corporation recently completed the final feasibility report for a new general ledger accounting system. It has hired a consulting firm to program and install the new system. The consulting firm is charging $350,000 for the remaining tasks to be performed. These tasks are to be performed over the next 10 months as detailed in the Gantt chart on the next page. The consulting firm is extremely concerned with the project staying on schedule because it is receiving a flat fee. The release of the final payment is contingent upon the system performing as stated in the contract and upon Peabody receiving appropriate documentation of the system.

Required:
a. Prepare a PERT diagram and indicate the critical path.
b. What happens to the time frame of the implementation of the project if the manufacturer is four weeks late shipping the hardware?
c. What happens if the data conversion does not go smoothly and takes an additional three weeks?
d. Who should conduct the post-implementation review? What activities should be conducted during this review? Do you think enough time has been allotted for this activity?

10. PERT and Gantt Charts
The lottery commission of a state with about $500 million a year in revenue has looked to modern technology for increasing lottery sales. The strategy is to place self-service sales machines

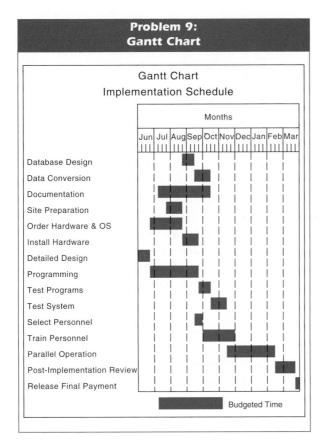

**Problem 9:
Gantt Chart**

Gantt Chart
Implementation Schedule

Months

	Jun	Jul	Aug	Sep	Oct	Nov	Dec	Jan	Feb	Mar

Database Design
Data Conversion
Documentation
Site Preparation
Order Hardware & OS
Install Hardware
Detailed Design
Programming
Test Programs
Test System
Select Personnel
Train Personnel
Parallel Operation
Post-Implementation Review
Release Final Payment

Budgeted Time

mainframe is expected to take four weeks, with an additional three weeks once the sales machines have been received. Another two weeks of testing by the state gaming commission is expected. The design of the databases is expected to take only two weeks. Not much data transfer is expected to be necessary, so only three weeks is budgeted for this task.

An estimated 20 employees need to be hired and trained to install and maintain these machines around the state. The hiring process is expected to take six weeks, and the training should take an additional six weeks. The documentation should be completed before the training of the new employees. The documentation should take about three months. As soon as the gaming commission signs off on the programs, the 15 machines are to be installed at test sites around the state. Four weeks are allotted for this installation procedure. A one-week testing period is planned, with commission employees going to the sites and using the machines. An additional week is planned to review the results of these tests. The pilot test then begins and runs for eight weeks. The data will be analyzed for four weeks after the pilot test. The final order for the additional machines will be placed after the data analysis is conducted and the demand for the number of machines is more accurately determined.

Required:

a.   Prepare a PERT chart for the above process. Identify the critical path.

b.   Prepare a Gantt chart for the above process.

11. Accountants understand their jobs very well. Programmers also understand their jobs. Unfortunately, accountants are rarely programmers and programmers are rarely accountants. While an accountant does not need to program, the accountant must be able to communicate his requirement to the programmer, an individual who may not understand the intricate needs of the accountants. To bridge this knowledge gap, the accountant may be called on to produce pseudocode—a set of detailed instructions written in English without syntax rules. Suppose you need a programmer to prepare code that will read sales information from an input screen, compute extensions for items sold, compute a total of these extensions, and update inventory balances, the sales ledger account, and accounts receivable as well as any subsidiary accounts. Prepare pseudocode for the programmer.

around the state. Customers simply fill out the bubbles on the form and insert the form into the computer. If they wish, they may enter their numbers directly in to the computer and skip the form altogether. The machine accepts cash and automatic teller machine cards. The lottery commission is very excited about this project because it thinks it could boost lottery ticket sales by as much as 30 percent.

The systems department has finished the final feasibility report and has determined the following estimates for implementing the system. It plans on purchasing a larger, more powerful mainframe computer to handle the processing of the transactions. The manufacturer has promised a delivery date of three months from the time the order is placed. The lottery sales machines must be special ordered and require a lead time of five months. The plan is to initially order 15 machines and test them for 12 weeks. If all goes well, the lottery commission will order a total of 500 machines, with 20 delivered and installed each month. This order will not be placed until the results of the pilot test have been analyzed.

The writing of the programs is expected to take six weeks. The testing of the programs on the

12. CMA 786 5-Y6
PERT Chart

Silver Aviation assembles small aircraft for commercial use. The majority of Silver's business is with small freight airlines serving areas where the airport does not accommodate larger planes. The remainder of Silver's customers are commuter airlines and individuals who use planes in their businesses. Silver recently expanded into Central and South America and expects to double its sales over the next three years.

To schedule work and keep track of all projects, Silver uses the program evaluation and review technique (PERT). The PERT diagram for the construction of a single cargo plane is shown on the following page. The PERT diagram shows that there are four alternative paths, with the critical path being ABGEFJK.

Bob Peterson, president of Coastal Airlines, has recently placed an order with Silver Aviation for five cargo planes. At the time of contract negotiations, Peterson agreed to a delivery time of 13 weeks (five working days per week) for the first plane, with the balance of the planes being delivered at the rate of one every four weeks. Because of problems with some of the aircraft Coastal is using, Peterson has contacted Grace Vander, sales manager for Silver Aviation, to ask about improving the delivery date of the first cargo plane. Vander replied that she believed the schedule could be shortened by as much as ten working days, or two weeks, but the cost of construction would increase as a result. Peterson said he would be willing to consider the increased costs, and they agreed to meet the following day to review a revised schedule that Vander would prepare.

Because Silver Aviation has assembled aircraft on an accelerated basis before, the company has compiled a list of crash costs for this purpose. Vander used the data shown in the Crash Cost Listing table below, to develop a plan to cut ten working days from the schedule at a minimal increase in cost to Coastal Airlines.

Upon completing her plan, Vander was pleased that she could report to Peterson that Silver would be able to cut 10 working days from the schedule. The associated increase in cost would be $6,600. Presented below is Vander's plan for the accelerated delivery of the cargo plane starting from the regularly scheduled days and costs.

Required:
a. PERT is a form of network analysis.
   1. Explain how the expected regular times for each activity are derived in using PERT.
   2. Define the term *critical path* and explain why path ABGEFJK is the critical path in this situation.
b. Evaluate the accelerated delivery schedule prepared by Grace Vander.
   1. Explain why Vander's plan as presented is unsatisfactory.
   2. Revise the accelerated delivery schedule so that Coastal Airlines will take delivery of the first plane two weeks (ten working days) ahead of schedule at the least incremental cost to Coastal.
   3. Calculate the incremental costs Bob Peterson will have to pay for this revised accelerated delivery.

13. Detailed Systems Design
On page 718 is an ER diagram for the expenditure cycle.

Required:
a. List the entity database tables and describe which entities need representing from an AIS perspective.
b. For each item identified as relevant to AIS, prepare a list of database tables along with primary and embedded foreign keys.
c. Prepare database tables showing attributes in normalized form.

14. Conceptual Design
Vince Malloy and Katy Smith, both systems personnel at Shamrock Steelworks, are designing a new expenditure cycle system. Vince has worked for Shamrock for 12 years and has been involved in many systems development projects. Katy recently began working for Shamrock. She has four years of experience in systems development with another comparably sized organization. Yesterday, Vince and Katy met to determine their plan for approaching the conceptual system design. Below is an excerpt of some dialogue that occurred in that meeting.

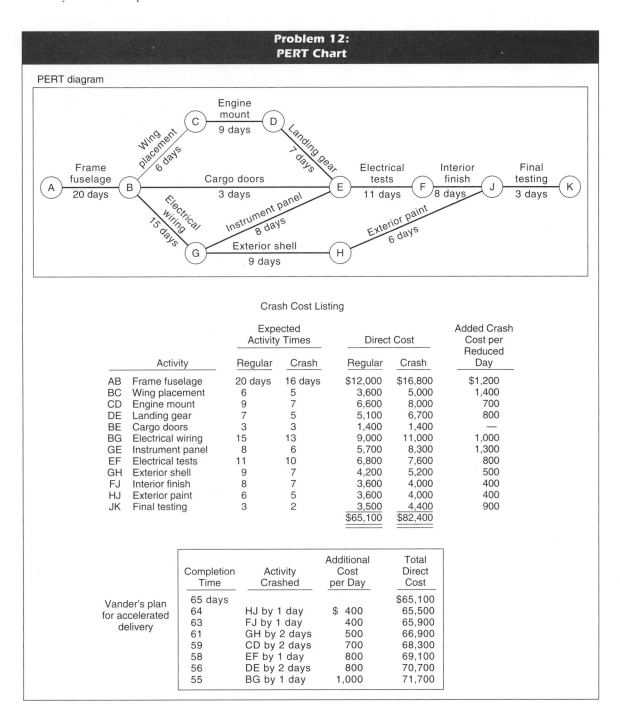

Problem 12: PERT Chart

PERT diagram

Crash Cost Listing

Activity		Expected Activity Times		Direct Cost		Added Crash Cost per Reduced Day
		Regular	Crash	Regular	Crash	
AB	Frame fuselage	20 days	16 days	$12,000	$16,800	$1,200
BC	Wing placement	6	5	3,600	5,000	1,400
CD	Engine mount	9	7	6,600	8,000	700
DE	Landing gear	7	5	5,100	6,700	800
BE	Cargo doors	3	3	1,400	1,400	—
BG	Electrical wiring	15	13	9,000	11,000	1,000
GE	Instrument panel	8	6	5,700	8,300	1,300
EF	Electrical tests	11	10	6,800	7,600	800
GH	Exterior shell	9	7	4,200	5,200	500
FJ	Interior finish	8	7	3,600	4,000	400
HJ	Exterior paint	6	5	3,600	4,000	400
JK	Final testing	3	2	3,500	4,400	900
				$65,100	$82,400	

	Completion Time	Activity Crashed	Additional Cost per Day	Total Direct Cost
Vander's plan for accelerated delivery	65 days			$65,100
	64	HJ by 1 day	$ 400	65,500
	63	FJ by 1 day	400	65,900
	61	GH by 2 days	500	66,900
	59	CD by 2 days	700	68,300
	58	EF by 1 day	800	69,100
	56	DE by 2 days	800	70,700
	55	BG by 1 day	1,000	71,700

Katy: I really think that the new system can be designed more efficiently if we use an object-oriented design approach. Further, future enhancements and maintenance will be easier if we use an object approach.

Vince: The method you are suggesting is a creation of modules. I do not have a problem with that concept in general. I just prefer using a top-down approach to design the system. We have been using that system for the past 12 years, and it has worked out OK.

Katy: Sure, your systems have worked for you, but perhaps they can be developed more efficiently, not to mention maintaining them. Further, we have approximately a two-year backlog of projects. Changing to a more efficient design system may help us to reduce that wait.

Vince: We may not end up with the system we want if we do not consider the "big picture." I am afraid if we get too tied to using existing modules for future projects, that we may design suboptimal systems that will require more maintenance and have shorter lives in the long run. What good will the more "efficient" system do us then?

Required:

Prepare a response by Katy, and develop a strategy for systems design that will address both of their concerns.

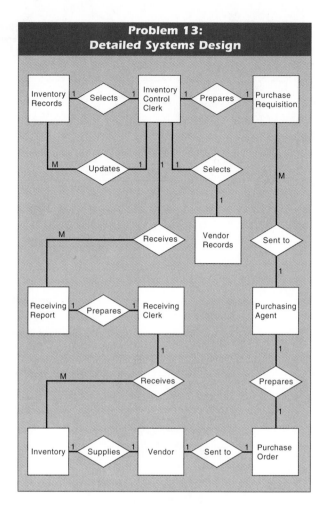

SYSTEMS DEVELOPMENT CASES

Several systems development cases that draw upon the material in this and the next chapter are available online at http://hall.swlearning.com.

chapter 15

IT Controls Part I: Sarbanes-Oxley and IT Governance

LEARNING OBJECTIVES

After studying this chapter, you should:

- Understand the key features of Sections 302 and 404 of the Sarbanes-Oxley Act.
- Understand management and auditor responsibilities under Sections 302 and 404.
- Understand the risks of incompatible functions and how to structure the IT function.
- Be familiar with the controls and precautions required to ensure the security of an organization's computer facilities.
- Understand the key elements of a disaster recovery plan.

This chapter provides an overview of management and auditor responsibilities under Sections 302 and 404 of the Sarbanes-Oxley Act (SOX). The design, implementation, and assessment of internal control over the financial reporting process form the central theme of these sections. Our study of internal control follows the Committee of Sponsoring Organizations of the Treadway Commission (COSO) control framework. Under COSO, IT internal controls are divided into application controls and general controls. Because of the extensive nature of the material and its importance to accountants, this and the remaining two chapters are devoted to the subject. This chapter presents controls and tests of controls related to IT governance including organizing the IT function, controlling computer center operations and designing an adequate disaster recovery plan. Chapter 16 deals with the security and access controls over operating systems, databases, and networks. Chapter 17 addresses systems development, program changes, and application control issues. As background material, the appendix to this chapter contains a brief overview of auditing concepts and principles.

OVERVIEW OF SECTIONS **302** AND **404** OF THE SARBANES-OXLEY ACT

The Sarbanes-Oxley (SOX) Act of 2002 established new corporate governance regulations and standards for public companies registered with the Securities and Exchange Commission (SEC). Whereas the act contains many sections, this chapter and the two following chapters concentrate on internal control and audit responsibilities pursuant to Sections 302 and 404.

Section 302 requires corporate management (including the CEO) to certify financial and other information contained in the organization's quarterly and annual reports. The rule also requires them to certify the internal controls over financial reporting. The certifying officers are required to have designed internal controls, or caused such controls to be designed, and to provide reasonable assurance as to the reliability of the financial reporting process. Furthermore, they must disclose any material changes in the company's internal controls that have occurred during the most recent fiscal quarter.

Section 404 requires the management of public companies to assess the effectiveness of their organization's internal controls over financial reporting. Under this section of the act, management is required to provide an annual report addressing the following points: (1) a statement of management's responsibility for establishing and maintaining adequate internal control (2) an assessment of the effectiveness of the company's internal controls over financial reporting (3) a statement that the organizations external auditor has issued an attestation report on management's assessment of the company's internal controls (4) an explicit written conclusion as to the effectiveness of internal control over financial reporting[1] and (5) a statement identifying the framework used by management to conduct their assessment of internal controls.

Regarding the final point, the SEC has made specific reference to the Committee of Sponsoring Organizations of the Treadway Commission (COSO) as a recommended control framework. Furthermore, the PCAOB's Auditing Standard No. 2 endorses the use of COSO as the framework for control assessment. Although other suitable frameworks have been published, according to Standard No. 2, any framework used should encompass all of COSO's general themes.[2] The key elements of the COSO framework, which is the basis for SAS 78, were discussed in Chapter 3. Our focus at this point is on IT controls (a subset of control activities), which were not previously discussed. This aspect of the COSO framework is used to present control and audit issues in this and the following two chapters.

RELATIONSHIP BETWEEN IT CONTROLS AND FINANCIAL REPORTING

The financial reporting processes of modern organizations are driven by information technology. Automated systems initiate, authorize, record, and report the effects of financial transactions. As such, they are inextricable elements of the financial reporting processes considered by the Sarbanes-Oxley Act and must be controlled. COSO identifies two broad groupings of information system controls: *application controls* and *general controls*. The objectives of **application controls** are to ensure the validity, completeness,

---

1   Management may not conclude that internal controls are effective if one or more material weaknesses exist. In addition, management must disclose all material weaknesses that exist as of the end of the most recent fiscal year.

2   A popular competing control framework is *Control Objectives for Information and related Technology* (COBIT®) published by the IT Governance Institute (ITGI). This framework maps into COSO's general themes.

and accuracy of financial transactions. These controls are designed to be application specific. Examples include:

- A cash disbursements batch balancing routine that verifies that the total of payments to vendors reconciles with the total postings to the accounts payable subsidiary ledger.

- An account receivable check digits procedure that validates customer account numbers on sales transactions.

- A payroll system limit check that identifies employee time card records with reported hours worked in excess of the predetermined normal limit.

These examples illustrate how application controls have a direct impact on the integrity of data that make their way through various transaction processing systems and into the financial reporting process. Application controls are examined in detail in Chapter 17.

The second broad group of controls identified by COSO is **general controls.** They are so named because they are not application-specific but, rather, apply to all systems. General controls have other names in other frameworks including **general computer controls** and **information technology controls**. Whatever name is used, they include controls over IT governance, IT infrastructure, security and access to **operating systems** and databases, application acquisition and development, and program changes.

Whereas general controls do not control specific transactions, they have an effect on transaction integrity. For example, consider an organization with poor database security controls. In such a situation, even data processed by systems with adequate built-in application controls may be at risk. An individual who is able to circumvent database security (either directly or via a malicious program), may then change, steal, or corrupt stored transaction data. Thus, general controls are needed to support the functioning of application controls, and both are needed to ensure accurate financial reporting.

AUDIT IMPLICATIONS OF SECTIONS 302 AND 404

The material covered in the remainder of this chapter and the following chapters assumes a basic understanding of the audit process. Specifically the reader should:

1. Be able to distinguish between the attest function and assurance;
2. Understand the concept of management assertions and recognize the relationship between assertions and audit objectives; and
3. Know the difference between a test of controls and substantive tests and understand the relationship between them.

The appendix to this chapter contains a brief overview of these topics. Those lacking this knowledge should review the appendix before continuing with this section.

Prior to SOX, external auditors were not required to test internal controls as part of their attest function. They were required to be familiar with the client organization's internal controls, but had the option of not relying on them and thus not performing tests of controls. The audit could, and often did, therefore consist primarily of substantive tests.

SOX legislation dramatically expands the role of external auditors by mandating that they attest to management's assessment of internal controls. This constitutes the issuance of a separate audit opinion in addition to the opinion on the fairness of the financial statements. The standard for this new audit opinion is high. Indeed, the auditor is precluded from issuing an unqualified opinion if only one material weakness in internal control is detected. Interestingly, auditors are permitted to simultaneously render a qualified opinion on management's assessment of internal controls and an unqualified opinion on the financial statements. In other words, it is technically possible for auditors to find internal controls over financial reporting to be weak, but conclude through substantive tests that the weaknesses did not cause the financial statements to be materially misrepresented.

As part of the new attestation responsibility, the PCAOB's Standard No. 2 specifically requires auditors to understand transaction flows, including the controls pertaining to how transactions are initiated, authorized, recorded, and reported. This involves first selecting the financial accounts that have material implications for financial reporting. Then, auditors need to identify the application controls related to those accounts. As previously noted, the reliability of these application controls rests on the IT general controls that support them, such as controls over access to databases, operating systems and networks, and so on. The sum of these controls, both application and general, constitute the relevant internal controls over financial reporting that need to be reviewed. Figure 15-1 illustrates this IT control relationship.

Compliance with Section 404 requires management to provide their external auditors with documented test results of functioning controls as supporting evidence for assertions in its report on control effectiveness. These tests would likely be performed by the organization's internal audit function or a specialized SOX group. Hence, management must actually perform its own tests of controls prior to the auditors performing theirs.

Section 302 also carries significant new auditor implications. In addition to expressing an opinion on management's annual assessment of internal control, auditors have responsibility regarding management's quarterly certifications of internal controls. Specifically, auditors must perform the following procedures quarterly to identify any material modifications in controls *over financial reporting*:

- *Interview management regarding any significant changes in the design or operation of internal control that occurred subsequent to the preceding annual audit or prior review of interim financial information*

- *Evaluate the implications of misstatements identified by the auditor as part of the interim review that relate to effective internal controls*

- *Determine whether changes in internal controls are likely to materially affect internal control over financial reporting*

Finally, Standard No. 2 places new responsibility on auditors to detect fraudulent activity. The standard emphasizes the importance of controls designed to prevent or detect fraud that could lead to material misstatement of the financial statements. Management is responsible for implementing such controls and auditors are expressly required to test them.

With this backdrop in place, the scene is set for viewing control techniques and test of controls that might be required under SOX. PCAOB Auditing Standard No. 2 emphasizes that a one-size-fits-all approach to the design and assessment of controls is inappropriate. Rather, the size and complexity of the organization needs to be considered in determining the nature and extent of controls that are necessary. The reader should recognize, therefore, that the controls presented in the remainder of this text describe the needs of a generic organization and may not apply in specific situations.

IT GOVERNANCE CONTROLS

IT governance is a broad concept relating to the decision rights and accountability for encouraging desirable behavior in the use of IT. Though important, not all elements of IT

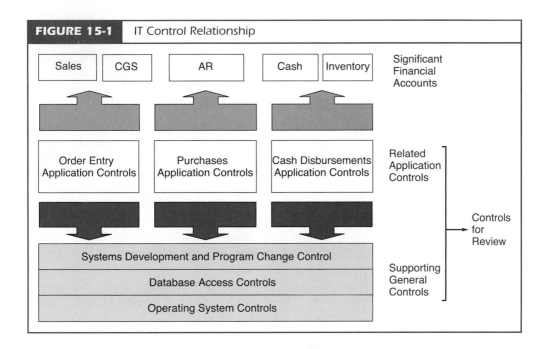

FIGURE 15-1 | IT Control Relationship

governance relate specifically to control issues addressed by SOX and outlined in the COSO framework. In this chapter we consider three governance issues that do: organizational structure of the IT function, computer operations, and disaster recovery planning.

The discussion on each of these governance issues begins with an explanation of the nature of risk and a description of the controls needed to mitigate the risk. Then, the audit objective is presented. This establishes *what* needs to be verified regarding the function of the control in place. Finally, example tests of controls are offered, which describes *how* auditors might gather evidence to satisfy the audit objective. These control objectives and associated tests may be performed by internal auditors providing evidence of management's compliance with SOX or by external auditors as part of their attest function. In this regard, we make no distinction between the two roles.

ORGANIZATIONAL STRUCTURE CONTROLS

Previous chapters have stressed the importance of segregating incompatible duties within manual activities. Specifically, operational tasks should be separated to:

1. Segregate the task of transaction authorization from transaction processing
2. Segregate record keeping from asset custody
3. Divide transaction-processing tasks among individuals so that fraud will require collusion between two or more individuals

The tendency in an IT environment is to consolidate activities. A single application may authorize, process, and record all aspects of a transaction. Thus, the focus of segregation control shifts from the operational level (transaction processing tasks now performed by computer programs) to higher-level organizational relationships within the IT function. The interrelationships among systems development, application maintenance, database administration, and computer operations activities are of particular concern.

The following section examines organizational control issues within the context of two generic models—the centralized model and the distributed model. For discussion purposes these are presented as alternative structures; in practice the IT environments of most firms possess elements of both.

SEGREGATION OF DUTIES WITHIN THE CENTRALIZED FIRM

Figure 15-2 presents an organizational chart of a centralized IT function. A similar organizational chart was presented in Chapter 1 to provide the basis for discussing IT tasks. It is reexamined here to study the control objectives behind separating these tasks. If the positions represented in this chart are unfamiliar, you should review the relevant sections in Chapter 1 at this time.

Separating Systems Development from Computer Operations

The segregation of systems development (both new systems development and maintenance) and operations activities is of the greatest importance. The responsibilities of these groups should not be commingled. Systems development and maintenance professionals acquire (by in-house development and purchase) and maintain systems for users. Operations staff should run these systems and have no involvement in their design and implementation. Consolidating these functions invites fraud. With detailed knowledge of an application's logic and control parameters along with access to the computer operations, an individual could make unauthorized changes to application logic during execution. Such changes may be temporary ("on the fly") and will disappear with little or no trace when the application terminates.

Separating the Database Administrator from Other Functions

Another important organizational control is the segregation of the database administrator (DBA) function from other IT functions. The DBA is responsible for a number of critical tasks pertaining to database security, including creating the database schema, creating **user views** (subschemas), assigning access authority to users, monitoring database usage,

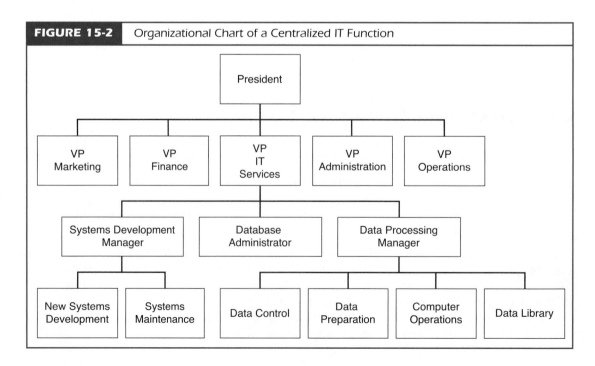

| FIGURE 15-2 | Organizational Chart of a Centralized IT Function |

and planning for future expansion. Delegating these responsibilities to others who perform incompatible tasks threatens database integrity. Figure 15-2 shows how the DBA function is organizationally independent.

Separating the DBA from Systems Development. Programmers create applications that access, update, and retrieve data from the database. Chapter 9 illustrated how database access control is achieved through the creation of user views, which is a DBA responsibility. To achieve database access, therefore, both the programmer and the DBA need to agree as to the attributes and tables (the user view) to make available to the application (or user) in question. If done properly, this permits and requires a formal review of the user data needs and security issues surrounding the request. Assigning responsibility for user view definition to individuals with programming responsibility removes this need to seek agreement and thus effectively erodes **access controls** to the DBMS.

Separating New Systems Development from Maintenance

Some companies organize their systems development function into two groups: systems analysis and programming. This organizational alternative is presented in Figure 15-3. The systems analysis group works with the user to produce a detailed design of the new system. The programming group codes the programs according to these design specifications. Under this approach, the programmer who codes the original programs also maintains them during the maintenance phase of the SDLC. Although a popular arrangement, this approach promotes two potential problems: inadequate documentation and fraud.

Inadequate Documentation. Poor-quality systems documentation is a chronic IT problem and a significant challenge for many organizations seeking SOX compliance. There are at least two explanations for this phenomenon. First, documenting systems is not as interesting as designing, testing, and implementing them. Systems professionals much prefer to move on to an exciting new project rather than document one just completed.

The second possible reason for poor documentation is job security. When a system is poorly documented, it is difficult to interpret, test, and debug. Therefore, the programmer who understands the system (the one who coded it) maintains bargaining power and becomes relatively indispensable. When the programmer leaves the firm, however, a new programmer inherits maintenance responsibility for the undocumented system. Depending on its complexity, the transition period may be long and costly.

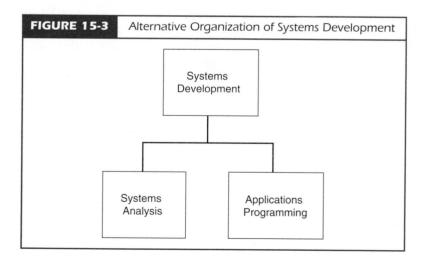

FIGURE 15-3   Alternative Organization of Systems Development

Program Fraud. When the original programmer of a system also has maintenance responsibility, the potential for fraud is increased. Program fraud involves making unauthorized changes to program modules for the purpose of committing an illegal act. The original programmer may have successfully concealed fraudulent code among the thousands of lines of legitimate code and the hundreds of modules that constitute a system. For the fraud to work successfully, however, the programmer must be able to control the situation through exclusive and unrestricted access to the application's programs. The programmer needs to protect the fraudulent code from accidental detection by another programmer performing maintenance or by auditors testing application controls. Therefore, having sole responsibility for maintenance is an important element in the duplicitous programmer's scheme. Through this maintenance authority, the programmer may freely access the system, disabling fraudulent code during audits and then restoring the code when the coast is clear. Frauds of this sort may continue for years without detection.

A Superior Structure for Systems Development

Figure 15-2 presents a superior organizational structure in which the systems development function is separated into two independent groups: new systems development and systems maintenance. The new systems development group is responsible for designing, programming, and implementing new systems projects. Upon successful implementation, responsibility for the system's ongoing maintenance falls to the systems maintenance group. This structure helps resolve the two control problems described previously.

First, documentation standards are improved because the maintenance group will require adequate documentation to perform their maintenance duties. Without complete documentation, the formal transfer of system responsibility from new systems development to systems maintenance cannot occur.

Second, denying the original programmer future access to the application code deters program fraud. Fraudulent code in an application, which is out of the perpetrator's control, increases the risk that the fraud will be discovered. The success of this control depends on the existence of other controls that limit, prevent, and detect unauthorized access to programs such as source program library controls discussed in Chapter 17. Whereas organizational separations alone cannot guarantee that computer frauds will not occur, they are critical to creating the necessary control environment.

THE DISTRIBUTED MODEL

Chapter 1 examined the impact on organizational structure of moving to a distributed data processing (DDP) model in which IT services are controlled by end-user departments. The effect of this is to consolidate some computer functions that are traditionally separated and to distribute some activities that are consolidated under the centralized model. In spite of the many advantages provided by DDP, the approach carries IT control implications that management and accountants should recognize. These are discussed in the following sections.

Incompatibility

Distributing responsibility for the purchases of software and hardware can result in uncoordinated and poorly conceived decisions. Organizational users, working independently, may select different and incompatible operating systems, technology platforms, spreadsheets, word processing, and database packages, which can impair internal communications.

Redundancy

Autonomous systems development activities throughout the firm can result in the creation of redundant applications and databases. Programs created by one user that could be used with little or no change by others will be redesigned from scratch rather than shared. Likewise, data common to many users may be reproduced, resulting in a high level of data redundancy.

Consolidating Incompatible Activities

The redistribution of IT functions to user areas can result in the creation of many very small units. Achieving an adequate segregation of duties may be economically or operationally infeasible in this setting. Thus, one person (or a small group) may be responsible for program development, program maintenance, and computer operations.

Acquiring Qualified Professionals

End users are typically not qualified to evaluate the technical credentials and relevant experience of prospective IT employees. Also, because the organizational unit into which these candidates are entering is small, opportunities for personal growth, continuing education, and promotion are limited. For these reasons, distributed IT units may have difficulty attracting highly qualified personnel.

Lack of Standards

For the above reasons, standards for systems development, documentation, and evaluating performance tend to be unevenly applied or nonexistent in the distributed environment.

CREATING A CORPORATE IT FUNCTION

The completely centralized and the fully distributed models represent extreme positions on a continuum of structural alternatives. The needs of most firms fall somewhere between these end points. For these firms, the control problems associated with DDP can, to some extent, be overcome by implementing a **corporate IT function**. Figure 15-4 illustrates this organizational approach.

The corporate IT function is a leaner unit with a different mission than that of the centralized IT function shown in Figure 15-4. This group provides technical advice and expertise to the various distributed IT functions, as represented by the dotted lines in Figure 15-4. Some of the support services provided are described in the following section.

Central Testing of Commercial Software and Hardware

The corporate IT group is better able to evaluate the merits of competing vendor software and hardware. A central, technically astute group such as this can evaluate systems features, controls, and compatibility with industry and organizational standards most efficiently. After testing, they can make recommendations to user areas for guiding acquisition decisions.

User Services

A valuable feature of the corporate group is its user services function. This activity provides technical help to users during the installation of new software and in troubleshooting hardware and software problems. The creation of an electronic bulletin board for users is an excellent way to distribute information about common problems and allows the sharing of user-developed programs with others in the organization. User services staff often teach technical courses for end users, which raises the level of user awareness and promotes the continued education of technical personnel.

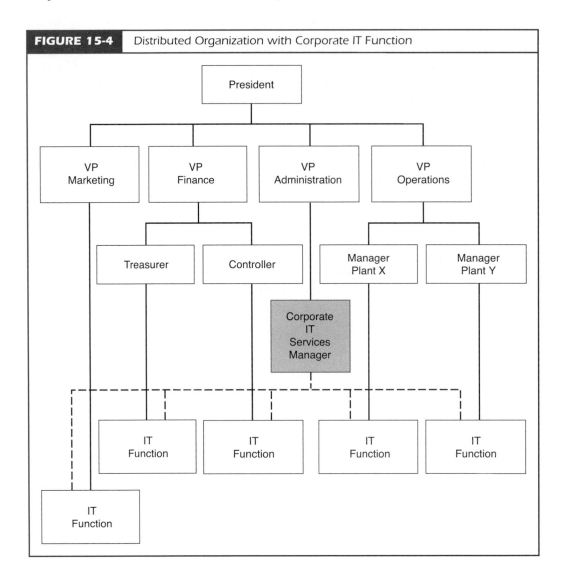

FIGURE 15-4 Distributed Organization with Corporate IT Function

Standard-Setting Body

The relatively poor control environment common to the distributed model can be improved by establishing central guidance. The corporate group can establish and distribute to user areas appropriate standards for systems development, programming, and documentation that will be compliant with SOX requirements.

Personnel Review

The corporate group is better equipped than users to evaluate the technical credentials of prospective systems professionals. Although the prospective IT hires will work for the distributed user groups, the involvement of the corporate group in hiring decisions can render a valuable service to the organization.

AUDIT OBJECTIVES RELATING TO ORGANIZATIONAL STRUCTURE

The auditor's objective is to verify that individuals in incompatible areas are segregated in accordance with the level of potential risk and in a manner that promotes a working environment. This is an environment in which formal, rather than casual, relationships need to exist between incompatible tasks.

AUDIT PROCEDURES RELATING TO ORGANIZATIONAL STRUCTURE

The following tests of controls would enable the auditor to achieve the control objectives.

- Obtain and review the corporate policy on computer security. Verify that the security policy is communicated to responsible employees and supervisors.

- Review relevant documentation, including the current organizational chart, mission statement, and job descriptions for key functions, to determine if individuals or groups are performing incompatible functions.

- Review systems documentation and maintenance records for a sample of applications. Verify that maintenance programmers assigned to specific projects are not also the original design programmers.

- Through observation, determine that the segregation policy is being followed in practice. Review operations room access logs to determine whether programmers enter the facility for reasons other than system failures.

- Review user rights and privileges to verify that programmers have access privileges consistent with their job descriptions.

COMPUTER CENTER SECURITY AND CONTROLS

Fires, floods, wind, sabotage, earthquakes, or even power outages can deprive an organization of its data-processing facilities and bring to a halt those functions that are performed or aided by the computer. Although the likelihood of such a disastrous event is remote, the consequences to the organization could be serious. If a disaster occurs the organization not only loses its investment in data-processing facilities, but more importantly, it also loses its ability to do business.

The objective of this section is to present computer center controls that help create a secure environment. We will begin with a look at controls designed to prevent and detect threats to the computer center. However, no matter how much is invested in control, some disasters simply cannot be anticipated and prevented. What does a company do to prepare itself for such an event? How will it recover? These questions are at the heart of the organization's disaster recovery plan. The next section deals specifically with issues pertaining to the development of a disaster recovery plan.

COMPUTER CENTER CONTROLS

Weaknesses in computer center security have a potential impact on the function of application controls related to the financial reporting process. Therefore, this physical environment is a control issue for SOX compliance. The following are some of the control features that contribute directly to computer center security.

Physical Location
The physical location selected for a computer center can influence the risk of disaster. To the extent possible, the computer center should be located away from human-made and natural hazards, such as processing plants, gas and water mains, airports, high-crime areas, flood plains, and geological faults.

Construction

Ideally, a computer center should be located in a single-story building of solid construction with controlled access (discussed in the following section). Utility (power and telephone) and communications lines should be underground. The building windows should not open. An air filtration system should be in place that is capable of excluding pollens, dust, and dust mites.

Access

Access to the computer center should be limited to the operators and other employees who work there. Programmers and analysts who occasionally need to correct program errors should be required to sign in and out. The computer center should maintain accurate records of all such events to verify the function of access control. The main entrance to the computer center should be through a single door, though fire exits with alarms are necessary. To achieve a higher level of security, access should be monitored by closed-circuit cameras and video recording systems.

Air Conditioning

Computers function best in an air-conditioned environment. For mainframe computers, providing adequate air conditioning is often a requirement of the vendor's warranty. Computers operate best in a temperature range of 70 to 75 degrees Fahrenheit and a relative humidity of 50 percent. Logic errors can occur in computer hardware when temperatures depart significantly from this range. Also, the risk of circuit damage from static electricity is increased when humidity drops. High humidity, on the other hand, can cause molds to grow and paper products (such as source documents) to swell and jam equipment.

Fire Suppression

The most common threat to a firm's computer equipment is from fire. Half of the companies that suffer fires go out of business because of the loss of critical records, such as accounts receivable. The implementation of an effective fire suppression system requires consultation with specialists. Some of the major features of such a system are listed in the following section.

a. Automatic and manual alarms should be placed in strategic locations around the installation. These alarms should be connected to a permanently staffed fire-fighting station.
b. There must be an automatic fire-extinguishing system that dispenses the appropriate type of suppressant (carbon dioxide or halon) for the location. For example, spraying water and certain chemicals on a computer can do as much damage as the fire.
c. There should be manual fire extinguishers placed at strategic locations.
d. The building should be of sound construction to withstand water damage caused by fire-suppression equipment.
e. Fire exits should be clearly marked and illuminated during a fire.

Fault Tolerance Controls

Fault tolerance is the ability of the system to continue operation when part of the system fails because of hardware failure, application program error, or operator error. Various levels of fault tolerance can be achieved by implementing redundant system components. Redundant disks and power supplies are two common examples.

Redundant arrays of independent disks (RAID). RAID involves using parallel disks that contain redundant elements of data and applications. If one disk fails, the lost data are automatically reconstructed from the redundant components stored on the other disks.

Uninterruptible power supplies. In the event of a power supply failure, short-term backup power is provided to allow the system to shut down in a controlled manner. This will prevent data loss and corruption that would otherwise result from an uncontrolled system crash.

Implementing fault tolerance control ensures that there is no single point of potential system failure. Total failure can occur only in the event of the failure of multiple components.

Audit Objectives Relating to Computer Center Security

The auditor's objective is to evaluate the controls governing computer center security. Specifically, the auditor must verify that (1) physical security controls are adequate to reasonably protect the organization from physical exposures; (2) insurance coverage on equipment is adequate to compensate the organization for the destruction of, or damage to, its computer center; and (3) operator documentation is adequate to deal with routine operations as well as system failures.

Audit Procedures for Assessing Physical Security Controls

The following are tests of physical security controls.

Tests of Physical Construction. The auditor should determine architectural plans that the computer center is solidly built of fireproof material. There should be adequate drainage under the raised floor to allow water to flow away in the event of water damage from a fire in an upper floor or from some other source. In addition, the auditor should assess the physical location of the computer center. The facility should be located in an area that minimizes its exposure from fire, civil unrest, and other hazards.

Tests of the Fire Detection System. The auditor should establish that fire detection and suppression equipment, both manual and automatic, are in place and are tested regularly. The fire-detection system should detect smoke, heat, and combustible fumes. The evidence may be obtained by reviewing official fire marshal records of tests, which are stored at the computer center.

Tests of Access Control. The auditor must establish that routine access to the computer center is restricted to authorized employees. Details about visitor access (by programmers and others), such as arrival and departure times, purpose, and frequency of access, can be obtained by reviewing the access log. To establish the veracity of this document, the auditor may covertly observe the process by which access is permitted.

Tests of Fault Tolerance Controls.

RAID. Many RAID configurations provide a graphical mapping of their redundant disk storage. From this mapping, the auditor should determine if the level of RAID in place is adequate for the organization, given the level of business risk associated with disk failure. If the organization is not employing RAID, the potential for a single point of system failure exists. The auditor should review with the system administrator alternative procedures for recovering from a disk failure.

Power Supplies Backup. The auditor should verify from test records that computer center personnel perform periodic tests of the backup power supply to ensure that it has sufficient capacity to run the computer and air conditioning. These important tests and their results should be formally recorded.

Audit Procedures for Verifying Insurance Coverage

The auditor should annually review the organization's insurance coverage on its computer hardware, software, and physical facility. The auditor should verify that all new acquisitions are listed on the policy and that obsolete equipment and software have been deleted. The insurance policy should reflect management's needs in terms of extent of coverage. For example, the firm may wish to be partially self-insured and require minimum coverage. On the other hand, the firm may seek complete replacement-cost coverage.

Audit Procedures for Verifying Adequacy of Operator Documentation

Computer operators use documentation called a *run manual* to run certain aspects of the system. In particular, large batch systems often require special attention from operators. During the course of the day, computer operators may execute dozens of computer programs that each process multiple files and produce multiple reports. To achieve effective data processing operations, the run manual must be sufficiently detailed to guide operators in their tasks. The auditor should review the run manual for completeness and accuracy. The typical contents of a run manual include:

- The name of the system, such as "Purchases System"

- The run schedule (daily, weekly, time of day)

- Required hardware devices (tapes, disks, printers, or special hardware)

- File requirements specifying all the transaction (input) files, master files, and output files used in the system

- Run-time instructions describing the error messages that may appear, actions to be taken, and the name and telephone number of the programmer on call, should the system fail

- A list of users who receive the output from the run

Also, the auditor should also verify that certain systems documentation, such as systems flowcharts, logic flowcharts, and program code listings, are not part of the operator's documentation. For reasons previously discussed, operators should not have access to the operational details of a system's internal logic.

DISASTER RECOVERY PLANNING

Some disasters cannot be prevented or evaded. Recent events include hurricanes, widespread flooding, earthquakes, and the events of September 11, 2001. The survival of a firm affected by a disaster depends on how it reacts. With careful contingency planning, the full impact of a disaster can be absorbed and the organization can still recover.

A **disaster recovery plan (DRP)** is a comprehensive statement of all actions to be taken before, during, and after a disaster, along with documented, tested procedures that will ensure the continuity of operations. Although the details of each plan are unique to the needs of the organization, all workable plans possess common features. The remainder of this section is devoted to a discussion of the following control issues: *providing second-site backup, identifying critical applications, performing backup and off-site storage procedures, creating a disaster recovery team,* and *testing the DRP.*

PROVIDING SECOND-SITE BACKUP

A necessary ingredient in a DRP is that it provides for duplicate data processing facilities following a disaster. The viable options available include the **empty shell**, recovery operations center, and internally provided backup.

The Empty Shell

The **empty shell** or "cold site" plan is an arrangement where the company buys or leases a building that will serve as a data center. In the event of a disaster, the shell is available and ready to receive whatever hardware the temporary user needs to run essential systems. This approach, however, has a fundamental weakness. Recovery depends on the timely availability of the necessary computer hardware to restore the data processing function. Management must obtain assurances (contracts) from hardware vendors that in the event of a disaster the vendor will give the company's needs priority. An unanticipated hardware supply problem at this critical juncture could be a fatal blow.

The Recovery Operations Center

A **recovery operations center** (**ROC**) or "hot site" is a fully equipped backup data center that is shared by many companies. In addition to hardware and backup facilities, ROC service providers offer a range of technical services to their clients who pay an annual fee for access rights. In the event of a major disaster, a subscriber can occupy the premises and, within a few hours, resume processing critical applications. September 11 was a true test of the reliability and effectiveness of the ROC approach. Comdiso, a major ROC provider, had 47 clients who declared 93 separate disasters on the day of the attack. All 47 companies relocated, and worked out of Comdisco's recovery centers. At one point 3,000 client employees were working out of the centers. Thousands of computers were configured for clients' needs within the first 24 hours, and systems recovery teams were on site wherever police permitted access. By September 25, nearly half of the clients were able to return to their facilities with a fully functional system.

A problem with this approach is the potential for competition among users for the ROC resources. For example, a widespread natural disaster, such as a flood or earthquake, may destroy the data processing capabilities of several shell members located in the same geographic area. All the victims will find themselves vying for access to the same limited facilities. The situation is analogous to a sinking ship that has an inadequate number of lifeboats.

The period of confusion following a disaster is not an ideal time to negotiate property rights. Therefore, before entering into a ROC arrangement, management should consider the potential problems of overcrowding and geographic clustering of the current membership.

Internally Provided Backup

Larger organizations with multiple data-processing centers often prefer the self-reliance provided by creating internal excess capacity. This permits firms to develop standardized hardware and software configurations, which ensure functional compatibility among their data processing centers and minimize cutover problems in the event of a disaster.

Pershing, a division of Donaldson, Lufkin & Jenrette Securities Corporation, processes more than 36 million transactions per day, about 2,000 per second. Pershing management recognized that a ROC vendor could not provide the recovery time they wanted and needed. The company, therefore, built its own remote **mirrored data center.** The facility is equipped with high-capacity storage devices capable of storing more than 20 terabytes of data and two IBM mainframes running high-speed copy software. All transactions processed by the main system are transmitted in real time along fiber-optic cables to the remote backup facility. At any point in time the mirrored data center reflects current economic events of the firm. The mirrored system has reduced Pershing's data recovery time from 24 hours to one hour.

IDENTIFYING CRITICAL APPLICATIONS

Another essential element of a DRP involves procedures to identify the critical applications and data files of the firm to be restored. Eventually, all applications and data must be restored to pre-disaster business activity levels. Immediate recovery efforts, however, should focus on restoring those applications and data that are critical to the organization's short-run survival. In any disaster scenario, it is short-term survivability that determines long-term survival.

For most organizations, short-term survival requires the restoration of those functions that generate cash flows sufficient to satisfy short-term obligations. For example, assume that the following functions affect the cash flow position of a particular firm:

- Customer sales and service

- Fulfillment of legal obligations

- Accounts receivable maintenance and collection

- Production and distribution

- Purchasing

- Communications between branches or agencies

- Public relations

The computer applications that support these functions directly are critical. Hence, these applications should be so identified and prioritized in the restoration plan.

Application priorities may change over time, and these decisions must be reassessed regularly. Systems are constantly revised and expanded to reflect changes in user requirements. Similarly, the DRP must be updated to reflect new developments and identify critical applications. Up-to-date priorities are important, because they affect other aspects of the strategic plan. For example, changes in application priorities may cause changes in the nature and extent of second-site backup requirements and specific backup procedures.

The task of identifying and prioritizing critical applications requires the active participation of management, user departments, and internal auditors. Too often, this task is incorrectly perceived to be an IT issue and delegated to IT professionals. Although the technical assistance of systems personnel is required, this is primarily a business decision and should be made by those best equipped to understand the business problem.

PERFORMING BACKUP AND OFF-SITE STORAGE PROCEDURES

All data files, application documentation, and supplies needed to perform critical functions should be specified in the DRP. Backup and storage procedures to safeguard these critical resources should be routinely performed by data processing personnel.

Backup Data Files

The state-of-the-art in database backup is the remote mirrored site, described previously, which provides complete data currency. Not all organizations are willing or able to invest in such backup resources. As a minimum, however, databases should be copied daily to tape or disks and secured off site. In the event of a disruption, reconstruction of the database is achieved by updating the most current backup version with subsequent transaction data. Likewise, master files and transaction files should be protected.

Backup Documentation

The system documentation for critical applications should be backed up and stored off site in much the same manner as data files. The large volumes of material involved and constant application revisions complicate the task. The process can be made more efficient through the use of CASE documentation tools.

Backup Supplies and Source Documents

The firm should maintain backup inventories of supplies and source documents used in the critical applications. Examples of critical supplies are check stocks, invoices, purchase orders, and any other special-purpose forms that cannot be obtained immediately.

CREATING A DISASTER RECOVERY TEAM

Recovering from a disaster depends on timely corrective action. Failure to perform essential tasks (such as obtaining backup files for critical applications) prolongs the recovery period and diminishes the prospects for a successful recovery. To avoid serious omissions or duplication of effort during implementation of the contingency plan, individual task responsibility must be clearly defined and communicated to the personnel involved.

Figure 15-5 presents an organizational chart depicting the possible composition of a disaster recovery team. The team members should be experts in their areas and have assigned tasks. Following a disaster, team members will delegate subtasks to their subordinates. It should be noted that traditional control concerns do not apply in this setting. The environment created by the disaster may necessitate the breaching normal controls such as segregation of duties, access controls, and supervision. At this point, business continuity is the primary consideration.

TESTING THE DRP

The most neglected aspect of contingency planning is testing the plans. Nevertheless, DRP tests are important and should be performed periodically. Tests provide measures of the preparedness of personnel and identify omissions or bottlenecks in the plan.

A test is most useful in the form of a surprise simulation of a disruption. When the mock disaster is announced, the status of all processing affected by it should be documented. This provides a benchmark for subsequent performance assessments. The plan should be carried as far as is economically feasible. Ideally, this will include the use of backup facilities and supplies.

AUDIT OBJECTIVE ASSESSING DISASTER RECOVERY PLANNING

The auditor should verify that management's disaster recovery plan is adequate and feasible for dealing with a catastrophe that could deprive the organization of its computing resources. The following tests focus on the areas of greatest concern.

AUDIT PROCEDURES FOR ASSESSING DISASTER RECOVERY PLANNING

Second-Site Backup

The auditor should evaluate the adequacy of the backup site arrangement. The client should possess vendor contracts guaranteeing timely equipment delivery to the cold site. In the case of ROC membership, the auditor should obtain information as to the total number of members and their geographic dispersion. A widespread disaster may create a demand that cannot be satisfied by the backup facility.

Critical Application List

The auditor should review the list of critical applications and ensure that it is current and complete. Missing applications may result in failure to recover. On the other hand, restoring noncritical applications diverts scarce resources to nonproductive tasks.

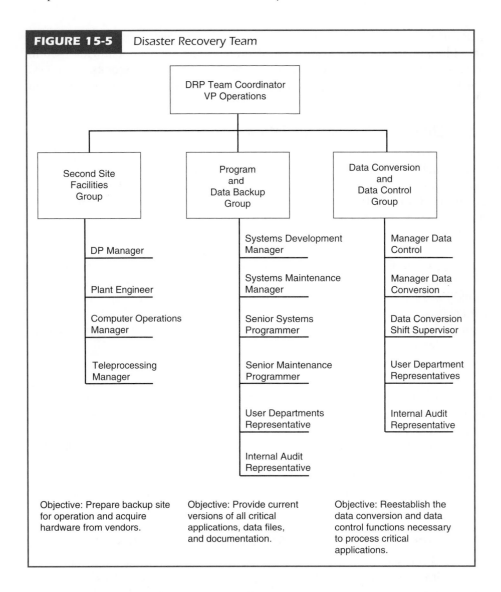

FIGURE 15-5   Disaster Recovery Team

Backup Critical Applications and Critical Data Files

The auditor should verify that the organization has procedures in place to back up stored off-site copies of critical application's and data. Evidence of this can be obtained by selecting a sample of data files and programs and determine if they are being backed up as required.

Backup Supplies, Source Documents, and Documentation

The system documentation, supplies, and source documents needed to restore and run critical applications should be backed up and stored off site. The auditor should verify that the types and quantities of items specified in the DRP exist in a secure location.

The Disaster Recovery Team

The DRP should clearly list the names, addresses, and emergency telephone numbers of the disaster recovery team members. The auditor should verify that members of the team are current employees and are aware of their assigned responsibilities. On one occasion, while reviewing a firm's DRP, the author discovered that a team leader listed in the plan had been deceased for nine months.

SUMMARY

This chapter examined some of the internal control issues and audit issues that have arisen out of Sections 302 and 404 of the Sarbanes-Oxley Act (SOX). It began with a review of management and auditor responsibilities under SOX. Then the (COSO) control framework recommended by the PCAOB and the SEC was examined. Next, the chapter presented exposures that arise in connection with organizational structure. In these general areas, exposures are controlled through important segregation of incompatible duties. The chapter reviewed computer center threats. To ensure the physical security of its computer equipment, a firm must choose a location that is not susceptible to human-made or natural hazards. The building that houses the computer equipment must be soundly and strategically constructed and equipped with systems that regulate air filtration, temperature, and humidity. An adequate fire-suppression system is also required, because fire is the most common threat to the computer center. Finally, the chapter presented the key elements of a disaster recovery plan. Several factors need to be considered in such a plan, including providing second-site backup, identifying critical applications, performing backup and off-site storage procedures, creating a disaster recovery team, and testing the DRP.

APPENDIX

Recent developments in information technology (IT) have had a tremendous impact on the field of auditing. In this text we have seen how IT has inspired the reengineering of traditional business processes to promote more efficient operations and to improve communications within the entity and between the entity and its customers and suppliers. These advances, however, have introduced new risks that require unique internal controls. They have engendered the need for new techniques for evaluating controls and for assuring the security and accuracy of corporate data and the information systems that produce it. This appendix presents an overview of alternative audit approaches and presents the general structure of an audit.

ATTEST SERVICES VERSUS ASSURANCE SERVICES

An important starting point for this body of material is to draw a distinction between the auditor's traditional attestation function and the emerging field of assurance services. The attest service is defined as:

> an engagement in which a practitioner is engaged to issue, or does issue, a written communication that expresses a conclusion about the reliability of a written assertion that is the responsibility of another party. (SSAE No. 1, AT Section 100.01)

The following requirements apply to attestation services:

- Attestation services require written assertions and a practitioner's written report.
- Attestation services require the formal establishment of measurement criteria or their description in the presentation.
- The levels of service in attestation engagements are limited to examination, review, and application of agreed-upon procedures.

Assurance services constitute a broader concept that encompasses, but is not limited to, attestation. The relationship between these services is illustrated in 15-6.

Assurance services are professional services that are designed to improve the quality of information, both financial and nonfinancial, used by decision makers. The domain of assurance services is intentionally unbounded so that it does not inhibit the growth of future services that are currently unforeseen. For example, assurance services may be contracted to provide information about the quality or marketability of a product. Alternatively, a client may need information about the efficiency of a production process or the effectiveness of its network security system. Assurance services are intended to help people make better

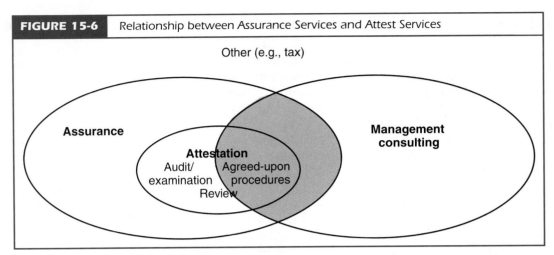

| FIGURE 15-6 | Relationship between Assurance Services and Attest Services |

SOURCE: Based on the AICPA *Special Committee Report on Assurance Services.*

decisions by improving information. This information may come as a by-product of the attest function, or it may ensue from an independently motivated review.

The evolution of the accounting profession is expected to follow the assurance services model. All of the big four professional services firms have now renamed their traditional audit functions "Assurance Services." The organizational units responsible for conducting IT audits usually have the words "Risk Management" in the title, such as: *IT Risk Management, Information Systems Risk Management,* or *Global Risk Management* and typically is a division of assurance services.

The material outlined in this appendix relates to tasks normally conducted by risk management professionals while performing an IT audit. In the pages that follow we examine what constitutes an audit, who performs audits, and how audits are structured. Keep in mind, however, that in many cases the purpose of the audit task, rather than the task itself, defines the service being rendered. Therefore, the issues and procedures described in this appendix apply to the broader context of assurance services, which include, but are not limited to, attest services. They also relate directly to the internal audit function.

WHAT IS AN EXTERNAL FINANCIAL AUDIT?

An external financial audit is an attestation performed by an expert—the auditor—who expresses an opinion regarding the presentation of financial statements. The audit objective is associated with the presentation of financial statements; in particular that in all material respects, the statements are fairly presented. The external auditor is an independent auditor, and is a certified public accountant (CPA). The SEC requires all publicly traded companies to be subject annually to a financial audit by an independent auditor. CPAs represent the interests of outsiders: stockholders, creditors, government agencies, and the "public." Public confidence in the reliability of the company's internally produced financial statements rests directly on the statements being evaluated by an independent auditor.

The external auditor must follow strict rules in conducting financial audits. These authoritative rules have been defined by federal law (Sarbanes-Oxley Act, 2002), the SEC, the Financial Accounting Standards Board (FASB), and the AICPA. Until recently, the SEC has delegated most of that authority to the AICPA and FASB, the majority of whose members are CPAs. The Sarbanes-Oxley Act of 2002 established the Public Company Accounting Oversight Board (PCAOB) to oversee much of the guidelines and standards of financial auditing, which potentially could replace the function served by FASB, and some of the functions the AICPA, including reprimands and penalties for CPAs who are convicted of certain crimes or guilty of certain infractions.

The public expression of the auditor's opinion is the culmination of a systematic audit process that involves three conceptual phases: (1) familiarization with the organization's business, (2) evaluating and testing internal controls, and (3) assessing the reliability of financial data. The specific elements of the audit process are examined later in this appendix.

AUDITING STANDARDS

The product of the attestation function is a formal written report that expresses an opinion about the reliability of the assertions contained in the financial statements. The auditor's report expresses an opinion as to whether the financial statements are in conformity with *generally accepted accounting principles.* External users of financial statements are presumed to rely on the auditor's opinion about the reliability of financial statements in making decisions. To do so, users must be able to place their trust in the auditor's competence, professionalism, integrity, and independence. Auditors are guided in their professional responsibility by the ten *generally accepted auditing standards (GAAS)* presented in Table 15-1.

Auditing standards are divided into three classes: general qualification standards, field work standards, and reporting standards. GAAS establishes a framework for prescribing auditor performance, but it is not sufficiently detailed to provide meaningful guidance in specific circumstances. To provide specific guidance, the American Institute of Certified Public Accountants (AICPA) issues Statements on *Auditing Standards (SASs)* as authoritative interpretations of GAAS. SASs are often referred to as *auditing standards,* or *GAAS,* although they are not the ten generally accepted auditing standards.

Statements on Auditing Standards

The first SAS (SAS 1) was issued by the AICPA in 1972. Since then, many SASs have been issued to provide auditors with guidance on a spectrum of topics, including methods of investigating new clients, procedures for collecting information from attorneys regarding contingent liability claims against clients, and techniques for obtaining background information on the client's industry.

Statements on auditing standards are regarded as authoritative pronouncements because every member of the profession must follow their recommendations or be able to show why an SAS does not apply in a given situation. The burden of justifying departures from SAS falls on the individual auditor.

TABLE 15-1	**Generally Accepted Auditing Standards**	
General Standards	**Standards of Field Work**	**Reporting Standards**
1. The auditor must have adequate technical training and proficiency.	1. Audit work must be adequately planned.	1. The auditor must state in the report whether financial statements were prepared in accordance with generally accepted accounting principles.
2. The auditor must have independence of mental attitude.	2. The auditor must gain a sufficient understanding of the internal control structure.	2. The report must identify those circumstances in which generally accepted accounting principles were not applied.
3. The auditor must exercise due professional care in the performance of the audit and the preparation of the report.	3. The auditor must obtain sufficient, competent evidence.	3. The report must identify any items that do not have adequate informative disclosures.
		4. The report shall contain an expression of the auditor's opinion on the financial statements as a whole.

EXTERNAL AUDITING VERSUS INTERNAL AUDITING

External auditing is often called **independent auditing** because it is done by certified public accountants who are independent of the organization being audited. External auditors represent the interests of third-party stakeholders in the organization, such as stockholders, creditors, and government agencies. Because the focus of the external audit is on the financial statements, this type of audit is called a *financial audit*.

The Institute of Internal Auditors defines **internal auditing** as an independent appraisal function established within an organization to examine and evaluate its activities as a service to the organization.[3] Internal auditors perform a wide range of activities on behalf of the organization, including conducting financial audits, examining an operation's compliance with organizational policies, reviewing the organization's compliance with legal obligations, evaluating operational efficiency, detecting and pursuing fraud within the firm, and conducting IT audits.

The characteristic that conceptually distinguishes internal auditors from external auditors is their respective constituencies: external auditors represent outsiders, and internal auditors represent the interests of the organization. Nevertheless, in this capacity, internal auditors often cooperate with and assist external auditors in performing financial audits. This is done to achieve audit efficiency and reduce audit fees. For example, a team of internal auditors can perform tests of computer controls under the supervision of a single external auditor.

The independence and competence of the internal audit staff determine the extent to which external auditors may cooperate with and rely on work performed by internal auditors. Some internal audit departments report directly to the controller. Under this arrangement, the internal auditor's independence is compromised, and the external auditor is prohibited by professional standards from relying on evidence provided by the internal auditors. In contrast, external auditors can rely in part on evidence gathered by internal audit departments that are organizationally independent and that report to the board of directors' audit committee. A truly independent internal audit staff adds value to the audit process. Internal auditors can gather audit evidence throughout a fiscal period; external auditors can then use this evidence at year end to conduct more efficient, less disruptive, and less costly audits of the organization's financial statements.

WHAT IS AN INFORMATION TECHNOLOGY (IT) AUDIT?

An IT audit focuses on the computer-based aspects of an organization's information system. This includes assessing the proper implementation, operation, and control of computer resources. Because most modern information systems employ information technology, the IT audit is typically a significant component of all external (financial) and internal audits.

The Elements of Auditing

To this point, we have painted a broad picture of auditing. Let's now fill in some details. The following definition of auditing is applicable to external auditing, internal auditing, and IT auditing:

> Auditing is a systematic process of objectively obtaining and evaluating evidence regarding assertions about economic actions and events to ascertain the degree of correspondence between those assertions and established criteria and communicating the results to interested users.[4]

This seemingly obtuse definition contains several important points that are examined in the following sections.

A Systematic Process. Conducting an audit is a systematic and logical process that applies to all forms of information systems. Though important in all audit settings, a systematic approach is particularly important in the IT environment. The lack of physical procedures that can be visually verified and evaluated

---

3   Institute of Internal Auditors, Standards of Professional Practice of Internal Auditing (Orlando, Fla.: Institute of Internal Auditors, 1978).

4   AAA Committee on Basic Auditing Concepts, "A Statement of Basic Auditing Concepts," *Accounting Review*, supplement to vol. 47, 1972.

injects a high degree of complexity into the IT audit. Therefore, a logical framework for conducting an audit in the IT environment is critical to help the auditor identify important processes and data files.

Management Assertions and Audit Objectives. The organization's financial statements reflect a set of management assertions about the financial health of the entity. The task of the auditor is to determine whether the financial statements are fairly presented. To accomplish this, the auditor establishes **audit objectives**, designs procedures, and gathers evidence that corroborate or refute management's assertions. These assertions fall into five general categories:

- The **existence or occurrence** assertion affirms that all assets and equities contained in the balance sheet exist and that all transactions in the income statement actually occurred.
- The **completeness** assertion declares that no material assets, equities, or transactions have been omitted from the financial statements.
- The **rights and obligations** assertion maintains that assets appearing on the balance sheet are owned by the entity and that the liabilities reported are obligations.
- The **valuation or allocation** assertion states that assets and equities are valued in accordance with generally accepted accounting principles and that allocated amounts such as depreciation expense are calculated on a systematic and rational basis.
- The **presentation and disclosure** assertion alleges that financial statement items are correctly classified (e.g., long-term liabilities will not mature within one year) and that footnote disclosures are adequate to avoid misleading the users of financial statements.

Generally, auditors develop their audit objectives and design **audit procedures** based on the preceding assertions. The example in Table 15-2 outlines these procedures.

Obtaining Evidence. Auditors seek evidential matter that corroborates management assertions. In the IT environment, this involves gathering evidence relating to the reliability of computer controls as well as the contents of databases that have been processed by computer programs. Evidence is collected by performing tests of controls, which establish whether internal controls are functioning properly, and substantive tests, which determine whether accounting databases fairly reflect the organization's transactions and account balances.

TABLE 15-2	Audit Objectives and Audit Procedures Based on Management Assertions	
MANAGEMENT ASSERTION	**AUDIT OBJECTIVE**	**AUDIT PROCEDURE**
Existence or Occurrence	Inventories listed on the balance sheet exist.	Observe the counting of physical inventory.
Completeness	Accounts payable include all obligations to vendors for the period.	Compare receiving reports, supplier invoices, purchase orders, and journal entries for the period and the beginning beginning of the next period.
Rights and Obligations	Plant and equipment listed in the balance sheet are owned by the entity.	Review purchase agreements, insurance insurance policies, and related documents.
Valuation or Allocation	Accounts receivable are stated at net realizable value.	Review entity's aging of accounts and evaluate the adequacy of the allowance for uncorrectable accounts.
Presentation and Disclosure	Contingencies not reported in financial accounts are properly disclosed in footnotes.	Obtain information from entity lawyers about the status of litigation and estimates of potential loss.

Ascertaining the Degree of Correspondence with Established Criteria. The auditor must determine whether weaknesses in internal controls and misstatements found in transactions and account balances are material. In all audit environments, assessing *materiality* is an auditor judgment. In an IT environment, however, this decision is complicated further by technology and a sophisticated internal control structure.

Communicating Results. Auditors must communicate the results of their tests to interested users. Independent auditors render a report to the audit committee of the board of directors or stockholders of a company. The audit report contains, among other things, an **audit opinion**. This opinion is distributed along with the financial report to interested parties both internal and external to the organization. IT auditors often communicate their findings to internal and external auditors, who can then integrate these findings with the non-IT aspects of the audit.

THE STRUCTURE OF AN IT AUDIT

The IT audit is generally divided into three phases: audit planning, tests of controls, and substantive testing. Figure 15-7 illustrates the steps involved in these phases.

Audit Planning

The first step in the IT audit is **audit planning**. Before the auditor can determine the nature and extent of the tests to perform, he or she must gain a thorough understanding of the client's business. A major part of this phase of the audit is the analysis of audit risk (discussed later). The objective of the auditor is to obtain sufficient information about the firm to plan the other phases of the audit. The risk analysis incorporates an overview of the organization's internal controls. During the review of controls, the auditor attempts to understand the organization's policies, practices, and structure. In this phase of the audit, the auditor also identifies the financially significant applications and attempts to understand the controls over the primary transactions that are processed by these applications.

The techniques for gathering evidence at this phase include questionnaires, interviewing management, reviewing systems documentation, and observing activities. During this process, the IT auditor must identify the principal exposures and the controls that attempt to reduce these exposures. Having done so, the auditor proceeds to the next phase, where he or she tests the controls for compliance with preestablished standards.

Tests of Controls

The objective of the **tests of controls** phase is to determine whether adequate internal controls are in place and functioning properly. To accomplish this, the auditor performs various tests of controls. The evidence-gathering techniques used in this phase may include both manual techniques and specialized computer audit techniques.

At the conclusion of the tests of controls phase, the auditor must assess the quality of the internal controls. The degree of reliance the auditor can ascribe to internal controls affects the nature and extent of substantive testing. The relationship between tests of controls and substantive tests is discussed later.

Substantive Testing

The third phase of the audit process focuses on financial data. This involves a detailed investigation of specific account balances and transactions through what are called **substantive tests**. For example, a customer confirmation is a substantive test sometimes used to verify account balances. The auditor selects a sample of accounts receivable balances and traces these back to their source—the customers—to determine if the amount stated is in fact owed by a bona fide customer. By so doing, the auditor can verify the accuracy of each account in the sample. Based on such sample findings, the auditor is able to draw conclusions about the fair value of the entire accounts receivable asset.

Some substantive tests are physical, labor-intensive activities such as counting cash, counting inventories in the warehouse, and verifying the existence of stock certificates in a safe. In an IT environment, the information needed to perform substantive tests (such as account balances and names and addresses of individual customers) is contained in data files that often must be extracted using computer-assisted audit tools and techniques (CAATTs) software.

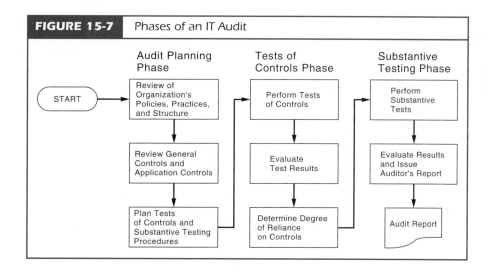

FIGURE 15-7   Phases of an IT Audit

ASSESSING AUDIT RISK AND DESIGNING TESTS OF CONTROLS

Audit risk is the probability that the auditor will render an unqualified (clean) opinion on financial statements that are, in fact, materially misstated. Material misstatements may be caused by errors or irregularities or both. Errors are unintentional mistakes. Irregularities are intentional misrepresentations to perpetrate a fraud or to mislead the users of financial statements. The auditor's objective is to minimize audit risk by performing tests of controls and substantive tests.

AUDIT RISK COMPONENTS

The three components of audit risk are inherent risk, control risk, and detection risk.

Inherent Risk

Inherent risk is associated with the unique characteristics of the business or industry of the client.[5] Firms in declining industries have greater inherent risk than firms in stable or thriving industries. Auditors cannot reduce the level of inherent risk. Even in a system protected by excellent controls, financial data and, consequently, financial statements can be materially misstated.

To illustrate inherent risk, assume that the audit client's financial statements show an accounts receivable balance of $10 million. Unknown to the auditor and the client, several customers with accounts receivable totaling $2 million are about to go out of business. These accounts, which are a material component of the total accounts receivable balance of $10 million, are not likely to be collected. To represent these accounts as an asset in the financial statements would be a material misstatement of the firm's economic position.

Control Risk

Control risk is the likelihood that the control structure is flawed because controls are either absent or inadequate to prevent or detect errors in the accounts.[6] To illustrate control risk, consider the following partial customer sales record, which is processed by the sales order system.

Quantity	Unit Price	Total
10 Units	$20	$2,000

Assuming the Quantity and Unit Price fields in the record are correctly presented, then the extended amount (Total) value of $2,000 is in error. An AIS with adequate controls should prevent or detect such an

---

5   Auditing Standards Board, AICPA Professional Standards (New York: AICPA), 1994 AU Section 312.20.
6   Ibid.

error. If, however, controls are lacking and the value of Total in each record is not validated before processing, then the risk of undetected errors entering the data files increases.

Auditors reduce the level of control risk by performing tests of internal controls. In the preceding example, the auditor could create test transactions, including some with incorrect Total values, which are processed by the application in a test run. The results of the test will indicate that price extension errors are not detected and are being incorrectly posted to the accounts receivable file.

Detection Risk

Detection risk is the risk that auditors are willing to take that errors not detected or prevented by the control structure will also not be detected by the auditor.[7] Auditors set an acceptable level of detection risk (planned detection risk) that influences the level of substantive tests that they perform. For example, more substantive testing would be required when the planned detection risk is 1 percent than when it is 5 percent.

THE RELATIONSHIP BETWEEN TESTS OF CONTROLS AND SUBSTANTIVE TESTS

Tests of controls and substantive tests are auditing techniques used for reducing total audit risk. The relationship between tests of controls and substantive tests varies according to the auditor's risk assessment of the organization. The stronger the internal control structure, the lower the control risk and the less substantive testing the auditor must do. This is because the likelihood of errors in the accounting records is reduced. In other words, when controls are strong, the auditor may limit substantive testing. However, the weaker the internal control structure, the greater the control risk and the more substantive testing the auditor must perform to reduce total audit risk. Evidence of weak controls forces the auditor to extend substantive testing to search for misstatements in financial data caused by control errors as well as business problems inherent to the organization. Because substantive tests are labor-intensive and time-consuming, they are expensive. Increased substantive testing translates into longer and more disruptive audits and higher audit costs.

KEY TERMS

access controls (727)

corporate IT function (729)

disaster recovery plan (DRP) (734)

empty shell (734)

fault tolerance (732)

mirrored data center (735)

off-site storage (734)

operating system (723)

recovery operations center (ROC) (735)

redundant arrays of independent disks (RAID) (732)

uninterruptible power supplies (733)

user view (726)

REVIEW QUESTIONS

1. The Sarbanes-Oxley Act contains many sections. Which sections are the focus of this chapter?

2. What control framework is recommended by the PCAOB?

3. COSO identifies two broad groupings of information system controls. What are they?

4. What are the objectives of application controls?

5. Give three examples of application controls.

6. Define general controls.

7. How do automated authorization procedures differ from manual authorization procedures?

8. Explain why certain duties that are deemed incompatible in a manual system may be combined in a CBIS environment. Give an example.

9. What are the three primary CBIS functions that must be separated?

10. What exposures do data consolidation in a CBIS environment pose?

---

7   Ibid.

11. Differentiate between general and application controls. Give two examples of each.

12. What are the primary reasons for separating operational tasks?

13. What problems may occur as a result of combining applications programming and maintenance tasks into one position?

14. Why is poor-quality systems documentation a prevalent problem?

15. What is the role of a corporate computer services department? How does this differ from other configurations?

16. What are the five control implications of distributed data processing?

17. List the control features that directly contribute to the security of the computer center environment.

18. What is fault tolerance?

19. What are redundant arrays of independent disks (RAID)?

20. What is the purpose of an audit?

21. Discuss the concept of independence within the context of an audit.

22. What is the meaning of the term *attest services*?

23. What are assurance services?

24. What are the conceptual phases of an audit? How do they differ between general auditing and IT auditing?

25. Distinguish between internal and external auditors.

26. What are the four primary elements described in the definition of auditing?

27. Explain the concept of materiality.

28. What tasks do auditors perform during audit planning, and what techniques are used?

29. Distinguish between tests of controls and substantive testing.

30. What is audit risk?

31. Distinguish between errors and irregularities. Which do you think concern auditors the most?

32. Distinguish between inherent risk and control risk. How do internal controls affect inherent risk and control risk, if at all? What is the role of detection risk?

33. What is the relationship between tests of controls and substantive tests?

34. List 4 general control areas.

35. What types of documents would an auditor review in testing organizational structure controls? Why is it also important to observe actual behavior?

36. What are some tests of physical security controls?

DISCUSSION QUESTIONS

1. Discuss the key features of Section 302 of the Sarbanes-Oxley Act.

2. Discuss the key features of Section 404 of the Sarbanes-Oxley Act.

3. Section 404 requires management to make a statement identifying the control framework used to conduct their assessment of internal controls. Discuss the options in selecting a control framework.

4. Explain how general controls impact transaction integrity and the financial reporting process.

5. Prior to SOX, external auditors were required to be familiar with the client organization's internal controls, but not test them. Explain.

6. Does a qualified opinion on management's assessment of internal controls over the financial reporting system necessitate a qualified opinion on the financial statements. Explain.

7. The PCAOB's Standard No. 2 specifically requires auditors to understand transaction flows in designing their test of controls. What steps does this entail?

8. What fraud detection responsibilities (if any) are imposed on auditors by SOX?

9. A bank in California has 13 branches spread throughout northern California, each with its own minicomputer where its data are stored. Another bank has 10 branches spread throughout California, with the data being stored on a mainframe in San Francisco. Which system do you think is more vulnerable to unauthorized access? Excessive losses from disaster?

10. Compare and contrast the following disaster recovery options: empty shell, recovery operations center, and internally provided backup. Rank them from most risky to least risky, as well as from most costly to least costly.

11. Who should determine and prioritize the critical applications? How is this done? How frequently is it done?

12. Discuss the differences between the attest function and assurance services.

13. Define the management assertions of existence or occurrence, completeness, rights and obligations, valuation or allocation, and presentation and disclosure.

14. An organization's internal audit department is usually considered an effective control mechanism for evaluating the organization's internal control structure. Birch Company's internal auditing function reports directly to the controller. Comment on the effectiveness of this organizational structure.

15. Discuss why any distinction between IS auditing and financial auditing is not meaningful.

16. Discuss how the process of obtaining audit evidence in a CBIS is inherently different than in a manual system.

17. Some internal controls can be tested objectively. Discuss some internal controls that you think are relatively more subjective to assess in terms of adequacy than others.

18. Give a specific example, other than the one in the chapter, to illustrate the relationship between exposure, control, audit objective, and tests of control.

19. Discuss the subjective nature of auditing computer center security.

MULTIPLE-CHOICE QUESTIONS

1. Which of the following is NOT a requirement in management's report on the effectiveness of internal controls over financial reporting?
   a. A statement of management's responsibility for establishing and maintaining adequate internal control user satisfaction.
   b. A statement that the organizations internal auditors has issued an attestation report on management's assessment of the companies internal controls.
   c. A statement identifying the framework used by management to conduct their assessment of internal controls.
   d. An explicit written conclusion as to the effectiveness of internal control over financial reporting.

2. Which of the following is NOT an implication of Section 302 of the Sarbanes-Oxley Act?
   a. Auditors must determine, whether changes in internal control has, or is likely to, materially affect internal control over financial reporting.
   b. Auditors must interview management regarding significant changes in the design or operation of internal control that occurred since the last audit.
   c. Corporate management (including the CEO) must certify monthly and annually their organization's internal controls over financial reporting.
   d. Management must disclose any material changes in the company's internal controls that have occurred during the most recent fiscal quarter.

3. Which of the following statements is true?
   a. Both the SEC and the PCAOB require the use of the COSO framework.
   b. Both the SEC and the PCAOB require the COBIT framework.
   c. The SEC recommends COBIT and the PCAOB recommends COSO.
   d. Any framework can be used that encompass all of COSO's general themes.
   e. Both c and d are true.

4. Which of the following is NOT a control implication of distributed data processing?
   a. redundancy
   b. user satisfaction
   c. incompatibility
   d. lack of standards

5. Which of the following disaster recovery techniques may be least optimal in the case of a widespread natural disaster?
   a. empty shell
   b. ROC

c. internally provided backup

d. they are all equally beneficial

6. Which of the following is NOT a potential threat to computer hardware and peripherals?

   a. low humidity

   b. high humidity

   c. carbon dioxide fire extinguishers

   d. water sprinkler fire extinguishers

7. Computer accounting control procedures are referred to as general or application controls. The primary objective of application controls in a computer environment is to

   a. ensure that the computer system operates efficiently.

   b. ensure the validity, completeness, and accuracy financial transactions.

   c. provide controls over the electronic functioning of the hardware.

   d. plan for the protection of the facilities and backup for the systems.

8. Which of the following is NOT a task performed in the audit planning phase?

   a. reviewing an organization's policies and practices

   b. determining the degree of reliance on controls

   c. reviewing general controls

   d. planning substantive testing procedures

9. Which of the following risks is least controllable by the auditor?

   a. inherent risk

   b. control risk

   c. detection risk

   d. all are equally controllable

10. Which of the following would strengthen organizational control over large-scale data processing center?

    a. requiring the user departments to specify the general control standards necessary for processing transactions.

    b. requiring that requests and instructions for data processing services be submitted directly to the computer operator in the data center.

    c. having the database administrator report to the manager of computer operations.

    d. assigning maintenance responsibility to the original system designer who best knows its logic.

    e. none of the above.

PROBLEMS

1. Physical Security

Avatar Financials Inc., located on Madison Avenue, New York, is a company that provides financial advice to individuals and small to mid-sized businesses. Its primary operations are in wealth management and financial advice. Each client has an account where basic personal information is stored at a server within the main office in New York City. The company also keeps the information about the amount of investment of each client on a separate server at their data center in Bethlehem, Pennsylvania. This information includes the total value of the portfolio, type of investments made, the income structure of each client, and associated tax liabilities.

In the last few years, larger commercial banks have started providing such services and are competing for the same set of customers. Avatar, which prides itself in personal consumer relations, is now trying to set up additional services to keep its current customers. It has recently upgraded its website, which formerly only allowed clients to update their personal information. Now clients can access information about their investments, income, and tax liabilities that is stored at the data center in Pennsylvania.

As a result of previous dealings, Avatar has been given free access to use the computer room of an older production plant. The company feels that this location is secure enough and would keep the data intact from physical intruders. The servers are housed in a room that the production plant used to house its legacy system. The room has detectors for smoke and associated sprinklers. It is enclosed with no windows and has specialized temperature controlled air ducts.

Management has recently started looking at other alternatives to house the server as the plant is going to be shut down. Management has major concerns about the secrecy of the location and the associated measures. They want to incorporate newer methods of physical data protection. The company's auditors have also expressed a concern that some of the measures at the current location are inadequate and newer alternatives should be found.

Required:
Answer the following questions:

1. Why are the auditors of Avatar stressing the need to have better physical environment for the server? If Avatar has proper software controls in place, would that not be enough to secure the information?

2. Name the six essential control features that contribute directly to the security of the computer server environment.

2. Internal Control

In reviewing the process procedures and internal controls of one of your audit clients, Steeplechase Enterprises, you notice the following practices in place. Steeplechase has recently installed a new computer system that affects the accounts receivable, billing, and shipping records. A specifically identified computer operator has been permanently assigned to each of the functions of accounts receivable, billing, and shipping. Each of these computer operators is assigned the responsibility of running the program for transaction processing, making program changes, and reconciling the computer log. To prevent any single operator from having exclusive access to the tapes and documentation, these three computer operators randomly rotate the custody and control tasks every two weeks over the magnetic tapes and the system documentation. Access controls to the computer room consist of magnetic cards and a digital code for each operator. Access to the computer room is not allowed to either the systems analyst or the computer operations supervisor.

The documentation for the system consists of the following: record layouts, program listings, logs, and error listings.

Once goods are shipped from one of Steeplechase's three warehouses, warehouse personnel forward shipping notices to the accounting department. The billing clerk receives the shipping notice and accounts for the manual sequence of the shipping notices. Any missing notices are investigated. The billing clerk also manually enters the price of the item, and prepares daily totals (supported by adding machine tapes) of the units shipped and the amount of sales. The shipping notices and adding machine tapes are sent to the computer department for data entry.

The computer output generated consists of a two-copy invoice and remittance advice and a daily sales register. The invoices and remittance advice are forwarded to the billing clerk, who mails one copy of the invoice and remittance advice to the customer and files the other copy in an open invoice file, which serves as an accounts receivable document. The daily sales register contains the total of units shipped and sales amounts. The computer operator compares the computer-generated totals to the adding machine tapes.

Required:
Identify the control weaknesses present and make a specific recommendation for correcting each of the control weaknesses.

3. Distributed Processing System (CMA Adapted)

The internal audit department of Hastone Manufacturing Company recently concluded a routine examination of the company's computer facilities. The auditor's report identified as a weakness the fact that there had been no coordination by the data processing services department in the purchase of PC systems used by individual departments of Hastone. Six different hardware manufacturers supply the computers that use different operating systems. In addition, several different software vendors provide spreadsheets, word processing, and database applications, along with some networking applications.

PCs were acquired in the operating departments to allow employees in each department to conduct special analyses. Many of the departments also wanted the capability to download data from the mainframe. Therefore, each operating department had requested guidance and assistance from the data processing services department. Data processing, however, responded that it was understaffed and must devote full effort to its main priority, the mainframe computer system.

In response to the internal audit report, the director of data processing services, Stan Marten, issued the following memorandum.

TO: All Employees
FROM: Stan Marten, Director
REFERENCE: Microcomputer Standardization

Policies must be instituted immediately to standardize the acquisition of PCs and applications software. The first step is to specify the spreadsheet software that should be used by all personnel. From now on, everyone will use Micromate. All PC hardware should be Microsoft compatible. During the next month, we will also select the standard software for word processing and database applications. You will use only the user packages that are prescribed by the data processing services department. In the future, any new purchases of microcomputers, hardware, or software must be approved by the director of data processing services.

Several managers of other operating departments have complained about Marten's memorandum. Apparently, before issuing this memo, Marten had not consulted with any of the users regarding their current and future software needs.

Required:

a. When acquiring PCs for various departments in an organization, describe the factors related to:

   1. Computer hardware that needs to be considered during the initial design and set-up phase of the microcomputer environment.

   2. Operating procedures and system controls that need to be considered.

b. Discuss the benefits of having standardized hardware and software for microcomputers in an organization.

c. Discuss the concerns that the memorandum is likely to create for the microcomputer users at Hastone Manufacturing.

4. Internal Control

Gustave, CPA, during its preliminary review of the financial statements of Comet, Inc., found a lack of proper segregation of duties between the programming and operating functions. Comet owns its own computing facilities. Gustave diligently intensified the internal control study and assessment tasks relating to the computer facilities. Gustave concluded in its final report that sufficient compensating general controls provided reasonable assurance that the internal control objectives were being met.

Required:
What compensating controls are most likely in place?

5. Disaster Recovery Plan

The headquarters of Hill Crest Corporation, a private company with $15.5 million in annual sales, is located in California. Hill Crest provides for its 150 clients an online legal software service that includes data storage and administrative activities for law offices. The company has grown rapidly since its inception three years ago, and its data processing department has expanded to accommodate this growth. Because Hill Crest's president and sales personnel spend a great deal of time out of the office soliciting new clients, the planning of the IT facilities has been left to the data processing professionals.

Hill Crest recently moved its headquarters into a remodeled warehouse on the outskirts of the city. While remodeling the warehouse, the architects retained much of the original structure, including the wooden-shingled exterior and exposed wooden beams throughout the interior. The minicomputer distributive processing hardware is situated in a large open area with high ceilings and skylights. The openness makes the data processing area accessible to the rest of the staff and encourages a team approach to problem solving. Before occupying the new facility, city inspectors declared the building safe; that is, it had adequate fire extinguishers, sufficient exits, and so on.

In an effort to provide further protection for its large database of client information, Hill Crest instituted a tape backup procedure that automatically backs up the database every Sunday evening, avoiding interruption in the daily operations and procedures. All tapes are then labeled and carefully stored on shelves reserved for this purpose in the data processing department. The departmental operator's manual has instructions on how to use these tapes to restore the database, should the need arise. A list of home phone numbers of the individuals in the data processing department is available in case of an emergency. Hill Crest has recently increased its liability insurance for data loss from $50,000 to $100,000.

This past Saturday, the Hill Crest headquarters building was completely ruined by fire, and the company must now inform its clients that all of their information has been destroyed.

Required:

a. Describe the computer security weaknesses present at Hill Crest Corporation that made it possible for a disastrous data loss to occur.

b. List the components that should have been included in the disaster recovery plan at Hill Crest Corporation to ensure computer recovery within 72 hours.

c. What factors, other than those included in the plan itself, should a company consider when formulating a disaster recovery plan?

6. Separation of Duties

Transferring people from job to job within the organization is the philosophy at Arcadia Plastics. Management feels that job rotation deters employees from feeling that they are stagnating in their jobs and promotes a better understanding of the company. The computer services personnel typically work for six months as an operator, one year as a systems developer, six months as a database administrator, and one year in systems maintenance. At that point, they are assigned to a "permanent" position.

Required:

Discuss the importance of separation of duties within the information systems department. How can Arcadia Plastics have both job rotation and well-separated duties?

7. Disaster Recover Service Providers

Visit SunGard's web site, http://www.sungard.com, and research its recovery services offered for the following classes: High Availability, System Recovery, and End-User Recover. Write a report of your findings.

8. Audit Committee

Micro Systems, a developer of database software packages, is a publicly held company and listed with the SEC. The company has no internal audit function. In complying with SOX, Micro Systems has agreed to establish an internal audit function and strengthen its audit committee to include all outside directors. Micro Systems has held its initial planning meeting to discuss the roles of the various participants in the internal control and financial

reporting process. Participants at the meeting included the company president, the chief financial officer, a member of the audit committee, a partner from Micro Dynamics' external audit firm, and the newly appointed manager of the internal audit department. Comments by the various meeting participants are presented below.

President: "We want to ensure that Micro Systems complies with the SOX. The internal audit department should help to strengthen our internal control system by correcting problems. I would like your thoughts on the proper reporting relationship for the manager of the internal audit department."

CFO: "I think the manager of the internal audit department should report to me because much of the department's work is related to financial issues. The audit committee should have oversight responsibilities."

Audit committee member: "I believe we should think through our roles more carefully. The Treadway Commission has recommended that the audit committee play a more important role in the financial reporting process; the duties of today's audit committee have expanded beyond mere rubber-stamp approval. We need to have greater assurance that controls are in place and being followed."

External audit firm partner: "We need a close working relationship among all of our roles. The internal audit department can play a significant role in monitoring the control systems on a continuing basis and should have strong ties to your external audit firm."

Internal audit department manager: "The internal audit department should be more involved in operational auditing, but it also should play a significant monitoring role in the financial reporting area."

Required:

a. Describe the role of each of the following in the establishment, maintenance, and evaluation of Micro Systems' internal control.
   Management
   Audit committee
   External auditor
   Internal audit department

b. Describe the responsibilities that Micro Systems' audit committee has in the financial reporting process.

9. CMA 1290 4-Y8
Role of Internal Auditor

Leigh Industries has an internal audit department consisting of a director and four staff auditors. The director of internal audit, Diane Bauer, reports to the corporate controller, who receives copies of all internal audit reports. In addition, copies of all internal audit reports are sent to the audit committee of the board of directors and the individual responsible for the area of activity being audited.

In the past, the company's external auditors have relied on the work of the internal audit department to a substantial degree. However, in recent months, Bauer has become concerned that the objectivity of the internal audit function is being affected by the nonaudit work being performed by the department. This possible loss of objectivity could result in more extensive testing and analysis by the external auditors. The percentage of nonaudit work performed by the internal auditors has steadily increased to about 25 percent of the total hours worked. A sample of five recent nonaudit activities is presented in the following section.

- One of the internal auditors assisted in the preparation of policy statements on internal control. These statements included such things as policies regarding sensitive payments and the safeguarding of assets.
- Reconciling the bank statements of the corporation each month is a regular assignment of one of the internal auditors. The corporate controller believes this strengthens the internal control function because the internal auditor is not involved in either the receipt or the disbursement of cash.
- The internal auditors are asked to review the annual budget each year for relevance and reasonableness before the budget is approved. At the end of each month, the corporate controller's staff analyzes the variances from budget and prepares explanations of these variances. These variances and explanations are then reviewed by the internal audit staff.
- One of the internal auditors has been involved in the design, installation, and initial operation of a new computerized inventory system. The auditor was primarily concerned with the design and implementation of internal accounting controls and conducted the evaluation of these controls during the test runs.
- The internal auditors are sometimes asked to make the accounting entries for complex transactions as the employees in the accounting department are not adequately trained to handle such transactions. The corporate controller believes this gives an added measure of assurance to the accurate recording of these transactions.

Required:

a. Define objectivity as it relates to the internal audit function.

b. For each of the five nonaudit activities presented, explain whether the objectivity of Leigh Industries' Internal Audit Department has been materially impaired. Consider each situation independently.

c. The director of internal audit reports directly to the corporate controller.

   1. Does this reporting relationship affect the objectivity of the internal audit department? Explain your answer.

   2. Would your evaluation of the five situations in question (b) change if the director of internal audit reported to the audit committee of the board of directors? Explain your answer.

10. Internal Control and Distributed System

Until a year ago, Dagwood Printing Company had always operated in a centralized computer environment. Now, 75 percent of the office employees have a PC. Users have been able to choose their own software packages, and no documentation of end-user-developed applications has been required. Next month, each PC will be linked into a LAN and to the company's mainframe.

Required:

a. Outline a plan of action for Dagwood Printing Company to ensure that the proper controls over hardware, software, data, people, procedures, and documentation are in place.

   Discuss any exposures the company may face if the above plan is not implemented

b. Discuss any exposures the company may face if the above plan is not implemented.

chapter 16

IT Controls Part II: Security and Access

LEARNING OBJECTIVES

After studying this chapter, you should:

- Be able to identify the principal threats to the operating system and the control techniques used to minimize the possibility of actual exposures.
- Be familiar with the principal risks associated with electronic commerce conducted over Intranets and the Internet and understand the control techniques used to reduce these risks.
- Be familiar with the risks to database integrity and the controls used to mitigate them.
- Recognize the unique exposures that arise in connection with electronic data interchange (EDI) and understand how these exposures can be reduced.

This chapter continues the treatment of IT controls as described by the COSO control framework. The focus of the chapter is on SOX compliance regarding the security and control of operating systems, database management systems, and communication networks. This chapter examines the risks, controls, audit objectives, and tests of controls that may be performed to satisfy either compliance or attest responsibilities.

CONTROLLING THE OPERATING SYSTEM

The **operating system** is the computer's control program. It allows users and their applications to share and access common computer resources, such as processors, main memory, databases, and printers. If operating system integrity is compromised, controls within individual accounting applications may also be circumvented or neutralized. Because the operating system is common to all users, the larger the computer facility, the greater the scale of potential damage. Thus, with more and more computer resources being shared by an ever-expanding user community, operating system security becomes an important control issue.

OPERATING SYSTEM OBJECTIVES

The operating system performs three main tasks. First, it translates high-level languages, such as COBOL, C++, BASIC, and SQL, into the machine-level language that the computer can execute. The language translator modules of the operating system are called **compilers** and **interpreters**. The control implications of language translators are examined in chapter 17.

Second, the operating system allocates computer resources to users, workgroups, and applications. This includes assigning memory work space (partitions) to applications and authorizing access to terminals, telecommunications links, databases, and printers.

Third, the operating system manages the tasks of job scheduling and multiprogramming. At any point, numerous user applications (jobs) are seeking access to the computer resources under the control of the operating system. Jobs are submitted to the system in three ways: (1) directly by the system operator, (2) from various batch-job queues, and (3) through telecommunications links from remote workstations. To achieve efficient and effective use of finite computer resources, the operating system must schedule job processing according to established priorities and balance the use of resources among the competing applications.

To perform these tasks consistently and reliably, the operating system must achieve five fundamental control objectives.[1]

1. The operating system must protect itself from users. User applications must not be able to gain control of, or damage in any way, the operating system, thus causing it to cease running or destroy data.
2. The operating system must protect users from each other. One user must not be able to access, destroy, or corrupt the data or programs of another user.
3. The operating system must protect users from themselves. A user's application may consist of several modules stored in separate memory locations, each with its own data. One module must not be allowed to destroy or corrupt another module.
4. The operating system must be protected from itself. The operating system is also made up of individual modules. No module should be allowed to destroy or corrupt another module.
5. The operating system must be protected from its environment. In the event of a power failure or other disaster, the operating system should be able to achieve a controlled termination of activities from which it can later recover.

1   F. M. Stepczyk, "Requirements for Secure Operating Systems," Data Security and Data Processing, vol. 5; Study Results: TRW Systems, Inc. (New York: IBM Corporation, 1974): 25–73.

OPERATING SYSTEM SECURITY

Operating system security involves policy, procedures, and controls that determine who can access the operating system, which resources (files, programs, printers) they can access, and what actions they can take. The following security components are found in secure operating systems: *log-on procedure, access token, access control list,* and *discretionary access privileges.*

Log-On Procedure

A formal **log-on procedure** is the operating system's first line of defense against unauthorized access. When the user initiates the process, he or she is presented with a dialog box requesting the user's ID and password. The system compares the ID and password to a database of valid users. If the system finds a match, then the log-on attempt is authenticated. If, however, the password or ID is entered incorrectly, the log-on attempt fails and a message is returned to the user. The message should not reveal whether the password or the ID caused the failure. The system should allow the user to reenter the log-on information. After a specified number of attempts (usually no more than five), the system should lock out the user from the system.

Access Token

If the log-on attempt is successful, the operating system creates an **access token** that contains key information about the user, including user ID, password, user group, and privileges granted to the user. The information in the access token is used to approve all actions attempted by the user during the session.

Access Control List

Access to system resources such as directories, files, programs, and printers are controlled by an **access control list** assigned to each resource. These lists contain information that defines the access privileges for all valid users of the resource. When a user attempts to access a resource, the system compares his or her ID and privileges contained in the access token with those contained in the access control list. If there is a match, the user is granted access.

Discretionary Access Privileges

The central system administrator usually determines who is granted access to specific resources and maintains the access control list. In distributed systems, however, resources may be controlled (owned) by end users. Resource owners in this setting may be granted **discretionary access privileges**, which allow them to grant access privileges to other users. For example, the controller, who is the owner of the general ledger, may grant read-only privileges to a manager in the budgeting department. The accounts payable manager, however, may be granted both read and write permissions to the ledger. Any attempt by the budgeting manager to add, delete, or change the general ledger will be denied. The use of discretionary access control needs to be closely supervised to prevent security breaches because of its liberal use.

THREATS TO OPERATING SYSTEM INTEGRITY

Operating system control objectives may not be achieved because of flaws in the operating system that are exploited either accidentally or intentionally. Accidental threats include hardware failures that cause the operating system to crash. Operating system failures are also caused by errors in user application programs, which the operating system cannot interpret. Accidental system failures may cause whole segments of memory to be "dumped" to disks and printers, resulting in the unintentional disclosure of confidential information.

Intentional threats to the operating system are most commonly attempts to illegally access data or violate user privacy for financial gain. However, a growing threat is destructive programs from which there is no apparent gain. These exposures come from three sources:

1. **Privileged personnel who abuse their authority.** Systems administrators and systems programmers require unlimited access to the operating system to perform maintenance and to recover from system failures. Such individuals may use this authority to access users' programs and data files.

2. Individuals, both internal and external to the organization, who browse the operating system to identify and exploit security flaws.

3. Individuals who intentionally (or accidentally) insert computer viruses or other forms of destructive programs into the operating system.

Operating System Controls and Test of Controls

This section describes a variety of control techniques for preserving operating system integrity. If operating system integrity is compromised, controls within individual accounting applications that impact financial reporting may also be compromised. For this reason, the design and assessment of these controls are SOX compliance issues. In this section, controls and associated tests over the following areas are examined: *access privileges, password control, virus control, and audit trail control.*

Controlling Access Privileges

User access privileges are assigned to individuals and to entire workgroups authorized to use the system. Privileges determine which directories, files, applications, and other resources an individual or group may access. They also determine the types of actions that can be taken. Recall that the systems administrator or the owner of the resource may assign privileges. Management should be concerned that individuals are not granted privileges that are incompatible with their assigned duties. Consider, for example, a cash receipts clerk who is granted the right to access and make changes to the accounts receivable file.

Overall system security is influenced by the way access privileges are assigned. Privileges should, therefore, be carefully administered and closely monitored for compliance with organizational policy and principles of internal control.

Audit Objectives Relating to Access Privileges

The objective of the auditor is to verify that access privileges are granted in a manner that is consistent with the need to separate incompatible functions and is in accordance with organization policy.

Audit Procedures Relating to Access Privileges

- Review the organization's policies for separating incompatible functions and ensure that they promote reasonable security.

- Review the privileges of a selection of user groups and individuals to determine if their access rights are appropriate for their job descriptions and positions. The auditor should verify that individuals are granted access to data and programs based on their need to know.

- Review personnel records to determine whether privileged employees undergo an adequately intensive security clearance check in compliance with company policy.

- Review employee records to determine whether users have formally acknowledged their responsibility to maintain the confidentiality of company data.

- Review the users' permitted log-on times. Permission should be commensurate with the tasks being performed.

Password Control

A **password** is a secret code entered by the user to gain access to systems, applications, data files, or a network server. If the user cannot provide the correct password, the operating system should deny access. Although passwords can provide a degree of security, when imposed on nonsecurity-minded users, password procedures can result in end-user behavior that actually circumvents security. The most common forms of contra-security behavior include:

- Forgetting passwords and being locked out of the system

- Failing to change passwords on a frequent basis

- The Post-it syndrome, whereby passwords are written down and displayed for others to see

- Simplistic passwords that are easily anticipated by a computer criminal

Reusable Passwords. The most common method of password control is the reusable password. The user defines the password to the system once and then reuses it to gain future access. The quality of the security provided by a reusable password depends on the quality of the password itself. If the password pertains to something personal about the user, such as a child's name, pet's name, birth date, or hair color, it can often be deduced by a computer criminal. Even if the password is derived from nonpersonal data, it may be *weak*. For example, a string of keystrokes (such as A-S-D-F) or the same letter used multiple times can easily be cracked. Passwords that contain random letters and digits are more difficult to crack, but are also more difficult for the user to remember.

To improve access control, management should require that passwords be changed regularly and disallow "weak" passwords. Software is available that automatically scans password files and notifies users that their passwords have expired and need to be changed. These systems also use extensive databases of known weak passwords to validate the new password and disallow weak ones. An alternative to the standard reusable password is the *one-time* password.

One-Time Passwords. The **one-time password** was designed to overcome the problems just discussed. Under this approach, the user's password changes continuously. This technology employs a credit card-sized smart card that contains a microprocessor programmed with an algorithm that generates, and electronically displays, a new and unique password every 60 seconds. The card works in conjunction with special authentication software located on a mainframe or network server computer. Each user's card is synchronized to the authentication software, so that at any point in time both the smart card and the network software are generating the same password for the same user.

To access the network, the user enters the PIN followed by the current password displayed on the card. The password can be used one time only. If, for example, a computer hacker intercepts the password and PIN during transmission and attempts to use them within the one-minute time frame, access will be denied. Also, if the smart card should fall in to the hands of a computer criminal, access cannot be achieved without the PIN.

Another one-time password technique uses a *challenge/response* approach to achieve the same end. When the user attempts to log on, the network authentication software issues a six-character code (the challenge) that can be either scanned optically by the card or entered into the card via its built-in keypad. The card's internal algorithm then generates a one-time password (the response) that is entered by the user through the keyboard of the remote terminal. If the firewall recognizes the current password, access is permitted.

Audit Objectives Relating to Passwords

The auditor's objective here is to ensure that the organization has an adequate and effective password policy for controlling access to the operating system.

Audit Procedures Relating to Passwords

The auditor may achieve this objective by performing the following tests:

- Verify that all users are required to have passwords.

- Verify that new users are instructed in the use of passwords and the importance of password control.

- Review password control procedures to ensure that passwords are changed regularly.

- Review the password file to determine that weak passwords are identified and disallowed. This may involve using software to scan password files for known weak passwords.

- Verify that the password file is encrypted and that the encryption key is properly secured.

- Assess the adequacy of password standards such as length and expiration interval.

- Review the account lockout policy and procedures. Most operating systems allow the system administrator to define the action to be taken after a certain number of failed log-on attempts. The auditor should determine how many failed log-on attempts are allowed before the account is locked. The duration of the lockout also needs to be determined. This could range from a few minutes to a permanent lockout that requires formal reactivation of the account.

Controlling against Malicious and Destructive Programs

Malicious and destructive programs are responsible for millions of dollars of corporate losses annually. The losses are measured in terms of data corruption and destruction, degraded computer performance, hardware destruction, violations of privacy, and the personnel time devoted to repairing the damage. This class of programs includes viruses, worms, logic bombs, back doors, and Trojan horses. Because these have become popular press terms in recent years, we will not devote space at this point to define them. Section A of the appendix to this chapter, however, contains a detailed discussion of this material.

Threats from destructive programs can be substantially reduced through a combination of technology controls and administrative procedures. The following examples are relevant to most operating systems.

- Purchase software only from reputable vendors and accept only those products that are in their original, factory-sealed packages.

- Issue an entity-wide policy pertaining to the use of unauthorized software or illegal (bootleg) copies of copyrighted software.

- Examine all upgrades to vendor software for viruses before they are implemented.

- Inspect all public-domain software for virus infection before using.

- Establish entity-wide procedures for making changes to production programs.

- Establish an educational program to raise user awareness regarding threats from viruses and malicious programs.

- Install all new applications on a standalone computer and thoroughly test them with antiviral software prior to implementing them on the mainframe or LAN server.

- Routinely make backup copies of key files stored on mainframes, servers, and workstations.

- Wherever possible, limit users to read and execute rights only. This allows users to extract data and run authorized applications, but denies them the ability to write directly to mainframe and server directories.

- Require protocols that explicitly invoke the operating system's log-on procedures to bypass Trojan horses. A typical scenario is one in which a user sits down to a terminal that is already displaying the log-on screen and proceeds to enter his or her ID and password. This, however, may be a Trojan horse rather than the legitimate procedure. Some operating systems allow the user to directly invoke the operating system log-on procedure by entering a key sequence such as CTRL + ALT + DEL. The user then knows that the log-on procedure on the screen is legitimate.

- Use antiviral software (also called *vaccines*) to examine application and operating system programs for the presence of a virus and remove it from the affected program. Antiviral programs are used to safeguard mainframes, network servers, and personal computers. Most antiviral programs run in the background on the host computer and automatically test all files that are uploaded to the host. The software, however, works only on known viruses. If a virus has been modified slightly (mutated), there is no guarantee that the vaccine will work. Therefore, maintaining a current version of the vaccine is critical.

Audit Objective Relating to Viruses and Other Destructive Programs

The key to computer virus control is prevention through strict adherence to organizational policies and procedures that guard against virus infection. The auditor's objective is to verify that effective management policies and procedures are in place to prevent the introduction and spread of destructive programs, including viruses, worms, back doors, logic bombs, and Trojan horses.

Audit Procedures Relating to Viruses and Other Destructive Programs

- Through interviews, determine that operations personnel have been educated about computer viruses and are aware of the risky computing practices that can introduce and spread viruses and other malicious programs.

- Verify that new software is tested on standalone workstations prior to being implemented on the host or network server.

- Verify that the current version of antiviral software is installed on the server and that upgrades are regularly downloaded to workstations.

System Audit Trail Controls

System audit trails are logs that record activity at the system, application, and user level. Operating systems allow management to select the level of auditing to be recorded in the log. They need to decide on their threshold between information and irrelevant facts. An effective audit policy will capture all significant events without cluttering the log with trivial activity. Audit trails typically consist of two types of audit logs: (1) detailed logs of individual keystrokes and (2) event-oriented logs.

Keystroke Monitoring. **Keystroke monitoring** involves recording both the user's keystrokes and the system's responses. This form of log may be used after the fact to reconstruct the details of an event or as a real-time control to prevent unauthorized intrusion. Keystroke monitoring is the computer equivalent of a telephone wiretap. Whereas some situations may justify this level of surveillance, keystroke monitoring may also be regarded as a violation of privacy. Before implementing this type of control, management and auditors should consider the possible legal, ethical, and behavioral implications.

Event Monitoring. **Event monitoring** summarizes key activities related to system resources. Event logs typically record the IDs of all users accessing the system; the time and duration of a user's session; programs that were executed during a session; and the files, databases, printers, and other resources accessed.

Setting Audit Trail Objectives

Audit trails can be used to support security objectives in three ways: (1) detecting unauthorized access to the system, (2) facilitating the reconstruction of events, and (3) promoting personal accountability.

Detecting Unauthorized Access. Detecting unauthorized access can occur in real time or after the fact. The primary objective of real-time detection is to protect the system from outsiders attempting to breach system controls. A real-time audit trail can also be used to report changes in system performance that may indicate infestation by a virus or worm. Depending on how much activity is being logged for review, real-time detection can add significantly to operational overhead and degrade performance. After-the-fact detection logs can be stored electronically and reviewed periodically or as needed. When properly designed, they can be used to determine if unauthorized access was accomplished, or attempted and failed.

Reconstructing Events. Audit trail analysis can be used to reconstruct the steps that led to events such as system failures, or security violations by individuals. Knowledge of the conditions that existed at the time of a system failure can be used to assign responsibility and to avoid similar situations in the future.

Personal Accountability. Audit trails can be used to monitor user activity at the lowest level of detail. This capability is a preventive control that can influence behavior. Individuals are less likely to violate an organization's security policy when they know that their actions are recorded in an audit log.

A system audit log can also serve as a detective control to assign personal accountability for actions taken such as abuse of authority. For example, consider an accounts receivable clerk with authority to access customer records. The audit log may disclose that the clerk has been printing an inordinate number of records, which may indicate that the clerk is selling customer information in violation of the company's privacy policy.

Implementing a System Audit Trail

The information contained in audit logs is useful to accountants in measuring the potential damage and financial loss associated with application errors, abuse of authority, or unauthorized access by outside intruders. Audit logs, however, can generate data in overwhelming detail. Important information can easily get lost among the superfluous details of daily operation. Thus, poorly designed logs can actually be dysfunctional. Protecting exposures with the potential for material financial loss should drive management's decision as to which users, applications, or operations to monitor, and how much detail to log. As with all controls, the benefits of audit logs must be balanced against the costs of implementing them.

Audit Objectives Relating to System Audit Trails
The auditor's objective is to ensure that the established system audit trail is adequate for preventing and detecting abuses, reconstructing key events that precede systems failures, and planning resource allocation.

Audit Procedures Relating to System Audit Trails

- Most operating systems provide some form of audit manager function to specify the events that are to be audited. The auditor should verify that the audit trail has been activated according to organization policy.

- Many operating systems provide an audit log viewer that allows the auditor to scan the log for unusual activity. These can be reviewed on screen or by archiving the file for subsequent review. The auditor can use general-purpose data extraction tools for accessing archived log files to search for defined conditions such as:
  - Unauthorized or terminated user
  - Periods of inactivity
  - Activity by user, workgroup, or department
  - Log-on and log-off times
  - Failed log-on attempts
  - Access to specific files or applications

- The organization's security group has responsibility for monitoring and reporting security violations. The auditor should select a sample of security violation cases and evaluate their disposition to assess the effectiveness of the security group.

CONTROLLING DATABASE MANAGEMENT SYSTEMS

Controls over database management fall into two general categories: access controls and backup controls. **Access controls** are designed to prevent unauthorized individuals from viewing, retrieving, corrupting, or destroying the entity's data. **Backup controls** ensure that in the event of data loss due to unauthorized access, equipment failure, or physical disaster the organization can recover its files and databases.

ACCESS CONTROLS
Risks to corporate databases include corruption, theft, misuse, and destruction of data. These threats originate from both unauthorized intruders and authorized users who exceed their access privileges. Several database control features that reduce these risks are reviewed in the following sections.

User Views
The **user view** or subschema is a subset of the total database that defines the user's data domain and restricts his or her access to the database accordingly. Figure 16-1 illustrates

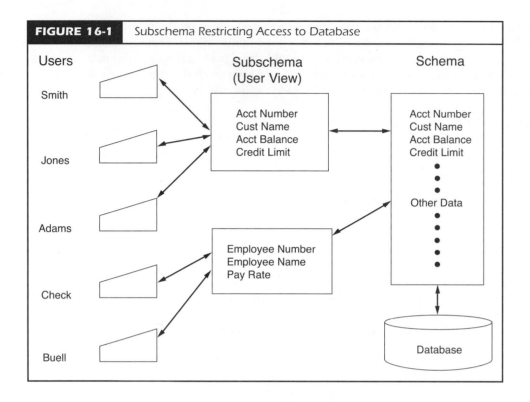

FIGURE 16-1 | Subschema Restricting Access to Database

the role of the user view. The database administrator (DBA) typically is responsible for defining user views. The auditor is concerned that such access privileges are commensurate with the users' legitimate needs.

Although user views can restrict user access to a limited set of data, they do not define task privileges such as read, delete, or write. Often, several users may share a single user view but have different authority levels. For example, users Smith, Jones, and Adams in Figure 16-1 all may have access to the same set of data: account number, customer name, account balance, and credit limit. Let's assume that all have read authority, but only Jones has authority to modify and delete the data. To achieve this level of restriction requires additional security measures, discussed next.

Database Authorization Table

The **database authorization table** contains rules that limit the actions a user can take. Each user is granted certain privileges that are coded in the authority table, which is used to verify the user's action requests. For example, the authorization table in Figure 16-2 shows that of the three users, only Jones has the authority to modify and delete the data.

User-Defined Procedures

A **user-defined procedure** allows the user to create a personal security program or routine to provide more positive user identification than a password can. For example, in addition to a password, the security procedure asks a series of personal questions (such as the user's mother's maiden name), which only the legitimate user is likely to know.

Data Encryption

Many database systems use encryption procedures to protect highly sensitive data, such as product formulas, personnel pay rates, password files, and certain financial data.

FIGURE 16-2	Database Authorization Table				
Dept	Accounts Rec			Billings	
User	Jones	Smith	Adams	Check	Buell
Password	Bugs	Dog	Katie	Lucky	Star
Authority: Read Insert Modify Delete	Y Y Y Y	Y N N N	Y Y N N	Y Y Y N	Y N N N

Data encryption uses an algorithm to scramble selected data, thus making it unreadable to an intruder "browsing" the database. In addition to protecting stored data, encryption is used for protecting data that are transmitted across networks. Various encryption techniques are discussed later in this chapter.

Biometric Devices

The ultimate in user authentication procedures is the use of **biometric devices,** which measure various personal characteristics such as fingerprints, voiceprints, retina prints, or signature characteristics. These user characteristics are digitized and stored permanently in a database security file or on an identification card that the user carries. When an individual attempts to access the database, a special scanning device captures his or her biometric characteristics, which it compares with the profile data stored internally or on the ID card. If the data do not match, access is denied.

Audit Objectives Relating to Database Access

The auditor's objectives are: (1) to verify that individuals who are authorized to use the database are limited to accessing only the data needed to perform their duties; and (2) that unauthorized individuals are denied access to the database.

Audit Procedures for Testing Access Controls

Responsibility for Authority Tables and Subschemas. The auditor should verify that database administration (DBA) personnel retain sole responsibility for creating authority tables and designing user views. Evidence of compliance can come from three sources: (1) by reviewing company policy and job descriptions, which specify these technical responsibilities; (2) by examining programmer authority tables for access privileges to data definition language (DDL) commands; and (3) through personal interviews with programmers and DBA personnel.

Appropriate Access Authority. The auditor can select a sample of users and verify that their access privileges stored in the authority table are consistent with their organizational functions.

Biometric Controls. The auditor should evaluate the costs and benefits of biometric controls. Generally, these would be most appropriate where highly sensitive data are accessed by a very limited number of users.

Encryption Controls. The auditor should verify that sensitive data, such as passwords, are properly encrypted. This can be done by printing the file contents to hard copy.

BACKUP CONTROLS

Data can be corrupted and destroyed by malicious acts from external hackers, disgruntled employees, disk failure, program errors, fires, floods, and earthquakes. To recover from such disasters, the organization needs to reconstruct the database to pre-failure status. This can be done only if the database was properly backed up in the first place. Organizations must, therefore, implement policies, procedures, and techniques that systematically and routinely provide backup copies of critical data. This section examines backup controls used in the database environment. Legacy systems that use a flat-file structure present a different set of issues that are discussed in Section B of the appendix to this chapter.

Large-scale database management systems employ a backup and recovery procedure similar to that illustrated in Figure 16-3. This system provides four backup and recovery features: database backup, a transaction log, checkpoints, and a recovery module. Each of these is described in the following section.

Database Backup. The backup feature makes a periodic backup of the entire database. This is an automatic procedure that should be performed at least once a day. The backup copy should then be stored in a secure remote area.

Transaction Log (Journal). The transaction log feature provides an audit trail of all processed transactions. It lists transactions in a transaction log file and records the resulting changes to the database in a separate database change log.

Checkpoint Feature. The checkpoint facility suspends all data processing while the system reconciles the transaction log and the database change log against the database. At this point, the system is in a "quiet state." Checkpoints occur automatically several times an hour. If a failure occurs, it is usually possible to restart the processing from the last checkpoint. Thus, only a few minutes of transaction processing must be repeated.

Recovery Module. The recovery module uses the logs and backup files to restart the system after a failure.

Audit Objectives Relating to Database Backup
The auditor's objective is to verify that database backup controls are adequate to facilitate the recovery of lost, destroyed, or corrupted data.

Audit Procedures for Testing Backup Controls
Database backup should be a routine activity.

● The auditor should verify from system documentation that production databases are copied at regular intervals (perhaps several times an hour).

● The auditor should verify from documentation and observation backup copies of the database are stored off site to support disaster recovery procedures.

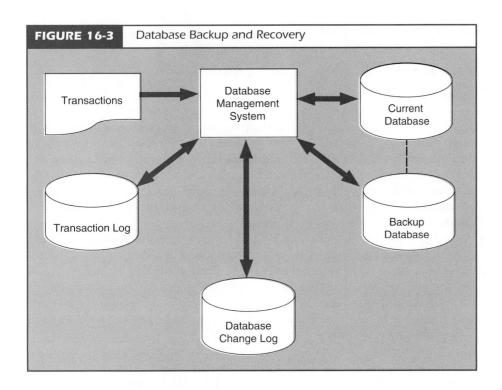

FIGURE 16-3 | Database Backup and Recovery

CONTROLLING NETWORKS

Chapter 12 examined the operational characteristics of several network topologies used in Internet and Intranet communications. Network topologies consist of various configurations of (1) communications lines (twisted-pair wires, coaxial cable, microwaves, and fiber optics), (2) hardware components (modems, multiplexers, servers, and front-end processors), and (3) software (protocols and network control systems). The technology of network communications are subject to two general forms of risk:

1. *Risks from subversive threats.* These include, but are not limited to, a computer criminal intercepting a message transmitted between the sender and the receiver, a computer hacker gaining unauthorized access to the organization's network, and a denial of service attack from a remote location of the Internet.

2. *Risks from equipment failure.* For example, transmissions between senders and receivers can be disrupted, destroyed, or corrupted by equipment failures in the communications system. Equipment failure can also result in the loss of databases and programs stored on network servers.

CONTROLLING RISKS FROM SUBVERSIVE THREATS

Firewalls

Organizations connected to the Internet or other public networks often implement an electronic "firewall" to insulate their Intranet from outside intruders. A **firewall** is a system that enforces access control between two networks. To accomplish this:

● All traffic between the outside network and the organization's Intranet must pass through the firewall.

- Only authorized traffic between the organization and the outside, as specified by formal security policy, is allowed to pass through the firewall.

- The firewall must be immune to penetration from both outside and inside the organization.

Firewalls can be used to authenticate an outside user of the network, verify his or her level of access authority, and then direct the user to the program, data, or service requested. In addition to insulating the organization's network from external networks, firewalls can also be used to insulate portions of the organization's Intranet from internal access. For example, a LAN controlling access to financial data can be insulated from other internal LANs. Some commercially available firewalls provide a high level of security whereas others are less secure but more efficient. Firewalls may be grouped into two general types: network-level firewalls and application-level firewalls.

Network-level firewalls provide efficient but low security access control. This type of firewall consists of a **screening router** that examines the source and destination addresses that are attached to incoming message packets. The firewall accepts or denies access requests based on filtering rules that have been programmed into it. The firewall directs incoming calls to the correct internal receiving node. Network-level firewalls are insecure because they are designed to facilitate the free flow of information rather than restrict it. This method does not explicitly authenticate outside users.

Application-level firewalls provide a higher level of customizable network security, but they add overhead to connectivity. These systems are configured to run security applications called *proxies* that permit routine services such as e-mail to pass through the firewall, but can perform sophisticated functions such as user authentication for specific tasks. Application-level firewalls also provide comprehensive transmission logging and auditing tools for reporting unauthorized activity.

A high level of firewall security is possible using a *dual-homed* system. This approach, illustrated in Figure 16-4, has two firewall interfaces. One screens incoming requests from the Internet; the other provides access to the organization's Intranet. Direct communication to the Internet is disabled and the two networks are fully isolated. All access is performed by proxy applications that impose separate log-on procedures.

Choosing the right firewall involves a trade-off between convenience and security. Ultimately, organization management, in collaboration with internal audit and network professionals, must come to grips with what constitutes acceptable risk. The more security provided by the firewall, however, the less convenient it is for authorized users to pass through it to conduct business.

Controlling Denial of Service Attacks

When a user establishes a connection on the Internet through TCP/IP, a three-way handshake takes place. The connecting server sends an initiation code called a *SYN packet* to the receiving server. The receiving server then acknowledges the request by returning a *SYN/ACK packet*. Finally, the initiating host machine responds with an *ACK packet code*. Computer hackers and crackers have devised a malicious act called a *denial of service attack*, in which the attacker transmits hundreds of SYN packets to the targeted receiver but never responds with an ACK to complete the connection. As a result, the ports of the receiver's server are clogged with incomplete communication requests that prevent legitimate transactions from being received and processed. Organizations under attack have been prevented from receiving Internet messages for days at a time.

If the target organization could identify the server that is launching the attack, the firewall could be programmed to ignore all communication from that site. Such attacks,

FIGURE 16-4   Dual-Homed Firewall

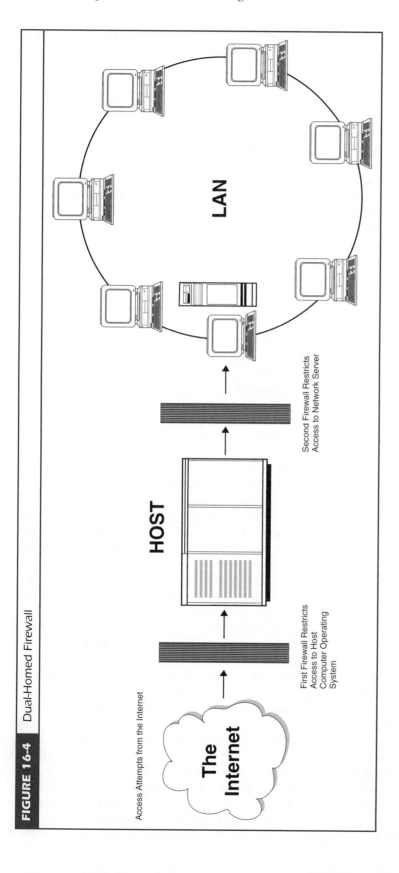

however, are often difficult to prevent when IP spoofing is used to disguise the source of the messages by randomizing the IP address of the attacker. Therefore, the receiving site views these transmissions as coming from all over the Internet when, in fact, they are coming from a single disguised location.

Denial of service attacks can severely hamper an organization's ability to use the Internet to conduct commerce. IT management and accountants can take two actions to limit the exposure. First, Internet host sites must engage in a policy of social responsibility. The firewalls at the source sites can be programmed to block the transmission of messages with non-internal IP addresses. This would prevent attackers from hiding their locations from the targeted site and would assure the organization's management that no undetected attacks could be launched from its site. This strategy will not, however, prevent attacks from areas of the Internet that do screen outgoing transmissions.

Second, security software is available for the targeted sites that scan for half-open connections. The software looks for SYN packets that have not been followed by an ACK packet. The clogged ports can then be restored to allow legitimate connections to use them.

Encryption

Encryption is the conversion of data into a secret code for storage in databases and transmission over networks. The discussion here pertains to transmitted data, but these basic principles apply also to stored data. The sender uses an encryption algorithm to convert the original message called cleartext into a coded equivalent called ciphertext. At the receiving end the ciphertext is decoded (decrypted) back into cleartext. The encryption algorithm uses a **key,** which is a binary number that typically is from 56 to 128 bits in length. The more bits in the key the stronger the encryption method. Today, nothing less than 128-bit algorithms are considered truly secure. Two general approaches to encryption are *private key* and *public key* encryption.

Private Key Encryption. **Data encryption standard (DES)** is a private key encryption technique designed in the early 1970s by IBM. The DES algorithm uses a single key known to both the sender and the receiver of the message. To encode a message, the sender provides the encryption algorithm with the key, which is used to produce a ciphertext message. The message enters the communication channel and is transmitted to the receiver's location, where it is stored. The receiver decodes the message with a decryption program that uses the same key employed by the sender. Figure 16-5 illustrates this technique.

The primary problem with the DES approach is that a perpetrator may discover the key and intercept and decipher the message. The more individuals who need to know the key, the greater the probability of it falling into the wrong hands.

Triple-DES encryption is an enhancement to standard DES that provides considerably improved security. Two forms of triple-DES encryption are EEE3 and EDE3. **EEE3** uses three different keys to encrypt the message three times. **EDE3** uses one key to encrypt the message. A second key is used to decode it. The resulting message is garbled because the key used for decoding is different from the one that encrypted it. Finally, a third key is used to encrypt the garbled message. The use of multiple keys greatly reduces the chances of breaking the cipher. Triple-DES encryption is thought to be very secure and is used by major banks to transmit transactions. Unfortunately, it is also very slow. The EEE3 and EDE3 techniques are illustrated in Figure 16-6.

All private key techniques suffer from the same problem. They are effective only when used within small exclusive groups. If outsiders know the keys, messages can be intercepted, interpreted, and altered. Encrypting data transmitted between large numbers of relative strangers (such as Internet transactions between businesses and customers) needs a different approach. The solution to this problem is public key encryption.

FIGURE 16-5 | The Data Encryption Standard Technique

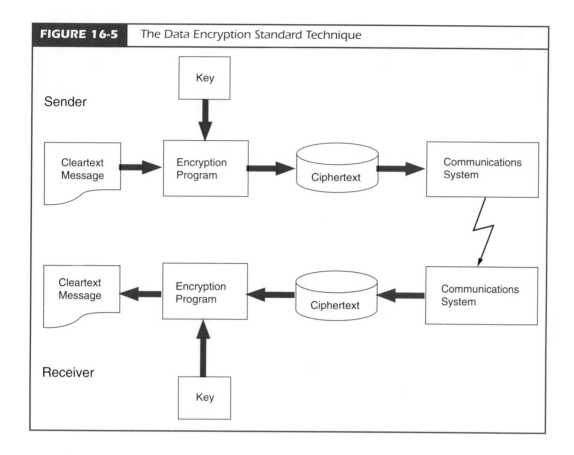

Public Key Encryption. The **public key encryption** technique uses two different keys: one for encoding messages and the other for decoding them. Each recipient has a private key that is kept secret and a public key that is published. The sender of a message uses the receiver's public key to encrypt the message. The receiver then uses his or her private key to decode the message. Users never need to share their private keys to decrypt messages, thus reducing the likelihood that they fall into the hands of a criminal.

RSA (**Rivest-Shamir-Adleman**) is a highly secure public key cryptography method. This method is, however, computationally intensive and much slower than standard DES encryption. Sometimes, both DES and RSA are used together in what is called a **digital envelope.** The actual message is encrypted using DES to provide the fastest decoding. The DES private key needed to decrypt the message is encrypted using RSA and transmitted along with the message. The receiver first decodes the DES key, which is then used to decode the message.

Digital Signatures

A **digital signature** is electronic authentication that cannot be forged. It ensures that the message or document transmitted by the sender was not tampered with after the signature was applied. Figure 16-7 illustrates this process. The sender uses a one-way hashing algorithm to calculate a **digest** of the text message. The digest is a mathematical value calculated from the text content of the message. The digest is then encrypted using the sender's private key to produce the digital signature. Next, the digital signature and the text message are encrypted using the receiver's public key and transmitted to the receiver. At the

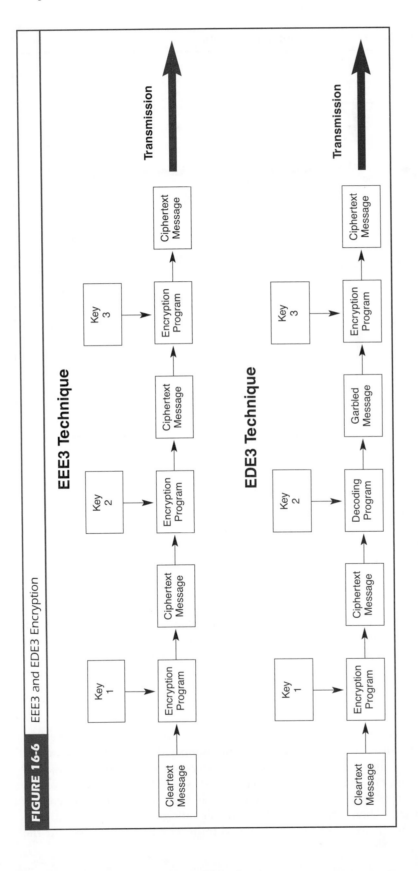

FIGURE 16-6   EEE3 and EDE3 Encryption

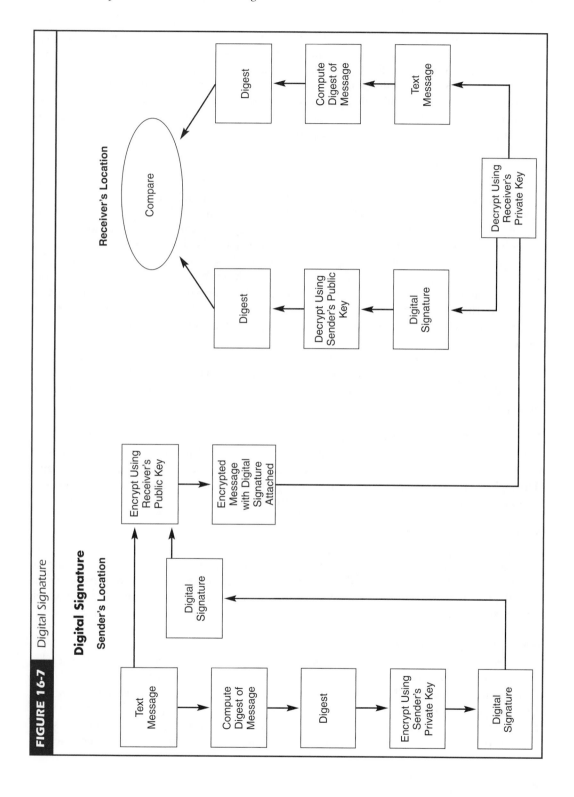

FIGURE 16-7   Digital Signature

receiving end, the message is decrypted using the receiver's private key to produce the digital signature (encrypted digest) and the cleartext version of the message. The receiver then uses the sender's public key to decrypt the digital signal to produce the digest. Finally, the receiver recalculates the digest from the cleartext using the original hashing algorithm and compares this to the decoded digest. If the message is authentic, the two digest values will match. If even a single character of the message was changed in transmission, the digest figures will not be equal.

Digital Certificate

The above process proves that the message received was not tampered with during transmission. It does not prove, however, that the sender is who he or she claims to be. The sender could be an impersonator. Verifying the sender's identity requires a **digital certificate,** which is issued by a trusted third party called a **certification authority** (CA). A digital certificate is used in conjunction with a public key encryption system to authenticate the sender of a message. The process for certification varies depending on the level of certification desired. It involves establishing one's identity with formal documents such as a driver's license, notarization, and fingerprints and proving one's ownership of the public key. After verifying the owner's identity the CA creates the certification, which is the owner's public key, and other data that have been digitally signed by the CA.

The digital certificate is transmitted with the encrypted message to authenticate the sender. The receiver uses the public key of the CA, which is widely publicized, to decrypt the sender's public key attached to the message. The sender's public key is then used to decrypt the message.

Message Sequence Numbering

An intruder in the communications channel may attempt to delete a message from a stream of messages, change the order of messages received, or duplicate a message. Through **message sequence numbering,** a sequence number is inserted in each message, and any such attempt will become apparent at the receiving end.

Message Transaction Log

An intruder may successfully penetrate the system by trying different password and user ID combinations. Therefore, all incoming and outgoing messages, as well as attempted (failed) access, should be recorded in a **message transaction log.** The log should record the user ID, the time of the access, and the terminal location or telephone number from which the access originated.

Request-Response Technique

An intruder may attempt to prevent or delay the receipt of a message from the sender. When senders and receivers are not in constant contact, the receiver may not know if the communications channel has been interrupted and that messages have been diverted. Using **request-response technique,** a control message from the sender and a response from the receiver are sent at periodic, synchronized intervals. The timing of the messages should follow a random pattern that will be difficult for the intruder to determine and circumvent.

Call-Back Devices

As we have seen, networks can be equipped with security features such as passwords, authentication devices, and encryption. The common weakness to all of these technologies is that they apply the security measure *after* the criminal has connected to the network server. Many feel that the key to security is to keep the intruder off the network to begin with.

A **call-back device** requires the dial-in user to enter a password and be identified. The system then breaks the connection to perform user authentication. If the caller is authorized, the call-back device dials the caller's number to establish a new connection. This restricts access to authorized terminals or telephone numbers and prevents an intruder masquerading as a legitimate user.

Audit Objectives Relating to Subversive Threats

The auditor's objective is to verify the security and integrity of financial transactions by determining that network controls (1) can prevent and detect illegal access both internally and from the Internet, (2) will render useless any data that are successfully captured by a perpetrator, and (3) are sufficient to preserve the integrity and physical security of data connected to the network.

Audit Procedures Relating to Subversive Threats

To achieve these control objectives, the auditor may perform the following tests of controls:

1. Review the adequacy of the firewall in achieving the proper balance between control and convenience based on the organization's business objectives and potential risks. Criteria for assessing the firewall effectiveness include:

   - *Flexibility.* The firewall should be flexible enough to accommodate new services as the security needs of the organization change.

   - *Proxy services.* Adequate proxy applications should be in place to provide explicit user authentication to sensitive services, applications, and data.

   - *Filtering.* Strong filtering techniques should be designed to deny all services that are not explicitly permitted. In other words, the firewall should specify only those services the user is permitted to access, rather than specifying the services that are denied.

   - *Segregation of systems.* Systems that do not require public access should be segregated from the Internet.

   - *Audit tools.* The firewall should provide a thorough set of audit and logging tools that identify and record suspicious activity.

   - *Probe for weaknesses.* To validate security, the auditor (or a professional security analyst) should periodically probe the firewall for weaknesses just as a computer Internet hacker would do. A number of software products are currently available for identifying security weaknesses.[2]

2. Review security procedures governing the administration of data encryption keys.
3. Verify the encryption process by transmitting a test message and examining the contents at various points along the channel between the sending and receiving locations.
4. Review the message transaction logs to verify that all messages were received in their proper sequence.
5. Test the operation of the call-back feature by placing an unauthorized call from outside the installation.

---

2   Examples include Security Administrator Tool for Analyzing Networks (SATAN), Internet Security Scanner (ISS), Gabriel, and Courtney.

CONTROLLING RISKS FROM EQUIPMENT FAILURE

Line Errors

The most common problem in data communications is data loss due to **line error.** The bit structure of the message can be corrupted through noise on the communications lines. *Noise* is made up of random signals that can interfere with the message signal when they reach a certain level. These random signals may be caused by electric motors, atmospheric conditions, faulty wiring, defective components in equipment, or noise spilling over from an adjacent communications channel. If not detected, bit structure changes to transmitted data can be catastrophic to the firm. For example, in the case of a database update program, the presence of line errors can result in incorrect transaction values being posted to the accounts. The following two techniques are commonly used to detect and correct such data errors before they are processed.

Echo Check. The **echo check** involves the receiver of the message returning the message to the sender. The sender compares the returned message with a stored copy of the original. If there is a discrepancy between the returned message and the original, suggesting a transmission error, the message is retransmitted. This technique reduces, by one half, throughput over communications channels. Throughput can be increased by using full-duplex channels, which allow both parties to transmit and receive simultaneously.

Parity Check. The **parity check** incorporates an extra bit (the parity bit) into the structure of a bit string when it is created or transmitted. Parity can be both vertical and horizontal (longitudinal). Figure 16-8 illustrates both types of parity. Vertical parity adds the parity bit to each character in the message when the characters are originally coded and stored in magnetic form. For example, the number of 1 bits in the bit structure of each character is counted. If the number is even (for instance, there are four 1 bits in a given eight-bit character) the system assigns the parity bit a value of one. If the number of 1 bits is odd, a 0 parity bit is added to the bit structure.

The concern is that during transmission, a 1 bit will be converted to a 0 bit or vice versa, thus destroying the bit structure integrity of the character. In other words, the original character is incorrectly presented as a different yet valid character. Errors of this sort, if undetected, could alter financial numbers. They can be detected at the receiving end by a parity check. The 1 bits are again counted by the system and should always equal an odd number. If a 1 bit is added to or removed from the bit structure during transmission, the number of 1 bits for the character will be even, which would signal that an error has occurred.

The problem with using vertical parity alone is the possibility that an error will change two bits in the structure simultaneously, thus retaining the parity of the character. In fact, some estimates indicate a 40 to 50 percent chance that line noise will corrupt more than one bit within a character. This problem is reduced by using horizontal parity in conjunction with vertical parity. In Figure 16-8, notice the parity bit following each block of characters. The combination of vertical and horizontal parity provides a higher degree of protection from line errors.

Audit Objectives Relating to Equipment Failure

The auditor's objective is to verify the integrity of the electronic commerce transactions by determining that controls are in place to detect and correct message loss due to equipment failure.

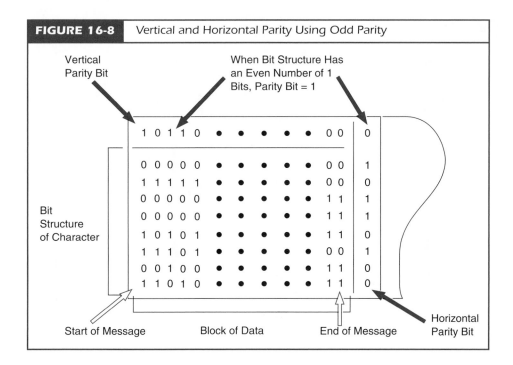

FIGURE 16-8 | Vertical and Horizontal Parity Using Odd Parity

Audit Procedures Relating to Equipment Failure

To achieve this control objective the auditor can select a sample of messages from the transaction log and examine them for garbled contents caused by line noise. The auditor should verify that all corrupted messages were successfully retransmitted.

ELECTRONIC DATA INTERCHANGE CONTROLS

EDI substantially changes the way companies do business and creates unique control issues that accountants need to recognize. Before examining these issues, let's first review the EDI concept. Figure 16-9 illustrates the data flow through the basic elements of an EDI system that links two trading partners—the customer (Company A) and the vendor (Company B). When Company A wishes to place an order with Company B, Company A's purchases system automatically creates and sends an electronic purchase order to its EDI translation software. The translation software converts the purchase order from Company A's internal format to a standard format, such as ANSI X.12. Next, the communications software adds the protocols to the message to prepare it for transmission over the communication channel. The transmission may be either a direct connection between the trading partners or an indirect connection through a value-added network (VAN). At Company B, the process is reversed, yielding a sales order in Company B's internal format, which is processed automatically by its sales order system.

The absence of human intervention in this process presents a unique twist to traditional control problems, including ensuring that transactions are authorized and valid, preventing unauthorized access to data files, and maintaining an audit trail of transactions. The following techniques are used in dealing with these issues.

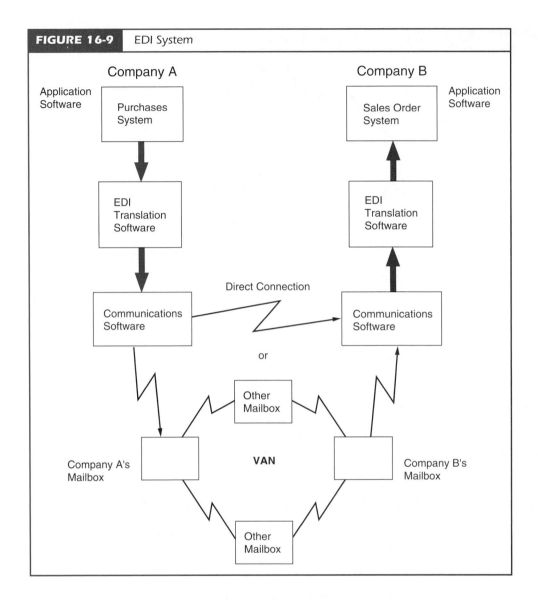

FIGURE 16-9 EDI System

TRANSACTION AUTHORIZATION AND VALIDATION

Both the customer and the supplier must establish that the transaction being processed is to (or from) a valid trading partner and is authorized. This can be accomplished at three points in the process.

1. Some VANs have the capability of validating passwords and user ID codes for the vendor by matching these against a valid customer file. Any unauthorized trading partner transactions are rejected by the VAN before they reach the vendor's system.
2. Before being converted, the translation software can validate the trading partner's ID and password against a validation file in the firm's database.
3. Before processing, the trading partner's application software can validate the transaction by referencing the valid customer and vendor files.

ACCESS CONTROL

To function smoothly, EDI trading partners must permit a degree of access to private data files that would be forbidden in a traditional environment. The degree of access control in place will be determined by the trading partner agreement. For example, it may permit the customer's system to access the vendor's inventory files to determine if inventories are available. Also, trading partners may agree that the prices on the purchase order will be binding on both parties. The customer must, therefore, periodically access the vendor's price list file to keep pricing information current. Alternatively, the vendor may need access to the customer's price list to update prices.

To guard against unauthorized access, each company must establish valid vendor and customer files. Inquiries against databases can thus be validated, and unauthorized attempts at access can be rejected. User authority tables can also be established, which specify the degree of access a trading partner is allowed. For example, the partner may be authorized to read inventory or pricing data but not change values.

EDI AUDIT TRAIL

The absence of source documents in EDI transactions eliminates the traditional audit trail and restricts the ability of accountants to verify the validity, completeness, timing, and accuracy of transactions. One technique for restoring the audit trail is to maintain a control log, which records the transaction's flow through each phase of the EDI system. Figure 16-10 illustrates how this approach may be employed.

As the transaction is received at each stage in the process, an entry is made into the log. In the customer's system, the transaction log can be reconciled to ensure that all transactions initiated by the purchases system were correctly translated and communicated. Likewise, in the vendor's system, the control log will establish that all messages received by the communications software were correctly translated and processed by the sales order system.

Audit Objectives Relating to EDI

The auditor's objectives are to determine that (1) all EDI transactions are authorized, validated, and in compliance with the trading partner agreement; (2) no unauthorized organizations gain access to database records; (3) authorized trading partners have access only to approved data; and (4) adequate controls are in place to ensure a complete audit trail of all EDI transactions.

Audit Procedures Relating to EDI

To achieve these control objectives, the auditor may perform the following tests of controls.

Tests of Authorization and Validation Controls. The auditor should establish that trading partner identification codes are verified before transactions are processed. To accomplish this, the auditor should (1) review agreements with the VAN facility to validate transactions and ensure that information regarding valid trading partners is complete and correct and (2) examine the organization's valid trading partner file for accuracy and completeness.

Tests of Access Controls. Security over the valid trading partner file and databases is central to the EDI control framework. The auditor can verify control adequacy in the following ways:

1.   The auditor should determine that access to the valid vendor or customer file is limited to authorized employees only. The auditor should verify that access to this file is controlled by password and authority tables and that the data are encrypted.

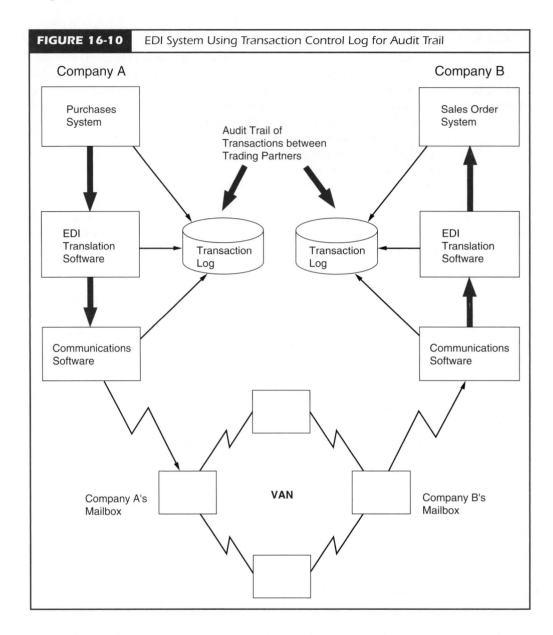

FIGURE 16-10   EDI System Using Transaction Control Log for Audit Trail

2. The degree of access a trading partner should have to the firm's database records (such as inventory levels and price lists) will be determined by the trading agreement. The auditor should reconcile the terms of the trading agreement against the trading partner's access privileges stated in the database authority table.
3. The auditor should simulate access by a sample of trading partners and attempt to violate access privileges.

Tests of Audit Trail Controls. The auditor should verify that the EDI system produces a transaction log that tracks transactions through all stages of processing. By selecting a sample of transactions and tracing these through the process, the auditor can verify that key data values were recorded correctly at each point.

SUMMARY

This chapter continues the discussion of IT general controls and audit tests begun in Chapter 15. It examined the risks and controls over operating systems, database management systems, networks, and EDI systems. The principal threats to the operating system are (1) unauthorized access, (2) intentional or unintentional insertion of viruses, and (3) loss of data due to system malfunctions. Unauthorized access to the database can be effectively controlled through the use of well-designed user views, authorization rules, user-defined procedures, and data encryption. Backup and recovery techniques can be used to safeguard data against system malfunctions. Networks and communication links are susceptible to exposures from both criminal subversion and equipment failure. Subversive threats can be minimized through a variety of security and access control measures including firewalls, data encryption, and call-back devices. Equipment failure usually takes the form of line errors, which are caused by noise in communications lines. These can be effectively reduced through echo checks and parity checks. The discussion then turned to EDI, where firms are faced with a variety of exposures that arise in connection with an environment void of human intermediaries to authorize or review transactions. Controls in an EDI environment are achieved primarily through programmed procedures to authorize transactions, limit access to data files, and ensure that transactions processed by the system are valid.

APPENDIX

SECTION A: MALICIOUS AND DESTRUCTIVE PROGRAMS

VIRUS

A **virus** is a program (usually destructive) that attaches itself to a legitimate program to penetrate the operating system and destroy application programs, data files, and the operating system itself. An insidious aspect of a virus is its ability to spread throughout the host system and on to other systems before perpetrating its destructive acts. Often a virus will have a built-in counter that will trigger its destructive role only after it has copied itself a specified number of times to other programs and systems. The virus thus grows geometrically, which makes tracing its origin extremely difficult.

Personal computers are a major source of virus penetration. When connected in a network or a mainframe, an infected PC can upload the virus to the host system. Once in the host, the virus can spread throughout the operating system and to other users. Virus programs usually attach themselves to the following types of files:

1. An .EXE or .COM program file
2. An .OVL (overlay) program file
3. The boot sector of a disk
4. A device driver program

Mechanisms for spreading viruses include e-mail attachments, downloading of public-domain programs from the internet, and using illegal "bootleg" software. Because of the general lack of control in PC operating systems, microcomputers connected to mainframes pose a serious threat to the mainframe environment as well.

WORM

The term **worm** is used interchangeably with virus. A worm is a software program that "burrows" into the computer's memory and replicates itself into areas of idle memory. The worm systematically occupies idle memory until the memory is exhausted and the system fails. Technically, worms differ from viruses in that the replicated worm modules remain in contact with the original worm that controls their growth, whereas the replicated virus modules grow independently.

LOGIC BOMB

A **logic bomb** is a destructive program, such as a virus, that is triggered by some predetermined event. Often a date (such as Friday the 13th, April Fool's Day, or the 4th of July) will be the logic bomb's trigger. They have also been triggered by events of less public prominence, such as the dismissal of an employee. For example, during the customary two-week severance period, a terminated programmer may embed a logic bomb in the system that will activate six months after his or her departure from the firm.

BACK DOOR

A **back door** (also called a *trap door*) is a software program that allows unauthorized access to a system without going through the normal (front door) log-on procedure. Programmers who want to provide themselves with unrestricted access to system that they are developing for users may create a log-on procedure that will accept either the user's private password or their own secret password, thus creating a back door to the system. The purpose of the back door may be to provide easy access to perform program maintenance, or it may be to perpetrate a fraud or insert a virus into the system.

TROJAN HORSE

A **Trojan horse** is a program whose purpose is to capture IDs and passwords from unsuspecting users. These programs are designed to mimic the normal log-on procedures of the operating system. When the user enters his or her ID and password the Trojan horse stores a copy of them in a secret file. At some later date, the author of the Trojan horse uses these IDs and passwords to access the system and masquerade as an authorized user.

SECTION B: DATA MANAGEMENT CONTROLS IN A FLAT-FILE ENVIRONMENT

BACKUP CONTROLS IN THE FLAT-FILE ENVIRONMENT

The backup techniques employed in legacy systems will depend on the media and the file structure. Sequential files (both tape and disk) use a backup technique called grandparent-parent-child (GPC), which is an integral part of the master file update process. Direct access files, on the other hand, use separate backup procedures. Both methods are outlined in the following section.

GPC Backup Technique. Figure 16-11 illustrates the **grandparent-parent-child** (GPC) backup technique that is used in sequential file batch systems. The backup procedure begins when the current master file (the parent) is processed against the transaction file to produce a new updated master file (the child). With the next batch of transactions, the child becomes the current master file (the new parent), and the original parent becomes the backup (grandparent) file. The new master file that emerges from the update process is the child. This procedure is continued with each new batch of transactions, creating generations of backup files. When the desired number of backup copies is reached, the oldest backup file is erased (scratched). If the current master file is destroyed or corrupted, processing the most current backup file against the corresponding transaction file can reproduce it.

The systems designer determines the number of backup master files needed for each application. Two factors influence this decision: (1) the financial significance of the system and (2) the degree of file activity.

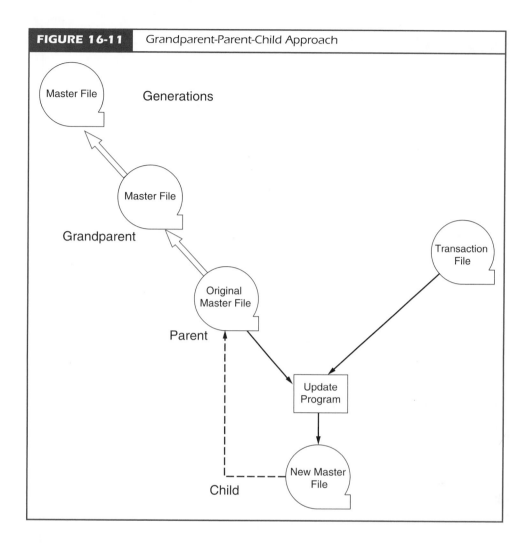

FIGURE 16-11 Grandparent-Parent-Child Approach

For example, a master file that is updated several times a day may require 30 or 40 generations of backup, whereas a file that is updated only once each month may need only four or five backup versions. This decision is important, because certain types of system failures can result in the destruction of large numbers of backup versions within the same family of files.

Direct Access File Backup. Data values in direct access files are changed in place through a process called *destructive replacement*. Therefore, once a data value is changed, the original value is destroyed, leaving only one version (the current version) of the file. To provide backup, direct access files need to be copied before being updated. Figure 16-12 illustrates this process.

The timing of the **direct access backup** procedures will depend on the data processing method being used. In batch systems, backup is usually scheduled prior to the update process. Real-time systems pose a more difficult problem. Because transactions are being processed continuously, the backup procedure takes place at prespecified intervals throughout the day (for example, every 15 minutes).

If the current version of the master file is destroyed through a disk failure or corrupted by a program error, it can thus be reconstructed from the most current backup file using a special recovery program. In the case of real-time systems, transactions processed following the last backup and prior to the failure will be lost and will need to be reprocessed to restore the master file to current status.

FIGURE 16-12   Backup of Direct Access Files

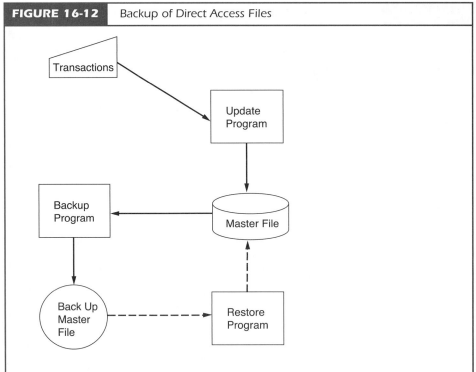

Real-Time Processing System

Real-time systems use timed backup. Transactions processed between backup runs will have to be reprocessed after restoration of the master file.

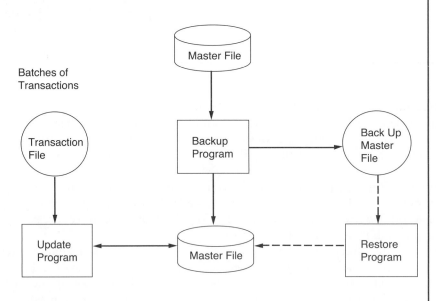

Batch Processing System

In a batch processing system using direct access files, the master file is backed up before the update run.

REVIEW QUESTIONS

1. What are the five control objectives of an operating system?
2. What are the three main tasks performed by the operating system?
3. What is the purpose of an access control list?
4. What are the four techniques that a virus could use to infect a system?
5. What is an access token?
6. Explain discretionary access privileges.
7. What is event monitoring?
8. What is keystroke monitoring?
9. What is a vaccine and what are its limitations?
10. What are the four basic backup and recovery features necessary in a DBMS? Briefly explain each.
11. What are the risks from subversive threats?
12. What are the risks from equipment failure?
13. What is a firewall?
14. Distinguish between network-level and application-level firewalls.
15. What are the most common forms of contra-security behavior?
16. What is a three-way handshake?
17. What are denial of service attacks? Can they be thwarted?
18. How does public key encryption work?
19. What is a digital envelope?
20. What is a digital signature?
21. Categorize each of the following as either an equipment failure control or an unauthorized access control.
    a. Message authentication
    b. Parity check
    c. Call-back device
    d. Echo check
    e. Line error
    f. Data encryption
    g. Request-response technique
22. Will a vertical parity check always catch a data transmission error? Why or why not?
23. At what three points in an electronic data interchange transaction and validation process can authorization and validation be accomplished?

DISCUSSION QUESTIONS

1. Why is human behavior considered one of the biggest potential threats to operating system integrity?
2. A bank in California has 13 branches spread throughout northern California, each with its own minicomputer where its data are stored. Another bank has 10 branches spread throughout California, with the data being stored on a mainframe in San Francisco. Which system do you think is more vulnerable to unauthorized access? Excessive losses from disaster?
3. Why would a systems programmer create a back door if he or she has access to the program in his or her day-to-day tasks?
4. Discuss the issues that need to be considered before implementing keystroke monitoring.
5. Explain how an access token and an access control list are used to approve or deny access.
6. Explain how a Trojan horse may be used to penetrate a system.
7. Discuss six ways that threats from destructive programs can be substantially reduced through a combination of technology controls and administrative procedures.
8. Explain the three ways that audit trails can be used to support security objectives.
9. Explain how poorly designed audit trail logs can actually be dysfunctional.
10. Many authorities believe that 90 percent of all computer fraud acts are not prosecuted by the employer. What do you think accounts for this lack of prosecution? Discuss the importance of the establishment of a formal policy for taking disciplinary (or legal) action against security violations.
11. Why is it risky to allow programmers to create user subschemas and assign access authority to users? What unethical technique do programmers sometimes use when they are not allowed to assign access authority to users?

12. Is access control of greater concern in the flat-file or database file environment?

13. How can passwords actually circumvent security? What actions can be taken to minimize this?

14. Explain how the one-time password approach works.

15. End-user computing has become extremely popular in distributed data processing organizations. The end users like it because they feel they can more readily design and implement their own applications. Does this type of environment always foster more efficient development of applications? Explain your answer.

16. Explain the grandparent-parent-child backup technique. Is it used for sequential files or direct access techniques? Explain.

17. Distinguish between data access and access privileges. Give an example by designing and explaining a database authorization table.

18. What are the objectives of auditors in auditing data management?

19. What are some tests of data communications controls?

20. Discuss some of the risks from subversive threats and how they can be controlled.

21. Discuss the risks from equipment failure and how they can be controlled.

22. Does every organization that has a LAN need a firewall?

23. Why might an individual launch a denial of service attack on a company's Internet connection?

24. Discuss the various ways in which data encryption may be used. Which way provides the most control?

25. What is RSA encryption?

26. Explain the triple-DES encryption techniques know as EEE3 and EDE3.

27. Distinguish between a digital signature and a digital certificate.

28. Describe a digest within the context of a digital signature.

29. What is a digital envelope?

30. Why is inadequate segregation of duties a problem in the personal computer environment?

31. Why is the request-response technique important? Discuss the reasons an intruder may wish to prevent or delay the receipt of a message.

32. Is backup redundancy inefficient?

33. Discuss how the widespread use of laptop and notebook computers is making data encryption standards more easily penetrable.

34. Discuss the unique control problems created by EDI.

35. "In an EDI system, only the customer needs to verify that the order being placed is from a valid supplier and not vice versa." Do you agree with this statement? Why or why not?

36. Discuss how EDI creates an environment in which sensitive information, such as inventory amounts and price data, is no longer private. What potential dangers exist if the proper controls are not in place? Give an example.

MULTIPLE-CHOICE QUESTIONS

1. The database attributes that individual users have permission to access are defined in the
   a. operating system.
   b. user manual.
   c. database schema.
   d. user view.
   e. application listing.

2. An integrated group of programs that supports the applications and facilitates their access to specified resources is called a (an)
   a. operating system.
   b. database management system.
   c. utility system.
   d. facility system.
   e. object system.

3. The purpose of a checkpoint procedure is facilitate restarting after
   a. data processing errors.
   b. data input errors.
   c. the failure to have all input data ready on time.
   d. computer operator intervention.
   e. echo check failures.

4. A user's application may consist of several modules stored in separate memory locations, each with its own data. One module must not

be allowed to destroy or corrupt another module. This is an objective of

   a. operating system controls.

   b. data resource controls.

   c. computer center and security controls.

   d. application controls.

5. A program that attaches to another legitimate program but does not replicate itself is called a

   a. virus.

   b. worm.

   c. Trojan horse.

   d. logic bomb.

6. Which of the following is NOT a data communications control objective?

   a. maintaining the critical application list

   b. correcting message loss due to equipment failure

   c. preventing illegal access

   d. rendering useless any data that are successfully captured by a perpetrator

7. Reviewing database authority tables is a(n)

   a. access control.

   b. organizational structure control.

   c. data resource control.

   d. operating resource control.

8. Hackers can disguise their message packets to look as if they came from an authorized user and gain access to the host's network using a technique called

   a. spoofing.

   b. spooling.

   c. dual-homed.

   d. screening.

9. Transmitting numerous SYN packets to a targeted receiver, but not responding to an ACK, is

   a. a DES message.

   b. the request-response technique.

   c. a denial of service attack.

   d. a call-back device.

PROBLEMS

1. Operating System and Network Control

Describe a well-controlled system in terms of access controls for a major insurance company that equips each salesperson (life, property, and investments) with a laptop. Each salesperson must transmit sales data daily to corporate headquarters. Further, the salespeople use their laptops to connect to the company's e-mail system.

2. Operation System Controls

In 2002, Mr. Rollerball started Mighty Mouse Incorporated, a small, 75-employee firm that produces and sells wireless keyboards and other devices to vendors through its manufacturing plant in Little Rock, Arkansas. In its first two years of business MM saw a substantial growth in sales and now current capacity was unable to keep up with demand. To compete MM enlarged its manufacturing facilities. The new facility increased employs to 250 people. During this period of expansion, MM Inc. has paid little attention to internal control procedures.

Security:

Recently, systems problems and hardware failures have caused the operating system to crash.

Mr. Rollerball was extremely concerned to discover that confidential company information had been printed out on the printers as a result of these crashes. Also, important digital documents were erased from storage media.

Malicious programs such as viruses, worms, and Trojan horses have plagued the company and caused significant data corruption. MM has devoted significant funds and time trying to fix the damage caused to its operating system.

Out of necessity to get the job done, as well as for philosophical reasons, system administrators and programmers have provided users relatively free access to the operating system. Restricting access was found to inhibit business and impede recovery from systems failures. From the outset, an open approach was regarded as an efficient and effective way to ensure that everyone obtained the information they needed to perform their jobs.

Required:

a. What internal control problems do you find?

b. How can MM improve internal controls?

3. Internal Control and Fraud

Charles Hart, an accounts payable clerk, is an hourly employee. He never works a minute past 5 PM unless the overtime has been approved. Charles has recently found himself faced with some severe financial difficulties. He has been accessing the system from his home during the evening and setting up an embezzlement scheme. As his boss, what control technique(s) discussed in this chapter could you use to help detect this type of fraud?

4. Internal Control and Fraud

Stephanie Baskill, an unemployed accounting clerk, lives one block from Cleaver Manufacturing Company. While walking her dog last year, she noticed some ERP manuals in the dumpsters. Curious, she took the manuals home with her. She found that the documentation in the manual was dated two months previous, so she thought that the information must be fairly current. Over the next month, Stephanie continued to collect all types of manuals from the dumpster during her dog-walking excursions. Cleaver Manufacturing Company was apparently updating all of its documentation manuals and placing them online. Eventually, Stephanie found manuals about critical inventory reorder formulas, the billing system, the sales order system, the payables system, and the operating system. Stephanie went to the local library and read as much as she could about this particular operating system.

To gain access to the organization, she took a low-profile position as a cleaning woman. By snooping through offices and guessing at passwords, watching people who were working late type in their passwords, and ultimately printing out lists of user IDs and passwords using a Trojan horse virus, Stephanie was able to obtain all the necessary passwords she needed to set herself up as a supplier, customer, systems operator, and systems librarian. Further, as a cleaning woman, she had access to all areas in the building.

As a customer, she was able to order enough goods so that the inventory procurement system would automatically trigger a need for a purchase of raw materials. Then, as a supplier, Stephanie would stand ready to deliver the goods at the specified price. She then covered her tracks by adjusting the transaction logs once the bills were paid. Stephanie was able to embezzle, on average, $125,000 a month. About 16 months after she

began working at Cleaver, the controller saw her arrive at a very expensive French restaurant one evening, driving a Jaguar. He told the internal auditors to keep a close watch on her, and they were able to catch her in the act.

Required:

a. What weaknesses in the organization's control structure must have existed to permit this type of embezzlement?

b. What specific control techniques and procedures could have helped prevent or detect this fraud?

5. CMA 686 5-2

Input Controls and Networking

Intex Corporation is a multinational company with approximately 100 subsidiaries and divisions, referred to as reporting units. Each reporting unit operates autonomously and maintains its own accounting information system. Each month, the reporting units prepare the basic financial statements and other key financial data on prescribed forms. These statements and related data are either mailed or telexed to corporate headquarters in New York City for entry in to the corporate database. Top and middle management at corporate headquarters use the database to plan and direct corporate operations and objectives.

Under the current system, the statements and data are to be received at corporate headquarters by the 12th working day following the end of the month. The reports are logged, batched, and taken to the data processing department for coding and entry into the database. Approximately 15 percent of the reporting units are delinquent in submitting their data, and three to four days are required to receive all of the data. After the data are loaded into the system, data verification programs are run to check footings, cross-statement consistency, and dollar range limits. Any errors in the data are traced and corrected, and reporting units are notified of all errors by form letters.

Intex Corporation has decided to upgrade its computer communications network. The new system would allow a more timely receipt of data at corporate headquarters and would provide numerous benefits to each of the reporting units.

The systems department at corporate headquarters is responsible for the overall design and implementation of the new system. It will use current computer communications technology by installing smart computer terminals at all reporting units. These terminals will provide two-way computer communications and serve as microcomputers that can use spreadsheet and other applications software. As part of the initial use of the system, the data collection for the corporate database would be performed through these terminals.

The financial statements and other financial data currently mailed or telexed would be entered by terminals. The required forms would initially be transmitted (downloaded) from the headquarters computer to the terminals of each reporting unit and stored permanently on disk. Data would be entered on the forms appearing on the reporting unit's terminal and stored under a separate file for transmission after the data are checked.

The data edit program would also be downloaded to the reporting units so the data could be verified at the unit location. All corrections would be made before transmitting the data to headquarters. The data would be stored on disk in proper format to maintain a unit file. Data would either be transmitted to corporate headquarters immediately or retrieved by the computer at corporate headquarters as needed. Therefore, data arriving at corporate headquarters would be free from errors and ready to be used in reports.

Charles Edwards, Intex's controller, is very pleased with the prospects of the new system. He believes that the data will be received from the reporting units two to three days faster and that data accuracy will be much improved. However, Edwards is concerned about data security and integrity during the transmission of data between the reporting units and corporate headquarters. He has scheduled a meeting with key personnel from the systems department to discuss these concerns.

Required:

Intex could experience data security and integrity problems when transmitting data between the reporting units and corporate headquarters.

a. Identify and explain the data security and integrity problems that could occur.

b. For each problem identified, describe a control procedure that could be employed to minimize or eliminate the problem. Use the following format to present your answer.

Problem Identification and Explanation	Control Procedure and Explanation

6. Preventive Controls

Listed below are five scenarios. For each scenario, discuss the possible damages that can occur. Suggest a preventive control.

a. An intruder taps into a telecommunications device and retrieves the identifying codes and personal identification numbers for ATM cardholders. (The user subsequently codes this information onto a magnetic coding device and places this strip on a piece of cardboard.)

b. Due to occasional noise on a transmission line, electronic messages received are extremely garbled.

c. Due to occasional noise on a transmission line, data being transferred is lost or garbled.

d. Important strategic messages are being temporarily delayed by an intruder over the telecommunications lines.

e. Electronic messages are being altered by an intruder before being received by the user.

7. Operating System Exposures and Controls

Listed below are five scenarios. For each scenario, discuss the potential consequences and give a prevention technique.

a. The systems operator opened a bag of burned microwave popcorn directly under a smoke detector in the computing room where two mainframes, three high-speed printers, and approximately 40 tapes are housed. The extremely sensitive smoke detector triggered the sprinkler system. Three minutes passed before the sprinklers could be turned off.

b. A system programmer intentionally placed an error into a program that causes the operating system to fail and dump certain confidential information to disks and printers.

c. Jane, a secretary, was laid off. Her employer gave her three weeks' notice. After two weeks, Jane realized that finding another job was going to be very tough, and she became bitter. Her son told her about a virus that had infected the computers at school. He had a disk infected with the virus. Jane took the disk to work and copied the disk onto the network server, which is connected to the company's mainframe. One month later, the company realized that some data and application programs had been destroyed.

d. Robert discovered a new sensitivity analysis public-domain program on the Internet. He downloaded the software to his microcomputer at home, then took the application to work and placed it onto his networked personal computer. The program had a virus on it that eventually spread to the company's mainframe.

e. Murray, a trusted employee and a systems engineer, had access to both the computer access control list and user passwords. He was recently hired away by the firm's competitor for twice his old salary. After leaving, Murray continued to browse through his old employer's data, such as price lists, customer lists, bids on jobs, and so on. He passed this information on to his new employer.

8. Database Authorization Table

The following information is stored in two relational database files:

Employee Master File
Social Security number
Name
Address
Date hired
Hourly wage rate
Marital status
Number of exemptions

Weekly Payroll
Social Security number
Hours worked
Deductions
Bonuses

Required:

a. Bogey works in personnel and Bacall works in payroll. Prepare a database authorization table that you feel is appropriate for Bogey and Bacall for these two files.

b. Discuss any potential exposure if the right prevention devices are not in place or if Bogey and Bacall collude.

9. Security and Control Assessment

Brew Bottle Company (BBC) is in the process of planning a more advanced computer-based information system. Slavish & Moore, LLP, BBC's consulting firm, have recently been provided with an overview of their proposed plan:

The Brew Bottle Company Information System (BBCIS) will be created with the help of its employees so that the system will function effectively. This helps ensure that the end product will perform the tasks that the user wants. System construction will begin with prototyping, CASE Technology, and Gantt Charts. From here, systems professionals and a systems administrator who will work full time for BBC will create data models of the business process, define conceptual user views, design database tables, and specify system controls. Each user in each department will submit a written description of their needs and business problems to the systems professionals. Systems professionals will then perform analysis of feasibility and system design. Each aspect of the system will be properly documented for control reasons; this will help if problems arise in the future stages of development and is essential to long-term system success.

The new systems administrator will determine access privileges, maintain the access control list, and maintain the database authorization table. Anyone requesting access will fill out a petition which must be approved and signed by the systems administrator. The administrator will have sole access to the transaction log which will be used to record all changes made to a file or database. This information will help detect unauthorized access, reconstruct events if needed, and promote personal accountability. The systems administrator will also be responsible for updating virus protection weekly so that the system will not be damaged by viruses planted intentionally or accidentally. One of the most important tasks of the systems administrator will be to copy databases and system documentation for critical applications to tape or disk on a daily basis. These disks and tapes will be stored in a secure location away from the company property.

Employees requiring computer access will be given a user name and password that will be entered when logging on to their computer terminal. A dialog box will appear when the system is turned on and this information will be entered.

Correct entry of information will give the user access, if information is entered incorrectly, the user will not be granted access. Furthermore, if a computer terminal is left idle for more than five minutes, a password will be needed to regain access. For security reasons, users will be required to change their passwords once every year.

Hardware will be purchased from Bell Computer Company with the advice of in-house systems developers. With the exception of basic applications, computer software will be purchased by user departments and added to the system.

BBCIS will run off of a computing center located in the company's administration building adjacent to the factory. Access to the computing center will require formal authorization. When entering the room there will be two security guards, the authorized employee will need to swipe their ID card to pass though security. Times will be recorded when the employee swipes their card for entrance and exit. The actual room that houses the computer systems will have an advanced air conditioning and air filtration system which will eliminate dust and pollens. There will also be a sprinkler system to minimize damages in event of a fire.

Required:
Based on Brew Bottle Company's plans for the implementation of a new computer system, describe the potential risks and needed controls. Classify these according to the relevant areas of the COSO framework.

IT Controls Part III: Systems Development, Program Changes, and Application Controls

LEARNING OBJECTIVES

After studying this chapter, you should:

- Be familiar with the controls and audit tests relevant to systems development process.
- Understand the risks and controls associated with program change procedures and the role of the source program library.
- Understand the auditing techniques (CAATTs) used to verify the effective functioning of application controls.
- Understand the auditing techniques used to perform substantive tests in an IT environment.

This chapter concludes our treatment of IT controls as outlined in the COSO control framework. The focus of the chapter is on SOX compliance regarding systems development, program changes, and applications controls. This chapter examines the risks, controls, audit objectives, and tests of controls that may be performed to satisfy compliance or attest responsibilities. The chapter concludes with a discussion of embedded audit modules and generalized audit software used for substantive testing.

SYSTEMS DEVELOPMENT CONTROLS

Chapters 13 and 14 presented the systems development life cycle (SDLC) as a multi-phase process by which organizations satisfy their formal information needs. An important point at this juncture is that specific SDLC steps will vary from firm to firm. In reviewing the effectiveness of a particular systems development methodology, the accountant should focus on the controllable activities common to all systems development approaches. These are outlined in the following section.

CONTROLLING SYSTEMS DEVELOPMENT ACTIVITIES

This section and the one that follows examine several controllable activities that distinguish an effective systems development process. The six activities discussed deal with the authorization, development, and implementation of new systems. Controls over systems maintenance are presented in the next section.

Systems Authorization Activities

All systems should be properly authorized to ensure their economic justification and feasibility. This requires a formal environment in which users submit requests to systems professionals in written form.

User Specification Activities

Users need to be actively involved in the systems development process. User involvement should not be stifled by the technical complexity of the system. Regardless of the technology involved, the user should create a detailed written description of their needs. The creation of a user specification document often involves the joint efforts of the user and systems professionals. However, this document must remain a statement of user needs. It should describe the user's view of the problem, not that of the systems professionals.

Technical Design Activities

The technical design activities translate user specifications into a set of detailed technical specifications for a system that meets the user's needs. The scope of these activities includes systems analysis, feasibility analysis, and detailed systems design. The adequacy of these activities is measured by the quality of the documentation that emerges from each phase. Documentation is both a control and evidence of control and is critical to the system's long-term success. Specific documentation requirements including designer, operator, user, and auditor documentation were discussed in Chapter 14.

Internal Audit Participation

To meet the governance-related expectations of management under SOX, an organization's internal audit department needs to be independent, objective, and technically qualified. As such, the internal auditor can play an important role in the control of systems development activities. The internal auditor can serve as a liaison between users and the systems professionals to ensure an effective transfer of knowledge. An internal audit group, astute in computer technology and possessing a solid grasp of the business problems to be solved, is invaluable to the organization during all phases of the SDLC. Internal auditors should therefore become formally involved at the inception of the systems development process to oversee the definition of user needs requirements and appropriate controls. Furthermore, this involvement should continue throughout all phases of development and maintenance activities.

Program Testing

All program modules must be thoroughly tested before they are implemented. Figure 17-1 shows a program testing procedure involving the creation of hypothetical master files and transactions files that are processed by the modules being tested. The results of the tests are then compared against predetermined results to identify programming and logic errors. For example, a programmer testing the logic of the accounts receivable update module illustrated in Figure 17-1 might create an accounts receivable master file record for John Smith with a current balance of $1,000 and a sales order transaction record for $100. Before performing the update test, the programmer concludes that a new balance of $1,100 should result. To verify the module's internal logic, the programmer compares the actual results obtained from the test with the predetermined results. This is a very simple example of a program test. Actual testing would be extensive and involve many transactions that test all aspects of the module's logic.

The task of creating meaningful test data is time consuming. This should not, however, be considered a single-use activity. As we shall later see, some aspects of application control testing require test data. To efficiently meet future **audit objectives**, test data prepared during systems implementation should be preserved. This will give the auditor a frame of reference for designing and evaluating future audit tests. For example, if a program has undergone no maintenance changes since its implementation, the test results from the audit should be identical to the original test results. Having a basis for comparison, the auditor can thus quickly verify the integrity of the program code. On the other hand if changes have occurred, the original test data can provide a baseline for assessing

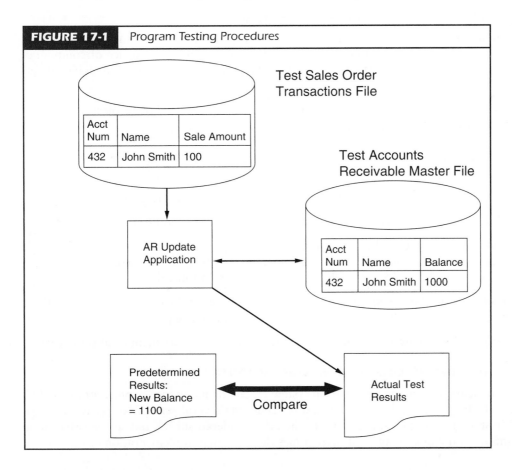

FIGURE 17-1 | Program Testing Procedures

the impact of changes. The auditor can thus concentrate tests of application controls on areas where computer logic was changed.

User Test and Acceptance Procedures

Prior to system implementation, the individual modules of the system need to be formally and rigorously tested as a whole. The test team should comprise of user personnel, systems professionals, and internal auditors. The details of the tests performed and their results need to be formally documented and analyzed. Once the test team is satisfied that the system meets its stated requirements, the system can be transferred to the user.

Many consider the formal testing and acceptance event to be the most important control over the systems development process. This is the last point at which the user can determine the system's acceptability prior to it going into service. Whereas discovering a major flaw at this juncture is costly, discovering it during day-to-day operations may be devastating.

Audit Objectives Relating to Systems Development

The auditor's objectives are to ensure that (1) systems development activities are applied consistently and in accordance with management's policies to all systems development projects; (2) the system as originally implemented was free from material errors and fraud; (3) the system was judged necessary and justified at various checkpoints throughout the SDLC; and (4) system documentation is sufficiently accurate and complete to facilitate audit and maintenance activities.

Tests of Systems Development Controls

The auditor should select a sample of completed projects (completed in both the current period and previous periods) and review the documentation for evidence of compliance with stated systems development policies. Specific points for review should include determining that:

- User and computer services management properly authorized the project.

- A preliminary feasibility study showed that the project had merit.

- A detailed analysis of user needs was conducted that resulted in alternative conceptual designs.

- A cost-benefit analysis was conducted using reasonably accurate figures.

- The detailed design was an appropriate and accurate solution to the user's problem.

- Test results show that the system was thoroughly tested at both the individual module and the total system level before implementation. (To confirm these test results, the auditor may decide to retest selected elements of the application.)

- There is a checklist of specific problems detected during the conversion period, along with evidence that they were corrected in the maintenance phase.

- Systems documentation complies with organizational requirements and standards.

CONTROLLING PROGRAM CHANGE ACTIVITIES

Upon implementation, the information system enters the maintenance phase of the SDLC. This is the longest period in the SDLC, often spanning several years. Most systems do not remain static throughout this period. Rather, they undergo substantial changes that often constitute, in dollars, an amount many times their original implementation cost.

Little is served by designing and implementing controls over systems development activities if control is not continued into the maintenance phase. Maintenance access to systems increases the risk that logic will be corrupted either by the accident or intent to defraud. To minimize the risk, all maintenance actions should require, as a minimum, four controls: *formal authorizations*, *technical specifications*, *testing*, and *documentation updates*. In other words, maintenance activities should be given essentially the same treatment as new development. The extent of the change and its potential impact on the system should govern the degree of control applied. When maintenance causes extensive changes to program logic, additional controls, such as involvement by the internal auditor and additional user test and acceptance procedures may be necessary.

SOURCE PROGRAM LIBRARY CONTROLS

Even with formal maintenance procedures in place, application integrity is threatened by individuals who gain unauthorized access to programs. The remainder of this section deals with control techniques and procedures for reducing this risk.

In larger computer systems, application program modules are stored in source code form on magnetic disks called the *source program library (SPL)*. Figure 17-2 illustrates the relationship between the SPL and other key components of the operating environment. This material presumes an understanding of the program compilation process. If you are uncertain about the meaning of the terms *source program*, *compiler*, and *load module*, review the section on language translators on the book's web page located at http://hall.swlearning.com.

Executing a production application requires that the source code be compiled and linked to a load module that the computer can process. As a practical matter, programs in

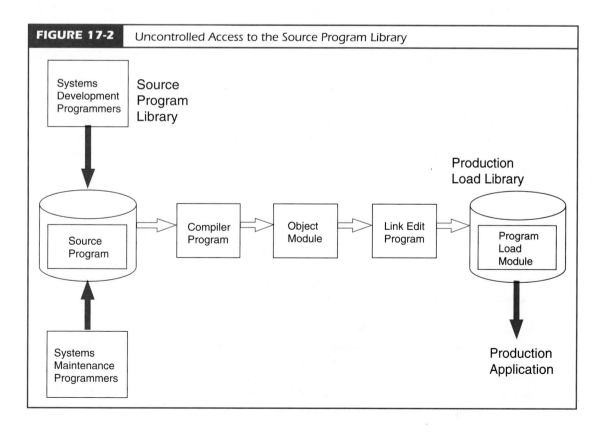

FIGURE 17-2   Uncontrolled Access to the Source Program Library

their compiled state are secure and free from the threat of unauthorized modification. At this point the source code is not needed for the application to run. In fact, we could destroy it if no future changes were ever to be made to the application. To make such a change, however, requires changing the logic of the source code on the SPL. This is then recompiled and linked to create a new load module that incorporates the changed code. Clearly, protecting the source code on the SPL is central to protecting the production application.

THE WORST CASE SITUATION: NO CONTROLS

Figure 17-2 shows the SPL without controls. In this situation, access to application programs is completely unrestricted. Legitimate maintenance programmers or others may access any programs stored in the library, which has no provision for detecting an unauthorized intrusion. Because these programs are open to unauthorized changes, no basis exists for relying on the effectiveness of controls designed into them. Even testing these controls proves only that they work now, but says nothing about how they worked last week or last month. In other words, with no control over access to the SPL a program's integrity during the period in question cannot be established.

A CONTROLLED SPL ENVIRONMENT

Controlling the SPL requires SPL *management system (SPLMS)* software. Figure 17-3 illustrates this approach. The black box surrounding the SPL signifies the SPLMS, which controls four critical functions: (1) storing programs on the SPL, (2) retrieving programs for maintenance purposes, (3) deleting obsolete programs from the library, and (4) documenting program changes to provide an audit trail of the changes.

You may have recognized the similarities between the SPL management system and a database management system. This is a valid analogy, the difference being that SPL software manages program files and DBMSs manage data files. SPLMS software may be supplied by the computer manufacturer as part of the **operating system** or may be purchased through software vendors.

The mere presence of an SPLMS does not guarantee program integrity. Again, we can draw an analogy with the DBMS. To achieve data integrity, the DBMS must be properly used; control does not come automatically—it must be planned. Likewise, an SPL requires specific planning and control techniques to ensure program integrity. The control techniques discussed in the following section address the most vulnerable areas and should be considered minimum SPL controls.

Password Control

Password control over the SPL is similar to password controls in a DBMS. Every financially significant program stored in the SPL can be assigned a separate password. As previously discussed, passwords have drawbacks. When more than one person is authorized to access a program, preserving the secrecy of a shared password is a problem. Because responsibility for the secrecy of a shared password lies with the group rather than with an individual, personal accountability is reduced.

Separation of Test Libraries

Figure 17-3 illustrates an improvement on the shared password approach through the creation of separate password-controlled libraries (or directories) for each programmer. Under this concept, a strict separation is maintained between the production programs that are subject to maintenance in the SPL and those being developed. Production programs are copied into the programmer's library for maintenance and testing purposes

| **FIGURE 17-3** | Source Prgram Library under the Control of SPL Management Software |

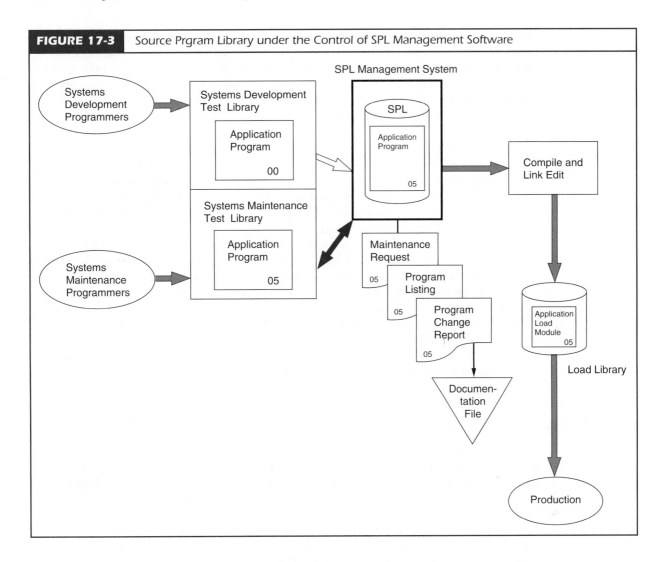

only. Direct access to the production SPL is limited to a specific librarian group that must approve all requests to modify, delete, and copy programs.

An enhancement to this control feature is the implementation of program naming conventions. The name assigned to a program clearly distinguishes it as being either a test or a production program. When a program is copied from the production SPL to the programmer's library, it is given a temporary "test" name. When the program is returned to the SPL, it is renamed with its original production name. This technique greatly reduces the risk of accidentally running an untested version of a program in place of the production program.

Audit Trail and Management Reports

An important feature of SPL management software is the creation of reports that enhance management control and support the audit function. The most useful of these are program modification reports, which describe in detail all program changes (additions and deletions) to each module. These reports should be part of the documentation file of each application to form an audit trail of program changes over the life of the application.

During an audit, the reports can be reconciled against program maintenance requests to verify that only approved changes were implemented. For example, if a programmer attempted to use a legitimate maintenance event as an opportunity to commit program fraud, the unauthorized code changes would be documented in the program modification report. These reports can be produced as hard copy or digital and can be governed by password control, thus limiting access to management and auditors.

Program Version Numbers

The SPLMS assigns a version number automatically to each program stored on the SPL. When programs are first placed in the libraries (at implementation), they are assigned version number zero. With each modification to the program, the version number is increased by one. For instance, after five authorized maintenance changes, the production program will be Version 05, as illustrated in Figure 17-3. This feature, when combined with audit trail reports, provides a basis for detecting unauthorized changes to the application program. An unauthorized change is signaled by a version number on the production load module that cannot be reconciled to the number of authorized changes. For example, if ten changes were authorized but the production program is Version 12, then two possible control violations may have happened: (1) authorized changes occurred, which for some reason went undocumented or (2) unauthorized changes were made, which incremented the version numbers. We will discuss this issue in more detail later.

Controlling Access to Maintenance Commands

Powerful maintenance commands are available for most library systems that can be used to alter or eliminate program passwords, alter the program version number, and temporarily modify a program without generating a record of the modification.

There are a number of legitimate technical reasons why systems designers must sometimes use these commands. If not controlled, however, maintenance commands open the possibility of unauthorized, and perhaps undocumented, program modifications. Hence, access to the maintenance commands themselves should be password controlled, and the authority to use them should be controlled by management or an IT security group.

Audit Objectives Relating to Systems Maintenance

The auditor's objectives are to determine that (1) maintenance procedures protect applications from unauthorized changes, (2) applications are free from material errors, and (3) program libraries are protected from unauthorized access.

The **tests of controls** necessary to achieve each of these objectives are examined in the following section. The discussion assumes that the organization employs source program library (SPL) software to control program maintenance. Without such software achieving the audit objectives may be impossible. The procedures described below are illustrated in Figure 17-4.

Audit Procedures for Identifying Unauthorized Program Changes

To establish that program changes were authorized, the auditor should examine the audit trail of program changes for a sample of applications that have undergone maintenance. The auditor can confirm that authorization procedures were followed by performing the following tests of controls.

Reconcile Program Version Numbers. The permanent file of the application should contain program change authorization documents that correspond to the current version number of the production application. In other words, if the production application is in its tenth version, there should be ten program change authorizations in the

---

FIGURE 17-4 | Auditing SPL Software System

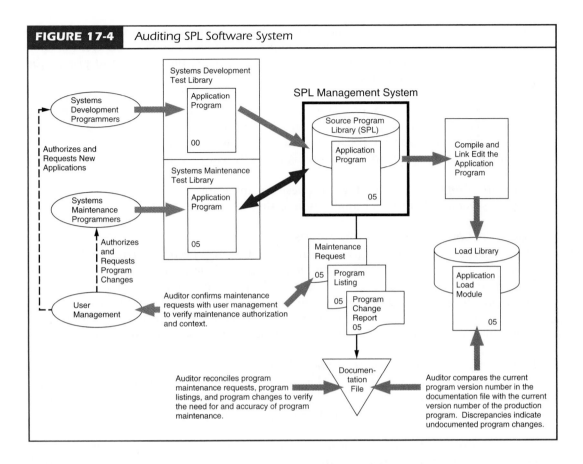

---

permanent file as supporting documentation.[1] Any discrepancies between version numbers and supporting documents may indicate that unauthorized changes were made.

Confirm Maintenance Authorization. The program maintenance authorization should indicate the nature of the change requested and the date of the change. It should also be signed and approved by the appropriate management from both computer services and the user departments. The auditor should confirm the facts contained in the maintenance authorization and verify the authorizing signatures with the managers involved.

Audit Procedures for Identifying Application Errors
The auditor can determine that programs are free from material errors by performing three types of tests of controls: reconcile the source code, review the test results, and retest the program.

Reconcile the Source Code. Each application's permanent file should contain the current program listing and listings of all changes made to the application. These documents describe in detail the application's maintenance history. In addition, the nature of the program change should be clearly stated on the program change authorization document. The auditor should select a sample of applications and reconcile each program change with the appropriate authorization documents. The modular approach to systems design

---

1   In most systems, a program in its original (unmodified) state has a version number of 00. Thus, ten changes will give a version number of 10.

(creating applications that comprise many small discrete program modules) greatly facilitates this testing technique. The reduced complexity of these modules enhances the auditor's ability to identify irregularities that indicate errors, omissions, and potentially fraudulent programming codes.

Review Test Results. Every program change should be thoroughly tested before being implemented. Program test procedures should be properly documented as to the test objectives, test data, and processing results. The auditor should review this record for each significant program change to establish that testing was sufficiently rigorous to identify any errors.

Retest the Program. The auditor can retest the application to confirm its integrity. We examine several techniques for application testing later in the chapter.

Audit Procedures for Testing Access to Libraries

The existence of a secure program library is central to preventing errors and program fraud. One control method is to assign library access privileges only to system librarians. Their function is to retrieve applications from the program libraries for maintenance and to restore the modified programs to the library. Thus maintenance programmers test applications in their "private" libraries but do not have access to the program library. The auditor may assess program library security by performing the following tests of controls.

Review Programmer Authority Tables. The auditor can select a sample of programmers and review their access authority. The programmer's authority table will specify the libraries a programmer may access. These authorizations should be matched against the programmer's maintenance authority to ensure that no irregularities exist.

Test Authority Table. The auditor may test the programmer's access privileges by violating the authorization rules in an attempt to access unauthorized libraries. Any such attempts should be denied by the operating system.

APPLICATION CONTROLS

In addition to IT general controls, SOX requires management and auditors to consider application controls relevant to financial reporting. Application controls are associated with specific applications, such as payroll, purchases, and cash disbursements systems. These fall into three broad categories: *input controls*, *processing controls*, and *output controls*.

INPUT CONTROLS

Input controls are programmed procedures (routines) that perform tests on transaction data to ensure they are free from errors. Input control routines should be designed into the system at different points, depending on whether transaction processing is real time or batch. Input controls in real-time systems are placed at the data collection stage to monitor data as they are entered from terminals. Batch systems often collect data in transaction files where they are temporarily held for subsequent processing. In this case, input control tests are performed as a separate procedure (or run) prior to the master file update process. In any case, transaction data should never be used to update master files until the transactions have been tested for validity, accuracy, and **completeness**. If a record fails an input control test, it is flagged as an *error record*. Later, we will see how to deal with these records. The following are examples of input controls.

Check digit. Data codes are used extensively in transaction processing systems for representing such things as customer accounts, items of inventory, and general ledger accounts in the chart of accounts. If the data code of a particular transaction is entered incorrectly and goes undetected, then a transaction processing error will occur, such as posting to the wrong account. Two common classes of data input errors cause such processing problems: *transcription errors* and *transposition errors*.

Transcription errors are divided into three categories:

1. *Addition* errors occur when an extra digit or character is added to the code. For example, inventory item number 83276 is recorded as 832766.
2. *Truncation* errors occur when a digit or character is removed from the end of a code. In this type of error, the inventory item above would be recorded as 8327.
3. *Substitution* errors are the replacement of one digit in a code with another. For example, code number 83276 is recorded as 83266.

Transposition errors are of two types. *Single transposition errors occur* when two adjacent digits are reversed. For instance, 83276 is recorded as 38276. *Multiple transposition errors occur* when nonadjacent digits are transposed. For example, 83276 is recorded as 87236.

These problems may be controlled using a **check digit**. This is a control digit (or digits) added to the data code when it is originally assigned that allows the integrity of the code to be established during subsequent processing. The check digit can be located anywhere in the code, as a prefix, a suffix, or embedded someplace in the middle. The simplest form of check digit is to sum the digits in the code and use this sum as the check digit. For example, for the customer account code 5372 the calculated check digit would be:

$$5 + 3 + 7 + 2 = 17$$

By dropping the tens column, the check digit 7 is added to the original code to produce the new code 53727. The entire string of digits (including the check digit) becomes the customer account number. During data entry, the system can recalculate the check digit to ensure that the code is correct. This technique will detect only transcription errors. For example, if a substitution error occurred and the above code were entered as 52727, the calculated check digit would be 6 ($5 + 2 + 7 + 2 = 16 = 6$), and the error would be detected. However, this technique would fail to identify transposition errors. For example, transposing the first two digits yields the code 35727, which still sums to 17 and produces the check digit 7. This error would go undetected.

A popular check digit technique for dealing with transposition errors is modulus 11. Using the code 5372, the steps in this technique are outlined next:

1. *Assign weights.* Each digit in the code is multiplied by a different weight. In this case, the weights used are 5, 4, 3, and 2, shown as follows:

Digit		Weight
5	–	5 = 25
3	–	4 = 12
7	–	3 = 21
2	–	2 = 4

2. *Sum the products.* ($25 + 12 + 21 + 4 = 62$).
3. *Divide by the modulus.* We are using modulus 11 in this case, giving $62/11 = 5$ with a remainder of 7.
4. *Subtract the remainder from the modulus to obtain the check digit.* ($11 - 7 = 4$ [check digit]).
5. *Add the check digit to the original code to yield the new code:* 53724.

Using this technique to recalculate the check digit during processing, a transposition error in the code will produce a check digit other than 4. For example, if the code above was incorrectly entered as 35724, the recalculated check digit would be 6.

Missing data check. Some programming languages are restrictive as to the justification (right or left) of data within the field. If data are not properly justified or if a character is missing (has been replaced with a blank), the value in the field will be improperly processed. In some cases, the presence of blanks in a numeric data field may cause a system failure. When the control routine detects a blank where it expects to see a data value, the error is flagged.

Numeric-alphabetic check. This control identifies when data in a particular field are in the wrong form. For example, a customer's account balance should not contain alphabetic data and the presence of it will cause a data processing error. Therefore, if alphabetic data are detected, the error record flag is set.

Limit check. Limit checks are used to identify field values that exceed an authorized limit. For example, assume the firm's policy is that no employee works more than 44 hours per week. The payroll system input control program can test the hours-worked field in the weekly payroll records for values greater than 44.

Range check. Many times data have upper and lower limits to their acceptable values. For example, if the range of pay rates for hourly employees in a firm is between 8 and 20 dollars, This control can examine the pay rate field of all payroll records to ensure that they fall within this range. The purpose of this control is to detect keystroke errors that shift the decimal point one or more places. It would not detect an error where a correct pay rate of, say, 9 dollars is incorrectly entered as 15 dollars.

Reasonableness check. The error above may be detected by a test that determines if a value in one field, which has already passed a limit check and a range check, is reasonable when considered along with data in other fields of the record. For example, an employee's pay rate of 18 dollars per hour falls within an acceptable range. This rate is excessive, however, when compared to the employee's job skill code of 693; employees in this skill class should not earn more than 12 dollars per hour.

Validity check. A validity check compares actual field values against known acceptable values. This control is used to verify such things as transaction codes, state abbreviations, or employee job skill codes. If the value in the field does not match one of the acceptable values, the record is flagged as an error.

This is a frequently used control in cash disbursement systems. One form of cash disbursement fraud involves manipulating the system into making a fraudulent payment to a nonexistent vendor. To prevent this, the firm may establish a list of valid vendors with whom it does business exclusively. Thus, before payment of any trade obligation, the vendor number on the cash disbursement voucher is matched against the valid vendor list by the validation program. If the code does not match, payment is denied, and the transaction is reviewed by management.

Processing Controls
After passing through the data input stage, transactions enter the processing stage of the system. Processing controls are programmed procedures and may be divided into three categories: *Batch controls, run-to-run controls,* and *audit trail controls.*

Batch controls are used to manage the flow of high volumes of transactions through batch processing systems. The objective of batch control is to reconcile output produced by the system with the input originally entered into the system. This provides assurance that:

- All records in the batch are processed.

- No records are processed more than once.

- An audit trail of transactions is created from input through processing to the output stage of the system.

Batch control begins at the data input stage and continues through all data processing phases of the system. Batch control involves grouping together into batches similar types of transactions (such as sales orders) and controlling them as a unit of work throughout data processing. To achieve this, a batch control record is created when the batch of transactions is entered into the system. This may be a user department action or a separate data control step. The control record contains relevant information about the batch, such as:

1. A unique batch number.
2. A batch date.
3. A transaction code (indicating the type of transactions, such as a sales order or cash receipt).
4. The number of records in the batch (record count).
5. The total dollar value of a financial field (batch control total).
6. The total of a unique nonfinancial field (hash total).

Figure 17-5 depicts a batch control record in relation to the batch of transactions it describes. The data in the control record are used to assess the integrity of the batch during all subsequent processing. For example, the batch control record in the figure shows a batch of 50 sales order records with a total dollar value of $122,674.87 and a hash total of 4537838.

Run-to-run control is the use of batch figures to monitor the batch as it moves from one programmed procedure (run) to another. Thus at various points throughout processing and at the end of processing, the batch totals are recalculated and compared to the batch control record. This ensures that each run in the system processes the batch correctly and completely.

Figure 17-6 illustrates the use of run-to-run control in a sales order system. This application comprises four runs: (1) data input, (2) accounts receivable update, (3) inventory update, and (4) output. At the end of the accounts receivable run, batch control figures are

FIGURE 17-5	Batch Control Record

	Batch Control Record					Batch of Sales Order Transactions		
Batch Number	Transaction Code	Date	Record Count	Hash Total	Control Total			
12403	019	01152006	50	4537838	12267487	Record1	*******	Record 50

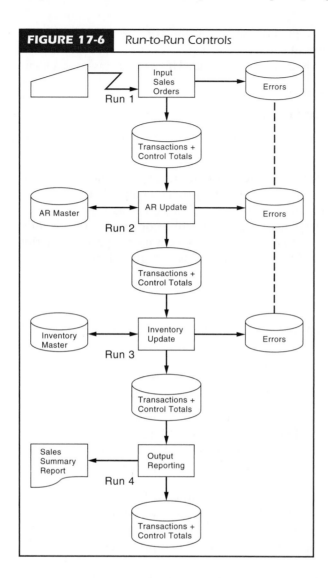

FIGURE 17-6   Run-to-Run Controls

recalculated and reconciled with the control totals passed from the data input run. These figures are then passed to the inventory update run, where they are again recalculated, reconciled, and passed to the output run. Errors detected in each run are flagged and placed in an error file. The run batch control figures are then adjusted to reflect the deletion of these records.

Notice from Figure 17-6 that error records may be placed on the error file at several different points in the process. In a separate procedure (not shown), an authorized user representative will make corrections to the error records and resubmit them as a special batch for reprocessing. Errors detected during processing require careful handling, because these records may already be partially processed. Simply resubmitting the corrected records to the system at the data input stage may result in processing portions of these transactions twice. Two methods are used to deal with this complexity. The first is to reverse the effects of the partially processed transactions and resubmit the corrected records to the data input stage. The second method is to reinsert corrected records into the processing stage at which the error was detected.

The term **hash total**, which was used in the preceding discussion, is the summation of a nonfinancial field to keep track of the records in a batch. Any numeric field, such as a customer's account number, a purchase order number, or an inventory item number, may be used to calculate a hash total. In the example below, the sales order number (SO#) field for an entire batch of sales order records is summed to produce a hash total.

```
SO#
14327
67345
19983
  •
  •
  •
  •
88943
96543
4537838    (hash total)
```

Let's see how this seemingly meaningless number can be of use. Assume that after this batch of records is created, someone replaced one of the sales orders in the batch with a fictitious record of the same dollar amount. How would the batch control procedures detect this irregularity? Both the record count and the dollar amount control totals would still balance. The hash total calculated by the batch control procedures would, however, not balance. The irregularity would thus be detected.

Audit Trail Controls in an IT environment ensure that every transaction can be traced through each stage of processing from its economic source to its presentation in financial statements. The following are examples of audit trail control.

Transaction Logs. Every transaction successfully processed by the system should be recorded on a transaction log, which serves as a journal. Figure 17-7 shows this process. Two reasons underscore the importance of this log. First, the transaction log is a permanent record of transactions, though the input transaction file is typically a temporary file. Once processed, the records on the input file are erased to make room for the next batch of transactions. Second, not all of the records in the input file may be successfully processed. Some of them will fail tests during subsequent processing and will be passed to an error file. A transaction log contains only successful transactions—those that have changed account balances. The transaction log and error files combined should account for all the transactions in the batch. The validated transaction file may then be scratched with no loss of data.

Log of Automatic Transactions. Some transactions are triggered internally by the system. For example, when inventory drops below the reorder point the system automatically generates a purchase order. To maintain an audit trail of these activities, all internally generated transactions must be placed in a transaction log.

Transaction Listings. The system should produce a (hard-copy) transaction listing of all successful transactions. These listings should go to the appropriate users to facilitate reconciliation with input. In addition, the responsible end user should receive a detailed listing of all internally generated transactions.

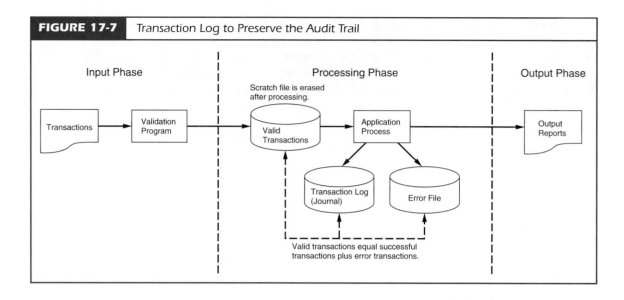

| FIGURE 17-7 | Transaction Log to Preserve the Audit Trail |

OUTPUT CONTROLS

Output controls are a combination of programmed routines and other procedures to ensure that system output is not lost, misdirected, or corrupted and that privacy is not violated. Exposures of this sort can cause serious disruptions to operations and may result in financial losses to a firm. For example, if the checks produced by a firm's cash disbursements system are lost, misdirected, or destroyed, trade accounts and other bills may go unpaid. This could damage the firm's credit rating and result in lost discounts, interest, or penalty charges. If the privacy of certain types of output is violated, a firm could have its business objectives compromised, or could become exposed to litigation. Examples of privacy exposures include the disclosure of trade secrets, patents pending, marketing research results, and patient medical records. This section examines output exposures and controls for both hard copy and digital output.

Controlling Hard Copy Output

Batch systems usually produce hard copy, which typically requires the involvement of intermediaries in its production and distribution. Figure 17-8 shows the stages in this output process and serves as the basis for this section.

Output Spooling. In large-scale data processing operations, output devices such as line printers can become backlogged with many programs simultaneously demanding limited resources. This can cause a bottleneck and adversely affect system throughput. To ease this burden, applications are often designed to direct their output to a magnetic disk file rather than print it directly. This is called **spooling**. Later, when printer resources become available, the output files are printed.

The creation of an output file as an intermediate step in the printing process presents an added exposure. A computer criminal may use this opportunity to:

1. Access the output file and change critical data values (such as dollar amounts on checks). The printer program will then print the fallacious output as if it was produced by the system.
2. Access the file and change the number of copies of output to be printed. The extra copies may then be removed without notice during the printing stage.

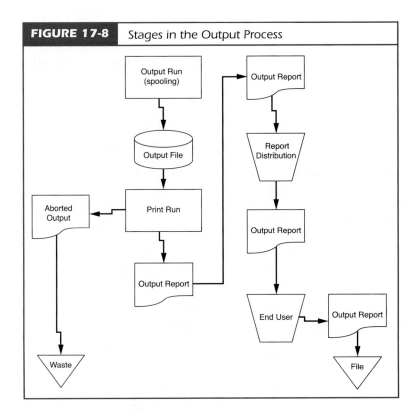

FIGURE 17-8   Stages in the Output Process

3. Make a copy of the output file to produce illegal output reports.
4. Destroy the output file before output printing takes place.

The management and auditors need to be aware of these potential exposures and ensure that proper access and backup procedures are in place to protect output files. File access and backup controls were discussed in Chapter 15.

Print Programs. When a printer becomes available, the print run program produces hard-copy output from the output file. Print programs are often complex systems that require operator intervention. Four common types of operator actions are:

1. Pausing the print program to load the correct type of output documents (check stocks, invoices, or other special forms).
2. Entering parameters needed by the print run, such as the number of copies to be printed.
3. Restarting the print run at a prescribed checkpoint after a printer malfunction.
4. Removing printed output from the printer for review and distribution.

Print program controls should be designed to deal with two types of exposures present in this environment: (1) the production of unauthorized copies of output and (2) employee browsing of sensitive data. Some print programs allow the operator to specify more copies of output than the output file calls for, which allows for the possibility of producing unauthorized copies of output. One way to control this is to employ output document controls. This is feasible only when dealing with prenumbered invoices for billing customers or prenumbered check stock. At the end of the run, the number of copies specified by the output file should be reconciled with the actual number of output documents used.

To prevent operators and others from viewing sensitive output, special multipart paper can be used, with a grayed-out top copy to prevent the print from being read. This type of product is often used for payroll check printing. An alternative privacy control is to direct the output to a special remote printer that can be closely supervised.

Waste. Computer output waste is a potential source of exposure. Aborted reports and the carbon copies from multipart paper need to be properly disposed of. Computer criminals disguised as janitorial staff have been known to sift through trashcans searching for carelessly discarded output that is presumed to be of no value. From such trash, computer criminals may obtain information about a firm's market research, credit ratings of its customers, or even trade secrets, which they can sell to a competitor. Computer waste is also a source of passwords that a perpetrator may use to access the firm's computer system. To control against this threat, all sensitive computer output should be passed through a paper shredder.

Report Distribution. The primary risks associated with the distribution of sensitive reports include their being lost, stolen, or misdirected in transit to the user. The following control techniques can be used:

1. The reports may be placed in a secure mailbox to which only the user has the key.
2. The user may be required to appear in person at the distribution center and sign for the report.
3. The report may be delivered to the user by a security officer or special courier.

End-User Controls. Once in the hands of the user, output reports should be examined for correctness. Errors detected by the user should be reported to the appropriate computer services management. Such errors may be symptoms of an improper systems design, incorrect procedures, errors inserted by accident during systems maintenance, or unauthorized access to data files or programs. Once a report has served its purpose, it should be stored in a secure location until its retention period has expired and then shredded.

Controlling Digital Output

Digital output can be directed to the user's computer screen or printer. The primary output threat is the interception, disruption, destruction, or corruption of the output message as it passes across the communications network. This threat comes from two types of exposures: (1) exposures from equipment failure and (2) exposures from subversive acts. Techniques for controlling communications exposures were discussed in Chapter 16.

TESTING COMPUTER APPLICATION CONTROLS

The appendix to Chapter 15 described how audit objectives are derived from management assertions such as *existence or occurrence, completeness, accuracy, rights and obligations, valuation or allocation,* and *presentation and disclosure.* Depending on the type of account being considered, a particular **management assertion** has different implications for the audit objective to be developed. Once developed, achieving the audit objectives requires designing **audit procedures** to gather evidence that either corroborates or refutes the underlying management assertions. Generally, this involves a combination of tests of application controls and substantive tests of transaction details and account balances.

This section deals essentially with the test of application controls, but at the end we will briefly review techniques for performing substantive tests. Tests of computer application controls follow two general approaches: (1) the black box (around the computer) approach and (2) the white box (through the computer) approach. First, the black box approach is examined. Then, several white box testing techniques are reviewed.

BLACK BOX APPROACH

Auditors performing black box testing do not rely on a detailed knowledge of the application's internal logic. Instead, they seek to understand the functional characteristics of the application by analyzing flowcharts and interviewing knowledgeable personnel in the client's organization. With an understanding of what the application is supposed to do, the auditor tests the application by reconciling production input transactions processed by the application with output results. The output results are analyzed to verify the application's compliance with its functional requirements. Figure 17-9 illustrates the black box approach.

The advantage of the black box approach is that the application need not be removed from service and tested directly. This approach is feasible for testing applications that are relatively simple. However, complex applications—those that receive input from many sources, perform a variety of complex operations, or produce multiple outputs—often require a more focused testing approach to provide the auditor with evidence of application integrity.

WHITE BOX APPROACH

The white box (through the computer) approach relies on an in-depth understanding of the internal logic of the application being tested. The white box approach includes several techniques for testing application logic directly. Typically these involve the creation of a small set of test transactions to verify specific aspects of an application's logic and controls. In this way, auditors are able to conduct precise tests, with known variables, and obtain results that they can compare against objectively calculated results. The most common types of tests of controls include the following:

1. **Authenticity tests**, which verify that an individual, a programmed procedure, or a message (such as an EDI transmission) attempting to access a system is authentic. Authenticity controls include user IDs, passwords, valid vendor codes, and authority tables.
2. **Accuracy tests**, which ensure that the system processes only data values that conform to specified tolerances. Examples include range tests, field tests, and limit tests.

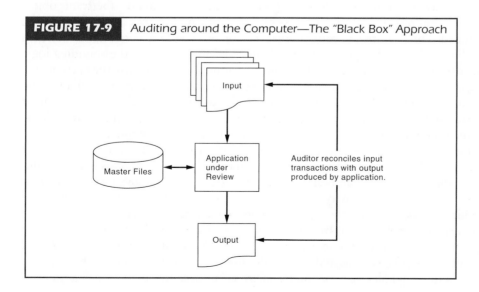

FIGURE 17-9   Auditing around the Computer—The "Black Box" Approach

3. **Completeness tests**, which identify missing data within a single record and entire records missing from a batch. The types of tests performed are field tests, record sequence tests, hash totals, and control totals.
4. **Redundancy tests**, which determine that an application processes each record only once. Redundancy controls include the reconciliation of batch totals, record counts, hash totals, and financial control totals.
5. **Access tests**, which ensure that the application prevents authorized users from unauthorized access to data. Access controls include passwords, authority tables, user-defined procedures, data encryption, and inference controls.
6. **Audit trail tests**, which ensure that the application creates an adequate audit trail. This includes evidence that the application records all transactions in a transaction log, posts data values to the appropriate accounts, produces complete transaction listings, and generates error files and reports for all exceptions.
7. **Rounding error tests**, which verify the correctness of rounding procedures. Rounding errors occur in accounting information when the level of precision used in the calculation is greater than that used in the reporting. For example, interest calculations on bank account balances may have a precision of five decimal places, whereas only two decimal places are needed to report balances. If the remaining three decimal places are simply dropped, the total interest calculated for the total number of accounts may not equal the sum of the individual calculations.

Figure 17-10 shows the logic for handling the rounding error problem. This technique uses an accumulator to keep track of the rounding differences between calculated and reported balances. Note how the sign and the absolute value of the amount in the accumulator determines how the customer account is affected by rounding. To illustrate, the rounding logic is applied to three hypothetical bank balances (see table on page 814). The interest calculations are based on an interest rate of 5.25 percent.

Failure to properly account for the rounding difference above can result in an imbalance between the total (control) figure and the sum of the detail figures for each account. Poor accounting for rounding differences can also present an opportunity for fraud.

Salami Fraud. Rounding programs are particularly susceptible to the so-called **salami fraud**. This fraud tends to affect large numbers of victims, but each in a minimal way. The fraud scheme takes its name from the analogy of slicing a large salami (the fraud objective) into many thin pieces. Each victim gets one of these small pieces and is unaware of being defrauded. For example, a programmer, or someone with access to the rounding program in Figure 17-10, can perpetrate a salami fraud by modifying the rounding logic as follows: at the point in the process where the algorithm should increase the current customer's account (that is, the accumulator value is > +.01), the program instead adds one cent to another account—the perpetrator's account. Although the absolute amount of each fraud transaction is small, given the hundreds of thousands of accounts that could be processed, the total amount of the fraud can become significant over time.

Most large public accounting firms have developed special audit software that can detect excessive file activity. In the case of the salami fraud, there would be thousands of entries into the computer criminal's personal account that may be detected by the audit software. A clever programmer may disguise this activity by funneling these entries through several intermediate accounts, which are then posted to a smaller number of intermediate accounts and finally to the programmer's personal account. By using many levels of accounts in this way, the activity to any single account is reduced and may go undetected by the audit software. There will be a trail, but it can be complicated. The auditor can also use audit software to detect the existence of unauthorized (dummy) files that contain the intermediate accounts used in such a fraud.

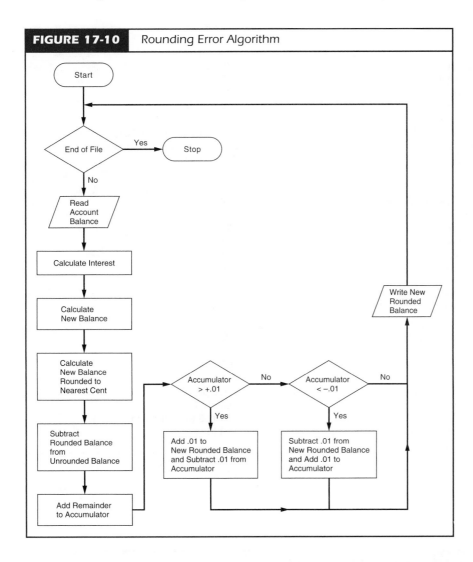

FIGURE 17-10 | Rounding Error Algorithm

WHITE BOX TESTING TECHNIQUES

To illustrate how application controls are tested, this section describes five **computer-assisted audit tools and techniques (CAATTs)** approaches: the *test data method*, **base case system** *evaluation, tracing, integrated test facility*, and *parallel simulation*.

Test Data Method

The **test data method** is used to establish application integrity by processing specially prepared sets of input data through production applications that are under review. The results of each test are compared to predetermined expectations to obtain an objective assessment of application logic and control effectiveness. The test data technique is illustrated in Figure 17-11. To perform the test data technique, a copy of the production version of the application must be obtained by the auditor. In addition, test transaction files and test master files must be created. As illustrated in the figure, test transactions may enter the system from magnetic tape, disk, or via an input terminal. Results from the test run will be in the form of routine output reports, transaction listings, and error reports. In addition, the auditor must review the updated master files to determine that account

Record 1

Beginning accumulator balance	.00861
Beginning account balance	2,741.78
Calculated interest	143.94345
New account balance	2,885.72345
Rounded account balance	2,885.72
Adjusted accumulator balance	.01206 (.00345 + .00861)
Ending account balance	**2,885.73 (round up 1 cent)**
Ending accumulator balance	.00206 (.01206 − .01)

Record 2

Beginning accumulator balance	.00206
Beginning account balance	1,893.44
Calculated interest	99.4056
New account balance	1,992.8456
Rounded account balance	1,992.85
Adjusted accumulator balance	−.00646 (.00206 − .0044)
Ending account balance	**1,992,85 (no change)**
Ending accumulator balance	−.00646

Record 3

Beginning accumulator balance	−.00646
Beginning account balance	7,423.34
Calculated interest	389.72535
New account balance	7,813.06535
Rounded account balance	7,813.07
Adjusted accumulator balance	−.01111 (.00646 − .00465)
Ending account balance	**7,813.06 (round down 1 cent)**
Ending accumulator balance	.00111

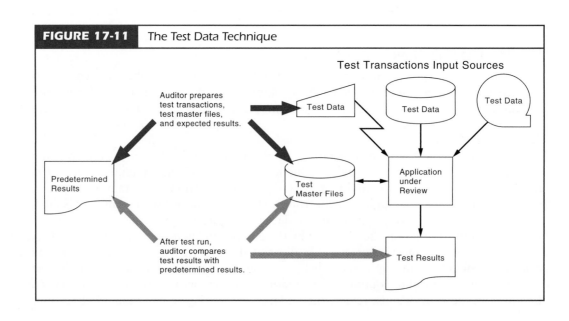

FIGURE 17-11   The Test Data Technique

balances have been correctly updated. The test results are then compared with the auditor's expected results to determine if the application is functioning properly. This comparison may be performed manually or through special computer software.

Figure 17-12 lists selected hypothetical transactions and accounts receivable records prepared by the auditor to test a sales order processing application. The figure also shows an error report of rejected transactions and a listing of the updated accounts receivable master file. Any deviations between the actual results obtained and those expected by the auditor may indicate a logic or control problem.

FIGURE 17-12 | Example of Test Data and Test Results

Test Transaction File

REC NUM	CUST NUM	CUSTOMER NAME	PART NUM	DESCRIPTION	QNTY	UNIT PRICE	TOTAL PRICE
1	231893	Smith, Joe	AX-612	Water Pump	1	20.00	20.00
2	231893	Azar, Atul	J-912	Gear	3	15.00	45.00
3	245851	Jones, Mary	123-LM	Hose	20	20.00	400.00
4	256519	Lang, Tony	Y-771	Spacer	5	2.00	10.00
5	259552	Tuner, Agnes	U-734	Bushing	5	25.00	120.00
6	175995	Hanz, James	EA-74	Seal	1	3.00	3.00
7	267991	Swindle, Joe	EN-12	Rebuilt Engine	1	1,220.00	1,220.00

Original Test AR Master File

CUST NUM	CUSTOMER NAME	CUSTOMER ADDRESS	CREDIT LIMIT	CURRENT BALANCE
231893	Smith, Joe	1520 S. Maple, City	1,000.00	400.00
256519	Lang, Tony	18 Etwine St., City	5,000.00	850.00
267991	Swindle, Joe	1 Shady Side, City	3,000.00	2,900.00

Updated Test AR Master File

CUST NUM	CUSTOMER NAME	CUSTOMER ADDRESS	CREDIT LIMIT	CURRENT BALANCE
231893	Smith, Joe	1520 S. Maple, City	1,000.00	420.00
256519	Lang, Tony	18 Etwine St., City	5,000.00	860.00
267991	Swindle, Joe	1 Shady Side, City	3,000.00	2,900.00

Error Report

REC NUM	CUST NUM	CUSTOMER NAME	PART NUM	DESCRIPTION	QNTY	UNIT PRICE	TOTAL PRICE	EXPLANATION OF ERROR
2	231893	Azar, Atul **X**	J-912	Gear	3	15.00	45.00	CUSTOMER NAME does not correspond to CUST # 231893
3	245851 **X**	Jones, Mary	123-LM	Hose	20	20.00	400.00	Check digit error in CUST # field
5	259552	Tuner, Agnes	U-734	Bushing	5	25.00	120.00 **X**	Price extension error
6	175995 **X**	Hanz, James	EA-74	Seal	1	3.00	3.00	Record out of sequence
7	267991	Swindle, Joe	EN-12	Rebuilt Engine	1	1,220.00 **X**	1,220.00 **X**	Credit limit error

Creating Test Data. Creating test data requires a complete set of valid and invalid transactions. Incomplete test data may fail to explore critical branches of application logic and error checking routines. Test transactions should be designed to test all possible input errors, logical processes, and irregularities.

Gaining knowledge of the application's internal logic sufficient to create meaningful test data may demand a large investment in time. The efficiency of this task can, however, be improved through careful planning during systems development. The test data used to test program modules during the implementation phase of the SDLC should be saved for future use by the auditor. If the application has undergone no maintenance since its initial implementation, current audit test results should equal the original test results obtained at implementation. If the application has been modified, the auditor can create additional test data that focus on the areas of the program changes.

Base Case System Evaluation

Base case system evaluation (BCSE) is a variant of the test data approach. BCSE tests are conducted with a set of test transactions containing all possible transaction types. These are processed through repeated iterations during systems development testing until consistent and valid results are obtained. These results are the base case. When subsequent changes to the application occur during maintenance, their effects are evaluated by comparing current results with base case results.

Tracing

Another type of the test data technique called **tracing** performs an electronic walkthrough of the application's internal logic. The tracing procedure involves three steps:

1. The application under review must undergo a special compilation to activate the trace option.
2. Specific transactions or types of transactions are created as test data.
3. The test data transactions are traced through all processing stages of the program, and a listing is produced of all programmed instructions that were executed during the test.

Figure 17-13 illustrates the tracing process using a portion of the logic for a payroll application. The example shows records from two payroll files—a transaction record showing hours worked and two records from a master file showing pay rates. The trace listing at the bottom of Figure 17-13 identifies the program statements that were executed and the order of execution. Analysis of trace options indicates that Commands 0001 through 0020 were executed. At that point, the application transferred to Command 0060. This occurred because the employee number (the key) of the transaction record did not match the key of the first record in the master file. Then Commands 0010 through 0050 were executed.

Advantages of Test Data Techniques

Test data techniques have three primary advantages. First, they employ through-the-computer testing, thus providing the auditor with explicit evidence concerning application functions. Second, if properly planned, test data runs can be employed with only minimal disruption to the organization's operations. Third, they require only minimal computer expertise on the part of auditors.

Disadvantages of Test Data Techniques

The primary disadvantage of test data techniques is that auditors rely on the client's IT personnel to obtain a copy of the production application under test. The **audit risk** here is that the IT personnel may intentionally or accidentally provide the auditor with the wrong version of the application. Audit evidence collected independently is more

FIGURE 17-13 | Tracing

Payroll Transaction File

Time Card #	Employee Number	Name	Year	Pay Period	Reg Hrs	OT Hrs
8945	33456	Jones, J.J.	2004	14	40.0	3.0

Payroll Master File

Employee Number	Hourly Rate	YTD Earnings	Dependents	YTD Withhold	YTD FICA
33276	15	12,050	3	3,200	873.62
33456	15	13,100	2	3,600	949.75

Computer Program Logic

```
0001    Read Record from Transaction File
0010    Read Record from Master File
0020    If Employee Number (T) = Employee Number (M)
0030        Wage = (Reg Hrs + [OT Hrs x 1.5] ) x Hourly Rate
0040        Add Wage to YTD Earnings
0050        Go to 0001
0060    Else Go to 0010
```

Trace Listing
0001, 0010, 0020, 0060, 0010, 0020, 0030, 0040, 0050

reliable than evidence supplied by the client. A second disadvantage is that these techniques produce a static picture of application integrity at a single point in time. They do not provide a convenient means for gathering evidence of ongoing application functionality. High cost of implementation is a third disadvantage of test data techniques. The auditor must devote considerable time to understanding program logic and creating test data. The following section shows how automating testing techniques can resolve these problems.

THE INTEGRATED TEST FACILITY

The **integrated test facility** (ITF) approach is an automated technique that enables the auditor to test an application's logic and controls during its normal operation. The ITF involves one or more audit modules designed into the application during the systems development process. In addition, ITF databases contain "dummy" or test master file records integrated among legitimate records. Some firms create a dummy company to which test transactions are posted. During normal operations, test transactions are merged into the input stream of regular (production) transactions and are processed against the files of the dummy company. Figure 17-14 illustrates the ITF concept.

ITF audit modules are designed to discriminate between ITF transactions and production data. This may be accomplished in a number of ways. One of the simplest and most commonly used is to assign a unique range of key values exclusively to ITF transactions. For example, in a sales order processing system, account numbers between 2000 and 2100 are reserved for ITF transactions and will not be assigned to actual customer accounts. By segregating ITF transactions from legitimate transactions in this way, routine reports produced by the application are not corrupted by ITF test data. Test results are produced separately in digital or hard-copy form and distributed directly to the auditor. Just as with the test data techniques, the auditor analyzes ITF results against expected results.

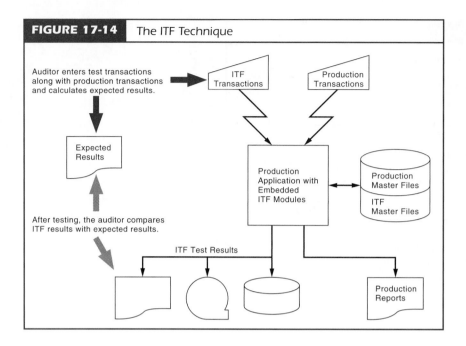

FIGURE 17-14 The ITF Technique

Advantages of ITF
The ITF technique has two advantages over test data techniques. First, ITF supports ongoing monitoring of controls as recommended by COSO. Second, ITF enhanced applications can be economically tested without disrupting the user's operations and without the intervention of computer services personnel. Thus, ITF improves the efficiency of the audit and increases the reliability of the audit evidence gathered.

Disadvantages of ITF
The primary disadvantage of ITF is the potential for corrupting data files with test data that may end up in the financial reporting process. Steps must be taken to ensure that ITF test transactions do not materially affect financial statements by being improperly aggregated with legitimate transactions. This problem can be remedied in two ways: (1) adjusting entries may be processed to remove the effects of ITF from general ledger account balances or (2) data files can be scanned by special software that remove the ITF transactions.

PARALLEL SIMULATION

Parallel simulation requires the auditor to create a program that simulates key features or processes of the application under review. The simulated application is then used to reprocess transactions that were previously processed by the production application. This technique is illustrated in Figure 17-15. The results obtained from the simulation are reconciled with the results of the original production run to establish a basis for making inferences about the quality of application processes and controls.

Creating a Simulation Program
Simulation packages are commercially available and are sometimes a feature of generalized audit software (GAS).[2] The steps involved in performing parallel simulation testing are outlined in the following section.

---

2   Although generalized audit software (GAS) can be used for testing internal controls, it is primarily a substantive testing technique. For this reason, this technology is discussed in the section that deals with substantive testing.

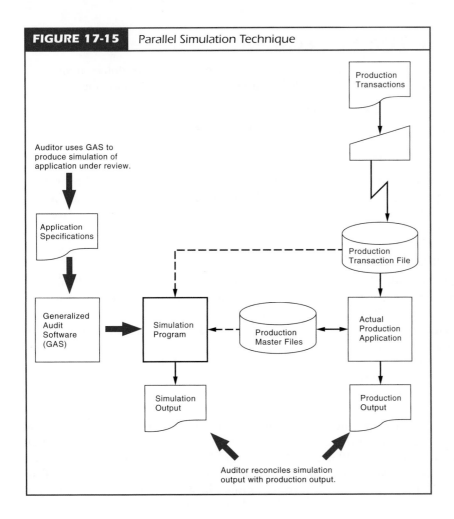

FIGURE 17-15 Parallel Simulation Technique

1. The auditor must first gain a thorough understanding of the application under review. Complete and current documentation of the application is required to construct an accurate simulation.
2. The auditor must then identify those processes and controls in the application that are critical to the audit. These are the processes to be simulated.
3. The auditor creates the simulation using a fourth-generation language or generalized audit software.
4. The auditor runs the simulation program using selected production transactions and master files to produce a set of results.
5. Finally, the auditor evaluates and reconciles the test results with the production results produced in a previous run.

Simulation programs are usually less complex than the production applications they represent. Because simulations contain only the application processes, calculations, and controls relevant to specific audit objectives, the auditor must carefully evaluate differences between test results and production results. Differences in output results occur for two reasons: (1) the inherent crudeness of the simulation program and (2) real deficiencies in the application's processes or controls, which are made apparent by the simulation program.

SUBSTANTIVE TESTING TECHNIQUES

Substantive tests are so named because they are used to substantiate dollar amounts in account balances. Substantive tests include but are not limited to the following:

1. Determining the correct value of inventory.
2. Determining the accuracy of prepayments and accruals.
3. Confirming accounts receivable with customers.
4. Searching for unrecorded liabilities.

Before substantive tests can be performed, these data must first be extracted from their host media and presented to the auditor in usable form. The two CAATTs examined in this section assist the auditor in selecting, accessing, and organizing data used for performing substantive tests.

THE EMBEDDED AUDIT MODULE

Embedded audit module (EAM) techniques use one or more programmed modules embedded in a host application to select for subsequent analysis transactions that meet predetermined conditions. This approach is illustrated in Figure 17-16.

As the selected transaction is being processed by the host application, a copy of it is stored on an audit file for subsequent review. The EAM approach allows material transactions to be captured throughout the audit period. Captured transactions are retrieved by the auditor at period end or at any time during the period, thus significantly reducing the amount of work the auditor must do to identify significant transactions for substantive testing.

To begin data capturing, the auditor specifies to the EAM the parameters and materiality threshold of the transactions set to be captured. For example, assume that the auditor establishes a $50,000 materiality threshold for transactions processed by a sales order processing system. Transactions equal to or greater than $50,000 will be copied to the audit file. From this set of transactions, the auditor will select a subset to be used for substantive tests. Transactions that fall below this threshold will be ignored by the EAM.

Though primarily a substantive testing technique, EAMs may also be used to monitor controls on an ongoing basis as recommended in the COSO framework. For example, transactions selected by the EAM can be reviewed for proper authorization, completeness and accuracy of processing, and correct posting to accounts.

Disadvantages of EAMs
The EAM approach has two significant disadvantages. The first pertains to operational efficiency and the second to EAM integrity.

Operational Efficiency. From the user's point of view, EAMs decrease operational performance. The presence of an audit module within the host application may create significant overhead, particularly when the level of testing is high. One approach for relieving this burden from the system is to design modules that may be "turned on and off" by the auditor. Doing so will, of course, reduce the effectiveness of the EAM as an ongoing audit tool.

Verifying EAM Integrity. The EAM approach may not be a viable audit technique in environments with a high level of program maintenance. When host applications are undergoing frequent changes, the EAMs embedded within the hosts will also require

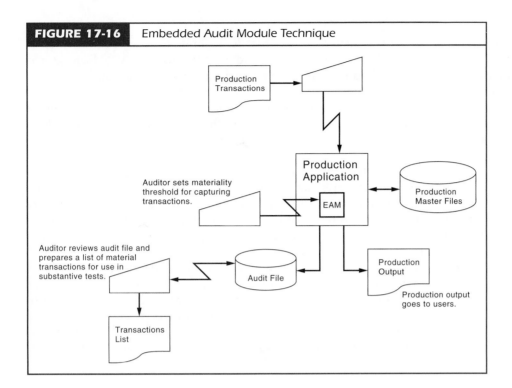

FIGURE 17-16   Embedded Audit Module Technique

frequent modifications. The integrity concerns raised earlier regarding application maintenance apply equally to EAMs. The integrity of EAM directly affects the quality of the audit process. Auditors must therefore evaluate the EAM integrity. This would be accomplished in the same way as testing the host application controls.

GENERALIZED AUDIT SOFTWARE

Generalized audit software (GAS) is the most widely used CAATT for IS auditing. GAS allows auditors to access electronically coded data files and perform various operations on their contents. ACL and IDEA are currently the leading products but others exist with similar features. The following audit tasks can be performed using GAS:

1. Footing and balancing entire files or selected data items.
2. Selecting and reporting detailed data contained on files.
3. Selecting stratified statistical samples from data files.
4. Formatting results of tests into reports.
5. Printing confirmations in either standardized or special wording.
6. Screening data and selectively including or excluding items.
7. Comparing two files and identifying any differences.
8. Recalculating data fields.

The widespread popularity of GAS is due to four factors: (1) GAS languages are easy to use and require little IT background on the part of the auditor, (2) GAS may be used on any type of computer because it is hardware independent, (3) auditors can perform their tests on data independent of client IT professional, and (4) GAS can be used to audit the data files of many different applications (in contrast with EAMs, which are application specific).

Using GAS to Access Simple Structures

Accessing flat file structures (such as a text file) is a simple process, as illustrated in Figure 17-17. In this example an inventory file is read directly into the GAS, which extracts key information needed for the audit, including the quantity on hand, the dollar value, and the warehouse location of each inventory item. The auditor's task is to verify the existence and value of the inventory by performing a physical count of a representative sample of the inventory on hand. Thus, on the basis of a materiality threshold provided by the auditor, the GAS selects the sample records and prepares a report with the key information.

Using GAS to Access Complex Structures

Gaining access to complex structures, such as VSAM files and object-oriented database files poses more of a problem for the auditor. Most DBMSs, however, have utility features that will reformat complex structures into flat files. In such cases, rather than accessing the complex structure directly, an intermediate flat file is produced, which the GAS then accesses. Figure 17-18 shows this technique.

To illustrate the file flattening process, consider the complex database structure presented in Figure 17-19. The database structure uses pointers to integrate three related files—Customer, Sales Invoice, and Line Item—in a hierarchical model. It would be difficult, if not impossible, to extract audit evidence from a structure of this complexity using GAS. A simpler flat file version of this structure is illustrated in Figure 17-20. The resulting single text represents the three record types as a sequential structure with variable length records that can be easily accessed by GAS.

Audit Issue Pertaining to the Creation of Flat Files

When auditors may rely on client IT personnel to produce a flat file from their database, they run the risk that database integrity will be compromised. For example, if the auditor is confirming accounts receivable, certain fraudulent accounts in the original database may be intentionally omitted from the flat file provided to the auditor. Auditors skilled in relational and object database technology can avoid this problem. Not surprisingly, public accounting firms are aggressively seeking employees with strong computer skills to accompany their accounting training.

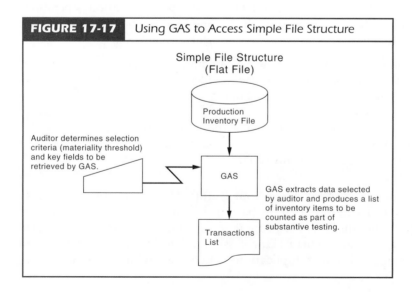

FIGURE 17-17   Using GAS to Access Simple File Structure

FIGURE 17-18   Using GAS to Access Complex File Structure

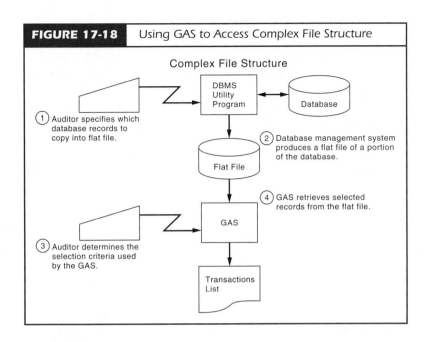

Complex File Structure

① Auditor specifies which database records to copy into flat file.

DBMS Utility Program ↔ Database

② Database management system produces a flat file of a portion of the database.

Flat File

④ GAS retrieves selected records from the flat file.

GAS

③ Auditor determines the selection criteria used by the GAS.

Transactions List

FIGURE 17-19   Complex Database Structure

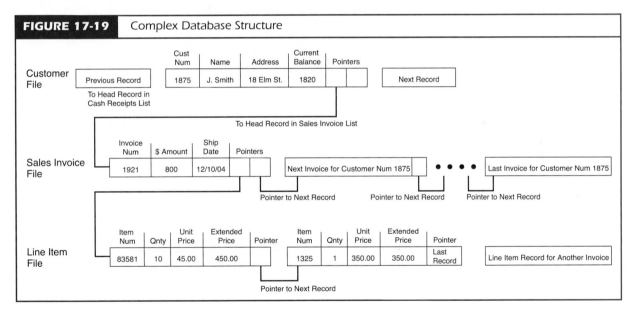

Customer File

Previous Record	Cust Num	Name	Address	Current Balance	Pointers		Next Record
	1875	J. Smith	18 Elm St.	1820			

To Head Record in Cash Receipts List

To Head Record in Sales Invoice List

Sales Invoice File

Invoice Num	$ Amount	Ship Date	Pointers		Next Invoice for Customer Num 1875	• • • •	Last Invoice for Customer Num 1875
1921	800	12/10/04					

Pointer to Next Record   Pointer to Next Record   Pointer to Next Record

Line Item File

Item Num	Qnty	Unit Price	Extended Price	Pointer	Item Num	Qnty	Unit Price	Extended Price	Pointer	Line Item Record for Another Invoice
83581	10	45.00	450.00		1325	1	350.00	350.00	Last Record	

Pointer to Next Record

FIGURE 17-20   Flat Version of a Complex File Structure

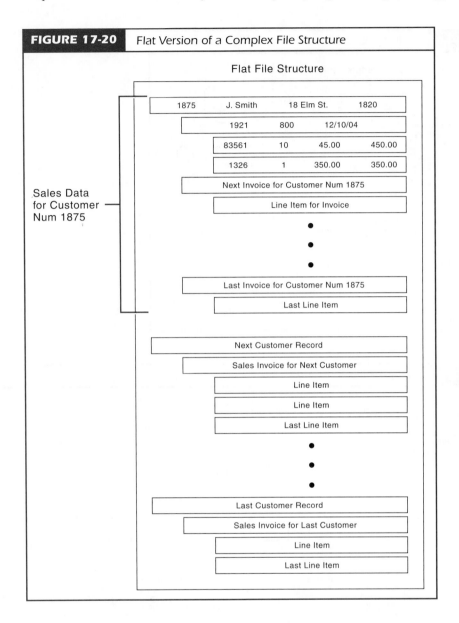

SUMMARY

Sarbanes-Oxley (SOX) legislation requires management to design, implement, and certify controls over financial reporting. Similarly, external auditors are required to attest to management's assessment of controls. This chapter dealt with the business risks, IT controls, and test of controls pertaining to three areas of specific concern to SOX: systems development, program change procedures, and computer applications. The integrity of financial data is directly dependent on the accuracy of the applications that process them. Likewise, the integrity of those applications depends on the quality of the systems development process that produced them and on the program change procedures through which they were modified. Lack of control over these areas, or inconsistency in their function, can result in unintentional application errors and program fraud. The systems development and maintenance controls and the test of controls described in this chapter apply both to management's SOX-compliance objectives and the auditor's attest responsibility. To test specific application controls, auditors (internal and external) use several CAATT techniques, including the test data method, the integrated test facility, and parallel simulation. This chapter concluded a discussion of two popular CAATTs (embedded audit module and generalized audit software) used for substantive testing.

KEY TERMS

access tests (812)

accuracy tests (811)

audit objectives (795)

audit procedures (810)

audit risk (816)

audit trail tests (812)

authenticity tests (811)

base case system evaluation (BCSE) (816)

completeness (802)

completeness tests (812)

computer-assisted audit tools and techniques (CAATTs) (813)

embedded audit module (EAM) (820)

existence or occurrence (810)

generalized audit software (GAS) (821)

integrated test facility (ITF) (817)

management assertions (810)

operating system (798)

parallel simulation (818)

presentation and disclosure (810)

redundancy tests (812)

rights and obligations (810)

rounding error tests (812)

salami fraud (812)

substantive tests (820)

test data method (813)

tests of controls (800)

tracing (816)

valuation or allocation (810)

REVIEW QUESTIONS

1. List the six systems development controls discussed in the chapter. List the two systems maintenance controls.
2. Explain how program testing is conducted and the importance of test data.
3. List the control features that directly contribute to the security of the computer center environment.
4. What is the purpose of a valid vendor file?
5. What are the broad classes of input controls?
6. Give one example of an error that is detected by a check digit control.
7. What are the primary objectives of a batch control?
8. What are the categories of processing controls?
9. If all of the inputs have been validated before processing, then what purpose do run-to-run controls serve?

10. What is the objective of a transaction log?

11. How can spooling present an added exposure?

12. What tests may be conducted for identifying unauthorized program changes?

13. What tests may be conducted for identifying application errors?

14. What is meant by auditing around the computer versus auditing through the computer? Why is this so important?

15. What are some white box tests?

16. What is an embedded audit module?

17. Explain what GAS is and why it is so popular with larger public accounting firms. Discuss the independence issue related to GAS.

18. What is the purpose of a limit check?

19. What is the purpose of a range check?

20. What is a reasonableness test?

21. What is a validity check?

22. What is a run-to-run control?

23. What information would a batch control record contain?

DISCUSSION QUESTIONS

1. Discuss how a controlled SPL environment can help to deter unauthorized changes to programs. Can the use of maintenance commands mitigate these controls?

2. What types of output would be considered extremely sensitive in a university setting? Give three examples and explain why the information would be considered sensitive. Discuss who should and should not have access to each type of information.

3. What are the classes of transcription errors?

4. What is the purpose of a check digit?

5. Does a hash total need to be based on a financial data field? Explain.

6. Discuss the three common methods of handling errors in transaction files.

7. Why is computer waste disposal a potential internal control issue?

8. Why would a systems programmer create a back door if he or she has access to the program in his or her day-to-day tasks?

9. The systems development life cycle is a methodology. Why are auditors responsible for evaluating the controls in this process?

10. What factors do you think might cause an auditing team to spend more time than average on tests to identify application errors? For unauthorized program changes?

11. Explain how an embedded audit module works.

12. Compare and contrast the following techniques based on costs and benefits:
    - test data method
    - base case system evaluation
    - tracing
    - integrated test facility
    - parallel simulation

13. What is the control issue related to reentering corrected error records into a batch processing system? What are the two methods for doing this?

MULTIPLE-CHOICE QUESTIONS

1. Computer applications use routines for checking the validity and accuracy of transaction data called
   a. operating systems.
   b. edit programs.
   c. compiler programs.
   d. integrated test facilities.
   e. compatibility tests.

2. How does a direct access file processing system edit individual transactions?
   a. takes place in a separate computer run
   b. takes place on-line mode as transactions are entered
   c. takes place during a backup procedure
   d. is not performed due to time constraints
   e. is not necessary

3. Which of the following is an example of an input control?

   a. making sure that output is distributed to the proper people

   b. monitoring the work of programmers

   c. collecting accurate statistics of historical transactions while gathering data

   d. recalculating an amount to ensure its accuracy

   e. having another person review the design of a business form

4. A control designed to validate a transaction at the point of data entry is

   a. recalculation of a batch total.

   b. a record count.

   c. a check digit.

   d. checkpoints.

   e. recalculation of hash total.

5. In a computer system, how are accounting records posted?

   a. master file is updated to a transaction file

   b. master file is updated to an index file

   c. transaction file is updated to a master file

   d. master file is updated to a year-to-date file

   e. current balance file is updated to an index file

6. The controls in a computerized system are classified as:

   a. input, processing, and output.

   b. input, processing, output, and storage.

   c. input, processing, output, and control.

   d. input, processing, output, storage, and control.

   e. collecting, sorting, summarizing, and reporting.

7. An employee in the receiving department keyed in a shipment from a remote terminal and inadvertently omitted the purchase order number. The best systems control to detect this error would be a

   a. batch total.

   b. completeness test.

   c. sequence check.

   d. reasonableness test.

   e. compatibility test.

8. In an automated payroll processing environment, a department manager substituted the time card for a terminated employee with a time card for a fictitious employee. The fictitious employee had the same pay rate and hours worked as the terminated employee. The best control technique to detect this action using employee identification numbers would be a

   a. batch total.

   b. record count.

   c. hash total.

   d. subsequent check.

   e. financial total.

9. Sarbanes-Oxley legislation calls for sound internal control practices over financial reporting and requires SEC-registered corporations to maintain systems of internal control that meet SOX standards. An integral part of internal control is the appropriate use of preventive controls. Which of the following is not an essential element of preventive control?

   a. separation of responsibilities for the recording, custodial, and authorization functions

   b. sound personnel practices

   c. documentation of policies and procedures

   d. implementation of state-of-the-art software and hardware

   e. physical protection of assets

10. Which of the following is NOT a test for identifying application errors?

    a. reconciling the source code

    b. reviewing test results

    c. retesting the program

    d. testing the authority table

11. Which of the following is NOT a common type of white box test of controls?

    a. completeness tests

    b. redundancy tests

    c. inference tests

    d. authenticity tests

12. An electronic walkthrough of the application's internal logic is called

    a. a salami logic test.

    b. an integrated test.

    c. tracing.

    d. a logic bomb test.

PROBLEMS

1. Input Validation

Describe the types of application control used for the following data in a payroll system.

a. Employee name
b. Employee number
c. Social Security number
d. Rate per hour or salary
e. Marital status
f. Number of dependents
g. Cost center
h. Regular hours worked
i. Overtime hours worked
j. Total employees this payroll period

2. Computer Fraud and Controls

Although the threat to security via external penetration is often seen as the greatest threat, many threats are internal. Computer frauds include (1) input manipulation, (2) program alteration, (3) file alteration, (4) data theft, and (5) sabotage.

Required:

For the five types of fraud identified above, explain how each is committed. Also, identify a method of protection against each. The same protection method should not be used for more than one type of fraud. Use the following format.

Type of Fraud	Explanation	Description of Protection Methods
a.		
b.		
c.		
d.		
e.		
f.		

3. Processing Controls

A well-designed system can prevent both intentional and unintentional alteration and destruction of data. These data controls can be classified as (1) input controls, (2) processing controls, and (3) output controls

Required:

For each of the three control categories listed, provide two specific controls and explain how each control contributes to ensuring the reliability of data. Use the following format for your answer.

Control Category	Specific Controls	Contribution to Data Reliability

4. Input Controls and Data Processing

You have been hired by a catalog company to computerize its sales order entry forms. Approximately 60 percent of all orders are received over the telephone, with the remainder either mailed or faxed in. The company wants the phone orders to be input as they are received. The mail and fax orders can be batched together in groups of 50 and submitted for keypunching as they become ready. The following information is collected for each order:

- Customer number (if customer does not have one, one needs to be assigned)
- Customer name
- Address
- Payment method (credit card or money order)
- Credit card number and expiration date (if necessary)
- Items ordered and quantity
- Unit price

Required:

Determine control techniques to make sure that all orders are entered accurately into the system. Also, discuss any differences in control measures between the batch and the real-time processing.

5. Audit Plan

Rainbow Paint Company, a medium-sized manufacturing firm, has no internal auditing department. It recently hired a new accounting firm to perform the external audit.

Required:

Outline an audit plan to examine operating system control, program maintenance controls, and organizational system controls. Include in your plan the audit objectives, exposures, necessary controls, and test of controls. Also include any documentation the auditors should request.

6. Audit Plan

The auditors for Golden Gate Company have a gut feeling that liabilities may be unrecorded. Their initial suspicions stem from a radical decline in accrued liabilities from last year. Golden Gate's records are all computerized.

Required:

Devise a plan to search the data files to perform a substantive test for identifying unrecorded liabilities.

7. Exposure Identification and Plan of Action

Two years ago an external auditing firm supervised the programming of embedded audit modules for Previts Office Equipment Company. During the audit process this year, the external auditors requested that a transaction log of all transactions be copied to the audit file. The external auditors noticed large gaps in dates and times for transactions being copied to the audit file. When they inquired about this, they were informed that increased processing of transactions had been burdening the mainframe system and that operators frequently had to turn off the EAM to allow the processing of important transactions in a timely fashion. In addition, much maintenance had been performed during the past year on the application programs.

Required:

Outline any potential exposures and determine the courses of action the external auditors should use to proceed.

8. Exposure Identification and Plan of Action

The internal auditors of Brown Electrical Company report to the controller. Due to changes made in the past year to several of the transaction processing programs, the internal auditors created a new test data set. The external auditors requested that the old data set also be run. The internal auditors embarrassingly explained that they overwrote the original test data set.

Required:

Outline any potential exposures and determine the courses of action the external auditor should take.

9. Exposure Identification and Plan of Action

As the manager of the external audit team, you realize that the embedded audit module only writes "material" invoices to the audit file for the accounts receivable confirmation process. You are immediately concerned that the accounts receivable account

may be substantially overstated this year and for the prior years in which this EAM was used.

Required:

Explain why you are concerned because all "material" invoices are candidates for confirmation by the customer. Outline a plan for determining if the accounts receivable are overstated.

10. Audit Objectives and Procedures

As an auditor, discuss any concerns that you would have, and any actions that you would take, in the following situation:

You are conducting substantive tests on the accounts receivable file to verify its accuracy. The file is large, and you decide to test only a sample of the records. Because of the complexity of the database structure you cannot access the database directly. The client's systems programmer uses a utility program to write a query that produces a flat file, which he provides for testing purposes.

11. Systems Development and Program Changes

Avatar Financials Inc., located on Madison Avenue, New York is a company that provides financial advice to individuals and small to mid-sized businesses. Its primary operations are in wealth management and financial advice. Each client has an account where basic personal information is stored at a server within the main office in New York City. The company also keeps the information about the amount of investment of each client on a separate server at their data center in Bethlehem, Pennsylvania. This information includes the total value of the portfolio, type of investments made, the income structure of each client, and associated tax liabilities.

Avatar decided to purchase software for asset management from specialized vendors. This software allows them to run analytics on the portfolios and run detailed simulations of market trends and is called Siman (*SIM*ulation *ANa*laytics). V-Dot Solutions, another contractual company that is customizing and installing Siman has sent a team of six systems analysts to carry out this task. They anticipate additional hardware installations to run the simulation analytics on Siman.

V-dot's setup requires them to train two people from Avatar who will be responsible for minor issues and basic maintenance of the system. Major problems and issues will be dealt with by special consultants from V-Dot. It takes four weeks to completely have the system operational and integrated into Avatar's existing computer system. The testing phase of the project has been readjusted to allow the two employees of Avatar to run these tests and ensure compatibility.

A year after the installation of the simulation software Siman, Avatar finds it very useful. To further upgrade the systems to the next level, they decide to another data source company for raw market data feed which is used to run the simulations. However, this requires changes to the source code of Siman. Fortunately, within its analytics department that uses Siman, Avatar has two programmers who are well versed in the programming language that Siman was written in. These programmers are able to implement the changes that will allow the new data feed to be used by Siman-II.

To remain competitive, Avatar has placed the programmers under a tight time constraint. To expedite the process, the documentation process is shortened with the intention that it will be looked into once the systems are running. The programmers also will be deployed back to the maintenance operations once the project is complete. The contract with original vendor of Siman, V-Dot, has expired and the company does not want to extend their maintenance services for another year. Instead it feels that these two programmers will be able to perform the same tasks for less money.

Required:
Answer the following questions:

a. Discuss the major internal control issues in Avatar's system development approach.

b. Comment on the duties performed by the two programmers of Avatar. Are systems maintenance and program development extensions of the same responsibility?

c. Identify potential issues that might arise due to weak internal controls.

12. Generalized Audit Software (CMA Adapted)

The internal audit department of Sachem Manufacturing Company is considering buying computer software that will aid in the auditing process.

Sachem's financial and manufacturing control systems are completely automated on a large mainframe computer. Melinda Robinson, the director of internal audit, believes that Sachem should acquire computer audit software to assist in the financial and procedure audits that her department conducts. The types of software packages that Robinson is considering are described in the following section.

- A generalized audit software package that assists in basic audit work, such as the retrieval of live data from large computer files. The department would review this information using conventional audit investigation techniques. Specifically, the department could perform criteria selection, sampling, basic computations for quantitative analysis, record handling, graphical analysis, and the printing of output (confirmations).

- An integrated test facility package that uses, monitors, and controls dummy test data through existing programs and checks the existence and adequacy of program data entry controls and processing controls.

- A control flowcharting package that provides a graphical presentation of the data flow of information through a system, pinpointing control strengths and weaknesses.

- A program (parallel) simulation and modeling package that uses actual data to conduct the same systemized process by using a different computer-logic program developed by the auditor. The package can also be used to seek answers to difficult audit problems (involving many comparisons and computations) within statistically acceptable confidence limits.

Required:

a. Without regard to any specific computer audit software, explain to the internal auditor the general advantages of using computer audit software to assist with audits.

b. Describe the audit purpose facilitated and the procedural steps to be followed by the internal auditor to use a(n)

1. generalized audit software package.
2. integrated test facility package.
3. control flowcharting package.
4. program (parallel) simulation and modeling package.

13. Audit of Systems Development (CMA Adapted)

Andre Co's chief information officer, Robert Ganning, has been asked to present a plan for the development and implementation of a new system. Peter Martin, an internal auditor for Andre Co, has been asked to review the plan to ensure its validity.

"I think it would be better if we worked together throughout the process," Martin told Ganning. "I see three distinct review phases that should be handled as consecutive elements in the process of developing the new system: specification, design, and system. Each phase should be completed and reviewed before the next phase is begun."

Martin defined the three phases as follows:

- *Specification review.* A review of the system definition to determine if the system provides for the internal control objectives of authorization, recording, safeguarding assets, and substantiation.
- *Design review.* A review of the detailed design to ensure that the system procedures and controls will accomplish the requirements established and approved in the specification review.
- *System review.* A trial run of the actual system during implementation to ascertain the presence of the original objective. Errors or omissions in translation of the designed system to an actual, implemented system would be detected.

Ganning and Martin agreed that a three-phase review approach would be both effective and efficient, and they proceeded on that basis.

Required:

a. Identify and discuss the considerations that should be part of the specification review process.

b. Recommend procedures that would help to validate the system development activities in the
    1. design review.
    2. system review.

c. Formulate an acceptance test as a final verification of the system's adequacy and integrity.

14. Payroll Application Control

Using the supplemental information below analyze the flowchart shown on the following page.

- The personnel department determines the wage rate of all employees. Personnel starts the process by sending an authorization form for adding an employee to the payroll to the payroll coordinator George Jones. After Jones enters this information into the system, the computer automatically determines the overtime and shift differential rates for the individual, updating the payroll master files.

- Employees use a time clock to record the hours worked. Every Monday morning. George Jones collects the previous week's time cards and begins the computerized processing of payroll information to produce paychecks the following Friday. Jones then reviews the time cards to ensure that the hours worked are correctly totaled; the system determines overtime and/or any shift differential.

- All other processes displayed on the flowchart are performed by Jones. The system automatically assigns a sequential number to each payroll check produced. The check stocks are stored in a box next to the computer printer to provide immediate access. After the checks are printed, Jones uses an automatic check-signing machine to sign them with an authorized signature plate that he keeps locked in a safe.

- After the check processing is completed, Jones distributes the checks to the employees, leaving the checks for the second- and third-shift employees with the appropriate shift supervisor. Jones then notifies the data processing department that he is finished with his weekly processing, and data processing makes a backup of the payroll master for storage in the computer room.

Required:

Identify and describe:

a. Areas in the payroll processing system where the internal controls are inadequate.

b. Two areas in the payroll system where the system controls are satisfactory.

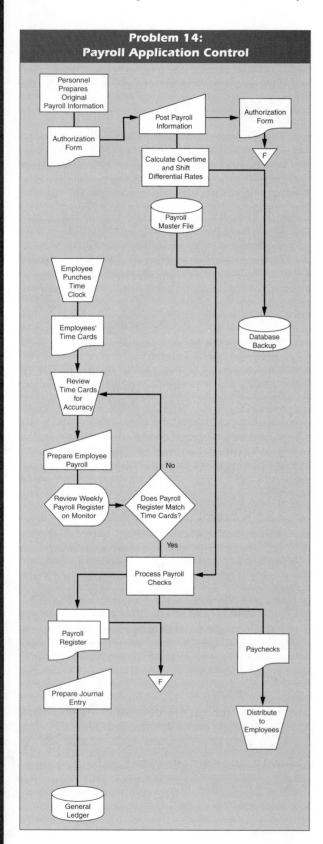

Problem 14:
Payroll Application Control

Glossary

The chapter in which the term is first defined is set in parentheses following the definition.

A

Access controls: Controls that ensure that only authorized personnel have access to the firm's assets. (3)

Access method: The technique used to locate records and to navigate through the database. (2)

Access tests: Tests that ensure that the application prevents authorized users from unauthorized access to data. (17)

Accounting information systems (AIS): Specialized subset of information system that processes financial transactions. (1)

Accounting record: A document, journal, or ledger used in transaction cycles. (2)

Accounts payable pending file: File containing a copy of the purchase requisition. (5)

Accuracy tests: Tests that ensure that the system processes only data values that conform to specified tolerances. (17)

Activities: Work performed in a firm. (7)

Activity-based costing (ABC): Accounting technique that provides managers with information about activities and cost objects. (7)

Activity driver: Factor that measures the activity consumption by the cost object. (7)

Agents: Individuals and departments that participate in an economic event. (1)

Alphabetic codes: Alphabetic characters assigned sequentially. (8)

Alphanumeric codes: Codes that allow the use of pure alphabetic characters embedded within numeric codes. (8)

American National Standards Institute (ANSI): The most popular EDI standard in the United States. (12)

Archive file: File that contains records of past transactions that are retained for future reference. (2)

Association: The relationship among record types. (9)

Attendance file: File created by the timekeeping department upon receipt of approved time cards. (6)

Attributes: Equivalents to adjectives in the English language that serve to describe the objects. (9)

Audit opinion: Opinion of auditor regarding the presentation of financial statements. (15)

Audit planning: Stage at which the auditor identifies the financially significant applications and attempts to understand the controls over the primary transactions that are processed by these applications. (15)

Audit risk: Probability that the auditor will render unqualified opinions on financial statements that are, in fact, materially misstated. (15)

Audit trail: Accounting records that trace transactions from their source documents to the financial statements. (2)

Auditing: Form of independent attestation performed by an expert who expresses an opinion about the fairness of a company's financial statements. (1)

Authenticity tests: Tests verifying that an individual, a programmed procedure, or a message attempting to access a system is authentic. (17)

Authority: The right to make decisions pertaining to areas of responsibility. (8)

Automated storage and retrieval systems (AS/RS): Computer-controlled conveyor systems that carry raw materials from stores to the shop floor and finished products to the warehouse. (7)

B

Backbone systems: Basic system structure on which to build. (1)

Base case system evaluation (BCSE): Variant of the test data technique, in which comprehensive test data are used. (17)

Batch: A group of similar transactions accumulated over time and then processed together. (2)

Batch control: Effective method of managing high volumes of transaction data through a system. (17)

Batch control totals: Record that accompanies the sales order file through all of the data processing runs. (4)

Batch systems: Systems that assemble transactions into groups for processing. (2)

Benchmarking: Comparison of key activities with similar activities elsewhere in the firm or in other firms. (7)

Big bang: An attempt by organizations to switch operations from their old legacy systems to the new system in a single event that implements the ERP across the entire company. (11)

Bill of lading: Formal contract between the seller and the shipping company that transports the goods to the customer. (4)

Bill of materials: Document that specifies the types and quantities of the raw materials and subassemblies used in producing a single unit of finished product. (7)

Biometric devices: Devices that measure various personal characteristics, such as fingerprints, voice prints, retina prints, or signature characteristics. (16)

Blind copy: A copy of the purchase order that contains no price or quantity information. (5)

Block code: A coding scheme that assigns ranges of values to specific attributes such as account classifications. (8)

Bolt-on software: Software provided by third-party vendors used in conjunction with already-purchased ERP software. (11)

Bus topology: Nodes in the topology that are connected to a common cable. (12)

C

Call-back device: Hardware component that asks the caller to enter a password and then breaks the connection to perform a security check. (16)

Cardinality: The numerical mapping between entity instances. (2)

Carrier sensing: Random access technique that detects collisions when they occur. (12)

Cash prelist: A list of all cash received by the mail room. (4)

Cells: Configuration of several different types of CNC into one complex machine. (7)

Centralized database: Database retained in a central location. (9)

Certification authorities (CAs): Trusted third parties that issue digital certificates. (12)

Chart of accounts: A listing of an organization's accounts showing the account number and name. (8)

Check digit: Method for detecting data coding errors. A control digit is added to the code when it is originally designed to allow the integrity of the code to be established during subsequent processing. (17)

Check register: A record of all cash disbursements. (5)

Client-server model: A form of network topology in which a user's computer or terminal (the client) accesses the ERP programs and data via a host computer called the server. (11)

Client-server topology: Topology involving the distribution of data processing between the user's application—the client—and the server. (12)

Closed database architecture: A database management system used to provide minimal technological advantage over flat file systems. (11)

Cohesion: Number of tasks a module performs. (14)

Cold turkey cutover: Process of converting in which a firm switches to a new system on a particular day and simultaneously terminates the old system. (14)

Compilers: Language translation modules of the operation system. (16)

Completeness tests: Tests identifying missing data within a single record and entire records missing from a batch. (17)

Computer-aided design (CAD): Use of computers to design products to be manufactured. (7)

Computer-aided manufacturing (CAM): Use of computers in factory automation. (7)

Computer-aided software engineering (CASE): Technology that involves the use of computer systems to design and code computer systems. (14)

Computer-integrated manufacturing (CIM): Completely automated environment. (7)

Computer numerical control (CNC): Computer-controlled machines that replace skilled labor. The computer contains programs for all parts being manufactured by the machine. (7)

Conceptual systems design: The production of several alternative designs for the new system. (1)

Conceptual user views: Description of the entire database. (14)

Control activities: Policies and procedures used to ensure that appropriate actions are taken to deal with the organization's risks. (3)

Control environment: The foundation of internal control. (3)

Control risk: Likelihood that the control structure is flawed because controls are either absent or inadequate to prevent or detect errors in the account. (15)

Conversion cycle: Cycle comprising the production system and the cost accounting system. (2)

Cookies: Files containing user information that are created by the Web server of the site being visited and are then stored on the visitor's own computer hard drive. (12)

Corrective controls: Actions taken to reverse the effects of errors detected in the previous step. (3)

Cost-benefit analysis: Process that helps management determine whether (and by how much) the benefits received from a proposed system will outweigh its costs. (13)

Cost center: Organizational unit with responsibility for cost management within budgetary limits. (8)

Cost driver: Cause of the cost. (7)

Cost objects: Reasons for performing activities. (7)

Coupling: Measure of the degree of interaction between modules. (14)

Credit memo: Document used to authorize the customer to receive credit for the merchandise returned. (4)

Critical success factors: Items of such importance that failure to meet any one of them would cause the firm to fail. (7)

Customer open order file: File containing a copy of the sales order. (4)

Customer order: Document that indicates the type and quantity of merchandise being requested. (4)

Cutover: Process of converting from the old system to the new system. (14)

Cycle billing: Method of spreading the billing process out over the month. (4)

D

Data: Facts, which may or may not be processed (edited, summarized, or refined) and have no direct effect on the user. (1)

Data collision: Event that occurs when two or more signals are transmitted simultaneously. (12)

Data currency: When the firm's data files accurately reflect the effects of its transactions. (9)

Data definition language (DDL): Programming language used to define the database to the database management system. (9)

Data dictionary: Description of every data element in the database. (9)

Data encryption: Technique that uses an algorithm to scramble selected data, making it unreadable to an intruder browsing the database. (16)

Data encryption standard (DES): Approach that uses a single key known to both the sender and the receiver of the message. (12)

Dataflow diagram: Diagram that uses a set of symbols to represent the processes, data sources, dataflows, and process sequences of a current or proposed system. (2)

Data manipulation language (DML): Language used to insert special database commands into application programs written in conventional languages. (9)

Data mart: A data warehouse organized for a single department or function. (11)

Data modeling: The task of formalizing the data requirements of the business process as a conceptual model. (10)

Data normalization: Process that promotes effective database design. (9)

Data redundancy: The state of data elements being represented in all user files. (9)

Data structures: Techniques for physically arranging records in a database. (2)

Data warehouse: A database constructed for quick searching, retrieval, ad hoc queries, and ease of use. (8)

Database: Physical repository for financial data. (1)

Database administrator (DBA): The individual responsible for managing the database resource. (9)

Database authorization table: Table containing rules that limit the actions a user can take. (16)

Database lockout: Software control that prevents multiple simultaneous access to data. (9)

Database management system (DBMS): Software system that controls access to the data resource. (1)

Deadlock: A "wait" state that occurs between sites when data are locked by multiple sites waiting for the removal of the locks from the other sites. (9)

Deletion anomaly: The unintentional deletion of data from a table. (9)

Depreciation schedule: Record used to initiate depreciation calculations. (6)

Detection risk: Risk that auditors are willing to take that errors not detected or prevented by the control structure will also not be detected by the auditor. (15)

Detective controls: Devices, techniques, and procedures designed to identify and expose undesirable events that elude preventive controls. (3)

Digital certificate: A sender's public key that has been digitally signed by trusted third parties. (12)

Digital envelope: An encryption method where both DES and RSA are used together. (12)

Digital signature: An electronic authentication technique that ensures the transmitted message originated with the authorized sender and that it was not tampered with after the signature was applied. (12)

Direct access files: Files in which each record has a unique location or address. (2)

Disaster recovery plan (DRP): Comprehensive statement of all actions to be taken before, during, and after a disaster, along with documented, tested procedures that will ensure the continuity of operations. (15)

Distributed databases: Databases distributed using either the partitioned or replicated technique. (9)

Document flowchart: Flowchart that shows the relationship among processes and the documents that flow between them. (2)

Documentation: Written description of how the system works. (14)

Drill-down: Operations permitting the disaggregation of data to reveal the underlying details that explain certain phenomena. (11)

E

Echo check: Technique that involves the receiver of the message returning the message to the sender. (16)

Economic order quantity (EOQ) model: Inventory model designed to reduce total inventory costs. (7)

Electronic data interchange (EDI): The intercompany exchange of computer-processable business information in standard format. (4)

Embedded audit module (EAM): Technique in which one or more specially programmed modules embedded in a host application select and record predetermined types of transactions for subsequent analysis. (17)

Employee file: A file used with the attendance file to create an on-line payroll register. (6)

Employee fraud: Performance fraud by non-management employees generally designed to directly convert cash or other assets to the employees' personal benefit. (3)

Empty shell: Arrangement that involves two or more user organizations that buy or lease a building and remodel it into a computer site, but without the computer and peripheral equipment. (15)

Encryption: Technique that uses a computer program to transform a standard message being transmitted into a coded (ciphertext) form. (16)

End users: Users for whom the system is built. (1)

Enterprise resource planning (ERP): A system assembled of prefabricated software components. (7)

Entity: A resource, event, or agent. (2)

Entity relationship (ER) diagram: Documentation technique used to represent the relationship among activities and users in a system. (2)

Ethics: Principles of conduct that individuals use in making choices in guiding their behavior in situations that involve the concepts of right and wrong. (3)

Events: Phenomena that affect changes in resources. (1)

Expenditure cycle: Acquisition of materials, property, and labor in exchange for cash. (2)

Exposure: Absence or weakness of a control. (3)

F

Financial transaction: An economic event that affects the assets and equities of the organization, is measured in financial terms, and is reflected in the accounts of the firm. (1)

Firewall: Software and hardware that provide a focal point for security by channeling all network connections through a control gateway. (12)

Flat-file approach: An organizational environment in which users own their data exclusively. (2)

Formalization of tasks: When organizational areas are subdivided into tasks that represent full-time job positions. (8)

G

Gantt chart: Horizontal bar chart that presents time on a horizontal plane and activities on a vertical plane. (14)

General ledger change report: Report that presents the effects of journal voucher transactions on the general ledger accounts. (8)

General ledger history file: File that presents comparative financial reports on a historic basis. (8)

Generalized audit software (GAS): Software that allows auditors to access electronically coded data files and perform various operations on their contents. (17)

Goal congruence: The merging of goals within an organization. (8)

Grandparent-parent-child technique: Backup technique used in sequential batch systems. (16)

Group codes: Codes used to represent complex items or events involving two or more pieces of related data. (8)

H

Hash total: Control technique that uses non-financial data to keep track of the records in a batch. (17)

Hashing structure: Structure employing an algorithm that converts the primary key of a record directly into a storage address. (2)

Hierarchical data model: A database model that represents data in a hierarchical structure and permits only a single parent record for each child. (9)

Hierarchical topology: Topology where a host computer is connected to several levels of subordinate smaller computers in a master-slave relationship. (12)

I

Independence: The separation of the record keeping function of accounting from the functional areas that have custody of physical resources. (1)

Indexed random file: Randomly organized file that is accessed via an index. (2)

Indexed sequential file: Sequential file structure that is accessed via an index. (9)

Indexed structure: A class of file structure that use indexes for its primary access method. (2)

Information: Facts that cause the user to take an action that he or she otherwise could not, or would not, have taken. (1)

Information overload: When a manager receives more information than can be assimilated. (8)

Inherent risk: Risk that is associated with the unique characteristics of the business or industry of the client. (15)

Inheritance: Each object instance inherits the attributes and operations of the class to which it belongs. (14)

Insertion anomaly: The unintentional insertion of data into a table. (9)

Instance: Single occurrence of an object within a class. (14)

Integrated test facility (ITF): Automated technique that enables the auditor to test an application's logic and controls during its normal operation. (17)

Intelligent forms: Forms that help the user complete the form and that make calculations automatically. (14)

Internal control system: Policies a firm employs to safeguard the firm's assets, ensure accurate and reliable accounting records and information, promote efficiency, and measure compliance with established policies. (3)

Internal view: The physical arrangement of records in the database. (9)

Interpreters: Language translation modules of the operation system that convert one line of logic at a time. (16)

Inverted list: A cross reference created from multiple indexes. (9)

Investment center: Organizational unit that has the objective of maximizing the return on investment assets. (8)

IP spoofing: A form of masquerading to gain unauthorized access to a Web server and/or to perpetrate an unlawful act without revealing one's identity. (12)

Islands of technology: An environment where modern automation exists in the form of islands that stand alone within the traditional setting. (7)

J

Journal voucher: Document sent to the general ledger for posting. (4)

Journal voucher listing: Listing that provides relevant details about each journal voucher received by the GL/FRS. (8)

Just-in-time (JIT): Philosophy that attacks manufacturing problems through process simplification. (7)

L

Labor distribution summary: A summarization of labor costs in work-in-process accounts. (6)

Lapping: Use of customer checks, received in payment of their accounts, to conceal cash previously stolen by an employee. (3)

Local area network: Network generally confined to a close geographical area. (12)

Logic bomb: Destructive program, such as a virus, that is triggered by some predetermined event. (16)

Logical key pointer: A pointer containing the primary key of the related record. (2)

M

Management by exception: The concept that managers should limit their attention to potential problem areas rather than being involved with every activity or decision. (8)

Management control decisions: Technique for motivating managers in all functional areas to use resources as productively as possible. (8)

Management fraud: Performance fraud that often uses deceptive practices to inflate earnings or to forestall the recognition of either insolvency or a decline in earnings. (3)

Management information system (MIS): System that processes nonfinancial transactions that are not normally processed by traditional accounting information systems. (1)

Management reporting system (MRS): System that provides the internal financial information needed to manage a business. (1)

Manufacturing resources planning II (MRP II): System that incorporates techniques to execute the production plan, provide feedback, and control the process. (7)

Master file: File containing account data. (2)

Materials requirements planning (MRP): System used to plan inventory requirements in response to production work orders. (7)

Materials requisition: Document that authorizes the storekeeper to release materials to individuals or work centers in the production process. (7)

Mnemonic codes: Alphabetic characters in the form of acronyms that convey meaning. (8)

Monitoring: The process by which the quality of internal control design and operation can be assessed. (3)

Move ticket: Document that records work done in each work center and authorizes the movement of the job or batch from one work center to the next. (7)

N

Navigational model: Model that possesses explicit links or paths among data elements. (9)

Network model: Variation of the hierarchical model. (9)

Network topology: Physical arrangement of the components. (12)

O

Object class: Logical grouping of individual objects that share the same attributes and operations. (14)

Object-oriented design: Building information systems from reusable standard components or modules. (14)

Object-oriented programming (OOP) language: Programming language containing the attributes and operations that constitute the object modules represented in the ER diagram at the implementation phase of the SDLC. (14)

Objects: Equivalent to nouns in the English language. (14)

On-demand reports: Reports triggered by events. (8)

On-line analytical processing (OLAP): An enterprise resource planning tool used to supply management with real-time information and also permits timely decisions that are needed to improve performance and achieve competitive advantage. (11)

On-line transaction processing (OLTP): Events consisting of large numbers of relatively simple transactions such as updating accounting records that are stored in several related tables. (11)

One-time password: A network password that constantly changes. (16)

Operational control decisions: Technique that ensures that the firm operates in accordance with preestablished criteria. (8)

P

Packet switching: Messages that are divided into small packets for transmission. (12)

Packing slip: Document that travels with the goods to the customer to describe the contents of the order. (4)

Parallel operation cutover: Process of converting in which the old system and the new system are run simultaneously for a period of time. (14)

Parallel simulation: Technique that requires the auditor to write a program that simulates key features of processes of the application under review. (17)

Parity check: Technique that incorporates an extra bit into the structure of a bit string when it is created or transmitted. (16)

Partitioned database: Database approach that splits the central database into segments or partitions that are distributed to their primary users. (9)

Password: Secret code entered by the user to gain access to the data files. (16)

Payroll imprest account: An account into which a single check for the entire amount of the payroll is deposited. (6)

Payroll register: Document showing gross pay, deductions, overtime pay, and net pay. (6)

Personnel action form: Document identifying employees authorized to receive a paycheck; is used to reflect changes in pay rates, payroll deductions, and job classification. (6)

PERT chart: Chart that reflects the relationship among the many activities that constitute the implementation process. (14)

Phased cutover: Process of converting to the new system in modules. (14)

Point-of-sale (POS) system: A revenue system in which no customer accounts receivable are maintained and inventory is kept on the store's shelves, not in a separate warehouse. (4)

Pointer structure: A structure in which the address (pointer) of one record is stored in the field on a related record. (2)

Polling: Popular technique for establishing communication session in WANs. (12)

Post-implementation review: Step in implementation phase that measures the success of the system. (8)

Preventive controls: Passive techniques designed to reduce the frequency of occurrence of undesirable events. (3)

Primary key: Characteristics that uniquely identify each record in the tables. (9)

Proactive management: Management that stays alert to subtle signs of problems and aggressively looks for ways to improve the organization's systems. (13)

Product documents: Documents that result from transaction processing. (2)

Production schedule: Formal plan and authorization to begin production. (7)

Profit center: Organizational unit with responsibility for both cost control and revenue generation. (8)

Program flowchart: Diagram that provides a detailed description of the sequential and logical operations of the program. (2)

Programmed reports: Reports that provide information to solve problems that users have anticipated. (8)

Project feasibility: Analysis that determines how best to proceed with a project. (13)

Protocol: Rules and standards governing the design of hardware and software that permit network users to communicate and share data. (12)

Prototyping: Technique for providing users a preliminary working version of the system. (14)

Pseudocode: English-like code that describes the logic of a program without specific language systems. (14)

Public key encryption: Technique that uses two keys: one for encoding the message, the other for decoding it. (12)

Purchase order: A document based on a purchase requisition that specifies items ordered from a vendor or supplier. (5)

Purchase requisition: A document that authorizes a purchase transaction. (5)

R

REA (resources, events, and agents) model: An alternative accounting framework for modeling an organization's critical resources, events, and agents and the relationships between them. (10)

Reactive management: Management that responds to problems only when they reach a crisis state and can no longer be ignored. (13)

Real-time systems: Systems that process transactions individually at the moment the economic event occurs. (2)

Receiving report: Report that lists quantity and condition of the inventories. (5)

Recovery operations center (ROC): Arrangement involving two or more user organizations that buy or lease a building and remodel it into a completely equipped computer site. (15)

Redundancy tests: Tests that determine that an application processes each record only once. (17)

Reengineering: The identification and elimination of nonvalue-added tasks by replacing traditional procedures with those that are innovative and different. (4)

Reference file: File that stores data that are used as standards for processing transactions. (2)

Remittance advice: Source document that contains key information required to service the customers account. (4)

Reorder point: Lead time times daily demand. (7)

Replicated database: Database approach in which the central database is replicated at each site. (9)

Request-response technique: Technique in which a control message from the sender and a response from the sender are sent at periodic synchronized intervals. (16)

Resources: Assets of an organization. (1)

Responsibility: An individual's obligation to achieve desired results. (8)

Responsibility accounting: Concept that implies that every economic event affecting the organization is the responsibility of and can be traced to an individual manager. (8)

Responsibility center: Organization of business entities into areas involving cost, profit, and investment. (8)

Responsibility reports: Reports containing performance measures at each operational segment in the firm, which flow upward to senior levels of management. (8)

Reusable password: A network password that can be used more than one time. (16)

Revenue cycle: Cycle comprising of sales order processing and cash receipts. (2)

Ring topology: Topology that eliminates the central site. All nodes in this configuration are of equal status. (12)

Risk assessment: The identification, analysis, and management of risks relevant to financial reporting. (3)

Robotics: CNC machine used in hazardous environments or to perform dangerous and monotonous tasks that are accident prone. (7)

Rounding error tests: Tests that verify the correctness of rounding procedures. (17)

Route sheet: Document that shows the production path a particular batch of product follows during manufacturing. (7)

Run: Each program in a batch system. (2)

Run-to-run controls: Controls that use batch figures to monitor the batch as it moves from one programmed procedure to another. (17)

S

Safety stock: Additional inventories added to the reorder point to avoid unanticipated stockout conditions. (7)

Salami fraud: Fraud in which each victim is unaware of being defrauded. (17)

Sales order: Source document that captures such vital information as the name and address of the customer making the purchase; the customer's account number; the name, number, and description of product; quantities and unit price of items sold; and other financial information. (4)

Scalability: The system's ability to grow smoothly and economically as user requirements increase. (11)

Scheduled reports: Reports produced according to an established time frame. (8)

Schema: Description of the entire database. (9)

Screening router: A firewall that examines the source and destination addresses that are attached to incoming message packets. (16)

Segregation of duties: Separation of employee duties to minimize incompatible functions. (3)

Sequential codes: Codes that represent items in some sequential order. (8)

Sequential files: Files that are structured sequentially and must be accessed sequentially. (2)

Sequential structure: A data structure in which all records in the file lie in contiguous storage spaces in a specified sequence arranged by their primary key. (2)

Servers: Special-purpose computers that manage common resources, such as programs, data, and printers of the LAN. (12)

Shipping notice: Document that informs the billing department that the customer's order has been filled and shipped. (4)

Slicing and dicing: Operations enabling the user to examine data from different viewpoints. (11)

Source documents: Documents that capture and formalize transaction data needed for processing by their respective transaction cycles. (2)

Span of control: Number of subordinates directly under a manager's control. (8)

Spooling: When applications are designed to direct their output to a magnetic disk file rather than to the printer directly. (17)

Stakeholders: Entities either inside or outside an organization that have direct or indirect interest in the firm. (1)

Star topology: A network of IPUs with a large central computer at the hub, which has direct connections to a periphery of smaller computers. (12)

Steering committee: An organizational committee consisting of senior-level management responsible for systems planning. (13)

Stock release: Document that identifies which items of inventory must be located and picked from the warehouse shelves. (4)

Strategic planning decisions: Planning with a long-term time frame and that is associated with a high degree of uncertainty. (8)

Structure diagram: Diagram that divides processes into input, process, and output functions. (14)

Structured design: Disciplined way of designing systems from the top down. (14)

Structured problem: Problem in which data, procedures, and objectives are known with certainty. (8)

Substantive tests: Tests that determine whether database contents fairly reflect the organization's transactions. (15)

Subsystem: A system viewed in relation to the larger system of which it is a part. (1)

Supervision: A control activity involving the critical oversight of employees. (3)

Supplier's invoice: The bill sent from the seller to the buyer showing unit costs, taxes, freight, and other charges. (5)

Supply chain management (SCM): A class of application software that supports the set of activities associated with moving goods from the raw materials stage through to the consumer. (11)

System: Group of two or more interrelated components or subsystems that serve a common purpose. (1)

System development life cycle: The formal process by which in-house development is accomplished. (1)

System flowcharts: Flowcharts used to show the relationship between the key elements—input sources, programs, and output products—of computer systems. (2)

System survey: Determination of what elements, if any, of the current system should be preserved as part of the new system. (13)

Systems analysis: Two-step process that involves a survey of the current system and then an analysis of the user's needs. (13)

Systems development life cycle (SDLC): Formal process consisting of two major phases: new systems development and maintenance. (13)

T

Tactical planning decisions: Planning performed by the middle-level manager to achieve the strategic plans of the organization. (8)

Test data method: Technique used to establish application integrity by processing specially prepared sets of input data through production applications that are under review. (17)

Tests of controls: Tests that establish whether internal controls are functioning properly. (15)

Third normal form (3NF): The normalization that occurs by dividing an unnormalized database into smaller tables until all attributes in the resulting tables are uniquely and wholly dependent on (explained by) the primary key. (9)

Third-generation languages: Procedural languages in which the programmer must specify the sequence of events used in an operation. (14)

Three-tier model: A model where the database and application functions are separated. (11)

Token passing: Transmission of a special signal (token) around the network from node to node in a specific sequence. (12)

Tracing: Test data technique that performs an electronic walkthrough of the application's internal logic. (17)

Trading partners: Category of external user, including customer sales and billing information, purchase information for suppliers, and inventory receipts information. (1)

Transaction: An event that affects an organization and that is processed by its information system as a unit of work. (1)

Transaction authorization: Procedure to ensure that employees process only valid transactions within the scope of their authority. (3)

Transaction file: Temporary file that holds transaction records that will be used to change or update data in a master file. (2)

Transaction processing system (TPS): Activity comprising three major subsystems—the revenue cycle, the expenditure cycle, and the conversion cycle. (1)

Transcription error: Type of error that can corrupt a data code and cause processing errors. (17)

Transfer Control Protocol/Internet Protocol (TCP/IP): The basic protocol that permits communication between Internet nodes. (12)

Transposition error: Error that occurs when digits are transposed. (17)

Trojan horse: Program that attaches to another legitimate program but does not replicate itself like a virus. (16)

Turnaround documents: Product documents of one system that become source documents for another system. (2)

Turnkey systems: Completely finished and tested systems that are ready for implementation. (1)

Two-tier model: A model where the server handles both application and database duties. (11)

U

Universal product code (UPC): A label containing price information (and other data) that is attached to items purchased in a point-of-sale system. (4)

Unstructured problem: Problem for which there are no precise solution techniques. (8)

Update anomaly: The unintentional updating of data in a table, resulting from data redundancy. (9)

URL (Uniform Resource Locator): The address that defines the path to a facility or file on the Web. (12)

User view: The set of data that a particular user needs to achieve his or her assigned tasks. (9)

V

Valid vendor file: A file containing vendor mailing information. (5)

Validation controls: Controls intended to detect errors in transaction data before the data are processed. (16)

Value-added banks (VAB): Banks that can accept electronic disbursements and remittance advices from its clients in any format. (12)

Value-added network (VAN): Network that provides service by managing the distribution of the messages between trading partners. (12)

Vendor-supported systems: Custom systems that organizations purchase from commercial vendors. (1)

Virus: Program that attaches itself to a legitimate program to penetrate the operating system. (16)

Voucher register: A register reflecting a firm's accounts payable liability. (5)

W

Walkthrough: Analysis of system design to ensure the design is free from conceptual errors that could become programmed into the final system. (14)

Wide area network: Network that exceeds the geographic limitations of a local area network. (12)

Work order: Document that draws from bills of materials and route sheets to specify the materials and production for each batch. (7)

Worm: Software program that "burrows" into the computer's memory and replicates itself into areas of idle memory. (16)

Index

intellectual property, 115

intelligent control agents, 590

intelligent forms, 675

internal auditing, 37

internal business process perspective, 631

internal controls, 133–44

   and Sarbanes-Oxley (SOX) Act, 136–37

internal financial transactions, 13

internal users, 11

internal view, 435

International Computer Security Association (ICSA), 587

International Standards Organization, 569

Internet, 198, 563

   addresses, 566–67

   business models, 574–76

   commerce, 564–78

   and crime, 580

   protocols, 569–73

   risks, 580–83

   service providers, 564

Internet Explorer, 564, 566, 570

Internet Message Access Protocol (IMAP), 569

interpreters, 756

intranet, 578–79

intra-organizational networks, 564, 592–00

inventory, 18

   alternative ordering procedures, 254

   coding, 382

   cost, 338

   physical, 46

   records, 235, 237

   reducing costs of, 337–38

   reduction of, 352–55

   status report, 447

   subsidiary file, 249

   subsidiary ledger, 167, 168, 178

   table, 498, 500

   updating from sales orders, 207

   usage, 339

   valuation, 237

inventory control, 242, 243, 249

   advantages of automating, 257–59

   main functions in production process, 335

   manual system, 247

   objective, 335

inverted list, 440

investment center, 408, 409, 411

investments, capital, 302

invoice, 167, 237

IP address, 567

IP spoofing, 582, 770

IPUs (information processing units), 24

islands of technology, 346

ISPs (Internet service providers), 564

IT auditing, 36–37, 742–44

IT controls, 141, 721–53

   and financial reporting, 722–23

   security and access, 755–92

   systems development, program changes, and application controls, 793–832

iterative design approach, 668

IT function, 729–30

IT governance, 721–53

IT projects, 631–42

J

JavaScript, 582

J.D. Edwards & Co., 16, 33

JIT. *See* just-in-time (JIT) manufacturing

job security, 727

job tickets, 284, 287

journals, 50–52

   cash receipts, 173, 175

   digital, 200

   sales, 167

   special, 178

manual accounting systems, 180–86

manual process accounting model, 27, 48–53

manufacturing environment

    allocation of costs using ABC method, 359

    automation of, 345–51

    changes, 355–63

    controls, 340–43

    flexibility in world-class environment, 344–45

    just-in-time (JIT) manufacturing, 354–55

    traditional, 331–43

manufacturing resources planning (MRP II), 348–50

    integration with manufacturing/financial systems, 352

    production capability planning modules, 353

Manugistics Inc., 535

marketing, 20

markup languages, 571

masquerading, 131

mass-production, 343

master file record, 56

materials and operations requirements, 334

materials management, 18, 20

materials requirements planning, 348–50

materials requisition, 333–34

materials return ticket, 334

matrices, 703

MCI, 564

measurement, performance, 406

message sequence numbering, 774

message transaction log, 774

methods, 665

Microsoft, 554–55, 564

middle management, 4

MIM Health Plans Inc., 542

mirrored data center, 735

MIS. *See* management information systems (MIS)

mission, 625

mnemonic codes, 386

modular system design, 676–77, 680–81

modules

    standard, 665

    and system design, 676–77

monitoring, 140–41

morale, 397

motivation, 397

move ticket, 333, 334, 335

MRP. *See* materials requirements planning (MRP)

MRP II. *See* manufacturing resources planning (MRP II)

MRP system, 351

MRS. *See* management reporting system (MRS)

multidimensional database, 536

N

navigational database models, 432–33, 468

needs analysis, 691

negligent hiring liability, 580

net present value analysis, 644–45

Netscape Navigator, 564, 566, 564

network control, 597, 767–77

network database models, 432, 433, 470, 472

networking, 365, 578

network interface card (NIC), 593

network layer protocols, 606–607

network-level firewalls, 586, 768

Network News Transfer Protocol (NNTP), 570

network topologies, 592–97

networks, intra-organizational, 564

NNTP (Network News Transfer Protocol), 570

nondiscretionary reporting, 11

noneconomic events, 503

nonfinancial transaction, 9

nonrepudiation, 590

normalization, 445, 447–53, 473–79, 536, 668

    and accountants, 453

    and foreign keys, 457–59

    importance of, 447–48